CULTURE AND POLITICAL CRISIS IN VIENNA

CULTURE AND POLITICAL CRISIS IN VIENNA

Christian Socialism in Power, 1897–1918

JOHN W. BOYER

THE UNIVERSITY OF CHICAGO PRESS
CHICAGO AND LONDON

John W. Boyer is dean of the College and professor of history at the University of Chicago. He is coeditor of the *Journal of Modern History,* and general editor, with Julius Kirshner, of the nine-volume *University of Chicago Readings in Western Civilization.*

The University of Chicago Press, Chicago 60637
The University of Chicago Press, Ltd., London
© 1995 by The University of Chicago
All rights reserved. Published 1995
Printed in the United States of America
04 03 02 01 00 99 98 97 96 95   1 2 3 4 5
ISBN: 0-226-06960-5 (cloth)
          0-226-06961-3 (paper)

This publication has been supported by a grant from the National Endowment for the Humanities, an independent federal agency.

Library of Congress Cataloging-in-Publication Data
Boyer, John W.
    Culture and political crisis in Vienna : Christian socialism in power, 1897–1918 / John W. Boyer.
        p.   cm.
    Includes bibliographical references and index.
    1. Vienna (Austria)—Politics and government.   2. Austria—Politics and government—1867–1918.   3. Radicalism—Austria—Vienna.   4. Christlichsoziale Partei.   5. Vienna (Austria)—Cultural policy.   6. Socialism, Christian—Austria—Vienna.
I. Title.
DB854.B67   1995
320.9436′13′09034—dc20   94-36240

This book is for Dominic, Alexandra, and Victoria.

CONTENTS

PREFACE

The present volume is a sequel to my previous book which I published some years ago on the early history of the Christian Social movement in Vienna and should thus be read in the context of the arguments of that contribution.[1] But this book differs from that earlier study in several substantial and important respects. First, it deliberately does not restrict itself to the history of the Christian Social party or the party's social-interest groups on the municipal level, for in many ways that story is less interesting and less compelling after 1897 than the party elite's contribution to regional and national (that is, state-level) policy debates. Nor does this volume claim to be a history of all regional Christian Social party organizations in German-speaking Austria, for the history of local and regional politics outside of Vienna and Lower Austria has only begun to be researched, both for the Empire and the First Republic. Rather, the story that is told here concerns the emergence of the Christian Social party as an agent of state-level politics in Vienna and the significance of some of its more important contributions to the political, social, and cultural fate of the Monarchy in the last decades of its existence. This makes the present volume much less a contribution to the social history of *Mittelstand* politics, and much more a contribution to the political history of *Mittelstand* society and its role in the policy-making process of late Imperial Austria, than its predecessor.

I should also alert the reader that, in lieu of an extended recapitulation of the arguments of *Political Radicalism* at the beginning of the present volume, I offer some synoptic reflections about the history of the party in the extended analysis that constitutes the Conclusion (Chapter 8). I have done so to avoid writing what would inevitably become two conclusions, one at the beginning and the other at the end of the present book. But it will be useful to offer a few brief reflections on why the study of the Christian Social party is of interest to historians of nineteenth- and twentieth-century Central European history, as we stand poised at 1897–98, between the processes through which the Christian Socials gained power and the means by which they manipulated and exploited it.

As a powerful electoral movement centered in a burgeoning metropolitan area, Christian Socialism offered some remarkable parallels (as well as contrasts) to urban and regional politics elsewhere in late nineteenth-century Central Europe. Recent work on Hamburg and Württemberg, for example, suggests the importance of the struggles of local and regional political movements to control administrative mechanisms and to define and defend the political space they needed to secure a meaningful role in the state constitutional order.[2] Indeed, it is not too large a claim to argue that the later nineteenth century saw both the redefinition and the reinvention of local and regional government throughout Central Europe, as substate political and administrative units became accustomed to the constitutional regimes established in the 1860s and moved simultaneously to defend and to expand their scope of governance, including important areas of social welfare policy.[3] To the extent that a "bourgeois public" was constituted in Central Europe in the nineteenth century, this happened much more forcibly after 1867 than before 1840. The pre-liberal *Gemeinde* had long preceded the liberal *Staat* throughout Central Europe, but within its local institutions and places of governance new patterns of political values and new *bürgerlich* social movements emerged after the onset of constitutional absolutism, giving these communities the opportunity to experiment with competitive political identities and to renew their public administrative rationality. Some of these movements were expressive of imagined futures, others of remembered pasts, but all were confident that they could and should improve on the status quo.

As a movement with both cultural ambitions and interest-based prerogatives, the Christian Social party clearly paralleled other regional and metropolitan movements set in fertile juxtaposition to established national political institutions. The history of Austrian Christian Socialism demonstrated that it was possible for a bourgeois protest movement to be both radically emancipatory and decisively conservative, within the general confines of the late nineteenth-century *Rechtsstaat*.[4] The Christian Social movement exposed the historical dilemma addressed by the now famous debate between a group of younger English historians interested in the local and regional dimensions of modern German history and the representatives of the so-called Bielefeld school, who have been seen as viewing the national administrative state and its affiliated "pre-modern" elites as historical actors that were fiercely influential in weaving the special and damaged fabric of German history.[5] If we leave aside the special *kleindeutsch* terms in which this debate has been pursued, it has raised two broader issues. First, to what extent must we understand modern German history as having both a compelling horizontal dimension, with a single and necessary end for many contingent beginnings, and a compelling vertical dimension, in which power is either produced and determined from below or constituted and exercised from above? Second, to what extent did the cultural peculiarities and liabilities of the German *Bürgertum*—however one defines that elusive target—predispose the course of German history in the nineteenth century in favor of one or both of these dimensional realities?

Transposing this debate into the Hapsburg arena, one gains a healthy respect for the limits of historical modeling, for what is sometimes overlooked in the work of the Bielefeld group and their English critics is that the terms that undergird their research agendas are not all that dissimilar. They may appear antinomic, but they are ultimately reconcilable. If one observes the history of late Imperial Austrian politics, a strong and persuasive case for administrative manipulation and hegemonic control by the liberal-absolutist central state can be made easily—far more easily than for Wilhelmine Germany. After all, Austria had a dynasty that possessed enormous cultural force and public respect, and a state bureaucracy that commanded an equivalent level of sturdy civic legitimacy—this is the other, less ironic and less magic side of Kafka's Castle. The Austrian *Bürgertum,* for all its differentiated values and capacities, depended upon this administrative state for the moral and institutional ground rules of its political culture—that is, for its way of thinking about civic life and its way of behaving within the sphere of public power.[6] Hence the preoccupation of so many talented Austrian politicians and political theorists at the turn of the century with questions of administrative reform, which they saw not only as a possible substitute for constitutional reform, but also as a desirable alternative to it.

Yet the history of later Imperial Austrian politics also showed the apparent collapse of political liberalism with far more devastating effect than in Germany—a collapse that called into question the permanence of the hybrid, liberal-absolutist state of 1867 that was built upon the liberal tradition. This in itself was not peculiar to Austria, for the undermining of the traditional bourgeois-dynastic state occurred everywhere in Europe between 1890 and 1930. Yet what was fascinating about the Austrian case was that the crisis of political liberalism was the result of the incursions of emancipatory civic movements like the Christian Socials and the Young Czechs who were themselves representative of "middling" bourgeois strata in late nineteenth-century Central European society.[7] Both parties were based on social *and* national movements with strong local and regional affiliations within what I have called the *Mittelbürgertum.* Both had robust political organizations with strong constituency support. Their adherents would fit very uneasily into portraits stressing the timidity and the passivity of the Central European *Bürgertum.* Yet while both parties first challenged and stymied the administrative state, each was eventually co-opted by that state, using institutions of regional and municipal governance both to express and to enhance their newly constituted social authority. Indeed, their unabashed exploitation of the Austrian administrative state and their eventual co-optive partnership with that state might be seen as confirming that it was possible in Central Europe to constitute *bürgerlich* power "from below" and then find entry into the world "of above," merging administrative domination and political empowerment in one extraordinary, if highly unstable, mode of governance.[8]

Much of the political history of modern Austria might be seen as affording a special model of the interaction of state and society which, because it added an all-important independent variable—politicized nationality—to the anti-liberal, anti-absolutist brew of social emancipation, produced new forms of bourgeois power *within* the context of a dynastic state system. To be "German" or "Czech" or "Polish" in Austria after 1900 gave one a special "ethnic" political license that allowed one not only to draw upon the constitutional and administrative prerogatives of the 1860s, but to blend those privileged identities into the new material and class interests of the 1890s. Like the Young Czechs and like some elements of the Polish Club, Karl Lueger's movement thus had one special advantage over parallel bourgeois protest movements in the Bismarckian Empire—it was self-consciously, if passively, "German" in an Empire where a citizen's constitutional standing and a group's political authority could only profit from invoking ethnicity in the calculus of state power. Yet it was also aggressively a-national (or perhaps post-national) in a multiethnic capital city that was both provincial *Vaterstadt* and imperial *Residenzstadt*, a city dominated by privileged *Stadtbürger* in the name of all Hapsburg *Staatsbürger*.[9] The nationality conflict in Austria was not merely the destructive, centrifugal process that usually appears in the historiography. It was also an emancipatory, centripetal process that reshaped the 1867 state in ways that allowed all bourgeois ethnic groups to be agents, as well as subjects, of their political destiny. That some—particularly Austro-German extremists before and during the First World War—rejected this competitive constitutional culture and sought to recreate univocal German control over other political peoples in the Hapsburg Monarchy was an indisputable fact, but it was only one possible model of constitutional rule in late Imperial Austria. As we will see in subsequent chapters, the Christian Social party offered another (admittedly unstable and only partially successful) model, seeking to balance the interests of class and nation in ways that would preserve rather than destroy the multinational character of that Empire.

The history of Austrian Christian Socialism also reminds us of the necessity of regional differentiation in the context of the moral dimensions of the debate about a German (or Austrian) *Sonderweg*. A recent publication on Austria's participation in the National Socialist regime insists that the years 1938 to 1945 in Austria must be seen "as a part of German as well as Austrian history."[10] The adjective "German" here implies a moral indictment as much as it denotes ethnicity—Austrians were and are deeply responsible for the National Socialist terror regime. This is undeniably true, but in spite of the misery and deep culpability of Austria's involvement in the Nazi catastrophe, and by implication, in the authoritarian, quasi-Fascist regime that preceded it, the fundamental questions to be asked of Austrian history in the late nineteenth century and twentieth century remain somewhat different from those usually articulated for *kleindeutsch* German history. Guilt is a prior and perennial problem in Austrian history, but it is as much a product of collective as it is of individual responsibility. If one sees 1918 as the "end" of Austrian history rather than 1934 (or 1938), the stakes are not only different but perhaps somewhat higher as well. If German history is the narrative of power gone awry, then Austrian history is the story of power gone away. It is precisely because the Imperial state proved so fragile in 1917–18 that we should seek to understand what that state was, what made it function as long as it did, what contributed to its stability amidst the remarkable economic growth and equally remarkable political crises of the late Empire, and what consequences its destruction had for the powerful mass political traditions like Christian Socialism and Social Democracy that it had nurtured so effectively.

The history of the Christian Social party is not only an important part of the history of the late Imperial state; it is also exemplary for other half-marginalized, half-hegemonic bourgeois political movements in Central Europe that walked a perilous line between noisy stability and silent revolution in the two decades before and after the First World War. Does its history betray merely one black thread of political irresponsibility, leading from prewar anti-Semitism to the disaster of Austro-Fascism? Or must we pay equal attention to the democratic and genuinely emancipatory traditions of the party? How easy is it to read the famous *Lager* of interwar Austrian history backward into the Empire? How are we to think about a Seipel or a Dollfuss in the context of a Lueger or a Gessmann? How powerful were the authoritarian traditions of the party, and how different were these traditions from those of the party's various domestic competitors? How, ultimately, are we to connect 1913 with 1919 or 1889 with 1934?[11] There are far too many silences in modern Austrian history, and answers for these questions will surely require a more subtle and flexible research agenda than ascribing "guilt" to any single political tradition or postulating a single, special "way" that Austrian history and its multiple political subcultures had to take before 1918.

Finally, just as a concern with the middle classes has properly generated much fascinating research in recent German history, much can be learned from an examination of Austrian parallels.[12] Questions of cultural identity—material and intellectual—and of political authority necessarily converge in the study of the Central European *Bürgertum*. As an agent of and sponsor of radical *bürgerlich* politics, the Christian Social movement depended on the constant and (until the crisis of 1914) seemingly bottomless reservoir of well-being within the Austrian *Bürgertum*. By well-being I mean more than just satisfied voters, often drawn from disparate and even incongruent social strata, whose material prosperity and behavioral stability guaranteed relatively predictable electoral outcomes. For the Christian Socials also sought to sustain levels of cultural certainty and moral authority that presumed an effective linkage between their social policies and the needs and expectations of their constituents. One of the surprising and patently "modern" features of Lueger's party was its realization that the task of an effective party organization was not merely to react to popular expectations but to shape and to mold them as well. Not only did the Christian Social party try to represent the material interests of the increasingly complex "middling" sectors of urban and rural civil society; by means of its political aesthetics and its various cultural policies the party also tried to ensure constancy in the political socialization and cultural reproduction of its voters.

Yet material stability and cultural perception also depended on relational social consciousness, for claims or expectations to one set of identities also signified counterclaims and expectations *not* to share in other identities. The social and cultural history of Viennese politics after 1897 showed only too well that the history of the *Bürgertum* must be read in dynamic conjunction with the histories of competing strata in civil society, and especially with a constant view of the leaders and the constituents of Austrian Social Democracy. Within the mythically cosmopolitan and ethnically "universalist" yet hermetically sealed world of fin-de-siècle Vienna, it was none too easy to presume, much less to sustain, the isolated *Lager* mentality that later histories of Austrian politics would espouse. This was a world fraught with cultural confrontations in the midst of interclass and transethnic social interactions, where opposites tended toward sameness in spite of heroic partisan efforts to the contrary. How else are we to account for the remarkable parallels between Christian Socialism and Social Democracy in Vienna? It is in this context that the history of late Imperial Viennese politics alerts us to the importance of context and convergence, to the frustrations of sameness as well as the luxury of difference, to relational consciousness as well as ideological insularity in the everyday practice of bourgeois *and* socialist politics. However uncomfortable this may be for historians on either side of the great Austrian political divide, young or old, postmodern or happily traditional, one cannot understand Karl Lueger without Victor Adler, and one cannot comprehend Otto Bauer without Ignaz Seipel. This is not a question of equity or evenhandedness—although both are ultimately warranted—but of (historiographical) common sense in the face of incredibly complex social realities.

Earlier versions of some parts of the present book previously appeared in other publications. These include "The End of an Old Regime: Visions of Political Reform in Late Imperial Austria," *Journal of Modern History,* 58 (1986), © 1986, The University of Chicago; "Austrian Catholics and the World: Facing Political Turmoil in the Early Twentieth Century," in *The Mirror of History: Essays in Honor of Fritz Fellner* (ABC-Clio: Santa Barbara, 1988); "Christian Socialism under the Empire: Some Reflections," in *Geschichte zwischen Freiheit und Ordnung. Gerald Stourzh zum 60. Geburtstag* (Verlag Styria: Graz, 1991); and "Religion and Political Development in Central Europe around 1900: A View from Vienna," *Austrian History Yearbook,* 25 (1994). I gratefully acknowledge the permission of the publishers to use this material.

Michael Geyer, Lothar Höbelt, David S. Luft, James J. Sheehan, and Gerald Stourzh were kind enough to read the whole of the present manuscript and offer helpful suggestions for revision, as well as correcting a number of mistakes. Those blunders that remain are mine alone. I am also grateful to Jules Kirshner, my fellow editor at *JMH,* for many stimulating discussions involving my work, and to Alan Bullock, Kathleen N. Conzen, John E. Craig, Constantin Fasolt, Fritz Fellner, Margarete Grandner, Barry D. Karl, Friedrich Katz, William H. McNeill, Anton Pelinka, Carl E. Schorske, and Karl J. Weintraub for advice and comments about individual sections of my manuscript.

The research and writing of this book were in part supported by fellowships from the National Endowment for the Humanities, the Alexander von Humboldt Foundation, and St. Catherine's College, Oxford. I am also grateful to the Division of the Social Sciences and to the College of the University of Chicago, where my colleagues and friends Edward O. Laumann, Donald N. Levine, Tetsuo Najita, and Ralph W. Nicholas provided important support for the project.

One of the special pleasures of this project was the chance it afforded me to test my ideas with graduate students who are also interested in Central European history. Over the last fifteen years a number of graduate students have assisted me with my work on this project, some of whom are now faculty members at other universities and colleges. They include Jonathan Sperber, Paul Silverman, James Melton, John Roth, Steven Lestition, Suzanne Marchand, Cate Giustino, Gary Finder, Anthony Steinhoff, Kay Schiller, Franz Henne, Matthew Berg, Greg Eghigian, Robert Beachy, Karl Bahm, Andrew Bouvet, Michelle Mayer, Robert Hogg, David Ellis, and Maureen Healy. And I am especially grateful to Christine Young for her unflagging support in Vienna.

I am deeply grateful to the archivists of the many archives that I cite on pp. 645–48 for their patience and assistance. Rudolf Jeřábek, Elisabeth Springer, and Lorenz Mikoletzky of the Austrian state archives; Annemarie Fenzl of the archdiocesan archives; and Peter Csendes of the archive of the city of Vienna were especially kind and helpful to me.

I also want to offer special thanks to Anton Staudinger, who was kind enough to share with me his transcripts of CS parliamentary protocols for 1917–18; to John Craig, who provided copies of several letters in German archives; to Arthur Lux, who helped me with the complexities of German stenographic script; and to Gabriella Hauch, who has undertaken the arduous task of producing a computerized transcription of the records of the Social Democratic Executive for the period 1898–1918. I had first worked with the latter documents in the *Verein für Geschichte der Arbeiterbewegung* in Vienna, and so I know how challenging Dr. Hauch's accomplishment is.

Finally and above all, I want to thank my wife, Barbara A. Boyer, for her love and support during the long period of this book's gestation.

Chicago, March 1994

ONE

The Christian Social Consolidation of Power,
1897–1905

Introduction

The challenges and opportunities facing the Christian Socials in the aftermath of their victories in 1895 and 1896 in Vienna were momentous. With modest financial and intellectual resources Karl Lueger and his colleagues had broken thirty years of Liberal rule in the capital, representing perhaps the most extraordinary shift in voter loyalties ever experienced in a major Central European city before the First World War. A political movement which scarcely ten years before had consisted of a motley, ill-organized group of ward politicians, most of whom had little or no formal experience in regional politics *or* in public administration, now found itself forced to assume responsibility for managing a major European capital and for directing the second most important provincial administration (aside from that of Bohemia) in the Hapsburg Empire.[1] The conversion of untested political energy into more conventional modes of administrative rule became a characteristic feature of the history of Austrian Christian Socialism after 1897. The exercise of power through public bureaucracies inevitably forced the party onto the defensive and imposed upon it a sense of accountability and even predictability from which it could hardly escape. This conservatism of power was both dangerous and advantageous. On the one hand, if the Christian Social party failed in its task of managing the burgeoning Viennese metropolitan area, if it was found incompetent or even unimaginative in offering alternatives to the Liberal regime, retribution from the voters for the gap between promise and accomplishment would not be long in coming. On the other hand, if the party seized the instruments of power and initiated substantial changes in local and regional government in harmony with its campaign promises, while not violating the ideological constraints imposed by the petty bourgeois social interests that the Christian Socials represented, then Lueger might hope not merely for the survival of his party but perhaps for its permanent hegemony in Vienna.

The high-tension style of politics developed by the Christian Socials in the early 1890s had raised expectations that Lueger's regime in Vienna would provide good government but also *different* government, and that new levels of political and administrative resources would be brought to bear to change the direction of municipal and *Land* policies as they affected the social interests of the Viennese *Bürgertum.* The basic question Lueger faced in 1897 was how to translate the impressive moral force behind his achievement into a policy program that was both revolutionary and socially conservative. For the Christian Socials assumed power at precisely that period of Austrian history when the massive forces of Austrian Social Democracy had commenced their drive for recognition and position, and inevitably the violently anti-bourgeois thrust of socialist political aesthetics, tactics, and policy ends influenced the Christian Socials in defining their own mission. For the Social Democrats, the Christian Socials symbolized all that they found distasteful about bourgeois society: not only was much of the Christian Social party's electoral base *kleinbürgerlich,* thus meriting socialist arrogance and contempt, but it also attracted a strong middle- and even upper-bourgeois following, which established it as a classic anti-Marxist obstacle to Social Democratic success. Given the clerical and anti-Semitic facade of the party and its undeniable success in recruiting a mass following of its own—in some ways beating the socialists at their own game— it was not surprising that Austrian Social Democrats reacted with such ferocity to Lueger's movement. In the face of the socialist challenge the Christian Social party faced a double paradox after 1897: it had to find ways to improve *bürgerlich* society institutionally and culturally, strengthening the economic resources and political opportunities of its *Mittelstand* voters, without disturbing conventional patterns of wealth and income accumulation (e.g. curbing new taxation) and without expending too many public resources on sectors of the burgeoning metropolitan community that were inherently hostile to the Christian Socials' survival. It also had to develop a policy program that claimed to represent the "public interest" in an aggressive way while defining the meaning of the "public" to serve the interests of a *Bürgertum* that was experiencing demographic growth and occupational diversification (as a result, among other factors, of the increasing prominence of the white-collar service sector).

A third consideration for the party was the fragile nature of its voting base. Christian Social success in 1895–96 had come as a result of massive disillusionment with Austrian Liberalism on the part of gentile voters in Vienna and Lower Austria, but the varied and often inharmonious nature of the Christian Social coalition made it necessary that the party give thought to revising the rules of the Viennese electoral game. To enhance the Christian Social party's security, the 1890 municipal charter (*Gemeindeordnung*) and its Liberal-designed franchise (*Wahlordnung*) would be replaced with instruments more easily manipulable by the party elite. What the party wanted was not merely political success but also the predictability of success in large and generous terms. To meet these expectations the curial system would be revised to enable the Rathaus to counterbalance possible dissidence by key voter groups within existing electoral curias.[2] Lueger had no ardent desire to abolish the privileged curias; but he did want a system in which the middle strata of the *Bürgertum* would dominate both the First and the Second Curias, and one in which no single interest group (such as the civil servants in the Second Curia) dominated a whole curia. The party's control over private interest-group demands—either those known in the present or those anticipated in the future—could be sustained only if it had the flexibility to play off such interests *within* each curia.

The impact of participation in institutions of public power also changed the organizational and financial structure of the party, exposing it to the dangers of rigidity and stagnation but also providing it with powerful financial and professional resources. Both Karl Lueger and his chief lieutenant, Albert Gessmann, realized that the party had to dominate the municipal and provincial bureaucracies of Vienna, but they also saw the benefits that a peaceful and harmonic détente between party and civil service might bring. In the *Magistrat* of the city of Vienna the party controlled the second largest "state" bureaucracy in Austria, with hundreds of highly qualified civil servants who might "voluntarily" assist the party in its legislative and policy programs.[3] Lueger quickly decided that controlling and assimilating the traditional Liberal civil service of Vienna was far preferable to displacing or destroying it.

A similar strategy of reconciliation with and gradual co-option of the professional bureaucracy was implemented on the state level, but with less predictable consequences.[4] Collaboration between the Lower Austrian *Statthalterei*[5] and the Rathaus over the city statute in 1900, which continued during the loan negotiations of 1901–2 and the debate over the Lower Austrian school laws of 1904, slowly won the Christian Socials the grudging respect, if not always the admiration, of the ministerial bureaucracy. Lueger's municipal administration proved to be neither as raucous nor as incompetent as the anticlerical Josephist civil servants might have feared, and the party's anti-socialist potential made it a force to be reckoned with by the end of Koerber's Cabinet in December 1904. In return, key elements within the party elite began to consider the possibility of joining the Cabinet, which would open up to the party the patronage and financial resources that Cabinet-level representation usually brought with it. But such a strategy was premature until after 1906. Albert Gessmann, who eventually designed the new *Reichspartei* patterned after selected elements of the German *Zentrum*, could only justify to Lueger (and his voters) a ministerial role for the Christian Socials by imposing on the party the role of mediator between conflicting Czech and German bourgeois parties. This controversial assignment in turn presumed the sponsorship of a bourgeois *Sammlung* strategy directed against Austrian Social Democracy. Both calculations were to be possible after the advent of universal manhood suffrage in 1907.

Once in place (with Lueger's grudging acceptance), Albert Gessmann's double strategy of uniting the Alpine Catholic conservatives with the Viennese and Tyrolean Christian Socials into one massive German *bürgerlich* party and of accepting the role of *Regierungspartei* by entering into the Cabinet in late 1907 had long-term consequences for the party in Vienna and for the Austrian political system more generally. On the positive side, after 1907 the party was the largest single political movement (in parliamentary seats and in popular vote) in Cisleithanian Austria, exceeding even the Social Democrats. Not only did the Christian Socials gain access to high-level Cabinet positions and ministerial patronage, they also became significant actors in shaping national legislation, especially on matters involving finance, commerce, and transportation, as well as regional revenue and administrative reforms. On the negative side, the Viennese Christian Socials joined a powerful agrarian alliance, for which they would pay dearly during the 1911 parliamentary elections. Just as the integration of the local municipal party into the resource and tax network of the Viennese administration prevented (and made unnecessary) the development of strong, party-based organizational structures, so too did the party suffer from its overachievement of wealth and power after 1907, losing its coherence as a "radical" party and relying on past laurels and on the manipulation of Lueger's name to keep its own internal affairs in order.

When Lueger died in March 1910 and the brutal inflation in domestic consumer prices and rising levels of urban unemployment led many Christian Social voters to desert the party in 1911, Lueger's successors faced the enormous tasks of internal restructuring and external political defense. The rise to power of Richard Weiskirchner in the Viennese party and his efforts to restructure the local party organizations found no parallel on the national level, where the *Reichspartei* was paralyzed by urban/rural conflicts and a weak, rotating leadership group in parliament. On the national level the party suffered grievous embarrassments with the estrangement of the Vienna organization from the new elite of rural and Catholic politicians who dominated the parliamentary club after 1911 and who often seemed more interested in the affairs of their provinces than of the state as a whole.

In the last years before the war little could be done to counteract these tendencies toward provincialization. The coming of the war, and its consequent "depoliticization" of all party politics, exacerbated the structural inadequacies of the *Reichspartei* concept. The rise of new, more Catholic-oriented radicals in the Vienna party (Leopold Kunschak, Richard Schmitz, Heinrich Mataja, and finally Ignaz Seipel) who were dissatisfied with the corporatist, bastion mentality of Lueger's *Bürger* politics in Vienna and who wanted to broaden the social basis of the party and to instill a more doctrinaire (and Catholic) ideological tone suggested that the Christian Social party faced fateful decisions about its electoral strategies and administrative assumptions by 1918, with or without the problems which the collapse of the Dual Alliance entailed. The last year of the war saw the success of this new generation of party activists, associated with the *Katholischer Volksbund,* as they claimed both moral hegemony and political authority in the Viennese party. Their irreverent criticism of the heritage of Lueger and their demands for internal reconstruction paralleled their break with Weiskirchner and the parliamentary club on *Octroi* war aims and state constitutional reform. The Revolution of 1918 brought this new elite to power not merely in the party but in the Republic as well, although in circumstances more radical and, for Vienna, more unfavorable than anyone in 1914 could have imagined. The great chasm in modern Austrian history between bourgeois Christian Socialism and laborite Social Democracy, which has defined the constitutional imagination of the state down to the present, now assumed more irreconcilable symbolic forms. Red Vienna stood counterposed to the Black countryside, translating Viennese cultural conflicts onto a national republican scale, and far surpassing both the ideological and class conflict between the two parties *within* Vienna before 1914.

Christian Social Hegemony in Vienna: The Municipal Revolution, 1898–1905

The first necessity of the Christian Social party in 1897 was to consolidate its power base in Vienna, exploiting the city as the primary focus of its electoral strength. Consolidation implied a threefold process of developing imaginative programs to enlarge the scope and efficiency of municipal services by placing them under the proprietary control of the city and using them to generate new revenue for the municipal budget (Lueger's program of municipal socialism); ensuring the party's permanent control of the instruments of power in Vienna by redesigning the municipal charter and franchise in 1899–1900 to eliminate those aspects of the 1890 documents that the Christian Socials found inconvenient; and subjecting the city's communal bureaucracy (and the civil service of the *Land* administration of Lower Austria as well) to explicit political sanctions that would serve the party without causing chaos in the day-to-day administration of the city or inviting the intervention of the Imperial Cabinet.

Each of these processes involved the party in extensive negotiations with the Cabinets between 1897 and 1905 (those of Badeni, Gautsch, Thun, Clary, and, most importantly, Koerber) and with the Lower Austrian *Statthalter,*

Count Erich Kielmansegg, who began the period with a marked suspicion of the Christian Social party but who became, some private quibbling and jealousies aside, one of those most appreciative of the anti-socialist thrust of Christian Social politics. Rather than opposing or curbing the party in any of its projects, the various Cabinets—however different they were in other respects—shared one common attribute. They proved remarkably willing to suffer insolence from and (in Gessmann's case) manipulation by the Christian Socials in return for the party's self-appointed role as a buffer against violent national strife and against the incursions of Austrian Social Democracy in the Empire's capital. Ernest von Koerber exploited this Janus-faced image of the party in different ways than had Badeni, but both confirmed the success of the Christian Socials' strategy of avoiding overt governmentalism (manifested in Lueger's disdain for formal participation in the affairs of the Cabinet) while stressing the party's anti-socialism and national moderation. After 1906 it became apparent that Lueger's localist and regionalist stance was both too little and too much—too humble to be able to shape advantageous public policy on the state level and too subject to the autocratic whims of Josephist bureaucrats on larger, constitutional issues (such as Koerber's plan in late 1904 to reform local and regional government in the Monarchy, which the Christian Socials found both administratively unsound and politically dangerous). Only then did the party consciously break out of the corporatism of Vienna and seek to enlarge its own electoral base by redefining the national political system in which it had to work.

Lueger's much-vaunted program of municipal socialism, beginning with construction of a new, city-owned gasworks in 1896–99 and control of the street railways and electrical works (in two stages, with final socialization coming in 1902) and ending with such later refinements as a city mortgage bank in 1906 was impressive on its own terms as a show of political will and economic achievement. Other massive construction projects, like the water-provisioning network (*Zweite Hochquellenleitung*) that finally opened in December 1910 and the dramatic development of the *Zentralfriedhof* (including the construction of a new church named in honor of Karl Lueger), were complementary feats with strong functionalist overtones. This is not to insist that Vienna was a leader in municipal socialist enterprises in Europe. A German investigation in 1908 on the pace of municipal ownership in Europe concluded that Austria as a whole was "at approximately the same stage of municipalization as is Germany."[6] With his flair for controversy, however, including a well-publicized feud in 1897–98 with the Viennese banking world and its journalistic supporters, Karl Lueger managed to convert what in other Central European cities were commonplace institutional and organizational changes into political symbols of the first order. The gasworks especially, since its municipalization oc-

curred early in his tenure as mayor, was touted as exemplifying Christian Social "anti-capitalism" at its best.[7] Yet Lueger eventually made his peace with
the Viennese banking community, and after 1902 had no problems in generating support for municipal loans, especially through mediation of the *Länderbank,* whose director, August Lohnstein, was a confidant of Lueger.[8] Although
on the level of campaign rhetoric the Christian Socials might tout their municipalization schemes as "anti-capitalist," from another perspective, given the
businesslike rationale of public ownership that undergirded these projects, they
were more properly an expression of state capitalism.

Stephan Koren has observed that the question of whether public industries
should be conceived as not-for-profit (*gemeinnützig*) or profit-making
(*gewinnstrebend*)—that is, whether they should be oriented primarily toward
public service or toward showing a healthy annual surplus—has been quite
thorny in Austrian history.[9] Although the distinction is arbitrary and often
blurred in the minds of those operating such industries, in Christian-Social
Vienna municipal socialism was enthusiastically *gewinnstrebend*. The search
for profit was of paramount importance, for profits not only demonstrated the
"maturity" of the party in its handling of public affairs but also offered to other
propertied interests in the city the specter of reduced or at least constant rates
of direct taxation. The various district associations of landlords (*Hausherren*),
many of them filled with Christian Social ward politicians, especially appreciated the happy combination of rising rental income and enhanced public revenues as one practical result of Lueger's schemes.

They were not disappointed, at least in terms of the economic success of
the municipal ventures. Although Liberal and socialist opponents criticized
both the extravagance and presentmindedness of the projects—financed as
they were by huge loans that became a disastrous burden for the city in the
1920s—the performance of the new municipal utilities after their first decade
of operation seemed to show such criticism to be arbitrary and unfair. So successful were the projects that they not only covered interest on and amortization of the loans but generated additional revenues for the city treasury. During
its first ten years of operation the municipal streetcar system earned 330 million crowns, with a net profit of 104.5 million. Of the latter, 22.6 million
crowns were transferred to the city's treasury as new income.[10] Based on a
review of the city's budget in May 1908, the Finance Ministry concluded that

> it must be stated emphatically that the financial condition of the mu-
> nicipality of Vienna, despite all of the demands it has taken upon itself
> in the last decade, is still quite favorable. Regular income has in-
> creased from 72 million crowns in 1897 to 125 million crowns in
> 1906, for which the city's municipal industries are substantially re-

sponsible; in 1906 they will show a pure profit of 11.6 million
crowns. . . , a level of performance that, one can be predict, will be
even higher in 1907.

Evaluating Vienna's financial condition in 1908 the report concluded: "one can
hardly argue that the city would be too deep in debt or that it would have
difficulty in meeting its obligations."[11] Equally important, the huge construction budgets of the various utilities were effective pump-priming devices for
the local Viennese economy. Of the 120 firms or craft shops that participated
in the construction of the city electrical works in 1900–1902, for example,
almost all were based in or near Vienna. The total labor and material expenditures for a project of this scale—it cost 36 million crowns—could not help but
boost the local economy, providing thousands of new jobs and ensuring the
short-term economic well-being of dozens of local industrial establishments.

Municipal socialism had other advantages for the party apart from maintaining the city's financial solvency and its economic stability, most notably the
affective imagery that the program offered to that "public" anxiously awaiting
Lueger's activism in the wake of a putative Liberal "decline." Municipal socialism was supremely attractive to Lueger for three reasons. It gave the party an
immediate, large-scale object on which to focus public attention as proof of
the party's "revolution" in municipal government, and its propaganda value
was therefore enormous. It also generated vast amounts of political patronage
(both direct and indirect) and, over time, important new revenues that the city
could use to cover new or expanded municipal services generated by Vienna's
demographic pressures. Finally, the municipal socialism program assisted the
party, by trial and error, in defining for itself the practical limits of the word
"social" in its title.

With the city's revenue coffers full and its politicians pretentiously trying
to insinuate themselves into upper bourgeois and Court circles (however cynical their actual reception), the first decade of the twentieth century in Vienna
provided a unique example of the normative reappropriation and assimilation
of older bourgeois cultural ideals by upstart social groups, who transformed
such ideals to serve their own vested political interests. The Christian Socials
saw their municipal socialist projects as emulating the Liberal-*Grossbürger*
building achievements of the third quarter of the nineteenth century, but on
different terms. They undertook these projects not on behalf of themselves as
a privileged "capitalist" class, but on behalf of their city as a bastion of traditional *bürgerlich* morality and dynastic social stability. This was what Lueger
meant when he proudly referred to Vienna, in the manner of a late medieval
patrician, as *unsere Vaterstadt,* combining local pride with a sense of proprietary corporatism. But this was a pride that was very much embedded in the late

nineteenth century, for it combined an assertive and competitive boosterism with a pride in the best that new technologies could bring to Vienna.[12]

Lueger's comments before the general assembly of the Viennese *Bürgervereinigung* in November 1904 were a perfect expression of these values, offered in the context of a fulminating attack on the Social Democrats.[13] Citing the accomplishments of his administration—especially its new technologically progressive municipal utilities and its parks—Lueger argued that they served all the inhabitants of the city. But he also reminded his audience who was responsible for these deeds, and to whose honor they must be accounted: "those who are out in the street marching and protesting are not the masters [*Herren*] of Vienna, but rather those who pay the direct taxes, those who are born here, who have their property in Vienna and love the city with all their heart—they are the ones who have a voice in its affairs."

In addition to the legally constituted *Bürger,* younger men would also play a role in defending the city—the sons of the *Bürger* [*Bürgersöhne*] "who are determined to take up the inheritance of their fathers." Lueger's discourse was defined by proprietary concepts—of the *Herr* (as in *Hausherr* or landlord) who possessed a disposable, but sacred share (*Erbteil*) as a form of cultural property in the city—and by intergenerational (and intraclass) bonds of familial loyalty. Youth by itself, outside of a strong family nexus, could expect no independent or natural role in the *Bürgertum;* only by co-option and familial sponsorship did one merit a place in the Christian Social universe.

The group before whom Lueger spoke—the *Bürgervereinigung*—was an invention of Christian Social publicists in the aftermath of the 1900 franchise reforms, which brought together men who held the honorific status of belonging to the official *Bürger* of the city and who held a privileged vote in the Second Curia. The concept of the *Bürgerrecht* in Vienna was freighted with corporate and exclusive connotations. During the Liberal era this "right" was granted sparingly, largely for individual achievement. Under Lueger it retained its social prestige but also became a way of infiltrating party loyalists into the Second Curia, thus transforming what was ostensibly a "municipal" institution into a patently party-political one and demonstrating how fluid was the boundary between public and private for the Christian Socials. Nomination remained a much coveted honor, and those receiving the *Bürgerrecht* after 1900 were eligible to become members of Lueger's *Bürgervereinigung,* an association that epitomized the symbolic appropriation of the cultural heritage of the Viennese *Bürgertum* by the Christian Social machine.[14] Lueger once called these men his "grenadiers of social order." In his view their mandate was "to support with determination those who want to hold fast to the traditional order, to defend the law and customs of our forefathers."[15] The statistical data on who received this honor between 1897 and 1910 are illuminating. Of the 9,301 men made

Bürger, over 94 percent were married, and over 96 percent declared themselves Roman Catholics. Extremely few unmarried men were given the honor, and status as a widower was apparently only slightly more acceptable. No Jews were accepted and only a small number of Protestants. The age and occupational structure was also predictable—over 56 percent were between 51 and 70 and another 33 percent between 41 and 50. Almost 70 percent of the nominees were "independents" (business or property owners) in crafts or industry, and the remainder were owners in commerce and trade. Of the 7,017 who were appointed between 1901 and 1910 only 8 percent were white-collar employees.[16] Most of the nominees were lower- and middle-bourgeois types, usually at least prosperous, if not moderately wealthy (the fee for appointment was 50 crowns, a not inconsiderable sum), culturally established, married, and of the correct religion. In sum, *they* were Karl Lueger's "people."[17]

At the same time that they proclaimed the glories of an imagined *Stadtbürger* past, Christian Social pronouncements on the municipal utilities sounded a second, seemingly discordant theme, namely, the modernity and progressiveness of their technological achievements.[18] Throughout Europe and America at the end of the nineteenth century urban planners were blinded by a new faith in the possibilities of technological innovation and managerial skill.[19] The Christian Socials were no exception. Each propaganda statement on the various city improvements touted the party's commitment to the most "modern" and technologically progressive instruments of urban management and technical services. The party had no opportunity to create a second Ringstrasse and thus to emulate the Liberal party's strategy in the 1870s and 1880s, as brilliantly demonstrated by Carl Schorske, to secure their fame and reputation in huge stone buildings.[20] However, this was not an entirely bad thing, for the few attempts of the Christian Socials to sponsor large, representational structures ended up producing heated conflicts in which the divergences of taste and aesthetic sensibility among various party leaders were set before an amused public. Although Leopold Steiner, Victor Silberer, and Robert Pattai were able to secure their colleagues' grudging consent in the Lower Austrian Diet to Otto Wagner's plan for the church at the Am Steinhof sanitarium in November 1903, no similar consensus could be found in the City Council for any of Wagner's several designs for a monumental city museum.[21] Approved by the City Council in July 1900 as a tribute to the Emperor's seventieth birthday, the city museum project combined the worst vicissitudes of Viennese aesthetic and electoral politics. Wagner's 1907 scheme for a building on the Karlsplatz merited Karl Lueger's personal support but ran up against opposition among his colleagues in the City Council (as well as among the Viennese artistic community more generally).[22] When the Council shifted the site of the museum to the Schmelz in the Fifteenth District and reopened the competition, the final winners in June 1913 were two younger architects, Karl Hoffmann and Emil Tranquillini. Their traditional design, praised for its ability to engender "beautiful feelings" and to encourage "ideal and restful thoughts," won out against a revised version of Wagner's plan.[23] In one party leader's words, the city museum competition had become "a battlefield for conflicting artistic opinions"; but it was also typical of what Leon Botstein has described as the many "criss-crossed alliances, friendships, quarrels and divergences in the modernist ferment of fin-de-siècle Vienna."[24] In their divided sympathies about modernist architecture Christian Social politicians simply reaffirmed the extraordinary difficulty of assigning fixed and consistent coordinates to "traditional" and "modern" in Vienna after 1900.[25]

In lieu of such grandiose buildings Lueger was able to bring about more dynamic and utilitarian forms of symbolic representation—street railways and electrical works—and more traditional forms of public aesthetics—the "garden belt" around the city that fulfilled a generations-long Austrian idealization of the "garden"—that were nonetheless monumental, larger than life, and immediately flattering to the city as a traditional cultural unit.[26] Not surprisingly, here too the *Vaterstadt* motif emerged in full force. Heinrich Goldemund, the city planner who helped to work out the implementation of the *Wald- und Wiesengürtel,* conceived of the project (according to a later Christian Social biographer) as a "hymn of love to the *Vaterstadt.*"[27] For Goldemund the garden belt was an aesthetic achievement on a par with monumental architecture, for he believed that "the beauty of a city is not secured in its works of architectural and artistic monuments alone, but equally in the charm of its landscape. . . . it is necessary to set limits on building construction which has the interests of only the individual and not the whole of society in mind."[28] Nor were other, more institutional innovations immune from this rhetoric. Commenting with pride on the fact that local suppliers and manufacturers were responsible for the construction of the new municipal electrical works in 1901–2, a city publication stressed that "with few exceptions it is Viennese and Brünn industrial establishments and Viennese industriousness which have created a beautiful monument [*Denkmal*] in the municipal electrical works."[29] Traditional *bürgerlich* values—a much-touted Viennese artisanal industriousness—coupled with technological modernity produced the new utilities.

With the exception of some rather tedious church buildings, the Christian Socials thus had no occasion to flatter themselves by using new architectural objects as historicist metaphors. Indeed, the municipality devoted some attention to historic preservation, even assigning a section of the huge 360-million-crown loan that was authorized in 1908 for the acquisition of older houses as a component of orderly city planning.[30] For the Christian Socials the city of Vienna was both past and future, a living and changing organism that was also an object of proprietary devotion. As "owners" (since only the self-defining *Bürgertum* owned the city) they would both conserve and improve, defend and elaborate. Their public-works programs were the mirror image of their own *bürgerlich* ideals, and in their uneasy balancing of traditionalism and modernism they paralleled many similar efforts at cultural harmonization between Vienna's single imagined past and its many anticipated futures. As Karl Wächter observed in 1909, rather than the Christian Social city fathers being backward in technological innovation, "far more can one accuse them of being too impetuous with innovations and costly experiments, of pursuing technological progress in too extravagant a manner."[31]

The same party that voted to subsidize a new edition of the works of Abraham a Sancta Clara and that patronized the musical romanticism of Franz Schubert was also eager to ensure its *Vaterstadt*'s prosperity with the fruits of technical progress—gasworks, waterworks, even subways.[32] Yet these instruments would reconcile, on congenial and defensible terms, traditional political and social values with newer opportunities for economic expansion and demographic growth. The new street railways offered an excellent case in point. Since the streetcars connected the center of the metropolis to its more garden-like suburbs, Christian Social city planners saw an advantageous conjunction of modern economic profit and traditional cultural pleasure as technology intruded into the "garden." Not only would the new electrified streetcar (*Strassenbahn*) system encourage investors to consider the semirural periphery of the city for new housing construction (an area known for its "beautiful and healthy landscape"), but the rail system would also result in increased building activity and thus would "increase the property values" of the area.[33]

The reference to "beautiful and healthy" suggested Christian Social attentiveness to the kind of demographic growth that municipalities throughout Central Europe would have to cope with in the immediate postwar period. The Green Belt was not merely decorative but embodied conscious social-ecological aims as well.[34] Yet the marriage of beauty to profit—the notion that beauty would enhance property—also marked the moral limits of Christian Social city planning. The party would not assume responsibility for the quality of individual or mass social reproduction; nor did it view city government as having a duty to provide decent housing for all of its inhabitants.[35] However frustrated individual party leaders may have been with the intransigence of the Viennese property owners, the landlords remained one of the most powerful interest groups within the Christian Social party down to 1914.[36]

To the extent that profits from the new utilities held direct tax rates constant and generated new sources of income, they would square the circle of Austrian municipal administration. Economic "progress" might be allied with, rather than directed against, older political privileges and cultural values. The Christian Socials' middle-bourgeois Jacobinism—claiming that the whole of the public was more virtuous than any of its parts and then defining its own electorate as the "whole"—was a logical substratum for the party's rationale on behalf of municipal socialism.

The Viennese municipal socialist ventures must also be seen in the context of a more general movement among European and American city governments to view communal ownership as a way of combining efficiency with morality.[37] Yet the Christian Social program of municipal improvement differed from the American Progressive model in two important ways. Rather than diminishing the role of partisan politics in city government, municipal socialism in Vienna both validated and strengthened the control of a single, hegemonic political party by handing it an enormous spoils system; and, rather than replacing private interests with the more rational and moral interests of the public at large, the Christian Social model integrated the private interests of selected bourgeois electoral groups into the renewed moral virtue of the proprietary city. What was good for the party was good for society, because the voters of the party also "owned" the city. Ultimately the two—the party and municipal government—were simply different incarnations of the same object: the Viennese *Bürgertum* as an archetype of imagined cultural stability and dynastic loyalty. Lueger's machine combined some features of the American "Boss" system and other features of American reform Progressivism into one unstable model of success (see below, Chapter 5).

Their municipalization program thus exposed the meaning of the words "public" and "people" for the Christian Socials. For Karl Lueger and his colleagues the "public" and the mass of individuals who happened to reside in Vienna were not identical or overlapping entities. Municipal socialist ventures served each, but in different ways. The "public" for Lueger was the body of tax-paying, law-abiding citizens, generally centered on the *Bürgertum* and its affiliated client groups (such as the governmental servants and white-collar employees in the service sector). This was a political-cultural as well as economic entity, having not merely the right of "active" citizenship (in the sense used by Abbé Sieyès), but also the social prestige to underwrite its proprietary control of the city. Lueger often referred to the "Christian People" (*christliches Volk*), which he used in the same restrictive, moral-political sense to define his own electoral constituency. Improvements in municipal utilities that provided job contracts and generated revenue to underwrite other special-interest subsidies for *bürgerlich* occupational groups (such as Christian Social training programs and subsidy schemes to assist the craft trades) profited the Christian Social "public" in direct and immediate terms.[38] The remainder of society—a more ill-defined object, including social strata who voted for the party's major opposition, the Social Democrats—could not expect such direct sponsorship. Characteristic was the frank statement of a Christian Social municipal report on the range of social services the city would provide to the poor: "municipal care of the poor is limited by law to the provision of those things absolutely necessary to sustain life. Anything beyond that limit remains the responsibility of the private sector."[39] Equally direct was Felix Hraba's critique of the idea that the city should build and subsidize more public kindergartens: "I must emphasize that the city has no responsibility in this area and that up to now it has been left to private charitable institutions. I urge that we keep it this way, since the financial situation of the city does not allow for additional spending here."[40]

The Christian Socials accepted the premise that service to all of society was a reasonable obligation of any ruling party in the city and province, but only in the passive sense that all who dwelled within the city's boundaries would have access to (and pay user fees for) better streetcars, better water provisioning, and larger and more aesthetically planned parks. The expensive political pageantry subsidized by the party would also stimulate local pride, although most party leaders were convinced that only members of *their* electorate were capable of affection for the *Vaterstadt*. What the Christian Socials did not mean by "service," however, was welfare in the socialist sense of redistributing massive public resources on behalf of the less fortunate members of society. Nor did they believe, as their socialist competitors eventually did come to affirm, that government should manage or accept ultimate responsibility for the quality of individual well-being. Paternalistic social rhetoric aside, Karl Lueger and his colleagues believed in the market and, for better or worse, they believed in families. When asked by a party journalist in 1907 whether he was worried that landlords in the city were planning various rent increases, Lueger showed no concern, arguing that the housing market operated by the principle of supply and demand and that, in any event, there were plenty of unrented apartments in Vienna.[41] Similarly, Hermann Bielohlawek could oppose the construction of more baths in public schools on the grounds that "the family must care for its children, and, even if it is poor, the family must decide when the child needs to be bathed and how it is to be cared for."[42] Christian Social progressiveness thus came to a sudden and uncompromising halt when matters of individual property or the traditional family were involved. Party practice was not necessarily indebted to the influence of Catholic social theory, but it was certainly complementary with such theory. Lueger felt that government intervention in society should be occasional at best and that where it occurred it must pay political dividends. It was hardly accidental that the largest and most publicized achievements of the party in social welfare came on behalf of the very old and the very young, client groups not in a position to fulfill the canons of self-help. In all other respects Lueger insisted that city businesses be managed on a market-oriented basis, utilizing labor codes for city workers not more (but also not less) generous than those in equivalent larger private concerns.[43] All municipal industries must show a profit for the city, rather than subsidizing their use by poorer elements of the population by offering public service at a reduced cost. In this sense the Vienna municipality was more conservative than some of its counterparts in Germany, where debates evolved over the appropriateness of city-subsidized services.[44]

The range of social values operative in the Rathaus was evident from the resources devoted to the extensive entertainment schedule (receptions, tours, banquets, exhibitions) undertaken or supported each year by the Mayor's Office.[45] Substantial sums of money were devoted to beautification schemes throughout Vienna, particularly the construction of gardens and fountains (often in districts where the party's base vote lay) that would enhance the fame and glory of the Imperial *Vaterstadt.* Associational subsidies provided by the city went to groups loyal to the party (or at least not meriting its current disfavor), not necessarily those that offered social services to the poor or less fortunate.[46] The municipal poor-care system, staffed by over 2,000 volunteer councillors (*Armenräte*) drawn from the ranks of the modestly propertied classes (typically master artisans, senior schoolteachers, and, in many cases, house owners), dealt with the poor in transactions that were at best paternalistic and at worst cruelly insulting.[47] It was neither surprising nor accidental that in Lueger's *Vaterstadt* poor-care councillors were addressed by those seeking assistance as "Herr Armenvater"—the motif of paternalist hierarchy and dependency extending to the very bottom of the municipal social system. Although Lueger and many of his colleagues were generous and often successful in trying to raise private contributions for the poor, their practical attitudes often contradicted the spirit of that benevolence. When Felix Hraba, Lueger's financial spokesman in the City Council, proposed that municipal poor councillors should wear uniforms and carry whips to protect themselves against aggressively greedy poor-care recipients, whom he described as belonging to a socialist clique, he only said publicly what many of his colleagues thought privately.[48] The uproar that followed Hraba's remarks—the Social Democrats obstructed approval of the 1909 municipal budget—was not merely the result of his gratuitous insult to the socialist party. It also reflected rival notions of the legitimacy of poverty on the one hand, and rival conceptions of who spoke for (and controlled) the poor, on the other. Christian Social charity was predicated on the assumption that support was given downward, by betters to lessers as acts of mercy. As Kenneth Prewitt has recently observed, unlike modern conceptions of philanthropy, late nineteenth-century charity implied merely "ameliorative action to reduce the felt pains of poverty or disease or illiteracy."[49] The charitable practice of *bürgerlich* groups like the Christian Socials did not seek to set in place structural solutions that would eliminate the "root causes" of such poverty. Such charity, offered under the benevolent guise of paternalist mercy, was doubtlessly useful to many impoverished people, but as the *Arbeiter-Zeitung* insisted about Lueger himself, it was always given with a sense of proper social distance between the giver and the receiver.[50] And because the poor-care councillors—who by occupation and social networks were likely to be loyal Christian Social activists with at least some level of political consciousness—had such intimate contact with and significant custodial responsibilities toward those whom the Social Democrats viewed as their "natural" constituents, neither were their charitable roles strictly "private" in nature. Authority-oriented encounters between Christian Socialism and Social Democracy were not restricted to election day, for in the local poor-care institutes of Vienna two thousand Christian Social voters exercised significant social disciplinary power over tens of thousands of Social Democratic clients on a daily basis.[51]

Two Christian Social initiatives—old-age annuities for small groups of poor schoolchildren and the Lainz home for the elderly—exemplify the values embedded in the party's public cultural practices. In 1898 the city created a municipal life-insurance company, the *Städtische Kaiser Franz Josef-Jubiläums-Lebens- und Rentenversicherungsanstalt,* named on the occasion of the jubilee of the Emperor.[52] As a way of dramatizing the party's social consciousness, the city decided that each year eighty-four poor children were to receive annuity policies—old-age income for the boys, dowry income for the girls—from the interest income generated by the initial founding grant of 500,000 fl. Short-term financial exposure for the taxpayers was nonexistent, since the policies would not reach maturity until long after the event. Yet if these modest transactions offered little immediate gain to the recipients, they did provide the occasion for political self-approbation for the donors. Indeed, the annuity policies were to be given over to the children in a "solemn public ceremony" to be held each year on the Sunday following December 2, the anniversary of the Emperor's accession to the throne. Conducted in the Festsaal of the Rathaus, over the years the Christian Social children's celebrations (*Kinderfeste*) became propaganda spectacles of the first order, attended not only by the party elite but also by high-ranking government officials, church dignitaries, and local school officials. The celebration held in December 1905 was typical. Josef Porzer, Lueger's vice-mayor who also chaired the board of the Insurance Institute, welcomed the guests, informing them that the gift of free annuities to the poor children was an excellent chance to advertise the work of the Institute itself: "this day is not merely a festival for the children, it is a festival of the municipal Institute . . . today is the day when the Institute can through its representatives come before the whole public and say something about its effect, its activity, and its development." According to Porzer, the outstanding financial success of the Institute was due to the trust that the population had in its programs and especially to the trust they had in the Christian Social municipal administration and in the "vigorous rule of our Mayor."

Lueger then distributed the policies to the children, remarking that he hoped the populace would view it as a "obligation of honor" to place their life insurance with the city Institute (as opposed to private companies). After one young girl recited a pious "Kindesdank" written especially for the occasion by M. G. Heimel-Purschke, a Christian Social primary-schoolteacher, a team of children then performed a patriotic pageant, *Die Spinnerin am Kreuz,* written by another schoolteacher, Mathilde Melkus. Her saga of family loyalty and heroic redemption was set in 1222 on the Wienerberg, where Edeltraut and her children anxiously await the return of their husband and father, the Knight Hermann, who has been captured by the enemies of Christianity while returning from the Crusades. Even though she is from a prosperous household, Edeltraut spins wool in an effort to earn sufficient means to replace a wooden cross marking the new boundary of the city with one of stone, thereby fulfilling a promise she has made to God in order to persuade Him to help her husband. In the meantime the brave *Bürger* of Vienna have recently received a charter from Archduke Leopold, enhancing their liberties, and there is much to celebrate. In the midst of a guild festival, where leading guild masters and their families rejoice in the prosperity of their city, Hermann in the company of his loyal friend Gottfried escapes his captors and returns to his faithful Edeltraut. The play concludes with the blessing of the reunited couple by the Genius of Happiness, who celebrates a world populated by "men of proud, heroic freedom and women of devout and quiet virtue."[53]

Thus the Viennese Christian family was secure against hostile forces; a virtuous, courageous, and industrious wife with her sensible children had been rewarded with the return of her heroic husband and father; the free citizens, proud of their urban freedoms, loyally celebrated their Lord; and, in the end, a vaguely "Christian" good triumphed over evil. The play was, in the words of one reviewer, "a patriotic apotheosis of Austria and the Emperor," but it was also a celebration of the virtues and vitality of a mythic Viennese petty patriciate. Confident in their urban liberties and conscious of their own moral and political identity, these historic characters played out an optimal world for early twentieth-century *bürgerlich* Austrians, a world of secure gender identities in which wives obeyed husbands but also retained important personal and cultural influence and in which established social and familial hierarchies guaranteed that the owners and masters of the city received due respect and reverence from the young and the poor. The poor were not outside of and thus not independent of civil society; they simply resided marginally, respectfully, and quietly within it. An agnostic medievalism steeped in a heavily secularized religious aura thus fashioned an ideal world where even the poor—including those with city annuity policies—might make their way, as long as they did so silently and with respect for their betters.

Lueger closed the celebration by calling the play a "homage to our fatherland Austria" and solemnly promising the Emperor that "even if others are untrue to him, the Viennese will remain loyal. We promise that we will never forget him." Coming on the heels of the great socialist electoral demonstration of November 28, 1905, Lueger's comments were also brave words in a dark night. The whole spectacle was an act of homage to Lueger and to the cultural values of paternalism, social subordination, and political exclusivity that he embodied so well. Since it symbolized baroque paternalism (with Imperial and dynastic overtones) toward clients of imputed moral innocence, Lueger's staff at the Rathaus often exploited the aesthetic motif of devoted children in arranging other political events. The performative "child" gave the party a claim to manipulate and thus overdetermine the future. The Christian Social present thus had no reason to fear for the Christian Social future.

If the *Kinderfest* demonstrated how eighty inexpensive insurance policies could be molded into a theatrical culture of an anti-socialist universe, where the Viennese bourgeoisie demonstrated both its patriotism and its social solidarity, all the while congratulating itself on its fiscal probity and financial conservatism, the Lainz *Versorgungsheim* afforded even more munificent aesthetic opportunities to a party in search of social esteem and material security. The Lainz home was opened in June 1904 amid much pageantry by the municipality, including a pompous, self-serving speech by Lueger in the presence of the Emperor who eight years before had rejected him as unfit for office.[54] Lueger announced that the home was the "pride" of the city, which had built the huge complex in only two years and equipped it with "modern technology." Its existence warranted the "protection of the Highest One" over the settlement, and, appropriately, the city had responded by building a church as the centerpoint of the settlement where the poor "could pursue their Christian duties." Franz Joseph responded to Lueger by noting that now, as in the past, he expressed "My interest and My good wishes on the many policies which the municipal government of My capital city has undertaken to improve the general welfare." The question of which man could more properly claim the proprietary adjective "My" was not settled by the exchange.

Touted as a comprehensive welfare settlement, Lainz was a huge old-people's home cum poorhouse that replaced less adequate facilities elsewhere in the city that were more costly to maintain. In 1907 over 70 percent of its occupants were sixty years old or older, and its mortality rate for the year was an astounding 1,402 persons.[55] Its existence was an excellent testament to the Christian Socials' fiscalism. According to the municipal official who supervised the project, Lainz was needed in order to reduce the city's direct grants to needy individuals which, he argued, could lead to "unjustified claims."[56] The architectural genesis of Lainz reflected the values and economic interests of its sponsors. The project consisted of twenty-nine buildings on a large tract of land near Hietzing, on the southwestern edge of the city. Construction contracts for the project were carefully apportioned among dozens of politically well-connected building contractors and firms and hundreds of Christian Social craft masters. Lueger was justified in bragging about its technology, for not only was Lainz totally electrified, including lighting systems and electric elevators, with the most modern telephonic and signal network anywhere in Vienna, but in addition it had its own light railway for food and freight distribution which connected all the buildings in the complex. Most of these units were institutional facilities for the care of the elderly poor (including a mortuary), but the symbolic centerpiece of the project (and counterpoint to the images of modern technology) was the church, dedicated to St. Charles Borromeo. Built in a neo-Romanesque style, the church's interior decoration was provided by gifts from private donors, most notably the leadership of the Christian Social party. Lueger and his vice-mayors provided stained-glass windows, and the Christian Social district leaders (*Bezirksvorsteher*) contributed the stations of the cross. The city proudly announced that this ornamentation had been paid for by dignitaries who, as members of respectable social circles (*Bürgerkreise*), were known for their civic consciousness. The church had numerous decorations, including a huge triptych behind the main altar in which one observed the remarkable sight of Karl Lueger, dressed "in the old German manner," kneeling before a figure of the Virgin Mary. The poor, sick inhabitants (*Pfleglinge*) would be encouraged to pursue a Christian life, but they must never forget who had paid for this particular Christian charity.[57]

Nor were the trade guilds forgotten. The interior walls of the church were lined with the emblems of the various Christian Social trade guilds—130 in all—representing the old corporate *Bürger* community which now offered private, yet collective, charity to the municipality.[58] Telephones and medieval guilds, electric elevators and Karl Lueger kneeling before the Virgin Mary: the Lainz home captured the improbable alliance of archaism and modernity, history and progress which the Austrian Christian Socials so effectively represented before 1918.

Ventures like Lainz were definitely charity and not social welfare, since the party was both politically and philosophically hostile to spending public monies to subsidize services for able-bodied adults within society, as opposed to gifts to the weak on the fringes. Economic protectionism for the master artisans was a different matter entirely, for this involved legal and political restrictions on behalf of productive and industrious groups who deserved support as economic producers. It was not "something for nothing," which the Christian Socials usually associated with the socialists' programs. When Lueger stirred socialist outrage in October 1904 by calling the workers noisy vagabonds, he meant the noun as much as the adjective.

Christian Social public works projects not only generated (and saved) revenue for the city and enhanced its *bürgerlich* pride (as well as putting the "others" of society in their place); they also evinced the slow reconciliation of the

party with the state bureaucracy. Administrative files on the negotiations over
the organization of the streetcar system and over approval of the large loans
that the city utilized to underwrite the municipalization program (and other
major projects like Lainz) show the increasing cooperation, both technical and
political, that Lueger and Weiskirchner were able to achieve with the various
Cabinets over time. In the negotiations conducted in early 1899 with the Railway Ministry and the Finance Ministry over the terms of the concession which
the city of Vienna, working with the *Bau- und Betriebsgesellschaft* controlled
by the German firm of Siemens and Halske, would receive for constructing
the new electric streetcar system—involving the length of tax exemptions
(whether for 15, 20, or 25 years); their applicability (whether only to the municipality or to Siemens and Halske as well); and their extensiveness (whether
for newly constructed electrified lines only or for the existing tracks with
horse-drawn cars which were to be converted to electricity as well)—the Finance Ministry adopted a tough negotiating stance to wring concessions from
Lueger. Hence the ministerial team which met with Vienna's representatives
on January 20, 1899, offered the city only a 15-year tax exemption, and that
only for the newer lines; and it offered no concessions at all to Siemens and
Halske.[59] Although the Finance Ministry eventually modified its objections,
the fact that the city's negotiators left the first meeting with government negotiators "astounded" at the government's seeming intransigence suggested a spirit
of authoritarian paternalism. Ultimately Lueger got most of what he asked for,
but only at the cost of playing games with Josephist financial administrators.
Indeed, it did not hurt Vienna that the Finance Minister in 1899 was the Young
Czech deputy Josef Kaizl, one of whose staff reminded him that the city of
Prague was also seeking similar concessions.[60]

In the Cabinet's handling of the 1902 loan one saw, however, a new sense
of accommodation to, or at least tolerance for, the municipality's institutional
and fiscal planning. Although he raised questions about the vagueness with
which the actual costs of many of the projected expenditures were estimated
(116 of the 285 million crowns was to go for the street railways, but much of
the rest was for minor projects), Ernest von Koerber recommended Imperial
approval not merely because of the advantages to the population from improved rail service but also because of his expectation that "the profit which
the city expects from the management of the streetcar system will constitute
the most essential factor for service of the interest and amortization of the
total loan."[61]

By 1914 the relationship between the city and the Finance Ministry had
become so accommodating (in light of the economic success of the city utilities) that Mayor Weiskirchner dared to ask for approval of another massive
loan to construct an underground subway system, even though the municipality
had not yet used the full amount of a loan from 1908 and even though the city

refused to state the technical specifications under which the loan would be announced and floated. Weiskirchner simply promised that the terms would be reasonable and that he would request subsequent administrative concurrence from the Finance Ministry about these details as soon as he found it practical to do so. The Cabinet accepted this arrangement and recommended that the loan be sanctioned, an expression of trust that might have been surprising when the party began its municipalization program in 1897.[62]

If Lueger's municipal socialism and his city beautification schemes, together with the city's commitment to modest if arbitrary social services, brought Vienna notability and recognition, the second major front of party activities—the reconstruction of the local franchise—brought permanent Christian Social hegemony in the Viennese polling place. This issue involved the reform of the charter and franchise of 1890. The files in the *Verwaltungsarchiv* and *Landesarchiv* on the construction and final approval of one of the most famous (or, from the socialist point of view, infamous) of Austrian electoral codes suggest that, compared with the electoral geometry and political manipulations pursued by Lueger and his colleagues, the Liberals' efforts in 1890 were naive child's play.

Lueger wanted a new city charter for Vienna in 1899 for several reasons. He had promised during earlier election campaigns that the Christian Socials would abolish the oligarchical *Stadtrat*[63] and restore more power to the City Council as a plenary body, and he felt obliged to make at least a token effort to replace the *Stadtrat* with a more democratic mode of executive decision-making, even though it was apparent throughout the negotiations with the Imperial government that this was one point on which the Emperor would not compromise.[64] More important, four explicitly political considerations arose that made a new statute and its accompanying electoral law both desirable and unavoidable. First, in 1898 a new national income-tax law went into effect. Thousands of men who had previously not been taxed now entered the tax rolls of Vienna and could expect that they would also be registered as voters on the city's electoral rolls. Unfortunately for the Christian Socials, many of these new income-tax voters were relatively prosperous workers or low-ranking white-collar types, some of them Jews, who clearly would not be inclined to vote for anti-Semites. The threat they posed was not dangerous, and their presence would mainly be felt in the traditionally anti-Semitic Third and Second Curias, but the Christian Socials had no desire to incorporate these people into the existing electoral system without building additional safeguards to ensure their future hegemony. In 1899 the party went so far as to threaten, on the basis of legal opinions of sympathetic municipal bureaucrats, to exclude all income-tax voters from the election system, since the original 1890 franchise had made no provision for voters who simply paid a direct income tax.[65] Second, the Council elections of 1898 (for the First Curia) had not brought the party any additional gains beyond those achieved in 1896. It had not lost seats, but it had failed to dislodge the remaining Liberals from traditional bastions of Liberal power, such as the Innere Stadt and the Leopoldstadt. The chance to write a new election code would provide the opportunity to inflate the First Curia with other kinds of wealthy voters, such as high-ranking state officials and middle-level landlords, upon whom the party could depend to bring the First Curia over to them.[66] Third, in the elections of 1895 and 1896 the Christian Socials had been forced to depend on the support of a subset of German nationalist politicians, a number of whom ended up in the anti-Semitic coalition in the City Council. The majority of these politicians settled down into comfortable, mutually opportunistic if not always strictly loyal attitudes toward the new regime, and between 1896 and 1900 they simply became a part of the larger Christian Social *Bürgerklub*. But a few—particularly Michael Gruber and Karl Fochler—remained wild cards whose support could never be taken for granted. Eleven of these politicians had broken with the anti-Liberal coalition in October 1896, and organized their own club in the City Council. In the immediate aftermath of Schönerer's anti-dynastic revanchism and following Lueger's bitter confrontation with Wolf during parliamentary consideration of the financial settlement (*Ausgleich*) with Hungary in November 1897, the mayor found the chance to write a new franchise and manipulate voter registration in the crucial Second Curia, where the bulk of nationalist sentiment was located, as a convenient way to intimidate the more obnoxious German nationalists and eventually drive them from the City Council.[67]

Finally, Lueger had always insisted that once in power the Christian Socials would work toward a more equitable municipal election system, perhaps on a noncurial basis, which would enfranchise the working classes in some way. The old Democrat in Lueger collided here with his own party's self-interest. Lueger knew that the best tactic he could adopt was not actually to give the workers a full share of the communal franchise, but to *appear* to try to give them some finite share. The party's final solution, to create a token Fourth Curia of twenty seats to be elected on a universal, noncurial basis, was a perfect response to this dilemma.

The negotiations between the party and the state bureaucracy were long and tangled but ultimately successful. The party brought into the City Council a first draft of a new statute, prepared by Richard Weiskirchner and Karl Lueger himself, in March 1899 which simply proclaimed universal manhood suffrage in Vienna by abolishing the curial system, but it imposed a five-year residency requirement. This draft was no one's first choice and the Cabinet deemed it to be completely unacceptable.[68] The City Council passed this version, however, sending it to the Lower Austrian Diet for final approval. *Statthalter* Erich Kielmansegg realized that Christian Social leaders wanted him to announce that the government would not accept this draft so that they could then withdraw it, blaming the Cabinet for the perpetuation of the undemocratic franchise. Shrewdly, Kielmansegg refused to issue an official opinion during initial hearings on the bill, although it was clear that he found the proposal extremely unattractive. Opposition quickly emerged within the ranks of the party itself, with Ernst Schneider and others openly negative. Finally, in mid-April the Christian Social majority on the Diet's election reform committee suddenly announced that they were withdrawing their support, allegedly because of government hostility.[69]

The party leadership then constructed a second, revised bill that retained the curial system, based on tax and educational status, but added to it the additional fourth curia with a five-year residency requirement.[70] In addition, Weiskirchner (the author of the second draft) engineered substantial shifts in the makeup of the three existing curias. For example, he shifted middle-sized property owners and higher-ranking state officials from the Second into the First Curia, substantially increasing its size, on the assumption that the party would be more likely to win a solid majority from the middle-ranking landlords (the poorer property owners who were left in the Second Curia) and the gentile civil servants than from the wealthiest segments of the property owners, some of whom still continued to support the Liberals. Men holding the honorary title of *Bürger* in Vienna were now allowed to vote in the Second Curia, giving the party a control device should the state officials left in the Second Curia become unreliable or rebellious. Both Gessmann and Lueger felt that the civil servants, on whom they had based their victories of 1895–96, were less predictable than the property owners and the artisans. As a precaution against possible political turmoil among the master artisans who voted in the Third Curia, however, party leaders also included various categories of servants (*Diener*) and other petty employees in the state, regional, or municipal bureaucracies in that Curia—men theretofore excluded from the franchise but who could easily be manipulated into voting for the party. Over time, this reshuffling of the traditional party-base vote influenced the kinds of strategies used in appealing to the electorate. By 1914, for example, campaign handouts for Third Curia voters in Rudolfsheim were addressed to "our worthy master artisans, employees of our state offices, and private employees in Vienna," who together were "the strongest pillars of our state."[71] No longer could the artisans, the classic protest group of the early 1890s, claim hegemony even in their own electoral curia.[72]

Weiskirchner tried to create a balance of forces within each curia, so that the party could spread its gains (and losses) over a larger number of interest groups and would no longer have to rely exclusively on one large bloc of votes (such as the civil servants in the Second Curia). This did not mean the party was prepared to repudiate its traditional base vote, but it did give Lueger the flexibility to deal more effectively with the demands of various interest groups, listening to all but becoming a hostage to none. The reform was not anti-*Bürger,* but rather pro-party. In a letter to Kielmansegg justifying the revised draft, Lueger implied that at last the city had an electoral system which reflected the social and cultural balance of power in Vienna.[73] The curial system would no longer serve the higher bourgeoisie and the intelligentsia at the expense of the *Kleinbürgertum,* since the center of power would shift to the middle sectors of *Bürger* society, those of commerce and industry and of the civil service and free professions. The workers would receive a limited role in the municipality by means of the twenty seats in the Fourth Curia, which, in Lueger's mind, was what they justly deserved. The new franchise epitomized the Christian Social ideal of Vienna as a bastion of the honest, God-fearing, property-owning *allgemeiner Bürgerstand,* whose members would now dominate all three major curias of the electoral system. The "middling" sectors of the Viennese *Bürgertum* now became the exemplary agents of political action, while the very poor and the very rich were left on the fringes.[74]

This version, which was passed on May 27, 1899 by the Lower Austrian Diet over ardent socialist and Liberal protests (each objecting for different reasons), still maintained the provision that the *Stadtrat* be abolished. It also contained an even more daring challenge to the government in its simple outright denial of any vote (except in the Fourth Curia) to those paying only income tax. It is debatable whether Gessmann and Lueger actually expected to obtain Imperial sanction of law for these provisions, but they were useful bargaining chips in their ensuing negotiations with the government to obtain approval of the rest of the bill, which had already provoked angry Social Democratic demonstrations. Following a series of confidential negotiations in the late fall and winter of 1899–1900 the Diet met in late February 1900 and passed yet another version of the law, retaining the *Stadtrat* and conceding the curial vote to men who paid a direct income tax.[75] In most other respects the party was satisfied with the outcome. Income-tax voters were distributed through the system in a more oligarchical fashion than was used with other taxpayers (the base line for voting in the Third Curia, for example, was set at 8 crowns in trade taxes for master artisans, but at 20 crowns for income-tax voters), and City Council seats were more equitably distributed throughout the city than under the 1890 franchise (the Innere Stadt henceforth had 11 seats, as opposed to 21 in 1890).[76] Weiskirchner later recalled that he had met with Erasmus von Handel, the government's chief negotiator, one fine winter's day to work out the final terms of the compromise bill, while the rest of the party waited for the results in the Diet.[77]

Emperor Franz Joseph sanctioned the legislation in late March 1900 over strident protests by the Liberals and the Social Democrats. Ernest von Koerber's report to the Emperor, in which Koerber recommended that the law be sanctioned, illuminated the motives of the government and of the Emperor in accepting the Christian Social revisions. After reviewing in detail the law's contents and the maneuvers that had preceded the final draft, Koerber admitted that the Cabinet was now handing Vienna over to Lueger and his party, since the new franchise severely handicapped what remained of the Liberal movement in the city and would never allow more than a token presence for radical nationalists or for the Social Democrats. But precisely the latter point was what Koerber found so attractive. In his concluding arguments he implied that political reality in the city now dictated that the state must accept the Christian Socials, for the only conceivable forces capable of displacing them were "social and economic currents whose encouragement could not be reconciled with the goals of a conservative *Staatspolitik,* in so far as the latter have not undergone an essential purification and control." From the Emperor's pencilled notations on the original report, it is clear that he agreed.[78] Koerber did not have to mention that by accommodating Lueger on this legislation he had bought his government the support (or at least tolerance) of the Christian Socials on other significant issues. Following the sanction of the statute the Emperor granted Lueger a personal audience, which the mayor turned into a propaganda coup against both the pan-Germans and the Social Democrats. The Emperor was alleged to have said after the meeting that "there may be much about the behavior of Dr. Lueger that is regrettable, but one thing is undeniable and that is that he thinks in a very patriotic fashion, and that is praiseworthy."[79]

As it was implemented in the municipal elections of 1900, 1902, and 1904 the new franchise gave the Christian Socials all they had expected and more.[80] In 1900, for example, the party swept all contested seats in the Third Curia and took 42 of 46 seats in the Second Curia as well.[81] The new cadres of property owners and state officials who were pushed into the First Curia made it possible for the Christian Socials to conquer 30 of the 46 seats in this curia in 1904, winning all but those in the Innere Stadt, Leopoldstadt, Alsergrund, and Döbling. By 1904 they held 136 of the 158 seats in the City Council. With their overwhelming hegemony in the Second and Third Curias, and with their remarkable success in fighting off the socialists in the Fourth Curia (of the 20 seats contested in the first Fourth Curial election in May 1900, the Christian Socials won 18, the Social Democrats 2), the party now had a virtual stranglehold over the city's politics, to be broken only by the revolutionary events of 1918–19.[82] If political immortality could be measured in votes, Karl Lueger could now rest assured of his place in the pantheon of Austrian politics.

A third feature of Lueger's municipal revolution complemented the first two—the moral and political appropriation of the communal and provincial bureaucracies by the Christian Socials and the effect this had on the municipal officials and the party. Recent work on the relationship of the Nazi movement to the German state system and civil service by such scholars as Jane Caplan, Dan P. Silverman, Tim Mason, and Martin Broszat has considered the extent to which a mass bourgeois movement, intent on imposing an essentially anti-legal normative framework (nationalist anti-Semitism on a racial basis) in German society and using violence and discretionary terror to implement its policies, dominated and yet paradoxically left intact much of the traditional German civil state.[83] Top Christian Social leaders like Lueger, Weiskirchner, and Gessmann were not racial anti-Semites, nor were they committed to the theory or practice of political violence. To compare occasional street-fighting around Viennese polling places with pogroms is to misunderstand completely the milieu of late nineteenth-century electoral politics in Vienna.[84] Counterfactual arguments to the effect that if the Imperial government had not been present, the Christian Social party would have plundered the Viennese Jewish community administratively and politically are ultimately unconvincing, even if offered with a strong moralizing voice. If there is an imagined continuity between pre-1914 Vienna and interwar politics, the line would run from Lueger to Dollfuss, not to Hitler, and even *that* presumed linkage is riddled with many contradictions.[85] Karl Lueger was a firm, if passive, adherent of the nineteenth-century concept of rule of law and never seriously tried to deprive the Viennese Jewish community of its civil rights.[86] Even without the protective cover of the Austrian Imperial state, it is doubtful whether Lueger himself would have wished to repudiate Jewish constitutional or economic rights as guaranteed in the legislation of 1867. At the same time Lueger was unreasonably, even paranoically sensitive to criticism from a newspaper community staffed largely by liberal Jews, and he was capable of expressing feelings of revulsion against the behavior of eastern, oriental Jews (feelings which were shared by many assimilated Viennese Jews as well).[87] Lueger's own public anti-Semitic rhetoric was crude, insulting, and quite often heartless, and its emotional effects could certainly be used by others, even within his party, for more nefarious purposes. Nor should we doubt that among many of the rank and file of the party hatred of Jews as ethnic as well as political "others" did in fact obtain, just as the latent anti-Semitism among many Social Democratic (and gentile Liberal) voters was a fact of which all competing political parties in Vienna were fully aware.[88] Indeed, as Anton Pelinka has pointed out, professed hatred of Jews was perhaps most intense and extreme among the small "left" within the Christian Social party, led by Leopold Kunschak.[89] But for Lueger and most of the top leadership of the party, public Jew-baiting was a preeminently political act. That this was a dreadful practice, that it imposed psychological burdens on innocent people far in excess of the needs of competitive politics, and that it set models for future politicians who might have a stronger bent toward literalism and far less common sense or flexibility than Lueger and his generation of ward politicians, is a burden that Austrian Christian Socialism shall forever have to bear.[90]

Even discounting his own assimilationist cravings, Arthur Schnitzler thus was probably correct when he insisted of Lueger that "at heart, even at the height of his popularity, he was no more anti-Semitic than he had been in the days when he had played tarot at the home of Dr. Ferdinand Mandl, with his brother Ignatz and other Jews."[91] Testifying at a libel trial in 1912 Alois Heilinger, a Christian Social municipal official close to Albert Gessmann who later ran afoul of the machine and who managed to survive the electoral debacle of June 1911, responded to the following question from the Christian Social attorney Heinrich Mataja about Lueger's views of Jewish civil rights:

> *Mataja*   in your [party's] political program is a requirement that the so-called constitutionally guaranteed equality will be protected, which you as a civil servant pledged to respect under all circumstances. Do you find a contradiction between this guarantee of equality and the anti-Semitic program of Lueger?

> *Heilinger*   The party has many different shades of opinion. [Ernst] Schneider, for example, has totally different views than I and Vice-Mayor Hierhammer. The differences within the party are so great that I myself would have to ask you what your views are . . .

> [Mataja repeated his question about Lueger]

> Dr. Lueger was not all that anti-Semitically inclined. He was a man who was for general social harmony. I never observed a personal act of hatred against the Jews on his part. On the contrary I observed in parliament that he frequently associated with Jews. I saw very little in the way of practical anti-Semitism on Lueger's part. To be sure, I saw that he was opposed to the domination of the Jews, but then we all are.

> *Mataja*   What was the nature of his political and programmatic anti-Semitism?

> *Heilinger*   I repeat, Lueger was really not an anti-Semite. He often associated with the enemies, not in a hate-ridden manner, like perhaps Schneider, but from the standpoint of equality. How often did I discuss this issue with him! . . . In so far as the [party] program is concerned, that is something else. Facts are in the end decisive, not words.[92]

Heilinger did not offer these comments to defend Lueger's reputation—indeed, such comments might have impugned the late mayor in some party circles—but rather to suggest Lueger's ability to sustain endless disjunctions between words and deeds, between object-oriented rhetoric and subject-oriented practice. Words governed the public world, and generated and authenticated the political power necessary to control. Deeds belonged to the private world, constructed out of endless individual transactions.

Yet in spite of Heilinger's insistence that Lueger did not wish to harm the Jews, we know that the politicians on the Christian Social *Stadtrat* both practiced and tolerated economic discrimination against Jews (especially in public contract awards) and that they employed an overt policy of occupational discrimination against Jews in the municipal and provincial civil services. Why was this the case and what purpose did it serve, aside from reserving job contracts and opening up administrative positions to trusted political clients of the party? Equally important, to what extent did the party preserve the administrative rationality and lawfulness of the civil bureaucracy, a bureaucracy which had been established and staffed by Liberal politicians for whom the party had no special sympathy?

The civil bureaucracy that Karl Lueger inherited in Vienna consisted of over two thousand civil servants in the city administration itself, plus hundreds of other job positions in city-controlled enterprises (a sector which was to expand drastically under Christian Social rule).[93] With the growth of municipal socialist projects, Lueger controlled, directly or indirectly, over 30,000 full-time positions (including worker and servant categories), and thus, next to the state, he was the single largest employer in the Monarchy. From the massive body of employment records of the *Magistrat* preserved in the *Stadtarchiv* it is evident that Lueger conducted no large-scale purge of the city service after taking power. By and large the internal rationality and job organization of the municipal service were left untouched, although various reforms were undertaken to improve task allocation and efficiency and to achieve a more equitable system of promotion and salaries.[94] Promotions within the *Magistrat* continued to be decided by the senior administrative officials meeting in collegial assembly (*Magistrats-Gremium*) and were usually approved by the *Stadtrat* and Lueger with few revisions. Political directives were rarely issued (at least in writing) to city administrative offices, except in cases where the bureaucracy knowingly and willfully overstepped what the party felt to be the line between policy development and policy implementation. In 1907, for example, the *Stadtrat,* composed of twenty-seven of the most powerful Christian Social city councilmen, sent the *Magistratsdirektor* (Richard Weiskirchner) a directive charging that certain offices had been disregarding public contract decisions approved by the *Stadtrat* and had been issuing contracts to firms of their own selection. The memorandum reminded the *Magistrat* that the awarding of public works contracts was a prerogative of the *Stadtrat;* the role of the *Magistrat* was simply to implement its instructions in an orderly fashion.[95] Given the party's intimate relationships with local merchants and manufacturers who received contracts and who in turn could be expected (if not actually forced) to contribute to the party's campaign funds, the *Stadtrat*'s sensitivity was hardly surprising.[96] When the *Magistrat* behaved autocratically toward workers employed by the city, however, just as it had in the Liberal era, the *Stadtrat* found less reason to complain. The social values motivating older officials and newer spoilsmen were far closer than many had assumed.[97] Leopold Kunschak's newspaper noted this when it complained in 1900 that the *Magistrat* "is still operating far too much in the routines of the old Liberal politics. It finds itself unable to accept the fresh, social spirit that is now moving through the municipal administration, and so constitutes a very serious obstacle to any reform that would be favorable to the workers."[98]

For the bourgeois politicians on the *Stadtrat,* of course, this situation was optimal. Since many of them distrusted Kunschak and his movement, their willingness to keep former Liberal officials in office is even more understandable.[99] In social values little stood between the old officials and the new rulers. Indeed, the technological innovations that the Christian Socials achieved in their municipal socialist enterprises would have been impossible without the enthusiastic cooperation of former Liberal officials, who took pride in their work and were genuinely excited over the possibility of launching dramatic enterprises which would enhance their professional bureaucratic standing still further. In Vienna, as in larger German cities, the explosion in numbers of professional salaried positions that resulted from the new municipal social services was accompanied by an enhanced professional consciousness on the part of municipal officials, which the Christian Socials had no reason to view as dangerous to their political interests.[100]

For most of the rule of the Christian Socials up to 1918 the senior councillors (*Magistratsräte*) in the city service were persons who had actually begun their careers before 1896. Virtually all of the top officials in the city administration during Lueger's tenure were thus men who were first appointed by and in many cases who had received important promotions under the Liberal regime. Yet the record suggests that they not only served Lueger loyally and responsibly but did so with discretion and even genuine enthusiasm as well. In view of the fact that they enjoyed job tenure (although no guarantee of further promotion) one may well ask how the party obtained their loyalty as swiftly and as easily as it actually did.

One perversely ironic factor in this process was Christian Social anti-Semitism, used both as a form of coercive disciplining and political co-option. The number of Jews (defined by religious affiliation) employed in the city government in 1896–97 was quite small. Perhaps two dozen or so were spread throughout the higher *Magistrat,* with even fewer in the subordinate clerical office positions.[101] Beginning with the promotion lists of 1897, Jewish civil servants began to be excluded from further professional advancement by the *Stadtrat.* When challenged in June 1901 by a Liberal city councilman, Alfred

Mittler, Lueger implicitly acknowledged the policy's existence but excused himself with the plea that he was not all-powerful and that his associates on the *Stadtrat* were ultimately responsible for municipal employment and promotion decisions.[102] Ferdinand Klebinder, a Liberal councilman who was also a member of the Jewish community, admitted in December 1908 that Lueger had tried to intervene on behalf of some of these officials, apparently against the wishes of his colleagues.[103] But whether or not Lueger or his more vociferous cronies on the *Stadtrat* were to blame for blocking the careers of some Jews, the actual process of discrimination presumed the co-option of non-Jewish officials. Indeed, party leaders must have either forced or "encouraged" the senior Liberal-appointed councillors in the screening committee to undertake the exclusion of Jewish candidates for promotion, since the names of Jewish officials were sometimes eliminated from the lists before the final recommendations were presented to the *Stadtrat*. Whether the councillors acted from passive acquiescence or active belief is difficult to determine.[104]

Aside from fulfilling an old Christian Social campaign promise about driving the Jews from the city service and thus opening up employment opportunities for newer officials who might be loyal to the new regime, the *Stadtrat* used these measures as a clever way both to discipline and to co-opt the rest of the city bureaucracy. Discrimination against Jews was both a political tactic and a control device that demonstrated to the rest of the service just how far the party was prepared to go—and how manipulable the senior councillors were—if political conformity was not demonstrated by party members. Nor was it accidental that in the midst of the *Stadtrat*'s anti-Jewish policy Lueger was also issuing warnings to dissident Christian civil servants who were complaining about salaries and work conditions.[105] Having used the civil servant issue against Mayor Prix and the Liberals, the Christian Socials knew exactly how far they were prepared to tolerate similar tactics against themselves. Lueger made it clear that he would reward the communal officials with benefits and salaries more generous than those received by their state counterparts, but he would also crush any dissidence if they refused to maintain political discipline. Jewish municipal officials were a convenient political liability; they suffered not because Lueger wanted to persecute them as individuals, but because in punishing them for what by Christian Social political logic they could not help but be—Liberals—the *Stadtrat* sent a forceful signal to their gentile colleagues. In a private interview with the Jewish musicologist Guido Adler in 1909, Lueger seemed to regret that his party had stymied these officials' careers, although he reported that they left municipal service with generous settlements.[106] The case of Ludwig Klaar, a Jewish physician who eventually did find patrons and was appointed to a senior municipal post after Lueger's death, showed that exceptions might be made, but only at psychic cost and humiliation to the candidate.[107]

The party's policy on the (non) promotion of Jewish officials should be seen in the context of a purposeful and public attempt to use administrative procedures for partisan advantage. Earlier Liberal practice also expected ideological cohesion and personal patronage in allocating appointments, so that screams of outrage from the surviving Liberal councilmen after 1897 encountered accusations of blatant hypocrisy by Lueger's forces.[108] But the Christian Socials took Liberal practice out of the shadows of private informality into the indiscreet glare of the public realm. When challenged about the political implications of appointments and contract decisions taken by the *Stadtrat,* the Christian Social spokesman for education, Leopold Tomola, made no bones about whose interests he represented:

> In regard to my position on the *Stadtrat,* I must emphasize that neither my voters nor the Christian Social party appointed me to the *Stadtrat,* in order to represent the views of Herr Jordan [a dissident Liberal teacher]. Rather, I was sent to the *Stadtrat* to work for the interests of the Christian Social party, who elected me. Yes, gentlemen, can you imagine for a moment that a party strives to attain power, in order to implement the principles of the party it has just defeated? That happens nowhere in the world, and you [Liberals] did so the least of all.[109]

The Christian Socials used explicit political criteria for appointments to the city service, and their public denials of that fact were contradicted in their own private deliberations. For example, in 1917, when the party faced the need to broaden the responsibility for wartime governance and voted to appoint two Liberal councilmen to the *Stadtrat* (one of whom, Oskar Hein, was a Jew), thus ending the comfortable regime of silence under which the Christian Socials could engineer their appointment discussions, Tomola had to warn his colleagues that, since the opposition now had a voice and a vote in such matters, "it will no longer be possible, as was done previously, to use exclusively party-oriented criteria in making appointment and promotion decisions. Rather, one must now also take time-in-service and the qualifications of the applicant into consideration."[110]

Hence, under Lueger's regime new appointees normally had to show personal sponsorship from a party notable or sympathizer to obtain a job. This was true for most entry-level positions, from lowly office servant to university graduates with law degrees seeking policy-making positions in the higher service. Eventually the city even developed a cover sheet for job applicants with a blank for the name or names of the person's sponsors. Usually these were party politicians, but on occasion wealthy party contributors from the business world or members of the aristocracy also served the role. Often more than one sponsor helped, as in the case of the energetic Julius Hofbauer, who not only had his father write a letter (the father was a senior teacher in the municipal schools) but also got a recommendation from Princess Fanny Liechtenstein and, in addition, managed to get supporting signatures from three Christian Social politicians on the *Stadtrat.* Needless to say, he got a job. Nor were paternal pride and influence absent in the hiring process, as in the case of Friedrich Haimböck, whose father Johann Haimböck (who held the title of "kaiserlicher Rat") managed to arrange a personal interview with Lueger to lobby for a city job for his son.[111] Although political sponsorship does not seem to have been made retroactive, especially for promotions of older civil servants to the more senior positions (where the *Stadtrat* generally used the individual's performance and time in service, rather than political considerations), the existence of such sponsorship could not have been lost on the older officials.[112] Nor could they have ignored the unduly high rate of nepotistic appointments, which offered the oppositional press targets for exposés, especially when the son or nephew or brother ended with his hand in the public till.[113] Not all petitioners got what they hoped for, however, as Franz Preinerstorfer learned after asking Richard Weiskirchner and Heinrich Schmid to waive the age limit for new city employees so that he could leave his job as a coal dealer and join the city electrical works. To insure that his request would be granted, Preinerstorfer even contributed 50 crowns to the Christian Socials' election chest. However, to his dismay the age limit was not lifted and he received a refund of his money.[114]

On rare occasions Lueger also allowed promotions of younger men out of sequence to higher positions or titles to demonstrate the value the party accorded to administrative and political competence. The most notable of such cases was that of Richard Weiskirchner, promoted over older officials to *Magistratsdirektor* in 1903, but others might be cited as well (such as Karl Pawelka, who directed Section XIX in the *Magistrat,* where municipal and state elections were supervised—a very sensitive post indeed).[115] Such promotions, though certainly not the rule, highlighted the practical rewards available for political cooperation. Files in the Party Archive for the 1905–6 universal suffrage bill reveal that Gessmann and Weiskirchner relied on various senior councillors from the *Magistrat* for policy papers and practical advice during the discussions with the Cabinet, even though such work may have had little or nothing to do with the "regular" duties of these bureaucrats.[116] In view of the fact that such men were competent administrators and, in many instances, trained jurists, the Christian Socials would have been foolish not to exploit their talents. On the more practical level of ward politics, party officials used the resources of ward administrative offices for partisan purposes, especially around election time.[117] Nor were officials in the Rathaus immune from party blandishments. In 1911, for example, the vice-director of the municipal office responsible for assembling voter lists was Karl Bader, a former assistant in Robert Pattai's law firm. Was it accidental that Bader had this particular job?[118]

Given the cultural conservatism and anti-Marxism of the Christian Socials and the ambitious scale of their municipal socialist schemes, which for local officials must have been very flattering (many of whom now found themselves occupying administrative positions of enhanced power and authority), it was hardly surprising that many civil servants simply decided to support the new regime in the city for sound personal *and* ideological reasons. The Nazi case is, thus, different from the Viennese, both in procedure and in ethos. Far more legal and moral continuity existed between the Liberals and Christian Socials than between Brüning and Hitler. Rather than using the public service to commit extra-legal acts, the Christian Socials used it to create a new municipal socialist haven. The party did discriminate against Jewish officials, but rather than dismissing them (and then murdering them), it nudged them into retirement. Aside from this truly disgraceful policy (about which Lueger seemed embarrassed at the end of his career), the normative and legal assumptions of the city bureaucracy established during the Liberal era remained generally unchanged. From the majority of municipal civil servants the party asked only for passive cooperation, and generally received it. The minority of communal officials who did become "political," especially those working on election matters, did so voluntarily and, no doubt, received appropriate rewards.

Another motive explains the collusion between the party and the bureaucracy. The files of the *Magistratsdirektion* contain fascinating memoranda from 1905 on the reaction of the higher officials in the *Magistrat* to Ernest von Koerber's critique of local government in the Monarchy, which was part of the Minister-President's general critique of the Austrian administrative system published in December 1904. In his *Studien* Koerber argued that local administrative elites, particularly in the statutory cities like Vienna, frequently manifested a "lack of objectivity" in their duties, since they had become politicized by contact with local political elites. Koerber proposed broad changes in the division of administrative labor that would have restricted the activities of the *Magistrat* in some areas and subjected it to closer state supervision in others.[119] Concerned senior officials in the *Magistrat* drafted commentaries and sent them to Richard Weiskirchner, denying the validity or accuracy of many of Koerber's criticisms and suggesting ominous consequences for Austrian local and regional administration if his plans were implemented.[120] Josef Harbich argued that if the reforms were instituted "the organization of the *Magistrat,* developed over time, meeting the sundry needs of the population and divided into various areas of administrative activity, would almost be made superfluous." Against Koerber's cost-benefit analysis that the Imperial civil service was over twice as effective as the *Magistrat,* measured by crowns spent per capita

on administrators' salaries, Harbich invoked the civic generosity and farsight-
edness of the municipal political authorities, in this case the Christian Social
party: "the city of Vienna has spared no effort to fulfill its lawful administrative
responsibilities by the creation of objective institutions and the recruitment of
a body of civil servants who in every respect meet their responsibilities in an
exemplary fashion."[121] Wilhelm Hecke, while acknowledging that Koerber was
correct in some of his criticisms, denied their applicability to the city of Vienna
and insisted that the general impulse behind the *Studien* was an admiration for
Prussian centralization, which had often misled Austrian policymakers in the
past: "Prussian laws have often brought forth envy on the part of our government and led us to imitation in instances where the preconditions and the disposition of our people have not provided a fruitful basis for the state to proceed. This accounts for the fact that some of our laws have not taken hold in
reality and lead a fictitious existence."[122] Also noteworthy were the more practical comments of Heinrich Demel, who argued that the government could do
whatever it wanted to the smaller towns but had better leave Vienna alone, thus
manifesting the proper Christian Social spirit: "I do not believe that we should
break our heads to protect the others. What do we care about the rural communes [*Landgemeinden*]? We only have to protect our own political turf."
Rather than reduce municipal prerogatives, Demel wanted to push for more
autonomy: city authorities should be given control over the police force in
Vienna.[123]

Transactions such as the *Studien* affair provided the elite-level politicians in
the Christian Social party with happy opportunities to play the role of sympathetic bystanders, assuring municipal officials that the party would protect their
interests from harmful changes in the structural relationship between state and
local government. But such episodes also reminded the higher communal bureaucrats in Vienna just how closely their fortunes as a special interest group
had become linked to those of the Christian Socials. One official, Wenzel Kienast, confirmed the symbiosis of prestige and position operative between the
party and the municipal bureaucracy by 1905 when he justified the *Magistrat*
by citing the achievements of Lueger's various social and economic programs.
Kienast also predicted that Koerber's reforms would mean "without doubt the
abolition of autonomy in its current sense and the absorption of policy agendas
by offices of the state," which in turn would diminish local political prerogatives and provoke "the most decisive opposition in the autonomous political
bodies."[124] If the Imperial Cabinet reduced the prerogatives of municipal administration as a way of "de-politicizing" urban politics, not only would the
Christian Social party lose power, but in addition the professional officials in
the *Magistrat* would experience an even greater humiliation.[125]

Finally, the issue of reciprocal enrichment—political loyalty in return for
salary increases—clearly played an enormous role in influencing many civil

servants. In 1898 the City Council reorganized the City Building Office (*Stadt-bauamt*), increasing the number of salaried officials attached to it. On December 21, 1898, Lueger held an "Eideserinnerung" in the chambers of the City Council, in the presence of many local politicians, for officials of the office who had been promoted as a result of the new arrangement. He reminded them that "[t]he civil service of the city of Vienna has always held it to be its duty to do justice to the interests of the city. And it is a consequence of their corresponding gratitude when the City Council sees it as its duty to improve the [salary] situation of the municipal officials."[126] Masked only slightly by this formalistic rhetoric was a clear political covenant—if the officials would support the Christian Social "city," they might expect appropriate material considerations in return. And the party took seriously its side of the bargain, for the various categories of municipal officials did receive a series of advantageous salary and retirement benefits, as well as a new promotion system more progressive than that operative in the state service, between 1898 and 1907.[127] At a time when state-level officials were aggressively pressing collective demands, the professional club of Viennese municipal officials, the *Verein der Beamten der Stadt Wien,* which had a membership by 1908 of almost 1,800 men, enjoyed a comfortable relationship with city authorities. It was often able to obtain approval of its requests and petitions, so that the few rebels who did try to push it into confrontations with party officials failed.[128]

The support that the ex-Liberal municipal bureaucracy gave to the party was vital, for Christian Social management of Vienna between 1897 and 1918 was, by any reasonable and fair account, efficient and responsible. In his authoritarian and patriarchal manner Lueger referred to the municipal civil servants as "his officials," and they did not fail him.[129] Vienna under Lueger and his successor, Richard Weiskirchner, enjoyed a city government that was technically progressive and reasonably successful in those areas of public policy in which it chose to venture. Although it was marred by many episodes of minor corruption, Christian Social rule did succeed in bringing the technical management of the city on a par with that of similar large cities in the German *Reich.* Even political opponents of the party admitted, if only grudgingly, that the technical implementation of policy in the city was sound, however much they might decry the specific content of such policy—or, in the case of the socialists— the lack of policy in social areas such as housing reform and child welfare.[130]

With the accommodation between (and, in some cases the integration of) bureaucracy and party, the structure of the local party apparatus in Vienna also became more complex. Service in one of the *Magistrat*'s district offices (*Bezirksämter*)—where civil servants inevitably worked in close proximity to and in cooperation with the local Christian Social district leader (*Bezirksvorsteher*), who was both an administrative official of city government and usually a senior party leader of the Christian Social district political organization[131]—

meant that local communal officials came into contact with the exigencies of ward politics. But the informal merger of tasks and interests between party and bureaucracy on both the ward and city levels also meant a shift in power away from the various Christian Social or anti-Semitic clubs and into the hands of the district leader and his party cronies on the local election committee. Lueger preferred to use the leaders of the twenty districts that the party controlled (Leopoldstadt remained in Liberal hands) as his principal contacts with local subelites, rather than dealing on an individual basis with each of the dozens of clubs and associations in the city. Gradually these men became little czars, with enormous influence and patronage. Only the power of the men who sat on the *Stadtrat* rivaled theirs.[132]

Not until after 1907 did the party actually begin to develop a formal party bureaucracy. Lueger distrusted such an apparatus as a threat to his own power, even though Albert Gessmann recruited an informal staff of party organizers from the communal and provincial bureaucracies to help the party on a part-time basis. Lueger's personal reaction to a possible party bureaucracy was the view that *"I am the organization."*[133] But Lueger's prerogatives were not the only reason for the lag in developing an internal apparatus. With effective staff support from the *Magistrat,* many party leaders felt no need for an independent cadre of bureaucrats. On the ward level the local bosses found in the district committee (*Bezirksvertretung*) and the district office (*Bezirksamt*) powerful resources for election mobilization and spoils. Thus, as late as Lueger's death in 1910 the party's fortune continued to hinge on the personal organizing abilities of the various district leaders and their cronies. So informal were procedures that after Lueger's demise party officials found it difficult to lay their hands on a copy of the original charter of the Christian Social *Bürgerklub.*[134]

The structure of the party elite also became more complex over time as new men made their way into the Council, the Lower Austrian Diet, and the central parliament and as more interest groups became affiliated with the Christian Social coalition. The tripartite scheme of the party elites as it existed in the early 1890s was modified in several ways. The sheer number of men involved in party life once the Christian Socials won Vienna was much greater, especially on the tertiary, subelite level. Within the various offices of urban and regional government prominent party members began to establish networks of personal influence apart from Lueger (such as Julius Prochazka, who took charge of the city employment bureau; and Leopold Steiner, who ran the provincial poor-care system), so that the "horizontal" structure of the party elites before 1896 was supplemented and modified (although never replaced) by a second, more fragmented "vertical" network of patronage and clientage relations after 1897. The district leaders and the members of the *Stadtrat,* who held salaried positions in city government but spent much of their time making what could only be conceived of as "political" decisions, assumed positions of prominence in the secondary, city-level elite—because of their egregious role in contract distribution. That the majority of both groups came from the "independent," propertied, commercial, and free professional sectors, rather than from the ranks of white-collar or service employees both explained (and reflected) the conservative, property-oriented attitudes of the party leadership after 1900.[135] Gradually a system of informal party representation evolved through the district election committees chaired by the district leader, to which each Christian Social, Catholic, or anti-Semitic club sent delegates. By 1907 these committees were somewhat larger than they had been in the *Kampfzeit* of the early 1890s, with more diverse interests demanding recognition by the Rathaus. More clubs and affiliated societies had joined the party after its successes in 1896–97, creating new rivalries in each district. The party also had to cope with the presence of semi-independent organizations, like Leopold Kunschak's Catholic Labor movement and Josef Stöckler's Lower Austrian *Bauernbund,* whose views about patronage and social action did not fit easily into the older Vienna-based paradigm. Indeed, in the *Bauernbund* the party faced an organization that was almost a party unto itself and that after 1908 formed the basis of the Christian Social movement in rural Lower Austria.

Over this complex network of spoils, patronage, and political machination stood Karl Lueger. Extremely jealous of his primacy, Lueger dealt with sundry cronies on specific policy issues but retained the moral authority of the city's premier *Herr im Haus.* Lueger was a superb political showman who was also (at least up to 1906) far more accessible to his constituents than previous mayors had been—the chronicle of weddings and funerals that he attended, the confirmation ceremonies that he sponsored, the schools and churches that he dedicated, the social and philanthropic events that he hosted would have made even a sturdy Irish-American political boss blanch.[136] Yet it was precisely because Lueger crafted such a forceful public personality and because he enjoyed such widespread public sympathy (even among some working-class circles) that he was able by the force of that personality to impose discipline, while relying on others for the day-to-day management of party business and for campaign mobilization at election time.

The role of principal second in the machine fell to Albert Gessmann, the tactician of the movement since the 1880s. Gessmann was for long Lueger's loyal second-in-command, and his political career bore many of the same marks that his patron's did. Coming from a modest *bürgerlich* family in the Neubau in Vienna (his father was a mid-level civil servant in the defense ministry), Gessmann attended the university, where he studied history and geology. Among his most influential teachers was Eduard Suess, the noted geologist who was also active in national Liberal politics.[137] Like Lueger, Gessmann broke into municipal politics as a young liberal democrat, but he joined Lueger's anti-Semitic, anti-liberal fronde in the early 1880s. A man of some literary and journalistic abilities—he served as a staff member of the university library until 1906 and became co-owner of the *Reichspost*—Gessmann deliberately avoided becoming entrapped in the municipal bureaucracy after 1897, even forgoing appointment to the *Stadtrat*. Rather, he exploited the dominance that the Christian Socials now exercised in the Lower Austrian Diet[138] and used his position on the Provincial Executive Committee (*Landesausschuss*) of Lower Austria after 1896 to create a semi-independent realm of political authority.[139] The last decades of the Hapsburg Empire saw a revolutionary (and highly controversial) expansion of the role of the Crownlands in the state's political system, as the autonomous provincial governments expanded their activities in funding the public school system, in furthering agricultural and industrial development, and in providing health and welfare services, all policy areas that were eminently amenable to political patronage and political networking.[140] The German constitutional theorist Georg Jellinek went so far as to call the Austrian Crownlands "state-like fragments," in view of their semi-sovereign pretensions and capacities.[141] So powerful was this decentralizing trend that both the Imperial civil service and the Army High Command would use the temporary collapse of politics in the first years of the First World War to try (unsuccessfully) to reduce the operative scope of provincial and municipal autonomy. Given the increasing policy responsibilities and financial influence of the Crownlands (which, to some experts, meant a dangerous erosion of the authority of the central state itself), Gessmann's decision to concentrate on provincial politics proved of enormous importance for the future of the Christian Social movement.[142] Although each of the six deputies on the Committee had a specific portfolio of administrative responsibility, Gessmann quickly expanded his particular area—the public school system—into one of the most politically powerful. Moreover, following a major staff reorganization of the Committee in 1902 Gessmann functioned as de facto executive director, since he had now gained control over all personnel and staff matters; the Committee's staff director, Dr. Heinrich Misera, reported directly to him.[143] Long before his crony Prince Alois Liechtenstein succeeded Abbot Frigdian Schmolk as *Landmarschall* in 1906, Gessmann effectively controlled the Lower Austrian provincial government.[144]

Although Lueger regularly consulted other notables on selected policies, Gessmann was the only other leader who had a sense of the whole panorama of party operations. Lueger's fate and that of Gessmann were inextricably intertwined. Lueger could not have won or sustained power without the tactical genius of Gessmann, yet Gessmann's views of the party's future ran in rather different directions from those envisioned by Lueger. Because of the absence of detailed party records before 1907 it is difficult to chart the exact formation of factions on the issue of parliamentarization based on an expansion of the party beyond Vienna. Clearly Gessmann was one of the major Christian Social politicians moving in this direction, going beyond the more cautious and municipally oriented Lueger to argue that the party must involve itself in state-level, ministerial politics as a mediating agent for bourgeois nationality conflicts and as the core of a defensive bloc against Austrian Social Democracy, and that to do so it must expand its base in the vast rural hinterland.[145] As early as January 1901 Gessmann's paper, the *Reichspost,* had called for the development of "a unified Imperial organization [*Reichsorganisation*] for the Christian Social party" that would span all the provinces with a central administrative executive based in Vienna. Gessmann's introduction of a Christian Social press service for local newspapers in all of the German-speaking Crownlands under Friedrich Funder's management was a humble first step in this direction.[146] Even if this rhetoric reflected the anxieties over the results of the 1901 parliamentary elections in Vienna, the desire to move beyond the capital was to prove a fateful turning point in the history of the Christian Social movement.

Gessmann had long had an interest in organizing the Lower Austrian peasantry, and even before 1896 he had spent part of his summer vacations touring rural villages in order to give political speeches at rallies sponsored by local Catholic political notables.[147] After 1896 Gessmann's power in the Lower Austrian school system gave him a wide network of rural political contacts and many opportunities to favor party clients in the staffing of school positions. Inevitably these experiences gave Gessmann a different perspective on the future of the party from that of Lueger. Contacts with Catholic-oriented, Lower Austrian political notables easily translated into contacts with similar groups in the Alpine lands. Not surprisingly, as early as 1904 Gessmann was involved in negotiations with various leaders of the Alpine-Catholic conservatives about the possibility of merging the two political blocs into one large German-Christian "peoples' party" (*Volkspartei*).[148] Although nothing came of these discussions in the short run, they were to have momentous consequences after 1906.

Christian Socialism and the Breakdown of the National Political System, 1897–1905

The preceding section discussed the process by which Lueger and his colleagues successfully charted the consolidation of the party's municipal power by 1905. Unfortunately for the Christian Socials, however, not all of their problems could be resolved by intimidating municipal officials or rewriting electoral codes. Two important cultural-political rivalries intervened after 1897 to confront the party with some fateful decisions. These were Georg von Schönerer's *Los von Rom* movement and Victor Adler's Austrian Social Democracy. Both were state-level political crusades, but both had important consequences for Viennese politics. If political Liberalism was effectively subdued in Vienna after the 1900 franchise, the Christian Socials could hardly rest on their laurels, for they now faced, in place of the Liberals, potent challenges from Schönerian cultic radicalism and Social Democratic electoral aggression.

The socialist and pan-German attacks on Christian Socialism in Vienna occurred under the aegis of a national political system that proved itself woefully inadequate, especially for a bourgeois, social-interest party like the Christian Socials wanting "bread and butter" social and economic legislation for the Austrian *Mittelstand*. The polarization of state parliamentary politics in Austria wrought by the Badeni crisis of 1897, which was not settled until after 1900 and then only on temporary and unstable terms, engendered a poisonous atmosphere of strident nationalism which the Christian Socials found disconcerting. Indeed, for the Christian Socials state and local politics seemed to be running in opposite directions after 1897. Lueger gained strength in Vienna, but his modest parliamentary delegation (26 deputies in 1898 in a House with 425 members) found itself adrift on a sea of acrimony and suspicion, too big to be ignored but far too small to make any difference in resolving ethnic hatreds. In an unpublished section of his private diaries, Joseph Baernreither described the obvious embarrassment of the Christian Social delegation in parliament in 1897 during the anti-Badeni protests staged by various German national groups. Baernreither took an almost sadistic joy in seeing the Christian Socials "squirm" over the issue of obstructing parliament. They did not want to betray their German-speaking colleagues, but at the same time they desperately wanted to preserve a working parliamentary system.[149] Baernreither's *Schadenfreude* was indeed Lueger's misfortune, for one of the few real political beliefs that Karl Lueger held throughout his life was a conviction that the Austrian parliament had to function in regular and predictable modes, not only to protect the "people" against the state but also to protect the state against the "people." Parliament, as an institution of interest articulation and political compromise, was the one viable mediator between violent social conflict on one side and bureaucratic authoritarianism on the other. Lueger viewed the parliament as a co-equal partner with the civil service in managing the Austrian political system. He worried less about the actual parliamentarization of the civil service and more about preserving the integrity of parliament as a consultative, policy-approving body that would set out the boundaries of action for the civil service on a broad range of social and economic agendas. Article-14 governments were bound to be seen as tyrannical and retrograde, not only because of their arbitrary nature but also because of their inevitably restricted purview. It was in both the government's and the parties' best interest, therefore, to preserve a functioning parliament, and one that would concentrate on social and economic reforms.[150]

Lueger did agree, after considerable pressure from more nationalist-minded colleagues (especially Ambros Opitz, the fiery, north-Bohemian German cleric who edited the *Reichspost* until 1903), to take the party into the opposition against Badeni's pro-Czech speech ordinances.[151] Lueger loyally signed and consistently supported the so-called Whitsun Program of the German bourgeois parties in May 1899.[152] He did this neither with enthusiasm nor with doctrinaire intent, as the German *bürgerlich* groups in Bohemia and Moravia claimed to do, but in an effort to freeze the German position and thereby prevent it from slipping into further extremism. Lueger looked to the Cabinet for leadership and endorsed the program of social blandishments (canals, waterways, rail and road construction) that Ernest von Koerber tried to use to distract the feuding national parties in 1901–2.[153] Lueger was, for example, an active and eager participant in the negotiations for the construction of a Danube-Oder canal, defending Vienna's interests with every trick of political intrigue known to him.[154] The Christian Socials supported this initiative not simply because they needed Koerber's cooperation at home but also because investment programs to enhance the economic infrastructure of the Monarchy were consonant with the self-image of the Christian Socials as a "social reform" movement.[155]

Koerber's mode of ostensible "nonpolitical" rule became a liability for the Christian Social party only in 1904, when he began to articulate plans to diminish the power of local and regional administrative and political authorities. Although formally an attack on the incompetence of these authorities (as opposed to political party management per se), Koerber's plans would have led to a radical reduction in the discretionary power of provincial and municipal political organizations. Movements like the Czech nationalist notable and petty notable parties and the Christian Socials, which held bastions of semi-independent administrative power in Bohemia and Lower Austria, would be weakened in their own electoral constituencies. In effect, Koerber sought to force local and regional politics into the same kind of advisory, consultative mode that national parliamentary politics (in the best of times) had assumed since the mid-1890s. This Lueger would never permit.

The Christian Socials bore little direct responsibility for Koerber's decision to resign in late 1904, an act that reflected his profound exhaustion and despair over the persistence of the nationality conflict as much as the vote of no confidence which he received in the parliamentary budget committee on December 9, 1904.[156] In fact, Christian Social press reaction was rather directed against the vindictive, scheming, and selfish nationalists on all sides who refused to compromise and who were so intent on destroying Austrian parliamentary life. Koerber fell because the Cabinet was deserted by the German national parties after being crippled in parliament by Czech obstructionism. It was true that since the embarrassment surrounding the Lueger birthday incident in October 1904 (see below), many in the party felt a deep ambivalence towards Koerber, which, if it did not alienate the party apparatus from him, at least gave the

Christian Socials less reason to support him when the other bourgeois parties had turned against the Cabinet. Some felt that Koerber's five years of brilliant scheming and studied fence-sitting, as well as his manipulation (and bribery) of parliament, had run into the ground. Others, although grateful for Koerber's political generosity towards the city, felt that their party was poised to move beyond the concerns of the municipality and that the time had now come for it to play a more emphatic role in state policy.[157] This might be facilitated by Koerber's removal and his replacement by someone more pliable and more sympathetic, such as Paul von Gautsch (the new nominee for Minister-President who not only enjoyed the Young Czechs' backing but also worked in the first months of his regime to establish good relations with Lueger and Gessmann).[158] Yet if one compares Karl Lueger's comments, given at a summit meeting of German party leaders with Koerber in mid-November 1904, with those of German spokesmen like Julius Derschatta, Gustav Gross, and Josef Baernreither, two different trajectories and two distinct goals were evident. Whereas the German national leaders grilled Koerber in defensive and even accusatory tones about possible concessions to the Czechs and other non-German ethnic groups, Lueger was more detached, suggesting ways to restore peace and avoid further public conflicts with the Germans. After the meeting Lueger characterized the session as "miserable" (*jämmerlich*), but the insult was not merely directed toward Koerber alone, as Baernreither wanted to believe.[159] It was Austrian politics that was miserable, but if Koerber was no longer up to the challenge of his job, then Lueger had no reason to continue to support him.

Since they could play no realistic role in shaping state politics before 1905, the Christian Socials viewed their relationship to the government and their role in state politics from a local perspective. How would pressures and problems generated or encouraged by state-level trends be transposed into Vienna? As consumers of the Minister-President's clever patronage and tolerance, the party had little to complain about. Rather the primary connection between state and local politics came in the collective and competitive presence of two other political movements in Vienna which pursued state-level agendas in the context of Viennese local politics. These were the pan-Germans and the Social Democrats.

In 1898 Georg von Schönerer decided to capitalize on a wave of radical national sentiment among German *bürgerlich* voters (and many workers as well) in the aftermath of Badeni's regime and proclaimed his *Los von Rom* campaign. The *Los von Rom* movement comprised a twofold attack on Austrian Catholicism and on Viennese Christian Socialism, arguing that both were part of a scheme to despoil the purity of German culture and to undermine the resolve Austro-Germans needed to resist Czech political imperialism.[160] Schönerer's strategy combined extreme nationalism and extreme anticlericalism in one unified, ideological format. Indeed, one might argue that the new wave of radical anticlericalism that characterized Austrian politics after 1900 began with the *Los von Rom* movement. Schönerer assayed his own political future with insight, since his days as a legitimate "social reformer" were long over; whatever political success remained to him would come only by playing the guttersnipe of Austrian cultural politics.

Even though the movement was soon weakened by a split between those like Schönerer, whose preoccupation with folkish *or* evangelical religion was only opportunistic, and those like Pastor Paul Bräunlich, who saw *Los von Rom* as a legitimate chance to enlarge the Austrian Protestant community at the expense of the Catholics, it outraged the Christian Socials.[161] Before 1898 the Christian Social party was not in any formal sense a "clerical" party, even though lower-order priests were active in its coalition practices. Lueger was now made responsible not only for an alleged anti-Austrian "ultramontanism" that would damage both the Dynasty and the Monarchy, but for the feudal-minded bishops who had fiercely opposed his party in the mid-1890s![162] By stigmatizing the party as "clerical" and anti-national and by forcing the party to defend the Church against a flood of some of the most vicious (and tasteless) political literature ever seen in Austrian politics, Schönerer helped to create the very object which he sought to destroy. Internal Catholic resistance to *Los von Rom* marked the beginning of stronger and self-willed Austrian Catholic action committees (exemplified politically by the *Piusverein,* organized in 1905 to subsidize Catholic journalism, and emotionally in the more aggressive, confident spirit of the participants at the 1907 and 1910 Catholic Congresses).[163] A new sense of political confidence was also manifested by the Austrian episcopate on public policy involving the schools, evident in the confidential deliberations of their annual meetings after 1901. Indeed, a catalogue of the "wishes" of the episcopate relating to the school system prepared by Archbishop Michael Napotnik of Lavant in 1906, based on a poll of his fellow bishops, called for little less than a total reconfessionalization of the public school system, a goal which even the Christian Socials would have rejected.[164] But the city and party also found themselves co-opted: Lueger's much-publicized attempt in 1899 to loan local churches in Vienna construction funds was in part a political reflex action against the demagogy of the Schönerians, just as his final justification for city support for the Church was centered on the local churches as buildings of civic and patriotic, as well as religious, interest to society.[165] Having linked his party to the Church, Schönerer placed Lueger in a position in which he inevitably had to defend the Church along with his party.

Even though Lueger realized that the practical impact of Schönerer's conversion campaign was not great (the number of conversions to Protestantism was less than 600 annually in Vienna, and sank drastically after 1905), *Los von*

Rom insulted Lueger's ego and the image of "his" city as a bastion of dynastic conservatism.[166] That Protestant money and missionaries flowed from Prussia and Saxony into Austria was also grating for a politician whose loyalty to the *Dreibund* was lackluster at best. In early 1902 Lueger escalated the issue by declaring *Los von Rom* an "international scandal," warning that "we want to cooperate with the German *Reich,* but we urgently wish and demand, however, that several of the individual German states abstain from meddling in Austrian affairs."[167] More important were possible electoral implications, since Koerber had clearly failed to gauge the enthusiasm that the new pan-German crusade was able to assemble outside of Vienna. The January 1901 parliamentary elections showed an unexpected surge of radical, German-national voting support among *bürgerlich* groups in Bohemia, Moravia, and other key areas. In Vienna the Christian Socials lost two close races in the Fifth Curia to the Social Democrats, and although the pan-Germans went away empty-handed, Lueger had no desire to wait and see if Schönerer could set more nationalist brushfires with anticlerical matches.[168] As an effort to secure conversions, *Los von Rom* might be marginal, but could it have more subtle, spillover effects on white-collar voters? Koerber's unwillingness to suppress overtly the *Los von Rom* diatribes, arguing that direct intervention by the Cabinet would simply enhance Schönerer's credibility, became a point of contention between the Christian Socials and the Minister-President.[169] Karl Lueger found himself caught in a crossfire between irate clerics and pan-German extremists, with many clerics feeling that the party was laggard in helping them.[170] Koerber's seeming lassitude on *Los von Rom* led Albert Gessmann to believe that unless the party shared in state policy-making it would always exist at the sufferance of the Cabinet. More important, Schönerer's paranoiac fear of universal suffrage, which he knew would destroy the precious world of pan-German sectarianism, made the franchise reform of 1907 all the more attractive.

Much more ominous for the Christian Social party was its confrontation with a second state movement, Austrian Social Democracy. Schönerer's thrust against the Christian Socials was coordinate with the first wave of Social Democratic agitation in the public school system and in the municipal electorate, giving many Christian Socials the sense that Victor Adler was in collusion with Schönerer on trying to destroy their party (which was not true) and that the socialists were hoping to exploit the embarrassment of the party over *Los von Rom* (which was true). The years between 1898 and 1905 saw growing discord between the two mass movements, culminating in the violent demonstrations against Lueger himself on the eve of his sixtieth birthday celebrations in October 1904. The stakes were high, since, as the party secretariat openly asserted at the 1903 socialist party congress, the Social Democrats were the only party left in Vienna that might curb the ascendancy of Lueger's forces.[171]

In the electoral arena the Social Democrats made at best slow headway against the Christian Socials. The oligarchical voting system utilized for municipal elections consigned the Social Democrat party to a token representation in the City Council. Even after the franchise reform of 1900, which established a Fourth Curia of twenty seats based on universal suffrage, the socialists won only two seats from the Christian Socials since the latter continued to win support not only from their core *bürgerlich* voters but also from petty employees, waiters, servants, janitors, and even some craft laborers who had fluid notions (or no notions at all) about their class position.[172] Only in bastions of deep socialist loyalty like Ottakring, Favoriten, and, later, Floridsdorf could the Social Democrats hope to surpass the Christian Social machine. In the 1901 parliamentary elections Victor Adler's forces demonstrated considerable energy, increasing their share of participating voters over the level of the 1897 elections and managing to pick off two seats in the Viennese Fifth Curia.[173] But in both cases the socialists won only narrow margins of victory; and the fact that the Christian Socials had trouble motivating their voters to go to the polls for the Fifth Curia voting, did not offer the Social Democrats the prospect of sweeping the city's Fifth Curia seats.

Nor did the results of the hard-fought campaign for the Lower Austrian Diet in October and November 1902 bring any more solace. Since the Diet franchise in Vienna was based on the most generous component of the current municipal ordinance (the new Fourth Curia that was launched in 1900), the size of the enfranchised electorate for the 1902 elections jumped from 89,811 in 1896 to 251,348, only slightly lower than the eligibility pool for the 1901 Fifth Curia state elections.[174] Even here, with the Christian Socials offering the Social Democrats the opportunity to compete for a greatly expanded pool of voters, the socialists won none of the 21 seats contested. Only in suburban Floridsdorf did Karl Seitz pull the Social Democrats to victory. Liberal hopes that the Christian Social experiment would prove a fluke (which seemed plausible after the results of the January 1901 parliamentary races) collapsed as Lueger's forces swept 46 of the 55 seats contested in urban and rural election districts throughout the Crownland.[175] The *Neue Freie Presse* was beside itself in outrage, even to the point of complaining that of the seventy members of the Christian Social election commission in the First District "not a single one holds an academic title."

Were the Social Democrats to be consigned to a permanent outcast status against the Christian Social machine, even though their popular vote averaged a respectable 22 percent? In many districts Christian Social margins of victory were not as lopsided as Lueger would have liked, but the end result was the same. The quiet fear that haunted Social Democratic voters and leaders alike after 1900—that in spite of a more open (and thus more legitimate) franchise they would *still* be marginalized within the regional and municipal political system—was bound to have substantial consequences for both mass parties.

In the short run, election campaigns became even more bitterly contested. All Viennese parties were capable of garden-variety electoral corruption; but the fact that 74 out of 115 persons arrested for attempted electoral falsifications in the 1902 Diet elections were Social Democrats suggests that at least some socialist activists felt an urgency that led them to emulate the bad habits of their Christian Social competitors.[176] Equally significant was the unruliness of Social Democratic crowds in Favoriten in early November 1902, following Victor Adler's defeat in a Diet run-off election against Julius Prochazka. Rhetorical violence and aggressive acts in front of Christian Social campaign locales were commonplace by Social Democratic election organizers (and vice versa), but rock- and bottle-throwing by a socialist crowd at the *Arbeiterheim,* resulting in this case in twenty-six injured workers and twelve injured police agents, revealed how hard-pressed the socialist party leadership was to control the escalation of hope they engendered in their own voters.[177] Yet even hope could not be taken for granted, for such chaos masked (and reflected) deep frustration on the part of many working-class voters. When combined with the apparent deadlock over universal suffrage on the state level, electoral losses in Vienna were bound to cast shadows over the legitimacy and wisdom of Victor Adler's strategy of procedural legalism. How realistic was the painful preoccupation of the Social Democratic leadership with parliamentary strategies for achieving politically credible social reform?[178] It is true that during these years the Viennese party made great strides in developing its "house and street" organization system, which was to pay substantial dividends after 1907.[179] Yet, as Hans Mommsen and other historians of the party have observed, the mood of the national leadership between 1900 and 1905 was often bleak, with many organizers feeling, in the words of Oswald Hillebrand, that "at every turn we encounter a level of indifference that could really push us to despair."[180]

If the Social Democrats presented Lueger with a less immediate electoral threat, socialist dissidence in the school system was more immediate and more troubling. The *Jungen* movement was perhaps the most provocative cultural-political challenge that the Christian Social party encountered in the first years of its rule. Its adherents were a small yet extremely articulate and courageous cadre of socialist teachers led by Karl Seitz, who attracted considerable popularity among the provisional teachers (*Unterlehrer*) in the school system in the 1890s. Many of the teachers sympathetic to their views were not themselves Social Democrats, but Seitz's ability to combine mundane, interest-group demands, such as improved tenure and better salary raises, with larger, socialist *Kulturarbeit* perspectives was appealing nonetheless. As I noted in *Political Radicalism,* he and his colleagues sought not merely to improve the "internal" social and fiscal resources of the school system but also to use the schools as a vanguard to initiate a moral transformation of working-class society. That the *Jungen* were violently anticlerical was a matter of record.[181]

Karl Lueger prided himself on his devotion to the public schools, but his devotion was measured by bricks and mortar on the one hand and by sustaining conservative social values on the other. Between 1897 and 1908 dozens of new school buildings were opened in Vienna. Class size by 1908 was still large—50 students per class—but the municipality did try to keep pace with Vienna's demographic growth (to over two million in 1910), which was Lueger's primary concern. In spite of these efforts overcrowding in the school system remained a sore point.[182] Within the schools Lueger wanted simple, pious, and utilitarian instruction, combining basic literacy skills with a heavy dose of moral education for the impressionable young dynastic citizens. Schooling on the elementary level would not necessarily promote social mobility or economic prosperity; that, if it could be achieved, would come through individual initiative or by family support for more specialized schooling beyond the level of elementary education or by patronage or business connections within public and private hierarchies. The life histories of top party leaders like Lueger, Gessmann, or Weiskirchner (and those of subelite leaders like Heinrich Hierhammer or Hermann Bielohlawek, not to mention younger protégés like Richard Schmitz, Eduard Heinl, and even Ignaz Seipel), who combined petty bourgeois social resources with individual ambition and hard work and (in some cases) with advanced education, became obvious models for the society the Christian Socials wished to reproduce in the future.[183] The lower schools should promote acceptance of one's place in life and tolerance for those of better or lower position. This is what Gessmann meant when he openly asserted that he could not conceive of an "orderly and socially stable integration of people" without "positive [religious] belief," which necessitated religious instruction in the schools. The *Jungen* were victimizing younger teachers by encouraging "an unbelievable class hatred, indeed class hegemony, a brutality in regard to individual social groups which cannot be imagined even in the worst feudal state." According to Gessmann, the socialists wanted to "poison the hearts of the young and undermine the sense of duty of the teachers."[184]

In expressing such opinions Gessmann merely reflected the concerns of his electorate. Status and standing in *bürgerlich* society might come in several ways: by familial subsidization of middle-school or university education, which was necessary to gain entry into the middle ranks of the civil service; by familial inheritance (often a factor in families who owned income-producing property, as in the case of a landlord); by sons assuming their fathers' occupations (as was sometimes the case among Christian Social guild masters and merchants) or by their obtaining even more desirable jobs as a result of their fathers' business connections; by employment in the lower ranks of the public bureaucracies, which presumed fortuitous social contacts or previous service in the Army more than formal educational attainment.[185] Lower-level, elementary schools should provide literacy, but they should not upset the naturally plural "orderliness" of society, nor should they call into question the polity's cultural values. Rather than serving as instruments of revolutionary social transformation, the schools should provide an institutional defense of moral values shared in the past and treasured in the present. In Rudolf Hornich's words, the schools should guarantee tradition and authority in a society tottering on the brink of cultural self-destruction.[186] The school system should encourage discipline as well as hard work, loyalty to corporate norms as well as individual achievement. And in a multi-ethnic cultural environment, it should also guarantee the peaceful assimilation of children into the mores and language of the Viennese *Vaterstadt*. The poor were both in and out of this system—in it because they would be taught to accept the Christian Social polity and its civic culture as having sole legitimacy, but out of it because they had no right to participate either in the governance of the city or in the regulation of the market and thus no right to understand, much less to protect, their own social lives.

In contrast to this wished-for world of order, the young socialist teachers taught in schools where poverty and hunger, shabbiness and despair signified vast social problems that were anything but orderly.[187] The world as manifested in their schools was one of social marginality and material impoverishment, of family disorganization and individual despair. In his unpublished memoirs Karl Seitz recalled his own experience of facing dozens of hungry, unkempt children on a daily basis:

> I was a young teacher working in Favoriten in a public school in the Quellenstrasse and there I got a frightening impression about the situation of proletarian children, an impression that was the same every day when at 10 in the morning I was supposed to distribute food tickets [*Speisemarken*] for a warm midday meal to the 40 or 50 children who had asked for them. I had three, in the best of cases five tickets to give out. The other children went away with nothing. This was 1888, and that stimulated me to work on behalf of the proletariat and proletarian children.[188]

Otto Glöckel had similar experiences in his school in Rudolfsheim, where the majority of his ten-year-old pupils did not have their own bed to sleep in and many fell asleep in class because they were forced to work early-morning or late-night jobs.[189] For Seitz and Glöckel, Christian Social admiration of "family life" was little more than cruel, pseudo-romantic rhetoric that bore no relationship to the harsh realities they faced each day in their classrooms. They and their compatriots soon came to believe that neither the school system itself nor the living conditions of the children lodged in it would improve without radical changes in larger social and political power relationships. This fundamental insight led many of them to the Social Democratic party and to a natural if non-theoretical affinity with Marxist political practice.[190] Their own material impoverishment as provisional teachers gave them a personal source of driving self-interest and group identity. Yet their preoccupation with the schools also made them include in their social pedagogy transformational goals for the present society, rather than mere prophecies for the society of the future. Their work as cultural pedagogues, and not merely as Social Democratic advocates, should thus not be underestimated. As practitioners of Marxist politics, they acknowledged the inevitability of class conflict and a materialist interpretation of history, but as socialist *Bildungspolitiker* they wanted to attend to the here and now of workers' lives. Seitz and his colleagues thus brought into the Social Democratic movement a robust appreciation of ideational and cultural products since, as Seitz later put it, "backward, ill-educated workers are a lead weight on the intelligent working class that is involved in life and death struggles, one that obstructs their cultural ascent."[191] Anticlericalism was a natural component of their crusade, not only because the *Jungen* decried the normative and behavioral agenda of the Catholic Church in the education of young people but also because it allowed the young socialists to position themselves as defenders of one important heritage of the Liberal state. That they read the 1869 Imperial School Law with *very* different strategic concerns from those which its Liberal authors had brought to the bill was merely one unintended consequence of the *Jungen's* attempt to co-opt one part of the Liberal tradition, which they did only for the purpose of inserting it into a post-Liberal, socialist order.[192]

The "School Program" that the *Zentralverein der Wiener Lehrerschaft,* the professional organization of the *Jungen,* adopted on April 10, 1898, in Vienna merged economic and social progress with cultural emancipation.[193] Insisting on the power of *Bildung* (a word quite explicitly chosen for its rich classical and idealistic connotations and its combination of the notions of school-based education and personal cultural development) to release the repressed energies of the poor, Seitz argued that the public school system was the captive of existing "moralist, religious, and political views" that served the interests of the propertied classes. The latter wanted to educate submissive, intellectually diminished children who, as adults, would be unable to know their own social interests. The reform of education would not only open the fund of human knowledge to current and future generations of the poor but it would help to ameliorate class conflict as well:

> The fact that science has been placed in the service of the ruling classes, and that our educational system only allows the rich to obtain higher *Bildung,* condemning the great mass of the poor to *Unbildung,* intensifies the class opposition between the propertied and non-

propertied by additional differences in *Bildung,* which [in turn] leads
to the further intensification of class conflict. The monopoly of *Bildung* by the rich, and the kind of forced, tendentious education that
they endure, leads to the intensification of conflicts . . . this situation
is not simply an injustice against the poor but also damaging for both
rich and poor. If one wants to moderate as far as possible the ordained
class conflicts in our society, which are themselves unavoidable, the
educational system must strive for an equal *Bildung* for poor and rich,
based only on the criteria of the personal abilities of the individual,
and not act in a biased manner.[194]

Not all of the dissident teachers lived up to these high ideals; and a few
stooped to scurrilities little better than the worst that a Josef Gregorig or
an Ernst Schneider could proffer. Eduard Jordan, for example, the bitterly
anticlerical editor of the *Österreichische Schulzeitung* and a public schoolteacher in the First District, was officially reprimanded in 1900 for having published a fictive public letter which, he reported, the president of the *Deutsch-
österreichischer Lehrerbund* had sent to all its members. In this letter teachers
were asked to spy on local clerics in their parish houses and, among other
things, to pay special attention to whether female servants (cooks, etc.) spent
undue amounts of time in the clergyman's presence and whether the clergyman
had a "niece" living with him in the parish.[195] Seitz and most of his colleagues
were more high-minded, but even their critique of conservative educational
values often led to overkill and unfair caricature. [196]

   Nor would it be fair to impute an attitude of indifference or apathy toward
the intellectual welfare of schoolchildren to a teacher merely because he or she
was a Christian Social party sympathizer or a member of the Christian Social-
sponsored *Verein der Lehrer und Schulfreunde,* the teacher association created
by Gessmann in early 1899 to serve as a semi-official party interest group and
which was populated by teachers carrying a variety of personal and professional motives.[197] Indeed, the majority of the Viennese teaching corps long
after 1897 consisted of teachers trained in Liberal-dominated pedagogical institutes (parallel to the city bureaucracy). The pious rhetoric of the Catholic
School Association should not be confused with the views of practicing teachers in the school system nor with the theoretical assumptions of teaching super-
visors after 1900. Lueger himself was quite clear about the fact that he was not
sympathetic to a reconfessionalization of the Austrian public school system.
When Kaspar Schwarz, the chairman of the Catholic School Association, decided to advocate reconfessionalization of the schools at the Fifth Austrian
Catholic Congress in Vienna in November 1905, Lueger threatened not to receive its dignitaries at the Rathaus.[198]

   Seen from the perspective of 1914, if not that of 1927, the fact that the first major institutional collision between Social Democrats and Christian Socials in Vienna occurred over public education had far-reaching consequences. For the *Jungen* never masked the hope that *their* praxis would have social and political consequences in bridging the gap between subject and society. That is, educational reform would assume dynamic potentialities far exceeding literacy skills or even personality development that would be of direct import for the present society and of revolutionary value for the coming society. In a curious if inchoate way the socialist teachers were the first "Critical Theorists." The dynamic, instrumental quality of *Bildung* that they espoused prepared the way for the cultural and legal theory that the first generation of Austro-Marxists accomplished a few years later.[199]

In attacking Christian Social hegemony in the schools the socialist teachers not only challenged the party's control of an important institutional and electoral *politicum* but threatened the Christian Socials with massive ideological humiliation as well. Both reasons must be kept in mind to understand the ferocity of Lueger's and Gessmann's counteroffensive after 1898. For forty years the Liberals in Vienna had touted the municipal schools as an example of the force of Liberal culture in the face of heinous "clericalism." The Christian Socials simply reaffirmed a belief in the political currency of public education by confirming the Liberals' earlier politicization of the system, albeit on more crass and opportunistic terms.[200] When Lueger appointed Josef Gregorig, the feisty Marxist-baiter from the Neubau, as a member of the Municipal School Board, he was simply stressing, in the most expressive way conceivable, that the schools, like everything else in the city, belonged to the taxpaying *Bürgertum*. Control of the school system meant control of the political loyalties of teachers, an articulate and numerous group who could cause all manner of trouble for any ruling political party should they enter the ranks of the electoral opposition. This was of special importance in the small towns and villages of Lower Austria, where teachers (or priests) were often the only notables suitable to direct election commissions and perform other semi-public functions.[201]

Hegemony in the schools also meant a self-confirming legitimation of the party's blend of a mild clericalism and a moderate anti-Semitism, coupled with a strong emphasis on the traditional family, on the work ethic (or at least its less rigorous Austrian incarnation, one that was often distorted into crude anti-socialism), and on traditional social structures and social interrelationships (especially the acceptance of the inevitability of one's fate as a member of the working class or of the *Bürgertum*). From this perspective accusations by the Social Democrats that the Christian Socials were pedagogical reactionaries were not so much wrong as irrelevant. One of the school system's roles was to help to educate children in literacy skills, but that role could not be the most politically significant one. Rather, the system was widely viewed as a powerful instrument for general cultural reproduction, one that validated the present world of the fathers (and mothers) as much as it constructed the future world of the children. This multigenerational reification of public education in Vienna characterized all three of the political regimes between 1848 and 1934. In their revolutionary reconstruction of education as a form of ersatz public politics the interwar Social Democrats fell squarely within the Viennese tradition.

Seeking to exploit the opportunities of professional representation that were already part of the Austrian public educational system, the young socialist teachers campaigned for election as the teachers' representatives to the Municipal School Board.[202] Such representation was an unusual prerogative that most school teachers elsewhere in Central Europe did not enjoy. Several *Jungen* ran in the June 1897 elections and two—Seitz and Sonntag—were actually elected in run-off elections in October, but Viennese and Lower Austrian school authorities raised procedural hurdles and they were seated only after a decision by the Austrian Administrative Court (*Verwaltungsgerichtshof*) in April 1899. The Christian Socials were not long in retaliating, resorting to both legal and extra-legal means to repress socialist-inspired dissidence within the ranks of the younger teaching corps (virtually none of whom were Jewish). In September 1897 Lueger fired five young teachers who lacked tenured status, and over the following months and years the city initiated other disciplinary actions against those, like Seitz, who had permanent jobs.[203] Thus began a reign of intermittent political harassment that lasted to 1914, with dozens of reprimands, salary reductions or freezes, and other acts of administrative chicanery dogging the heels of the surviving *Jungen*.[204] Nor were these machinations confined to the private venues of administrative justice. At the ceremony where he welcomed new teachers Lueger made it a point to issue a stern warning that neither Social Democrats nor Schönerians would be tolerated on the city payroll. In this tactic the party earned the sympathy of the Imperial government. Kielmansegg himself felt that Lueger's anti-socialist employment edict was understandable, even if in the long run it would also be ineffective, given the "extreme, inappropriate behavior of some of the younger teachers who are damaging the reputation [of the profession]."[205]

Only occasionally did the government intervene to moderate the disciplinary actions taken by the city authorities, and usually for reasons of political convenience more than civil libertarian conviction. In April 1901, for example, Gessmann moved in the Lower Austrian Provincial School Council (*Landesschulrat*) to have Karl Seitz dismissed as a tenured schoolteacher, because his raucous behavior at a meeting of the Municipal School Board a month earlier had "damaged the reputation of the teaching corps in a most offensive manner."[206] Karl Rieger, a Lower Austrian school inspector, offered an alternative motion to give Seitz both an official reprimand and a demotion, with the provision that future radical behavior would result in immediate termination. The competing motions resulted in a tie vote, which Bishop Godfried Marschall broke in favor of Rieger. The latter's motion was then adopted by the full Council.[207]

Often tenured teachers who had been disciplined, having no luck in administrative appeals to the Lower Austrian School Council or to the Ministry of Education, took their cases to the Administrative Court. One such teacher, Rudolf Hawel, was a popular writer who had authored *Die Politiker,* a play mocking Christian Social politicians that the Raimund Theater staged in 1904. He now submitted an eloquent defense of his various political activities, arguing that he had acted out of moral conviction and had been unjustly held back in salary raises and benefits. But the court refused to intervene, reflecting a lack of sympathy with the ends and means of these political activists.[208]

Within the party Lueger relied on Gessmann to manage the campaign of repression. Gessmann did this with great zeal. By 1903, when the quadrennial elections among Viennese schoolteachers were held for their professional representatives to the Municipal School Board, Gessmann had managed to coerce or entice a sufficient number of older and higher-ranking teachers into voting for the Christian Social slate by threatening to hold up long overdue salary raises if the teachers refused to comply. The socialist slate went down in humiliating defeat.[209] In addition, Gessmann recruited rural clergy in Lower Austria to serve as a network of political eyes and ears to watch for dissidence among teachers in the villages and small towns.[210] A socialist report on the politicization of the Viennese teaching corps in 1908 insisted that nearly 30 percent of the promotions accorded to public schoolteachers in Lower Austria between 1900 and 1908 were awarded out of proper sequence, without proper seniority, simply at the political convenience of the party.[211]

While many of these accusations were correct, not all teachers who were denied promotion or salary raises were persecuted for political reasons, even though the aggrieved might mask their disenchantment with cries of foul play. Socialist accusations that *all* Christian Social personnel decisions smacked of corruption and cover-up were certainly an exaggeration. Even his status as an anti-Semitic city councilman did not protect Ferdinand Rauscher, a school principal in Hernals who had been convicted of public drunkenness and slander, from demotion in 1899 by the Lower Austrian School Council to the rank of ordinary teacher and transfer to another school.[212] Many of the disciplinary cases that ended up in the Ministry of Education reflected genuine pedagogical incompetence or failure to meet normal professional obligations. It was a curious feature of the period that the same Red-baiting Christian Social appointees to the Municipal School Board (*Bezirksschulrat*) who delighted in hounding socialist teachers were also capable of exercising care in conducting other disciplinary cases.[213] Indeed, the most frequent cause of disciplinary action was mistreatment of students, usually by beatings or sexual harassment. It says much about the moral priorities of those concerned, however, that a teacher "guilty" of Social Democracy was treated as having erred equally (or even more) seriously than one guilty of physical brutality.[214]

The conflict over the schools reached its climax in October 1904 when Albert Gessmann strengthened Christian Social control over the Viennese and rural Lower Austrian school systems with a package of four laws that revised the educational system established in the province in 1869.[215] Gessmann submitted his laws to the Diet suddenly and without warning on October 18, 1904, forcing them through over the angry objections of the few remaining Liberals and of Karl Seitz, the lone Social Democrat. The legislation had a covert prehistory: Gessmann had actually negotiated with Hartel and Kielmansegg for a month before he announced the bills in public, so that their ultimate sanction (a few revisions in late December aside) was a foregone conclusion.[216] The laws provided generous salary increases for both Viennese and rural Lower Austrian teachers, but in return it subjected the teachers to a series of disciplinary and political restrictions: Catholic priests were given permanent membership on all local school boards; members of district boards were required to take an oath of secrecy (thus depriving the Social Democrats of one important source of information on school politics); lower-ranking teachers with less than five years of continuous service were excluded from voting for the teachers' professional representatives on the Municipal School Board; and teachers were now accountable, in disciplinary proceedings, for private behavior outside of school hours, leverage that Gessmann could use to intimidate teachers who dared to engage in oppositional politics on their own time. Financial and staffing responsibility for the municipal *Pädagogium,* the famous institute for pedagogical training in Vienna founded by the Liberal party in 1868, was transferred to the Lower Austrian government, which created a special teachers' academy (*Lehrerakademie*) for continuing education for tenured schoolteachers and combined this institution with a Lower Austrian Teacher Seminar.[217] Rudolf Hornich and August Kemetter, professional educators and political supporters of Gessmann, assumed leadership of the *Pädagogium,* which soon became a center for the pedagogical doctrines of Otto Willmann, a distinguished Austrian Catholic educator influenced by Herbartian theory.[218] Gessmann thus combined all phases of professional training and development of teachers under a single party-sponsored roof. That the new teachers' academy was distasteful to Social Democratic educational practitioners was obvious, but their unhappiness should not mask the fact that men like Hornich and Kemetter were serious educators and not mere party hacks.[219]

The debates in the City Council and the Diet on the 1904 legislation conveyed a powerful message to the teachers: the taxpayers were sick of the dissidence provoked by the *Jungen* and would consent to salary raises only if such provocations ended. Given the generous size of the salary increases (the total package would cost the province over 4 million crowns annually), it was understandable that the majority of teachers accommodated themselves to Gessmann's strategy. By the end of two grueling days of debate, in which he offered the only credible opposition to the bills, Seitz found himself mocked by the Christian Social deputies, who wondered aloud if the poor man were not tired after so much pointless talking.[220]

The Social Democratic leadership in Vienna may have been dismayed by Gessmann's countercultural hegemony, but they soon found appropriate revenge. Two weeks earlier (on October 5), during an angry debate over the introduction of half-day instruction in rural Lower Austrian schools, Karl Lueger had exchanged insults with Karl Seitz about the moral and social status of their respective electoral constituencies, during which Lueger insisted that many of the socialist parents of poor schoolchildren in Vienna sold their children's clothes to old clothes dealers for money. To prove his more general point about where the Lumpenproletariat's political home lay, Lueger opined that the socialist workers who marched and demonstrated on May Day in the Prater were a band of noisy (and apparently) ill-dressed tramps.[221] Even in Vienna, with its tradition of histrionic political rhetoric and its fluid disjunction of meaning and discourse, this was going too far. Lueger's arrogant insults were a declaration of war. The Social Democrats responded not through economic sanctions but by attacking the living symbol of the Christian Social movement, Karl Lueger himself.

On October 24, 1904, Karl Lueger was to celebrate his sixtieth birthday. The Christian Social leadership planned several mass demonstrations including a party rally and a public mass at the Votivkirche on Monday, the 24th, but the culmination would come on the evening of the 23d when party loyalists would symbolically take back the site of the Ring from the Social Democrats by marching with lampions and flags—the famous Lueger torchlight procession (*Fackelzug*). Ostensibly organized to honor Lueger the man, the ceremonies would also glorify the movement that he had led for so long. The official sponsor of the parade was the erstwhile *Bürgervereinigung,* which not only planned the festivities but also in good mercantile terms paid for them by printing commemorative medallions with Lueger's portrait, which the party then forced municipal bureaucrats to sell (and to purchase themselves) at inflated prices.[222] A *Festschrift* in honor of Lueger was also printed (including a pious biography authored by Leopold Tomola), to be given away by the School Board to all Viennese school children at a cost of 33,000 crowns. Not only did party functionaries expect municipal officials to make financial contributions (and keep detailed lists of who did and who did not give money), they also asked for volunteers to serve as guides for the parade.[223] The Christian Social public was also expected to subsidize a new charitable foundation, the Karl Lueger-Stiftung, as a permanent memorial to the man and his work.[224] One official in the Municipal Construction Office proudly reported to Lueger's ward boss in

Währing, Anton Baumann, that he had given 60 crowns to the *Stiftung* and that all the other employees in his office had also given their share. Baumann organized a house-by-house collection scheme, dividing his ward into 76 sections and sending subordinates to visit between 40 and 60 houses in each section. Nor was he sheepish about approaching wealthier contributors—Julius Meinl, for example, gave 1,000 crowns for the endowment.[225] Members of the *Bürgervereinigung* gave a total of 20,000 crowns and total contributions to the endowment by the party faithful amounted to almost 400,000 crowns, suggesting that the constituency base of the Christian Social party was slowly moving beyond the class of archetypal small artisan masters into more complex realms of patronage, clientage, and wealth.[226] Yet the most critical role that fell to the ward bosses like Baumann was to mobilize participants for the march on the Ringstrasse. By mid-October about 130 clubs and groups had announced they would send representatives on the 23d when the *Altwiener Bürgertum* would reclaim the Ring. Much was at stake, for a poor turnout would subject the party to socialist ridicule.

The Social Democratic leadership decided that no more fitting insult could be offered to Lueger than to make a mockery of the event. They immediately drafted plans to disrupt it.[227] In the week before the *Fackelzug* various local Christian Social leaders found their houses or businesses surrounded by crowds of screaming workers, demonstrating against Lueger and giving the anti-Semites (and the police) a foretaste of what was to come on October 23.[228] At one rally two hundred socialists surrounded the residence of Josef Stary, the Christian Social district leader of Alsergrund; at another they hung two huge red flags which bore the motto "Down with Lueger, long live the working class!"[229]

These intimidation tactics succeeded twice over. Not only did the Police President, on Koerber's instructions, order the Christian Socials on October 19 to cancel the *Fackelzug* for fear of public disorder, but files on the work of the executive committee suggest that ward leaders were finding it difficult to obtain the support of *bürgerlich* participants by the final week of preparations.[230] The *Deutsches Volksblatt* valiantly insisted that Lueger's supporters would not be intimidated by the specter of Red terror, but this was not altogether accurate, for the total number of individual and group-sponsored commitments for the *Fackelzug* was less than 8,000, a pathetic figure measured against the tens of thousands of activists the Social Democrats could put on the Ringstrasse at will.[231] The Christian Social party had little trouble raising large sums of money through "voluntary" political contributions, but promises to show up and face screaming socialist crowds were more difficult to obtain.

Lueger may have been outraged that the police dared to interfere with "his" birthday celebration, but, in fact, Count Wedel reported to Berlin that the police decision was actually triggered by a request from several "influential leaders" of the party (most likely Gessmann and Weiskirchner) that the police *should* prohibit the *Fackelzug,* since they realized the party was heading for a catastrophe.[232] Of course the party had to roast the government in the Lower Austrian Diet on October 21, portraying itself as the victim of a weak, cowardly state and an insolent, brutal Social Democracy, but what disturbed Lueger most was not his humiliation in being denied the *Fackelzug,* but the de facto toleration which the police had to show to the huge socialist crowds who gathered on the Ringstrasse on the afternoon and evening of the 23d to scream obscenities and to mock him.[233] Not only had the Christian Socials been deprived of their parade, but in addition the police permitted tens of thousands of Social Democrats to seize de facto control of the Ringstrasse at their pleasure.

The Social Democrats had not only embarrassed the party before the government and the Viennese public, making them seem incapable of managing their own political theatricality, but also and more importantly they showed that while Lueger might well control the Rathaus, *they* still controlled the Ring. When 200,000 Social Democratic sympathizers took over the Ringstrasse in November 1905 in support of universal suffrage, the memory of socialist intimidation tactics in October 1904 still rankled the Christian Socials. Even Lueger knew there were limits beyond which the huge Red crowds could not be pushed, and if any among the Christian Social elite had second thoughts about suffrage reform, the conjunction of anti-Semitic weakness and socialist strength on the Ringstrasse impressed reality onto the Rathaus. At the same time, Lueger possessed one enormous advantage: if he could not persuade innocent *Bürger* to face socialist agitators in street confrontations, he did control a pliant municipal bureaucracy and a well-funded club system that knew how to manipulate public opinion and voter lists in order to win elections. Not the least of the motives behind Lueger's final decision in favor of universal suffrage in 1905–6 was his ardent desire to beat the Social Democrats at their own game, but on his own political territory—if not on the Ringstrasse, then in the polling place.

Lueger's birthday fiasco showed that by 1905 the hatred between the two mass parties and their social clients far surpassed simple economic or class dimensions. The gap between Christian Social and Social Democratic loyalists had widened to form a chasm in Viennese society, encompassing religion, education, law, and dynastic privilege. In their celebration of organized, machine-like power and in their contempt for sectarian political minorities, however, the two parties did have powerful shared attributes. To the extent that both tried to subordinate "national" rhetoric and emotions to the strategic needs of the social policy prerogatives and aspirations of their constituents, they sought to define the past in terms of the future rather than, as Schönerer and the rabid nationalists did, to enchain the future in the mythology of the past. Both preferred spectacle to myth.

Upon the fall of Koerber's government, political power in Vienna by early 1905 thus stood in uneasy equilibrium between the Christian Socials and the Social Democrats. The Christian Socials were in full command of the machinery of government in the city and were confident of future electoral supremacy, but they were also worried that their hegemony might be disrupted by the "terror" tactics of the Social Democrats. For the Social Democrats, temporary loss of the schools was counterbalanced by the perverse pleasure they took in denigrating Lueger and being able to stage mass demonstrations. After 1905 many of the younger socialist pedagogues—Seitz and Glöckel were the most prominent—moved beyond the school system (from which they had been either fired or placed on inactive service) to other, more significant roles within the Social Democratic hierarchy. A new field of opportunity opened in 1907, when Karl Seitz and Otto Glöckel were elected to the new "peoples'" parliament from Vienna and Seitz became executive secretary of the Social Democratic parliamentary delegation. The anticlericalism that these young teachers had preached with such little success in the Lower Austrian school system could now be revived and applied to larger social concerns. The pedagogical anticlericalism of the *Jungen* would, when married with the more academic anticlericalism of young Austro-Marxist theorists like Max Adler and Otto Bauer, become a defining force in Social Democratic policy by 1911.

All of these factors—the confidence and self-satisfaction of the Christian Social party after almost a decade of absolute rule in Vienna; its willingness to face the socialists in a showdown battle for control of parliament; and its deep hatred for those "Jewish-led freethinkers" who despoiled the *Vaterstadt* under the benevolent protection of a "weak" government (from whose "weakness" the party also profited handsomely)—were of critical import in the decisions that the party leadership would take in supporting universal suffrage in 1906.

In early 1905, as both feuding Czech and German national politicians from Bohemia celebrated their "victory" in ridding themselves of Ernest von Koerber, the Christian Social *Deutsche Zeitung* insisted that one important aspect of the collision between feuding national groups and Koerber had heretofore been ignored:

We must emphasize one point that has up to now been ignored in the press. The [German] Left would not have allowed itself to be pushed into such a false direction if the influence of the city of Vienna had been able to make its mark felt more effectively. That has not happened. Vienna represents approximately 20 per cent of the German population of Austria, but its influence in no way corresponds to this numerical ratio. In the Auersperg era [the 1870s] it was the German Casino in Prague that commanded the Germans of Austria and to which everyone, from the Great Mountains [in northern Bohemia] to the Adriatic, had to submit if they did not want to be accused of being a "traitor" to the German cause. The Casino is now deposed, but now one allows Eger and Reichenberg and the suburbs of Graz to bully Vienna and to terrorize on occasion the totality of the Germans. Whether that is a healthy relationship is beside the point. But it is clear that if Vienna's voice and votes had been decisive, Dr. Karel Kramář would not be posing today as a man of triumph.[234]

In setting the world of municipal politics in Vienna on a national stage, the universal suffrage reform of 1907 would respond decisively to these complaints. The two largest party blocs in parliament after 1907 were both molded in the context of Vienna's political culture, and both would seek to impress upon the Hapsburg state paths to political and social modernity radically different from those of the curial-national parliaments of the past forty years. Bypassed by "state" politics for almost a half-century, Vienna finally took possession of the state.

TWO

Universal Suffrage and the Founding of the Reichspartei, 1905–1907

The Party in 1905

By 1905 the Christian Socials were justifiably proud of their political and administrative victories, even if events like those surrounding Lueger's birthday imposed limits on their escalating ambitions. In the course of less than a decade they had recast municipal politics in Vienna, seizing control of the administrative apparatus of the city and launching large-scale public works programs that generated favorable publicity for Vienna throughout Europe. Lueger settled into the role of an esteemed *Bürger* patrician, a role that he had craved all his life and that he now, with only a few years remaining to him, played to the hilt. The jealous comments of Erich Kielmansegg about Lueger's egregious vanity on public occasions when the Emperor or Kielmansegg were present merely confirmed Lueger's pride in his city and in himself epitomizing the *christliches Volk*.[1] A journalist close to Lueger's nemesis, Karl Hermann Wolf, acidly described the archaic rhetoric and the inflated "imperial" pretensions that surrounded Lueger's public appearances:

> When "He" [Lueger] undertakes official ceremonies, everything must be decked out with flags, with young girls dressed in white dresses presenting him with bouquets of flowers. . . . And now the newest item. On the occasion of the dedication of the Laimgrubenkirche, the Municipal School Board issued an edict that the Emperor and the Mayor were to be jointly cheered by the local schoolchildren and the teachers. But we are not yet finished. The *Deutsches Volksblatt* of the 8th of the month announced: "at the dedication of the new ward administration building in the Twentieth District Herr Alois Swoboda had the honor to be introduced to Mayor Lueger [wurde die Ehre zu-

teil dem Bürgermeister Dr. Lueger vorgestellt zu werden]." What differentiates Dr. Lueger indeed from a Monarch? In his own mind he imagines himself to be an imperial ruler in any event, and those who live from "his grace" are legion.[2]

But Lueger's arrogance was not wholly self-serving, for he was supremely conscious of the fact that his growing list of titles and honors also enhanced the respect he could wring from Court officials or bureaucratic paper pushers. Hence Karl Seitz's account of Lueger's joy at receiving the title of *Geheimrat:*

Do you realize that when we are invited to the Hofburg, the Police President of Vienna sits at the head of the table, because he is Baron Brzesowsky? Who, however, is of greater importance for the city of Vienna: the Mayor or the Police President? From the point of view of Vienna's interests I have always felt quite bitter about the fact that I must always sit at the low end of the Imperial table. Now it will be different—I am a Privy Councillor of His Majesty, and therefore an Excellency. I, as Mayor of Vienna, will sit near the head of the table, and that will be an honor for the city of Vienna.[3]

With the passage of the 1904 school laws and the equally noteworthy passage and sanction of the incorporation of Floridsdorf into the city, which Lueger pushed through in late 1904 and which increased the territory of Vienna by over 50 percent, the party seemed to stand at the pinnacle of success.[4] But for some in the party, especially men of ambition like Albert Gessmann and Friedrich Funder, the success the party merited was merely the first step on the ladder of Imperial honor and power to which the Christian Socials might aspire. As long as the party thought of itself as merely an urban, municipal party, using its modest delegation in parliament to protect the city's interests, its potential was limited to that of a regional movement. Lueger had mobilized Vienna as his power base, cajoling and intimidating the Imperial government into supporting his policies. This in itself resolved one fundamental weakness of the old Liberal regime in the city, which had to depend on outside political support for its defense. But what would happen if the party were to build upon such a superb base of power, find allies and confederates elsewhere among the German-speaking *Bürgertum,* and earn for itself a greater share of power on the state level? Gessmann realized—this was an undercurrent in his fulminous attacks against Koerber for the latter's forbearance toward the socialists in November 1904—that without such an expanded role the Christian Social party would always be at the mercy of the administrative policy-makers who had risen to prominence since Badeni. The Cabinet might be manipulated on particular issues of local interest to the party, but unless the Christian Socials actually won membership in the Cabinet and forced a parliamentarization of national affairs they would have no control over the government on *state* legislation (such as canal investments or social insurance). Without such power the Christian Socials might end up being held accountable by their own voters for policies over which they had no direct control, simply because they now presented a "governmental" image of their own, albeit on the *Land*, as opposed to the state, level.

Such restlessness reflected the rising expectations in which top Christian Social leaders were happily entrapped by 1905. When the party had assumed power in 1896 many in its leadership were probably fearful that Count Badeni's predictions would prove true—that Lueger and his colleagues would make such a mess of municipal and regional government that either the Imperial government or the voters themselves would soon throw them out of office. But, in fact, exactly the opposite had happened. Not only did Leopold Steiner, Robert Pattai, Albert Gessmann, and others who obtained top municipal and provincial administrative positions find that they enjoyed the power and perquisites that went along with public life, but they also felt that they had been successful in meeting their administrative responsibilities. Utilizing the professional staffs of the various public bureaucracies, the party had done a credible if churlish and often self-interested job of administrative rule.[5] Nor was the contrast between the relatively stable political environment of Vienna and Lower Austria on the one hand and the chaos in the central parliament and in the Bohemian Diet on the other lost on Christian Social publicists. Hence could Josef von Baechlé, a wealthy local party leader from the First District, proudly inform a meeting of the *Verein "Christliche Familie"* in December 1903 that

> instead of trying to improve the people politically and economically by vigorous work and to pave the way for solving the great problems of modern life, our fatherland has been brought to the brink of disaster. . . . Only in Vienna and more recently in Lower Austria do we see a party in control which does not view its role as stirring up the people, but rather in strengthening their productive energies; one that does not pose chimerical programs directed toward the destruction of the state, but one that holds strongly to the Dynasty and to the Austrian state idea; one that is interested not in weakening, but in enhancing the state.[6]

Gadfly critics like Joseph Schöffel might recount individual instances of Christian Social mismanagement, but since the Liberal party had also faced many such accusations, the Christian Socials lost no sleep over such commentaries.[7] Opponents like the Social Democrats criticized the accumulation of offices and salaries and the double and even triple job distribution among the party elite, but this merely encouraged those concerned to think in more expansive terms. When Albert Gessmann boldly called for "reconstruction of the state" in early 1904, he certainly anticipated that his own party would play a substantial role in that process.[8]

These ambitions paralleled a slow process of cultural maturation accompanying the civic hegemony of the last six years of Lueger's rule in Vienna. Between 1897 and 1904 Viennese politics had seen a series of dramatic provocations as the Christian Socials made the transition from opposition tribunes to power-holders. Lueger's attempt to channel public funds toward the construction of Catholic churches, which led to Lucian Brunner's fronde against the city before the Administrative Court; the controversy in 1898 over the Municipal School Board's attempt to allow Jewish and Catholic schoolchildren in ten public schools to be assigned to confessionally designated classrooms (which the Ministry of Education severely restricted); the debacle of the Kaiser-Jubiläums-Stadttheater, which began as an "Aryan" theater in 1898 and ended up after 1904 as a conventional, market-oriented enterprise; Hermann Bielohlawek's folk drama in December 1902 in which he threatened the annihilation of the Jews; Ernst Schneider's ritual-murder fantasies; Josef Gregorig's and Josef Scheicher's discursive effluvium—the account book overflowed with crude language and outrageous behavior, even if some of it was offered for histrionic purposes.[9] Yet slowly a greater realism and sobriety took shape. In part this may have reflected the confidence that came from holding power, with Schönerer contained, the socialist schoolteachers politically marginalized, and party leaders more comfortable about their electorate. The outcome of the City Council elections for the First Curia in May 1904, where the Christian Socials swept all seats except for the First, Second, Ninth, and Nineteenth Districts, was particularly satisfying, since it reaffirmed the continued ability of the party to co-opt (or intimidate) former gentile Liberal voters into the new regime. Anti-Semitism had now reached its functional apogee, since as the *Reichspost* told its readers "the complete political separation between Judaism and Christianity has now been completed, and even Liberals begin to feel uncomfortable about being elected by Jews."[10] But even here, exceptions could be and were made, for a quiet (and extremely sensitive) theme of post-1900 politics in Vienna was the phenomenon of some Jews choosing to vote for Christian Social candidates.[11] We have evidence that this happened in the Diet election between Lueger himself and Eduard Jordan held in the Leopoldstadt in November 1902; and again in the April 1910 municipal elections when the Christian Social ward boss of the Josefstadt, Johann Bergauer, negotiated with local Jewish leaders to persuade their voters in the First Curia to support his party's candidate, Karl Stahlich, against the renegade journalist Ernst Vergani. The Jewish electors apparently complied, feeling that it was a question of the lesser of two evils.[12]

When Joseph Bloch, the feisty Jewish journalist, mocked Lueger in 1904 for continually violating his professed creed of "Kauft nur bei Christen" by extending lucrative municipal contracts to Jewish suppliers, there was both irony and truth in the observation.[13] Nor did anti-Semitic zealots have an easy time in overriding normal patterns of interchange between gentiles and Jews in the marketplace, in spite of the boycott campaign instigated by Prince Alois Liechtenstein and others, since as late as 1904 the president of the *Verein "Christliche Familie"* was expressing irritation about the "extraordinary divergence between the language and the behavior of so many Christians, between complaining about the Jews and yet shopping at Jewish stores."[14] By 1907 this association, which was created in the early 1890s in support of local artisans and which published a "Wegweiser" to encourage Christian Social customers to boycott Jewish merchants and to patronize party-affiliated "Christian" merchants, was in deep financial and organizational trouble, with public doubts being expressed about the effectiveness of its tactics and one leader admitting that "in the case of many district groups much remains to be desired. All too many are in need of revival." Not surprisingly, the frustrated leaders blamed the Christian Social party leadership, whom they saw as not sincerely interested in supporting their "economic program" of retail anti-Semitism.[15] By 1910 Sigmund Mayer, a local Jewish merchant who was also a community leader and political activist, would report that "now the Christian Social party is moving gradually to another point of view. Its leaders have become convinced about the impossibility of destroying the Jews economically. They have given up this effort and now are worried only about themselves and their constituents. There is little doubt that sooner or later the party will have to give up struggling against the Jews altogether."[16]

Having used "the Jews" discursively and emotionally to define a new political universe for all others in the city, many party leaders saw private arrangements with Jewish individuals or even groups that ranged beyond (or stopped short of) electoral politics as being tolerable and, within the limits of discretion, politically cost-free. For some observers it was time to put the issue where it belonged, on the back burner. Hence Anton Bach argued candidly in 1906 that

> It may be time to put the problem [of anti-Semitism] in its proper place as a secondary issue and to give up the eternal *Antisemitenriecherei* as well as the eternal *Judenriecherei*. The Christian Socials especially go on and on with verbal Jew-hatred, and for the Jews they are a bête noire, a red flag. And yet anyone who knows the real circumstances knows that neither the Jews nor the Christian Socials, viewed as individuals or as groups, do each other much harm. They not only make the very best deals with each other, but Lueger even brags with

pride that his administration does not differentiate according to nation, race, and confession, and, in fact, the first avenue [of appeal] for every poor Jew who feels that a city agency has done him an alleged wrong is the Mayor, who often enough intervenes [on their behalf].[17]

The slow but certain marginalization of old-line true believers like Ernst Schneider and Josef Scheicher within the ranks of the party leadership also became a matter of record. In Scheicher's case this resulted in bitter personal attacks on Albert Gessmann, embedded in Scheicher's voluminous autobiography, *Erlebnisse und Erinnerungen.*[18] In Schneider's case it culminated in his defeat for reelection to parliament in May 1907 and his repudiation by a majority of his colleagues in his bid to join the Lower Austrian Provincial Executive Committee in January 1908.[19] Soon thereafter Richard Weiskirchner would write to Lueger complaining that "unfortunately Ernst Schneider has been behaving in an extremely irresponsible manner and is throwing stones in all directions."[20] The dramatic purge of Josef Gregorig by the Christian Social *Bürgerklub* in early February 1904 for having complained too loudly about the inauthenticity of the anti-Semitism of many party leaders, as well as about alleged influence peddling by some members of the *Stadtrat,* was also suggestive. For Gregorig a new standard of political correctness was necessary: "at the next elections we will ask these gentlemen directly whether or not they indeed are anti-Semites. If one of them replies that they are Christian Socials, we will respond: that's not enough! For under that label the greatest charlatans have come into the party. They must clearly and cleanly confess themselves to be anti-Semites—otherwise they face a fight to the finish!"[21] An official investigative commission organized by Lueger found it difficult to refute charges Gregorig leveled later in the same month against Ludwig Zatzka: that Zatzka, a member of the *Stadtrat* and a wealthy building contractor, had influenced the allocation of official contracts; that he had facilitated real-estate transactions in which he had a personal interest; that he had helped his son-in-law, who worked for the city, to gain a lucrative management contract; and that various of his actions had damaged the city's financial interests. The commission's failure paralleled the inability of the party to disprove Gregorig's accusations about the careless opportunism of its anti-Semitism.[22]

In a very different direction the promotion of Hermann Bielohlawek to important administrative positions—especially as a member of the Lower Austrian Executive Committee, where he was the czar of regional social welfare in Lower Austria and the sponsor of commercial development for small trades—was a signal that changes were at hand. Unlike Schneider and Gregorig, Bielohlawek was a resilient ward heeler of considerable native talent and with a taste for verbal political combat who, once on the escalator of ascending power, gradually matured as a politician and as a person. Having been

first elected to the parliament along with Lueger in the democratic Fifth Curia
in 1897, Bielohlawek had a penchant for flippantly humorous as well as nox-
ious rhetoric, and he was known (and in the party considerably admired) for
his rhetorical bluster and combativeness. His infamous speech in the City
Council in 1902, in which he threatened to destroy the Jewish community, has
long served as a benchmark of the party's anti-Semitism.[23] Bielohlawek's early
populist connections with the *Angestellten* movement eventually lost attractiveness for him, however, and under Gessmann's patronage he was elected to
the *Stadtrat* in October 1901 and to the Lower Austrian provincial government
in May 1905. Since Bielohlawek also edited a newspaper, the *Österreichische
Volkspresse,* local businessmen in search of public contracts soon proved a
boon for the paper's advertising income. In 1907 Bielohlawek maneuvered
himself into a more comfortable parliamentary seat from the Parkviertel in the
First District, where his constituents were among the wealthiest in the city, if
not the Monarchy. To the chagrin of his critics he not only began to wear fancy
clothes, but he drove around Vienna in a handsome coach, ate at the best restaurants, learned to speak passable French, and even quoted Euripides, and he
proved himself a clever and able administrator.[24] His witty barbs against the
Liberals merited him Karl Kraus's tag of "Der Hanswurst des Liberalismus."[25]
By any reasonable accounting his stewardship of Lower Austrian health-care
facilities was fair and balanced, just as his work on behalf of youth protection
was dedicated and effective, evaluations shared at the end of his career even
by his political enemies in the civil service, the Social Democratic party, and
in the Liberal press.[26] As the liberal-democratic *Neues Wiener Tagblatt* observed when he died in 1918, Bielohlawek "made an effort in the course of the
years to polish up his original manner as an agitator and by self-education and
self-discipline to achieve what he had set as his life goal—to be able to administer the governmental positions he achieved in an objective and professional
manner."[27] During the War he played a valuable role in sustaining public mo-
rale in the face of hunger and other deprivations.[28] Upon his death even his
most ardent opponents, the Viennese Social Democrats, were generous in their
evaluation of his later career.[29]

The life of Heinrich Hierhammer also exemplified the upward mobility of
marginal *kleinbürgerlich* types into positions of power and influence, which
encouraged them to assume roles of moderation and respectability toward all
members of the urban community.[30] Born into a humble petty bourgeois family
in 1857, Hierhammer attended an *Unterrealschule* and had a number of modest
white-collar jobs before establishing a small printing business. In his role as
an amateur actor and entertainer he first encountered Lueger at a charity event
in the later 1880s. He soon became involved in the anti-Liberal movement in
the early 1890s, first as a loyalist of Schönerer and as an editor on Ernst Vergani's *Deutsches Volksblatt,* and then, after breaking with Vergani, as an orga-

nizer for Lueger and Pattai—Robert Pattai gave him 100 fl. to help out in the 1891 parliamentary elections and then steered lucrative printing contracts to Hierhammer's firm. Soon Hierhammer's economic situation took a dramatic turn for the better. He considered himself and his family well situated, with a business that produced a "handsome profit" and left him the free time to be elected to the City Council from the wealthy First Curia in Margarethen in 1898. From a modest *Kleinbürger* in 1890 Hierhammer felt he had joined the well-situated *Mittelbürgertum* by the turn of the century. From there, it only required Lueger's personal favor to be selected for the position of third vice-mayor in 1905, a record of social and political ascent of which Hierhammer was extremely proud. He later recalled of the office he occupied as *Vizebürgermeister* and of those who paid him congratulatory visits:

> All of this constituted a kind of backdrop to the status, the position, to the social level that I now occupied in public life. The step from simple businessman and modest city councilman to vice-mayor of the capital of the Empire, the elevation of a former ordnance sergeant to the [protocol] rank of a Major General (which I assumed on occasions at which the Emperor or some other member of the Court appeared), was indeed a powerful upward leap.[31]

Also noteworthy about Hierhammer's personal circumstances was that his wife, Leopoldine, was Jewish, and that Hierhammer himself avoided the kind of raucous anti-Semitism practiced elsewhere in the party.[32] It was not surprising that at the funeral of the actor and former *Burgtheater* director Adolf Sonnenthal in April 1909 the Jewish community leader and Liberal city councilman Wilhelm Stiassny would direct conciliatory words toward Hierhammer, while both of them stood at Sonnenthal's grave.[33]

Even the *Österreichische Wochenschrift* recognized during the 1904 communal elections that anti-Semitic rhetoric had become careless ritual. Complaints to the party headquarters by aggrieved and believing anti-Semites (of whom the party certainly continued to have a goodly share) about municipal contracts awarded to Jewish suppliers and merchants suggest that the economic consequences of "official" anti-Semitism may have diminished over time, even if Jew-baiting remained a ready tool in times of stress, as the dramatic events of the autumn of 1905 would show. Richard Weiskirchner, who was always close to Lueger in his politics, went so far as to give a public interview to a journalist in 1907 in which he insisted that "when I served as the director of charitable affairs in the city administration, my justice and evenhandedness were recognized even by our enemies. I provided assistance to poor and needy Jews in the same way as to poor, oppressed Christians. Charity, like human misery, knows no boundaries."[34] Whether or not Weiskirchner actually meant what he said is certainly important, but the most notable feature of this claim was the fact that he was willing to make it in public. By 1905 Lueger himself felt confident enough to take the heat that his nomination of Josef Porzer to become the second vice-mayor of the city of Vienna generated in racial anti-Semitic circles, for Porzer's mother was Jewish and he himself strongly identified with Catholic, as opposed to more secular, anti-Semitic interests in the party.[35] Against the pan-German screams of treachery and betrayal, the Christian Social press was uncharacteristically silent.[36] Nor was Porzer's an isolated case: not only was Heinrich Hierhammer's wife Jewish, but so too was the mother of the young Christian Social lawyer and politician Victor Kienböck, who became a leading figure in interwar Austrian politics. The Hierhammer and Porzer cases led the venerable Social Democratic politician Franz Schuhmeier to heap sarcasm on the Christian Socials:

> Gentlemen! In the Viennese City Council the descendant of a Jew has become the second vice-mayor, and the husband of a Jew is about to become the third vice-mayor. It seems to me that the pastors of the churches in Vienna will not be able to handle all the Jews who will come to them to be baptized, because they think that they can become something in the Lueger administration. If not vice-mayor, they can at least hope to become a provincial deputy or a member of the Provincial Committee or a member of the *Stadtrat*.[37]

Lueger himself would later insist to Guido Adler in 1909 that he had steered his party "three years ago" onto a more moderate course, one that it would not depart from in the future.[38] Upon Lueger's death in 1910 the socialist *Arbeiter-Zeitung* candidly admitted that "in the final period of his life he [Lueger] demonstrated a clear effort to stop or at least to weaken the injustices to which his party was all too easily inclined."[39]

Nor was this muddying of the anti-Semitic front done out of the good nature or moral conviction of these politicians. It was part of a larger process of maturation that drew the Christian Social party into the grasp of the formerly hated "plutocrats" and "capitalists" and won it substantial, government-mediated support from large industry and the banking sector. One clear measure of this trend was the willingness of senior party leaders to accept positions as directors on the corporate boards of various industrial and commercial enterprises, where they often found themselves sitting side by side with Jewish fellow directors. By 1910, for example, Gessmann, Ebenhoch, Hierhammer, Morsey, Fink, Fuchs, Schraffl, Baumgartner, and Hagenhofer served as *Verwaltungsräte*. Morsey's firm, the Leykam-Josefstal Aktiengesellschaft, was Jewish-owned.[40] Another indicator was the comfortable relationship that the city administration developed with the large Viennese banks, in whose direction wealthy Jews played a prominent role. When the anti-Semitic *Stadtrat* issued a statement in June 1908 commending the support provided by the *Bodencreditanstalt* and the *Länderbank* in placing a new 360-million-crown loan, local Social Democrats led by Jakob Reumann observed that this was a highly unusual way to fight "Jewish capital." Unperturbed by these rhetorical darts, Victor Silberer replied for his party that "Dr. Lueger and the whole anti-Semitic party have never had a bigger triumph than today. Now we have obtained the trust which the Liberals have denied us . . . and this trust expresses itself in the splendid terms given to us on a silver plate by the Viennese, the Jewish financial world."[41] A third factor was the utility of anti-socialist collaboration for wealthy gentiles and Jews, an exercise in which the Christian Socials necessarily played a leading role after 1907. Was it surprising that *Die Industrie,* the journal of the *Zentralverband der Industriellen Österreichs,* would assure its readers in early 1908 that "the fact that the future minister of labor in Austria, Dr. Gessmann, does not sympathize with Social Democracy, is sufficient, in and of itself, to assure him the trust of Austrian producers and employers"?[42]

None of these trends meant that Christian Social voters were any less anti-Semitic, although in some district elections just before the war these same voters received campaign literature in which little or no trace of anti-Semitism was evident, an extraordinary change from the 1890s.[43] Nor can they mean that Viennese Jews felt either happy about or satisfied with their marginalized political status, or with Lueger's arrogant, off-again-on-again paternalism toward them, or with the emotional defensiveness into which they were frequently forced.[44] As the re-eruption of gutter anti-Semitism in Vienna in the middle and later stages of the First World War clearly demonstrated, deeply rooted cultural attitudes were involved here that could be manipulated again, should changed economic or political circumstances make this necessary or even desirable.[45] What is important to note, however, is that in the last decade before the war the Christian Social party *as a structural ensemble* had begun to pursue a different, more multifaceted agenda. And, as Anton Bach observed, this implied possible tensions between issues that worked on the municipal level in Vienna and those that worked beyond Vienna. Upper Austrian or Tyrolian peasants were probably no less inclined toward knee-jerk anti-Semitism than many of their fellow Viennese voters, but the issue itself did not have the same valence in their socioeconomic worlds, and attempting to marginalize Jews was not something on which they would be inclined to spend much political capital.[46]

On the gender front one also observed the fascinating efforts of party arrivistes clamoring for approval and social influence. The first Christian Social women's organization, the *Christlicher Wiener Frauenbund,* began in March 1897 as little more than a crude lobbying group with raucous political aims.[47] Its female supporters had played an important theatrical role in the process leading up to Lueger's confirmation, and it is fair to say that Christian Social party leaders were conscious of the potential influence that married women from the lower and middle *Bürgertum* might exercise over their husbands' political choices throughout the period before 1914.[48] The kind of discourse employed in its weekly newspaper (the *Österreichische Frauen-Zeitung*) and that articulated in the group's public rallies and meetings stressed the role of women in nurturing children, caring for and/or managing the home, and guaranteeing civility, decency, and religious values.[49] Yet the day-to-day practices of the association also assumed that these women did have the capacity to hold opinions about public issues, and that the party (and in a more subordinate sense the Church) was responsible for shaping and sustaining these opinions. This does not mean that the Christian Social party advocated or supported active political rights for women. But it does suggest that there was both male and female consensus about the propriety of supportive roles for women in affirming certain kinds of political choices.[50] The regular appearance of politicians and clerics as speakers before assemblies of these women gave them a real, if shadowy, existence as a legitimate political audience, as did the regular attendance at party rallies by wives of local politicians or other local loyalists. The passivity of the role should not lead us to minimize the importance of the process of inching adult women into the realm of political discourse and political opinions, whatever the particular content of those opinions might be. To the extent that "the family" was idolized by Christian Social propagandists and to the extent that junior members of many Christian Social families profited from official or unofficial nepotism and from network patronage mediated by their fathers or mothers, this also made families into semi-public household units in which political roles were distinct but political values and conversation were doubtlessly shared.

But organizations like the *Christlicher Wiener Frauenbund* and the *Verein "Christliche Familie,"* along with a myriad of other small clubs and voluntary associations, also played private roles throughout the period by brokering local, neighborhood sociability and organizing modest charitable events to benefit the local poor.[51] The half-public "maternalist" practices of the Christian Social women ran parallel to the city's official philanthropic paternalism—both sought to help the poor, but on terms designed to ensure the psychological security and status superiority of the benefactors.[52] Of special note was the ability of many of the *Frauenbund*'s *Ortsgruppen* to organize social events that brought circles of friends and acquaintances of both sexes together on a regular basis, usually in the context of an amateur musical performance or a banquet or a short journey, occasions where few traces of formal "political" behavior were evident but where leisure was nonetheless politically constituted and legitimated.[53] The longer the Christian Socials remained in power the more complex these networks of semi-private sociability became; their constituents, many of whom thought of themselves as members of petty, ward-level social elites, clearly had a level of material and temporal resources to devote to leisure that marked them as different from their Social Democratic interlocutors.

Eventually, however, more complex sets of gender-related activities and resources were brought into play. The performative rituals of the *Ball der Stadt Wien*, for example, became occasions for the Christian Social political *Prominenz*, together with their wives, to mingle with established agents of Viennese high or at least higher society and to accomplish breathtaking, if self-deluding, social climbing. The May corso in the Prater, on which Lueger's administration bestowed substantial moral patronage, was a similar integrative event on a broader scale where members of the high and higher aristocracy, wealthy bourgeois ladies (some of them Jewish), and Christian Social women all played complementary, if unequal, roles.[54] Society columns in the *Reichspost* and *Deutsches Volksblatt* reporting the style and color of the dresses worn by these women at such semi-public social gatherings marked a slow revolution in status and prestige, as important in its own way as the vote totals Lueger's cronies produced on election day. By 1905 women associated with the Christian Social party were participating in large-scale charitable activities, like the *Wiener Kinderhilfstag*, along with women drawn from aristocratic and high bourgeois social circles.[55] Bertha Weiskirchner, spouse of the *Magistratsdirektor* who was Lueger's putative political heir, was widely known for her aggressive self-advancement in higher social circles, and even for her dreams of becoming "Frau Ministerpräsident."[56] Heinrich Hierhammer was equally proud of his wife's service as a representative of the city: "with the greatest satisfaction and inner gratification I observed that my wife had successfully taken on the role of the wife of the vice-mayor of Vienna and understood how to represent herself in that capacity, for which her education and natural disposition served her well."[57] Eduard Heinl later recalled the surprise and satisfaction that he felt as a poor nobody from an impoverished family on entering these circles:

> Among other things I still remember being presented to the spouse of the *Statthalter* of Lower Austria, Frau Anastasia Kielmansegg, who was the head of countless charitable organizations. I, the son of a concierge woman, learned how to get along in these circles. I believe that it proved not all that difficult, for soon I had laid my shyness aside, and in any event I was not frightened by the allure of these elegant circles. One only had to approach them with a kind of decisive firmness.[58]

Certainly the first as well as the second society of Vienna continued to think of most of these people—Christian Social politicians and their spouses—as outsiders. Ironically, in this realm of social "allure" the Christian Social upstarts were cast in roles not unlike those they tried to force upon the Viennese Jews. Both groups, the one with enormous political power and little claim to "taste," the other with great intellectual and (for a small elite) financial power but (after 1897) no claim to "politics," found themselves simultaneously tolerated *and* snubbed.

Political Modernism and Corporate Protectionism in 1907

Three major legislative efforts approved by the parliament in early 1907 illuminated the new aggressiveness of the Christian Social party and demonstrated its anxious claims to exert a more prominent role in state affairs: the universal manhood suffrage law, the reform of the *Gewerbeordnung,* and salary-reform legislation for state officials. All three bills showed how far the party had come since its strict oppositional period of the early 1890s and how far Austrian parliamentary life was able to rebound from its nadir in the Koerber era. But while the first law was a bold act of political modernism that reshaped the landscape of Austrian electoral politics and, indirectly, that of Imperial public life, the second and third laws were more traditional responses, undertaken to shore up voter support for the party in the coming days of universal competition. All three bills demonstrated that parliament had emerged, if only temporarily, from the self-destructiveness of the Koerber period, and all three had powerful unintended consequences both for the Austrian state and for the Christian Social party over the long haul.

The most important single national policy action in which the Christian Socials played a formative role after 1897 was without doubt the enactment of universal manhood suffrage.[59] The story of the introduction of universal suffrage in Austria has been related before, but the central role played by the Christian Social party in achieving the reform has not been fully recognized. Indeed, early historians of the Social Democratic party studiously ignored the contributions of their best-hated rivals in completing the reform.[60]

The storm over universal suffrage revealed both the opportunities and the constraints that all large bourgeois political movements faced in Austria in 1905. For eight years Austria had been embarrassed and victimized by a deadlocked political system, at the center of which stood a parliament which one recent historian has characterized as a "dying institution."[61] Touted as a panacea that would both revive Austrian parliamentary life and resolve the intransigent nationality question by bringing new, social-oriented voters into the polling place, the enactment of universal manhood suffrage in Austria in 1906 was an enormous gamble. By 1914 it was judged by contemporaries (and has continued to be judged by later historians) as a failure. Yet this viewpoint is perhaps too one-sided, for to the extent that suffrage reform encouraged more powerful party machines and more coordinated German national coalition groups (such as the *Deutscher Nationalverband*) it was in fact a modest success.[62] More significant was the law's effect in opening up the system to younger politicians like Josef Redlich, Wilhelm Miklas, Michael Mayr, Leopold Kunschak, Karl Renner, Ferdinand Skaret, and Otto Glöckel, all of whom first entered parliament and state-level politics in 1907. Other *novi homines* who had already served in parliament gained new responsibilities, such as Karl Seitz, who became the secretary to the Social Democratic parliamentary delegation. The political elites of the First Republic earned their spurs in the parliament of 1907. There were no fewer parties in the parliament after 1907 (in fact, there were more), but they felt themselves able to represent their "house" interest groups and constituents more effectively before various governmental agencies.[63] And it is important to remember that the democratically elected parliament of 1907–14 was (in a rump version) responsible for the peaceful transition in power that took place in Austria in November 1918, in sharp contrast to the violent upheavals endured by Hungary, which lacked such publicly legitimate representational systems.

Still, Austrian party structures were sorely tested by the enormous expectations and opportunities generated by universal suffrage. More complex forms of political partisanship evolved, not all of which assumed the form of "national" contentiousness. A powerful yet unexplored issue during this period was, for example, the emergence of informal coalition groups of rural-agrarian and urban-industrial interests, cutting across national, ethnic, religious, and on rare occasions even class lines. Equally important may have been the reform's opening of parliament to men with more varied, and often less formally educated social backgrounds, individuals who some commentators felt would be more inclined to put self-interest before the general interest.[64] Both trends—a more coherent organization of political representation and an increased sensitivity by the party leaders to the need of acknowledging the particularistic interests of their colleagues while at the same time cloaking them in more universal forms of eudaemonistic discourse—resulted in new forms of party-government interaction: actual parliamentary representation in the Cabinet during the period 1907–9 and for 1909–11 governments with a mix of civil servants and party members that had a closer appreciation than Koerber had demonstrated before 1904 of the need for negotiations with and consensus among the larger centrist parties (German, Polish, and Czech).

During much of 1905, domestic political opinion in Austria and especially within the Christian Social party focused on the constitutional turbulence in Hungary, with the Christian Socials attracting public sympathy as one of the most vigilant anti-Magyar groups in Austrian politics. If nothing else the Hungarian crisis was a welcome change from the endless ethnic bickering that had marked Austrian parliamentary politics in 1904. Albert Gessmann was not alone in using the threat of chaos in Hungary to emphasize the need for reconciling Germans and Czechs in restoring working order to the Austrian parliament, but such rhetoric was an important forecast of his party's looming agenda.[65] Certainly the party welcomed Emperor Franz Joseph's vague threat that he might impose universal suffrage in Hungary and thus destroy the monopoly of gentry power unless the Hungarian Independence party retreated from its extreme demands on the army, the economy, and the constitutional system.[66] Hence it was not surprising that when Gessmann engineered a meeting of the Lower Austrian party cadres in September 1905 at Eggenburg, a small town 60 kilometers northwest of Vienna, he combined an attack on the "Judeo-Magyar clique" in Budapest with a rebuke against the Cabinet in Vienna led by Paul von Gautsch, both of which opposed introducing universal suffrage in Hungary.[67]

The Christian Socials' resolution that passed at Eggenburg on September 17 was cautiously silent, however, about a similar program of electoral reform for the western half of the Empire. The first dramatic push for reform came from the Left, but even here the protocols of the Social Democratic leadership suggest that Victor Adler and his lieutenants did not anticipate how far they could realistically push the issue until after the Russian Revolution exploded in late October.[68] When parliament reopened on September 26, 1905, several groups of deputies submitted motions of urgency requesting suffrage reform in Austria. Speaking for his party on October 2, Karl Lueger committed the Christian Socials to support these motions, arguing that electoral reform might break the hold of the Magyar gentry in Hungary and denationalize parliamentary feuding in Austrian politics.[69] At this stage, however, the issue was still highly speculative and Lueger gave no sense that the party was prepared to fight uncompromisingly. He also noted, in a preview of party strategy, that the Christian Socials could accept universal suffrage only with a high (five-year) residency requirement and a law prescribing compulsory voting—the first intended to disenfranchise tens of thousands of seasonal laborers in Vienna, the second to compensate for the more effective party machinery of the socialists by forcing bourgeois voters to exercise their franchise or face legal penalties.

At a meeting of the Joint Ministerial Council in Ischl in August 1905 Gautsch had expressed serious reservations about General Fejérváry's reformist plans for Hungary because of their possible overflow into Austria, declaring that "Austria was not yet ready for universal suffrage."[70] Gautsch's decision in early November 1905 to reverse his earlier opposition reflected the pressures generated by the revolution in Russia, the street violence between socialists and the police on the evening of November 2 (which threatened to escalate unless governmental concessions were forthcoming), and the decision of the Emperor himself, who ordered the Cabinet on November 3 to take up the issue of election reform.[71] The Christian Socials played no role in these events, but these weeks saw the jelling of a coalition of interest within the party leadership in favor of reform. Already in mid-October the "Konservative Korrespondenz," a Catholic-oriented news service, had published an anonymous appeal that Lueger organize a new party, presumably to be based on universal suffrage, that would cut across nationalistic issues and unite different ethnic groups. Whereas the anti-Semitic *Deutsches Volksblatt* roundly rejected the idea, Gessmann's mouthpiece, the *Reichspost,* was sympathetically evasive.[72] By early November Albert Gessmann and others, like Leopold Kunschak, who were interested in expanding the party beyond (and within) Vienna had firmly joined the reform bandwagon.[73]

Yet it was precisely the impact of the reform on Vienna's curial traditions that tempered Lueger's enthusiasm. He candidly admitted in an interview on October 20 that

> with regard to the effect of electoral reform in Austria, I believe that neither my party [in Vienna] nor the Liberals would gain much from it. On the other hand, I believe that the conservative [Catholic] parties would emerge from such a reform greatly strengthened. In any event, a party would emerge that would operate exclusively on the basis of economic reform issues. The present parties have only a modest interest in economic reform and pursue for the most part nationalist aspirations.[74]

To his credit Lueger resisted those of his colleagues who urged that his party negate or compromise the reform. But as the Social Democratic juggernaut began to gain steam, there was little that the Christian Socials could do to maintain a position of parity. In spite of a public rally in support of reform that had been called for the 26th, Lueger's forces still found themselves standing on the sidelines along with the rest of Vienna, envious and outraged, while the Social Democrats took control of the Ringstrasse with their famous parade on November 28, 1905.[75] Lueger himself admitted to Erich Kielmansegg that the government could not prevent the socialist parade, unless they wanted to provoke violence; and reports from Kielmansegg's office show that the final parade was the product of weeks of negotiations among the police, the *Statthalterei,* the Christian Social municipal authorities, and the socialist party leadership. Everyone concerned knew exactly what was at stake and what roles were to be played.[76] The theater of the streets in Vienna also required rehearsals.

But Karl Lueger's common sense and pragmatism as a municipal administrator made it no easier him for to concede his *Vaterstadt* to socialist spectacles.[77] Victor Adler's theatrical triumph must have deeply rankled. That the socialists' tactics on the 28th profoundly embarrassed the Christian Socials was also apparent in the unusually bitter speeches denouncing Red "terrorism" given by local party leaders in the days following the event. The rhetoric of the leaders reflected the anger of their constituents, many of whom had covered their shop windows and closed their doors, complaining that they had been intimidated into doing so by fear of stone-throwing workers. One industrialist, J. L. Herrmann, reported to Kielmansegg that the Social Democratic clerks' association had circularized Viennese shopkeepers and businessmen strongly urging that they close their establishments until 2 P.M. on the 28th. For Herrmann this was "coercion and a disguised threat," which showed that the socialists were becoming "ever bolder and more extravagant." Herrmann fulminated that "it has come to this in our beloved fatherland, that we businessmen have to let ourselves be subject to such an insult," and he demanded the government take strong action to curb such "terrorism."[78] Voices like Herrmann's, deeply anxious about the leading proponents of universal suffrage, were overwhelmed by the chorus of optimism that accompanied the reform, but we would be wrong not to acknowledge the suspicion evident among Viennese *bürgerlich* circles, remembering that Karl Lueger had to take this resistance into account. Among older Christian Social anti-Semitic politicians in Vienna like Robert Pattai and Ernst Schneider, suffrage reform raised grave doubts and covert resistance, as it did for the sometime clerical "democrat" Josef Scheicher.[79] To the nationalist *Herrenhaus* member Karl Auersperg, himself a bitter opponent of the reform, Pattai complained privately in December 1906 that "our party, which had in its first incarnation a truly national and therefore also conservative orientation, has since then been more and more pushed in a democratic direction and others will profit."[80] Not only would this new "democratic direction" of the Christian Social party have to compete with aggressive Social Democrats (not the inept conservatives Schöpfer faced in Tyrol), but in addition universal suffrage was bound to enhance the claims of Leopold Kunschak to a larger share of the Viennese delegation's seats. Either way the older *bürgerlich* leaders and their voters stood to lose.

Compounding the party's perceived "insult" of having been upstaged by Red "terrorists" and embarrassed before its own voters was the fact that a small band of socialist university students, some of whom were Jews, had joined the workers' parade and had exchanged insults with their anti-Semitic, nationalist rivals who were badgering them from the ramp of the university.[81] The result was a brief skirmish that the intervention of the police quickly stopped, but one that was widely reported in the Christian Social press.[82] Christian Social ward agitators and journalists spread real or fictional stories about Jews taking special pride in the socialist parade.[83] To eager and frightened anti-Semitic minds the connection was now all too apparent: not only were the "Reds" inciting terrorism, but Jews were aiding and abetting that effort as well. That journalists writing for the big Liberal dailies were extravagant in their coverage of the march was simply more salt in the Christian Socials' wounds.

Lueger had to respond in some way to the alarm of his voters. During the chaos on October 31, when news had arrived in Vienna of the Czar's constitutional concessions, several prominent socialist orators had played on and exploited the Russian motif. Alluding to the possible use of a general strike, Wilhelm Ellenbogen told his party's congress that if need be the "congenial and sensible Austrian proletariat will learn to speak Russian, for we have no right to hold back the inflamed passions of our brothers in the factories, if they want to rise in order to struggle for equal rights." Karl Seitz told workers massed before the parliament building on the Ring that "we owe it to our brothers in the East; we owe it to the thousands who have shed their blood on the streets of St. Petersburg and Moscow; we will storm against this ramshackle House until it fulfills the only duty that history has left to it—to kill itself and to allow itself to be replaced by a parliament of the people, based on universal equal suffrage."[84] Speaking before the Christian Social "Donaustadt" Association on December 5, Lueger painted a picture of socialist intimidation and lawlessness, and complained that the authorities made no effort to protect peaceful taxpayers against Social Democratic threats. With timely organization it might have been possible to protect Viennese shopkeepers from being forced to close their stores on November 28, but "the authorities had no time to protect peaceful shopkeepers, for they had to protect the Red flags [on the Ringstrasse]." Lueger then cleverly turned the "Russian connection" back upon the Social Democrats and added the ever-effective ingredient of anti-Semitism to make the discursive maneuver work. He compared them to the revolutionaries in Russia. Like their counterparts in Russia, the Social Democrats depended on the Jews, a form of collaboration which had provoked anti-Semitic outbreaks in the east. Let the Jewish community of Vienna know that there were limits beyond which the Viennese would not allow themselves to be pushed, and those limits had been established in Russia. The Jews should take care, therefore, in supporting the Social Democratic "revolutionaries" in Vienna, lest what happened in Russia be repeated in Vienna: "We in Vienna are anti-Semites, but it is not in our nature to kill and maim. But if the Jews should threaten our *Vaterland,* then we will know no mercy. . . . If one preaches peace and order to us, we will gladly follow these commands, but only if others follow these doctrines."[85]

Lueger's threats produced an outcry from the press, and while he slowly backpedaled by insisting that he had meant no harm to the Viennese Jewish community, the Christian Social press delighted in its opportunity to insult the Social Democratic leadership by roping the bourgeois press into covert allegiance with them. Lueger's bellicose warning to the Viennese Jewish community must be situated in the context of his own and his constituents' frustrations over Red control of the Ring, and considered in light of their fears of what universal suffrage might bring. The speech's real audience were Lueger's embittered and frightened constituents. He was certainly not deliberately inciting a persecution of Jews. Rather, Lueger's remarks were a well-calculated, if blatantly irresponsible reaction to the political risks he faced in supporting universal suffrage.

On the one hand, Lueger sought to discredit or at least minimize socialist political power by invoking anti-Semitic prejudice—it was the "Jews" and not the workers that his *bürgerlich* followers really had to fear—and in so doing he attempted to reassert the discursive ability of his party to protect its own constituents. But, on the other hand, Lueger also sent a warning to the Jewish community, particularly to the more propertied elements of that community and to their press, that they would support the Social Democrats at their own risk. When Lueger insisted at a meeting of the City Council on December 7 that it was rare in the history of a political party that "the most moderate was also the leader" and that Jews would receive equal and equitable treatment under his municipal government, he was not far from the mark. But again he repeated a warning that "it will not be good if the Jews bind themselves to revolutionaries and Social Democrats."[86] Franz Schuhmeier, who knew Lueger quite well, easily connected the Ringstrasse march and Lueger's revival of anti-Semitism: "this demonstration proved Lueger's rule to be bankrupt. Up to now Lueger has been able to claim that 'I am the master of Vienna.' Now he can no longer do this. So he has to turn to his old pastime—the Jews."[87]

Lueger's hope that even if socialists did control the Ring the Christian Socials could still maintain hegemony in the city using a combination of anti-Marxist, traditional patriotic, and anti-Semitic appeals was not shared by some of his more emotional colleagues, but it anticipated the later Janus-faced pragmatism of the party's strategy on the franchise reform. Should the party not run even with the socialists on this issue, while simultaneously demanding structural (gerrymandering or residency) concessions from the Cabinet in the construction of the suffrage, it might face retribution if the Cabinet succeeded in pushing the bill through against the party. Moreover, previous election results in the municipal Fourth Curia had demonstrated that the Christian Socials could hold their own against the Social Democrats in Vienna; and to accept such changes conceded nothing about the future of the municipal franchise. With universal suffrage the Christian Socials also stood an excellent chance of sweeping most seats in rural Lower Austria and Tyrol, thus giving the party a much stronger presence in the new parliament. At the same time, to defer to and rely so heavily on the Austrian peasant voter would constitute a decisive turning point in the history of the Christian Social movement. To tolerate universal suffrage in Vienna in order to gain rural seats was to trade one kind of certainty for another and to shift the locus of sovereignty in the party. No longer would the party's urban seats be the "safest" seats of the machine. In 1907 this tactic seemed worth the gamble, but by 1911 many urban Christian Socials had second thoughts.

Hence the Viennese Christian Social delegation made a fateful commitment to support the final legislation sponsored by Minister-President Max Vladimir von Beck (who had succeeded Gautsch in April 1906). Along with Adler's Social Democrats and the Czech parties the Christian Socials became one of the three major blocs that pushed the law through parliament in December 1906, defeating attempts to weaken or to eviscerate it by attaching plural voting, corporatist occupational schemes, and other obstructionist devices.

The new Alpine wing of the Christian Socials which had evolved in Tyrol and Vorarlberg in the later 1890s, led by Aemilian Schöpfer, Josef Schraffl, and Jodok Fink, also vigorously favored universal suffrage.[88] These men had assembled a coalition of lower clerical, peasant, and artisan supporters and, replaying the original Christian Social model of the late 1880s, had made significant strides against traditional Catholic political elites. Although they had only four deputies in parliament in 1905, the fact that Albert Gessmann assigned several of the major speeches during the parliamentary debates on suffrage reform to Schöpfer, Schraffl, and Fink suggests the value he accorded to their views.[89]

In his memoirs Erich Kielmansegg conceded that Gessmann played the crucial role in the negotiations with the Cabinet on this bill, serving with Leopold Steiner and Jodok Fink as the principal Christian Social representative on the parliamentary committee for electoral reform (*Wahlreformausschuss*).[90] Gessmann's ascendancy reflected not only his skillful assessment of the current balance of forces in the Cabinet but also the fact that Karl Lueger, who had been suffering for years from several ills, including diabetes, became much worse in 1906 and was forced to leave Vienna for long periods of time for recuperation. The disease severely impaired Lueger's sight, and although important party policies were cleared with Lueger by telegram or by means of personal emissaries, day-to-day negotiations between the party and the Cabinet and the supervision of countless mundane party affairs were left in Gessmann's hands, who came to exercise a level of power almost equal to that of Lueger himself.

Gessmann's influence in the Ministry of Internal Affairs and his participation in the electoral reform committee were crucial to the success of the bill.[91] Alois Liechtenstein duly noted this fact in a confidential letter to Beck asking that Gessmann be awarded a (previously promised) title of *Hofrat* in return for his services during the electoral negotiations.[92] Gessmann relied on the Viennese *Magistrat* for many of the position papers he brought to the ministerial negotiations and subsequently to the committee sessions. According to Kielmansegg, Gessmann also persuaded the Minister of Internal Affairs, Arthur Bylandt-Rheidt, to rely on the advice of various civil servants sympathetic to

the party.[93] The Christian Socials were less interested in the division or allocation of seats by nationality (in Lower Austria this would not concern them at
all) and much more worried about the technical regulations governing the voting process itself. Gessmann fought hard, for example, to retain control of the
supervision of balloting by local governmental authorities in Austrian cities,
knowing that as long as the Viennese *Magistrat* ran elections in Vienna (controlling voter registration and deregistration procedures) and as long as the
Christian Socials controlled the *Magistrat,* the party was well situated for close
contests.[94] Initially Gessmann supported Lueger's demand for a five-year residency requirement, but he relented when Richard Bienerth (Beck's Minister
of Internal Affairs and the government's chief negotiator) and Victor Adler
consented to the Christian Social map for apportioning seats in Vienna and to
a provision allowing provincial Diets to enact compulsory voting (*Wahlpflicht*).[95] The new pattern of seat distribution, based on a one-year residency
requirement, gave Vienna 33 seats to be distributed over its 21 districts.
Smaller districts with substantial middle- or lower middle-class populations
and long traditions of voting Christian Social in the Third and Fourth city Curias, like Mariahilf (66,838 people in 1906) and Neubau (76,760), were
awarded the same number of seats (two per district) that traditional Social
Democratic strongholds like Ottakring (173,761) and Favoriten (145,530) received. With Bienerth's covert assistance Gessmann also dictated how and
where the election boundaries would fall within each district.

The election reform of 1906 constituted a test case for the survival of the
Austrian political system. In October 1905 Karl Lueger had cynically predicted that the parliament was incapable of accomplishing anything, much less
a major election reform, and opined that the *Verwaltung* would have to break
the existing constitution and impose by fiat a new reform on both sides of the
Monarchy.[96] Lueger only suggested this because he knew Gautsch would never
dare to do it, but the frustration evident in his remarks reflected similar currents
flowing in Austrian and Hungarian politics in later 1905. The Thronfolger,
Franz Ferdinand, was beginning to adopt a more forceful and destabilizing
posture toward Austrian public life and party politics. Many in his entourage
thought in terms of a *Staatsstreich.* Unlike Lueger, they took such rhetoric
seriously.

The Christian Social party had both the misfortune and the opportunity
to be associated closely with Max von Beck's ministry between 1906 and
1908 and simultaneously to establish close relations with the camarilla around
Archduke Franz Ferdinand. Eventually these two alliances worked at cross-
purposes, and the party found itself caught in the middle of a vehement struggle for power between Beck and the Archduke. The most successful manipulator of the Austrian political system since Taaffe, Beck sought to discredit the
radical pessimism voiced by Franz Ferdinand and his aristocratic cronies.

Gessmann's and Alfred Ebenhoch's collaboration with Beck showed the new respectability of the party in more conservative, Court circles, but it ultimately enraged Franz Ferdinand, whose egregious disdain for those who served him ultimately came to include a cynical appraisal of most of the Christian Social leadership. The Thronfolger genuinely admired and feared Karl Lueger, however, and as long as Lueger held him at arm's length his ability to manipulate the party was limited. The party's ambivalent relations towards Franz Ferdinand are the subject of an analysis later in this book.[97]

Following the passage by the *Abgeordnetenhaus* of the new national franchise in December 1906 (the *Herrenhaus* followed suit in January 1907), politicians of all parties scrambled to strengthen their political bases for the parliamentary elections scheduled for May 1907. For the Christian Socials this meant attending to two of their largest and most prized voter constituencies, the Viennese artisans and the state civil servants. The interventions of the party bore fruit in the commercial code of 1907 and in white-collar salary legislation, but in both cases the later history of the party's relationship to these occupational strata showed the increasing complexity of the choices the party had to make as it assumed greater levels of political responsibility.

Certainly the first group that felt itself entitled to action was the artisan community. For years artisan groups had complained about the inadequacies and shortcomings of the 1883 commercial code (*Gewerbeordnung*).[98] Although several initiatives circulated in parliament between 1897 and 1904, including a proposal submitted by the Ministry of Commerce to the chambers of industry and the trade guilds in 1901 for preliminary review, all of them foundered, in large part because of a lack of consensus about how much additional protectionism was justifiable.[99] Some of this resistance was self-interested, but much of it reflected honest doubts in industrial and academic circles as to how effective additional restrictive legislation against larger competitors would actually prove for the artisans' own cause. Even Joseph Di Pauli, the clerical Catholic who served as Minister of Commerce in 1899 and who might have been sympathetic to artisan demands for more legislation restricting competition, was heard advocating more cooperative self-help and less reliance on government protection.[100] Finally, in December 1904, the Ministry of Commerce submitted its own version of possible revisions to the code, and the commercial committee of the *Abgeordnetenhaus* held hearings on this proposal during 1905, completing its work in February 1906.[101] The committee revised the government's draft in several key respects, and the full House adopted its version in July 1906. As of October 1906, however, the bill was still stalled in the *Herrenhaus,* and Ernst Schneider asked pointedly at a meeting of Viennese guild leaders in November whether Gessmann's new-found prominence in the electoral reform process might not be leveraged to help get the bill through to Imperial sanction.[102] Since the curial parliament was set to expire in late January, and since many doubted whether the new parliament would be prepared to adopt "reactionary" trade legislation, it was essential to get the bill through quickly. In the midst of its own misgivings about universal suffrage the *Herrenhaus* passed a revised version of the bill in late December, which mitigated some of its most radical anti-industrial features. The *Abgeordnetenhaus* then swallowed its pride and voted to accept the *Herrenhaus's* version on January 17, 1907, two days before the upper House finally acceded to Beck's electoral reform.

The amendments to the commercial code repaid political debts that the Christian Socials had owed to the Austrian *Gewerbestand* for two decades. The new law substantially tightened and expanded several regulatory clauses of the 1883 code.[103] Section 38a of the code, for example, which regulated the production of custom-made clothing and shoes, was changed to minimize competition from large-scale clothing manufacturers and dealers against smaller hand-work artisans (although, since the new clause was not made retroactive before January 1, 1907, it had little immediate effect during the remainder of the Imperial period). Section 104 created a more formal and empirically verifiable process for testing the competence of journeymen who wished to become independent masters. Equally important, the political and legislative "clout" of the anti-Semitic trade guilds was enhanced by sections of the law that provided opportunities for artisan leaders to serve as official government consultants on matters requiring certification and licensing policies.[104] Artisan leaders now received important new prerogatives as advisers of the *Magistrat* and the Ministry of Commerce, not only demonstrating the new-found respectability that the Christian Social party was able to lend its allies but also according the guilds significant consultative influence over the determination of wage and hours agreements, over the approval of new trade licenses, and over the apprentice system.[105]

Christian Social leaders stood at the center of efforts to get this bill through, making it a condition of their support for Beck when he became Minister-President in mid-1906.[106] Yet it was perhaps not without irony or deliberate purpose that few of them showed up for the final vote on the *Herrenhaus's* compromise draft in mid-January. Ostensibly most were distracted by the propaganda visit of a delegation of Rumanian politicians to the Rathaus, but press reaction in the party also suggested that the leadership felt it had gone as far as was possible or desirable toward meeting the demands of Schneider and his cronies.[107] The February 1907 law was, as many party leaders realized, the end of protectionism for the handicraft trades, in the sense that a practical legal maximum had now been attained. If the artisan trades continued to founder (as many did during the commercial recession of 1911–12), other kinds of answers to their problems would have to be found outside the range of prohibitory legislation. Not only did the inherent "anti-capitalist" proclivity of many in the party elite decline as a result of their exposure to the exigencies of managing a modern "industrial" system in the city of Vienna, but key Christian Social leaders like Gessmann and Weiskirchner who had to confront state-level economic policy planning in the Cabinet between 1907 and 1911 realized that additional protectionism was a luxury that neither the party nor the city could afford, if it injured Austria's competitive posture in foreign markets and produced consumer outrage, price inflation, and unemployment at home.[108] Given the robust expansion of the Austrian economy in these years, leaders of big business were not shy in associating their interests with those of the state.[109] Even Lueger was heard to grumble that "in order to help the artisans, one has to have a mountain of money."[110] Representing a party of consumers as well as a party of small and medium producers—after all, the "new" Third Curia created in 1900 had expressly counterbalanced artisans against public and private employees—and interested in maintaining a base of support in the new Fourth Curia where men of very modest income voted, party leaders now came to view more stringent protectionism as politically risky and economically unjustified. In addition to continuing its indirect subsidization of artisan crafts through city and provincial contracts, the party thus concentrated its energies after 1907 on *Gewerbeförderung* projects whose long-term goal was to help the craft trades become competitive in the market.[111] This program was run with largesse and political sensitivity by Hermann Bielohlawek with the help of Eduard Heinl, another protégé of Gessmann (and for a time, Gessmann's private secretary) and a future commerce minister in the First Republic, who became a full-time director of craft support for the Lower Austrian government in 1910.[112] Richard Weiskirchner's efforts during his tenure as Minister of Commerce between 1909 and 1911 to strike a balance between the needs of large industry and small hand-work artisans, instead of discriminating in favor of the latter as opponents of the Christian Socials had predicted, suggested a more conservative trend among the party elite, as did the frequent (and symbolically noteworthy) appearances by top party leaders at official ceremonies involving the Viennese big business community.[113] Appearing at a trade exhibition of leather and shoe products in August 1908, Gessmann urged that small firms modernize their production facilities if they expected to compete in the market.[114] The *Reichspost* went so far in July 1907 as to announce that the Christian Socials saw their goal as one of finding "a common platform between the *Mittelstand* and industry," for what was most needed was an "economic program that would try to encourage ideas of bourgeois solidarity [*bürgerliche Solidaritätsgedanken*]."[115]

Moreover, instances of cooperation between artisan leaders and representatives of larger firms in the face of the rapid growth of (and more aggressive tactics of) the Social Democratic unions in Vienna after 1900 revealed that "anti-capitalist" rhetoric was becoming both murkier and less reliable. During the lock-out of *Tischlergehilfen* by their artisan employers in 1909, for example, the masters sought the support of the wholesale wood dealers, men whom they had formerly labeled as "usurers" and "capitalists."[116] By 1914 the Christian Social party had slowly shifted from the extremism of artisan protectionism to a more balanced program of encouraging cooperation, craft modernization, and industrial self-help, using the generous resources of the Lower Austrian budget.

The co-option of influential artisan leaders into prominent political and social positions (such as service as a Councillor at the Chamber of Commerce) also had an effect on the propensity of key artisan leaders toward political radicalism.[117] It was hardly surprising that the party leadership curbed Ernst Schneider by easing him out of the leadership of the craft movement after 1907 and by organizing a new political-interest organization parallel to the *Bauernbund* movement, the *Deutsch-österreichischer Gewerbebund* in July 1908. Yet in contrast to the dynamic presence of the peasant leagues, the *Gewerbebund*'s complacent leadership seemed to match the distaste for further *Kleingewerbe* extremism on the part of top party leaders.[118] Heavily subsidized by the Christian Social secretariat (it became a continual drain on the party treasury), the *Gewerbebund* espoused less radical and more conciliatory views of commercial affairs. Thus its *spiritus rector* Eduard Heinl could later offer a quite negative opinion about Ernst Schneider's beloved compulsory trade guilds: "the trade guilds [*Gewerbegenossenschaften*] bore a compulsory character, membership in them was often felt to be burdensome, and there were few master craftsmen who had the idealism to be able to use and exploit these compulsory organizations as an instrument of economic policy."[119]

Dominated as it was by older, more established artisan leaders, the *Gewerbebund* could not guarantee total political unanimity within the craft sector. Personal animosities and status rivalries continued to provoke dissidence, particularly the feeling of younger guild chairmen that they were not given sufficient access to the patronage and spoils that their predecessors had enjoyed. During the feuds after Lueger's death, the frustration of some guild leaders came to the surface, amid accusations that the party leadership had not been sufficiently aggressive in opposing the Social Democrats' attempt to abolish the *Arbeitsbuch* and had also tolerated revisions in store hours that would prove unfavorable to small businessmen. When Hermann Bielohlawek openly challenged the effectiveness of compulsory trade guilds and protective legislation in a parliamentary speech in June 1910, he merited abusive criticism from many guildsmen.[120] Yet when artisan renegades revolted against the Rathaus during the June 1911 elections, they did so by running "independent" Christian Social artisan candidates rather than by deserting wholesale to vote for the Social Democrats or the Liberals (as did many fixed-income, white-collar employees and state officials).

As the party became entrenched in the Rathaus it was inevitable that its leaders would have to respond to the multiple constellations of interest and loyalty on which the party depended for its support. Membership in the powerful *Stadtrat* or in the district administrations thus offered a perspective different from that of the oppositional period before 1896. The cohort of local politicians who had rode on Lueger's coattails into municipal prominence in 1897— Karl Renner was not altogether wrong to call them "ward corporals playing the role of generals"—was forced to see that the economic or social interests of one bourgeois interest group might easily conflict with those of another, even though both belonged to the "christliches Volk," and that they could not function effectively by ignoring the multiplicity of interests on which the party's welfare resided.[121] Party leaders who achieved regional and national prominence like Gessmann, Weiskirchner, and Steiner faced even more complicated balancing acts in playing the role of interest mediators, especially as social and occupational boundary lines became more complicated and fluid within the urban *Bürgertum*. The Christian Social party was exposed to the peril that all parties face once in power: its elites might slowly grow distant from the respective interest groups with which they had been associated before taking power, and on all levels—local and national—the party leadership might assume a logic and a history of its own. Inevitably this institutionalization of power meant that the relationship between political identity and economic-occupational identity became more complicated and that positions of power came to be allocated not merely on the basis of occupational criteria but also on a person's standing within relevant *political* networks as well. The Christian Social election slate in Vienna for the 1907 elections merely confirmed this point. Candidates were drawn from a variety of bourgeois occupations, and very few men ended up on the list who did not have substantial local political identities beyond their specific occupational roots. If guild leaders expected that in such a dynamic environment they would automatically gain a lion's share of the seats, they were sadly mistaken.[122] Of 33 seats in Vienna, only 7 were accorded to guild representatives, although the vast majority of the other candidates were men of *bürgerlich* standing and occupation who might be expected, on class terms, to appeal to artisan voters. The February 1907 *Gewerbe* law was one final attempt to repay these voters and reaffirm lines of loyalty between the party and the master artisans, but it could not defuse the jealousies and personal animosities that might emerge among their leaders as the guilds slowly ceased to be the be-all and end-all of Christian Social politics.

The most potent anxiety for the Christian Social artisans remained their hatred of Leopold Kunschak's labor movement. For the growth of the Christian Social Laborite faction inevitably provoked conflicts between the older business sections of the party and the "upstart" Kunschak organization.[123] After 1900, when his forces gained a foothold in the Christian Social organization by winning several Fourth Curia City Council seats, Kunschak demanded more representation for his club in the parliamentary and Diet delegations, to Lueger's dismay. Feuds that erupted between the artisan masters and the Kunschak forces over the distribution of seats in the 1907 parliamentary elections caused headaches for the Rathaus in finalizing the election slate in several districts of the city.[124] After the elections, tensions continued over the new Lower Austrian commercial education law, a law which Kunschak sponsored in October 1907 that protected apprentices against being forced to attend school late at night or early on Sunday morning. When *Mittelstand* interests in the party obtained the consent of the Diet to repeal key features of the law in January 1909, Kunschak was left humiliated before his own supporters.[125] Not surprisingly, he became one of the strongest advocates of expanding the municipal franchise system to break the grip of *bürgerlich* economic interests.

The second electoral interest group to which the Christian Socials had to accord special attention in 1907 was the Austrian state civil servants. Because of their tradition of syndicalist aggressiveness dating from the 1890s and because of the patronage accorded them by all competing national and social movements, the state officials were a crucial link between the older curial election system and the new, less predictable universal system. True, many voters under the older system could be accounted for under the new system as well: journeymen in craft trades who had voted for the socialists in the Fifth Curia in 1897 and 1901 would hardly be inclined to change their votes now; similarly, master artisans in Vienna, although they grumbled about being forgotten by the party leadership, could probably be expected to remain near if not in the Christian Social camp. But with the thousands of civil servant voters in the city and with the even larger masses of governmental servants and part-time employees, not to mention the growing masses of the private commercial employees, a rather different set of behavioral calculations had to prevail.

In September 1898 after years of agitation the Austrian civil servants had gained a comprehensive improvement of their salary conditions when the Emperor finally sanctioned legislation passed by parliament in 1896.[126] Rather than serving to dampen civil service radicalism the 1898 reforms only inspired higher expectations. The years between 1898 and 1906 thus saw, however, a further radicalization of the civil servants' movement (*Beamtenbewegung*) along several lines.[127] Organizations representing individual groups and levels of officials and teachers competed with each other in identifying deficiencies that the 1898 salary settlement had left unresolved. Even politicians sympathetic to the civil servants had difficulties in figuring out where the political jurisdiction of one group ended and that of the next group began. More importantly, in 1901 a number of larger civil servant organizations, led by the *Verein der Staatsbeamten,* united to form a broad coalition lobbying group, the *Zentralverband der österreichischen Staatsbeamtenvereine.*[128] In 1905–6 a series of angry congresses of civil servant representatives took place, voicing demands for higher salaries and benefits from the government and, more significantly, demanding fundamental changes in the structural organization of the civil service hierarchy—guarantees of promotion as determined by time in grade (*Zeitavancement*) and a modern code of rights and responsibilities for officials (*Dienstpragmatik*).[129]

Gessmann and other Christian Social leaders realized that the party would never survive in Vienna if the thousands of gentile, white-collar voters employed on all levels of public service in the city and region became alienated from the party. On the municipal and provincial levels, where the party had direct control over employment conditions, salaries could be adjusted to the political requirements of upcoming elections, which meant that employees in these sectors were generally better off than their colleagues in the state bureaucracy. Lueger bragged openly about this imbalance, telling a congress of state officials in late 1905 that Viennese municipal officials already had the concessions that the state officials sought from the Imperial government. After months of pleading with Beck on behalf of the state officials, during which time postal officials threatened to start a passive resistance movement by working to regulations during the autumn of 1906, Gessmann finally persuaded Beck that action had to be taken before the elections to pacify the state civil servants.[130]

As the lower House prepared to vote on the amendments to the *Gewerbeordnung* and less than two months before the opening of the election campaign, Beck allowed two bills to be brought before parliament providing modest increases in cost-of-living allowances for civil servants, establishing new incremental salary scales for the seven lowest ranks of state officials (for the lowest three ranks, time-in-grade requirements were also shortened), and lowering the service time for a full pension from forty to thirty-five years.[131] Whereas none of the top leadership had bothered to show up for debates on the commercial code on January 17, they appeared in full force on January 19 for these bills. Indeed, the bills were submitted under a motion of urgency in Leopold Steiner's name and Gessmann gave the principal report. For Gessmann, the law was vital because "one must pay a state official in a reasonable manner. He must be able to lead a humanly worthy life, or he will not be able to manage his duties in the appropriate manner."[132]

These concessions may have contributed to the Christian Socials' success in winning seats in the *bürgerlich* wards in Vienna in May 1907.[133] Significantly, this law was the last opportunity the Christian Socials were to have to pose as the tribunal defenders of the Austrian state officials. By joining the Cabinet after 1907 the party lost its freedom of action on this issue, and when it accepted into its ranks a large number of agrarian (and clerical) delegates the very composition of the party on the state level suggested a possible hostility to urban consumer concerns. When the price inflation of 1908–11 incited massive voter protests in Austrian cities, the Christian Socials found themselves caught in a cascade of white-collar and fixed-income protests that became harshly anti-agrarian, in spite of the fact that the Christian Socials had adopted the conciliation of urban and rural economic interests as the fundamental rationale of their party.

Both of these corporate legislative initiatives—protection for small businessmen to isolate them from the market, and financial largesse for state officials to enhance (albeit phrased in more modern twentieth-century terms) their status in civil society—stood in glaring contrast to the spirit of the universal suffrage legislation of 1907. It was one of the ironies of Austrian parliamentary history that all three bills were passed within a week of each other.[134] Although both corporate initiatives bore political fruit in the short run, both called into question the party's ability to manipulate a system of expensive, interest-based rewards to anticipate all contingencies that might emerge in the electorate. Many in the party soon realized that if the Christian Socials wanted order in civil society, they would first have to construct order within the political party itself, and that the party's energy and money would be better spent in strengthening bonds of party loyalty and party affinity than in simply running on the perpetual treadmill of interest-group solicitations. While he supported the 1907 civil service bill, Albert Gessmann also observed in parliament that a more fundamental reform of the civil service would be necessary in order to make it more efficient and reduce costs. Then the state would be able to pay higher salaries to the officials without added expense to the taxpayer.[135] Yet as Gessmann's friend Josef Redlich also argued, any such administrative reform would have to originate from the new party system, for the civil service could hardly be expected to reform itself. If the administrative state could not adequately control (and would not relinquish) the anarchy of interest-group politics, then the strong political parties would have to do so. This fundamental insight was a part of the heritage of the Imperial political system for the political culture of the First Republic.

The Elections of 1907 and the Establishment of the Reichspartei

Having prepared the groundwork so carefully, the Christian Social party fared well in the parliamentary elections of 1907. The main elections (*Hauptwahlen*) on May 14, 1907, brought eighteen victories in the city and twenty-one in the Lower Austrian countryside. The runoffs (*Stichwahlen*) on May 23 increased the total in Vienna to twenty, giving the party hegemony in Lower Austria. Most of the Christian Social victories in Vienna came in the smaller interior districts with substantial *bürgerlich* majorities. A recent analysis of this campaign, comparing it to the races in Prague, has argued that the Christian Socials' support came mainly from business and propertied voters and secondarily from civil servant and other white-collar and petty governmental employee groups and from fringe groups that were working-class in material circumstances but not in cultural or political self-identification (such as the *Hausbesorger,* postmen, and petty municipal employees like the *Diener*). The party received only a very modest share of male "working-class" votes.[136] This interpretation makes sense in terms of previous alignments of the city vote, beginning with the 1897 parliamentary elections, and is consistent with qualitative data on the structure of the campaign itself.

The efficiency of the Social Democratic street and house system greatly helped that party's campaign in the city; in addition socialist agitators occasionally left their own turf and invaded Christian Social rallies. The Christian Socials in turn exploited an extremely unpopular bakers' strike in April against the unions to great effect. In the end the traditional Christian Social voting blocs held firm. Minor dissidence manifested itself among several of the guild masters—mainly grumbling against Kunschak and his protégés such as Adolf Anderle and Franz Spalowsky—which Gessmann was able to control. Although the *Verein der Beamten und Angestellten Österreichs* mounted independent candidacies in seven races, arguing that only civil servants could properly represent other civil servants, in all seven contests the Christian Socials ran up solid majorities, with strong support among white-collar and government employees.[137] Voter turnout was remarkably high—91 percent of the electorate observed the new *Wahlpflicht* law and voted. Erich Kielmansegg later estimated that this had worked, as Gessmann had predicted, to the advantage of the Christian Socials, since their "return" rate on lazy *bürgerlich* voters was as high as 14 percent in some wards, whereas the Social Democrats, already possessing a superb political organization, received less than a 7 percent increase.[138]

The final vote totals were impressive in demonstrating not merely the logic of Gessmann's gerrymandering but also the latent power of Social Democracy. Compared with the Christian Socials' 49 percent of the popular vote, the socialists won a respectable 39 percent.[139] They pulled in eight seats in the primary elections in Vienna and won two more in the runoffs—all in the big working-class districts like Ottakring and Favoriten. More importantly, several of the "safe" bourgeois seats that the Christian Socials had thought impervious to challenges were pulled to victory against the Social Democrats only by modest margins. The election confirmed that Vienna was a city of two "legitimate" worldviews and would remain so in the future, each party maintaining a large "base vote" of loyalists defined by a varying (and flexible) mix of class, cultural, or employment-based motives. But it also suggested that small shifts by swing voters, particularly the unsettled civil servants, whose existence in Viennese elections was by now a notorious fact, might have important consequences for the security of each party. For the Christian Socials the results could not help but affect future party strategy. If 49 percent of the popular vote was the most the party could achieve in an election conducted under highly favorable economic and ministerial circumstances, what would happen if key elements of their *bürgerlich* coalition became unsteady?

The most dramatic change wrought by the elections did not occur in Vienna, however. The 1907 elections saw the leaders of the *Niederösterreichischer Bauernbund* swept into office with huge majorities on the first ballot in the twenty-one Lower Austrian rural districts (*Landgemeinden*). Josef Stöckler, Karl Jukel, Karl List, Karl Fisslthaler, Alois Höher, and others now entered parliament and places of influence in the Christian Social party hierarchy. Whereas the city organization had won only 49 percent of the Viennese vote, the peasant leaders, running with virtually no credible opposition, garnered 79 percent of the rural popular vote. Stöckler's career was paradigmatic of that of many of these men.[140] Born in 1866 (he was thus twenty-nine when Lueger had started his battle to be confirmed as mayor of Vienna), Stöckler had worked his way up the rural political hierarchy of his village to win the mayorship of St. Valentin (near Amstetten) in 1898. The local *Bezirkshauptmann* described him in 1907 as a "wealthy" peasant of substantial holdings, an autodidact who possessed only a grade-school education but who was deeply interested in the political press. His natural cunning and ambition, combined with an interest in agricultural modernization (his own holdings were viewed as models of progressive cultivation techniques) had brought him into contact with provincial agricultural officials and eventually to the attention of Albert Gessmann. Gessmann encouraged Stöckler to run for the Lower Austrian Diet in 1902 and arranged his appointment as vice-president of the Lower Austrian *Landeskulturrat* in 1906.[141] In the same year Stöckler was elected chairman of the Lower Austrian *Bauernbund*. His colleagues tended to be equally well-placed—confidential reports on the Christian Social victors consistently noted that they were prosperous peasants, usually owning medium-sized farms with one or more houses, sometimes managing a *Gasthaus,* and that they possessed cash reserves. Some, like Karl Jukel, had obtained an education in progressive agricultural techniques before assuming their proprietary or management responsibilities.[142] All were local notables—typically either the mayor of their village or chairman of a local public-service committee. They were articulate, crafty and, as was reported of Stöckler, "a personality on the rise who will definitely play a prominent role."[143]

This was a different type of peasant leader than the downtrodden creatures Josef Scheicher had tried to help in the late 1870s and early 1880s. When Stöckler displaced Scheicher as a member of the Lower Austrian Provincial

Executive Committee in 1909 it was clear that long-term service to the party during its early *Kampfzeit* now counted for very little indeed. Many of these peasant politicians had been mere adolescents or in early adulthood at the beginning of the Christian Social movement, but they now had control of substantial family resources (in some cases personally assembled in the later 1880s and 1890s, when the agricultural recession that had so preoccupied Vogelsang and Scheicher had eased). Scheicher, who both admired and felt jealous of these new leaders, concluded that government subventions, new methods of cultivation, and the rural cooperative movement had "transformed the peasants into a self-conscious corporate group. Whoever today is familiar with the *Bauernbund* with its vigorous organization would not be able to imagine that ten or twenty years ago the peasants were nothing but bondsmen, who were harassed and exploited and who were considered beyond the protection of the law."[144] As the autocratic force on the Lower Austrian Provincial Executive Committee, Gessmann used his patronage to sponsor their mobility from village politics to the larger world of the province. Fisslthaler especially was described in confidential government reports as a "Vertrauensmann Gessmanns" and, not surprisingly, this won him certain perquisites—his son was employed as a Lower Austrian government official and he himself became the postmaster of his village.

Stöckler and his colleagues had behind them the 46,000-member *Niederösterreichischer Bauernbund*. Modeled on Schöpfer's Tyrolean *Bauernbund*, this group was established in June 1906, uniting existing local peasant associations in Lower Austria that had begun to emerge in the 1890s into one powerful (and wealthy) interest group.[145] Appropriately, the featured speaker at the founding ceremony was Albert Gessmann, who noted the profound significance of the election reform for Austrian rural society. The putative "representatives" of the peasantry in the nineteenth century had been their social "betters"—the nobles of the *Grossgrundbesitz*. With the abolition of such privileged curias in 1907, the peasants could now organize and take politics into their own hands. To do so effectively they had first to assemble a powerful organizational infrastructure.[146] The peasants took Gessmann at his word, and with the stubborn persistence and group discipline that characterized their future behavior within the parliamentary club they established the single most efficient interest group in the Christian Social party. Their election program of May 1907 accepted Gessmann's slogan of a higher harmony between the rural and urban middle classes, but their detailed demands for special tax concessions, exemptions from military service, more government investment in agriculture, improved military contract allocations, and more favorable (that is, more protectionist) tariffs suggested that the peasants had a collective mind and a rationale of their own and would not easily be manipulated by anyone, including Gessmann. In their attempt to balance cultural tradition and economic development the peasant leaders constituted an appropriate parallel to the mother party in Vienna itself.[147] Yet their particularist, anti-Vienna political values would be deeply felt in the future, especially after the elections of 1911.

For Baron Beck the results of the elections were satisfactory, indeed, even "quite favorable," as he reported to *Statthalter* Carl Coudenhove in Bohemia, although he regretted that his Minister of Education, Gustav Marchet, had failed to retain his seat in Lower Austria. Beck had worked long and almost as hard as Gessmann to achieve results acceptable to the large centrist parties, including playing host to a last-minute summit meeting of leaders of all the German *bürgerlich* parties, at which the Christian Socials agreed to support their nationalist colleagues in some run-off races with the Social Democrats. Beck joked with Coudenhove that the "feverish activity that I have been doing in the last few days would outshine a regular party election office."[148] Never before had an Austrian Minister-President intervened so directly and personally in a general election campaign. Some years earlier Franz Joseph had complained to Philipp Eulenburg that, in contrast to Hungary, he had found it impossible to influence elections in Austria.[149] Even in 1911 the Minister of Internal Affairs, Max Wickenburg, would complain bitterly about the estrangement of local administrative officials from local voters in the *Bezirkshauptmannschaften* which, he argued, made it impossible in Austria for the Cabinet to influence elections in a predictable way. Beck's praxis in 1907 belied these excuses. He was successful precisely because of his ability to force the party leadership cadres of the various *bürgerlich* factions to make concessions and honor agreements. Rather than simply imposing subordinate officials on the electorate, Beck felt sufficiently comfortable with the party system to work directly with its leaders on a parity basis. He was, thus, consistent in his appeals to Coudenhove and other provincial governors that they should ensure the fairness and honesty of actual balloting, all the while engaging in interparty bargaining on behalf of the government's sympathizers.

Beck was also fortunate to have so skillful and unscrupulous an administrative assistant as Rudolf Sieghart, whose talents in the dispensation of titular and material patronage were long fabled (and condemned) among contemporaries.[150] Gessmann reported to a meeting of the party leadership in June 1910 that he required a personal fund of 150,000 crowns a year to manage party business effectively. Elections cost even more. Some of this money could be raised privately—Alois Liechtenstein had donated over a half-million crowns to the party from his private fortune by 1910.[151] But the enormous powers of the Minister-President's office were not to be dismissed. Money could be solicited directly, from big industrial and commercial interests anxious to minimize Social Democratic gains, but it could also flow through more subterranean channels as party leaders were appointed to *Verwaltungsrat* positions in big banks and capital industries.[152] Count Wedel reported to Berlin that Beck had collected large sums of money in 1907 from Austro-German industrialists and had channeled these funds to Christian Social election committees in Lower and Upper Austria.[153] Alfred Ebenhoch admitted to Franz Ferdinand that Sieghart had "always shown great largesse toward our party from the resources that the Cabinet regularly has available."[154] Together, Beck and Sieghart achieved a new level of voluntary manipulation of the political system by the Cabinet, not by their adherence to traditional Josephist administrative values but because they were occasionally willing to cast such values to the winds.

In view of the exceptionally positive results, most of which were achieved without having to depend on runoff compromises (a good indicator of any party's core strength), Gessmann and others like Alois Liechtenstein made a virtue of necessity and argued that the fact that the Christian Socials had done so well in Vorarlberg and Tyrol meant that the party must become a true *Reichspartei,* diversifying its voting strength and expanding its scope by prudent mergers with affiliated parties. That the party had done far better in percentage terms in the provincial areas of Lower Austria than in the city itself was yet another reason to accentuate its rural potential by looking for like-minded parties to the West. Gessmann's enemies in Vienna (most notably Ernst Vergani) might argue that their worst fears had been confirmed and that Beck's suffrage law had simply created a Frankenstein monster, but for the time being this was a minority position in the Viennese leadership. In the new *Abgeordnetenhaus* the party held 66 seats, making it the second largest party behind the Social Democrats. With such size came accountability: if legislation to resolve key *Mittelstand* social demands (including those of the civil servants) failed to get through a parliament with such pronounced Christian Social strength, the party could no longer hide behind others' political skirts.

Lueger, for one, seemed uneasy about the new-found prominence of the party. In a candid interview in the *Reichspost* in May 1907 he suggested that the supreme need of the party was to maintain its political independence by not joining the Cabinet: "as long as I have something to say, the party will remain independent, and once one has ministers [in the Cabinet], one is dependent on others."[155] For a few months such a policy seemed defensible, but the announcement in June 1907 by Alfred Ebenhoch that he and other German clerical conservative leaders from Upper Austria, Salzburg, and Styria had voted to seek union with the Christian Social party cast the future in a radically different light. In a settlement tolerated by Lueger but devised by Gessmann and Ebenhoch, thirty Alpine Clericals joined the Christian Social parliamentary delegation, making it the largest faction in Cisleithanian politics. With 96 seats in parliament, almost one-fifth of the Austrian *Abgeordnetenhaus* now stood under Karl Lueger's uncertain control.

The history of this unification was complex, involving as it did ten tumultuous years of German Catholic politics in Austria between 1897 and 1907. In

November 1897, as noted above, Lueger decided to take the Christian Socials into the formal opposition against Badeni and joined the coalition of German parties opposing the government's language ordinances.[156] He did this with regret and at the last possible moment, but once the Christian Socials had sided with nominally "anticlerical" German *bürgerlich* parties against the Cabinet, there was no turning back from explicit oppositional status and from a break with the Alpine conservatives. Speaking for the Christian Social club in the *Abgeordnetenhaus* on 19 November 1897, Leopold Steiner castigated the Alpine Catholics for refusing to join the opposition and reminded them that it was fully possible for the Christian Socials to storm the positions of the Catholics.[157] The Catholic conservative faction under Joseph Di Pauli of Tyrol and Alfred Ebenhoch of Upper Austria had decided, after tortuous negotiations in October 1897 within their own party club in which Di Pauli came close to persuading his colleagues to withdraw from the Cabinet's informal coalition, to remain loyal to Badeni and his Slavic-clerical ring.[158] When Joseph Baernreither resigned as Minister of Commerce in the fall of 1898, in protest against the failure of the Cabinet to offer a satisfactory, equitable response to the Germans, Count Thun chose Di Pauli as his replacement, thereby giving the clerical conservatives representation in the Cabinet. The Germans from the Bohemian lands considered this decision tantamount to national treason, yet the nationality question looked rather different to men from Innsbruck and Linz than to those from Reichenberg and Brünn, and the conservatives valued the ideological advantages to be gained by staying with the coalition. In contrast to the Christian Socials, they were also loath to ally themselves with their historic enemies, the Sudeten German Liberals.[159]

As long as the Thun Cabinet survived (until October 1899), tensions between the two groups persisted. They were intensified when several younger Tyrolean conservatives, led by Aemilian Schöpfer, decided in March 1898 to secede from the *Katholische Volkspartei* when the latter refused to support the indictment of former Minister-President Badeni for his alleged mishandling of official affairs.[160] A young priest with excessive ambitions who saw the radicalism of his fellow clerics in Vienna as a model, Schöpfer established a Christian Social Association in Innsbruck in April 1898, beginning the famous *Bruderkampf* which tore Tyrolean Catholicism apart until its final denouement after the 1907 parliamentary elections.[161] At first Schöpfer and his small group of supporters (most notably Josef Schraffl and Martin Thurnher) were a symbolically welcome but hardly significant gain for the Viennese party; but when they began to trounce their conservative opponents in regional and national races, as Schraffl did brilliantly against Di Pauli in the parliamentary elections in 1901, Lueger and Gessmann found they had on their hands a movement in whose success they now had a vested interest. Schöpfer was hardly in the Viennese "Catholic" mold—he was a priest whose cultural beliefs were as orthodox and integralist as those of the conservatives with whom he battled. He shared with the Viennese party, however, an unwillingness to be manipulated by the arch-conservative episcopate and a frenetic confidence in the virtues of electoral democracy in a province with a solidly Catholic *and* predominantly rural voting base. As Josef Wackernell, the leader of the Tyrolian conservatives, bemoaned in 1903, Schöpfer's party "values only the will of the people, not ecclesiastical authority."[162] With his lifelong dedication to the Austrian peasantry and his (and Schraffl's) organization of the Tyrolean *Bauernbund* as a mobilization device for his anti-conservative fronde, Schöpfer's impact was soon felt beyond his own province. Rural Christian Socials used the Tyrolean peasant league as a model for establishing a powerful peasant wing for their party in Lower Austria. Even before the merger with the other Alpine Catholics, therefore, the Christian Socials already had an influential rural base. More than half of the 64 seats which the party won in 1907 came from rural electoral districts.[163]

Once the Thun government collapsed and the conservatives no longer found themselves burdened with ministerial status, relations between the two parties became more casual. If not amity, then at least points of common interest could emerge when neither had a vested interest in the status quo of Cabinet power. This second period in their history reflected the constraints and problems generated by the *Los von Rom* movement in both Vienna and in the Alpine lands. A critical assumption of the Alpine Catholics' strategy in cooperating with Badeni and Thun had been that the national issue could be held in a relatively stable and even subordinate status in their home territories, but the results of the 1901 parliamentary elections showed that this had been a serious misjudgment. Ebenhoch and several colleagues went down in defeat as a wave of German nationalist sentiment swept through the Alpine lands.[164] When Ebenhoch managed to reenter parliament in a by-election in 1903, he was a much sobered and more responsive politician anxious to accommodate the winds of political change.[165]

By 1904 the more progressive of the Alpine politicians, centered around Ebenhoch, began to send cautious signals to Vienna that they would consider a program of political cooperation. Ebenhoch himself had a long record of association with Lueger, whom he considered to be a personal friend.[166] In the fall of 1904 Ebenhoch actually proposed such a coalition at a meeting of conservative party leaders in Linz, but he was stymied by other colleagues, many of whom found it difficult to imagine an era of Christian Social comity and conciliation.[167] In Vienna a similar mood of isolation prevailed. The determined campaign in 1904 by the Viennese to prevent the appointment of Josef Altenweisel as bishop of Brixen showed how inflexible both the Viennese and Tyrolean wings had become in their relations with the conservatives.[168]

Yet signs of change were inescapable. Following the Christian Socials' crushing victory in the Viennese Council elections in the spring of 1904, the *Reichspost*, most certainly speaking for Gessmann, proudly announced that

> the Christian Social party must not stop with its possession of Vienna. She, like no other party, can assert that she possesses the capacity for municipal governance and that the future of urban life in Austria lies in her direction. . . . The Christian Socials must therefore move out into the Crownlands. The beginnings are already there to make her into a party of the Empire [*Reichspartei*], a fate to which she is destined because of her farsighted economic program which will reconcile the nationalities and because of the brilliant ability of her leaders.[169]

Events elsewhere pushed in the same direction. In Styria in 1904 conservatives and Christian Socials established a temporary regional coalition in preparation for Diet elections in which, for the first time, seats for a curia based on universal suffrage would be contested among the Social Democrats, the German nationalists, and the "Christian" coalition. The results—the Christian coalition won 51,650 votes against 33,241 for the socialists and 17,415 for German nationals—suggested that the concerted program of collaboration may have saved both parties from disaster.[170]

Finally, a third period of integration emerged in 1905–6 with the struggle over universal manhood suffrage. This issue did two things for the Catholic conservatives. Politically it divided them into an intransigent majority which supported such anti-democratic measures as a plural franchise, and a radical minority, led by Ebenhoch, which saw that in their small-town and rural electoral context (of the thirty-two districts in which Catholic conservatives won seats in May 1907, thirty were rural) they had little to fear from universal suffrage and that a more consciously populist strategy toward peasant voters might even enhance their electoral opportunities. More importantly, because Beck's legislation did pass both houses of parliament, it created technical means for the Ebenhoch minority to seize the initiative from more recalcitrant conservative regional organizations. Only those who survived the litmus test of universal competition in May 1907 would be in a position to dictate future party policy.

When Ebenhoch announced his intention to vote for universal suffrage in February 1906 he took the first step towards what became, in retrospect, an inevitable merger of the two parties.[171] The defeat of the plural franchise amendment (offered by Johann Tollinger from Tyrol, one of Schöpfer's rivals) on November 21, 1906, when Ebenhoch resisted bitter pressure from conservative nobles in Upper Austria and supported the Christian Socials, sounded the death knell of traditional Alpine politics.[172] Speaking at a meeting of the Upper

Austrian *Volksverein* in Wels on November 12, Ebenhoch suggested that the upcoming campaign for new elections "must find the Christian *Heerlager* united."[173] His comments could be read as a call for a mere electoral coalition rather than a permanent fusion of the two parties, but various Viennese politicians were also speculating about the long-term consequences of the modernization of the franchise.[174] Indeed, the autumn was filled with hysterical "bloc" rhetoric as bourgeois politicians on all sides scurried to adapt and thus to survive. Strident demands were voiced within the German *bürgerlich* camp for the creation of an electoral bloc among the four big nationalist parties before the onset of the elections. In several regional party congresses of the *Deutsche Volkspartei* in October calls were heard for a "united national political party," although interfactional suspicions and the negative reaction of the *Freialldeutschen* precluded any serious cooperation until after the May elections.[175] The German *Landsmannminister* in Beck's Cabinet, Heinrich Prade, further fueled these appeals in early December by suggesting that a union between the Catholic conservatives and the Christian Socials was all but inevitable and that the German bourgeois parties must also be prepared to transform themselves.[176] The Liberal press in Vienna, always ready to view the world of German politics through its own distorted glass, urged the creation of such a "Liberal" bloc as a protection against a future "Catholic bloc" of Christian Socials and conservatives. National defense required anticlericalism as well.[177]

The first indication that a union of the two groups was feasible came in the early stages of the election campaign. Although the Christian Socials held their own political congress in Linz in late March, local Christian Social partisans indicated their willingness to defer to Ebenhoch's conservatives and thus avoid the electoral fratricide that marked Tyrolean politics in 1907.[178] Ebenhoch, for his part, issued an election statement that demonstrated a new-found sensitivity toward the national issue, declaring that the Germans could rely on his party to defend true German values on all relevant issues and noting that on ideological issues little separated his party from the Christian Socials.[179]

On March 31 the Christian Socials announced their decision to avoid overlapping contests in Upper Austria and in Salzburg. They mounted candidatures in four urban districts in Upper Austria which the Catholic conservatives chose not to contest, and in turn the Christian Socials supported the latter in the other eighteen Upper Austrian electoral districts. In Salzburg the party also ran no independent candidates in rural areas, but in Styria local forces on both sides were unable to reach a similar level of cooperation. On May 2 Ebenhoch suggested at his party's congress in Linz that the conservatives faced two strategic options following the elections: either they could enter a large national bloc of all German parties or they could merge with the Christian Socials, providing them with a "strong group of vigorous fighters."[180] The *Reichspost,* representing Gessmann, replied the next day, judging the first option as unlikely given the fragmentation of German bourgeois politics in the Monarchy, but endorsing the second.[181] The paper insisted that little separated the two traditions in programmatic terms and that Alpine regional autonomy—always a major concern of westerners anxious to avoid the hegemony of "Vienna"—had been preserved for the Tyroleans who had joined the party in 1898–1901. Both arguments were slightly disingenuous. There *were* cultural differences between the two groups that rhetoric could not bury and that would ultimately return to haunt the party after 1911, but the artfulness of the *Reichspost*'s discourse reflected the anxiety of both factions to conceal possible divergences.

The final results of the elections—seventeen conservatives elected in Upper Austria, four in Salzburg, twelve in Styria, and one in Carinthia—were sufficiently impressive to lead Ebenhoch to push for a merger. The Christian Socials had swept 13 of 18 Tyrolean contests, including all of the rural seats, which meant that the conservatives disappeared from the scene. The *Bruderkampf* could no longer be exploited to disrupt unity talks. Following the runoff elections the *Reichspost* announced that Ebenhoch would lead his seventeen-man delegation over to the Christian Socials before the new session of parliament opened in mid-June. Anxious (and vindictive) commentaries in *Vaterland* suggested that the merger was indeed imminent. The last week of May saw secret talks between Gessmann and Ebenhoch on necessary technical arrangements.[182]

Finally, on June 1 Victor von Fuchs of Salzburg hosted a meeting of all clerical delegates at which Ebenhoch and the Upper Austrians announced that they would join the Christian Socials, even if the others refused. Fuchs had serious reservations about the union, preferring a looser form of inter-bourgeois coordination among all German parties.[183] The Styrians, led by Franz Morsey and Franz Hagenhofer, were equally uneasy, and published reports on the conference could not mask the fact that several hours of debate were required before Ebenhoch's views won out. A grudgingly unanimous decision was taken to merge with the Christian Socials, subject to the explicit defense of provincial autonomy and the independence of the provincial parties on regional issues and, for rural interests, economic self-determination.[184]

Negotiations immediately commenced between the Alpine leaders and Lueger and Gessmann. The constraints imposed by Ebenhoch were congenial to Lueger as well. Because his was a Vienna-centric view of Austrian politics, he could appreciate regionalist paranoia on the part of others. More important, a party without centralized, bureaucratized leadership would be heavily dependent on his own personal, charismatic control.[185] Gessmann, in contrast, sought a more centralist structure for the party, to make it something other than a parliamentary club, but against Lueger's resistance he had found it difficult to do more than establish a small party secretariat in Josefstadt on Hamerlingplatz Nr. 9 and staff it with younger supporters like Eduard Heinl, Konrad Rumpf, and Richard Wollek, as well as with his son, Albert Gessmann, Jr.[186] What emerged in late May 1907 was a Christian Social parliamentary *Vereinigung*, not an organizationally centralized party, even though Gessmann's secretariat provided some national policy coordination. A new club statute was drafted by Gessmann, Weiskirchner, and Jodok Fink which responded to the particularist sensitivities of the rural delegates by giving them a special subplenary body to review party agrarian policy and recommend decisions to the plenum. It was also understood that both urban and rural delegates had the right to "vote their constituencies" on economic issues where the leadership could not prevent urban-rural contestations and where it was unwilling to impose absolute discipline.[187]

The Viennese leadership approved of the arrangement, and on June 10, after a short, enthusiastic speech by Alois Liechtenstein, both parliamentary groups officially sanctioned the deal. In the aftermath of Lueger's death in 1910 various enemies of Gessmann insisted that Lueger had agreed only with hesitation to take more extreme clericals like Franz Morsey into the party. This is confirmed by a plaintive letter of Morsey to Baron Beck on June 2, condemning Ebenhoch's abandonment of "the old program" of the Conservatives and noting that the Viennese were now refusing to accept him (Morsey) into the party.[188] Although much of this had to do with Morsey's intractable personality,[189] it also reflected Lueger's uneasiness with extreme clerical agitators. Gessmann himself later admitted that Lueger had always been suspicious of agrarian politicians; Leopold Steiner confessed in 1910 that Lueger often made hostile, sarcastic comments about the Lower Austrian provincial government.[190] But if Karl Lueger did have doubts, he failed to act on them.

As if to stress that the Christian Socials were not selling their souls to "clericalism," the club passed simultaneously a resolution welcoming future cooperation on all national issues with other "pure" German parties. The adjective "pure" was an early warning to Sudeten German factions in the *Volkspartei* and the *Fortschrittspartei* that the cost of the Christian Socials' cooperation would be the exclusion of the small band of radical Viennese Liberals (Paul von Hock, Camillo Kuranda, and Julius Ofner) from any role in German national politics.[191] On June 18 the new assemblage of *Reichspartei* delegates constituted itself. Karl Lueger was elected chairman, with Gessmann and Liechtenstein from Vienna and Schraffl, Ebenhoch, and Fuchs from the Alpine *Länder* as deputy chairs (*Stellvertreter*). A similar *Proporz* allocated the parliamentary secretary assignments: Axmann and Steiner from Vienna, Fink from Vorarlberg, Stöckler from rural Lower Austria, and Franz Hagenhofer from Styria. Day-to-day affairs of the club would be governed by an executive committee (*Leitungsausschuss*) and by a parliamentary commission. Alfred Ebenhoch voluntarily withdrew his name as a candidate for the presidency of the *Abgeordnetenhaus*, leaving the way open for Lueger's choice, Richard Weiskirchner, to be elected. Ebenhoch had wanted and perhaps even expected this position and had written privately to Lueger on June 3 asking for it. Lueger insisted on Weiskirchner, however, whom he had chosen in February to succeed him as mayor of Vienna, as a sign that the center of power, if not of ideology, still lay in the Rathaus.[192]

Just as ardent Alpinists like Franz Morsey scrupled about throwing away their particularist and Catholic programs to join the Christian Socials, the merger was not unanimously favored among the more *kleinbürgerlich* and nationalist sections of the Vienna party. Predictably, the center of such resistance lay with the *Deutsches Volksblatt* where Ernst Vergani editorialized that the fusion would lead to a watering-down of the standard anti-Semitism of the Christian Socials and to an extension of Alpine clericalism into Vienna, heretofore immune to such influences. A more articulate correspondent argued in a public letter in the *Volksblatt* that the Christian Socials had never been a clerical party and that their former role as a mediator between the bourgeois *freiheitlich* parties and the rural clericals would now be compromised if they were viewed as a clerical instrument.[193] For others simple proprietary jealousy stood in the way of accommodation. When Michael Mayr, an arch-Catholic university professor from Innsbruck, published a lead essay on "Our Party and Our Press" in the *Reichspost* in late June, many of the Viennese *Altkämpfer* might shudder at the shift in proprietary discourse—if the Christian Social party now "belonged" to men like Mayr, what was left for those who had founded it?[194] The bitter opposition of local Viennese district leaders like Paul Spitaler of the Landstrasse to the introduction in Vienna of local branches of the Upper Austrian *Ostmark,* a clerical nationalist organization founded by Josef Schlegel in Linz in 1909, revealed persistent organizational anarchism that Gessmann's overarching structures only temporarily repressed.[195]

Inevitably, the merger produced a cacophony of contradictory justifications. Alfred Ebenhoch insisted that the history of the two parties made the *Reichspartei* idea inevitable and that on ideological grounds little separated them.[196] Gessmann argued, more compellingly, that the new party was the only agent capable of resisting Social Democratic hegemony in the new parliament: "one of the major arguments for this decision . . . was that we intended at any price to prevent the Social Democrats from becoming the largest party in the House."[197] Three years later Ebenhoch said much the same in a private letter to Bishop Altenweisel of Brixen, arguing that the need to create a large, anti-socialist party had been foremost in his mind.[198] Other commentators insisted that it had been fear of a similar union among the German *bürgerlich* parties of Bohemia and Moravia, who would have outnumbered and isolated the two Austrian "Christian" factions, that had forced the decision, one in which Beck had taken a personal interest and which the Cabinet had covertly encouraged. The latter interpretation, although chronologically plausible—the German *bürgerlich* leaders of the *Volkspartei*, the *Fortschrittspartei*, the *Agrarpartei*, and the *Freialldeutschen* (representing among them 80 parliamentary seats) summoned a meeting in early June in Vienna to discuss the establishment of a *Deutscher Nationalverband*—was probably not completely accurate.[199] Lueger was convinced that the various German factions had always been their own worst enemy and that any union they might achieve would be temporary at best. As for government pressure, doubtlessly Beck did support the unification, on both parliamentary and ideological grounds. The *Reichspost* constantly emphasized that in the new parliament only large parties would have any significant role; this was clearly the Cabinet's view as well.

Political defensiveness and tactical opportunism played a role, but larger strategic aims were also involved. Divided, the parties could achieve much less to affect the social policy issues relevant to their constituents. It was not entirely propagandistic make-work when the party delegation in the first days of the new parliamentary session brought in dozens of proposals for a range of social welfare programs and government reorganizations, most for the benefit of the two parties' middle-class clientele.[200] Aside from their divergent relationships to Catholicism and anti-Semitism, few matters of programmatic substance prevented such a union. Both parties had always based themselves on lower- and middle-bourgeois social strata; both were intensely patriotic and dynastic, even if they occasionally engaged in anti-aristocratic diatribes. Both were militantly anti-socialist, not simply on economic but on cultural grounds as well. Both shared a fundamentally different perception of the nationality question from that of the northern German parties, stemming from their roles as spokesmen either for predominantly German lands where the nationality question was as much an issue of structural autonomy as one of ethnic collectivity (the Alpine conservatives) or for a city in which mass immigration and the overriding presence of intra-ethnic class conflict dictated a measured stance toward the Czechs. The two principal negotiators—Gessmann and Ebenhoch—both sought positions in the Cabinet (Rudolf Sieghart would write cynically to Beck referring to the party's "Portefeuillehunger" in the summer of 1907),[201] not only for their own personal advancement but from an enterprising conviction that the Christian Socials should control those areas of state policy for which they would be held accountable by their voters (such as, in Ebenhoch's case, agricultural tariffs). Lueger was no longer strong enough to resist such pressures.[202]

Bitterness between some members of the two camps endured long after 1907. It was apparent in negotiations between Friedrich Funder and various Catholic aristocrats over a merger of *Vaterland* and *Reichspost* in 1912 and in the private comments of various older bishops who felt deprived of any political role by the Christian Socials. Among privileged noble elites a residue of resentment against their displacement was also apparent. When Archduke

Franz Ferdinand accused Ebenhoch, as agricultural minister in 1908, of setting the peasants against traditional authorities, he was simply responding to his and his fellow nobles' detestation of the franchise reform that had put Ebenhoch in the Cabinet in the first place.[203]

The principal architect of this new scheme was Albert Gessmann, and its principal journalistic spokesman was Friedrich Funder. In a series of campaign speeches in late 1906 and early 1907 Gessmann articulated his belief that the upcoming elections would signal a fundamental change in the constitution of Austrian politics. He was hardly so naive as to believe that the nationality problem would disappear, but he argued that an even greater menace now confronted all *bürgerlich* parties, whatever their national identity. The massive cadre organization of Austrian Social Democracy menaced not only private property and capitalist investment in Austria but traditional Austrian culture as well. Gessmann was not the only Christian Social politician using such bourgeois-front rhetoric. As early as November 1905 the *Deutsche Zeitung* had argued that the specter of universal suffrage made interbourgeois cooperation imperative: "The educated and property-owning classes among the Czechs, the Poles, the Italians and the South Slavs will be as little inclined to allow political power to fall into the hands of the homeless proletariat as will be the Germans. In this context a silent alliance among the educated and patriotic elements of all the nationalities must come into existence."[204] But where the newspaper displayed indiscriminate hostility against working-class voters, Gessmann was more subtle in concentrating his fire on the workers' political spokesmen. Nor was this a surprising turn in his career. As early as the "Social Course" of the *Leo-Gesellschaft* in August 1894 Gessmann had called attention to the formidable potential of Social Democracy to disrupt Austrian civil society.[205] Yet, ironically, it was only through anti-Marxism that the true interests of the Germans could be served:

> we were and are Germans and must therefore view as one of our primary obligations that the German people in Austria should suffer no injury from this new political order. It is . . . a well-known fact that I have always viewed the struggle against Social Democracy as the principal object of my life's work, and will continue to do so in the future because I am absolutely convinced that the final goal of the socialist program, a number of justified individual demands aside, would lead to the destruction of our national culture and of our whole social order.[206]

German *bürgerlich* politicians in Bohemia and Moravia who ignored this fact, and who dared to collaborate with the socialists against the Christian Socials in run-off elections, giving in to older *freiheitlich* values against class unity, were dangerous to themselves and to the national cause.

At the Christian Social party congress in Vienna on March 11 Gessmann developed these ideas in a more elaborate fashion. The Christian Social party was, he insisted, a true trans-class party encompassing peasants, the urban bourgeoisie, and the workers, and only such a party could offer an effective alternative to Social Democracy.[207] The party was also a legitimate national party, although its policies would not abridge the legitimate cultural development of other linguistic groups. And the Christian Socials were a *Reichspartei,* capable of mounting electoral candidacies across the Monarchy. Gessmann then read the party election manifesto, which was certainly his own work. This document gave further meaning to the concept of *Reichspartei* by presenting the socialist threat and the nationality conflict in the context of the Hungarian problem and by cleverly transforming anti-Magyarism into a covert pro-Slavism and pro-Germanism. The Christian Socials stood for a "total Reich" (*Gesamtreich*) with Vienna as its center, and for a *Reich* which also gave to each of its peoples "freedom and justice." The humiliation of Austria was only possible because its individual nations had been set against one another (presumably by the Hungarians). The Christian Socials condemned this "artificial incitement of national conflict," although they would also defend German "goods and interests."

Although Gessmann's speeches hardly contained a convincing or workable policy for dealing with Hungary (which became his rhetorical foil for everything wrong in modern politics), they did contain a dual message for domestic consumption. German bourgeois politicians had to recognize the Social Democrats as the primary enemy; and ideology based on class conflict, not on inherited Liberal anticlericalism, had to determine the future Austrian political universe. But this logic led in another direction as well: German *bürgerlich* parties had to view their situation and that of the Czechs and the South Slavs in the context of the Empire as a whole. Such a connection would not only legitimate the Christian Socials' long-standing support of repressed Slavic minorities in Hungary and justify their cautious support for Trialism (although always with Vienna as the linchpin); it would also open the door for a more conciliatory policy toward the Czechs. Since the Social Democrats were the major political enemy (and, implicitly, not the Czechs), the major defense of the Imperial state had to be constructed on social and not national terms.

Party policy aimed at shaping the 1907 election campaign was guided by the *Reichspartei* program. The leadership did nothing to counter Liberal rumors of a future "Catholic bloc" before May 14, but the elections were fought on their own terms, leaving a decision about structure until the Rathaus saw the final vote totals. As early as January 15, 1907, the party leadership issued a pronouncement in the *Reichspost* declaring that its campaign would extend throughout the Empire—not merely concentrating on Vienna or Lower Austria but also running candidates in each Crownland. In practical terms this meant that the party supported merely nominal candidates in several German districts of Bohemia and Moravia who had no realistic chance to win.[208] Putting up nominal candidates was not completely pointless, however. At the very least the party might exercise some influence in runoff agreements. The invasion of traditional "nationalist" territory was also a punitive response to talk of a national bloc by German politicians like Heinrich Prade and Paul Hofmann von Wellenhof.[209] When the *Deutsche Volkspartei* complained late in the campaign that the Christian Socials were pushing too hard and endangering future collaboration, the latter could gleefully cite proclamations by the *Volkspartei*'s leadership that their bloc would of necessity also be anticlerical.[210] However, Baron Beck intervened during the critical runoff election negotiations to ease the way for compromises between the Christian Socials and other German parties in several Bohemian districts so that, campaign skirmishing aside, the final results would allow each side to live with the other in the upcoming coalition.[211] Occasionally the Christian Socials were confronted with circumstances that threw logic to the winds: Beck was not averse to putting pressure on Gessmann to throw the party's support, in the event of a runoff election in Eger between a socialist candidate and Georg von Schönerer, to the former.[212]

Reichspartei rhetoric and a national slate of candidates were not mere window-dressing, however. During and after the campaign the Gessmann-controlled *Reichspost* published various programmatic essays that spelled out a new future for Austrian parliamentary politics. Gessmann's colleagues Josef Schraffl and Victor Kienböck suggested that the future of Austrian Christian Socialism lay in a more ambitious and lofty program of exploiting political democracy, not in resisting it, as the German bourgeois parties in Austria had been wont to do. In an essay worthy of the Social Democrats Schraffl argued that democracy would bring to the fore articulate, mass expressions of economic interest and reduce intra-Austrian national conflict. Kienböck in turn prophesied a "renewal" of the total Monarchy, whose new mass democracy in the west would become a beacon to the "oppressed" nationalities in Hungary. More importantly, several essays eloquently praised the German *Zentrum* as a party that the Austrian Christian Socials would do well to imitate. The *Zentrum* was a model "Volkspartei" worthy of emulation because, Funder argued, it was able to force its voters to rise above interest-group particularism and to persuade middle-class Catholic voters in Germany to support, on occasion, even working-class candidates.[213] In spite of the slightly fallacious image of the *Zentrum* offered here, and its even more opportunistic Austrian interpretation, the connection was clear: of all modern western European political parties, the German Catholic *Zentrum* was clearly the most congenial model for Gessmann's group within the Christian Socials.

This interpretation became more compelling after the elections. In a lead article three days before Ebenhoch made his announcement on unification, the *Reichspost* reviewed a recent pamphlet by Martin Spahn on the history of the *Zentrum*.[214] It was not the Catholic image of the *Zentrum* that appealed to the reviewer so much as its organizational and political influence on national policy priorities, an ability, the *Reichspost* argued, that was owing to the evolution of the *Zentrum* from a specifically confessional party to a mass *Volkspartei* concentrating on social and economic legislation. Austrians also needed a "unified, strong, socially reformist Christian-German party." The muted attention to the *Zentrum* as a specifically Catholic party was not accidental: Gessmann did not want the Christian Socials loaded with too heavy a "Catholic" image. What he did want was a disciplined national party, with a refined commitment to social and economic reform, rising above petty national squabbles to offer Austrian Germans an alternative to previous political typologies. Duncan Gregory of the British embassy caught this subtle difference when he noted that Gessmann's tactic "was to distinguish between the appellation 'Christian' and 'Catholic' . . . and to repudiate the notion that it is a Clerical party on the lines of the German Centre party."[215]

Appropriately, Gessmann's ambitions for his party included a final step which the German *Zentrum* never dared (or was allowed) to take—the acceptance of ministerial power. This was to prove the most significant difference between the two Christian parties in Central Europe before 1914. The Christian Socials cast their fate with a project of ministerial parliamentarization, whereas the *Zentrum* reserved its energies for a more discrete, interest- and pressure-group strategy of political maneuver.[216] That Albert Gessmann had an abiding respect for the Center was evident in his and Funder's long-standing professional cooperation with Matthias Erzberger, who wrote for the *Reichspost* before 1907 and who used his Viennese connections for various peace projects during the First World War. Gessmann was also acquainted with Martin Spahn, who visited him in the early autumn of 1908 while attending the International *Mittelstand* congress organized in Vienna.[217] Finally, Gessmann had a personal connection with the *Zentrum* in Vienna in these years. One of his closest political contacts was Friedrich Gaertner, a young Viennese economist who had studied with Eugen Schwiedland at the Technical University in Vienna and with Alfred Weber at the University of Heidelberg. His studies of various economic policy fields—including social insurance (*Sozialversicherung*) and commercial credit for small businesses—reflected Gessmann's own thinking. Gaertner's career began as an informal political operative for Gessmann while he worked in Vienna as a correspondent for the German Catholic newspaper *Germania*. Along with Eduard Heinl, Gessmann's private secretary, Gaertner helped to draft the legal statutes for the Lower Austrian *Bauernbund;* and, according to Kielmansegg, Gaertner functioned as Gessmann's agent in setting up the operations of the new Ministry of Public Works in early 1908. His skillful public policy studies and his sensitivity to the economic models that Germany could provide Austria made him an ideal interlocutor for Gessmann. With Gessmann's patronage Gaertner entered the civil service in November 1907, working first at the *Arbeitsstatistisches Amt* in the Ministry of Commerce and in 1910 moving to the powerful *Ministerratspräsidium,* where he attained the title of *Sektionsrat* at the age of thirty-five. During the First World War his influence soared as commissioner of food distribution at the *Kriegsgetreideverkehrsanstalt.* So able did Gaertner prove himself that he was charged with conducting high-level negotiations with German political authorities on behalf of the Monarchy to secure needed foodstuffs.[218]

Gaertner was a man of talent, discretion, and good judgment, combining the best traditions of Austrian administrative rationality with a shrewd sense of political power. He was not the only young, university-trained Catholic intellectual to enjoy Gessmann's patronage—Richard Schmitz, Josef Sigmund, Richard Wollek, Wilhelm Miklas, Alfred Schappacher, and August Kemetter also rose in the party with Gessmann's help—but Gaertner's admiration for the *Zentrum* and his moderate, reformist views on social welfare legislation, including a *Zentrum*-like agenda of subsidizing anti-socialist *Mittelstand* politics, were especially close to Gessmann's own.[219] In several insightful articles published in *Germania* between 1905 and 1907 Gaertner argued that any future progress in the realm of Austrian politics would depend on a revolutionary reshaping of the electoral order, away from the segmented, interest-group curialism of the past and toward what he hoped would be a more competitive, economically oriented free market of universal suffrage. Gaertner believed that two great blocs would dominate Austrian parliamentary life, one led by the Christian Socials, the other by the Social Democrats. In the former ensemble the other German bourgeois parties would have to cooperate, as would Slavic *bürgerlich* politicians. In such an atmosphere of intrabourgeois economic cooperation "a *Kulturkampf* appears to be virtually excluded."[220] Gaertner did not believe that the nationality conflict would disappear, but he thought that it could be superseded by an agenda of other, more important policy issues and that the new democratic parties would be better placed to compromise with each other on national issues.[221] He also affirmed the conscious modeling of the Christian Social *Reichspartei* on the German *Zentrum:* "[since they are] now more than ever before similar to the German *Zentrum,* the Christian Socials intend to inaugurate social politics (*Sozialpolitik*) in a grand manner."[222]

This vision of the Christian Social party as a national *Volkspartei* that would cut across regional and class interests, basing itself upon the urban and rural middle classes and uniting Germans while reconciling Slavs, was ambitious and daring. It was not surprising that Gaertner would soon become the bête

noire of Ernst Vergani, who detested Gaertner's visions for the Christian Socials, and who, in the midst of his fronde against Albert Gessmann in 1910,
would roast Gessmann for using Gaertner as his chief political adviser.[223] But
this vision was also an invitation to paralysis, if not outright disaster, unless
secular economic growth and internal party discipline were maintained. The
success of the *Reichspartei* hinged on the ability of the leadership to hold together a party that would be both rural *and* urban in its economic constituencies and that would cut across class lines in Vienna to permit the retention of
a core of middle-class seats in the capital. On paper this strategy was logical
in that it reflected the regional proportions of Austrian electoral districts as
they were distributed in the 1907 suffrage bill among German-speaking constituencies. Of the 152 parliamentary seats contested in the new system in the
six Crownlands of Lower Austria, Upper Austria, Tyrol, Salzburg, Styria and
Vorarlberg, 43 were in large urban areas (including Vienna) whereas 28 were
in smaller cities and towns, and 81 were defined as rural.[224] The final result of
the balloting in May 1907 produced a Christian Social party that reflected, in
very rough proportions, the first and third components of these ratios: 20 delegates from large urban districts (all from Vienna) and 40 from rural *Gemein-
den.* The party's weak point was in the second category, smaller cities and
towns, where it received only 6 seats. The anchorage of the party in the urban
areas lay almost exclusively in Vienna. In other large German-speaking cities
like Linz, Graz, and Salzburg and in the smaller industrial cities like Wiener
Neustadt outside Vienna, the party fared much less well, consistently losing
seats either to the Social Democrats or to German nationalist factions like the
Volkspartei. After the merger the agrarian accent of the party became even
more demonstrable: 27 city seats against 69 rural seats. The numerical disparity of votes was not so extreme (252,623 urban voters against 466,756 on the
land) but because of the peculiarities of the 1906 legislation and the absence
of proportional voting or proportional allocation of seats on the basis of population, the final result made the party seem unduly rural.[225] This meant that the
Reichspartei was both a Viennese party, in the mold of Lueger, and a strongly
rural-agrarian party with no tertiary sectoral strength.

For many in the leadership these two facts were interrelated. Since the majority of population in these six lands still lived in districts that the Austrian
census defined either as small-town or rural (a fact which many younger Viennese Liberals consciously ignored in their dreams for a "New" Liberalism after
1907), the success of the new *Reichspartei* in gaining a stranglehold on rural
seats might be seen as a gain or at least as a tolerable fallback against a socialist
victory in Vienna. Richard Charmatz's long, eloquent plea in June 1907 on
behalf of a "new Liberalism" suggested that future Liberals should encourage
modern industrial development and greater industrialization and urbanization

in Austria.[226] Compared to such futurism (and for the time, utopianism), Gessmann's strategy at least had the merits of taking Austria as it was, and not as he wanted it to become.

This then became the principal gamble of the *Reichspartei:* could urban and rural interests live in peace and harmony and could their cohabitation be marketed successfully to each side's voters? The German *Zentrum* had succeeded in balancing rural and urban interests in its party (however tenuously), in spite of the fact that the leaders of the *Zentrum* also had to contend with powerful centrifugal and regionalist ambitions. But what held the *Zentrum* together and provided it with logical and substantive coherence was not merely its economic rationality but also the cultural isolation of German Catholics within the wider framework of German society. Even if the progressive Rhenish faction of the *Zentrum* insisted that it was a party and not a confessional organization, a majority of *Zentrum* voters still employed religious self-consciousness as a form of self- and group identification. Were such integrative devices available to the Austrians?

As the descriptions of the *Zentrum* in the *Reichspost* and as the criticisms of the Vergani faction made clear, they were not. Even an old *Hetzkaplan* like Josef Dittrich, now an exceptionally popular pastor (and chairman of the district election committee) in the Leopoldstadt, was aware of Viennese sensibilities. He refused to accept nomination for a parliamentary seat in 1907 since "the Christian Socials must avoid giving their enemies any occasion of arguing that, even in their external organization, they are a clerical party."[227] Rather than serving as a bridge or link for the party, the "clericalism" issue might tear it apart, given the different views of religion between the Viennese and the Alpine ruralists. "Clericalism" was an issue that might be used as a secondary weapon against the party, but its other, positive self—"political Catholicism"—was unsuited as the primary *positive* integrative device for the party. Gessmann was correct therefore in thinking that overt religious consciousness had to be integrated into a broader, anti-socialist ideology.

Another conventional "currency" of bourgeois politics in Austria was, of course, nationalism. Hence the insistence of the *Reichspost* that the *Reichspartei* was not merely a urban/rural "peoples' party" but also a "German" party. But this formula also had its dangers, if pushed too far. Converting the party into a *völkisch* cadre organization threatened to make it indistinguishable from other German nationalist factions (a danger which came to pass under Richard Weiskirchner's leadership in the First World War). Such a strategy might also undercut the appeal of the party to Austrian Slavs in general and to assimilated Czech voters in Vienna in particular.

A final possibility was anti-socialism, and given the limitations of other integrative themes it is not surprising that Gessmann chose to make this his strong suit. It also made the most sense in Vienna, and Gessmann was as much a Viennese politician as Lueger. But where Lueger saw the party's future in consolidation under his personal rule in Vienna, Gessmann had a more ambitious vision of intraclass expansion and coalition beyond the city. In a personal demonstration of this urban-rural habitus, Gessmann had himself elected to parliament in two districts—from Neubau in Vienna and from the rural city district of Mistelbach in Lower Austria—and then accepted the latter seat as an act of solidarity with the Lower Austrian *Bauernbund*. What Gessmann failed to see was that both groups of leaders and voters—Viennese and Alpine—may have been ardently anti-socialist, but "socialism" meant something quite different to each side. In rural Tyrol it was a distant object of hatred but not a serious object of electoral competition. Hating socialism did not mean having to organize against it, and, more importantly, it did not mean tailoring one's social and national-economic policies to compete with it.

Writing in the *Reichspost* in January 1904 the Prague theologian Karl Hilgenreiner argued that, since issues of church and state were relatively settled in Austria and since public attention was directed toward other problems like the nationality question, it made no sense to create a uniform and unified Catholic party: "A concentration of Catholic political parties was not even achieved at a time [in the 1870s] when to be Catholic could and should have given us a trump card; it is even less likely now, when for a long time church-state issues have not been present on the agenda of state politics."[228]

What differentiated January 1904 from June 1907 was the sudden, explosive, and successful intervention of Austrian Social Democracy and its cultural as well as economic agendas into the matrix of Austrian state politics. Hilgenreiner's world—the world of the Prague Germans and of Bohemian Catholicism—presumed the exclusive hegemony of national tensions and intrabourgeois rivalries on the menu of Austrian politics. All of this had changed by 1907, as the two Viennese-based mass social movements now collided in competition for state policy and ultimately for cultural hegemony. Yet, for better or worse, that diversity within the "Catholic" camp that Hilgenreiner noted was not superseded by the new *Reichspartei*. Rather the final stylization of the *Reichspartei* was a creative hybrid: a bourgeois *Volkspartei*, swinging opportunistically between images of "Christian" and "Catholic," based in the urban middle class and peasantry and yet sensitive to potential client groups within the working classes, conciliatory of both rural and urban interests, and standing as the final defense against Austrian Social Democracy. It was not, as Ernst Vergani would later argue, a party made in Vienna for the interest of the rural "clericals." Quite the contrary, this was a party made out of the stuff of Viennese bourgeois anti-socialism, attempting to universalize its doctrines by adding to them the territorial and moral presuppositions of the adjectives "Christian" and "German." Observing this artful and flexible combination of roles and values in 1908 in an essay published in *Hochland,* Martin Spahn could pay the Christian Socials the ultimate compliment of hoping that the German *Zentrum* would become more like them.[229] When Spahn then sent a copy of this article to Albert Gessmann, he received a predictably warm and appreciative response.[230] In their imperialistic tactics the Christian Socials paralleled remarkably their bitter enemy, for the Viennese Social Democrats also saw the Austrian political world through their own temporal spectacles.

THREE

The Reichspartei and the Era of Ministerialism, 1907–1911

The Christian Socials and the Beck Era

The immediate occasion for the decision of the Christian Social leadership to join Minister-President Max von Beck's coalition Cabinet in November 1907 was the *Ausgleich* with Hungary. Beck's remarkable success in eliciting from a weak Hungarian government final agreement on the economic *Ausgleich* has been discussed in considerable detail.[1] The logic of Beck's strategy was clear. First, he aborted Hungarian hopes of joining military demands to an economic settlement by refusing to negotiate any military concessions in the context of the *Ausgleich*. Second, by attempting to secure only a decennial settlement that would be in effect until 1917, Beck was able to limit the range of controversy and establish politically safe choices for his Hungarian partners. Although his failure to push for a twenty- or even thirty-year treaty was later seen as having contributed to the economic and political instability of the Monarchy during the First World War (since the settlement's renewal in 1916–17 gave Stefan Tisza an excellent pressure point against Austrian constitutional and administrative reforms) Beck decided that less was more in 1907, and that Austria's greatest priority lay in ending the period of pseudo-constitutional "reciprocity" that had governed the economic relations between Austria and Hungary since 1899 (when the last legally negotiated settlement had expired).[2] Beck's principal difficulty—and it was both genius and luck that he avoided it—was that the *Ausgleich* had a political double life. It was a complex fiscal and legal document that deserved the complex, assiduous negotiations of the experts; but it also served as a hostage for the Thronfolger and for Hungarian nationalists, both of whom used it as a weapon with which to attack the constitutional status quo. Julius Andrássy's *Junktim* between the *Ausgleich* and the guarantees for the Hungarian constitution articulated in 1906, the separatist implications of which Beck was able to weaken but not eliminate in his accord with Andrássy in September, was only the most overt of these impulses. Beck's decision to force a settlement was the last step in the dissolution of his formerly amicable relationship with the Thronfolger.[3] Henceforth the Belvedere became a government in internal exile, conspiring to bring Beck down.[4]

In October 1907, after fourteen months of intensive negotiations, the two sides reached provisional agreement on a draft treaty.[5] The bill was introduced into the Austrian *Abgeordnetenhaus* on October 16.[6] It offered a balanced package of modest victories and equally bearable losses for the Austrian side. The Hungarians consented to raise their rate of contribution to the joint budget (the *Quote*) by 2 percent, from 34.4 to 36.4 percent. They also agreed to a downward adjustment in the capitalization rate of the state debt (which lowered Austrian contributions to this budget line) and agreed to a rail connection from Carinthia through Hungarian (Croatian) territory to Dalmatia. The question of more equitable railway fees for Austrian goods shipped on Hungarian railways was also resolved in Austria's favor. In return Beck had to concede the word "Vertrag" rather than "Bündnis" as characterizing the agreement, signifying the relationship of two sovereign states rather than one state in two administrative parts, and was forced to make concessions on the acceptability of Hungarian securities for Austrian *Sparkassen* investments and Hungarian access to consumption tax revenues. The final product was a classic compromise from which neither side emerged as a clear winner or loser.[7]

Beck immediately commenced negotiations with the bourgeois parties to secure their support. The attitude of the Christian Socials would be critical. No other German faction would vote for the *Ausgleich* without assurances that Lueger would support it, and no agrarian faction of any party would support it unless they were certain that the agrarian majority in the Christian Social club would not use the bill to embarrass them. Throughout the autumn the party's press had sustained a vicious anti-Magyar line, expostulating against Hungarian chauvinism and warning against concessions in the negotiations. Would Lueger and his colleagues dare to sacrifice one of their cardinal issues for the sake of Beck?

The most blatant way to secure Christian Social support was to co-opt the party into the ministry by transforming the Cabinet into a multiethnic, bourgeois coalition. In mid-September Josef Schraffl broached the issue of joining the Cabinet in a speech in Innsbruck, noting that no decision had yet been made and that the party would not support a bad settlement with Hungary, but that in the event it did enter the Cabinet it would want a powerful role in shaping future governmental policy, not simply token ministerial positions.[8] Rumors spread in the press that Gessmann sought the creation of a new ministry of labor (*Arbeitsministerium*) with important controls over Austrian social policy as the price of the party's support for the *Ausgleich*.[9] The party leadership offered unconvincing denials of these rumors. Schraffl had forecast the course of the next two months—the party would construct propagandistically a "good" settlement out of a "bad" settlement, in return for substantial control over the future Beck Cabinet. In late September Beck spoke with Lueger about appointing Ebenhoch as Minister of Agriculture, receiving no firm commitment.[10] Ebenhoch himself opened a new tactical route in a lead article in the *Reichspost* on September 21, praising Beck for his resolve and determination, while painting an ominous portrait of the consequences of failure to agree on a settlement. The provisional decrees of September 1899 establishing a regime of reciprocity expired on December 31, 1907, which would result in a de jure if not de facto state of economic independence for each side of the Monarchy and the end of the legal basis of the Austro-Hungarian Bank. Ebenhoch also alluded to the uproar this would cause in Austrian foreign affairs, particularly with the *Dreibund,* and to the anxiety of the German government that the crisis be quickly and permanently resolved.[11] Introducing the critical issue of time, Ebenhoch relativized the problem and enabled his party to rationalize an agreement in the name of "saving the Monarchy as a whole."

Gessmann too had more partisan reasons for cultivating Beck's sympathies. In September 1907 he introduced a franchise reform bill in the Lower Austrian Diet which expanded the provincial franchise substantially, creating a general curia of 58 seats of which 48 were assigned to Vienna and 10 to the rest of the province, but which also retained privileged and tax-based seats in existing curias outside of Vienna. The bill almost doubled the number of seats (from 78 to 127). His work was based on complex negotiations with Beck and Kielmansegg over the summer, in which the limits of his party's toleration of "democracy" had become apparent.[12] For the agrarians the final revised draft was especially appealing since it offered them a plurality of seats (and, with the large landowners, close to a majority of seats) against Vienna—a conscious effort by Gessmann to reinforce the rural "fall-back" position of the party should the Social Democrats ever sweep Vienna. Whereas Vienna had a majority (33) of the 64 Lower Austrian seats in the *Abgeordnetenhaus,* in the Diet it would now have only 48 of the 104 seats that were publicly contested (23 seats were reserved for the *Grossgrundbesitz,* for the Chamber of Commerce, and for a few honorific notables like the archbishop of Vienna [*Virilisten*]). Following stormy protests by the Social Democrats, the Diet voted this reform in late September 1907. Gessmann expected the quick approval of Beck and the Cabinet for this bill, which even Kielmansegg recognized as tantamount to handing the province into the permanent possession of the Christian Socials (he estimated that with this franchise the party would, at a minimum, control 80–90 seats at any given time).[13] It is not unlikely that an informal understanding was reached between the two on the party's "reasonableness" toward the *Ausgleich* in return for permanent hegemony in Lower Austria.[14]

Others in the parliamentary delegation might favor joining the Cabinet, but Lueger was not so quick to join the bandwagon. But even he gradually tempered his discourse. He might declare in late September that "I can say quite definitely that if the *Ausgleich* is not favorable and satisfactory to us in every respect, it will not be passed by parliament," but this simply begged the question of what was favorable.[15] Beginning in the second week of October, Beck conducted secret meetings with top Christian Social leaders. Although favoring entry into the Cabinet, Gessmann implied on October 14 that the party would consider this possibility only after the legislation had gone through parliament. That is, a deal for the party's support would be arranged beforehand, but the existing ministers would be left with the onus if the final draft proved politically unmarketable.[16]

Initial reaction by the leadership to the *Ausgleich* legislation was cautiously favorable (the *Reichspost* grudgingly admitted this was the best agreement Austria had seen in forty years, but added that that was also not saying very much), and a meeting of the parliamentary club on October 21 adopted a stance of cautious independence, as did most other parties with the exception of the Social Democrats. That the *Ausgleich* secured economic advantages for Austria at the cost of juristic concessions to Hungary was acknowledged in the public comments by Christian Social spokesmen.[17] An ostentatiously favorable article on the final settlement in the October 1907 issue of *Österreichische Rundschau* characterized it as a "justly balanced settlement" with which both Austria and Hungary should be satisfied.[18] Alfred Ebenhoch tried to provoke a decision from the party with an encouraging evaluation on October 20 in the *Reichspost,* but not before he had privately acknowledged to Lueger ten days earlier that the mayor would make the final decision on the party's entering the Cabinet.[19]

When debate on the first reading opened on October 25 Lueger, although very ill, appeared in parliament as the principal Christian Social speaker. Listing himself as an oppositional speaker, he presented comments that were complex and, for Beck, bewildering. Lueger reported that in spite of several days of debate in the club, no agreement had yet been reached on how the party should vote. It had decided, therefore, to take no final position but to await the debates in the *Ausgleich* committee and to seek clarification of various points in the original draft.[20] The socialists interpreted this performance as a crude gambit by the Christian Socials to blackmail Beck into further concessions; he had already arranged for the Imperial sanction of the Lower Austrian franchise on October 11, which was made public on October 30. Lueger's comments at his birthday celebration on October 24, where he appealed for party unity and professionalism ("Unity is more necessary that ever before"), reflected genuine debate in the party not over whether it would eventually vote for the bill but over what price it would demand. Economic pressure from Austrian industrial circles pointed toward acceptance, and at a meeting on October 25 of the *Freie industrielle Vereinigung*—an ad hoc group of urban parliamentarians interested in industrial issues to which several prominent Christian Socials belonged—sympathies ran strongly in favor of accepting the settlement.[21] The issue, then, was not one of theory versus practice but one of authority and leadership. Entrance into the Cabinet would diversify authority in the party and legitimate Gessmann's *Reichspartei* as a vehicle independent of the Vienna organization. It was a step the aging and sick Lueger could take only with great ambivalence.

At this point an external crisis in the sitting Cabinet forced both Beck's and Lueger's hands. Since early October negotiations had been conducted in Prague among the various Czech parties to create a single Czech parliamentary club, parallel to the Gessmann-Ebenhoch *Reichspartei*. One roadblock to such a body was the existing distribution of ministerial seats. The Young Czechs presently held both of the Czech ministerial positions, even though they had suffered substantial losses in the 1907 elections against the emergent Czech Agrarian party. The latter, reflecting a process of mass conservatism on a democratic basis similar to that which now sustained the Alpine part of the *Reichspartei,* represented a potentially more powerful (and culturally conservative) segment of the Czech electorate than did the Young Czechs. Negotiations for unity eventually deadlocked, but in the process the Young Czech Club pulled both of its ministers, Bedřich Pacák and Josef Fořt, out of the Cabinet, alleging that Beck was unwilling to cooperate with Czech nationalist demands. In fact, they could no longer count on the support of the other Czech factions, most of which were more sympathetic to the Agrarians. The *Ausgleich* conundrum also played a role: even though they were ministerial colleagues of Beck, the Young Czechs dared not support the settlement with Hungary unless assured that the other Czech factions would not repudiate it. That various independent agrarian lobbying groups like Ritter von Hohenblum's *Agrarische Zentralstelle* had come out in opposition to the *Ausgleich* made unilateral action all the more difficult for any bourgeois party.

By early November Karel Prášek, the leader of the Czech Agrarians, had gone public with demands that his party be given ministerial representation as the price Beck would have to pay for the *Ausgleich*.[22] He also made it no secret that he coveted the Ministry of Agriculture, then occupied by Leopold Auersperg, a professional civil servant who was accounted to the German side. What began as an intra-Czech patronage crisis—which of the Czech factions would merit representation in the Cabinet?—thus set off a mad scramble for places in what would now have to be a reconstructed Beck ministry, whether Beck intended it to be such or not. The following seven days saw the most intensive and, for many, the most perverse minister-trading that ever occurred in modern Austrian politics, belying the conventional wisdom that only the Emperor made ministers.[23] For the German *bürgerlich* parties, the notion of Prášek, a former army corporal with a primary school education, as agricultural minister was nothing less than horrendous, and they persuaded the Christian Socials to lobby Beck against making such a crude concession. The Czechs, in turn, threatened obstructionism against the *Ausgleich* without a suitable resolution of the Cabinet question. Beck was now faced with the worst of all Austrian political nightmares—ethnic feuding between Czechs and Germans inserted into the Austro-Hungarian constitutional conflict. He had two alternatives—either insert the Christian Socials in the reconstruction of the Cabinet and thus force both the Czechs and the Germans to submit more modest claims, or dismiss the House and implement the *Ausgleich* by means of Article 14.

On the evening of November 6 Beck visited Lueger at the Rathaus and offered the Christian Socials two positions in the Cabinet, the actual assignments not yet designated. After considering the alternatives Beck sketched out (either Article 14 or the dismissal of parliament and a new round of elections that his party would be hard-pressed to afford), Lueger gave in and accepted Beck's offer. To Brosch the following day he justified his decision with what was doubtlessly the true explanation. He was convinced that parliamentary sanction of the *Ausgleich* was of tremendous importance, both for parliament itself and for the Hapsburg state.[24] If he was anything, Lueger was consistent in his valuation of the authority of parliament, whatever its collective institutional foibles, against both dynastic autocracy and nationalist chauvinism. If the Austrian government were to maintain the interests of the western half of the Monarchy against the Magyars, it had first to preserve its own public integrity. To vote against the *Ausgleich* now would have severely damaged that integrity and would simply repeat the vicious circle of Hungarian moral hegemony over Austria that had begun in 1898–99. Hungary had a functioning parliament; Austria, in spite of its new "democracy," had administrative autocracy and chaos.

To this end Lueger set aside his personal doubts and consented to allow his party into the government. Lueger was still very ill in the autumn of 1907 and his role in the *Ausgleich* crisis was his last major action on behalf the Christian Social party before his death in 1910. Ultimately, his decision joined practical value, contextual rationality, and political responsibility, the mark of a true statesman. For all his cultural Magyarphobia, Lueger recognized that the interests of the *Reich* as an economic unit deserved rational support from both sides of the Monarchy, since both sides profited from their mutual integration. Gessmann's younger ally, Friedrich Gaertner, offered a similar, economic justification in a long essay on the *Ausgleich* finished in June 1907 for Max Weber's *Archiv für Sozialwissenschaft*. For Gaertner it would be "a mistake against all economic rationality . . . if one separated two [state] areas that complement each other so splendidly. Today one sees a clearly observable tendency to construct larger economic arenas."[25]

That entrance into the Cabinet was not a price Beck was obliged to pay for the Christian Social party's support of the *Ausgleich* was made clear by the *Reichspost* on November 9, which noted that the party had decided to vote for it anyway and only thereafter to raise the issue of governmental participation.[26] This suggested that Gessmann and Ebenhoch had not been able to persuade Lueger to accept Cabinet membership until after the Czech-German cabinet crisis had reached perilous limits.

Once Lueger had agreed to move, intense negotiations began that produced hourly shifts in possible Cabinet combinations over the next two days, as an astonished Viennese public looked on.[27] Gessmann would have preferred to claim the powerful Ministry of Commerce, but Beck's need to separate feuding Czech and German agrarians made it imperative that a Christian Social, Ebenhoch, be placed in the Ministry of Agriculture. Since an unwritten rule of Austrian cabinet politics dictated that the same ethnic camp could not have both Agriculture and Commerce, the Czechs claimed the Ministry of Commerce. Beck then persuaded Gessmann to enter the Cabinet as minister without portfolio, promising him a new ministry, the *Arbeitsministerium,* that had been touted two months earlier and was to be created by transferring important policy agendas out of the Ministries of Agriculture, Internal Affairs, and Commerce. Since the new Ministry seemed to promise Gessmann vast authority over future Austrian social policy, he gambled that it would actually be preferable to Commerce and accepted it. That this would prove a fateful mistake and that Beck would be unwilling or unable to fulfill his promises only became apparent later.

The resulting Cabinet, announced on November 10, thus reflected the new realities of Austrian politics after the May 1907 elections. All three major bourgeois blocs—Czech, German national, and Christian Social—were now represented in the government. Gessmann's and Gaertner's dream of a *Sammlung* of bourgeois parties seemed on the verge of reality, a fact that may explain the venomous bile the Social Democrats threw at Gessmann in their press. Not merely his person, but his anti-Marxist bloc theories as well seem at last to have come of age.[28] Significantly, rather than one agrarian the new Cabinet now had three. Although it was the largest party in the House, the Christian Socials had the smallest number of ministers—a reflection of the curious fact that esteem in Austrian parliamentary politics was measured above all in the negative power to obstruct, not in the positive power to vote. Small, obstreperous factions needed ministers too—systemic weakness in party structure translated into chronic weaknesses of Cabinet authority.

Lueger thus brought the party into the Cabinet at the urgent request of Beck and under the pressure of his ambitious subordinates, although to Richard

Weiskirchner several months later he would insist that he had always had reservations and had done so against his own better judgment.[29] In any event, Beck had paid the agreed-upon price for the party's sanction of the *Ausgleich,* which was made easier for the Christian Socials by virtue of a working alliance with the German national parties in the form of a twelve-person coordinating committee (*Zwölferausschuss*). Neither side trusted the other, but together they might approve the *Ausgleich* without fear of back-biting or revenge. On December 12 the final reading of the bill passed the *Abgeordnetenhaus,* after a series of self-justifying rallies in Vienna where the Christian Socials portrayed their vote as both rational (the *Ausgleich* was not as bad as it seemed; indeed, it was better than all previous agreements) and as patriotic (failure to approve it would lead to the legal equivalent of civil war in the Monarchy, which no one wanted). The triumph was Beck's, but it was also his swan song.

Alfred Ebenhoch moved into the Ministry of Agriculture, which he had long coveted and for which he was supremely prepared. His tenure was, from the small and medium agriculturalist's perspective, both successful and salutary.[30] When the party leadership decided to pull him out of the Cabinet in late 1908 his agrarian colleagues in the party delegation could offer genuine expressions of regret, if not outrage, at the move. Not all of his views were popular, and not all of his Ministry's policies were his own. Ebenhoch found himself defending the government's trade agreements against the aggressive network of agrarian protectionism organized by Alfred von Hohenblum; and he earned the growing displeasure of the Right in the *Herrenhaus* and of their patron Franz Ferdinand by his insistent support for the rights of small peasant landowners.[31]

It was with Gessmann and the putative *Arbeitsministerium,* however, that Beck had made his most controversial choice. Not only was Gessmann, in his own words, a professional "agitator" of long-standing, whom the Social Democrats and radical Liberals in Vienna held in greater contempt than any other single bourgeois politician, but Beck also himself found Gessmann's new ministerial role problematic. His aggressive partisanship on behalf of his party made him a fierce opponent, and one far more dangerous than most of the hapless conspirators Beck dealt with on the ministerial level. They did not have mass political constituencies behind them; they could not claim to speak in the name of Karl Lueger. Even if much of Gessmann's power was derivative from Lueger, he was the first mass-based political figure to enter the Austrian cabinet service and the first to have his own substantial political base. His view of politics came from the rally hall, not the academy; he had no sympathy for or loyalty to Josephistic traditions of Austrian administrative management. He was impatient and cruel, the closest approximation (next to his friend Rudolf Sieghart) to a Machiavellian that Austrian politics had ever produced. Beck was dealing with a radically new kind of Cabinet official. Brosch reported to the Thronfolger that the Minister-President found the notion of Gessmann as one of his ministers not quite "agreeable."[32]

The first six months of the new Cabinet were consumed by cultural, constitutional, and institutional-organizational issues, none of which succeeded in bringing it down, but all of which combined over time to discredit it in Christian Social eyes. Ironically, the great accomplishments of Beck's regime preceded rather than followed the advent of full parliamentary ministerialism, even though most of those acts were taken in the name of achieving such governance. For Gessmann the first order of business was to establish the new *Arbeitsministerium* that he had accepted as the Viennese niche in the Imperial order. He had agreed to this nonexistent ministry on the basis of what he thought were Beck's assurances that he would be allowed to make it into a novel and powerful experiment in governmental reorganization and social modernization, one that would also offer the Christian Socials a central base for shaping future Austrian social and economic policy. When the Imperial rescript authorizing the new ministry was finally issued in late March 1908, however, after four months of acrimonious debate and inordinate delay, the result was far different from what Gessmann and his allies had intended.

Beginning in late November Gessmann formulated ambitious plans for the *Arbeitsministerium,* which became the target of sharp debate. The very name of the Ministry, which could be interpreted to mean either a "Ministry of Labor" or a "Ministry of Public Works," suggested that Beck's practice of creative ambiguity was again operative. Was this to be a ministry of social policy (insurance, labor conditions, employment, emigration, etc.) or was it to be a "technical" institution in support of the other "political" ministries, preoccupying itself with more mundane assignments like public construction, mines, and technological innovation? From party press reports and Gessmann's own statements before sundry economic-interest groups as he canvassed Vienna for support, a vision of his views emerged that comprised *both* a ministry of social resources and a ministry of industrial, technical, and construction services.[33] In early January 1908 the *Neue Freie Presse* obtained a draft of his program and published its details, which amounted to nothing less than a "super-ministry" claiming many of the most significant social policy agendas of the Austrian state.[34] Gessmann envisaged a five-section ministry, consisting of Industry and Social Policy; Public Contracts; Roads and Buildings; Canals, Rivers, and Harbors; and Mines and Energy. Especially controversial was the fact that most of these agendas were to be taken away from existing ministries. In the first section, for example, Gessmann wanted to take labor law and the supervision of labor organizations from the Ministry of Commerce, and emigration and housing development from the Ministry of Internal Affairs. In the second section Gessmann would not only gain a general stranglehold over public contracts, but also obtain a specially privileged position in supporting small-business development, the latter stripped from Commerce. The plan had both an institutional and a political logic that reinforced each other. By gaining control of most of the valuable agendas of *Sozialpolitik,* especially union supervision and social insurance, Gessmann would put his party in a superb position to curb the influence of the Social Democrats in local social welfare agencies. More importantly, he would gain a powerful lever with which to fulfill the many campaign promises of the Christian Socials in their posture as the social reform party par excellence. Had the plan gone through, for example, control of the new system of *Sozialpolitik* agendas in industrial and technical development would have gained the Christian Socials meaningful access to the world of big industrial capitalism, a strategy that became one of the critical values Gessmann would seek to impose on his middle-class movement over the next four years, and would have provided the party with a "modernistic" image that would have encouraged Austrian economic progress.[35]

Even before the *Neue Freie Presse* exploded its bombshell (which the Christian Social media did not even bother to deny), labor circles in Vienna had reacted with outrage to the possibility of the Christian Socials assuming supervision of the Austrian unions and industrial labor relations. The specter of Gessmann, the "conqueror" of socialist teachers in Vienna and Lower Austria and the author of the 1904 Lower Austria school laws, as the Minister in charge of labor policy sent the Social Democrats into paroxysms of anger. A meeting of representatives from large industrial and commercial firms in Vienna on November 15 suggested that they too had qualms about Gessmann's meddling, although most were willing to hand *Sozialpolitik* over to him. A curious game of political football thus ensued in which some capitalists sought to make the new Ministry a narrow "labor ministry," where Gessmann's talents as an antisocialist would be well utilized (Alfred Lenz, a prominent industrialist, favored a ministry of social policy with Gessmann in charge since in this way "the all-too-great influence which the socialists have in the past exercised on all Ministries can be broken");[36] while the Social Democrats made it clear to Beck that anything more than an equally narrow "technical" public works ministry would constitute a casus belli.[37] An issue of special concern to the industrialists was Gessmann's control of state procurement policy. In view of the way the Christian Social *Stadtrat* had manipulated municipal contracts in Vienna, the prospect of having to deal with Gessmann for state contracts was not altogether pleasant.

Between December and February negotiations took place among and within existing ministries, particularly the Ministry of Commerce and the Ministry of Internal Affairs, over the surrender of portfolios to the *Arbeitsministerium.* Gessmann encountered resistance from professional civil servants entrenched in these Ministries and from their political patrons in parliament and in the Cabinet. The current Minister of Commerce, František Fiedler, was a Young

Czech. Removing policy agendas from his Ministry and giving them to a "German" (Gessmann) might be viewed by the Slavic parties as tantamount to betrayal. Leading German bourgeois deputies like Karl Chiari and Stefan Licht, while supporting the establishment of an anti-socialist social welfare ministry, opposed handing over substantial commercial or industrial responsibilities to the Christian Socials.

Beck thus found himself in the midst of a remarkable street fight, as Josephist civil servants conspired with socialist and *bürgerlich* politicians on both sides of the ethnic divide to subvert the Christian Socials' quest for power. In contrast to Gessmann's or Lueger's previous confrontations with the government, from which they had emerged victorious (over the 1900 city statute and the 1904 school laws), the party was now playing for higher stakes but with less leverage. To demand partisan franchises or educational laws for their own province was one thing; to antagonize the Social Democrats on the state level by discrediting the facade of "neutral" Josephist bureaucratism was another. The Christian Socials might claim to "own" Vienna, but they did not (yet) own the state.

Indeed, a remarkable feature of the late Imperial system was the quiet confidence that the Social Democrats placed in the state-level Ministries, both as institutional incarnations of absolutist *and* central power and as expressions of dynastic right. If all else failed, the socialists assumed they could count on a minimal level of respect from these agencies based on the proceduralism of the Austrian administrative service, on the modulation implicit in the ethos of the centralistic Josephist state of law, and, ironically, on the slow but perceptible acknowledgment by the socialists of Franz Joseph's equitable style of governance. Hence the willingness of the socialist party leadership to show up in formal dress for the traditional Imperial audience that opened the new parliament in June 1907, although this caused an uproar in some more "progressive" sections of the party. Such representations neither repudiated the theoretical republicanism of the movement, nor did they signify dynastic nostalgia. But they did suggest that the socialist party could coexist with the Imperial system as long as certain political equities were maintained. The Social Democrats were not certain that these expectations would be honored by Franz Ferdinand, and hence they viewed his impending succession with apprehension. What their German brethren already took for granted—the bankruptcy of "their" dynasty—the Austrians had only to anticipate.

Within the Cabinet a process of informal consultation and collaboration with the socialists had begun in the later 1890s, becoming most obvious during Koerber's ministry. Its persistence under Beck merited him furious diatribes by *Herrenhaus* members who accused him of sympathizing with or even encouraging the Social Democrats.[38] That the trend reflected a combination of institutional pressure and Josephist administrative rationality, not mere personal whim, was evident in the increasingly close relationships that developed among the Social Democratic party and union organizations and the various Ministries during the war. These relationships developed not just in the context of socialist involvement in war regulatory work and the eventual invitation for socialist membership in the Cabinet, but also in more subtle cultural concessions. When subordinate officials in the military government issued an order in 1915 allowing Catholic chaplains in war hospitals to forbid patients' access to Social Democratic literature, Adler and Seitz had no difficulty in getting the War Minister to overrule his subordinates' actions immediately.[39] Would Beck so aggravate Victor Adler by acceding to Gessmann's demands that the socialist leader might take his party into parliamentary obstruction, heretofore a "bourgeois" political sin from which the Social Democrats had abstained?[40]

Ironically, Albert Gessmann's position was the more "modern," since in his view a parliamentary ministry was precisely that—a ministry in which the party in power assumed control and exercised its right to control policy. His background in Viennese ward and machine politics, and later in Lower Austrian regional administration, made these assumptions self-evident to him. The Social Democrats had little access to such background experiences. Before 1914 their self-image was far more closely tied to that of their historic persecutor and eventual "protector"—the centralistic, administrative state. Of the two pre-war parties, the Austrian Social Democrats were the more "Josephist" as long as they were lodged in a minority position. This role would be reversed in the First Republic in Vienna.

The feasibility of Gessmann's plans ultimately turned on a critical but minor procedural issue. How would they be implemented: by Imperial decree or by legislative action in parliament? The Christian Socials favored the former; the Social Democrats demanded the latter. If Beck submitted Gessmann's proposals for parliamentary consideration in the *Abgeordnetenhaus,* any hope of pushing so many diverse policy agendas into one "monster ministry" (as the Liberal press tagged it) would be lost. Every major economic interest group in the Monarchy could mobilize at least one political faction to delay if not to obstruct such legislation.

Less than a week after the new Cabinet was in place, the *Reichspost* published two articles by an anonymous "expert" arguing that Austrian constitutional law prescribed no unilateral solution to the question of how a new ministry was to be established and noted that the most recent precedent, the Railways Ministry in 1896, was established by decree rather than parliamentary vote. The author admitted, however, that this was more a political than a constitutional issue and that doubtlessly parliament would have to play a role, although this might be restricted to approving specific policies and interventions undertaken by the new Ministry once established, rather than to approving its actual existence.[41]

These essays were an ill-disguised effort by the Christian Socials to bypass parliament, and this strategy met with decisive rejections from both the Social Democrats and the Viennese academic establishment. Edmund Bernatzik, the distinguished Austrian constitutionalist, published an essay in the *Neue Freie Presse* arguing that the creation of a new Ministry which had the authority to impinge upon the general rights of the citizens constituted de facto a revision of the constitutional settlement of 1867 and had to be approved by parliament. By late January the delays in formulating a clear plan of action for the new Ministry were becoming a major embarrassment for the Christian Socials.[42]

By the end of January Beck's stalling forced the party leadership to act. On January 25 it issued an official communiqué noting its "growing mistrust" of the situation and threatening to withdraw from the Cabinet if "certain demands" were not met.[43] Beck then complicated matters when, in informal remarks on January 29 before the Budget Committee, he promised that legislation for the new Ministry would be submitted to parliament for approval. Yet, when the transcripts of the meeting were published the following day, Beck was reported as not making such a specific assurance. The Social Democrats and several bourgeois deputies like Otto Steinwender immediately accused him of backing down before Christian Social pressure and of having falsified official transcripts.[44]

The situation was now sufficiently critical for Gessmann to arrange a summit meeting with Lueger and Beck to force the Minister-President to live up to what the *Reichspost* termed "binding assurances." Although Gessmann made one last effort to secure the creation of the Ministry by Imperial decree, Beck's comments on January 28 seemed to foreclose that option, creating what the Liberal press joyously termed a "dam against the energetic agitation for a large-scale *Arbeitsministerium*."[45] The *Reichspost* issued ominous-sounding pronouncements, suggesting that "neither Dr. Gessmann nor his party are willing to back down on their demands that the new Ministry have a substantial socio-political policy scope." But when the final decision on the competencies of the new Ministry was taken by the Cabinet, Gessmann ended up with a much truncated version. He would get agendas like mines, electrification, and bridge construction but only one social agenda, craft development, which, since it related primarily to encouraging the technological modernization of small and medium-sized industrial firms, constituted no threat to the Social Democrats.[46] Appropriately, the name *Arbeitsministerium* was now jettisoned in favor of *Ministerium für öffentliche Arbeiten*. The one concession Beck had secured for Gessmann was to attach vocational educational institutes to the craft portfolio, a modest field of political patronage. The party camouflaged its disappointment, but even the *Reichspost* admitted in a classic understatement that the Ministry "does not comprise all of the sociopolitical range of policies that would have been desirable."[47] Further, as Funder complained on February

7, both the *Deutscher Nationalverband* and the Christian Socials often found themselves learning of decisions taken by Beck from reading the opposition press. This was the beginning of a profound disenchantment on both Gessmann's and Ebenhoch's part over the value of their ministerial presence.[48] Later in the month, Weiskirchner, who was already uneasy with Beck's waffling before the Social Democrats, complained to Lueger that "a number of deals are being arranged of which our ministers know nothing."[49]

In the end, Beck did arrange for an Imperial decree, issued on March 21, announcing the new Ministry, but parliament was still left with the responsibility of approving the transfer of existing policy portfolios and authorizing the budget. Since the work of the Budget Committee extended into mid-March, Gessmann had to wait until early April for the plenum of the *Abgeordnetenhaus* to take up this legislation. In the interim, tensions between the Christian Socials and more anticlerical members of the German *bürgerlich* group over the Wahrmund Affair spilled over into the *Arbeitsministerium*, with some German members of parliament asking whether Gessmann should be allowed a free hand in naming his own section heads or whether guarantees should be demanded that nonpartisan officials would be appointed. This insult, among others, led Beck to summon a meeting of the two party leaderships on February 21, where, according to Ebenhoch, the Germans apologized and agreed to work with, rather than against, the Christian Socials. Such interfactional fighting hardly boded well for the future of the Cabinet.[50] Weiskirchner thought that it would not survive the spring.

When the legislation for what had become a ministry of public construction rather than labor came up for discussion in parliament on April 8, it was pushed into plenary consideration without prior committee discussion by a majority motion of urgency. Speaking as the principal opponent of the bill, Victor Adler admitted that a ministry of public works might be a valuable addition to the state administrative apparatus and that, to the extent that it encouraged technical modernization in mining and other industrial sectors, it would be a salutary innovation. But over all else loomed the person of Albert Gessmann. For Adler the only positive feature of the Ministry was what it had failed to include, a covert admission of the success of Social Democratic pressure on Beck. In the end Adler simply could not vote for a ministry controlled by so nefarious a socialist-hater as Gessmann.[51]

For the Christian Socials Karl Drexel presented an inept defense of his leader, but the most surprising commentary was that of Josef Redlich, who spoke on behalf of the German national parties. For Redlich, approval of the proposal was axiomatic for precisely the same reasons Social Democrats found it offensive. Austria stood on the threshold of parliamentary ministerialism in the Western European sense, and Albert Gessmann, as floor leader of the largest party in parliament, deserved the *Arbeitsministerium*. Personal motives or jejune biographical details were irrelevant. Redlich's frankly *Realpolitik* perspective, which would sanction virtually anything to achieve parliamentary stability, did not deny that the proposal was intrinsically meritorious. Against Liberal journalistic accusations that the Ministry was a hodgepodge thrown together to please Gessmann, Redlich argued that its proposed table of organization had at least as much rationality and procedural logic as the existing Austrian Ministries. The state administration suffered considerably from interministerial rivalries provoked by overlapping jurisdictions in the older Ministries that had evolved helter-skelter over time. Redlich hoped that Gessmann's initiative would be the beginning of a new era of administrative reform, in which a renewed parliamentarism would force organizational and personnel reforms onto the civil service.[52] Redlich's later preoccupation with administrative reform between 1911 and 1914 is discussed below, in Chapter 6, but his speech on behalf of Gessmann and the Christian Socials in 1908 already anticipated both the creativity and the frustrations of that reform effort.

Redlich's sober views demonstrated a remarkable convergence of personal and political interests between this brilliant Liberal constitutionalist and the Christian Socials' parliamentary leader. Redlich owed his appointment as professor of administrative and constitutional law at the Technical University in Vienna to Gessmann's patronage. The establishment of a Ministry of Social Welfare during the First World War would show that Gessmann's views about the desirability of rationalizing state control of social security were timely and convincing.[53] Indeed, the war ended with this Ministry under the control of Ignaz Seipel, an ironic continuity in the history of the Christian Social party. But the practical advantages of the parliamentarism that Redlich so decisively espoused were already becoming uncertain for many of the Christian Socials by the spring of 1908. Gessmann was left with a ministry whose structure, once it began functioning in July 1908, proved profoundly disappointing. By late March the Wahrmund scandal had sufficiently enraged clerically oriented Alpine deputies in the *Reichspartei* that a minority favored voting against the Cabinet when the Budget Committee reviewed the budget of the Ministry of Education. Only the intervention of Lueger and heavy lobbying by Gessmann and Ebenhoch prevented the anticlerical scandal from embarrassing the Cabinet.[54]

More serious, however, was the pressure the party felt from the Belvedere to jettison Beck. Given the Thronfolger's intense interest in thwarting the Hungarian Independence Party's demands for army reform, he eagerly exploited both militarism and Hungarian pretensions in pressuring the Christian Socials. The decision of the party to vote for the *Ausgleich* did not mean it had repudiated the "Hungarian card."[55] Indeed, that card soon came back into play under the aegis of military preparedness. Christian Social support for the Imperial Army was useful not only to hammer Hungarian revanchism but to attack the

Social Democrats on one of their weakest points. Hence the enthusiasm of the party leadership for military armaments and especially for new marine construction, which would not only create new jobs but whose representational imperialism would satisfy the patriotism of all good Austrian *Kleinbürger,* including many who happened to be Social Democratic workers. Josef Schlegel, the party's spokesman for naval development, was especially energetic in combining economic and patriotic arguments to justify big-ship construction.[56] The municipality contributed to this new popular militarism by sponsoring a program of after-school training for young boys which included military drills. A city-subsidized *Knabenhorte* association was established in late October 1907 in a competitive response to the program founded in 1906 by one Captain Franz Opelt, a retired Army officer who drew support from private sources, and which eventually incorporated dozens of groups across the Monarchy. In late June 1907 Opelt cleverly displayed his youthful charges at a parade attended by members of the high aristocracy and by Army leaders led by Field Marshal Beck. Thirty thousand spectators cheered as three thousand boys marched around the Trabrennplatz accompanied by a band playing patriotic hymns.[57] Obviously this was a field of public interest—given the lack of parental supervision in after-school hours that led far too many Viennese school children into delinquent behavior—which the Christian Socials could not ignore. At the same time both party and educational leaders felt uneasy about the overly militaristic ethos purveyed by Opelt, and the city's *Zentralverein zur Errichtung und Erhaltung von Knabenhorten* sought to encourage other aspects of the children's social and cultural development.[58]

Given the popularity of civil-military spectacles like the Trabrennplatz parade, the eagerness of Christian Social politicians in 1907–8 to play the role of a pro-military lobby made perfect sense, whether this meant granting members of veterans' organizations the right to bear weapons or obtaining wage increases for the regular enlisted cadres of the army.[59] The Christian Socials were not merely aping their *Zentrum* cousins to the north in using the army as an anti-Marxist issue, for they had the inestimable advantage of having both an army and an Emperor that enjoyed wide popularity in the Austrian electorate, even if the heir to the throne was not viewed in the same light. The *Zentrum* might vote credits for the fleet from what Karl Bachem once ambiguously referred to as its "loyale Politik," but it still endured the abuse of the German Navy League. The Christian Socials had a far easier task in supporting Austrian military appropriations.[60] The military issue entered Christian Social discourse not as a compensatory argument to demonstrate the *kaisertreu* views of the party, as was the case with the *Zentrum,* but to show the absence of such values among their principal enemies: first the Magyars and then the Social Democrats. When Josef Schraffl spoke grandly at a session of the Delegations in February 1908 of the three *Eisenklammern* that held together the *Gesamt-*

staat—the Army, the Dynasty, and Catholicism—he had achieved a discursive zenith from which to batter Austrian Social Democracy. Ironically, however, the presence of the "Magyars" as the partial target of such discourse before 1914 also worked to defuse that discourse and make it less threatening for the Austrian socialists.[61]

In early November 1907, a month before parliament approved the *Ausgleich,* Leopold Steiner submitted a motion demanding that the Cabinet negotiate with the joint Ministries of Defense and Finance so that legislation would be submitted at the next Delegation meeting providing wage increases for the officers and enlisted men in the Austro-Hungarian Army.[62] Salaries were an issue that War Minister Schönaich was eager to resolve, since the War Ministry agreed that the increases were justified. At a joint Ministerial Council in late October 1907 the Hungarian Minister-President, Sándor Wekerle, had seemed to be flexible about a compromise that would allow for officers' salary raises (although these might be linked to concessions such as the introduction of Hungarian as the language of command in units composed mainly of Hungarian soldiers; the revision of emblems worn by Hungarian soldiers; and the revision of flags and emblems carried by Hungarian units to reflect a more specific Magyar identity).[63] When the Delegations met in early 1908, however, the Hungarian government was unwilling to agree to any adjustments. For the Christian Socials the issue now moved from embarrassing the Social Democrats to flaying the Hungarian chauvinists. Based on the constitutional arguments of Professor Heinrich Lammasch, who distinguished between military base salaries which were clearly a "joint" budgetary responsibility and emergency assistance grants which, he argued, could be seen as a purely Austrian agenda, Josef Schraffl formulated a motion urging the Austrian government to proceed with unilateral wage increases for enlisted men and officers serving on its territory. These increases would take the form of extraordinary allowances for living expenses rather than increases in base pay.[64] Count Vinzenz Latour, a member of the *Herrenhaus,* had submitted a parallel motion for officers' salaries; and in late February 1908 the two motions were fused into one joint proposal, the Schraffl-Latour motion.

The Austrian Delegation approved the Schraffl-Latour motion on February 25, but a week later their Hungarian counterparts in Budapest poured cold water on the whole scheme.[65] This might have provoked a major interministerial upheaval, with the Beck Cabinet caught in the middle. But Karl Lueger intervened via Liechtenstein to order his party colleagues not to provoke a crisis, and Beck and Gessmann presided over a compromise whereby Schönaich and Aehrenthal committed the government on March 10 to recall the Delegations in late May, with the further assurance that the government would work vigorously to insert salary increases into the joint military budget for 1909, with retroactive increases for 1908.[66]

Throughout the episode Archduke Franz Ferdinand was convinced that Beck was negotiating military concessions to the Hungarians based on secret agreements concluded during the *Ausgleich.* The Thronfolger's paranoia passed its always low threshold in January 1908 when, in hysterical tones, he ordered Brosch to intervene with Lueger so that the Christian Socials would put pressure on Beck to prevent possible concessions to Hungary.[67] Unfortunately, Brosch found little to report to Franz Ferdinand in early February about the imminence of such concessions.[68]

When the Delegations concluded their work in mid-March, Beck and Schönaich had backed themselves into a corner. Franz Ferdinand was so enthusiastic about the Christian Socials' apparent victory that he summoned Ebenhoch and gave him a long, unctuous account of Lueger's greatness as a political leader.[69] That it had been Lueger who kept the party behind Beck in March does not seem to have occurred to the Thronfolger. Beck clearly would have preferred that the matter of military salary raises be buried, but when the Joint Ministerial Council met in late May to thrash out the collision of interests, Beck waged an impassioned if ultimately ineffective campaign to honor the government's promises to the Christian Socials.

This meeting of the Council must count as one of the more remarkable sessions of that ill-fated institution. It certainly belied conventional wisdom that the Joint Ministries were little affected by domestic political pressures. When the Council opened on May 17, the Hungarian Minister-President Wekerle was unbending in his resistance to the concessions Schönaich and Aehrenthal had offered the Austrians in March. Wekerle believed that they had gone far beyond what the Hungarian Cabinet either could or would tolerate and that the Hungarians were being asked to repudiate their earlier demands for a *Junktim* between salaries and military concessions. To find themselves faced with a *Diktat* from the Austrian parliament as to how and when these salary increases would be implemented would push the Cabinet into a difficult, if not catastrophic, situation in Budapest. Wekerle would have none of it.

Wekerle's intransigence through two unusually acrimonious sessions of the Ministerial Council revealed complex psychological pressures that conditioned Austro-Hungarian relations even on the highest level. Wekerle did not hesitate, for example, to exploit the concessions Beck had won in the *Ausgleich* negotiations: "in Hungary people are saying that Austria can afford to be generous [with the salaries], since the cost of the raise will be paid for by the increase in the Quote won from Hungary." But ultimately the issue did not turn on money (which Beck realized—"es handle sich für Ungarn kaum um 2 Millionen"); wounded pride and the sense that Beck had been put up to embarrassing Budapest by the Christian Socials were the stumbling blocks. When Beck presented a four-point program that reflected the Christian Socials' expectations, Wekerle responded contemptuously that if he were to agree to such demands he would be "gone in eight days." Wekerle did offer, however, an alternative proposal which would eventually become the basis for a settlement—the Hungarians agreed to a modest immediate increase in officers' salaries, but rejected wage increases for the enlisted ranks for the next two years, substituting for the latter a modest improvement in food allotments.[70]

During the three-day interim between the two sessions both Wekerle and Beck consulted with their respective Cabinets to see if a further basis for compromise might be established. On May 21 Wekerle reported no change in sentiment or policy. Beck then tried, using his considerable powers of flattery and charm, to force a deal. He would accept the Hungarian compromise on the salary agenda if Wekerle would agree to a recall of the Delegations in early June. Beck then recounted his painful negotiations with the Christian Socials. Lueger and Liechtenstein had visited him on May 20. Beck had given them an enthusiastic account of how generous the Hungarians actually were, urging them to accept what might seem to be a formal failure in return for getting substantial practical results. Lueger wavered, and Beck was certain he might have been persuaded, but in the end both leaders refused to concede anything. Beck then spoke with Josef Schraffl, who bluntly told Beck that the party might be able to live with the delay in salary increases, but they desperately needed the June Delegation sessions: "for God's sake we have to have the session in June." The Christian Socials were as much if not more dependent upon histrionic politics and chauvinistic symbols as their Hungarian counterparts.

Yet Wekerle refused to accede. The Hungarian *Reichstag* would still be in session in June, he argued, and it would be suicidal for any Hungarian Cabinet to hold Delegation sessions while the *Reichstag* was sitting. In spite of Aehrenthal's last-minute appeal, the Hungarian remained firm on not recalling the Delegations until the autumn. Since Beck had already agreed to the salary compromise, Wekerle ended up winning on all fronts. The end result of the Council was, as Beck himself characterized it, an across-the-board defeat for the Austrian Cabinet and the Austrian parliament: "people will point out that he [Beck] as well as the parliament were not able to achieve a complete success in any direction." Beck's last-minute invocation of the image of the poor Emperor who should be spared the "difficulties" of the Council's collision left Wekerle totally unimpressed, as did Beck's plea that his domestic political situation was far more fragile than was Wekerle's. The marathon session ended with this spectacle of the Austrian Minister-President having to beg political support from his Hungarian counterpart and then being turned down cold.[71]

Even more embarrassing was the fact that both the Austrian and Hungarian governments would introduce legislation in their respective parliaments to provide similar limited salary improvements for the *Landwehr* and *Honvéd*. Since by law military salary scales had to be the same for regular line troops and standing reserve forces, in effect this meant that in Austria the Coalition would be voting *against* the Schraffl-Latour motion and for the Hungarians' own version of the compromise, a situation which the *Reichspost* understandably characterized as "discrediting our parliamentarians before the electorate."[72]

This unforeseen turn of events placed the Christian Social party in a quandary. If they supported or even publicly tolerated the compromise, they would seem to be backing down before the Hungarians and would expose themselves to Social Democratic ridicule. Beck was already in deep political trouble over internal squabbles within the German national parliamentary group. During a preliminary vote on the *Landwehr* budget on May 13 a sizable minority in the German bourgeois parties deserted the Coalition, leading Brosch to report to the Thronfolger that Beck's position "is without doubt shaken."[73] Brosch immediately initiated a pressure campaign on Christian Social deputies to create havoc in the Cabinet's ranks by rejecting the compromise that Beck was negotiating in the Ministerial Council. By May 22 Brosch thought he had the agreement of Gessmann and Fuchs, obtained "not without difficulties," that the party would condemn the May 21 compromise and thus provoke a Cabinet crisis.[74] Fuchs, who was the President of the Austrian Delegation, published a harsh attack on Aehrenthal and Beck in the *Reichspost* on May 23, accusing them of failing to consult with the leaders of parliament before undertaking these agreements (which was a blatant lie) and characterizing his colleagues' reaction to the agreement as "depressed and embittered" (which was the unvarnished truth).

In the interim Schönaich and Aehrenthal both offered pro forma resignations to the Emperor, based on their nominal support for Beck against Wekerle, which Franz Joseph peremptorily rejected on May 25. The intervention of the Crown in support of the compromise, which the Emperor termed a "harmonious, binding agreement," raised the political stakes still further. Funder came as close as he dared to direct criticism of the Crown when he noted caustically of this declaration that "with deep respect the Austrian citizen stands before the Throne, but what he defends are not merely dynastic interests but also the homeland which he and his ancestors before him cultivated, and everything that makes up the essence of the fatherland. Loyalty to the Dynasty cannot release the citizen from his responsibilities to the fatherland."[75]

Beck responded with an equally effective pressure campaign, threatening the party leadership with new elections or, worse, with the succession to the Minister-Presidency of Franz Thun, who was known for his lack of sympathy toward the Christian Socials. He also—at least according to Brosch— energetically promised personal rewards to individual members of the parliamentary delegation. In the end, Gessmann and Ebenhoch could not be persuaded to abandon the Cabinet and a weak and ill Lueger, according to Brosch, was too willing to defer to Beck.[76]

Finally, Brosch turned to Weiskirchner, from whom he got vague assurances of sympathy—Beck would last no more than a few months anyway—but no ready agreement to go against his colleagues. On May 25 Jodok Fink, representing a majority of the party, entered a mild challenge in parliament, asking Beck to explain the discrepancy between the March agreement and the Hungarian version of the May 21 Council meeting.[77] Beck's response to Fink at a session of the army committee of the lower House on May 27 was a model of obfuscation, insisting the compromise was not a "defeat" since officers' salaries would be raised and the enlisted ranks would receive their proper share of salary increases at some point in the future, although "how this will be accomplished is still an open question and will have to be settled later by the military administration." The *Arbeiter-Zeitung* noted of Beck's "victory" that "hypnosis is only effective when the candidate is willing to be hypnotized."[78]

The so-called *Gagenfrage* in itself did not undermine Max von Beck's rule, but it once again raised serious doubts in the minds of party leaders about the advantages they were obtaining from the Coalition. The fiasco was admittedly of the Christian Social party's own making, for it had employed bullyboy tactics on a policy agenda over which Beck had only limited control, humiliating the Minister-President before Wekerle and his fellow Ministers and itself before the electorate. This was the first, bruising confrontation of the party leaders with the harsh realities of high-level Cabinet politics in Austria, and they came away with a new-found respect for the intractability of the "heinous" Magyars.

Beck's Fall

Rather than losing control of the Cabinet as a result of the Army issue, Beck was the victim of the one area of policy he had assiduously sought to avoid over the previous two years—the nationality question. But his political demise in early November 1908 was also owing to the decision of the *Reichspartei* to abandon him at a critical juncture of his Ministry's history. Having been the first to preside over a formal parliamentarization of the Austrian ministerial system, Beck now had the dubious honor to fall victim to what was probably the first vote of no confidence by members of a governing coalition in Austrian political history.

From March 1906 until early 1908 Beck had been able to focus public attention away from the language question in Bohemia and Moravia. The long, tense negotiations for universal manhood suffrage consumed most of 1906 and provided a temporary respite from the intensity of national conflict in parliament. The popularity of the election reform among most Czechs distracted them from pursuing a radical program of national rights, and Beck's ability to persuade the Czech and German parties to join in a ministerial coalition in 1907–8 reflected assumptions on both sides that the *bürgerlich* forces should stand together against social and class radicalism. Gessmann's *Reichspartei* structure was the child of this mentality and, as events were to show, heavily dependent upon it for legitimacy.

In early 1908 Beck decided that, having pushed through the *Ausgleich* and the election reform, he would now confront the nationalities question. He intended to bring into parliament and into the Bohemian Diet a series of laws on language use and on the administrative and political organization of the Bohemian provincial government.[79] In early April 1908, speaking before the Budget Committee, he reported that the submission of the language law was imminent, but political difficulties in midyear, including the death of the German *Landsmannminister* Franz Peschka and feuding among the German nationalists over his replacement, led to further delays. By the summer of 1908 Beck had decided to start his campaign on the provincial level, using the autumn session of the Bohemian Diet to introduce legislation revising the provincial franchise (expanding and democratizing it by establishing a general curia in both Czech and German districts) and creating a permanent Czech-German commission to negotiate a modus vivendi on those thorny issues (court organization, administrative personnel policies, district administrative boundaries) that defined ethnic conflict in the province.[80]

Unfortunately, Beck's initiative came too late. Ethnic conflict in Bohemia— a myriad of local and regional political rivalries, ethnic hatreds, and interest-group collisions—reemerged with full force during 1908, placing the Cabinet on the defensive for the first time since 1905. Trouble began in the winter of 1908 in the Bohemian court system, where some judges in German-speaking judicial districts refused to entertain motions or appeals submitted in Czech.[81] At the same time Czech administrative officials and jurists on regional and local levels in both Bohemia and Moravia began a deliberate campaign to use Czech as an inner official language (*innere Amtssprache*) by composing documents for inner-administrative use in Czech. This procedure was technically illegal since the withdrawal of the Gautsch *Sprachenverordnungen*.[82] Beck found himself caught in the middle of an intractable cultural struggle, urging that official regulations governing the use of German be adhered to, but seeking to avoid embarrassment of his Czech ministers, which would make the situation only worse.[83] Once it was apparent, moreover, that Beck was serious about pursuing a legislative solution to the Bohemian problem, both sides became more imperialistic, attempting to establish as many precedents as possible before a final settlement might be imposed.[84] By the summer of 1908 the majority Czech and German parliamentary factions, still nominally members of the same Coalition, were now clamoring for government intervention against each other.

During the summer session of parliament several German-Bohemian deputies led by Anton Pergelt initiated an obstructionist campaign to blackmail Beck into punitive actions against the Czechs.[85] Their strategy collapsed when the full *Deutscher Nationalverband* refused to go along, but the irascibility of the politicians in Vienna found serious parallels in the provinces. Popular unrest in Bohemia seethed throughout the summer, finally breaking forth in bloody clashes in various German and Czech towns. The names Bergreichenstein and Schüttenhofen became code words for outraged Germans who now insisted that "state authority" could no longer protect them.[86] Regular Sunday riots between German university students and Czech mobs in Prague also punctuated the summer and fall; and in late September 1908 the ethnic violence spread south to Carniola, where three days of anti-German rioting among the Slovene majority in Laibach led to the intervention of the army.[87] The violence reached its apogee on September 20 when two men were killed and nine wounded by an ill-disciplined troop of soldiers. These riots were particularly disturbing since they occurred in a city governed by a Slovenian mayor and a Slovenian-dominated City Council, and where the local police force was for the most part Slovene. As German shops were broken into and individual inhabitants insulted or beaten up, local police frequently did nothing to restrain those responsible. The ineffective and biased behavior of local security forces—a situation repeated in many Czech-controlled towns in Bohemia—and the manifestation of ethnic hatred in "official" police behavior led many Germans to decry what Heinrich Prade, the German *Landsmannminister,* called the "collapse of state authority" under Beck's regime. Yet, unlike the Zabern Affair in Germany, the force of national hatred was so irresistible that each ethnic camp easily fell into condemnations of the other, rather than of the army unit that had perpetrated the killings.[88]

Thus the Bohemian Diet opened its autumn session in Prague in mid-September in a most inauspicious context. Scandal ensued even before the Diet had begun substantive work when the new, pro-Czech *Oberstlandmarschall,* Ferdinand Lobkowitz, incensed the Germans with his manipulative use of the Diet's code of procedure to set the agenda for the session. The Germans began formal obstruction of the Diet on September 24.[89] In spite of Beck's arduous and patient attempts to control the crisis, including sending both Czech and German ministers to Prague (which probably hurt rather than helped restore order), the Germans would not be conciliated. Inevitably, their ire turned against Beck. On September 30 Adolf Bachmann and other local German nationalists attacked Beck personally and urged their compatriots to rethink the *Deutscher Nationalverband*'s involvement in the Cabinet.[90] Rather than closing the Diet session immediately, as the Germans wanted, Beck insisted on bringing in his franchise reform proposals on October 9, three days after the Bosnian annexation crisis exploded onto the Austrian domestic scene. The franchise proposals further outraged many within the German *bürgerlich* contingent, for they saw the new general voter curia as a covert reward for Czech and German Social Democrats, who would now flood into the Diet en masse.[91] Gradually German hatred of the Czechs was transformed into dissidence toward Beck as well, and serious questions were raised by responsible German leaders over the survivability of the Beck coalition. Heinrich von Tschirschky was not alone in his judgment when he reported to Berlin that "there can now be no doubt that the Beck ministry is finished."[92] By mid-October the Diet had degenerated into a circus of petty violence—Czechs and Germans spitting at each other, ripping each other's clothes, throwing books, ink wells, and furniture, as well as engaging in fistfights on the floor of the Diet. Finally, Beck summoned his Cabinet on October 16 and, supported by a majority vote of the Germans and Poles against the two Czech ministers, closed the Diet immediately.[93]

The closure of the Bohemian Diet on October 16 led immediately to a Cabinet crisis. The Czech ministers Fiedler and Prášek tendered their resignations on October 17, and the Czech political press announced that when parliament reopened in November the Czech parties would retaliate with their formal obstructionism, thus sabotaging the parliamentary coalition. Beck told Tschirschky that these protests were merely "formal" and that he would be able to master the situation and persuade the Czechs to stay on, a judgment he repeated to Gustav Gross on November 1.[94] But this was a vastly overoptimistic view of the crisis. By mid-October Tschirschky reported that rumors had already begun to circulate that Beck would be replaced by Richard Bienerth, long a favorite of the Thronfolger, whose detestation of Beck now found renewed purpose. The Emperor refused to accept or reject Fiedler's and Prášek's resignations in the two weeks that followed, as the Bosnian crisis reached its zenith and his attention was diverted to foreign affairs. Beck thus had a grace period in which to negotiate with both German and Czech interests to obtain an agreement for a reconstructed ministry that would master the national crisis.

Beck now ran up against a third and even more formidable enemy, for during October the Christian Social leadership slowly came to the decision to withdraw the party's support for Beck in favor of Bienerth. When this repudiation occurred was less controversial than why it happened, but both problems have been buried in the morass of conspiracy. Funder and the more clerical wing of the party had been disillusioned with Beck since July because of the Cabinet's uncertain handling of the Wahrmund Affair,[95] but Beck's indifference to clerical mania would hardly have justified Gessmann or Lueger in undercutting his rule. Ebenhoch valued his role as Agricultural Minister and wanted to retain his position in the Cabinet. He had already admitted confidentially in February 1908 that Beck had "done all that was possible" in handling the Wahrmund Affair (see below, Chapter 4) and again in March that Beck "has been quite serious in trying to ease our political position."[96] There is no reason to doubt that Gessmann felt any differently; and the distrust felt by the Tyroleans or Styrians against Gustav Marchet would not, in itself, have been sufficient reason to pull out of the Cabinet.[97]

Pressure from the Belvedere to drop Beck was a long-standing concern for the leadership, but Brosch's heavy-handed pressure of May was not repeated in October. When Brosch visited Lueger in mid-October he encountered the mayor's resistance against leading an anti-Beck fronde. According to Lueger, the only thing that could bring Beck down would be the Emperor's loss of confidence. Lueger then noted cryptically that he personally felt Beck no longer had an effective majority behind him in parliament and that the Emperor should be told this.[98] Although Franz Ferdinand jumped at this hint and wrote to Franz Joseph demanding Beck's resignation, Ebenhoch's correspondence in late October suggests that neither Lueger nor Gessmann had made a final decision on Beck's fate before November 1.[99] Beck met Lueger in Vienna on November 2 and felt reassured that he could continue to count on the Christian Social party's support in reconstructing his Cabinet.[100] When the leadership of the parliamentary club met on November 5, however, sentiment was running strongly against Beck. The Minister-President himself judged the *Reichspost*'s communiqué on the conference, published on the morning of November 6, as an indication that he must resign.[101] Gessmann provided a swan song for the Beck cabinet in a speech at Oberhollabrunn, arguing that "the existence and functioning of the parliament" must be the highest priority for all German parties and that, in spite of the current crisis, the idea of an inter-bourgeois coalition with ministerial responsibility should be retained, because it was "fundamentally healthy and politically fruitful."[102]

This change in the direction of party policy was engineered, Beck later argued, by Gessmann and Weiskirchner. Seriously negative signals against Beck began to emerge in late October around the issue of the government's broken promises involving army reform. Since the party had played so formidable a role in the Schraffl-Latour motion, it was predictable that when the Austrian Delegation finally assembled in late October that the *Gagenfrage* would re-emerge. On October 21 Julius Axmann delivered a tough speech in the military committee of the Austrian Delegation attacking Beck and Schönaich for their failure to keep the Christian Socials informed about the government's change of plans.[103] Axmann claimed to speak "in the name of my party" in threatening Beck that he could no longer count on the Christian Socials if "things continue as they have done in the past." Beck made a stupid mistake when he responded to Axmann in a way that made it clear that he considered Axmann childish and self-indulgent whereas he, Beck, had grave responsibilities and could not afford such grandstanding.[104] This minor transaction was important for two reasons: it suggested that Gessmann's forces in the club had decided to move against Beck (Axmann was usually a mouthpiece for Gessmann); and it also contributed some sense of why they would want to do so.

Axmann's criticism of Beck was intentionally directed not at the failure of the government to honor its March promises, since everyone recognized that Beck had little control over the financial decisions taken by the Joint Ministerial Council, but at Beck's presenting the party with a fait accompli that exposed it to embarrassing Social Democratic propaganda. The theme of Beck as an unreliable and politically erratic leader who often broke promises was a frequent one in the *Reichspost* and the *Deutsches Volksblatt* in the late autumn of 1908. Propaganda value aside, the motif did have a real target—both Gessmann and Weiskirchner, each for different personal reasons, wanted a change in regime by November 1908, and each saw in Beck not merely a leader whose time had passed but also one with whom continuing cooperation was inadvisable, perhaps even dangerous. Weiskirchner held supreme ambitions for his career; he ardently desired a ministerial position, even though Lueger preferred to keep him in the municipal government. The only way Weiskirchner could achieve his goal was by supporting Gessmann in overthrowing the Cabinet.

For Gessmann, in turn, by the late autumn of 1908 this act had become a personal and professional necessity. When the *Arbeitsministerium* was finally constituted in July, Gessmann soon came to rue the day he ever agreed to take the post of public works minister. Rather than controlling a powerful Ministry of Social Affairs with considerable revenue resources, he was stuck with a minor technical ministry with an unsatisfactory budget. Throughout the spring and summer of 1908 he was besieged with job petitioners, many of whom came with "proper" political credentials, to wit, letters from sponsors in the party hierarchy.[105] Although Gessmann made some effort to accommodate his colleagues, his patronage resources were limited, and this led to bitterness on the part of his fellow deputies. Moreover, Gessmann was overwhelmed with hundreds of dubious funding and subvention requests, many of them from erstwhile electoral clients.[106] Many of these too he had to reject, thus engendering still more bitterness. Also problematic was the attitude of the professional civil servants in the new Ministry, who found Gessmann's frankly political criteria for policy formation and subventions to be grating.[107] Gessmann thus found himself besieged from without and subverted from within and he quickly became disillusioned.

Burdened with such an albatross, a ministry that consumed huge amounts of his time and subjected him to the animosity of traditional Christian Social voter groups, Gessmann had all the while to continue compensating for Lueger's inability to lead the party organization. As the autumn approached and the party geared up for the critical Diet elections in October, matters came to a head. The elections of 1908 were to prove the last great victory of the Christian Social party in prewar Austria. Gessmann ceremoniously refused an election alliance with local German national groups and fought a two-front war against the Social Democrats in the new Viennese general curia and against the *Deutschbürgerlichen* in the small towns outside Vienna.[108] In both cases the results were extremely satisfying. The party crushed both the Social Democrats (taking 43 of the 48 Viennese seats) and the nationalists and seized a total of 93 out of the publicly elected 104 seats in the Diet. The brilliance of Gessmann's reform of the Diet's suffrage had been demonstrated beyond doubt.[109]

But trouble loomed on the horizon. Only with great difficulty had Leopold Kunschak been persuaded not to provoke dissidence by holding to his demands for an equitable share of the Viennese mandates. Kunschak participated loyally at the Christian Social regional party congress on October 3, but he then proceeded to summon an executive council of Laborite leaders on October 12 to criticize his treatment by the city organization and to demand a "reorganization of the whole party." As the police noted in observing Kunschak's troubles, "a sharp conflict exists between the party leadership and the Christian Social workers. The latter feel they have been disadvantaged in terms of candidatures, since they are only allowed to run in districts where the Christian Socials are expected to lose."[110] Lueger's illness and Gessmann's absences from Vienna on government business were beginning to take their toll on party discipline. While celebrating the Christian Social triumph on October 27, Funder announced that in the future the party must pay more attention to leadership and organization:

> the electoral triumph today should not lead the party to feelings of self-satisfaction. Quite the opposite . . . gaps in the party must be filled, especially those that are not apparent only because of the weakness of our opponents. Our party organization, which in Vienna rests on an aging foundation, must be modernized and ways must be found to recruit a new generation of skilled party workers. . . . The great work of the party must not, as has previously been the case, remain the responsibility of only a few men.[111]

Funder's commentary reflected Gessmann's concern, later made explicit in their private correspondence, that Lueger and the Viennese *Bürgerklub* were living on borrowed time, operating in the world of mass politics with antiquated techniques, outdated programs, and archaic ideas against an increasingly skillful socialist organization.[112] Equally significant was Funder's reference to a need for a "Vertiefung der Ideen und Grundsätze" of the party. Gessmann's term as minister had proven a powerful learning experience. He came to realize that older *Kleingewerbe* protectionist programs, up to 1905 a staple concern of party propaganda, were of dubious value for both their putative clients and for the Austrian economy at large.[113] With this shift in his economic views came the realization that the party needed to rethink its social programs and electoral constituencies and to expand what it understood by the legitimate *Bürgertum,* forging new alliances with both the industrial capitalist establishment above and the mass of white-collar workers below (or next to) the traditional Viennese artisan *Mittelstand.* By the conclusion of the campaign a now-exhausted Gessmann had decided that the future prosperity of the party would require accommodating newer and younger personalities and conciliating the Laborites and the rural faction under Josef Stöckler and that therefore he must return to full-time political work and resign the onerous and unrewarding ministerial position. Funder would later justify Gessmann's resignation by citing the need to restore effective leadership of the party: "the life interests of the Christian Social party demand that Dr. Gessmann . . . dedicate himself totally to the party."[114]

Some progress in organizational modernization had been made. During the 1908 election campaign, with so many candidates running for office, Gessmann's secretariat had published a long reference handbook for them to use in preparing their speeches, *Die christlichsoziale Partei im Niederösterreichischen Landtage 1902–1908.* For the Social Democrats, such (for the time) sophisticated election tools were already available in the 1907 elections, but for the Christian Socials this was a novel and ambitious undertaking.[115] But the very solution also reemphasized the problem—the party was growing too large and too diverse, with too many ideological factions and generational segments, to leave its supervision to a small group of inexperienced clerks. Someone needed to make decisions. Small constraints became major problems as when Beck, responding to complaints from parliament about the nonappearance of ministers at what often proved to be long plenary sessions, assigned to each member of the Cabinet specific times of the week when he would have to be present in the *Abgeordnetenhaus,* so that at least four ministers would be in attendance at all times. Gessmann ended up with five morning or afternoon assignments, listening (as did his fellow ministers) to the endless tedium that consumed the vast majority of each parliamentary session. In addition he had to participate in the many other ministerial and Cabinet meetings that marked the final stages of the crisis perplexing Beck's government. How was he to run the largest political party in Austria under such constraints?[116] To Martin Spahn he complained that "I am so preoccupied on the one hand by agitational work for the still-to-be held Diet elections in rural Lower Austria, and on the other by the frequent ministerial meetings which have resulted from the impending Cabinet crisis, that even with the best of intentions I do not have a minute of free time left over."[117]

A second issue that preoccupied Gessmann and Weiskirchner also reinforced this decision. On November 3, 1908, three days before Beck fell, the Cabinet submitted to parliament its long-awaited draft legislation on social insurance. This momentous law had been in the works since late 1904, when Koerber proposed an Austrian version of the German old-age and disability insurance system, which would consolidate and expand Austrian social-welfare coverage for industrial workers.[118] Initial action on this program fell victim to the turmoil of 1905–7, and only after the general elections of 1907 was the government ready to move on the issue. In the interim both the Christian Socials and the Social Democrats had made a comprehensive social insurance plan a key component of their electoral platforms, although with a profound difference in objectives. The Social Democrats sought an improved version of welfare benefits for the clientele of the existing sickness and accident insurance laws from the 1880s—the industrial working class. The Christian Socials insisted, in contrast, that "Independents" (*Selbständigen*)—small and medium-sized shopkeepers and master artisans, as well as property-owning peasants (and their rural laborers)—be included in the coverage for retirement insurance.

Work on the final draft was completed in late 1908 by a ministerial committee chaired by Bienerth but dominated by Gessmann.[119] Gessmann succeeded in obtaining Bienerth's agreement to the party's demands for "Independent" coverage, and the final draft included businessmen and farmers in what was one of the most integrated and progressive social insurance schemes ever proposed in prewar Europe. Existing programs of sickness and accident insurance adopted in the 1880s were modernized and consolidated into a larger administrative organization that would also provide old-age and disability insurance on the basis of a combination of mandatory participant contributions and outright state grants to the elderly.[120] The inclusion of major Christian Social electoral groups in the old-age component of the plan irked the Social Democrats, as did Christian Social attempts to reduce the autonomy and shift the political orientation of the local insurance boards by allocating representation to employers and independents as well as to workers, which meant in effect that the socialists would lose and the Christian Socials gain influence.

The next four years of parliamentary consideration of the bill saw bitter (yet intellectually quite stimulating) wrangling over the very concept of "social insurance" as opposed to "worker insurance" (to adopt the distinction offered in the *Arbeitsbeirat* by the Christian Social jurist Victor Kienböck), with the Christian Socials taking what proved (after 1945) to be the more prescient conception of state guarantees for the whole of society rather than largesse for partial societal segments. Gessmann was extremely proud of this bill, viewing it as a major weapon for his party's survival against the Social Democratic onslaught. By including favored *bürgerlich* groups and by integrating farmers and urban business interests in the plan, the Gessmann-Bienerth insurance laws became a legislative metaphor of the *Reichspartei* idea, a paradigm for a new society of social guarantees in which urban and rural blocs would see the social and cultural bonds that joined them, in contrast to the economic interests that divided them.

Rather than denying the political, interest-group dimensions of the bill, Gessmann's protégé Friedrich Gaertner explicitly celebrated them in an analysis that he published in the prestigious *Archiv für Sozialwissenschaft*.[121] Gessmann saw a special advantage in the party's support for the master artisans—social insurance for the industrial *Mittelstand* would be an attractive incentive that might persuade artisans to give up their dependence on protectionist legislation and to modernize their production methods and strengthen their commitment to the market. Hence Gessmann wanted the insurance bill pushed through parliament quickly; later commentaries in the *Reichspost* stressed that this was his highest legislative priority for the party, and not merely for the subjective good it would deliver to its prospective consumers. Friedrich Funder argued that all *bürgerlich* parties, Czech as well as German, needed the legitimacy that these laws would provide: "those parties that want to preserve the current social order and defend it against Social Democracy are with every element of their lives bound up with this great work."[122] Richard Weiskirchner insisted that social insurance would be the "most imposing and important responsibility of the new parliament" and that it would give universal manhood suffrage a "monument more impressive than one can imagine." Among Gessmann's peasant allies the insurance plan met with unrestrained enthusiasm, suggesting that he had at last found an issue that might bridge the gap between the urban and rural factions of the party.[123]

The looming nationality battles which threatened to disrupt the autumn session of parliament might make consideration of the social insurance package impossible. Given their growing mistrust of Beck's reliability, and the evident fact that Beck was not the man to resolve the Czech-German conflict, Gessmann and Weiskirchner decided on a radical step. Beck would be pushed aside in favor of Bienerth, who would use his standing as a "new man" to reconstitute the *bürgerlich* coalition and buy time for the *Reichspartei* by promising a judicious settlement of the nationalities question *after* the social insurance legislation had gone through parliament. Given Bienerth's previous dependence on Gessmann, the latter doubtlessly conceived of his coup as a double act of parliamentarist control—not only would the Christian Socials bring down Beck, but they would also appoint his successor, who would then become a willing tool of the party hierarchy.

The plan was, in retrospect, both vague and bold, but it combined the virtues of extricating Gessmann from the *Arbeitsministerium* while offering Weiskirchner his long-sought chance to join a new Bienerth Cabinet. Gessmann decided that he would replace Alois Liechtenstein as Lower Austrian *Landmarschall*, a more prestigious and powerful position than that of a junior cabinet minister, and use his position to consolidate and modernize the party organization.[124] The plan also had the virtue of cooperating with the Belvedere, although for reasons independent of Franz Ferdinand's paranoia toward Beck.

On November 1 Beck informed Gustav Gross that he was determined to reconstruct his Cabinet on lines similar to those of the past. However, his negotiations with both the Germans and the Czechs soon suggested that the Christian Social reaction on November 5 that Beck "is no longer up to resolving the Bohemian problem" (which became the party's "official" justification for dumping him) was not far from the mark. Tschirschky's evaluation for Berlin was similar: "from the moment Beck made the settlement between the Czechs and the Germans the highest priority of his ministry, the ground began to shake under his feet." Without the autumn riots, Beck might have endured the crisis, but Laibach and Prague "made the Minister-President's challenge unsolvable."[125] On November 5 the executive committee of the Young Czechs in Prague voted to pull out of the Cabinet, and although it did not foreclose the possibility of joining a third Beck ministry, it would do so only after certain demands had been met, most of which the Germans found loathsome.[126] Similarly, on November 6 the Germans submitted to Beck a secret four-page list of demands that he must meet if they were to remain in the Cabinet—including the division of Bohemia into nationally demarcated *Kreise,* the use of German as the *innere Amtssprache* through a state language law, and the acceptance of ratios based on nationality for the appointment of provincial and local officials.[127] These points were completely unacceptable to the Czechs. With the discussions so gridlocked, Beck had no future. Whether Gessmann and Weiskirchner were aware of the German desiderata is uncertain; had they known of the list, it would have been all the more reason to proceed against Beck. If he was to fall, it was in the Christian Socials' interest to sacrifice one man for a program. When the leaders of the *Verband* met with Lueger on November 12 to solicit his support for their list, all they came away with was his agreement to appoint three Christian Social representatives to a joint German-Christian Social commission to establish a "common platform on the Bohemian question."[128] Clearly the Christian Socials felt uncomfortable with their conationals' intransigence. But their gamble in dispensing with Beck now raised a new question: could Bienerth do any better?

On November 7 Beck held his last Cabinet meeting, which voted its collective resignation, and the next day the Emperor commissioned Bienerth to form a new ministry. The same day that Beck resigned, Gessmann met with Chiari, Pergelt, and Sylvester, claiming to represent Bienerth.[129] He proposed to these German national leaders that they cooperate with the Christian Socials in forming a new parliamentary ministry under Bienerth, which would have a generous complement of German members: Internal Affairs would go to Stürgkh, Education to Pergelt, and Justice to Sylvester. The Czechs would obtain Agriculture and Gessmann's own Ministry, and the Poles would receive Finance. The Christian Socials would take what remained—Commerce and Railways. The proposed distribution was a covert attempt to favor the more nationalist members of the *Verband* against anticlerical *Freisinn* types. Gessmann cleverly combined vengeance against Gustav Marchet, satisfying the clericals in his own party, with a reaffirmation of the party's loyalty to the German *Gemein-bürgerschaft*. Gessmann argued that the new Cabinet's immediate agenda would include securing approval of the provisional budget, as well as legislation covering the Bosnian annexation and the Serbian and Rumanian trade agreements. Then it would preoccupy parliament with "great economic assignments" and "repress the national question" altogether. Preeminent among the former would be the social insurance laws. Gessmann's solution to Beck's troubles was, thus, to ignore them, buying off both Czechs and Germans with palliative social legislation.

Albert Gessmann's strategy was intelligible in terms of the overriding importance he attributed to the social insurance legislation. Indeed, the *Reichspost* judged Bienerth's competence to succeed Beck precisely in the terms of his co-parentage, with Gessmann, of these laws: "a good omen for the new Cabinet may lie in the remarkable circumstance that its leader is the man from whose *Ressort* the social insurance laws emerged." Yet Richard Bienerth's selection as Minister-President was neither remarkable nor accidental. Brosch reported to Franz Ferdinand as early as May 1908 that the Christian Socials held Bienerth "in complete trust" as a possible successor to Beck, a judgment that was fully consonant with the Thronfolger's own views. Bienerth's political relations with Gessmann and Lueger dated from his service as vice-president of the Lower Austrian School Council between 1900 and 1905, where he assiduously supported Gessmann's purge of socialist teachers and the party's politicization of school personnel policies. Erich Kielmansegg even insisted that Bienerth owed his appointment as Minister of Internal Affairs in June 1906 to Gessmann, since the Christian Socials wanted a congenial and manipulable minister during the drafting of the universal suffrage legislation.[130] Franz Ferdinand did not "impose" Bienerth on Gessmann or on the Emperor, as at least one historian has argued. If anything the reverse was the case.[131] Gessmann wanted a pliable, yet reasonable and effective leader who, once basic trade and foreign-policy legislation was out of the way, would implement the laws that Gessmann felt would ensure the popularity of his party against the Social Democrats. Social insurance for all would be political insurance for a few.

The same day that Gessmann visited Sylvester and Chiari the *Reichspost* published further details of his plan: Alfred Ebenhoch would become President of the *Abgeordnetenhaus* in place of Weiskirchner, Liechtenstein would join the new Cabinet, and Gessmann would succeed him as *Landmarschall*. Gessmann's disillusionment with ministerial life would also find an appropriate resolution. As *Landmarschall* Gessmann would assume a position in the province equivalent to that of Lueger in the city, becoming political czar of the third largest Crownland. Gessmann also had substantial ambitions to expand the Christian Social party into Bohemia, and he planned a major electoral drive in both Czech and German areas once relieved of the burdens of office.[132]

Gessmann was certainly aware of Lueger's health problems; this shift would guarantee him the mantle of party leadership once Lueger had left the scene. At a Christian Social party congress held immediately before the Lower Austrian Diet elections in mid-October, Lueger had referred to Gessmann as the "conqueror of Lower Austria" for his work on the new provincial franchise. The comment was slightly ironic, for Lueger made it immediately before recounting why, since it was legally impossible for Vienna to seek *reichsunmittelbar* status, urbanists and peasants in Lower Austria should learn to live with each other in a marriage of convenience against the Social Democrats. The contrast with Gessmann's peasant strategy in Lower Austria was painfully apparent. For Lueger the program of the party was its "deeds in the past," not Gessmann's social welfare schemes of the future.[133]

Finally, by placing Weiskirchner at Commerce the party would not only gain control of a more prominent Ministry than Public Works, but it would also position one of its most talented leaders for a future Minister-Presidency and make a gesture to its urban middle-class constituencies who were disgruntled by the prominence of the new agrarian faction. All in all, this seemed to be a rational strategy, and one that the party could have pursued with or without the Thronfolger's support.

Having been handed a prepackaged strategy by Gessmann, Bienerth was supposed to execute it. He initiated negotiations with the Czechs and Germans on November 9. From the first he diverged from Gessmann's scenario, however, showing himself capable of independent, if wrongheaded, political decisions, by insisting that a preliminary modus vivendi on the Bohemian question be agreed upon *before* the Cabinet was launched. This proved both naive and impractical, and the vague proposals that he offered to the Germans did little more than restate the Stremayr language *Verordnungen* of 1880. They met with categorical rejection on November 12.[134] Three days of fruitless negotiation failed to resolve a crisis that grew more convoluted with each passing hour. Bienerth was handicapped by the divisions within the feuding blocs, and the absence of strong, disciplined leadership in both the German and the Czech parties contributed to the failure of the negotiations.[135] On November 12 the German leaders presented Bienerth with their demands, which were an updated version of the desiderata Beck had received a week earlier.[136] Bienerth was unwilling to accept either the specificity or the timetables demanded by the Germans. Instead he planted an unusually frank article in the semi-official *Fremdenblatt* implying that the government would not hesitate to dismiss par-

liament and summon new elections if the national parties were not more cooperative. He also argued, in retrospect rightly, that the negotiations had become
a turning point in Austrian political history and that the unparalleled chance of
the parties to rule the state—for the first time in thirty years—was about to be
lost, with power reverting to the civil service.[137]

Heinrich von Tschirschky remarked to his superiors in Berlin that no Austrian premier had ever spoken in such terms to the Viennese political public;
but the effect was nil.[138] On November 13 a marathon negotiating session of
all the major parties was held, at which Lueger, Gessmann, and Weiskirchner
represented the Christian Socials. This conference lasted eighteen hours and
reached a preliminary agreement between the Germans and Czechs that the
language question would be brought before parliament for legislative regulation in the coming year and that Bohemian election reform would again be
placed on the agenda of the Diet.[139] But once the discussion moved from such
generalities to the specific contents of the legislation the group quickly fell
into disagreement. The Czechs also raised the issue of establishing a second
Czech university, to be located in Moravia, which the Germans declared to be
a "casus belli." Gessmann tried to eliminate this problem by proposing that
two new universities be built in Moravia, one German and one Czech, but both
sides rejected this out of hand. Karel Kramář, representing the Young Czechs,
suggested that his side was "in principle" willing to consent to a regulation of
civil service appointments (the issue of national ratios) but did not want it
rushed. Finally, in the face of insurmountable national hostilities, Weiskirchner
restated a modified version of Gessmann's original strategy of November 7:
both sides would drop all of their specific demands, recognize the status quo
of the language question provisionally, and agree to join the coalition on the
basis of a vague commitment by Bienerth that he would submit legislation to
parliament on the nationality question as soon as was reasonably possible. In
the interim parliament would proceed with the social legislation. This the
Czechs rejected totally, while the Germans were willing to go along only if the
Cabinet established a specific timetable for the nationalities law. At this impasse the conference ended, having accomplished nothing other than to exhaust the participants and bring home to the Christian Socials how erroneous
their calculations had been. Having had his plea for a six-month armistice between the warring national groups in Bohemia rejected, a plan which he
thought "would also be in the interest of the bourgeois parties," Karl Lueger
left the meeting, telling a journalist at the door that "I'm going home. What's
happening in there is rhetoric without end—a deluge of speeches, from which
nothing much will result."[140]

Ernst Vergani blasted Albert Gessmann's fruitless strategy in a lead article
on November 13: "who is responsible that the current crisis broke out, without
having gauged the problems which a parliamentarization of the ministry would

face; who is responsible for the fact that the former Cabinet was destroyed, without obtaining agreement among the German parties on the national question and without the consent of all the parties about the reconstruction of the Cabinet?"[141] Gessmann's largesse with new universities and Weiskirchner's complacency about nationalist defense showed their lack of interest in who got what from whom in Bohemia or Moravia. German national press communiqués on the meeting might tout the loyalty shown by the Christian Socials, and especially Lueger, to their German colleagues, but it was clear that the Christian Social leadership cared little about the details of the language or civil servant questions in Bohemia, other than wanting them resolved. With the collapse of the talks, Bienerth had no alternative but to appoint a temporary ministry of civil servants (*Beamtenministerium*) and to tread water. Not only was Beck's experiment in interethnic coalition politics dead, but so too was Albert Gessmann's assumption of Alois Liechtenstein's position as *Landmarschall.* Since Liechtenstein could not be unceremoniously dumped, Gessmann was left with nothing, as was his erstwhile co-conspirator Richard Weiskirchner.

Josef Redlich complained to Baernreither in early December that "Gessmann has committed one blunder after another in recent weeks."[142] Redlich's scorn was understandable and yet it was slightly off target. A standard explanation of Beck's fall has imputed the determining cause to the relationship between the party and the Thronfolger.[143] This was clearly Beck's own interpretation. He wrote bitterly to Coudenhove soon after the event that he had been brought down by an ominous conspiracy: "I am only the victim—to speak plainly—of an arranged political assassination, which was the final result of a well-conceived plot, whose final skeins lay in the hands of a high authority."[144] Rudolf Sieghart, Beck's chief of staff, also supported this view, even though most Christian Socials readily distinguished between Beck and Sieghart. While willing to dump the former they went to great lengths to sustain their connections with the latter.[145] Another interpretation has seen the Wahrmund Affair as the determining force, and certainly the *Reichspost* offered appropriate evidence for making such a connection when it insisted on November 8 that as early as June 1908 the "anarchy in the universities confirmed in all politically oriented people a final judgment on Beck's system. One can argue by the first week of July [1908] Beck's Cabinet was already dead."[146]

However, although having some validity, both explanations fall short of comprehending Christian Social motives. It was Gessmann, rather than Lueger, who played the major role in orchestrating the anti-Beck coup (which Beck only realized after the fact), and he had more significant motives than toadying to Franz Ferdinand or patronage for a clerical fronde. Not only did Gessmann feel disillusioned by Beck's failure to live up to sundry promises (the *Arbeitsministerium,* military salaries, and others), but he also believed that Beck, as a result of the disastrous course of the Bohemian Diet session in October and the street violence in Slavic cities and towns, was no longer a creditable Minister-President. The decisions of the Young Czech executive council on November 5 and of the Germans on November 6 made the political crisis inescapable, whatever the Christian Socials did or failed to do. Beck might have fallen without Gessmann's intervention; Gessmann sought to make a virtue out of a vice and to plot the script for a new coalition ministry before the old one had died.

The interventions of Gessmann and Weiskirchner on November 7 and November 13, as recorded in Gustav Gross's memoir, suggested that Gessmann's major motive was to replace what he held to be an imperfect form of parliamentary governance with an improved reincarnation in hopes of pushing through the legislation which would leave his and his party's permanent mark on Austrian public life. Eager to define a self-enhancing comparison with Austria's neighbor to the north, the *Reichspost* insisted that Gessmann's legislative scheme would far surpass the current German system of *Alters- und Invaliditätsversicherung*. Bienerth, who had loyally allowed Gessmann virtual carte blanche in the ministerial committee drafting the final version of these laws, seemed an appropriate replacement for Beck, someone who would dodge the nationality issue by concentrating the attention of parliament on the social legislation. The *Reichspost*'s verbal attacks on Beck's unreliability and haplessness throughout October may thus be read as reflecting an independent source of concern within the party, and not merely as Funder's parroting of the Belvedere. Even Lueger, who was more well disposed toward Beck than others were, realized that Beck no longer had a credible parliamentary majority. The actions of the party leadership cannot be construed as having been dictated by the Belvedere, although, once agreed upon, they were coordinated with the Belvedere. Confusion about the party's behavior has always arisen from the conflation of this vital distinction.[147]

The critical weakness in Christian Social strategy was that it underestimated the intractability of the nationality problem in Bohemia and Moravia. Neither the Czechs nor the Sudeten Germans were moved by Gessmann's social legislation ploys, just as they had systematically rejected Ernest von Koerber's pork-barrel tactics five years earlier. Bienerth also proved to be less predictable and less tractable than either Gessmann or Weiskirchner had expected. He too could cultivate the Belvedere and could do so independently of the Christian Socials. Gessmann thus was left bearing the responsibility not only for having weakened his own public position but also and more importantly, for having undermined the very foundation—parliamentary ministerialism—on which he had designed the *Reichspartei* structure. The near-hysterical lead articles in the *Reichspost* as the negotiations wound their way toward the abyss suggested that the critical consequences of the coup were finally hitting home. On November 13 the paper published an interview with a "prominent Christian Social parliamentarian" who castigated both the Germans and the Czechs for sacrificing parliamentarism to "crass egotism, crude eccentricities, and inflexible pettiness" and noted that the principal victim of a cabinet of civil servants would be the new social insurance laws.[148] If this was not Gessmann himself, it was his ghost. The party's fronde against Beck was launched not out of willful perversity, but as an ill-considered exercise in *va banque* politics with the fortunes of the state, and its failure was catastrophic. Bienerth's inability to conjure up a reincarnation of the Beck coalition in November 1908 soon became an accepted status quo, and a party whose collective identity was anchored in the presumption of ministerial influence and *bürgerlich* social activism now found itself languishing. What had begun as a partnership under Beck would end in a captivity under Bienerth.

The Aftermath: The Christian Socials and the Bienerth Regime

Although he managed to survive for almost three years, a not undistinguished record as Austrian premiers went, Richard Bienerth's regime failed to merit the respect of his contemporaries or to provoke the imagination of later historians.[149] Bienerth's work as Minister of Internal Affairs in the Beck Cabinet had given him frequent opportunities to collaborate with the Christian Socials. The party's eager support for his candidacy in late 1908 to be Minister-President reflected their estimation that he was competent and energetic as well as pliable. Unfortunately, as the party leadership learned to their dismay over the next two years, once ensconced in the premiership Bienerth was none of these things. His most enduring (and problematic) characteristic may well have been that, of all late Imperial occupants of the office, Bienerth proved to be the most congenial to Archduke Franz Ferdinand—a bond that was made possible not only by Bienerth's unctuous deference before the Thronfolger and his artful ability to avoid entrapment in the on-going power struggles between the Emperor and his impatient successor but also by his willing acquiescence to the Thronfolger's insistence that there should be no significant structural changes in the Austrian governmental system until after the latter's succession to the Throne.[150]

Bienerth's first months in power were marked by turmoil in and out of parliament. Less than a month after assuming office he was forced to declare martial law in Prague because of rioting and looting by angry Czech nationalists. Parliament reopened on November 26, 1908, to a flood of Slavic and German obstructionist motions. The lower House was able to pass a provisional budget for 1909 only on December 15 when the government agreed to end martial law in Bohemia in return for the Social Democrats joining the German and Polish parties to allow the budget to come before the House on the basis of parliamentary urgency.[151] The socialists then came close to embarrassing the new regime by proposing a "democratic constitution" for the newly annexed regions of Bosnia and Herzegovina, failing only because the Christian Socials and the *Deutscher Nationalverband* stood together to defend Aehrenthal's foreign policy.[152] As if to prove that Gessmann had been correct in arguing that Beck's language law would only destroy parliamentary unity, Bienerth insisted on bringing in national legislation which owed much to previous efforts by Koerber and Beck, and the predictable happened—obstruction by Czech radicals and fistfights and other acts of petty violence between Czech and German deputies on the floor of parliament on February 5, 1909.[153]

After two months of experimentation with a provisional cabinet of civil servants, Bienerth moved to break out of the obstructionism by placing his government on semiparliamentary footing in mid-February 1909.[154] He invited several key German and Polish leaders into the Cabinet. For the Christian Socials Richard Weiskirchner became Minister of Commerce and for the Poles Leon Biliński received the most important Ministry, Finance. Karl Stürgkh and Victor von Hochenburger were awarded Education and Justice respectively. A German large landowner and former civil servant who had adamantly opposed the introduction of universal suffrage in 1905–6 and who had been appointed to the *Herrenhaus* in 1907, Stürgkh was "accounted" to the Germans, although his tenure at the Ministry of Education had rude surprises ahead on matters of church-state relations. Hochenburger, a jurist from Styria, was similarly considered "German," although he had retired from active politics in 1901 and had no parliamentary affiliation. Gustav Schreiner, a militant German nationalist, became German *Landsmannminister.* The Czechs were allotted the Agriculture Ministry (which was given to Albin Bráf, a university professor with past connections to the Old Czechs who was already a member of the *Herrenhaus*), and Johann Zacek was appointed as Czech *Landsmannminister.* None of the major Czech parties received substantive portfolio representation in the Cabinet. As Tschirschky reported to Berlin, the new ministry had the aura, if not the reality, of being the long-awaited German-Christian Social-Polish combination against the Czechs. This regime was not what Gessmann had originally envisaged in November 1908 in his conspiracies against Beck, since it lacked both the character and the power of a true coalition ministry.[155]

Bienerth claimed that his new Cabinet would differ from Beck's in that he would no longer manipulate or buy votes on critical issues, as Beck had repeatedly done. His would be a government of, but not by or for, the parties, in the interests of the general welfare. Such "strong man" rhetoric had been heard ten years before—Casimir Badeni was fond of similar self-stylizations—and it proved no more convincing or successful for Bienerth. The new Cabinet was not certain of a parliamentary majority on any bill of importance; and the major

Czech factions, excluded from Cabinet patronage and political placement (which continued apace under Bienerth, just as it had under Beck), had every motive to bring down the government at the first opportunity. The "middle way" between party and civil servant rule which Bienerth proudly asserted that he would follow led in circles.[156]

Three unhappy parliamentary sessions followed the appearance of this Cabinet in 1909, each with a track record more dismal than its predecessor. Bienerth proved to be a weak, lackluster personality who followed events rather than guiding them. His survival in office reflected the stubborn unwillingness of the aged Emperor to tolerate change of any kind (a character trait from which Karl Stürgkh, Bienerth's successor, would profit enormously) and the fact that several of his key Cabinet ministers, notably Biliński and Weiskirchner, were able to compensate for his lack of energy with policy initiatives of their own. Although many of his problems could be traced to Bienerth's ignorance of the intricacies of parliamentary culture (Redlich described to Baernreither in December 1908 a scene at a meeting of the chairs of the various parliamentary parties in which Bienerth had proven so hapless that Weiskirchner, as President of the House, had to take charge of the meeting), the systemic instability of the major Czech and German parties, lacking disciplined leadership the Christian Socials enjoyed in the person of Lueger or the Social Democrats could summon in their collective hierarchy, made it seem that the parties and not Bienerth were culpable for every failure.[157] Hence Bienerth became the first Minister-President to enjoy a curious exemption from accountability, to reap more rewards for failure than for success. He had neither the flexibility and cunning of a Beck nor the autocracy and energy of a Stürgkh. No Minister-President generated more varied rumors of his impending fall; yet none remained more doggedly in office. Austrian politics had at last received a leader worthy of its own disgrace.

Christian Social policy during the Bienerth Cabinet was consistent with the party's intrinsic, self-defining need to restore a workable standard of parliamentary accountability and to push through Gessmann's program of social legislation. At a meeting of the parliamentary club on June 30, 1909, the deputies voted unanimously to seek all possible ways around Slavic obstructionism in order to resume work on the social legislation stalled in committee. In early July 1909 Lueger and Gessmann even risked embarrassment to persuade the other German parties to accept tougher antigovernmental language in a motion of urgency drafted by Ivan Šusteršič on the Bosnian Bank controversy (established by Imperial order in April 1909 with Hungarian, rather than Austrian capital), in order to prevent the collapse of the session by South Slav and Czech obstructionists.[158] In the end Lueger and Gessmann could not force a compromise on Bienerth, and the Christian Socials, already under pressure from the Emperor not to support what he viewed as an anti-Hungarian maneuver and domestic meddling in the competence of the Joint Ministries, saw their efforts go down in defeat. Having barely passed the budget for 1909, the House was swamped with South Slav motions of urgency and, as an English observer noted, "complete deadlock ensued: parliamentary work became impossible. . . . Many important measures were lost, the chief being the bills for commercial treaties with the Balkan states and for the creation of an Italian university in Vienna. Numerous projects for the improvement of internal communications for the furtherance of home industries were also frustrated."[159]

During the parliamentary crisis of December 1909, in contrast, the Christian Socials encountered more success. Because of the Cabinet's decision to sanction the German-national protection laws (*Schutzgesetze*) (see below, Chapter 4), a rush of Ruthenian and Czech obstructionist motions on minority schools and national minority rights paralyzed the House, preventing consideration of the basic agenda of fiscal legislation, most notably the provisional budget for 1910. Josef Redlich noted in his diary that many in Vienna saw this as the beginning of the end for Bienerth, expecting either a radical reconstruction of the ministry or—as the Czechs hoped—its disembowelment in favor of a coalition cabinet of national parity. Even Gessmann admitted to Redlich that he had lost sympathy with his erstwhile colleague because of Bienerth's blundering; Weiskirchner was so frustrated that he urged the use of Article 14 to enact the budget.[160] Redlich himself proposed to Aehrenthal a radical reconstruction of the Cabinet including the temporary elimination of both Czech and German *Landsmannminister* positions to defuse tensions.[161] Many hoped that Bienerth's days were numbered. Dreams of minister-making filled the coffeehouses—Paul von Gautsch waited in the wings, and Richard Weiskirchner was only too happy to describe to friends the membership of his impending Cabinet.

After several days of fruitless debate on the Czech demands for the protection of Slavic minorities and on state aid to minority schools, the last of the motions of urgency was voted down on December 2.[162] To avoid Bienerth's closing the session and executing the budget with Article 14, the Slavic Union refrained from entering new obstructionist motions and allowed the budget to pass through the House. Following the first reading of the provisional budget on December 11, the next significant issue on the agenda was the commercial treaties bill which implemented the industrial and agricultural trade agreement signed with Rumania earlier in the year and which also authorized the government to conclude similar agreements with the other Balkan states and put them provisionally into effect.[163] The first component, which raised the level of permissible meat imports from Rumania to Austria in return for Rumania lowering import tariffs on Austrian industrial goods, produced a fascinating convergence of national and economic interest-group opposition. Most agrarians in the House—German and Slavic—opposed the bill, even though the Cabinet had tried to buy off all but the most militant opposition with companion legislation to establish a 54-million-crown fund to subsidize domestic meat production over the next nine years. On December 15 the Czechs suddenly overwhelmed the House with fifty-seven new motions of urgency, all with the purpose of stopping the commercial treaties bill.

It had been apparent in Christian Social club debates in June 1909 that the Alpine and Lower Austrian agrarians had serious reservations about the trade agreement. Their intractability toward what the Viennese delegates obviously considered a major political issue led to short tempers and recriminations, in spite of Aemilian Schöpfer's appeal that the trade agreement was "a question not of agriculture or industry, but of the Monarchy. If the Christian Social party, as the largest in the House, cannot find a way out of the impasse, then it will offer the public a very poor testimonial." Disregarding Schöpfer's and Gessmann's appeals for party unity, Johann Hauser and other agrarian leaders announced on June 30 that they would vote against the bill. Only Bienerth's closing of the House on July 15 postponed the consequences of their decision until December. The Rumanian trade agreement thus became the first crisis to test Gessmann's assumption that the *Reichspartei* would rise above particularistic urban-rural economic conflict; and the party barely sustained its credibility. But the Christian Social agrarians still observed the larger discipline of party loyalty and agreed not to initiate obstructionism.[164]

When parliament assembled on December 15, it immediately verged on disaster. The Social Democrats sought to break the agrarians' will with a remarkable marathon session (*Permanenzsitzung*) that lasted eighty-six hours from December 15 to 18. Victor Adler thought that if one could not persuade the obstructionists to stop talking, one might exhaust them into submission. During this session a plan emerged, first with the Slovenian Clericals led by Janez Krek and then in a more refined form with Karel Kramář of the Young Czechs, to provide the President of the House (the Christian Social Robert Pattai) with radical but temporary procedural powers to curb obstruction by sharply restricting the use of motions of urgency for the next twelve months. Surprisingly, the plan gained the support of the Slavic Union, which saw it as a brilliant way to embarrass Bienerth by demonstrating both the putative good will of the Czechs and, more importantly, their power to control parliament.[165] The Krek-Kramář motion took both the Social Democrats and the German *bürgerlich* parties by surprise—and so outraged Bienerth that he sought the Emperor's assent to close parliament. Adler and Lueger both threw the support of their parties behind the motion, however, and on December 18 the reform passed with the Christian Socials, the Social Democrats, the Poles, and the Czech and Italian *bürgerlich* factions voting against the Germans, some Czech radicals, and the Ruthenians. The German *bürgerlich* leadership refused its support unless the Slavs first agreed to abandon their obstruction. The Christian Socials thought such pettiness inappropriate when important social and economic legislation was at stake. As Gessmann explained to Redlich: "we couldn't stand back, otherwise the electorate would throw us all out of here."[166]

In two reports to Berlin, Heinrich von Tschirschky reacted to what he saw as the national treachery of the Christian Socials before a wave of "Slav terror": the Kramář motion symbolized the "progressive repression of the prominence of the Germans and the growing slavicization of Austria."[167] In fact, it did neither. Explaining the Christian Socials' decision to leave the other German parties in the lurch, Tschirschky saw a creeping clerical conspiracy—Gessmann was a "long-standing, bitter enemy not only of German liberalism, but of every facet of the German national character" and Liechtenstein was a "clerical demagogue" sympathetic to the Slavs. From one perspective he was not altogether wrong, for both did oppose integral nationalism. A more reasonable explanation, however, may be seen in Josef Redlich's comments about his own dilemma. Redlich was forced to speak against the Kramář motion out of party loyalty, but he admitted privately that it was basically a good idea and that he was glad it had passed. However, he also noted that it would have a long-term effect only if it were replaced by permanent reform of parliamentary procedure and, more importantly, if the more rational parliamentarians had the courage to resist obstructionist bullying. The debates in the Christian Social parliamentary club on December 17 demonstrated that the party was aware of the dubious precedent it was setting in opposing the German *bürgerlich* factions, but, in the end, sustaining a working parliament outweighed ethnic fraternity.[168] In mid-May 1910, as the House commenced debate on such a permanent code of procedure, Gessmann eloquently articulated a similar vision of co-equal "cooperation" between the parties and the bureaucracy in which neither nation—German nor Czech—would "hold the state up" for shameful and selfish national demands. It was this hope for political rationality, and not "clericalism," that motivated his party's acquiescence to the Slavic initiative.[169]

Richard Bienerth owed a great deal to this temporary reform of procedure put through in late December. Until December 21 the Cabinet had little to show for its first year in office. Now the commercial treaties bill finally passed its first reading (with urban and rural members of both the Christian Socials and the *Deutscher Nationalverband* splitting on the vote). Legislation on the working conditions of commercial employees (the *Handlungsgehilfengesetz*) and on accident insurance in construction trades, as well as amendatory legislation to the criminal code, were also passed in late December. When parliament reassembled in late February 1910 a revised version of the financial plan (*Finanzplan*) that had been introduced in October 1909 by Leon Biliński to eliminate the state's budget deficit through increases in several categories of direct and indirect taxation (in the expectation that this would also permit direct grants to the budgets of the chronically underfunded provincial governments and the passage of expensive new social-welfare legislation) finally received its first reading in parliament, but then it quickly stalled as each major economic interest group in the Monarchy found one or another section of the plan objectionable.[170] The package of laws on sickness, accident, and old-age pension insurance introduced in November 1908 still languished in committee, although the Social Democrats had the committee declared "permanent" so that it could work in spite of the turmoil in the plenum. Final committee work on this legislation was not concluded until March 1911, immediately before Bienerth dissolved parliament. These laws, which the Christian Socials desperately wanted to crown their image as a social reformist party, then fell victim to the Cabinet's insouciance and the state's miserable financial situation.[171]

Nonetheless, the first six months of 1910 saw more productive work by the parliament than at any time since late 1907, with Bienerth getting parliamentary approval of a major loan (for 182 million crowns) in mid-April and parliament also voting the first reading of the long-awaited career regulations (*Dienstpragmatik*) for state officials in which all the major bourgeois parties had a profound interest.[172] A Social Democratic attempt in the Finance Committee in May to embarrass Bienerth by delaying final consideration of the budget until the government had provided information on its plans to purchase four new dreadnoughts was beaten back when the Czech deputies agreed to leave the room, so that the Christian Socials and German nationals could vote down the Social Democrats.[173] After capping two relatively successful quarters of work with parliamentary approval of the budget on June 23, however, Bienerth ran up against a series of obstructionist initiatives, the last by the Polish Club which demanded guarantees that Koerber's plans for internal canal and river development from 1901 would be revived and funded. This Bienerth found unacceptable, preferring to close the session rather than risk an open break with the Poles.[174]

If Gessmann and Weiskirchner wanted to push Bienerth into reconstructing the Cabinet to accommodate the Slavs—Czech politicians expected such a move in early 1910—the internal party crisis provoked by Lueger's death and by the Hraba and Vergani Affairs in the spring and summer of 1910 ended all such plans. Redlich reported in June that Weiskirchner's previous expansiveness and ambition had given way to depression.[175] On most legislation the Christian Socials now had no option but to follow Bienerth's "leadership," as was evident in May and June 1910 when the Budget Committee finally took up the Cabinet's proposals for establishing an Italian Law Faculty in Vienna. Italians demanded the faculty be located in Trieste, which the government, the Army, and the Thronfolger adamantly opposed.[176] The only alternative was Vienna, which put the Christian Socials at the center of the controversy, particularly since the *Deutscher Nationalverband* rejected the Faculty's presence in the capital city. On June 17 the Christian Socials accepted a *provisorium* of Vienna (according to which the faculty would be located there for the first four years, its ultimate location likely to be Gradisca) as long as the German national parties went along.[177] In itself the bill was of little interest to the party, but Gessmann thought that by minimizing controversy on such tangential if symbolically explosive issues he might gain more leverage with Bienerth on legislation of substance.

Yet this proved to be impossible. In return for such pliability on national and military issues, the party gained little in social policy. When Bienerth failed to control further obstructionism in July 1910 and ordered what Gessmann privately called "this shameful adjournment," a rare manifestation of anger erupted in the club against the Cabinet. For the first time many members questioned what the party was gaining by its tractability and cooperation with a regime that was so incompetent.[178] August Kemetter thought that "these repeated annual closings of parliament point to a system under which the government does not want parliament to become powerful enough to control the country. We approve everything the Cabinet wants, and in return we get nothing." Kemetter wanted the party to pull Weiskirchner out of the Cabinet and to assume an independent position in parliament like the Social Democrats. His views were extreme, but others of a more moderate persuasion were equally frustrated. Leopold Kunschak even raised the explosive issue of whether the party should stay so closely tied to the *Deutscher Nationalverband.* Perhaps a Christian Social-Slavic tactical alliance would be preferable: a view not uncongenial to Gessmann but now, following Lueger's death, unlikely. Others in the leadership, like Jodok Fink, thought this alternative was not desirable, but the mere fact that the question could come up was significant. In a conversation with Tschirschky in early 1911 Bienerth even admitted that his "sober" style of rule handicapped centrist parties like the Christian Socials which were interested in social and economic issues, since they received little that was tangible to present to their voters.[179] National radicals, in contrast, who complained and threatened obstruction, gained both recognition and occasional concessions. While Bienerth recognized the problem, he had neither the inclination nor the ability to respond to it.

The problems facing the party by mid-1910 were deeper, moreover, than Richard Bienerth's lack of parliamentary finesse. In the wake of Lueger's death an explosion of petty scandals and personal feuds in the Vienna organization shook the party and made it the laughingstock of Austrian parliamentary life.[180] Inevitably these scandals, although their locus was purely Viennese, had their effect on the party's ability to function on the national level, especially since they led to a personal estrangement between Gessmann and Weiskirchner. Aemilian Schöpfer warned in late November 1910 that the Christian Socials risked becoming a "negligible factor" in state politics because of backbiting within the club.[181] Lacking Lueger's moral authority, which had previously served as his legitimizing principle in times of crisis, Gessmann's tactical skills, although considerable, were insufficient to hold the club together. As leadership became consensual rather than autocratic, sessions of the club became longer and more convoluted, and gradually attendance at plenary meetings of parliament suffered. The very fact that the club began to keep formal stenographic records of its debates, which Lueger had long refused to tolerate, signalled that Gessmann's long sought-after bureaucratization of the party was both real *and* chimerical. Between April and November 1910 the club spent more time discussing internal party discipline and local scandals than it did on any substantive legislative issue. In remarkable sessions on June 21–22, for example, reflections upon the financial probity and honor of the party elite were recounted in detail (discussed below in Chapter 5). Gradually a loss of nerve manifested itself which would be devastating the following year. Brosch reported to the Thronfolger in September that Gessmann was "tired of politics" and that Weiskirchner was isolated from "a great part of his former supporters."[182]

The party was weakened not by these animosities alone but also by their conjunction with one of the most serious inflations in consumer food prices in modern Austrian history. A modern economic history of the so-called price inflation (*Teuerung*) of 1909–11 in Austria has yet to be written, but it would show an inflated level of meat and cereal prices beginning in 1908 and reaching its zenith in later 1911, resulting from the conjunction of both natural catastrophes (the droughts of 1909 and 1911) and import shortfalls.[183] This inflation was also of continental proportions—similar trends occurred in many German cities, producing similar social disruptions. Average consumer prices in Vienna for meat, bread, milk, sugar and petroleum increased by 20–30 percent (in the case of meat by almost 50 percent), producing violent consumer reactions in the marketplace and ultimately in the streets. In early October 1910 the Social Democrats organized mass protests against food prices in Vienna, and a year later the worst street excesses in the city's modern history erupted. By 1911 even the stolid leaders of the *Bürgerklub* admitted the city found itself in the midst of a minor crisis. The economic reporter on the *Stadtrat,* Josef Rain, reported to a session of the Congress of Austrian Cities: "in recent years an increase in prices has been charted that includes all important consumer products and that is almost unbearable, both for the *Mittelstand* and for the working classes, since it is no longer possible to bring their household expenditures in balance with their incomes."[184]

The extraordinary pressures caused by the food-provisioning crisis in major urban areas produced rifts in the *Reichspartei* that neither Gessmann nor the more responsible Alpinists were able to control. This was a classic urban versus rural dichotomy and it had a prehistory of potent acrimony. In December

1909 the Christian Social agrarians had come close to revolting against the leadership over the commercial treaties bill; by September 1910 Brosch had to inform Franz Ferdinand that tensions between the urban and agrarian wings of the party made a consistent anti-Hungarian policy impossible.[185]

Throughout 1910 popular pressure mounted for the Cabinet to take decisive steps against the food price inflation. Because the issue of retail meat prices was so volatile and easily targetable, the Social Democrats concentrated their fire on meat import tariffs, demanding large increases in the importation of both frozen Argentinian meat and fresh meat from neighboring Balkan lands and permanent reductions in the level of tariff charges on all meat products. Austrian agrarians in response mobilized their strident and well-funded professional interest groups, most notably the fiercely protectionist *Zentralstelle* led by Alfred von Hohenblum.[186] The problem came to a head when the Social Democrats brought a motion (in the name of Jakob Reumann) before the parliament's Inflation Committee (*Teuerungsausschuss*) in November 1910 requiring the government to authorize the importation of overseas meat in unlimited quantities and to eliminate tariffs on all imported meat. Leopold Kunschak offered an alternative motion, considerably more vague, that would have limited the authorization of Argentinian meat imports to one year and that said nothing about permissible quantities of such meat or about the volatile tariff question. A majority on the Committee voted for Kunschak's motion, but both drafts came before the House for plenary debate which opened on November 30. Attempting to quell the uneasiness that the issue had generated among the Cabinet's majority and implicitly supporting Kunschak's motion, Richard Weiskirchner delivered one of the worst speeches of his career on November 25. He first trivialized the problem of meat scarcity and, then, after suggesting that the government would do what was necessary to prevent a provisioning crisis with overseas meat, intimated that Vienna would first have to secure the agreement of the Hungarian government before any additional foreign meat could be allowed in the Monarchy.[187]

This fumbling performance set the socialists off on a crucifixion of Weiskirchner. They recounted the abysmal record of the Cabinet's negotiations with Serbia for a trade agreement, involving an alleged "sell-out" of Austrian commercial and urban interests by the government and by Count Aehrenthal to the Hungarians in March 1909.[188] Two days later Weiskirchner's counterpart in Budapest, von Hieronymi, observed in the Hungarian parliament that his government had no intention of approving Austrian imports of overseas meat. Now even members of the *Deutscher Nationalverband* felt it necessary to distance themselves from Weiskirchner. Otto Lecher pointedly demanded that "just as the agrarians have a right to an effective Minister of Agriculture, I demand that we have an effective Minister of Commerce and that you [Weiskirchner] stand at our side."[189]

When the Reumann and Kunschak motions were considered on December 1, the *Deutscher Nationalverband* offered a substitute motion for Kunschak's (in the name of Arthur Stölzel) that came closer to Reumann's by proposing unlimited imports of foreign meat without deadline and adjusting tariffs where necessary.[190] After a rancorous twelve-hour session Stölzel's motion passed on a roll-call vote of 223 against 202, with the Christian Social agrarians voting against it and the urbanists voting for it. As a point of practical policy the resolution meant little—the government was not bound by it, and emergency shipments of Argentinian meat were hardly likely to make an impact on the current crisis. But the debate outlined the quandary faced by a party like the Christian Socials that claimed to be both inter-regional and trans-class. The German parties in the *Deutscher Nationalverband* did not face the same kind of crisis, since none of them claimed to belong to the same integral political unit. The *Deutscher Nationalverband* never claimed to be more than an instrument of parliamentary coordination for distinct regional/class parties, the majority of whose members were based in Bohemia and Moravia. The German agrarians might remain within the *Verband,* therefore, and still vote against the Stölzel motion in good conscience. For the Christian Socials, in contrast, the situation was more frustrating, since the *Reichspartei* claimed to be able to reconcile urban-rural conflicts *within* its own structure and then present a common front to the outside world. For the first three years, in a period of sustained economic growth, this had been possible. In the midst of an enveloping economic crisis, such internal unity was more problematic.

Karl Drexel, who was the principal Christian Social to speak against the Stölzel motion on December 1, confronted the conundrum of interest versus structure when he argued that "it is very seldom that a politician has voters and others of only one class [in his district]. My concept of a parliamentary delegate is much more idealistic. . . . I believe that a parliamentarian represents the whole people [*das ganze Volk*], that he must keep the needs of the state as a whole in mind in all of his actions, as well as the needs of his particular district."[191] The practicality and suitability of such discourse, consistent with Gessmann's and Ebenhoch's conception of the *Reichspartei* in 1907, was increasingly dubious by 1910–11. Even Drexel, while admitting that Kunschak's motion would pass, acknowledged that many ruralists were loath to support even that limited engagement of the problem: "some of them are not willing to take on the burden of having voted for it, and then some other agrarian politician comes into their district and tells the voters 'your representative is guilty of having lowered your prices'."[192]

Since Stölzel's more comprehensive motion passed the House, Kunschak's petition was not brought up for a vote and the Christian Socials were able to avoid revealing the discord into which they had talked themselves during the last week of November. In late November the party delegation tried to work out a compromise that would be acceptable to all of its factions. Many agrarian deputies wanted to allow each delegate to vote his constituency, an idea which Gessmann and other centrists like Schöpfer found dubious: "by splitting up our votes the party would offer an absurd spectacle. One wing will be manipulated by the Social Democrats, another by the German Agrarians. Then we will no longer be a party, and we will simply be ignored."[193] Kunschak and Drexel appealed to their agrarian colleagues to support the motion, admitting (far more frankly than had Weiskirchner) that Vienna was enduring a major food crisis that had to be mitigated. But some ruralists were not convinced: Matthias Bauchinger of Lower Austria stated that he would vote for Kunschak's motion only if three of its key points were revised or stripped away. Alois Höher, a leader of the Lower Austrian *Bauernbund*, articulated what most of the peasant delegates were thinking: "it really comes down to whether one thinks the economic or the political loss would be the greater."[194] To support the motion would endanger the well-being of his peasant voters (and possibly his own seat at the next election); to vote against it might embarrass and cripple the Viennese contingent of the party. After days of such inconclusive and impatient debate, the club decided on November 30 not to impose unanimity on its members. Without saying so explicitly, Josef Stöckler hinted at how most of the Christian Social agrarians intended to vote if the Kunschak motion came up: "the passage of the motion is certain. The agrarians will have it easier if they can say that they were outvoted."[195] Pleas for class unity and party discipline by Kunschak and Gessmann had been to no avail in the face of harsh economic realities. Quite possibly even Lueger would have been unable to hold the party together on such a vote. Yet the invocation of "economic necessity" to justify political disunity was as, Aemilian Schöpfer wisely observed, quite dangerous, since "economic questions nowadays make up 90 percent of politics, and with such freedom [of voting] the party would cease to be a factor of power, and simply end up in chaos. . . . Such freedom would destroy the unity of the party, which the gentlemen themselves don't really want to do."

The meat import issue hardly signified the death of the *Reichspartei*. Indeed, the debates of November 24–30 had revealed a widespread respect for and loyalty to the idea of a united, comprehensive "peoples' party." Those who voted against the party on December 1 did so with genuine regret, not from cynicism over its future. On the majority of national economic and social issues the party was still able to stand in reasonable harmony.[196] But the glaring division over food imports and Weiskirchner's unfortunate comments, which received more applause from the agrarians than from his own urban constituents in Vienna, planted a time bomb in Vienna that the Social Democrats could explode at will.

The economic tensions of 1910 not only handed the socialists a ready-made cudgel, but they also fed and gave intellectual substance to past rivalries and jealousies that Lueger had been able to control, if not repress. 1910 saw enterprising attempts by the Social Democrats and splinter Liberals in Vienna to exploit the economic crisis among traditional pro-Christian Social electoral groups, particularly the master craftsmen. In June 1910 municipal artisan groups, many of them affiliated with the Christian Socials, called a rally at the Rathaus to protest the failure of parliament to pass export trade legislation favorable to their crafts as well as the inflation that had devastated the market for personal and small industrial products in Vienna.[197] The party was caught by surprise by this meeting, which had been summoned without its consent. Only through clever last-minute maneuvers did the Rathaus gain control of the meeting's agenda and thus prevent the artisans from turning it into an anti-governmental propaganda festival. Weiskirchner viewed the gathering as a personal affront, but such dissidence was inevitable, if only because his Ministry, which had responsibility for commercial regulations as well as trade agreements, was the logical target of the artisans' unhappiness.[198] Later in the year, Alois Heilinger, an ambitious Christian Social official in the municipal bureaucracy who had been elected to parliament in 1907 as a self-styled expert on artisan affairs, decided to exploit such *Mittelstand* unrest by propagating an opportunistic anti-agrarian platform. Heilinger's intemperate accusations about Weiskirchner's "selling out Austrian tradesmen to the Hungarians and the agrarians" forced the parliamentary delegation to censure him in February 1911, which in turn led to his secession from the party.[199] The feud might have been banal and trivial, except that thousands of artisan voters, the bedrock of the Christian Social base vote in the capital, wondered if Heilinger were not correct in his observations.

The troubles posed by Heilinger were paralleled by another, more ominous quarrel provoked by Ferdinand von Pantz and August Kemetter.[200] Pantz was a hot-tempered but articulate member of the Styrian delegation, first elected to parliament in 1907 from the rural district of Gröbming. Concerned about the need to sustain the productivity and profits of his own constituents—Alpine dairy farmers who also produced meat for urban markets—he argued in 1909 that Austrian cereal producers were to blame for the shortages in domestic meat production. By keeping import tariffs on feed grains high, they endangered local meat production and ultimately exposed dairy and meat producers to the kinds of anti-rural propaganda spread by the Social Democrats. Gessmann tried to prevent a split between Pantz and the more "orthodox" Styrian Christian Socials represented by Michael Schoiswohl in late 1909, and he even obtained Pantz's and Schoiswohl's signatures to a private protocol that stated that "there had been a whole series of misunderstandings which had produced bitterness on both sides, but which were not grounded in facts."[201] Unfortunately, they *were* based on substantial differences. When Pantz continued to speak out in 1910, the powerful Lower Austrian ruralists in the party, who represented (and some of whom personally were) cereal producers, became outraged. In March 1910, immediately before Lueger's death, the party leadership again tried to paper over the conflict, with Gessmann warning the agrarians that only the Social Democrats would profit from such intraparty feuding, but this did not prevent Josef Stöckler and his colleagues in the Lower Austrian *Bauernbund* from bringing a formal protest to the parliamentary leadership, demanding that Pantz be stopped from "coming to Lower Austria with his theories" and threatening to use "all available means" against him.[202]

Pantz was undeterred by such bellicosity, informing Gessmann that "we, as representatives of voters whose economic interests are severely damaged by the high cereal prices, will not be hindered in our struggle against high tariffs." In parliament on November 30 Pantz urged that cereal production be viewed as a dying industry in the Austrian Crownlands and demanded a reduction of import tariffs on feed grains.[203] In early December, together with August Kemetter, the director of the Lower Austrian Teachers' Institute and a former protégé of Gessmann, Pantz founded the *Österreichischer Wirtschaftsverein*, a small propaganda association to spread his anti-agrarian tariff programs. He did so without the party's approval, which forced the central leadership to act to retain the support of the Lower and Upper Austrian cereal producers in the *Bauernbund* movement. Ironically, Leopold Kunschak also threw his Laborite faction against Pantz and Kemetter, ostensibly to preserve party unity but in fact to gain the support of the rural Lower Austrians in his continuing tribulations with the Rathaus. On December 16, 1910, the parliamentary commission voted to condemn the *Österreichischer Wirtschaftsverein*, giving its leaders until mid-January to back down.[204] Pantz refused to do so, and in late 1911, after a year of recriminating letters and petitions, the now-dominant agrarian faction forced their expulsion from the club. Pantz and Kemetter, together with another aggrieved Styrian who also opposed entrenched peasant interests, Raimund Neunteufel, eventually constituted themselves as the small yet vociferous *Deutsches Zentrum*, providing another example of discord among colleagues which, in the context of their shared cultural values, was unfortunate (Kemetter and Neunteufel were, for example, devout Catholics).[205]

The Heilinger and Pantz episodes—the former arising from unrest among Viennese master artisans, the latter reflecting irreconcilable theoretical and regional differences among the agrarians themselves—illuminated the difficulties that the economic crisis had wrought for the *Reichspartei* structure. The intensity of vendettas and feuding was such that by March 1911 Friedrich Funder, as chief editor of the *Reichspost,* had to send the party leadership a letter asking for instructions on the etiquette of dealing with senior politicians who were trying to insult each other in the pages of the paper.[206] Weiskirchner's presence in the Cabinet compounded the party's loss in credibility before the electorate. On some issues he was able to defend the party's interests; for example, his opposition to Biliński's beer tax as part of the *Finanzplan* helped kill the measure.[207] Weiskirchner was also helpful on matters of patronage, although even here, perhaps because of his Viennese background, he was not as effective as he should have been as the representative of a party spanning six different provinces. After Bienerth reconstructed his ministry in early January 1911, keeping Weiskirchner on as Minister of Commerce, the Alpinists insisted that more attention be paid by the Cabinet to their patronage needs.[208] Positive accomplishments were harder to come by. Weiskirchner's pet project of modernizing Austrian maritime navigation, to which he justifiably devoted great attention, died when Bienerth dismissed parliament in March 1911.[209] After the fiasco of December 1910 the party seemed to be left with its opposition to ameliorative trade and tariff legislation for urban consumers as its major "achievement" in two years of Cabinet governance.

By early 1911 the Christian Socials thus found themselves boxed in by economic woes, internal bickering, and a hapless Minister-President, while the Social Democrats repeatedly outmaneuvered them on the floor of parliament. In February 1911, after a gratuitous discussion about the role of women in politics, the club was forced to agree to vote for the Social Democratic bill amending the 1867 Associations Law (which, among other novelties, permitted women to join political clubs), simply because it could conceive of no effective alternative.[210] Such defensiveness was troublesome for a party accustomed to putting its opponents in such predicaments. As Gessmann lamely explained to the club in January, the Christian Socials had reached the point where they seemed to be playing a zero-sum game: they could not go into opposition against the government without destroying parliament and hence had to remain loyal to Bienerth, even though the party "is often forced to adopt positions which are actually against its intentions." They were stuck with a ministry which, in Redlich's words, was "without plans, without talent, without ideas."[211]

In March 1911 Bienerth tried a desperate move to break the deadlock of renewed oppositionalism in which his Cabinet was entrapped. On March 31 he announced that he would dissolve parliament and call new elections in June, two years before the House's normal term. He then proceeded to use Article 14 to implement critical fiscal legislation. His decision came after a month of bickering with the *Deutscher Nationalverband* over the budget (caused in part by the jealousy of leaders like Julius Sylvester and Otto Steinwender in having been passed over in the latest ministerial lists) and after renewed attempts by the Czechs to bring down the Cabinet by obstructing the Budget Committee.[212] Bienerth's political *Staatsstreich* shocked the German bourgeois parties, and it was violently opposed by the Christian Social leadership. Gessmann reported to a session of the club on March 29 that he had tried to dissuade Bienerth from this rash act, but that the party now had too little influence to stop it. In response Victor Silberer asked cynically what one could expect of a Minister-President who had said of the Christian Socials that they were "easy to have." Robert Pattai insisted that Bienerth's actual words had been "the relationship is ideal," but in either version it seemed to many that Gessmann's policy of accommodation had seriously damaged the party.[213]

Bienerth's decision stunned Vienna. Why would he summon new elections in the midst of a major recession when the result could only be the loss of bourgeois seats to the Social Democrats? It said much about his status as a political novice that Bienerth actually thought the opposite would occur. In a conversation with Heinrich von Tschirschky, Bienerth articulated his reasons for the break with parliament. He admitted that with sufficient concessions in late March it might have been possible to buy off the Czech and Ruthenian obstructionists and to keep parliament working, but he now saw himself as a defender of German interests in the Monarchy that were threatened by the powerful Slavic majority. No government could rule against the Slavs, but his Cabinet had become a permanent target of Czech pressures for parliamentarization that would force him out in favor of someone like Gautsch. Bienerth expected the next House to have a similar national makeup, and even admitted that Czech moderates would lose seats to their more radical nationalist colleagues, but he also thought that a careful policy of electoral compromises between the *Deutscher Nationalverband* and the Christian Socials would ensure an increase in seats for both of the big *bürgerlich* groups and a repression of the Social Democrats: "if the Christian Socials and the German bourgeois parties hold together, Baron Bienerth hopes to deprive the socialists of a not inconsiderable number of seats and thus give him the necessary power to continue the current governmental system."[214]

This remarkable strategy—which also saw Bienerth asking that Berlin urge the National Liberals and the *Zentrum* to pressure their Austrian counterparts into cooperation (which a shocked Tschirschky refused to recommend)—showed Bienerth's inability to gauge either the depths of popular economic distress in Vienna or the hatred of the Christian Socials by local Jewish *bürgerlich* groups and the Liberal Viennese press.[215] Bienerth's last-minute conversion to an anti-socialist *Sammlungspolitik* had resonances of Beck's strategy of 1907–8, but it manifested critical differences as well. Beck had sought in the elections of 1907 to minimize discord between all bourgeois parties, Czech and German, not simply among the Germans themselves. His strategy was simultaneously anti-socialist *and* national-coalitional. Bienerth, in contrast, had neither the imagination nor the courage to force the German parties to accept a parliamentary partnership with the Czechs on the Cabinet level. Josef Redlich, who found his intransigence on this point outrageous, thought that a strong, decisive leader would have been able to construct such a ministry. Instead, with his "sober" (according to Tschirschky) style of rule, Bienerth insisted that reconciliation must first be attained on the regional level between the Czech and German factions in the Bohemian Diet before ministerial reconstruction could be considered. The collapse of the German-Czech *Ausgleich* negotiations in Prague in late 1910 foreclosed this option. Left with no other alternatives, Bienerth's election campaign was simply an effort to reconstitute a German-Polish bloc—his customary, if unreliable, working majority between 1909 and 1911—by beating up the Social Democrats. In electoral strategy he had come full circle, returning to the views of the man he had spent the last two years mocking: Max von Beck. But rather than substituting class conflict for national conflict, as Beck had sought to do, Bienerth simply *added* class conflict to national conflict in a supreme escalation of Austrian political discord. The results for himself and for his erstwhile allies would be catastrophic.[216]

FOUR

Religion and Nation in Viennese Politics, 1907–1914

The Terms of the Debate

Religion and nation were two aspects of the Austrian cultural universe that Karl Lueger and most other party leaders recognized, supported, and yet viewed with some skepticism and occasionally even with trepidation. Neither Lueger nor any other member of the party elite wanted to disassociate the party from either Catholicism or German culture in Vienna, but the party wore its religion lightly—it was as much "Christian" as it was "Catholic"—and Lueger had little patience with extremists in the German or Czech national camps who for the sake of obstructionist national grandstanding would sacrifice the benefits that would accrue from a parliament that could pass "neutral" social and economic legislation. The party's official line—and on these two issues the official was also the actual line—was that Vienna was both a German and a Catholic city. But having ceremoniously declared that fact, the Christian Socials proceeded to define their own purpose in terms of neither attribute, but rather exclusively as the servant and executor of the "Christian people," of the *Reichshaupt- und Residenzstadt Wien* in which men and women of various nationalities and Christian sects presumably could be included.

This was most clear, perhaps, in the politics of city employment as managed by the *Magistrat.* Applicants were required to list both religion and national identity on a screening form, but in fact anyone who was not a Social Democrat, a pan-German, a Jew, or a person who had officially rejected membership in a recognized religion (*konfessionslos*) was realistically eligible for employment. The number of men appointed and promoted in the city bureaucracy or in municipal service industries with Czech, Slovak, and Polish names was considerable, although for Lueger's purposes they were all good "Germans"— by which the party meant that they could speak and write German, they were loyal to the party, and they agreed with the general postulate that Vienna was a German city. On the state level, Christian Social "Germanness" was a license to be taken seriously. It was an organic link to the powerful constitutional assemblages of the 1860s, affording a splendid entree into the prerogatives and possibilities of the 1867 liberal-absolutist state. But it did not mean the exact replication of the terms of 1867, for the Christian Socials—and this was a fundamental difference from older Austro-Liberals—did not require the sterilization of other national political movements and institutions for their own identity. The identity of the Christian Social party was forged in the ferocious political marketplace of the 1890s, not in the salons of the 1860s. Brutal, yet pragmatic variation, not univocal idealism, defined their political universe.

As the need for a formal anti-Semitic facade for the party diminished after 1905, the weight given to "Christianity" as a counter-issue that could be used to domesticate anti-Semitism might have declined as well.[1] Speaking in December 1926 at a celebration in memory of P. Heinrich Abel, the Viennese Catholic leader Jakob Fried would look back to 1896 and compare the then wayward commitment to religion on the part of Christian Social party leaders with the staunch visage presented by Ignaz Seipel's party:

> If the Christian Social party today is a party whose structural conception is one totally different from that of thirty years ago [in 1896], then that was accomplished by men who worked in this party, and whose accomplishment it was that the Christian Social party today is no longer merely a party thrown together on a Christian-political basis for the sake of appearance and for opportunism, but rather that it is a party which wants to serve the Christian idea. Pater Abel can claim much more of the credit for this development than can the men who at that time were the political leaders of the party.[2]

Similarly, Lueger's purge of pan-German city councilmen in the 1900 elections suggested that he would have been only too happy to put and keep the national issue on the back burner of Viennese politics. But in fact the dynamics of Austrian politics after 1900 and especially after 1907 carried the party into new and more intense cultural conflicts, involving both religion and German nationalism. Both issues threatened to become independent variables with logics of their own.

In the case of religion this was the Christian Social party's own fault, for Lueger and others in the party shamelessly used religious observance and religious patronage as political cudgels with which to beat down Austrian Social Democracy. Once the party was in power, Catholic clerics gained seats on local school boards and a few were even elected to the City Council and the Lower Austrian Diet (where they enthusiastically participated in and often led the purges of socialist teachers); Gessmann organized clerics as political agitators and contact men; and the city gave beneficent and ostentatious subventions to local Catholic charitable and educational associations, while withdrawing or reducing similar subsidies held by groups associated with the Liberal party. Perhaps most grating for the Social Democrats was Lueger's use of religious ceremonies to buttress his political machine. Each new public school opening in Vienna was marked by a mass celebrated by a Catholic priest at an altar installed in the school gymnasium.[3] Similarly, the dedication of church buildings offered valuable performative opportunities to meld the elites of the state, the nobility, and the city. When the foundation stone was set for the new Canisiuskirche in October 1899, for example, an elaborate ceremony was attended not only by Lueger and other Christian Social notables and by various Church leaders but also by members of the Court and high nobility, along with Erich Kielmansegg, Wilhelm Hartel, Richard Bienerth, the Viennese Police President Habrda, and other high-ranking civil servants. The "feudal" Court, the Josephist state, and arriviste *Kleinbürger* society all performed their assigned roles in a single orchestrated pageant. At a dinner following the ceremony Lueger openly admitted the instrumental purposes behind these events: "I love to appear at festivities such as the present one precisely to demonstrate that I want to proceed aggressively against those elements who want to disturb our peace."[4]

Yet for all the noise and animation with religious symbols and cultic performances, the party leadership in Vienna did not, at least in Lueger's time, conceive of itself as a confessional party by seeking to impose a dominant *religious* identity on civil society. Indeed, this was precisely the point that Jakob Fried was alluding to in 1926. Rather, its use of religion was more politically pluralistic and more culturally utilitarian, as the iconography in the Lainz church showed. This is not to say that the years after 1897 lacked signs of a religious revival among the lower and middle strata of the *Bürgertum* which the party had to take into account, and which, in the collective agency of an association like the *Katholischer Volksbund,* would slowly influence the party's basic character. Walter Sauer has chronicled the increase in small Catholic and Christian associations in the city after 1880, observing rightly that this growth suggests a revival of public and private interest on the part of at least some local inhabitants toward religion.[5] Jakob Fried's celebration of the urban mission work of Pater Heinrich Abel was certainly justified. Abel's Marian congregations and his annual pilgrimages to Mariazell constituted important new venues for a semi-public Catholicism beyond the confines of everyday church ritual, and contributed new (and strengthened older) forms of public devotion, as did many Catholic family and especially women's associations that sprang up after 1890–95.[6] Nor should the increase of devotion among lower-middleclass women and men under the aegis of Catholic prayer associations be ignored.[7] But the Marian movement and the noisy civic religiosity of the *Christlicher Wiener Frauenbund* must be placed at one end of a broad spectrum of cultural values, at the other end of which would lie the largely male ward organizations and especially white-collar voters associated with the party, for whom religion was a subordinate if important part of the *bürgerlich* stability and the traditional order that Lueger wanted to affix to his *Vaterstadt*.[8] The Christian Socials approved of and defended Christian religious identities but did not emphasize "Catholicism" as an independent political variable deserving decisive and exclusive prominence on its own. Nor did the Christian Socials pay much attention to the wishes or needs of the Austrian bishops before 1910, unless those needs also served the party's own tactical interests; in turn, Cardinal Gruscha and a number of his older colleagues remained suspicious of Lueger down to the mayor's death.[9] Party electoral propaganda for the first municipal elections held in Vienna under the new franchise in May 1900 abstained from explicit references to Catholicism or Catholic institutions, preferring the vaguer term of "Christian."[10] Indeed, it was precisely this shyness toward "Catholicism" on behalf of "Christianity" that Austrian Catholic conservatives originally found so dubious about the Christian Social movement. For the conservative Dominican theologian Albert Maria Weiss, who was a longtime opponent of Lueger, it appeared in retrospect as if

> the Christian and the Catholic might be two different religions, or even stand in direct contradiction to each other. . . . The danger was all the greater in the circumstances obtaining in old Austria. Under the influence of Josephinism and Liberalism a kind of Christianity purged of all ultramontane and Catholic characteristics had evolved, whose nature no one really understood. . . . one imagined a Christianity existing without the Church, without the sacraments, without liturgical services, a kind of deism with Christian names.[11]

German Catholic journals also noticed this peculiar, on-again, off-again stance manifested by Austrians for whom Christianity was somehow less "clerical" than Catholicism:

> one cannot deny the fact that some well-meaning Catholics, apart from the liberal Catholics who are Catholic by virtue of their baptismal certificates [*Taufscheinkatholiken*], have lost a sense of the total power and significance of Catholic belief. Otherwise it is difficult to explain the deliberate avoidance of the word "Catholic" and the fear of being associated with decidedly Catholic activities.[12]

Long after the party's accession to power in 1897 the competing streams of "Christian" and "Catholic" orientations remained in balance, with Lueger himself perhaps more sympathetic to the first.[13] For many activists it was perfectly plausible to be "Catholic" on some occasions and "Christian" on others; and it was equally possible, as Reinhold Knoll has rightly observed about Lueger himself, to be both pious *and* anticlerical.[14] Nor were Christian Socials from the Alpine lands insensitive to the cultural differences between their Catholicism and the "Christianity" of their Viennese brethren. Josef Schraffl admitted in July 1911 that he opposed a strong confessional emphasis in a statement of party principles because "it is of no value to the Tyroleans and it would hurt the Viennese," and affirmed that in this assessment "he was in agreement with Exz. Gessmann."[15] To try to categorize rigidly the Viennese under the Empire in terms of a single kind of Catholic religious identity and practice would be as frustrating as attempting to define what a "worker" was in late nineteenth-century French politics. A party that had its "white" as well as its "black" sides did much of its cultural painting in gray.

Events took place after 1900, however, which encouraged (or forced) some Christian Social leaders to seek a more actively "religious" profile for the party. The vulgar anticlericalism that accompanied the pan-German *Los von Rom* movement put the party into a highly defensive position toward the Church and encouraged the growth of militant Catholic journalistic and social organizations such as the *Piusverein,* which, although not formally associated with the Christian Social party until after the reorganization of 1910–11, inevitably assumed a more prominent role in its intellectual and cultural circles. To the extent that *Los von Rom* introduced a newly imagined Austrian Protestantism, pastoral agitators like Paul Bräunlich inadvertently helped to constitute a "new" Catholicism. Further, desacralizing pressures from young socialist militants like Seitz and Glöckel, whose very raison d'être was an acute combination of anticlericalism and class conflict, had a profound impact on younger party leaders, especially those younger Catholics with secondary and university training who had been influenced by Heinrich Abel's mission movement. Nor should we forget the extraordinary indifference that slowly grew into active hatred of the institutions of the Catholic Church by many Viennese working-class men and women, even if some of those workers continued to harbor religious sentiments in a private, familial context.[16] The Viennese clergy became special targets for socialist abuse, which was only magnified as priests allowed themselves to be co-opted by Gessmann and other leaders in support of Christian Social electoral agitation against the Social Democratic party.[17] Conversely, as working-class men entered the public realm as voters and marchers, the utility, if not the actual vitality of "Christianity" for many Christian Social loyalists increased, if only as an additional marker by which they might assert (and protect) their own respectability and stability, while marginalizing and stigmatizing their enemies.

As a party in the municipal opposition, limited to the mundane satisfactions of ward politics, the earlier anti-Semites had had little need for "intellectuals" in their ranks. If such individuals existed they were either secularly inclined journalists and lawyers like Theodor Wähner (Wähner's *Deutsche Zeitung* represented the more nationalist and secular wing of the party) and Robert Pattai or Catholic clerics like Ambros Opitz and Franz Schindler, who played leading roles at the *Reichspost*. Contemporary German evaluations of Austrian Catholicism remarked on the lack of devotion and religious identity on the part of many educated or even "half-educated" persons.[18] But the appointment of Friedrich Funder, a strongly orthodox Catholic layman, as chief editor of the *Reichspost* in 1902 and the recruitment of young intellectuals (some from the University of Vienna) who did have strong Catholic identities, for its editorial staff shifted the balance of cultural emphasis, if not actual power, in the party's press toward a more Catholic orientation. Once the *Reichspost* came to enjoy the patronage of the camarilla around Archduke Franz Ferdinand, its supremacy within the party's journalistic establishment was only a matter of time. In 1907 it absorbed the *Deutsche Zeitung* (which was abolished). With the collapse of *Vaterland* in 1911 the *Reichspost* became the only credible spokesman for the *Reichspartei*.[19] The ascendancy of Albert Gessmann (who was part-owner of the paper) strengthened the Catholic faction, even though Gessmann himself did not always affirm Catholic values in his personal political views.[20] This shift in power toward those within the party interested in giving the Christian Socials a more openly Catholic profile was substantially enhanced by the party's electoral growth in the Alpine lands after 1907. If the Viennese did not fully appreciate the Catholic sensibilities of their western brethren, the Wahrmund scandal brought home to them the fact that the merger of 1907 required give as well as take.

To the extent that church-state issues were the subject of governmental deliberation in Vienna, the decision-making ethos was shaped by the senior members of the *Magistrat,* who were not necessarily affiliated with Catholic viewpoints. Rudolf Sieghart commented in his memoirs that Lueger "defended absolutely his independence [vis à vis the clergy], and the Viennese *Magistrat* was during his regime predominantly German-national in orientation."[21] The co-option of ex-Liberal municipal civil servants and former anti-clerical schoolteachers thus strengthened the party's "white" side. Although he was a personal friend of Franz Schindler and other clerics and a man of religious conviction, Richard Weiskirchner represented this side of the party.[22] A talented municipal civil servant intent on avoiding harsh partisanship, Weiskirchner was Lueger's personal choice to succeed him as mayor in 1910. As mayor Weiskirchner was not beyond trying to dampen quietly both the anti-Semitic and "clerical" posture of the party, much to Funder's and Heinrich Mataja's dismay during the First World War.[23] However, the fact that men like Friedrich Funder, Eduard Heinl, Victor Kienböck, Richard Schmitz, Josef Sigmund and others with strong Catholic credentials rose in journalistic and associational circles meant that a new elite of Catholic educated individuals was also making its presence felt.

Finally, the Social Democrats and the new Fabian Left-Liberals helped through initiatives like the *Freie Schule* to create what they insisted they wanted to destroy—a truly *Catholic* Christian Socialism. In an earlier essay on the self-understanding of late nineteenth-century Viennese Liberals, I characterized political culture in Vienna after 1897 as experiencing a renaissance of conflicting beliefs, many of which had little direct impact on social policy but which provided a fascinating spectacle of new and untried moral perspectives.[24] Rather than "killing off" alternate views of polity and society, as they claimed they could and would do, the Christian Socials seemed to generate new oppositional forms at every turn. The striking presence of Lueger's power—his arrogance, ruthlessness, and ostentatiousness—begged for challenges. That these challenges occurred in a reasonably free political environment, at a time when governmental censorship was slowly withdrawing its control over political expression, testified both to the mediatory power of the Imperial administration and to the pleasure which all sides took in the theatricality of the new rhetoric.

One of the most vital components of the political revolution in Vienna between 1897 and 1914 was the new anticlericalism. Among the main body of the Social Democratic party, anticlericalism was a long-standing belief and a reliable tool; but when faced with a major opponent who combined religious posturing with *kleinbürgerlich* anti-Marxism, anticlericalism was not just a necessity—it was a godsend. Hence the socialist preoccupation with religion in Catholic Austria may be seen as paralleling French liberal phobias about religion in Catholic France. Just as for Gambetta or Ferry clericalism was the enemy, in the sense that the French Catholic Church recapitulated in its history, memory, and contemporary power a hundred years of anti-revolutionary praxis, so too did Lueger's revitalization of political religion seem to revive the worst features of Josephism and baroque Catholicism in Austria, combining state and church in new, far more potent forms that signified the self-emancipation of *bürgerlich* civil society from the administrative and dynastic state.[25] Just as killing the Church for the French would accomplish the long-awaited act—of ending the French Revolution—killing Viennese clericalism in its new bourgeois form would be a signal that the final stage of revolutionary progress in the socialist epoch had begun.

Yet, the clericalism issue carried with it a far more complicated agenda for Austrian Social Democrats than mere tactical convenience. Indeed, for the *Jungen* like Karl Seitz and Otto Glöckel and for those who joined the *Los von Rom* and *Freie Schule* movements, anticlericalism assumed a life of its own. The Austro-Marxist preoccupation with religion and anticlericalism reflected two wider differences from the Marxism of their German comrades to the north.[26] The first lay in the propensity of younger Austrian socialists to privilege theories of political personality development in a multi-ethnic empire, applauding strategies that would enhance cultural and ethnic individuality while maintaining legal and economic solidarities. The second lay in their equally strong instrumental evaluation of ethical forces as being able to shape the context in which class struggle would be pursued. The impassioned front mentality that the younger Austro-Marxists practiced with such zeal was a component of their larger quest to empower "new men" and "new women" with revolutionary cultural identities. For some, like Max Adler, a new society of purely secular, humanistic values in which religious expression would be erased from the public (and perhaps also from the private) scene might accompany and perhaps even precede a fundamental transformation in the relations of material production. Since bourgeois culture and religious morality seemed to affirm existing class relations in Austria, their socialist counterparts should be turned against those class relations. They might help to modify, if not overcome, class repression, since socialist humanism could be offered not merely to the proletariat but also to Austrian society at large, including the middle and lower bourgeoisie.

One of the most fundamental characteristics of interwar Austro-Marxism was the revolutionary value that the Viennese socialists accorded to changes in education (*Bildung*) and in manners (*Gesittung*), as opposed to mere reconstruction of tax codes and housing systems.[27] Coming out of an epoch of prewar political conflict in Vienna, in which the primal enemy of the party was an ostentatiously "Christian" movement that brandished religion as a tool for spectacle and political combat, the younger socialists understandably defined political success in counterreligious terms. Catholicism functioned for the Austro-Marxists in much the same way as the bogeyman of the "Junkers" (or the Hohenzollern Dynasty) served for their German counterparts. In part this was a generational matter. The Social Democratic movement in Austria had a long history of opposition to publicly endowed and privileged religion and especially to Catholicism. The work of Paul Zulehner, Helmut Konrad, Gerhard Steger, and many other scholars has demonstrated the fiercely anticlerical background of early party leaders. Yet Victor Adler's generation earned their political spurs in the 1880s and 1890s when the basic issue of the Social Democratic party was survival and its principal achievements would be institutional and political—the development of a coherent, unified party structure, the achievement of universal suffrage, and the establishment of a successful union movement.[28] The official position of the party—as articulated by Victor Adler—was that socialists should not be co-opted into proto-bourgeois, anticlerical frondes, either on behalf of Protestantism or more general anticlerical German nationalism. Hence Adler's open repudiation in 1899 of the *Los von Rom* movement.[29] Adler's position was not the only possible view—others within the party like Engelbert Pernerstorfer had more flexible views about the organizing role of cultural experience—but in the decade preceding the securing of universal manhood suffrage in 1905 the party had other fish to fry than engaging in anticlerical crusades.

This preoccupation with electoral tactics and simple survival began to change in the face of Christian Social provocations. The heritage of ten years of persecution in the Vienna school system, and the revulsion against Christian Social manipulation of the school system as manifest in the 1904 school laws led some leaders—most notably Pernerstorfer and Schuhmeier—into open support for a *Los von Rom* movement among the Viennese working classes.[30] For younger members of the party, especially those who had suffered personal setbacks because of Christian Social persecution, politicized religion now assumed new and more ominous forms. The old "enemy" of the socialists—the state itself—now seemed to defer to the anti-Marxism of the large bourgeois political parties. Traditionally the neo-Josephist administration (*Verwaltung*) had provided the fail-safe mechanism against overarching religious ambition in Austria, but now the socialists found themselves confronting an independent political movement which not only intimidated that administration but also appropriated from the Austrian state its prerogative of supervising (and exploiting) public religion. Moreover, the slow dampening of conflict between church and state in Austria—a trend evident by the latter 1880s which led some commentators to assert by 1914 that there was no "church-state" problem in the Monarchy—made it unlikely that the state would seek to block such political appropriation in the name of curbing or limiting the powers of the Church in civil society.[31] Not only was post-Josephist anti-clericalism losing its identity—indeed later anticlericals like Ernst Victor Zenker insisted that the state bureaucracy and the courts made every effort to accommodate the Church in spite of the interconfessional legislation of the 1870s—but many of the positive prerogatives that Josephist pattern of state regulation of church (*Staatskirchentum*) (and its reconstituted successor after 1874) exercised toward the Church (funding support, patronage, political sponsorship) were being taken over on the regional and local levels by more clearly politicized authorities, which in Vienna and Lower Austria meant the Christian Social party.[32] The federal revolution in Austrian state governance, so much debated and decried in the last decade before the war, was bound to have an effect on the ability of individual Crownland administrations to privilege or to marginalize cultural and social institutions at will.[33]

The intellectual and political world of the younger socialists was that of Lueger triumphant; of Gessmann, the Imperial Hofrat and Cabinet Minister; of the *Piusverein* and networks of politicizing clerics, who condemned socialism from the pulpit on Sunday and in catechism classes during the school week; of the *Reichspost,* prosperous and confident of financial help from conservative Court circles and from Austrian industry, mediated through Rudolf Sieghart. Their world was also one of nationalist crisis, in which their own party threatened to degenerate into feuding national wings. The level of brilliant theory which this generation of socialists attained was not a little owing to the gap between expectation and concrete achievement wrought by earlier generations' political and institutional strategies. This gap invited new experiments in national-cultural mediation, among the most notable of which were Renner's and Bauer's contributions, and a new emphasis on anticlerical culture and on mass education as positive and unifying modes of progressive socialist politics. Not surprisingly, this new socialist "attention" toward religion and especially Catholicism did not go unnoticed among the Christian Socials. Josef Scheicher argued in May 1907 that

> Social Democracy—or Socialism—was from the very beginning conceived of by its founders as a social party, a social system. . . . The socialists of the 1870s still had, so far I remember, a social program and sought to effect social improvements. That has changed fundamentally today [1907]. Social goals and initiatives swim at best like specks of fat in a bowl of cheap soup, lonely and abandoned on a sea of hatred for church and religion.[34]

For all that divided the various Austrian socialist factions after 1907, one issue on which they could unite was anticlerical *Bildung.*[35] Secular humanism might join what linguistic identity put asunder, as well as correct the deficit that younger members of the party elite like Otto Bauer and Robert Danneberg saw in the absence of a self-generating political consciousness among Austrian working-class circles.[36] Socialist preoccupation with *Bildung* after 1907 thus took many forms and had overlapping constituencies. Again, the ironic parallel between the Christian Social and Social Democratic experiences was obvious, for the Christian Socials sought in much the same way to exploit anti-socialism as a bridge over bourgeois nationality squabbles. Karl Renner was more correct than he imagined when he called the Christian Socials "our most intimate enemy."[37] Both mass parties viewed the Empire through the prism of Viennese politics.

In this chapter I discuss three instances of cultural combat in early twentieth-century Vienna that resulted from this collision of radical *bürgerlich* politics with the renewed anticlericalism on the one hand and with growing nationalist sensibilities on the other. All three instances involved various facets of the premier cultural *politicum* of Austrian Liberalism—public education in the schools and in the universities.

The Politics of Ethical Positivism:
The Verein "Freie Schule"

Perhaps the most controversial experiment in secular, anti-religious moral renewal, used as a political bludgeon against the Christian Social party, was the *Freie Schule*. In March 1905, following the Emperor's sanction of Albert Gessmann's school laws for Lower Austria, a group of radical Liberal, German national, and Social Democratic politicians and educators met to establish the *Verein "Freie Schule,"* an educational association devoted to combatting the "clerical menace" threatening Austrian public education.[38] The *Freie Schule* inadvertently brought together elements of the prior alliance over *Los von Rom;* Engelbert Pernerstorfer gave one of the principal speeches at the founding ceremony, along with German national students and local anticlerical university professors. The *Freie Schule* was chaired by Paul von Hock, a Liberal jurist on the Administrative Court; its secretary was Ludo Moritz Hartmann, a Social Democratic historian active in a series of anticlerical educational causes. The list of initial supporters of the association contained predictable names: Julius Ofner, Karl Seitz, Josef Enslein, Anton Menger, Stefan Licht, Emil von Fürth, Max Burckhard. This was a last gasp of Viennese Liberal *Freisinn,* leaning heavily on the Social Democrats, for most of the audiences at the association's protest meetings consisted of their working-class clientele.[39] Numerous bourgeois dignitaries, many from the Austrian universities, signed the initial charter, although over time enthusiasm for the association waned so that it became the preoccupation of a small group of dedicated radicals like Ofner, Hock, and Hartmann. Among the Viennese teaching corps the *Freie Schule* met with a modest, but enthusiastic response—a rally in February 1906 attracted approximately four hundred teachers to hear Ofner and several socialist teachers condemn Christian Social manipulation of the schools.[40] Although Catholic claims that the association was the property of Viennese freemasons seem exaggerated, there is little doubt that the ethos behind the *Freie Schule* owed much to masonic sponsorship, both financial and intellectual.[41] The association's numerical growth was steady, but not impressive. By 1910 it had 26,000 dues-paying members throughout the German and Bohemian lands of the Monarchy.[42]

The *Freie Schule* conducted a wide-ranging program of agitation and protest on various educational policy issues. In a speech given in March 1906 Baron Hock insisted that he and his colleagues were not against religion, but only against its political abuse by the Christian Socials and the Catholic Church.[43] However, both the politics of the association and the logic of its practices belied this claim. Underlying the *Freie Schule*'s cultural-revolutionary practice was a hostility to all organized religions, and especially to the Roman Catholic Church. Most of its bourgeois leaders were ethical humanists with varying degrees of social reformist commitment; a minority were militant freemasons who detested Roman Catholicism. Most were committed to struggle not merely with ecclesiastical authorities but against any orthodox religious belief as proffered by and represented by those authorities. In urging Ernst Mach in 1912 to join him in publicly declaring *konfessionslos* status, Ludo Hartmann insisted that "the Church is an enormous power in Austria and millions of people still doze in its mystical darkness gladly and thoughtlessly." Only a vigorous and powerful counterorganization could hinder its growth. Hartmann admitted that it was unlikely that the association would generate a mass exodus from the Church (*Massenaustritt*), but he felt compelled by "social responsibility" to take the act himself.[44]

Friedrich Jodl, a professor of philosophy at Vienna since 1896, articulated this need to promote a moral alternative to Catholicism in a talk sponsored by the *Freie Schule* in May 1909 on the fortieth anniversary of the Imperial School Law.[45] Jodl was an ethical positivist with a deep interest in the work of Hume and Feuerbach who devoted his life to public education and to a naturalistic, monistic anticlericalism.[46] In a 1893 essay on "Religion and Modern Science" in *The Monist* he had announced the absolute irreconcilability of, and the "profound intellectual abyss" between, religious and scientific modes of thought and ethics. The world of the later nineteenth century was marked by a collision of rival groups which "no longer understand each other, which no longer speak the same language, and which live in totally different worlds of thought and sentiment." Efforts by theological modernists to bridge the gap were logically and conceptually absurd. The notion of a God who conjoined and reconciled ethics and nature had been destroyed by modern science. All that remained for man was to take the stark division of nature and ethics as a given and to fall back upon the "spirit of humanity" in an effort to develop humanistic ethical systems appropriate to man's secular being.[47]

In 1909 Jodl was even more explicit about the legal consequences of these views. Although he applauded and defended the integrity of the Imperial School Law of 1869, Jodl noted that even this legislation reflected the conceptual and political limitations of the time. In its first paragraph it directed that all children were to receive a compulsory "moral-religious" instruction by representatives of the recognized state confessions, whether Christian or Jewish. Forty years later modern society had changed profoundly, and a new kind of education in secular morality was needed to complement, if not ultimately to replace, the formal religious instruction provided for by the early Liberals. Jodl argued that "we know today, and it belongs to the basis of our beliefs, that moral and religious education are two different things, oriented toward different goals, working with different means." He admitted that it might be politically impossible to revise the school law to eliminate the word "religious," but he suggested that the appropriate clause be reworded to read "moral and religious" instead of "moral-religious," emphasizing the epistemological and scientific difference between the two. Jodl despaired that no major political party in Austria was either interested in or capable of pursuing such a goal but recognized that educational associations like the *Freie Schule,* which might create the intellectual basis for a new party in defense of culture (*Kulturpartei*), must nonetheless work to liberalize Austrian culture.

Jodl's revisionism bespoke the high moral intent, combined with revolutionary cultural expectations, of the Viennese bourgeois intellectuals who followed the banner of the *Freie Schule.* But it also explained their isolation. For nowhere in his talk did Jodl concede the necessity of cultural reform as a prelude to economic egalitarianism *and* social transformation. His was a judicious but narrowly idealistic view that would ultimately be unable to defend itself against Austro-Marxist theory and practice. It also imputed to the wide range of enemies of his ideal "free school" an affinity with "clericalism," an accusation that was not only self-deluding but self-fulfilling as well. To the extent that the *Freie Schule* attacked the Christian Socials as a "clerical" party, they created the object of their imputation. For in fact Lueger and Gessmann had no desire to "clericalize" the schools in the manner assumed by men like Jodl. Religion for them was a necessary part of the traditional acculturation of young children who would become the *Vaterstadt's* adults in the future, and it was thus a necessary component of the curriculum, ensuring loyalty to the Dynasty and discipline for civil society. This functionalist view of religion may have been objectionable, but it was not necessarily "ultramontane" in the sense explicated by the *Freie Schule.* For Christian Social politicians the *Freie Schule* was a covert Social Democratic political organization with freemasonic and bourgeois ethical decoration. It was an electoral threat and a political insult, not a "moral idea" in Jodl's sense.

Not surprisingly the *Freie Schule* took the lead in resisting the new *Schul- und Unterrichtsordnung* issued by the government in September 1905, which prescribed compulsory attendance at church exercises as part of the moral-religious instruction of children required by Austrian law.[48] Since the Christian Socials took these provisions literally and issued fines against parents who refused to allow their children to attend religious services, the *Freie Schule* had yet another cause célèbre with which to roast the city administration.[49] The association provided legal assistance for parents seeking to remove their children from religious exercises, but, as Paul Speiser noted in 1908, the government steadfastly ignored such appeals. One parent whose children attended the

Freie Schule's school wrote plaintively to Karl Seitz in early 1909 urging that a rally be held to protest harassment by the municipal authorities and the hours parents had to spend being interviewed by petty civil servants at the School Board. Nothing suggested better the legal (and political) isolation in which these people found themselves and in which they were involving their children.[50]

The most notable accomplishment of the *Freie Schule* was, however, its experiments in school management and curricular design, based on its organization of private primary-school classes that used modern, indeed revolutionary pedagogical methods. In 1906 the *Freie Schule* opened model school classes by taking over two private educational institutes established in 1902 by Josef Enslein, a young socialist teacher who had attended the same orphanage as Karl Seitz and who graduated from the St. Pölten teacher training seminar a year after Seitz. Like his fellow *Jungen,* Enslein ran afoul of the Municipal School Board for his professional activities, including his service as the first editor of the *Freie Lehrerstimme.* He compounded his political isolation by repudiating his nominal membership in the Catholic Church and declaring himself *konfessionslos* in 1906, an act he took "not for the purposes of political propaganda but out of the deepest personal conviction."[51] Under Enslein's leadership the schools undertook several progressive innovations, including a limitation on class size to 16–20 students per room, freedom of movement in the classroom, and the teaching of developmental skills, all of which foreshadowed the innovations that Otto Glöckel would undertake on a more massive scale in interwar Vienna.[52] Although Josef Enslein was willing to offer religious instruction in his schools, he insisted that this not be "confessional" in nature, that Church authorities had no right to supervise or dictate what this instruction might be. The school's experimentation with special instruction in ethics and morality could easily be interpreted as a challenge to the formal program of Roman Catholic catechetical practice approved by the Archdiocese of Vienna.[53]

Inevitably, given his broader cultural goals, Enslein's anticlericalism ran up against the Christian Social-dominated Municipal School Board and the Lower Austrian Provincial School Council, which spent several years in legal battles trying to close the school. Finally, in February 1909, the city administration did precisely that, arguing that the association had employed teachers of religion not approved by the Archdiocesan authorities and had thereby violated both the 1868 law on religious instruction in the schools and the 1869 Imperial School Law (*Reichsvolksschulgesetz*).[54] An appeal to the Ministry of Education met with an equally unfavorable decision in August 1909. Although the association assembled persuasive interpretations of the relevant laws to argue that private schools should be held exempt from the certification requirements placed on public institutions,[55] the clauses in question permitted variant readings. In such cases political discretion inevitably played a major role, and the Christian Socials brought pressure to bear when Richard Weiskirchner entered Bienerth's second ministry in February 1909 for the government to settle the *Freie Schule* issue. Moreover, Bienerth's Minister of Education, Count Karl Stürgkh, was increasingly a *persona grata* in Christian Social circles as well as at the Belvedere.[56] The timing of the final administrative decision against the *Freie Schule,* released by the Ministry in August when most politicians were on vacation, suggested that it had not been drafted on the spur of the moment.

The *Freie Schule* appealed the Ministry's decision to the Administrative Court. On July 8, 1910, the Court delivered a Solomonic decision to the effect that Imperial school laws did not require the prior agreement of a given church or other religious body to offer religious instruction before a private school was actually opened. But once the school was opened and operating, the recognized religions had to have the opportunity to appoint religion teachers of their own choice, if they chose to do so. The Court was careful to argue that the state could not compel the Catholic Church (or any other religious group) to do this, just as the Church in turn had no right to screen the fitness of teachers in private schools who were responsible for other instructional areas or even to screen those teachers who, by default, would have to teach religion should the Church decide not to appoint its own catechist. But the director of the school was obliged to make certain that the Church had the opportunity to appoint its own religion instructor. Since Enslein and his *Freie Schule* had not given the Archdiocese of Vienna that option, the local school authorities were justified in closing down the school.[57]

Josef Enslein eventually decided to compromise in order to keep his schools open, and in September 1910 he notified the authorities of the number of Roman Catholic students enrolled.[58] The Archdiocese in turn assigned a catechist, Father Josef Wolny, who was a professor of religion at a local Viennese gymnasium, to provide religious instruction to the children.[59] From the first, Enslein gave Wolny virtually no cooperation, treating him as a pariah. In the spring of 1911, for example, Wolny had to file an official complaint with the Municipal School Board that Enslein was refusing to provide a room where the children could gather before proceeding to a local church for confession and communion and that Enslein also refused to provide supervision for the children during these devotional exercises.[60] One can imagine that the schoolchildren, the progeny of good, free-thinking parents, hardly had a higher or more sympathetic view of their new religion teacher than Enslein did.[61] Nor was Wolny's presence a boon for Enslein's enrollments, for Enslein insisted that one-third of the (nominally) Roman Catholic children enrolled in 1910 dropped out after Wolny began his catechetical labors.[62] The final straw came when Enslein refused to pay Wolny for his services, on the grounds that Wolny's presence had been imposed on Enslein's school and that he was thus under no legal obligation to compensate the priest. Wolny, in contrast, insisted that Enslein owed him over 600 crowns in unpaid salary.[63]

Did Father Wolny ever receive his money? Beginning in 1911 Josef Wolny ran the gamut of Imperial justice searching for someone to help him. With the help of the Archdiocese he went first to the Imperial school authorities, but they determined that they had no standing to assist him since "it is not in the area of competence of the Provincial School Council to decide whether and to what extent the owner of a private school is obliged to compensate someone who is charged with providing religious instruction at his school."[64] By defining the employment relationship between Wolny and Enslein as having a "private-legal" (*privatrechtlich*) status, the government essentially washed its hands of the claim. Wolny then turned to the civil courts, filing suit in the District Court of the Eighth District in Vienna (Josefstadt) to secure his wages. This court, however, refused to grant relief, arguing that no contract was involved (Enslein could not be regarded as Wolny's employer, since Wolny had been forced on Enslein) and that Enslein made no profit from Wolny's services.[65] Wolny then appealed his case to the Regional Court (*Landesgericht*) and the Supreme Court (*Oberster Gerichtshof*), both of which not only dismissed the case but also charged Wolny with court costs.

Finding himself caught in a backlash of negative decisions and owing Enslein several hundred crowns in court fees and his own attorney even more in legal fees, Wolny proceeded to the Administrative Court as a last resort. The Court's decision of June 6, 1914, is of interest in light of its previous arguments of July 8, 1910.[66] Now the Court admitted that Wolny only found himself teaching in the *Freie Schule* because in 1910 it had confirmed the public right of the Church to provide religious instruction in a private school. To that limited extent, Wolny's situation was embedded in a transaction involving public law. At the same time, the Court found that "the responsibility based in public law to make religious instruction possible cannot also include the duty to compensate such instruction, since one cannot argue that without such compensation religious instruction would not be provided." If current practice required that the state compensate catechists who taught in public schools—a stipulation provided by the law of June 17, 1888—this did not apply to private schools. Hence the Court found Wolny had no claim to his 660 crowns of salary. The Church might be able to impose itself on "private" society, but it could not make that society pay for it.

This minor and modest decision, delivered two months before the First World War enveloped the old Empire, was a sign of good times and bad. The laws that the Court enforced were laws created by the Liberal party of the 1860s and early 1870s. They defined church-state relations at a time when the kind of transaction that it now found before it—a militantly anti-socialist and anti-Semitic priest battling a militantly anticlerical, socialist pedagogue—

could hardly have been anticipated. Wolny's frustration is easily imaginable. He had been asked to perform instructional services to which the Catholic Church had a public claim and which, in political terms, it *had* to provide. In this sense Wolny was caught in the "public" of both law and politics. However, once on the premises of Enslein's school, he enjoyed no protection from "public law," but was at the mercy of Enslein's private generosity or lack thereof. Indeed, to work as a catechist in Josef Enslein's school amounted to acting as a domestic missionary, serving *pro bono* among "inhabitants" who did not want to know the true Faith and who would certainly not pay to hear about it.

The narrative of this petty conflict becomes more fascinating when one learns that Josef Wolny was also a Christian Social city councilman (representing Alsergrund) and a deputy in the Lower Austrian Diet, and that he was thus a functionary in the party that pushed through the 1904 Lower Austrian schools laws, thus provoking the *Freie Schule*'s crusade in the first place. Josef Wolny was not a simple parish priest but rather a living embodiment of that union of radical *bürgerlich* politics and politicized religion that the Christian Social party so exquisitely represented. Josef Enslein, in turn, was not simply an innovative teacher but also a member of the Social Democratic party since 1895 and the first editor of the socialist-oriented *Freie Lehrerstimme*. A longtime friend and compatriot of Karl Seitz, the interwar mayor of Vienna who was also a victim of Christian Social teacher persecution, Enslein became the president of the union of municipal employees under the Social Democratic regime of Red Vienna, as well as a member of the Municipal School Board. He too was a "public" person.

The leaders of the *Freie Schule* were delighted by Father Wolny's legal misfortunes in 1914, yet if looked at in a broader context, it was not Wolny who had lost. The Archdiocese made other arrangements to compensate him (Cardinal Piffl agreed to cover his court costs) and, after all, in 1917 he also received a much valued appointment as Canon (*Domherr*) of the Cathedral of St. Stephan.[67] Perhaps we may see that honor as a kind of belated battle pay. The fact that the Christian Social-run municipal administration of Vienna and of the province of Lower Austria had the political muscle and legal acumen to keep this small school on the ropes for so long—entangled in a continuous round of litigation from 1906 to 1914—and to impose a violently anti-socialist priest on its students, suggests that they too could play the Liberal school laws to great effect. The political transactions targeting the *Freie Schule* were part of a restructuring in cultural-political power relations in Austria that had taken place between 1869 and 1914. In 1869 the Church was left to its own devices to oppose the legal incursions of a new Liberal state which claimed to represent all of civil society. In 1914 the Church was sheltered by that same state, using those same laws. But it was not merely a "clericalized" civil service or the

Emperor that now stood ready to protect the Church. Rather, the Liberal political system had again shown itself capable of generating the instruments of its own destruction, in this case a radical *bürgerlich* movement that grabbed onto the institutions of regional and municipal self-governance created by the Liberals. The Church was thus protected (and exploited) both by a new mass party, which was the bastard offspring of the Liberal movement, *and* by a code of older Liberal laws that proved congenial and accessible to that party's political and administrative manipulation.

The Enslein-Wolny feud transpired in a small private elementary school and was undertaken by two men who detested each other. Yet their professional and personal lives represented not merely different conceptions of the good for society and different party programs to effect that good but also what Ignaz Seipel would later call incommensurable "worldviews."[68] Their mutual vindictiveness demonstrated the extent to which, by 1914, religion—as a moral code, as a culture of identity and discipline, and as a realm of clerical authority and sacral practice—had become both a target and a weapon in the gang wars of early twentieth-century mass politics.

The freethinker (*Freidenker*) mentality characteristic of the bourgeois proponents of the *Freie Schule* was replicated in other small circles in Vienna after 1900.[69] Josef Redlich was suspicious of their presumption and arrogance, noting in his diary that they were "un-Viennese" and that they represented no one other than the *Neue Freie Presse* and the Concordia (the Liberal journalist's guild in Vienna).[70] One of the most self-indulgent freethinkers was Ernst Victor Zenker, an itinerant journalist, amateur historian, self-taught sociologist, freemason, leader of the local marriage-law reform movement, and supporter of the *Freie Schule*. In 1907 Zenker ran for parliament in the Landstrasse on the program of a "Radical Party," one of whose central tenets was "that we condemn all attempts to encourage outdated and anti-social privileges by regenerating the medieval autonomy of the provinces. We oppose the autonomy of the Crownlands with a program of autonomy of peoples and modern self-government."[71] Given such views, it is not difficult to imagine how the Rathaus could "read" a political agenda into the agitation of the "*Freie Schule.*"

Although he was defeated in 1907, the next round of elections brought Zenker more success. With massive Social Democratic electoral support he managed to defeat Heinrich Schmid, the Christian Social candidate in the Wieden in 1911, for a seat in parliament, running on the platform of what he now styled as the "Independent Economic Party."[72] His social theories were, however, anything but sympathetic to orthodox Marxism. In addition to topical books on Austrian Church-State relations and the history of Viennese journalism, Zenker wrote long, rambling analyses of modern social relations and ethics.[73] He was especially influenced by the work of Ludwig Gumplowicz and

Gustav Ratzenhofer, and he owed to them his combination of deterministic social mechanics and anticlerical ethical positivism.[74] Inevitably his attempts to reconcile (or override) class conflict by the assumption of transsocial ethical unities gave rise to logical problems in his work, as more orthodox German socialist commentators were quick to point out.[75] Zenker posited a society of humanity moving slowly toward ethical rationality and cultural integration, leaving behind the trail of ignorance, religious superstition, and mental torture sponsored by the Church. Yet his society was marked not so much by class conflict as by the natural contestations between the "masses," whose behavior was emotional, unreflective, and controlled by natural forces, and a select number of independent ethical personalities, who from birth had the talent and energy to assist the masses to move toward a higher order of reason. Although he denied that he was a Nietzschean, Zenker set forth a moral hierarchy of the rational few against the emotional many that must have made the Austro-Marxists exceedingly uncomfortable.[76]

Zenker confidently believed that the small groups of freethinkers, Ethical Society agitators, and Freemasons in Vienna were the vanguard of a final epoch of social integration and social reason.[77] He was vague on how this insinuation of a higher, rational ethics into the emotionally active masses would occur. Perhaps it was not surprising that at the end of his life in the 1930s he could view Hitler and the German National Socialists with respect, not merely because of their anti-Semitism (Zenker later insisted that he too had harbored anti-Semitic attitudes, even within the Viennese Freemason movement) but also because of their ability to impress hegemonic cultural unity on German society against "reactionary" cultural pluralities like the churches. Zenker's attempt to reconcile anti-clericalism, anti-Semitism, and moral action was merely one feature of the peculiar balance of forces obtaining among "progressive" Liberals in fin-de-siècle Vienna.[78]

The reaction of the majority of the German bourgeois politicians to Zenker's fanaticism ranged from indifference to suspicion. When after his election to parliament in 1911 he tried to join the *Deutscher Nationalverband,* his petition was rejected, in part because of the pressure of the Christian Socials.[79] But Zenker's status as an outsider was not merely owing to his ferocious anticlericalism, which, since it read the Christian Social party out of the legitimate spectrum of national parties, ran against the larger state-political interests of the Austrian Germans. Zenker's studious dismissal of a pragmatic, interest-based approach to politics also played a role. The first attribute—greater sensitivity to culture than to nation—was shared by all Viennese politicians. But Zenker's belief that politics existed to train a society in morality, not to respond to particularistic needs, ran against the practical necessities of modern parliamentary life. The result was double isolation. Zenker could speak neither to German issues nor to issues of power and material interest. He was neither a legislator nor a politician but an ethical dilettante, thrust into politics with borrowed votes and living there on borrowed time.

Zenker's own emphasis on culture as opposed to nation or class as the defining variable of progress made it easy for him to project transnational schemes of ethnic conciliation. In October 1912, for example, he spoke in parliament proposing *Reichsunmittelbar* status for the great port cities in the south, an idea which the South Slav and Czech delegates viewed with enthusiasm.[80] He reported with considerable pride to Robert Seton-Watson in March 1913 that his espousal of trialistic schemes had led him to be viewed as a "traitor to the German cause." He also admitted that he and his radical progressive colleagues from Vienna were so estranged from the mainstream of German bourgeois politics that they were "a small world unto ourselves."[81]

The general reaction of the major German political factions to the *Freie Schule* paralleled their reception of Zenker. Ludo Hartmann complained bitterly to Jodl in 1905 that many bourgeois politicians and intellectuals were either indifferent to the *Freie Schule* or they were fearful of retribution and hence refused to support the association.[82] In 1906 Paul Hock wrote to Gustav Marchet urging that the German progressives sign a statement of public support for the *Freie Schule*. Like Hartmann, Hock admitted to Gustav Marchet that he encountered "little inclination to go public." This made it all the more necessary that the *Verein* find a strong leader to direct the vast "army" of anticlericals in Austrian society. If only one strong man would emerge, the fortunes of the movement would be assured.[83] Marchet passed the letter to his party's executive committee, which decided not to sign the statement. Their reaction reflected in part their sensitivity to Court circles, but Marchet also shared Redlich's reaction about the futility of such posing. To Moritz Benedikt, Redlich argued in 1912 that only years of strong economic development would restore to Liberalism a functional role in Austrian politics; he had no sympathy for anticlerical politics "à la Hock."[84] Hock himself complained in 1906 that the association faced serious problems of credibility with the Viennese middle classes, encountering "a lack of participation, a narrow-minded indifference, and a lack of interest from the broad, influential sections and the prosperous circles of the bourgeoisie."[85] By 1908 Hock was plaintively calling for "a little more courage" on the part of his German political friends.[86]

Outside of Vienna the association faced similar problems, especially in areas where nationalist associations like the *Südmark* already commanded the loyalty, time, and money of *bürgerlich* voters. As one unlucky *Freie Schule* agitator in Mödling reported to Karl Seitz in 1908, most of the bourgeois voters were already preoccupied with existing *völkisch* or anti-Semitic associations ("the *Freie Schule* can expect nothing from the local bourgeoisie") and the local workers already had "enough associations and therefore enough to pay." The only promising constituency seemed to be some local students ("with some effort I am able to keep a few students interested in the local group").[87] Hock's army was more fictive than real.

The reaction of many German *bürgerlich* politicians to the *Freie Schule* reflected their suspicions about a movement that seemed to include not merely German but also Czech freethinkers. Unlike the earlier *Los von Rom* movement, which was soon recognized as a negative vehicle of pan-German extremism, the perception was widespread in Austrian government circles that the freethinkers were a more ambitious and more nationally complex lot, given the range of their anticlerical and antimilitaristic agenda and the fact that Czech freethinkers used anticlericalism to intensify rather than to temper national identity. In the summer of 1907 the Cabinet faced the dilemma of whether to prohibit an international *Freidenker* congress from meeting in Prague (Ernst Victor Zenker and Julius Ofner attended from Vienna).[88] After balancing his options Beck decided not to prohibit the affair, although he instructed the Bohemian *Statthalter* to try to isolate it. Still, the acting mayor of Prague demonstrated a shrewdly ambivalent attitude towards the congress, and the city of Prague granted the organizers a subvention of 1,000 crowns for a banquet.[89] A report on the meeting's aftermath noted that the freethinkers were making inroads into the Czech middle classes (particularly among the teachers), a signal to Vienna that the movement provided yet another cultural cover for national dissidence.[90] Beck was sufficiently worried about the effects of the movement in the Czech lands to ask his Minister of Internal Affairs, Bienerth, in April 1908 to explore ways to limit subsequent manifestations.[91]

Once the First World War commenced, the *Freie Schule* suffered from the same problems of declining membership and income as most other voluntary organizations. When the *Verein* held its annual business meeting in March 1916, its financial condition was problematic. Paul Speiser reported that the group had lost tens of thousands of members in recent years and that it had spent 30,000 crowns to print brochures attacking the Eucharistic Congress in 1912. Most telling, however, were the arguments of the plenary speaker, Otto Glöckel.[92] Glöckel discussed the future of the *Freie Schule*'s postwar programs. From his comments it was clear how far the *Verein* had moved toward integration into the Social Democratic party by 1916. Unlike the controlling discourse of the *Freie Schule* in 1905–9, which still valued the Imperial School Law as the epitome of Liberal virtue, Glöckel now pronounced the 1869 school law "in ruins." An originally progressive law had become so compromised by clerical influences that it was useless and needed to be replaced by modern socialist school policies. Rather than modify the clause "moral-religious," as Jodl had proposed in 1909, Glöckel now demanded as part of the "new program" that the clause be dropped completely and that a "complete separation of the activity of the school and that of the Church" be enacted. In addition, education at all levels was to be free ("education shall not be the privilege of the wealthy") and a common, integrated middle school (*Einheitsschule*) for children aged ten to fourteen would become the norm, replacing the division of children between mediocre public schools and more exclusive *Gymnasien* and *Realschulen*. Education would be compulsory until the age of eighteen, and the system of teacher education would be radically transformed. Finally, the "Geist" of the schools would be revolutionized, treating children not as "objects" of learning but as creative participants in whom the love of learning must be instilled. Glöckel was confident that the war itself would force changes in Austrian education, given the shortcomings of noncommissioned officers in the army and the cultural "Tiefstand" of peasants with six years of crude education, who knew how to charge exorbitant prices but who were too stupid to produce reasonable crop levels. Like the French Radicals of the 1870s, Glöckel used the crisis of war to legitimate a new era of public education.

Glöckel, whose views were seconded by Ludo Hartmann in a second assembly of the *Freie Schule* in March 1916, had presented the core of the school program which he was later to implement in Red Vienna.[93] The *Freie Schule* had moved beyond the ethical idealism of men like Jodl and Hock to view the schools as the motor for the social and economic transformation of a class-based society. What the intrinsic success (and value) of *that* program could not disguise, however, was that as an instrument of liberal bourgeois *Kulturkampf* the *Freie Schule* was an abysmal failure. In his autobiography twenty years later Zenker bitterly accused the German bourgeois groups of having handed the *Freie Schule* over to the Social Democrats, who "exploited it demagogically and turned it into a branch of their own party."[94] Zenker claimed that his hope to gather "all the forces opposing clericalism into one large organization . . . collapsed before the eccentricities of the persons and groups involved, because of the jealousy of petty leaders . . . and because of the secret evasions of the parties." But this explanation evades the issue of the intellectual substance and cultural appropriateness of the freethinkers' creed. Josef Redlich came closer to the mark when he insisted to Hermann Bahr in 1918 that Ludo Hartmann, whom he thought a "fanatic and a political antipode," represented a fusion of Prussian-Protestant *freisinnig* ideals and an adoration of the "ideas of 1789." Inherent in Zenker's and Hartmann's critiques of late Imperial Austrian society was a peculiar blend of German national liberalism and French Radicalism.[95] Both represented essentially individualistic and meta-idealistic paradigms at a time when political collectivism with mass social-interest agendas had assumed a guiding role in shaping Austrian civic culture. "Individualism" could survive only under the patronage of an anti-Semitic *bürgerlich* movement that took every opportunity to insult the French revolutionary tradition. "Liberty," in turn, could be sustained only through the patronage of a second collectivist movement that demanded, as Otto Bauer was later to insist, the material self-emasculation of the bourgeoisie as the price of cohabiting a world of anticlerical honor and grace.

The Wahrmund Affair

The *Freie Schule* represented both a last gasp of Liberal anticlericalism and a first expression of socialist pedagogy in Vienna, targeted on the public school system. If Karl Lueger initiated the process of Liberalism's decomposition from without by undercutting the political alliances and patronage systems on which Viennese Liberals had so comfortably depended, Paul von Hock and Ernst Victor Zenker finished it from within. In 1921 the whole project of the *Freie Schule* was subsumed organizationally and financially into the Austrian Social Democratic party.[96] This melding of bourgeois and socialist anticlericalism between 1905 and 1918, although not without a certain charm, did mark a new stage in Austrian political history. The terms and the timing of this transformation of generational and ideological politics were illustrated by a second and far more influential Austrian political scandal involving both the Christian Socials and the Social Democrats, the Wahrmund Affair. For the Christian Socials and the Beck Cabinet the Wahrmund Affair was both destabilizing and destructive; for the Social Democrats it helped to define the choices and options to be considered in constructing a socialist-sponsored *Kulturkampf*. Like most good Austrian scandals, it began with a pathetic anti-hero unworthy of the passions he generated.

On November 16, 1907, Karl Lueger delivered one of the most controversial speeches of his career at the Sixth Austrian Catholic Congress in Vienna. Violence by pan-German student groups had occurred at several Austrian universities earlier in the year, most notably at the University of Graz in late October where the promotion ceremony of a Catholic theologian, Johannes Ude, was blocked by violent protests on the part of German national students.[97] A chain reaction ensued in which local Styrian Christian Socials appealed to Lueger for support, with the result that on October 24 Lueger led a protest delegation of Christian Social Styrian parliamentary deputies to visit Minister-President Beck.[98] In mid-November violent clashes between German national and Italian students shook Graz and Vienna, with the result that both universities had to be closed on November 13. Appearing at the opening of the Catholic Congress on the evening of the 16th Lueger went public with his complaints about the student disorders. Bragging that the public school system in Vienna had ceased to be a scene of conflict, he asserted that what was now needed was the "conquest of the university for the Christian people." Although Lueger also complained about the appointment of too many Jews to the faculty of the University of Vienna, the tone and substance of the Congress speech could be seen as advocating the infusion of Catholic religious values in the university system much more than as expressing Lueger's homespun, rhetorical anti-Semitism.[99] The opposition had come to expect the latter, but the former seemed both novel and more ominous, given the new presence of the Christian Socials in the Beck ministry. And Lueger's remarks took on a special significance because of his explicit reference to the successful politicization of the Lower Austrian and Viennese public school systems between 1897 and 1905. Having seized control of the public schools, did the Christian Socials now intend to grab the universities as well?

The object of Lueger's incursions was especially sensitive, given the status of the universities as the epitome of Liberal hope in Austria. The universities in German-speaking Austria before 1914 were one of the last bastions of a civil, "non-statist" Austrian Liberalism. They were, if only in the most idealistic terms, the closest institutional embodiment of forms of liberal values which in western European lands had been diffused far more thoroughly throughout civil society. As corporations the universities claimed to represent neutral and liberal science (*Wissenschaft*) in a political culture suffused with national antagonisms among conflicting and privileged elites of educated (*Gebildeten*). They were staffed with professors and subordinate faculty most of whom (national differences aside) found themselves in ideological perplexity over their inherited status as "liberals" and their need to organize themselves against both statist and partisan political manipulation. It was hardly surprising that some of the most aggressive proponents behind the organization of the German congress of university teachers (*Hochschullehrertag*) in Salzburg in September 1907 were Austrian academics led by Ludo M. Hartmann, who thought that this organization would preserve the "independence of the universities" against both bureaucratic meddling by state authorities and clerical pressures from the Church.[100] Nor can the striking odyssey of a young historian like Heinrich von Srbik after the revolutionary events of 1918–19 be appreciated without a sense that the comfortable setting in which science could be pursued was now endangered by alien forces heretofore excluded from the academy.[101]

At the same time the universities were plagued by rival student factions that were destined—however mutually divergent they were—to repudiate the Liberal heritage of 1867. Universities like Vienna, Graz, and Innsbruck were dominated by pan-German student groups who were among the most illiberal and politically immature in Central Europe. But after 1900 the same universities also saw the growth of Catholic, socialist, and Zionist student associations claiming social as well as academic recognition.[102] The fractured image of the University of Vienna in 1907—an artifact of a (now) bygone age of political Liberalism whose students advocated post-liberal forms of cultural and political reproduction—paralleled the imbalance between past and future that marked the debates in parliament over universal suffrage.[103] As John Haag has recently pointed out, Karl Lueger afforded protection to Catholic student groups at Vienna, just as Victor Adler encouraged young socialist academics.[104] Why permit German nationalist students to monopolize political discourse at the universities? Why allow "liberal" professors to coexist disingenuously (if silently) with one kind of radical politics while they arbitrarily condemned other kinds?[105] Lueger's linguistic taste may have been poor, but his logic was incontrovertible, and Christian Social pressure on the universities cannot be separated from other trends in both Germany and Austria to subject the universities to the normative constraints of contemporary civil society.[106] Unlike their colleagues in the Prussian universities, many Austrian academics seemed to long for a strong Althoff-type regime that would protect them from the vicissitudes of mass political partisanship, an ironic role-reversal of the preceding generation's professional pride and moral certainty in the 1860s and 1870s.[107] Other academics sought safety in schemes of professional self-defense.[108] Both demonstrated the public marginality of university academics in a civic culture supercharged with national and cultural partisanship. Any suggestion that they could be "conquered" by the "clericals" simply exposed the isolation of the professorial elite. This sense of shame and fear, as much as Lueger's vulgarities, exploded into controversy.

Lueger's motives in making the speech were unclear. Heinrich von Tucher, the astute Bavarian legate in Vienna, thought that either Lueger was suffering the long-term effects of his illness and could no longer be relied on to exercise good judgment, or that the spoiler in Lueger's personality had come to the fore and that he could not resist causing his newly "ministerial" colleagues Gessmann and Ebenhoch embarrassment. That less than two weeks later, at an assembly honoring the fiftieth anniversary of the death of Field Marshall Radetzky, Lueger delivered an equally embarrassing speech attacking Italian irredentist elements who were allegedly bent on the Monarchy's destruction— a speech so provocative that the Ballhausplatz had to issue a public disavowal—lends credence to Tucher's argument.[109] Lueger's predictability and tactical judgment may well have decreased as his illness progressed, but he also may have wanted to reassert his authority by claiming yet another major cultural institution for his new "state" party.[110] If the affirmation of his party's power was Lueger's purpose, the timing of his speech—less than two weeks after the party had joined the Cabinet—could not have been worse.

German national leaders like Otto Steinwender and Julius Sylvester warned that the working parliamentary coalition among the German *bürgerlich* parties that Gessmann and Liechtenstein wanted would be impossible if the Christian Socials opened new ideological wounds.[111] H. Wickham Steed, no more sympathetic to the (as he saw it) "Jewish" press of Vienna than to the "clerical" Lueger, speculated that Lueger's political lieutenants like Gessmann "would sorrowfully but truthfully declare that the Burgomeister's own 'tongue of flame' often blazes forth in a manner embarrassing if not dangerous to his party."[112] The Social Democrats even accused the Christian Social parliamentary club of issuing an official interpretation of Lueger's speech that downplayed any "clerical" implications.[113]

Outraged university professors at the University of Vienna summoned a protest meeting against Lueger, denouncing the threat to their academic freedom and urging vigilance by the state against a possible attack on the universities by the Christian Socials. Friedrich Jodl gave the principal address, lambasting Lueger for wanting to become an Austrian Althoff, a general inspector of the Austrian universities, but without Althoff's enlightenment.[114] These tirades were mounted in spite of the fact that, as Karl von Amira, a prominent Liberal jurist in Munich, admitted to Lujo Brentano, Lueger's speech "contained a great deal that was true" and even though concerted action against Lueger could only undermine the status of Gustav Marchet as the Minister of Education.[115] The Liberal press in Vienna, many of whose editors hated the collaboration between the Christian Social party and the German nationals, exploited Lueger's ill-tempered remarks with enormous satisfaction. The stage was set, therefore, for fireworks that might seriously impair the work of Beck's Cabinet.

On November 22, 1907, Thomas Masaryk brought in a motion of urgency before parliament, demanding that the Cabinet offer guarantees that the Christian Socials would not be allowed to conquer the universities.[116] The motion was signed by twenty-five members, most of them associated with small factions like the Viennese democrats, the Ruthenians, the Zionists, and the Czech national socialists. Neither the Social Democrats (who brought in a harsher motion a few days later) nor any of the German national leadership signed the motion. Parliament debated the motion for three days in early December, and the Christian Socials cleverly defused the issue by voting with the majority of the House to approve discussion of the Masaryk motion and then moving to amend a critical section to eliminate any reference to the Christian Socials. The final version crafted by Karl Drexel simply enjoined the government to protect the academic freedom of the universities against any threats, from whatever political quarter they might emerge. The government parties then obtained unanimous approval of this draft. Masaryk felt upstaged and outmaneuvered.[117]

The parliamentary debates on the Masaryk motion presented a full range of Liberal opinions on freedom of learning and on the alleged incompatibility of Catholicism and modern research. Most strident was Masaryk himself, who argued that Lueger intended a moral and intellectual Catholicization of the university system and not merely its political subjection to the Christian Social party.[118] For Masaryk, culture was as important an object of public policy as social or economic affairs, and the Christian Socials were a threat to modern culture. Cultural problems involving religion were and should be beyond ethnic particularity, for these were issues that should unite freethinking men of all nationalities. The vote on his motion would establish whether "the majority [of the Austrian parliament] is proclerical or anticlerical." Masaryk dreamed of a new Comtean age of scientific, humanistic religion. He was, as he properly argued, not an atheist and not an enemy of religion. Rather he wanted a new age of progressive, modern religious values that would sweep society clear of the tangled webs of superstition and Catholic medievalism.[119]

As a government based on a complex and delicately designed program of interest accommodation, the last thing the Cabinet needed was a recorded vote on who was or was not "clerical" in the *Abgeordnetenhaus*. Aside from the obvious political tussles that would result, the terms of the dichotomy must have seemed naive in the context of the subtle interactions and negotiations that were the staple fare of the Josephist administrators in the Ministry of Education, for whom collisions between church and state were neither desirable nor necessary.[120] Gustav Marchet replied for the Cabinet that guarantees of freedom of teaching and research were built into the Austrian constitutional laws of 1867 and that Masaryk's motion was thus superfluous.[121] Marchet was technically correct but beside the point, since Masaryk's intervention was designed for its political force, not its constitutional logic. Josef Redlich entered the debate with an eloquent elucidation of the many difficulties which Jews encountered in obtaining senior posts in Austrian higher education. Admitting that the current cultural atmosphere in Austria was starkly different from the "materialist" ethos of the 1880s, Redlich suggested that a collision with the new, more absolutist and idealistically oriented systems of thought was perhaps inevitable. All that could be hoped for was tolerance and pragmatism on both sides.[122]

The Christian Social position was defended by two articulate Alpinists: Michael Mayr, a Catholic university professor from Innsbruck, and Karl Drexel, a young clerical secondary-schoolteacher from Vorarlberg.[123] Their new prominence in the party as spokesmen for cultural affairs suggested one of the long-range effects of the union of the Viennese Christian Socials with the Alpine Catholic parties. On matters of culture these more conservative westerners could inevitably expect some measure of support from their more secular Viennese brethren, who in cases such as the Masaryk motion were probably just as happy *not* to have to rise to defend positions with which they felt only the vaguest sympathy.[124] Mayr and Drexel argued that Catholics wanted equality and equitable treatment in the management of the universities and an end to the system of intellectual and social nepotism that locked up appointments and promotions against known Catholic applicants.[125] The only other Christian Social to speak was Karl Lueger himself, who claimed that his motives for attacking the universities were political—defending Catholic aspirants against

Jewish-Liberal cliques—and had nothing to do with infusing them with clerical values or attacking their independence.[126] The contrast between Mayr and Drexel on the one side and Lueger on the other was striking, a younger generation of energetic conviction and "principles" arrayed against an older one of custom and pragmatism. But in this round both shared a common objective, namely, that the controversy should be settled as quickly as possible.

With the compromise resolution the Masaryk-Lueger affair seemed to be over, and the parliament resumed its work on the *Ausgleich* with Hungary (which passed in a final reading on December 17). Masaryk's injection of anticlerical *Kultur* into Austrian parliamentary politics was short-lived. But both Mayr and Drexel had mentioned in passing the name of Professor Ludwig Wahrmund as an example of an academic who held up Catholicism as an object of indifference and even outright contempt. Lueger's Congress speech soon paled into insignificance against the furor generated by Ludwig Wahrmund, who became the test case for the survivability of Gessmann's strategy of religious accommodation among the divergent factions of the Austrian Cabinet.

Wahrmund was a scholar of canon law and ecclesiastical history who had served since 1896 as a member of the Faculty of Law in the University of Innsbruck, an appointment he obtained with the support of Catholic ecclesiastical and political leaders like Bishop Simon Aichner and Theodor Kathrein in Tyrol.[127] The Tyroleans soon had cause to regret their patronage, for Wahrmund was anything but conventional in his theological opinions. Although these were unsystematic and often frustratingly vague—Wahrmund was more adept at polemic than theological precision—he adopted liberal Protestant views of ecclesiology and Christology after 1900, influenced by his admiration for Kant, Schleiermacher, and Harnack. He came to believe that religion was a matter of subjective feelings based on cultural and ontological inadequacy. To be religious meant to long for a state of unattainable perfection and security. In this sense religion might properly be called an "illusion," although one justified by man's moral being. Religion required and admitted little in the way of formal institutional doctrine and discipline. Hence Roman Catholicism, especially in its present "subjection" to an ignorant papacy, was a profound distortion of a collective existential illusion. It played upon the weak by offering them a false sense of security through fantasies of moral and theological objectivity.[128] Wahrmund presented these assertions in cantankerous literary forms which the British diplomat in Vienna, Duncan Gregory, aptly characterized as "offensive in every respect, even to the un-denominational forms of Christianity" and as "an inferior production by a man of inferior ability."[129]

A querulous person with a self-righteous vision of a new, revisionist theology, Wahrmund found himself increasingly at odds with the Church whose law he was hired to teach. His intellectual tirades represented the most sensitive of all academic freedom cases: a self-indulgent academic who attacked the public

corporation which had provided him with his initial moral and scholarly legitimacy. Professionally, as a tenured university professor, Wahrmund was an employee not of the Catholic Church but of the state. Under any reasonable reading of the Austrian constitution his freedom to teach or write anything he
wished seemed self-evident. Had not the government said as much in its response to Lueger's flippant remarks? But Wahrmund's case was difficult to
adjudge precisely because it raised with painful clarity a characteristic dilemma for Austrian church-state relations at the beginning of the twentieth
century: how far would the state extend the mantle of academic freedom into
the heartland of theological scholarship? Did academic freedom guarantee not
only freedom of research on theological subjects but the freedom to use that
scholarship to attack the Church as a political institution in the media and at
political rallies?[130] Would the state allow one set of opinion makers—the
Christian Socials—to exploit religion politically, while denying to others the
right to attack religion in the political marketplace? Could one use the "cover"
of scholarship to make statements which, under any other circumstances,
might be seen as a violation of Section 303 of the Austrian criminal code
(which protected "recognized religions" from slander)? Where was the boundary between scholarly research and political polemic, and how would the state
set and enforce that line? For Thomas Masaryk, as a professor of philosophy
in the philosophical faculty of the University of Prague, to utter scandalous
remarks about the Church might be unexceptional (especially when he did so
under official immunity as a member of parliament). For a "Catholic" professor of canon law, responsible for the professional education of future jurists
and clerics, to make similar statements in the local Innsbruck branch of the
Verein "Freie Schule" was, from the point of view of many Catholics, something quite different.

As early as 1902 Wahrmund had clashed with a local Tyrolean political
leader, Georg Jehly, characterizing Jehly's deeply conservative cultural values
as the products of "intellectual impoverishment and blind fanaticism."[131] His
initial foray into political scandal merited Wahrmund a rebuke by Koerber's
Minister of Education, Wilhelm von Hartel, in parliament in March 1902.[132]
Wahrmund's scholarship on ecclesiastical marriage legislation, which ultimately led him to believe in the dissolubility of the marriage contract and the
morality of divorce, and his dismay over the anti-modernist crusade of Pius X,
particularly the Syllabus of July 1907 and the encyclical Pascendi condemning
modernism in September 1907, led Wahrmund back into the fray. In late 1906
he accepted the chairmanship of the newly founded Innsbruck branch of the
Verein "Freie Schule," speaking at its dedication about the backwardness of
current theology in Rome.[133] Michael Mayr's unflattering discussion of him in
the Lueger debate in late 1907 further outraged Wahrmund. He sent Mayr a
public letter in early December in which, among other niceties, he called Cath-

olic students at the University of Innsbruck "moles and parasites."[134] Matters came to a head when Wahrmund delivered his famous lecture on *Katholische Weltanschauung und freie Wissenschaft* at a session sponsored by the *Freie Schule* in Innsbruck on January 18, 1908.[135] This talk, parts of which were later suppressed by the Austrian courts as slanderous against Catholicism, was a rage-filled condemnation of the papacy and its recent theological pronouncements.

News of the speech immediately polarized Austrian politics. Catholic Conservatives in Tyrol, eager to embarrass their Christian Social rivals in the provincial government, demanded that the government discipline Wahrmund by removing him from his professorship. This, together with their own distaste for Wahrmund, made it inevitable that the Christian Social Alpinists would put pressure on the Viennese leadership of the party. Initially Beck and Marchet hesitated to intervene publicly, hoping that the storm would blow over, even though Beck himself realized that it was in the interest of Tyrolean conservatives not to let the matter subside.[136] As Minister of Education Marchet felt particularly compromised, since he was the representative of the German progressives in the Cabinet. His later handling of the affair was marked by a paralyzing sensitivity to the scandal's conflation of academic freedom and political reality.[137] That the affair did not subside was owing to the ability of minority interests to force the major German political blocs both in and out of the Cabinet to react to their extremist tactics. Counterposed to hysterical cries for Wahrmund's dismissal coming from Tyrolean peasant and student groups were proclamations by the anticlerical Liberal press in Vienna depicting Wahrmund as a glorious crusader for freedom of speech.

The Cabinet thus found itself caught in a crossfire in which, as Masaryk was later to complain, the reaction of all serious politicians was to run for cover. Initial reaction by Austro-German parliamentary deputies was cool to Wahrmund, as a statement by Karl Chiari in mid-March in *Die Zeit* demonstrated.[138] Encouraged by the press to act in place of their "cowardly" political representatives, pan-German and other "liberal" student groups at the universities became the motive force behind the controversy, showing once again their ability to combine political immaturity with generational negativism. Some cynics, like the German Ambassador Tschirschky, blamed the longevity of the affair on the perversity of the *Neue Freie Presse*'s hope to disrupt the "German block" of Christian Socials and German nationals.[139] As a guild the university professors again found themselves targets of abuse, and, posturing about academic freedom aside, many felt that Wahrmund was expendable. Writing to Lujo Brentano in late March 1908, Karl von Amira reported that he had encountered a lack of sympathy for Wahrmund among many academics in Munich, with some arguing that the professor had transgressed the permissible bounds of discretion and decorum.[140]

By mid-March 1908 Beck and Marchet faced protest rallies in Tyrol and counterdemonstrations in Vienna and Graz. But before they could agree on a plan of action, another scandal rocked the city. The Papal Nuncio, Granito di Belmonte, gave an interview to an editor of *Vaterland* on March 17 in which he revealed that he had visited Foreign Minister Aehrenthal on March 3 and demanded Wahrmund's expulsion from the law faculty at Innsbruck. Aehrenthal in turn sent a private note to Marchet, bringing the Nuncio's intervention to his attention but arguing that since Belmonte had acted privately without authorization from Rome, the government had no cause to make an official response.[141] Belmonte rejected this gloss, insisting in a second interview in *Vaterland* that his was an official representation to which he expected an answer. His intervention was fuel for the fires of anti-ultramontanist paranoia— was this not solid evidence of papal meddling in Austrian affairs? Even the Christian Socials quickly disavowed the tactless behavior of the Nuncio.[142] The Austrian Foreign Ministry's request that Belmonte be recalled to Rome met a stiff rejection by the Vatican, producing a diplomatic standoff that was not resolved until 1911.

Beck now strove for a compromise solution to end the affair before it could disrupt the approaching session of parliament (which was to open on April 2). Beck hoped that this session would bring him the third star in his political triple crown—not only the *Ausgleich* and universal suffrage, but also the first general budget debated and passed by a popularly elected parliament in Austria. Since approval of Gessmann's new Ministry of Public Works was an early item on the House's agenda, the Viennese Christian Socials had no interest in seeing the affair endure. Only the extreme pressure felt in the Rathaus from the Tyrolean delegation forced the party into a confrontational stance. In late March 1908 Marchet offered the Christian Socials the establishment of a second chair in canon law at Innsbruck, to be filled by a known Catholic partisan, in return for their acquiescence to Wahrmund's staying on in Tyrol.[143]

In the meantime Wahrmund had left Austria on a two-month vacation, giving the Cabinet the fleeting hope that the danger had been contained. Popular resentment in Tyrol continued unabated, however, and in the face of pressure from the Crown and from Tyrolean political leaders Gustav Marchet engineered a decision by the Innsbruck faculty to suspend the lectures which Wahrmund was scheduled to give during the summer semester.[144] This proved to be a decisive mistake—too little to intimidate Wahrmund, but enough to outrage his supporters. Student protests erupted at Innsbruck, Vienna, and Graz; and a further compromise proposed by the rector of the University of Innsbruck, Rudolf von Scala, that would permit Wahrmund to lecture on subjects other than canon law fell flat. On May 16, 1908, a band of 200 peasants led by the Styrian Christian Social leader Franz Hagenhofer tried to battle their way into a promotion ceremony for a Catholic student, Michael Aldrian, at the University of Graz to which pan-German students refused them access.[145]

At this point (mid-May) the Christian Social leadership felt itself losing control over the situation. Weiskirchner had reported to Lueger in late February that he and others had been able to persuade the Alpinists not to raise the issue of a Catholic legal faculty in Salzburg, which at present would only cause the party "difficulties."[146] But slowly pressure mounted among the more clerical-minded Alpinists for decisive action against Wahrmund, or, failing that, against Gustav Marchet, whom they condemned for his passivity. In early April Baron Morsey wrote to Beck, reporting that he was under irresistible pressure from his constituents in Styria to "choose between us and the Freemason Marchet."[147] Finally, in mid-May Morsey went public, publishing a diatribe in the *Reichspost* against Marchet which argued that Beck had been mistaken in appointing a weak, indecisive academic to the critical post of Minister of Education and that the post should now go to a more "objective and forceful" administrator (which might have led to the withdrawal of the Germans from the Cabinet).[148] Morsey insisted that his party had great respect for Beck but that the affair had now become so serious as to call into question the existence of the Cabinet. Such imputations signalled potential discord within the Christian Social elite and demonstrated why many Viennese politicians were so suspicious of ideologues like Morsey.

To save both the unity of the party and the Cabinet itself, Gessmann and Lueger now put pressure on Beck for a realistic settlement. On May 20 the *Reichspost* published a communication of the parliamentary delegation that demanded that the government apologize for the insulting statements made by the rectors of the universities of Vienna and Graz against Catholic student and peasant groups and threatened that the party would vote against the budget line of the Ministry of Education unless satisfaction was given to the peasants and order was restored immediately.[149] That the relatively measured tone of this announcement left the more extremist Alpine Catholics disappointed was implied by a commentary that the *Reichspost* published next to it. This second statement argued that the party communication actually meant that the Christian Socials now wanted Marchet's resignation and his replacement by a neutral official (Max von Hussarek) in the Ministry of Education. Although this was not the official position of the Rathaus, it brought the Christian Socials perilously close to a public break with the German national leadership. Tschirschky might argue that this would be disastrous for the German cause in Austria, but it was a project to which Archduke Franz Ferdinand had committed his not inconsiderable resources.[150]

The demarche worked: later in the day on May 20 Beck gave the Christian Social leadership a firm assurance that Wahrmund would not lecture in Innsbruck during the summer. Further student disruptions, including a nationwide strike of the universities beginning on June 3, then led Beck to construct what became the final settlement, which Marchet and Beck bullied Wahrmund into accepting and which Beck then presented to Lueger, Gessmann, and Weis-kirchner on June 16.[151] Wahrmund would be transferred to a professorship at the German university in Prague beginning in the fall semester, with generous financial inducements involving research leave and pension status to make the move acceptable. Also on June 16, anticlimactically but with great effect, Emperor Franz Joseph publicly chastised Marchet for having allowed the affair to drag on.[152] Transferred to Prague, Wahrmund tried unsuccessfully to obtain a professorship at Vienna in 1909 and eventually disappeared into a cloud of unintended anonymity with his career in relative shambles.[153] To Karl von Amira in Munich he complained in mid-July 1908 that he had suffered so many insults in Austria that he could no longer work there and that "the behavior of the so-called liberal parties has been in fact deplorable [*jämmerlich*], as was that of most of my colleagues."[154]

The scandal produced only a limited resonance in the *Abgeordnetenhaus* until early June. Then, in the midst of the special debate on the budget, Thomas Masaryk gave a trenchant defense of Wahrmund that forced the big German parties to respond in kind. Masaryk admitted that Wahrmund's literary style was crude and perhaps even professionally inappropriate, but he insisted that the affair had to be seen in the light of larger, more universal questions.[155] Ludwig Wahrmund's behavior was only superficially at issue. Rather, this was a test case of the resolve of the Austrian state to support more progressive forms of cultural and social evolution. The present epoch was a transitional one in which no compromise could be tolerated toward the vestiges of past cultural corruption. A new, higher form of individual morality was struggling to be born against traditional religious intolerance. The inevitable *Kulturkampf* would be salutary, and Masaryk had no doubt which side would be victorious. Religion was, thus, not a *Privatsache*. For the Liberals to treat it as such was to allow the Church to infiltrate the agencies of civil institutional power that monitored and, in Austria, even sponsored cultural growth. Masaryk also condemned attempts to reconcile national conflicts on the basis of accommodative economic and class interests, while holding questions of religious culture in abeyance. National identity and social liberty could be achieved only when joined to full ethical freedom. Catholicism in its traditional institutional forms was incompatible with such freedom and hence antithetical to true national progress.

Masaryk's speech was a powerful critique of the premises of Austrian church-state relations, even though his references to actual policy were fleeting. Its most devastating effect was on the German and Czech progressives for whom the affair had been a considerable embarrassment. For Masaryk called into question the two assumptions that governed political logic in the Beck ministry: that a coalition of all bourgeois parties, including the Christian Socials, was justifiable on the grounds that "nation" and "religion" were distinct and separable cultural entities; and that national unity would be served by participation in a parliamentary ministry in which interest-based negotiation replaced stark power-confrontations. By sacrificing the heritage of anticlericalism for the false consciousness of economic realism, Masaryk implied, bourgeois liberals of all national groups had betrayed the ethical wellsprings of their political history. Masaryk's challenge was formidable: could one be a "progressive"—Czech or German—without being an anticlerical?

On June 10, Josef Redlich, who had supported Masaryk in his earlier confrontation with Lueger, rose to defend Marchet and German progressive behavior during the crisis. He provided a second interpretation of the Wahrmund crisis, one that diverged from the ethical absolutism of Thomas Masaryk.[156] Redlich was not an unabashed defender of Beck's virtues—he admitted that the Minister-President only listened to the parties on an irregular basis—but he rejected the "atomistic" politics that informed Masaryk's logic. Redlich agreed that Wahrmund himself was perhaps the least significant player in the whole affair. His anticlerical rhetoric had long been familiar and its banality would have been unlikely to cause controversy if the crisis had been better handled by the university rectors. Redlich disassociated himself from Wahrmund's insulting comments about religious belief and implied that the professor had surpassed the defensible boundary of scientific research to engage in political mudslinging.

The significance of the affair lay elsewhere, namely, in its meaning for the relationship between the Austrian universities and the Austrian civil service. Redlich insisted that he too affirmed freedom of research and university autonomy, but that it was naive to think that such values could be sustained in a political and administrative system so paternalistic and unimaginative, as unresponsive to talent and creativity, as the Austrian. The real danger facing Austrian progressives was not their traditional nemesis, clericalism, but a living cancer that was destroying the nerve centers of Austrian society—the passivity and self-serving conservatism of the Austrian bureaucracy. Better that the energies lavished on the Wahrmund Affair be redirected to improve the conditions of higher education; which, in turn, would require fundamental changes in the way in which the Austrian administration dealt with the universities. Fundamental reforms in the administrative service were necessary to make it more effective and more humane, and these could be achieved only by the will and force of large national political groups in the *Abgeordnetenhaus*. The Wahrmund Affair and Masaryk's commentary trivializing the accomplishments of instrumental politics simply played into the hands of the enemies of parliamentary life in Austria.

For Redlich, the conflict of nationalities in Austria was only resolvable by interest-based negotiations between large, disciplined national political units in a modern parliamentary framework. A parliament consisting of dozens of small, feuding factions would accomplish nothing. Where Masaryk mocked Beck's pressure on parties to unite in larger blocs, Redlich thought that only the formation of large coalition parties among the *bürgerlich* groups would give Austria the chance to develop a modern parliamentary system. And only such large coalition units, working in harness within an effective parliamentary structure, could drag the Austrian administration into the twentieth century. Clericalism, Redlich seemed to imply, paled into insignificance when one considered the moral and legal inefficiencies of the administration.

Redlich's approach was consistent with his general support of Christian Social–German nationalist cooperation and with his long-standing interest in both the prerogatives of and limitations on administrative rule in Central Europe.[157] Redlich was opposed not so much to the efficacy of administrative rule as he was to its inefficient, overly politicized and corrupt operations that undercut the public good. Indeed, Redlich's progressivism lay in his ability to imagine a dual political system for Austria which would integrate parliamentary and administrative authority. In his own way he diverged as sharply from conventional political expectations as did Masaryk, signaling the new complexity of circumstances faced by all German bourgeois politicians in the aftermath of the 1907 suffrage reforms. For Masaryk, Liberalism could survive only by reviving and intensifying a discourse of cultural combat defined by ethical absolutes; he went far beyond the complacent, statist anticlericalism of the 1860s and 1870s. Redlich in turn also modified the assumptions of etatist rule in which Josephist Liberals had taken consolation for decades. Administrative power would find perfect legitimacy only in concord with democratic rule, not in conflict with it. Rather than functioning as an authoritarian instrument of German-national hegemony, the civil service would be transformed into a beneficent system of expert social governance controlled by a new democratic parliament.

The significance of the Wahrmund Affair was apparent in the discord that it produced within both Christian Social and German national parliamentary ranks, with, as Duncan Gregory observed, "the extreme wings of each party have been pulling vigorously in opposite directions."[158] Sir Edward Goschen correctly judged that the affair had disrupted Gessmann's strategy for the Christian Socials, which was "to avoid identifying themselves with a completely Clerical policy . . . and to explain that they are a Christian (or anti-Semitic) and a German rather than a Catholic party."[159] Goschen thought that the Wahrmund crisis would force the Christian Socials into declaring themselves either Christian or Catholic, but he oversimplified the categories available to the Viennese leadership. Lueger had shown that he could combine

"Christianity" and "Catholicism" at will when doing so served his political ends. Goschen also exaggerated the timing of the affair's intellectual impact, since the movement toward a more Catholic profile for the party was possible only after the catastrophe of June 1911. But the connection Goschen drew was useful nonetheless. Neither Gessmann nor Lueger wanted a Christian Social-sponsored *Kulturkampf* in 1908, and neither, for different reasons, was prepared to submit party policy to the dictates of the Alpine Catholic forces or to take orders from the Vatican. Attempts by the Thronfolger's agent, Major Brosch, to use the crisis to discredit Beck failed. Gessmann later commented on the religious bigotry that started the anti-Modernism crusade when he warned Friedrich Funder that the "splendid Catholic circles among our aristocrats and bishops are ignoring the abyss which threatens to engulf them in the very near future." For Gessmann the times were running against authoritarian solutions, and the "rashness of the Roman state chancellory since the death of Leo XIII has done its share to damage the Catholic Church in the worst possible way."[160]

The survival of Gessmann's *Reichspartei* assumed accommodations within the various regional power centers of the Christian Social party as well as a mediatory role between the Czech and German bourgeois parties. Alois Liechtenstein restated these assumptions on June 1 when he commented that continued Christian Social cooperation with the *bürgerlich* German national parties would make possible an eventual agreement with the Czechs and South Slavs, "[f]or our unity makes us sufficiently strong to secure from the Slavs in the north and south of the Empire a peace that is for both sides advantageous, honorable, and lasting."[161] The question for the Christian Social leadership thus became how to limit the damage caused by the affair so that informal cooperation with the German nationals could be sustained. The June 1910 deal succeeded in doing this temporarily, but deeply felt distrust remained among the Alpine Catholics against Marchet and Beck. When Gessmann and his collaborators in Vienna decided to withdraw the party's support for Beck in late 1908 for quite different reasons, they did so in the mistaken assumption that they could kill two political birds with one well-aimed stone: replace Beck with a more stable coalition ministry and satisfy their Catholic colleagues' desire for vengeance.

The Wahrmund Affair thus demonstrated both the fragility of the *Reichspartei* and the challenges of integrating it into a broader network of intrabourgeois coalitions. For both presumed a downplaying of national and cultural provocations in favor of advantageous economic and social programs. Gessmann was correct about the compatibility of his party's economic goals and those of the various German factions. Even an ardent anticlerical like Emanuel Weidenhoffer admitted during the Wahrmund debates that the two *bürgerlich* groups shared virtually identical economic platforms.[162] But Weidenhoffer also felt that "clericalism" was a specter that even economic fraternity could not dispel, and he feared that the Christian Socials were becoming a clerical party. The Wahrmund Affair did not, as many feared (or hoped), destroy the informal coalition between the German parties, but it raised the question of whether the particularistic interests of each group would allow a permanent working relationship on the open stage of Cabinet politics. Occasional cooperation in parliament on specific items of legislation was easy, but with official representatives in the Cabinet the responsibility each carried for the other's special interests was much more substantial.

For the Social Democrats the affair had even more important consequences. In early June Victor Adler condemned the betrayal of the German nationals and the pathetic behavior of Marchet, warning that anticlericalism had deep roots in the Austrian working class and that it was an issue which the German bourgeois parties could not ignore.[163] Adler admitted his personal ambivalence about exploiting *Kulturkampf* rhetoric, not because the tactic failed to work but because it worked too well. He cautioned that "it lies neither in our wishes nor in our interest to distract the working class into a fight against clericalism" when serious economic and political struggles loomed ahead. Why expose the working classes to every bourgeois renegade wearing anticlerical colors who came along? Adler was consistent in this policy of non-collaboration—even Ludo Hartmann's initiatives initially suffered from Adler's suspicion of bourgeois-staffed educational initiatives for the workers.[164] Nonetheless, Adler vigorously defended the ideal of academic freedom in the universities, given its exemplary importance for thousands of public-school teachers and in light of the working-classes' sensitivity to the issue of cultural enlightenment more generally.

Adler's views were supplemented by two younger socialists, Otto Glöckel and Karl Renner. Glöckel reiterated Adler's concern for the school system, insisting that the Wahrmund Affair showed the consequences of the government's having delivered the public schools to the "clericals."[165] Education was of a piece. What had happened in the schools could easily happen in the universities, since the insidious feature of the clericals' power was that it thrived upon "an unfree, backward, and superstitious people." Although he did not offer a specific commentary on his party's tactics, Glöckel was clearly far more concerned about the future religious-ideological struggle than was Adler.

Karl Renner provided, however, a more complex and powerful interpretation of the affair, that implicitly outlined the options of the Social Democratic party in addressing the religious question during the final years of the Empire.[166] For Renner the Wahrmund question showed the historic isolation and defensiveness of the Austrian bourgeoisie and its perverse dependence on older cultural forms to protect it against the rising working class. With Wahrmund the bourgeoisie signaled its repudiation of *Wissenschaft* and of academic freedom, because these had become commodities dangerous to the material privileges of the capitalist social hierarchy. The bourgeoisie now viewed the intelligentsia not as its prototypical mediator and spokesman, as in the 1860s and 1870s, but rather as a subservient service group to be kept in financial and ideational bondage.

Renner surmised that the Christian Socials had secretly welcomed the Wahrmund scandal as a way to distract attention from the rival economic interests within their own party. Social Democracy had the right—indeed, the obligation—to sponsor more progressive views of culture, and Renner foresaw the day when the party's cultural vision of a classless society of humanity and freedom would gain ascendancy. An unintended problem in Renner's presentation was, however, a tension between content and method. If both parties could legitimately employ cultural strategies (however high or low their motives), then the difference between these cultural worldviews had to be judged in terms of relative ethical content. This brought Renner to the question of religion in private and public affairs.

Renner reiterated the classic position of his party—that religion was a *Privatsache,* a matter of private opinion—and argued that the Social Democrats had no intention of starting a crusade against private religious belief. The socialists did not want a *Kulturkampf,* but rather a *Klassenkampf,* and their immediate objectives in parliament would concentrate on economic and social questions (an ironic parallel to Gessmann's views). But this avoidance of *Kulturkampf* was possible only if religion as a moral and ethical phenomenon was accepted solely as a *Privatsache*—that is, as an object beyond the interests of or the political reach of the state. Religion as a phenomenon of individual belief was uncontroversial. The party did advocate, however, the divorce of religion from organizations of public sponsorship, such as the schools and the universities.

Renner's (and implicitly Victor Adler's) tentative divorce of *Kulturkampf* from *Klassenkampf* was not accepted by all of his generational peers in the Viennese party. The Wahrmund Affair opened a serious and, in its long-range implications, significant debate within the Social Democratic party on the uses and ends of anticlericalism as a political tactic and as an epistemological strategy. In the context of the affair a series of articles appeared in *Der Kampf* discussing the value of continued participation by the Social Democrats in the *Verein "Freie Schule."* Two articulate non-Viennese members, Michael Schacherl of Styria and Josef Strasser of Bohemia, presented trenchant critiques of the *Freie Schule* movement and insisted that the Social Democrats should divorce themselves from it.[167] Schacherl argued that the Wahrmund Affair, as well as the recent history of the *Freie Schule* itself, had revealed the moral bankruptcy and political cowardice of the German Liberal movement in Austria. He contended that the socialists were disgracing themselves and wasting precious moral and economic resources in collaborating with groups who were intrinsically unsympathetic to the socialists' class position but who did not even have the courage of their supposed convictions. According to Schacherl, one of the assumptions of the *Freie Schule* was that it would provide a cultural bridge between socialist and bourgeois interests, demonstrating that common ground could be established that would mitigate interclass tensions. His experience had shown that this was an illusion. Most *bürgerlich* politicians and their voters had no desire to collaborate with the socialists on any terms, and those few who were dedicated anticlericals had little influence on the great majority. For Schacherl, thus, anticlericalism was not a solvent of class conflict, but simply masked its perpetuation.

Two months later Josef Strasser reiterated Schacherl's arguments, but he added a more internal justification for stopping collaboration. Most of the cadre support for the *Freie Schule* came from working-class members who often neglected their own union and party organizations to find time for the *Freie Schule*'s agitatorial work. Strasser believed that many Austrian workers still held *kleinbürgerlich* democratic (as opposed to Marxist-collectivist) moral values, which led them to personalize and thus to trivialize class conflict. This made it difficult for the party to instill a systematic, disciplined socialist perspective. Their petty bourgeois mentality led many workers to seize upon the Church as the preeminent "power of darkness" responsible for their misery, exaggerating its "demonic power" in a manner which Strasser could only describe as "superstitious." Ironically, they were victimized by the same cultural traits they sought to attack. This political personalism and ideological naiveté, coupled with an almost irrational fear of the Church, led the workers into compromising associations with fringe bourgeois groups who claimed to be anticlerical, but in fact simply exploited the workers' good intentions. Strasser found this situation disturbing, not merely because of the workers' exaggerated image of the Church and their naive conviction that the bourgeoisie could be trusted, but also because they were distracted from setting their own proper political and intellectual priorities. Contact with bourgeois anticlericalism, therefore, was not just strategically useless; it was intellectually poisonous as well. It discredited the Social Democratic party to be associated with bourgeois radicals who, in moments of crisis, were only too willing to betray the socialist cause.[168]

Strasser (who, perhaps not surprisingly, was one of the founders of the Austrian Communist party after 1919) and Schacherl had formulated critiques that clearly reflected the domestic political environments in which they worked— the Alpine and Czech provinces—where to be a German "liberal" by 1908 meant to be a German national and where anticlericalism as a political "bridge" between the classes had little meaning. But in Vienna the younger socialists encountered a somewhat different situation. It not only had a large and increasingly self-conscious Jewish community whose votes they clearly coveted; it was also a city whose occupational structures were slowly being transformed by modern industrial and commercial rationalization, producing new and potentially sympathetic client groups for whom "class" position and hence "class consciousness" were still unanswered questions. White-collar *Angestellten* in the burgeoning urban service industries were a prime example.

Freisinn in Vienna also meant something quite different than it did to the mainline German national parties after 1907. The radical liberalism of fringe politicians like Ofner, Hock, Friedmann, Zenker, and others, who counted heavily on a combination of socialist and Jewish voters for their election successes in 1907 and especially in 1911, could be viewed as a phenomenon peculiar to Vienna, and therefore as warranting special collaborationist dispensations. Could not anticlericalism provide a solvent for class antinomies in Vienna, where the national question was of less importance and where culture could confront class head-on without interference from other political variables?

Karl Seitz responded to Schacherl's essay on behalf of the Viennese party. True to his heritage as leader of the *Jungen,* Seitz defended the *Freie Schule* as an educational and political organization which, though still in its infancy, might nevertheless do useful work in enlightening and reinforcing that part of the bourgeoisie that was still anticlerical.[169] He admitted that the majority of bourgeois voters might already be beyond the pale, but he insisted that the Social Democrats might profitably collaborate at least with the majority of the intelligentsia and with other "free elements" and thus prevent their ensnarement (*Umgarnung*) by bourgeois proclerical leaders. Even in the event that the *Freie Schule* movement failed, the socialists would have demonstrated to all "morally free people that their place is with us, that they can only participate in the great, forthcoming *Kulturkampf* against clericalism in this century in the ranks of the antipodes to Clericalism, in the ranks of Social Democracy."

This final argument, added almost as an afterthought, raised more problems than it solved. Did Seitz mean that Austrian socialism might rely on cultural weapons such as anticlericalism as trans-class devices to unite workers and intellectuals in a crusade against clericalism while papering over real economic divergences (which Marxists like Strasser found improbable)? Or was this merely a temporary stage of political education after which the bourgeoisie would be subsumed into the belief structure of the Social Democratic party and would accept its economic programs? What value did anticlericalism hold, therefore, against economic and class divergences? Was it a warrant for *bürgerlich* voters to betray their class interests? Schacherl (and subsequently) Strasser denied that the device could function in this way, but Seitz, in at least one reading of his position, seemed to postulate the imminent *Kulturkampf* as having so powerful a valence as to pull all "morally free" people into socialism.

Such views came close, in many respects, to the radical idealism of Masaryk, and it was not surprising that Karl Renner found them troublesome. Writing against Max Adler in the summer of 1909, Renner took exception to Adler's intimation that a *Kulturkampf* could function as an active variable in determining the outcome of class conflict.[170]

It remained for Otto Bauer to attempt to resolve these issues with more precision. In doing so Bauer laid the intellectual groundwork for socialist *Kulturkampf* tactics against the Christian Socials in Vienna between 1909 and 1914, which in turn set a powerful precedent for socialist self-understanding in Vienna during the interwar years. Bauer's arguments also showed how much power the younger socialists accorded to "culture" as a semi-independent political variable for the transformation of mass public opinion by revolutionary education, and they made clear why younger Christian Social activists like Richard Schmitz sought to counter the Austro-Marxists with an intensified political Catholicism.

Bauer wrote two critiques, one against Schacherl and a second against Strasser.[171] In his first essay, in June 1908, Bauer sought to find a middle way between Schacherl's isolationism and Seitz's collaborationism by suggesting that Schacherl's warning against illusions about bourgeois eudaemonism was both timely and valid but that the particular construction of bourgeois reality in Europe gave rise to promising opportunities for ideological *and* class collaboration which could not be ignored. Bauer differentiated two epochs of bourgeois economic development in the nineteenth century. In the first epoch, ideological opposition against the Church was shared by the bourgeoisie and the recently organized working classes, although the former merely sought to strengthen the powers of the constitutional (and bourgeois) state against the Church, whereas the latter believed that religion was a *Privatsache* and sought to expunge it entirely from the instrumentalities of public life. In the second and more recent epoch, however, the propertied classes, frightened by the extraordinary growth and political presence of the working class, had retrenched and sacrificed their class ideology (anticlericalism) for materialistic class interests, and they now advocated intraclass alliances against the proletariat by all segments of the bourgeoisie, clerical and nonclerical alike. In Austria the nationality conflict had given further impetus to this inversion of values, since the primacy of national over other cultural values dictated the special desirability of intraclass collaboration among the bourgeois factions of various national groups. But Bauer also saw within the Austrian bourgeoisie new elements who no longer possessed the necessary economic resources and class qualities to justify their putative "bourgeois" status: the intelligentsia (following Renner's arguments, although with a different conclusion) and especially the new *Mittelstand,* who were only separated from the working class by inherited status presumptions and other archaic prejudices. Anticlericalism, especially if presented in an integrated socialist ideological framework, might have the salutary effect of destroying this false consciousness by illuminating the true material bonds that joined these occupational groups to the working classes. A community of ideology (*Gemeinschaft der Ideologie*) would reveal to these members of the new middle class their existential membership in the socialist community.

With this formulation, Bauer, in spite of his disclaimers, had both adopted and clarified Seitz's position. More importantly, he had tailored anticlericalism to the locus classicus of Austrian Social Democratic politics—the city of Vienna. Bauer insisted that economic conflict was still the primary object of socialist politics, since class repression was the primary motor of contemporary social evolution, but at the same time he transposed anticlericalism into a cultural-ideological antidote for those inherited ideological distortions that prevented the new *Mittelstand* from accepting its fate as a member of the socialist community. Thus, the struggle against clericalism would clarify and bring reason to those exploited bourgeois classes who, by the logic of history and the necessity of their material condition, were in fact members of the working classes: the private employees, state white-collar workers, and the bulk of the intelligentsia. Culture would be proffered not as a substitute for class conflict but as a reinforcement for and supplement to such conflict. It would not mask class differences, but it would show that in many cases such differences were illusory. In a word, it would be a tool for mass political education.

Against Strasser Bauer faced a more difficult assignment, since Strasser had impugned the capacity of socialist workers to associate themselves simultaneously with anticlericalism and more basic economic issues, as well as questioned the desirability of their doing so. Bauer argued that in its confrontation with religion as an experienced social phenomenon the proletariat might be divided into three distinct groups. Each group was at a distinct stage of evolutionary progress tending toward intellectual and emotional liberation from the social constraints that religion imposed on the individual. Workers who had only recently escaped from the impoverished moral economy of *kleinbürgerlich* or rural occupations were inevitably in the first stage characterized by great deference toward traditional religious symbols and superstitions. The attitude of the party toward these people would be one of paternalist patience. It would avoid insulting their motives or beliefs since, by an inexorable process of historical-cultural evolution, they would eventually move into a second stage of secularization, in which love of religion would turn to hatred and devotion to bitter antagonism. Bauer believed that this second stage of active and intense hatred of religion comprehended a substantial minority of the contemporary Austrian working-class movement, as well as, significantly, most of its subelite cadre structure, explaining the excesses of anticlericalism to which these particular leadership groups were often prone (and about which Strasser was so worried). Finally, Bauer postulated a final stage, the result of perfect dialectical confrontation between love and hate, by which the individual worker and his family would become completely indifferent to religious symbols and ritual, neither hating nor loving them, and hence arriving at a perfect intellectual and political objectivity. On this final level socialist political action would be directed only against the Church as an institution and against the intrusion of religion into the realm of public order. Here the conventional doctrine of *Religion ist Privatsache* made sense as a practical policy, not just as an ideal. Bauer clearly considered himself and many of his elite colleagues to have attained this level of intellectual and emotional maturity.

But because the second stage played so critical a role in Austrian socialism, and because hatred of the Church and of religion was so extraordinarily pervasive throughout Austrian working-class culture (according to Bauer), the party should and could do nothing to alter it. Those in the third stage might look askance at the adolescent excesses of their brethren in the second stage, but the party as an institution apparently had no educational obligation to force these people to a higher and more balanced plane of indifference. In fact, according to Bauer, the party should do all it could to satisfy the instinctual urges of this group, who would move to the third stage in a natural, evolutionary manner when the time came. The effectiveness of this scheme as a tactical rationalization for *Kulturkampf* anticlericalism lay in its combination of instinctual liberty and revolutionary resignation. For those workers (who conveniently happened to be a large and influential mass of the party) for whom hatred of religion was a true necessity of the heart (*wahres Herzensbedürfnis*), the party had to concede and even tolerate institutional contexts to support their behavior. For the mature, elevated types, who were beyond such hatred, the party reserved its doctrine of religion as a *Privatsache*.

Together the two essays contained a contradiction: in the first, anticlericalism was seen to be part of an educative program in class self-understanding, whereas in the second (among people who already recognized their standing in the working class) it was more natural and evocative. But a mutually reinforcing functionalism between the two roles was also apparent: whereas anticlericalism would outbid other bourgeois ideologies and link the potential companion groups in the bourgeoisie to the proletariat, it would also satisfy important emotional and psychological urges within the socialist cadre organization. Anticlericalism was a perfect combination of necessity and opportunity that would link diverse economic groups within the "proletariat" and establish consensual unity out of the throes of cultural hatred.

In the short term, the less imaginative but more practical orientation preferred by Victor Adler and Karl Renner seemed to be ascendant.[172] The socialists found themselves constrained by their interest in passively encouraging a formation of bourgeois parties that would gain ministerial power against the

Austrian bureaucracy and Court. The 1909 Social Democratic party congress in Reichenberg made it clear that the fall of Beck was seen by the socialists as a historic failure of the Austrian bourgeoisie, one that the socialists claimed to regret, even if they condemned the circumstances under which it occurred. Hence they were unwilling, as a matter of general policy in 1907–8, to disrupt the bourgeois coalition. This may generally be said to be Renner's and Adler's policy of directing party work toward practical, economic and social issues. Such flexibility did not mean, however, that the party viewed with equanimity the "realism" of men like Josef Redlich. In his speeches in April 1908 supporting Gessmann's *Arbeitsministerium* and in June attacking Wahrmund's indiscretions, Redlich signaled the initial success of Gessmann's *Reichspartei* strategy, if not in achieving its cultural aims, then at least in its frank celebration of the convergence of class and power. The danger that Redlich's mentality posed for the socialists was this: "clericalism" had always been seen by socialist theorists as characteristic of a feudal epoch, a state of cultural backwardness and administrative connivance that would pass when the true bourgeois revolution completed its course. Such was the case in France, and, in certain respects, in Germany as well. But in Austria "clericalism" seemed to take on new life and support just as Austria entered a new age of democratic legitimacy and parliamentary control. In Germany the SPD never had to face, on the national level, the specter of *Zentrum* politicians pursuing anti-socialist cultural policies within state ministries. With the entry of Gessmann and Ebenhoch in the Cabinet, followed by the Wahrmund Affair, the Austrian Social Democrats could not be certain what would follow. Bourgeois political hegemony seemed to bring forth cultural relics of past epochs as well as the desired "modernization" of the Austrian political system. The world of 1908 failed to conform to socialist strategy in a most unhappy way. Perhaps it was only to be expected that some of their younger theorists would make a virtue of a vice and try to short-circuit both processes—"clerical feudalism" and anti-Marxist class hegemony—by conflating the processes of cultural and political modernization and by turning "clericalism" against its putative new sponsors. In one knockout blow Gessmann's *bürgerliche Sammlung* would be both fragmented and discredited.

Should Gessmann's vision of bourgeois ministerialism show signs of weakness, as it did under Bienerth's regime, the Social Democrats had nothing to lose by combining *Kulturkampf* rhetoric with social and class issues. The strategy of the party after 1911 tended in this direction, if only because the 1911 election could be read as a retroactive fulfillment of the views of Max Adler and Otto Bauer. Bauer contended as much in a short commentary published immediately after the June election in which he justified the temporary cultural alliance between the Social Democrats and the bourgeois *Freisinn* as the only way to "break the superiority of clericalism" and to destroy the "social demagogy" of a party that claimed to transcend class antagonisms.[173] Once Christian Socialism was out of the way, a purer and more class-oriented politics of *Klassenkampf* would resume, so that in supporting the Social Democrats the anticlerical bourgeoisie in Vienna was positioning itself as the primary target for the Left. Bauer was not incorrect in his second assumption. In the parliamentary elections in February 1919 for the National Assembly in Vienna Otto Bauer was a member of the socialist slate in the combined electoral district of *Innen-Ost.* Among his bourgeois opponents was Ernst Victor Zenker whose candidacy was crushed by the Social Democratic machine, the same Zenker who used and then repudiated socialist crossover votes to win in the Wieden in 1911. The moral expediency of 1911 was resolved in the socialist landslide of 1919.

Bauer's theory of the exploitative value of anticlericalism for undercutting and co-opting bourgeois *Freisinn* thus was consistent and, in the short run, successful. But unfortunately for Bauer (and for his party) the Social Democrats never succeeded in killing off the Christian Socials, so that the *Kulturkampf* strategies became a perennial component of socialist politics in German Austria, rather than a temporarily expedient alliance with the German *Bürgerlichen.* And it became something more as well.

Given the prominence of the nationality conflict in the prewar Austrian Social Democratic party and given Victor Adler's determination to concentrate all of the party's energies before 1907 on winning the franchise and attacking *all* bourgeois parties of whatever stripe, socialist anticlericalism was only one issue among many. But anticlericalism eventually blossomed as one of the major leitmotifs of modern Austrian politics—not simply because the socialists "appropriated" bourgeois anticlericalism as a political weapon but also because of their rigorous efforts to use it as a revolutionary cultural weapon to initiate and sustain material-social transformation. Bauer's emphasis on electoral struggle as a form of revolutionary enlightenment—including the propaganda of *Kultur*—was simply a more general statement of this conception, which his erstwhile colleagues in the socialist freethinker movement pushed into a direct connection between moral revolution and social transformation. Where Bauer (as a reasonably orthodox Marxist) saw mere tactical expediencies, others like Otto Glöckel and Ludwig Wutschel saw organic and generative linkages.

In a study of Karl Leuthner, Roger Fletcher has recently argued that that prewar Austrian socialist manifested the same "negative integrationist" mentality that marked many of his German collaborators to the north—that they adopted, in spite of themselves, the forms and values of bourgeois society.[174] Leuthner, a right-wing Austrian revisionist who owed more to Nietzsche and various ethical Darwinists than to Marx, was certainly a creative proponent of the Austrian socialist *Kulturkampf.* But the presence of neo-Kantian radicals like Otto Bauer and Max Adler and of *Jungen* like Otto Glöckel and Karl Seitz among the most vigorous sponsors of the "struggle over culture" suggested that this was an issue that cut across revisionist-orthodox lines and gave to the Social Democratic party a special, unifying identity. Because Glöckel and Seitz saw the *Kulturkampf* as a necessary first step in the material reconstruction of society, opening up education and law to the masses and allowing the masses to appropriate and construct their own worlds of intellectual and moral power, Austro-Marxist anticlericalism was not merely a mindless element of "negative integration." The *Kampf* exchanges of 1908 revealed a self-consciousness about what was new and old in the *Kulturkampf.*

All socialists agreed that what was new was the conceptual and political link between discursive anticlericalism and the revolutionary transformation of social institutions, not merely for the proletariat but also for potential allies and partners among the bourgeoisie who might be "eased" into socialism by enlightened *Bildungsarbeit.* In spite of Otto Bauer's admonitions in Linz in 1926 against the danger of viewing a freethinker crusade as having an independent epistemological force, the idea of a specifically socialist *Kulturkampf* became for many younger tacticians in the party both a means and an end.[175] The dialectical challenge facing interwar Social Democracy, which the debates on the 1926 Linz Program vividly illustrated (although they did not satisfactorily resolve it), was how to make the end serve the means, while preventing the means from betraying the end.

Anson Rabinbach has recently demonstrated how "culture" came to have a semi-autonomous significance in Austrian Social Democratic politics in the twenties, possessing illusory properties which alternately served to provoke and to avoid true revolutionary praxis.[176] In this strategy the Austro-Marxists seemed to fulfill one of the cardinal tenets of their neo-Kantian theory, which, in Ernesto Laclau's words, "allowed Marxists to conceive the infrastructure as a terrain whose conformation depended on forms of consciousness, and not upon the naturalistic movement of the forces of production."[177] The "temptation" of culture as a meaningful, mass electoral issue first confronted the Social Democratic party in 1907–8; on the heels of its formidable entry into the mass parliamentary scene, and if the party did not succumb entirely to the blandishments of anticlericalism as a thing unto itself, that path was at least sketched out.

The Wahrmund Affair was thus an important symbolic event in late Imperial Austrian politics. In its wake the principal proprietors of the anticlerical strand of Austrian Liberalism had become the Austrian Social Democrats. Before Wahrmund, other bourgeois parties could still claim to represent cultural "liberalism." But after June 1908 only the Social Democrats could sensibly adopt this posture, claiming anticlericalism as their own and using it as a primary component of consciousness for the new ideological man/woman that

Austro-Marxism sought to gestate. Just as the Christian Socials had succeeded Austrian Liberalism in 1897 in political, corporatist, and class-economic terms, now the second "nature" of the Liberal tradition was appropriated by one of the two great Austrian parties of the twentieth century. Not class, but culture was the Liberal heritage that devolved upon the Austro-Marxists.

This more powerful conception of what socialism was to do, and of the means it was to use, was not lost on the generational peers of the younger Austro-Marxists in the conservative *Lager.* In 1928 a fascinating exchange between Heinrich Mataja and Ignaz Seipel illuminated the transformational capacities of the Austro-Marxist tradition by debating ways to combat them. Mataja wrote to Seipel arguing that the Christian Socials needed a stronger and more vigilant ideological profile against a party which crept up on the individual in his role as a "producer, as a consumer, as a father, as a bearer of a world view, as a tourist, as a musician, as a cyclist, and approached him in the form of a labor union, a legal defense organization, a vocational guidance center, a credit association, a *Schutzbund,* a gymnastic society, a choral society, an animal protection league.... In a superb way the Social Democrats attempt to combine the three [necessary] elements of an organization: passion, self-interest, and terror."[178] If the Christian Socials were to compete effectively, was it not necessary to move beyond the crude bourgeois political organizations developed under Lueger and create a modern party that would have "a spiritual movement, positive accomplishments, and a strong organization"?

Surprisingly, Seipel refused to follow Mataja's argument. He granted that Mataja had a point, but he thought that the correct response lay in a different realm, beyond the conventionally "political."[179] According to Seipel the Christian Socials had a different view of the relationship of the individual to the state than did the Marxists. Since Austrian socialism's own collectivist party structures reflected the Austro-Marxists' larger views that individual initiative and will should be subsumed by the state—both following and anticipating the ideal state—Seipel held that it would be morally and politically impermissible for the Christian Socials to try to create such collectivist organizational structures. But Seipel then went further and noted something that Mataja had glossed over. Austro-Marxism was not simply or not even a "party" in the traditional sense of the word. Rather, for Seipel it was a community with a worldview (*Weltanschauungsgemeinschaft*) whose only parallel, at least in Austria, was the Roman Catholic Church. The political, financial, and cultural instruments of power of the Austro-Marxists were means to achieve a new moral world of social and political values. Where Mataja's perception of the Social Democrats was colored by political instrumentalities, Seipel viewed the same phenomenon from the point of view of its moral intentions and ideological dynamics. From this perspective Austrian socialism was not only an organizational machine but also a "community with a common worldview," seeking not merely material revolution but cultural and psychological transmutation as well. Hence the only fitting agency to combat it was its institutional equivalent in cultural power and resilience, the Catholic Church.

Seipel's perceptive comments on the Austrian socialists—which even Otto Bauer might have found flattering—revealed the condition of the Austrian political terrain in the late 1920s and constituted the terminus of a process that had begun in the years 1905–11. Lueger had never viewed the Church as the exclusive agent for anti-socialist cultural combat. This was properly the responsibility of the party and more importantly of the civic community—the *Vaterstadt*—in which all loyal Viennese lived. But after 1907 two things changed: the self-understanding of the younger Christian Socials, for whom formal Catholic religious values were a compelling political currency, and the self-categorizations of the younger Austro-Marxists, for whom anticlericalism now became a premier political objective in their search for a revolutionary *Kulturkampf.* Whereas Christian Social Vienna may have played the role of "father" in the Empire, in the later 1920s Mataja clearly saw that the role of fatherhood had been subsumed by the Social Democratic party. For Seipel, therefore, only the Catholic Church could combat the cultural imperialism of the Social Democrats. The putative target of the Social Democrats—the Church—now became its only worthy opponent.

The National Temptation: The Christian Social Party and the Lex Axmann-Kolisko

If religion proved to be a destabilizing phenomenon for the center of the Christian Social party in Vienna, given the ease with which the Wahrmund Affair could set the more extreme clericals from the west on edge and the eagerness of Viennese socialists to exploit anticlericalism as an electoral weapon, nationalism also proved to be a problem more intractable and persistent than Albert Gessmann had imagined in the heady days of the *Reichspartei*'s founding. The functional and instrumental parallels between the two cultural fields were important. According to Gessmann's original vision the *Reichspartei* was designed to minimize anticlericalism *and* integral nationalism, concentrating the public's imagination on social and economic issues and forcing bourgeois politicians of all parties to abandon political discourses that may have been appropriate to the older curial parliament, but that the new "democracy" of 1907 would make anachronistic. Gessmann's vision was extraordinary in its ambition, for national identity was the cardinal state-building technique of nineteenth-century Europe. As suggested earlier, the traditional strategy of the Viennese Christian Social party had been to deal with nationalism by treating it as a paradox: the Rathaus acted as if, by magic, the conflict of nationalities did not apply to Vienna, all the while insisting that the Christian Socials were a *German* party that could be relied upon to defend German interests. This turn of thought paralleled a seeming non sequitur, namely the party's combination of a vigilant anti-Dualism, which would privilege non-dominant peoples in Transleithania, with its putative defense of a German-based Imperial centralism in Cisleithania. Hence the party's simultaneous support for anti-Slavic policies, such as the annexation of Bosnia-Herzegovina in 1908 (although their anti-Serbianism was as much a function of Austrian cultural chauvinism as it was of a specifically "German" consciousness), *and* for vague federalist (or at least anti-Dualistic) schemes which might have enhanced the public rights of non-German groups within the *Gesamtmonarchie*.[180] Such creative flexibility with what were for many other Austrian Germans sturdy and inviolable principles lay at the heart of Christian Social party policy on the nationality question, and it had its own instrumental rationality.[181] Not only did part of the Christian Social electorate in Vienna consist of assimilated Bohemian and Moravian "Czech" voters whom no one wanted to alienate with irresponsible hate rhetoric, but in addition the problems of the northern Austrian Germans seemed sufficiently distant as to be only slightly irksome.[182] What possible evidence might be presented to suggest that the party was not faithful to Germandom in its own domain? Did not the city spend substantial sums of money each year on celebrations dedicated to German culture—a policy that found one remarkable expression in 1909 when the *Verein für Sozialpolitik* convened in Vienna, being welcomed both by Weiskirchner and Lueger?[183] Did not the party welcome visiting "German" dignitaries on a regular basis with appropriate panache and largesse? Did not the oath taken by those who were chosen to join the Viennese *Bürgerschaft*—party loyalists and wealthy local notables whom the party either wanted to reward or control (many of whom had suspiciously Czech-sounding names)—contain a promise to defend the "German character" of the city?

Not all German observers in Vienna were convinced by this facade. The German Ambassador Wedel was deeply suspicious of Lueger, viewing with considerable skepticism the latter's commitment to nationalist values.[184] And in at least one respect Wedel was right. Lueger did not equate German national identity with loyalty to or deference for Germany's interests—hence his vigorous repudiation of Theodor Mommsen's famous letter of November 1897, attacking Austrian softness toward the Czechs; hence his much publicized trip to Bucharest in June 1906, taken in contravention of the wishes of the Ballhausplatz, to lend his support to Rumanian nationalist aspirations against the Magyars, a people that Philipp Eulenburg thought to be the most loyal friends of Germany in the Hapsburg Monarchy. The negotiations sponsored by Gessmann and Weiskirchner for the support of Croatian economic interests in Bosnia-Herzegovina grew out of similar feelings.[185] In his dedication to a specifically Austrian form of German culture, neither bound to *Reichsdeutsch* values nor in sympathy with the extremism of the Sudeten Germans, Karl Lueger pursued a line of policy that ran directly to Ignaz Seipel and that might be said to foreshadow the painful search for a specifically "Austrian" identity that would preoccupy the founders of the Second Republic between 1945 and 1955. Put in contemporary terms, the Christian Socials were among the first German-speaking political groups in the Monarchy to acknowledge political nationality and ethnic language as related yet distinguishable spheres. One might be a good German and still recognize that "Germanness" in fact conveyed a multiplicity of meanings and consequences. To be "German" in Vienna or in St. Pölten was not necessarily to be "German" in Leitmeritz or Prague.[186]

Forced during the 1907 election campaign to respond to accusations that his party was "soft" on the national question, Albert Gessmann pointed out that Vienna was a magnet for internal Austrian immigration, much of it Slavic, given the role of the city in the national labor market. Gessmann sarcastically criticized the supposition that nationalist propagandizing could stop this immigration: "We face the immigration each year in Vienna of between 40,000 and 50,000 people, most of whom are not of the German nationality. If perhaps the gentlemen [the pan-Germans] have a way to prevent that, we are ready to make use of their recipe!" For Gessmann, the true achievement of the party had been its ability to keep assimilationist mechanisms working to integrate these people, while maintaining the economic growth of the city so that its German-speaking population would remain prosperous and culturally dominant, presenting newcomers with a level of success which they would try to emulate by learning the local language. Gessmann thought that the only realistic national policy was an effective economic policy coupled with cultural conciliation and patience: "What kind of a national policy is it when one confronts those who speak a different language with a fist under the nose and simply provokes them to resistance? One doesn't need to fear such resistance if one treats these people speaking a foreign tongue decently and induces their assimilation to our own nation [in a voluntary way]."[187]

As noted in Chapter 1, city employment policies for the thousands of jobs controlled by the city bureaucracy were based primarily on political loyalty to and patronage from the party machine, not on nationalist standards as such. Leopold Tomola bluntly admitted this in a session of the *Bürgerklub* in July 1917, when he plaintively informed the club that, because of the political opposition gaining seats on the *Stadtrat,* one would no longer be able hire or promote individuals according to the usual criterion of party loyalty.[188] Under Lueger candidates had to certify that their principal language of communication (*Umgangssprache*) was German, but this did not mean that men who were bilingual or even, in rarer cases, those whose first language was Czech but who had then mastered German were excluded. *Umgangssprache* was, as theorists of Austrian nationality law were well aware, a highly subjective (and often unreliable) mode of determining national identity on a collective or individual basis.[189] It was neither psychologically nor sociologically equivalent to "ethnicity," and Lueger's comments in parliament in 1901 on why he introduced the requirement prove that he viewed it in an instrumental rather than in a racial manner. He expected all officials of the city to be able to conduct the city's business (however important or trivial) in German and he wanted their ability *and* willingness to do so certified publicly.[190]

The *Umgangssprache* requirement was born of the contortions of the Badeni period, and Lueger saw it as a concession to prevent something worse: employment on the basis of ethnic nationality rather than language competency. Until after 1910, when Lueger was dead and the party in factional disarray with "nationalism" becoming a cudgel for intraparty gang wars, little effort was made to ascertain whether an individual had even told the truth on such questionnaires. When Minister-President Bienerth in August 1909 sought to assure Brockdorff-Rantzau of the German Embassy of the effectiveness of Viennese assimilationist mechanisms in securing the city's German culture, he had only to point out that the municipal bureaucracy actually employed various Czechs, some in "superior positions," but all of whom had been assimilated into Viennese culture.[191] Brockdorff-Rantzau may not have been appeased, but Bienerth, who knew the Christian Social party's employment policies intimately, had made a valid point. The party was unwilling to use ethnicity as a rigid and uncompromising standard to measure qualifications for office. Rationally it would have been absurd for the municipal bureaucracy in a city the size of Vienna, with a Czech community numbering over 100,000 inhabitants, not to employ some bilingual (and bi-ethnic) officials, even if the party did not brag about this openly.

The consequences of these practices did not go unnoticed, however, in pan-German circles. One German national journalist found Lueger's purging of pan-German schoolteachers and his simultaneous willingness to employ assimilated Czechs in the municipal services little less than outrageous:

> According to Dr. Lueger's most open admission no honorable German nationalist will be hired for a city job, but in contrast crowds of grim enemies of the Germans, the Czechs, streaming from their starving *Heimat*, find the door of city employment wide open at the streetcar system, at the gasworks, and at other municipal enterprises. The city employment assistance service has just about become a breeding ground for Czech journeymen, and the city's premises in the *Stadtpark* are made available to unscrupulous and provocative Slovenes and Slavs.[192]

Nor did Czech ethnic identities prevent prominent political careers within the Christian Social party itself. When Anton Nagler—along with Adolf Gussenbauer, one of the few unregenerate "nationalists" in the Christian Social *Bürgerklub*—tried to prevent Franz Hoss of Floridsdorf from being elected vice-mayor of Vienna in May 1910 by citing evidence that Hoss was of Czech extraction and his wife was a Czech, he was voted down by a huge majority of the club on the grounds that such arguments were "not worthy of a German man."[193] And in moments of crisis, even out-and-out political deals with nationalist Czechs could not be excluded, as occurred in mid-June 1911, when a desperate Christian Social leadership negotiated with Viennese Czechs for votes in the parliamentary run-off elections in return for concessions in regard to the Komenský school movement.[194]

But even such concepts as "dual ethnicity" or "partial assimilation" (the actual psychological incidence of which in Austria were perhaps larger than formalistic statistical mechanisms can measure) does not explain the Christian Socials' ambivalence.[195] As Viennese, Lueger and Gessmann believed that their city was both a moral and political world unto itself and that it had a personality all its own. One was a "Viennese" before one was a "German," and conversely, anyone deemed a loyal Viennese was automatically a good German. Their way of thinking about civil society was as much corporate as it was "national," and it reflected deeply rooted imperatives based upon the pluralistic constitution of identity in Viennese history since the late eighteenth century.[196] When Wilhelm Miklas defended the party's support of nationalist protection laws in parliament in November 1909, he resorted to the metaphor of a landlord (*Hausherr*) to describe its self-consciousness. The German inhabitants of the city and province were landlords who practiced (and, implicitly, controlled and protected) regional customs which each new guest must respect.[197] The party did not seek to prevent Czech immigration; and it did not define itself as a superior race. But as good landlords its members did insist that newcomers acknowledge and accept the values and cultural practices set down by the original owners. The peculiar combination of pre-modern proprietary values and democratic instrumentalities manifested by the Christian Socials in other social policy areas also found expression in their dealing with Slavic "others." Interpretations of the Viennese "nationality problem" that fail to set its public rhetoric in the context of the city's political culture miss the values that informed the day-to-day practices of men like Gessmann and Lueger.[198] Yet was Vienna's peculiar and provincial imperialism suitable for the rest of the Monarchy? And if Vienna became the linchpin of the state political system—a role to which it was tending after 1907—how long could the problems plaguing the rest of the Monarchy be held at bay in Vienna? This was the critical problem the Rathaus faced after 1907.

Lueger's treatment of local Czechs varied between indifference and paternalism. To argue that his first ten years in office saw an increasing persecution
of and violence against the Viennese Czechs is an exaggeration.[199] Many of the
protests against the Czech community brought in the City Council between
1897 and 1909 came from German national or Liberal politicians, and those
that did emanate from the Christian Social *Bürgerklub* tended to come from a
small group of councilmen led by Adolf Gussenbauer, whose racist agenda
was not shared by the majority of his colleagues.[200] Such occasional petty violence as did occur involving local Czech cultural groups was almost exclusively the work of pan-German university students or other *Alldeutsch* agitators, whom Lueger and most of his party thoroughly despised. The ethnic
provision inserted in the municipal *Bürgereid* (the candidate had to swear to
preserve the "German character of the city," as well as its character as the Imperial *Reichshaupt- und Residenzstadt*) was a reaction to the aftermath of the
Badeni riots and the tactical need of the party to defend itself against attempts
to exploit its conciliatory position in national politics (a favorite tactic of the
Neue Freie Presse). The actual formula adopted was Lueger's alternative to
the original proposal by Michael Gruber in January 1899—an errant German
nationalist whom Lueger eventually evicted from the Council in the elections
of 1900—that would have demanded adherence to "German nationality."
Lueger's discursive requirement was inexpensive and clearly attuned to his desire to protect his own party against pan-German accusations of being secret
sympathizers of the Slavs; and it is not accidental that the oath's endorsement
of the German character of the city followed, rather than preceded, its endorsement of the Imperial and Austrian character of the city.[201] This is not to minimize the fact that party leaders did believe adamantly that Czechs arriving in
Vienna from Bohemia and Moravia for the purposes of work and residence
should assimilate to the local German-speaking culture. But so did most
Czechs living in the city. Even residential patterns encouraged this assimilation
for, as Michael John has recently demonstrated, the segregation index of
Czechs in Vienna was half that of the Jewish community.[202] To describe their
individual or familial decisions to assimilate as errors of moral judgment or
failures of ethnic courage is to insult them, not to explain their history.[203]

Rather than viewing the national problem in terms of defensive territorial-
ism and minority ethnic sensitivities, as most Bohemian Germans were wont
to do, the Christian Socials perceived it largely in terms of functional assimilation. They viewed Vienna as a majority culture tolerant of cultural "others" as
long as the latter integrated themselves by learning and using the language and
by affirming loyalty to local cultural practices. This was the sense in which
most Christian Social leaders understood themselves to constitute a "German"
party, sincerely believing that others would accept their assumption that the
"nation" was subordinate to the cultural character of the city, not the reverse.

Lueger's persistent invocation that "Vienna is a German city" must be understood in the context of his wider values.[204] If he considered Vienna a "German" city, he also considered it an "Austrian" and a "Christian" city. The triadic juxtaposition was not accidental.[205] But even pluralism had its limits, as the summer of 1909 would demonstrate.

During the summer of 1909 a collision of nationalist violence and intra-Cabinet bickering sorely threatened the Christian Socials' attempt to hold the national issue "constant" in Lower Austria under the guise of a Vienna-specific assimilationism. Controversy centered first around the efforts of the Komenský School Association to expand its network of private Czech language schools in Vienna and Lower Austria; and second on a series of ugly riots provoked by anti-Czech agitators which embarrassed the Christian Socials into doing what they had always sought to avoid—taking legislative actions against a Slavic constituency group within their own electorate.

The Komenský school was a privately funded institution that did not enjoy public certification (*Öffentlichkeitsrecht*) to operate as a full legal alternative to the public schools.[206] Since the government allowed the association to send its Viennese students to Lundenburg, on the Moravian border, for annual testing, however, the school could be used by Czech parents as a practical, if inconvenient, substitute for the public system. German was taught, but the principal language of instruction was Czech. The first Komenský school had been opened in the district of Favoriten in 1883 and was tolerated, although not encouraged, by Liberal city authorities. By 1900 it enrolled 840 pupils in seven classes. In the context of a municipal school system with over 200,000 students, such an institution was hardly a threat to German culture. After taking power in 1897 the Christian Socials allowed the Favoriten school to operate. But they also discouraged by means of chicanery and bureaucratic obstreperousness any expansion of the school, partly from their conviction about the importance of linguistic assimilation but also because of Lueger's determination to bring the whole primary school system under the control of his party. As different as their objectives were, the Rathaus distrusted both the *Freie Schule* and the *Komenský Schule* as errant ventures; it was not surprising that a prominent Christian Social politician like Johann Hauser would link the two.[207] But Lueger's compulsive political pragmatism also worked in the other direction. As he informed his parliamentary colleagues in June 1909, he had serious doubts about providing resources to German-language defense groups if such funds ended up in the hands of known opponents of the Christian Social party.[208]

The Czech community that the Komenský Association served was an ambivalent patron for this anti-assimilationist institution. Nominally the community comprised 98,430 people out of a city of almost two million (according to the 1910 census, measuring *Umgangssprache*).[209] Since Austrian census statistics did not measure nationality, but only national language, and since most individuals of Czech birth or ancestry probably listed German as their principal language on the census, it is difficult if not impossible to estimate with precision the size of the assimilated as opposed to the nonassimilated sectors of the community. Using contemporary studies of the 1890 and 1910 censuses, Monika Glettler suggests that for every four persons of Czech descent in Vienna three would have been considered by the Austrian Statistical Office to be "German." A demographic portrait of those 98,430 who indicated Czech as their primary language is more easily established; it approximates immigrant communities elsewhere in Central Europe. It was younger than the city population as a whole, and it had a significantly higher percentage of younger males than Vienna as a whole. The community was occupationally diverse, but within predictable limits; the majority consisted of workers or apprentices in the huge Viennese personal goods industries, or, in the case of women, of servants in domestic households. For a minority, residence in the city had brought the outward symbols of success: craft masterships, lower white-collar positions, and occasionally even secure occupations like schoolteachers and municipal or state civil servants. In some industrial occupations in Vienna like shoemaking or wood processing, Czechs—assimilated and unassimilated together— may have outnumbered the resident Germans. Wilhelm Winkler estimated that in 1910 there were 3,221 master artisans in the city in the trades of shoe production and tailoring who had listed Czech as a principal *Umgangssprache*.[210] If one accepts Glettler's ratio as even minimally valid, the number of master artisans owning smaller shops or firms who were first or second generation Czechs (using either German or Czech as their principal language) would be much higher. One can see why the Christian Social party, with its original base in the Third electoral Curia of master artisans and shopkeepers, could be scorned by the pan-Germans as the party of the "Czechs."

But the use of *Umgangssprache* itself as a determinant of assimilation or nonassimilation is only partially valid. The complex cultural realities and role definitions behind the decision of a family to write "German" or "Czech" on a census questionnaire were hardly comprehended by such simplistic categories, if in fact individual family members ever filled out the questionnaire.[211] Statistics on the population of the city's primary schools in 1907 demonstrated the assimilation that was occurring among their school-age children. Of 232,196 students in the system, 218,999 claimed German as their mother tongue, whereas only 11,538 listed Czech as their primary language.[212] Obviously the schools continued to function as a powerful motor of assimilation, either encouraging children to identify themselves culturally as "German" or, perhaps more rarely, actually teaching them the language effectively. This was the context in which the advocates who pushed the Komenský private schools undertook their work. They saw that unless Czech schoolchildren were exempted from the powerful assimilationist processes of the public school system, subsequent generations would lose their linguistic identity and the integral Czech community that the radicals valued would fail to emerge from the shadows.[213]

Thus, the public schools in Vienna were a microcosm of larger cultural passions and social conflicts. Membership in and support for the Komenský school involved differentiated roles and expectations. In view of the fact that the school enrolled less than 900 students, participation in it was the exception rather than the rule, even among the unassimilated Czechs. Petitions to the Imperial government in 1901 requesting that Czech public schools be opened in Vienna drew approximately 3,000 signatures.[214] Even allowing for the vagaries that affected such petitions, this was not an impressive number in a city with almost four hundred thousand people with some share of Czech descent. Some parents sent their children to the Komenský school simply because they could learn German more easily in a Czech-language environment. For them, Komenský was not an alternative to assimilation but a more circumspect route toward it. For the more nationalist-minded elite who financed and ran the school, however, other purposes were evident. The Czech school official František Bělehrádek who visited the Favoriten school in 1910 made the alternatives clear: either assimilation or "the retention of a Czech nationality in Vienna."[215] Even here nuances were evident. Some Czech activists dreamed of maintaining an identifiable Czech consciousness in Vienna but were realistic enough to admit the necessity of integration into the wider world. For these people the antimony "assimilation versus nonassimilation" was too stark, yet their delicate balancing act frequently resulted only in organizational paralysis. For others, such as the radical Jan Janča, who espoused extreme nationalist values, the very fact that Viennese Czechs were *not* embattled was a sign of moral failure. Janča felt that Vienna should become a *zweisprachige* city and that the Viennese Czech community should work toward ethnic particularity as a first step toward achieving national, state-level parity.[216]

When the leaders of the Komenský Association decided to expand by opening a branch in the Landstrasse in Vienna and another in the small Lower Austrian town of Unter-Themenau, they encountered a concerted campaign of obstructionism by Christian Social school authorities. Based on unfavorable administrative recommendations by local school councils, the Lower Austrian Provincial School Council ordered both ventures closed in early January 1909, on the ostensible grounds that sanitary and physical conditions in the buildings used were inadequate. The result was the inauguration of a five-year legal and administrative struggle, involving the city, the province, the state, the high courts, and the local Czech community, which ended in 1914 with the nominal, but empty and unenforceable victory of the Komenský school forces.[217]

In the summer of 1909 the Komenský Association decided that it would open additional private classes in two other Viennese districts, further challenging both the city administration and the Ministry of Education.[218] Reaction by Christian Social district politicians was exceptionally negative, with the Meidling district committee voting to condemn any effort to open a Czech primary school in its ward. Liberal newspapers spread rumors to the effect that the Komenský Association was planning "a systematic agitation against the German character of the capital."[219] Parliament having been closed by Slavic obstructionism in mid-July, the political season was over and most local politicians were about to leave the city or had already left. For the small yet vociferous bands of local German nationalists in Vienna and Lower Austria the issue seemed heaven-sent. Here was the "proof" that Gessmann's assimilationism was a charade. Here was an invitation for German nationalist gadflies in parliament and in the Lower Austrian Diet to exploit the traditional August hiatus when good political news was hard to come by and when the tempers of "professional" defenders of Germandom could be cooled by generous amounts of alcohol. On July 23 a German national wire service published a commentary warning of impending "Czech advances" in the city, blaming the situation in part on the "benevolent neutrality" which local school authorities (a not very subtle swipe at the Christian Social municipal administration) had shown over the years to the Viennese Czech community.[220] Other German politicians soon joined what quickly became a minor bandwagon born of public ignorance and moved by appropriate measures of ethnic viciousness and alcoholic excess. In the last week of July several public gatherings were staged against the Czechs. At one rally in Meidling a member of the Diet, Friedrich Leupold von Löwenthal, raised the issue of the *Lex Kolisko* and demanded that the Cabinet sanction the law as a reasonable defense against the Czech "attack." This was one of the first reported connections between the *Lex Kolisko* and the Komenský school crusade in 1909; it would not be the last.[221]

The Meidling rally was hardly impressive—sympathetic newspaper coverage did not print the numbers in attendance, always a bad sign. Lueger sent a tactical telegram to the conveners, excusing his absence and declaring that he would do "whatever is in my power" to keep Vienna German. From the Christian Socials' view this was a tempest in a teapot. Yet the *Neue Freie Presse* devoted a substantial allocation of editorial space in July and August to hysterical articles on how and why the city would soon be lost to the Czechs. That this was done to embarrass the Christian Socials was apparent when the newspaper editorialized that

> the Czech question is an awkward chapter in the history of the Christian Social party. The leaders of the party that have come to power in Vienna have a quite iniquitous past [on the national question]. The Czechs repeatedly recall the help which the Christian Socials sought from small Czech tradesman against the Liberal regime in Vienna,

and of the promises that were made in return for Czech electoral support. To be sure, Dr. Lueger has sought to cover up this past by all sorts of nationalist flourishes.[222]

On August 3 an essay appeared by Rudolf Kolisko, a former German nationalist deputy in the Lower Austrian Diet, arguing that the only effective defense against Czech pressure on the schools was the bill, named after himself (the *Lex Kolisko*) which the Lower Austrian Diet had repeatedly passed between 1898 and 1909.[223] The *Lex Kolisko* mandated that the official language of classroom instruction (*Unterrichtssprache*) in all Lower Austrian and Viennese public schools would be German. First passed by the Diet in December 1898, it had been opposed consistently by every Cabinet from Thun to Beck and denied Imperial sanction, as government jurists had insisted that it violated Section 19 of the constitutional law on the General Rights of Citizens (which guaranteed to each citizen the right of instruction in a language understandable to him, as long as it could be justified as *landesüblich* in the province) and Section 6 of the Imperial School Law (which invested regional school authorities with the power to determine the local language of instruction based on local conditions).[224] The Law was thus seen by the government as unconstitutional and, more importantly, as an attempt by a provincial legislature to tamper with the administrative prerogatives of the civil service. For practical reasons the Kolisko Law would not have prevented the establishment of private schools not possessing the *Öffentlichkeitsrecht*, since such schools were strictly speaking not "public" in character (which even Kolisko admitted). And since the Austrian Imperial Court had already ruled in October 1904 against demands by local Czechs in Vienna that they be guaranteed access to Czech-language primary schools that enjoyed *public* status, on the grounds that the Czech communities in Vienna and Lower Austria did not meet the legal requirements for recognition as a *Volksstamm* and that German was the conventional language of social and economic intercourse in Vienna (the *landesübliche Sprache*), the law itself might be said to be both too little and too much. It would neither abolish the private Komenský schools, nor could it add anything more to existing defenses of German culture provided by the courts.[225] In point of fact, the issue was more political than legal-theoretical. Discussing the *Lex Kolisko* with Brockdorff-Rantzau in August 1909, Richard Bienerth casually admitted that if the Cabinet had wanted to sanction the law, it could have found administrative jurists to manufacture an appropriate constitutional justification.[226] But the Cabinet did not wish to do so, not only because of the Emperor's opposition, but also because it would be a gratuitous insult to the Bohemian Czechs, bearing all the marks of German hysteria during the Badeni-Thun period.

However marginal the *Lex Kolisko* might have been, the violence of the summer of 1909 returned it to the public's imagination, not as a realistic legal defense against the Czechs, but as a symbolic concession to be wrung from the Cabinet by the manipulation of radical German pressure groups. Not what the Law did but what it implied became its critical valence.[227] Law and public disorder joined hands to disrupt the government's equilibrium.

Simultaneously with these events, conflicts also erupted in several small towns outside of Vienna that contained small but less assimilated and more culturally self-conscious Slavic immigrant communities. These people worked in a diversity of lower- and lower-middle-class occupations—as railway employees, craft artisans, farm workers, semi-skilled industrial laborers—in both semi-urban and rural contexts. In 1900 in the administrative district of Mistelbach 8,250 Czech speakers lived among a German population of 101,821; in Gmünd there were 4,107 Czech speakers against a German population of 57,717.[228] In Unter-Themenau, a small town in northeastern Lower Austria with the unusual situation of having a majority of Czech speakers, the Komenský Association had tried to establish a small private school with 135 students, but its operations were hampered by local and regional school authorities. When the Komenský Association decided to hold a meeting in late July in Rottenschachen to encourage the creation of other schools in the area, a crowd of angry Germans from the countryside responded by gathering in a local tavern to hear speeches prophesying the doom of Germandom. Tensions mounted throughout August in these small towns. In Schwechat (with a 10 percent Czech-speaking population) local members of the *Miromil* club, a friendly association whose younger members had recently adopted a more pronounced Czech nationalist tone, tried to hold a harvest festival on August 1, only to find that streams of nationalist "defenders," most of them from Vienna, had encamped in a tavern across the road and began hurling insults and rocks during the festivities. Two hundred Czechs confronted several thousand Germans, separated only by a line of police with bayonets.

Finally in mid-August the violence entered central Vienna. A Czech tourist club planned a river tour through the Wachau on a ship from the *Donau-Dampfschiffahrts-Gesellschaft*, traveling up the Danube from Vienna to Melk. When the ship departed its dock in Vienna on the evening of August 14, hundreds of demonstrators gathered to hurl insults at the travellers.[229] After the ship left, crowds of young hotheads carrying German colors and screaming the *Wacht am Rhein* ran through the city, insulting passersby and breaking windows until after midnight. A police report described the constituency involved: "youthful supporters of the German national party who were joined by many morally doubtful and drunken individuals who were intent only on provoking trouble—the ilk who form a typical street mob." In Melk a similar crowd heard inflammatory speeches by nationalist deputies Vinzenz Malik and Emanuel Weidenhoffer. Local German nationalists like Franz Pittner who, after months of languishing in the Lower Austrian Diet, now found themselves with a usable issue, published statements condemning the Christian Socials for "making deals with the Czechs in Vienna in order to destroy the liberal elements."

In Vienna, riots in Fünfhaus and Rudolfsheim in early September finally produced the bloodshed the police had feared. Insults escalated to fistfights and property damage, and on September 3 a young apprentice teacher, Wilhelm Mintnich, fell to his death from a rampart on the *Stadtbahn* while running from mounted police. The riots recurred with monotonous consistency. Nationalist politicians would organize protest rallies attended by men from diverse occupations—university and gymnasium students, craft apprentices, and shop attendants—for whom rhetoric eased the way to collaborative violence. Given the heat and the alcohol, these smaller crowds were soon joined by hangers-on, unemployed laborers, and others with a taste for street combat, and a few taunts or rocks would set the mass off. The arrest record for the night of September 2 was typical: of thirteen arrestees brought up on charges, one was thirty-five, one twenty-seven, one twenty-two, and the others were between sixteen and twenty years old.[230] A leading police official in Vienna, Baron Gorup, described the riots as starting out as harmless political rallies but soon losing control to street violence.[231] To argue that the hatred manifested even by those rioters who might be designated "nationalist" (probably a minority) was typical of the broader adult population of Vienna would be silly. But window smashing and brawling, coming during an increasingly lucrative tourist season and threatening to continue into the autumn, clearly disturbed local businessmen. To the extent that the Christian Socials finally acted to regain control, this was owing to constituency pressure within their electorate as much as to the Rathaus' anger at being upstaged by petty nationalists. In Lueger's world only one man held a warrant for demagogy in the *Residenzstadt Wien.*

In mid-August the Christian Social party leadership returned to Vienna for a meeting of the parliamentary commission to discuss the initiative of Stanislaus Glombinski, the leader of the Polish Club, to revive work in parliament and to end Slavic obstruction.[232] They enthusiastically voted to support Glombinski, in contrast to the German *bürgerlich* factions, whose leaders made cynical remarks about the Pole's motives.[233] The commission reacted to the street riots by issuing a communiqué denouncing the *Neue Freie Presse* in Vienna for having manipulated public emotions; indeed, Gessmann suspected that the German nationalist agitation was "directed not against the Czechs, but rather only against us." When a group of parliamentary chairmen met on August 17 to discuss Glombinski's proposals, Lueger personally guaranteed the safety of Czechs living in the city or of Czech politicians traveling there on business.[234] His initial reaction was to try to contain the situation by words of conciliation alone.

The persistence of the riots, and especially the death of Mintnich on September 3, made it clear that words alone could not curb the violence. Equally important, the riots were focusing unflattering attention on the city—was Vienna to become another Prague? Czech parliamentary deputies announced at the end of August that they would take turns remaining in the capital, even though parliament was not in session, in order to protect the local Czech community. Pan-German politicians gleefully seized on the chance, denied to them for the past ten years, to meddle in Viennese politics.

On September 6 the Christian Social party leadership again assembled in Vienna for the opening of the fall Diet session and initiated a two-front strategy to end the nationalist violence.[235] Abandoning their earlier hesitation, the leaders voted to make a publicly respectable effort to obtain the sanction of the *Lex Kolisko* in Lower Austria and to support similar legislation in the provinces of Upper Austria, Salzburg, and Vorarlberg (even though it was clear that the Cabinet was extremely unsympathetic). In return, the party expected that the local German nationalists would abandon the *Abwehr* movement and cease provoking crowds in Vienna. The official communiqué of the conference stressed once again that the only effective national defense was economic growth. Gessmann stated this forcefully at a rally at Zistersdorf, arguing that unless economic conditions for German-speaking agricultural laborers in Lower Austria were improved they would continue to emigrate and, in turn, would continue to be replaced by even poorer Czechs.[236]

Yet Gessmann's arguments highlighted the party's dilemma. If the Christian Socials took an intransigent stance on the *Lex Kolisko* and forced the Cabinet to sanction the law, they could be accused of fueling Czech obstructionism in parliament. The decision to take the "legislative route" was problematic and reflected diverse pressures on the Rathaus from within the municipal administration and lower elites in the party organization. Business and craft leaders associated with the party demanded relief from the riots and from Czech counteragitation. Later in September an embarrassing feud erupted in Vienna when Christian Social ward functionaries Paul Spitaler and Anton Nagler in the Landstrasse refused to allow the party secretariat to organize a local branch of the *Ostmark,* a Catholic organization for the defense of German culture that was based in Upper Austria. Richard Wollek then sought to discipline Nagler and Spitaler, but other Viennese ward bosses joined them, protesting against the "clericalization" of the party by men like Wollek and Josef Schlegel (whom they derisively referred to as the "Gessmann-Germanen").[237] Lueger was able to paper over the tussle, but only temporarily. The conflict was about territoriality and not about nationalism, but it did reinforce the need of the Rathaus to stop the *Abwehr* controversy as quickly as possible.

Pressures for a settlement also mounted in the Cabinet. A few days after the Ministry of Education's negative decision on Enslein's *Freie Schule* became public in late August, the Ministry's parallel decision to affirm the closing of the Komenský schools in the Landstrasse and Unter-Themenau also became known. That these decisions were politically connected was certain, all the more so since the *Neue Freie Presse* adamantly denied any parallel between the two. Local Czechs proceeded, again with the help of Bohemian parliamentary deputies, to organize a school strike in Unter-Themenau. Prominent Czechs visited Bienerth on September 2, demanding that the government grant the schools a temporary deferment from the Ministry's decision while they appealed to the Administrative Court.[238] German politicians, in turn, appealed to Bienerth to stand firm against the Czechs. On September 16 Stürgkh issued an order exempting both the *Freie Schule* and the Komenský schools from his Ministry's decisions until the Court ruled. This *Junktim* bought the Cabinet time, but Bienerth still found himself threatened by prominent Czech and German politicians immediately before critical negotiations to reopen the Bohemian Diet were to take place.[239]

Bienerth also faced personal conflicts within his Cabinet. The two Czech members, Johann Žáček and Albin Bráf, were unalterably opposed to the *Lex Kolisko,* but so was Count Stürgkh, nominally a "German" minister. Stürgkh resented the intrusions of provincial politics into the administrative prerogatives of his Ministry. Gustav Schreiner, the German *Landsmannminister,* informed Joseph Baernreither in late September that differences of opinion between Stürgkh and himself were so severe that he might be forced to "draw the consequences" (namely, resign).[240] The situation was even more complex in that Schreiner, a strident German nationalist, was intensely disliked by many in the Christian Social party leadership, whereas Stürgkh enjoyed considerable sympathy.[241]

In contrast to Schreiner moderate *bürgerlich* politicians like Josef Redlich admitted that the *Lex Kolisko* raised grave constitutional and political problems.[242] When Gustav Marchet sent Redlich drafts of two possible alternatives to the original *Lex Kolisko,* Redlich replied that the first—which simply restated the law while allowing exemptions for a few Czech communities— faced "an obstacle in Section 6 of the Imperial School Law which can scarcely be overcome." Redlich also noted, as the Social Democrats were later to argue, that enforcing the German language as the only customary (*landesübliche*) language in Lower Austria by means of a provincial law might have grave consequences for Germans living in majority Czech lands like Moravia. Redlich thought it best that the Lower Austrian Diet confine itself to a law defining the working language (*Amtssprache*) of local school bureaucracies as German. Anything more might be excessive. Marchet agreed, writing to Baernreither that "Redlich has justifiably raised the question of whether we should do this at all."[243]

Both the Christian Social parliamentary club and the Diet club met on September 16 to set party strategy. After hours of discussion, in which the possibility of revising the Kolisko law to make it acceptable to the Cabinet was discussed, the members finally agreed to continue to pursue the original version of the *Lex Kolisko*. Lueger would initiate the strategy with a motion of urgency requesting (but not demanding) information from Kielmansegg on why the government had not sanctioned the bill.[244] When the Diet opened, Lueger gave an uninspired speech introducing his motion of urgency, which was as much a repudiation of the German *Abwehrbewegung* as it was a critique of Czech aspirations ("the German people will not be saved by swinging clubs or other nonsense").[245] Seitz and Renner responded for the Social Democrats, delivering *ad hominem* attacks on Gessmann. For Seitz the fact that the Christian Socials now had to pander to cheap nationalist sentiment, after years of ignoring the problem, was a signal that the *Reichspartei* "had gone to the devil." Renner noted that if German Crownlands approved the *Lex Kolisko* a similar tactic could be used against the Germans in lands with Slavic majorities. Gessmann replied with an equally unflattering portrait of Seitz, but he made it clear that the party saw its actions in instrumental terms as a way out of the controversy. Hermann Bielohlawek then gave a speech which made little reference to the *Lex Kolisko,* and much more to the local nationalists who were trying to embarrass the Christian Socials by putting them on the spot. After listening to hours of such banality, Lueger's patience wore thin: "I am absolutely astounded that such a debate could have occurred about the motion I have just made."[246] His motion then passed unanimously, after the Social Democrats had left the chamber. They would not vote for, but dared not vote against it. Of the Christian Socials' low-energy performance, the *Neue Freie Presse* observed that "during the debates one missed on the part of the Christian Social speakers that tone of unbending determination with which they are, in other circumstances, accustomed to support their demands."[247] The *Lex Kolisko* had become everyone's political albatross.

At a meeting of the City Council the next day Victor Silberer resubmitted a motion to amend the Council's code of procedure to read that the only language of discussion and debate would be German. In spite of the severity of his illness, which had almost immobilized him, Lueger chaired the session and was openly unhappy with this last-minute attempt to introduce a version of the *Lex Kolisko* in his own domain. He replied sarcastically: "No mayor of the city of Vienna would ever dare to allow a language other than German to be used here. I don't need ordinances and laws; I do what I think is right and good."[248] Power would determine the sovereignty of language, not pieces of paper.

After the Diet debate on September 16 passions began to cool in Vienna, since the local German national leaders were now implicated in the Christian Socials' tactics and had to stop provoking the crowds. The brutal treatment accorded the most recent rioters by the police had also had a sobering effect. For two weeks Bienerth refused to allow Kielmansegg to respond to Lueger's initiative, in part because the Cabinet committee appointed to deal with the situation—Stürgkh, Schreiner, and himself—could come to no agreement, and in part because the negotiations in Prague over the reopening of the Bohemian Diet reached their climax in the last week of September and the first week of October.

By early October it was clear that the Prague negotiations would collapse. The failure of these negotiations meant that political attention immediately returned to Vienna. From a modest sideshow the *Lex Kolisko* became the principal event, the second act in a drama whose first act had just closed in Prague. To sanction the law would indicate the Cabinet's partisanship for the Germans; to refuse to do so would reward the Czechs for their intransigence. What had begun as a local symbol for street bullies now illuminated government priorities in the state-nationality conflict.

Bienerth finally bit the bullet and informed Gessmann and Lueger on October 1, 1909, that he would not recommend the sanction of the law in its existing form.[249] But the question became one of alternatives—would the Cabinet accept substitute language? The first week of October was spent in delicate discussions of possible ways out of the impasse. By October 5 Albert Gessmann was able to inform Josef Redlich that he had drafted alternative legislation, specifying German as the mandatory language of instruction for Lower Austrian teacher-training institutions and requiring that all teachers graduate from such institutions, and that the Christian Socials would offer this in place of the *Lex Kolisko*.[250] Redlich immediately wrote to Baernreither reporting that Bienerth had agreed to accept this compromise.[251]

Other Germans were also looking for alternatives. On October 5 Baron Freudenthal, acting for the *Grossgrundbesitz* delegation in the Lower Austrian Diet (possibly under the guidance of Gustav Marchet, who had been urged by Redlich to suggest an *Amtssprache* law to the nobles), submitted two supplementary motions urging the passage of laws which would declare German the official language of business in the Lower Austrian government and in the Diet and which would similarly mandate German as the language of business in all autonomous governmental agencies in the province.[252] No action was taken on Freudenthal's motions, but two days later the senior leaders of the German parties (the *Deutscher Vollzugsausschuss*) met in Vienna to hear Karl Urban and Anton Pergelt present a review of the controversy that included a proposal for a general *Schutzgesetz* to be offered in the four German-speaking Crownlands (Lower Austria, Upper Austria, Salzburg, and Vorarlberg) in place of the *Lex Kolisko*. The intervention of the senior German leaders, several of whom had just returned from Prague, was critical. No longer were the Christian Socials dealing with local nationalists whom they despised. No longer could they explain the whole affair away as a concoction of the *Neue Freie Presse*. Sentiment among the Germans was evidently as suspicious of the Christian Socials' motives as Lueger was of theirs, but it is also likely that Urban and Gross shared Redlich's concerns that what might help Germans in Lower Austria could later be used against them in Bohemia.[253] Sensing that it would be excluded from secret coalition talks, the Liberal press now screamed that the Rathaus was planning to substitute a cadaver for the *Lex Kolisko,* which the Cabinet would happily bury after a decent period of stalling.[254]

On October 8 Kielmansegg read the government's reply to Lueger's original motion of urgency, using the Imperial School Law as the reason for non-sanction (thereby avoiding a determination about the law's intrinsic unconstitutionality). But Kielmansegg also indicated the government's willingness to continue negotiating on the broader problems raised by the law. Debate then commenced on a motion offered by Lueger, based on Gessmann's draft, which specified German as the official language of instruction in teacher-training institutions in Lower Austria. The diet also voted to create an ad hoc twenty-member committee on national affairs that would study the possibilities alluded to by Kielmansegg.

Armed with Gessmann's alternative drafts, Lueger decided to prevent possible backbiting in the German camp by calling a summit between his own party and the major German spokesmen.[255] The conference that met in Lueger's rooms in the Rathaus on October 9 was remarkable.[256] Karl Urban presented a long, complex justification of his draft of a national protection law that declared German the *Landessprache* of the four Crownlands. Urban's draft replicated the two motions offered by Freudenthal in the Lower Austrian Diet on October 5.[257] Opinion among representatives of the German parliamentary factions as to what exactly the new draft would accomplish was divided. Urban insisted that the Cabinet's arguments against the *Lex Kolisko*'s constitutionality were not tenable but that a more pragmatic strategy to approach the problem of Czech schools "at least indirectly" would be to establish German as the *Landessprache* of Lower Austria. He was vague about the practical effects of this law (suggesting cryptically that, if not the law, then at least political common sense might make it desirable to allow the Czech communities in Lower Austria the possibility of maintaining public schools). Ernst Jäger argued that the draft would have no effect on the problem of the *Unterrichtssprache,* whereas Anton Pergelt had insisted that the law would cover both public and private schools, an assumption Gustav Gross delicately denied. None of the Christian Social delegates participated in the legal wrangling, and the comments of Richard Weiskirchner (who declared flatly that with this new draft the *Lex Kolisko* was no longer under consideration) and Gessmann (who asked Urban pointedly whether a special law on the *Unterrichtssprache* problem would be necessary) suggested impatience to end the scandal.

Weiskirchner recommended that the Czech communities in Lower Austria with a majority Czech population be exempted from the law. When Gustav

Gross admitted that the best defense against the Czechs would be a concerted German cultural program, the debate had moved onto ground more sympathetic to Christian Social interests. Several members sought to justify their intervention in Lower Austrian affairs; and Eduard von Stransky even apologized for the dissidence which the Viennese Liberal press was trying to sow between the Germans and the Christian Socials. The absurdity of this sentiment must have astounded everyone in the room. But Julius Sylvester had touched the most critical issue when he urged at the beginning of the meeting that whatever was decided had to be supported unanimously by all parties in the four Crownlands. This summit was not exactly a gathering of comrades, but it had gone more smoothly than anyone could have anticipated.

After the discussion of Urban's draft, Lueger adjourned the meeting until the participants could meet with Bienerth and Stürgkh the following day. Bienerth was noncommittal about the specific text of the proposals, but he was sufficiently encouraging to permit Lueger to call a second session of the group to finish the editorial work. Gessmann later (in January 1910) asserted that Bienerth had indicated his willingness to recommend sanction of the drafts, on the understanding that these new laws would replace the *Lex Kolisko* and that the German parties would agree not to revive that troublesome law.[258] The result was a twofold package of legislation that combined Gessmann's school law with Urban's version of the Freudenthal initiative of October 5. In the first law, German was declared the official language of instruction in teacher-training institutes; in the second, it was declared the official language of the Lower Austrian Diet, of the Provincial Executive Committee, and of the statutory cities. The Lower Austrian law varied from the others by essentially exempting several Czech communities from German in local official use. Neither law made mention of German as a general *Unterrichtssprache,* and it was clear to everyone, as Karl Seitz observed (comparing the new laws to the original *Lex Kolisko*), that it was not a case of the Christians Socials having poured water in their wine, but rather that only water was left in the glass.[259] The so-called protection laws simply sanctioned and gave legislative force to the linguistic status quo. In Lower Austria, for example, German was already the only language used in official business and in teacher training. No one, with or without these laws, would have dared to use any other language. Further, the laws did not prevent the creation of more Komenský schools, nor could they prevent the Ministry of Education from granting the *Öffentlichkeitsrecht* to those schools. They were a symbolic tour de force, but one that was still to prove expensive for Bienerth in provoking Czech outrage.

The Lower Austrian Diet passed this legislation on October 14, in its third set of nationalism debates within a month. The arguments for and against had by this time become stale; Karl Seitz made a halfhearted effort to trivialize the legislation; Karl Renner accused Gessmann (not incorrectly) of wanting to buy German national votes for run-off contests in the next parliamentary elections. But even the Social Democrats were not exempt from ritualistic politics. Seitz offered an amendment that would have allowed Czech-speaking petitioners to conduct personal business in Czech. Only after the amendment's defeat did the socialists abstain.[260] The few nationalists in the Diet halfheartedly assented to the compromise, although they doubtlessly felt they had been betrayed. What had begun in July as a *völkisch* crusade ended as a theatrical parade in October.

The question then became what the Cabinet would do. The Czech press in Prague had followed the protection laws in painstaking detail; their passage elicited thundering condemnations from Czech politicians and journalists. When a delegation of Czechs appeared before Bienerth on October 14 to protest the laws, the hotheaded Czech journalist working in Vienna, Jan Janča, threatened Bienerth with vague allusions to violence if the laws were sanctioned.[261] Bienerth abruptly terminated the meeting, but the incident made a highly unfavorable impression on the Emperor, giving credence to pan-German charges of linguistic terrorism in the capital.

Rumors abounded that the Czech ministers in the Cabinet would be forced to resign should Bienerth recommend Imperial sanction. He wavered for two weeks and at a meeting with Lueger and other German leaders on October 28 even suggested the possibility of delaying sanction in hope of successfully reopening parliament, but he was persuaded to honor his previous agreement.[262] On October 30, after heated debate between Schreiner and the two Czech ministers, the Cabinet voted to recommend the sanction of the protection laws. The same day the Czechs resigned, causing havoc in parliamentary negotiations and forcing Bienerth to delay the opening of parliament by almost a month.[263]

Was, therefore, the support of the Christian Social party for the 1909 protection laws an irresponsible act that destabilized the national parliamentary system? As noted in Chapter 3, Czech agrarians would most likely have initiated obstructionist tactics in 1909 even lacking the protection laws as an excuse; and in the aftermath of their sanction parliament was able to overcome the avalanche of obstructionist motions entered in late November and early December. Not all of the obstructionism behind these motions was ethnic. All of the agrarian parties in the House—German and Slavic—bitterly opposed the Rumanian trade agreement. Even the Christian Social ruralists were tempted to provoke serious trouble for Bienerth until they were restrained by their party leadership.[264] The willingness of the Christian Socials to join with Karel Kramář and the Young Czechs and also with the Social Democrats to push through important new powers for the President of the *Abgeordnetenhaus* in late December saved the session and paved the way for the relatively fruitful period of parliamentary work that followed in the spring of 1910. That Lueger and Gessmann aligned their party with the social and national "opposition" against their erstwhile class-coalition partners among the Germans suggested that they valued parliamentary productivity more than the cardboard facade of national unity in cases where some *reasonable* alternative to German intransigence existed.[265] In the face of Bienerth's inability to shape an effective parliamentary majority it would be disingenuous to suggest that the Christian Socials' support for the protection laws undermined Bienerth's leadership. It was difficult to subtract something from nothing even in the contorted world of Austrian politics.

For the Christian Social party the protection laws helped to ensure the continuation of the inter-German bourgeois coalition and to end the violence of the late summer. But both Gessmann and Lueger definitely saw the laws as the end and not the beginning of the national defense movement. Gessmann felt that the administrative-political avenues open to the party in Lower Austria—controlling the Provincial School Council and having a sympathetic forum in Stürgkh's Ministry of Education—were more than sufficient to control the kind of national imperialism being hawked by Jan Janča. Nationalism was a temptation which the party could ill afford, if it expected to compete successfully with the Social Democrats in Vienna. If in addition to ending the party's operational problems in the region the protection laws also forced the Emperor to effect a positive change of Cabinet, that would be acceptable. Rather than signaling a significant shift in policy on the nationality problem, the passage of these laws was an artful attempt to restore the political status quo in Lower Austria.

The protection laws did not end the party's trouble with this issue, however. In early January 1910 Edmund Hofbauer, a member of the small German nationalist contingent in the Diet, decided to repudiate the deal that Lueger and Gessmann had made with the German leadership on October 9–10—that no further action would be taken beyond the protection laws without the unanimous agreement of all the German parties—and to reintroduce the *Lex Kolisko* (now renamed the *Lex Hofbauer*). Gessmann felt betrayed and had Lueger summon a second summit of German *bürgerlich* and Christian Social leaders on January 17 in parliament to settle accounts. Although a few participants like Eduard von Stransky insisted that no explicit deal had been made with Bienerth in October, the majority accepted Gessmann's interpretation, and Gustav Gross drafted a communiqué announcing that the joint leadership felt further consideration of the *Lex Kolisko* to be "inadmissible" at that time.[266] A special "committee of nine" (*Neunerausschuss*) was established—including Gessmann and Jodok Fink—to discuss the future of the law.

In spite of this last-minute intervention the local German nationals would not relent, and Hofbauer brought into the Diet a motion to renew the *Lex Kolisko*. Gessmann replied on January 21 with a vituperative speech condemning the nationalists' dishonesty.[267] When the *Neunerausschuss* met on February 6 he again denounced the "equivocations and perfidies" of the nationalists. Gessmann assured his audience that his party would remain loyal to the German cause. But if the conference should decide that further consideration of the law was "not opportune," which "in view of the current political situation may well be the case," the nationalists must cease their propaganda attacks against the Christian Socials. The committee then decided, on a motion of Karl Urban, to request further information and more material and "only after examination of this material will the *Neunerauschuss* decide on further action in this direction." Gessmann thought this dodge was silly since everyone knew that the German parties already had all the material they needed, and he insisted for the record that the *Lex Kolisko* not be resurrected in the current session of the Diet.[268] Even Gross was forced to admit that "we are all agreed that our goal must be to prevent the opening of public Czech schools in the four German Crownlands. The *Lex Kolisko,* however, offers no practicable way to achieve this goal."

A further meeting of the committee on May 10 confirmed Gessmann's logic. Urban and Gross admitted that the target of the *Lex Kolisko,* since it involved the Imperial School Law, could be dealt with only on the parliamentary level and that the 1909 protection laws had put the Lower Austrian Diet "at the limits of its authority." According to Urban, "in order to secure influence over the [Czech] private schools, it would be necessary to change the Imperial school law." He then contradicted his October 1909 sentiments, admitting now that unless the Czech-speaking communities in Lower Austria were exempted from the *Lex Kolisko* the law would be unconstitutional. Gessmann then happily reemphasized his standing argument that the national conflict was essentially economic in its dynamics: "the economic moment is the most important. We often see that, for example, master craftsmen find it difficult to obtain credit in a German bank, while Czech-owned institutions respond to them in the most accommodating fashion." Finally, Hofbauer, who had caused so much trouble, gave a miserable and yet honest confession of his true motives: "Hofbauer reported that he had brought the *Lex Kolisko* back into the Diet without any ulterior motives, but that he was not fully informed about the current situation; now he realizes the significant difficulties which the matter would encounter. One needed something for external purposes to calm the German *Volk*."[269] The law had been a propaganda exercise all along.

Was it altogether surprising, then, that when Hofbauer again routinely submitted his *Lex Hofbauer* in the spring session of the Diet in 1912 he not only found the Christian Socials suddenly sympathetic but also saw the law ripped out of his hands by the majority and brought before the house with a Christian Social rapporteur, Karl Fisslthaler, on the last day of the session (after all the serious business had been accomplished)?[270] The Christian Socials were tripping over each other to support a law which Gessmann had wanted to kill three years earlier and which the Christian Socials had even denounced in a propaganda pamphlet as German national treachery. With the crucial campaign for City Council elections a month away, the Rathaus desperately needed to eke out every possible vote in the Second Curia, where nationalist rhetoric might win some white-collar voters away from the Social Democrats. Had the socialists allowed themselves the luxury of sympathizing with Czech school demands, this would have exposed them to the accusation of national betrayal.[271]

Karl Seitz battered the hypocrisy of the Christian Socials' new "German" strategy:

> I understand quite well why you deploy Herr Fisslthaler here reciting in the deep tones of his former Bismarckian and Schönerian past, and why you also suddenly stand here, as if you were pure, genuine, ancient Germans wearing bearskins, and would not think of anything else before the City Council elections except, exclusively and solely, how are we going to save the German folk in Lower Austria from the deluge of Czechs and from the Czech school children?

For Seitz the Christian Socials were doubly deceitful: they stole from the nationalists to outflank and to mollify them; and they geared up local election machinery to embarrass the Social Democrats by turning the old tactic used by the *Neue Freie Presse* against the Christian Socials in 1909—"softness on the Czechs"—against the socialists in 1912.[272]

For once the Social Democratic insults bore an uncanny resemblance to the truth. The principal defender of the Christian Socials was Richard Weiskirchner, who delivered a smug, platitude-laden speech on why the previous Cabinet (of which he had been a member) had refused to sanction the law. He then offered an ancillary motion that the Diet also recommend that parliament consider a law revising the Imperial School Law to give the provinces explicit jurisdiction over regional *Unterrichtssprachen*.[273] Clearly no one in the party elite had changed his view of the constitutional limitations or the propagandistic possibilities of the *Lex Kolisko*. By the spring of 1912, however, Lueger was dead, Gessmann in disgrace, and party unity shattered. As we shall see, the principal architect for the reconstruction of the Viennese party after its devastating defeat in June 1911 was Richard Weiskirchner; and it was also Weiskirchner who undertook a concerted campaign to attract white-collar voters back to the Christian Socials by infusing diluted nationalist discourse into the party's conceptual armory as protection against the Social Democrats.

The riotous debate that accompanied this particular meeting of the Diet saw one Christian Social deputy, Ritter von Troll, pour a glass of water over the head of Alois Heilinger, a renegade who had split from the party after Lueger's death and had spent the session taunting his ex-comrades. The socialist Johann Pölzer then screamed: "I'd like to see Lueger's reaction to someone doing something like that!"[274] Christian Social "nationalism" had become a part of the larger conceptual disorganization from which the *Reichspartei* suffered in the wake of Lueger's death. It was an effect, not a cause, of that disintegration, and its pathetic reappearance in 1912 suggested both the foreignness of the concept and its marginal value for rescuing a party foundering in emotional self-destruction.

That the socialists, verbal posturing aside, found themselves in a dilemma not very different from that of the Christian Socials showed how powerful were the effects of Vienna's corporate culture on both parties. The Social Democrats were loath to take any action to alienate Czech-speaking voters in city districts like Favoriten and Meidling and in the countryside. Yet many of Victor Adler's colleagues in Vienna considered the Komenský school movement a provocative distraction by Czech nationalists that would profit the Czechs little and would provoke counterreactions among the party's majority German clientele.[275] As on many other issues, the two ideological enemies in Vienna were not nearly as far apart as their respective propagandists insisted. A roll-call vote in the *Abgeordnetenhaus* in June 1910 on the motion of František Staněk to give the Viennese Komenský school a subvention of 100,000 crowns saw German-speaking Social Democrats voting with German-speaking Christian Socials *against* Czech-speaking socialists to defeat the measure. Even more than the Christian Socials, the socialists suffered from divisiveness within their party caused by nationalist confrontation. Czech socialist demands that they be allocated a parliamentary seat in 1907 from Favoriten in Vienna met with Victor Adler's stubborn refusal, contributing in a small but measurable way to the self-destructive nationalism that tore the Imperial party apart. According to Adler, "the Czech comrades cannot possibly demand from us that we engineer conquests for the Czechs on the territory of Vienna. A tactical advantage for the Czech comrades in this case would mean a terrible injury for the German party along the whole front."[276]

Yet the Austro-German socialist leadership was sensitive to its lack of resolve and consistency. At the party congress in Reichenberg in late September 1909, Josef Strasser criticized the willingness of Pernerstorfer and Glöckel to send telegrams of greeting to the annual convention of the "chauvinistic" *Deutscher Schulverein* and the decision of socialist city councilmen in various communities to vote for a subvention for Peter Rosegger's *Schutzstiftung* for

German schools. Pernerstorfer's self-justification was vacuous, and Otto Bauer finally admitted that Strasser's criticisms had merit.[277] If local Social Democrats in Vienna seemed slightly more pro-Czech after 1909, this was largely because the Christian Socials were inching in the other direction. Neither side believed in the reality of a Czech "takeover"; but neither was interested in helping the Czechs to develop as a distinctive ethnic group. The Czech community in Vienna had become a pawn in larger struggles over which it had no control.

FIVE

The Collapse and Reconstruction of the Christian
Social Party, 1911–1914

Lueger's Death

On March 10, 1910, Karl Lueger died. He had endured years of suffering and ultimately near blindness as a result of diabetes, kidney disease, and other ills.[1] His afflictions began to take their toll as Lueger neared the zenith of political success—he had been proudly reelected to another six-year term as mayor in April 1903—and by 1906 they had become so serious as to be life-threatening. So ill was he in 1906 that he had to abandon an active role in the 1907 campaign, delegating all the strategic planning and most of the day-to-day supervision of party affairs to Albert Gessmann and, in an important division of labor, leaving the supervision of the city government to Richard Weiskirchner. In his last years Lueger's involvement in party and municipal affairs was erratic, although he was well enough to return to full-time work in late 1909 and early 1910, chairing the party delegation in parliament and the Diet.

In January 1910, in one of his last public appearances, Karl Lueger delivered a remarkable eulogy at the funeral services of Ferdinand Klebinder, a Liberal city councilman from the Leopoldstadt who was also an active member of the Viennese Jewish community. Speaking before an audience of Liberal politicians and Jewish community officials, Lueger argued that

> everyone will agree if I insist that he who stands at the head of the city, who holds the highest honor that the citizens [*Bürger*] can bestow, is bound in the face of the majesty of death to put aside party differences, and to honor a man who has fulfilled his duty responsibly and honestly. Ferdinand Klebinder was a city councilman in the fullest sense of the word. He was always completely responsible and reliable. He was always objective, and if I did not always agree with him, I

was always eager to consult with him and, indeed, often followed his advice. . . . I thus feel obliged to express my gratitude and the admiration that I held for him.[2]

If the occasion was surprising, Lueger's words and sentiments were not. Did he now, at what he certainly knew to be the end of his own career, regret the slanders he had leveled at the leadership of the Viennese Jewish community? Even taking the *Arbeiter-Zeitung*'s insistence—noted above in Chapter 2— that the final years of Karl Lueger's regime had seen an effort to avoid injustice and achieve compromises, such an assumption would be dubious, running against what we know of the man. We cannot doubt that Lueger did feel friendship and camaraderie with a fellow political professional like Klebinder and yet believed that the world of party politics and the world of ordinary civil relations were two separate entities. Politics was war, and "the Jews" were by definition partisans of the enemy. Yet Klebinder was not only a Liberal and Jew, but also a political professional and a citizen of the *Vaterstadt*. Within the confines of war, codes of battle had to be sustained and professional credentials respected. Indeed, as he had done with Wilhelm Stiassny and several other prominent Jews who had expertise in urban affairs, Lueger clearly (if quietly) valued and exploited Klebinder's advice throughout his regime. As mayor, Lueger could consult and even esteem Klebinder, even if, an ambitious politician, he could isolate and marginalize him. If it was to Lueger's credit that this political Manichaeism allowed him to keep open avenues of communication with the Jewish community throughout his rule, it was to his much greater debit that he did not and perhaps could not appreciate the anxiety and the dismay that his confrontational politics caused for individual Jews. The Klebinder funeral says much about the integrative links as well as the disintegrative rifts between Jews and gentiles in Vienna on the eve of the war. Lueger's death two months later brought quiet, if sincere, expressions of condolence from the leadership of the *Israelitische Kultusgemeinde,* which Arthur Schnitzler regarded as humiliating.[3] Not everyone was capable of such political or personal generosity, however. Ludo Moritz Hartmann, for example, wrote to Stephan Bauer reporting Lueger's death, confident that the darkness lay behind them and that the new age beckoned.[4]

Lueger's passing marked a turning point in the history of Christian Socialism and more generally for Austrian politics. Of the numerous obituaries published on Lueger, two of the most illuminating were those that appeared in the *Arbeiter-Zeitung* in Vienna and in the Social Democratic *Kommunale Praxis* in Berlin. For the lead writer of the Austrian socialist daily Lueger had to be understood as a man motivated by a unique and successful "will to power," one that allowed him to achieve in Vienna what had proven almost impossible elsewhere in Central Europe: "to organize the *Kleinbürgertum* politically and

to constitute them as an independent party."[5] Lueger was perhaps the first bourgeois politician to "take the masses into account, who moved the masses, who
sank the roots of his power deep in the ground." He produced a "profound
upheaval," for Lueger

> snatched up everyone below the high bourgeoisie and above the prole-
> tariat who struggled for deliverance and who seemed capable of view-
> ing him as the liberator. He united these disparate elements who had
> no economic homogeneity or shared cultural interests—hard-pressed
> small artisans and businessmen, lower-ranking civil servants, and
> white-collar employees—into his party, he organized and disciplined
> them, and he made out of those whom the Liberal snobs arrogantly
> despised as the *kleinen Mann* the rulers of this city.

The Austrian socialist commentary was preoccupied with Lueger's will to
power over the masses—viewing Lueger as the man who constituted and educated a new, anti-socialist civil society far more powerful (and therefore far
more dangerous) than the Liberal regime that had preceded him. In contrast,
the evaluation of the Berlin socialist writer was more concerned with Lueger
and the state, paying tribute to Lueger as a strong, forceful professional politician who, unlike most German big-city mayors, refused to conform to the role
of an "ordentlicher und rechtlicher Verwaltungsbeamter."[6] Lueger was a leader
who forced his will upon the Austrian civil service and, when necessary, the
Crown itself. Rather than criticizing Lueger for this posture, the author thought
that it was actually "sein höchster Ruhm" that he had politicized the office of
mayor, not because the policies of the Christian Socials were either morally
correct or sympathetic to Viennese socialism (which they were not), but because the Austrian civil service would never be able to turn the clock back
to an age when political values and issues were subservient to the whims of
professional bureaucrats.[7] The implication of the essay was evident: the Austrian Social Democrats were fortunate not only in having had an enemy of
heroic proportions, worthy of the *agon;* they were also lucky to have had an
enemy not entirely different from themselves. For Lueger had provided a
model of political accomplishment and a process of civic-structural reform
within Austria upon which Social Democrats could build to assert *their* right
to political participation and rule. Indeed, the author could not help speculating
how Lueger would have crushed the arrogant officials in Prussia who hamstrung communal politics in the *Reich:*

> Let us imagine for a moment a situation in which Lueger's plans for
> a ring of parks and open spaces around Vienna encountered the oppo-
> sition of a minister of the quality of the Prussian gentleman Herr von

Arnim and his two gun-loaders Wrobel and Wesener, who without any understanding of the needs of the city's development, without any concern for the health of future generations, had dared with brutal crudeness and with a grim thirst for power to sell off the most beautiful parts of the environs. . . . what would Lueger had done with these puffed up gentlemen? He would have, figuratively speaking, given them such a kick that they would have been chucked head over heels from parliament and from their offices and would have landed in a blessed community for pensioners.

Even with this occasional wishful thinking the *Kommunale Praxis* essay was a sensitive appreciation of the man and his regime.

Ultimately the two socialist perspectives were complementary. Karl Lueger and his lieutenants had mobilized bourgeois public opinion in Vienna, building on older Liberal political traditions, but enlarging the clientele for those traditions to include the lower and the middle *Bürgertum* and empowering them to seek public policy consonant with their social and economic interests. They had also forced a historic revision of power relations in the Austrian governmental system not merely in Vienna, but in the other German-speaking Crownlands as well. Exploiting the mechanisms of autonomous administration (*Selbstverwaltung*) available to regional and big-city governments under the Austrian constitutional laws of the 1860s, Lueger had created a second tier of political power that offered an alternative to the failed parliamentary life on the Imperial level. The easy transition in 1918 between Empire and Republic on the provincial and municipal levels was in part owing to the fact that the Christian Socials under Lueger's leadership had spent twenty years carving out of the Imperial administrative system "spaces" of partisanship in the provinces and in Vienna. These spaces offered new and more flexible opportunities for administrative-political interaction than theretofore had been available in either Austria or Prussia.[8]

But by assuming power in such a forceful and personalized way and by politicizing local and regional bureaucracies in Vienna, Karl Lueger left his party facing a double dilemma. On the one hand, no single member of the Christian Social elite could easily replace Lueger, for Lueger, like big-city machine leaders in American politics, had no interest in grooming a successor to himself while he still held power. On the other hand, because Lueger had had the resources of the city and provincial bureaucracy at his beck and call and had integrated the earlier "petty notable" framework of Viennese club politics into the district administrations of the city, the party now faced the problem of constructing a formal party apparatus to maintain discipline and coordinate party planning. Since future Christian Social mayors would be unlikely to have the charisma necessary to deal with the party subelites in so personal a fashion, some independent, *neutral* control center was needed to coordinate party policy. By force of personality Lueger could control the various ward bosses and protect them against each other; a less charismatic leader might need the resources of a professional staff of party officials to ride herd on the rival associational and personal disputes that were (and are) part of any big-city political organization. And the two issues were connected, because until the issue of Lueger's successor as mayor and party head was settled, no effort could be expended on the structural reorganization of the party.

Lueger had played many roles in the party: head of the parliamentary delegation and hence head of the *Reichspartei* itself; mayor of Vienna; official head of the Diet delegation; chief of the municipal party organization; and charismatic spokesman for and embodiment of the party before Austrian society at large. In many respects he was a "boss" in the American sense of the term, although his political views and his administrative policies manifested some features of that Progressive mentality which in late nineteenth-century America was often opposed to "unreconstructed" bossism. A comparative view of his position in the context of American urban politics illustrates both the utility and the limitations of applying the same interpretive model to two quite different political cultures.[9]

The Boss in American urban politics was part of a system of political and administrative governance used for a rapidly urbanizing society of immigrant newcomers. Bossism represented a model of one-man rule, sometimes visible, often (to borrow Charles Merriam's term) "invisible," in large cities with unstable and rapidly changing ethnic foundations. The Boss employed distinctively antidemocratic and often arbitrary administrative methods, while basing his popularity, legitimacy, and electability on a democratic voting base.[10] Indeed, as Amy Bridges has recently argued, the emergence of machine politics in the United States cannot be understood without reference to the conjunction of new social conflicts attendant on industrialization and widespread manhood suffrage.[11] Bossism has also connoted a system of politics in which public power not only rests on and is exercised according to distinctively "private" standards, but in which the fluid that operates the system is a network of covert, discretionary "private" rewards (and punishments), commonly known as "corruption," distributed to circles of loyalists associated with the Boss. Of course, neither personalist rule nor a system of patronage and "corruption" was necessarily inefficient (frequently the opposite was the case), although many Progressive reformers seemed to equate immorality with inefficiency. Finally, Bossism represented a form of equalitarian political and economic power frequently at odds with established business groups in the cities and alien to the cultural worlds of the middle and upper middle classes, although big-city machines were willing to collaborate with businessmen as long as such interactions occurred on the machine's terms and to its advantage. In many instances the line between cooperation and exploitation was easily overstepped.[12]

Michael Frisch has delineated two categories of "progressive" theorists among opponents of the party machines who offered alternative visions of reform governance in the cities. Both (ironically) derived from variant readings of European urban governmental practice.[13] "Cultural-organicist" theory advocated by Albert Shaw, Frank Parsons, and others portrayed the city as a closed, autonomous corporation to be run independent of partisan political control by a moral aristocracy of businessmen and disinterested professional managers.[14] The corruption of machine politics and the private monopolists could be remedied only by cutting the cities off from state control, by providing them with substantial home-rule legislative powers, and by encouraging municipal socialist ventures as well as corporatist and, in Parsons' case, mutualist values in city governance.[15] In contrast, modern administrative theorists like Frank Goodnow argued that the solution to the corruption of the machine was not more home-rule and autonomy, which they held to be merely transitory remedies, but rather a more bureaucratized integration of city and state. Hence Goodnow proposed a reform that would not isolate the city from the state but infuse the city with the authority of state administrative values. This was not, as some critics have argued, a radical bureaucratization and depoliticization of city government, since Goodnow supported elected councils on a ward basis. But the activities of the City Council would be recognized for what they were—implementation of higher administrative power.[16]

Given the propensity of both groups of reform theorists to look to Europe as a source of inspiration, it is not surprising to find features of the Christian Social regime in Vienna that would have interested the American reformers and offered models of what they sought to export to the States (although Albert Shaw thought Lueger was a demagogue who was bent on disturbing sound urban government by misleading the electorate).[17] Variant readings of Lueger's regime might produce a more Bosslike or a more Progressive image, depending upon which features are accentuated. One might argue, for example, that Lueger was a "Boss" in every sense. He ruled the city autocratically and arbitrarily, yet constantly justified his actions by citing his interest in and respect for the "people." By the final years of his regime there is no doubt that, with his popularity at its zenith, his autocracy had a genuinely "democratic" base. Lueger also played the role of a patrimonial *Herr im Haus,* both tolerating and often covering up corruption within his own party and using a closed system of cronyism to govern the party on the district level. Finally, to the extent that it was a program of municipal rights against private "capitalism," his regime might be said to merit the rubric "anti-big business" as well. From the American perspective, Lueger's municipal socialism could at the same time be considered a Progressive policy, and his view of city industries and services as profit-making businesses to be run by rational management standards might have found sympathetic consent from those reformers whom James Weinstein has called the "Corporate Liberals."[18] Lueger served not merely as elected mayor, but as the chief administrative officer of the city (as head of the *Magistrat*), and he had substantial state responsibilities given Vienna's dual-track public administration. Hence Lueger had the unique opportunity to play the roles both of "Boss" and of "decentralizing reform bureaucrat," a combination rare in American urban history.

Lueger and his American machine counterparts shared a common need to manipulate administration to serve partisan politics and an occasional willingness to channel party ambitions to secure administrative efficiency (again, two categories that are not mutually exclusive). Fundamental tactical differences emerged, however, from the divergent legal and cultural contexts in which they operated. Vienna, like many large American cities, was a city of immigrants, and the party's deference to its "Czech" electoral clientele has been noted above. But neither was the Christian Social party absolutely dependent upon these people nor did it style itself as the principal protector of their rights and prerogatives. Quite the contrary. This was a party with a trenchant commitment to the *Heimat* and it defended a curial voting structure in the municipality that was impervious to "democratic" practice, however much Lueger or his colleagues might invoke the *Volk*. When Lueger spoke of the *Volk* he usually meant the "people" loyal to and rooted in Vienna's corporatist history, "people" who assented to and applauded the conception of Vienna as an Imperial *Vaterstadt*. Class-based ideological conflict established a different set of constraints than in American cities, making the municipal political system both more rigid and less open. When Lueger insisted in his political will that the party take particular note of the interests of white-collar, educated strata he revealed his own personal affection for the real Christian Social *Volk*.

The party of lower-class "immigrants" (in the American urban sense) in Vienna was the Social Democratic party, not the Christian Socials. By 1910 Lueger's party was one of landlords, property owners, industrial interests, civil service groups, and prosperous taxpaying artisans and merchants (even those who were first- or second-generation migrants from Bohemia or elsewhere). Were Vienna transposed to the United States, the Christian Socials' electorate might have served as the basis for a potentially fruitful Progressive-Reformist movement *against* Bossism. Lueger's demands that newcomers submit to "Germanization" were closer to those Progressive impulses in the United States for "Americanization" than to American machines which accepted the immigrants on their own cultural terms, just as his party's worship of Crownland autonomy against "centralism" was closer to late nineteenth-century currents in America where, in Barry Karl's apt phrase, "the words 'local autonomy' had become a code signal, not of democracy for all, but of democracy for some."[19] Where the Christian Socials differed from the American reformers was in their lack of interest in providing positive assimilative mechanisms—such as the settlement house movement—for the immigrants, preferring a more Darwinistic view that those who survived and who prospered economically by their own efforts would eventually want to vote for the Christian Socials, and those who did not would probably fall to Social Democrats in any event. If Lueger shared Frank Parsons' confidence in municipal socialism, he did not share his moralistic Fabianism. The rigid ideological configuration of European urban politics thus provided rival political camps with a false sense of certainty and predictability based on presumed class political behavior.

This does not mean that newcomers to Vienna might not want to vote for the Christian Socials, but in municipal elections few *could* vote for the party until they had established social and economic credentials and manifested considerable social mobility, since the curial election system was heavily biased in favor of established propertied elites. Democratic theory was much more appropriate for national elections, but here the party arrived at the paradox forced by Albert Gessmann's modernism. For the party to play a consistently democratic role in Vienna would have meant consigning much of its authority to the Christian Social Workers' movement, just as the democratic *Reichspartei* privileged peasants against the urban *Mittelstand*. For the petty notables of the *Bürgerklub* the first was unacceptable, the second barely tolerable. It was not accidental that the first successful initiative for modern proportional voting procedures in Lower Austria was sponsored in 1914 by Josef Stöckler's agrarian faction for the province's rural communities.[20] Weiskirchner and the Viennese, in contrast, held proportional voting to be an idea filled with "significant danger."[21] Stöckler and his colleagues felt greater certitude about the political behavior of voters with modest means in Lower Austria than they could about Christian Social merchants or property-owning artisans plagued with union disputes and walkouts organized by the Social Democrats in Vienna.

One fundamental difference between American and Austrian machine politics—whether Christian Social or, after 1918, Social Democratic—was the objective reference for their proprietary rhetoric. American urban politicians might speak of the political party as "their" possession, and only because they owned the party (as inherited through generations of nepotistic and cronyistic effort) could they claim to rule the city. Only because their party (in the most recent American experience, usually the Democratic party) was the most powerful, best organized, and most socially effective in the city was their rule legitimate. Power might be absolute, but it was sustained by achievement, not by ascription. Machine parties emerged in nineteenth-century American politics as assimilative spokesmen for the immigrants and workers against older, privatized, and paternalist conceptions of late eighteenth-century urban govern-ment. Even contemporary political rhetoric suggested the political party shared a combination of accessibility and territoriality—New York democracy of the mid-nineteenth century was the "true home of the working classes."[22] Thus the image of a theoretically pluralistic society constituting the city—the "people" of any populist's dreams—was valid for all citizens without distinction of race or economic status. As historians of American progressivism have noted, resis-tance against "outsiders" to the city came more from Progressives than from their machine opponents, who whatever their other failings, did have a crude but effective view of social pluralism and a belief in the naturally sovereign rights of the political party (a tradition always stronger in America than in Europe).[23]

In Vienna the reverse occurred. The Christian Socials were close to the older Liberal elites they had defeated (and then co-opted) in their paternalist and corporatist views. They too were property owners, they too were *Stadt-bürger* as opposed to *Staatsbürger.* Only because Lueger claimed to own the city could he justify the hegemonic control of his party in the curial election system. Vienna was the property (*Eigentum*) of the traditional owners of the city—the taxpaying bourgeoisie—just as its houses were the property of Christian Social landlords who dominated the inner sanctums of the party. This view of the city as a closed corporation and of the party as the reflection of that private world paralleled the image of Vienna as a bastion against "others" rather than as a mecca for "others." The consistency of this defensive posture throughout the literary hagiography of Vienna is remarkable, infecting Liberal, Christian Social, Nazi, and Social Democratic histories of the city.[24] Not the opportunities afforded to immigrants, nor the pluralism of the society which would welcome them (and the city was in fact both open and pluralistic, in spite of its governors), but suspicion of them and demands for the cultural and ideological conformity of the newcomers dominate the literature. This was the dark side of Lueger's nationalism: Czechs were welcome, but they must first become Viennese. Jews would be tolerated, but they must cease to be Jews. Although he disliked Lueger, Albert Shaw's vision of autonomous, corporatist municipalities, what Frisch refers to as "dairy democracies," was not incompat-ible with Christian Social posturing about Vienna.[25]

Finally, Vienna was not merely a city with a political "machine" but also a capital city integrated into and functioning within a long-standing Josephist administrative context. Municipal autonomy in Austria was not autonomy from machine parties in state houses, but autonomy from powerful, hege-monic, and meddlesome central ministerial bureaucracies located down the street. It was the reverse of what many American reformers sought. When Lueger took power in 1897 he found a reasonably efficient city bureaucracy. He did not hesitate to acknowledge the competence of the Liberal-appointed civil servants whom he inherited. As he said of Stephan Sedlaczek, a high-ranking official who joined the *Magistrat* in 1880 and who retired in 1907 because of ill-health: "I deeply regret Dr. Sedlaczek's retirement, and I would prefer that he could still be a very active official because those like him who have served for a long period of time have had an opportunity to gain a more intensive knowledge of the city's conditions."[26] Lueger's job as a reformer was not to enhance the autonomy of the local civil service but to make it more pliant. To a remarkable extent he succeeded in doing so. But try as they might, the Christian Socials were forced to observe the rules of a larger political-bureaucratic system written by someone else. Inevitably the supervision of the Imperial bureaucracy had an effect. The Christian Socials might select and appoint young men to the city bureaucracy on the basis of party connections and personal patronage, but they had to have educational credentials similar to those expected by the state civil service. On the higher levels of the *Magistrat*, the new employees had to be able to pass the Imperial civil service qualifying examination within three years of entering the city bureaucracy.[27] This does not mean that the Christian Socials blindly followed Imperial bureaucratic orders. On the contrary, the party's enormous strength in Vienna usually intimidated the bureaucrats in the state and regional ministries, who were only too happy to please Lueger whenever possible.[28] Nor could the government compel the city to enforce decrees or judgments without encountering such procrastination as to make the efforts ludicrous. This became clear in 1912–14 when the city consistently refused to follow the Administrative Court's injunctions on allowing a second Komenský school to open in the Landstrasse, leading one prominent jurist to complain that in Austria judges could decide the law, but certainly not enforce it.[29]

In this sense *Kommunale Praxis* was correct: from a Central European perspective, the Christian Socials assembled an enormous anti-bureaucratic political basis, which they did not scruple to use to pressure the state civil service, just as the Slavic parties, particularly the Poles and Czechs, also tried to bully the central ministries on affairs involving municipal home rule. But in exercising this electoral power, the party did accept the legal framework of municipal government provided in the Austrian constitutional laws of the 1860s, which meant that the party worked with and controlled a city government of professional civil servants, many of whom continued to assert their "value-freedom" and political neutrality but who, in practice, like the young Richard Weiskirchner, were only too happy to support the political party that paid their salaries. A report from a local civil service leader, Josef Dworak, to Weiskirchner in 1914 indicated that approximately one-eighth of the provincial and communal civil servants in Vienna were actively involved in Christian Social–influenced political organizations.[30] Most of the remainder were likely to be dependable voters for the party and were sympathetic to its policy interests. Dworak wanted to increase the ratio of activists, but the party leadership may in fact have found the current percentage of active as opposed to passive supporters more attractive: too much professional and political activism might lead to the municipal officials developing pretensions about an independent role in the party and the municipality, as often happened in American urban governments in the twentieth century. Yet sufficient partisans could be recruited from the local bureaucracies (Eduard Heinl and Konrad Rumpf, for example, who served on Gessmann's staff in the *Reichspartei* secretariat, were taken from the municipal and provincial bureaucracies) to enable the Christian Socials to pit one bureaucracy against another—city against state. In accepting "professionalism" and then forcing its conformity, the Austrians actually engineered a more powerful model of urban politics than was possible in an America that lacked a strict ideological dimension to its urban conflicts and that made a fetish of structural reform. Austrian urban government did not experience that process which Martin Schiesl has seen in America where "reform bureaucracies . . . constituted the new power centers in urban affairs and were more entrenched than the bases of power of the political machine." When the director of the *Magistrat*, Karl Appel, in speaking at Lueger's funeral asserted that the municipal bureaucracy had seen the mayor as an "emissary [from God] sent to wipe away the sins of the past and to elevate the hopes of the Christian people of Vienna," the Christian Socials could be justifiably proud of their political assimilation of the local civil service.[31]

The administrative supervision of Viennese municipal administration by the Lower Austrian *Statthalterei*, especially in those policy areas where the city exercised the delegated authority of the state, and by the *Polizei-Direktion*'s network of police inspectors and spies also limited the amount of corruption that could take place and ensured continued provision of effective communal services, no matter how much "honest graft" was or was not paid. Opponents of the Christian Social regime had a field day of self-righteous pomposity after Lueger's death, when scandals about corruption in the party broke in the spring and summer of 1910. Felix Hraba's improbable odyssey as a "reformer" will be considered in a later section of this chapter, but the generic issue of corruption in Austrian politics is one of a more general import and also lends itself to a comparative perspective of Bossism and machine life in America.

Ernest Griffith has argued that the height of corrupt practices in American cities occurred in the 1880s and early 1890s.[32] The enormity of this corruption can be explained by the demography of large American cities of the period, by their enormous institutional growth, and by the weakness of indigenous civil service traditions, but it was also a function of the wide range of jurisdictions American cities already possessed or shared with equally corrupt state governments. Big-city governments in the United States often had powers that simply invited corruption—the power to regulate the liquor trade and saloons, to authorize huge corporate franchises, to exercise local police jurisdiction, to regulate gambling, to set closing hours for shops. Municipal civil and criminal court jurisdictions, staffed with elected judges and district attorneys connected to the local machine, serving under the regulation of state governments often dependent on machine practices, were equally susceptible to corrupt practices. Many of these structural properties were simply nonexistent or radically different in Vienna. Police and courts were "national" and subject to Imperial ministries in the city, beyond local political control. Judges were Imperial officials, appointed for life; juries were selected from the voter and tax roles and had to be approved by the Imperial courts. Similarly, the city of Vienna had little control over closing laws and no responsibility for regulating the operational side of the liquor trade (although it did, as a delegated authority, collect liquor taxes). Hence the possible scope of "corrupt" behavior was narrower and more peripheral than in most American cities. Because the Viennese Christian Socials both dominated and yet, as politicians in a city with its own legally recognized charter, had a certain distance from their "state legislature" (the Lower Austrian Diet), there was less of the vertical, intraparty corruption that characterized relationships between big-city machines and statehouses in the United States. Indeed the most "corrupt" period of Vienna's history was the so-called *Gründerzeit* under the Liberals in the 1870s, which saw massive institutional expansion using private franchising; it was not Lueger's tenure, during which municipal socialist schemes were pushed through against private utility holders.

Much of what Lueger's critics touted as corruption was influence peddling for political gain: the allocation of jobs, stipends, and other spoils to friends and cronies of the party in return for loyalty and support at election time. This kind of influence peddling was common among politicians of all the bourgeois parties, and the Liberal journalists and politicians who lambasted Lueger certainly knew the conditions in their own camp. Hence the Christian Social reaction to Liberal moralisms was mere cynicism, especially when "good" Liberals like Gustav Marchet engaged in similar practices.[33] In the *Marchet Nachlass* one finds, for example, a thick file of "Interventionen"—letters to Marchet from people seeking jobs, scholarships, favors, and other expressions of Marchet's influence. Marchet's ability to get jail sentences commuted to less onerous monetary fines was, apparently, especially well known, as was his ability to arrange for reexaminations for candidates who needed to pass a given state examination for a specific civil service office and had failed it the first time through.[34] Nothing that Marchet did was illegal, and he did not take money for his interventions. But he was not above accepting a well-paying position on a bank board arranged for him by loyal friends. Rudolf Sieghart's cunning as a bureaucratic manager of Austrian parliamentary politics hinged on his ability to manipulate titles and other, more material rewards, such as *Verwaltungsrat* positions, in return for political compliance. Money was not at issue; Sieghart does not seem to have profited personally from any of these transactions, but it is clear that such horse-trading was rampant throughout the Austrian administrative and political system. As Josef Redlich later noted, it served to make Sieghart's *Ministerratspräsidium* into a "super-ministry" by which the Austrian higher civil service kept a tight rein on the various political parties after 1900.[35]

This kind of subjective favoritism lies at the heart of any political machine, but the Christian Socials practiced it on a wider scale and with considerably less discretion than did Liberal lawyers or university professors. Virtually no one in late Imperial Austria got anywhere of moment or significance in public life without some form of *Protektion,* a situation which, some local critics would argue, has not changed very much in Vienna today. In a culture in which personal deference and sociability were seen as necessary complements to standards of rational work-performance and "output," it is hardly surprising that personal patronage became so vital and integral a part of any public official's cursus honorum. Hanns Schlitter's private diaries, kept during his time as director of the *Haus-, Hof- und Staatsarchiv* between 1913 and 1918, contain instances of Schlitter's willingness to bend the rules to arrange (or deny) sinecures for men with whom he felt personally comfortable (or uncomfortable) working.[36] Reliability and accountability could best be established by a system of subtle social guarantees, which a system of social and cultural patronage afforded. When talented young men with advanced educational standing were in a surplus, as was the case throughout late nineteenth-century Germany and Austria, other criteria beyond educational credentials were necessary to make "rational" selections possible.

This expectation of both minimum technical competence and proper political connections was not characteristic only of inbred Viennese cultural systems, whether Liberal, Christian Social, or Social Democratic. As one local politician in the Daley machine in Chicago noted, politics in his world was essentially "without records," conducted in a culture of verbal, nonwritten exchanges. A man's word is his bond. Decisions taken today might have long-term consequences down the road, and often the truth value of anyone's motives—measured by intention or consequence—is apparent only after arbitrary choices have long been made. The most realistically valid and reliable credentials in such circumstances are personal and subjective appraisals which emerge from personal proximity and dependency. This is essentially what one colorful old ward politician in Chicago meant when he observed, "We don't want nobody nobody sent."[37] Lueger would have warmly agreed, for he valued personal loyalty as a supreme virtue. As he said in 1907 in a tribute to his fellow Landstrasse politician and personal friend of thirty years, Karl Hörmann, "you are one of the men on whose word one can always rely, in whom one can always put total loyalty."[38]

A second and more easily defined form of corruption involved money for personal gain. Here the record of the Christian Social party was less ambitious than the worst excesses of American machine politics, but damaging nonetheless. Again, distinctions must be made between appearance and reality. The Axmann case, which some local wags called the "Christian Social Panama," was perhaps the most notable instance of money corruption in the party.[39] Julius Axmann was the leader of the Christian Social commercial clerks' (*Handlungsgehilfen*) association in the 1890s, and the chairman of the journeymen's committee (*Gehilfenausschuss*) of his guild. Facing severe pressure from clerks loyal to the Social Democratic slate, led by Karl Pick, Axmann secretly channeled 34,000 crowns which had been accumulated to build a convalescent home for sick employees into his personal election fund. Had Axmann maintained control, he would have been able to cover up the misappropriation, but in the election conducted in April 1902 Pick's forces defeated him and the Social Democrats were in a position to gain access to the organization's financial records. Karl Lueger then intervened to obtain an equivalent amount of money which was deposited in the city treasurer's office on behalf of the clerks (from sources never revealed) and forced Axmann and a colleague, Heinrich Frass, to resign from the curatorium regulating the endowment. The story only broke years later, when Felix Hraba and Ernst Vergani conspired to embarrass Gessmann and Axmann by releasing its details to the public in the summer of 1910. Gessmann discussed the incident at a parliamentary club meeting in July 1910, confessing that several members of the party leadership had known of Axmann's misdeeds, but out of respect for Lueger they had kept quiet.[40] Axmann was forced to resign from the party and the parliamentary club and he disappeared from public life.

The most ironic aspect of the affair is that Axmann clearly did not take the money for himself—the theft was for political and not personal ends. Because of this wrinkle his colleagues in the party seemed to accept his action as regrettable but necessary, given the poverty of party finances in the 1890s, just as his exclusion was equally regrettable but necessary. Axmann was unlucky to have gotten caught, though not by the law, as the victim of a political vendetta against his patron, Albert Gessmann.

Not all cases of local corruption were so impersonal. The control the party exercised over the *Stadtrat* and the Provincial Executive Committee, which were responsible for approving bids on purchases of goods and services in the city and in the Crownland, inevitably led to questionable decisions and, in some cases, scandal.[41] Even in the parliamentary club speculation about improprieties emerged. Franz Morsey reported in June 1910 that he had been unable to obtain an order for paper products in city offices on behalf of the firm he represented (as a member of its board of directors), even though the firm had submitted the lowest bid, because *Protektion* was functioning.[42] It is difficult to estimate the extent of this corruption, since the Justice and Internal Affairs Ministries seemed to have maintained a paternalistic indifference towards the party's financial peccadilloes in Vienna and in Lower Austria, conducting no systematic investigations even after Lueger's death. This might suggest that such corruption was sufficiently modest to allow the Ministries to rationalize that the political costs of alienating and embarrassing the party were greater than preventing a few "deals"; or, conversely, that the corruption was so enormous that, for the sake of the state's image, it was best left untouched. Those instances of corruption in public contracts that became widely known usually surfaced during private libel trials or in resentful memoirs, not in the context of state investigations. But it does seem likely that the politicians on the *Stadtrat* and Provincial Executive Committee played leading roles in either undertaking or at least tolerating these abuses (perhaps explaining the inordinate desire of local politicians to get elected to these bodies), even though the amounts of money or other commodities changing hands were often so small as to be embarrassing for a typical American machine boss. The *Arbeiter-Zeitung* was a particularly vigilant observer of Christian Social contracts and patronage manipulations, and its perpetual claim—"the city administration of Vienna stands alone among all municipal administrations in its unlimited possibilities for corruption"—while exaggerated had some core of truth.[43] Certainly the party's election fund profited handsomely from a regular infusion of contributions solicited from local industrialists and merchants who wanted to obtain (or retain) municipal contracts.

Lueger himself never took a crown of honest graft; and reasonably objective assessments of other top leaders like Gessmann and Weiskirchner asserted the same.[44] This was perhaps because they found it unnecessary, given the multiple offices to which they managed to get themselves elected or appointed. Weiskirchner's annual salary as a municipal civil servant was 4,000 crowns in 1896; twelve years later it was over 50,000 crowns—all of it legal—as Minister of Commerce, member of parliament, member of the Diet, and *Magistratsdirektor* in retirement.[45] This multiplicity of offices was much envied by lesser lights in the party, but was intelligible in view of the dearth of ministerial talent among the first generation of party leaders. This situation may explain the paradoxical divergence in values between the relatively honest elite of the Christian Socials and the envious and self-indulgent subelite that lodged itself with Lueger's and Gessmann's approval in marginal, but still lucrative, positions in local government. Those who could assemble wealth legally, using talent, education, and social patronage did so; those arriviste ward politicians without administrative capabilities or Court social graces did so in more sordid ways.

A third form of corruption of which the party was frequently accused was electoral manipulation. As the local administrative authority responsible for conducting elections and tabulating the results, the *Magistrat* was viewed by the Social Democrats as an ersatz political cadre of the Christian Social party, stealing votes and penalizing the opposition parties by disenfranchising their voters.[46] Since the *Magistrat*'s supervisory powers over provincial and national elections were delegated to it by the state, the Imperial government had the right to investigate socialist complaints of vote fraud in the 1907 parliamentary and 1908 Diet elections. Inquiries undertaken by the Lower Austrian *Statthalterei* suggested that some corruption certainly existed on the ward level, although the extent to which the *Magistrat* actively cooperated with it was debatable. Erich Kielmansegg concluded that administrative disorganization and poor record-keeping, together with the confusion of having to assemble on a short-term basis lengthy voter registration lists based on the new system of universal suffrage, were far more to blame for faulty voter lists than willful manipulation by local officials.[47] A second investigation in March 1914 by Richard Bienerth (who had replaced Kielmansegg as *Statthalter* in 1911) similarly exonerated the municipal bureaucracy.[48] On the other hand, the extent to which these second-level administrators were themselves exposed by these accusations and tried to minimize irregularities is difficult to judge, but it should not be discounted. Certainly the Social Democrats believed that Kielmansegg and his staff bore some of the blame.

As for corruption in the polling place, the Christian Socials had their rightful share. The Christian Social party archive reveals, for example, the charming story of Stanislaus Wagner, a local party operative who sent a plaintive letter to the party secretariat in 1914 asking that the party provide him with a personal subsidy.[49] To justify this unusual request Wagner gave his story. An unemployed commercial clerk, he had just spent a month in prison for an election fraud violation and could not find employment. During the 1913 parliamentary runoff election in the Leopoldstadt, Wagner had successfully voted seven times in the same ward, using various forged voter-registration cards. Apparently a man who took pride in his work, Wagner went back for an eighth attempt. On his way out of the polling place he had the misfortune to get into a fistfight with socialist poll watchers, who summoned a policeman. When the policeman found a voter identity card on Wagner made out in the name of "Josef Schimmel," his career as a political operative for the Christian Socials came to a sudden halt. Wagner did not explain how the officials of the *Magistrat* who were supposed to be supervising the voting allowed the same man to obtain seven different identity cards. When faced with such evidence one must conclude that, in spite of Kielmansegg's obfuscations, socialist complaints about a politicization of the municipal bureaucracy had some substantial basis in fact. But it would also be naive to think that the Liberals and Social Democrats did not engage in similar practices, albeit with less success. The number of Social Democratic election agitators arrested by the police because of voting irregularities in Viennese elections after 1900 was sufficiently high to suggest more than police overscrupulosity. Following the 1912 municipal election a Liberal city councilman, Alois Moissl, was also convicted of election bribery.[50] If corruption marked Viennese electoral politics, it was systemic and not peculiar to one ideological faction.

The issue of corruption involved complex questions of self-perception and self-definition: what actually was "corrupt" according to the internal standards of the party itself or according to contemporary political morality? For example, Albert Gessmann was severely criticized for his involvement in the *Baukreditbank,* a private bank founded by Gessmann and other investors in 1909–10 to assist developers and building contractors in assembling capital for new construction, a policy arena in which Gessmann became interested during his service as Minister of Public Works. Vergani and others anxious to undercut Gessmann's reputation in the party intimated that he was taking care of his friends financially—which may or may not have been true—and that he was "immoral" for involving himself in a "capitalist" undertaking that charged "usurious" transaction rates.[51] The stated assumption—whatever his enemies' actual motives—seemed to be that a "reform" politician like Gessmann who established private banks and got himself and his colleagues lucrative positions on boards of directors must be "corrupt" because he was betraying his party's own principles.

The morality and propriety of Christian Social parliamentarians accepting well-paying seats on industrial and financial boards of directors became the subject of an exceedingly provocative party discussion on June 21, 1910.[52] Since the party had begun its life on an "anticapitalist" platform in the 1880s, that so many members served on industrial boards (or as bank owners) might be seen as a betrayal of public trust. Several reform-minded members like August Kemetter and Leopold Kunschak demanded that restrictions be placed on such involvements, to the extent that the boards not be those of public-service corporations and the seats not based on personal stock ownership. Inevitably, the discussion commenced with a review of the connections of the party to Rudolf Sieghart and his cronies in the Viennese banking world. Kemetter was convinced of the evil machinations of Rudolf Sieghart—he had provoked a minor scandal in parliament in March 1910 when he exposed a deal in which Sieghart was apparently involved whereby a certain official in the Railways Ministry by the name of Siegmund Sonnenschein was to get control of a powerful new bureau—and he now demanded that the party demonstrate its independence. But Alois Liechtenstein reminded his colleagues that "Sieghart has helped the party a great deal through five ministries." Gessmann seconded this view, arguing not only that Sieghart himself was respectable, discreet, and a man of his word (an unusual set of virtues in Imperial Vienna), but that beggars were not in a position to be choosers: "a party that is not able to raise money by its own resources has to find other sources, since the contributions of the membership are by no means sufficient." The discussion might have ended on this ruthlessly pragmatic note, but other members moved the debate onto the level of principle, asserting that anticapitalism was no longer morally or operationally tenable for the Christian Social party. Several leading Alpine deputies made surprising confessions of having been converted to see the morality and efficacy of the capitalist system. Aemilian Schöpfer now thought that the party could no longer survive simply by depending on its old anticapitalist rhetoric. Industrial capitalism was not in itself immoral, and the party must concentrate on gaining access to capitalist circles and working for reform from within, not on attacking capitalism from without. Schöpfer added, in a remark so sensitive that Gessmann had to remind everyone of the confidentiality of the meeting, that "anti-Semitism is found only among nations that have little business sense" and that the party would have to engage in "educational work" to change its voters' opinions—presumably anticapitalism and perhaps even anti-Semitism might have to be jettisoned if the party were to modernize itself. Victor Fuchs of Salzburg added that party involvement in industrial elites would help the "small people" (its petty bourgeois electorate), since the party would then play a role of influence and leadership in industrial and banking circles: "We also must play a role in the money markets." Gessmann had already insisted at a meeting in mid-May 1910 that the party needed a closer relationship to industrial capitalism if it were to survive against the Social Democrats: "Today the party could use capitalism, especially to support a party newspaper . . . our craft policies using the *Befähigungsnachweis* as a political idiom are bankrupt—we need to attract capitalistic circles to support our organization."[53] Even Kemetter admitted that he had been persuaded by the liberal Catholic theologian Franz Martin Schindler to accept some forms of investment and participation in industrial capitalism as morally legitimate.

The May and June meetings constituted nothing less than a formal repudiation of the ideological origins of the party in the 1880s. For Schöpfer, involvement with big capitalism or high finance per se could not be corrupt, since the capitalist system itself was not immoral. The issue was not whether politicians belonged on boards of directors, but what kinds of moral choices they made in these roles. The propriety of such commitments could be examined only on a case-by-case basis, not by totalistic enactments. The danger in Schöpfer's approach was twofold. First, it was politically volatile in Vienna, as long as the party continued to depend on the curial system of voting (had Gessmann's critique of the *Kleingewerbe* become public it would have seriously compromised the party within its artisan voting base). Second, by encouraging the party to involve itself with the leaders of big industry, it inevitably exposed members to the kinds of corruption rampant in Austrian business circles in the late nineteenth and early twentieth centuries. That the party ultimately took this route under Seipel in the 1920s, evincing procapitalist sympathies toward Austrian big business, is a matter of record; this transformation occurred when the party ceased to be dependent on the Viennese lower-middle-class electorate as the principal source of its identity and institutional power. But this process began well before the First World War, and as the June debates suggested, it resulted from a conscious shift in the strategy of the party elite that had begun even before Lueger's death.

The Crisis in Succession, 1910–1911

Immediately following Lueger's death, a crisis in the succession to the office of mayor occurred, which had long-lasting repercussions for the party over the next eight years. When a severe attack of diabetes and kidney disease in early 1907 had made it seem unlikely he would survive, Lueger had dictated, in the presence of a small circle of cronies (including Gessmann and Liechtenstein) his so-called "political testament," in which he nominated Weiskirchner as his personal choice to succeed him as mayor of Vienna and, implicitly, as head of the Viennese party organization as well.[54] The testament was noteworthy since Lueger urged his colleagues to keep the party's attention on the smooth administration of Vienna as the centerpoint of Christian Social politics and to maintain a careful balance between all interest groups in the party, paying as much attention to the urban population and especially to the white-collar electorate in Vienna as to the rural electorate, with the strong implication that the party not become solely an agrarian movement. Lueger saw that without the centripetal weight of Vienna, the party might disintegrate into a collection of feuding regional principalities; and if the party should lose Vienna, the remainder—peasants and small townsmen—would be loath to protect those Viennese bourgeois interests that were closest to Lueger's heart. Hence the not-so-subtle slap at Gessmann: the position of mayor would go to a Viennese civil servant, a politician with reasonably urbane and secular tastes who would ensure that Vienna continued to exercise its proper share of power within the movement.

From Gessmann's subsequent correspondence with Friedrich Funder it is apparent that the relationship between Gessmann and Lueger was, at least after 1907, not without serious tensions.[55] Following Lueger's death, Victor Silberer observed that "even if we have lost our Bismarck, we still have our Moltke, and that person is Gessmann."[56] The analogy was imperfect, but it summed up well the contradictory roles and different visions of the two leaders. Gessmann disliked the informality and personalism of Lueger's style of rule and his preoccupation with Vienna and Vienna's problems as a moral world exclusive of state-level interests. To Funder he complained that "thanks to the unhappy state of the character of our 'great' Lueger and the absence of character that he encouraged in others, we are all done for." For Gessmann, Vienna was the linchpin for what he described to Funder as a "Sammlung der bürgerlichen Parteien" against the Austrian socialists.[57] The two visions were not necessarily mutually exclusive, and on many issues, such as nationalism and fear of socialism, Lueger and Gessmann shared common ground. But where Gessmann saw Vienna as an agent and instrument of state-level renewal, Lueger saw it as a corporate organism unto itself. The final object—the stability of *bürgerlich* society in Austria—was similar, but the means favored by the two men differed. By himself, without the pressure of Gessmann, Beck, and Ebenhoch, Lueger might have been satisfied with the status quo of 1905—the Christian Socials would cooperate with the Alpine parties on an issue-by-issue basis, without launching a new movement. This was clear by late 1909 when, as the Christian Social parliamentary delegation grappled with its members' divergent reactions to the Balkan commercial treaties, Karl Drexel argued that "the club should debate the great questions involving agriculture in a systematic fashion. That we have not done. Then we also need to educate our voters, just as the German Center party has itself done. Our party needs a professional staff center [*Geschäftsstelle*]." Lueger's reaction was quick and brutally to the point: "Such a staff center would cost a lot of money, and that we don't have. The fundamental reason lies in our lack of money. . . . Our party is different from the German *Zentrum*. We have to be patient."[58] For the elderly Lueger, four months before his death, Gessmann's vision of the Christian Socials as a Hapsburg version of the Center had been found wanting.

Gessmann also found Lueger's tolerance of the foibles of the local party elites frustrating, not because he was more self-conscious than Lueger about corruption, but because he hated the inefficiency, selfishness, and tactical irrationality of ward politics. His problem was not a lack of democratic imagination, but a lack of democratic consistency, for Gessmann knew that the party in Vienna had to depend on an antidemocratic curial system, and yet he insisted on the virtues of electoral democracy on both the provincial and state levels.[59]

Lueger in turn came to resent and perhaps even to fear Gessmann's power. Felix Hraba's enemies thought that Lueger had put Hraba up to trying to curb Gessmann's near absolute power over financial expenditures in the Lower Austrian provincial government.[60] The 1907 Lower Austrian suffrage reform was almost exclusively Gessmann's work, undertaken during Lueger's absence, and it was no accident that the agrarian interests ended up with more seats than the city of Vienna. Although in the end their conflict may have been more personal than ideological, it was all the more intractable for that. Lueger's pride was

wounded when he faced his own superannuation by a formerly deferential lieutenant, who had both the physical health and political audacity that Lueger had
lost by 1908–9.[61]

Gessmann reacted to Karl Lueger's death with efficiency and dispatch
within the parliamentary club. On March 15 Prince Alois Liechtenstein as *Landmarschall* of Lower Austria was immediately named chief of the *Reichspartei*
and of the Viennese organization (the *Wiener Parteileitung*) to replace Lueger.
Liechtenstein in turn, citing his frailty and ill-health, nominated Gessmann to
head the parliamentary club.[62] Gessmann then pushed through a more formal
structure of collective control, dominated by himself as the new parliamentary
club chairman.[63] Under Lueger membership in leadership of the *Reichspartei*
was fluid and informal, with Lueger inviting to meetings of top party leaders a
shifting membership; the same casual openness was true of the leadership of
the Viennese party proper and of the central election committee (*Zentralwahl-
komitee*) that approved or disapproved candidates' nominations.[64] In May 1910
the parliamentary club formalized and gave permanent membership to a
Reichsparteileitung, consisting of the leader of the party, party members serving as Imperial ministers, the fourteen-member parliamentary commission, the
chairmen of the provincial party organizations, the Christian Social provincial
governors (where applicable), the mayor and three vice-mayors of Vienna, and
various party secretaries. Consonant with the ethos of Lueger's testament, Vienna retained its hegemony with almost half of the 33 seats. A five-man executive committee (Liechtenstein, Gessmann, Ebenhoch, Weiskirchner, and Neumayer) assumed temporary control of party affairs in place of Lueger until such
time as a permanent party directorate could be established.[65] Alfred Ebenhoch
presented this transitional structure to the general party conference summoned
in June 1910.[66] In addition to establishing these categories of party representation, the plan also expanded and formalized the purview of the party secretariat, dividing it for administrative purposes into two interconnected parts. The
first part was a secretariat for the parliamentary club itself, consisting of a
"wissenschaftlicher Konsulent," who was a deputy drawn from the party's delegation, and an administrative head of the secretariat. The former was Karl
Drexel, elected from Vorarlberg; the latter was Josef Sigmund, also from
Vorarlberg. Sigmund was to play an increasingly important administrative role
in the party, particularly during World War I. Both were sympathizers of Albert
Gessmann. The second part was the party secretariat proper, in which Eduard
Heinl, Konrad Rumpf, Richard Wollek, and others took responsibility not only
for the work of the party, but also for the administration of the Lower Austrian
Bauernbund and other party-affiliated organizations.[67] When the Christian Social Diet Club met on March 16, Gessmann was elected chairman of that club
also. On both national and regional levels, Gessmann's intentions were trans-

parent: Liechtenstein was to be the figurehead leader, while Gessmann would actually run the party.[68]

In contrast to the transition on the state and provincial levels, the succession to the Rathaus led to political disaster. Gessmann conspired to replace Weiskirchner as the party's mayoral candidate even before Lueger was dead. He told Redlich several days before Lueger's death that he expected to be the next mayor.[69] Over the course of 1910 and 1911, details of the complex events following Lueger's death sputtered forth in trickles of rumors, the veracity of which was then (and is now) extremely difficult to demonstrate. From the records of the party leadership, however, the main lines of the drama emerge. Weiskirchner visited Gessmann in late February 1910 and proposed a deal: he no longer considered himself bound by Lueger's wishes and even claimed as of February 1909, when Weiskirchner entered the Cabinet, Lueger's testament was no longer valid. Weiskirchner told Gessmann that he preferred to remain at the Ministry of Commerce, where he expected soon to succeed Bienerth as Minister-President, and offered to support Gessmann's candidacy for the Rathaus.[70] After some hesitation Gessmann accepted the proposal and began to conspire to negate Lueger's will. On the day of Lueger's death, a key group of party leaders met in the Palais Liechtenstein to hear Weiskirchner disavow his interest in the mayorship and also warn against a "provisorum." In spite of Leopold Kunschak's importunities that he take the job, Weiskirchner held firm, and at the end of the meeting Gessmann announced that he was grateful to Weiskirchner for his statement, "for without this I would have refused to even think about a candidacy [for mayor]."[71]

However, a series of blunders, for some of which Gessmann was responsible, made the deal impossible. Gessmann hoped to prevent the publication of Lueger's political will, and launched his campaign for the mayorship two weeks before Lueger's death by having the *Reichspost* publish the account of a private interview between Lueger and himself in which Lueger was alleged to have urged Gessmann "to keep my people together," a statement which those present in the room later denied Lueger had made.[72] Soon after this interview was published, Heinrich Hierhammer gave Ernst Vergani, the renegade editor of the *Deutsches Volksblatt,* a copy of Lueger's will. Vergani then rushed news of its existence into print as Lueger lay on his deathbed, thereby preventing a simple transition *in camera.*[73] Gessmann's attempt to negotiate directly with Vergani, whom he actually visited, proved useless.[74] Gessmann's plans included a round of rewards or consolation prizes for those who were to be passed over; Josef Neumayer, for example, was to be promoted "out" of the city administration by being ennobled and receiving a seat in the *Herrenhaus.* Others of the old guard were in line for largesse in the form of secondary offices; Leopold Steiner was allocated the position of second vice-mayor, for example. The *Stadtrat* would be enlarged to include members of Kunschak's Laborite faction and possibly even of the small *bürgerlich* Liberal opposition (both presumably to be mobilized against intractable party loyalists in the showdown vote on the mayorship). One of those to be rewarded was Julius Axmann, the former *Handlungsgehilfen* leader, to whom Gessmann would turn over his seat on the Lower Austrian Provincial Executive Committee.[75]

Gessmann was intensely feared by many in the Vienna faction of the party who disliked the universal suffrage law of 1906, who felt threatened by the *Reichspartei*, and who were envious of Gessmann's having accumulated so many offices. Lueger had left the ward bosses alone, and had protected them against Gessmann's aspirations to create a central party bureaucracy.[76] Eduard Heinl, a young Viennese municipal official whom Gessmann recruited to work for the party, recorded in his autobiography an awkward scene where one local district leader, enraged at the putative transgressions of Gessmann's protégés, bellowed that the party needed no officials since it had men like himself to run its affairs![77] Indeed, as Lueger's illness took its course, the ward bosses had chafed under the discipline of the *Magistrat* and the political control of the *Stadtrat*, protesting against the intrusions of the city hall "bureaucracy" in their bailiwicks. In late 1909 the Christian Social district leaders created their own conference in the *Bürgerklub,* meeting regularly to exchange complaints about "the Rathaus." [78] With Gessmann as mayor these politicians would face even greater coercion, not merely from the municipal bureaucracy, but from a new party bureaucracy as well. They would have none of it.[79]

Once Vergani got hold of Lueger's testament (which was in all the Viennese newspapers by the morning of March 11), he cleverly initiated a series of anti-Gessmann articles designed to encourage others to oppose the deal. Resistance coalesced around the party elders in the *Stadtrat,* led by Heinrich Hierhammer, one of Lueger's vice-mayors, and Vincenz Wessely, the influential chairman of the Christian Social *Bürgerklub*.[80] Since the Cabinet supported Gessmann's candidacy, Bienerth was anxious to have the mayoral vote in the City Council held on March 19, but the anti-Gessmann faction in the *Stadtrat* and in the *Bürgerklub* quickly voted to delay the election for six weeks, allegedly out of respect for Lueger, but actually to permit opposition to coalesce.[81]

By March 13 it was clear to Gessmann that his attempt to circumvent Lueger's will was in trouble. The best that Gessmann might hope for in an open election in the City Council was 70 to 80 votes. Although this slight majority would have been sufficient, he decided that the process would be both personally demeaning and divisive of party unity.[82] Gessmann's withdrawal—which the *Reichspost* portrayed as a nonevent, claiming that in fact Gessmann had never been an official candidate—was taken as an additional blunder by his supporters, who, like Victor Silberer, felt that he should have fought the contest out to the bitter end.[83]

Gessmann was furious over Weiskirchner's behavior during the crisis. Rather than supporting Gessmann wholeheartedly, Weiskirchner soon adopted a quixotic, "statesmanlike" pose, issuing a communiqué on March 14, rejecting the mayoral office "for now" but asserting that when his services were no longer needed by the Crown, he would gladly accept it.[84] In late March Weiskirchner left Gessmann totally in the lurch by journeying to Brioni for a holiday, where he managed to obtain an ostentatious interview with the Thronfolger.[85]

Given Gessmann's decision to take himself out of the running, the question then became who would substitute for Weiskirchner. A private conference on Sunday, March 13, attended by Gessmann and Weiskirchner, led to a decision that the second vice-mayor, Josef Porzer, who was an ardent Catholic (and whose mother's side of the family was Jewish), would be nominated as the interim mayor, with Weiskirchner agreeing to accept the office after an interval of at least two years. This news immediately provoked strong opposition by Gessmann's enemies in the *Bürgerklub*. When an assembly of party notables met on March 14 to set the stage for this transition, however, an angry Leopold Steiner—who resented the innuendos circulating concerning his part in the conspiracy—unexpectedly disclosed the details of the pact between Gessmann and Weiskirchner, including the latest twist involving Porzer. Not only was Gessmann forced to issue a public denial of his own candidacy, but Weiskirchner now waffled and announced that he could support Porzer if he were the candidate of the *Bürgerklub*, but that Josef Neumayer, the senior vice-mayor, also had a strong claim on the interim appointment. An old-guard nationalist from the Innere Stadt and one of the leaders of the anti-Gessmann faction in the *Stadtrat,* Neumayer was hated by the agrarians in the party. Alfred Ebenhoch announced with considerable embarrassment that the selection of the mayor was, of course, only a matter for the local Viennese organization, and not a responsibility of the *Reichspartei* leadership.[86] Thus foundered Gessmann's attempt to use the *Reichspartei* to co-opt the office of *Bürgermeister.* This was the first, self-inflicted wound to the *Reichspartei*'s dignity in 1910–11; it would not be the last.

The *Stadtrat* was dominated by the old guard of the Christian Social *Bürgerklub*—of the 27 elective seats on the *Stadtrat* in 1908, 18 were held by politicians who were first elected to the City Council in the *Kampfzeit* of the Christian Social movement before 1896.[87] Many of these politicians—such as Leopold Tomola, Vincenz Wessely, Felix Hraba, and Sebastian Grünbeck— had received seats on the *Stadtrat* as sinecures in return for their work in the wards during the political struggles of 1891–97. These men resented Porzer almost as much as Gessmann and insisted that Neumayer be selected.[88] Porzer's potential support lay with councilmen not on the *Stadtrat:* with those who had joined the Council after Lueger's ascension to power, especially with

Kunschak's Laborite faction, and with those who were also members of the parliamentary delegation and who therefore had a wider vision of the party. Finally, at a meeting of Viennese party leaders on March 21, Porzer, faced with the intractable opposition of the *Stadtrat,* withdrew his name, whereupon Neumayer acknowledged that he would serve at Weiskirchner's pleasure.[89]

Neumayer's victory signaled the political hegemony of the *Stadtrat* within the *Bürgerklub,* its members now assuming the role of an ersatz privy council in the party, and, more important, the victory of the most conservative politicians, men who hated not only Social Democracy but any kind of democracy. Leopold Kunschak met with little sympathy from these men in the next eight years. It also boded ill for the cooperation of rural and urban interests in the party. When Neumayer was sworn in as mayor on May 3, his one lively remark in an otherwise tedious speech was to condemn the "price gouging" of the Austrian peasantry, a statement which led angry peasants to assemble at a protest rally in Wolkersdorf on May 23 where prominent Christian Social agrarians led by Johann Mayer denounced the new mayor.[90]

Neumayer's selection in late March came on the heels of a scandal provoked by one of the principal spokesmen for the anti-Gessmann faction on the *Stadtrat,* Felix Hraba.[91] A specialist in municipal financial affairs, Hraba had a long record of disagreements with Gessmann and others in the party elite. It was Hraba who had prevented Franz Morsey from using his political connections to drum up business within the city administration, and it was Hraba who opposed placing city funds on a short-term, deposit basis in the *Länderbank,* for which Josef Strobach and other Lueger cronies received ample rewards from the bank's director, August Lohnstein. Hraba was angered by Gessmann's ambitions, and especially by Gessmann's idea of enlarging the *Stadtrat.* Since Porzer appeared to have at least an outside chance of defeating Neumayer (Heinrich Hierhammer suspected as late as March 18 that Gessmann himself still coveted the mayorship, using Porzer as a stalking-horse), Hraba decided to speak out. On March 19 he gave a blistering speech in Hietzing denouncing Gessmann and the *Reichspartei,* claiming that the latter had become a thoroughly agrarian instrument against Vienna that was now meddling in the *Bürgerklub*'s prerogatives. Hraba charged that many of those who claimed fealty to Lueger had long stood in Lueger's disfavor, and that Lueger himself had regretted his support for the *Reichspartei.* He then condemned Gessmann's plans for a new spoils system of municipal patronage, alluding to the projected ten new seats on the *Stadtrat* and various other changes.

Finally, after grumbling about the audacity and irreverence of those "vultures" who dared to divide Lueger's heritage even before the mayor was dead, Hraba threw some real incendiaries. He charged that instances of improper and perhaps even illegal behavior by party functionaries had taken place in the municipality and in the Lower Austrian government. He neither named names nor gave specific instances of corruption; he merely indicated that in a budget as large as that of the city of Vienna, it was always possible to skim something off if one had the power and the intent. He was particularly harsh in judging the financial practices of the Lower Austrian Provincial Executive Committee, arguing that, unlike the city of Vienna, the Lower Austrian government had no independent office of audit to supervise the expenditure of public funds. When he had tried to persuade the Diet to introduce such an office, he met with fierce hostility from Gessmann. He concluded by threatening the retribution of the *Bürgerklub* against these "wolves in sheep's clothing," who were the bane of the party and who worshiped only one God, the "Gott 'Nimm'."[92]

Although filled with improbable arguments that placed Hraba himself in a bad light (if financial irregularities had occurred, why had not Hraba exposed them, rather than keeping silent for so long?), the speech contained a sufficient core of truth to justify the political explosion that followed. The peroration set off a chain reaction of fear and revenge, and events assumed a life of their own. Even Hraba's colleagues on the *Stadtrat* were dismayed that one of their own would undercut party unity so blatantly and endanger them by loose, ill-targeted accusations. For Gessmann, coming as it did in the wake of his humiliation over the mayorship, the speech was a gross insult, and he demanded that accounts be settled. On March 21 Liechtenstein summoned an emergency meeting of the Viennese members of the Christian Social Diet Club, who denounced Hraba but stopped short of punitive measures.[93]

When the Christian Social *Bürgerklub* met on April 6 to ratify Neumayer's candidacy for mayor, the Hraba speech became the Hraba affair. Sensing that this was an irresistible issue with which to embarrass all of the *bürgerlich* factions, Leopold Kunschak demanded that it be discussed openly and that if Hraba refused to name names and give details, he should be expelled from the party.[94] Quickly other supporters of Gessmann joined in, and even Hraba's erstwhile allies in the *Stadtrat* found little reason to defend his breach of confidentiality (although four did vote against his exclusion).[95] Most of those present seemed less concerned with the veracity of Hraba's charges than with the gratuitous embarrassment he had caused. Hraba at first refused to respond to Kunschak's demand, urging that the club not force him to make his evidence public and offering to submit his complaints to a "party court" of twelve men who would hear his evidence privately. But after abusive attacks from Kunschak, Gessmann, Victor Silberer, Hermann Bielohlawek, and others who demanded that Hraba "name names," he did so, mentioning Julius Axmann and Bielohlawek as two of the culprits to whom his March 19 speech had made reference. Upon this the club then voted to throw Hraba out of the party and to request that Axmann and Bielohlawek initiate libel actions against Hraba to vindicate their reputations.

Three days later, the Christian Social Diet Club also voted Hraba's exclu-

sion, but this time eighteen members of the club, mainly from Vienna, boycotted the session. As Gessmann's forces tried to gather signatures on a petition
supporting a collective libel action against Hraba, many of those who had initially voted against Hraba hesitated to sign.[96] The split in the Viennese organization that had undermined Gessmann's mayoral candidacy was now replicat-
ing itself in the Hraba affair. Eventually most city councilmen were persuaded
or coerced into supporting the action, but many did so against their better judgment—Josef Neumayer later insisted that he had been opposed to a public libel
action, urging instead a Council investigative commission, but was outvoted.[97]

Gessmann's understandable desire for personal vengeance against Hraba
was a serious tactical mistake. Had the majority ignored him or forced a recan-
tation and apology by private negotiations, the bloodletting that ensued might
have been avoided or at least minimized and kept from public view. Hraba
himself had second thoughts about the consequences of his "villainy," sending
a semi-apologetic letter to the Diet Club on April 9 regretting that "I expressed
myself in so extreme a manner."[98] Weiskirchner's relations with Gessmann now
degenerated, the former urging a compromise with Vergani and Hraba, citing
Lueger's policy of "bridging differences" and keeping party conflicts out of
the newspapers, the latter accusing Weiskirchner of secretly putting Vergani
and Hraba up to their mischief.[99]

Bielohlawek, Axmann, and Liechtenstein (acting for the Lower Austrian
provincial government, whose integrity Hraba had also impugned) filed law
suits against Hraba on April 22. Robert Gruber, Hraba's attorney, announced
that Hraba had collected a huge file of evidence and was prepared to submit it
to the courts at a trial which all Vienna eagerly awaited. Bienerth complied
with Gessmann's wishes by obtaining an order from the Emperor officially
closing the Diet, so that Hraba's immunity as a provincial deputy would expire
and he would be subject to criminal prosecution.[100]

The months of April and May also saw Ernst Vergani stepping up his fronde
against Gessmann in the *Deutsches Volksblatt*. Gessmann repaid Vergani's de-
vious behavior on March 10–11 by having the party central election committee
refuse to approve the latter's candidacy for a City Council seat from the Josefstadt in the by-elections scheduled for late April. Vergani ran anyway, but
Friedrich Funder compounded the insult by printing favorable comments about
his rival, Karl Stahlich, in the *Reichspost* and ignoring Vergani. Stahlich won,
and Vergani was beside himself.[101] Soon thereafter he launched a major press
campaign to tar Gessmann with corruption and clericalism and ruin his career.
Gessmann might appeal to his colleagues for "honesty, conciliation and calm,"
but the Liberal and Social Democratic press had a field day retelling one scandalous rumor after another and demanding a public investigation into the
Christian Social cover-up.[102] As party unity crumbled, local ward heelers be-

came anxious for their own survival, and pressures increased on the Rathaus to stop the scandal short of an open trial. A meeting of Christian Social associational leaders on June 8 demanded that a congress be summoned to restore party unity.[103] The new *Reichsparteileitung* held its first semipublic session on June 10, with the propriety of *Verwaltungsrat* positions as the main subject on its agenda. A worse tactic than this fumbling behavior could scarcely have been possible.[104]

The Hraba libel trial was set to open in late June. Since early May several attempts had been undertaken to arrive at a compromise, all of which failed because of Hraba's and Gessmann's obstinacy. No one wanted a trial, however, and on its eve several of Hraba's colleagues from the Hietzing ward organization (Hraba's home district) were able to negotiate a settlement with the party leadership, with Richard Weiskirchner playing the role of chief mediator.[105] The result was a deal, ratified by the party leadership on June 17, by which Hraba agreed to issue a communiqué through the *Stadtrat* indicating that he had spoken rashly, and that he had not intended to accuse anyone of corruption but had merely been offering positive suggestions, admittedly in an inappropriate way, for improving the efficiency of administration in the city and province. Although he denied accusing Liechtenstein or any member of the Provincial Executive Committee of corruption, he did not offer a public apology.[106] In return the party leadership agreed to withdraw the lawsuits. Vergani and the Liberal press spread rumors that the party had submitted to other "requirements," such as allowing Hraba to keep his position on the *Stadtrat* and not opposing his reelection to the City Council when his term expired in 1912, but the records of the parliamentary club meeting of June 22 show that these may have been fabrications. Indeed Gessmann and many of the Alpinists thought Hraba had gotten off too easily.

At a meeting of the parliamentary club on June 22, August Kemetter regretted that the party had not appointed an investigative commission to look into Hraba's charges, but a majority peremptorily rejected this idea, thinking it could now bury the affair. Franz Rienössl argued that a commission would have only "spread the scandal further," and Schöpfer, speaking for the Alpine deputies, thought that the club should stop wasting its energy on the affair.[107] Unfortunately the scandal refused to die.

When the *Bürgerklub* met on June 23, little generosity was manifest toward Hraba. Under Gessmann's pressure, the club refused to readmit Hraba to membership and moved to strip him of all administrative responsibilities on the *Stadtrat*, with the implication that he would be denied reelection to the Council in 1912.[108] This petty vengeance set the whole affair off again. Hraba angrily insisted that he cared nothing about readmission to the party, but that he had only agreed to the public communiqué if he were left as spokesman for finance on the *Stadtrat*. On July 1 he issued a declaration to the morning newspapers accusing the party leadership of having broken promises given to him before he agreed to the settlement.[109]

Hraba's malevolence was well known, and most members of the elite found him disagreeable. Ernst Vergani, however, was another story. Vergani had tried to split the parliamentary club with his campaign against Gessmann, but two meetings in late May showed that this was impossible, since virtually everyone present defended Gessmann.[110] On June 17 Vergani offered Liechtenstein a compromise, negotiated by Karl Jedek without the club's authority, whereby Vergani would be allowed to attend meetings of the parliamentary leadership and enjoy various other concessions in return for ending his attacks on Gessmann in the *Deutsches Volksblatt*. Vergani also insisted on a "settlement of the Axmann matter" as a final blow to Gessmann before the armistice would commence. When the club refused to accept Vergani's demands (Josef Schraffl insisted that Vergani was simply trying to blackmail the party into lucrative monetary concessions and urged resistance) he resumed his hate articles.[111] In view of Vergani's persistence, however, the party leadership finally agreed in early July on two decisions: Julius Axmann, whose theft of funds was the most damaging evidence in Hraba's possession, would be asked to resign from the party. Axmann did this in a letter to Alois Liechtenstein on July 7 (although the reasons for the resignation were kept secret).[112] Overturning party policy of late June, the *Bürgerklub* then voted on July 8 to establish a public investigative commission in the City Council with bipartisan membership to examine Hraba's evidence of corruption and make a report to the city. To give the impression of impartiality, the Liberal and Social Democratic factions in the Council not only were allowed membership on the commission but were allowed to nominate their own representatives. The Lower Austrian Diet followed suit three days later, establishing its own commission under Anton Baumann.[113]

This second installment of the Hraba scandal sent shock waves through the party. Relations between Gessmann and Weiskirchner deteriorated into open enmity, with Gessmann suggesting in a semipublic remark at the *Bürgerklub* meeting on July 8 that Weiskirchner had long known of Axmann's transgressions and that it was unfair to exonerate him from prior knowledge of the scandal.[114] In reply Weiskirchner claimed to have evidence proving that he, in contrast to Gessmann and Leopold Steiner, had argued with Lueger that Axmann should be exposed. Josef Neumayer promised to present this memorandum to the *Bürgerklub*, but Gessmann managed to have it repressed.[115] So critical was the situation by early July that Konrad Rumpf reported to Funder that other resignations by party prominents, including those of Steiner and Josef Rain, were imminent.[116]

Both investigative commissions scheduled their hearings for late September. The Christian Social majority in the Council commission voted to restrict its inquiry to only those sections of Hraba's speech that referred to the municipality. Hraba refused an invitation to appear before the commission, sending instead a long letter to Josef Porzer, the chair of the commission. In it he recounted in painful detail Gessmann's efforts to seize the mayorship and reiterated his charges about loose financial practices in the Provincial Executive Committee, but he presented no solid evidence of financial wrongs.[117]

Franz Schuhmeier, who represented the Social Democrats on the commission, insisted that the group should expand its purview and conduct a broad investigation into the history of public contract allocations by the Christian Social *Stadtrat,* but none of the warring factions in the Rathaus were that suicidal. The majority refused to budge from its "mandate" and peremptorily declared the commission closed, judging that Hraba had not offered any evidence to validate his "reckless" accusations.[118] In its final report to the City Council on October 18, the majority implicitly validated Hraba's revelations about Gessmann's projected spoils system, declaring such practices as "not desirable from the standpoint of the municipal administration," although not illegal. The report also excused the city's connections with the *Länderbank* by noting that these were initiated by Lueger himself, out of gratitude for August Lohnstein's support for the municipal socialist projects, in the late 1890s, when all other major Viennese banks refused their support.[119] The party was thus forced, once again, to appeal to Lueger for its questionable legitimacy, and while declaring itself innocent of having violated the law, it stood embarrassed at having been caught in that gray area between legality and criminality that patronage spoils inevitably occupy.

The Diet's investigative commission that met on October 13, 1910, acted along similar lines, but here the party came off looking even worse, because in contrast to the Council commission's agenda the bulk of the discussion centered on the circumstances by which public contracts were let to suppliers for provincial construction projects (rather than political patronage as such).[120] Hraba had implied that lucrative (and illegal) commissions or fees had been paid to members of the provincial government to secure contracts for politically sympathetic firms—a charge that was probably true, but that was impossible to prove without access to the actual purchasing files. Hraba consented to appear before the commission but again refused to go beyond his previous vague pronouncements on "faulty accounting methods and controls" in provincial finances, with the predictable result that the Christian Social majority again exonerated itself of any wrongdoing.

When the commission's report came before the plenum of the Diet on October 20, it included a request by Karl Seitz that the provincial government provide the commission with relevant documents on recent public-works construction, particularly the records of the Steinhof sanatorium project, which had generated substantial cost overruns, and other documents pertinent to the issue of corruption.[121] Steinhof's initial construction began in 1904 when Leopold Steiner held the dossier for public welfare as a member of the Lower Austrian Provincial Executive Committee, but the sanatorium was not completed until 1907. Since Hermann Bielohlawek had replaced Steiner in May 1905, he found himself behind the socialist eight ball. Moreover, Bielohlawek had spent the middle of September in an embarrassing libel trial against a friend of Hraba's, Franz Zipperer, who had accused Bielohlawek of corruption at a political rally on August 5.[122] Although an examination of the records on Steinhof might have demonstrated what Kielmansegg's investigators found in examining municipal election files, that is, disorganization and sloppiness more than actual corruption, the socialists were off on a grand fishing expedition from which they could not possibly return empty-handed. When the majority refused to make the records available, Renner compared the corruption of the former Liberal regime to that of the present occupants of the Landhaus: "The old Liberals, whom you often accused in the past as being the quintessence of corruption, could not hold a candle to you people. Never during the Liberal regime were public funds managed so badly."[123] As general spokesman for the majority, Josef Porzer thought the Social Democrats either naive or perverse in their quest for the documents, noting that officials who took bribes would certainly not be stupid enough to leave records in the files.[124] But the spectacle of the majority who self-righteously reprimanded Hraba while refusing to examine his charges appeared to the Social Democrats to be an unprecedented manifestation of moral turpitude. Karl Seitz caustically described the scene as one in which "the accused has pronounced himself innocent."[125]

The Hraba scandal thus reached its banal conclusion in October 1910. It had presented Vienna with the remarkable portrait of a once hegemonic and unified party squabbling bitterly about petty corruption and mismanagement in its own ranks for more than seven months. The two investigative tribunals, rather than establishing either the facts behind Hraba's charges or the justice of them, left public opinion seriously troubled by the imputation of scandal. Although Hraba himself could hardly be credited as a "reformer," the damage to the party's collective reputation was severe. Much of the damage was self-inflicted, resulting from Gessmann's overly personalized handling of the case as he tried first to use the courts to achieve personal vengeance, and then to use public commissions for a whitewash. Coming immediately after the crisis in succession at the Rathaus, the scandal not only destroyed working friendships and professional relationships and discredited Gessmann as a Viennese party leader; more important, the cannibalism that ensued prevented the orderly transition of power after Lueger's death. At a meeting of the Diet Club in late September, the pathetic state of party organization in the city and province was the topic of heated discussion, though no one present had a magic solution.[126] When Richard Wollek attempted to devise a formal *Statut* for the club (which, while Lueger was alive, it had never possessed), he ran into opposition from both agrarian and urban factions over petty details that simply masked far more profound tensions.[127] And, in view of the tensions between Gessmann and Weiskirchner, between the Gessmann forces on the Lower Austrian Provincial Executive Committee and the Neumayer clique on the Viennese *Stadtrat,* between the agrarians in the *Reichspartei* and Neumayer, and between Kunschak's Laborite faction and the majority of the *Bürgerklub,* it is doubtful that anyone, including Lueger, could have salvaged unity before June 1911.

The Rathaus was now governed by an elderly nationalist (Neumayer was sixty-six) whose gaffes only increased over time. Not only had he managed on his first day in office to alienate the powerful *Bauernbund,* meriting a personal chastisement from Gessmann, but in October 1910 Neumayer undertook a highly publicized journey to Hungary to visit the mayor of Budapest, ostensibly to discuss common interests, but also to negotiate a joint strategy for the importation of cheap foreign meat. This journey, which the Liberal press found as fascinating as the party's own press found it embarrassing, outraged the agrarian majority in the *Reichspartei.* Long Lueger's bête noire—he specifically urged vigilance toward Hungary in his political testament of 1907—were the Magyars now to enjoy Christian Social patronage and courtesy? At a dinner in his honor Neumayer toasted his hosts, noting that he had formed many friendships with Hungarians as a university student and that he had never lost his "feelings of friendship" towards Hungary.[128] Closer contacts between Austrian-German and Hungarian cities were desirable to establish a network of mutual political interests. The impression of the visit was thus one of manifest anti-agrarianism and latent anti-Slavism: Germans and Magyars hand in hand against Austrian peasants and Slavs.[129] In his revival of a modest German nationalism and in his outbursts against the peasantry, Neumayer pursued a double attack against Gessmann's *Reichspartei.* The increasingly anti-Czech tone of the city administration between April 1910 and Weiskirchner's succession as mayor in early 1913 was one immediate consequence of having Neumayer in power.[130] Lacking either charisma or imagination, as mayor Neumayer was hapless and as party boss a disaster. What influence he had within the Council he used to obstruct Gessmann's plans. For example, a projected rise in the Lower Austrian beer tax in October 1910, which Gessmann and Porzer thought both necessary and politically acceptable to cover salary increases for public school teachers, had to be abandoned because Neumayer maneuvered the *Bürgerklub* into rejecting it.[131]

In the midst of the Hraba scandal and at the conclusion of Neumayer's "friendship" visit to the Magyars, another public spectacle took place which, when viewed in the context of the self-flagellations of the Christian Socials, promised more evil in the months ahead. On October 2, 1910, a crowd of over a hundred thousand demonstrators organized by the Social Democrats marched along the Ringstrasse from the Schwarzenbergplatz to the Rathaus to protest the inflation in consumer prices.[132] The day was sunny and temperate, the crowd in a good mood, the parade filled with colorful banners and signs denouncing Weiskirchner as a tool of the agrarians and displaying other appropriate themes. Unlike during many Ringstrasse demonstrations sponsored by the socialists, the police had no trouble this day. But the theme of the parade and its enormous popularity could hardly comfort the ruling elites in the Rathaus. For not only had the parade enjoyed joint sponsorship by the Social Democrats and the local *bürgerlich* Liberals, but the sidewalks lining the Ring were filled with thousands of men and women cheering in support. As the *Neue Freie Presse* rightly noted, this was a march of consumers, not ideologues, and their outrage in October against exorbitant meat and bread prices would produce by the following June inexorable pressure with which Lueger's party, even in the best of times, would have had difficulty coping. These two sets of autumnal images—the Christian Socials wallowing in recriminations and scandalmongering within the Rathaus and the "public" protesting living conditions without—set the tone of the 1911 elections.

The Elections of 1911

The final section of Chapter 3 discussed the events that led Richard Bienerth to gamble with his political career in the early spring of 1911 and summon national elections three years ahead of schedule. Bienerth hoped to weaken Slavic obstructionism by expanding the electoral base for a renewed German-Polish bourgeois coalition including the Christian Socials. Albert Gessmann fought hard to dissuade Bienerth, arguing that these elections would prove catastrophic for the Christian Social party in Vienna. Bienerth felt, however, that his government had been so disabled by the national tensions that the elections were a last welcome chance to force a realignment of party factions in parliament and foster a new, stronger Cabinet coalition.

Party and state files on the 1911 elections show that Gessmann again tried to assume command of the Christian Social campaign. At a special session of the parliamentary club in late March, Gessmann insisted that in politics the only thing that counted was success and that he had a track record of success.[133] In an attempt to maintain control over the Viennese party organization, Gessmann also summoned a special congress on March 19 to ratify an organizational statute which created a new, twenty-seven-member party leadership for the city itself (*Wiener Parteileitung*).[134] Yet paradoxically Gessmann's character became the campaign's most critical issue, as Ernst Vergani published more scurrilous and defamatory articles in the *Deutsches Volksblatt* against the

Christian Social leader. Vergani dredged up the "dirt" from the Lueger succession crisis a year before and concocted new fables as the campaign wore on, with Gessmann finally bracketed in early June as the "reptile" in that viper's nest of agrarian and clerical corruption which was now the Christian Social *Reichspartei*. Gessmann fought back with outraged public letters in the *Reichspost,* detailing both Vergani's lies and the latter's dubious stock and property manipulations, but that the truth was largely on Gessmann's and not Vergani's side was completely beside the point.[135] To the electorate, accustomed to an insolent, indeed brazen Gessmann, such exchanges could not help but suggest that he had lost his nerve. The architect of the *Reichspartei* had now become its principal liability. Awkward "unity" performances between Gessmann and his rivals in the *Bürgerklub* like Vice-Mayor Heinrich Hierhammer, who on June 10 managed after painful obfuscations to deliver a lukewarm endorsement of Gessmann, were hardly calculated to convince voters. By the final days of the race Gessmann was being treated like a pariah by the Viennese ward leaders—no one wanted to be seen with him on a rally platform.[136]

The party did not lack for money, since Bienerth wanted it to maintain its current strength and encouraged generous party support among Austrian industrial circles. This was one election, however, that neither money nor Albert Gessmann's fabled organizational talents could win. In the provinces, preliminary reports from the various *Statthaltereien* to the Cabinet indicated that the party would fare well, although the reoccurrence of feuding in Tyrol threatened two seats in Kufstein and Lienz.[137] The regional campaign assumed novel dimensions, revealing logics which varied from province to province. Whereas Social Democrats and Christian Socials were at each other's throats in Vienna, in Upper Austria the two parties actually conducted secret negotiations about mutual support (or at least mutual abstention) in runoff elections against the German *Bürgerlichen.*[138] In general, however, the strategy of the Social Democratic leadership was to support all those *bürgerlich* candidates in run-off elections who were deemed to be in opposition to Bienerth's Cabinet.

Predictably, the results for the party in the provinces were good. In rural Lower Austria the Christian Socials again swept all twenty-one seats, although their aggregate vote was smaller than in 1907.[139] In Tyrol and in Styria the party lost one seat, but in Salzburg and in Upper Austria it maintained its delegate strength and even enhanced its standing by winning a second Upper Austrian city district. At the conclusion of the runoffs on June 20, the Christian Socials had retained 73 seats outside of Vienna. In Vienna, in contrast, the news was catastrophic. Just as the elite had quarreled in the Rathaus, so too did subelite cadres turn on each other out in the wards. In most districts of the city squabbles broke out among rival clubs and organizations, each claiming the right to nominate the "official" candidate of the district. In Neubau in mid-April, for example, nine different local notables demanded party sponsorship for one race. Neither Gessmann nor Mayor Neumayer could control such anarchy. At a meeting of the Viennese party leadership on April 12 to discuss the allocation of candidacies, serious tensions were evident between *bürgerlich* and Laborite interests. The mood was at best desultory, with Gessmann reminding his colleagues that "a party that fails to take the workers into account cannot expect to achieve much in a general election."[140] By the first week of May the party still had no official slate of recommended candidates, and a week before the election it was still trying to curb secessionist candidacies within several important wards.[141] When election day arrived, Gessmann had managed to obtain official slots for only three Laborite candidates (Kunschak, Anderle, and Hemala), the latter two being opposed by dissident *bürgerlich* forces in their own wards. Three other Laborites (Görner, Spalowsky, and Krikawa) were allowed to run against regular party candidates, but the end result was that the Christian Socials lost all six seats to the Social Democrats.

The worst breaches in discipline occurred among the artisans and the civil servants. Small groups of dissident Christian Social artisans, angry over their "neglect" by the Rathaus and by the party-sponsored *Deutsch-österreichischer Gewerbebund,* launched independent candidacies in eight election districts. Some of the renegades ran with the backing of an ad hoc *Gewerblicher Zentralausschuss,* whose propaganda was printed and paid for by a local Liberal election committee funded (in part) by Jewish industrialists.[142] The case of Leopold Engelhardt was characteristic of many of the renegades. The chairman of the butchers' guild, Engelhardt was a resident of Leopoldstadt, but he negotiated with a group of Jewish butchers in Mariahilf to nominate him to run as an independent candidate against Robert Pattai. Engelhardt and his predecessor, Georg Hütter, had long been at odds with the municipality. The price inflation had brought past tensions to a head, with the Rathaus criticizing the butchers for victimizing customers. Engelhardt aspired to larger roles in city politics, and the upheavals of 1910–11 offered him a perfect opportunity to kill three birds with one stone: exonerate his guild by destroying the career of a prominent Christian Social politician, gain a parliamentary seat himself, and force the Christian Socials back into greater dependence on their traditional supporters from the 1890s, the master artisans. In Pattai's case Engelhardt had a convenient target, since the *Arbeiter-Zeitung* published exposés of the fortune in real estate and legal consultancy contracts which Pattai had assembled since 1900.[143]

Envy was a powerful motive in these feuds. That these "anti-Semites" drew support from Jewish sources to pursue their civil war bothered them not in the least, for consistency never had a high value in Viennese politics. In most cases the renegades ran as independent Christian Socials, and in the critical run-off elections that occurred between Christian Socials and Social Democrats, they and their followers usually returned to the fold. However much they might resent the Rathaus, these petty propertied types were not likely to give their votes to the Social Democrats.

In the case of the civil servants and other white-collar employees, however, a more profound shift in sentiment took place. As in 1907 several civil servant candidates came forward (Leopold Waber, Wilhelm Pollauf, Karl Neugebauer), but this time they combined German national or Liberal appeals with civil-service blandishments. In other districts more conventional Liberals or, as in Zenker's and Hock's case, *Kulturkampf* radicals, gave special attention to the civil servant question, as did the Social Democrats, who now portrayed themselves as the truest friends of the civil service in a parliament which had "done nothing for the officials."[144] The campaign was punctuated by dozens of uproarious rallies for civil servants where the Christian Socials and Gessmann in particular were excoriated for having failed to force Bienerth's acceptance of the *Dienstpragmatik* and an accompanying salary raise. Such complaints were current in 1907, but now, in the midst of an inflation which had hit status-anxious officials on fixed incomes hard, they had a compelling, indeed irresistible force. Opinion in leading civil servant organizations ran strongly against the Christian Socials and in favor of German national or even local progressive candidates.[145] Among lower-ranking state groups, like postal officials and various categories of civil servants, the Social Democrats made inroads. Even among the local employees in the city and provincial bureaucracies Christian Social party agitators detected unrest. Leopold Tomola admitted that Waber's agents had been able to collect 1,400 crowns for his election chest in the offices of the Lower Austrian finance directorate; and the Social Democrats now for the first time gained defiant expressions of support within the ranks of the municipal employees. Lueger's dictum that he would tolerate no Social Democrats on the city payroll seemed, if only covertly, defunct. Even the schoolteachers, who had recently received a salary raise in August 1910, now found either the courage or the opportunity to complain of political manipulation within their ranks (typically, the 1910 raise had given the Lower Austrian School Council generous discretionary powers to evaluate a teacher's "performance" before certifying him or her for such raises).[146]

One index of the direction the election would take was the propaganda the two sides distributed. The Christian Social gang wars of 1910 offered hack journalists from the Social Democratic and Liberal camps a fund of scurrilities. Vergani's literary calumnies soon found their way into pamphlets (which the Christian Socials persuaded the Justice Ministry to confiscate), but the Liberals and the Social Democrats also flooded the city with handbills preaching against Christian Social corruption and "clericalism" and dumping responsibility for the price inflation on the "agrarian" Rathaus. A small broadsheet, the *Wiener Blitzlichter,* carried no less than three long articles on corruption in an eight-page issue ("Dr. Weiskirchner und der Lloyd: ein Raubzug auf die

Taschen der Steuerträger"; "Bielohlaweks Glück und Ende"; and "Die Korruption im allgemeinen und die des Baron Engel im besonderen"), all of which
contained exaggerations and distortions but rested on a core of publicly acknowledged facts.[147]

Fighting a two-front war against Vergani *and* the Liberals and Reds, the
Christian Socials responded by renewing their pose as a state-supporting
(*staatserhaltende*) party. Gessmann organized a special election broadsheet of
his own, *Der Reichsratwähler,* that countered Vergani's charges with a formu-
laic list of the party's municipal accomplishments for the "Weltstadt Wien."
But what was most striking about this pamphlet was its tedious, defensive tone.
Little mention was made of corruption (what could Gessmann say?), and there
were few ways in which he could portray the new gasworks and the new waterworks as attractive issues for white-collar voters with shrinking budgets. In
desperation Gessmann was even forced to cite a small, Jewish-Liberal periodical, *Das Forum,* where Gustav Morgenstern had urged his readers (i.e., Jewish
bourgeois voters) not to support the Social Democrats. When the all-powerful
Christian Social electoral machine found itself reduced to quoting Jewish pamphlets to sustain a coherent electoral image, voters might sense that something
was profoundly wrong in Lueger's *Vaterstadt.*[148]

The first round of voting on June 13 told a dismal story. Of thirty-three
district races the Christian Socials won only two, while the socialists took
seven and the Liberals one. In the run-off elections on June 20 the party salvaged one additional seat, losing twenty-two to the Social Democrats and ersatz Liberals (most of whom were elected because the Social Democrats threw
their support to them in the run-off elections). All of the major party leaders—
Gessmann, Weiskirchner, Pattai, Liechtenstein, Steiner, Bielohlawek, and the
rest—went down in humiliating defeat. Characteristically, two of three Christian Socials who survived the June massacre (Wenzel Kuhn and Franz Rienössl) were local politicians who had close ties to local sentiment, and thus
were able to disassociate themselves from the party *Bonzen.*

Statistically, the party lost over 30,000 votes on the first ballot in Vienna
from its zenith in 1907 (from 159,000 to 128,000).[149] Voter dissidence could
also be measured in the enormous number of empty ballots turned in (over
16,000), which was twice as high as in 1907. More special interests emerged,
but the Christian Socials' losses, aside from the thousands of voters who turned
to artisan "independents," clearly benefited the Social Democrats and the ragtag group of Liberals, although in different ways.[150] The Social Democrats
increased their share of the vote by 18 percent (from 125,000 to 146,000),
whereas the *bürgerlich* vote increased 15 percent (from 30,000 in 1907 to
38,000 in 1911) for the assorted groups of "Liberals" or "nationalists." These
tended to fall into one of three main groups: the older anticlerical progressives,
who by now included a substantial Jewish voter bloc concentrated in the Innere

Stadt, Leopoldstadt, and Alsergrund; the German nationalists, who were anti-Semitic, nationalist, and largely white-collar civil servant voters and scattered throughout the city but with special strength in Landstrasse, Hernals, and Währing; and the supporters of Zenker's *Wirtschaftspolitische Reichspartei,* which was his own creature but which also played directly to the white-collar vote in Wieden. This diverse group of non-Christian Social *Bürgerlichen,* whose internal "labels" often signified little in voter attachment or ideological conviction, gained new importance in close runoff contests between Christian Socials and Social Democrats; and it is important to note for the future of Christian Social strategy in Vienna that the majority of the 8,000 vote increase in the *bürgerlich* domain between 1907 and 1911 fell to the German national-ist, as opposed to the anticlerical progressive, camp.

Those voters who had voted Christian Social in 1907 and who shifted either to the socialists or to one of the Liberal or nationalist factions in 1911 seem to have been in the main civil servant voters or lower-ranking white-collar and service workers, including employees in the formerly sacrosanct municipal workforce. Master craftsmen, in contrast, were more likely to support their own candidates (or one of the token poseurs Vergani ran). A similar pattern emerged in the runoffs on June 20. The Social Democrats also seem to have profited from an unusually large number of new voters having entered the lists in Leopoldstadt and in Hietzing, which had elected Christian Socials in 1907.

Following the main elections, Gessmann managed to negotiate a compro-mise agreement for the runoff elections with the leaders of the *Deutscher Na-tionalverband,* but within twenty-four hours this was a worthless piece of pa-per.[151] The Sudeten nationalists wanted Christian Social support for Bohemian and Moravian interests but could offer the party little in Vienna. The Liberal press, led by the *Neue Freie Presse,* reacted in outrage and the agreement col-lapsed. Jewish voters and other bourgeois dissidents in Vienna who did not support Albert Gessmann were no more inclined to follow Gustav Gross or Karl Chiari. The *Gewerblicher Zentralausschuss* did a quick turnabout for the runoff elections, urging artisan voters not to cross over to support the Social Democrats.[152] No such appeals were heard from the civil-servant interest groups, however. Indeed the omnipresence of pro-civil-servant and employee rhetoric in the Social Democratic camp in the week between the primary elec-tions and the runoffs confirmed Friedrich Funder's later assessment that the Christian Socials had lost many races because they had been deserted by a small, but in the context of the runoff elections, significant number of national-ist voters, who were often private employees and petty state officials. The cam-paign brought its own ironies for the Jewish community. So great was the ha-tred of the Christian Socials that Jewish voters were willing to support Leopold Waber in Währing, who in addition to his civil-service platform was known for his nationalist anti-Semitism.[153]

The 1911 election for parliament was in some respects a fluke. In subsequent elections for the Fourth Curia of the City Council in 1912 the Christian Socials won a surprising eleven out of twenty-one seats, much more favorable results than a year earlier. In the parliamentary by-election in Leopoldstadt in October 1913, the party won back from the Social Democrats an important seat—important because this was a district with a heavy Jewish and working-class population, where the party could have done badly. Instead, Heinrich Mataja won the seat for the Christian Socials by attracting back some of the white-collar vote they had lost in 1911 and by negotiating a compact with local German nationals for additional support. Mataja's victory suggested that with the easing of the inflation, the stabilization of consumer prices, and the careful reorganization of the Viennese party under Richard Weiskirchner, the Christian Socials could still expect to enjoy an impressive base of support among Viennese middle- and lower-middle-class voters. Had Bienerth allowed parliament to run until May 1913, it is conceivable that in elections held under more stable circumstances the Christian Social party would have maintained a small majority of total parliamentary seats in the city.[154]

Social Democratic interpretations of the victory varied in emphasis, but common themes among younger socialist commentators were the new hegemony of anticlerical *Kultur* and bitter hatred of the Christian Socials.[155] The generational fault line apparent in socialist discussions of the Wahrmund Affair in 1908 was again manifest in the rhetoric of 1911. Victor Adler might speak at a socialist rally in Währing, urging laborers to vote for Leopold Waber and William Pollauf as crossovers, but his heart was hardly in his task. Adler offered no assurance of their personal honor or reliability. They had only one qualification—namely, that they were not Christian Socials. Socialists should vote for them not because of who they were, but because of who they were not ("the question is not for whom I want to vote, but against whom I want to vote"). What bound the two sides together was not grand anticlerical enthusiasm but the utility of survival: "We do not demand from them that they love us, that they share our principles. But we do expect that they will show a minimum level of reason" against the corruption of the Christian Social machine.[156] Adler's truer sentiments emerged at a meeting of party representatives on June 28, where he proudly announced that "black Vienna has now become to a large extent red Vienna," and that victory had occurred because of the self-reliance and courage of the party itself.[157]

For some of his younger colleagues, however, more ambitious perspectives seemed to beckon. In a runoff speech in the Josefstadt, Ludo Moritz Hartmann argued that Social Democrats and Nationalists held two important values in common. Both were devoted to preserving national identity, and both were dedicated to modern *Bildung*. Citing the German experience, Hartmann insisted that the *Bürgerlichen* would have to recognize and respect the socialist contribution to *Bildungsarbeit:* "That Social Democracy has fulfilled a *Bildungsmission* among the people has been recognized even in the German *Reich* by leading intellectuals and professors." Following his remarks the Fabian Michael Hainisch, claiming to speak for the local intelligentsia, sang Hartmann's praises: "On a series of cultural problems Austria, represented by Dr. Hartmann, marches at the head of the line. . . . Every serious person, who in truth is concerned with the welfare of the people, must do everything they can to put Hartmann in parliament." Anticlericalism provided not merely a common enemy, but, implicitly, a common program of values.[158]

Similar views informed the analysis of another young socialist, Karl Leuthner, who won a seat in Mariahilf by defeating Robert Pattai in the runoffs. Although admitting the role that corruption and inflation had played, Leuthner believed he had found the key to the Social Democratic/progressive alliance in cultural *ressentiment*. Military metaphors defined his analytic framework. Since 1907 two great parties had sought to dominate Vienna, struggling again and again with ferocity. Leuthner compared the parties to "two enemy camps," which in countless battles had "continually looked each other in the whites of their eyes." In 1911 the battle began in the main elections and ended only in the runoffs. Thousands of Jewish voters voted against the Christian Socials, but more surprising were the thousands of former Christian Social anti-Semitic voters who deserted their own party. What could explain this remarkable phenomenon? Leuthner had an answer:

All this [dissidence] was nourished from a deeper source. That is the sharpness of the hatred, which is only found in the political life of countries where a Clerical or Clerically-colored party is hegemonic. The Clerical manifests a force of repulsion against all intellectually richer, culturally interested social circles. Even in the days of their greatest triumph, the Christian Socials always held the intelligentsia at a distance.

It was this alliance with "obscurantism" and this "hatred for modern ideas and science" that provided the ultimate death blow to the Christian Socials. For Leuthner, therefore, the final explanation and the most powerful and overriding electoral motive in 1911 was anticlericalism.[159] Only anticlericalism had the power to pull together workers and owners, propertied and nonpropertied, to break the grasp of the Christian Social party.

Leuthner and Hartmann were not alone in seeing June 1911 as a victory of anticlericalism over clericalism, of cultural progress over cultural reaction. In the *Arbeiter-Zeitung* Friedrich Austerlitz pronounced that "for all that separates the bourgeoisie and the working class, both are rooted in modern economic life, in urban culture [*Kultur*] and in the spiritual life of our times."[160]

For both groups clericalism was a common enemy, a relic of the Counter-Reformation that imposed outdated forms of authority on modern man. The most elegant, if self-contradictory, celebration of the elections came, however, from Renner's Austro-Marxist competition in 1908, Max Adler. Adler argued that the elections showed the moral and intellectual bankruptcy of the Christian Social party by demonstrating that it was neither truly Christian nor even proximately socialistic. Religion had long since become for the Rathaus a mere "cover to legitimate electoral corruption." The future historian of the political culture of the bourgeoisie in the early twentieth century would, according to Adler, find intriguing the spectacle of this degradation of religion into mere sloganeering, "this unparalleled confusion over the concept of Christianity." Adler admitted that "Christian" for many Christian Socials was merely a shorthand way of saying "don't vote Jewish," but he did not elaborate how such a proposition could be consistent with his own party's view of the Christian Socials as "clerical." He insisted that if the Christian religion signified "the illuminating founder of the religion and his evangelism, a teaching of consolation for the tired and poor, but also . . . a passionate attack on the rich and the oppressors of the folk," then the Christian Socials bore no relationship to a "religious" party. Ironically, the Social Democrats did, for in Adler's mind the only residue of "religious" force in Vienna belonged to the socialist movement:

> the Social Democrats have magnificently taken up this duty of any religion which wants to win social power and become a people's religion, and [its teachings] are now embedded with almost religious fervor in the inner convictions of its believers, with the difference that they are connected to a beautiful intellectual labor, as can only emerge from a scientifically reinforced conviction.

Christian Socialism was dead, but "Social Democracy will arise, and cast off the chains of Mammon. In her ranks stir those eternal muses of divine progress which the Church has buried under the flowers of earthly trinkets. She calls forth into the world: all must be made new, all must be made different!"[161]

Max Adler's remarkable conflation of science and religion imputed to the Social Democrats not merely the agency of material liberation but the more important project of cultural transformation. For Max Adler the victory of 1911 authorized the Social Democrats to undertake both simultaneously, indeed perhaps to privilege the second over the first. Red successes also illuminated the quasi-religious traits of a scientific and secular socialism which would build a new world of moral virtue on the rubble of Christian Social lies and infamy. In 1908 Friedrich Austerlitz had published a scorchingly negative but brilliant portrait of Gessmann in *Der Kampf,* rightly suggesting that Gessmann represented the second stage of the Christian Social movement, away from the localism of Lueger and toward class conflict on a grand, state scale.[162] Gessmann's political "death" in 1911 and the alleged demise of his party now seemed to signify the opening of a third epoch, in which Social Democracy could go on the offensive against a confused and dispirited *Bürgertum*, using cultural as well as class weapons.

Election-day enthusiasm aside, it is more likely that the 1911 socialist victories resulted from consumer distress over inflation and contempt for the Christian Socials' intraparty feuding and for their blatant opportunism than they did from voter interest in the prospect of a new, anticlerical yet curiously "religious" Viennese *Urmensch*. Heinrich von Tschirschky caught the "anti-" flavor of the campaign when he wrote that

> the result so far has been a more negativistic one, that is the defeat of the Christian Social big shots. The voters have not racked their brains over who and what they have put in the place of the conquered party and its leaders, and really don't care if they have, by the election of so many socialists, driven out the Devil with Beelzebub. The mass of voters, following their emotions more than their political conviction, had only one goal in mind: bring down the rich Christian Social big shots.[163]

Interestingly, when Wilhelm Pollauf returned Victor Adler's compliment and journeyed to the neighboring district of Hernals to urge (in his and Leopold Waber's name) *Beamten* to vote for Leopold Kunschak's socialist opponent, he stressed not the clericalism of Kunschak (to which he made a fleeting reference) but rather Gessmann's manipulation of the school system, Christian Social persecution of nationalist civil servants, and the party's prohibition of nationalist *Turnvereine* from using public school facilities.[164] Pollauf wanted vengeance, not ideological coalitions. In the Josefstadt Alois Heilinger successfully defended his seat against Hartmann's blandishments to bourgeois voters by disassociating himself from Christian Social "agrarianism" while insisting that he was still a Christian Social party member, which suggests the "clericalism" issue had a finite appeal in engendering bourgeois revolt.[165]

Nor did the election results mean the death of the Christian Social party in Vienna. In the worst of circumstances, lacking effective municipal or national leadership, the ward organizations had still managed to generate 125,000 votes in the city. By depriving the Christian Social party of its Vienna contingent in parliament, however, the voters of June 1911 did initiate fundamental processes of reform within the Viennese party, as well as a categorical shift in power within the *Reichspartei* toward the western Alpine lands.

Attempts at Reconstruction of the Viennese Party, 1912–1914

The June losses had immediate repercussions on the leadership of the Christian Social party. Because he had insisted on the right of control during the campaign, the major share of guilt for the disaster inevitably fell on Gessmann. Profoundly tired after years of political combat, Gessmann resigned most of his party offices (he even transferred his share of the *Reichspost* to Funder), vowing never to return to a leadership position within the party. To Max von Beck, whose political career he had undermined three years before, Gessmann now wrote complaining of the injustice and misfortunes of politics, which in Austria tended to "ruin one's character." He insisted that the results of the elections were not surprising, and that he had predicted as much to Bienerth months before.[166] Gessmann did retain his seat in the Diet and on the Provincial Executive Committee, and he felt bitter about the pressure which Weiskirchner brought to bear to force him to resign that as well. Henceforth, until the collapse of the Monarchy in 1918, an animosity existed between Gessmann and Weiskirchner which had adverse effects on the party's resilience during the First World War.[167]

A second immediate effect of the collapse was that Richard Weiskirchner resigned his cabinet post in the Bienerth government (which itself collapsed on June 28). For the next twelve months Weiskirchner devoted his attention to rebuilding the shattered political organization in Vienna. He faced an enormous challenge, for in July 1911 the latent civil war between the Gessmann and Hraba-Vergani factions spilled out into the streets and rally halls of Vienna, with open clashes occurring between Kunschak's supporters and the more nationalist faction of the party under Robert Pattai, Adolf Gussenbauer, and Anton Nagler. Unless someone restored order, the party faced certain disaster in the 1912 Council elections. Weiskirchner rose to the occasion and took on the role of mediator and conciliator of both sides. His low profile in the 1911 campaign (during which Weiskirchner, for once, gladly deferred to Gessmann) and his claim to the mayorship, based on Lueger's posthumous recognition, allowed Weiskirchner a second lease on his damaged career.

In mid-July 1911 the *Bürgerklub* voted to set aside the organizational plan for the Viennese Christian Social party concocted by Albert Gessmann in March and created instead a nine-man directorate to plan the future of the Viennese party. This committee, which had only one Laborite member (Kunschak) and which was thus heavily dominated by *bürgerlich* interests, authorized Weiskirchner and Steiner to write a new party statute, which was discussed by the full *Bürgerklub* in October 1911. This document provided a clear division of authority within the party between the center and the wards. Weiskirchner also organized a separate *Sekretariat* for the Viennese party, staffed by several capable young officials loyal to him personally (Liechten-stein remained the nominal Chairman, but Weiskirchner was in control). This secretariat was to play an important role in coordinating the work of rebuilding the party's electoral apparatus. At a party congress called in January 1912 to ratify the statute (which had been reviewed by various constituent groups of the party in late 1911), Weiskirchner signified his intention to reclaim the of-fice Lueger had bequeathed to him.[168] Facing a revolt in the *Bürgerklub* be-cause of his sheer incompetence, and under heavy criticism from the Social Democratic delegation in the City Council, Josef Neumayer was finally forced to resign as mayor in December 1912, and Weiskirchner was immediately con-firmed as his successor, taking office in early January 1913.[169] Weiskirchner's dominance in the party (along with his erstwhile ally Leopold Steiner, who had taken over the chairmanship of the *Bürgerklub*) reestablished a situation similar to Lueger's union of the positions of party boss and mayor.

The statute adopted by the 1912 congress established a three-tiered system of representation in the party.[170] The basic unit of the party continued to be the district political club, and party membership now became contingent on membership in one of the clubs in each district. Each club now had a right to send to the district election committee (*Bezirkswahlkomitee*) a specific number of delegates based on its relative membership against all other clubs in the district. The election committee in turn was now organized on a permanent basis, to be chaired by the local district leader in each district, and was respon-sible for recommending nominees to run for local offices. The twenty-one election committees in the city would each elect three delegates to the *weiterer Parteirat,* a sixty-three-member party council in which official policy and strategy would be set and which also functioned as a central election commit-tee. The *weiterer Parteirat* in turn elected a nine-man executive committee (*eng-erer Parteirat*) that was charged with the actual administration of party affairs. The mayor of Vienna and the Lower Austrian *Landmarschall* (in 1913, Weis-kirchner and Liechtenstein respectively) sat on the *engerer Parteirat* ex officio.

Under Lueger party leadership tended to focus on Lueger himself and on a small group of elite colleagues with whom Lueger arbitrarily chose to share his power and authority. The new statute created, at least in theory, a more orderly and representative framework of authority. Because the election com-mittee was to include all delegates of the district associations and local not-ables on a permanent, elective basis, the power of the district leaders would be institutionalized and legitimated within a wider circle of associational inter-ests. They would be no less powerful, but they would now be more publicly accountable for their actions. The purpose of the statute was, therefore, not to reshape the existing network of power and authority in the party. Instead it was to establish principles of accountability for all in the party elite and to force them to deal in a reasonably open and equitable fashion with competitive factions within each ward, as they were represented in the election committee. Weiskirchner sought not to displace Lueger's system but make it more rational and predictable by bureaucratizing it.

Lacking Lueger's personal authority as the source of legitimacy for the party, the system itself, in its new hierarchical *and* representational structure, would carry with it a self-sustaining legitimacy. Rather than saying "Lueger wants x to do y," Weiskirchner could now argue that "the party" wanted the same course of action. In theory at least, each occupational or social faction in each district would have some measure of representation on the district committee, although Weiskirchner was under no illusions that the petty oligarchies around the district leaders would share their prerogatives. The most glaring problem was the relative representation of interests on the district election committees. In almost all the districts, older *bürgerlich* factions maintained a solid grip on the election committees by refusing to publish accurate membership lists of their clubs (which were frequently smaller than Kunschak's labor associations and had more overlapping members) and simply claiming, by prior right, majority control. Since no one in the Rathaus had either the power or the motivation to force such publication, the status quo frequently remained unchanged.[171] Kunschak's subordinates in the Leopoldstadt asked plaintively in December 1912, "how is it possible that the *Bund der deutschen Antisemiten* [a local nationalist club, which local *bürgerlich* leaders allowed to affiliate with the party], which on paper has a membership of about 600, gets 17 representatives on the district election committee, and the Christian Social labor organizations, which have about 4,000 members . . . get only 12?"[172] Weiskirchner had no evident or satisfactory answer for them.

The new municipal party secretariat in the Josefstädter Strasse in turn assumed a wide-ranging series of seemingly mundane tasks, which were crucial to reorganizing the party and preparing it for future competition with the socialists. Henceforth much of the propaganda used in Council, Diet, and parliamentary elections was written in the secretariat, printed at party expense, and only then distributed to the various ward bosses and their electoral committees or to the party press.[173] The secretariat also assumed responsibility for allocating political operatives and agitators before each election, finding appropriate local election headquarters, shifting party loyalists from one district to another as the need arose, and renting a fleet of automobiles on election day for the ward organizations.[174] This office also administered party funds and conducted regular (and successful) contribution drives to replenish the party's election chest, targeting especially larger suppliers to the city government who wanted municipal contracts. The secretariat also organized a speaker's bureau, assigning rally speaking assignments to local and regional politicians, and ensured that local candidates got publicity by arranging for appropriate newspaper coverage of their public appearances. Weiskirchner also encouraged each ward organization to create a Christian Social district newspaper and subsidized these papers directly as well as arranging advertising contracts from municipal industries.[175] Conferences for editors of metropolitan and ward newspapers were held to discuss party policy and special articles the leadership wanted written. A major source of intraparty journalistic feuding disappeared when Ernst Vergani turned the editorial control of the *Deutsches Volksblatt* over to a new consortium of investors and withdrew from the paper. By early 1914 the secretariat would note with satisfaction that the newspaper was now loyally following the mayor's line. Weiskirchner thus reimposed a tentative, but workable univocality on the Christian Socials in Vienna, eliminating what Friedrich Funder had once called the internal "stinkbombs of calumny" which had so tarnished the party's collective presence in 1911.

Perhaps most important, Weiskirchner used the secretariat as a neutral agency to try to mediate and resolve local ward feuds, a chronic problem of the post-Lueger period. The archives of the party after 1912 are filled with sundry reports of mutually antagonistic local notables complaining about each other's "treachery" and asking the Rathaus to intervene in favor of this or that side. Most of the feuding concerned conflicting claims for positions on the slates for municipal offices, but some arose over the number of seats allotted to rival clubs and organizations on the district election committee and over insignificant but ferocious questions of job patronage.[176] From the protocols that the secretariat drafted to try to resolve such disputes (which usually contained accounts of their genesis), it is also apparent that most involved the kinds of petty—yet all the more bitter—personality clashes that have typically affected large political machines in the United States.[177] Weiskirchner could not eliminate these aggravations, but by establishing a central clearinghouse for complaints he could at least monitor the undercurrents of disaffection, asserting the secretariat as the final mediating authority.

The effect of the new organizational network was already apparent in the spring 1912 Council elections, when the crucial Second and Fourth Curias were scheduled to vote. Liberal and Social Democratic papers had visions of a second Christian Social catastrophe of the magnitude of June 1911, which might even shake the party's control of the Rathaus. Both groups employed propaganda similar to that of 1911—charges relating to corruption, clericalism, and inflation—but they were sorely disappointed.[178] After some initial lassitude on the part of old ward leaders who were unaccustomed to (and deeply resented) the discipline the secretariat was trying to impose from above, the new party apparatus was set in motion, and the work of the winter now paid off. The city was blanketed with hundreds of paid agitators; voters were brought to the polling places in special vehicles; special agitation centers were opened in key locations in each district to coordinate the campaign on a street-by-street basis. The secretariat supported over 400 political rallies in the weeks preceding the polling.[179] The party retained 11 seats of the 21 seats in the general Fourth Curia and swept a large number of the Second Curia seats (39 out of 46), thus retaining a stranglehold on the Council.[180] In spring of 1914 the elections for the Third Curia showed a similar result—the party won all 46 seats contested, crushing its opposition. In a private letter to Weiskirchner in March 1914 even Albert Gessmann acknowledged the major role of the new mayor in bringing the party back from chaos.[181]

Some of the success Weiskirchner enjoyed in 1912–14 was due to a stabilization in retail food prices that helped to neutralize the price inflation, for which the mayor was not responsible but from which he profited handsomely.[182] Another factor, however, was his willingness to cultivate and cooperate with local German nationalist leaders in Vienna and with their nationalist mentors outside the city as well. Electoral compacts between the party and the various small nationalist organizations in the city were negotiated in 1912–13, bringing back to the party the "swing" vote of white-collar voters who were willing to give Weiskirchner a chance to set a more centrist, anti-agrarian, and secular mode of *Bürger* politics for the party.[183] In contrast to the rural Lower Austrians under Josef Stöckler, who had declared war on the German nationalists in their districts, Weiskirchner adopted precisely the opposite policy.[184] Still, Heinrich Mataja, who profited from such compromise negotiations in his 1913 by-election from the Leopoldstadt, had to admit that "in many party circles there is a suspicion that this rapprochement will injure our party's principles."[185]

The negative publicity generated in September 1911 by food riots in Ottakring, Josefstadt, Neubau, the Innere Stadt, and elsewhere also aided Weiskirchner in his strategy to recapture the *bürgerlich* votes lost in June. In mid-September the Social Democrats staged what they thought would be conventional protest marches against the inflation and against the decision of the government to prohibit the importation of foreign meat from Argentina, but the crowds got out of hand, and at the end of two riotous days, 263 people had been arrested, 52 were wounded, and 4 people lay dead in the streets. The age distribution of the arrestees—at least 152 were under twenty-five, and 197 were unmarried—suggested that this too was a typical Viennese riot of unemployed and "Jungen" rather than of regular union or party members, but the extensive damage done to property (350 private shops were attacked, with considerable losses from plundering) made it difficult for the socialists to escape responsibility. The violence of September 1911 terrified good *Kleinbürger* types and thus served to undercut Karl Leuthner's prediction that anticlericalism would now constitute the new, hegemonic idiom of Viennese politics. Although he condemned the riots, Weiskirchner was doubtlessly delighted with them, for they forced public attention away from the "culture" and corruption issues and back on the economy, and on terms that put the Social Democrats on the defensive. As the German embassy reported to Berlin, "September 17 brought a political catastrophe for the socialist leadership, from which the Christian Socials may certainly profit, by bringing back before the consciousness of the lower and middle *Bürgertum* in Vienna the gulf that separates them from the Social Democrats."[186]

Municipal administration under Weiskirchner in the immediate prewar period of 1913–14 changed little from that under Lueger. The party's unwillingness to take serious steps in policy areas, such as housing reform, that many of its most wealthy *Bürger* voters found anathema continued to create tensions between Weiskirchner's supporters and the Kunschak wing.[187] After the Viennese agreed in early 1914 (with serious misgivings) to tolerate the Lower Austrians' demands for proportional suffrage in small-town elections, the Christian Social Laborites brought pressure to bear for a similar concession for Vienna, but Weiskirchner was stubbornly resistant.[188] Indeed the Christian Social Laborites' record in supporting proportional suffrage on a list basis for all elections—communal as well as regional and national—was as respectable as that of the Social Democrats.

If Weiskirchner's administrative policies did not differ substantially from those of his mentor, his public persona did. He portrayed himself as the man who would reconcile hostile bourgeois elites in Vienna to Christian Socialism, preparing the way for a reversal of June 1911 in the next national elections. Greetings flowed from the Rathaus to prominent Liberal politicians, including Eduard Suess and Ernst von Plener; and Weiskirchner took special care to style his leadership as pro-industrial and pro-foreign trade, welcoming gatherings of big industrialists to Vienna by announcing the city's (and party's) amity toward such groups.[189] The party's enforcement of the policy for anti-Semitic public contracts continued to be spotty. As long as peace and prosperity continued, such "softness" on anti-Semitism was tolerated; once the war began Weiskirchner would pay a price for his tactical "liberalism" on this issue. At the same time the party's traditional artisan voters were not forgotten. For example, Weiskirchner ostentatiously announced to the City Council in early March that he had urged the Lower Austrian financial directorate to adopt a lenient policy toward businessmen in arrears on their taxes because of the economic downswing of the last years, thus proving himself a "friend" of the small and medium-sized propertied interests in the city.[190] The results of the Third Curia elections in 1914, when many of the dissident artisans of 1911 returned to the Christian Social fold, suggested the initial success of this policy.

Weiskirchner also maintained a cautious distance from his neighbors in Lower Austria. When a group of Christian Social activists based in the smaller cities and towns of the province proposed in late 1912 that the Viennese party leadership (*Parteileitung*) participate in a coordinating committee with them and with Stöckler's Lower Austrian *Bauernbund*—thus reestablishing the semblance of a unified party organization in the province—Weiskirchner hesitated, citing (through the secretariat) the "well-known political circumstances" that made this inadvisable. The Viennese "already have a sufficiently arduous struggle with our enemies, without making this even more difficult for ourselves."[191] Toward the Church Weiskirchner adopted a sympathetic, yet slightly distant stance. Subventions to Church organizations continued with great largesse, but it was Josef Porzer, and not Richard Weiskirchner, who gave one of the opening addresses to the 1913 Catholic Congress held in Linz.

Finally, Weiskirchner gained an important ally when Richard Bienerth succeeded Erich Kielmansegg as *Statthalter* in mid-1911. Bienerth was no more energetic as *Statthalter* than he had been as Minister-President, but he eagerly consulted with Weiskirchner on sensitive policy issues (according to Kielmansegg, Bienerth even sent important documents to the Rathaus for Weiskirchner's vetting). With such leverage, enhanced in 1914 when Weiskirchner got himself appointed as Liechtenstein's *Landmarschallstellvertreter,* Vienna's position was improved in the Lower Austrian government.[192]

The Christian Social Party in the Stürgkh Era, 1911–1914

If the party in Vienna seemed to rebound, at least tentatively, from its defeat in 1911, its relations with the national party leadership seemed to grow more tenuous and strained over time. The Social Democrats also emerged from 1911 to find their parliamentary structure in trouble—when parliament reconvened, three distinct national clubs of socialists now replaced the formerly unified party—but the crisis of the Christian Socials differed profoundly from that of their ideological opponent. Regional loyalties and occupational biases, not ethnic identities, played havoc with the latter, and on the critical social and economic issues that Gessmann had always seen as the central matrix of party policy, the club was less capable of unified, predictable responses than the Social Democrats were even in their worst nationalist fratricide. Unlike the Social Democrats, whose divisions were the product of pride and ambition, the Christian Socials found themselves demoralized by scandal, shame, and fear.[193]

The destruction of the Viennese parliamentary contingent left eight urbanists (three from Vienna, five from provincial urban districts) arrayed against sixty-five members elected from rural election districts. Following Gessmann's resignation from his party offices on June 21, 1911, the Christian Social parliamentary club elected Alfred Ebenhoch as chairman of the parliamentary delegation, while Liechtenstein continued in the now purely honorific role of general party chairman. When the delegation met for the first time after the election on July 4, a long debate ensued in which Josef Stöckler demanded that the rural Lower Austrian delegates (who were frightened by the loss of three seats in the small-town curia in the June elections) be allowed their own separate representation in the club. As he put it, "the connection with Vienna has caused the Lower Austrians difficulties."[194] Stöckler also claimed to have heard rumors that the city delegates also wanted a separate section (if not a separate party), and he moved that the club be renamed the *Verband deutsch-christlicher Abgeordneter,* eliminating the old name "Christian Social" altogether. "Verband" would imply a much looser, associative relationship among semi-independent sovereignties. The three Viennese who survived the elections—von Baechlé, Rienössl, and Kuhn—were only too happy to accommodate Stöckler, but saner heads, led by the Christian Social Alpinists Jodok Fink and Josef Schraffl, intervened. As Schraffl cautioned, "one should avoid replacing unthinkingly something of proven value with something novel but untested." Fink pleaded "at this moment, let's have no separation." Finally an agreement was worked out whereby the Viennese rump was permitted to organize a separate lobby for city interests, and the Lower Austrian *Bauernbund* delegates, though constituting a distinct unit from the Viennese, declared their loyalty to the *Reichspartei.* Henceforth the official title of the club was the "Christian Social Union of German Deputies," with the adjective "German" inserted to protect the party against pan-German sniping on the right.[195] The Lower Austrians further insisted upon a new seven-man directorate (*Vorstand*) which would represent the delegation to the outside world, only one member of which ended up coming from Vienna. Stöckler's desire to put as much tactical distance between his colleagues and those responsible for the June catastrophe was the first expression of many future tensions between the various agrarian interests and those of Vienna. When Ebenhoch decided to retire from politics because of ill health in late 1911, the club had no permanent chairman but selected a temporary chair each month from the septemvirate.[196]

The club was now dominated by a group of younger, rural-based parliamentarians, among whom Fink, Schraffl, Stöckler, Miklas, and Schöpfer were particularly influential. Just as the Viennese worked after 1912 to reorganize their "provincial" organization (for in view of the de facto secession of the Lower Austrians, Vienna was now treated as if it were a separate Crownland—ten years before the city received such status under the Republic), so too did the various Alpine parties work at enlarging the scope of their operations. The *Landesparteitag* rather than the *Reichsparteitag* became the principal vehicle of Christian Social political mobilization; a renewed consciousness of rights and prerogatives marked the internal relationships of one provincial party to another.[197] Having been wounded or at least frightened when compelled to defend a univocal party in 1911, many politicians now seemed to feel there was weakness, not strength, in unanimity. The debates conducted by the club in mid-July on a parliamentary program demonstrated a similar confusion, with hours being devoted to the formulation of a short, six-point statement which, in the past, Gessmann would simply have drafted and imposed on the party.[198] Better prudent particularism than strong centralism. Inevitably this meant a diminution of the *Reichspartei* secretariat organized by Gessmann in 1906, which soon lapsed into insignificance against the Viennese secretariat. Typically, when the party had the chance to nominate a vice-president for the *Abgeordnetenhaus,* the Lower Austrians claimed the job for one of their own, and after some acrimony the club was forced to elect Karl Jukel.[199] Although most of the new agrarian leadership continued to acknowledge the idea of a *Reichspartei,* they naturally viewed the party from their own regional perspectives and expected that the parliamentary club would serve the economic interests of their rural constituencies above all else. A few were not averse to plotting more serious modifications. Josef Stöckler was rumored to have tried (unsuccessfully) to jettison Vienna altogether in the autumn of 1911 by uniting the agrarian sections of Christian Socials and the Bohemian-based *Deutsche Agrarpartei* into one rural coalition which, among other things, would put Stöckler in the Ministry of Agriculture. Observing such events from his temporary political exile in France, Albert Gessmann could not resist writing to Funder: "how pitiably have the short-sighted and petty plans of these intriguers collapsed."[200]

Inevitably the lack of representation in the parliamentary delegation hurt Vienna. In June 1913 city and parliamentary leaders were forced to hold a summit to clarify "a long list of misunderstandings" which had grown up between them.[201] The suspicions of the Lower Austrians about Viennese particularism seemed confirmed in the summer of 1911 when voices like those of Robert Pattai and Anton Nagler were heard to argue for a new Christian-German national party excluding contact with the agrarians altogether.[202] Fortunately Weiskirchner was able to overcome this kind of defeatism, but the image of the Viennese party as it struggled in late 1911 and early 1912 to reform itself was hardly an attractive one. The conflicts out of which the revised statute of 1912 emerged, with the *Bürgerklub* seeking to ensure its hegemony in the party against Kunschak's "clerical mafia," led many in the *Reichspartei* to doubt Vienna's long-term survival in the Christian Social universe. Alois Liechtenstein, still longing for the more ambitious, imperial ideals of 1907, characterized the *Bürgerklub*'s new statute for the Viennese party as written "von Spiessern für Spiesser."[203] Gessmann was convinced that the party in Vienna needed an infusion of new, younger men, who would replace the "Old Guard ruined under Lueger's system." Until this happened Gessmann was convinced that "our immediate future lies above all out in the Crownlands."[204] Josef Schraffl summed up the perceptions of many Christian Social Alpinists, when he noted in October 1911, "In Lower Austria panic is everywhere; they are frightened that new elections might occur. Formerly the Rathaus was the center of the Christian Social party; now the [parliamentary] *Reichspartei* will have to constitute the center, since the [party] organizations have all become localist-oriented."[205]

The party's state-level profile in the years between 1912 and 1914 lacked sharpness and on most important pieces of legislation was reactive. In July 1911 the club announced that it was adopting a politics of the "free hand" in dealing with the interim Gautsch ministry, suggesting the possibility of a more independent and antagonistic position vis-à-vis the government than either Lueger or Gessmann had found desirable. In part this reflected the tolerance that Gautsch seemed to demonstrate during the first months of his ministry toward the Social Democrats, and the Christian Socials' justified suspicions that a minority within the *Deutscher Nationalverband* would be only too happy to collaborate with the socialists in future runoff elections. But it was also the natural consequence of the club's own lack of a consistent, aggressive program and of a profound disillusionment with the effects of Gessmann's ministerialist ideas. Johann Hauser, the influential Upper Austrian prelate who succeeded Ebenhoch as *Landeshauptmann* in Linz, went so far as to insert in his last will and testament in mid-July 1911 a plea that the Christian Socials never again "send someone into the Cabinet or engage themselves for the policy of the government. . . . Nothing has damaged our party more than its 'ministeriability'."[206] During a remarkable session in late October, the club debated participating in a "working majority" under Gautsch (provoked by Gautsch's negotiations with the Czechs for a parliamentarization of the Cabinet). When Josef Schraffl asserted that the party had a strong interest in keeping parliament functioning, he encountered surprising resistance from those who saw such rhetoric as a stalking horse for a government coalition. Johann Mayer was surprised that "tendencies toward a friendship with the government are now coming to light," while Alfred Ebenhoch insisted that the party had gained virtually nothing from its participation in previous ministries. By playing free agent and by demanding concessions "from one issue to the next" it might achieve more from the Cabinet.[207] However therapeutic such talk may have been, its implausibility was amply demonstrated when Mayer suggested that the party would as a free agent become the "conscience of the House." The very occasion of the debate, five days after Ebenhoch had angrily reported to his colleagues that Gautsch had initiated negotiations with the Czechs without even informing the Christian Socials, suggested that the party's isolation in 1911 had little to do with its attachment or nonattachment to a given Cabinet. Instead its situation owed much to the fact that as a moderate and centrist party the Christian Socials had no choice but accommodate the regime. Schraffl thus contradicted himself (as Ebenhoch pointed out) when he supported the "free hand" while simultaneously urging that the party do everything possible to keep parliament functioning. Given the extremes of Austrian politics, the second often excluded the first.

This became the supreme irony of the late Imperial Christian Social party. It was forced into responsible behavior in spite of itself. In the context of the Austrian system, "responsibility" meant collaboration, if not outright promiscuity. At the same time the putative failure of parliamentarization, resulting from the party's inability to control the Cabinets in which it held membership, but for which it was accountable to the voters, now became a critical challenge to the state-level identity of the Christian Socials. The lack of focus that the *Reichspartei* manifested over the next seven years emerged not only from internal collisions between urbans and rurals on ad hoc policy priorities, but from a lack of clarity about the role that a large, centrist political party should play in the national administrative system. Should it degenerate into a band of self-seekers whose principal object was petty patronage for themselves and their interest-group clients—the model that drove other Austro-German factions—or should it maintain a statesmanlike posture by articulating and trying to implement new social policies? How could it do the latter—Gessmann's model—if it lacked power in or even the respect of the Cabinet?

Once Karl Stürgkh replaced Gautsch in November 1911 as the last peacetime Minister-President, the party, while nominally maintaining its free-agent posture, swung back toward the government, not least because Stürgkh named as Minister of Education a prominent Catholic civil servant, Max von Hussarek, thereby reassuring the Catholic majority in the parliamentary club.[208] Stürgkh also adopted a more vigilant line against the Social Democrats, a relief to the embattled survivors of June 1911 who, unlike in the epoch of Beck-Bienerth, now found themselves beset by the unruly opportunism on the part of the other German *bürgerlich* parties. Stürgkh's willingness, even his avidity some argued, to dismiss parliament and rule by Article 14 must have intimidated politicians unaccustomed to resisting the Cabinet even on minor issues.[209] On those few policies where the Christian Socials dared to cross Stürgkh, such as the income tax laws of 1914, he had no trouble humiliating them. In the end, until the coming of the war, they needed him more than he did them. The club's long, tedious debates on minor pieces of legislation pending in committee and before the plenum, which rarely generated more than banalities, suggested a parliamentary group lacking in dynamic leadership and using rhetorical consensus as a substitute for a clear sense of purpose. The agrarian majority in the club set party policy on domestic economic issues such as the *Teuerung* with a ruthlessness that occasionally led the few Viennese representatives to wonder if they were actually members of the same party. Roll-call votes on measures to resolve the inflation in food prices in July and in mid-November 1911 and again in March 1912 saw the agrarians voting consistently against the Austrian urban electorate, whose most articulate spokesmen were now lodged in the *Deutscher Nationalverband* and the Social Democrats.[210] On November 22, 1911, the majority of the club even repudiated a harmless motion to increase overseas meat imports brought before the parliamentary committee on the inflation (*Teuerungsausschuss*) by Anton Jerzabek, a Christian Social physician who lived in Vienna (he was employed by the municipality) but who had been elected to the Bohemian urban constituency Rumburg-Georgswalde in June 1911.[211]

The urbanists' deficit in power within the club was apparent in the fall of 1912, when a minor bill on salaries for railway employees put party loyalty to the test. In mid-December 1911 the *Abgeordnetenhaus* had adopted a motion first submitted by the Social Democrat Josef Tomschik urging the government to raise base salaries for 240,000 employees in the state railway system by 38 million crowns in order to compensate for inflation.[212] Stürgkh refused, but he did allow an additional 21 million crowns to be allocated for emergency salary relief. When the House's Budget Committee reviewed the provisional budget in July 1912, Tomschik and Otto Glöckel again attempted to raise the railway employee salaries by attaching an amendment that would have inserted into Section 2 of the 1912 budget the 17 million crowns deleted by Stürgkh. The Budget Committee split seventeen against seventeen, with the Christian Social members voting against the allocation. When the issue came before the House and the party found itself threatened with another embarrassing roll-call vote, a strong majority of the parliamentary club was inclined to support the bill, since by now both the Social Democrats and Kunschak's Laborites had made the railway salaries a test case for the white-collar electorate. But Stürgkh's pressure and their own second thoughts led the Christian Social agrarians to hold a second club discussion on July 2, 1912. Here they decided not only to oppose the bill but to enforce this decision by declaring party discipline (*Klubzwang*).[213] A small minority, including the soon-to-be renegades Ferdinand Pantz and August Kemetter, announced that they would break with the party and vote with Tomschik and the Social Democrats. On the same day the Social Democratic bill was voted down in the plenum 192 to 136, with the Christian Social agrarians opposing it.[214]

The last act occurred in the fall of 1912. Popular opinion in Vienna reacted strongly against the Christian Socials' opposition to the Tomschik amendment. The Social Democrats staged dozens of strident rallies in support of the railway employees, all carefully monitored by the police.[215] In late October 1912 Pantz and Kemetter again broke ranks with their erstwhile colleagues and submitted to the House a motion almost identical with Tomschik's, calling for the expenditure of the now famous "17 million" during the 1913 budget year.[216] Christian Social labor organizations throughout the Monarchy flooded the parliamentary club with letters and petitions demanding support for the railwaymen.[217] Jodok

Fink found Pantz's behavior not "loyal," however, and insisted that party members be free to vote their constituencies. In response to what they felt to be shabby treatment, Pantz and Kemetter reaffirmed their resignation from the Christian Social party in early December 1912.[218] When Tomschik's and Pantz's motions came before the *Abgeordnetenhaus* on December 28, the club allowed freedom of voting, and the agrarians helped to vote both motions down—this in spite of a direct appeal from the Christian Social railway workers' league.[219]

The railway employees' concerns were valid in the Viennese perspective, but the episode showed how agrarian indifference to high-profile urban issues could compromise Vienna. Not only were the thousands of railway workers in the metropolitan area a potent electoral force in whose ranks Kunschak had managed to gain support, but the railway employees included white-collar workers as well as manual workers, which made them an attractive target for the white-collar politics that both the Social Democrats and the Christian Socials were eager to pursue. For the socialists, support for the *Eisenbahner* was an access point into the moral and economic world of petty civil servants; for the Christian Socials it would constitute strong evidence of the party's interest in the welfare of lower-ranking white-collar workers and public service personnel. In either case what was in fact rather a minor issue—the additional 17 million crowns would have had little practical impact on the salary scale of the railway bureaucracy—escalated into a major symbolic conflict.

Nor was all public policy debate colored by the urban-agrarian fault line. When Gautsch brought before the parliament the question of locating an Italian Legal Faculty in Vienna in October 1911, Viennese urbanists and Lower Austrian agrarians united in opposing the Faculty in the capital, even on a temporary basis. Similarly, when Stürgkh reactivated a part of Koerber's plans for canal construction in December 1911, but omitted the Danube-Oder canal, six Lower Austrians, including Josef Stöckler, Karl Jukel, and Karl List, were willing to join with the Viennese in arguing that the canal would critically enhance Vienna's prosperity and, thus, that the original plan from June 1901 should be implemented.[220]

Not all legislative activity during the Stürgkh era brought the party such conflict, however. Most of the agrarians in the club showed themselves surprisingly sympathetic toward the comprehensive social insurance package first proposed by Gessmann and Bienerth in 1908. Even Josef Stöckler, usually the last to give the Viennese anything gratis, urged that it would be prudent to support the bills, if only for tactical reasons.[221] Such consensus was not surprising, since the controversies plaguing the social insurance laws were more class- than region-oriented. The necessary fiscal expenditures involved could be justified by the inclusion of urban *and* rural *Mittelstand* groups under the coverage, since all German *bürgerlich* parties supported the inclusion of economic "independents" in the mandatory coverage (which the Social Democrats opposed). They also hoped to weaken the self-administrative mechanisms of the plan in favor of stronger state administrative controls (to prevent the socialists from lodging the administration of the new system in existing *Krankenkassen*). As Johann Hauser of Upper Austria coarsely put it in June 1913, in commenting on the party's stance toward draft legislation regulating the working hours of bakery workers, "in the first instance we are a party that must take care of the interests of the employers."[222] Such bluntness, however embarrassing it might be for Kunschak, illuminated the one vital link that held the party together and that would keep it together throughout the First Republic. Policy issues did exist on which the peasants, urban artisans, and property owners could find shared class interests. Gessmann was thus not completely wrong in postulating class rather than nation as a principal focus of the party; ultimately, under Seipel, his vision of a conservative *bürgerlich* party would be vindicated. Unfortunately, in the 1920s this strategy would be directed against Vienna rather than being directed toward the city's interests.

The Christian Socials also proved pliable allies of Stürgkh in June 1912 when the Austrian Cabinet rushed the long-awaited Army Law, the most controversial military legislation of the decade, through parliament. First considered by the Austrian parliament in 1903 to replace the outdated manpower law of 1889, the army bill had served as the focal point of Hungarian nationalist chauvinism for years before Stephan Tisza pushed it through the Hungarian parliament in June 1912. The law reduced the term of service for some categories of enlisted ranks from three to two years (although the government could make exceptions) but raised annual recruiting levels from 139,000 to 181,000 men, while providing for further automatic increases up to 236,000 by 1918. The latter provision meant that both parliaments relinquished control of army manpower levels for at least twelve years.[223] The Christian Socials' accommodation toward a bill that met few of its demands and whose provenance was humiliating in the face of the party's anti-Magyarism (the Austrian parliament appeared as the tail on the Hungarian dog) was intelligible not only in light of the club's view that Imperial patriotism was good politics against the Social Democrats; it also made sense in the context of its desire to gain concessions from Stürgkh on a *Kriegercorpsgesetz* which, among other things, would have authorized veterans to bear arms on ceremonial occasions.[224] The latter project reflected the interest of several Viennese party leaders led by Josef von Baechlé to extend Christian Social patronage to a new Austrian veterans' movement, in the expectation that a new field of electoral clientage would emerge. They believed that the veterans' movement would also provide an effective antidote to integral nationalism since, as a petition they sent soliciting the Thronfolger's support argued, the veterans' movement would encourage an "Austrian patriotic spirit."[225]

Following the victory of Heinrich Mataja in a by-election in the Leopoldstadt in October 1913, the Viennese delegation finally had an aggressive spokesman within the club, and coordination between the Viennese party and the parliamentary delegation improved.[226] Weiskirchner was able to persuade the club to support Vienna's demands about tax reform and civil service salaries in 1913–14, perhaps the last major legislative package considered by the Austrian parliament before the war. The most controversial legislation of the 1911–14 parliamentary session, the so-called *kleiner Finanzplan*, was the distillation of an ensemble of initiatives for tax reform which had preoccupied the government since 1908. The most controversial segment of this plan was a bill that would have increased personal income tax rates and that finally came up for parliamentary action in June 1913. Its political weight was all the heavier, since Stürgkh decided to hold up approval for the new civil service personnel code (*Dienstpragmatik*) passed by parliament in late December 1912 until the tax legislation went through, a strategy which the bourgeois parties openly accepted.[227] This in turn led to heavy pressures on these parties from the major civil servant organizations to go along with the regime's tax bill, whatever the political consequences.

Both political and interparliamentary conflicts were at issue in the personal income tax fight. The German *bürgerlich* parties, who still depended on the older curial system to maintain their hegemony in municipal and regional legislative bodies, wanted to apply higher tax rates to lower- and medium-income brackets, since this would increase the number of enfranchised voters from the working class. Special debate on the bill commenced on November 25, 1913, and on December 10 the lower House adopted legislation that set the minimum level of taxable income at 1,600 crowns (up from the existing tax threshold of 1,200 crowns) and applied progressively higher rates only to income levels over 10,000 crowns.[228] The *Herrenhaus* then passed a bill on December 29 restoring the minimum to 1,200 crowns but introducing higher comprehensive rates on *all* levels. The next day the *Abgeordnetenhaus* accepted the 1,200 threshold but held out against generalizing the rate increases. This divergence led to a fifty-two-member interparliamentary conference which convened on January 12, 1914, where the upper House agreed to raise the minimum to 1,600 crowns but demanded in return that the higher rates apply to all incomes. This the Social Democrats were willing to do, since the resulting increase in income taxes paid by more prosperous workers would increase their share of Third and possibly even Second Curial voters in Vienna and other large Austrian cities.[229]

The conference proposal set off a firestorm in the Rathaus. Weiskirchner and the *Bürgerklub* were furious, for the bill as amended would have enfranchised workers in the Third Curia earning at least 2,000 crowns.[230] The Alpinists in the party, represented by Fink and Schraffl, had accepted the inter-House compromise on January 12, but Weiskirchner brought heavy pressure to bear to change their minds. The result was a club decision, seconded by some deputies in the *Deutscher Nationalverband,* to repudiate the compromise, even though the powerful civil servant lobby hysterically demanded that both parties submit so that the Cabinet would release the *Dienstpragmatik.*

Finally, Josef Redlich provided a possible exit by offering a new compromise formula that accepted higher rates on incomes between 1,600 and 10,000 crowns but delayed their implementation until 1915, at which time they would be used only in years when the total annual revenue of the income tax was less than 120 million crowns.[231] The Christian Socials agreed to a modified version of the Redlich formula that Gustav Gross brought into the *Abgeordnetenhaus* on January 17. At a club meeting the same day, Johann Mayer described the political corner into which the party had backed itself, urging that "we have to try to bring this thing to an end as quickly as possible." The reaction of the Cabinet (and the Viennese Liberal press) was negative, however, and one by one the various *bürgerlich* factions in parliament gave way to Stürgkh's pressure and agreed to the compromise the *Herrenhaus* had originally proposed. On January 21 Karl Seitz delivered a damning critique of the Christian Socials' hypocrisy in claiming to protect the poor against higher taxes, and he assured Weiskirchner that if he needed to protect the Third Curia, he had only to appoint more (manipulable) city employees who would then vote as they were told. In end the Christian Social party stood very much alone in rejecting the tax package.[232]

Redlich himself characterized the panic-stricken behavior of the Christian Socials during the negotiations as being preoccupied with "trivialities and follies." Not only was the party unable to gain what it wanted, but it found itself abandoned by the *Deutscher Nationalverband* and the Czech urbanists as well. The club lost whatever remaining leverage it had with Stürgkh, and it handed the Social Democrats yet another issue with which to assault them in the Viennese Second Curia—as the party which endangered the rights of civil servants for the sake of the political privileges of the artisan masters. When the government sanctioned the new tax law on January 23, it simultaneously approved the *Dienstpragmatik,* but the net effect of the previous week's machinations was to make it seem as if the civil servants owed their long-awaited personnel code and accompanying salary raises *not* to the Christian Socials, but to the Social Democrats![233] As the last critical issue decided by parliament before the war, the *Finanzplan* showed a party so captivated by archaic electoral strategies that it would compromise its own reputation before one of the most powerful and articulate constituency groups in Austrian politics. At the same time the willingness of Weiskirchner and his colleagues to stand up for what could only be termed party-political desiderata, as opposed to toadying to the pressure politics of the *Beamten,* was an important stage in the Christian Social party's internal development. The party's goals that were involved may have been reactionary and even benighted, but at least they were the *party's* goals, and might be said to be a step in a progressive direction.

When Stürgkh decided to prorogue the Austrian parliament in March 1914 and rule by Article 14, he found surprising understanding from the Christian Social party. The motives informing Stürgkh's actions will always remain as opaque as his timing was transparent. On January 30, 1914, Stürgkh informed the Cabinet that the Emperor had signed the necessary documents for the prorogation of parliament, which he set into effect as a way of intimidating the Czechs, who had launched a systematic obstruction in protest against the government's handling of the Bohemian situation.[234] In late February he then changed course and asked Franz Joseph to recall parliament for March 5. Upon the reoccurrence of even more bitter dissent in parliament on March 11–13, Stürgkh used his warrant a second time, the ostensible rationale being the inability of parliament to enact critical legislation.[235] But reports of the sessions of the Cabinet in January and March raise doubts about how determined Stürgkh was to secure a compromise with the Czechs on ending martial law in Bohemia and calling new elections for the Bohemian Diet.[236] From the very beginning of his rule Stürgkh had made no secret of his contempt for the philandering qualities of Austrian parliamentarism, and the half-hearted attempts made by the Cabinet to manage the Bohemian *Ausgleich* negotiations between the Czechs and Germans were a sign not only that the government was unwilling to make compromises to sustain parliament, but that Stürgkh was only too happy to rid himself of parliament altogether. Joseph Baernreither even insisted that Stürgkh wanted the Bohemian negotiations to fail, fearing the power of a new German-Czech condominium against him. If Stürgkh had been listening to the urgings of the Thronfolger, Baernreither was probably correct. Karl Bardolff, Franz Ferdinand's chief aide, sent Stürgkh a confidential memorandum in August 1913 reporting that the Thronfolger opposed any piecemeal settlement of the Bohemian question, even one using Imperial decrees.[237] As Leopold Berchtold also surmised when the Hungarian-Rumanian *Ausgleich* negotiations stumbled in January 1914, Bardolff (and implicitly Franz Ferdinand) wanted no major structural reform anywhere in the Monarchy until after Franz Joseph's death.[238] In view of the aged Emperor's illness in the spring of 1914, from which he barely recovered, that passage of power seemed only a matter of time.

Certainly the Emperor's unusually provocative comments to Berchtold in March ("Man muss endlich fertig werden") and to Heinrich von Tschirschky ("In Österreich ist überhaupt mit einem parlamentarischen Ministerium nichts zu machen") suggest that Stürgkh was acting with and not against Imperial consent in disregarding parliament.[239] Unlike Beck he refused to prostrate himself before the parties; and unlike Bienerth he refused to humiliate himself by making false threats. Whatever other faults might be attributed to Stürgkh—

Baernreither would speak of him as "an invention of Aehrenthal, who tolerates no man of independent thought"—he had at least the courage of his own stubbornness.[240] His suspicion of parliament and his search for "strong" solutions were appropriate in the final year of peacetime politics, during which the continuing debility of the Emperor and the perceived imminence of Franz Ferdinand's grand *Staatsstreich* accompanied public pressure for confrontational strategies on many fronts. Count Berchtold encountered similar pressures in the Austrian Delegation in December 1913, facing charges of aimlessness in Austrian foreign policy and demands for greater vigor in defending Austrian interests in the Balkans.[241] Stürgkh made his response in March, Berchtold his in July 1914, but both were of a piece. Incompetence, enriched by equal portions of ambition and fear, struck blindly against phantom and real enemies. Rarely has the inevitable coupling of *Innenpolitik* with *Aussenpolitik* found a more vengeful expression than in the Vienna of 1914.

Jodok Fink and Wilhelm Miklas were authorized at the last club meeting on March 17, 1914, to write the party communiqué reacting to Stürgkh's closure of parliament. They argued that the prorogation was "regrettably necessary" and was welcomed by the population as "an act of salvation." The Christian Social party expected that the Cabinet would now use its (Article 14) power not merely for necessary financial legislation but to support other programs to stimulate trade and commerce. Even a permanent reform of the parliamentary code of procedure (to replace the temporary measure passed under Bienerth) would be desirable.[242] That those who had proudly fought to maintain the status of parliament and outmaneuver obstructionists now consented—indeed, even applauded—such autocracy demonstrated how far the party's public purpose had degenerated. Under Karl Lueger's leadership even such an implicit approbation of Article 14 would have been unthinkable.

But it also suggested how far the collapse of the illusions of 1906–7 had penetrated the Austrian polity. Even among the Social Democrats—as the debates of the 1913 socialist party congress showed, where one full day was devoted to the possibility of socialist obstruction of parliament—frustration and disillusionment over the powerlessness of the Austrian parliament gave rise to what Stephan Licht termed "a form of desperado sentiment."[243] One might well argue that the beginning of the end of the Imperial state occurred on March 17, 1914, when the two principal supporters of the franchise of 1907, which was designed to free Austria of political and administrative autocracy and restore credibility to a "people's parliament," lost confidence in the system of parliamentary politics they had designed, and in so doing followed a vast shift in public sentiment *against* parliament.

Stürgkh was rumored to plan the recall of parliament in the autumn, but his negotiations with Czech and German party leaders in the late spring and early summer of 1914 failed to generate the ironclad assurances for the reopening of the Bohemian Diet and restoration of the provincial administration that he now demanded.[244] Indeed, the Bohemian conundrum became a nightmare for the central state in ways that surpassed the violence and obstruction of the 1897–1913 period. In demanding of the major parties a self-generated agreement on Bohemia *before* parliament would ever be reopened, a pact that countless negotiations since 1900 had failed to produce, Stürgkh was refereeing a game whose outcome was a foregone conclusion. Stürgkh refused to participate actively in the negotiations, but he still expected a "formal agreement of all parties" on a concrete plan. Julius Sylvester, a lackluster German *Volkspartei* deputy from Salzburg who had succeeded Robert Pattai as President of the *Abgeordnetenhaus* in 1911, thus found himself saddled with the responsibility for the Czech-German compromise.[245] Sylvester wrote to Baernreither in May begging for help. He did not feel competent to lead a conference to negotiate an agreement between the Germans and Czechs in Bohemia, noting "I am not sufficiently familiar with the situation in Bohemia that I can direct the conference successfully."[246] Against such competition Stürgkh had little to fear. Ernst von Plener even found him "full of satisfaction" over the disgrace of parliament.[247]

The Christian Socials' hopes for a beneficent utilization of Article 14 also proved illusory, for although Stürgkh himself differentiated between a narrower and more latitudinarian interpretation of Article 14 (its use for "necessities of state" or for other desirable social and economic legislation), his Cabinet proved remarkably unimaginative (or perhaps too prudent) to recommend anything other than a string of relatively modest decrees, many of which the Cabinet gauged would be politically popular.[248] This was hardly a *Staatsstreich* ministry in purpose or will. Similarly, Stürgkh's intervention in Bohemia in 1913, dismissing the autonomous Provincial Executive Committee and imposing an Imperial commission to manage the province's affairs, was an exercise in constitutional attentism, not coup d'état politics. Austria would enter what was to prove the last war of its history lacking either a sitting parliament or a central bureaucracy intent on (or even capable of) reforming the system and exercising effective governance of society. With both of the mass political parties that had designed the new parliamentary system of 1907 in organizational and moral disarray, the state had stalled; merely marking time, it was waiting for a deus ex machina to save it from itself.

Writing in the second edition of his *Geschichte Österreichs* in 1913, the young Otto Bauer aptly described the relationship between immobility and chaos which characterized the Austrian state:

the Austrian parliament lurches powerlessly back and forth between parliamentary coalitions, which fall apart over the national conflict, and the bourgeois dictatorship [of the *Verwaltung*], which provokes national obstruction. The bourgeoisie cannot overcome this dead point [in its history]. Without a supersession of the national conflict by national autonomy, no lasting, working majority can be created in parliament. But the bourgeoisie lacks the power to revolutionize the state constitution. Only great historical events will this time push the political development further.[249]

What Bauer failed to note, of course, was that his own party was as plagued with national disruptions as was the hypothetical "bourgeoisie" on whom he heaped such scorn. And rather than awaiting a future of objective, revolutionary circumstances, many Austrians had another agent in mind as eyes shifted to the Thronfolger.

SIX

The Party, the Church, and the Thronfolger, 1911–1914

The Volksbund and the Renewal of Viennese Political Catholicism

The years between 1911 and 1914 were times of frustration and despair for the Viennese Christian Social Party and especially for those in the party who considered themselves Catholic both in ideology and political choice. Feuding was rife and tensions were particularly acute between Leopold Kunschak's Laborite wing and the parent party controlled from the Rathaus. In his personal bitterness Gessmann even blamed Lueger for the catastrophe of June 1911, since Lueger's "truly hostile attitude toward the party" (by which Gessmann meant the party organization), his selection of subordinate leaders, and his self-destructive tendency toward the party had finally led to the fulfillment of a prediction that, according to Gessmann, Lueger had once made privately to him: that when he was gone "it would be all over" for the party.[1] However biased his personal judgment, Gessmann's arguments had an inherent logic consistent with his own *Reichspartei* rhetoric: of the various segments of the urban party, only Kunschak and the younger Laborites now seemed to represent a vision of universal politics and transclass social reconciliation.[2]

Not surprisingly, many younger and (in relative terms) more progressive members agreed with Gessmann that the party was now in drastic need of reform and reinvigoration. It seemed that the Christian Socials were standing between two worlds, unable to decide in which they wanted to live: would they fight to preserve the old curial voting system in Vienna, continuing to depend on exclusivist *bürgerlich* interest groups, or would they abandon such nineteenth-century artifices, support proportional suffrage, and confront the Social Democrats with a new social strategy of mass electoral democracy?[3] Would the party endorse wide-ranging administrative reforms to make the civil service more efficient and more representative, or would it view such reforms as impinging on its own regional and local prerogatives? These questions were never completely resolved before 1918, when the Revolution imposed its own solutions. But the last years before the war saw conflicts among the Christian Socials between those who wished to sustain the older assumptions of corporate privilege and those who wished to discard them for a more creative, if a more dangerous, future. This chapter discusses several developments which, although occurring on the flanks of the party, were to prove of great import for its long-term history.

Of critical importance to the Christian Social movement and for Austrian conservatism in general was the emergence of a generation of younger politicians and religious activists after 1907. Writing in the *Sozialistische Monatshefte* in July 1911, the Austrian socialist Karl Leuthner had argued that the Christian Socials lacked any serious commitment to ideas in general and to the Viennese intelligentsia in particular. But by 1914, when these younger activists had become more established in the party, this was certainly no longer the case.[4] Leopold Kunschak and his followers were among this younger Christian Social vanguard.

Kunschak's Laborites had played only a marginal role in the Christian Socials' June 1911 loss; the party leadership had allocated only three of the thirty-three Viennese seats to Christian Social Laborite candidates, upon which Kunschak ran three additional independent laborite candidates as a protest. Following that debacle Kunschak began an intensive campaign for fundamental changes in the party's allocation of political resources, demanding a more disciplined approach to electoral politics, a larger role for his faction in candidate selection, and a more Catholic and social orientation for the party.[5] The *Deutsches Volksblatt* might characterize such views as those of a "clerical mafia," of a "paid mob," and of "sworn enemies of the German bourgeoisie," but Kunschak had the courage of his convictions. His tenacity in leading a crowd of Catholic workers to break up a rally of older Christian Social notables in late July 1911, at which Robert Pattai and other older *bürgerlich*-nationalist politicians tried to assert their hegemony in the party, was appropriate both tactically and ideologically. If the *Reichspartei* had to be infused with some ideological coherence beyond the vapidity of Gessmann's anti-Marxism (and many party activists saw this as the lesson of 1911), then social Catholicism was preferable to integral nationalism.[6]

Yet his dilemma remained essentially the same as it had been before 1911 — Kunschak could postulate hordes of potential Christian Social voters among the workers in the Viennese districts, but no one could be sure how numerous these supporters were and how resistant they might be to socialist blandishments. The results of the Fourth Curia elections for the City Council in April 1912 offered hope that a strategy of emphasizing commitments to the worker/

white-collar employee clientele of the party as well as to the property/trades sectors might succeed. In the twenty-one races that Christian Social candidates—many of them associated with or at least sympathetic to Kunschak—contested, they managed to win an average of 44 percent of the popular vote. This was no mean achievement, given the modest level of financing of the *Arbeiterpartei* and the halfhearted support often accorded to its candidates by *bürgerlich* voters.[7] However, Christian labor union membership levels remained unimpressively low, with rates of growth far smaller than those enjoyed by the Catholic unions in Germany. Indeed, some of what Kunschak claimed as the "labor" vote was in fact a very soft base of more traditional Christian Social propertied voters who, when faced with the choice of a Social Democrat or a Christian Social Laborite, would grudgingly vote for the latter.

Another group proved to play a more important role, however, in the long-term reconstitution of the party than did Kunschak's Laborites with their minimal sustenance of marginal working-class votes in Vienna. This was a younger generation of Catholic intellectuals and administrators in Vienna after 1907, who adopted the Christian Social party as their own and in turn came to feel that they should be allowed more authority and responsibility in its operations. An ideological transformation occurred in the course of this generational shift on both clerical and lay fronts. Among the lower clergy, the slow, painful modification of the brand of activism urged by Joseph Scheicher was already apparent by 1907. The isolated self-help mentalities of the 1880s changed with the success of the Christian Social machine, with the creation of new Catholic associational opportunities, and with more aggressive leadership by the episcopate. Some lower clerics withdrew into self-contented illusions and lethargy; others reaped indirect yet real psychological and political rewards by collaborating with Lueger's party and by participating in new Catholic or Christian Social party organizations. The participation of local clerics in ward political clubs or in district meetings of the *Christlicher Wiener Frauenbund* offered them new interactive venues in which they encountered potentially sympathetic audiences, but in which they had to win the respect and attention of these audiences in more dynamic, competitive, and semi-secular environments. Still other clerics came to see their pastoral work in more self-consciously professional terms, requiring expertise and but also meriting public respect. Emblematic of this new concern for "scientific" expertise was the emergence of programs for Catholic catechetical training, developed under the aegis of a special catechetical section of the *Leo-Gesellschaft*.[8] The *Correspondenzblatt für den katholischen Clerus Oesterreichs,* once a hotbed of lower clerical ire, became a more predictable professional journal after 1907.

Josef Scheicher was one of those most responsible for shaping earlier Catholic attitudes in the Christian Social party. His career had epitomized the urgency of the generation of younger clerics in the 1880s and early 1890s who had supported Karl Lueger's struggle for power.[9] Once the party was in power, Scheicher and his clerical colleagues experienced both the good and the bad results of political success. Some of the aggrieved *Cooperatoren* of the 1880s were secure in comfortable and even prosperous parish pastorates or other ecclesiastical offices by the 1900s. The list of members of the various organizational committees for the 1912 Eucharistic Congress in Vienna—many of them local priests—suggested that the fruits of generational succession, coupled with appropriate sponsorship by the Christian Social leadership, may have offered ways for some clerics to resolve the interest-based and ideological concerns that had first stimulated the lower clerical protest movement. Albert Gessmann's school legislation, which the Lower Austrian Diet passed in 1904, enhanced the local clergy's role in the Lower Austrian school system (under the supervision of the party) and thus may have helped to mitigate their grievances toward the educational system. The Christian Social purge of Social Democratic teachers highlighted a system of collaboration that heightened the institutional prestige, if not always the independent discretion, of the clergy. Personally, Scheicher prospered, being elected to the Lower Austrian Provincial Executive Committee and commanding a modest level of authority and popular affection.

But with his loose tongue and irascible temper Josef Scheicher was never accepted as a leader in inner-party circles, and even his status in rural Lower Austrian politics was eclipsed after 1907 by the success of the *Niederöster-reichischer Bauernbund* under Josef Stöckler. It was perhaps a tribute to Scheicher's lonely defense of the peasantry in the 1870s and 1880s that his putative protégés—many of them comfortably situated proprietors by the 1900s—now attained the political maturity to be able to surpass the style of unpredictable gadflies like Scheicher. To his dismay, Scheicher found that the "Ministerial" party of Albert Gessmann and Alfred Ebenhoch needed the talents of *Altkämpfer* and anti-Semitic agitators less and less, especially of those given to citing Karl von Vogelsang's neoromantic social theory. More out of resentment than principle Scheicher questioned the universal suffrage reforms of 1906, and in his autobiography, *Erlebnisse und Erinnerungen,* he vented his spleen against those who, he argued, had betrayed the party by changing it in ways he refused to comprehend, selling its soul to the rich and propertied while diminishing its anti-Semitic impulse and its commitment to *Mittelstand* protection. The autobiography was filled with contradictions, a record of the logical perplexities its author experienced throughout his career.[10]

Scheicher's swan song had come, however, in the realm of his own professional interests: the clergy. In an effort to restore his colleagues' honor and dignity and to pressure both government and episcopate into more vigilant defenses against Georg von Schönerer's *Los von Rom* movement, Scheicher had helped to organize the general congress of Austrian clergy (the *Clerustag*) which met in Vienna in August 1901.[11] The Congress transcended the localized synodalism exhibited by the clerics of 1848 to engineer a multinational priestly collective for professional action. Over 450 priests from all over the Monarchy journeyed to Vienna to attend.

The Congress featured speeches and discussions on the *Los von Rom* movement and the clergy, the salary situation, and the clergy's desire for enhanced legal protection. The most controversial speech was Scheicher's own. He recited a long list of ills that clerics endured—from meagre incomes to *Los von Rom* libel. He blamed several factors for the weak social position of the clergy and its lack of popular respect. The state filled better-paying positions in the Church hierarchy with "men of its own confidence," and exploited clerics by imposing tedious secular duties on them, but then insisted that the Church sustain its own "self-defense and independence" when it was attacked by atheists and anti-Christians. The relationship between bishops and priests was not "evangelical in nature." A sense of "byzantinism" conditioned the behavior of many clerics and offered *Los von Rom* agitators an excellent basis for criticism that they could use in spreading discontent. Scheicher also made what was, in retrospect, the most notable remark of the whole affair. He demanded a "reformatio in capite et membris" among the clergy. Bishops must cease to act autocratically; priests must cease to be recruited solely from poorer families whose only motivation was to obtain a higher education for their offspring. The priesthood must not become a "caste." Rather, it should work in partnership with the laity.[12]

The clerical Congress, and especially Scheicher's speech, caused a sensation in Vienna. His use of phrases that alluded to reform Catholicism, at a time when the writings of German theologians like Herman Schell and Josef Müller had already been condemned for their provocative reformism, was a direct challenge to the Austrian episcopate. In November 1901 the bishops met in Vienna and refused to approve the staging of further clerical congresses, compromising the future of the new institution. In July 1902 the official diocesan newspaper of Vienna published a notification of this prohibition of a second congress, reporting that "the episcopate does not approve of the general congresses of priests, and the individual bishops will offer their clergy an opportunity . . . to make their wishes and complaints known in the channels prescribed by canon law."[13] The bishops' actions generated substantial outrage, particularly since the clerics planning the second congress for August 1902 had no official warning of the condemnation. Letters protesting the arbitrariness of the episcopate's action found their way to the *Reichspost* and other papers. Robert Breitschopf, a Benedictine active in organizing the Lower Austrian peasantry, wrote that the bishops' decree had come like a "bolt out of the blue." The clerics whom Breitschopf knew took the prohibition as a "moral slap in the face." Another priest argued that if the bishops refused to allow their clerics to meet at national congresses, the clergy should withdraw from all external political activity and confine themselves to purely pastoral tasks.[14] This may not have been a realistic threat, since such abstention was probably the reaction many bishops hoped for.

The repression of the Congress was part of a larger strategy by the Austrian episcopate after 1901 to regain control of its often unruly subordinates. A lower clerical associational movement in Bohemia—the *Jednota,* established by Czech priests, some of whom had attended the Viennese *Clerustag*—was repressed in 1907, over an issue involving an institutional and political dynamic that surpassed the boundaries of national identity. Nor was lower clerical activism merely an Austrian problem. In 1907 Pius X's famous antimodernist encyclical *Pascendi* placed severe, almost draconian restrictions on clerical congresses organized by priests. Scheicher and his colleagues had no alternative but to back down, and Scheicher did not mask his disappointment and even bitterness. His career as a leader of the lower clerical avant-garde was drawing to a close.[15] Defeat had come not simply because the general tenor of ecclesiastical culture had changed with the onset of Rome's profound suspicions of "liberalism" and with the Austrian government's renewed interest in clerical discipline, but also because Scheicher and his collaborators had dared to transfer institutions with a secular political aura into the realm of ecclesiastical authority. As long as they directed the major force of their political radicalism toward helping the anti-Semitic movement—the major emphasis of their praxis of the later 1880s and 1890s—they were relatively safe; once they began touting congresses of priests apart from the bishops (and the party), they were on thin ice. The *Reichspost* was sympathetic, but Gessmann had other goals in mind than sustaining Scheicher's synodal pyrotechnics. Although he welcomed agitational support from the lower clergy at election time, Gessmann's support for Bishop Franz Nagl as the successor to Cardinal Gruscha showed that he was willing to support a tough disciplinarian as archbishop of Vienna— as long as the archbishop was personally sympathetic to the Christian Social party. As younger appointees to the episcopate drew closer to the Christian Social party and realized how useful a mass, government-oriented political party could be for the interests of the Catholic Church—thus closing the gap between the bishops and the party leadership that had dated from 1890–95— the rationale for the kind of anti-Josephist, anti-hierarchical bluster that made Josef Scheicher credible evaporated. Intelligent and aggressive hierarchy working in cooperation with the new governmental *Reichspartei,* not clerical democracy bound to street-corner anti-Semitism, seemed to be the order of the day after 1907. This transformation also suggests how useful the heritage of Liberalism ultimately proved to be for the Austrian Catholic Church by 1914. On one hand, the Church learned to live with, and profit from, the flexible rules governing Church-state relations set down by the Austrian Liberals, rules that were administered after 1890 by high civil servants not unsympathetic towards much of the Church's social and political mission. On the other hand, the Church profited from the political collapse of Liberalism and from its reincarnation—electorally speaking—in the cadres of the Christian Social party after 1900. Once that party gained Cabinet membership in 1908 and could itself exert further pressure toward administrative accommodation, the circle of exploitation of "Liberalism" by Catholicism had indeed come full circle. A Church that seemed to have no effective external protectors in 1874 had both the regime and the counter-regime on its side by 1914.

Scheicher's failure did not close down all opportunities for lower clerical interventions in public life, but it did suggest the lower-order clerics would have to adopt new forms of discourse and organization. The career of Franz Martin Schindler demonstrated both the success of a politics of cooperative, institutional mobilization *within* the hierarchical Church through the modality of modern social and theological science and the importance of a new Catholic intelligentsia for the future of the Christian Social movement.[16]

In many respects Schindler was Scheicher's logical opposite. They were contemporaries who both served as young advocates of the Christian Socials in the late 1880s and early 1890s, but Schindler attained the university professorship that Scheicher never reached. Both men were sympathetic to the moral and jurisdictional problems of liberal Catholic theologians like Albert Ehrhard (whom Schindler brought to Vienna as a professor of church history in 1898, only to lose him to Freiburg four years later); but Schindler's own scholarship, as it related to social and economic issues, evolved in liberal Catholic directions, whereas Scheicher's economic views remained mired in the anti-Semitic corporatism of the 1880s. As professor of moral theology at the University of Vienna from 1888 until 1917, Schindler continued to work behind the scenes for the Christian Socials. He chaired the board of the *Reichspost,* where he influenced Gessmann's views on social issues and guided Funder's editorial policy. In 1907 he was rewarded for his long service to the state, which also included membership on the *Arbeitsbeirat,* with a seat in the *Herrenhaus.* In his work as the founder and general secretary of the *Leo-Gesellschaft,* the learned society of Austrian Catholics, Schindler organized, as Franz Zehentbauer later noted, "the whole Catholic lay intelligentsia" of Vienna.[17] But Schindler's greatest contribution to Austrian conservatism in the twentieth century may have been the young clerics he influenced in his lectures and seminars on moral theology and Christian social doctrine (*Gesellschaftslehre*) and in special events like the popular Social Course of 1894. The most prominent of these clerics was Ignaz Seipel, but they also included other interwar Catholic clerical intellectuals like Jakob Fried and August Schaurhofer.[18]

Schindler's social thought had a clarity that Josef Scheicher's lacked. His admission of the value of political and economic corporatist structures might seem to approximate notions of Vogelsang and Scheicher; but in his refusal to condemn finance capitalism, in his acceptance of political competition as the primary basis of legitimacy in a polity of universal suffrage, and in his opposition to far-reaching state control of the economy Schindler moved far beyond the neoromantic posture, toward a liberal Catholic analytic framework. In 1905 Schindler published a major work, *Die soziale Frage der Gegenwart,* which signaled his formal break with the traditions of Vogelsang.[19] He rejected Vogelsang's anticapitalist, state-interventionist theories, his condemnation of interest on money, and his view of the immorality of the wage-labor contract, arguing instead for a more pluralistic view of society and economy in which the state would regulate and guarantee (but would avoid massive intrusions against) the principle of private property. *Die soziale Frage* demonstrated the qualities that were critical to Schindler's personal influence: his comprehensive knowledge of contemporary social science and the pluralism of his interpretive views. Michael Pfliegler later reported that Schindler was one of the first major theologians in Central Europe to "include in his discipline [of moral theology] the sociological and economic problems raised by [the process of] industrialization."[20]

Schindler's students were the successors of the *Hetzkapläne* of the 1880s, but their self-understanding was different from that of aggrieved parish priests suffering indifference and insults in the anticlerical Viennese wards. They were university-educated theologians conscious of the wider intellectual and policy issues in which Christian Socialism was caught up and (as the life of August Schaurhofer demonstrated) more willing to experiment with varying solutions to the labor question. Their attachment to Catholicism was no less orthodox or intense than that of the clerics of the 1880s, but it was manifested in different kinds of concerns and was less parochial and less narrowly professional. Most important, the views of these young clerics had been informed by progressive Catholic theology (although none of them were Modernists), and by the second-generation impact of *Rerum Novarum,* which was a stimulus not merely to recognize the "social question" but to bring to bear the weapons of modern social science and economics to resolve it with a Catholic science of society.[21] It was hardly surprising that Schindler's most important student, Ignaz Seipel, would publicly oppose the Integralism purveyed by Franz Eichert and Richard von Kralik in their journal *Der Gral.*[22] Unlike Scheicher's generation, which had never ceased to be preoccupied with the ghosts of Austrian Liberalism (hence Joseph Scheicher's almost paranoid ambivalence about the Josephist administrative state), Schindler's students realized that twentieth-century Catholics could ill afford to disown capitalism by subsidizing archaic, anti-industrial interests as they battled Austrian Social Democracy. Their enemy lay on the left, not in the center.

Franz Schindler called no congresses of priests; his honored place in late

Imperial politics was diametrically opposed to Scheicher's status in 1911 as political outsider. Schindler was appropriate for a party that had claimed state-preserving pretensions, but he also had the delight of training younger "sociological" clerics who would seek to push the party in directions Lueger had never imagined.

Interest in the social question among Catholic circles at the University of Vienna was not confined to Schindler's clerical students, however. Similar interests were evident among Catholic laymen who often collaborated in the work of Schindler's clerical protégés and who were often members of one of the Catholic university student groups that emerged with such fervor and combative pride after 1900. Some of these young laymen, such as Friedrich Funder, editor of the *Reichspost,* and Franz Hemala, the editor of the *Christlichsoziale Arbeiterzeitung,* were profoundly influenced by lectures Schindler organized. The early public career of Richard Schmitz, who was to play a critical role in the ideological partisanship of the First Republic, epitomized the aggressive, self-conscious maturation of this generation of younger Catholic lay intellectuals, whose view of Viennese politics diverged sharply from that of the generation of Karl Lueger and Albert Gessmann and who, because of their lay status, had more flexibility than did clerics in defining agendas of social action.

Schmitz was born in Moravia in 1885—the year Lueger was first elected to parliament and four years before Schmitz's family moved to Vienna. From his father, an unemployed artisan who eventually won a minor functionary position in the administration of the city of Vienna, Schmitz gained a powerful admiration for Karl Lueger. During his attendance at the Elisabeth Gymnasium the young Schmitz revealed a propensity toward formal religiosity, joining a Marian congregation and thus becoming a part of the new wave of public religiosity that Heinrich Abel stimulated in Catholic *Mittelstand* circles after 1890.[23] In 1905 he joined one of the Catholic student societies at the University of Vienna, the *Norica,* where he made professional and intellectual contacts that would shape his career. Schmitz seemed more interested in journalism and radical political agitation than in continuing his studies, and by 1905–6 he was speaking at local party rallies in favor of universal manhood suffrage. Eventually he caught the eye of Albert Gessmann, who sent him to Bohemia in 1906 to work as a party organizer for the Diet elections. Schmitz also befriended Kunschak and Hemala and served for a short time as an editor on their newspaper, thus acquiring practical contacts within the Christian Social labor movement. A short sojourn followed in the Tyrol, where Schmitz helped to found and edit a Catholic newspaper in Innsbruck during the height of the Wahrmund controversy.[24] Schmitz was profoundly impressed by the intensity and emotional force of Alpine Catholicism, and the impact of such devotion had a lasting effect. Much of his later "un-Viennese" rigidity on matters of cultural politics and state religious policy may have resulted from this exposure to Tyrolian puritanism.

In 1910 Friedrich Funder brought Schmitz back to Vienna, offering him a position as economics editor on the *Reichspost*. Funder promised Schmitz that he would find the money necessary for his salary from industrial circles, since "we [the *Reichspost*] already have valuable contacts with financial circles, which only need to be exploited in order to secure considerable editorial advantages for us." Such comments suggested the ambivalence that Funder qua social reformer would experience more than once in his career.[25] Finally, in the summer of 1911 Schmitz joined the newly reorganized *Volksbund der Katholiken Österreichs*. This organization—first called the "Nichtpolitische Zentralorganisation der österreichischen Katholiken"—had emerged in 1905 in the midst of the critical institution-building among Austrian Catholics during the first decade of the century. By June 1910, using the model of the German *Volksverein für das katholische Deutschland*, a group of clerical activists led by Schmitz's friend Gregor Gasser and Franz Schindler's former student August Schaurhofer had transformed the slumbering group into a militant cadre organization to oppose Catholicism's enemies, particularly Austrian Social Democracy.[26]

Originally Schmitz feared that the new *Volksbund* was simply another feudal vehicle to humor the Catholic aristocracy, but he was soon persuaded that it had the potential to revitalize both Viennese Catholicism and Christian Socialism and, indeed, that intellectual renewal in the Church was a necessary precondition to the success of the party. Only by articulating a new program of transclass social reform and more militant Catholic values could the losses of June 1911 be overcome. In July 1911 Schmitz became an administrative director of the *Volksbund* and also assumed a leading editorial role in its journal, *Volkswohl*. In 1913, upon the early retirement of August Schaurhofer, Schmitz became the principal director of the *Volksbund*.

These biographical details illuminate a slow but subtle transformation in the composition of the elite and subelite of the Viennese Christian Socials. As the party embedded itself in the terrain of establishment politics and attracted more prosperous sources of material support after 1900, it began to acquire, through a simple generational change, a younger cadre of literate and intellectually articulate gymnasium- and university-educated supporters, most of whom were members of Catholic university student societies. Some of these new *Gebildeten* went into the city, provincial, and state bureaucracies or into law firms, eventually attaining positions of influence and power from which they could assist the party in its cultural and financial feuds with the socialists after 1919. The Christian Social lawyer and financial expert Victor Kienböck is a good example of this career pattern.[27] Others—like Schmitz, Funder, and

Hemala—went into new Catholic associations and journalistic enterprises, from which they assumed positions of political prominence in the First Republic. Such younger *Gebildeten* were unlikely to emerge from the pan-German student circles that dominated the prewar Austrian academic scene; nor, certainly, were their origins to be found in Jewish or socialist student groups. Rather (to the extent they committed themselves to an ideological profile) they came from those groups of Catholic students who survived the climate of contempt and indifference toward Catholic values that prevailed in many academic circles in Vienna before the war.[28] Josef Scheicher noted in his memoirs that Albert Gessmann was especially inclined to recruit younger party talent from these circles of Catholic students.[29] Their foundation in the university world made them prime candidates for co-optation into the powerful, if intellectually barren, world of Viennese Christian Socialism. A tremendous field of opportunity thus presented itself to young enthusiasts like Schmitz and other educated laymen and laywomen whose political behavior after 1914 reflected cultural convictions and professional aspirations already in place before the war. They were personally committed to a more reformist and ideologically aggressive social Catholicism, and they saw the Christian Social party not as a collection of "anti-" interest groups but as the bulwark of a specifically Catholic mentality of the kind that older leaders like Lueger and even Gessmann might have found overly doctrinaire.[30] It was hardly accidental that the *Volksbund* thought of itself as an analogous organization to the *Volksverein,* and that its leaders would invite Heinrich Brauns from München-Gladbach to open the "Social Week" that the *Volksbund* organized in Vienna in September 1911 as a declaration of intellectual independence from the Christian Social past.[31]

Under Schmitz's leadership membership in the *Volksbund* grew from 4,200 in 1910 to over 28,000 in 1914, as the group developed a broad-based program of organizational and educational activities throughout German-speaking Austria. Schmitz insisted on the virtues of organization and on regularized membership roles, an emphasis which was more characteristic of the Austrian socialists than of his Christian Social predecessors. In the tradition of the *Volksverein* the *Volksbund* defined itself as a mass organization built on direct memberships by individuals, not as a cover organization for other subsidiary clubs and associations.[32] An occupational profile of the organization in 1912 revealed its social foundations: of the 14,547 regular members (11,350 in Vienna and in Lower Austria), 3,850 were workers, 2,751 were white-collar employees, 2,661 were master craftsmen, and 1,549 were agriculturalists. Many of the remaining members (whose occupations were not identified) may have been either university students or women.[33] Even from such general statistics, the shift away from the traditional social profile of the mainline Christian Social electorate was apparent: *Kleingewerbe* artisans, on whom the parent party in Vienna still depended as the bedrock of its vote in the existing curial system, were outnumbered by both working-class and white-collar contingents. The *Volksbund* devoted considerable efforts to spreading its message of Catholic activism among the university students, developing a separate periodical series for students (*Der soziale Student*) and creating a *Sozialstudentische Zentrale* in Vienna in 1913. The latter was dedicated to stimulating "practical social labor" for "positive Christianity" by students among the populace, including the working class. Admittedly, the initial yield was painfully small—a *Sozialer Kurs* for university students held in February 1914 attracted only 112 participants, suggesting the problems these activists faced in the metropolitan area.

Schmitz saw his work with the *Volksbund* as a way to increase the programmatic intensity and structural precision of the Christian Social party—a party heretofore dominated by demagogic leaders, known mainly for their rhetorical elasticity and willingness to sacrifice principles for momentary advantage. Catholicism in Vienna, Schmitz noted privately in his diary, faced an apocalyptic threat: "The thousand-year struggle of the enemies of Christ against His Holy Church flares up with terrible power especially at the present."[34] Programmatic weaponry had to be forged to confront the socialists effectively; the *Volksbund* could play a critical role in educating a new, ideologically adept party elite. The informality of the Lueger era had to be succeeded by systematic social and cultural education, which should not be left in the hands of the party itself. It was rather the *Volksbund* that had the intellectual resources necessary to make such training effective, just as the *Volksverein* provided the German *Zentrum* with a reliable resource for elite and mass "Aufklärung und Schulung."[35] As Otto Maresch put it in describing the aspirations of the new organization, political consolidation needed more than changes in party tactics. Much more did it require that ideological education and cultural affirmation precede effective political work: "Up to now it has not been sufficiently appreciated that, in the end, the party movement can only be the external manifestation of a more deeply rooted development, that the strength of a group devoted to a specific worldview cannot be guaranteed by external political success, but only by its capacity to influence the masses through social-pedagogic means."[36] Special attention also had to be paid to the Christian Social working-class organizations. The labor wing of the party had to overcome its atavistic self-conceptions and cease playing a token role of (unsuccessful) political activism; it had to engage a wider range of economic, educational, and ideological problems. To do this, the labor faction had to establish a more professional organizational network based on union cadres, thereby obtaining the kind of political leverage that only strong economic-interest representation allowed.[37]

In early September 1911 August Schaurhofer and his colleagues, including Richard Schmitz, staged the *Soziale Woche*—a lecture symposium that expressed these aspirations in a way that made older secular politicians in the party uneasy.[38] It was perhaps fortuitous that the *Woche* occurred simultaneously with the Ninth Party Congress of Kunschak's *Arbeiterpartei*, where dissidents, led by Karl Bittner, moved to secede from the main Christian Social movement and to establish a distinct *Christlichsoziale Arbeiterpartei Deutschösterreichs* which would develop independent policy agendas for workers and lower-level employees. Kunschak beat back the secessionists and kept the *Arbeiterpartei* an integral unit of the Christian Social party, but it was clear that he blamed the *bürgerlich* majority for the disorganization that had followed the June catastrophe and that he expected fundamental structural changes to remedy the weakness of the party's organization. The structural revisions undertaken by the party in 1912 might be seen as a partial, if inadequate, response to Kunschak's demands in the fall of 1911.[39]

Not only did the *Volksbund* exclude the senior leaders of the party from the actual program of the *Soziale Woche,* but several speeches presented what the organizers themselves characterized as "a completely new orientation of the prevailing views of Christian social reformers in Austria." Ten lectures were given on subjects involving social reform and the working classes to an audience of several hundred clerics, workers, and white-collar employees, and the close attention given to these proceedings by the *Reichspost* and the unusually pointed reaction by the Social Democratic *Der Kampf* suggested that this was not simply a routine propaganda effort.[40] Indeed, the papers by Heinrich Brauns on "Economic and State Activity in the Nineteenth Century," "Goals and Methods of Social Reform Work," and "The Union Question," and those by Leopold Kunschak and Franz Sommeregger on (respectively) "The Improvement of the Working Class as a Cultural Problem" and "Directions and Goals of Austrian Agrarian Policy since the *Grundentlastung*" provoked genuine intellectual controversy in a party not noted for its ideological self-consciousness since the days of Karl von Vogelsang.

Predictably, Heinrich Brauns dominated the symposium.[41] Brauns had spent the last eight years of his tenure as a leader of the German Catholic *Volksverein* embroiled in the Catholic struggle over the confessionalism of the union movement (*Gewerkschaftsstreit*), a battle within German political Catholicism over the legitimacy of interconfessional trade unions that pitted the more progressive Rhenish faction of the *Zentrum* against the combined forces of the "Berlin faction" (*Berliner Richtung*) and some members of the German episcopate, particularly Cardinal Kopp of Breslau. The terms of this struggle were not easily replicated in Austria, given the immaturity and disorganization of the Christian trade unions in Vienna. The importance of Brauns's visit to Vienna was primarily symbolic. It was significant that a prominent German cleric with impeccable credentials, a moderate liberal (or progressive conservative), would journey to Vienna to give encouragement to his Viennese brethren and, implicitly, to support them in their vision of the Christian Social party as a social Catholic reform movement. This was an ironic reversal of the original terms on which the German *Gewerkschaftsstreit* had been fought: the Germans had sought to defend a more liberal and latitudinarian view of their labor movement against Catholic integralism, whereas the younger Austrians had first to establish the very Catholicity of their own party.

Brauns's lectures in Vienna must be seen in the context of his experiences during the union struggle. He argued that Austrian Catholics had to alter their understanding of the economic structures of modern society and come to terms with that society through a pragmatic program of social reform.[42] Neoromantic illusions about the inevitable evil of capitalism had to be disregarded. Not only was the modern world inextricably bound up with capitalist structures of production in its pursuit of sustained domestic and international economic growth, but in addition these structures in themselves were morally neither good nor bad. The modern industrial system, slowly encroaching on the agricultural sector, confronted the imaginations of Europeans in the new century. To the state would fall a growing level of intervention and social supervision. Brauns envisaged a century in which economic growth would slow and new technological and political mechanisms would be developed in European societies to moderate the pressures and dislocations of the industrial epoch. The twentieth century would be one not of continued economic upheaval but of rational "consolidation" in which a "new order" would result from the efforts of states and interstate alliances to regulate and control the changes wrought by nineteenth-century industrialization.

It followed from these assumptions that Catholic strategies for social reform had to reflect the new industrial society of the future rather than nostalgic remnants of the past. Capital and labor were inevitably separate entities. In his approach to the social question, Brauns had little sympathy for romantic notions of a hierarchically integrated, corporate (*ständisch*) society.[43] Rather, he believed that capital and labor found themselves pitted in an unavoidable, partial opposition of interests. Union organization was a functional and justifiable economic necessity, and one's position toward unions could not be based primarily on noneconomic considerations. Hence the Church had to acknowledge independent forms of interest representation among the workers. Critical to a reasoned Catholic response was an aggressive exploitation of such modern organizational forms: not simply pietistic "workers associations" led by local priests but independent Christian labor unions, equipped if necessary with the right to strike. The clergy's role was one of cooperation, not of paternalist hegemony. Brauns implied that religious identity and laborite activism were not necessarily separate categories of cultural experience, but that they were certainly distinct categories of organizational power and purpose.

Brauns did not articulate a higher or final level of institutional integration by which class and interest conflicts might be eliminated (as Catholic social theory was wont to do through theories of a neocorporate order based on occupational status [*berufsständische Ordnung*]). But in according prominence to the modern state with its regulatory and supervisory roles Brauns seemed to be proposing a bureaucratically guaranteed theory of social equilibrium. In contrast to other Catholic social theorists of the late nineteenth century who sought structural guarantees to curb the mammon-like strivings of "capitalism," Brauns seemed more willing to see industrial society as a field of play for opposing social forces, where relative power would determine economic equilibrium. Social balance would emerge through the dynamics of competitive industrial politics rather than through prescriptive structures, but always under the guidance and protection of a socially responsible state.

In these presentations Brauns violated several traditional Austro-Catholic pieties: he subordinated the clergy to the unions; he admitted the inevitability, if not of class conflict, then at least of class negotiations; and he repudiated the intellectual world of Karl von Vogelsang and the 1870s. By acknowledging modern industry's right to exist, Brauns enhanced the justification for labor unions and Catholic labor movements, as even the recognition of the conflict between capital and labor implied the legitimacy of both against older corporate forms of production. Brauns's views reflected the bitter struggle over the successful Christian labor movement in Germany, as well as the threat of papal intervention against the *Volksverein* and against the Christian unions' organizational independence and religious interconfessionalism. They also illustrated the emergence among the German Catholic laity of a political self-consciousness that would function as an independent variable in *Zentrum* politics.[44]

In Vienna, however, his remarks struck different chords. Leopold Kunschak's paper on the improvement of the working class as a problem of culture contained points of both convergence with and divergence from Brauns.[45] Tactically, the embattled positions in 1911 of the *Volksverein* and the Austrian Christian Social Laborites were in some respects comparable. Both men asserted the final validity of Catholic Christianity as a system of moral values, but, ironically, it was Kunschak who came across as the more vigilant Catholic, decrying the secularizing tendencies of the epoch that had so weakened Catholicism. Kunschak's vision of society was also marked by a harsher view of the social consequences of industrial capitalism—a variation in emphasis that Brauns was quick to note in the discussion that followed. Kunschak described the continuing misery of the Austrian working classes and—perhaps externalizing his own beleaguered position in the Christian Social party—their need to gain access to the levers of cultural and administrative power. Inevitably, Kunschak was more interested in policy strategies involving the control and exploitation of state power than in the more systemic trade-unions strategy Brauns advocated. This was not merely because Brauns could take the powerful (and Catholic) *Zentrum* for granted whereas in Kunschak's case Austria had yet to develop a truly Catholic political party; his opinion also reflected different cultural perceptions of the proper role of the state in society. For Kunschak the Josephist state was not merely a guarantor of the market; it was also a positive agent whose legislative and administrative prerogatives in social welfare policy had to be exploited to the full.

In the general discussion after Kunschak's talk, Brauns said that Kunschak's views reminded him of the rhetoric of German Catholics in the 1860s and 1870s—the world of Ketteler (if not of Vogelsang)—and argued that many of the features that Kunschak seemed to regard as essential to and constitutive of the capitalist system were merely attendant phenomena (*Begleiterscheinungen*) which would pass away.[46] Capitalism had also brought positive advantages to the working class; it had made the workers "active, more knowledgeable [and] independent." Kunschak, in turn, hotly denied that he believed in reactionary theories that sought to turn back the economic clock. He did admit, however, that Austria, as a more agrarian state, had yet to reach the level of industrial development found in Germany. From this difference in referential milieus came an inevitable disjunction in analytic emphasis, although Kunschak insisted that he and Brauns were "moving on the same theoretical path."[47]

As different as these presentations were, their authors nonetheless shared some important sensibilities. The very fact that Kunschak associated himself with Brauns's practical acceptance of the modern capitalist system was a remarkable departure from standard Christian Social party propaganda, which had publicly favored anticapitalism to please its lower-middle- and middle-class clientele even while the party elite enjoyed the fruits of accommodation with Austrian industrialists. The more frankly procapitalist stance of the interwar Christian Socials under Ignaz Seipel had already found its expression, one might argue, in the *Soziale Woche* of 1911.[48] Kunschak's noticeable lack of sympathy—again paralleling Brauns—for the obstreperous and limitlessly self-indulgent handicraft masters suggests that he (like Richard Schmitz) realized that the Viennese *Arbeiterpartei* needed different enemies as well as different friends. As he wrote to Friedrich Funder in February 1912, Albert Gessmann had come to a similar conclusion after visiting France and Switzerland. He was now convinced that "this panicky, suicidal *Kleinbürgertum* has no understanding of the really important achievements in the economy which we have undeniably accomplished . . . our economic program needs to experience a complete revision in favor of the Christian workers and, hence, in the direction of a reformed *Manchestertum*." Yet Gessmann feared that because it could not adapt to the modern world, the Austrian Catholic "worldview" was fated to decline. What Gessmann argued privately in political exile, Brauns and Kunschak anticipated publicly in Vienna.[49]

It was also apparent, however, that each side could use the same theoretical concepts for very different ends. Brauns came from a uniformly and self-consciously Catholic party with an energetic, articulate laity in a religiously divided state; Kunschak, from a vaguely "Christian" party in a society disdainful of "clericalism" and in a uniformly Josephist-Catholic state. To the Viennese Catholics it was clear that Brauns's München-Gladbach ethos could not—and should not—be exactly replicated in Austria. A confidential memorandum that the *Volksbund*'s sympathizers wrote in late 1913 for presentation to Archbishop Piffl, defending the *Volksbund* against the attacks of Austrian integralists like Anton Mauss and Anton Orel, stressed precisely this point. Austrian Catholics, who nominally constituted 91 percent of the Austrian population, did not need the kind of interconfessional political or ecclesiastical strategies that German Catholics, only 36 percent of their state, had to develop.[50] What they needed was a clearer concept of their Catholicism than the vaguely "Christian" ethos attached to Viennese Catholic traditions, a form of collective cultural identity the "liberal" German tradition simply took for granted. For Heinrich Brauns, Catholic union organization in western Germany was a critical point both of intellectual contention and of pragmatic survival. Kunschak, in contrast, faced not only political indifference from his party leadership but also a radically different clientage structure in the electorate. "Christian unions" would be of less help in Vienna where the socialists were better organized and the pace of industrial development was far slower than in the west German cities with which Brauns regularly dealt. It was not accidental that Kunschak's erstwhile "laborite" colleague, Julius Prochazka, spent most of his time in the *Abgeordnetenhaus* after 1907 as the spokesman for groups of civil servants and white-collar employees whose political consciousness was different from and more unpredictable than that of classic working-class client groups.[51] Even Albert Gessmann, with all his sympathy for social Catholicism, thought that in the face of the "brutal ascent" of Austrian Social Democracy the most immediately valuable strategy that the Christian Socials could pursue would be his long-sought bourgeois front. Gessmann, like many others, saw the problems of the future but could respond only with ideals of the past.[52]

If the *Volksbund* could differentiate itself from the *Volksverein* on grounds of clientele and culture, it could not—and beyond a certain point would not—do so on grounds of intellectual spirit. The controversies raised by the *Soziale Woche* were part of a larger challenge that the *Volksbund* posed for party and ecclesiastical traditionalists. To the older *Mittelstand* party leaders, Schmitz's irreverent remarks on their efforts to forge alliances with local German national groups in 1912–14 must have seemed outrageous. But until the outbreak of the war the actual impact of the *Volksbund* circle on practical Christian Social politics was limited, even if Ernst Vergani and other nationalists feared the organization as a secret cadre out to clericalize the Viennese Christian Social party. Vergani insisted in October 1911 that the "nonclerical bourgeois elements" in Vienna were being terrorized by Kunschak's Laborites, and that "be-hind them stands the *Katholischer Volksbund* under the direction of Cardinal Nagl, who now wants to get the Viennese Christian Social party totally under his control."[53] Schmitz's skepticism about party compromises with anticlerical nationalists was, however, consistent with a heritage of the party from the early days of Lueger—a heritage whose legitimacy Ignaz Seipel would restore by the later stages of the war. In this special sense, Seipel's followers among the interwar Christian Socials were lineal descendants of Lueger's movement not only in what they advocated but also in what they opposed. However different their perspectives on religion and the economic role of Vienna in national poli-tics, both groups rejected integral nationalism—hence the Viennese party's un-easiness at Social Democratic *Anschluss* rhetoric in 1918–19.[54]

More serious for the *Volksbund* circle were the accusations of modernism and liberalism raised against them by the Austrian Integralist movement be-tween 1910 and 1914. Older feudal aristocratic Catholics resented the upstart organization. But in Anton Orel's neoromantic criticism of modern capitalism and his espousal of the tradition of Vogelsang, and in the scurrilous journalism of Anton Mauss, the *Volksbund* encountered opposition that recalled the bitter-ness and factionalism of the German *Gewerkschaftsstreit,* even if it lacked the political coherence of the latter.

Orel was a young, university-educated leader who sought to mobilize Cath-olic youth organizations in Vienna to promote a revival of Vogelsang's antica-pitalist social theory. He first surfaced in Viennese politics in 1904 as an advo-cate of Catholic apprentice groups, cooperating with Kunschak in opposing the hegemony of *bürgerlich* commercial and industrial interests in the Chris-tian Social party. His natural extremism led to a break with Kunschak in No-vember 1909, which followed Orel's attack on the Christian Social party for the antilabor trade school amendment adopted by the Lower Austrian Diet in January 1909 and from his conviction that Kunschak had become a toady to bourgeois interests. Orel arrayed his *Verband der christlichen Jugend Öster-reichs* against Kunschak's *Reichsbund der christlichen Arbeiterjugend Öster-reichs,* and in January 1913 he founded the *Karl von Vogelsang Bund* (with the journal *Die Volksbewegung*).[55] Between 1909 and 1913 Orel collided with Kunschak and Schmitz on a wide range of ideological and status issues. At the Austrian Catholic Congress in Linz in August 1913, Orel's public legitimacy was undercut when the *Volksbund* was selected as the location for a central secretariat of all Austrian Catholic youth organizations.[56] Orel and his protégés fought back bitterly, attacking the *Volksbund* as a stalking horse for "the total dominance of Gladbach Liberalism in Catholic Austria." They charged that the *Volksbund* imported "social political wisdom from the Prussian Gladbach"—a crude appeal to the latent anti-Prussianism that lay close to the hearts of many Austrian Catholics. For Schmitz, Kunschak, and their allies, in contrast, Orel and his small circle of devotees were fanatical visionaries. Ironically, the warring factions shared some common values: both repudiated the ideological vapidity they thought characteristic of the older Christian Social party; both opposed the tendency of the Rathaus to sanction electoral compromises with local German nationalist elements in Vienna and to toy with "Germanic" rhetoric; both were, in their own manner, deeply committed to programs of serious social reform directed against the *bürgerlich* milieu of the *Reichspartei*.[57] The intellectual war between the two movements was, thus, as much a case of political proximity as of theoretical difference, but it nonetheless caused much embarrassment to the *Volksbund,* even after Friedrich Piffl committed himself publicly in support of their organization at its third congress in October 1913.[58] For the socialists, the intra-Catholic feuding was an endless source of delight.

In Mauss—an errant priest born in the Rhineland who ended up in Vienna—the *Volksbund* faced an even more problematic enemy. Mauss founded his *Österreichs katholisches Sonntagsblatt* in 1910, using it to attack the *Kölner Richtung* in German Catholic politics and to excoriate local Austrian Catholics for their putative association with it. Mauss's attacks on local Catholics, including members of the *Volksbund,* led several Catholic associations to protest to Cardinal Nagl and to demand that Mauss be disciplined for his insults. But Mauss had powerful supporters in Rome.[59] Petitioners condemning Mauss found it difficult to deny having *any* sympathy for or connection with the *Kölner Richtung,* and for this very reason the project that Mauss nurtured epitomized, in its crudity and simplicity, the Modernist experience in Central European Catholicism. Mauss projected a horrific vision of the papal Church threatened by heretics, by men who would undermine the dogma of papal infallibility and who undertook "open struggle against Rome"—men hostile to the Roman curia who sought to nationalize and thereby relativize Roman Catholicism by integrating it into a secular and, even worse, Protestant cultural environment. In Mauss's mind the *Volksbund* was nothing less than the local Austrian center for the evils of the *Kölner Richtung.*[60]

With the accession of Friedrich Piffl to the Viennese archiepiscopal throne in 1913, the *Volksbund* Catholics gained an outspoken supporter (more so than Nagl, who tended to trim and equivocate on accusations involving Modernism),[61] but Piffl found it difficult to curb the abusive behavior of Orel and Mauss. Even the aged Emperor sided with Piffl.[62] With such support, Schmitz and his colleagues continued their offensive in 1913–14. Schmitz, Alfred Schappacher, and Franz Sommeregger undertook an extensive lecture series and gave various courses in German Bohemian and Alpine cities in 1913, establishing a reputation for the *Volksbund* and causing bewilderment among local Social Democrats. In one industrial center in northern Bohemia, Schmitz organized the first Catholic political rally ever held in the town, defying an audience filled with jeering nationalists and Social Democrats.[63] On these occasions Schmitz's message was consistent with his earlier tenets: the *Volksbund* did not seek to replace other Catholic organizations, but it did seek to provide a coherent, scientific social leadership and an ideological direction that had heretofore been lacking. In contrast to German Catholics, who were a numerical minority, Austrian Catholics were potentially an immense majority, but one hampered by "laxity, vapidity, and open unbelief."[64]

Schmitz's emphasis on the scientific objectivity of the new Catholic avantgarde was both self-justificatory and self-defining. Social reform would be wedded to and shaped by Catholic ideological values. Rather than ignoring modern social science education, Catholics should welcome the weapons it offered. Schmitz's lectures on economic policy were particularly intriguing, for although he insisted that the *Volksbund* was indebted to the *Volksverein* only for its operational methodology, his themes could easily have been found in the work of Heinrich Brauns or August Pieper. Modern industrial development must be accepted; the principle behind industrial capitalism was essentially "profane" in nature and had to be judged on its own functional merit. It was less important to challenge the modern capitalist system itself than to reform the particular evils and to meet the special dangers that accompanied it. The greatest threats facing Catholics were the materialistic and rationalistic impulse and the mania for acquisition and profit which marked the new system. Individuals, especially those who were economically weak, faced uncertainty and marginality. Hence the development of mass-interest organizations (like unions or peasant associations) was critical, since individuals organized in collective groups achieved a more equitable sharing of resources. Yet their success raised, in turn, another significant danger: the possibility of class conflict. How could one sustain economic-interest representation and social justice without succumbing to the class-oriented blandishments of Social Democracy? For Schmitz only a double strategy would be successful. On the one hand an "intensive cultivation of religious life" would instill in Catholics the moral responsibility for conscientious cooperation among all members of society; on the other, the social education and organization of the masses would create that "feeling of solidarity," that recognition of the "large connections of social and economic life" Schmitz believed intrinsic to a Catholic view of modern society.[65]

It might well have seemed that these arguments simply mimicked the recent expostulations by Gessmann and others on the need to upgrade party economic programs, but a sharp difference was immediately apparent in Schmitz's political intentions. Schmitz did not seek to accommodate Viennese Liberal or Sudeten *bürgerlich* groups, but rather to differentiate Catholicism from them. Modern Catholic culture would become an exclusive, normative bastion of political and moral virtue. Schmitz's unease over *bürgerlich* front tactics with local German nationalists and his grouping of Liberalism with Social Democracy signaled a new militancy that superseded the intellectual worlds of either Gessmann or Weiskirchner.[66] Rejecting economic integralism—Schmitz and the *Volksbund* were opponents of interwar neoromanticists—Schmitz substituted a cultural and political agenda that diverged from Gessmann's bourgeois coalitionism as well as from Weiskirchner's nationalist coalitionism. His thought contained both particularistic and unifying features, masking a peculiar tension between political democracy and economic progressivism on the one hand and rigid cultural conservatism on the other. Whether Schmitz's fusion of pluralism and antipluralism would ultimately prove tenable was, in the late Empire, an untested proposition. In the First Republic it became a critical issue of state survival.

Writing in *Volkswohl* in early 1914, in an essay dedicated to Adam Trabert, a recently deceased Catholic writer who had participated in the early stages of the Christian Social movement in the 1890s, Schmitz demonstrated the exclusionary perspectives that infused his generationalist consciousness. Schmitz argued that just as Trabert had had to free himself from the narcosis of an empty liberal democracy before he could recall his native Catholic belief, so German Austria had to throw off the liberal anticlericalism for which Josephism had prepared the ground. He then suggested that

> the work at present, even more than in the times of the energetic Trabert, has to be pursued in two directions: the powerful surge of the Christian people's movement in the last twenty years makes laying a principled foundation for it the indispensable prerequisite for its further existence and success; out of its ruins, decaying liberalism's pernicious seed has sprung up among the fresh crops, among the propertied classes as a readiness to enter struggle for culture, within the working class as Social Democracy. As our enemy changes, so must our weapons. . . . The present generation often fights with new weapons against an old enemy wearing a new mask. What unites us with the past is the commonality of principles, of ideology, of goals. For we young people [*Jungen*], who assume the heritage of the now aged champions with humble veneration, but also with the joy of struggle and with the unbroken creative power of those who are young, Adam Trabert will always shine as a model of staunchness in outlook and strength of character.[67]

This generational shift in the cultural perspectives of younger party activists was a momentous event in the history of Austrian Christian Socialism. Lueger's generation of party notables had maintained a consciously opportunistic view of religion: it did not belong in all areas of party policy and public life, and when it was included it had to serve the secular interests of the party rather than be an end unto itself. In contrast, religious values were central to the political project of the succeeding generation, who thus completely inverted the logic and rationale of their elders' work. The younger Christian Socials paid the Austro-Marxists the ultimate compliment of wanting to emulate them, not merely organizationally, but also epistemologically. Cultural values were weapons of enormous power that both appropriated and transcended more mundane issues involving economic interest. It was hardly surprising that Schmitz confessed in his private diary that his service in Innsbruck during the Wahrmund Affair had been the beginning of his intellectual and religious transformation.[68]

In the short term, as often happens in cases of generational tensions, the *Volksbund* was somewhat isolated. The Mauss and Orel episodes came at a time when Integralism and Modernism were code words used to destroy men's reputations and careers. Both the *Volksbund* and the Christian Social Laborites found themselves on the defensive at precisely the time that their energies should have been directed toward securing their status within their own party. Thus they were forced to fight rearguard actions instead of combating the external enemy of Austrian Social Democracy, thereby confirming the absence of the core of effective Catholic values that Richard Schmitz wanted to establish in Viennese Catholicism. Not surprisingly, Schmitz was quite frustrated over the failure of Rome to repress the slander campaign against the *Volksbund*.[69]

At a congress of the Christian Social party in January 1914 a minor incident revealed the gap between present and future generational assumptions. Karl Angermayer, the leader of the Viennese branch of the nationalist, anti-Semitic *Ostmark,* suggested that the party should organize a special section for the education of its personnel, giving them instruction in social and economic policy issues to improve their competitive standing against the Social Democrats. Angermayer clearly wanted a party-run agency, not a religious academy. Richard Schmitz then took up the issue of political education in a long essay in the *Reichspost* several days later.[70] Schmitz thought the idea commendable but argued that the party should not involve itself in the arduous task of managing a school, since it had more immediate problems involving electoral strategy and political governance to contend with. Rather, just as the German *Zentrum* had given responsibility for "soziale Bildungsarbeit" to the *Volksverein,* so too could the *Volksbund* serve in Austria as an academy that would teach the principles of Catholic social theory. Instruction in social Catholic *Wissenschaft* would be become a staple element in the training of future Christian Social leaders; the *Volksbund* would provide "the permanent social school" of the Christian people.

For Mayor Richard Weiskirchner and the older leaders of the Christian Social *Bürgerklub,* such rhetoric represented a formidable challenge. Why in-

volve the party in the turbulent waters of Catholic social theory at a time when
Schmitz himself was being accused of heretical views in Rome? Equally important, for the men of the *Bürgerklub* the acquisition of political skills was a
product of conventional occupational training (as lawyers or businessmen) and
of involvement in the Christian Social polis itself. The governance of the city
was a business, and its voters were the shareholders of the corporation. One
learned politics informally and personally by doing politics and advanced by
meriting the casual, but very meaningful, approbation of one's elders and sponsors. Personal patronage led to promotion and seniority led to power. The party
did not need doctrinaire programs—had this not been Lueger's message?
Hence the party's encouragement of clubs of younger party members who were
active supporters, or at least sympathizers, with the machine—the *Verbände
der Bürgersöhne* and the various nationalist *Jungherrenklubs* and the *Meister-
söhnevereinigungen*. Some natural overlapping between the two sources of
leadership aside, would it be more to the party's advantage for the new generation to emerge from the old party elite and subelite and from party-associated
commercial and civic interest groups, or from the world of Catholic voluntary
organizations? In 1914 this was still an open question, and the feisty, impatient,
and undeferential political Catholicism of Schmitz and the *Volksbund* was not
a universally recognized model of political virtue throughout the Christian Social party.[71]

Although it was a minority influence in the party at the beginning of the
war in 1914, the *Volksbund* had attained a far more prestigious status by the
time the war ended in 1918. For not only did the *Volksbund* groups nurture the
leaders of interwar Austrian conservatism, but its principal rivals in the Viennese Christian Social party found their reputations and their policies discredited by the last year of the war. The crisis of 1918–19 opened opportunities for
the new generation of Catholic professionals, and they were not long in seizing
a prominent role in the Viennese party. A significant part of the political and
intellectual elite of the interwar party, at least in Vienna—Seipel, Kunschak,
Schmitz, Mataja, Funder, Kienböck, to name only a few—was loyal to the
values of Catholic social theory and the *Volksbund* tradition.[72] Ignaz Seipel,
interwar leader of the Austrian Christian Socials, described to Alfred Missong
in the early 1930s the importance of the *Volksbund* movement for wartime
Christian Socialism: upon Seipel's permanent return to Vienna in 1917 he
"came into a closer alliance with the *Volksbund* than [that sustained by] most
of the other Christian Social politicians, at least internally and spiritually. This
alliance had the greatest significance immediately after the revolution in November 1918. At that time the cultural organization of the Catholics supplemented the almost nonexistent political organization of the Christian Social
party most effectively."[73]

Before the opening of the provisional National Assembly on October 30,

1918, thousands gathered in front of the Lower Austrian Landhaus in the Herrengasse in Vienna to hear various politicians speak before the beginning of the Assembly's deliberations. When Richard Weiskirchner, the wartime mayor of the now lost war, tried to speak, he was shouted down (according to police reports) with cries of protest. Not only did Weiskirchner's control of the party leadership in Vienna begin, in symbolic terms, to decline that day, but the moral hegemony of his and Gessmann's generation of Christian Social politicians also crumbled with that of the dynastic state with which they had been so intimately associated. It was therefore not surprising when Victor von Fuchs, the elderly leader of the Salzburg Catholics, wrote to Count Otto Harrach in early December 1918 arguing that the days of Weiskirchner and the "Rathauspartei" were numbered, but also observing that "in Vienna a quite energetic and vigorous Catholic life is stirring, which opposes the vague Christian party program [of Weiskirchner] with a strongly principled, incisive program of Catholicism. . . . The circles around Professor Seipel represent this direction, namely the 'Katholischer Volksbund' which began before the war and which enjoys the special and dedicated support of Cardinal Piffl."[74] Schmitz, Seipel, and Mataja were no less "monarchic" than Weiskirchner or Gessmann, but they were fresh, new faces, unencumbered by past failures and miscalculations, ambitious to implement their vision of Christian Socialism, and sufficiently courageous to do so on terms of ideological and political parity with Austrian Social Democracy.

The Episcopate Ascendant: Nagl and
the Eucharistic Congress of 1912

As important as the loyalty of the lower clergy and the ambitions of other religious activists were for the Christian Social party, the political maturation of a younger and more aggressive episcopate was of equal consequence. The appointment of Franz Nagl in January 1910 as coadjutor bishop and finally as archbishop of Vienna in 1911, in succession to the aged Cardinal Gruscha, symbolized the coming to power of a new generation of bishops in Austria, men for whom the problems of church and state in the early twentieth century were more complex and for whom the older terms of "ultramontane" and "Josephist," which had defined the intellectual parameters of Josef Scheicher's world, were simply too crude to describe either their administrative tactics or political imagination. Nagl had long been on good terms with leaders of the Christian Social party, who supported his candidacy for the Viennese post. One important exception was Karl Lueger himself, who undertook an embarrassing, last-minute intervention with the Pope on behalf of Godfried Marschall.[75] Nagl also enjoyed strong patronage from the Thronfolger, Archduke Franz Ferdinand. Immediately following the successful outcome of the 1907 elections, Albert Gessmann wrote to Nagl, then bishop of Trieste, arguing that the elections had brought with them a "profound shift in the political center of gravity" in the Austrian political system and implying that the party was willing to support the candidacy of someone whom it felt would share the new aspirations and ambitions of the *Reichspartei* leadership. Gessmann was certain that a bishop who had so "renowned an understanding about the social question and about the modern age" as Nagl would agree with his strategy for the Christian Social party.[76] Nagl himself openly supported the Christian Social party, although he also had frank and unapologetic expectations for an enhanced role for the clergy in civil affairs. Speaking at the Lower Austrian Catholic Congress held in Wiener Neustadt in November 1911, in the presence of numerous Christian Social dignitaries, Nagl announced that a regenerated Church would make a conscious effort to mediate tensions between rival national groups in the Monarchy (not to deny, as had previous generations of bishops, that the "nationality question" even existed).[77] It was possible to combine good Austrianism, good Catholicism, and loyalty to one's own national ethnic group, according to Nagl, whose talk sounded as if it had been drafted in the Christian Social party secretariat. This process of reconciliation and regeneration was the public responsibility of the clergy, a duty that, Nagl argued, was the heritage of Karl Lueger ("the great regenerator of our public life," against whom, since he was dead, Nagl apparently held no grudge). The public no longer needed to fear "that in the process the clergy would take control." Practical success would eliminate traditional popular anticlericalism: "If the clergy carries the banner of a true *Volksaufklärung*, why should one fear the clergy?" Catholic laity must defend and support the clergy. The Viennese intelligentsia especially must again be won for the Catholic cause.

Such rhetoric was strikingly different from Cardinal Gruscha's usual somnolence. Nagl's appointment as archbishop of Vienna signaled a new militancy by the Church toward the party. Speaking before a meeting of the Church Building Association in January 1912, Nagl noted with satisfaction that at least some Christian Social leaders, in the aftermath of June 1911, seemed to recognize the need to reemphasize religious values as part of their effort to regain supremacy in Vienna. What the party had formerly viewed with some skepticism as a possible hindrance (too close an association with the formal hierarchical organization of the Church) would now be viewed as an asset, a development that could not help but redound in favor of the Church, or so Nagl hoped.[78]

Nagl's strategy of a Church militant led by the higher clergy (and not by the *Hetzkapläne*), working in partnership with the Christian Social party and deriving public approbation from its new aggressiveness, found supreme expression in the Viennese Eucharistic Congress of September 1912. Nominally a religious festival held under the joint sponsorship of the Catholic hierarchy in Austria and prominent members of the Hapsburg Dynasty, the Congress epitomized both the defensive confidence and the embattled self-satisfaction of the later Imperial Church, while illuminating in practice the episcopate's arguments about the new public utility of religion.[79] The Congress also suggested, by its logistics and cultural iconography, the moral hegemony of the episcopate over the lower clergy. Nagl may have been more attuned to contemporary mass politics than Gruscha, but for that very reason he was able to exercise a strict, almost authoritarian discipline over the clergy. A renewed sense of hierarchy was evident in Austrian ecclesiastical culture, even in small, circumstantially petty things. In the solemn procession around the Ringstrasse that ended the Congress, the archbishops and cardinals rode in ornate carriages, warm and comfortable, while the masses of priests and bishops walked in a cold rain.

In most Catholic countries international eucharistic congresses, although exploiting mass spectacle and pageantry, were usually "internal" affairs of the local Church, organized to arouse eucharistic devotion and to express loyalty to the papacy. The early eucharistic congress movement, which began in Lille in 1881 and which for many years reflected the isolation and emotional frustration of the Catholic Church in France and Belgium against state anticlericalism, eventually evolved into an impressive international ritual, with annual congresses occurring in London, Madrid, Montreal, Cologne, Malta, and Vienna between 1908 and 1914.[80] The Congress held in Vienna, although drawing upon elements from previous assemblages (particularly the Cologne Congress of 1909) had a special identity and symbolic value which went far beyond the usual practice of ecclesiastical politics in Austria.[81] The Congress was not the work of the Christian Social party, whose leaders and journalists often found themselves in relatively subordinate roles on the various organizing committees, but without the material and administrative resources that the municipality of Vienna put at the disposal of the organizers (especially a direct cash subsidy to underwrite local expenses), the Congress could hardly have been staged. Neither were the *Volksbund* or any of the other associational structures in which the lower clergy had found a political home directly involved in the proceedings. Indeed, the talks relating to social and youth affairs at the Congress were timid, consensus-oriented presentations, quite different in tone and substance from the usual programs of the *Volksbund.* Josef Redlich found Albert Gessmann in a foul mood over the affair, Gessmann intimating that the Congress's supporters were motivated by an unctuous desire to impress Archduke Franz Ferdinand.[82] Although supportive of the Congress, Friedrich Funder ran afoul of Nagl over accusations that he placed the printing order for the Congress's *Festschrift* with a "freemasonic firm."[83]

The Eucharistic Congress was a production of the Austrian episcopate and the higher Viennese clergy.[84] Nagl exercised close executive control over the planning through a central administrative committee of higher diocesan clerics, who in turn were assisted by prominent members of the Austrian high aristocracy, government officials, and even members of the Hapsburg family in arranging the Congress's logistics and securing its propaganda and funding. Indeed the Congress afforded a new opportunity for publicity to the Catholic Right in Austria, which had so bitterly contested the rise of the Christian Social party in the 1890s and then found itself eclipsed by Lueger's legions (and which now felt itself once again embattled by the new avant-garde of radical younger Catholics in the *Volksbund*).

Crucial to the Congress's prestige was the Emperor's decision to accord his official *Protektorat*.[85] As a later chronicler was to note, no previous international eucharistic congress had so favorable a milieu. In stark contrast with the French congresses, this assemblage would confirm the status of Catholicism as the public, if not legal, religion of the Austrian state. The Imperial *Protektorat* became an ideological opportunity for everyone concerned, pro and con. For it not only provided the Dynasty's personal endorsement of the Congress, but it enabled the Cabinet to participate in the lavish spectacle on an official basis. For the socialists, the *Protektorat* simply confirmed their long-standing accusations about the efficacy of "clericalism" as a public force in Austrian life. The aggressive integration of partisan religious culture and dynastic political power revealed, they argued, the antipluralistic bias of the Austrian state in matters cultural. Since the line between state administration and Dynasty was so fluid and so delicate, independent administrative neutrality was virtually impossible. For the Catholics this was precisely the point they wished to drive home: religion, particularly *their* religion, was not a *Privatsache,* but a critical nerve system of the state itself. By receiving the official protection and active participation of both the Emperor and the Thronfolger, they would demonstrate at an international level that Catholicism was a force superior to nationalism as a cultural bond for the Empire. It was hardly accidental that the Congress's organizers arranged to have large contingents of Catholic faithful from all the ethnic groups of the Monarchy participate in a grand procession, which was to be a "parade of peoples." The Congress presented the Church as the last bastion of "Austrianism," not only an institutional fortress but a metapolitical bulwark which, while respecting ethnic diversity, provided a centripetal force for political unity. The Congress showed a Church on the moral and political offensive which could assemble in Vienna hundreds of thousands of pilgrims. With the support of the Imperial bureaucracy and the city government, it could take possession of the Ringstrasse for a triumphant eucharistic procession by 150,000 people. What the Christian Social *Reichspartei* had tried and failed to accomplish in 1911, the bishops with the help of the Dynasty seemed to achieve effortlessly in 1912.

The Congress was thus not simply the feudal relic that the socialists sought to make it out to be.[86] Rather it assumed, as Seipel did subsequently, a new *Grossösterreich* in which a fusion of dynastic *and* popular religion became a cultural nexus for transethnic loyalty and thereby helped the Church to legitimate and earn its prestigious "official" position. No longer, Nagl argued, did the Church demand privileges simply on the basis of secular historic right or because of its intrinsic "truth," for it had now a public, instrumental value that all could see.

The Congress therefore presumed that the relationship of the state to civil society would be mediated by religion. Socialists sought to relegate religion to the status of a *Privatsache,* if not actually to expunge it from Austrian culture by a process of secular state Enlightenment; Catholics wanted to convert their cultural values into hegemonic ties to bind the Empire (Republic) together against the menace of socialism by penetrating the administrative apparatus. The two sides shared three critical features: both challenged existing conventions that presumed the civil service's formal neutrality in cultural affairs; both did so by developing new, totalistic schemes to unify the Empire through ersatz, cultural substitutes in place of ethnic antagonisms; and both were prepared to alter the form and content of dynastic rule in Austria to suit their own purposes.

Contemporary estimates suggested that, in spite of adverse weather, the Church succeeded in attracting several hundred thousand people, including visitors from abroad, participants from elsewhere in the Monarchy and (most numerous of all) bystanders from the city itself, managing them with a logistical skill worthy of the Austrian socialists at their best.[87] Anticipating possible disruptions from Social Democratic agitators and crowds, the government had stationed thousands of troops in the city, but it found it need not have bothered—police reports on the Congress submitted to the Lower Austrian *Statthalter* noted that the proceedings ran with machinelike efficiency.[88] Count Berchtold found the Thronfolger "very satisfied," and Franz Ferdinand was usually not one to be enthusiastic about other people's handiwork.[89] Was this actually the same city that slightly more than a year before had seemed to repudiate "clericalism" and deliver itself to the socialist party?

The internal, religious, and theological side of the Congress—its innumerable rhetorical variations on the eucharistic theme, its mobilization of thousands of schoolchildren (who conveniently happened to be on school holiday) for mass communion services; its extensive series of theological lectures and speeches by prominent clerics, university professors, and lay activists; the majestic entry into the city by a papal legate (who had traveled to Vienna in a special train of the Imperial Court)—all of this was sustained by the political character of the events. Not only did the Christian Social municipality place dozens of public-school buildings at the disposal of the Church to house visitors, but the Austrian military administration set up special kitchens to provide free meals for those who traveled to the city on specially discounted rail tickets offered by the Austrian railway administration. When the eucharistic procession left St. Stephan's Cathedral on Sunday morning, September 15, and marched around the Ringstrasse, the Imperial carriage transporting the Eucharist was followed by carriages carrying the Emperor, the Thronfolger, and other members of the Court. As Cardinal Nagl observed, this was a Corpus Christi procession to the nth degree, combining official dynastic and governmental support with mass acclamation.[90]

Anticlerical opponents of the Christian Social party in Vienna reacted to the Congress with desultory protests and, one suspects, embarrassed frustration. At enormous cost (which almost led to its bankruptcy), the *Freie Schule* printed two million copies of an anticlerical brochure, the *Josefsblätter für das deutsche Volk in Oesterreich*, with a section of anti-Jesuitical and anticlerical remarks attributed to Emperor Joseph II and essays by socialist and Liberal intellectuals on the heinous dangers of clericalism.[91] Attempts to distribute the brochure on street corners in Vienna ended in the impressive spectacle of various socialist politicians being detained by the police. But the editors of the brochure were perceptive in their iconographic choice: what would Emperor Joseph II have thought, what should his contemporary heirs in the state administration think, about the sponsorship of this "papal" religious rite by the Austrian civil service? Was it not predictable that proponents and opponents of Catholicism would try to play historic components of the Dynasty off against each other? If the Archduke Franz Ferdinand, with his patronage for the Catholic School Association, was at one extreme, then was not Joseph II at the other?

The *Freie Schule* also held a protest meeting attended by 3,000 people where Hock, Zenker, Glöckel, and other professional anticlericals offered a serenade of anti-Catholic refrains. Noting the market opportunism of the Viennese, Zenker reported that Jewish shopkeepers who were eager to gain the pilgrims' business had hung eucharistic pennants in their shop windows, and implied that the Catholics proved equally accommodating by patronizing the Jewish shops. Zenker rightly concluded that Christian Social anti-Semitism was a charade, but he avoided the other logical conclusion that many Viennese were uninterested in *any* doctrinairism, whether pro- or anti-clerical. Glöckel thought that Austria had now arrived at the final epoch of clerical hegemony, one in which the Minister of Education (Max von Hussarek) had dishonored his office by repudiating the traditional anticlericalism of the Josephist civil service and welcoming the Congress on behalf of the Cabinet.[92]

The *Arbeiter-Zeitung* also tried to trivialize and disparage the Congress, but when the newspaper resorted to silly arguments about the obvious discrepancy between the charity and humanity of the Apostolic Age and the conditions of modern Catholicism, readers could sense that the battle had already been lost.[93]

Ernst Victor Zenker complained bitterly that the Liberal newspapers treated the Congress as a media event, legitimizing it in spite of their editors' own anticlerical intentions. A congress of proponents of crematoria which met in Vienna at the same time was totally ignored by the Liberal newspapers. Zenker also thought the unholy silence of the *Deutscher Nationalverband* about the Congress proved the bankruptcy of traditional Austrian Liberalism.[94]

Because of the official patronage of the Emperor and Archduke Franz Ferdinand, the Social Democrats faced limits in their ability to castigate the proceedings. When a group of socialist parliamentarians brought a protest before parliament, their main objection was the support accorded to the Congress by the government, not the legitimizing role of the Emperor himself. An "international demonstration of Clericalism under the title of a Eucharistic Congress" had been favored by the government in "a conspicuous manner."[95] The army, the railways, the hospitals, and even the public schools had been misappropriated by the Cabinet and the Christian Social municipal administration to the advantage of the Clericals. State officials had been given special leaves of absence from their jobs to participate in the Congress, whereas such behavior would never have been tolerated if Social Democratic party congresses or pan-German rallies were in question.

Yet it would be a mistake to exaggerate socialist fears, for if the Church took possession of Vienna and of the Ringstrasse for four days, this was hardly the death knell of socialism's cultural assault on political Catholicism. Much of what passed as popular support for the Congress was mere curiosity or native Viennese sympathy for public spectacle. The same people who lined the street curbs watching Victor Adler's cadres march in November 1905 may have lined the streets watching Franz Nagl's clergy and aristocrats march in September 1912. From the official account of the procession on the Ring, actual lay participation in the parade from Vienna itself was probably not more than 20,000 people, including many who were children and students, and some individuals under institutional care.[96] In the context of a city of almost two million people these statistics show the need for caution in evaluating the hyperbolic reactions for and against the Congress in both political camps.[97] Neither side could legitimately claim advantages or disadvantages from such a spectacle that could easily translate into winning or losing votes. The strange and unpleasant fact was that no precise connections between religious identity and political choice could be posited by any Viennese politician before 1914, unless perhaps in certain sections of the Jewish community, where options were more limited in terms of acceptable choices. And even Jewish voters were divided by 1912 as a result of factional and nationalist feuding.[98] This does not mean that voters were not interested in anticlerical (or clerical) rhetoric. At the margin, when more fundamental economic and social issues failed to finalize voter choice, a repeated infusion of such rhetoric might have had an impact. Neither the 1907 nor the 1911 elections in Vienna, however, turned on the problem of religion. Schönerer had been unable to breach Vienna with *Los von Rom;* to the extent that critical voter groups abandoned the Christian Socials in 1911, contemporary evidence suggests that was because of voter discontent with the economy, and also with the internecine warfare within the Christian Social party.

The new anticlericalism of the younger socialists and *Freie Schule* adherents and the new *Catholic* Christian Socialism of men like Schmitz, Funder, and Kienböck may have been, therefore, premature. Indeed it was an open question before 1914 whether such inflexible cultural strategies could have succeeded in transforming Viennese political life. The question might be fairly put: if, in a counterfactual sense, the First World War had not interrupted the slow generational evolution of municipal politics in Vienna by spreading mass impoverishment throughout its society, would the inflexibility demonstrated in Schmitz's "Märzwahlen" article in April 1914—rejecting political compromise and demanding an internally consistent Catholic programmatic stance for the party—have sustained itself over time? Would the *Kulturkampf* mentalities of interwar Vienna, resting as they did on a painful symbiosis of cultural partisanship and economic deprivation, still have dominated Vienna's political world? Or did the *Kulturkampf* of the 1920s reflect a situation sui generis, legitimated by the devastation of the war and the attendant economic and political collapse of ordinary *bürgerlich* society in urban Austria? More significantly, would the mutual dependence and reinforcement of political issues involving *Kultur* and *Wirtschaft* after 1918 have found toleration and credibility in a Viennese electorate not beset by disequilibrating social pressure?

It is in this analytic context that one must evaluate the significance of mass events like the Eucharistic Congress. Before 1914 discourse relating to religion and to the family was rapidly being transformed, becoming more complex and more dangerous to use with each passing year. The volatility of voter reactions to a range of new issues had yet to be measured effectively, and voter loyalty to all political groups was open to question. Evidence from early twentieth-century German elections involving the *Zentrum* and SPD may confirm this assumption. Unreliable swing voters, discretionary new voters, and older supporters loyal in some cases but disloyal in others complicated all of the German parties' predictive strategies after 1900.[99] The seesaw effect that the socialists and Christian Socials encountered in Vienna between 1911 and 1914, with a substantial (if only in relative terms) core of voters shifting back and forth between the two big parties or between their subsidiary client groups, offered little consolation. In Richard Schmitz's mind the way to prevent such electoral instability was to increase the potency of dogma, which would polarize (and thus fix) the internal boundaries of the map of politics in Vienna.[100] But a boundary, as Lueger's generation knew, not only kept some people in but it kept others out. Early Christian Social electoral strategy up to 1897, and even in the transitional period between 1897 and 1905, was inclusive rather than exclusive in its motives and actions. Anyone who exhibited minimal personal loyalty to some section of the party elite and was not an unreconstructed socialist or Schönerian could be a member of the Christian Social party. Behavior, not belief, agency, not ideology, were the cardinal criteria of political affiliation. After the explosion of opportunity offered by the new national franchise in 1907, when the size of the potential electorate increased substantially, two reactions set in. Both sides assumed that an irrevocable transformation of the Austrian political system had been achieved—the mirage of parliamentarization—and both assumed that they would play leading, if not hegemonic, roles in making that system work. In 1907 both hoped to seize a majoritarian position by combining traditional issues (the economy, social welfare, loyalty toward or indifference to the Dynasty, class-based front rhetoric) with more aggressive party organization. The elections of 1907 hardly provoked on the policy front the type of innovations that they induced organizationally in the parties themselves. They proved to be tomorrow's war fought with yesterday's weapons, and all sides were disillusioned when the new electoral structures did not produce political magic overnight.

The lesson of 1907 was, moreover, that neither party could control Vienna unilaterally, and that new strategies were necessary to entice the other side's potential supporters. By 1908 each party commenced a fascinating process of evaluating its political means and ends (a process which, in the case of the Christian Socials, Lueger's death accelerated but which was evident even before his death) and of thinking about the ways by which voters might be attracted. But neither party was ready for the shock Richard Bienerth gave the Austrian political world when he sprang the June 1911 elections. Each side now realized that political survival would depend on expanding its range of possibilities by attracting swing voter groups. The question was, how were such groups to be defined and approached? Were they to be offered a broad coalition status, or were they to be asked to commit themselves to rigorous cultural values? In 1911 the socialists succeeded in raiding the other side, but this was hardly a test case for a new politics of ideology; and the assurance of the socialists in 1911 was simply copied by the Catholics in 1912. In both cases the confidence of the party propagandists exaggerated the meaning of 1911 and 1912.

Hence the remarkable logic under which a Social Democratic election association in the Josefstadt could publish an appeal in 1913 (among whose authors was Ludo Hartmann) asserting that its potential constituency in the district consisted either of middle-class intellectuals who had now concluded that a "socialist order" in society was inevitable, or of merchants and master artisans who had finally realized that "our current social order can no longer offer an effective protection against proletarianization."[101] To such voters the Social

Democrats offered useful representation, since the party was "not one which is concerned with the interests of individuals" and was not egotistical. This appeal could be read in one of two ways by prospective consumers: *either* that the socialists were the only effective protection for bourgeois voters against proletarianization *or* that middle-class and propertied Josefstadt voters would suddenly be willing to change their political self-understandings so radically that they were prepared to abandon class-based, interest-group politics in favor of a new moral, anticlerical collectivity. The two positions were not necessarily irreconcilable, and the arguments were appropriately vague so as to encourage variant readings, yet the first was a clear distortion of Marxist doctrine, while the second was futile utopianism, unjustified by later events. Either way, the Josefstadt socialists, in their ambition to make headway in new electoral territory, had wandered onto perilous ground, imputing illusions to others. Whether the middle-class electorate would accept a new age of univocal *Kulturkampf* discourse, once economic prosperity had returned, was in 1914 an open question made unanswerable by the First World War.

What the Eucharistic Congress of 1912 did suggest, ironically, was that the administrative state still controlled, in the sense of setting the permissible context of meaning and action, the limits of popular political aggression. The socialists may have been outraged by government (and dynastic) patronage, yet precisely the involvement of the state co-opted and bound the Congress. The 20,000 troops stationed to preserve order in the city bound in and limited the Catholics on parade, as much as they blocked out the socialists who sat in the editorial offices of the *Arbeiter-Zeitung,* writing with dismay about the procession on the Ring. Compared to the cultural violence of the 1920s and early 1930s, the Congress had a naive quality, according to which none of the participants—friend or foe—were ultimately responsible for the consequences of their actions. The Congress could be "filed" in police reports, laid to rest *ad acta,* just like meetings of socialist schoolteachers or of *Freie Schule* agitators. Mass cultural events subsidized by the administrative authority of the state could hardly prove Vienna to be Catholic, any more than temporary economic crises could prove it to be socialist. Both parties—the Red and the Black—left the Imperial epoch carrying with them more illusions than they cared to admit.

The Christian Social Party and the Thronfolger

The first two sections of this chapter discussed new intellectual and organizational forces that expanded the horizon of Christian Social politics after 1907. Both the *Volksbund* and the bishops sought to imagine and then to capture a new public. Both did so by pushing Catholicism as a programmatic and cultural force back into the public realm on mass-social terms. In so doing both presumed that religion had a vital role in defining public policy and in linking state and civil society, and both were thus strongly inclined to affirm the religious efficacy and the administrative constancy of the Dynasty. The *Volksbund* did this implicitly by its imperial, supra-nationalist, and historicist pretensions; the Congress explicitly by its invocation of the *Protektorat.* But the Christian Socials also encountered and negotiated with the Dynasty and the dynastic state in new ways after 1907 in processes made more provocative since they actually faced *two* rival Dynasties—the Emperor's and that of his impatient nephew. Christian Social politicians had to learn by trial and error that the world of democratic, competitive politics and the world of inherited dynastic privilege—even if that privilege was a tremendous asset for Catholic religious values—were not necessarily compatible. The next two sections will first discuss the relationship of the Christian Social party to the Thronfolger and then try to situate the autocratic politics of the Archduke in the context of the narrowing range of choices available to Christian Social politicians on the eve of the war. As we will see in the penultimate chapter, the Archduke's autocratic *Octroi* visions before 1914 found important emulators during the First World War itself, emulators whose political methods and goals were often not compatible with the organizational or religious interests of the Christian Social party.

To be Christian in Karl Lueger's world also meant to be Imperial and to be dynastic. Religion for the Christian Socials cannot be understood except as a component of a civic culture of reliance, discipline, and duty. This bonding between religious identity and political loyalty led inevitably to discrepancies. Lueger's regime had to be launched *against* the objections of the Emperor, but Lueger's *Vaterstadt* motif depended heavily on the Dynasty as a source of Christian invocation and as a moral telos toward which all public action should move. Hence the irony, observed in Chapter 2, of a Lueger who was both more imperial and more democratic than the Emperor himself. Similarly, Albert Gessmann's *Reichspartei* was also an amalgamation of mass democratic politics and quasi-religious dynasticism, claiming both to buttress the Monarchy and to draw authority and legitimacy from the Monarch. Both the *Vaterstadt* and *Reichspartei* were intrusive and exploitative—both claimed to "serve" the Emperor, but both also used Imperial images for the party's own practical purposes. With the aged Emperor the Christian Socials had a proper but hardly harmonious relationship.[102] Franz Joseph's two unintended "gifts" to the Christian Social party—his rejection of Lueger's mayoral appointment in 1895 and his support of universal suffrage in 1905–6—were as inconsistent as they were dramatic.

Yet Franz Joseph's putative successor also had interesting inconsistencies. Unlike his uncle, Franz Ferdinand violently opposed the democratic franchise of 1907, and his bellicose sponsorship of conservative cultural causes—such as the Catholic School Association—reflected an aggressively ostentatious Catholicism that the Emperor lacked. Yet Franz Ferdinand was equally, if unconsciously, protean in provoking change, for during the course of his long, impatient apprenticeship for power the Thronfolger afforded ambitious politicians—democratic and antidemocratic, from all walks of life—opportunities to imagine a world other than their own, one in which they could play leading roles. Rarely have the powerless been so easily co-opted by one who himself had but half a share of power—and not by winks and nods, but by garrulous insults and imperious ruminations. The Archduke Franz Ferdinand was graced with a character that ambitious politicians loved to hate.

A minor incident in 1913 involving a Catholic bishop and the Archduke affords a useful illustration of the complex relationship between the Thronfolger and the Christian Social party. In December 1913 Bishop Josef Gross of Leitmeritz appealed to Franz Ferdinand, asking that Albert Gessmann be nominated to a seat in the *Herrenhaus*.[103] Nominations to the Upper House of the Austrian parliament were sensitive instruments of government policy, all the more so since they involved the Crown in the workings of parliamentary politics. From the very beginning of parliamentary government in the 1860s, appointments to the *Herrenhaus* manifested political motivations; Eduard Taaffe had been especially adept at manipulating such appointments in the 1880s.[104] During the tense negotiations between Beck's Cabinet and the *Herrenhaus* over the universal suffrage bill in 1906–7, the power of the Crown to appoint new (and more favorably disposed) members to the Upper House provoked a conflict so serious that it threatened to undermine the whole reform project.[105] The *Herrenhaus* eventually got its way, and limits were established for the permissible number of government appointees, showing the *Herrenhaus*'s residual power in Austrian parliamentary life. Rather than "break" the *Herrenhaus*'s power, the Cabinet preferred to compromise. The Upper House was, moreover, not merely a brake on the "dynamic" lower House (as it was in other Western European states).[106] At several critical periods in modern Austrian politics the *Herrenhaus* became the center of political activism, for example, during the enactment of Liberal legislation on church and state in the 1870s, and most prominently during 1915–16, when pressures mounted for the reestablishment of parliamentary governance in the Monarchy. More important, since its members combined standing and influence in civil society with putative nonpartisanship, the *Herrenhaus* was, like the Army and the higher civil service, an institution which claimed to be able to rise above the divisive conflicts that often wrecked useful work by the *Abgeordnetenhaus*. The *Herrenhaus* thus saw itself as a forum where fundamental issues of public concern might be raised in an atmosphere of reasoned discussion and debate. And in the intimate world of Vienna that constituted the local setting for high politics in Austria, membership in the *Herrenhaus* could serve as a warrant to conspire and meddle on a prestigious, life-tenured basis, as Joseph Baern-reither proved so ably in the later stages of his career.

Gross's intervention was itself not without personal and political complications. He had been the favored candidate to succeed Cardinal Nagl as head of the Archdiocese of Vienna upon the latter's death in February 1913. Like Nagl before him, Gross enjoyed the strong support of the Christian Social party and especially of Gessmann, who remembered the energy that Gross had displayed in assisting local party operatives in the 1907 and 1911 elections in Falkenau and in Leitmeritz. Contemporary accounts (and later historical commentaries) even asserted that the final papers authorizing the presentation of Gross's name to the Vatican had been prepared for the Emperor's signature.[107]

Unfortunately for Gross, Archduke Franz Ferdinand had other ideas and, given the unfavorable publicity that attached itself to Gross's case, the Thronfolger was able to push Friedrich Gustav Piffl, the head of the Augustinian monastery of Klosterneuburg, as his personal choice to succeed Nagl. The Thronfolger had long been impressed with Piffl's intellectual and administrative talents and with his loyalty to the Dynasty. Piffl was also the personal choice of Max von Hussarek, the Minister of Education and Culture.[108] He gained the nomination and went on to a distinguished, if controversial, career as the episcopal counterpoint to Seipel in the Christian Social party in the First Republic.[109] Unlike both Funder and Gessmann, Piffl was not, at least in the Thronfolger's mind, associated with the putative pro-Sieghart faction in the Christian Social party after 1911. Sieghart, in turn, was closely associated with Max Beck, and Franz Ferdinand had never forgiven Beck for the successful opposition the latter had waged against the Archduke's reactionary politics in 1905–7.

The subject of Gross's appeal was not new to the Stürgkh Cabinet. In the immediate aftermath of the June 1911 debacle, Gessmann's name had been discussed as a possible *Herrenhaus* appointee, but at the time, in the midst of the civil war in Vienna, his enemies in the *Bürgerklub* and among the Lower Austrian agrarians lobbied Stürgkh against such an honor. Weiskirchner wanted no rivals in the municipality, and Josef Stöckler and other agrarians wanted no strengthening of the Viennese presence in the parliamentary *Reichspartei*. Both sides, as much as they might distrust each other, feared Gessmann more. The upshot was that Stürgkh appointed Prince Alois Liechtenstein to the *Herrenhaus,* whom no one feared.[110]

Gross's letter came at a time when the political debility of the party was evident to the Austrian political world at large, during the frustrating and unsuccessful guerrilla war conducted by the club in the *Abgeordnetenhaus* against the Imperial tax legislation of 1914, in the course of which the Christian Socials were betrayed by other German bourgeois groups and resolutely ignored by the Cabinet. However, it also followed a period of disenchantment by the Thronfolger with several of the party's leaders over issues of policy and personal judgment. Indeed, the historical (and historiographical) myth that the Christian Socials were the preeminent "Thronfolgerpartei" in late Imperial politics, so prevalent in commentaries of contemporaries like Josef Redlich and H. Wickham Steed, was never more dubious than for the period 1911–14.

Among the top party elite several members had run afoul of Franz Ferdinand's prejudices after 1908 and could hardly count themselves as members of a "Belvedere camarilla." Prince Alois Liechtenstein confided to Hanns Schlitter in March 1913 that he had last spoken with the Thronfolger five years previously, when he had presumed to urge a conciliatory approach toward Hungary, and had even dared to present a memorandum he had drafted to this effect. From that point forward he was considered *persona non grata* at the Belvedere.[111] Similarly, Alfred Ebenhoch had made the mistake of maintaining cordial relations with Beck and Sieghart during the autumn of 1908 when Court intrigues mounted against them—"treason" in the mind of the Archduke. In February 1909 Franz Ferdinand told his chief of staff, Major Brosch, that Ebenhoch was also responsible for inciting Austrian peasants against the feudal nobility during his tenure as Minister of Agriculture.[112] Albert Gessmann himself had a long but uneasy relationship with the Belvedere. During the brief period of his ministerial activity he was the addressee of Franz Ferdinand's imperious demands, even though the Archduke preferred to deal with Lueger since he felt that Gessmann was too strongly interested in maintaining his standing with Beck.[113] Following Beck's fall, when Gessmann blundered by playing into Franz Ferdinand's hands, his contacts with the Belvedere ran in more indirect channels, usually via Friedrich Funder. Gessmann's suggestion to the Archduke that tensions between Austria-Hungary and Italy should be improved by the negotiations on the issue of the papal *non expedite,* which prohibited state visits by Catholic sovereigns to Rome unless the sovereign first visited the Vatican, and that the Christian Social party was interested in arranging such a compromise, met with an abrupt and inflexible rejection.[114] By 1912 Gessmann was insisting to Josef Redlich that he, unlike others who sought to pander to the Archduke's tastes, was not a "clerical," and that clericalism had no future in Austria.[115]

Richard Weiskirchner enjoyed a more comfortable relationship with the Belvedere, partly because he consciously sought to play himself off against Gessmann for the Thronfolger's favor. Brosch noted in a letter to Franz Ferdinand in 1907 that Weiskirchner was one of the few men of talent in the party who could be relied upon. After Weiskirchner became Minister of Commerce he tried his best to ingratiate himself with the Archduke, with an eye to ensuring the Belvedere's support for a much-coveted Minister-Presidency. By the end of his tenure as minister in 1911, however, Weiskirchner too had fallen on uncertain times. Brosch evaluated Weiskirchner's ministership as a failure, and, according to Ludwig Pastor, the Archduke repeatedly expressed his "great dissatisfaction" with the new mayor of Vienna.[116]

Franz Ferdinand genuinely admired Lueger and was disturbed by his untimely death, but Lueger's views of the Thronfolger, although difficult to verify empirically, were probably marked by ambivalence. Lueger was not accustomed to submitting to the kind of imperious behavior that characterized any permanent relationship with the Archduke.[117] During his service as Stürgkh's Minister of Education, Max Hussarek complained that, in Redlich's words, "it is virtually impossible to administer anything, because he [the Archduke] is constantly meddling in everything." Lueger would hardly have tolerated such behavior.[118]

Only Funder himself managed to survive (on the whole) relatively unscathed, in large part because as the editor of the party's newspaper he had a more direct, instrumental value to the Belvedere. According to his own testimony, Funder first became involved in the Thronfolger's entourage in the summer of 1905, at the invitation of Major Brosch, who sought to influence the editorial policy of the *Reichspost*.[119] Funder gradually developed a close working relationship with Brosch, which carried over to include Franz Ferdinand's second head of chancellory, Colonel Karl Bardolff. Both men provided an "inside source" for daily news on Court and secular political issues that gave Funder a unique position among his colleagues in the ragtag world of Viennese journalism (a position resented in other Viennese editorial rooms). But with such information also came obligations, and Funder found himself called upon to report on the moral character of those who antagonized or simply interested the Archduke.[120] More significant, Funder often felt pressure to slant news to suit the Thronfolger's personal tastes, which he occasionally resisted (sometimes from disagreement, but also because of the contradictory implications of what the Belvedere demanded). On issues like the Hungarian constitutional question, Funder's natural inclinations toward a Vienna-based centralism and his willingness to sponsor trialistic political rhetoric in the *Reichspost* made cooperation easy (although in practice Funder was both more nationalistic and more ardently political than other members of the Belvedere's circle).[121] On issues that Funder felt involved his own journalistic integrity, he too proved intractable and uncooperative.

In March 1912, for example, following the closing of the old, aristocratic-sponsored *Vaterland* (from a combination of debt, lethargy, and indifference), the Archduke sought to stimulate a marriage of convenience between the feudal patrons who had supported *Vaterland* and the owners of the *Reichspost*.[122] This tactic must be seen in the context of the ventures sponsored by Franz Ferdinand to establish a new and more powerful daily newspaper in Vienna that would rival or surpass in wealth and circulation the *Neue Freie Presse*. Brosch would even insert in his final plans for the Thronfolger's assumption of

power the establishment of a "respectable press" as a primary requirement for
the success of the *Staatsstreich*. And Brosch was sufficiently cosmopolitan to
argue that the new press, while it could not be "Jewish," should also be neither
"Christian Social nor clerical" in order to establish its credibility and comprehensiveness.[123] These machinations occurred at a time when Funder found
himself embattled by the constant sniping of Vergani's *Deutsches Volksblatt*
and of some in the Viennese *Bürgerklub* who thought the "Catholic" paper to
be unrepresentative of their own more secular views.[124] Further, the *Reichspost*,
in spite of Funder's best efforts, had never been sufficiently capitalized to permit effective competition with the big Liberal dailies.

Together with Franz Schindler and Victor Kienböck, Funder met with a
delegation of Austrian Catholic aristocrats in March 1912 to review the various
programmatic assumptions that such a merger would presume. The meeting
showed that it was impossible to establish either collegial or ideological unity
between the two sides. Particularly interesting in Funder's private account of
these negotiations was the argument of the Feudals that the Christian Socials
were unduly sympathetic to the German *Zentrum's Kölner Richtung* in their
refusal to obey automatically the instructions of the Austrian episcopate and
that they rejected the imputation of being a "confessional" party, positions
which Funder made no effort to deny.[125] The negotiations fell apart when
Funder refused to concede any measure of ideological or political control to
the aristocrats, in spite of the interest that the Belvedere had in encouraging
such a fusion. The mythic portrait of Austrian Catholic unity presented by
Nagl's Eucharistic Congress later in the year was far less impressive when
viewed in the context of these ongoing suspicions and animosities between the
high nobility and the professional, Catholic-oriented politicians in the party,
not to mention those among the Christian Socials who were leery of any strong
connection with the Church.

Even Funder was not exempt, moreover, from the charges of the Belvedere's
rumormongers. In the spring of 1914 he found himself accused of having accepted a 600,000-crown bribe from Rudolf Sieghart, an accusation which, according to Alois Liechtenstein, emanated from a vengeful Alexander Spitzmüller.[126] Funder threatened to resign as editor of the *Reichspost* unless cleared
of the charge, and eventually the Belvedere had to admit his innocence. Coming as it did during the critical illness of the Emperor and immediately before
what everyone in Vienna assumed to be the imminent succession of Franz Ferdinand to the throne, the fiasco must have left Funder with mixed feelings
about Franz Ferdinand and the Belvedere's grand reformist schemes. Like
many others in Vienna in 1914, Funder found himself forced to repress his
ambivalence towards the man in favor of a desperate hope in the efficacy of
the revolution that the Thronfolger would impose on the state. As Josef Redlich
noted in his diary in May 1914, it was becoming increasingly difficult to ignore

the personality behind the programs ("Und dieser Herr soll ein Reformkaiser Österreichs im 20. Jahrhundert werden!").[127]

Even in the best of times the party's relations with the Thronfolger were thus unpredictable and subject to Franz Ferdinand's distaste for the changeable nature of Austrian party politics (especially the pernicious inconsistency of leading Austrian political figures, who rarely failed to maintain personal contacts with men from a diversity of ideological colorations). Bishop Gross's attempt to draw upon the Archduke's patronage in late 1913, following his own rejection for the post of Archbishop of Vienna and occurring in an atmosphere of mutual distrust between top party leaders and the Thronfolger, could hardly succeed.

This was not because Franz Ferdinand was disinclined to meddle in the process of *Herrenhaus* appointments. Max von Beck and Richard Bienerth had long made it a policy to keep the Archduke informed of their intentions, and in June 1912 Franz Ferdinand had even intervened with Baron Karl von Heinold, acting as chairman of the Cabinet in the place of Stürgkh (who was temporarily incapacitated by an eye infection), to secure an appointment to the *Herrenhaus* for Alexander Spitzmüller. According to the Archduke, parity demanded that Spitzmüller, as a director of the *Creditanstalt,* be accorded the same public honors as Rudolf Sieghart, the new Governor of the *Bodencreditanstalt.*[128] Heinold rejected this argument, noting that Sieghart occupied a more responsible position in his bank than did Spitzmüller, and that the Vice-President of the *Creditanstalt,* Moritz Faber, already sat in the *Herrenhaus.* As a professional civil servant with little hope of or desire for the Minister-Presidency, Heinold could afford to resist the Archduke's imperious demands. In the case of Gessmann, Stürgkh now shrewdly made his own recommendation conditional upon Franz Ferdinand's consent. Gross indicated that Stürgkh had told him that he must deal first with the Thronfolger before expecting action from the government. Rather than a *Herrenhaus* appointment that he did want, Franz Ferdinand would be given one that (apparently) no one wanted—Albert Gessmann.

Gross presented his appeal in the broadest terms possible. Not only did Gessmann's long service to the Christian Social party and to the Austrian state warrant an effort to recognize his loyalty, but the "ethical foundations of the Monarchy" as well as "the rights of the Church" had now come to depend upon the political fortunes of the Christian Social party more generally. It was an open secret, according to Gross, that the government and especially the higher civil service had failed to support the Christian Socials in their struggles with anticlerical and anti-dynastic forces, even though the party had sacrificed much of its earlier public esteem by joining the ministerial coalition in 1907. Indeed, Gross suggested that the poor standing of the current Cabinet among the electorate was owing to its inability to reward and to support those political movements that manifested dynastic loyalty, like the Christian Socials. As long as the Cabinet refused, for example, to fill key civil service posts with sympathizers of the party, it would find itself in the paradoxical situation of lavishing its patronage on an opposition that would then intensify its efforts to undercut the government. Gross obviously found this (common) Austrian practice of giving political gifts to enemies while ignoring friends to be both naive and dangerous.

For Gross the only way to break this vicious circle of negative reinforcement was for the Dynasty and the Cabinet to work to restore the Christian Social party to the level of prestige and financial support it had enjoyed before the catastrophe of 1911. The party desperately needed a strong, authoritarian leader to take charge of its disorganized cadre organization and to infuse new life into the regional party organizations. Only by restoring public confidence in its top leadership could the party play once again, with new financial reserves, its accustomed role in defending the Dynasty and the Church. Only Gessmann was capable of reviving the party in this way, but his political future depended upon his prior rehabilitation by the Cabinet with a *Herrenhaus* seat in 1914.[129]

Despite the exaggeration of its argument (Franz Ferdinand would certainly have found dubious the assertion that the Christian Social party was the principal defender of the Monarchy's ethical life), Gross's letter suggests how far the Austrian episcopate, and especially its younger and more aggressive members, had come since the mission of Cardinal Schönborn to Rome in the spring of 1895. Rather than viewing the Christian Social leadership as distasteful opportunists and interlopers, some members of the episcopate now welcomed them as allies in their own struggle against Austrian Social Democracy. Gross, like Nagl and Piffl, was a member of a new generation of Austrian bishops, born in the 1860s or 1870s, whose political tastes and opinions were shaped profoundly by the work of Joseph Scheicher and Franz Schindler. Gross was an admirer of Josef Scheicher, a friend of Ignaz Seipel, and a loyal colleague of Friedrich Piffl, with whom he shared not only cohort membership but a common set of ideological and strategic presuppositions. For these younger bishops cultural passivity was as dangerous as political debility; both sins could be avoided only by an alliance with a more Catholic Christian Social party. Gross's epistle reconfirmed the strategy articulated by Cardinal Nagl in 1911–12: not merely to support the Christian Social party passively but to encourage it to define itself with a more substantive ideological profile, a program ultimately fulfilled only after 1919.

Colonel Bardolff, who had discretion over such petitions, obtained two confidential estimates of Gessmann's previous political activities and current situation following his humiliation in 1911. The first was by Friedrich Funder, Gessmann's loyal friend.[130] Funder reacted to the possibility of Gessmann's

nomination to the *Herrenhaus* with enthusiasm, reciting a long list of his accomplishments. Most noteworthy he felt were Gessmann's activities on behalf
of the school system. As a member of the Provincial Executive Committee
Gessmann had taken charge of a school system disrupted by the "anarchistic"
behavior of many teachers. With an "iron hand" Gessmann had created order
and prevented the "political poison" of socialism and pan-Germanism from
spreading into society by way of the schools. Gessmann also merited a place
of recognition by his work in creating the Christian Social *Reichspartei* out of
the disparate city and rural constituencies of the party in 1907. Not only had
Gessmann possessed the courage and the vision to create such a new comprehensive organization where his colleagues had been content to maintain the
provincial fragmentation of the past, but the new *Reichspartei* had stimulated
other Austrian-German bourgeois politicians to think in terms of the need
for greater cohesion and collective discipline. Hence the founding of the
Deutscher Nationalverband was an indirect result of Gessmann's labor. Funder
implied that Austrian politics had profited from the suppression of small splinter political groups and their replacement by these two great political coalitions. Finally, Funder argued that only Gessmann had had the organizational
talents that had permitted the early Christian Social party to win its enormous
electoral successes in the later nineties. Gessmann's return to active politics
would, Funder felt, reinvigorate the Christian Social party.

　　Funder's comments apparently met with skepticism, for the Archduke noted
on his copy of Funder's statement that before making a final decision he required an additional evaluation of the case by someone less partisan and yet
equally knowledgeable about Austrian politics, who could explain why Gessmann had been forced to retire from public life in 1911–12. Bardolff responded
by interviewing Eugen Schwiedland, a Viennese economist at the *Technische
Hochschule* who had written various studies on the Austrian handicrafts industries (a subject of considerable interest to the Christian Socials) and who had
worked for Gessmann at the newly created Ministry of Public Works.[131] He
had also authored several essays for Franz Schindler's journal at the Catholic
Leo-Gesellschaft, Die Kultur. Over the years Schwiedland, who was formally
neutral in regard to party politics, had come to know Gessmann and other
Christian Social political figures well. His opinions were intelligent, if sometimes caustic.[132]

　　Schwiedland's evaluation was quite different from that of Funder.[133]
Schwiedland admitted that Gessmann had accomplished much in the Lower
Austrian school system, that though he had often acted in a partisan fashion to
advance the interests of his own party, he had restored the authority of the
state in educational matters. Gessmann had also worked with great energy and
assiduity in other policy areas of the Lower Austrian government, and he was
responsible for the *Reichspartei.* But in doing these things Gessmann had also

involved himself in an inevitable conflict of roles that had proved to be his undoing. According to Schwiedland, Gessmann had engineered the establishment of the Ministry of Public Works in the expectation that by gaining control of a huge new ministry with specifically urban and (in the case of the craft industries) *Mittelstand* policy prerogatives, the Christian Socials would be able to politicize the Austrian civil service and to channel valuable and often lucrative state subsidies and contracts to key electoral supporters. Once in power, however, Gessmann found that the situation was far more complex. The professional civil servants of the ministry (most of whom he had recruited from other existing ministries) were surprised by the overt political guidelines that Gessmann followed in allocating resources; and officials often found themselves hard-pressed to justify the uses to which Gessmann wanted to put public funds. The result was an ongoing tug-of-war between Gessmann and the permanent officials of his own Ministry, which was aggravated by Gessmann's frequent absences as he tried to continue his work as the Christian Social party's chief executive. Gessmann also found that styles of authority were not readily transferable between ministerial life and party operations. In the party Gessmann had been accustomed to consult widely among his colleagues in order to obtain consensus; when he tried the same manner of decision-making with the higher permanent officials of the Ministry, he simply opened himself to opposition from his own subordinates. On the side of the party Gessmann found an equally difficult set of challenges. Once in power Gessmann was inundated by special interests and pleadings, as various loyalists expected that the minister would respond to their own private needs. Since Gessmann found it impossible to meet most of the demands made upon him, not only for subsidies but for jobs, he quickly lost sympathy. Inevitably rivals capitalized on his predicament, and envy of the "good fortune" of the arriviste minister worsened Gessmann's already strained relations with subordinate party activists.

According to Schwiedland, this crossfire of administrative resistance and party hostility had led Gessmann to the personal decision to abandon Beck's Cabinet in November 1908, which in turn had such fateful consequences for late Imperial politics. Unfortunately, Gessmann's calculations proved erroneous and, although he contributed to Beck's fall, he found it impossible to undo the damage he had caused to himself and the party. His later involvement with schemes to establish a private mortgage bank, based on his own considerable wealth, simply fueled the fires lit by local rivals like Ernst Vergani. When Lueger died, Gessmann's role in the succession crisis was unsettling, and enhanced his image as a crass opportunist. The collapse of the party in June 1911 was simply the last stage of Gessmann's political devolution. Schwiedland admitted that Gessmann was not personally corrupt but noted that rumors abounded in Vienna that Gessmann had regularly persuaded various private firms to offer contributions to the Christian Social party treasury in return for arranging favorable state contracts.

Faced with two divergent references, Colonel Bardolff came down against Gross's recommendation. In doing so he argued that Gessmann's experience manifested the "typical characteristics of the fate of a minister who had emerged politically from a radical populist party." Given Gessmann's other liabilities, it was prudent to stop the affair. Gessmann was not the man to revive the fortunes of the Christian Social party. Presumably younger and less compromised men would have to assume that task.

Franz Ferdinand agreed with Bardolff, and a week later Bardolff wrote a polite but unequivocally negative letter to Bishop Gross indicating that "Gessmann no longer possesses the popularity" necessary to revive the party's fortunes.[134] Franz Ferdinand might be interested in sponsoring the nomination of a younger leader to the *Herrenhaus,* who would serve a longer and more effective period of service on behalf of the party and the Church. With that the matter ended. Before Gross could respond with other candidates, the Thronfolger was dead and the political situation transformed fundamentally. How unenthusiastic Franz Ferdinand actually was about Gross's meddling—the Archduke had, as Ludwig Pastor noted, a pronounced streak of Josephinism about him in his dealings with the Austrian episcopate—is not hard to imagine.[135]

The assiduous investigations of Bardolff and the cautious and, in retrospect, reasonable evaluation by Franz Ferdinand are interesting in themselves, since they suggest that the Thronfolger was more informed about Austrian public affairs, and could, on occasion, react with more foresight than has sometimes been recognized. Against H. Wickham Steed's accusations (based largely on private information which he had obtained from Thomas Masaryk and others) that Franz Ferdinand had degenerated by early 1914 into a raving psychotic who was unfit to rule his own passions, much less an Empire,[136] the Gross episode reveals a judgment about Austrian party politics that was close to the mark, even if it also demonstrated the prejudiced mindsets of the Archduke and his assistant. Neither Franz Ferdinand nor Bardolff doubted the justice or urgency of Gross's larger challenges; they simply felt the tactical problem of the party would have to be resolved in ways both more practical and more compatible with the Thronfolger's prejudices. Bardolff's jaundiced postulate on the incompatibility of political and administrative modes of power reflected the self-conscious isolation of the Dynasty (and especially of the Thronfolger). Whereas Schwiedland, as an academic civil servant, looked with unease on the intrusions of political norms into administrative decision-making, Bardolff allocated to this process an aura of pessimistic determinism and inevitability, which, consciously or not, foreshadowed Franz Ferdinand's understanding of his future role as Emperor. Given the enormous pressure generated by rival nationalist movements in the Monarchy, and given the resistance of the higher civil service to "political" values (other than its own internal interest-group demands) as the basis for policy decisions, perhaps party-based Cabinet government in Austria was an impossibility. If this was true, only the Dynasty could provide the leadership to integrate politics and administration.

Unlike Schwiedland, moreover, Bardolff seemed to attach no special blame to either side. He felt that as a group the civil servants were as selfish and particularistic as any conventional political party. This is also apparent from Bardolff's vitriolic views about the self-serving *Beamtenbewegung* and his arguments in 1913 that a general moral "Sanierung" of the officialdom must precede any systematic attempt at administrative reform.[137] According to Hanns Schlitter, the Archduke even ordered lists prepared detailing the affiliations of those civil servants who did choose to manifest partisan political sympathies.[138] Public officials, in the Archduke's sublimely Josephist view, should concern themselves neither with their own corporate concerns nor with the partisanship of party politics, but in a pure eudaemonistic sense with the affairs of the State itself. Like Joseph II before him, Franz Ferdinand found it difficult to separate the concept of the state from his own personality.[139]

Not the intransigence or duplicity of the professional civil service but the activism of a revitalized Dynasty led by Franz Ferdinand would resolve the grave problems in structure and leadership that threatened the Monarchy. In this context the plans for constitutional, administrative, and political revision of the Empire which Bardolff and his predecessor Brosch had commissioned for Franz Ferdinand's use after his succession to the throne—allowing for their many internal contradictions and systematic variations—suggested the need for the monarch to gain leverage against both the mass political parties and the emergent *Beamtenbewegung*. In their commentaries on these plans both Bardolff and Baron Eichhoff left no doubt about the need to insert a tough law controlling the political rights of civil servants. Both men opposed as the product of dangerous political opportunism the 1912 *Dienstpragmatik* which accorded more advantageous terms to civil servants on matters of regular salary raises and protection against arbitrary dismissal.[140] In drafting even more radical *Octroi* legislation during the war Eichhoff would insist that the active and passive franchise of civil servants must be abolished in order to put them on par with military personnel as corporate groups beyond the ken of political rights. In 1914 such action was not merely directed against "political" officials; it also chastised any independent spirit of administrative corporatism among Austrian civil servants, especially those who might feel that Schwiedland's distinction between politics and law was appropriate.

The Gross-Gessmann episode also illuminated the gap that separated party interests and those of the episcopate. At a time when the Christian Socials could survive only by collaborating on the broadest terms with other German bourgeois parties—the strategy Richard Weiskirchner would pursue before the war—Gross now sought to create a Christian Social party in the Church's own image and likeness. Rather than reduce intra-German political tensions on matters relating to culture and religion (which Gessmann was prepared to do), Gross sought to fashion a renewed pro-Catholic Christian Socialism as a first line of defense against cultural anticlericalism and administrative indifference. This dream of a reverse *Kulturkampf* was an ironic reversal of the episcopate's stormy relationship to the party in the 1890s. Then the bishops had mistrusted the party for its meager religiosity, even though the early party brought to the fore a genuine social reformist fervor on the part of the radical lower clergy. Now the episcopate sought to embrace a "new" Christian Socialism, but one which had become in fact far less idealistic and far less responsive to a putative general public interest. Gross also failed to acknowledge the regional limitations of the prewar Christian Socials. It was hardly accidental that Gross, a bishop in an intensely German nationalist area of northwestern Bohemia, conceived of the Christian Socials even before the war in such terms. For Gross the Christian Social party beckoned as one possible solvent of nationalist *and* anticlerical blockages in the state-level political system. Yet it was precisely in the lands of the northern part of the Empire—Bohemia, Moravia, Silesia— that the Christian Socials fared so poorly in 1907 and in 1911 against the other German *bürgerlich* forces. Seen in the perspective of an Imperial political system, in which the Christian Socials were but one possible German option, too close an adherence by the party to "Catholic" political norms might prove both tactically discomforting and electorally disabling. Once the Empire was gone, and the former German national parties were absorbed by the various successor states, the Christian Socials could contemplate fitting their older secular, interest-based clientele into a more systematic ideological format. With the Social Democrats as the only available enemy after 1918, bourgeois politics ceased to be an alternative to clericalism.

The third and perhaps most revealing aspect of the affair was the light it sheds on the transformation of Austrian party politics in the period after 1907. For on one point at least Funder and Schwiedland were in agreement: Gessmann's activities in the history of the Christian Social party were understandable only in terms of a profound shift in the relationship of individual politicians toward their own parties and the central state administrative apparatus. Lueger had resisted formal entrance into the Cabinet for precisely the reasons explicated by Schwiedland. Once radical politicians joined the Government as representatives of their parties, individual accountability became collective responsibility, and individual weakness became party catastrophe. Even if each party could rely in practice on a fragmented, interest-based electorate, each was placed after 1907 on the same competitive footing and was forced to adopt a similar discourse of eudaemonistic intent about civil society. What had formerly been the property of early Liberalism now became a structural feature of the system of politics itself. Public expectations of the effectiveness of the new parties swelled, the electorate taking the rhetoric of the new system literally, just as the level of their leaders' responsibility to the public increased. Eventually—and this became Gessmann's classic dilemma—the two functions collided. Public expectations of the Christian Socials, as a new mass people's party elected through universal suffrage, increased the accountability burden of the party's top leadership. At the same time, the same leaders, relying on their new prestige as spokesmen for "people's parties," were inclined (or urged) to assume levels of administrative responsibility that the existing political culture simply was not designed to tolerate. Rather than being viewed as regrettable, as Schwiedland and Bardolff were wont to do, Gessmann's attempt to combine mass-based political accountability and executive decision-making might have been applauded, if not for his motives, then at least for their possible consequences.

The Future of Austrian Politics in 1914: Parliamentary Governance, Administrative Reform, or Staatsstreich?

Why was this combination of roles so fragile? Writing in October 1918 during the last, desperation-filled weeks of the Monarchy's existence, Ignaz Seipel offered an eloquent defense of Imperial rule that sought to reconcile past and future—European absolutism with American Wilsonianism. Seipel argued that dynasticism could be integrated into democratic systems of governance by repudiating the traditions and power structures of the Josephist civil service. For Seipel the essence of Hapsburg imperialism had always been the defense of cultural and popular freedom (the Emperor as *Anwalt und Schützer* of the freedom of the people). What had obscured the institution of monarchy in the nineteenth century was its linkage to and co-optation by an oppressive bureaucratic system. Seipel criticized the arbitrary hegemony of this bureaucracy, whose Germanness was an accident of history: "It is not true that the German nation ruled the other Austrian national groups; what is true, however, is that the Germans as well as the other national groups groaned under the weight of a bureaucracy which just happened to be German, but which did not act oppressively simply because it was German."[141] The postwar world, in contrast, might combine self-determining national democracy with populistic dynasticism to the apparent exclusion of bureaucratic hegemony.

Seipel may have been wrong in imputing such indifference toward cultural or political hegemony on the part of the Germans, but his comments on the intimate and eventually fatal collusion of the Germans with the state and especially the state administrative apparatus touched upon a critical factor in that community's fate. The Austro-Germans were by 1918 not the victors over the state but, rather, its victims. The first task of the historian as well as the statesman of 1918 was to comprehend the tragic history of the Austro-Germans not in terms of hegemony, but in terms of self-entrapping illusions and degradation. Indeed, the state itself had become a victim of its own bureaucratic power. Seipel's desire to retain a vestigial "great" Austria led him into a half-hearted acceptance of a "small" Austria, and his loyalty to dynasticism created suspicions of disloyalty to republicanism. In late 1918 controversies over state form worked against the conditions of state function.

Otto Bauer, Seipel's great antagonist in the First Republic, offered a radically different perspective on the dissolution of the state in October 1918. Bauer had emerged during the war as a preeminent spokesman for national autonomy on a state-political basis. As the ruins of the Empire began to settle in mid-October, he projected a new home, a new legal and moral context for the German Austrians, to wit, collaboration with and eventually outright merger into the new Social Democratic German republic. Writing in the *Arbeiter-Zeitung*, Bauer proclaimed the end of German imperialism and militarism and, with that, the collapse of the "system of power which subjected the German people themselves to the rule of the generals, the Junkers, the capitalists." Bauer looked with confidence toward the imminent day when the majority of German voters would "gather in the camp of Social Democracy," making "the Germany of tomorrow . . . a democratic Germany." [142]

Bauer prudently avoided a precise description of the mode of revolutionary transformation—it might occur, he argued, in sudden stormy upheavals or in quickly paced legal reforms, but one way or another it was inexorable. The victory of democracy, because it was a victory of the proletariat, opened new vistas for Austro-Germans as well. Bauer noted that these developments in Germany were of critical importance to Austrians because "the old Austria is dead" and

> we Social Democrats want to build a new one, a confederation of free peoples. But if the other nations of Austria do not want to join such a community, or if they only agree under such conditions and forms that would not protect our economic interests and right to national self-determination, then German Austria will be forced to decide whether it were not preferable to join the German Reich as a special federal state [*Bundesstaat*].

By reemphasizing the ineluctability of national self-determination with a seeming adherence to the ideals of revolutionary democratic nationalism,

Bauer had moved, as Hans Mommsen notes, beyond the intellectual and emotional perimeters of the Monarchy.[143]

What is ironic about both positions—the lost monarchism and Catholic universalism of Seipel and the ardent socialist transformationalism and *Anschluss* mentality of Bauer—is the range of issues on which they might find agreement, if only negatively. Viewed from the perspective of 1927 or even 1934 both visions were problematic: both presumed the unacceptability of a small, German-Austrian state per se, and both sought to anchor Austro-German national consciousness in the development of a new, more universal state formation that would surpass the limited vision of the nineteenth-century ideal of one bourgeois state, one democratic nation. In Seipel's case this came by virtually dismissing the hegemonic past of the Germans—implicitly by making them victims of their own hegemony. Bauer in contrast quickly and deftly subsumed what was left of a narrowly "Austro-German" national consciousness into the German *Reich,* but one that itself, Bauer hoped, would be fundamentally transformed into a new, socialist society.

Both views signaled the short-term repercussions and long-term consequences of the death of the Empire, necessitating a process of political decompression that would endure for at least a generation. And both positions brought forth with unusual clarity the dilemma *before* 1914 of what one might call "progressive" German political theorists in east-central Europe: could one protect the "Germans" as a national and ethnic group in the Monarchy not by guaranteeing to them a greater relative level of separate and discrete juridical resources or special territorially based political privileges but, rather, by strengthening the competitive and regulatory institutions of the state, seen as an independent locus of power beyond (yet based on) national prerogatives? Could one encourage the generation of a more diverse range of public policy issues distinct from the cultural interests of any nation (including the Germans), but which would inevitably allow the Germans cultural hegemony or at least competitive parity?

Twenty-five years ago, one historian, Andrew Whiteside, commented that "[Austro-] German national politics after 1879 were only a postscript to the great crisis. No new policies or events significantly changed the attitudes of the leaders or the masses."[144] If "German" here refers to the Sudeten tradition, this view is correct. If, however, one adopts a more capacious meaning for the adjective, one finds, especially in the period 1905–14, other fascinating visions of state reform policy undertaken or sponsored by what may fairly be called "German" political interests in the Monarchy.

It is clear that the views of Austro-Germans on their role as cultural and political hegemonists changed radically in the Monarchy between 1867 and 1918. They changed their views not merely in terms of the intensity of their defensiveness (which is the usual assertion about the behavior of the Germans as a collective political group). The period itself was punctuated by decisive shifts in the very constitutive framework and substance of what we must reasonably understand as defining "German" politics. After 1900 two major "German" parties emerged and tried to seize both the symbols and the organs of power in the Monarchy. Their preoccupation with German national issues was so different from anything that had preceded them as to call into question the assumption that by 1907 one can even speak of a single "German politics" or even a single German nationalism in the Hapsburg Monarchy.

Before 1900 Austro-German politics were bound up in a matrix of values of Liberals and was, as epitomized in the Whitsun Program of May 1899, a politics of language and territory on the one hand and specifically defensive provincial politics on the other. This was a politics executed in Vienna, but it was undertaken in the spirit of the great heartland of Liberal politics—in Bohemia, Moravia, and Silesia, and, to a lesser extent, selected Alpine bastions in Styria, Salzburg, and Carinthia. While Elizabeth Wiskemann argued nearly fifty years ago that in the 1860s and 1870s "Liberal rule was to a large extent Sudetendeutsch rule,"[145] it would be a mistake to argue that Austrian Liberalism was unilaterally "Sudeten" (to use an early twentieth-century term) in its cast of mind, or even to assume that all Bohemian Germans had a common and unified political program. Indeed, traditions of both centralism and regional particularism found strong advocates in the Sudeten camp. The larger agenda of German politics, however, as epitomized in the constitutionalist period of 1861–79, in the period of linguistic and cultural retrenchment from 1879 to 1896, and finally, from 1897 to 1914, the period of activist defense, was strongly influenced by German national concerns for the northern periphery. The role of Vienna and Lower Austria in state-level Austro-Liberal politics has yet to receive a definitive account. But it is fair to say that the city was more a discursive and symbolic object than an acting subject, stranded in a no-man's-land of pluralistic social and national interests (including an electorate composed of former Czechs as well as Germans) and surpassed in its political unorthodoxy only by the cultural immobility and religious conservatism of other Alpine Crownlands like Upper Austria or Tyrol.

German nationalist politics after 1879 were victimized by the curious dialectic in the evolution of the state's electoral and constitutional institutions. The German Liberals had designed a state and regional political apparatus that oppositionalist parties like the Young Czechs and the Christian Socials used to subvert the Liberals' hegemony. The Badeni Crisis of 1897–99 was the final, public act of the Germans' devolution and isolation. The Whitsun Program of May 1899, whose modesty far exceeded the ambitious Linz Program of two decades earlier, merely confirmed the new fortress mentality of a political group that could no longer think in terms of the state as a whole, but that quite consciously now styled itself as a particularist group seeking a minimum level of defense: the form and aesthetics of the Whitsun Program stood in indirect relationship to its lack of imagination and its loss of nerve.

The emergence of the two great mass parties of the twentieth century in Austria—Christian Socialism and Austrian Social Democracy—changed these calculations drastically. The slow mobilization of political opposition within the German camp resulted not only from social upheavals or transformations in mass values but also from the gradual expansion of the Austrian electoral system. Each decade significant new "actors," with new political or electoral constituencies holding no special consensus about former Liberal politics, were invited into the system. Not surprisingly, they not only bit the hand that fed them but began to cannibalize the body as well.[146] Both parties emerged (in their modern form) almost simultaneously in the 1880s, and both assumed the Viennese metropolis as the executive and visual center of their organizations. It is also evident that both, as much as they detested each other, also saw themselves as vanquishing the Austro-German Liberals. Both, in spite of such claims, inevitably assembled within their respective coalitions elements of older Liberal values and organizational techniques. For most of the century there have really been only two major social and organizational ensembles in modern Austrian politics, and from the beginning they have shared some remarkable affinities. Both were German parties: this was always the case for the Christian Socials and formally was the case for Victor Adler's cadres since 1911. Both were ultimately centralistic and imperial in their political and administrative values, but included strong autonomistic elements, not only in the provinces but also in Vienna itself. Each had a surprisingly subtle sense of opportunism in regard to the nationality problem, bowing and bending to it but always with a larger agenda of social and economic interests in mind. Each was based, in ethos if not in form, in Vienna, and each tended to measure victories and defeats in Vienna as constituting a prominent, if not categorical, mark of its larger legitimacy and success. Each viewed the Hapsburg political universe through the special prism of Viennese provincial cosmopolitanism, and each constituted a pattern of values in what Hermann Broch charmingly called the "value vacuum" in fin-de-siècle Vienna. Each emerged as a result of new voter enfranchisements in the electoral system—each had, thus, a sense of venturesomeness and movement, and was willing to and could conceptually understand politics as a form not of defensive attrition but of social aggression and ideological conquest.

The major policy agenda on which both had the opportunity to act and which constituted the fundamental legitimizing act of their new existence as Imperial parties of more than peripheral or regional significance was the universal suffrage law of 1906–7. As we saw in Chapter 2, Albert Gessmann, the principal parliamentary leader of the Christian Social party by 1905–6, was a vigilant defender of the bill, as were Christian Social Alpinists like Aemilian

Schöpfer, Josef Schraffl, and Jodok Fink. The final result of the reform law, as Gessmann argued in his analysis of the May 1907 elections, was to challenge bourgeois political groups of all nationalities: "For the government and for all the bourgeois parties these elections offer—as I often had the chance to argue in the parliamentary reform committee—the most serious warning to rally themselves in time, to disregard that which separates and to concentrate on that which unites." Gessmann then insisted that "social reform of the grandest style must be launched, in order that in place of national quarrels social-political work above all will be accomplished in the great new House. Only thus can the truly menacing danger of Social Democracy be met successfully."[147] Secular social reform, undertaken by reformed, disciplined mass bourgeois parties would thus kill two political birds with one interest-based stone: it would bring the rival nationalities together and preempt the disequilibrating power of the Social Democrats.

The election reform law thus became for Gessmann a unique opportunity to sanction an informal, defensive coalition strategy among all Austrian bourgeois parties, of which a natural leader would be the Christian Social *Reichspartei*. Gessmann's sometime parliamentary ally, Josef Redlich, argued in defense of the German-Czech-Polish bourgeois coalition in 1908 that "the present political system is based on a coalition of three great national party groups. . . . This system is the correct one for Austria, because it is the only way that a truly parliamentary government in Austria can be sustained. No people in Austria—including the Germans—is strong enough to sustain by itself such a parliamentary government." He was expressing ideals that Gessmann sought to implement in practice.[148]

The Social Democrats were equally, if in far more theoretical terms, supportive of universal suffrage. Nevertheless, in contrast to the ambitions of the Christian Socials, for whom the logic of the law would be the creation of a new German class politics, the Social Democrats viewed the law as a desperate attempt to preserve the semblance of mass, international unity within their own party and to create a system of democratized power that would enable processes of national autonomism to evolve within the Austrian polity. Moreover, as is apparent in Karl Renner's work, the socialists also held expectations similar to the Christian Socials' that the law would establish a new configuration of class- and economic-interest politics, beyond the range of older curial nationalist conflict. As early as 1901 Renner argued eloquently for universal suffrage in justice to the state and as a necessary precondition for the political survival of the Austrian bourgeoisie: "The bourgeoisie must learn to swim and really swim in the stream. A boat made out of legal privilege is merely a paper vessel, on which only fools would rely." Only with such reforms would economic/class conflict emerge in full clarity: "Economic classes strive not for separate [national] states but for a distinct, self-advantageous arrangement of the existing state; they split up nations and bind together similar economic strata of all the peoples to political parties." Lacking universal suffrage, the Austrian bourgeoisie did not view itself as an "economic class" but rather merely as a "supplier of civil servants." The reforms were justifiable not merely for the proletariat but also for the state itself.[149] Similar arguments emerged in his *Grundlagen und Entwicklungsziele* in 1906: with such a suffrage "the natural battle organization of the propertied classes will come into play." Eventually "alliances of the progressives of all nations, of clericals, the supporters of industry, of the agrarians of all nations must take place and bridge over the antitheses of nationality."[150]

Even more radical (and more aggressively orthodox) commentators, like the young Otto Bauer, admitted that the reform was both progressive and instrumentally useful (although it could not be a definitive end unto itself). He understood that the most recent evolutionary stage in Austrian bourgeois parliamentarism—political democracy—was the product of socialist militancy and that it afforded the Social Democrats, as the principal (and principled) opponents of bourgeois parliamentarism, timely opportunities for their critical work of ideological education. It also gave them full membership in the grid of state power, where they formed the primary opposition against an unstable bourgeois bloc.[151] Thus, Social Democratic support for the bill, beyond legitimate hopes for the positive consequences of opening up the system and the conciliation of national rivalries, can be read as an attempt by the Social Democrats to tolerate, if only grudgingly, the creation of a bourgeois-dominated parliamentary system, in the anticipation that some democracy was better than none and some parliamentarism better than the autocratic status quo.

Ironically, the Christian Socials and Social Democrats shared some motives on this subject (as on many other issues). For both, universal suffrage was nothing less than an institutional, etatist solvent that might reduce the tensions of nationality. Not only would these tensions be confronted with direct, democratically legitimated solutions and the parliament's attention shifted to social and economic issues, but, equally important, the national parties would be forced to act in a responsible, *independent* way vis-à-vis the civil service. Both sought to create a new political culture of disciplined mass parties and informed and active voters—Gessmann's insistence on laws making voting compulsory was a crude, but effective, tactic to force the Austrian bourgeoisie into successful competition with the Social Democrats.

The question remains, Why did this experiment fail? Its failure is often attributed solely to the nationalities dilemma, but this interpretation is too narrow, for the nationalities problem also generated new forms of political participation that might have strengthened the Hapsburg state. In an essay in *Der Kampf* in 1909, Otto Bauer argued that the future of parliamentarism (and ministerialism) in Austria had to be seen not merely in the context of the substantive struggle between Czechs and Germans or the foreign policy issues facing the Monarchy, but also as involving larger structural issues between democracy and bureaucracy:

> It is not a question of the struggle of Slav and German . . . but a new phase of an old altercation, which each parliament in Europe endured, of the conflict between parliament and government, between democracy and bureaucracy, between popular control and absolutism. Our first duty is thus: we must help the people to understand that the nations of Austria must themselves secure the democratic constitution of nationalities, if they do not want to open the way for a bureaucratic *Staatsstreich.*[152]

Gessmann's attempt (and for that matter, Victor Adler's) to fashion a large, independent, and bureaucratically skilled mass party across regional lines was more reminiscent of nineteenth-century American parties than of traditional Austrian conceptions of party organization and political style. It was not accidental that Josef Redlich, searching for an epithet for the Christian Social elite in Vienna, would summon the phrase "sie sind alle 'politicians' im amerikanischen Sinne."[153] Recent analyses of the political process in nineteenth-century America have observed the peculiar semiconstitutional role that American political parties came to play in the formation of the modern American state. In the United States mass parties preceded, rather than followed, mass bureaucracy and provided the nerve centers and instruments of democratic governance that later forced independent, executive, and managerial elites to maintain a constant adherence to political norms and to decentralized state practice. Mass parties served as broad popular instruments of both vertical and horizontal interest articulation and constituency representation in the American polity. The later growth of a modern, industrial-based central bureaucracy could not displace completely the representational power (and the implicit prerogative to influence, if not unilaterally determine, policy) that the political parties enjoyed in the multinational republican empire that was late nineteenth-century America.[154]

In the multinational dynastic empire that was Austria we know that the reverse obtained. An enduring tradition of bureaucratic management of the state long preceded any party system. The party system that evolved between 1870 and 1900 was necessarily limited by the curial, regional-ethnic particularism and political modesty with which the Austrian Liberals defined "their" version of the state. Rather than decisively resisting the bureaucratic state, the Liberals simply co-opted its managerial elites into their own narrow range of political values, the end result being a curious melange of party and administrative visions that made it possible to speak of "Josephist" Liberalism. The nascent

Czech national movements, one might argue, although formally attacking the system, also accepted many of its key assumptions—defensiveness, particularism, national hegemony—as cardinal values. The sinkholes of nationality, to which both German Liberal and Czech bourgeois parties soon fell victim, simply intensified the regional fractures and ideological narcissisms of the party system, making it seemingly impossible for mass-based interregional parties to sustain a serious hearing within the dynastic and administrative establishment.

The first decade of the Christian Social movement produced a modest change in these assumptions. Each of the major parties of the late Imperial period had dozens of prominent politicians who craved the same chance that Gessmann had to establish an independent, bureaucratically reinforced base of party political operations; and Beck's Cabinet and the Bienerth and Stürgkh ministries that followed allowed no happy alternative to the failure that Gessmann endured. If the election reform expanded the scope of the political system, a single law was incapable of creating instantaneous traditions of party discipline and order and of effective resistance against the blandishments of the administrative state. The various parties, when given the rare option, nominated unimaginative operators to represent them in the Cabinet who failed to establish any dominant political profile. Or they found themselves handed nationally stereotyped "representatives" from the Crown who in fact looked first to the needs of the ministerial bureaucracy (if they were not actually members of that bureaucracy) or to the material advantages of their own careers. When Franz Joseph quipped to Heinrich von Tschirschky, the German ambassador in Vienna, in 1914 that "it must be a very special pleasure to become a minister, since the deputies have no other goal in mind," he was alluding to the narcissistic self-service which attached itself to all Cabinets and demonstrating how such attitudes could arise in the first place.[155] The Emperor's cynicism and fondness for solid mediocrity controlled the quality of ministers who served him, few of whom had any serious interest in representing parliament as a body before the Crown.

In contrast to the Prussian system (which Jürgen Kocka, summarizing Otto Hintze, has described as the "straffe, starre, militärisch-bürokratische Struktur" of the Wilhelminian state), the cultural configuration of high-level ministerial hegemony in Austria was neither so antipluralistic nor so neofeudal that these "politicians" were even conscious of betraying the material interests of their constituents or of weakening the rationale of a sphere of political action independent of bureaucratic norms.[156] The very tradition of neoliberal, Josephist Cabinets into which they were co-opted bore none of the crassly antiliberal features normally imputed to Prussian power structures to the north. A happy medium of bureaucratic hegemony and political servitude might be sustained, under forms even more insidious than in Germany for their relative ideological modernity and social universalism.

Max Weber's insistence on a tension between political and bureaucratic modes of rule was, thus, less intelligible in Austria. Decades of the symbiotic integration of etatist and liberal values within the high ministerial service suggested that, at least on the level of norms if not also in the efficient exercise of power, the state officials could both "rule" and administer society. In Josef Redlich's words, in the final decades of his reign the Emperor Franz Joseph viewed the bureaucracy as "the sole bearer of state power qualified for the direction of governmental affairs."[157] A prescient observer of the Austrian civil service, precisely because he so often collided with it, Ignaz Seipel responded in 1930 to a friend's complaint about Austrian diplomatic officials—that they never cited the *Reichspost* and never masked their unease about the cleric-politician Seipel—by suggesting that such behavior had a historic explanation:

the higher *Beamtenschaft* is still liberal in its most basic values, which one cannot really blame them for. They date from the Monarchy and the Monarchy was itself thoroughly liberal since the time the Hapsburgs died out. The rulers from the House of Lorraine brought liberalism and bureaucratism with them from their homeland. Joseph II and Franz I were exemplars of this, but Franz Joseph represented the high point of both movements. . . . the Hapsburgs were great aristocrats, the Lorrainers honest civil servants. Their Liberalism was of the gentle Austrian sort that was compatible with personal faith, indeed even piety, and respected and protected the clergy, but that would only accept the higher clerics if the latter showed themselves to be worldly and if possible a little liberal. Our senior ministerial officials are still largely of this sort. They will put up with me, and even recognize much of what I have accomplished. But they properly feel me to be inwardly alien to them, and for that reason are uncomfortable with me. [158]

However loyal to the Dynasty, the Austrian civil service was always marked by a certain Josephist-Liberal spirit, which although not party-political, set clear boundaries to both feudalism and clericalism.

The constraints of the Austrian political system reflected, in turn, the limited range of political choices in strategy and in structure available to mass parties after 1907. Paradoxically, a system that was designed to encourage active, participatory control of the legislative process and active policy formation by large constituent blocs soon found itself playing an exclusively defensive role. Most major national parties were capable of little more than disruptive actions against legislation that seemed to pose disequilibrating effects for them or their national allies. In their inclination toward systemic negativism all shared a destructive desire to forgo positive choices for themselves in order to make negative choices *against* their rivals.

In a letter of black pessimism to Baernreither in August 1910, Josef Redlich described this negativist mentality at length:

> All of our parties and politicians have become in recent years—and this is true above all for we Germans—so oriented toward the negative, that I find it difficult to imagine how these elements are now suddenly supposed to work in a positive manner. The pressure of demagogy, and the Austrian habit to worry only about the next day, have brought the situation to the point where everyone remains attached to tried and true tactics, indeed if only this means not allowing a competing party or sect within one's nation a chance to seize a tactical advantage. This is the case with the Czechs, and also with the Germans, and it is characteristic that those who feel themselves to be the weakest—such as the so-called German Liberals in Bohemia—have most fallen prey to negative behavior and political rigidity.[159]

Yet a parallel to this antipolitics was the promiscuity of all political parties toward specific national client groups within the middle and lower ranks of the Austrian civil service, who enjoyed a unique status as the most symbolically significant "consumers" of the patronage that the parties could eke out of the higher civil service. On the one hand, this strange alliance resulted from the huge number of civil servant voters and from their superior interest-group organizations; on the other, from the curiously narcissistic inclination of Austrian bourgeois parties to see "victories" in official patronage as a substitute for parliamentary control and as a logical measure of their national and social standing within the state. Instead of viewing political power as a fluid and dynamic instrument to achieve positive legislative acts, the parties adopted the more passive, corporatist-proprietary criterion of ethnic employment rates in the civil service as a primary test of their access to the state. The language question simply intensified this issue, highlighting the value of *administrative* hegemony as the only salient sphere of political action. Rather than "taking" power and creating their own patronage, as the Christian Socials were able to do on the regional level, the bourgeois parties took an endless series of gratuities (*Trinkgelder*) on the state level. This process drastically narrowed the general interest representation of the parties. It also contributed to a pronounced shift in power within the central ministries toward the *Ministerratspräsidium,* which gradually exercised a "bureaucratic dictatorship" within the Cabinet as a whole.[160] The civil service thus became a contestant in and consumer of the "game" of patronage as well as the referee who set and manipulated the rules of that game. This vicious-circle form of political hegemony, undertaken not in the name of policy activism—since the Austrian civil service was little inclined to change anything in Austrian society—but on behalf of caste stabilization and conflict avoidance made it impossible for parliamentarians to develop a system of parallel relations under which parliament would maintain control of the bureaucracy.

Since the primary parliamentary role of an Austrian political party became the achievement of defensive attrition, rather than positive legislative cooperation, it was hardly surprising that each would measure its share of the state in material concessions and patronage for ethnically fragmented sectors of the civil service, if possible to the disadvantage of other competing ethnic civil service groups. This had several consequences, all of them problematic: the director of the Austrian postal and telegraphic service, Friedrich Wagner v. Jauregg, chastised Gustav Gross in 1914 for the way in which German politicians humiliated themselves before the Ministries, seeking endless petty favors and demands for their civil servant client groups, when, Jauregg argued, these people were simply exploiting the "national" issue for their own purposes and from his own experience in many cases had no serious "ethnic" consciousness at all.[161] Equally important, the lavish attention paid to the officials by the parties created serious problems of discipline for the higher ministerial-level service, since no minister or higher civil servant who hoped for a future in the system would dare alienate the parties by "abusing" (e.g., disciplining) errant public officials of one or another national group.

A typical example of this mutual reinforcement of negativism came in 1909 when Alexander Spitzmüller, at the time the vice-president of the Lower Austrian Financial Office, disciplined a subordinate official, Fritz Schmid, for making anti-governmental remarks in a civil-servant protest rally. Spitzmüller soon came to regret his professionalism, since politicians of all the major German parties saw his actions as dangerous, and leaders of the *Nationalverband* intervened with the Cabinet, forcing a curtailment of the proceedings against Schmid.[162] Looking at this situation in 1914 (from a clearly jaundiced Prussian perspective), Heinrich von Tschirschky saw a symbiotic process of mutual corruption between the parties and their client groups in the civil service, each party counting on the cooperation of "its" lower and mid-level civil servants and each group of officials ready to coerce its party. Tschirschky alleged nothing less than the "downfall" of the Austrian civil service: each petty official "now feels he has to court the favor of his nationality, his party, the member of parliament of his district. Bribery is rampant, since the disappearance of the old, centrally oriented German officials." Tschirschky blamed the new corruption on the entrance into the civil service of Slavs who constituted an educated proletariat from the Austrian *Mittelschulen,* but one might fairly argue that the process transcended national lines—the Christian Socials were the status equivalent of the Czech petty bourgeoisie, and they too managed to assemble powerful sources of partisan support from their civil servant clients.[163] Even Lueger was not above trying to bully Spitzmüller into dropping a tax corruption case against a wealthy Viennese industrialist (and friend of the Christian Social party) in return for help in getting ahead with his career (which Spitzmüller also refused to do).[164]

Given the extent to which parliamentarians were dependent upon administrative pleasure to fill the increasingly strident demands of their constituents, the Cabinet could easily fragment and atomize the various parties by playing members off against one another, even within the same party. Professional managerial elites and political leadership came to play dialectically perverse and mutually undermining roles. Lacking strong central leadership, no party could confront the state as a collective unit, and ministries could easily encourage disruptive, fragmentary behavior which undercut party discipline; but lacking support from the state, no party could generate central cadre control. Beck had tried to encourage more centralized forms of party discipline, one prominent result being the modern Christian Social party. The Social Democrats had tried to sustain such discipline even before 1907. But elsewhere, in other German bourgeois factions and among the Slavic clubs, the idea was less fruitful. The new franchise of 1907 was a technological innovation imposed on an archaic party system, and two national elections in 1907 and 1911 were hardly sufficient to construct a new system of party organization. Indeed, Stürgkh profited from the chaos of the parliamentary parties. Gessmann's own decision to withdraw from ministerialism in favor of Crownland administration and politics simply reinforced the dichotomy between centralistic Josephism and robust regional political autonomy that was so characteristic of the Austrian system by 1914.

Hence the significance of Jauregg's critique: if parties prostituted themselves before the *Beamtenbewegung,* and allowed professional bureaucracies the privileges of internal politicization coupled with external systemic anarchy, not only would they weaken their position vis-à-vis the government, they would discredit themselves before the electorate. In such a context, it was easy for an autocrat like Stürgkh to play the civil service off against the parties, using the nationalistic conflict in Bohemia as an excuse for what was a much larger and more profound dilemma in the system of Austrian politics itself. The weakness in state governance in the Hapsburg Monarchy in 1914 was not simply the nationality conflict in Bohemia and Moravia, but the insertion of that conflict into an unstable parliamentary and administrative system where the pressures of integral nationalism were simply intensified *and* institutionalized. The impasse in parliamentary governance in 1909–13, and its trivialization by Stürgkh in 1914, followed directly from this combination of ill-disciplined political parties locked in combat with the civil service, each claiming to serve the "people" but in fact each preoccupied with interest-group particularism within its own national sanctums. Ironically, the one "interest" that claimed to serve as a general representative of all society—the Austrian civil service—now co-opted the parties into its own national particularisms.

By 1914 many Austro-German commentators claimed that the reform of 1907 had failed. But if not parliamentarism, what else? The question was frequently posed by contemporaries in 1912–14, and among the diversity of responses two other routes to state survival emerged as worthy of contemplation: administrative reform as ersatz constitutional revision or a constitutional *Staatsstreich* by the Thronfolger himself. As the German ambassador in Vienna, Heinrich von Tschirschky, viewed the pessimism felt by Austrian politicians in early 1914, he inquired about solutions to or ways out of the crisis. Given the problems of immobility of the bureaucracy and its deadening weight on the system, together with the entanglement of the bureaucracy in politics, it is not surprising that some political theorists considered administrative reform a necessary first step. In a perceptive report to Berlin, Tschirschky duly noted that one reform program on the docket was that of the Austrian administrative reform commission.

This remarkable enterprise originated with a proposal in parliament in 1909 by Josef Redlich that the Cabinet appoint a high-level committee of distinguished experts to study the range of problems associated with the Austrian civil service—its organization, its cost-effectiveness, its rules of administrative procedure, and its personnel appointment policies.[165] In 1911 the government agreed to launch such a commission, the Imperial rescript appointing the commission charging it to propose ways by which opportune improvements in the existing administrative organization would make it more able to keep abreast of the growing needs of the population. Granted the commission's role was advisory to the Cabinet, its broad mandate allowed it to solicit information from a diversity of political and social interest groups in the Monarchy (for which it organized a major *Enquete* in 1912) and to examine problems of internal structure and administrative procedure in a fascinating series of publications. Its membership consisted of twenty-three high-ranking jurists, ex-Cabinet members, senior administrators, and distinguished university professors, of whom Edmund Bernatzik, Josef Redlich, Erwin von Schwartzenau, and Guido von Haerdtl were unusually active. Although the commission had high-ranking Slavic members, some of its most creative and significant work was undertaken by its German representatives. At the inaugural session of the commission on June 28, 1911, its chairman, Schwartzenau, presented an eloquent justification for the urgency of undertaking administrative reform. In contrast to others who might see such reforms as relating only to practical questions, such as the improvement of services and the reduction of costs, Schwartzenau saw the reforms as touching upon larger issues: the civil service in the twentieth century would be called upon, along with parliament, to fashion out of the existing state a new welfare state (*Wohlfahrtsstaat*). Only a civil service at the height of training, efficiency, and rationality could respond to the pressures and conciliate the rival interests generated by modern society. The civil service's final goal—"the welfare of the state itself and of the totality organized in it"—was an appropriately Josephist vision of the constitution of modern Austrian society.[166]

Hence Schwartzenau and many of his colleagues viewed the work of the commission as having wide, if only implicit, political consequences. Coming in the immediate aftermath of the 1911 elections, which had cast grave doubts about the viability of Beck's original scheme of parliamentary governance, the commission's mandate to forge a semi-independent initiative for administrative reform seemed all the more urgent. Schwartzenau did not explicitly mention the nationalities problem, but it formed a central concern of the commission. Although the commission rejected the possibility that the state administration could or should sustain "a national character," its final recommendations included proposals for inserting *Kreisregierungen* in the larger provinces, not merely to reduce the enormous workloads of the larger *Statthaltereien,* but to make the political administration more accessible to diverse national clients (as well as to use territorial demarcations within the state as boundaries that would open neutral "spaces" between contesting groups).[167]

Among the fascinating reports and recommendations generated by the commission, those by Haerdtl, Redlich, and Bernatzik were especially controversial. In their division of labor they comprehended three major issues of administrative governance in the Monarchy: the cost-effectiveness and labor productivity of the Austrian civil service—the issue of civil service personnel; the efficiency and rationality of existing structures of financial administration on regional and local levels—the issue of the rationality (or irrationality) of traditional administrative organization based on centralistic principles; and the effectiveness of existing systems of administrative justice to monitor and conciliate complaints against bureaucratic action (or nonaction), the latter an issue that impinged on the viability of the 1867 constitutional disjunction between political administration and the courts.

Of the three reports Haerdtl's was perhaps the most provocative. Shocked by the enormous growth in public expenditures for administrative services in the Monarchy (which between 1890 and 1911 increased by almost 200 percent, much of it attributable to new appointments rather than salary or benefits raises for existing personnel; tax revenues for the same period grew far more slowly) and by the inefficiency of university- and *Mittelschule*-trained officials, Haerdtl assembled some remarkable data on labor productivity of tenured juristic officials in the seven central ministries. His data demonstrated that of 370 officials in his sample, 32 percent processed on average less than one file a day, and 36 percent fewer than two files a day, whereas only a pitifully small minority actually seemed to put in a full working day (which itself was only 5.5–6 hours long). In the regional state offices, in contrast, working loads and days were both heavier and longer. When viewed in light of the fact that, according to the existing order of business, one file might easily be handled by several different officials, the absurdity of the situation was undeniable. That many officials employed in these positions merited their jobs as a result of political, national, or nepotistic patronage was self-evident.[168]

In order to achieve a greater efficiency and economy Haerdtl proposed a carrot-and-stick approach: the number of tenured, juristic positions in the ministries should be decreased, with the clerical support staff held stable or even increased, since much of the "work" the more senior officials claimed to do could actually be handled by officials with more modest educational credentials. Further, more use should be made of contractual or per diem employees. In return for a reduction of personnel and a complete reorganization of the order of work—reducing the number of paperwork exchanges, making lines of jurisdiction clearer, eliminating multiple jurisdictional claims—average salaries of the civil servants might be increased. Enhanced labor productivity would result, thus, by controlling manpower levels, by imposing inter- and intra-office rationality, and by making salary scales more attractive for those who remained.[169]

Haerdtl's timely if blunt comments generated outrage in the higher service, and, as Bardolff reported to Franz Ferdinand, the parties as well: "the guilt for the extraordinary expansion in officials . . . is placed on the influence of the politicians, who are always trying to get as many clients of their respective parties as possible employed in the ministries."[170] His critique hit at the collusion between political and national interest groups and the civil service on the sensitive matter of national patronage, and was doubly problematic. However much they might quarrel over *Protektion* and decry bureaucratic inefficiency, none of the big political parties, German or Czech, had any interest in reducing the number of officials in the state system, either in Vienna or in the provinces.

Josef Redlich, in contrast, produced a report that was massively detailed and on an opaque topic—the Austrian financial administration. He began with a survey of the existing structure of financial administration in the Monarchy, including a detailed description of its three-level hierarchy (district, province, and central ministry). Redlich identified numerous problems within the system, technical as well as political. The lines of jurisdiction between and within levels were frequently unclear, which, Redlich thought, could be traced back to the interpenetration of political and financial norms on the first and second levels. Local tax officials were subject to the sometimes arbitrary control of the political officials in the districts, which slowed collection procedures, increased paperwork, and grated on the locals' own status consciousness. Redlich argued that the district chiefs (*Bezirkshauptmänner*) functioned as objects of private manipulation and influence among local notables in their districts, and thus, tax departments attached to their offices were similarly affected. Regional offices functioned better but both kinds were unevenly staffed and usually dramatically over- or underworked: the typical workload of Lower Austrian financial officials was five times greater than that in Galicia measured in income tax returns reviewed per official. Many of the smaller regional directorates had manpower allocations unjustified by the tax revenues they managed to collect: the crassest case was Dalmatia, where the government spent 2.1 crowns in salaries and other expenses for its revenue personnel for every 1 crown they collected in direct taxes! Equally significant, the final level of jurisdiction, the Finance Ministry in Vienna, had grown enormously in the past thirty years, since it served not merely as a higher regulatory and policy-setting agency but continued to operate in an eighteenth-century mode as an executive, interventionist authority for judgment of individual cases. Redlich also noted, in this connection, the natural attractiveness of this particular ministry for political *Interventionen* by individual parliamentary deputies, a practice that he wanted to curb sharply.[171]

Redlich's prescriptions for change were as drastic as Haerdtl's. On district and provincial levels independent revenue authorities would be established, completely divorced from regular political administration. In addition to their responsibility for all direct taxes, they would also be responsible for the consumption tax and some administrative fees. The revenue inspection service, one of the most expensive and overstaffed in the whole civil service, would be divided into two administrative sections, its personnel reduced and placed under simpler administrative controls on the local and regional levels. A new scheme for distributing provincial directorates would consolidate and combine smaller provincial units (e.g., Moravia with Silesia; Lower Austria with Upper Austria and Salzburg) and accord to these supraregional units some of the elaborate appellate powers that were exercised by the Ministry in Vienna. The Finance Ministry, in turn, would suffer a diminution of its power to adjudicate appeals and to meddle in petty investigations, and its staff would be consolidated. In the future it would concentrate its activities on a more general supervision of the revenue process and, more importantly, on exercising more elaborate controls over the state budget (which Redlich found both static and ill coordinated), including the creation of a central inspection service for evaluating and auditing ongoing expenditures.[172]

The commission accepted Redlich's views, but they were never implemented by the Cabinet. For they struck not only at the sacred cow of comfortable, procedural anarchy in the central ministries—as his earlier commentaries in parliament on the state of Austrian administration foretold, Redlich saw the

Austrian ministries as poorly organized—but they also sought to redefine the basic purpose of central government. As Redlich stated,

> The essential and fundamental difference between the central admin-
> istration of a modern state and the old, customary centralistic admin-
> istrative methods lies in the fact that in the former, the central instance
> does not dominate, but rather directs, that the actual decision-making
> process concerning individual cases is accomplished fundamentally
> by the real executive authority (whether on the local or regional level),
> that central authority directly observes the total administrative activ-
> ity of its subordinate offices, not with the intention of dominating
> them, but above all in order to gather continuously the most precise
> information. [173]

Redlich thus sought to enhance the professional autonomy of regional administrators by freeing them from the tutelage of "Vienna" and redefined the basic
purpose of "centralization" in the Austrian civil service from one of executive
intervention to broad-scale inspection and supervision of delegated authority.
By weakening the prerogatives of the Finance Ministry over actual policy implementation and by undercutting the sacrosanctity of Crownland rights, the
total package of reforms would have (in theory) considerably reduced the opportunities for political meddling in the revenue process, either by parliamentary deputies via the Ministry or by local notables via the districts. By improving the accuracy, efficiency, and public scrutiny of the budget process,
Redlich's program would have given parliament far *more* power over the Cabinet. This was a kind of power, of course, which the Austrian parliament, in
contrast to its west European neighbors, was ill-fitted to exercise. The separation of finance from the political administration was yet another feature of
Redlich's interest in encouraging administrative autonomy. Autonomy, for
Redlich, was the technical, professional independence of a smaller number of
more efficiently utilized revenue officials, men with an enhanced esprit de
corps and improved salary levels, freed from partisan political manipulation.
Like Haerdtl, Redlich viewed administrative reform as an act of modern political engineering that would improve service, reduce costs, and mobilize public
confidence and sympathy for the "state" beyond the realm of explicit national
confrontations. Given Redlich's compulsive interest in economic modernization, it is also possible that he saw administrative reform as a way to link political efficiency with industrial entrepreneurialism.[174]

A third contribution, and intellectually one of the most complex, was that
by Edmund Bernatzik, a distinguished professor of law at the University of
Vienna.[175] Bernatzik concerned himself with a critical issue in Austrian admin-

istrative law—access by petitioners to appeals against administrative decisions taken by the civil bureaucracy. Existing systems of legal control within the Austrian administration provided for methods of internal administrative review in cases where individuals, institutions, or corporate bodies complained about decisions taken by one of the three instances of administrative authority (district, province, or ministry). These procedures enjoyed the quality and consequence of "justice" only in a very limited sense, however, since they remained internal, arbitrary acts of the civil service. As Bernatzik complained in 1912, the norms that had regulated administrative review were meager, and those that did exist had the character of internal instructions from the head of state to his underlings. They did not need to be and were not to be publicized. Whether officials actually observed them was no business of the petitioners; civil servants were accountable only to their immediate superiors in obeying or not obeying these regulations.[176]

Bernatzik sought to impose more equity and openness onto the administrative system and to accord the final determination of the administrative review process some of the qualities of judicial decisions. He proposed the establishment of an internal, quasi-judicial review process within the bureaucracy itself, the *Verwaltungsjurisdiktion*. This was a dualistic system of half-voluntary and half-professional review panels, consisting of professional civil servants and of lay councillors (*Beisitzer*), that were in part a product of Bernatzik's admiration of the English justices of the peace and the jury system: the draft would bring into the process of administrative justice "an entirely independent element, an element that is related to the institution of the jury. Its members will be taken from circles who do not belong to the civil service, and who will be elected by representatives of the people." On the level of the districts the review panel would consist of two individuals, an official of the Crown and a layman serving without pay (Bernatzik: "naturally the model of the English justice of the peace asserts itself here").[177] Final competitors for the position of voluntary *Beisitzer* would be selected by the provincial governor from a list of nominees prepared by the local district civil servants (thus giving the civil service a powerful role in their designation). But the final candidate would be elected by the mayors of the towns or communes voting in the district in an annual assembly. On the regional level a similar tandem would be established, and on the ministerial level a three-man panel created, where conflicting decisions would terminate (since tie votes would be impossible).

The *Verwaltungsjurisdiktion* would not constitute a civil court in the sense provided by the 1867 constitution, thus sparing in theory the distinction between administration and justice which lay at the heart of the Liberal separation of powers in 1867 (in practical terms, though, the *Jurisdiktion* would have made a profound impact on civil law by providing an alternative mode of public adversariness within society, and, appropriately, the draft adopted on a wholesale basis technical components of the Code of Civil Procedure, including verbal testimony and rules of evidence). The *Jurisdiktion* would also not function as an "administrative court," since Bernatzik feared that employing either professional administrative judges (independent of the actual civil service) or even honorary judges would result in a politicization of justice under the cover of nominal objectivity. Rather, Bernatzik insisted that the *Jurisdiktion* would be part of the *Verwaltung,* yet nebulously distinct from it, by creating a duality of roles on the part of active civil servants who, on an ad hoc basis, would constitute and enforce a functionally separate system of controls and norms over their own and their colleagues' official acts. For Bernatzik the Austrian state had to allow national and social "passions" a role, but to subordinate them to the civil service itself—to square the circle by reining them in by the controls and the veto of the political civil service as representatives of the interests of all society. Bernatzik was, thus, the perfect Josephist, seeking not to displace the civil service but to insert into its recognized realm of hegemony national and class representatives who would work in parity with professionals and who would also be subject to the latter's normatively nonpartisan veto.

Bernatzik's proposals, like those of Redlich, were remarkable both for their analytic radicalism and their political utopianism. Not only did his work challenge customary assumptions about the proper isolation of the civil service from society (and *its* political interests), and open up to society new modes of interlocution with the state, but it ultimately called into question the distinction between *Verwaltung* and *Justiz.* If Redlich threatened the central ministries with loss of executive authority and if Haerdtl threatened the bourgeois parties with loss of patronage, Bernatzik threatened the Social Democrats with an oligarchy of law. He admitted that the Austrian "gentry" did not possess a tradition of dedicated public service to the state. Yet his system of elected notables, resident in the district in unsalaried positions, might have implanted a social oligarchy into the civil service. Moreover, in the larger cities the mayor functioned in place of the chief of the local district administration, according him prerogatives for participating in the exercise of such "justice." In Vienna this would have enhanced the Christian Social machine's role in the administrative process. Rather than reducing partisanship in the civil service the ultimate effect would have been to increase it, as some of Bernatzik's colleagues on the commission duly noted.

Both the radicalism and the complexity (and resultant uncertainty) of its proposals turned the commission into a white elephant. Not only were the big political parties (including the Christian Socials) suspicious of its work, but the commission encountered dogged resistance within the higher ranks of the civil service itself. Certainly Karl Stürgkh had neither sympathy for the commission's work nor any urgent desire to implement its recommendations. When Colonel Bardolff discreetly inquired of the Minister-President about the status of Haerdtl's report in March 1913, Bardolff came away with the sense that Stürgkh harbored serious suspicions about the whole matter.[178] That Stürgkh made a deal with the political parties and traded the *Dienstpragmatik* for the government's *Finanzplan* in January 1914, in spite of sentiment on the part of some members of the commission that the *Dienstpragmatik* should become part of a rational and comprehensive reform of the inner service, probably demonstrated his lack of interest in the project. Redlich himself admitted publicly in 1914 that key political and administrative elites were hostile to its work. By the outbreak of the war the commission was languishing, and in January 1915 it was released from further responsibilities. As one prescient Catholic commentator noted in 1915, the commission had achieved "no practical success." Not surprisingly, as Karl Brockhausen argued in 1916, on matters involving nationality—as opposed to technical administrative reforms per se—the commission's consensus usually fell apart.[179]

Tschirschky, too, thought that the commission was doomed to failure. He argued, as others would during the war, that administrative reform within the given constitutional framework was illusory.[180] Like many commentators in Vienna in early 1914, Tschirschky was thus forced to turn back to the constitutional problems of the state and to the Thronfolger, Franz Ferdinand, who many hoped would be a deus ex machina for Austria's salvation.

The reform alternatives available to the Thronfolger were a curious melange of hyperbolic, but unfocused, friend-foe discourse and occasionally sensible policies for institutional change. Of the various collections of "plans" developed for the Archduke, two of the most ambitious were those attributed to Brosch from 1910–11 and to Eichhoff from 1913–14. As different in tone and details as these scenarios for the new regime were, their similarities were more striking. Both postulated the possibility of a period of semilawlessness in which the Archduke would, by negotiation or even selective military pressure, impose his constitutional supersovereignty on recalcitrant German, Czech, and Magyar politicians to achieve far-reaching structural changes in the Imperial system. Both bore an uncanny resemblance in their contempt for or ignorance of parliamentary and formal party political mechanisms. Brosch was most overt when he encouraged the Archduke to view possible parliamentary anarchy resulting from the Hungarian political coup d'état as an acceptable state of affairs, since previous interparty squabbling in the Austrian parliament had proven beyond doubt that, when the national parties fought among themselves, the rights of the Crown remained undisputed.[181] Eichhoff was more subtle, but his draft of an Imperial manifesto contained not less than three overt or covert criticisms of political parties and the existing political process in less than five pages.[182]

Both plans were also noteworthy in what they failed to address. Brosch devoted less than ten lines—in a document running to thousands of words—

to the Austrian nationality conflict, while offering an extremely detailed account of the necessity for new state emblems for the Austrian half of the Monarchy. A more literal and effective statement of the "emblematization" of public politics could hardly have been imagined. Was this perhaps because neither Brosch nor Bardolff and Eichhoff had any effective solutions? Bardolff soon proved himself to be an unabashed German nationalist, and Eichhoff's later chameleonic flights in constitutional praxis during the First World War hardly gave confidence in the realism of his views. At the heart of their theorizing lay serious doubts about the effectiveness of a party-based system of politics as a mode for the rational distribution of public resources. Rather, both seemed to presume a pseudohieratic conception of the state as a centralized haven of pure dynastic power, in which the Thronfolger had merely to will the corporate good, however speciously or contradictorily defined, in order to prove his constitutional superiority over other, rival political actors and values. A letter that Franz Ferdinand sent to Leopold Berchtold in 1913 conveys this hieratic feature of his self-portrait: he defended his meddling in Austrian foreign affairs since he always acted on the basis of intense study for the sake of the Monarchy, but then added that "through a special grace of God I have *always* been proven right in recent years."[183] Issues of concrete political management were simply irrelevant once one had curbed the civil servants and proffered a program of mystic animation in place of parliamentary negotiation. For Bardolff, administrative reform itself was not the first priority. Far more essential was the restoration of a *Verwaltungsmoral* producing a mood of "discipline and order," to be inspired by the Thronfolger himself.[184]

The *Staatsstreich* plans—even allowing for the fact that they were written for the Thronfolger and not by him—reflected a curious restatement of eighteenth-century Josephist German administrative centralism placed in the service of corporatist, high noble reverence for a hierarchically integrated, but socially compartmentalized, world. These plans may have been written in Vienna, but their moral habitat was that of Artstetten, of Konopischt and the dozens of other islands of moral tranquility in which feudalists like Franz Ferdinand both consoled and isolated themselves and their *Stand* from the twentieth century.[185] If, before, absolutism was the opponent of customary justice, absolutism now became the last haven of corporate privilege. Such privilege functioned as a device to mediate political partisanship and was now epitomized by the political-sacerdotal person of the Dynast. The Thronfolger had, in this sense, stood Joseph II on his head; appropriately, he intended to assume his throne with the name "Franz II," recalling the reactionary, as well as the administratively modern, features of the Austrian *Vormärz*.

This strange combination of authoritarianism and corporatism was most painfully evident in the Belvedere's harping against the politicization of the Austrian subministerial bureaucracy. For what the Archduke and his minions ultimately sought was a more "Prussian"-like civil service caste imbued precisely with those anti-democratic military virtues which Prussian Liberal theorists like Max Weber might decry as characteristic of the hegemony of neofeudal *Denkmodelle* in Germany. That such etatist militarism contradicted the long-standing disassociation of Austrian military and civil-political ruling elites—a primary cultural-political difference between Austrian and Prussian state traditions—was not irrelevant to the Belvedere. The military assumptions and ethos of the Archduke's *Staatsstreich* plans for civil society must be recognized in explicating the general features of his putative "system."

As different as their goals and methods were, however, the administrative reform commission and the Thronfolger's dossier shared some marked similarities. Both sought to confront state administrative issues not in the exclusive terms of the national right or national privilege of the Germans. They hoped to transcend the nationalities problem by identifying larger, systemic relationships between the bureaucracy and the political system, and between the Crown and civil society, which might be redesigned. Franz Ferdinand attacked the problem of state control of society by vast constitutional changes in the relationship of Austria and Hungary, to the end of factionalizing and trivializing ordinary interest-group and nationalist politics and concentrating all moral (and military) authority in himself. Redlich and his colleagues preferred to work from within by reforming first the civil administration, and then worrying about its relations with the parties and the nations in Hapsburg society. The first method implied a new and more powerful role for the Dynasty, the second recognized that in a modern state no single level or sector of government could assume total responsibility for political imagination or administrative management.

Having written tracts for the times which none of the major parliamentary parties nor the civil service itself would accept, the administrative reform commission was politically dead by 1914. If Austrian parliamentarism was undercut by administrative autocracy, attempts to modernize and depoliticize the civil service were equally compromised by the anarchy of the parties. A classic standoff ensued, each side insidiously enjoying the status quo, all the while denigrating the other's motives, capacities, and intentions. The last hope for serious organizational change in peacetime died with Franz Ferdinand in June 1914. Ironically the individual perceived by many to be "irrational" had become the last, however dubious hope for serious internal structural reforms in the Monarchy, a situation whose ambivalence disturbed many serious "liberal" theorists. So problematic was the Austrian polity by 1914 that order hinged on therapeutic chaos and liberalism depended on illiberal violence.

Following the Archduke's assassination, the English historian Robert Seton-Watson wrote to Friedrich Funder, with whom he had engaged in regular correspondence over the previous four years, offering his condolences.[186] Funder responded in early July 1914 with a brief note of gratitude, adding that "with each day that separates us from this disaster, our pain grows greater, for in the wake of the sullen despair we at first felt has come the clear perception of the total horror of this event and its causes. I have never wanted to die, but in these days I have asked myself a hundred times, why it could not have been my honor to die in place of these beloved [people]."[187] Funder's comments were required by his pose of loyalty to Franz Ferdinand before Seton-Watson, but the sentiments surpassed personal grief. Stunned apathy had led to a self-negating despair, with the one agent of state renewal, for whose constitutional program even the tribulations and insults meted out by the Belvedere could be endured, now gone. The last thread in Tschirschky's scenario for a reconstitution of the Imperial state was now severed, and Austria's future seemed consigned only to her past.

One also senses, however, the subtle initiation of a campaign for vengeance and scapegoatism—Funder's oblique reference to his perception of the causes (*Ursachen*) of the murders. In Funder's mind a logic of aggression toward the Serbians justified by reasons of state survival was painfully apparent, and one comprehends how Austrians could support war against Serbia, not out of love for Franz Ferdinand, but out of self-respect. The hysteric logic of a *Primat der Innenpolitik* was now ascendant in the one area of policy with which Austrian domestic politics had not yet succeeded in defiling itself: military imperialism abroad. Funder's dismay soon led to vicious anti-Serbian jingoism, which Seton-Watson condemned in a second, far less generous communication in late July.[188] By treating the issue only in juristic and diplomatic terms, however, arguing that evidence was not sufficient to warrant a punitive action against Serbia, Seton-Watson failed to comprehend the *Reichspost*'s antagonism. The assassination not only humiliated Austria abroad, but exposed once again the painful lack of options that thoughtful politicians of all parties faced in attempting to salvage an equitable and effective ruling system from the chaos of Stürgkh's autocracy.

In his last letter to the one-time leader of the now defunct Belvedere camarilla, Funder was caught in this dual spirit of despondency and militaristic bluster. To Brosch he wrote on July 13:

Your words of hopelessness, my dear Colonel, struck me like a knife in my breast. I think we must believe, we must always continue to believe in this Empire, to whom our whole way of life still belongs. We must not give ourselves up for lost. Precisely because the great man has just fallen, we must work twice as hard to prove ourselves worthy of him. The blow must be struck now, and I hope that it is already finally beginning to dawn on those bloodless brains that they must temporize no more. I hear that Ischl is already agreed upon the widest possible decisions, and that Berlin is also pressing. If only for once we would act, we will soon see the consequences.[189]

In this narrow, and yet profoundly felt sense, the First World War was fated to see desperate acts of political experimentation, executed not through the rationality of law and reason, or even through the legitimacy of religious dynasticism, but rather through the harsh realities of military coercion.

SEVEN

The Christian Social Party in the First World War

Mass Politics and the Impact of the War

The First World War not only signaled an abrupt and ruthless end to the tentative process of internal reconstruction that Richard Weiskirchner had tried to initiate after 1912 within the Viennese Christian Social party, it exploded the very political culture within which all Austrian political parties operated. Initial jingoism aside, the war was no more a Christian Social war than it was a Social Democratic war, but both parties paid a heavy price for their entrapment in its moral and economic degradation. For in Austria the First World War, as everywhere in Europe, exacerbated tensions embedded within the polity, especially those centered on generational conflict, on the antithesis between administrative and political reform, and on the cross fire of militant national expectations. But by discrediting profoundly the administrative state which before 1914 had been a fundamental source of political order and cultural rules, and by destroying the fragile balance of economic progress that had made it possible for that state to force political parties and social movements into compliance with those rules, the war also opened possibilities, even necessities for change, so dangerous and so unmanageable that stable political and social institutions in Austria were virtually impossible for the next thirty years.

The stresses of material deprivation and, by 1916, outright hunger, and the consequences of mass mobilization and changing demographic structures in the city affected both major Viennese parties in similar ways: the slow but certain disorganization of central party hierarchies, and a growing disillusionment among each party's electoral base with the autocracy of the national government, itself the willing victim of provocative military interventions in civil affairs. Both parties suffered severe factional disputes during the war over structures of governance and over the control of ideological mediation, conflicts emerging from tensions latent before 1914 that the excesses of the war brought to the open. Both party elites had grave problems in controlling their traditional cadre supporters, as they found themselves cut off from traditional sources of patronage and money. Both watched their regular district organizations become indolent, as younger activists were drained from the city by conscription into the army and as elderly party managers lost power owing to illness, death, and their own incompetence. Cut off from their electorates, lacking accurate gauges of public opinion, unable to organize traditional political rallies or other partisan events, party organizations gradually atrophied to the point where their behavior mirrored the *Burgfriede* syndrome that the Cabinet proclaimed as the only loyal form of public behavior. Because their party organizations had traditionally stood outside the nexus of state patronage and power, the Social Democrats endured the war in better organizational shape than did the Christian Socials, but by 1917 police reports on the mood of the Viennese working class showed substantial rank-and-file outrage over their leaders' indecision.[1] To the extent that their union organizations, always more closely integrated into the Austrian socialist party's leadership than was the case in Germany, were co-opted into ad hoc managerial arrangements by the military government to help ensure worker compliance with the war economy, the Social Democrats faced even greater risks than the Christian Socials.[2]

The declaration of war on Serbia on July 28 and the commencement of general hostilities six days later took both of the major Viennese parties by surprise. For each, the enthusiasm of the moment was soon tempered by problems of sustaining wartime politics. The Austrian Social Democrats were embarrassed by Friedrich Austerlitz's excessively patriotic, even jingoistic, editorials in the *Arbeiter-Zeitung;* Friedrich Funder would later ironically recall that in their tone they were not much different from what he was writing in the *Reichspost.*[3] In the Social Democratic Executive a bitter debate erupted over the newspaper's chauvinism, with Karl Seitz and Fritz Adler challenging Austerlitz's pretensions to speak for the party as a whole. Significantly, when Wilhelm Ellenbogen moved to publish an official declaration on the party's stance about the war, Karl Renner opposed the motion, foreshadowing the later split between Renner and Otto Bauer in 1917–18.[4]

During the first years of the war Victor Adler and younger right-centrists like Renner and Karl Leuthner defined the party's "official" views before the government and the military. Renner's wartime essays, which urged administrative reform coupled with enhanced national democracy, combined a *Realpolitik* recognition of Austrian administrative centralization with a covert appreciation of the instrumentality of the war in achieving political democracy.[5] In Redlich's apt phrase, Renner represented an "alloying of Karl Marx with Alexander Bach."[6] Although it would be a misreading of his position to suggest that it was either militaristic or imperialistic, for Renner the war represented not only a constitutionally tolerable but potentially transformational process that might lead to a new, democratic *Grossösterreich,* one that did not exclude either territorial adjustments in the East or possible *Mitteleuropa* projects. Between 1915 and 1917 Renner defended his views with alacrity and energy against challenges from Left pacifists like Robert Danneberg, Max Adler, and Rudolf Hilferding.[7]

Although the socialist Left was in a minority position in the Executive, their views became more relevant with Fritz Adler's assassination of Stürgkh in October 1916 and with the crisis of war governance that plagued Austria after the death of Emperor Franz Joseph a month later. Surrendering immediately after the murder, Fritz Adler faced trial in May 1917. Just as Karel Kramář had exploited his political trial sixteen months earlier to attack national repression, so Adler used his, conducted without a jury before a special senate of judges, to condemn the constitutional illegality and brutality of wartime jurisprudence. Yet Karl Stürgkh and his war government were not Adler's primary target. Condemning his fellow party members for lack of courage in resisting the war and for opportunistic illusions about the future of the Imperial state that were bereft of moral dignity (Renner was "a Lueger in the Social Democratic party"), Adler subjected his own party to a large measure of blame. He openly insisted that "a revolution in Austria will be achieved only against the party Executive. The party Executive is an agent for inhibiting revolutionary movements." Engelbert Pernerstorfer remarked to his colleagues on the Executive that the trial delivered to the Social Democratic party "the most terrible wound since its founding."[8] Count Wedel, who succeeded Tschirschky as German ambassador in late 1916, reported to Berlin in June 1917 that "Victor Adler, Renner, Seitz, Leuthner, Šmeral no longer enjoy the trust of broad sections of the population. It is rather Friedrich Adler, a condemned man, the murderer of the Minister-President, who is the hero of the day and the man of the people."[9]

The turning point, if one specific event can illuminate this complex personal and organizational process, came at the party congress in Vienna in October 1917, where the tensions that had simmered between moderates like Renner, who in December 1916 had assumed semiofficial status in the government as a member of the directorate of the Food Office (*Ernährungsamt*), and the pacifist Left broke into the open.[10] A minority of Left pacifists represented by Gabriele Proft, whose famous *Erklärung der "Linken"* was actually drafted by Otto Bauer, openly challenged the party tactics during the war.[11] Yet ironically, in spite of the vigorous defenses of the socialists' centrist strategy by Seitz, Ellenbogen, Austerlitz, and Victor Adler himself, general agreement emerged that the context for the party's strategy of mediation and instrumentalism was slowly changing and that the very course of the war, as much as any faction's motives during the war, now made a stronger antiwar profile necessary. This did not mean that socialists suddenly repudiated the kind of ambivalent cooperation with governing authorities that had already merited Renner and Adler invitations to join the Cabinet (which both men rejected). But the Austrian Left did not secede, precisely because of the new relevance of their views and because of Victor Adler's remarkable mediatory abilities in preserving unity.[12]

Nor did these ideological tensions lack generational overtones that were already evident before 1914. The young Otto Bauer privately trivialized the death of Franz Schuhmeier in 1913, writing to Karl Kautsky that "Schuhmeier's death means for Vienna the loss of a valuable agitator, nothing more. Within the party he has been a reactionary element for years."[13] The elderly Engelbert Pernerstorfer went so far in April 1915 as to condemn the "little band which consists not only of academics, but also exclusively of Jews," who were trying to take over the leadership of the party and, by failing to recognize the validity of German nationalism, to push it into a dangerous internationalism.[14] Pernerstorfer's death in January 1918 was little mourned by his younger colleagues. When Josef Redlich suggested to some younger Austro-Marxists that a memorial be established to the cofounder of their party, the idea left them cold.[15]

The most tragic figure in this factionalism was Victor Adler, who throughout the war was burdened with the conflicting duties of exercising authority on behalf of his party while trying desperately to defend the social interests of the Austrian working class. Despondent over the fate of his son, Adler was grateful to preserve the appearance of party unity. To Friedrich Ebert he would write stolidly in November 1917 that "we must unfortunately do more with very much less nowadays. But at least we have held the party together. And that was an achievement, and often no small one."[16] But to his close friend Adolf Braun, Adler seemed less confident: "The responsibilities are so monumental that people have the feeling they simply cannot accomplish anything decisive. I must also confess that I have often thought: what good does it do to try to plan something, for it will turn out differently in any event."[17] It said much of Adler's ambivalent situation in 1918 that he welcomed Otto Bauer back as his lieutenant, even though he was aware of Bauer's radical predilections.[18]

In contrast to their Marxist opponents, the Christian Socials felt less confounded by the coming of war. For many in the party leadership the assassination of the Thronfolger was a powerful indictment of the miserable course of Austrian foreign policy since 1909. Heinrich Mataja complained on July 2, 1914, that "up to now we have pursued a policy of leniency and indulgence, and the authority of the state and the life of the Archduke have fallen victim to this policy."[19] Throughout July the *Reichspost* crusaded to avenge the Sarajevo murders, arguing that the "guilt question" was not merely the external problem of Serbia's culpability but also a domestic manifestation of the weakness of Austrian leaders. Did Friedrich Funder and other party leaders actually want war, or was their aggressive domestic-political language—a discourse that certainly helped to back Berchtold into a desperate corner—simply imprudent bravado? If they indeed wanted war, which war did they want? At what point did they confront the dreadful realization that war with Serbia also meant war with Russia, and hence a world war? These questions, hinging as they do on the intended and unintended consequences of very disturbing choices, are probably unanswerable. But by the end of July, when a European war was inescapable, Funder greeted it in the name of an Imperial historical conscious-ness: Austria was united in a struggle for fatherland and home, and although the peoples of the Empire might speak many languages and constitute many nations, they had a common language that was "the language of enthusiastic membership in this venerable Empire for which their fathers have shed their blood in a thousand battles and which we, the generations of today, have not ceased to love with all our hearts."[20] The Viennese Catholic writer Richard Kralik shared a similar confidence that the war would renew and empower an explicitly Austrian state consciousness: "The first success [of the war] will be the strengthening of the Austrian state idea. Austria has proved itself in good and bad times an indestructible, necessary, highly spirited, and impressive political personality, an individual of unique significance in the totality of nations."[21]

Expressive of their insouciance towards possible long-term consequences, the Christian Social party leadership did not even meet to discuss the outbreak of hostilities. When the parliamentary club did reassemble briefly in Decem-ber, there was little for it to do, for Stürgkh refused adamantly for the next two and a half years to recall parliament. The Cabinet also rejected, on Statthalter Richard Bienerth's advice, appeals for the recall of the Lower Austrian Diet.[22] Stürgkh's conversion of the Reichsrat building on the Ringstrasse into a mili-tary hospital for wounded officers epitomized his trivialization of parliamen-tary life. With the immediate imposition of heavy newspaper censorship in August 1914, virtually all of the conventional arenas of "public" politics were closed to policy debate.[23]

Since they were the masters of the largest municipality in the state, the failure of the German short-war scenario by late 1914 had devastating conse-quences for the Viennese Christian Socials. As social deprivations and military intrusions in civilian life grew apace, the party in its bureaucratic incarnation found itself saddled with enforcing a wide range of extremely unpopular poli-cies involving manpower mobilization, reduced social services, housing re-strictions, and food rationing, and it earned enormous public abuse for doing so. What had formerly been the party's unique advantage—its control of the huge Viennese bureaucracy—now became its curse. As in Germany, the com-ing of the war was supposed to "end" partisan politics, but it did precisely the opposite, intensifying the conspiratorial and secretive dimensions of political partisanship by breeding simultaneous dissatisfaction and boredom.[24]

Under wartime exigencies Christian Social provincial leaders came to Vienna less frequently. The war thus gave informal support to already existing pressures for a federalization and provincialization of the Christian Social party by further weakening the moral standing of the Viennese center, a process coordinate with the pressures endured by the general state system. This relative vacuum of strong political leadership in the state enhanced Richard Weiskirchner's role as ersatz spokesman for the Christian Social *Reichspartei* in the capital, even if his colleagues in the parliamentary club resented his claim to speak for the party as a whole.[25] As mayor and chief executive officer of the largest city in the Monarchy, Weiskirchner played a prominent role as war official not because of his distance from the state administration but because of his implicit membership in it. Of the major leaders of the party only Weiskirchner found himself positioned to sustain a semiautonomous realm of publicity and political identity. Within weeks of the outbreak of hostilities, Weiskirchner appealed to the *Bürgerklub* to approve the grant to him of emergency powers to act on behalf of the city of Vienna on a wide range of financial and other policy issues without formal legislative approval by the City Council, for which he would then seek retroactive authorization "after the end of hostilities."[26] He then requested that both Stürgkh and Bienerth approve what Stürgkh indiscreetly called "a kind of general authority" over the city. This they were only too happy to do in September 1914, even though officials in the Ministry of Internal Affairs noted that there was nothing in the city charter to justify such an act.[27] Henceforth, until he agreed to summon occasional sessions of the City Council beginning in February 1916, Weiskirchner played a role not unlike that of Stürgkh on the state level: an autocrat presiding over an uneasy local *Burgfriede,* who was subject to bitter private complaints from dissident members within the *Bürgerklub* and increasing unpopularity with the public at large.[28]

Josef Redlich sarcastically observed Weiskirchner's new image in the pose of the all-prescient "Kriegsbürgermeister"; certainly Weiskirchner's name showed up on thousands of major and minor orders relating to war governance in the city, most of them in his capacity as head of the *Magistrat.*[29] Nor was Weiskirchner passive about constructing this new role. At his direction the Christian Social party secretariat prepared a propaganda brochure, *Die Gemeinde Wien während der ersten Kriegswochen,* and in the autumn of 1914 distributed over 60,000 free copies throughout the city and province. The brochure reported on the city's war mobilization efforts between August 1 and September 22, 1914, and although most of the policies listed reflected routine war planning by the state and municipal bureaucracies, in discursive terms Weiskirchner had appropriated the achievements of others by transforming them into acts of his own superior administrative will. A press release from the party secretariat proudly announced that the brochure proved that "there is no area of public administration or private charity which in some form has not been subjected to the solicitous consideration of our *Stadtoberhaupt* and his loyal assistants. After reading this brochure, one can understand how we in Vienna have felt virtually nothing of the war and its unpleasant consequences."[30]

The last line would return to haunt the Christian Social party. As the war continued and conditions of life in the city became more desperate, Weiskirchner's personal and the party's collective responsibility for Vienna became a gigantic political albatross. What Weiskirchner had so assiduously claimed in the "good" times of 1914—that he was personally responsible for the welfare of the Christian Social polis—he could not suddenly repudiate when food riots broke out two years later. When a vigorous movement among Austrian civil servants emerged in 1915–16 for preferential food allocation and emergency salary raises, it was the *Deutscher Nationalverband* that stepped in to play the role of principal patron of the officials. This was not merely because of its historic standing and interest affinity with the civil servants but because the *Verband*'s political rival within the German bourgeoisie, the Christian Socials, now found themselves saddled with responsibility for the abysmal food and housing situation in Vienna. Because none of the leaders of the *Verband* had any equivalent administrative authority, they did not constitute the same kind of negative target for civil servant unrest as did the Christian Socials, with their hegemony in Austrian regional government. Among the Christian Socials, in contrast, voices of criticism against the endlessly self-indulgent (but in terms of war inflation, probably justified) demands of the civil servants were manifest by mid-1916. If Gessmann and others in the parliamentary executive demonstrated more sympathy for a raise in *Congrua* rates for the lower clergy in 1916 than for additional largesse for the officialdom, it was perhaps because many in the club thought improbable Weiskirchner's predictions that the party would recapture the civil servant votes lost in 1911. Hence it was more important to obtain assistance for the clergy in order to strengthen the party's electoral apparatus in rural areas.[31]

As a substitute for regular meetings of the City Council, Weiskirchner did establish a conference of political leaders (*Obmänner-Konferenz*) including Christian Social, Liberal, and Social Democratic representatives, which met regularly to review policy decrees involving food and provisioning which municipal officials either intended to issue or were forced to issue by the government, and to offer suggestions on specific administrative policy areas.[32] Weiskirchner would occasionally make concessions to oppositional pleas or recommendations on issues of material provisioning and supply offered in this forum, although sometimes this simply meant assuring the participants that he would consult with Stürgkh or another member of the Cabinet. On questions of critical political concern, especially the reform of the municipal franchise and the membership on the *Stadtrat,* the conference became deadlocked by the opposition of the Christian Social *Bürgerklub* to serious structural concessions. Weiskirchner and Leopold Steiner did persuade their colleagues to make a token concession to the Social Democrats and Liberals in the autumn of 1916, offering them three seats on the *Stadtrat.* But the socialist delegation refused to be co-opted by Weiskirchner's offer, made "in the spirit of the *Burgfriede,*" which was a manifest attempt to draw the Social Democratic party into co-responsibility for unpopular municipal policies. Much to the Christian Socials' chagrin, the socialists rejected the proposal.[33] By 1918 the *Obmänner-Konferenz* had become a shadow body, and there was some sentiment among the Social Democrats to withdraw its representatives altogether.

The Christian Social *Bürgerklub* in turn held regular meetings to give informal consent and advice to Weiskirchner, but until 1918 these sessions too had a more therapeutic than substantial value. As older members of the party died or retired or fell sick, with no wartime municipal elections scheduled (Bienerth also opposed new Council or Diet elections), the *Bürgerklub* also became a smaller and more defensive body, its primary focus being concerns about better food provisioning and ways to limit negative political fallout against the party out in the wards.

Inevitably, the Christian Social party's reaction to the war hinged on its perception of the conflict's acceptance or at least toleration by the civilian population. Here too was a marked similarity to the Social Democrats, for both parties tended to judge the war less in terms of narrow ideological narcissism (as did their German national rivals) and more through a calculus of theory tested by practice. Ignaz Seipel found the talent and patience of typical Christian Social politicians for constitutional theorizing surprisingly low.[34] This was doubtlessly true, precisely because the party had enjoyed a comfortable, profitable relationship with the Imperial state. What did worry party leaders, however, were the deprivations inflicted by the state on their constituents. The Christian Socials' initial enthusiasm for the war thus tended to seesaw unsteadily between pessimism and optimism, as the leadership tried to gauge the unpredictable mood of the Viennese populace, using far less accurate mechanisms than they had heretofore possessed.[35] As early as January 1915 the party club heard an unsettling report by Gessmann on the acuteness of the food problem.[36] It became increasingly difficult to ignore the fact that the party's own political fate in the war was now substantially dependent on the availability of food.

As soon as it was apparent that the conflict was to be a long one, the war provoked among both the Christian Socials and the Social Democrats constitutional debates that could be comprehended only within the scope of prewar ideological and generational tensions. Constitutional debates during the war evolved amid intraparty crises of authority, as well as in the context of larger war-aims desiderata and uncertainty about the future structure of the state. Indeed, to speak of "war aims" in Austria is to raise a different set of issues than in Germany, and the radical nationalist Karl Hermann Wolf was right to characterize his principal concerns as involving "internal war aims."[37] For most Viennese politicians the "aims" of the war referred more to internal state reorganization and future electoral balance than to territorial aggrandizement or to schemes of *Mitteleuropa* imperialism.[38] In part this reflected their shared unease about the nationality problem. Neither of the mass Viennese parties found themselves able to exploit the nationality question as a dominant focus for wartime constitutionalist debate, presuming a single national group as hegemonic within the Austrian political system. For both parties the critical divide came in April 1917, when Heinrich Clam-Martinic succumbed to Czernin and the young Emperor and, abandoning plans for a pan-German *Octroi,* recalled the *Reichsrat* for the first time in over three years.

For the Christian Socials the first year of the war was spent in ideological uncertainty. Richard Weiskirchner's official position dictated his prowar, pro-German enthusiasm on public occasions; and his general inclination throughout the war was to cooperate with German national groups to achieve extraconstitutional changes before the recall of parliament, which would secure the cultural and political hegemony of Germans in the Monarchy.[39] But even Weiskirchner recognized certain limits to this collaborationist strategy. Like Stürgkh's careful balancing act between tolerance for pan-German mutations and cautious patience toward the Slavs (apparent in his behavior during the Kramář treason trial in late 1915 and early 1916), Weiskirchner's strategy was more concerned with preserving his own and the *Bürgerklub*'s autocratic power within the party and the region than with abstract ideological formulas.[40] He bridled, for example, at suggestions that the autonomy of the city be reduced during the war or that future mayors of the city should be appointed rather than elected. Dissidence over this guarded collaboration, which Redlich derisively called Weiskirchner's "insipid pan-Germanism of 1914–1918," emerged only gradually, in Catholic circles and among prominent individuals like Gessmann and, after his arrival in Vienna, Ignaz Seipel.[41]

Indeed, the war brought a temporary, if modest, revival of Albert Gessmann's fortunes in the Alpine-dominated parliamentary club.[42] In March 1915 Gessmann and Liechtenstein privately assisted Matthias Erzberger in seeking concessions from the Austrian Foreign Minister, Count Burián, to keep Italy out of the war, although the Tyrolean faction of the parliamentary club resisted any territorial solution involving South Tyrol.[43] That their informal intervention had any practical import was doubtful; the decision of the Imperial Crown Council on March 8 to enter into negotiations for the cession of Trentino resulted from more powerful variables, including pressure from Berlin. But the willingness of the Viennese to concede Tyrolean territory in order to keep peace with Italy suggested the party's new sobriety about the war by 1915.

Even so unreconstructed a nationalist as Robert Pattai could write to Weis-kirchner urging the party to pressure Burián into making the territorial conces-sions necessary to avoid war with Italy.[44] A similar effort by Gessmann and Funder, again with the participation of Erzberger, to secure concessions for their Rumanian clients in Hungary that would limit internal dissidence and minimize the advantages nationalists in Rumania might see in the war, was equally unsuccessful. A private conference staged by Gessmann and Liech-tenstein in early 1916 to propose a political settlement between the Hungar-ians and their Rumanian citizens, in which several of the members of the old Belvedere camarilla participated, only antagonized Tisza and earned Funder a dressing-down from Burián for meddling in Hungarian internal affairs.[45]

Both initiatives demonstrated the party's covert interest in limiting the spread of the war. When Gessmann was invited to a special meeting of the parliamentary club in January 1915 to report on the foreign situation, his report was pessimistic, including a critique of Prussian diplomacy toward the neu-trals; and when Heinrich Mataja delivered a similar report a month later, it was remarkable not merely for its candor in accepting a territorial solution to the Italian question but in its tacit questioning of the general conduct of Austrian foreign affairs.[46] In the private councils of the party, a refreshing lack of war jingoism and a contagious resentment against the attempted militarization of administrative life before 1917 became possible. Gessmann argued confi-dentially to Redlich in February 1916 that a quick peace with Italy would be highly desirable and could be purchased for "only three *Bezirkshaupt-mannschaften.*"[47] However improbable such calculations, they illuminated the growing uneasiness of the party elite over the war's consequences for their political fate.

Both the Christian Socials and the Social Democrats also faced constitu-tional and moral dilemmas concerning postwar reconstruction, the very terms of which changed radically as the fortunes of the state slipped from the naive haplessness of 1914 to the brutal disasters of 1918. By 1918 leaders in both movements had come to think the unthinkable, imagining a state without a supranational Dynasty and a nation without a multinational state. To the extent that the war demonstrated Austria's profound material and military dependance on Germany, it also illuminated a pervasive arrogance on the part of German political elites toward Austria and Austrians. Such postures were often ex-pressed in the German Supreme Command, provoking Field Marshal Conrad into a bitter diatribe on the "pettiness, self-importance, and bad faith of the leading German military authorities and the shamelessness with which they exploit, for the purposes of blackmail, our inadequate resources and our conse-quential dependence upon them."[48] Or the discourse of hegemony could oper-ate more covertly, as in the widespread and humiliating rhetoric of "sympa-thetic" Germans for the "poor" Austrians, which served merely to stir up a reciprocal hatred among Austrians for cultural images of "Prussia," not only in the public at large, but within the Imperial Court. Hence could a journalist who had spent a month and a half in Vienna in late 1915 inform the German Foreign Office that "it is of the greatest importance that people in Germany be conscious of how much mistrust there is for Germany on the part of the Austrian Emperor and his entourage, and how much Viennese Court circles fear that Germany could become all-too-strong and make Austria all-too-weak."[49] In the face of such perceptions both Viennese political parties had to address critical issues of "Austrianness" and to reconsider their previous covert toleration of a moderate German nationalism under the umbrella of a dynastic supranationalism.[50]

Politics now became privatized, involving small groups of conspirators, each attempting to marshal prewar contacts and influence to achieve minor favors from one or another Ministry or from the Army High Command. In the free play given to such private deals, the war simply intensified the worst attitudes of the Austrian party system toward the civil service before 1914. What was in Germany the *Burgfriede* became in its Austrian incarnation a *Verwaltungssumpf.* The lack of central war governance is one of the most peculiar features of wartime Austrian politics. For the first two years of the war, the civil service faced serious competition from the Army High Command, in part because Stürgkh refused to avail himself of a parliamentary counterweight. Multiple competitions for power—Tisza set against Stürgkh, Stürgkh against Conrad, each against the other in endless permutations—forced each major broker to appeal constantly to the elderly Emperor and his chancellory for mediation. War politics in the civil order became almost exclusively administrative politics—a trend even more extreme in Austria than in Germany. Conrad might boast in Teschen that, next to Tisza, he controlled Austria, but this underestimated the residual power of the civil administration. His machinations against Stürgkh and Tisza, for example, did not shorten their tenure in office, even though Conrad made no secret of his view that "if the Monarchy is not to collapse, a change in these [two] governments is urgently needed."[51]

In Germany, the civil administration found itself increasingly undermined by the Supreme Command, which was dominated after 1916 by the autocratic Ludendorff and Hindenburg. In contrast, the failure of the Austrian High Command's authoritarian constitutional schemes of 1915–16, the dismissal of Conrad in February 1917, and the parliament's repudiation in July 1917 of the militarization of civil justice that Stürgkh had tolerated all helped to undercut domestic military imperialism in Austrian politics.[52] With its insatiable claims to men, material, and transportation, the Army continued to exercise great power, but the higher civil service and the Crown retained ultimate political control (such as it was) in Austria during 1917–18. Rather than autocratic generals naming and dismissing chancellors, as Hindenburg and Ludendorff were wont to do in Berlin, Vienna saw Generals Schönburg and Bardolff futilely pursuing the scenario of a "Ministry of the iron hand" in February 1918, relying on the on-again, off-again support of the young Emperor Karl. Encountering foot dragging even from the War Minister, the generals soon found themselves entrapped in a conventional Viennese political conspiracy. In the murky world of Viennese Court politics, Schönburg and Bardolff were in over their heads.[53]

Coming on the heels of the initial period of political feuding after Lueger's death, the First World War introduced a second great period of intraparty turmoil from which the Christian Socials were hard-pressed to survive as a national party and which ultimately obliterated Vienna as the cultural and political center of the Christian Social movement. No history of the Monarchy to date has captured the extent to which the social history of the First World War was actually the urban history of the war, and, conversely, the way in which the war was above all a social revolutionary event that found expression in the cities. Not demographically, but imaginatively and symbolically, Austria became "urban" only after 1914. Paradoxically, the "Red Vienna" of the 1920s as a totalizing instrument of revolutionary hope and, for its opponents, as a universal metaphor of conservative crisis was possible only in the aftermath of the war, once the moral economy of Lueger's brand of patriarchal politics had been discredited. The war's profound social and psychological pressures revolutionized Viennese society; the upheaval of 1918–19 was merely its final expression.

Nationalist Conspiracies in Vienna, 1915–1917

Vienna began the war as the morally hegemonic and proud *Reichshauptstadt* but ended it as a degraded villain blamed by the rest of the state for commonly shared miseries. The Christian Social party, so dependent on contacts with the public and on image manipulation in the media and with a heavy contingent of regional politicians who did not live in Vienna, suffered more than the small left-Liberal or German national groups, whose prewar political conventicles were easily converted into private "political circles" during the war.[54] The emergence of a number of these semiconspiratorial groups among the nationalist *bürgerlich* parties was not accidental. Having no systematic party discipline before 1914, they did not scruple at political anarchism now. It said much about the Austrian political system's self-destruction that the new self-styled "hero" of Austro-German politics in Vienna was Karl Hermann Wolf.[55]

Among the Austro-German bourgeois parties the first serious war-aims efforts came not from the Christian Socials but from elements of the troubled

Deutscher Nationalverband. Only in the wake of German nationalist agitation did the Christian Socials abandon their uncertainty and assent to a serious, if ambivalent, war-aims program in September 1915. For the German *völkisch* parties of Bohemia and Moravia had the supreme advantage over the Christian Socials of knowing what they wanted—ethnic hegemony—and how to achieve it—an anti-Slavic *Staatsstreich,* if necessary in collaboration with the High Command.[56] When a German member of the Moravian Provincial Executive Committee, Wilhelm Freisler, wrote to Gustav Gross in March 1915 urging intervention with the War Ministry to protect the city commandant of Brünn, Eugen Pöschmann, against the *Statthalter* of Moravia (who disapproved of Pöschmann's anti-Czech views and sought to have him transferred), the moral superficiality and political hysteria of subelites in the German nationalist movement became painfully apparent. For Freisler, Pöschmann's dubious achievement of having intimidated the local Czech population justified Gross in conducting backdoor intrigues against the *Statthalter.*[57]

German nationalist opportunists hatched dozens of schemes during the first years of the war, sensing the chance for a final reckoning with the Czechs and Poles based on a rapid and decisive victory over the Russians by German arms. Gustav Gross, the chairman of the *Deutscher Nationalverband,* was typical when he wrote to his colleagues in late August 1914 announcing that even though it was unlikely that parliament would meet during the war (which he assumed would be of short duration), the forthcoming peace conference should serve as the occasion to transform the Austrian constitution in favor of German interests. Gross then listed his own agenda (German as the official language of the state, the creation of a commercial parliament between Germany and Austria, and the separation of Galicia and Dalmatia from the Cisleithanian parliament), inviting his colleagues to do likewise.[58]

Gross's anticipation of "war aims" as peace conditions was premature, and his leadership over his unruly flock was soon compromised by his lassitude and unimaginativeness and by the ambitions of younger men who saw the war as a chance to establish political track records of their own. It was inevitable, therefore, that more ambitious nationalists would outdistance Gross. Indeed, problems of generationalism were not restricted to the Christian Socials and Social Democrats. Even before the war Gross had been viewed as inept by younger, more militant deputies, who resented his collaboration with the Christian Socials. Otto Ganser of Lower Austria had resigned from the *Nationalverband* in April 1913 because the "faction is willing to make alliances with the Clericals."[59] Perhaps sensing a revival of such opposition, Gross hesitated to summon a full assembly of the *Nationalverband* to discuss war aims, hoping that preliminary work could first be done in small, informal committees. By October 1914 his plan resulted in complaints, like that of Stephan Licht to

Baernreither, that Gross was squandering precious time by his laggardness.[60] When Gross finally called a meeting of the *Verband* in late November, little was accomplished.

Pressure for a war-aims program more radical than Gross's musings was also generated by the intervention of the Pan-German League in Viennese politics. Heinrich Class, the secretary of the League since 1898, visited Vienna in late September 1914 to lecture Austro-German political leaders and intellectuals at the *Deutscher Klub,* an influential nationalist society that had been founded in 1907 by university men to provide a forum for their nationalist political views.[61] Disturbed by the group's political disorganization, Class urged his Austrian interlocutors to take heart and formulate their own war-aims program, presenting it as a modern version of the 1882 Linz Program.[62] Although he left Vienna with doubts about his erstwhile co-conspirators, Class's intervention and, more important, the bravado of local pan-Germans eager to rely on their big neighbor's help eventually had an energizing effect, especially among university professors and members of the *Altherrenverbände* close to the Radical party led by Karl Hermann Wolf and Raphael Pacher. In early November Pacher issued a call for a "new order of all political, national and economic-social relationships" and a "clear program for the immediate and distant future."[63] Soon thereafter Wolf and Pacher prepared a statement of domestic war aims that called for fundamental constitutional changes to guarantee the hegemony of Austro-Germans over their Slavic compatriots. They even traveled to Berlin in mid-December 1914, offering to submit their ideas to Arthur Zimmermann, the German Undersecretary of State.[64] Wolf's and Pacher's interventions were to have an impact on the escalation of pan-German theorizing over the next two years.

By early 1915 in Vienna at least four circles of German national and other *bürgerlich* politicians were meeting informally to work on "programs" for the postwar future of the Monarchy.[65] It said much about the constitutional uncertainty of the Christian Socials that, with the exception of Richard Weiskirchner, their leaders played little role in any of these groups. The most influential and moderate was the Liberal conventicle hosted by Gustav Marchet in weekly meetings which began in January 1915, where such lectures as Karl Urban's on the conversion of the international status of the German-Austrian alliance were heard and where Friedrich Naumann first discussed his *Mitteleuropa* plans in Vienna.[66] So many people were conceiving programs for the future (*Zukunftsprogramme*) by the winter of 1915 that Hermann Brass would circularize Marchet suggesting a committee meeting to coordinate the work of the various circles.[67] Urban, an experienced German parliamentarian from Prague who had been deputy speaker of the Bohemian Diet, made no secret of his dissatisfaction with the literati-like triviality of some of these discussions: "it is very easy to put forth programs of wishes, which summarize the dreams of the Germans in Austria for the future; but these things are for practical politics, so to speak, *Muster ohne Wert.*"[68]

Typically, the privatization of politics intensified the tangle of personal animosities that had entrapped German bourgeois parties in the last years of the Monarchy. When Marchet initially excluded Gross and Steinwender from his meetings, he was chastised by Josef Dobernig, the leader of his own circle of southern Alpinists, on the grounds that "the behavior of certain gentlemen of your circle does not encourage cooperation" and that "this group is hardly justified to declare that Gross and Steinwender are not qualified to participate."[69] With no electorate to worry about, the years 1914 through 1917 became the intellectual high point of many of these politicians' lives. Many behaved in a manner appropriate to their civil occupations—namely, as academics, the worst of politicians—having only themselves for a constituency. With some justice Josef Redlich had once complained to Gross that "the major pleasure in Austrian politics seems to lie in personal scandals."[70]

Among the first "war-aims" programs presented to Stürgkh in October 1914 was that prepared by Bohemian Germans led by Adolf Bachmann and Gustav Schreiner, which warned Stürgkh of insidious subversiveness among the Czech population in the province and urged vigilance against Slavs undermining the war effort.[71] Although the memorandum contained no structural proposals, its code of discourse—describing the treasonous and cunning Czech who endangered the honest, loyal German—could obviously be shifted to justify repressive measures by the state, wartime "self-defense" becoming the nominal excuse for permanent postwar ethnic exploitation. Such was the rationale of the work of a group of nationalist university academics led by Rudolf Much and Rudolf Geyer, who were university professors at Vienna; August Schachermayr, a local archivist and the head of the *Kyffhäuserverband* in Vienna; and by other representatives of the *Altherrenverbände der deutschen völkischen Studentenschaft* and of the *Deutscher Klub* in Vienna who began deliberating war-aims pronunciamentos in later 1914. In March 1915 Schachermayr, who had more nerve and more energy than Gross, succeeded in organizing a plenary conference of various extremist groups in Vienna to review a definitive war-aims program that the leadership of the *Deutscher Nationalverband* refused to attend.[72] Henceforth, in spite of a belated meeting between Gross and Schachermayr's supporters in May 1915, a unified programmatic front between the divergent camps of professionals and amateurs was impossible.[73]

Impatient with what they saw as the *Nationalverband's* moderation, Schachermayr and other nationalists began drafting their own *Forderungen der Deutschen in Oesterreich,* which in turn drew in part upon ideas articulated by Wolf and Pacher. In revised form their draft became the so-called *Osterbegehrschrift* of April 1916, one of the toughest pan-German war-aims statements to emerge in Austria during the war.[74] Simultaneously leaders of the various pan-German *Volksräte* in Carinthia, Lower Austria, Styria, and Trieste were busily at work, drafting documents of their own. The program of the *Deutscher Volksrat für Wien und Niederösterreich* in January 1915 was typical, including such gratuitous insults as the imposition of German as the exclusive language of the bureaucracy on all levels, German as the exclusive language of the state, and a new parliamentary franchise that would accord seats to national groups on the basis not of population but tax performance.[75] So vituperative were the Viennese sectarians in the *Deutscher Klub* that even some of their Sudeten brethren were astonished. The leaders of the German *Volksrat* for Bohemia wrote to Marchet with some skepticism in September 1915 reporting that the *Deutscher Klub*

> fears that by a division of Bohemia into two parts and by a separation of the rank lists of civil servants into two parts [the proposal of the *Volksrat*] the Czech part of the province will be lost to German influence. The gentlemen [in Vienna] suppose that it will be possible after the experiences of the war to impose German officials throughout the Czech areas and in this way have a denationalizing influence on the Czechs. We must confess, on the contrary, that it would indeed be difficult to assemble the power necessary to Germanize the Czech population living in Bohemia.[76]

As an integral corollary to these negative "war aims" (negative in the sense that their logic was not so much territorial aggrandizement as punitive, ethnic hegemony within existing Hapsburg territories), plans also emerged in 1915–16 for closer economic, fiscal, and military ties between Germany and Austria. The obverse of brutalizing the Czechs would be closer dependence on the *Reich;* perversely, the Nazis in March 1938 would reverse the process by brutalizing "Germans" to envelop the Czechs. In a report on a meeting in Berlin of the *Deutsch-österreichisch-ungarischer Wirtschaftsverband,* a group of German and Austro-Hungarian industrialists and public officials who met to discuss prospects of economic integration, one member of Marchet's circle, Wilhelm Medinger, enthusiastically argued that "a close integration with Germany by means of economic convergence can strengthen the state-conserving elements among us, and oppose the growing emigration from the East with a supply of industrious elements from the West."[77] But when the group assembled again in June 1915 in Vienna, the limits as well as the possibilities of such a strategy were apparent. Commenting in *Die Hilfe* on the results of the Vienna meeting, Friedrich Naumann had to admit that "there exist in Austria concerned individuals who cannot rid themselves of the fear that German industry is trying to compensate itself for markets lost abroad and in the West [of Europe] at the expense of our Austrian and Hungarian allies."[78]

In the winter of 1915 a small group of intellectuals, civil servants, and university professors including Heinrich Friedjung, Otto Lecher, Eugen Philippovich, Hans Uebersberger, Michael Hainisch, and Richard Riedl met regularly at Friedjung's apartment to draft a comprehensive war settlement that joined formulas for internal reconstruction with *Mitteleuropa* economic theory.[79] The result of these ambitious, if pathos-ridden, machinations was Friedjung's *Denkschrift aus Deutsch-Österreich* in July 1915, which not only argued for a Central European economic union (and thus anticipated the arguments of Friedrich Naumann's *Mitteleuropa,* which appeared four months later in Berlin), but which connected economic union with a military *Wehrverband* as well. Austria would be locked into a permanent, institutionally delineated structure of common defense with the Prussian army.[80] The tragedy of 1866 would be superseded not by a greater, multiethnic Austro-German empire—the world Friedjung had lost in his professional histories—but by the military marginalization and spiritual colonization of Austria by Prussia. Appropriately, the final section of the *Denkschrift* presented a list of inner-Austrian constitutional revisions that should accompany economic and military integration, all to be undertaken before the recall of the Austrian parliament.

Friedjung's hope to insert himself into the world of high politics as, in Joseph Redlich's words, "a kind of 'representative man' of the Germans of Austria," was manifest when he submitted a copy of the booklet to Minister-President Georg von Hertling of Bavaria in August 1915, solemnly reporting that if Bethmann Hollweg (to whom Friedjung had also sent a copy) or "your Excellence should require more detailed explanations, I will make myself available for personal consultations."[81] Hertling felt no need to consult with Friedjung, but Lerchenfeld, the Bavarian legate in Berlin, agreed to meet with him in early November. Lerchenfeld came away with a rather different impression of the project than that which Friedjung was proffering: "He [Friedjung] is very taken with his ideas, but if one questions him closely, Austrian pessimism becomes manifest even in him. He isn't even completely confident that the leading circles in Austria want to and could establish a closer connection with Germany."[82]

To Erzberger, Albert Gessmann might describe the *Denkschrift* as a work of men "without any political influence," but Gessmann was ignoring the significance of their motives, as distinct from their literary product.[83] For Friedjung and his collaborators were looking beyond the realm of political convention to articulate a moral utopia. Friedjung was prepared to make remarkable concessions toward military autocracy in civil affairs, if such could bring about *Mitteleuropa.* To Gustav Marchet, Friedjung wrote in September 1915 that since the army would doubtless play the leading role in future Austrian politics, "it is almost more important that these ideas are made known to be evaluated by high military circles than by the civilian-bureaucratic side."[84]

Given the pressure which the High Command brought to bear on the civil service's prerogatives in the first years of the war, and the loose talk in Vienna of a future ministry of generals, Friedjung's interest in a role for the military in state governance was not surprising, but it suggested how far he (and other Liberals of similar persuasions) had moved from the conventional assumptions about state-military relations in Austria. For Friedjung, political professionals like Gessmann were now men without influence, since the new political order in Austria presumed their degradation. By 1918, redundant politically and his grand designs in shambles, Friedjung would revert to simple scandal as a mode of self-affirmation, as in his vicious attack on Heinrich Lammasch in March 1918 (criticizing Lammasch for his peace address in the *Herrenhaus* where Lammasch suggested, among other things, that Austria had no business fighting a war to preserve German control of Alsace-Lorraine). Like many other amateur theorists of the *Staatsstreich*, Heinrich Friedjung became a nuisance in Austrian politics.[85]

Austrian war aims on the nationalist front thus swung between humiliating, self-deprecating submissions to an idealized German economic and political power (offered with a pathos and obsequiousness that many Germans found embarrassing), and grotesque attempts to crush Czech or South Slav independence within the Monarchy by creating a cultural apartheid between superior Germans and subservient Slavs. These aims constituted a curious inversion of the German war-aims process, which sought to seize new areas beyond the Reich to compensate for democratization within the empire. Of course not all Austrian-German intellectuals or industrialists subscribed to these schemes for economic union with Germany, but such resistance could not dispel the critical tactical and psychological dilemmas faced by the Austrians in their military and economic dependence upon the German Empire.[86] Commenting on a tough, self-interested speech that Gustav Stresemann had given at a meeting of German and Austrian industrialists in late 1915, the Austrian chargé d'affaires in Dresden observed to Stephan Burián that "even if the meeting ended on an unfortunate note and our representatives left Dresden in a mood that can hardly be described as rosy, so in retrospect I cannot help thinking that Stresemann did us a great service. Our industrialists will have to open their eyes to the true spirit that prevails here. They will perhaps now have to understand that German industry, as the economically stronger, will always strive to impose its will on us . . . on the assumption that we have no other choice but silently to accept their terms."[87] The former German minister of the interior, Clemens von Delbrück, noted in December 1916 that "if one explores the real reasons that they cite against a closer economic association with us, one finds that their extended arguments really mask an extraordinary confession of political and economic weakness." Delbrück then asked logically: "one cannot really understand how a state that feels itself too weak to remain at the side of a powerful ally would try, without that ally, to exercise great-power politics with a free hand."[88] A long, eloquent Austrian critique of pan-German agitation, written in late 1915 or early 1916 and submitted to the Imperial chancellory, made much the same point, arguing that economic union would subsidize a "Hungarian-Prussian" domination of the Hapsburg Monarchy.[89] Austro-German war-aims conspirators thus stood between the Scylla of destroying the liberal culture in Germany and Austria that erstwhile progressives like Friedjung and Baernreither claimed to be defending and the Charybdis of moral and political trivialization at the hands of a true great power.

The September 1915 Program

Gustav Gross's unwillingness to submit to the extreme nationalists—issues of prerogative and status aside—reflected a strategic decision by the senior leadership of the *Deutscher Nationalverband* that the only meaningful route to constitutional revision would be through a renewal of their prewar political alliance with the Christian Social party. The idea itself of a war-aims coalition was not Gross's. In mid-September 1914 Carl Beurle, a nationalist deputy from Linz, sent Gross a proposal urging that they initiate negotiations with the Christian Socials over a common platform on war aims. He enclosed a letter from his fellow Upper Austrian, Johann Hauser, the current chairman of the Christian Social parliamentary club and a Catholic cleric known for his sympathies toward the *Verband,* that expressed vague agreement to cooperate in such a strategy. As the possible basis for such negotiations, Beurle also enclosed a *Denkschrift* that bore the mark of its early date by proposing union with Germany to dominate Central Europe, but without explicit punitive actions against the Austrian Slavs.[90]

Gross took up Beurle's suggestion, adding to the latter's vision of *Mitteleuropa* his own domestic agenda for the Austro-Germans, and in late October 1914 Weiskirchner responded to Gross's invitation to nonbinding negotiations with a commitment by the Viennese party leadership to "the points raised during your visit."[91] Problems immediately arose, however, over intraparty jurisdictions between the Viennese and Alpine deputies, and Beurle had to write to Gross again in mid-November warning him that Hauser and the parliamentary club were suspicious that Gross was talking only with Weiskirchner and urging him to pay more attention to the parliamentary club.[92]

These talks had no immediate result. Under pressure from the radical nationalists like Schachermayr and Wolf to accept more vindictive schemes, however, Gross approached Weiskirchner in early March 1915 with a five-page draft statement on war-aims. This document had been approved by the leadership of the *Nationalverband* as a reasonable summary of nationalist aspirations and was eventually published in March 1916 as *Der Standpunkt des Deutschen Nationalverbandes zur Neuordnung der Dinge in Österreich.* It combined vituperative rhetoric against the Czechs ("the state must be released from the unbearable Slavic hegemony") with detailed practical suggestions, including proposals for laws establishing German as the inner language of service and communication (*innere Amts- und Verkehrssprache*) in all courts and administrative instances; regulations specifying that graduates in all state universities, including the Czech university in Prague, had to pass one of their state examinations in German; and, along with a general reform of the civil service, the creation of language-specific regional administrative areas in Bohemia that were synonymous with the long-standing German demand for linguistically demarcated *Kreise.* In addition, parliament would be recalled only after the laws were imposed by an Imperial *Octroi.* The "Entwurf" also contained ritualistic pleas for the "closest possible economic integration" of Germany and Austria, leading to an economic alliance in the future.[93]

After consulting with the leaders of the parliamentary club, Weiskirchner informed Gross that nothing could be done before the late spring of 1915. Serious negotiations began in the summer, when representatives of all three groups (the *Verband,* the Viennese leadership, and the Christian Social parliamentary club) considered the Germans' proposals. Gross's draft underwent substantial changes as Weiskirchner and others produced a shorter document, eliminating language directly offensive to the Slavs and restating the German demands in less antagonistic terms. Gone were the prescriptions about a Germanization of the school system, for example, as well as the plea for the use of German in all official bureaucratic instances.[94]

Even the July version apparently proved too strong for the tastes of the parliamentary club, however, and in early September 1915 the club executive under Victor von Fuchs of Salzburg agreed to yet another version, which now took the form of ten specific points offered not as "demands" but as "goals" towards which both major parties agreed to work, "while protecting their [own] party principles."[95] The tone of what became known as the "governing principles" (*Richtlinien*) was moderate. While urging the introduction of German as a language of communication (*Verkehrssprache*)—as opposed to a language of the state (*Staatssprache*)—this draft also conceded that the "linguistic needs of the non-German population in official instances and in the schools will be taken into account according to their real needs." Rather than malicious attacks on the Czechs, the final draft simply recommended "changes in the constitution in so far as they have proven themselves necessary, as well as a revision of the parliamentary code of procedure." Finally, the parliamentary club inserted a clause missing from all of the previous drafts, demanding as a concomitant of administrative reform "the elaboration of the autonomy of the provinces."[96]

The final version was clearly a compromise.[97] Gross got a vague assent to resolve the Bohemian question, while the Christian Socials reoriented the war aims away from a seeming attack on parliament and toward a reconfirmation of provincial liberties. No mention was made of the school system, none of the *Kreis* problem, and none of a permanent economic alliance with Germany (instead the final draft urged economic integration by progressive stages). On the Polish conundrum the Christian Socials agreed with pan-German demands that Galicia be accorded a special status and thus excluded from parliamentary representation in Vienna (which would have equalized power between German and Slavs in parliament), but at the same time they insisted that the exclusion of Galicia should allow for "the full protection of the interests of the Monarchy." Gross then accepted this draft, which Gross, Weiskirchner, and Fuchs formally presented to Stürgkh on September 30.[98]

Heinrich von Tschirschky, always attuned to currents of intrigue, reported to Berlin that a "highly significant and welcome agreement" between the two party groups had transpired which, he hoped, would have "for the future direction of the situation in Austria, internally and externally, great and useful significance." That Tschirschky received his information on the negotiations from Weiskirchner may explain the tenor of his remarks, but for others in the party leadership the "alliance" with the Nationals had a more pragmatic value. It offered the Christian Socials one more point of political leverage against the Cabinet on the critical question of food provisioning for Vienna. Although food issues were nowhere mentioned in the document, they provided a hidden agenda of which all participants were aware.[99] With the establishment of a tenuous consensus in the autumn of 1915, each of the contracting parties had to decide how to implement it (the document was not released to the newspapers until mid-January 1916).[100] Without some positive reaction from the Cabinet, the *Richtlinien* were worse than worthless—they were another chance for the Cabinet to humiliate the parties. Stürgkh had done just that in late October 1915 when key leaders of the three parliamentary factions of the *Herrenhaus* collaborated on a memorandum drafted by Baernreither that criticized the Cabinet's war governance in a plot to replace Stürgkh with Silva-Tarouca. Stürgkh easily crushed this conspiracy by appealing to the Emperor.[101]

The reaction of the Cabinet to such war-aims plans during the first eighteen months of the war was one of caution, as Stürgkh sought to play each side off against the other. In December 1914 Stürgkh issued an administrative order threatening to censor any newspaper daring to print the results of an informal poll of leading persons on how they viewed the impact of the war on the relationship of Austria to Germany in political, economic, and national terms.[102] Even harmless essays such as an article by Hermann Bahr on his friend Redlich's ideas of administrative reform fell victim to the imperious censor.[103] Such disdain enraged the Germans—Dobernig even accused Stürgkh of allowing Slavic newspapers the freedom to publish political essays while repressing their German counterparts, but their protests simply dramatized the politicians' helplessness.[104]

In fairness to Stürgkh, however, his suspicion of German war-aims vendettas resulted not merely from his sense that they were Trojan horses to allow the parliamentarians to regain lost ground but also from his Hungarian counterpart Tisza's resistance to schemes that would subjugate Austria to Germany. Tisza's blunt warning against pan-German conspiracies at the Joint Ministerial Council of June 18, 1915, where he argued that a customs union with Germany would mean Austria-Hungary's political captivity, was accompanied by pressure on Stürgkh to repress such discussions in Vienna.[105] Doubtlessly to assuage Tisza, Stürgkh actually issued a semiofficial condemnation of war-aims schemers in the *Fremdenblatt* in July. Wilhelm Medinger complained to Marchet that Stürgkh (whom he derisively called "our Potiorek of the civil service") "has refused to meet with a delegation of the *Wirtschaftsverband.*"[106] Nor did the resistance of the Crown and the Cabinet against *Mitteleuropa* visions go unnoticed in Berlin. Lerchenfeld, the Bavarian minister in Berlin, reported to Munich in November 1915 that the Austrians were making every effort "not to come into too great a dependence on Germany."[107] By December 1915 the absence of any systematic war-aims planning merited heated criticism from the Army High Command, with Conrad accusing the government of having wasted fifteen months of the war and still having no goals in mind.[108]

Yet in 1916 Stürgkh decided to show more flexibility towards the domestic elements of the nationalist program, if only for the sake of appearance. Joseph Baernreither later insisted that Stürgkh gave the leadership of the *Deutscher Nationalverband* assurances that he would consider the imposition of various constitutional changes by Imperial decree; and Stürgkh did allow the *Statthalter* of Upper Austria, Erasmus von Handel, to begin to draft such instruments in early 1916.[109] Stürgkh's encounter with *Octroi* legislation was not new, however. During 1915–16 the Minister-President had been the recipient of various proposals for radical constitutional reforms drafted by the Army High Command, most of which Stürgkh sent to his Cabinet ministers for evaluation and commentary. Their generally uncertain and often negative reactions probably anticipated Stürgkh's own.[110] A core principle of these drafts was to overturn the provincial revolution in Austria for which the Christian Socials had been partially responsible between 1895 and 1914. In their autocratic, antidemocratic ethos these plans—for which various high-ranking officers (especially Colonel Oskar Hranilović and General Alfred Krauss) and Johann Eichhoff, a high-ranking civil servant from the Ministry of Internal Affairs who served as an adviser at the headquarters of the High Command in Teschen, were responsible—surpassed even the administrative autarky of Stürgkh. These schemes were not unknown to the Viennese political public. In a letter to Bahr in July 1915 Redlich alluded to these machinations, but took consolation in the fact that "our autonomistic core parties—the Christian Socials and the so-called 'German nationals' in Styria, Carinthia, Salzburg, and Upper Austria are too strong [for the schemes to succeed]."[111]

Stürgkh's decision to use Handel—without a firm commitment as to when he would proceed to take action—probably represented an attempt to reassert himself against the Army on the one side and pan-German political circles on the other. Redlich might argue in January 1916 that Handel, whom he thought a tough opponent of provincial and local autonomy during his service in Linz and Zara, represented a conflation of interests between the high military and the upper civil service, and that the struggle for Austria would now be against the "ineradicable centralistic-bureaucratic inclinations of our military and the circles associated with them," but this view probably exaggerated the convergence of interests between the military and Stürgkh, even though on many technical issues (Crownland autonomy, and so on) consensus between the two power groups might be expected. Given his running feud with the Army in Bohemia and Conrad's ill-disguised attempts to embarrass him, Stürgkh had no special interest in allowing his Cabinet to serve as the help-mate of military autocracy.[112] Stürgkh's negative personal reaction to many of the more provocative acts of military justice should also not be discounted. Nor were the interests of the military schemers and their counterparts among the pan-German politicians necessarily congruent. For example, the Army placed great emphasis on curbing the future political power of Austrian civil servants, regardless of nationality, by excluding them from either the passive or active franchise. Yet within the German-speaking bourgeois electorate the civil servants were among the staunchest supporters of the parliamentary deputies who belonged to the *Deutscher Nationalverband.*[113]

Finally, Stürgkh's new flexibility may also have been affected by the start in January 1916 of formal negotiations between Vienna and Budapest for the renewal of the Austro-Hungarian *Ausgleich.* One component of the Austrian government's initial negotiating position was that the settlement of the *Ausgleich* should not preempt concurrent talks between Germany and the Monarchy on future economic integration, which may have been a facet of Stürgkh's larger strategy of playing off the Germans against the Hungarians.[114] When the German government proposed in mid-November 1915 that the two sides commit themselves to the long-term goal of an economic union, the initial Austrian response had been hesitant and uncertain, stressing the need to preserve its state sovereignty and economic independence.[115] By January 1916, however, given the increasingly dependent financial position of the Austrians, Stürgkh proposed that negotiations for the *Ausgleich* should be conducted in coordination with negotiations for an economic alliance with Germany. For the Hungarians, Tisza again rejected such a view, insisting that the new *Ausgleich* had to be finalized before negotiations began with Berlin. Stürgkh agreed to drop his plan for concurrent talks, but by appointing Handel to draw up constitutional drafts for the Austrian half of the Monarchy, Stürgkh gained additional leverage in the power struggles over the *Ausgleich* that took place from February to October 1916.[116]

Handel finished preliminary work on his constitutional drafts in mid-1916, producing a collection of radically centralist laws that responded to many of the concerns of the Germans, though they would have also compromised general political liberty in the process. But Stürgkh's promises were again of limited value. He refused to act on Handel's drafts until after the renewal of the *Ausgleich* with Hungary was finalized, which meant that an *Octroi*—if Stürgkh was ever really serious about this—would be effectively delayed until mid-1917 or beyond.[117] In the meantime, as the military fortunes of the Central Powers seemed less propitious, Handel himself began to have second thoughts about the drastic scope of his proposals, and arranged for a second set of more modest proposals in the late fall of 1916, which the Koerber Cabinet inherited after Stürgkh's assassination by Friedrich Adler.[118] Thus, until Stürgkh's death, no action was taken on either the coalition's *Richtlinien* or on Handel's various projections for constitutional reform.

Along with this intense intragovernmental maneuvering, dissidence erupted in the ranks of the German nationals over the agreement with the Christian Socials. In March 1916 Gross finally issued his official war-aims program— the *Standpunkt des Deutschen Nationalverbandes zur Neuordnung der Dinge in Österreich.*[119] During the same month Emil Pfersche went public with a scathing attack on Gross in the *Neue Freie Presse* for having accepted the Christian Socials' formulation of an expansion and protection of Crownland autonomy, arguing that this was nothing less than a betrayal of German interests in Bohemia.[120] Hermann Brass, a wealthy financier of German *völkisch* politics from Brünn, suggested to Gross that Pfersche's critique reflected the anxiety of Viennese freethinkers like Ernst Zenker and Max Friedmann and the editorial staffs of the big Viennese dailies that if a wartime coalition between the Christian Socials and German Nationals survived a peace settlement, the final result would be the defeat of the victors of 1911. Yet the executive committee of the *Fortschrittspartei* in Prague also proclaimed that it was not bound by the Christian Socials' autonomy clause.[121]

Redlich trivialized the plots of "the gentlemen professors of the Austrian universities, law professors who plan a pronouncement against the 'Autonomiefreundlichkeit' of the *Nationalverband*"; but, motives aside, Pfersche had raised a provocative issue.[122] How could German nationalists logically accept stronger Crownland autonomy in the Christian Social-dominated Alpine provinces without abandoning their efforts to undermine such institutions in Bohemia and Moravia? Structural guarantees against "Slavic hegemony" would be meaningless if existing autonomistic institutions were left untouched.[123] The only alternative would be a formal move to undercut democratic electoral insti-tutions, such as overt franchise discrimination against the Czechs in the Bohe-mian Diet. This the more moderate nationalists, who claimed at least some residual affiliation to "liberalism," were hesitant to do. But when Gross tried to explain away the alleged insignificance of the Crownland autonomy clause by arguing that what was meant was an expansion of the powers of the *Statt-haltereien* on the regional level, not those of the independent Provincial Execu-tive Committees, he simply showed the extraordinary gap between the needs of the Christian Socials and his own party.[124] For the Christian Socials most certainly understood "Ausgestaltung" to be synonymous with "Erweiterung." That which was to be defended and expanded were the elected, party-controlled administrative bodies—not merely the Provincial Executive Com-mittee but all semiautonomous regional and local administrative councils—in Vienna and in the Alpine provinces. As early as March 1908, at a session of the *Enquete* on the reform of provincial finances organized to discuss ways to resolve the chronic deficits plaguing Austrian regional administrations, Robert Pattai had warned the Cabinet that the Christian Social party would tolerate neither administrative nor financial reform that infringed on the prerogatives of the autonomous regional institutions.[125] That the issue had become highly sensitive by early 1916 was indicated by a motion offered by Albert Gessmann in April 1916 at a meeting of the Christian Social parliamentary club, urging the party leadership to resist Social Democratic or nationalist plans for under-cutting regional autonomy.[126] The autonomy issue was one on which all of the factional interests in the Christian Social party—Crownland vs. Viennese, rural vs. urban, anti-Semitic vs. philo-Semitic, "Christian" nationalist vs. Cath-olic—could easily and enthusiastically unite, and Gross's gloss on the meaning of the concept of autonomy did not bode well for the future of the bourgeois coalition.

Nor was the alliance with Gustav Gross without danger for the Christian Socials. The same Carl Beurle who had encouraged the Gross-Weiskirchner collaboration of 1914–15 would write to Gross in 1916 arguing that now was the time to establish a united, trans-class German political party because "we have the rare opportunity to entice away the voters of the Christian Socials and the Clericals."[127] To the chagrin of other nationalists, Beurle proceeded to found the *Deutsche Arbeitspartei* in the spring of 1916, a faction that attracted the support of the Christian Social renegades Pantz and Kemetter. Older na-tionalists like Karl Urban might hold aloof from Beurle in favor of Bohemian-Moravian nationalist interests, but the end result was one more step toward political anarchy on the part of the German bourgeoisie, subverting the ratio-nale that Weiskirchner had presented in 1915 to his fellow party leaders for the coalition.[128]

Gross's interest in coming to terms with the Austrian Social Democrats may have been a further reason for some Christian Socials to think twice about the *Richtlinien.* Christian Socials like Heinrich Mataja could justify collaboration with the German nationalists in anticipation of election compromises of the future, but Gross's negotiations with Karl Renner and Karl Seitz in May 1916 offered other visions of the next elections. Gross wrote to Seitz in mid-May seeking an accommodation with the Social Democrats on constitutional changes to be sought for Bohemia and the Empire. Simultaneously, Urban approached Josef Seliger, the leader of the German-Bohemian Social Democrats, with a similar message.[129] This initiative came several months after Victor Adler and Karl Renner had negotiated with the Austrian trade unions' leadership on possible terms for a closer "economic partnership" with Germany, even though Adler recognized that efforts towards an economic *Annäherung* could be exploited by others interested in a Central European defense league.[130] When a joint conference on economic relations was held in Berlin in January 1916, Adler found the Germans preoccupied with their own ideological quarrels ("the impression of the movement in Germany is in general not very favorable. The party struggle is continuing, and increasing in bitterness."), and he himself, in contrast to Karl Renner, was ambivalent about how much of their economic independence the Austrians should be prepared to sacrifice.[131]

Rather than refusing contacts with the German Nationals outright, as a minority in the socialist leadership was inclined to do, the Executive agreed to permit Adler, Seitz, and Renner to hold a nonbinding discussion that took place at the end of May. In their fear of Christian Social autonomism, the more conservative socialists, and especially Renner, had at least one point in common with Gross.[132] When the two groups met, Gross reviewed the *Verband*'s program for *Mitteleuropa* and its various political objectives, but the meeting ended "without any political consequence." The official position of the Social Democrats continued to be that constitutional revisions could only follow the recall of parliament, not precede it.[133] This meant that they could reject the *Richtlinien* on procedural, if not substantive, grounds, even though nationalist sentiment in the Executive was more diverse and mutable than party propaganda was willing to acknowledge. Nor were some members of the socialist party leadership totally averse to a limited *Octroi:* Baernreither for one was convinced that the Social Democrats would have accepted the imposition of a new code of procedure on the Austrian *Abgeordnetenhaus* by Imperial decree, in spite of their public statements to the contrary.[134]

In view of these events it was not surprising that doubts began to emerge within the Christian Social party about collaboration with the German nationalists. Gessmann told Redlich in late 1915 that he found the machinations of the *Nationalverband* to be "hopeless" and that the various *Mitteleuropa* union schemes were "unworkable."[135] When Gustav Gross sought to lure the Chris-

tian Social leadership to a joint meeting of Austrian and Reich German politicians to be held in Budapest in late January 1916 to affirm a joint statement of
military collaboration, they refused to attend, with Fuchs citing their unwillingness to support a military convention integrating the Austrian and German
armed forces.[136] At a closed party congress in mid-December 1915 Gessmann
delivered an impassioned attack on the Cabinet for refusing to recall parliament, arguing that the government's simultaneous exploitation of and repression of the German bourgeois parties was causing them serious and perhaps
irreparable harm among their electorate. Many voters assumed that unpopular
mobilization measures had the informal support of the Christian Socials. Until
parliament was restored or the war ended, the Christian Socials should avoid
contact with the government except in the most special cases, in order to be
able to call the Cabinet to account after the termination of hostilities. Gessmann was in fact criticizing the principal tactical assumption behind the *Richtlinien,* namely, that they would be implemented in the absence of parliament.
Gessmann believed that "even the most inferior parliamentarism is better than
none at all."[137]

The Christian Social leadership may have found Gessmann's critique unsettling, although the majority clearly desired the reestablishment of parliamentary life.[138] But the continuing intellectual confusion still present was demonstrated at a subsequent party conference in February 1916, when Heinrich
Mataja, a former proponent of pro-German policies, now criticized the "lack of
clarity" in the *Richtlinien's* conjunction of centralization and autonomy (Mataja
feared that autonomy would suffer), while still acknowledging the value of
future collaboration on economic and national issues with the *Nationalverband.*[139] Given that within a year Mataja would attempt a coup in the Viennese
party leadership against Weiskirchner, Weiskirchner's dependence on Mataja
for justifications of his wartime politics showed how fragile this course was.
Nor was there unalloyed enthusiasm among the Christian Socials for schemes
that would engender economic union with Germany. When asked in early 1916
to review a proposal of the German Center party outlining how such a union
might be effected, Heinrich von Wittek drafted a most unenthusiastic response,
arguing that "from the point of view of Austrian and even more Hungarian
industry . . . a general abandonment of tariff protection would, in face of the
many cases of overwhelming German competition, be quite alarming."[140]

There were other discordant voices as well. In late 1914 Albert Gessmann
organized his own study group to develop proposals for the political reconstruction of the Monarchy. According to Friedrich Gaertner, who along with
Josef Sigmund and Jodok Fink was a member of the group, Gessmann advocated the reconstruction of the Monarchy on the basis of a democratic, federal
system, proposing the introduction of proportional suffrage for parliamentary
elections and the creation of nationally demarcated electoral registers in areas

of mixed ethnic population, as well as according the Jews in Galicia and Bu-
kowina the status of a legal nation. Various drafts of some these plans, of which
Sigmund was the primary editor, have survived in the Christian Social party
archive and in the papers of Erasmus von Handel.[141] Gessmann and Sigmund
not only encountered indifference from the government (although Stürgkh did
send their draft of a new electoral code to Handel for vetting) but also met with
the outright hostility of German nationalist leaders from Bohemia and Moravia, who were unwilling to accept "responsibility for a solution that would
have accommodated in some ways the wishes of the Czechs."[142] This is not
surprising, since in his evaluation of the Gessmann-Sigmund proposal Handel
shrewdly noted that the principal gainers from the reforms would be the Social
Democrats and the Christian Socials (especially in Vienna, where the latter
would recover ten of the parliamentary seats they lost in 1911) and the principal losers would be the remaining bourgeois parties (Handel estimated that in
Vienna alone the German Progressive contingent would decline from seven to
two seats), an outcome that would strengthen the Christian Socials' claim to
be the central coordinating leader of the anti-socialist *bürgerlich* front in the
Abgeordnetenhaus.[143]

Gessmann was also involved with the new journal *Das Neue Österreich.
Monatsschrift für Politik und Kultur,* which began to appear in April 1916, the
same month pan-German agitation was peaking with the *Osterbegehrschrift.*
This journal was edited by one of Gessmann's political protégés, Rudolf Hornich, and enjoyed substantial support among the high nobility, one of whom,
Prince Ferdinand Zdenko von Lobkowitz, subsidized the venture. Its stance
toward the nationality question was diffuse, but basically *kaisertreu* and conciliatory toward the Slavs.[144]

In the same spirit of Gessmann's enterprise was Josef Sigmund's "The Goal
of the Germans in Austria," an elegant statement attacking war-aims nationalism.[145] A young politician from Vorarlberg who was the permanent secretary
of the parliamentary *Reichspartei* and an assistant to Gessmann and Fink, Sigmund argued for a "just constitution" for all nations based on a national-
democratic, federal state structure for the Monarchy in which the traditional
Crownlands would be preserved and regional autonomy expanded, but a national election register and national election curias would be created in each
province on the basis of size of ethnic population. Sigmund rejected immediate
economic or constitutional linkages with Germany, which would be feasible
only in the distant future: "Only when the Monarchy stands again on firm footing, in Hungary and in Austria, can we then seriously consider without timidity
the German plan for an economic federation extending from the North Sea
through the Balkans to the Indian Ocean." For Sigmund the Austro-Germans
would do well to use their temporary hegemony in a careful and generous sense
and not allow themselves to be duped by pan-German hysterics. Appropriately,

Sigmund concluded his essay with an appeal for the renewal of the consciousness of a specifically "Austrian fatherland," quoting the Hapsburg motto of
A.E.I.O.U. as the ultimate war aim that loyal Austrians could advocate.[146] Although their voices were drowned out in the cacophony of hatred in 1915–16,
Sigmund's and Gessmann's ideas anticipated those of Ignaz Seipel and the
Meinl group, containing all the tragic limitations of those attempts to resist
national disintegrative forces with a supranational, dynastic consciousness.

Vehement opposition to Christian Social "nationalism" also came from
Cardinal Piffl of Vienna. Piffl was so outraged by Weiskirchner's cooperation
with the *Deutscher Nationalverband* that he threatened to lead a secessionist
movement to found his own Catholic party at the conclusion of the war.[147]
Weiskirchner's later resentment of Ignaz Seipel's prominence as a new national
leader of the Christian Social party should be considered in light of this axis
of discord between the "secularists" and the "clericals" over war-aims politics
in 1915–17.[148]

War-aims conundrums also provided the opportunities for old enemies to
settle prewar grudges. In the autumn of 1915, for example, Gessmann was the
victim of a clever but scurrilous defamation plot concocted by Hans Bösbauer,
a minion of Catholic feudalist circles led by Count Ernst Silva-Tarouca. Bösbauer was the editor of the *Neue Zeitung,* a Viennese scandal sheet long financed by Catholic aristocrats who were at odds with the Christian Social leadership.[149] A secret party disciplinary commission chaired by Alfred Ebenhoch
in 1909 heard testimony portraying Bösbauer as an unscrupulous manipulator
who was adept at playing all sides against each other in the inbred world
of Viennese salon politics but who had a special enmity for Gessmann and
the center of the party.[150] Hoping to embarrass Gessmann and Funder while
pandering to the *Herrenhaus* circles hostile to Stürgkh, Bösbauer wrote an
anonymous memorandum, labeled as originating from a so-called "Gessmann
Group," in which he argued that Stürgkh should be deposed from power and
replaced by a conservative-Catholic coalition to be led by Baron Beck that
would (implicitly) oppose German war aims.[151] Bösbauer also wrote a counter-
memorandum, attacking his own fabrication in the name of outraged yet loyal
German Catholic circles, which he intended to pass off as the views of Silva-
Tarouca (who seems to have known nothing of the conspiracy). He then circulated both statements anonymously to dozens of key Austrian political leaders,
most of whom assumed Gessmann and Beck were behind a pro-Catholic (and
pro-Slavic) plot to overthrow Stürgkh. Although Gessmann was eventually
able to demonstrate his innocence, and Beck proved his ignorance of the affair
to his friends in the *Nationalverband,* such scandalmongering inevitably sul-
lied both men's reputations.[152]

Josef Redlich recorded a conversation in September 1916 where "Gessmann tells me that he sees the day coming soon when all patriots, including

leading representatives of the Social Democrats, will have to unite to save the state from ruin, and he counts me among these men."[153] Gessmann was certainly aware of Redlich's contempt for the pan-Germans and their plans, and of Redlich's equally strong desire for public office. If such talk seemed improbable in light of Gessmann's prewar Red-baiting, it did have a certain desperate logic. The only alternative to collaboration with the German frondeurs might be a tactical alliance with the Social Democrats. That this would ultimately happen in the coalition of 1918–19 showed his foresight, but Gessmann, now sixty-four years old, in extremely poor health, and hated by Social Democrats of all factions, was hardly the man to persuade the Christian Socials of the viability of this alternative.

Sigmund's and Gessmann's visions of an Austrian national patriotism did find ironic expression, however, when the party faced the initiative of *Herrenhaus* deputies in July 1916, led by Silva-Tarouca, to force Karl Stürgkh to recall parliament.[154] This initiative was rooted in the perception by aristocratic and other "Austrian" circles in Vienna that the Austrian war government was being dreadfully managed, and that the authority and the legitimacy of the state badly needed reinforcement. The recall of parliament, proponents thought, might respond to both issues by providing a vent for popular displeasure over the civil service's mismanagement of the war economy. On July 18, 1916, the Christian Social parliamentary leadership approved the party's participation in the conventicle and passed a general motion supporting the recall of parliament.[155] After such promising intrigue, however, the actual assembly at Silva-Tarouca's house on July 26 was anticlimactic. Karl Hermann Wolf, whom Redlich viewed as a proxy for Stürgkh (what better way to preserve the blissful acrimony of prewar parliamentary politics than to encourage Wolf's vindictiveness?), adamantly insisted that parliament never again meet until the Germans in Austria were given constitutional hegemony by the "supreme power." Wilhelm Ellenbogen for the Social Democrats demanded exactly the opposite, namely, that no constitutional changes be undertaken without the prior consent of parliament. Speaking for the Christian Socials, Josef Schraffl remarked that in its acrimony and lack of consensus the group had all the characteristics of a prewar session of the *Abgeordnetenhaus*. In principle his party supported the recall of parliament, but only if it received an effective code of procedure. Otherwise it might better, Schraffl argued, that parliament not be convened. Schraffl's ironic comments were noteworthy not in their superficial points of agreement with Wolf but in their divergent motives: the main objective of the Christian Social party in supporting the *Octroi* was to secure the imposition of a new code of parliamentary procedure and thus make possible the recall of the *Reichsrat*, not the national hegemony sought by Wolf and his cohorts.[156] Given the results of the session, Weiskirchner had no difficulty in persuading the parliamentary club in late August 1916 to abstain from further participation in such meetings.[157]

The Collapse of Octroi Politics

In spite of the failure of Silva-Tarouca's initiative, the increasingly desperate social conditions and the atmosphere of despondency over the food crisis forced politicians to continue to look to parliament as a way of curbing Stürgkh's wartime absolutism. The personal and official marginality of deputies in a government without a parliament was not lost on the Christian Social leaders. Josef Stöckler summarized this situation well in 1917 when he confessed that "We deputies owe our existence to parliament. The past three years have certainly made us aware of the fact that, without the parliament, we as deputies count for nothing!"[158] In early October leaders of the three parties in the *Herrenhaus* tried to secure at least the recall of the Delegations, while Julius Sylvester, former President of the *Abgeordnetenhaus,* invited Stürgkh to meet with party leaders of the lower House. But these initiatives merited only brusk rejections by Stürgkh, who refused to meet with the party leaders because he did not recognize them as an official *Instanz* of government.[159] The Emperor in turn told Max von Beck that he could not recall parliament because the Army High Command opposed doing so.[160] As food conditions, particularly in the capital, grew genuinely desperate in the autumn of 1916, exposing both the Christian Socials and Social Democrats to accusations of failing to defend the public's interest, pressure for the parties to act grew apace.

The Christian Social party was thus caught in a cross fire of public expectations that they should regain control of the political system and private, pan-German pressure to undermine the only institution possibly capable of doing precisely that. The paralysis of older Christian Social political leaders seemed to dictate continued, if uneasy, cooperation with the *Nationalverband.* Unable to find an effective scapegoat other than general "corruption," the leadership of the parliamentary delegation, under special pressure from Josef Stöckler and other agrarians, voted on October 10 to endorse recall, provided that "guarantees are created that would permit an effective functioning of the House, and prevent any possibility of damaging the image of the Empire abroad or at home."[161] At a meeting of the municipal *Bürgerklub* on October 16 Heinrich Mataja rejected Heinrich Schmid's objections that a return to parliamentary squabbling would weaken Austria's reputation abroad, insisting that "harsh criticism of the enactments of the military leadership is an everyday occurrence in all parliaments and the population would approve of this."[162] But the leadership was unwilling to cut its ties to the *Verband.* Three days later Josef Schraffl informed Gustav Gross that the Christian Socials would also be willing to meet again with the *Deutscher Nationalverband* to plan strategy.[163]

Whether Stürgkh would have eventually bowed to political pressure for the return of parliament is doubtful. Only the brutal act by a young scion of the Social Democrats, Friedrich Adler, broke the hold of wartime absolutism. Frustrated by what he felt to be his own party's covert support for the war and angered by a police order prohibiting a mass assembly that had been organized by several Vienna university professors to support the recall of parliament (at which it was rumored that the Christian Social Karl Jukel, in his capacity as a vice-president of the *Abgeordnetenhaus,* would also speak), Adler murdered Karl Stürgkh on October 21, 1916. In his own mind Adler thought himself "no less and certainly no more guilty of murder than the military officer who kills or orders others to kill in time of war."[164] Adler's tyrannicide and the appointment of Ernest von Koerber as Minister-President in late October called a temporary halt to the German national machinations, for Koerber emphatically supported the recall of parliament and rejected the *Octroi.*[165] The shock of Stürgkh's murder temporarily energized the parties, and a meeting of delegates of all the parliamentary parties on October 23 agreed overwhelmingly to support the recall of parliament.[166] On behalf of the Christian Socials Josef Schraffl sought to reengage prewar social issues and the fight against corruption as tasks that only parliament could handle. Nor was the party unsympathetic to Koerber, who immediately made conciliatory gestures toward the municipality of Vienna. But many of the German Nationals were not yet reconciled to the return of parliament without a prior imposition of the *Octroi,* and a near break in relations occurred when, during a joint meeting of the two parliamentary delegations on November 9 that had been called to coordinate economic issues, Gustav Gross offered a reactionary resolution demanding a "close political, military and economic union with Germany, the regulation of the language question in Austria and the introduction of a state language, as well as the special constitutional status for Galicia."[167]

The likelihood of a new era of parliamentary activity collapsed a week later. The death of the aged Emperor Franz Joseph on November 21 suddenly undercut Koerber's major basis of support. When the Emperor's young, inexperienced successor, Karl, was persuaded by Ottokar Czernin and Konrad Hohenlohe to dismiss Koerber on December 13 in favor of a Cabinet of German sympathizers, the final act opened on Austro-German war-aims conspiracies.[168]

Having welcomed the imminent recall of parliament without an *Octroi,* the Christian Socials now found themselves forced back into unsteady cooperation with a new Cabinet headed by Heinrich Clam-Martinic, which Karl Urban and Joseph Baernreither joined as representatives of the Germans with the understanding that the Cabinet would now move expeditiously on Handel's *Octroi* drafts. In club meetings in late December and early January, Christian Social party leaders agreed to support a limited *Octroi* of a code of parliamentary procedure, the German *Staatssprache*, and legislation equivalent to a settlement (*Ausgleich*) of Bohemian affairs, but they gave Gross and the Germans no binding commitments on Poland or on the Hungarian settlement. Since they expected that the *Octroi* would be confined largely to Bohemia, without implications for their home territories, and since they looked forward to the immediate recall of parliament, this probably seemed a reasonable compromise.[169]

Toward the new Minister-President, however, the party maintained a guarded position, and it is noteworthy that one of the first initiatives taken by the party toward Clam was to insist on appropriate compensation if prominent Jews like Moritz Benedikt and Louis Rothschild were appointed to the *Herrenhaus*.[170] This reassertion of covert political anti-Semitism, heretofore largely absent from party deliberations since 1911, followed the emergence of virulent popular anti-Semitism against both native Jewish traders and shopkeepers and recent immigrants from Galicia and Hungary in the various Viennese wards, which the police began to chart in their confidential reports as early as 1915.[171] Resentment against the Galician refugees attained rhetorical boldness in late 1914 when Leopold Steiner, on behalf of the Christian Social *Bürgerklub,* publicly urged Mayor Weiskirchner to seek the immediate repatriation of refugees from Galicia who had encamped in Vienna during the early months of the War.[172] The Christian Socials' hopes for a quick recall of parliament soon foundered, however, with dire consequences for the coalition. Gross reported to the *Nationalverband* in mid-January that Baernreither and Urban had been unable to get a firm deadline from Clam for the issuance of the *Octroi* laws; indeed, Baernreither was not even allowed to see Handel's working drafts until the end of January.[173] On January 24 the Christian Socials approved a revised version of the 1915 *Richtlinien* that formally renewed their compromise with the Germans, dropping the offensive word "Autonomie" in favor of a more precise and useful demand for "upholding the self-administration of the Crownlands and communes."[174] In return, they finally acceded to pan-German demands for the introduction of *Kreise* but specified that these structures were only for Bohemia, which had the effect of converting what had formerly been a general statement on war "hopes" into a program of Sudeten politics. In contrast to earlier German demands for a special status for Galicia, this document required that the Crownland receive an "expanded autonomy" that did not compromise the integrity of the Empire itself.[175] On January 30 Weiskirchner then convened a summit meeting of both sides at the Rathaus to ratify the new accord.[176] In his private diary Baernreither insisted that the meeting was both amicable and dignified, and that no overt animosity against the Czechs was evident. But Redlich, who knew Baernreither well, had a different view of Baernreither's pretensions of combining nonpartisanship with anti-Czech legalism. Already in 1916 he had noted that Baernreither "has become more anti-Czech than ever."[177] Baernreither also thought that he had undermined Christian Social autonomism, but Funder's commentary in the *Reichspost* when the *Richtlinien* were made public showed clearly that the party viewed the document's programmatic minimum as its own political maximum.[178]

Although the Christian Socials thus seemed to stand in formal agreement with what the *Octroi* laws would accomplish, everything depended on the *Nationalverband*'s ability to push the laws out with dispatch. When Baernreither at last obtained Handel's final drafts he found them useless and had to begin de novo to draft legislation for Bohemia and the Empire.[179] These materials included a law establishing German as the general language of Austrian administration and government throughout the Monarchy; a second law regulating the use of Czech and German in Bohemia (which abandoned the concept of two languages customary throughout the whole of the Crownland [*landesübliche Sprachen*] and allowed authorities to designate areas where "need" of bilingual officials was greater or less, so that some purely German parts would have no Czech-speaking officials at all);[180] a third law introducing homogeneous German and Czech *Kreise* in Bohemia, based on linguistic majorities; and a law restricting Crownland-level governmental responsibilities by relegating most business to new, ethnic *Kreis* diets and *Kreis* executive committees. In Baernreither's own words "what remained for the [Crownland] Diet had no political significance." In addition to this virtual division of the province into two political-administrative worlds, Baernreither also fashioned a new franchise for the Diet, dividing it into two electoral curias, one of 130 seats based on universal suffrage, and a second, also of 130 seats, representing big economic interest groups, one of which (not surprisingly) was Baernreither's own *Grossgrundbesitz*. The result was a shotgun marriage of feudal and grand bourgeois oligarchy with nationalist democracy. In addition, working with Robert Pattai and Jodok Fink, Baernreither also drafted a new code of procedure for the *Abgeordnetenhaus*.[181]

As long as Baernreither restricted himself to Bohemia, the Christian Socials were content with their role of interested bystanders. But Baernreither decided to go further, attacking past and present problems in the educational system as well. Like many Bohemian Germans, Baernreither thought that the most effective way to curb Czech influence on the school system would be to restrict the prerogatives of policy determination and personnel supervision enjoyed by the autonomous regional authorities and to enhance the powers of the state bureaucracy, especially the *Statthaltereien* and the Ministry of Education in Vienna, over local school systems.[182] Such vertical and horizontal centralization met with sympathy on the part of ministerial bureaucrats in Vienna, led by Max von Hussarek, who wanted the executive power of administrative authorities enhanced.[183] But since the kinds of changes Hussarek sought could not be arbitrarily applied to Bohemia, Baernreither was forced to draft universal instruments valid for all of the Crownlands. He also produced tough new disciplinary regulations against political dissidence by schoolteachers, and a law imposing the conditions set by the former *Lex Kolisko* throughout Austria.

These gratuitous initiatives put Baernreither on a collision course with the Christian Socials. He met with Weiskirchner and Gessmann, both of whom warned Baernreither to drop his plans for educational reform since they would be interpreted by the party as attacks on Crownland autonomy. Weiskirchner cynically told him in mid-February that "to lay a hand on provincial autonomy will make even the most indolent Viennese philistine into a revolutionary. Autonomy is the great protection of the bourgeoisie [in Austria]." Weiskirchner's corporatist view of autonomy (what undercut the German bourgeoisie in Bohemia protected the same bourgeoisie in Vienna) was matched by Gessmann's more politically subtle but equally negative dissent. Gessmann told Baernreither on February 9 that this was a most inopportune time to be attacking the autonomy of the school system, for "the people have made immense sacrifices [during the war] and one does not want to give the impression that we are now going to subject them to autocratic control."[184] Such advice actually intimidated Baernreither into suppressing his school drafts, but his attack on educational autonomy and rumors of other such initiatives offered Weiskirchner's rivals in the party an opening to press for the immediate recall of parliament. Leopold Kunschak published a long article in *Volkswohl* vigorously defending provincial control of public school systems; and in early January 1917 the *Reichspost* published an equally forthright justification of the sanctity of provincial autonomy more generally.[185] On February 7 Josef Stöckler summarized discussion in the parliamentary executive by declaring that the party would fight "the assault on autonomy, and as a means to this end will try to negotiate with the *Nationalverband;* if this has no success, the party will withdraw its support for Ministers Urban and Baernreither."[186] Finally in late February Gessmann drafted a second motion for the party executive demanding the immediate recall of parliament and "above all the most trenchant support by Ministers Baernreither and Urban for the creation of an effective code of parliamentary procedure." He said nothing about pan-German expectations for Bohemia.[187]

On March 7 the club met to discuss this resolution. The debate manifested intense conviction that parliament should be recalled, if only to help deflect public criticism of the Christian Socials.[188] When the Viennese press learned of this resolution, the Liberal newspapers screamed "treachery" and "felonious betrayal," but Johann Hauser, the current party chairman, wrote to Gross the same day informing him that the Christian Socials now put the highest priority on the immediate return of parliament, as urged by the "whole population" (meaning Christian Social voters).[189]

Moreover, the incident and the kinds of routinized and vacuous rhetorical responses the Christian Socials managed to generate revealed a critical issue that had heretofore been suppressed in the discussions. Throughout the early part of the war the future status of the Crownlands in a postwar constitutional settlement had been a lively subject of debate in Austrian legal and political circles. When the editors of the *Österreichische Zeitschrift für öffentliches Recht* polled fourteen university professors in 1916 on the desired future status of the Crownlands, a number of distinguished jurists attacked the quasi-political hegemony that the Crownlands had come to enjoy in the late Imperial period. Karl Brockhausen went so far as to argue that the Hapsburg state of the late seventeenth and the eighteenth centuries was fashioned against particularism of the Crownlands, and their reemergence as major political and policy actors between 1880 and 1914 had led to a situation where "the whole of the system of self-administration, from Crownland down to township, is becoming alienated from the state, indeed hostile to the state."[190] Yet, at the same time, it was precisely because of this new-found prominence that any attempt to meddle with provincial autonomy was a serious and perhaps treacherous venture. As Rudolf von Herrnritt admitted, the Crownland administrations brought to the fore

> men who are in regular contact with the people, who enjoy their trust or at least that of the larger political parties; personalities who also, in contrast to the leaders of the state civil service who mainly come from the ministerial offices, have strong support in the public and who represent political power. To be sure, these personalities—names do not need to be mentioned—feel themselves to be representatives of a certain Crownland particularism.[191]

Would such "personalities"—Herrnritt surely meant Christian Social politicians like Karl Lueger and Albert Gessmann—allow German nationalist ideologues to endanger a major structural basis of their party? The later preoccupation of Christian Social negotiators in drafting a constitution for the new Republic in 1919–20 with preserving and enhancing Crownland prerogatives followed on an equally stubborn, if less overt, attempt to defend provincial rights during the war.[192]

For the Christian Socials, the nationalist *Richtlinien* were thus "war aims" only in a most limited sense.[193] They did not offer a comprehensive program to reform the Monarchy because the party itself, divided into pro- and anti-nationalist factions as well as by regional and class rivalries, could not agree on what should constitute such a program. Leopold Kunschak's Laborite faction managed to write a serious proposal for structural reforms in the Monarchy in 1916, but it was ignored by everyone except the *Volkswohl* group.[194] The January 1917 version of the *Richtlinien* was, from the point of view of the *Gesamt-*

partei (Vienna and the Crownlands), an act of conflict avoidance, designed to shift the focus of imperial reform onto Bohemia, with the implicit assurance that nothing would be done to regional and local administrative institutions in the Alpine lands without the consent of parliament, which, for most of the regional leaders, meant closure on any serious reform.[195] Even Baernreither's blunders might have been contained—for in spite of the Stöckler-Gessmann resolutions, the party had not formally repudiated the *Richtlinien* or the strategy of an *Octroi*—had Baernreither and Urban been able to force Clam's hand on the Bohemian components of the package. But as the spring dragged on, Clam became less certain of both the contents and the prudence of the *Octroi*. In mid-March he even suggested to Baernreither a much reduced version of the legislation that the latter refused to accept.[196] Equally important, serious difficulties emerged in the Cabinet and between the two parties over the scope and substance of the special status to be accorded to Galicia: was the province to be excluded completely from the *Reichsrat,* and if so, how was the Hapsburg state to retain control of or access to the financial and fiscal resources of the new Polish "state"? As Baernreither admitted privately in his diary, even if the Bohemian *Octroi* had been issued, it could not have contained the new code of parliamentary procedure the Christian Socials demanded, since that presumed a final settlement of the Galician problem which by early April 1917 simply was not in place.[197] That a special meeting of the various interest groups within the Christian Social party voted at Gessmann's urging on March 8 to demand the use of proportional suffrage throughout the Empire for postwar elections (not merely in Vienna, to which Baron Handel wanted to restrict it) was a clear signal of where the party's priorities lay—not only for the recall of the existing parliament, but for a process to enhance the authority of the postwar parliament and its own hegemony within the German *bürgerlich* camp.[198]

Finally, outside events brought the *Octroi* strategy to bankruptcy. On March 8, 1917, revolution broke out in St. Petersburg, and just as the Revolution of 1905 had had profound consequences for the Austrian political system, the fall of the Romanovs in 1917 forced a reconsideration of pan-German autocracy. Not only were the Social Democrats emboldened to pressure Clam for a change of course (in late March Adler, Pernerstorfer, and Seitz met him for confidential political talks) but Karl Renner, as a newly appointed director of the *Ernährungsamt,* had an equally lengthy conversation with the Emperor.[199] The new Austrian Foreign Minister, Ottokar Czernin, who in January 1917 had stridently defended the idea of *Octroi* politics against Josef Redlich's objections, was both shocked by the Revolution and, ever the clever opportunist, ready to turn it to his own account.[200] As early as March 6 Czernin had hinted to Baernreither that foreign policy considerations might intervene to undermine the *Octroi*. Anti-democratic tactics in Austria seemed especially inappropriate following the stirring debates in the Prussian House of Deputies in mid-

March on the necessity of a democratic reform of the House's franchise, and the announcement by Bethmann Hollweg on March 14 that the Prussian government would initiate serious constitutional reforms. Nor had the Czechs sat idly while the Germans quarreled about their putative fate; Wedel reported to Berlin that they threatened a general strike in major armaments industries in Bohemia should the Cabinet go through with the *Octroi*.[201] Reviewing such pressures, and in hopes of exploiting the Austrian Social Democrats to mediate a separate peace with the new provisional government in Russia, Czernin decided in mid-April to repudiate the whole concept.[202]

Equally important, the young Emperor had begun his reign skeptical about the legality of the *Nationalverband*'s directives, and only his gentle incompetence, and the forceful voices of those advising him between December 1916 and February 1917, had permitted the German politicians to pursue their plans during the early winter of 1917. Karl's dismissal of Conrad as chief of staff in late February 1917 reflected his long-standing hostility toward Conrad's authoritarianism, his increasing pan-Germanism, and his meddling in civil politics, even if this action implied no clear idea of a positive reform program.[203] The fateful Sixtus negotiations—confirmed by Karl's letter of March 24, 1917, which sanctioned peace terms involving the restitution of Alsace-Lorraine to France and the reestablishment of independent Serbian and Belgian states— bespoke a vision of postwar Central Europe hardly congruent with earlier German *Mitteleuropa* assumptions.[204]

In an interview with Clam and Czernin in early March, Karl had become decidedly cool to the Germans' schemes.[205] The American declaration of war against Germany on April 6, following Wilson's address justifying the war in terms of national liberties, further sobered Vienna. Redlich wrote to Bahr on April 11 forecasting a possible recall of parliament, if only because of the "great confusion" now reigning in the Cabinet.[206] Finally, Polzer-Hoditz, the Emperor's chief of staff, gave Karl a long sermon on April 11 arguing for constitutional changes only via parliament and on criteria of strict national equity and personal autonomy, and suggesting the threat of proportional suffrage if the bourgeois parties refused to cooperate. According to Polzer's account, Karl accepted this logic, and although he later refused to issue a Manifesto enunciating such policies, he had decided against the *Staatsstreich*.[207]

As late as March 22 Baernreither and Urban reported to a joint committee of the Christian Social and Nationalist parliamentarians that most of the drafts were ready and would be issued "in a few days." But the Christian Socials' patience had already run out, for Johann Hauser reported at the same meeting that his party insisted on the recall of parliament, and, rubbing the salt of high-minded indifference into the wounds of the *Nationalverband,* added that "the fulfillment of the *Voraussetzungen* [the *Octroi*] should be seen as the duty of any government, and the German bourgeois parties were acting unintelligently if, by constantly repeating themselves, they made these questions into national demands."[208]

On April 12 Karl instructed Clam (through Polzer) to abandon the *Octroi*
and to set procedures in motion for the recall of the *Reichsrat,* orders that he
repeated personally to the Minister-President on April 15. The next day Clam
held a Ministerial Council at which Czernin expostulated on how the exigencies of Austrian foreign policy necessitated such a course, upon which Baernreither insisted that the Cabinet resign. Clam, to Baernreither's chagrin, refused
to resign, upon which Baernreither and Urban offered their individual resignations.[209] Bitterly, Baernreither observed that "we Germans have lost a battle.
Whether the failure to take care of the state language and the Bohemian issues
can later be reversed remains to be seen. For now the Czechs, the South Slavs,
the socialists and the Jewish circles affiliated with them have triumphed."[210]

Confusion now reigned in the German ranks. Although Urban and Baernreither eventually agreed to remain in the government (which endured until
late June, being succeeded by that of the career bureaucrat Ernst von Seidler)
the war-aims schemes of 1914–17 were dead, if not yet buried. On April 17
the Christian Social club met to hear Johann Hauser hold a surprisingly
apathetic funeral for the *Octroi.* Hauser suggested laconically that the new role
of the Christian Social party was one of statesmanlike mediation to prevent
German outrage over the fate of the drafts from turning against the Crown or
endangering the possibilities for peace.[211] At a joint meeting of German
National and Christian Social leaders the next day, Hauser bluntly reminded
them that "sentimentality does not constitute effective politics."[212] Appropriately, Weiskirchner led a delegation of shocked politicians out to Laxenburg to
meet the Emperor on April 19. Weiskirchner's address, in which he regretted
the fate of the *Octroi* and reiterated the importance of the Germans to the Monarchy, received a ceremonious response by Karl, who assured the politicians
that he was grateful for the loyalty of the Germans, viewing them as "one of
the pillars of the unity of the state in the future ordering of thé polity, which,
initiated during the war, must be accomplished with resoluteness after its conclusion." The *Reichspost,* following Hauser's dictum, might conclude that this
historic meeting renewed the "unshakeable trust in the future" of the German
leaders, based on their confidence in the Emperor's leadership, but this was
little more than a brave facade.[213] Parliament, recalled for May 30 after three
years of moral and physical exile, reassembled in the worst possible circumstances: it was decimated by deaths and arrests (since 1914 twenty-five deputies had died, and nine, including Karel Kramář, were sitting in Austrian jails);
led by Cabinets of mediocre, unimaginative bureaucrats; plagued by intransigent Slavic provocations and German counterprovocations; filled with politicians bereft of new ideas for the future; and set in a capital city suffering from
hunger and disease. The possibility of constitutional reform by parliamentary

action in the summer of 1917 was as utopian as the *Octroi* strategy that it was supposed to replace.

Ignaz Seipel and Later Constitutional Plans, 1917–18

The Emperor's decision to recall parliament produced little change in the reactive posture of the Christian Socials. Having been robbed of the *Octroi* which they did not need, they now obtained a parliament which they had no idea how to use. The programmatic addresses that opened the House on May 30, 1917, set a tone of bitter acrimony which would endure for the next fifteen months. The Czech spokesmen František Staněk and Antonin Kalina insisted upon the reconstruction of the Empire into a system of independent federal states, with borders guaranteeing Slavic majorities and thus the majority hegemony of the Bohemian and Moravian Czechs, within a mere nominal union under the Hapsburg Dynasty. Austria as an integrated administrative, military, and financial state—centralized or decentralized, autonomous or regional—would cease to exist.[214] Kalina also repudiated any moral support for the war ("we deny most emphatically any responsibility for this war, which was not only forced upon our people, but which was even directed against us. . . . The three years of war have been for all of us a time of absolutistic and terroristic domination"). Nor did he hesitate to claim the Allies as covert supporters of Czech freedom ("the whole world is fighting for our freedom"), and in painfully literal allusions to Wilsonianism he proclaimed the "natural right of self-determination of the people, which has become the law in the conscience of a new democratic world," as the logical parallel to the Bohemian *Staatsrecht* in underwriting a new Czech nation-state. That Kalina's conflation of Czech hegemony in Bohemia via the *Staatsrecht* with the theoretical self-determination of each ethnic group contained a grave contradiction might be tactically irrelevant, but it suggests how awesome the fragmentation in Austrian political discourse had become. As Hanns Schlitter noted, "Entente catchwords" had become fashionable in Austria.[215]

The German parties reacted to the Czech speeches with specious outrage. Appropriately, Wolf's ally Raphael Pacher delivered a tough defense of the German-dominated Dualistic state. But such bluster simply masked the Germans' bewilderment about where to turn and what to do.[216] Attempts by Polzer-Hoditz and Seidler in July 1917 to initiate constitutional reform on the margins of parliament by establishing a special State Conference to plan a new political-administrative system were vigorously opposed by the Christian Socials as undercutting parliamentary rule, yet the party adamantly refused— in spite of pressure from the Crown—to join either Seidler's or Hussarek's cabinets, which might have strengthened the link between war government and parliament.[217] Within parliament the possibility of a consensus-based constitutional settlement grew more doubtful as its working atmosphere was poisoned with national hatred. On the heels of disastrous labor unrest in January 1918, the chimerical "victory" of Brest-Litovsk might have intimidated the Slavs into sullen quietude for a few weeks in February and March, but it hardly engendered sympathy for the "old regime," and sensible observers realized that the tragedy was not over.[218]

The best the Christian Socials could manage was to resume their *staatserhaltende* pretensions for a state that was rapidly ceasing to exist. Appropriately, when Johann Hauser arose in the lower House on June 12 to offer the Christian Social party's official reaction to the recall of parliament, he carefully distanced himself from Pacher by avoiding any mention of German national goals in Bohemia, arguing instead for positive social and economic reform work that parliament should address.[219] In late February 1918, under the shadow of the Eastern settlement, the party even sought to initiate formal constitutional negotiations between the Germans and Slavs as a way of avoiding a parliamentary crisis over the 1918 budget. Although Hauser's personal intervention helped preserve a weak majority on March 7 for the Cabinet's provisional budget bill, their larger effort was stillborn.[220] Within two months Seidler had become the captive of the German radicals, closing parliament in early May with the intention of issuing a miniature version of the *Octroi* that imposed *Kreishauptmannschaften* on Bohemia along ethnic lines (four German as opposed to seven Czech *Kreise*).[221] The Christian Socials' frustrated immobility in the face of such banditry, which aimed a final blow at any rational state settlement, evinced their paralysis.[222] What might pass as marginally justifiable "statesmanship" before the war was now a desperate triage to save the individual organisms of a dying state.

More significant changes took place within the party leadership, however. In mid-May 1917 Franz Hagenhofer, the old Styrian peasant leader, wrote to Josef Sigmund urging him to encourage the hierarchy to select a permanent parliamentary leader in place of the rotating chairmanship that had brought the party such disrepute between 1911 and 1917.[223] Hagenhofer admitted that the new leader should be a resident of Vienna for reasons of both convenience and prestige. Alois Liechtenstein was not a member of the *Abgeordnetenhaus* and Victor Fuchs was too old for the job, and the only likely Viennese candidate was Heinrich Mataja, whom Hagenhofer respected, but whom he feared might try to import some of the "principles of the Social Democrats"—an allusion to Mataja's forceful centralistic views on party organization. The most important attribute of the leader must be, however, unimpeachable Catholicism. Although religious orthodoxy would disturb the Viennese (for them "einen recht schwierigen Standpunkt"), the new leader had to be a "positive Catholic" who would defend a new party program of clear and open Catholic principles.

Hagenhofer's views were supported by Jodok Fink and Josef Stöckler, but rather than Mataja, Johann Hauser was selected in mid-May to be the new permanent Chairman.[224] For the first time in the party's history a Catholic cleric now stood as its public leader, and a cleric not from Vienna but from Upper Austria. Hagenhofer's missive was significant not merely for its recognition of generational change—he was one of the first to explicitly acknowledge the need for reconstitution of the movement's leadership pool—but also for its insistence on both Catholicism and formal programs to revitalize the party. Demands for a party of "principles" became a standard leitmotif in intraparty polemics in 1917–18, comprehending both constitutional and societal issues.[225] The moral aimlessness that seemed to characterize the party under Weiskirchner and Gessmann must now be superseded by "scientific" planning; and the former self-conception of the party as one which did not need programs— Lueger's famous stance—now fell victim to young systematizers enthralled with theory. Not surprisingly, the group best situated to provide such codified, anti-Marxist prescriptions was Richard Schmitz's *Volksbund*. In May 1918 the *Volksbund* even modified the title of its monthly journal *Volkswohl*, adding to it, in overt emulation of the Austro-Marxists' *Der Kampf*, the subtitle of *Christlichsoziale Monatschrift*. A modern party needed not merely new blood and new ideas, but also a deliberative, "scientific" journal for its intelligentsia.[226]

For some older members of the party, especially in Vienna, the residue of nationalist collaboration was too strong to eradicate. Just as the extreme pan-Germans became more intractable in late 1917 and early 1918 (the German Radicals led by Wolf and Pacher seceded from the *Deutscher Nationalverband* in October 1917), so too did at least some of the older Christian Social leaders succumb to dreams of revanchist victory.[227] Weiskirchner welcomed the Brest-Litovsk settlement as a "bread peace" that would restore the city's collective well-being and his own reputation (to his huge embarrassment, however, the city's per capita bread ration was again cut by 50 percent in June 1918).[228] That a delegation of the City Council led by Weiskirchner constituted the audience for Czernin's bellicose speech against the French in early April 1918, which led Clemenceau to retaliate with the publication of the Sixtus correspondence on April 12 and thus discredit the Emperor, was an ironic finale to Weiskirchner's war-aims maneuvering.[229] For a few in the party even this posturing was an insufficient gesture on behalf of *Deutschtum*. Robert Pattai for one delivered a vigorous and explicit pan-German speech to the *Herrenhaus* in February 1918 (to which he, Weiskirchner, and Gessmann were appointed belatedly in May 1917) defending Brest Litovsk as a peace of victory ("we are the victors and we demand the palm of victory") and supporting territorial acquisitions by the Central Powers in the east and south.[230] When Heinrich Lammasch, a dignified Catholic jurist and peace advocate as well as a close friend of Seipel and

Redlich, responded by accusing Pattai of succumbing to the blandishments of the German *Vaterlandspartei*, Pattai shouted that its rallies had been a "splendid success!"[231] The Christian Social party leadership in the Rathaus quickly issued a statement repudiating any responsibility for Pattai's sentiments or proposals.[232]

Most of the parliamentary delegation thus felt uncomfortable at such extremism, but their lack of purpose was particularly striking when compared with the intellectual endeavors of the *Volksbund* group, centering on Ignaz Seipel. Seipel's career, especially during the First Republic, has been charted by two recent biographies, most eloquently in that of Klemens von Klemperer.[233] A young cleric with brilliant intellectual capacities, Seipel was a student and protégé of Franz M. Schindler at the Theological Faculty of the University of Vienna. Owing both to his intrinsic talent and to Schindler's patronage, he obtained a chair at Salzburg in 1912 and was called to Vienna to succeed Schindler as Ordinarius in moral theology in mid-1917. In 1916 he published his great work *Nation und Staat,* a systematic analysis of the limits as well as the value of national identity, which sought to repudiate the contemporary axiom that argued that nationalism must lead to and authenticate state formation, and, conversely, that monoethnic states were morally preferable to or more functionally desirable than multinational political units.[234] By subordinating the nation to the state on the level of both political organization and moral value, Seipel accorded to national identity one level of legitimacy in the organization of social and cultural space but withheld from it an exclusive claim to validate and authenticate sovereign (state) power. Seipel's authorization of an independent role for political organization above national particularism found more concrete expression in several wartime essays he wrote in Salzburg in 1916–17 on the constitutional future of the Hapsburg Monarchy. His concise overview of the possibilities of constitutional reform, *Gedanken zur österreichischen Verfassungsreform,* which he completed in August 1917, was to prove especially influential for his subsequent role in the party. [235]

Critical to Seipel's approach was a universalist perspective that posited all eight national groups in the Monarchy as equal in historic (as well as moral) value, even if in the actual organization of affairs inequities might prevail. In Seipel's view neither the interests of individuals nor those of large ethnic groups could be comprehended exclusively by nationalist criteria. Taking what seemed, in its scope and resonance, a Madisonian view of the multinational vitality of the Hapsburg Monarchy, Seipel argued that it was precisely the existence of a large and powerful configuration of conflicting social interests and ethnic needs that created a central market and afforded possibilities for competitive economic growth, as well as for unusual realms of cultural and intellectual enrichment. In this paradigm the state was not merely a central bureaucratic apparatus in instrumental terms, nor the sentimental dynastic cult in affective terms, but a curious subject of both rationality and affectivity, finding its final legitimacy in the sanctity of history itself. The Hapsburg state was an enduring product of history that had served over the centuries culture-preserving and culture-mediating roles, which in turn had spawned and given credence to the pretensions of the various nationalities. To abandon the "state" that was their rational and customary home was for Seipel to destroy the organic consciousness of history. Yet to fulfill its historic mission, this state of Crownlands and nations needed not merely a reformed bureaucratic superstructure and particular, regional substructures but also a frank recognition of the concept of national (personal) autonomy. A resolution of the nationality problem must originate, therefore, from two directions: a consensus by the nations of the value of state apparatus that could rise above national difference, and a recognition by that state of the special individual and group-cultural interests of the nations.

Upon his permanent return to Vienna in October 1917, Seipel renewed his connections with several small circles of pacifists and liberal constitutionalists anxious to change the course of Austro-German politics. His close friendship with Heinrich Lammasch and Hermann Bahr and his cordial relations with Josef Redlich and other members of the Meinl Group made him part of that notable "third way" in Hapsburg politics of 1917–18 whose history has yet to receive a comprehensive and sensitive account.[236] Ernst Karl Winter has described them as "standing on the Right, but thinking on the Left."[237] But it was within the Church and the Christian Social party that Seipel's main activity lay. He joined Schindler as a member of the board of the *Reichspost* and developed a close political friendship with Heinrich Mataja, the young Catholic nationalist who spent 1918 challenging Richard Weiskirchner's authority in the city party. With Lammasch, Mataja, and Franz Sommeregger, the young *Volksbund* activist, Seipel traveled to Zurich in late January 1918 to participate in the Second International Catholic Union, where he met Karl Muth, Matthias Erzberger, and other German Catholic progressives seeking an end to the Armageddon. Most important, Seipel became an influential voice in the *Volksbund* in late 1917, participating in various informal discussions among its leaders, including the so-called "Pucher evenings" that were attended by Hildegard Burjan, Jakob Fried, Oskar Katann, Victor Kienböck, August Schaurhofer, Richard Schmitz, Alma Seitz, and Franz Sommeregger.

Seipel saw the *Volksbund* as a venue to reeducate the Christian Social party hierarchy on the issues of war and peace. He wrote to Lammasch in late December 1917, announcing his intention to hold a lecture series in the *Volksbund* on "world peace and state organization" for "Christian Social deputies, journalists and local leaders. . . . The purpose would be to educate our people, who do not really stand on the ground of the papal Peace Note as of yet, as to what the issues really are."[238] In late January Seipel would describe the "substantial upheaval in views" that had begun to take hold of Christian Social leaders who now "feel that a new orientation is necessary" but who either could not comprehend or dared not accept the full implications of such changes. Even Funder, as ardently Catholic as he was, still wore the blinders of the past:

> One can talk with Funder. I was astonished at how reasonably he could discuss Wilson and the prospects of world peace . . . but in his deepest heart he holds firmly to that which he feels is patriotic. He has, to be sure, good will, but [he] would have to change his mental outlook, and is hindered in this by the party, but even more by his constant worry to adopt views which will please the Court.[239]

Ever the rationalist, Seipel had stumbled upon issues which even he could not resolve. Customary dynasticism and social conservatism left many party leaders dangling, conscious of the failure of the *Octroi* but unclear as to what the Court wanted and uncertain how to formulate their own views. As early as October 1917 Seipel had been consulted informally by party leaders on various options for constitutional reform, and when, in the midst of the budget crisis and seeming collapse of parliament in February 1918 the parliamentary club established a fifteen-man Constitutional Committee to study proposals relating to constitutional reform, it was only natural that Seipel was included.[240]

In late February Seipel produced a two-page memorandum, the *Grundgedanken zur Verfassungsreform* which he hoped would serve as an outline to a final settlement.[241] Building on the concept of national autonomy, Seipel insisted on six propositions: that all administrative and representative institutions, insofar as settlement patterns and economic rationality permitted, be divided on national lines, beginning with the local communes; that the communes be united into larger municipal administrative districts (*Obergemeinden*), which in turn might have special administrative interrelationships with Crownland-level authorities, depending on the ethnic composition of the Crownland (Seipel left open the possible insertion of *Kreise* in some Crownlands, depending on economic and administrative necessities); that in administrative areas of mixed population where formal divisions were not possible, the personality principle (national self-identification on a national register) would be operative and that these national electoral groups would elect in turn national curias in the Diet which would have substantial responsibility for the cultural affairs of each ethnic group, including the school system; that these national bodies would also have the right to form working relationships with like national units from other regions for joint policy development; that the central parliament be retained, but the *Herrenhaus* converted into a house of national-interest representation; and finally, that a comprehensive administrative reform accompany the other structural changes, deemphasizing the dual-track nature of Austrian public administration by creating "mixed committees" in which officials of the state, the autonomous Crownlands, and professional politicians would cooperate on large policy issues.

Seipel's *Grundgedanken* found a more elaborate articulation in the work of his colleague and friend Franz Sommeregger. In late 1917 Sommeregger was commissioned by the party to prepare for private circulation a memorandum on "Constitutional and Administrative Reform" that offered comprehensive proposals for imperial reform. It is evident that Sommeregger was profoundly influenced by Seipel's ideas, and that the final version of his memorandum was, in intellectual terms, as much the product of Seipel as of its author. According to Seipel's private diary, Sommeregger submitted the first draft of his proposal to Seipel for vetting, and Seipel and Sommeregger met regularly throughout the winter of 1917–18 to discuss constitutional and other political issues.[242] Also during the winter of 1918 Sommeregger published four long articles in the *Reichspost* on the problems of constitutional and administrative reform in the Monarchy that functioned as glosses on and explications of his draft.[243] These materials offered both a serious alternative and a worthy successor to the German-national orientation of Weiskirchner and Gross.

Sommeregger began with two critical assumptions that had been missing in earlier war-aims calculations: that the achievement of an equitable, consensus-based reconstruction of the Monarchy was a necessary condition for a successful peace settlement with the Allies; and that any such reconstruction must take as its a priori assumption the fact that no single ethnic group could be accorded political or administrative hegemony in the Monarchy.[244] With the selfish interests of pan-German theorists in mind, Sommeregger decoupled the Austrian war aims from German revanchism and repudiated the underlying assumptions of *Octroi* politics, namely, that the postwar world would be a haven for German hegemony. Sommeregger thus took a giant step toward reconnecting constitutional rationality with political reality in the winter of 1918. He further insisted that the idea of the Empire as a political and economic unit must remain unimpaired but that, in the classic conundrum of Liberal nationalist scenarios, national autonomy must be balanced against state centralization and traditional Crownland particularism. To accomplish this, Sommeregger constructed a system of precarious balances that rejected the extremes of pan-German hegemony and the Czech *Staatsrecht*. He also cleverly resolved the issue of constitutional versus administrative reform by collapsing the two in one large analytic project: *Verwaltungsreform,* by serving the interests of national autonomy, became ersatz constitutionalism; and *Verfassungsreform,* by creating spaces of political neutrality and equilibrium in place of national hatred, would prepare the way and provide the proper venue for modern administrative reform.

At the top of his system Sommeregger left the *Reichsrat* relatively untouched, with one important difference: the *Herrenhaus* would be converted into a modern upper house by severely restricting hereditary (aristocratic) appointments, in place of which the eight nationalities and occupational interest groups would find appropriate representation. Constitutionally, Sommeregger left the existing Crownlands in place, but his plan added to each Crownland with significant national minorities a system of personal identification (a national register, by which each adult would signify his or her national identity) and elected national curias, based in the Diet. To these national curias, constituted as independent subordinate corporations, would fall primary responsibility for and control over public school systems and other "cultural" institutions in the delineated territorial areas allotted to one or another nationality. The regional administrative mechanisms of those Crownlands with monolithic ethnic bases were left untouched, but power in the larger lands would be decentralized by a system of *Kreis* governance, both state-administrative and popularly elected. In Crownlands of mixed ethnicity these *Kreise* would be nationally demarcated. In the emphasis which he placed on the *Kreise* Sommeregger diverged from Seipel's earlier draft. He did accept, however, Seipel's idea of *Obergemeinden,* but subordinated them to Crownland and *Kreis.*

Equally important was Sommeregger's scheme for administrative reform. Arguing that the existing system of top-heavy state supervision and dual-track administration in the provinces was inefficient and prone to political lapses, he suggested that more of the agendas of policy-making and implementation be accorded to regional administration (from Vienna) and that in all Crownlands a system of what he called "mixed" authorities (*Gemischtbehörden*) be developed, which would bring together officials of the *Statthaltereien* and the autonomous Crownland bureaucracies in some regular and prescribed manner (which he did not elaborate). Rather than dualism, one would have a "mixed" system of administration. Like Seipel, Sommeregger also recognized ad hoc administrative organs (*Zweckverbände*) of a higher order to coordinate interregional ethnic policies.

Sommeregger's overview afforded a three-way compromise. To the Christian Socials he left the traditional prerogatives of their German Crownlands intact. The Sudeten Germans would receive their long-awaited national division of Bohemia into *Kreise,* but on terms that were less generous than those Baernreither had conceived and that might prove acceptable to the Czechs (the Diet as a plenary body would retain much of its existing financial and administrative authority); German *Mittelschule* students would be forced to study a second language (presumably Czech) in school; and minority schools in mixed-language areas were, at least in principle, guaranteed by law (thus eliminating the possibility of a *Lex Kolisko*). The reform of the *Herrenhaus* into a house representing national and corporate interests might also secure for the Slavs a more prominent role in national legislative development. In sum, Sommeregger's proposal was antithetical to Czech *Staatsrecht* claims, but it was also at odds with the spirit, if not entirely with the letter, of the *Octroi.*

Sommeregger's (and Seipel's) drafts were remarkable instruments of reform, even if they did contain various logical and substantive fallacies (Sommeregger, for example, skirted the issue of the internal official language [*innere Amtssprache*] of public bureaucracies on the Crownland level, leaving his discussion of the public status of various languages curiously inadequate). Their work on the Constitutional Committee ultimately came to nothing, however. Although it met regularly during the late winter and spring, by the summer of 1918 the committee was vegetating, as the majority of the party awaited events, unwilling to abandon long-held prejudices in favor of new ideas sponsored by Seipel. Even Mataja, who shared so many interests with Seipel, found it difficult to accept the full implications of Seipel's political pacifism.[245] To Seipel's dismay several leading Viennese Christian Socials led by Weiskirchner participated in Wolf's German *Volkstag* movement against the Austrian Slavs, organizing a rally in Vienna on June 16 where Weiskirchner denounced those spreading "treason and disloyalty."[246] Several days earlier Weiskirchner had proclaimed that the recent meeting of the two Emperors at the German military headquarters would ensure to the Austro-Germans "a leading role" in the Empire.[247] Such rhetoric clearly reflected the misleading glow of the early June 1918 military successes of the Central Powers—which, in the case of the Austrian front in Italy, soon proved quite chimerical—and Seipel trenchantly rebuked such collaborationism in *Volkswohl,* chiding the Germans for evincing a national chauvinism they had always condemned in the Slavs, and for placing the interests of their putative *Volk* over those of the *Gesamtstaat* as whole.[248] To Lammasch he could not disguise his shock over the moral failure of the Germans—many of them of his own party—to accept the desperation of their common condition: "Just how necessary it is that one now with all possible means commit oneself for the Emperor and thus for Austria, we saw yesterday once again at that totally monstrous *Volkstag.*"[249]

In August 1919 Ignaz Seipel drafted a private memorandum analyzing the failure of constitutionalist efforts in 1918. The German parties bore the greatest guilt, he insisted, and within the Christian Socials he cited the new chairman, Johann Hauser, as having been particularly intractable.[250] According to Seipel, Hauser exercised "passive resistance" against the committee, and when Seipel urged Hauser to put pressure on the Emperor to move ahead, Hauser openly refused, suggesting that nothing should be done until after the war or at least until the Cabinet was ready. Since Weiskirchner was equally ambivalent, the committee was doomed to fail. Later, beginning in April 1918, the Christian Socials and German Nationals held joint committee sessions on constitutional reform, but attendance was poor on both sides; Seipel again sought to convince his party colleagues of the unavoidability of national autonomy, but by the time he had finally succeeded, the fall of the Monarchy was imminent. Some, like Leopold Kunschak, profited from their war experiences. Against Weiskirchner's German nationalism the Laborite proclaimed in June 1918 that

> German Austrians must give up their *Lieblingsgedanken* of being the dominant nationality in Austria, and view their duty as trying to remain the leading nation; for today Austria is democratized and parliamentarized, and above all else numbers count, and before the law of numbers the Germans cannot prevail, since the majority of the voters are not German.[251]

But Kunschak remained, as usual, in the minority. Seidler's blundering also contributed to the chaos, and, although Seipel was too discreet to admit this, so too did the adolescent meandering through these complex issues by an Emperor whose earnestness everyone appreciated, but whose authority few took seriously.

Seipel and his *Volksbund* allies were not inactive, however, and, together with Heinrich Mataja, held meetings in the summer and early autumn of 1918 to discuss the one front where they might exercise influence, the internal reorganization of the Christian Social party.[252] Here too, until Weiskirchner and the *Bürgerklub* were discredited by the revolutionary chaos of the autumn, little could be done, but it was apparent from the new vigor and confidence manifested in the pages of the *Volkswohl* throughout 1918 that the young turks saw the day of their political and intellectual fulfillment as imminent.

Just as the Social Democratic Left gained vigor with each new disaster after January 1918, so too did the Christian Social "Left"—as ironic as it may be to associate Seipel and Mataja with such a rubric. In Otto Bauer's case, however, such energy had an immediate impact on the Social Democratic party hierarchy, whereas Seipel and his colleagues in *Volkswohl* did not break into the inner sanctums of party power until very late in 1918. Their "Left" was profoundly conscious of the valued weight of history and they, somewhat earlier than their Austro-Marxist peers, manifested a new sobriety of tone distinct from prewar social militancy. This transformation was inevitable in view of the fact that Seipel, Sommeregger, and Mataja sought to establish the intellectual groundwork for postwar reconstruction by emphasizing normative continuity rather than revolutionary discontinuity. A new spirit of progressive centrism in social policy, linked to a rigorous Catholicism *and* anti-Semitism in ideological terms, would form the core of bourgeois strategy against Austro-Marxism. Richard Schmitz, who like Otto Bauer had spent most of the war in military service away from Vienna, returned in April 1918 to resume his leadership in the *Volksbund*. In May 1918 Schmitz drafted a new theoretical program for the group, which he evidently hoped to impose upon the mother Christian Social party as well.[253] In addition to generous programs of labor protection, social welfare systems, land and housing reform, and redistributive taxation, Schmitz foresaw modern policies of *Mittelstand* credit and investment and state assistance to Austrian peasant cultivators. The former preoccupation of the *Volksbund* with the working and white-collar classes was now broadened to include former clients of the Lueger coalition.

Schmitz's rhetoric, moreover, now resembled that of Seipel's constitutionalism in its genteel corporatism and organicism. For Schmitz the postwar state would be infused with "an organic concept of community" against both the class conflict of the socialists and the anarchic individualism of the Liberals. Neither the individual nor the class, but the family and the supranational state of corporate peoples would define and defend human dignity and progress. Although he claimed this concept would also resolve the nationalities question, it was much more directly aimed at a state with a single ethnic base in which the major axis of conflict would be with the Social Democrats. Indeed the national premises of the program were the most puzzling. Schmitz admitted that no *Volkstum* could exploit or culturally absorb another, hence eliminating a linguistically integrated society, and that the richness of the supraethnic state (following Seipel) derived from its ethnic diversity. Yet he could not resist according to the Germans the role of leadership of the multiethnic state. Nor was Schmitz reticent in attacking the "new riches" of the war profiteers, most of them (he insisted) Jews. This incremental anti-Semitism constituted a transparent reversal of earlier *Volksbund* praxis that had downplayed Jew-hatred, and provided a sign that the group now measured its effectiveness in appeals to a more diverse (and in 1918 far more impoverished) middle-class audience.

Franz Sommeregger also assayed the future of postwar society in a critique of the analytic construct of "war-socialism." In tones of ambivalence similar to those of Rudolf Hilferding, Sommeregger admitted both the logic of an evolutionary development toward "moderate, relative state socialism" (against the "socialist utopian state"), but he emphasized also the independent reality of political force—what he called "the *Realpolitik* of life"—with which Catholics must concern themselves. If one set of "political power factors" (the new socialist party) could impose its vision on society, then Christian social theorists must sponsor their vision of what for Sommeregger was an organic, solidarist program of social planning for postwar reconstruction.[254]

Indeed what was so shocking about the approaches of Schmitz and Sommeregger, organicist theory aside, was their tactical similarity to certain strains of Central European Marxist thought. Like Hilferding, they measured the new society not by mere wage levels or tax reforms but as a subject to be constructed with specific ethical values. This made the collision between the

Volksbund and Austro-Marxists all the more explosive, for it accentuated the fact that the two sides were divided less on issues of "social planning" and social policy (although there were acrimonious differences) than on culture, law, and political values—or, in the context of the transitory symbolism of November 1918, on the alternative of Monarchy versus Republic.

The Party and the Home Front

For those who remained behind in Vienna, the experience of the war was as disruptive and traumatic as for those at the Front, but in more subtle, less violent ways. Whereas the outer front was defined by fear, exhaustion, and a pendulum of boredom and death, the "inner front" was marked by social displacement, malnutrition, hunger, and, for the middle classes, profound status anxiety.[255] From the first months of the war the Christian Socials realized that the food issue would determine their fate, and in a superficial sense the history of the war in Vienna was the history of municipal food provisioning. But other forms of deprivation soon matched the expressiveness of food loss, and other forms of social change soon bedeviled formerly stable and prosperous electoral constituencies of the Christian Socials, to the point where by 1918 no one, least of all the party leadership, could be certain that the *Bürgertum* of Lueger's epoch would actually survive the war, in discursive, economic, or political terms.

Food provisioning for the city suffered from the same disorganization, mismanagement, and faulty planning that characterized much of the Austrian domestic war administration.[256] Since early expectations were for a short war, no long-range planning for food procurement and distribution was in place in 1914. In late November 1914 price controls were established for cereal and flour, but not until 1915 did the Cabinet consent to introduce tougher regulatory measures aimed at controlling wholesale production of basic foodstuffs. When the need for such war economy measures was felt (spurred by runs on stores in early 1915 and incessant shortfalls in Hungarian and Galician grain and meat shipments to Austria), the Austrian response was a complex system of rationing and the establishment of control commissions with public power, but staffed by men drawn from the private sector, to regulate the procurement and wholesale distribution of food and other crucial consumer products (the so-called *Zentralen*): a system so haphazard and so improvisational that the cure was often felt to be worse than the disease. That some members of the latter commissions were wealthy Jewish merchants and bankers afforded the more malicious among the Christian Socials with perfect targets for abuse—by 1917 their popular signification was "schools for Jews."[257] Not until midway in the war, after intensive political rivalries between the various ministries had finally been overcome, was a central coordinating body for food procurement and price policy established, the *Amt für Volksernährung*.[258] This office, according to its historian, became a political football, having three different directors in less than two years and suffering from a lack of organizational independence, subject as it was to the office of the Minister-President for its authority. While Germany's *Kriegsernährungsamt* had dictatorial powers, the Austrian *Ernährungsamt* lived a dubious existence, fighting for its legitimacy against jealous civil servants in the older ministries and against imperious staff officers from the High Command.[259] The city administration, in turn, found itself trying to enforce the growing web of state regulations and administrative interventions in food procurement and distribution that Weiskirchner knew only too well would produce backlashes in public opinion. At the *Reichspost*, Funder tried to deflect criticism of the city by ranting against price gougers guilty of "high treason," but reliance on such rhetoric for long stretches of time was neither politically palatable nor successful.[260]

Equally significant, none of these control structures had any authority in Hungary, which steadfastly maintained a distinct war-economy administration. Austria had long been dependent on Hungary and Galicia to cover its own net domestic deficit in food provisioning. Not only did shipments from Galicia stop early in the war, but beginning in early 1915 Hungarian shipments to Austrian cities began to dwindle as well, leading Richard Weiskirchner to blast alleged Hungarian recalcitrance in a speech before the Landstrasse political club *Eintracht* in late March 1915.[261] It is undeniable that Hungarian deliveries of cereal products shrank drastically during the war, from 14,000,000 meterzentner in 1913 to less than 300,000 in 1917. Shipments of meat, dairy products, and potatoes suffered similar catastrophic declines.[262] Officially the Hungarians justified this collapse by citing the pressures of military provisioning and declines in domestic production. It was certainly the case that a series of disappointing harvests, together with bad climatic conditions in 1916 and 1917 and chronic shortages in agricultural manpower, created disadvantageous conditions that made many Hungarians miserable, both in Budapest and in the countryside.[263] Still, for many Viennese their "enemy" in the war lay not in the west or south but down the river in Budapest. Stung by a comment in July 1917 by the Hungarian Food Minister to the effect that it was the incompetence of the municipality that had led to severe food shortages in Vienna, the Christian Social city fathers reacted in outrage. By late 1917 Weiskirchner was regularly playing upon popular anti-Magyarism to excuse the city's inability to provide adequate food provisions:

> Our relationship with Hungary is untenable. One can see that by looking at the two ministers of food supply. The one from the other side of the Leitha [the Hungarian Johann Hadik] is a chubby, well-fed

man; our Minister Höfer looks like a withered almond. Hungary is said to have earned 15 million from Austria during the war, and out of spite they are more interested in seeing us starve to death than the English are. . . . The time has come to shout a serious warning across the Leitha: "take heed for the future: the war will not last forever."[264]

Retail prices for key commodities such as bread, potatoes, and milk more than quadrupled during the course of the war. For many products, supplies simply gave out: officially the city followed a "two meatless days" per week policy, but for many in Vienna the week consisted of seven such days. Until mid-1916 supplies from Rumania covered part of the shortfalls from Hungary, but with the declaration of war on Austria by Rumania in August this source of supply vanished. The years 1917 and 1918 thus became years of hunger and near-starvation. Average daily food consumption for adults in the city by mid-1918 was officially estimated at only two-thirds of that in Budapest, based on official ration allowances. These allowances were unable to provide even the minimal caloric values required by adults in nonstrenuous occupations (2,500 daily). Arnold Durig's investigations in later 1918 suggested that the maximum legal caloric value of an individual's food ration cards in Vienna (at a time when most available goods were rationed) was 716 calories per day. In Berlin and Munich, in contrast, the same ration cards provided almost 1,400 calories.[265] By 1918 the only possible means to supplement diet were illegal: the black market or other dubious transactions, such as lengthy trips into the countryside where truck farmers, who even in the face of legal retribution refused to bring their wares into market, sold food that Viennese consumers would "buy at any price."[266] A report on the food crisis submitted to the Military Chancellory in November 1917 argued that

> the general mood of the population is poor, no, it is miserable! And it is not only miserable among the working class, but especially among the middle classes, and indeed among military forces stationed in the interior. All the signs of a desperate resignation are evident, and the smallest provocation—a chance slackening in the supply of coal or potatoes—will be the last straw and lead to a conflagration, which will not be able to be contained by force, because force leads to counterforce.[267]

A police report on the market situation in the spring of 1918 would conclude that "a great part of the population is literally starving and finds itself defenseless before the greatest deprivations."[268] Food disturbances and eventually riots became the principal leitmotif in the confidential reports of the police on the mood of the population. More scarcities and surges of panic buying in February and March 1915 forced the introduction of bread and flour rationing. By January 1916 the police reported frequent disputes among customers in markets and stores, as people began to gather on cold winter nights at 2 or 3 A.M. before *Ankerbrotfilialen* to wait for the doors to open four hours later. Meat was "unobtainable" for most people, who now consumed mainly vegetables and coarse bread. The police noted ominously (for the Christian Socials) that "as a result of the conditions there exists an enormous dissatisfaction with the alleged inaction of the municipal officials and with the parliamentary deputies."[269] In the spring of 1916 rioting broke out in markets in Favoriten, Rudolfsheim, and other working-class districts, as angry women protested soaring prices and lack of supply. Such disturbances were repeated in September, as thousands of people left the shops each day having failed to purchase basic commodities. Workers in local factories began staging wildcat strikes over the food shortages, leading the Police President to warn that "in view of the existing mood of the population, it is not to be excluded that, if the unfavorable provisioning situation endures, serious disturbances and demonstrations on a large scale might take place."[270] A report of mid-March 1917 noted that in addition to the desperate food-supply situation, rumormongering had begun to the effect that a hunger typhus was about to plague the city. By the early spring of 1917 the police could not help but notice the parallels between events in Vienna and St. Petersburg, including frequent shouts of "Let's go into the [inner] city!"[271] At one food riot in Favoriten, exclamations were heard that "We don't want war! We are hungry and we want to eat!"[272] As a troop of captured Russian prisoners of war was escorted through the district of Meidling in mid-May, passersby began handing the prisoners money, and when the guards intervened to stop them, the crowd shouted "Pfui—down with the war, if there is nothing to eat!"[273] Even the Emperor was caught up in the turmoil. A crowd of sixty women tried to enter his residence at Laxenburg in early April 1917 to explain their grievances about food. When Karl began giving small gifts of food to villages around the palace, the police saw this as a dangerous precedent since it would provoke women elsewhere in the province to beg for food.[274]

The cumulative impression of such random events must be considered in explaining the sudden repudiation of the German-national *Octroi* strategy by Karl and Czernin in mid-April. The massive worker protests of mid-January 1918, where over 110,000 workers engineered a spontaneous general strike, were the climax of popular outrage over food shortages and the failure of the peace initiatives, even if detestation of the war was present in the Viennese mind long before the labor violence of January. The mass syndicalism of the January strikes, occurring without and in many cases against the Social Democratic leadership, challenged the leadership of both the socialists and the Christian Socials. For the former it dramatized the irrevocable need for peace on any terms; for the latter it signalled that the *Vaterstadt* no longer belonged to them.[275] Even the presence of the army in Vienna assumed new aesthetic dimensions. Franz Ferdinand's once proud source of state sovereignty and dynastic integrity was now "represented" in the spring of 1918 by impoverished enlisted men on leave in the capital who made nuisances of themselves by standing in front of the various public war kitchens, by making insulting remarks about their officers, and by begging for money door-to-door.[276]

The High Command's ruthless policies on food and matériel procurement contributed to the crisis, since military supply agencies intervened in domestic wholesale markets to snap up huge quantities of supplies, without effective coordination between them and their civilian counterparts. No prewar plans existed for such coordination in August 1914, and none were developed during the course of the conflict. Instead, a veritable administrative guerila war between the military and the *Amt für Volksernährung* developed for access to scarce supplies.[277] Inevitably the military seemed to come out ahead. Durig found that the nutritional state of the wounded and sick in Austrian military hospitals in Austria in 1918 was higher than that of the average civilian adult population of Austrian cities.[278] And police reports indicated that threats to draft striking workers into active military service were actually counterproductive, for many "agitators" actually preferred the relative prosperity of military provisioning to the desperate civilian rations they could obtain. Nor was food the only source of contention. Richard Weiskirchner found himself having to beg the High Command in 1917 to give back to the Viennese market a small percentage of the leather they had stockpiled, lest Viennese shoemakers go bankrupt.[279]

The war severely disrupted conventional retail sales markets and personal goods industries, as well as destabilizing the commercial housing market. The state's recognition of consumer organizations as agencies for food distribution—most notably the Social Democratic purchasing cooperatives and hundreds of war kitchens (*Kriegsküchen*)—and the introduction in late 1916 of compulsory distribution, based on place of residence (*Rayonierung*), through specified retail outlets led to the impoverishment and in many cases bankruptcy of small retailers, many of whom before 1914 had been reliable Christian Social voters.[280] By 1918 over 600 restaurants in Vienna had closed their doors. The system of rationing introduced in March 1915 (first restricted to bread and flour, but soon expanded to include meat, milk, potatoes, sugar, coffee, fats, and other key items) did not prevent the growth of a huge network of illegal peddlers and black marketeers, who also siphoned off conventional customers.[281] Declining food stocks, often of dubious quality, also led to dissension between the Christian Social party and its traditional client groups in the food-processing industries. Bread flour was consistently "devalued" by admixtures of maize and other near inedibles, so much so that by 1918 travelers in Vienna described local bread as being "nauseating."[282] When Mayor Weiskirchner chastised Viennese bakers in 1915 for producing bread that threatened their "fine old reputation," a representative of the bakers' guild angrily rejected the mayor's comments as gratuitous and implied that if Weiskirchner wanted better bread, he should provide the bakers with better flour.[283] Nor did the party escape regional political dimensions of the food crisis. When the Lower Austrian *Statthalterei* announced in 1916 tough enforcement procedures to force local farmers to market the grain that many of them were hoarding as a way of providing Vienna with more bread, the urban and rural interests of the Christian Social party headed in utterly divergent directions. Some of the most bitter criticism of the Imperial Austrian administrative state (and of the Dynasty behind that state) evident by 1918 emerged in Christian Social agrarian ranks.[284]

Shortages in wood, cloth, and leather led to underemployment or total production stoppages in other business sectors traditionally loyal to the Christian Socials. The artisan trades and small shopkeepers were especially hard hit. Clothing prices soared as stocks declined, with the cost of a man's suit rising fivefold between 1914 and 1917. Leather supplies became desperately low by 1917, and few new shoes were available for any price in Vienna (except in government offices, where senior civil servants managed to obtain stocks for purchase by their own subordinates).[285] Since military procurement officials preferred both the standardization and the volume of mass- or factory-produced items, even the "opportunities" of the war economy proved highly disadvantageous to older craft industries. Many small and medium-sized retail shops found their credit exhausted and could not afford to stock sufficient consumer articles even when they were available.[286] Nor were the artisans the only middle- or lower-middle-class victims of war mobilization. The imposition of rent controls on selected private apartment buildings in January 1917, ordered by the Cabinet to ease working- and lower-middle-class fears of massive housing displacements and the pressure of soaring rents (and as a goodwill gesture toward the tens of thousands of military dependents living in large cities), put the Christian Social landlords in a vicious mood.[287]

The distress of white-collar employees on fixed salaries, who faced the massive inflation in food, clothing, and (until 1917) housing costs, could be dealt with more directly, and most governmental agencies allocated their civil servants emergency salary supplements (*Kriegszulagen*). After foot-dragging by Stürgkh, who initially opposed across-the-board salary supplements, state employees received six such supplements (August 1915; February 1916; December 1916; June 1917; December 1917; and July 1918), while municipal employees received similar benefits.[288] Even so, many of these men remained embittered over the government's "favoritism" for the working classes, especially its special ad hoc concessions in wages and in food provisioning to workers in war-related industries. Typical was the complaint submitted to Gustav Gross in January 1916 that provincial authorities in Bohemia were privileging working-class *Konsumvereine* as opposed to individual members of the middle classes in the distribution of food.[289]

The very meaning of money changed, as the crown's value quickly became devalued and the pattern of prewar economic transactions collapsed, being replaced by new, arbitrary schemes of "privilege." A worker with "less" money might obtain "more" food or other goods than a *bürgerlich* family forced to stand long hours outside a market store, simply because of the organizational exigencies of the food distribution system, or because of the special ration allocations introduced for the poorest strata (*Mindestbemittelten*) in July 1917.[290] By April 1918 the police would argue that the mood of the middle classes was even more negative than that of the poorer elements.

> The most bitter complaints are found in the *Mittelstand*. Those on fixed salaries are always complaining that the worst burdens have been shoved off on them. The rich are, they argue, in a position to buy goods, even if at exorbitant prices, whereas the workers, who get continual wage raises and who are given access to food supplies, are also somewhat cared for. Only the *Mittelstand* finds no help. Oppressive hardship reaches up into the so-called "better circles" and displeasure over the unbearable circumstances spreads more and more.[291]

But the war's force was even greater, as it undermined or challenged status expectations and status presumptions. It became far more difficult for *bürgerlich* strata to maintain "proper" prewar social distance from the working class, in emotional or even basic physical terms. A bitter protest by various Christian Social civil servant organizations in Vienna to the Ministry of Internal Affairs in April 1918 over the "grave injustice" of giving food to the consumer organizations argued not only that this "privileged" system was characterized by "inequality and injustice"; the officials also insisted that their corporate authority (*Standesautorität*) and professional dignity prevented them or their family members from "queueing up" for food along with lower classes at public markets and that "we are no longer able to use servants for this purpose because of our poverty."[292]

Such protests signaled, moreover, a process of intraclass civil war which set one fearful, envious *Mittelstand* group against another, and individual members of the middle classes against the growing web of corporatist organization of civil society. When the government finally gave in to complaints of the civil servants and allowed them to establish their own collective purchasing and distribution organizations, merchant groups were outraged. The Chamber of Commerce in Brünn protested against the "most recent exemption of a large class of people from the general food supply plan" which was bound to injure local merchants, who had already lost their proletarian customers and who were now dependent on middle-class customers for their survival. Equally important, the artisans, small shopkeepers, and private officials would be discriminated against if other strata in the *Mittelstand* were given privileges denied to them.[293] As food and clothing grew more scarce in 1917 and 1918, each particular interest in the *Bürgertum* found reasons to justify seizing petty advantages over its former class colleagues. Surpassing other civil servant self-representations, the Viennese police force found an especially effective form of pressure: they insisted that they needed special food rations because, given their duty of inspecting retail markets for price conformity and preventing illegal trade, they could not be expected to undertake such tasks in a responsible fashion unless they were provided with extra food themselves.[294]

Seemingly petty issues illuminated the collapse of internal social "boundaries" in the metropolitan center. This was clear, for example, when a shortage of equipment and coal led to a substantial curtailment of public transportation in Vienna in early 1917. The *Strassenbahn* ran only a few hours a day, and the number of streetcar stops was also restricted. The upshot was not only that well-to-do and poor suffered the same constraints on their mobility but that, given the radical decline in private, horse-drawn coaches and automobiles, divergent social groups were now thrown together in massed, overcrowded public vehicles. Even operagoers now had to use the *Strassenbahn,* dressed in formal clothes as they sat next to charwomen and day laborers.[295] Ironically, the alternative to associating with workers was often to behave like workers. In January 1917 a group of *Mittelstand* women organized a common lunch kitchen, the *Gemeinschaftsküche des gebildeten Mittelstandes,* since they were unwilling to attend war kitchens frequented by women of the working class.[296]

As elsewhere in Europe, the threat to the *Bürgertum* was not merely class-based. As thousands of Viennese white-collar employees were conscripted into the army, the newspapers were filled with ads by employers seeking respectable employees for shops and businesses. Much of the slack in the labor force in the factories and in the commercial and mercantile sectors was taken up by women, leading both to uneasiness and even overt hostility toward women by traditional labor and political groups.[297] As women either joined the official labor force or labored "unofficially" by standing in queues for hours waiting for meager food allotments, women's attitudes changed drastically toward their social "betters." Popular resentment of aristocratic families and the newly enriched in Vienna who cheated on the rationing system was not concocted by wishful-thinking English intelligence agents.[298] The Viennese police acknowledged powerful resentment against wealthy women who still insisted on wearing jewelry and fancy accoutrements in public.[299]

Where poorer women were not available, employers could use school-children. Having lost over one-third of its municipal labor force to the army, the city was forced to send schoolchildren out into the streets to clear snow from streetcar tracks in early February 1917. The *Neue Freie Presse* might argue that this built character, but it was a sign of social disarray. Clothing prices reached such heights by 1917 that the police noted that many families could not clothe their children sufficiently to send them to school.[300] Confidential reports to the Cabinet charting a brutalization of the youth (*Verrohung der Jugend*)—high incidences of crime, sexual disturbances (homosexuality, prostitution, and other acts), and damage to property by adolescents and even children—offered a realistic portrait of the impact of the war on Viennese family life.[301] That such criminal behavior was now perpetrated by progeny of "good" *bürgerlich* families was yet another signal that the moral habitus of prewar society was being dissolved.[302]

The government's use of maximum price edicts not only failed to control market behavior but, when coupled with the overly complex system of ration cards, generated endless public cynicism about the force of administrative law. It also engendered a pattern of petty war profiteering in domestic retail items that the Christian Social newspapers loved to attribute to the Jewish refugees from the east who had fled to Vienna in 1914–15.[303] The presence of tens of thousands of these involuntary immigrants, who met with unceasing hostility (and occasional street violence) from the resident population, and the convergent myths (and often the reality) of price gouging and black marketeering were perfect stimuli to revive the liminal anti-Semitism that was a perennial part of the culture of the Viennese petty and middle bourgeoisie.[304] Even reform-oriented Christian Socials, like Leopold Kunschak, followed (and exploited) popular anti-Semitism. Kunschak insisted that "anti-Semitism is more justified now than ever before. Usury, price fixing and black marketeering are undertaken almost exclusively by Jews."[305] Corruption in food sales was not an exclusive responsibility of poor Jews, however. Even heavily censored Viennese newspapers carried regular reports of fraud in the food rationing system; it was an open secret that the wealthy in Vienna, more so even than in Berlin, could always find nourishing food on which to spend their war-inflated crowns. Nor was the civil service exempt from this morass. In October 1918 a *Hofrat* in the Railways Ministry, Johann Brejcka, was discovered to have "transferred" two railway cars of flour from Moravia to Vienna, where he intended to have it sold for 25 crowns per kilogram. Avarice was thus no stranger to the civil service.[306]

Those who suffered most were the very young and the very old. Although the study of wartime malnutrition and pediatric illnesses enhanced the collective, therapeutic role of Viennese medical science toward society, which the Social Democrats would greatly expand in the later 1920s, such scientific learning was possible (and necessary) only because of the extensive deprivations endured by children, adolescents, and the aged between 1915 and

1919.[307] Indeed, the war constituted nothing less than a biological catastrophe for the Viennese populace. Already in 1915 the birth rate began to drop sharply, while the civilian death rate soared. A birth deficit of 7,761 in 1915 rose to 25,443 in 1917 and 32,240 in 1918.[308] Malnutrition brought sundry diseases in its wake, most notably tuberculosis and rickets. Childhood mortality rates from tuberculosis more than doubled between 1914 and 1918; at the Viennese Children's Clinic tuberculosis was responsible for 69 percent of all deaths by 1918. Nine-tenths of all children admitted to the clinic in 1918 were officially classified as suffering from hunger.[309] The "hunger years" of 1917 and 1918 left a profound trail of social degeneration in their wake. Clemens von Pirquet's investigations into the health of 114,947 Viennese school children in 1920, undertaken in cooperation with the American Relief Administration, revealed the extent of the disaster: almost 80 percent of the children examined were seriously underfed, many on the verge of illness from chronic malnutrition. A similar investigation of 57,000 children in mid-1918 had arrived at virtually identical conclusions. One Viennese school teacher reported in despair the scenes in his classroom: "We teachers looked on helplessly while our students collapsed both psychically and physically. The fearful consequences of this dreadful war were brought home in our children: pallid faces, exhaustion, a shuffling pace, eyes without brightness, all these signs spoke of a lack of food, of bitter misery."[310] Class membership was a factor here too: the incidence of undernourishment revealed by Pirquet's investigations was greater as one moved from the inner districts and garden suburbs like Hietzing and Döbling to the working-class ghettos of Favoriten and Ottakring. When Austrian women gained the vote in 1919, the mothers of these hungry, sick children became a potent force at the polls.

The internal history of the Christian Social party in Vienna was closely associated with these social transformations in the temper of city life. Indifferent and overconfident in 1914–15, the party became progressively more acrimonious, divisive, and shame-ridden as the war dragged on. Weiskirchner's presence loomed large in the councils of the party throughout the period, but by late 1915 his bravado and tireless efficiency began to suffer under the strains of constant food shortages, and he now found himself on the defensive as his public pronouncements became both more contradictory and less credible. In their press and in the closed rallies they managed to hold, the Social Democrats cleverly began in mid-1915 to blame the Christian Socials for food shortages in Vienna. This was the first breach of the so-called *Burgfriede,* since it transformed the food problem from a question of administrative possibility into one of political volition. The socialist stratagem was also a covert means of regenerating their own faltering party organization by reviving one of their classic propaganda issues—hatred of the "clericals." Although the police were instructed to intervene if the attacks became too crude, the Christian Social party leadership officially protested in October 1915 that too little censorship was being imposed on the Social Democrats in their attacks on the municipality. The Christian Socials realized, however, that the censor could hardly protect them from the negative publicity concerning hunger; this was revealed by a secret meeting between the party and the leaders of the *Nationalverband* in November 1915 to find ways to remedy the Cabinet's bungling of the food issue.[311] The nationalists too were ready to make food a politicum, from their own self-interest and as repayment for the Christian Socials' accommodation on war aims in September.

But the events of 1915 dramatized the larger dilemma of the party in Vienna: how was it to react to a dreadfully unpopular war that the party had originally claimed was legitimate and for which it continued to bear administrative responsibility? Having less pride or place to lose, Leopold Kunschak and the Christian Social Laborites had a somewhat easier path to self-abnegation, and Kunschak, once arrogantly proud of Austrian war achievements, did not scruple in the autumn of 1917 to plead for an honorable and just but above all quick peace.[312] Richard Weiskirchner, however, was caught in the web of public expectations he had woven for himself early in the war. In April 1915 he could still publicly affirm his loyalty and "gratitude" to Stürgkh,[313] but by late 1915 he began to speak out against the Cabinet, trying now to assert a "middle" stance between the people and Stürgkh, without impugning the legitimacy of the war itself.[314] This led in turn to open distrust of the mayor by leading members of the Cabinet, for, as Burián remarked to Stürgkh, "Weiskirchner no longer has the courage to stand up against his party comrades (butchers, bakers, shopkeepers, etc.)."[315]

Weiskirchner seized upon the Jews as a convenient scapegoat, as did many other *bürgerlich* politicians, but his broader views of war politics were curiously inconsistent. His opponents in the party accused him of hypocrisy on the Jewish issue—denouncing Jewish corruption but consorting with wealthy Jews privately. He never ceased to insist, as he noted in 1916 before a gathering of Christian Social women, that "he would tolerate no politics in the war." Politics had ended in 1914.[316] This was not merely empty *Burgfriede* rhetoric; rather it became the essence of Weiskirchner's own political identity, for his ultimate excuse now became his status as an honest civil servant, worthy of public gratitude and even sympathy, buffeted by larger forces beyond his or the municipality's control.[317] A weak, indecisive government that hamstrung a well-meaning mayor and, as one of Weiskirchner's cronies argued, treated the city "like some obscure village" was the real source of Vienna's misery.[318]

Within his party Weiskirchner's recipe was "more of the same": hold fast to present institutions and avoid radical changes. Hence his defensive views on suffrage reform. Both the democratic aura of the war and the electoral message of June 1911 argued for the expansion of universal suffrage to the municipalities and for proportional representation by list voting. Yet when Gessmann and Liechtenstein proposed proportional voting in 1917, Weiskirchner and the Viennese *bürgerlich* faction gave their grudging support on the condition that Vienna's municipal franchise be exempted from any reform (beyond the Fourth Curia). Nothing could disrupt the curial system, even though its socioeconomic preconditions—a stable and predictable *Bürgertum*—were quickly going by the board. Later negotiations between the *Bürgerklub* and the socialist faction in the City Council for a reform of the municipal suffrage proved equally unproductive, given the intransigent stance adopted by the Christian Social negotiators.[319]

From one perspective Weiskirchner's views had a basic rationality since, as the police noted, most people in Vienna had long abandoned illusions of partisanship in preference to finding food for themselves. Many ceased to care about the war. The police reported in 1917 that "quite often one hears the expression that prolonging the war under such conditions is impossible, and the previous sacrifices have all been in vain . . . little attention is paid to the events at the Front." The Emperor's controversial amnesty proclamation in July 1917 was generally ignored in the city: "Only in the German-oriented and more intelligent circles of Vienna has the edict produced an outraged, indeed embittered reaction."[320] The Lower Austrian *Statthalter* reported in August 1917 that public "interest in the events of the war has dramatically receded. . . . Public opinion is thoroughly preoccupied with the [current] economic misery."[321] In May 1918 the police even reported substantial public sympathy for Emperor Karl in his "Sixtus Letter" conundrums, suggesting that it was mainly among the minoritarian "German-national" circles of the intelligentsia that he was discredited.[322] Since part of the putative clientele of the Christian Social party lay precisely in these "more intelligent circles," however, some militants felt that a more activist stance had to be adopted. More important, the continued incursions of the Social Democratic and the Liberal press against the party, which attained dramatic proportions after the police relaxed the controls on political rallies and censorship in mid-1917, suggested to many party leaders that the *Burgfriede* had become a cruel farce.[323]

In 1917 Weiskirchner's supremacy began to face serious internal challenges. At a conference of all elected officials of the party called in January 1917 to discuss the state of the party organization, Franz Spalowsky, one of Kunschak's lieutenants in the Laborite movement, delivered a stunning critique of the degeneration of party life.[324] Spalowsky admitted that objective circumstances existed that had led to difficulties: party activists had been drafted, thus reducing the effectiveness of many local organizations, and the party's elected officials were overburdened and exhausted by war work, which left them little time for or interest in party affairs. More important, the party was held responsible for the misguided policies of the state in food provisioning and other war sectors, leading to massive voter disenchantment with the Christian Socials. Still, such excuses could range only so far, and Spalowsky noted that "the present condition of the party is a strong admonition that we have to dedicate more attention to the work of the party in the future than we have in the recent past." Spalowsky then described the disarray into which the Vienna party had fallen under Weiskirchner's wartime leadership. In many districts of the city only one general assembly of party loyalists had been held since the beginning of the war (some districts had held no rallies at all). Also "the connections between the elected officials of the party and the voters are disappearing." In some wards the city councilmen had no idea what was happening in the district committees, and conversely, many instances occurred of local district notables making controversial decisions against the will of (or political interests of) the City Council. Local poor-care councillors who did not enjoy automatic membership on the district election committee were totally ignored by party higher-ups, even though they frequently had the most intimate connections with local voters and the best sense of popular moods. Spalowsky also noted, in what would become a constant refrain of the reformers, that the anarchy of rival political clubs in each ward did the party little good. Historic circumstances had led to each district having six or more competing political clubs, representing divergent factions or class interests in the ward. The 1912 party statute had simply confirmed these private preserves in their prerogatives and built a structure of bureaucratic control over them. But to the extent that their frequent feuds and petty enmities, as well as their questionable membership lists, wrought havoc in the work of the election committees, they were the Achilles' heel of the party.

Spalowsky thought that, ideally, all such clubs should be merged into one general political association in each ward; at the minimum, pressure should be brought to force coordinated planning by the clubs in place of the current "dirty competition" among them. Spalowsky's other suggestions were equally sensible—each election committee should be ordered to assemble on a monthly basis; each district should have regular party conferences; more frankly political agitation should begin, and the party should stop being deceived by the "slogan of the *Burgfriede*" that was simply self-deceptive. Finally, a more consciously programmatic orientation was needed to combat socialist propaganda, and this meant more emphasis on anti-Semitism, which was the most effective way to discredit the Social Democrats with their own voters: "Even the Social Democrats have not been able to dispel anti-Semitism from their voters." Anti-Semitism would become a magic wand to reconjure voter loyalty lost in the face of economic misery.[325]

Spalowsky's censures met with little response from Weiskirchner, who replied with banal comments on the value of sustaining party unity, loyalty, and friendship. Had such criticisms remained the sole property of the Laborites, who had their own vested interests in pushing structural reforms (a merger of all clubs in each ward, for example, would weaken the traditional *bürgerlich* elites who dominated the smaller organizations), nothing would have happened. But in the spring of 1917 another, more prominent member of the Viennese party became the spokesman for reform, Heinrich Mataja.[326] Mataja was a thirty-eight-year-old lawyer who had first entered Christian Social politics in 1906 by defending local politicians in libel trials. He was elected to the City Council in 1910 from the Landstrasse and was sufficiently ambitious to try (unsuccessfully) to win election as vice-mayor upon Josef Porzer's death in 1914. Although originally associated with German nationalist circles (he belonged to a nationalist fraternity at the University of Vienna, rather than a Catholic student club), Mataja caught Albert Gessmann's eye, and in line with his policy of sponsoring young university talent, Gessmann allowed Mataja to run in a Styrian district in the 1911 parliamentary elections. Although he lost miserably, Mataja's fine sense of political intrigue (Seipel once told him that he had a good "nose for politics") and immense energy merited him the chance to run in the parliamentary by-election in Leopoldstadt in October 1913. His victory showed both the initial success of Weiskirchner's reconstruction program and Mataja's ability to present himself as a forceful, dynamic spokesman for the Vienna party in national affairs.[327] Originally held in suspicion by Kunschak as yet another *bürgerlich* rival (in 1911 the Laborites had dismissed him as an opportunistic adventurer), Mataja proved to be a politician of greater ideological malleability than many Laborites had expected. He was genuinely religious, and the onset of the war led him to reemphasize his Catholic views, with which he managed to combine strident anti-Semitic rhetoric. He participated in both meetings of the International Catholic Union in Zurich, at the second of which he made contact with Ignaz Seipel. As noted above, he eventually broke with nationalist collaborationism, and by the spring of 1917 he was appealing for a more moderate and conciliatory war program toward the Austrian Slavs.[328] Mataja also advocated closer ties with the Alpine parties and the parliamentary club, and thus demonstrated that not all members of the Viennese party were necessarily afflicted with the "Rathaus" mentality of wanting or expecting to dominate the party from the center.[329] In his own peculiar way he was thus a "progressive" and a logical successor to Albert Gessmann, willing to bate the greedy civil servant groups who plagued the party during the war. His programmatic view of politics, however, including his rigid anti-Semitism, sharply separated him from both Weiskirchner and Gessmann.

Mataja had long been an advocate of party reform. As early as 1913 he published a pamphlet based on newspaper articles he had written on the need for reconstruction after the 1911 elections, which argued for a more comprehensive and effective organization than that existing under Lueger.[330] In February 1916 he presented a critique of the structural defects of the Viennese party at a closed party congress, which anticipated Spalowsky's later, more reproachful remarks. Like Spalowsky, Mataja thought that the clubs needed consolidation, but he went even further to argue that the party should have simply one association for the whole city.[331] Mataja also had a larger and more comprehensive sense of what should comprehend "politics." Similar to the Social Democrats (and to Richard Schmitz), Mataja thought the party was ignoring the potential of the sundry nonpolitical organizations to which its voters belonged. He had long believed that the party's membership base was too narrow, restricted as it was in formal terms to membership in a political club.[332] Mataja also urged the introduction of a "house system" in which each apartment house would have a designated Christian Social political operative who would report to and be held accountable by central party authorities, a plan that would deliver another blow to the exclusivity of the local clubs. Not unexpectedly, the most vociferous voices in support of Mataja's views came from the Christian Social Laborite leaders as well as the *Volksbund.* A natural convergence of "democratic" and "Catholic" interests was in the making.

As political life began to stir in January 1917 in the wake of Stürgkh's death and the onset of the *Octroi* machinations, Mataja wrote to Alois Liechtenstein, the nominal head of the Viennese party, urging that planning begin immediately to achieve necessary reforms, since "our enemies do not hesitate to pursue a covert but all the more intensive agitation from man to man . . . [while] the Christian Social party lacks an energetic emphasis on and implementation of its principles."[333] Neither Liechtenstein nor Weiskirchner took any immediate action, however, and by June 1917 Mataja initiated his own reform movement by inviting dissident leaders to a meeting to discuss ways to outflank the party leadership. Five sessions were held between June 23 and July 18 of this rump group, which consisted of marginal politicians (out of the fourteen people who attended the first session only one, aside from Mataja himself, was on the *Stadtrat,* and only three were city councilmen).[334] Beneath their extravagant "programmatic" discourse lay both greed and vanity. The most prominent renegades came from the Laborite faction, which was represented at several meetings by its leaders, Kunschak and Franz Hemala. Their discussions highlighted currents of bitterness that were doubtless representative of larger numbers in the party, but probably not of the party elite itself. Indeed Weiskirchner and the *engerer Parteirat* were objects of scorn throughout the meetings. Mataja declared openly on July 11 that

> I have changed my views since January. At that time I still believed that the *Parteileitung,* as it is presently constituted, could do something. Since then I have come to the conviction that among the leaders

there are those who have not the least interest in the fate of the party. We can't stop with sending a petition of protest; we have to try to work for a new party leadership.

This secessionist mentality was not supported by the majority—even Kunschak backed away from such brinkmanship—but the repudiation of Weiskirchner and the *Stadtrat* was explicit and intense. Schwarz from Maria-hilf complained on June 23 that "the way the party is presently led is a scandal and will lead only to its collapse. From the *Parteirat* one hears nothing at all." Rosenkranz from the Third District condemned as circuses the occasional meetings of officials that Weiskirchner summoned: "the greatest comedy is the party congresses. We need a man who has the courage to stand for anti-Semitism, then the masses will follow him. Weiskirchner's position is: after me the deluge!" Binder of the Landstrasse argued that "the current direction is really remarkable. One might note the letter of appreciation which District Leader Blasel [a Liberal from Leopoldstadt] sent to Weiskirchner—this gives one much to think about."[335] Resentment of Weiskirchner's accommodation towards wealthy Jewish circles in the city was foremost in the conspirators' minds, as well as demands that the "old program" of the party be restored, namely, anti-Semitism.[336]

This cult of anti-Semitism was notable, since in using it the "reformers" had to argue against and thus distort their own history. At the final meeting Franz Hemala summed up the inconsistency of this argument, since he admitted that the Christian Socials never had a real program of any kind, much less one based on anti-Semitism. What they had had was the person of Lueger:

The situation in which we find ourselves is the logical result of our circumstances. The party has no program, so that a candidate could always say "My program is Dr. Lueger." Had the party after Lueger's death developed a program, instead of engaging in personal squab-bles, things might not have gotten this bad. The party congresses are a lot of eyewash ... the only people who count for something in the party are those with official offices; the organizations are being re-pressed. The extent to which the mayor is deluded about the mood of the population is incredible. If one tries to tell him the truth, however, he sees this as a hostile gesture. . . . The party leaders must reestablish contact with the political organizations. If they are too tired and weak to do this, let them resign.[337]

Mataja's anti-Semitic fronde was a mélange of opportunism and conviction. To argue that Weiskirchner was insufficiently anti-Semitic was also to attack Lueger, since Lueger's evasiveness was simply emulated by his successor. But it was also to hit Weiskirchner at his weakest point, by pandering to the enormous outbreak of hatred of Jews in Viennese *kleinbürgerlich* circles in 1917 and 1918. Mataja's anti-Semitism was fueled by his ambition and unscrupulosity but also, apparently, by a genuine conviction that more Catholicism in the Christian Social party was logically consistent with more Jew-hatred. This was a grave heritage, shared in part by Ignaz Seipel, for the political culture of the First Republic.[338]

Mataja's own strategy in these meetings combined personal vindictiveness with proposals for substantive reform. It fell to Kunschak to urge that the dissidents try to work through conventional party channels, a tactic to which Mataja finally assented. Hence the group drafted a statement of protest which was sent to Liechtenstein in early September.[339] This memorandum, signed by leaders of fourteen associations as well as Kunschak for the Laborites, condemned the lack of anti-Semitism in the leadership ("in the Rathaus influential Jews and Jewish organizations enjoy the greatest influence"), as well as the "lack of energy of the party leadership" and urged the need for reform ("the life of the party is now totally foreign to the leadership. What is happening out in the wards . . . about that the leadership could not care less"). The memorandum became notorious when a copy of it got into the hands of a Liberal newspaper, the *Wiener Allgemeine Zeitung,* through the connivance of Leopold Blasel, Mataja's nemesis in Leopoldstadt politics. Within days all Vienna was speculating about a new round of gang wars in the party, similar to the Hraba-Vergani scandals of seven years earlier.[340] Even Weiskirchner and the elderly Liechtenstein now saw that the situation had gotten out of hand. The plenum of the party leadership met on September 11 and voted to summon a general party congress in January 1918 to discuss reforms to the party statute, as well as the creation of a formal statement of party principles.[341] Mataja seized control of the editorial process. He co-opted Franz Schindler to draft the statement of principles, while he personally rewrote the party statute, after soliciting suggestions from various party clubs and organizations in the late autumn of 1917. So diverse and mutually contradictory were these proposals, however, that the touted congress could not be held; the new program and statute were not ready until late February 1918.

Mataja's new statute sought to cure the ills of the party by merging authoritarianism and democracy into a leadership structure that Mataja recognized as provocative: this "more disciplined form of organization will meet strong resentment from many, many factions."[342] In a clever tactical move he left the existing club basis of the election committees untouched, but he forced onto the clubs public registration of membership, the records of which had to be submitted to the party leadership. For the first time in its history the Christian Social party would have an accurate measurement of its nominal membership, rather than the erroneous and often duplicitous "records" kept hidden in the various clubs. Membership on the district election committees would now be truly representative of relative numerical strength in the district, which would work to the advantage of Kunschak's forces. More important, Mataja seriously weakened the prerogatives of both the clubs and the election committees in favor of central party control from the Rathaus. Errant or rebellious clubs now might be expelled from the party; and the work of the election committees was made subject to strict supervision and investigation from the Rathaus, which might intervene to force laggard committees to take action. In place of the existing dual system of *weitere* and *engere Parteiräte,* Mataja weakened the former and abolished the latter, instituting a single *Parteileitung,* consisting of fifteen men, elected by a general party congress. The latter consisted of a delegation from each district election committee, whose size was based on the total number of club members in the district. The *Parteileitung* received virtual dictatorial powers in setting party policy and forcing discipline onto subordinate clubs and committees. The result, Mataja argued, would permit a "concentration of all forces in the party, which we desperately need to cope with the bitter struggles that lie before us."

In contrast to the novelty of Mataja's reforms, Schindler's program was a predictable mixture of the various platitudes that had served the Christian Socials so well over the past thirty years. It contained nothing novel, aside from an invocation of the necessity of allowing women into the political system (urged by the Laborites) and a plank on anti-Semitism that responded to the mob pressures of the war years by affirming the necessity of the general principle of resisting the influence of Jewry, but then restricting the focus of such opposition to "all legal means."[343] Although he was the intellectual father of more radical, programmatic thinkers, in 1918 Franz Schindler was a seventy-year-old prelate schooled in and loyal to Lueger's model of consensus and interest coalitionism. When called upon to bite the political bullet, he too fell back on past assumptions.

The reforms were debated by the *engerer* and the *weiterer Parteirat* beginning in March. At this point stalling commenced, and not until June were Mataja's and Schindler's drafts accepted for distribution to the ward election committees. Their reaction was predictably ambivalence or foot-dragging (especially on the issue of women's voting), and it was not until late August 1918 that the leadership felt itself in a position to move ahead.[344] In the interim Mataja had bullied Weiskirchner into supporting other minor reforms, such as establishing a party commission to hear public complaints about administrative failures of the *Magistrat* and imposing a tax on party functionaries to bolster the sagging revenues of the party's war chest (which met resistance in the *Bürgerklub*).[345] Weiskirchner gave in to Mataja's browbeating (including a remarkable incident of Mataja publicly chastising the mayor for publishing two newspaper articles in a "Jewish" newspaper, the *Wiener Tagblatt*).[346] Although Mataja planned a series of confirmatory meetings capped by a party conference in late September to launch his new statute, the collapse of the military front and the chaos of October intervened, making all such inner-party reform efforts moot. Mataja himself was appointed state secretary for internal affairs in the revolutionary government in late October and became preoccupied with the state crisis. The municipal party thus exited the war with the same deficient political structures that had been in place before 1914. More important, it ended the war having merited the censure, if not outright hatred, of the majority of the Viennese populace for their envelopment in the catastrophe. This was the profound illusion under which Heinrich Mataja and his co-conspirators suffered—organizational reforms, for all their persuasiveness, simply could not reverse by 1918 the currents of popular despair that the war had set in motion.

The November Revolution and
the Christian Social Party

The political history of the Austrian state in 1918 was both haphazard and demeaning, with one catastrophe following upon another. As Ernst von Seidler pushed a more "German" course in domestic politics—following that of Ottokar Czernin in foreign affairs after August 1917—his already fragile support in parliament drastically eroded. The young Emperor may have regretted this turn to the right, but in the aftermath of the Sixtus Affair he felt himself trapped.[347] Following the decision taken at Brest-Litovsk to award the Cholm district to the new Ukrainian state, the Polish Club rebelled against Seidler and went into the opposition, refusing to vote for the provisional budget. Christian Social leaders found that cooperation with more militant German national factions had little consequence for their most vital political concern—food. Their dilemma was apparent in the quietly dissenting tone that the Christian Social leadership took when Seidler adjourned parliament in early May 1918 and proceeded to poison the political well with his decree establishing the *Kreisregierungen* in Bohemia. In mid-June 1918 the Christian Social leadership once again split with the *Deutscher Nationalverband* by urging the Emperor to recall parliament immediately.[348] Parliament reopened in an atmosphere of chaos, with Wedel reporting to Berlin that he had been visited by several German nationalist hotheads, inquiring if they could count on German battalions to march into Austria in order to impose the kind of order they thought necessary.

Buffeted by intrigue among various German national groups and thoroughly discredited among Slavic politicians, Seidler finally resigned in late July 1918. He was succeeded by Max von Hussarek, a sober, clerically minded civil servant with long years of service as Minister of Education and informal connections to the Christian Social party. The pressures faced by Hussarek simply to keep basic administrative services functioning left him little room to maneuver. A conservative estimate by Wedel in mid-July suggested that two-thirds of the Austrian public openly or covertly favored the victory of the Allies.[349]

The collapse of Bulgaria on September 26, 1918, brought the revolution into full swing. Several days later Karel Kramář summoned a meeting of the Czech National Committee in Prague that ended in an official call for secession from the Empire. When parliament reopened in Vienna on October 2, the Czech and south Slav delegations were brutally critical of the Empire and supremely confident of independence. František Staněk spoke for his conationals when he asserted that "German and Magyar hegemony and coercion, which have so long repressed us, are already collapsing" and that "we want to be free of the dirt of Austro-Hungarian nationality politics. We want to save ourselves and our fellow nationals from this swamp. . . . We want to consolidate the energies of our people in our own political organization."[350]

For the Austro-Germans this meant inevitable segregation. On October 3 *bürgerlich* and Social Democratic deputies from both houses of parliament met to discuss a socialist resolution that affirmed the right of self-determination for other national groups but also demanded the "unification of all German areas of Austria into a German-Austrian state."[351] On October 8 the Christian Social leadership affirmed a similar statement, while also insisting on their "religious and dynastic conviction." Yet it was apparent from club debates that the majority of the parliamentary delegation viewed a German-Austrian state as a distinctly second-class alternative, and that they would accede to "self-determination" only if forced to do so by external events.[352] Nor were the socialists eager to rush forward. At a meeting of the party executive on October 11 Otto Bauer urged that it was "necessary that the party now explain clearly and specifically how, in the midst of disintegration, they imagine the new order [*Neuordnung*] of Austria." Karl Renner responded that "wide circles in the party would scarcely understand such a definitive decision" and urged that "we must therefore wait and see how the developments take place in the coming weeks."[353]

The final attempt of the Crown to stave off collapse came on October 16, when Karl issued his Peace Manifesto.[354] Hussarek was not enthusiastic, arguing that such a proposal was too little, too late, to satisfy the Czechs and Southern Slavs.[355] Although Hungary was exempted from the document, Budapest quickly declared that the legal basis of the 1867 Settlement had been rescinded.[356] Reactions in the press and among Austro-German political literati were harshly negative, but Wedel reported that many Viennese reacted with an air of bemusement, local wits calling the document the "Manischwach" rather than "Manifest."[357]

Although Hussarek was not responsible for the Peace Manifesto, its publication was the penultimate nail in his political coffin; Robert Lansing's note on October 19, recognizing a state of belligerency between the Czecho-Slovaks and the Austro-Hungarian Empire, nailed the lid down.[358] German nationalists screamed for Hussarek's head, even those who later hypocritically claimed that they would have been willing to coexist with Slavs in a federated state. Since the remaining Slavic politicians in Vienna also refused to work with Hussarek, the Emperor cast about for alternatives, including a remarkable offer of the Minister-Presidency to Karl Renner.[359] Finally, Heinrich Lammasch, a professor of international law at the University of Vienna and a confirmed Catholic pacifist throughout the war, replaced Hussarek on October 27. A decent, honest person, unfitted for the chicanery and pathos that was all that was left of the Imperial political system, Lammasch had long been connected with leading party figures. Along with several of his colleagues in the final Cabinet, notably Josef Redlich (Finance) and Ignaz Seipel (Social Welfare), Lammasch had been a key member of an informal circle of "loyal" opposition to the war led by Julius Meinl, a local businessman and civic leader.[360] Karl viewed Lammasch's appointment as a desperate chance to contain the explosions of nationalist particularism; Lammasch himself hoped only to preside over a more equitable territorial and military settlement. Yet the timing of the appointment rendered this goal absurd.

In the wake of the Emperor's Manifesto, the Czecho-Slovak National Council in Paris issued Masaryk's declaration of independence from the Empire on October 18. Even before this final blow, the Austrian Germans had decided to proceed on their own.[361] On October 21 the remaining German representatives of the *Abgeordnetenhaus* constituted themselves as a provisional National Assembly, establishing a twenty-member executive committee (*Vollzugsausschuss*) to make recommendations on the future constitution of the (rump) state. On October 30 this committee recommended that the National Assembly create a permanent German-Austrian State Council (*Staatsrat*). This Council in turn nominated the state secretaries of fourteen "state offices," most paralleling the old Imperial ministries. In effect, German-speaking Austria now had two sovereign governments.

The reaction of the Christian Social leadership to the events of late October and early November 1918 was predictably cautious.[362] The party followed a double strategy, bowing to democracy but seeking to avert the Republic. On the one hand it agreed to participate in the new provisional democratic government, nominating four Christian Socials as State Secretaries (Heinrich Mataja, Karl Jukel, Josef Stöckler, and Johann Zerdik), arguing that the Emperor's Manifesto of October 16 sanctioned the creation of provisional assemblies on a national basis.[363] On the other hand the leadership doggedly defended the monarchical principle as the best, if not the only, form of legitimate rule, refusing to acknowledge a Republic unless and until the new state was approved by the people by popular referendum or by a democratically elected Constituent Assembly. At the opening session of the provisional National Assembly on October 21, in the face of Victor Adler's call for a democratic Republic, Josef Schraffl read an official Christian Social declaration that his party would act "on the basis of a steadfast adherence to the monarchic form of government."[364] As late as the morning of November 10 Johann Hauser assured Cardinal Piffl that his party would resist voting for a republic.[365]

Yet the object that Piffl and the *Volksbund* wanted most—to preserve the Monarchy, if not the Empire—was impossible. During the fateful days that preceded the Emperor's semi-abdication on November 11, facts outpaced memories. Events in Germany and shifting public opinion in the Austrian provinces and in the streets of Vienna certainly provided a powerful incentive. Once it was clear that the Empire as a constitutional entity was lost, the compulsion many party leaders felt to defend the dynastic principle inevitably dissipated. Factions emerged, with provincial and especially agrarian politicians in the Christian Social party recalibrating the scope of their self-interest while also remembering the exploitation they and their constituents had endured at the military's hands during the war.[366] On October 22 the leaders or delegates of provincial governments who were present in Vienna met at the Lower Austrian Landhaus to affirm their role in the transition from war to peace which, given the "dissolution of the centralistic administrative apparatus," they thought all the more necessary.[367] As Anton Staudinger has observed, the logic of debates in the Christian Social club during the first week of November was not merely pro or contra a republic, but pro or contra a Vienna-based centralism.[368] In defending provincial autonomy against the recentralization purportedly coveted by the Social Democrats, the peasant representatives played out tensions that were inherent in the *Reichspartei* from the very beginning.

Although the oath of office taken by the new State Secretaries on October 31 had been taken "Im Namen des Staates Deutschösterreich," this could be read as a democratic rather than a republican concession. Indeed, Reinhard Owerdieck has recently argued that both the Christian Socials and the Social Democrats had agreed not to push for a definitive settlement of the constitutional question before the calling of a constitutive assembly.[369] The Imperial Cabinet judged the laws passed on October 30 as "making a good impression," and was pleased that the "attempt on the part on some sides to achieve the introduction of a republican form of government did not succeed, that in fact the question of the form of the state has been left open and that thus the hope for the preservation of the Monarchy has not suffered any damage."[370] Yet, that a principal Christian Social spokesman on October 30 was Josef Stöckler, who pointedly praised the advantages that the new democracy would bring in "exterminating the old privileges" under which peasants had suffered, boded ill for the future of the Dynasty.[371]

In the immediate aftermath of the announcement of the abdication of Kaiser Wilhelm II and the proclamation of the Republic in Berlin on November 9, the State Council voted on the morning of November 11 to submit to the provisional National Assembly a law establishing a democratic Austrian Republic as a part of the new German Republic.[372] The Council's historic decision (and its impending approval by the Assembly on November 12) meant that the Emperor's personal and constitutional status could no longer be deferred. A powerful factor in these decisions was the almost total collapse of Karl's public standing. As Wedel reported to Berlin, "he enjoys so little respect and trust that the question [of Karl's fate] is only viewed as a problem of the second rank."[373]

Seipel was confident as late as November 9 that the question of the form of the state and the fate of the Dynasty was still open, but sentiment in both the Social Democratic and German-national factions grew day by day in favor of the Republic.[374] Although difficult to chart with precision, it seems likely that public opinion in Vienna, especially among discharged soldiers and the working classes, now strongly supported the Republic.[375] As early as November 7 Victor Adler insisted in the Social Democratic executive that it was absolutely necessary that the issue of the Republic be clarified; on the morning of November 11 the Social Democratic leadership decided that if the bourgeois parties on the State Council should veto the Republic their delegates would immediately resign, provoking a crisis.[376] Socialist emissaries Karl Renner and Karl Seitz warned the Cabinet (and in particular Lammasch and Seipel) on the evening of November 10 that the provisional government was in no position to guarantee the Emperor's personal safety should he refuse to abdicate.[377] Rather than a formal abdication, however, the socialists agreed to the voluntary renunciation by Karl of the affairs of state, an indelicate attempt to circumvent the fate that his fellow monarch, Wilhelm II, had endured a day earlier.

There followed the remarkable morning session of the State Council on the November 11 at which Renner leveraged the Emperor against the Christian Social party. Even before news of the State Council's final decisions arrived at Schönbrunn, the Emperor was under heavy pressure from Lammasch to accept the document.[378] Knowing that the Cabinet had decided on the Emperor's "abdication" and that Karl was likely to accept the Cabinet's draft, Renner argued that "it would be for us a totally intolerable situation, we would be in the most untenable position before the people, if our declaration did not match that of the Court."[379] The Council therefore had to match the Emperor's generosity. Given the intention of the Allies to marginalize and deprive Austria of key territorial resources, the best insurance of future security was an open appeal to self-determination.[380] Renner's discursive tactics worked brilliantly. Although three of the six Christian Social members of the State Council voted against Renner's first motion—which signified approval of the Republic—the Christian Social chair of the Council, Johann Hauser, abstained. Since all but one of the party's delegates then voted for Renner's second motion—declaring German-Austria a "constituent part of the German Republic"—it was clear that sentiment in the Christian Social delegation had already come to terms— soberly and quietly—with a Republic. According to Richard Wollek, news arriving in Vienna describing the strong republican sentiment evident in Upper Austria and Tyrol helped to shift the attitudes of the rural leaders. When the new provisional governments of Carinthia and Tyrol voted on November 11 to support a republic, the final die had been cast.[381]

By November 11 the last defenders of the Monarchy left within the Christian Social party leadership were the leaders of the *Volksbund* group, especially Seipel and Funder, and their ally Cardinal Piffl.[382] Whereas Christian Social peasant leaders like Fink, Stöckler, and Schraffl acceded to (and in the cases of Fink and Stöckler quietly applauded) the Social Democrats' demand for a Republic, the Viennese Catholics were inflexible.[383] The Committee of Seven (*Siebener Ausschuss*), organized in mid-October by Schmitz, Funder, Seipel, Mataja and several others, functioned (according to Funder) as an ersatz "divisional general staff" for the party in Vienna. Meeting in the *Volksbund's* offices this group both coordinated rally and organizational work and provided a forum for discussions of future political and social policy in the German-Austrian state.[384] Seipel might later insist to Alfred Missong that the *Volksbund* was the only effective presence in the "just about nonexistent political organization of the Christian Social party" in October 1918, but this counted for nothing when the party leadership met on November 11 and 12 to decide how to vote on the Council's drafts.[385] Funder could appeal for restraint in a lead article in the *Reichspost* on the morning of November 12, but Johann Hauser declared that the party's consent to the Republic was inevitable once the revolution in Germany had begun. Even if the party had been able to stop the proclamation of the Republic in Vienna, this would only have led to civil war.[386]

This final victory of the provinces over Vienna overturned the logic embedded in the *Reichspartei* of 1907–14. But the intransigence of the Viennese was not merely a product of sentimentality or of their Vienna-centric views. It also resulted from their trepidation in losing the one mediatory institution that might privilege the culture of Catholicism in contests with urban anticlericalism, and the one agent that (from their perspective) could mediate corporate solidarity and democratic equality in a revolutionary epoch. Democracy without Dynasty—republicanism—was merely a "formal democracy," lacking either an authentic bond to the Austrian past or a legitimate guide to its cultural future.

Yet, as Ignaz Seipel's own intellectual compromises on the question of republicanism soon demonstrated, the Viennese were not without a realistic core. Four articles by Seipel, commissioned by Friedrich Funder and published in the *Reichspost* beginning on November 17, charted the way.[387] But Heinrich

Mataja had already alerted his party to the long-term consequences of such pragmatism in an article published in mid-October 1918. Transposing his local fronde against the "bureaucrat" Weiskirchner onto the state level, Mataja insisted that "the decision about the great questions which affect the interests of the German people in Austria is a matter for the political parties. Officials schooled in administration are not called upon and are not appropriate to provide leadership in this time of great political upheaval."[388] When Heinrich Mataja wrote these words, he still hoped that it would be possible to save the Monarchy. Yet his comments soon assumed a different significance, for they implied that whatever the outcome of the constitutional and diplomatic conundrums of late 1918, it would be the mass political parties and not the Dynasty or its civil servants that would make the final decisions about state form and state function. Once an upstart bourgeois protest movement which had dared to challenge the Crown, the Christian Socials were now (along with the Social Democrats) to decide the fate of the Crown in 1918. The strong, party-dominated political system in the First Austrian Republic is impossible to understand without remembering this great role reversal.

EIGHT

Conclusion:
Christian Socialism under the Empire

Under the revolutionary settlement of November 12, 1918, the provisional National Assembly determined that universal suffrage should be the norm for all future municipal elections in Austria. In the interim, municipalities were ordered to add an appropriate number of workers' representatives to the existing municipal Councils. In Vienna Richard Weiskirchner negotiated a temporary settlement between the Christian Socials and the Social Democrats, which reconstructed the city government of Vienna by giving the socialists 60 seats in the City Council (as opposed to 84 for the Christian Socials, 19 for the *Deutschfreiheitlichen,* and 2 for the pan-Germans) and one vice-mayoral position in the executive. Both major parties approved this agreement, the Christian Socials for fear that in the absence of a negotiated agreement the new provisional government for *Deutschösterreich* would impose a far more drastic and far less agreeable reform; the Social Democrats for reasons of strategic convenience. The new socialist minority could effectively block any substantial policy initiatives by the Christian Socials until new elections could be called on the basis of universal suffrage, at which time the socialists felt confident that they would win a huge majority in the Council by conventional means.[1] This decision by the Viennese socialists for a policy of legality in the aftermath of the Revolution was an index of the party's future behavior as well, in its effort to balance political constitutionalism on the one hand and radical social transformation on the other. That the Christian Socials were left holding the responsibility for the immediate postwar chaos in the city may also have been a consideration in socialist strategy.

On March 6, 1919, the municipality adopted a new suffrage law replacing the old corporate electoral system with universal suffrage. The formal transfer of power between the two movements occurred after the municipal elections of May 1919. On November 16, 1918 Weiskirchner had summoned a meet-

444

ing of the leadership of the Viennese Christian Social party to discuss the future, at which he and the Christian Social labor leader Franz Spalowsky spoke. Weiskirchner blamed Karl Stürgkh for Vienna's food misfortunes during the war, and, appropriating an enthusiasm for the kind of party reform that Heinrich Mataja had urged during the war, he insisted: "Our first duty is to constitute our district election committees. Into these we must bring young people. Energetic young people must cooperate with us in greater numbers. It is a question of the existence of our party on the one hand and of the Christian worldview on the other." But the traditionalist reemerged when he argued that the Christian Socials should fight the next elections on the basis of past accomplishments: "We remain Christian Social even now. We will enter the battle with our old flag flying; we will struggle and with God's help also be victorious."

Franz Spalowsky spoke in more sober tones. He noted that the entrance of women into the electorate would have momentous consequences and that "organizationally we have practically no contact with the women. . . . Men have no influence over women [in voting choices], while contrariwise quite a large number of women have a significant influence over the men." Surveying the rest of the party apparatus, Spalowsky was no more confident, and his comments on the youth problem bore a different accent than those of Weiskirchner: "Let's get rid of the old men, who are no longer agile. [Our] organizations must have new blood, new energies." The Christian Socials needed to do what they had hesitated to undertake for so long: "We must only understand the necessity of adapting our electoral machinery to the needs of the time, in such a way that we draw men and women from the broad masses of the population under the spell of our ideas."[2]

Unfortunately for the Christian Socials, it was Spalowsky and not Weiskirchner who spoke sense to the party. The May 1919 elections gave the Social Democrats a clear victory in which they seized 100 of the 165 seats in the new Council. The Social Democrats now had a stranglehold on Vienna which they retained until 1934 (and which, with the "exception" of 1934–45, they continue to hold to the present day). On May 22, 1919, the Council elected Weiskirchner's old Social Democratic nemesis in the *Obmänner-Konferenz,* Jakob Reumann, to succeed him as mayor. The electoral support for the Social Democrats in Vienna more than surpassed their constituency achievements in June 1911, as the Christian Socials found themselves repudiated not merely by men and women of the working classes but also by many now impoverished *bürgerlich* voters, who were ready for radical changes in the management of the municipality. Anti-Semitism did not, as some Christian Social party leaders had hoped in 1917–18, possess the magic force to counteract the social bitterness and moral defeatism of the electorate. The long-awaited structural reforms in the party came too late and with too little decisiveness to have a measurable effect. Yet in the Republic as a whole the Christian Socials, with their powerful voting reserves in the agrarian hinterland and small towns, stood almost evenly matched with the Social Democrats: the seesaw pattern of the initial national elections of February 1919 (SDAP with 41 percent; CSP with 36 percent) and those that followed in October, 1920 (SDAP with 36 percent; CSP with 42 percent) suggested that neither side could assume that there would be an exact correspondence between ideological hegemony and majority rule.

For the Christian Socials these profound events were a fitting conclusion to forty years of political turbulence. The caesura of 1918–19 naturally invites a review of the contribution and meaning of the Christian Social movement in the last decades of the Empire. Founded by Karl Lueger and Albert Gessmann in the late 1880s as an aggregation of *Mittelstand* interest groups, the party succeeded in winning control of Vienna in 1895–96. The electoral coalition that put Lueger into power—comprising disgruntled public officials, petty and mid-sized businessmen, property holders, private commercial employees, and other middle-class groups of one coloration or another—was widely disparate in its material needs and cultural ambitions. What seemed to link these groups was, on the one hand, a negative "push"—resentment about actual or imagined economic and social disadvantages that many voters were experiencing in the aftermath of the Great Depression, and anxiety over alleged Jewish predominance in business and the arts; and, on the other hand, a positive "pull"—the opportunity to gain a share of the civic spoils (not all of which were necessarily material in nature) attendant upon the governance of any major metropolitan center. The civic radicalism of the 1880s became the proprietary paternalism of Lueger's rule in the 1900s. The Christian Social party devoted the first ten years of its control of Vienna to defensive, assimilatory tactics such as revising the municipal franchise in 1900, bringing socialist schoolteachers and former Liberal municipal officials to heel, recasting Lower Austrian school laws, and building a series of proud and technologically progressive municipal utilities, which proved to be both economically efficient and tremendous sources of patronage. In all of this the actual structure of the party as party changed slowly: Lueger ruled the party and the city after 1897 just as he had ruled the party before 1897, relying less on formal bureaucratic structures of control than on informal cronyism and benign consultation (and often neglect). His ambitions were, in the long term, modest. Once in possession of Vienna and Lower Austria, Lueger seemed to have reached his natural limits of political aggrandizement.

Yet the breakdown of the national political system under Badeni and his successors and the decision of the Emperor to open it to new political forces in 1905 by supporting universal manhood suffrage introduced a second revolutionary stage in the history of the Christian Social party. From a modest, regionally based party with 25 deputies in parliament in 1901 the Christian Socials became with 96 members the largest party in the new parliament of 1907. And with universal manhood suffrage emerged a different and more ambitious vision of the party—that of the *Reichspartei,* encompassing not merely Vienna, but the peasant-dominated Alpine provinces as well. The real hero of Christian Social policies in the second epoch of its history was Albert Gessmann—one of the main architects of the new party structure—far more than Karl Lueger. Nor was this an inconsiderable achievement, for the establishment of universal suffrage was the first step toward breaking the hold of private realms of household power, based on personal status or personal taxation of individual property owners and producers, in the constitution of the liberal state, and engineering a more ambitious conception of the state as an interventionist force within a democratized civil society. However unwilling or ambivalent many of its *bürgerlich* members in Vienna may have felt about this evolution, the Christian Social party was clearly a major agent in this transformation of the Austrian state.

The destiny of the *Reichspartei* was ineluctably joined to the future of the parliamentary, interethnic system of bourgeois coalition politics which it logically and technically presumed. The experiences of the party in the Beck and Bienerth ministries from 1907 to 1911, when party influence in the Cabinet was at its height, suggested that the nationalities question was not controllable by modes of therapeutic social intervention (such as social insurance, craft reform, and public construction under the aegis of a new super Ministry of Labor that Gessmann originally envisaged) and that the traditions of Josephist administrative autocracy which had marked Austrian Cabinets since Taaffe were not nearly as accessible to mass political manipulation and accountability as many of the Christian Socials originally thought or hoped. Miscalculations by the party hierarchy, together with the profound divisions within the Viennese party and between Vienna and the provinces that followed Lueger's death in 1910, led to the political degeneration of the *Reichspartei* into a disunited and occasionally unpredictable participant in Stürgkh's regime between 1911 and 1914. These same squabbles and factional rivalries, coming as they did in the midst of a serious inflation in food and living costs in 1910–11, ruined the party's credibility with many of its former (or potential) electoral supporters among white-collar and business groups, and resulted in the electoral disaster of June 1911.

At the same time Gessmann's other calculation—that class could be made superior to cultural issues—fell apart under the pressure of continuing anti-clerical and nationalist tensions within and among the German- and Czech-speaking parties. The gradual co-optation of the *Freie Schule* movement in Vienna by younger Social Democrats and the sublimation of bourgeois anti-clericalism into Austro-Marxist *Bildung* qua *Kulturkampf* after the Wahrmund Affair demonstrated, long before the advent of "Red Vienna" in the First Republic, that the lines of battle in Austrian politics could not be drawn merely along social-interest or economic lines. Culture and moral consciousness remained independent variables in the Austrian political system. Before 1914 the Austrian administration thus found itself in the precarious and politically dangerous position of refereeing irreconcilable cultural conflicts, all the while representing a huge network of potential job patronage that the conflicting, class-based parties hoped to appropriate and control.

The final prewar years saw various attempts to rebuild the party, of which two were notable. Richard Weiskirchner sought to reconstruct and broaden the old Lueger coalition of white-collar voters and small and medium business interests and to retain the corporate system of elections against the Social Democrats, drawing on support from local German nationalist voters to do so. The party's technique might be "modernized," but its ethos would retain a careful balance that preferred political pragmatism to theoretical consistency, and, if anything, would shift toward greater collaboration with capitalist and industrial circles. In contrast, younger groups of ideologues centered in the *Volksbund* and Leopold Kunschak's Laborites viewed the rise of Austro-Marxism as an intellectual as well as organizational threat, but one that also offered tremendous opportunities if only the party could expand its audience and redefine its moral purpose. For Kunschak and Catholic radicals like Richard Schmitz and Franz Sommeregger, other kinds of franchise arrangements were at least conceivable, assuming that Catholicism could be persuasively proffered to the laboring masses. The advocates of the *Volksbund* movement sought to create a new, scientific Christian Socialism, to be sponsored and led by a Catholic intelligentsia (clerical and lay) and directed toward a more universal, socially responsible electorate. The problem of the party was not, as some thought, that it had too much "religion," but that it had too little.

The strange relationship of the party to Archduke Franz Ferdinand illuminated all of the ambiguities and problems of its condition in 1914. Having lost the credibility of Gessmann's ministerial strategy, suspicious of attempts at *Verwaltungsreform* which might impugn their jealously guarded prerogatives in the autonomous Crownlands, and living in humiliating bondage under Karl Stürgkh, some Christian Socials found themselves by 1914 anticipating the Thronfolger's possible *Staatsstreich* which, ironically, might have undermined the relatively open political system on which mass parties like the Christian Socials depended.

The coming of the war closed down all internal reform efforts within the party and ended the possibility of peacetime constitutional reform in the general Austrian polity. The war reprivatized politics, fragmenting the political and popular bases of support on which all the parties depended, enhancing the formal control of the Austrian civil service in public and private spheres of life, and, with considerable irony, setting the higher civil service in competition with the Austrian High Command over claims to speak on behalf of civil society. Stürgkh's uneasy relationship with Teschen, one that forced him to listen and respond to complaints by leading military figures who challenged his government's management of home-front society—a humiliating reversal of power relationships—merely demonstrated that wartime absolutism was a pluralistic rather than monolithic phenomenon and that those who claimed to possess absolute "power" could probably not be certain from day to day whether they were really able to exercise it.[3]

The war also forced all German parties to stake out positions for what would prove to be the final round of constitutional self-flagellations endured by the Empire. Bred to political irresponsibility before the war, many German bourgeois politicians could now give free reign to utopian dreams of hegemony over the Slavs by co-opting the legitimacy of military coercion, if not covert violence. War-aims schemes and conspiracies piled one on top of another as circles of Austro-German literati dreamed of refashioning the universe of Austrian politics. For the Christian Socials the first three years of the war demonstrated the party's confusion. As the war mayor whose public image alternated between strident bellicosity and defensive apologetics, Richard Weiskirchner seemed to define its image. By 1915–16 the party allowed itself to be co-opted into tacit and then explicit support for pan-German *Octroi* schemes, less because such plans offered meaningful advantages to the Christian Socials, and more because they could thereby control the damage that general constitutional reform might inflict upon the corporate and regionally autonomous bastions on which the party had depended before 1914 for its power and patronage.

But this strategy worked only to a very limited degree, for the party could not escape the political swamp into which the uneasy alliance of wartime military and civilian absolutism sank. As professional politicians the Christian Socials were no more immune to the insults and the machinations of the war government than were the other parties. Weiskirchner himself came to blame the central government for Vienna's misfortunes. Nor did the parliamentary party escape the cross fire of civil and military absolutism: Karl Niedrist, a Christian Social parliamentary deputy from Tyrol, so displeased the Austrian High Command by his efforts to defend the interests of his fellow peasant proprietors in 1915–16 that he was accused by Archduke Friedrich of being among those who were "inciting the people against the authorities" and who were "poisoning a people, whose love of the fatherland and whose loyalty to the Dynasty have become proverbial, with unhealthy ideas." Niedrist was ordered by a less than enthusiastic *Statthalter* Friedrich Toggenburg to leave his home province in early 1916.[4] Not surprisingly, when Josef Stöckler spoke in the provisional National Assembly on October 30 on behalf of the Christian Social Agrarians he described his constituents' reaction at having left the Empire in the optimistic terms of an escape from traditional bureaucratic hegemony: "We would consider it to be a great piece of fortune if, in addition to ending old privileges, the spiritually and emotionally destructive bureaucracy in Austria would be reformed."[5] The war offered renewed examples of the military and civil bureaucracies trying to tame or curb the political parties, a facet of life that the professional politicians of both major parties would not soon forget after November 1918.

True, the failure of the *Octroi* in April 1917 opened up possibilities for last-minute political renewal, which the Christian Socials initially welcomed but which they, along with the other German parties, soon squandered. More important, it set the stage for the revival of the fortunes of the *Volksbund* group and other younger Christian Social political intellectuals who now came to the fore with their own constitutional ambitions and social strategies. Ignaz Seipel, Richard Schmitz, Heinrich Mataja, Leopold Kunschak, Franz Sommeregger— all important leaders with a more "Catholic" or at least "principled" orientation in the Christian Social party—felt empowered by the vicissitudes of 1917–18, just as Austro-Marxists like Otto Bauer also tried to seize moral and ultimately tactical control of their party after Fritz Adler's murder trial in May 1917.[6] For both sets of activists, their theoretical odysseys during the war ended at unexpected destinations, forcing them to come to terms with a new constitutional order, that of the Republic.

In Vienna the ravages of war had led to growing disenchantment with both of the big parties. The January 1918 strikes were an implicit challenge to the traditional Social Democratic elite; and if within the Christian Socials no such overt "electoral" revolt could be charted, it was certainly present on a less ostentatious basis in the extensive economic deprivations and psychological grievances felt among the white-collar and small business circles of the party, as well as in the daily frustrations encountered by hungry consumers looking for food.[7] In April 1918 Heinrich Mataja warned his fellow party leaders that "the Christian Social delegates and representatives are continually besieged with complaints and grievances about the actions of organs of the Viennese *Magistrat*. Since the municipal administration is controlled by the Christian Social majority, the Christian Social party and especially the *Bürgermeister* are held responsible for the measures [people] object to."[8] Efforts by Mataja in a fronde against Weiskirchner to revitalize the Viennese party organization in 1917–18 and thus regain control of public opinion were interrupted by the crisis of late 1918. Here too the groundwork had been prepared for more doctrinaire postures than Lueger or Weiskirchner had been inclined to support, but the Christian Socials were about to find themselves in a pitiful minority status against the Social Democratic behemoth that would turn the Rathaus from "Black" to "Red."

By 1919 therefore the party's history had come full circle, a fact that the

Arbeiter-Zeitung sonorously celebrated: "for twenty-three years, a Christian Social has occupied the office of Mayor: Strobach, Lueger, Neumayer, Weis-kirchner. Now their hegemony has collapsed; it is over, completely and irrevocably over."[9] From a group of ragtag outcasts in the early 1880s who had risen to political prominence and power in the mid-1890s by assaulting with impunity the powerful Liberal party in Vienna, the Christian Socials now found themselves once again dispossessed and dishonored. A quarter century of political hegemony in Vienna had enabled the party to co-opt Liberal *bürgerlich* voters and ruling traditions, but had also exposed it to the same dangers of incipient democratization that the Christian Socials had exploited against the Liberals. The ways in which the Christian Socials appropriated and fulfilled the Liberals' vision of a civic corporate political culture are matched in irony only by the dialectical relationship of sameness and opposition that defined the great antinomy of modern Austrian politics in the twentieth century: Christian Socialism versus Social Democracy. By succeeding the Liberals in both class and civic terms, the Christian Socials found themselves forced to behave like a *staatserhaltende Partei*. This was Albert Gessmann's aspiration—his party would become the critical linchpin in a grand anti-socialist coalition that would launch it into parliamentary and ministerial power. Yet by accepting reasonable levels of "Christian" rhetoric as a civic religion for their party (Lueger always viewed the Church as a component of the civic legitimacy of the Hapsburg Dynasty and the Viennese *Residenzstadt,* and hence as one vital part of the composite portrait of Imperial—and bourgeois—Vienna), and by integrating into the party the vast agrarian hinterland between 1901 and 1907, Gessmann and his colleagues had shifted its identity in the direction of a modern Christian-conservative party of the post-1945 European variety. The frank realization by the party elite during 1910–11 that they must reconcile themselves to capitalism and seek support from industrial circles was simply the final step in cementing an alliance of property against nonproperty in a "Christian" ideological mode.

Yet within the party, as within Austrian Social Democracy, younger elites were emerging by 1907–11 who were dissatisfied with the routinization of parliamentary *Klassenkampf.* Among the Austro-Marxists this took the form of a new preoccupation with the *Endziel* of revolutionary utopia, but also of a new sensitivity toward the transformational power of anticlericalism, both as an electoral issue and as a mode of revolutionary education. Among the university-educated Catholic intelligentsia who, empowered by a different ethos from Lueger's generation, would take power in 1919, similar concerns about the lack of ideological discipline and social coherence were also at issue. For these circles Christian Socialism must become what earlier party leaders had always resisted, to wit, both Christian *and* Social. Karl Lueger's and Victor

Adler's generation had fashioned the axis between the two great *Lager,* but it took an Otto Bauer and an Ignaz Seipel to infuse the two with wholly irreconcilable identities.

Christian Socialism and the Continuities of Austrian History

One of the classic issues in German politics has been the alleged "failure" of the German Revolution of 1918, in which moderate elements of the German Social Democrats gained control of the machinery of state in November 1918 and then failed to push for a categorical social *or* administrative revolution while they tried to recast the constitutional order. Although the revolution in Austria eventually resulted in a reconstitution of critical forms of prewar administrative governance, the break with the imagined and encountered political past was more decisive there, not only because the multinational state of Imperial Austria had ceased in a territorial sense to exist, but also because even the history of (and historical consciousness about) the Imperial state now ceased to be an object of proprietary recognition. The absence of any independent "national" basis for the new state also accentuated its unwanted novelty. One might argue, therefore, that the early history of the First Republic, and the history of the Christian Socials in the early First Republic, must be seen through the image of radical discontinuity. Certainly the Christian Socials endured a powerful break in the constitution of their political elite, as many of the top leaders of the party in Vienna—Gessmann, Liechtenstein, Pattai, Bielohlawek, Schindler—died immediately before or within a few years after the end of hostilities. Other important local leaders went into political retirement.[10] The radical nature of Austro-Marxist theory and practice, whose practitioners and benefactors now gained a hegemonic hold on the city of Vienna and, for a short time, a share of the national government, might reinforce this image of discontinuity. In Berlin the socialists were forced to enter a coalition with the local bourgeois parties; in Vienna the break with the heritage of Christian Social-*bürgerlich* rule was more decisive. More important, the state into which both German Social Democrats and Centrists fitted was one governed by larger, institutionally fixed buffer zones and semi-independent institutional powers (such as the *Reichswehr*), making resource distribution and power sharing far more critical than the pursuit of absolute ideological models for the future society. This condition of overlapping public spheres of mutual material advantage has permitted one recent historian of the Weimar Republic, Michael Geyer, to characterize its political arena as an instrumental "system of procedures."[11] Only during the crisis of 1930–33 did the ideologically predictable (if not always stable) power cartel break down, leading to private intrigue and gang wars in the streets.

The parallel of such political "privatization" and anarchy first occurred in Austria not in 1930–33 but in 1914–18, when the conventions and the generation-based assumptions of Austrian politics collapsed so decisively that the two inheritor parties of the Republic could shape their policy agendas in far more value-laden and morally absolutist terms than was the case for their counterparts in the early and middle periods of Weimar. In Weimar ideological intractability and self-possession were situated at the extreme ends of the political spectrum (to the Right the National Socialists, to the Left the German Communists), but in Austria the albatross of ideological certainty (and the ambition to craft new patterns of social relations) hung squarely in the middle of the political system. In Austria an explicitly political revolution did take place, launched by and for the two great parties, and directed not only against the Crown but against the *Verwaltung* as well. Hence the true meaning of the revolution in Austria must be measured not merely by its often mixed programmatic appeals but also by the fact that it was yet another powerful step toward the creation of a democratically legitimated interventionist state, endowed with populist legitimacy and parliamentary sovereignty, a state whose potential *legal* ethos was remarkably pluralist, setting it beyond the bounds of petty ideological tyranny. As Robert Kann noted, the original 1920 constitution expressed a compelling normative relativism, even if it was only after 1945 that it was able to become "a common denominator . . . for the whole people of the state."[12]

Questions about the scope and impact of the revolution also suggest, however, the larger question of the continuities and discontinuities in the forms of Austrian public life. In what ways did the *Lager* mentality of the First Republic, in which Austro-Marxists battled a more ideologically combative Christian Socialism in a struggle of cultural ideology and class resources, reflect a continuity with the struggles pursued in the prewar period? How did prewar conceptions of state power, swinging between older, curial notions of corporate politics and more efficient and broad visions of a plebiscitary state, translate into post-1918 realities?

These are complex issues that can be considered only within the compass of a general history of Austria.[13] But even in a preliminary sense we must recognize that the lines of the formidable conflict between the worldviews and brilliant personalities of an Ignaz Seipel and an Otto Bauer were already etched into the terrain of Austrian politics before 1914. In an essay on Western European corporatism, Charles Maier has observed that "corporatist trends have generally centered on industrial-labor organizations that parallel the political party divisions between social democracy and Christian democracy (or other conservative parties)."[14] From the Austrian evidence this is certainly not surprising. Yet this parallelism of corporate politics between the parties is also exemplified in one ironic but fundamental continuity of Austrian politics, namely, the joint forms of political behavior employed by Christian Social and Social Democratic rule (in Vienna at least) in the period from 1897 to 1934: both parties shared a fundamental conception of the municipality (the *Gemeinde*) as a unit of functional governance which, although located within the traditional state power system, could effect momentous changes and mediate interests *in place of* that system. Max Adler's vigorous appropriation of the municipality in 1919 as one of the revolutionary "organs of socialization" that would help to create a new socialist society was perhaps an extreme idea, but it was one that fell within a paraconstitutional tradition established well before 1918.[15] Both parties viewed the city as a corporate unit which, when politicized by explicit partisan norms and controls, could represent a model society for the rest of the Monarchy (Republic). In Lueger's case this "modeling" was to be primarily symbolic by affirming through the paternal *Residenzstadt* the integrity of the Christian Social "people"—electorally, the Christian Social lower and middle *Bürgertum*—as the most loyal patrons of the Dynasty, as well as affirming the Dynasty as the most effective defender of the "people." Lueger's Vienna was a living testimony to this marriage of love and opportunism between the Christian Social electorate and the Hapsburg ruling establishment. In the socialists' case Vienna was to move beyond mere symbolic agency to become the actual proponent of social transformation, although in the epistemology of Austro-Marxist politics the symbolic could serve at times as a substitute for, and even an excuse for, avoiding action.[16] But in the case of both parties Vienna as a corporate political unit played an influential and independent role in the constitution of the modern Austrian state. For the Christian Socials Vienna was an autonomous corporate agency with which to challenge the "public" Imperial administration and thereby to enhance, even if quite unintentionally, the larger domain of legitimacy associated with a modern democratic state. The Social Democrats took this process one giant step farther and used the city as a weapon with which to try to reconstruct the very moral basis of the new post-liberal state. In each case the city as an economic unit was merged with the city as a cultural agent in the name of a larger political agenda and a more ambitious social program.

The ease with which both (reconstructed) parties after 1945 came to accept state-political corporatism—the corporatism of a strong, autonomous state undergirded by equally strong, semipublic interests—may reflect the fact that both parties were extensively involved before 1918–34 in developing or at least nourishing potential corporatist or paracorporatist institutions—either professional interest groups such as the unions and peasant leagues or state-sponsored consultative bodies for interest mediation in the legislative process.

But their acceptance of a common purpose for the post-1945 state—sponsorship of the public's *economic* welfare above all else—and their tolerance of competitive structural instruments to effect that sponsorship may also reflect their joint heritage in either managing or participating in the autonomous corporate power of the *Gemeinde Wien.* Once the network of corporatist institutions was (re-) established in Austria after 1945 as a mode of conflict resolution for discordant social and economic demands, and as a means to effect and constitute the new "economic" state, it functioned successfully only because of the *extensive* politicization of bureaucratic and managerial elites. One might argue that such intermediate institutions could formally claim to "dispense" with politics, precisely because they were so finely attuned to the political expectations and the limits of possible and permissible action, set by the big party blocs.[17]

Although both parties shared a common heritage resulting from their roots in the Viennese metropolitan center, two fundamental differences did obtain between the two big parties in Vienna in their pre- and postwar conflicts, and herein lay one of the decisive consequences of the Austrian revolution. Before 1918 the Christian Social movement was an amalgam of various kinds of ideological and geographic interests, with the agrarianism (and, in part, the Catholicism) of the Lower Austrian, Upper Austrian, and Tyrolean factions balanced against the urbanism and more secular, anti-Semitic profile of the Viennese mother party. Among German bourgeois groups the Christian Social party as a whole served a nationally defensive but socially progressive role, defined by its hegemony over the most secure bastions of the German-speaking electorate. The very image of the *Reichspartei,* although it papered over serious factionalisms within the party, connoted a centralistic cultural dedication to the Empire as a political project. These facts meant that the Social Democrats had for an opponent a party which, while radically different on any number of individual class or cultural issues, at least laid claim to occupying the same territory (Vienna) and to exercise the same kinds of policy interests (the welfare of Vienna, considered within an integral view of the Empire as a coherent and approved political entity). Tendencies that undercut the Christian Social party's balance between secularism and clericalism and between urbanism and ruralism were clearly evident before 1918, however, and it has already been stressed that some younger Christian Social leaders were already calling for a more formal dedication of the party to coherent ideological principles as extra insurance against the entrapments of Social Democracy. This push toward ideological rigor found its parallel among the Social Democrats with the politics of men like Otto Bauer and Otto Glöckel, whose anticlericalism seemed to be not merely a policy strategy but also an ethical and moral code.

Before 1914 an uneasy likeness or union bound both parties to the city—the Social Democrats because they claimed Vienna as their probable democratic heritage (of which they thought themselves deprived by their opponents' "undemocratic" franchise), the Christian Socials because of their actual structural hegemony in the city, based on an imagined Christian "folk" loyal to both the party and the Dynasty.[18] Once this balance had been swept away, once the Christian Socials in Vienna had ceased to play anything more than an embattled minority role in the City Council and had lost any possible pretence of majoritarian legitimacy, the focus of party policy inevitably became more distant from Vienna and its particular social needs. With the socialists claiming Vienna as their own in proprietary terms, to the exclusion of everyone else, bourgeois Viennese and non-Viennese, unable to "love" or even sympathetically relate to the paternalistic *Residenzstadt* which was Lueger's pride, now felt dispossessed from "their" own city. No other image of the rhetoric of the First Republic was so powerful and yet so disruptive to the civil order as that of "Red Vienna."[19] As the socialists tried desperately to build on Lueger's municipal autonomism and surpass it by recasting the political and economic structure of the city into a socialist utopia, they now entered their claims to formal proprietary control over the city as well. In his first announcement as mayor in May 1919 Jakob Reumann insisted that "the hope of the people must be fulfilled that life in this city of work will develop according to the needs and interests of the broad masses, not according to the *Geldsackinteressen* of small groups. Social revolution must follow the political upheaval. With the nationalization of the means of production, important responsibilities fall to the greatest municipality of the state."[20] When in their introductions to the celebratory work *Das Neue Wien* (1926) both Karl Seitz and Georg Emmerling juxtaposed the proud term "das neue Wien" with proprietary references to "unser Wien," the associative rhetorical patterns may have been unintended, but in broad political terms they signified that the newly created socialist Vienna was also a city that had become "our" Vienna. Hugo Breitner's discourse was more frankly confrontational but equally in this vein when he proclaimed in 1927 that "Vienna is red and must forever remain so!"[21]

Only because the Christian Socials had assumed that they "owned" the city in a corporate sense, as property owners and taxpaying members of the municipal *Bürgertum,* could they justify the oligarchical control their party exercised over the city. A similar combination of corporate exclusivity and ideological intolerance was replicated by the Social Democrats (political decisions in the First Republic swinging between functional "policy" per se and more absolute reflections of ethical righteousness and territorial proprietorship). Both interwar parties assumed generalized identities in the interests of a putative society of the whole, but, as Alessandro Pizzorno has noted of the developmental process of such mass parties, both established ideological goals that were "rigid and nonnegotiable" that also claimed to be formulated with a view of the interests of society as a whole.[22] Hence their collective identities could never be fully gratified by (or held accountable to) concrete interests. Just as Vienna before 1914 had "belonged" to the Christian Social "people," so now did the city belong to the socialist working class; and this ironic continuity in legal form created a fundamental discontinuity in political culture. Vienna, formerly the major battleground of Christian Socials and Social Democrats, the *Residenzstadt* in which the main impulse centers of both parties were located, now became a fortress from which an embattled Social Democracy looked out upon a ruralized Christian Socialism. Once the Christian Socials ceased to have hegemony in the city, as happened after 1919, a situation of extreme polarization had been created that was unprecedented in terms of the history of the two parties in the Empire.

Playing upon a distinction between the bourgeois society of the present and the socialist commonwealth of the future, Robert Danneberg might insist that "from the municipality, which as an administrative authority was often alien, indeed hostile to the masses of the people, is emerging under socialist influence a true commonwealth that encompasses everyone who lives within its walls and which follows the progress of the individual from the cradle to the grave, wherever it becomes necessary."[23] Yet it was precisely this conflation of moral and social totality with the practical results of majoritarian politics that was so striking about Red Vienna. For in spite of the (impressively) high ethical intentions of the Social Democrats, "their" city had ceased to be a *Gemeinde,* in the literal sense that it could function as a *communio* where all could come together and feel themselves as having a share in the community. After 1919 no longer was Vienna merely the location of the parties' conflict; rather it became a central subject of that conflict.

A second discontinuity in political form has already been suggested, which intensified the potency of the first, that of clericalism and anticlericalism. As early as the late Empire there appeared mentalities that can only be described eighty years later as examples of cultural fanaticism on both sides of the party divide: Paul von Hock's belligerent *Freie Schule* and Karl Seitz's anticlerical *Jungen* counterposed to the arrogant rhetoric of the Catholic *Schulverein* and Anton Orel's anti-Modernistic Romanticism. Before 1914 senior politicians in both parties had the power and, on some occasions, even the good sense to keep this genre of cultural bombast and posturing within certain boundaries. More important, the Imperial administration served, despite the suspicion of both sides, as a referee between partisans where cultural matters were concerned. After 1918 not only was it far more difficult for the administration to play this role, but in addition a new cohort of politicians came to the fore, anxious to try their hand at direct parliamentary management of the Austrian political system and bringing with them heightened expectations about the efficacy of culture as a weapon of state mobilization and control. The result, for the Twenties at least, was a far stronger dose of political responsibility for both major parties than they were perhaps ready to deal with. The surrender of political authority by the Crown shifted the control of the state, turned republican, onto the two mass political movements, and their antagonistic and divisive feuds on cultural and social as well as economic matters made the already awesome job of political management nearly impossible.[24] Ignaz Seipel was hardly alone in 1921 when he asserted that in relation to the *Kulturkampf,* "other questions are secondary."[25]

The next twenty years of Austrian history would be spent in the futile attempts of two great worldviews (however internally contested) to gain cultural hegemony and totalism in a political culture and an electorate almost evenly balanced between them. This too was a heritage of the crisis of culture and politics that emerged in the late Empire, and its lasting imprint would be resolved only by the catastrophe of Nazi occupation, in the final aftermath of which Austrians of both camps would abandon both totalistic national and cultural systems (pan-Germanism and either political Catholicism or Austro-Marxist *Kultur*) as organizing instruments of public power.

The Christian Socials and the Social Democrats thus found themselves saddled with the responsibility for designing and operating a new constitutional and political system which in its inner logic assumed the parliamentarism of power. Yet even aside from manifest ideological and class differences, both parties' prior experience with parliamentary authority was a two-edged sword. Both were able to provide a workable transition to republican governance, confident of their own prerogatives and of their own traditions; both affirmed, therefore, in principle the idea of an autonomous state power, governed by political norms. However, both parties had been bitterly disappointed with the parliamentary culture of the late Empire, because the national question was so impervious to instrumental solutions. Both were tempted to judge the Imperial system as having reached the point of bankruptcy because of objective features which no one could control and for which no one (certainly not themselves) was responsible. Although both mass parties were theoretically dedicated to "parliamentary democracy" in 1919, both were also susceptible to a fatalism in respect to *that* democracy's ultimate survival and both were only too willing to experiment with or—in the case of the Austro-Fascists—even to dishonor the very concept of parliamentary governance.[26] In doing so, both marshaled a full complement of contemporary excuses for their own failures to develop coherent and effective public policy, but their practical ambivalence toward parliamentarism may have had historically conditioned roots in the late Imperial period as well.

In the face of these stark burdens, the caesura of 1945 was painfully evident in the speeches of Karl Seitz, Leopold Kunschak, and Karl Renner honoring the reopening of the Austrian *Nationalrat* in December 1945. The nominal theme of the day was confidence in the future of Austria, but it was articulated

by three partisans who had been leading actors in the struggles of the 1920s
and who in the course of Nazi rule had been forced to recognize the mistakes
of their collective past. Looking back over a lifetime of political turbulence,
Seitz proclaimed to both socialists and Christian Socials (now renamed the
People's Party) that "we are Austrians, and we want to remain Austrians. . . .
We want to remain an independent people forever; to be able to develop freely
in this way and according to our own nature. Long live the Republic of Austria!" Kunschak spoke of suppressing partisanship in favor of national cohesion: "We stand together and put party interests aside, because we all feel the
duty, above all and with all our power and with all the devotion we have, to
serve the people and the fatherland." Both Seitz and Kunschak thus implicitly
posited a new state culture as the source of political stability and control. Karl
Renner captured the moment best, however, when after describing the loyalty
of the conservative western provinces to his provisional government in the
months after the occupation he announced: "Austria, taken for dead, condemned to death, erased even from the language of the books of international
law, was resurrected indubitably and unequivocally. From this moment forward
let it hold in truth and in imperishable reality: Austria will last forever!"[27] Renner's invocation of Austrianness, reflecting years of humiliation, guilt, and dis-
consolation, offered in the old chamber of the *Abgeordnetenhaus* where forty
years before as young, vitriolic Social Democrats, he and Seitz had battled
Christian Socials like Gessmann and Kunschak, marked a profound turning
point in Austrian history. The last representatives of those leaders who had
wrought a strong democratic state against the private political culture of the
nineteenth century, but who then failed to provide the electorate of that state
with an all-encompassing rationale to underpin either the state's legitimacy or
their own authority, had now, over a quarter century later, to make a new beginning, but one in which the terms of politics would be radically reconstituted in
favor of economic consensus, if not cultural cohesion among the state's political elites. This consensus not only accorded economic reconstruction primary
sway, but it also slowly came to depend on (and in turn helped to nurture) a
new Austrianness as an antidote to the ideological street wars of the interwar
period.

The history of late Imperial politics thus ended not in November 1918 but
in April 1945, and perhaps more fundamentally in May 1955, when the final
State Treaty was signed in the Belvedere. For the 1955 settlement not only
established an independent state from without, under the recognition of the
four occupying Powers, but it also assumed (although it did not mandate) an
internal political-cultural "neutrality" or at least "objectivity" from within as
well, one that presumed and was willing to reproduce a state of "citizens,"
rather than one of "Germans," "clericals," "anticlericals," "free-thinkers,"
"Reds," "Blacks," or any of the sundry groups created through tricks of

discourse by which Austrians before 1938 sought to order their public lives, dividing themselves from their neighbors across the hall or across the street.[28] The invocation, indeed the constitution of an "Austrian identity" and claims for the existence of a putative "Austrian nationality" are, from this perspective, analytically fascinating, for they imply that for the first time since the collapse of dynasticism in 1917–18 some universal categories of public *cultural* self-understanding exist which are not merely acknowledged but even respected by most members of Austrian civic society.[29] The democratic Austrian state of the mid-twentieth century had finally found a general cultural norm to sustain its universal claims of legitimacy and authority.

Christian Socialism and Its Heritage

How, then, are we to think about the Christian Social party as a leading component of modern Austrian political culture? From the outset this was a movement and a party apparatus buffeted by ironic and dangerous contradictions. Although its political discourse often sounded benighted, the party's conservatism was not so much reactionary as it was an expression of its search for social stability on behalf of those modestly privileged bourgeois client groups that constituted its primary electoral base. Herein lay the party's most critical dilemma—how much of the Liberal political past had to be (or could be) retained while confronting new social and economic issues? How far could the party "play" with political democracy without falling victim to the full expectations of social democracy? The Christian Socials had the electoral potential of a "mass" party, along with a clientele uncomfortable with that designation. Its cohabitation with Catholicism, at least in the first generation of its leaders, was also a function of its deeply rooted penchant for social and cultural stability as much as it was an explicit privileging of religious norms. The Catholicism of Lueger and his cronies was exemplified in the civic proprietorship memorialized by the church building in the Lainz *Versorgungsheim:* a church in whose construction and decoration the craft guilds and other party-affiliated organizations, as well as numerous individuals, collaborated with the municipality (and for which they took manifest civic credit), and in which Lueger's image, dressed in old German costume, stood in a painting above the altar.

The Christian Social party in Vienna was not "liberal" in cultural ethos, if one remembers that anticlericalism was a central, defining element within the genesis of Austrian Liberalism.[30] Certainly the party despised the ethos of Viennese *Freisinn,* its utopianism and political naiveté as much as its blatant anticlericalism. Nor can the Christian Socials' opportunistic provocation and exploitation of anti-Semitism afford them a claim to a truly liberal heritage; if anything, this arrogant ensemble of discriminatory rhetoric stood in stark contradiction to norms of individual humanity defended by nineteenth-century Liberalism. At the same time the party shared many earlier Liberal assumptions about the relationship of the administrative state to civil society, just as it recruited its electorate from middle- and lower-middle-class groups who in the past had voted or in the future might have voted Liberal. The inadequacy of conventional political language to mark out either the lateral or the forward boundaries of the party is apparent from the diversity of groups in the party's coalition which might be broadly designated as "bourgeois" but which themselves employed categories of social self-designation that surpassed or actually undercut a clear ordering by class or cultural identity. The party combined nativism, aesthetic radicalism, and a crude (and shrewd) anti-Semitism with formal (and genuinely felt) appeals to constitutional procedure, legal equity, and dynastic respectability. The party's basic belief that the liberal *Rechtsstaat* could be retained, but under new conceptions of social representation, new patterns of political clientage, and a new language of politics, marked it as a peculiarly early twentieth-century political phenomenon: a proponent of democratic cultural integration, but only on reductionist terms that immediately made marginal significant "democratic" components (the Jews, the Social Democrats, the poor, and so on) within the Christian Social polis.

The Christian Social party's historic contributions before 1914 were both exemplary and effective. Lueger's seizure of political power in Vienna was an important component of the construction of a modern, competitive party system in Austria, for it challenged the state to allow room for new social movements that would eventually call into question the legitimacy and autonomy of what might be called the "coalition absolutism" of 1867. That is, the Christian Socials must be seen not only as an anti-Liberal but also as an anti-absolutist force, in spite of their penchant for romantic, dynastic rhetoric. Yet, at the same time, the party became the last and perhaps "best" hope for an Austrian bourgeoisie threatened by the enormously attractive power of Austrian Social Democracy. Even more important, in seizing political power Lueger and his colleagues also gained valuable regional administrative prerogatives, which made them shareholders (however unwelcome or distrusted) in the state apparatus itself. By enhancing the corporate status of the city of Vienna, which enabled the party to play the role of producer and employer, and by vigorously defending the semi-autonomous economic and fiscal prerogatives of the Crownland of Lower Austria, the party anticipated in structural terms the curious organized capitalism that underlay the social revolution of Red Vienna in the 1920s. If the party seemed to play a dubious, relatively unimaginative role in the interminable debates over internal war aims between and within various German *bürgerlich* groups during the First World War—debates which threatened the institutions of regional and local autonomy—this only demonstrated how important those institutions had become to the Christian Socials by 1914.

Finally, with its strong support for universal suffrage in 1905–6, the Christian Social party not only contributed to the unraveling of the compromise between dynastic-bureaucratic absolutism and Liberalism that was the hallmark of the 1867 system: it also made a fundamental, if unintended, contribution to the creation of an independent sphere of public power unlimited by and uncontrolled by the world of private domestic (or personal) wealth. Its impact on the modern state had not merely an institutional-structural force but also a political-anthropological effect. The Christian Social party's major role in creating and legitimating the world of bipolar social and cultural hatreds that was sustained between 1918 and 1938 must be counterposed to the role of its successor party after 1945 in contributing to the success of the democratic parliamentarism and economic neocorporatism that eventually stabilized the new regime and overcame the operational consequences of interwar hatreds. In both instances the Christian Social party played out the roles of emancipatory provocation and functional self-interest that it had already articulated under the Empire. The history of the Christian Social party can be seen only within the limits of its time and judged in the context of its time.

NOTES

ÖKS Österreichs katholisches Sonntags-
      blatt
ÖW Österreichische Wochenschrift
ÖZP Österreichische Zeitschrift für Poli-
      tikwissenschaft
PA Politisches Archiv
PAAA Politisches Archiv des Auswär-
      tigen Amtes
PRO Public Record Office
RGBl Reichsgesetzblatt
Rp Reichspost
SMZ Sonn- und Montags-Zeitung
SP Stenographische Protokolle über
      die Sitzungen des Hauses der Abgeord-
      neten

SPNÖ Stenographische Protokolle des
      niederösterreichischen Landtages
UM Ministerium für Kultus und Unter-
      richt
V Vaterland
VGAB Verein für Geschichte der Arbei-
      terbewegung
VW Volkswohl
WF Wiener Familienfreund
WGGT Wiener Gewerbegenossen-
      schaftstag
WSLA Wiener Stadt- und Landesarchiv
ZVSV Zeitschrift für Volkswirtschaft,
      Sozialpolitik und Verwaltung

PREFACE

1. *Political Radicalism in Late Imperial Vienna: The Origins of the Christian Social Movement, 1848–1897* (Chicago, 1981).

2. Richard J. Evans, *Death in Hamburg: Society and Politics in the Cholera Years, 1830–1910* (Oxford, 1987); David Blackbourn, *Class, Religion and Local Politics in Wilhelmine Germany: The Centre Party in Württemberg before 1914* (New Haven, 1980); George Steinmetz, *Regulating the Social: The Welfare State and Local Politics in Imperial Germany* (Princeton, 1993). See also Lothar Gall, ed., *Stadt und Bürgertum im 19. Jahrhundert* (Munich, 1990), and, for general background, the essays in David Blackbourn and Richard J. Evans, eds., *The German Bourgeoisie. Essays on the Social History of the German Middle Class from the Late Eighteenth to the Early Twentieth Century* (London, 1991).

3. Wolfgang R. Krabbe, *Die deutsche Stadt im 19. und 20. Jahrhundert. Eine Einführung* (Göttingen, 1989), provides a helpful recent survey of the explosion of urban governmental agendas after 1880 in Germany. See also Brian Ladd, *Urban Planning and Civic Order in Germany, 1860–1914* (Cambridge, Mass., 1990); and, using the *Städtetag* movement as an example of the fragile self-empowerment of municipal governments, Hermann Beckstein's *Städtische Interessenpolitik. Organisation und Politik der Städtetage in Bayern, Preussen und im Deutschen Reich 1896–1923* (Düsseldorf, 1991).

4. The important work of Margaret Anderson on the Center party has raised a series of parallel questions about late nineteenth-century German politics. See especially *Windthorst. A Political Biography* (Oxford, 1981); "The Kulturkampf and the Course of German History," in *CEH*, 19 (1986): 82–115; and "Interdenominationalism, Clericalism, Pluralism: The *Zentrumsstreit* and the Dilemma of Catholicism in Wilhelmine Germany," *CEH*, 21 (1988): 350–78. On a related topic, the research of Celia Applegate has shown the power of the *Heimat* ideal, glorifying localist identities, among the late-

nineteenth-century German bourgeoisie. See "Localism and the German bourgeoisie: the 'Heimat' movement in the Rhenish Palatinate before 1914," in *The German Bourgeoisie*, pp. 224–54, as well as *A Nation of Provincials: The German Idea of Heimat* (Berkeley, 1990).

5. The principal articulation of the former position is David Blackbourn and Geoff Eley, *The Peculiarities of German History. Bourgeois Society and Politics in Nineteenth-Century Germany* (Oxford, 1984). Hans-Ulrich Wehler's various works are usually seen as typifying the latter approach, but see also Jürgen Kocka's recent restatement in "Bürgertum und bürgerliche Gesellschaft im 19. Jahrhundert. Europäische Entwicklungen und deutsche Eigenarten," in *Bürgertum im 19. Jahrhundert. Deutschland im europäischen Vergleich* (3 vols., Munich, 1988), 1: 11–76. For helpful assessments, see Robert G. Moeller, "The Kaiserreich Recast? Continuity and Change in Modern German Historiography," *Journal of Social History*, 17 (1983–84): 655–83; and Jürgen Kocka, "German History before Hitler. The Debate about the German 'Sonderweg'," *Journal of Contemporary History*, 23 (1988): 3–16.

6. See especially Waltraud Heindl, *Gehorsame Rebellen. Bürokratie und Beamte in Österreich 1780 bis 1848* (Vienna, 1991), pp. 329–33.

7. See most recently Robert Luft, "Politischer Pluralismus und Nationalismus. Zu Parteiwesen und politischer Kultur in der tschechischen Nation vor dem ersten Weltkrieg," *Österreichische Zeitschrift für Geschichtswissenschaften*, 2 (1991): 72–87, as well as Bruce M. Garver, *The Young Czech Party 1874–1901 and the Emergence of a Multi-Party System* (New Haven, 1978), and Gary B. Cohen, *The Politics of Ethnic Survival. Germans in Prague, 1861–1914* (Princeton, 1981).

8. These transactions were clearly part of larger processes involving the redefinition of what the "state" actually was in Central Europe in the late nineteenth and early twentieth centuries. See especially the insightful comments of Michael Geyer in "The State in National Socialist Germany," in Charles Bright and Susan Harding, eds., *Statemaking and Social Movements. Essays in History and Theory* (Ann Arbor, 1984), pp. 193–97.

9. For the cultural and political practices of the Central European *Stadtbürger*, see especially Hans-Ulrich Wehler, "Die Geburtsstunde des deutschen Kleinbürgertums," in Hans-Jürgen Puhle, ed., *Bürger in der Gesellschaft der Neuzeit. Wirtschaft—Politik—Kultur* (Göttingen, 1991), pp. 199–209; and *Deutsche Gesellschaftsgeschichte* (2 vols., Munich, 1989), 1: 177–92, 202–17; 2: 174–85. From a different perspective, see also the essays in *Stadt und Bürgertum im 19. Jahrhundert*.

10. Emmerich Tálos, Ernst Hanisch, and Wolfgang Neugebauer, eds., *NS-Herrschaft in Österreich 1938–1945* (Vienna, 1988), p. ix.

11. For two recent valuable efforts to think about links between the pre- and post-1918 epochs, see Donald L. Neiwyk, "Solving the 'Jewish Problem': Continuity and Change in German Antisemitism, 1871–1945," *Year Book of the Leo Baeck Institute*, 35 (1990): 335–70; and Robert Wohl, "French Fascism, Both Right and Left: Reflections on the Sternhell Controversy," *JMH*, 63 (1991): 91–98.

12. See especially the work of the Bielefeld *Bürgertum* project, as well as the series on *Bildungsbürgertum im 19. Jahrhundert* (Stuttgart, 1985–92), and Blackbourn and Evans, eds., *The German Bourgeoisie*. For Austria, see now Ernst Bruckmüller, Ulrike Döcker, Hannes Steckl, and Peter Urbanitsch, eds., *Bürgertum in der Habsburger-Monarchie* (Vienna, 1990).

CHAPTER ONE

1. The city of Vienna served both as capital of the western half of the Empire and as capital of the Crownland of Lower Austria. The population of the city in December 1910 was 2,031,498; Lower Austria as a whole had 3,530,698 inhabitants.

2. In Vienna, as elsewhere in the Empire, enfranchisement for males was based on either taxable income or personal and professional status. Until 1900 the city electorate was divided into three hierarchical curial groupings (*Wahlkörper*), each of which elected one-third of the city councilmen. For a discussion of the system, see my *Political Radicalism*.

3. The *Magistrat* was the appointed municipal bureaucracy, nominally chaired by the mayor, but in fact run by its own director (*Magistratsdirektor*). In this book I will retain the original German word, *Magistrat*, so as to avoid confusing the municipal civil service with the Imperial civil service. Civil servants of the higher ranks of the *Magistrat* were required to meet educational and training norms similar to those which state civil servants of equivalent ranks were held accountable.

4. I use the word "state" to mean both the central bureaucratic-ministerial-judicial apparatus in Vienna (the central ministries and the high courts), together with the Crown's regional and district administrative instruments (such as the *Statthaltereien* and the district courts); and the central parliament.

5. The *Statthalter* was the Crown's official representative in each of the larger Crownlands. His office, including his administrative staff, was the *Statthalterei*. In this book I will retain the original German word, *Statthalter*, rather than translate the word as "governor," which has an entirely different meaning in American English. Until 1911 this position was held by Count Erich Kielmansegg, who was then succeeded by Count Richard Bienerth. The *Statthalter* exercised general administrative authority on behalf of the Cabinet and the Crown throughout the Crownland, as well as managing the relations of the government with the Crownland's self-governing institutions of the Diet (*Landtag*) and the Provincial Executive Committee (*Landesausschuss*). Outside of Vienna, this control was exercised on the local district level with the assistance of Imperial civil servants called District Captains (*Bezirkshauptmänner*) who were appointed by the Crown and who reported to the *Statthalter*. Vienna, a large, self-governing administrative unit with its own charter, was exempt from such direct executive control. Indeed, the municipal administration functioned in lieu of a *Bezirkshauptmannschaft* as the Imperial administrative authority "of the first instance" (*politische Behörde erster Instanz*), with the elected mayor and the locally appointed city bureaucracy representing the city to the *Statthalterei* and being responsible for implementing Imperial decrees

and policies in the city. The city of Vienna was thus "local" and "political" when it acted in its own areas of policy responsibility (which Austrian jurists called its *selbständiger Wirkungskreis*), and it also served as a delegated Imperial administrative authority when exercising or implementing policy which was Imperial in origins and thus belonged to the *übertragener Wirkungskreis*. This latter facet explains why municipal civil servants in the *Magistrat* could be held to the same performance norms as those of their counterparts in the state civil service, since in some aspects of their jobs they were in fact "acting" as state officials.

6. See Carl Johannes Fuchs, "Die Entwicklung der Gemeindebetriebe in Deutschland und im Ausland," *Schriften des Vereins für Sozialpolitik in Wien*, 132 (1910): 65. For surveys of the development of the municipalization projects, as well as an objective evaluation of their financial successes, see Felix Czeike, *Liberale, christlichsoziale und sozialdemokratische Kommunalpolitik (1861–1934)* (Vienna, 1962), and Maren Seliger and Karl Ucakar, *Wien, politische Geschichte 1740–1934. Entwicklung und Bestimmungskräfte grossstädtischer Politik* (2 vols., Vienna, 1985), pp. 783–917. On the municipalization movement in Germany, see Brian Ladd, *Urban Planning and Civic Order in Germany, 1860–1914* (Cambridge, Mass., 1990), esp. pp. 236–51.

7. The municipal gasworks opened on 31 October 1899. The operations of the older *Wiener Tramway Gesellschaft* were replaced in late 1899 by the operations of the *Bau- und Betriebsgesellschaft* of Siemens, which was owned by the Deutsche Bank in Berlin. For these agreements, see *Vertrag welcher am 28. November 1898 . . . zwischen der Gemeinde Wien einerseits und der Firma Siemens & Halske andererseits abgeschlossen wurde* (Vienna, 1898). This was merely a temporary solution, and by April 1902 negotiations were concluded for the the city to take over the property rights and operate its own streetcar system. Municipal operations commenced on 1 July 1903. The municipal electrical works opened on 1 August 1902. On the city's loan problems, see *Die Zeit*, 8 January 1898, pp. 29–30; 29 January 1898, pp. 71–72.

8. Lueger relied on August Lohnstein, who was the General Director of the *Länderbank*, for financial advice and support throughout the period. See, for example, the report on the prospects for a new subway system for Vienna that Lohnstein sent to Lueger on 24 March 1908, I. N. 41544, *Handschriftensammlung*. That Lohnstein became one of Lueger's principal financial advisers was one of the many ambiguous facets of Christian Social anti-Semitism. For Lohnstein's involvement in the city's loan efforts, see *AZ*, 11 March 1900, pp. 6–7.

9. See Stephan Koren, "Die Industrialisierung Österreichs—vom Protektionismus zur Integration. Entwicklung und Stand von Industrie, Gewerbe, Handel und Verkehr," in *Österreichs Wirtschaftsstruktur. Gestern-Heute-Morgen*, ed. by Wilhelm Weber (2 vols. Berlin, 1961), 1: 367–68.

10. *Die Entwicklung der städtischen Strassenbahnen im zehnjährigen Eigenbetriebe der Gemeinde Wien* (Vienna, 1913), p. 147.

11. See the evaluation of Ministerialrat Dr. Pöschl in Z. 22051, 21 May 1908, *FM Präs.* Lueger himself insisted that the streetcar system "auch für die Zukunft eine reiche

Quelle von Einnahmen eröffnet, durch welche wieder andere dringende Bedürfnisse der Grossstadt befriedigt werden können." *Bericht des Referenten betreffend die Aufnahme eines Investitions-Anlehens von 285 Millionen Kronen . . ., Z.* 15. 142, ad Beil. Nr. 342 ex 1901, *Gemeinderat der Stadt Wien,* p. 9. For a similar evaluation, by an expert not sympathetic to the Christian Socials, see K. T. Wächter, "Die Gemeindebetriebe der Stadt Wien," in *Schriften des Vereins für Sozialpolitik,* 130 (1909): 213–18. For a typical Liberal critique of the programs, see Ludwig Vogler's discussion of the 1908 municipal loan in *NFP,* 9 January 1908 (M), pp. 2–3.

12. One might well argue that the Christian Socials' glorification of the *Vaterstadt* was a late nineteenth-century revival and reappropriation of that cult of local urban paternalism and corporatism that marked many Central European cities before 1848. Hans-Ulrich Wehler has called this earlier process one in which "das Identitätsgefühl des Stadtbürgers . . . allein mit seiner Stadt unauflöslich verbunden [war]." Wehler, "Die Geburtsstunde des deutschen Kleinbürgertums," p. 202. Yet the general fascination with technological modernity on the public scene that was manifest within the Christian Socials' ranks also calls at least partially into question Wehler's claim that "die mächtigen Kräfte der neuen Welt"—including technology and mass communications—were "von der unüberhörbar lärmenden Kulturkritik des Kleinbürgertums als wahre Greuel perhorresziert" (p. 207). A more nuanced way of exploring the social proclivities of at least some of these urban voters and their political leaders is clearly called for.

13. *Rp,* 29 November 1904, p. 9. Lueger would never admit that municipal socialism, by making the city budget depend on subsidies from the municipal utilities which the working classes did use, as opposed to more traditional direct taxation which they did not pay, undermined the very logic of the proprietary city concept. This eventually became one of the Social Democrats' most persuasive arguments against the curial system.

14. This process of appropriation and revival of traditional *bürgerlich* acts and words was apparent throughout the period up to 1914. For example, the Christian Socials decided in 1904 to revive the traditional Prater corso of the *Bürgertum,* as a challenge to the socialist May Day, using the *Bürgervereinigung* as its principal sponsor. See *NFP,* 10 May 1904 (M), p. 9; *NWT,* 18 June 1904, p. 9; *DZ,* 9 May 1905, pp. 5–6. A copy of the statutes of the association is in *H.A. Akten. Kleine Bestände,* Schachtel 1–4, *WSLA.* The legal and political consequences of the *Bürgerrecht* are described in *Statistisches Jahrbuch der Stadt Wien für das Jahr 1900,* pp. 98–99.

15. "Generalversammlung der Wiener Bürgervereinigung," *DZ,* 4 December 1905 (M), p. 2.

16. See the reports in *Statistisches Jahrbuch der Stadt Wien für das Jahr 1901,* p. 188; *Statistisches Jahrbuch der Stadt Wien für das Jahr 1905,* pp. 114–15; *Statistisches Jahrbuch der Stadt Wien für das Jahr 1910,* pp. 120–21.

17. A senior official in the Präsidialbureau of the *Magistrat,* Robert Jiresch, later recounted that the oath-taking ceremonies of the new *Bürger* were family affairs, since candidates brought their spouses and (often adult) children. According to Jiresch, these

events were among Lueger's favorite appearances ("Da war Dr. Lueger in seinem Element und es gab ebensoviele feierliche wie heitere Szenen"). This is from a memoir by Jiresch published in the *Rp* in 1930, quoted in Rudolf Kuppe, *Karl Lueger und seine Zeit* (Vienna, 1933), p. 573. Note also the comment in Marianne Beskiba, *Aus meinen Erinnerungen an Dr. Karl Lueger* (Vienna, n.d.), p. 88: "Bezeichnend für Lueger war es, dass seine intimen 'Freunde' sich ausschliesslich aus sehr bemittelten Leuten rekrutierten; arme Teufel und wenn dieselben von noch so hingebungsvoller Treue und Selbstlosigkeit, hielt er sich vom Leibe."

18. The gas and electrical works were "Meisterwerk der fortgeschrittensten Technik." *Rp*, 20 July 1904, p. 1. See also the celebratory descriptions of the progressiveness of the gasworks in the official guide, *Die Erbauung des Wiener städtischen Gaswerkes. Im Auftrage des Herrn Bürgermeisters Dr. Karl Lueger bearbeitet* (Vienna, 1901); and the comments on the streetcar system in "40 jähriger Bestand der Strassenbahnen in Wien," *Zeitschrift für Elektrotechnik*, Heft 42, 1905, p. 3: "So hat denn die technische Welt alle Ursache, sich des ausserordentlichen Aufschwunges zu erfreuen, welchen die Strassenbahnen in Wien genommen haben, was sie insbesondere dem zielbewussten Streben der jetzigen Gemeindeverwaltung und ihres gegenwärtigen Bürgermeisters Dr. Karl Lueger zu verdanken haben. . . ." Characteristic also was the two-volume guide to Vienna produced in 1905 by the *Österreichische Ingenieur- und Architekten-Verein* with a heavy municipal subvention, *Wien am Anfang des XX. Jahrhunderts.* Its subtitle was *Ein Führer in technischer und künstlerischer Richtung,* but most of the first volume related to the former subject, namely, the technological progressiveness of municipal developments.

19. As Arthur Mann has observed, "the social engineer had replaced the ward boss," at least in the imaginations of those who sought to confront urban reform in a revolutionary way. See his "British Social Thought and American Reformers of the Progressive Era," *Mississippi Valley Historical Review,* 42 (1955–56): 686. Lueger claimed in 1901 that technical progress only arrived in the city once he had attained political power: "Erst der jetzigen Gemeindeverwaltung war es vorbehalten, auf allen Gebieten des öffentlichen Lebens Wandel zu schaffen," including a gasworks which was the "Bewunderung der ganzen Welt." *Bericht des Referenten,* p. 1.

20. Carl E. Schorske, *Fin de siècle Vienna. Politics and Culture* (New York, 1980), pp. 24–115.

21. See the debates in the *SPNÖ,* 1903, pp. 1251–65. For the background, Elisabeth Koller-Glück, *Otto Wagners Kirche am Steinhof* (Vienna, 1984).

22. See Lueger's comments in *Rp,* 20 October 1907, p. 4; Peter Haiko and Renata Kassal-Mikula, eds., *Otto Wagner und das Kaiser Franz Josef-Stadtmuseum. Das Scheitern der Moderne in Wien* (Vienna, 1988), pp. 74–75.

23. *AB,* 1913, pp. 1838–39; Haiko and Kassal-Mikula, eds., *Otto Wagner,* pp. 90–102.

24. *AB,* 1913, p. 1820; Leon Botstein, "Music and Its Public. Habits of Listening and the Crisis of Musical Modernism in Vienna, 1870–1914." Dissertation, Harvard

University, 1985, p. 1082. For a commentary on the *Stadtmuseum* controversy, see Ludwig Hevesi, "Otto Wagners Stadtmuseum," in *Altkunst-Neukunst. Wien 1894–1908* (Vienna, 1909), pp. 254–59.

25. Efforts to think about, if not to resolve, the tensions between cultural tradition and technological modernity mark much of the literary work of the period, particularly that of Robert Musil. See especially David S. Luft, *Robert Musil and the Crisis of European Culture: 1880–1942* (Berkeley, 1980). Cate Giustino of the University of Chicago is now researching a Ph.D. dissertation on the cultural and administrative history of Prague in the late nineteenth century that will discuss these problems in a Czech context.

26. See *Der Wald- und Wiesengürtel und die Höhenstrasse der Stadt Wien* (Vienna, 1905). This pamphlet was published by the municipality at Lueger's direction. The author insisted that the band of parks and gardens would enhance a city "whose real magic lies in its combination of scenic charm and the structural magnificence of a modern city of millions" (p. 4). Not only would the gardens signify and unify past and future, but they would also conduct the traveler into the glories of Vienna's corporate and embattled role in history, for the Kahlengebirge recalled the "welthistorische Sendung" of the city (p. 25).

27. *Festschrift herausgegeben anlässlich der Hundertjahrfeier des Wiener Stadtbauamtes* (Vienna, 1935), p. 50.

28. Heinrich Goldemund, *Generalprojekt eines Wald- und Wiesengürtels und einer Höhenstrasse für die Reichshaupt- und Residenzstadt Wien* (Vienna, 1905), pp. 3–4.

29. *Die städtischen Elektrizitäts-Werke und Strassenbahnen in Wien* (Vienna, 1903), p. 82.

30. Heinrich Goldemund later recalled with pride in 1935 that the Christian Social administration had prevented overdevelopment of the Inner City by insisting on a balanced approach to economic modernization. See Heinrich Goldemund, "Der städtebauliche Werdegang Wiens," in *Festschrift*, pp. 74ff. See also *Die Gemeindeverwaltung der Stadt Wien in der Zeit vom 1. Jänner 1914 bis 30. Juni 1919* (Vienna, 1923), p. 73.

31. Wächter, "Die Gemeindebetriebe," p. 218. In his "Music and Its Public" Leon Botstein provides many examples of similar projects to bridge premodern and modern values in the Viennese musical world after 1890. See especially pp. 1410ff.

32. On the party and Abraham a Sancta Clara, see Johannes Eckardt, "Zum fünfundzwanzigjährigen Bestande der österreichischen Leo-Gesellschaft," *Das Neue Österreich* (February, 1917), p. 57, as well as Robert A. Kann, *A Study in Austrian Intellectual History. From Late Baroque to Romanticism* (New York, 1960), pp. 109–13. For the city's enthusiastic support of Schubert's music, see Botstein, "Music and Its Public," pp. 1033–34.

33. *Die städtischen Elektrizitäts-Werke und Strassenbahnen in Wien*, pp. 135–36.

34. For German parallels see Ladd, *Urban Planning*, pp. 67–73.

35. See most recently Michael John, *Hausherrenmacht und Mieterelend: Wohnverhältnisse und Wohnerfahrung der Unterschichten in Wien, 1890–1923* (Vienna, 1982);
Albert Lichtblau, *Wiener Wohnungspolitik 1892–1919* (Vienna 1984); Peter Feldbauer,
*Stadtwachstum und Wohnungsnot. Determinanten unzureichender Wohnungsversor-
gung in Wien 1848 bis 1914* (Vienna, 1977); and Wolfgang Hösl and Gottfried Pirhofer,
Wohnen in Wien 1814–1938. Studien zur Konstitution des Massenwohnens (Vienna,
1988).

36. In 1907, 82 of the 163 City Council members were property owners. The percentage was even higher for the *Stadtrat,* all of whose members were Christian Social
politicians, where 20 out of 31 members were property owners. *Hausherren* interests
in (and beyond) the party led the fight against a new *Bauordung,* which was still not
approved by the City Council when the war broke out in 1914. See the debates in the
AB, 1909, pp. 2583–86; as well as the commentaries in *AZ,* 30 October 1909, p. 9; 10
November 1909, p. 8; and 12 November 1909, pp. 7–8.

37. For the transmission of European municipal socialist models to an American
audience, see Albert Shaw, *Municipal Government in Continental Europe* (New York,
1895); and Frederic Howe, *The City, the Hope of Democracy* (New York, 1905) and
The British City: The Beginnings of Democracy (New York, 1907). Ernest Griffith captured the paradox of this kind of reform when he noted that "then, as now, there was
doubt about the relative operating efficiency of the city government as compared with
private operation, especially if the municipally owned utility (as frequently happened)
was to be looked upon as a happy hunting ground for the spoilsman." *A History of
American City Government. The Conspicuous Failure, 1870–1900* (Washington, D. C.,
1983), p. 193.

38. See Kuppe, *Karl Lueger,* pp. 400–401.

39. See *Die Gemeinde-Verwaltung der Stadt Wien im Jahre 1904* (Vienna, 1906),
p. 310.

40. *AB,* 1908, p. 2988.

41. "Ein Interview mit Dr. Lueger," *Rp,* 1 December 1907 (M), p. 4.

42. *AB,* 1908, p. 3082.

43. On the inadequacies of city labor codes and social welfare provisions for municipal employees, the best contemporary source is the Christian Social Laborites' own
newspaper: *CSAZ,* 23 June 1900, p. 1; 20 October 1900, p. 6; 8 September 1900, p. 3;
27 October 1900, p. 6; 9 March 1901, p. 5; 20 September 1901, pp. 1–2; 14 December
1901, pp. 1–2; 31 May 1902, p. 5; 10 January 1903, p. 5; 9 May 1903, p. 4; 23 May
1903, p. 5; 20 June 1903, p. 5. See also the commentary in *AZ,* 31 July 1907, pp. 6–7;
and Lueger's comments about how he would deal with city workers who did not behave
themselves in *AZ,* 4 July 1908, p. 5. For a modern evaluation, which stresses continuities between Liberal and Christian Social regimes on welfare and social policy, see Seliger and Ucakar, *Wien,* pp. 867, 911ff.

44. See, for example, Ladd, *Urban Planning,* pp. 201ff.

45. *Die Gemeinde-Verwaltung der Stadt Wien im Jahre 1904,* pp. 75–79, as well as Karl Seitz's acerbic comments in *SPNÖ,* 1904, pp. 86–92, 96–98. The *AB,* 1908, pp. 582–83 has a list of seven large subventions, amounting to over 98,000 crowns, which the party gave to various congresses held in the city. The 1907 Catholic Congress alone received 20,000 crowns.

46. See Robert A. Kann and Peter Leisching, eds., *Ein Leben für Kunst und Bildung. Eduard Leisching 1858–1938. Erinnerungen* (Vienna 1978), pp. 65–67, 112, for Christian Social harrassment of the *Volksbildungsverein.*

47. For the organization of poor care in Vienna in this period, see *Die Gemeinde-Verwaltung der Stadt Wien im Jahre 1902* (Vienna, 1904), pp. 315–19. For the attempt of one Christian Social *Bezirksvertretung* to rid itself of the poor altogether, by transferring a local asylum for vagrants from the Landstrasse to the periphery of the city, see *AZ,* 13 February 1908, p. 7. Michael John has drawn attention to the self-interested cases of landlords who were also poor-care councillors, and who were thus in a position to give aid so that their tenants could pay their rent! Michael John, "Obdachlosigkeit— Massenerscheinung und Unruheherd im Wien der Spätgründerzeit," in Hubert Ch. Ehalt, Gernot Heiss, and Hannes Stekl, eds., *Glücklich ist, wer vergisst. . . ? Das andere Wien um 1900* (Vienna, 1986), pp. 184–85, and the illustration preceding p. 177.

48. *AB,* 1908, p. 3192; *AZ,* 20 December 1908, p. 9.

49. Kenneth Prewitt, "Social Sciences and Private Philanthropy: The Quest for Social Relevance," p. 11. Unpublished paper, presented at the University of Chicago, September 1991.

50. *AZ,* 11 March 1910, p. 2.

51. The number of people involved in the system was considerable. In 1907, for example, 42,136 individuals sought temporary financial assistance from the public poor-care system. Many thousands more were dealt with by private associations, in which Christian Social *Mittelstand* voters also played key roles. The distribution of cases by district makes it clear that the greatest number of cases fell in districts like Ottakring, Favoriten, and Brigittenau, where the socialists had their strongest political roots. *Statistisches Jahrbuch der Stadt Wien für das Jahr 1907* (Vienna, 1909), p. 826.

52. *AB,* 1898, pp. 1575–87.

53. *DZ,* 5 December 1905, p. 4. The play, with revisions, even went into print: Mathilde Melkus, *Die Spinnerin am Kreuz. Ein Singspiel für die Jugend in einem Aufzuge. Musik von Josef Wenzl* (Leipzig, n.d.), *Wiener Stadtbibliothek.*

54. The speech is in *Die Gemeinde-Verwaltung der Stadt Wien für das Jahr 1904,* p. 303, and Jakob Dont, *Das Wiener Versorgungsheim. Eine Gedenkschrift zur Eröffnung im Auftrage der Gemeinde Wien* (Vienna, 1904).

55. *Statistisches Jahrbuch der Stadt Wien für das Jahr 1907,* pp. 863–64. Lainz served as a central screening point for all poor in need of institutional care. Those over seventy, and those who had special reasons to remain in Vienna, were generally kept at Lainz; others were transferred to other institutions. See *Die Gemeinde-Verwaltung der Stadt Wien im Jahre 1912,* p. 328.

56. Dont, *Das Wiener Versorgungsheim,* pp. 11, 15. For general policy background, see Seliger and Ucakar, *Wien,* pp. 850–68, as well as Gerhard Melinz and Susan Zimmermann, *Über die Grenzen der Armenhilfe. Kommunale und staatliche Sozialpolitik in Wien und Budapest in der Doppelmonarchie* (Vienna, 1991), pp. 154–59.

57. The Lainz settlement is described in detail in Dont, pp. 18–72. The altarpiece was painted by Hans Zatzka, the brother of a Ludwig Zatzka, who was a leading Christian Social politician on the *Stadtrat.* For a similar, if less striking example of the "bourgeoisfication" of sacral art see Flordius Rohrig's comment on Tom von Dreger's Last Supper from 1916 ("wo die Apostel fast wie eine bürgerliche Stammtischrunde wirken") in "Kirche und Staat in Österreich 1804–1918," in *Gott erhalte Österreich. Religion und Staat in der Kunst des 19. Jahrhunderts* (Eisenstadt, n. d. [1990]), p. 19.

58. See Jakob Dont, ed., *Der heraldische Schmuck der Kirche des Wiener Versorgungsheims* (Vienna, 1911).

59. See the ministerial negotiating strategies outlined in Z. 445, 14 January 1899; and their implementation in Z. 650, 20 January 1899, *FM Präs.*

60. Z. 650, 20 January 1899; Z. 2788, 24 March 1899, ibid.

61. Copy of the *Vortrag,* dated 16 February 1902, Z. 12142, ibid.

62. See Weiskirchner to the Finance Ministry, 20 May 1914, Z. 39092/1914; and the final determination in Z. 46961, 19 June 1914, and Z. 57686, 27 July 1914, ibid.

63. The *Stadtrat* was the elected executive committee of the municipality that was responsible for allocating public contracts, for managing the city budget, and for appointing all municipal officials and all city schoolteachers. It therefore had enormous power. In order to differentiate the *Stadtrat* from the City Council, I will retain its German title in this book. Unlike the other City Council members, who served *pro bono,* the men who sat on the *Stadtrat* received an annual administrative salary of 3,000 crowns. According to the municipal charter of 1890 the *Stadtrat* consisted of 22 members elected from the plenum of the City Council, plus the mayor and two vice-mayors. The charter of 1900 confirmed these arrangements. The number was enlarged in 1905 to 31, including the mayor and three vice-mayors. As the city's executive committee, it met far more frequently than did the Council. In 1906, for example, the City Council held only 29 meetings, whereas the *Stadtrat* met 134 times. Unlike the Council, its meetings were conducted in camera, with debates not published. Lueger's dislike of the *Stadtrat* was probably genuine, but the alternative he proposed in March 1899—to divide its duties among a larger number of politicians organized in four sections (*Abteilungen*)—would have been almost as oligarchical and just as secretive, but it would have enhanced his own authority as mayor against that of his cronies.

64. For Lueger's previous and often contradictory statements on the municipal suffrage, see *AZ,* 11 June 1899, pp. 2–3.

65. My assessment of the negotiations for the new 1900 franchise is based on the unpublished files in B2 ad 415/1899–1900, *Statt. Präs., NÖLA;* and Carton 1567, 11/1, *MI Präs.* For the general background, see the excellent overview in Maren Seliger and Karl Ucakar, *Wahlrecht und Wählerverhalten in Wien 1848–1932. Privilegien, Partizi-*

pationsdruck und Sozialstruktur (Vienna, 1984), as well as idem, *Wien,* pp. 753–66, which is based on published sources.

66. Not surprisingly the *Hausherren* who were already in the First Curia were fundamentally opposed both to the first version, which would have abolished their curia, and to the second, which would have expanded it. See the petition of the *Hausbesitzerverband,* dated 11 April 1899, B2 ad 415, *NÖLA.*

67. Clemens Weber, "Karl Hermann Wolf (1862–1941)." Dissertation, University of Vienna, 1975, pp. 105–7; Eduard Pichl, *Georg Schönerer und die Entwicklung des Alldeutschtums in der Ostmark* (3d ed., 6 vols., Oldenburg, 1938), 5: 404–5; and Karl Fertl, "Die Deutschnationalen in Wien im Gegensatz zu den Christlichsozialen bis 1914." Dissertation, University of Vienna, 1973, pp. 143–63.

68. The first draft from 1899 is in *H.A. Akten. Kleine Bestände* ("Gemeindeverfassung"), Mappe 1, *WSLA.* For Lueger's justification of this draft, see *AB,* 1899, pp. 698, 740–43. Various Liberal protests to the government are in B2 ad 415, 1900, *NÖLA.*

69. *AZ,* 28 March 1899, p. 2; 30 March 1899, pp. 1–2; 15 April 1899, p. l; 21 April 1899, p. l. Lueger adopted a stance of outraged innocence, blaming the government for the turnaround. *AB,* 1899, pp. 1082–83.

70. See *SPNÖ,* 1899, *Beilage* 115, and the debates held on 27 May 1899 in ibid., pp. 280–382. The City Council supported the new version in *AB,* pp. 1639–63.

71. See the campaign broadside in Z. 807, Carton 72, *CPW.*

72. A later, party-generated survey of the occupations of Third Curia voters in Landstrasse, Wieden, Neubau, Alsergrund, Hietzing, Hernals, and Währing from 1913 demonstrated the equilibrium of forces that eventually resulted. Of the 6,089 registered voters in Landstrasse, for example, 1,562 were master artisans, 2,704 were petty officials or *Diener* in public service, 1,085 were private employees, and 664 were workers. In Wieden, the artisans had a larger relative percentage (901 voters, as opposed to 588 for the servants, 630 for the private employees, and 156 for the workers), but even there they could no longer totally dominate the ward's politics. See Z. 512, Carton 72, *CPW.*

73. See Lueger to Kielmansegg, 27 June 1899, *NÖLA.* Lueger justified excluding *Personaleinkommensteuer* voters, other than in the Fourth Curia, since the city did not have access to this revenue, and hence, they did not contribute to the corporation: "Wenn Pflichten auch Rechte entsprechen sollen, würde daher diesen Steuerpflichtigen kein Gemeindewahlrecht gebühren." Gessmann spoke in the same vein on 23 June 1899: *AZ,* 24 June 1899, p. 4.

74. In his obituary of Lueger, Alfred Ebenhoch caught the mayor's own proclivities toward the middle sectors of the *Bürgertum* when he observed that "Er starb in durchaus mittelbürgerlichen Verhältnissen, obwohl er in der Lage gewesen wäre, sich zu bereichern." *Hochland,* 7 (1910): 231.

75. *SPNÖ,* 1900, pp. 53–127, 130–215, 218–65; *AB,* 1900, pp. 468–79. The changes Koerber and Kielmansegg demanded in the May 1899 draft are in B2 ad 415, 18 January 1900, *NÖLA.* The party complied with most of the demands in the version Gessmann and Weiskirchner presented to the Diet on 20 February (*SPNÖ,* 1900, *Beilage* 24), but held out until the last possible moment to reintroduce the *Stadtrat* on February

23. Immediately after the settlement Kielmansegg wrote to Lueger confidentially asking that he begin making preparations for the spring elections on the new model, since the administrative time required was at least two months. This suggests that a deal had already been worked out among Lueger, Kielmansegg, and Koerber that the new version would be sanctioned. Letter of 26 February 1900 (draft), B2 ad 415, Z. 1226, *NÖLA*.

76. For the final political maneuvering, see *AZ,* 23 February 1900, p. 5; 25 February 1900, p. 3. The Christian Socials left the schoolteachers in the Second Curia in the final bill, although in the 1899 version they had pushed them into the Third Curia. The franchise also introduced a three-year residency requirement in the new Fourth Curia, which would disqualify many potential socialist voters. Voters in the three privileged curias had a double vote, since they were also allowed to vote in the general Fourth Curia. The total number of city councilmen was now 158, up from 138 under the 1890 system.

77. Weiskirchner to Handel, 13 August 1919, Carton 2, *NL Handel.*

78. Koerber's *Vortrag,* with the Emperor's notations, is in Z. 1751, 16 March 1900, 11/1, Carton 1567, *MI Präs.* Koerber also accepted the Christian Socials' view that the poorer elements of the population did not deserve more than a modest presence in the Council since they contributed no direct taxes, while depending more on social services than did the bourgeois voters. Kielmansegg's report on the final bill is also in this file, Z. 1229, 1 March 1900. Lueger also had the advantage over the Cabinet of threatening to schedule elections for the Council in the spring of 1900 and then simply refusing to give the vote to any of the new income-tax voters, by citing the interpretations of the *Magistrat* of the 1890 franchise. Kielmansegg was obviously very worried about this, and informed Koeber in early January 1900 of Lueger's threat. Letter to Koerber, 8 January 1900, Z. 123, ibid. The final version of March 1900 was thus a compromise between the Cabinet, which did not want the precedent established of new elections without the participation of the new taxpayers, and the Christian Socials, who would allow them in only on the most disadvantageous of terms. See also Julius Ofner's later comments on the Liberals' defeat in *SP,* 1908, p. 4142.

79. Gustav Kolmer, *Parlament und Verfassung in Österreich* (8 vols., Vienna, 1902–14), 8: 46.

80. In order to inaugurate the new system, the Second and Fourth Curias were subject to complete renewal in 1900, with by-elections held to fill vacant seats in the First and Third Curias. The Third Curia then voted as a whole in 1902, the First as a whole in 1904. For these elections see *Statistisches Jahrbuch der Stadt Wien für das Jahr 1900,* pp. 104–7; *Statistisches Jahrbuch der Stadt Wien für das Jahr 1902,* pp. 210–12; *Statistisches Jahrbuch der Stadt Wien für das Jahr 1904,* pp. 118–20.

81. No independent pan-German politician survived the 1900 election in the Second Curia: "Jetzt sind im II. Wahlkörper die Wolf-Schönerer Männer und die Juden ganz hinausgefegt." *Rp,* 27 May 1900, p. 2; *DV,* 26 May 1900 (M), p. 2.

82. For an overview of the statistical results of municipal elections before 1914, see Seliger and Ucakar, *Wien,* pp. 923–63.

83. See Gerhard Hirschfeld and Lothar Kettenacker, eds., *Der "Führerstaat": My-*

thos und Realität. Studien zur Struktur und Politik des Dritten Reiches (Stuttgart, 1981), most notably in the essays by Tim Mason, Hans Mommsen, and Jane Caplan. See also Jane Caplan, *Government without Administration: State and Civil Service in Weimar and Nazi Germany* (New York, 1988), and Dan P. Silverman, "Nazification of the German Bureaucracy Reconsidered: A Case Study," *JMH*, 60 (1988): 496–539.

84. "Die heutige Generation hat keinen Begriff, mit welchen terroristischen Mitteln damals der Wahlkampf geführt wurde." Eduard Heinl, *Über ein halbes Jahrhundert. Zeit und Wirtschaft* (Vienna, 1948), p. 42. In his *50 Jahre Erlebte Geschichte* (Vienna, 1959), pp. 49–50, 63–68, Oskar Helmer gives a similar portrait of prewar electoral conflicts, seen from a Social Democratic perspective.

85. For Jewish attitudes toward the *Ständestaat,* see the judicious evaluation in Harriet Pass Freidenreich, *Jewish Politics in Vienna, 1918–1938* (Philadelphia, 1991), pp. 180–203. Freidenreich nicely summarizes the dilemma of the Viennese Jews: "Discrimination formally based on religious grounds, while scarcely desirable, was certainly preferable to discrimination based on racial principles. Austrian antisemitism one could live with, if necessary. Its German Nazi counterpart would not let you live" (p. 202).

86. The recent biography by Richard Geehr, *Karl Lueger. Mayor of Fin de Siècle Vienna* (Detroit, 1990), presents the counter-case on the issue of Lueger's relationship to the Jewish community. Aside from citations of individual examples of Lueger's anti-Semitic rhetoric, Geehr does not demonstrate (at least to my mind) that Lueger was intent on a systematic de-legalization of the Jews in Vienna. It would be extremely tempting to make analogies between Lueger's habitus and that of Hitler, but this does not seem to me to be sufficient, or even reasonable, for explaining the very complicated history of the Christian Social party. No one can excuse anti-Semitism, and Lueger must bear responsibility for what he did. But it is important to integrate Lueger's career in the context of the history of the Christian Social party viewed as a complex social organization which evolved over time and changed over time.

87. Lueger's disgruntlement with the Liberal press, which he consciously identified as being staffed by Jews, was evident in the late 1880s and early 1890s. See the quote cited in Robert S. Wistrich, *The Jews of Vienna in the Age of Franz Joseph* (New York, 1989), p. 222.

88. See the candid comments in Helmut Gruber, *Red Vienna: Experiment in Working-Class Culture, 1919–1934* (New York, 1991), pp. 25–27, and Robert S. Wistrich, *Socialism and the Jews: The Dilemmas of Assimilation in Germany and Austria-Hungary* (Rutherford, N. J., 1982), pp. 225–61. Jacques Kornberg's excellent new biography of Herzl, *Theodor Herzl. From Assimilation to Zionism* (Bloomington, 1993), offers powerful evidence of the prevalence of anti-Semitism among Liberal notables in fin de siècle Vienna. Hermann Bielohlawek, when faced with charges of Christian Social discrimination against Jewish officials, observed laconically: "Ein bisschen Antisemitismus muss auch schon in der Ära Prix gesteckt sein, weil eigentlich verhältnissmässig wenig Juden im Rathhause angestellt waren, und soviel ich von einigen liberalen Gemeinderäten erfahren habe, so ganz frei von dieser Krankheit war Prix

auch nicht." *AB,* 1908, p. 3078. Note also Karl Kraus's ironic comment in early 1901 that "[d]ie Zeit, da der Antisemitismus in Deutschösterreich parteibildend war, ist vorüber, seit der Antisemitismus so sehr Gemeingut aller deutschen Parteien geworden ist, dass ein Noske nirgends mehr Unterschlupf finden kann." *Die Fackel,* Nr. 64, January 1901, p. 2.

89. Anton Pelinka, *Stand oder Klasse? Die Christliche Arbeiterbewegung Österreichs 1933 bis 1938* (Vienna, 1972), pp. 215, 217; as well as the hard-hitting but fair evaluation of Kunschak in Bruce F. Pauley, *From Prejudice to Persecution. A History of Austrian Anti-Semitism* (Chapel Hill, 1992), pp. 158–63.

90. I believe that Bruce Pauley's recent contribution, *From Prejudice to Persecution,* pp. 45–49, supports this argument: even though opportunistic and, in and of itself, not of enormous material harm to the Jewish community, Lueger's use of anti-Semitic rhetoric presented a terrible model.

91. Arthur Schnitzler, *My Youth in Vienna.* Translated by Catherine Hutter (London, 1971), p. 120. Schnitzler's evaluation was shared by almost all other major and minor contemporaries who knew Lueger. They range from enemies on the Left and the Right, and former collaborators in the center. See, for example, Wilhelm Ellenbogen, *Menschen und Prinzipien. Erinnerungen, Urteile und Reflexionen eines kritischen Sozialdemokraten,* ed. Friedrich Weissensteiner (Vienna, 1981), pp. 65–66; Pichl, *Schönerer,* 5: 381–85; Rudolf Sieghart, *Die letzten Jahrzehnte einer Grossmacht. Menschen, Völker, Probleme des Habsburger-Reichs* (Berlin, 1932), pp. 315–16; Ernst Victor Zenker, *Ein Mann im sterbenden Österreich. Erinnerungen aus meinem Leben* (Reichenberg, 1935), pp. 73–74; and Alexander Spitzmüller, *" . . . und hat auch Ursach, es zu lieben"* (Vienna, 1955), p. 74. Note especially the observation by the Jewish community leader Sigmund Mayer (who knew Lueger well, but who opposed his policies categorically) that "Seine antisemitische Gesinnung war stets ganz und gar Heuchelei. Vor allem war bei ihm von dem physischen Rassenhass gegen die Juden gar keine Rede." Sigmund Mayer, *Ein jüdischer Kaufmann 1831 bis 1911. Lebenserinnerungen* (Leipzig, 1911), p. 296. See also the balanced evaluations in Peter Pulzer, *The Rise of Political Anti-Semitism in Germany and Austria,* rev. ed. (Cambridge, Mass., 1988), pp. 198–203; Robert S. Wistrich, *Between Redemption and Perdition. Modern Antisemitism and Jewish Identity* (London, 1990), pp. 43–54; Sigurd Paul Scheichl, "The Contexts and Nuances of Anti-Jewish Language: Were All 'Antisemites' Antisemites?," in Ivar Oxaal, Michael Pollak, and Gerhard Botz, eds., *Jews, Antisemitism and Culture in Vienna* (London, 1987), pp. 89–110; Leon Botstein, *Judentum und Modernität. Essays zur Rolle der Juden in der deutschen und österreichischen Kultur 1848 bis 1938* (Vienna, 1991); and Kornberg, *Herzl,* pp. 89–111.

92. *AT,* 17 February 1912, pp. 1–2; as well as *AZ,* 15 February 1912, p. 9; *DV,* 15 February 1912 (M), p. 9; *NFP,* 15 February 1912 (M), p. 14; *NWT,* 15 February 1912 (M), pp. 18–19. Mataja asked the question about Lueger's anti-Semitism to try to trap Heilinger—who was from Mataja's perspective a hostile witness—into contradicting himself.

93. A survey of city positions is in Z. 943, Carton 73, *CPW.* See also the "Personalstand in den einzelnen Ämtern am l. März 1902," Z. 968, 1902, Carton 66, *MD.*

94. The employment files, bound in huge, filthy packets, are in the archive of the *Magistrats-Direktion.* Major reforms in the municipal service occurred in 1898, 1902, 1906, and 1913. The details are in the appropriate volume of the *Die Gemeinde-Verwaltung der Stadt Wien* series. Salaries were adjusted in 1907 and 1911.

95. See Hierhammer to Weiskirchner, 11 April 1907, Z. 1506, Carton 107, *MD.* For socialist criticism of the *Stadtrat,* see *AZ,* 10 October 1908, pp. 9–10, 11 October 1908, p. 1; 15 October 1908, p. 8; 22 October 1908, p. 1; 22 November 1908, p. 10; 17 December 1908, pp. 8–10. For a good description of the administrative system under Lueger, see Karl Renner, "Ein Zerrbild der Autonomie," *K,* 5 (1911/12): 200–205.

96. For an example of how wealthy contractors or other businessmen subsidized municipal election campaigns, see the letters from contributors for the 1914 City Council campaign in Z. 861, Carton 73, *CPW.* The coordinator of the campaign fund was Heinrich Schmid who, not surprisingly, was a member of the *Stadtrat.* Unusually candid comments occurred about campaign contributions in the Lower Austrian Diet in January 1912, with allegations made about huge contributions having been offered in return for contracts. See *SPNÖ,* 1912, pp. 672–74.

97. A good example of such continuity was Lueger's *Präsidialvorstand,* Rudolf Bibl, who first joined the *Präsidialdienst* under Mayor Prix, but who loyally and enthusiastically served Lueger as well. See Bibl's "Erinnerungen an Dr. Lueger," *NWT,* 24 February 1935. See also *AZ,* 9 January 1900, p. 7, and 27 May 1903, p. 7, on Lueger's uneasiness in receiving delegations of city workers in his office with demands in hand. Jane Caplan points out that "in some influential quarters in the new regime, civil servants remained the objects of an unrelieved suspicion." *Der "Führerstaat,"* p. 180. This was much less the case with the Christian Socials, who welcomed the professional rationality of the *Magistrat.*

98. *CSAZ,* 23 June 1900, p. 2.

99. The Christian Social press tried its best to suppress reports of feuding between Kunschak's forces and the *bürgerlich* majority, but so wide was the gulf that this self-censorship was ultimately ineffective. See, for example, the angry report in the *Reichspost* on a protest by the Laborites in Margarethen against Sebastian Grünbeck, because the powerful *Hausherren* leader (and member of the *Stadtrat*) had openly opposed expanding the franchise to include the working classes. *Rp,* 26 February 1899, pp. 1–2; as well as *AZ,* 17 February 1899, p. 3; 23 February 1899, pp. 4–5.

100. This was especially true of the older, Liberal-appointed officials who were at the forefront of many of the modernization schemes executed during Lueger's tenure and at the same time were steadfastly loyal to the political needs of the Christian Social party. For German developments, see Krabbe, *Die deutsche Stadt im 19. und 20. Jahrhundert,* esp. pp. 129–39.

101. When they assumed power, the Christian Socials began to screen the religious background of all officials employed in the city who applied for or who were considered

for promotion, along with compiling information on their age and their seniority. These lists still exist in the *WSLA*. See, for example, Z. 590, 1898, Carton 48 and Z. 2863, 1898, Carton 50, *MD*. See also Karl Kraus's commentary on this issue in *Die Fackel,* Nr. 147, 21 November 1903, pp. 25–26. Kraus identified seven Jews out of 225 *Konzeptsbeamten,* and one Jew out of 159 *Stadtbauamtbeamten.* For various actions against Jewish officials, see Z. 768, 1897, Carton 43; Z. 590 15 March 1898, Carton 48; Z. 470, 1902, Carton 66; Z. 736, 1903, Carton 74; Z. 826, 1905, Carton 88; Z. 1974, 1907, Carton 110, *MD*.

102. *AB,* 1901, pp. 1099–1100.

103. "Einige dieser Beamten der Gemeinde, die vorzüglich qualifiziert waren und gegen die nichts vorgelegen ist, sind ja befördert worden, allerdings durch den Impuls des Herrn Bürgermeisters." Ibid., 1908, pp. 3095–96.

104. I found one case where a senior councillor questioned the implicit consent to professional anti-Semitism that his colleagues were giving, and that official (the aging Ferdinand Kronawetter, long Lueger's nemesis) was voted down. Z. 3012, 21 December 1897, Carton 43, *MD*. Doubtlessly there were other such cases, and it is certainly likely that at least some of the gentile officials felt sympathy for their Jewish colleagues.

105. See *Mitteilungen des Vereines der Beamten der Stadt Wien,* 27 November 1899, pp. 33–39.

106. Adler: "Werden nicht in Ihrem Rathaus die jüdischen Magistratsbeamten unverdient zurückgesetzt?" Lueger: "Es sind keine mehr da. Sie wurden alle—man kann sagen—in nobler Weise entschädigt. Nur einen der tüchtigsten Arbeiter unter meinen Beamten traf das Schicksal sehr hart und ich empfinde es heute noch als schwarzen Punkt, wenn ich an ihn und an sein Schicksal denke. Es gibt Trauriges, viel Trauriges in der Politik!" As reported in "Eine Erinnerung an Bürgermeister Dr. Lueger," p. 5 (1909), MS 769, Box 4, *Guido Adler Papers,* University of Georgia. For the background of this fascinating document, see Guido Adler, *Wollen und Wirken. Aus dem Leben eines Musikhistorikers* (Vienna, 1935), pp. 108–9. I am grateful to Leon Botstein for bringing this document to my attention. Karl Kraus also reports pension settlements for several of these individuals. *Die Fackel,* 21 November 1903, p. 26.

107. George Clare, *Last Waltz in Vienna. The Rise and Destruction of a Family 1842–1942* (New York, 1982), p. 23.

108. For example, the politicization of teacher appointments was widely acknowledged under the Liberal regime. Both Karl Seitz and Otto Glöckel owed their careers as teachers to Liberal political patrons.

109. *AB,* 1908, p. 3037.

110. "Verhandlungsschrift über die Sitzung des Bürgerklubs vom 18. Juli 1917," Carton 37, *CPW*. The transcripts of club or executive proceedings, on the parliamentary, regional, or municipal level for both the Christian Social and Social Democratic parties, of which I make substantial use in this book, were generally stenographic summaries of the actual debates. Like speeches reported in newspapers, they should be read as transcripted summaries, meant to convey the speaker's and/or author's basic meaning.

Unlike the proceedings of official bodies, however, such as the Diet or parliament, they were obviously not recorded on a word-for-word basis.

111. For a sample sheet, see Z. 1353, 1907, Carton 108, *MD*. The cases cited are also in Carton 108.

112. Rudolf Bibl reported that Lueger was accustomed to asking new officials at their oath-taking ceremony: "Wer hat denn Sie zum Magistrat gebracht?" Bibl, "Erinnerungen an Dr. Lueger." Yet it should also be noted that even Lueger could sometimes become disgusted by the extent of Christian Social nepotism, when it came to putting close family members on the public payroll. See Heinrich Hierhammer's recollections in Herta Hafner, "Heinrich Hierhammer. Vizebürgermeister von Wien, 1905–1918. Ein bürgerlicher Aufsteiger." Diplomarbeit, University of Vienna, 1988, p. 96.

113. See the case of Ferdinand Adam-Wessely, son of Vinzenz Wessely, who was a city councilman and guild leader. The younger Wessely obtained a job in the office supervising city election rolls, as well as the position of secretary in a craft guild. He was caught misappropriating 6,000 crowns in craft funds and forced to resign. *DR*, 29 November 1906, p. 5. Or the case of Emmerich Miklas, the brother of Wilhelm Miklas, a public-school teacher who was ranked low for a promotion even by the Christian Social-dominated school board, but who received it nonetheless. *AZ*, 20 June 1908, p. 8.

114. See Preinerstorfer's letter of 30 June 1914, Z. 992, Carton 73, *CPW*.

115. On Weiskirchner, see Karl Harrer, "Dr. Richard Weiskirchner." Dissertation, University of Vienna, 1950. Weiskirchner joined the municipal civil service in 1883, being first assigned to the department of the *Magistrat* that regulated public markets. He then worked in the statistical department, in the department for public health, and finally in the department responsible for poor care, before being appointed Vice-Director of the *Magistrat* in 1901. In 1889 he had joined the informal circle of anti-Liberal discussants that met at the Hotel "Zur goldenen Ente" under the direction of Franz Schindler, and he was one of the first municipal officials to join openly the Christian Social movement, a fact that was not unrelated to the fact that he was slated for a seat in parliament in 1897 and a seat in the Lower Austrian Diet in 1898.

116. Pawelka was singled out for an early award of the title of *Magistratsrat* in 1907 on the basis of his "geradezu ausgezeichnete Dienstleistung." Pawelka was an "überaus verwendbarer Beamter," which might or might not be a compliment, depending upon how one judged Pawelka's work in the municipal election office. Z. 845, 23 February 1907, Carton 107, *MD*.

117. For some striking examples in 1908, see *AZ*, 18 December 1908, p. 8.

118. Ibid., 20 June 1911, p. 4, arguing that Pattai had gotten numerous other former employees city or provincial patronage jobs.

119. For Koerber's memorandum, see Alois Czedik, *Zur Geschichte der k.k. österreichischen Ministerien 1861–1916* (4 vols., Teschen, 1917–20), 2: 419–51, esp. 421–22. For contemporary reactions, see especially *NFP*, 19 December 1904 (A), pp. 1–2, as well as the "Die autonomen Finanzen (Diskussion in der Gesellschaft Oesterreichischer

Volkswirte)," *Volkswirthschaftliche Wochenschrift,* 2 February 1905, pp. 81–87; and Rudolf von Herrnritt, "Zur Reform der inneren Verwaltung in Österreich," *Österreichische Rundschau,* 1 (1904–5): 645–49.

120. Kielmansegg transmitted Koerber's report to Lueger on 20 December 1904. Z. 26, Carton 87, *MD.*

121. Josef Harbich, "Studien über die Reform der inneren Verwaltung," 4 November 1905, pp. 6–7, Carton 87, *MD.* Georg Schmitz has observed that the officials in the central ministries always bore a certain jealousy toward regional and local government agencies, which was most clearly manifest in 1918–1920 when they "nunmehr angesichts des Erstarkens der Landesverwaltungen um ihre berufliche Existenz fürchtete." Georg Schmitz, *Der Landesamtsdirektor. Entstehung und Entwicklung* (Vienna, 1978), p. 24.

122. Wilhelm Hecke, "Referat über die 'Studien zur Reform der inneren Verwaltung'," 28 June 1905, Carton 87, *MD.*

123. *Mitteilungen des Klubs der rechtskundigen Beamten der Stadt Wien,* vol. 3, nr. 7, June, 1905, p. 4.

124. Wenzel Kienast, "Denkschrift 'Studien über die Reform der inneren Verwaltung'," 29 April 1905, Carton 87, *MD.*

125. Ernst von Plener, who was certainly no friend of the Christian Socials, correctly gauged the probable reactions of regional politicians like Lueger to a possible diminution of their prerogatives when he observed that, while such politicians might distrust involvement in the state goverment, on the *Land* level "[d]ort begreifen sie und üben sie die Empfindungen und Instinkte einer Regierungspartei vollkommen aus, haben den Mut und die Verantwortlichkeit, selbst für unpopuläre Massregeln einzutreten, welche sie im Interesse des Landes, seiner Verwaltung und seiner Finanzen für notwendig erachten." "Die autonomen Finanzen (Diskussion in der Gesellschaft Oesterreichischer Volkswirte)," *Volkswirtschaftliche Wochenschrift,* 2 February 1905, p. 82.

126. *Festschrift herausgegeben anlässlich der Hundertjahrfeier des Wiener Stadtbauamtes,* p. 27.

127. In 1906 the Council voted to institute "Zeitbeförderung," providing for regular steps in advancement apart from extraordinary promotions; and it also lowered the required number of years of service before retirement to thirty-five. Salaries were improved substantially in 1907. See *Die Gemeinde-Verwaltung der Stadt Wien im Jahre 1906* (Vienna, 1908), pp. 24–29; and *Die Gemeinde-Verwaltung der Stadt Wien im Jahre 1907* (Vienna, 1909), pp. 24–26; and Z. 2390, 1907, Carton 110, *MD.* The *Mitteilungen des Vereines der Beamten der Stadt Wien* contain detailed reports on various reforms undertaken between 1898 and 1914.

128. See, as examples, the incidents cited in *Mitteilungen des Vereines der Beamten der Stadt Wien,* 7 (1902): 43–45, and 13 (1908): 42.

129. Bibl, "Erinnerungen an Dr. Lueger."

130. *Kommunale Praxis,* 10 (1910): 321–23; Wächter, "Die Gemeindebetriebe," pp. 213–21; and Fuchs, "Die Entwicklung," pp. 65–72.

131. The district leader (*Bezirksvorsteher*) was elected by the ward's district committee (*Bezirksvertretung*), normally serving a six-year term. The ward committee consisted of between eighteen and thirty men who were elected by the district's voters, also for six-year terms. This committee was not the same as the district election committee (*Bezirkswahlkomitee*), which was a party, rather than a municipal agency, and which normally had a somewhat larger membership. But many of those elected to the district committee would also have been prominent members of the district election committee.

132. Heinl tells the charming story of trying to persuade a meeting of district leaders of the need for tighter party organization. Franz Rienössl, the *Vorsteher* of the Fourth District, replied: "Was wollen Sie denn da, junger Mann. Wir wissen, wie es im Bezirk aussieht, wir sind da, das genügt!" Heinl, *Über ein halbes Jahrhundert,* p. 18.

133. Ibid. See also Heinrich Mataja's allusion to Lueger's opposition to party reform in his letter to Ignaz Seipel, 3 April 1928, *NL Seipel.*

134. The *Bürgerklub* was the official name of the Christian Social parliamentary faction in the City Council. See the comments of Victor Silberer at the Hierhammer-Stahlich trial, *AZ,* 16 February 1912, p. 9, and the general reflections of Heinl, *Über ein halbes Jahrhundert,* pp. 15–18.

135. For the composition of the *Stadtrat,* see Seliger and Ucakar, *Wien,* p. 969. Similar distributions for the *Bezirksräte* can be calculated from data in the *Statistisches Jahrbuch der Stadt Wien für das Jahr 1907,* p. 128.

136. Kuppe, *Karl Lueger,* pp. 428–36, while not always reliable on details, offers many examples of this kind of political crowdsmanship.

137. From the lists of lecture courses Gessmann took, it is apparent that he found Suess's classes especially attractive. Gessmann Akten, *Universitätsarchiv,* Wien. See also Eduard Suess, *Erinnerungen* (Leipzig, 1916), p. 286.

138. Following the elections of 1896 the party controlled 33 out of 78 seats, exercising a de facto majority in cooperation with sympathetic German national and conservative aristocratic allies; in the elections of 1902 the Christian Socials seized 46 seats, thus exercising an absolute majority.

139. The *Landesausschuss* was elected by the members of the Diet. It consisted of six members, who essentially constituted a permanent executive committee for the Crownland.

140. For Lower Austria, see Leopold Kammerhofer, *Niederösterreich zwischen den Kriegen. Wirtschaftliche, politische, soziale und kulturelle Entwicklung von 1918 bis 1938* (Baden, 1987), and Georg Schmitz, *Die Anfänge des Parlamentarismus in Niederösterreich. Landesordnung und Selbstregierung 1861–1873* (Vienna, 1985), as well as the older work by Ferdinand Kant, "Der Niederösterreichische Landtag von 1902 bis 1908." Dissertation, University of Vienna, 1949. A modern introduction to the place of the Crownlands in Austrian political practice is contained in Wolfgang Pesendorfer, *Der Oberösterreichische Landtag. Historische Entwicklung, Wesen und Bedeutung einer Institution* (Linz, 1989).

141. Georg Jellinek, *Allgemeine Staatslehre*, 3d ed. (Bad Homburg, 1966), pp. 492, 647–60.

142. For the enhanced political and policy status of the Crownlands administrations, which provoked intense discussion and debate in juristic and government circles between 1897 and 1914, see Ferdinand Schmid, *Finanzreform in Oesterreich* (Tübingen, 1911), esp. pp. 3–41; Ernst Mischler, "Der Haushalt der österreichischen Landschaften," *Jahrbuch des öffentlichen Rechts der Gegenwart*, 3 (1909): 579–601; and debates in the *Stenographisches Protokoll der Enquete über die Landesfinanzen. 7. bis 12. März 1908* (Vienna, 1908). For the continuation of the controversy over the status of the Crownlands during the First World War, see the *Gutachten* of fourteen leading university experts on "Länderautonomie" in the *Österreichische Zeitschrift für öffentliches Recht*, 3 (1916): 3–199.

143. Gessmann's personal staff was thus substantially larger than that of any of the other members of the Committee. For many administrative purposes he *was* the Committee. See the detailed report concerning the new "Referats-Einteilung," Nr. 75.700/ 1902, *N. Öst. Landes-Ausschusss, NÖLA*. For the creation of the *Präsidialbüro*, see Schmitz, *Der Landesamtsdirektor*, pp. 10–12, 16.

144. "Der leitende Geist im Landesausschuss war damals und ist heute noch in der christlich-sozialen Partei überhaupt Dr. Albert Gessmann." Josef Scheicher, *Erlebnisse und Erinnerungen* (6 vols., Vienna, 1907–12), 5:105; a judgment confirmed by Schmitz, *Der Landesamtsdirektor*, p.18.

145. The *Arbeiter-Zeitung* observed upon Lueger's death in 1910 that the mayor rarely left Vienna to campaign elsewhere, even in Lower Austria. He remained a creature of the city all of his life. See *AZ*, 11 March 1910, p. 1.

146. "Christlich-Sociale, auf zur Organisation!" *Rp*, 18 January 1901, p. 1; Friedrich Funder, *Vom Gestern ins Heute. Aus dem Kaiserreich in die Republik* (Vienna, 1953), pp. 272–73.

147. Edeltrude Binder, "Doktor Albert Gessmann." Dissertation, University of Vienna, 1950, pp. 49–50; Scheicher, *Erlebnisse*, 5: 107–8.

148. See *Rp*, 6 September 1904, p. 2; 13 September 1904, p. 1; 18 September 1904, p. 2; 23 September 1904, pp. 1–2; 13 October 1904, pp. 1–2; 22 October 1904, pp. 1–2.

149. Baernreither Diary, Nr. 1, f. 54, Carton 4, *NL Baernreither;* for the Christian Socials' repudiation of Badeni in November 1897, see A 13864, 27 November 1897; A 13960, 29 November 1897; A 13969, 28 November 1897, Oest. 70/Bd. 31, *PAAA*. Two sensible reviews of the Christian Socials' behavior during the Badeni crisis may be found in Fritz Csoklich, "Das Nationalitätenproblem in Österreich-Ungarn und die christlichsoziale Partei." Dissertation, University of Vienna, 1952, pp. 56–80; and Berthold Sutter, *Die Badenischen Sprachenverordnungen von 1897* (2 vols., Graz, 1960–65), 2: 51, 126, 376–81. Csoklich and Sutter both place too great an emphasis on the events of 1897, alleging that they drove Lueger and the party in a pro-German direction. The Christian Socials did have to react to the risk of pan-German allures on their flanks

with an enhanced level of nationalist rhetoric, but the basic direction of the party as moderately pro-German, anchored in Vienna but also interested in Imperial harmony and comity, was evident before and after 1897.

150. In parliament in February 1901 Lueger argued that "es gibt gar keine frucht-bringende Tätigkeit und keine Möglichkeit einer gegenseitigen Annäherung, als bis wir uns wieder mit wirtschaftlichen Angelegenheiten befassen. . . . Wenn wir auf die wirkliche Brotfrage des Volkes zu sprechen kommen, wird es keinen Unterschied geben, ob jemand der einen oder der anderen Nationalität angehört, sondern jeder ist bestrebt, das möglichst Beste für das Volk zu finden." *SP,* 1901, p. 294.

151. Funder, *Vom Gestern,* pp. 200–203, and *Rp,* 1 February 1914, p. 5. For the background see Sutter, *Sprachenverordnungen,* 2: 124–26, 376–81. For an interesting evaluation of Opitz's influence, see also the observations of Franz Kordač, the Czech priest who in 1919 was appointed Archbishop of Prague, in A. K. Huber, ed., "Franz Kordačs Briefe ins Germanikum (1879–1916)," *Archiv für Kirchengeschichte von Böhmen-Mähren-Schlesien,* 1 (1967): 164–75.

152. For the *Pfingstprogramm* of 20 May 1899 see Czedik, *Zur Geschichte,* 2: 180ff., 453–64.

153. On Koerber's ministry, see Herwig Leitgeb, "Die Ministerpräsidentschaft Dr. Ernest v. Koerbers in den Jahren 1900–1904 und Oktober - Dezember 1916." Dissertation, University of Vienna, 1951; Alfred Ableitinger, *Ernest von Koerber und das Verfassungsproblem im Jahre 1900. Österreichische Nationalitäten- und Innenpolitik zwischen Konstitutionalismus, Parlamentarismus und oktroyiertem allgemeinem Wahlrecht* (Vienna, 1973); and the older survey in Kolmer, *Parlament,* 8: passim. On his investment program, see the report in A 7269, 15 May 1901, Oest. 86/1/Bd. 13, *PAAA;* as well as the modern evaluations in Alexander Gerschenkron, *An Economic Spurt That Failed. Four Lectures in Austrian History* (Princeton, 1977), pp. 76–110; and David F. Good, *The Economic Rise of the Habsburg Empire, 1750–1914* (Berkeley, 1984).

154. For Lueger's views of the canals, see his comments in the *Stenographische Protokolle. Wasserstrassenbeirath, III. Plenarversammlung am 31. Jänner 1903,* pp. 10–12, and his speech in *SP,* 1901, pp. 4496–4501.

155. Contemporary analysts also suggested that Lueger was eager to enhance the access of the city to cheap coal from the Moravian basin, and that by constructing this canal the monopoly enjoyed by the *Nordbahn* railroad in transporting coal to Vienna would be broken and the price of coal subjected to stronger competition.

156. Czedik, *Zur Geschichte,* 2: 346–52; Kolmer, *Parlament,* 8: 613–17. See also Tucher's report on the collapse of the ministry, Nr. 667, 28 December 1904, MAIII/2472, *BHSA.* For the Christian Socials and Koerber on the *Los von Rom* problem, see Czedik, 2: 344, as well as 347–48 for the role of Karel Kramář in Koerber's fall. See also *Rp,* 22 December 1904, p. 1 ("Der Protest des katholischen Volkes").

157. See "Nach Hause . . . ! Die christlichsoziale Partei und die Lage," *Rp,* 11 December 1904, pp. 1–2; "Dr. v. Koerber und die Stadt Wien," *DZ,* 3 January 1905, p. 6.

158. Josef Redlich, *Emperor Francis Joseph of Austria: A Biography* (New York,

1929), p. 458, argues that Kramář was instrumental in persuading Franz Joseph to accept Koerber's resignation by asserting that the Czechs would welcome Gautsch. Wedel raised the question of whether Koerber expected his resignation to be accepted. See A 269, 4 January 1905, Oest. 86/2/Bd. 14, *PAAA*. For Christian Social parliamentarist schemes, see the allusions in *Rp,* 11 December 1904, p. 1; and *DZ,* 1 January 1905, p. 1, as well as Wedel's discussion of the potential state significance of the Christian Socials as a reason for the Cabinet tolerating their foibles, which is probably based on his conversations with Koerber, in A 16885, 24 October 1904, Oest. 70/Bd. 42, *PAAA*.

159. See the "Resume der am 19. November 1904 abgehaltenen Besprechung," ff. 43–86, *NL Baernreither.*

160. On *Los von Rom,* see Lothar Albertin, "Nationalismus und Protestantismus in der österreichischen Los-von-Rom Bewegung um 1900." Dissertation, University of Cologne, 1953; and Andrew G. Whiteside, *The Socialism of Fools. Georg Ritter von Schönerer and Austrian Pan-Germanism* (Berkeley, 1975), pp. 243–62. On the conflict between the Protestant pastors and Schönerer, see Whiteside, *The Socialism of Fools,* pp. 251–59. See also the files "Los von Rom 1900–1910" in Carton 2146, 25, *MI Präs.*

161. The distinction between the political and religious sides of the movement is stressed by Gustav Reingrabner, "Der Evangelische Bund und die Los-von-Rom Bewegung in Österreich," in Gottfried Maron, ed., *Evangelisch und Ökumenisch. Beiträge zum 100jährigen Bestehen des Evangelischen Bundes* (Göttingen, 1986), pp. 258–71, as well as by Peter F. Barton, *Evangelisch in Österreich. Ein Überblick über die Geschichte der Evangelischen in Österreich* (Vienna, 1987), pp. 155–56.

162. This clever tactic was pursued by Karl Hron, *Habsburgische "Los von Rom" Kaiser. Eine Studie über die antiösterreichischen Tendenzen des ultramontanen Klerikalismus* (Vienna, 1901).

163. On the *Piusverein,* which was founded at the Fifth Catholic Congress in Vienna in November 1905, see Funder, *Vom Gestern,* pp. 314–21.

164. See the "Referat über die österreichische Volksschulgesetzfrage," August 1906, in *Protokoll der Bischöflichen Versammlung in Wien von 11. bis 18. Oktober 1906* (Olmütz, 1907), pp. 75–86, *EBDA*.

165. For Lueger and the church construction controversy, see *Rp,* 10 March 1899, pp. 1–2; 17 May 1899, pp. 1–2; 20 December 1899, pp. 1–3; as well as *AZ,* 1 February 1899, p. 6, and Alexander Täubler, "Christlichsoziale Kirche- und Klosterfürsorge," *K,* 5 (1911–12): 205–9. The City Council had voted a 30,000 fl. subvention for the St. Laurentius church project in December 1896, and also approved a grant of 100,000 crowns in February 1898 for the Jubiläumskirche under construction on the Erzherzog Karlplatz. It then agreed to participate on a 40 percent basis in February 1899 in a loan fund of 10 million crowns to assist in church construction in general. A Liberal councilman, Lucian Brunner, brought suit in the Administrative Court to stop these grants, on the grounds that they essentially compelled non-Christian taxpayers to support Catholic confessional projects. In two decisions, one in March 1899 and a second in December 1899, the Court found in favor of Brunner. See the *Sammlung der Erkennt-*

nisse des k.k. Verwaltungsgerichtshofes, 23 (1899), pp. 315–18, 1289–97. However, the public outcry against the Court's decision was so great, that, according to Funder, Lueger was able to intimidate it into softening its doctrinaire position about subventions. Following a subsequent decision by the Court in November 1906 (ibid., 30 [1906], pp. 1140–46), the city was able to resume some support for religious construction projects, if these could be presented as having substantial public-aesthetic and patriotic significance. See also Funder, *Vom Gestern,* pp. 234–37; and Robert Ehrhart, *Im Dienst des alten Österreich* (Vienna, 1958), pp. 102–4. It is important to note that Lueger's outrage over the Court's decision was more owing to what he thought a dangerous violation of Vienna's autonomy by the Court, than it was to any "Catholic" sensibilities on his part. As always, Lueger was interested in the practical exercise of power.

166. As a practical exercise, *Los von Rom* could hardly receive high marks. By March 1899 the police counted only a "relatively small" number of converts in Vienna, hardly the stuff from which a "mass" movement could be constituted ("Im Wiener Polizei-Rayon hat die Bewegung kaum besonderen Anklang gefunden"), 20 March 1899, J6 ad 494, Z. 2747, *Statt Präs., NÖLA.* Even many of Schönerer's most loyal voters in Vienna refused to make the final break with their legal, if wholly nominal, Catholic identities. The total number of conversions has always been a source of debate. See Reingrabner, "Der Evangelische Bund," pp. 259–62, as well as the annual reports in the *Evangelische Kirchenzeitung für Österreich.*

167. *Rp,* 8 January 1902, p. 9.

168. For the national elections of 1901, see *Statistisches Jahrbuch der Stadt Wien für das Jahr 1901,* pp. 190–91; *CSAZ,* 5 January 1901, pp. 1–2; and the police reports in E5 ad 94/1901, *Statt. Präs., NÖLA.* The number of registered voters in the Fifth Curia was 307,741.

169. For Koerber's official position, see his comments on 3 June 1901 in *SP,* 1901, pp. 4873–74. It is important to note, however, that lower-level state administrative authorities were well-placed to harrass the Protestants in more discreet ways. Between 1899 and 1901 the number of foreign (German) Protestant vicars who were accepted by the government authorities to work permanently in Austria declined precipitously. See Reingrabner, "Der Evangelische Bund," p. 264.

170. This was one issue on which the lower clergy and the bishops easily united, and for which the much-detested tradition of *Staatskirchentum* could be conveniently, if only temporarily, revived. The Austrian bishops sent two promemoria (dated 18 March 1899 and 20 December 1901) to the government, protesting an alleged lack of force in responding to the *Los von Rom* propaganda. A principal reason why the state should use the Austrian criminal code against *Los von Rom* propagandists was the traditional "dynastische Treue" of the Catholic clergy and their loyalty to the state. See the *Protokoll der Bischöflichen Versammlung in Wien von 12. bis 20. November 1901* (Brünn, 1902), pp. 30–33, *EBDA.*

171. "[D]ass die Sozialdemokratie sich als der einzige Gegner der Christlich-

Sozialen erwiesen hat, der bis auf weiteres überhaupt politisch ernstlich in Frage kommt. Der Kampf gegen den Klerikalismus liegt im wesentlichen auf den Schultern unserer Partei." *Protokoll über die Verhandlungen des Gesamtparteitages der Sozialdemokratischen Arbeiterpartei in Oesterreich. Abgehalten zu Wien vom 9. bis zum 13. November 1903* (Vienna, 1903), p. 14.

172. Franz Patzer, "Die Entwicklungsgeschichte der Wiener Sozialdemokratischen Gemeinderatsfraktion. Von ihren Anfängen bis zum Ausbruch des ersten Weltkrieges." Dissertation, University of Vienna, 1949, pp. 35–40. In 1900 the socialists won 56,720 votes against 77, 608 for the Christian Socials. In 1906 the respective totals were 98,112 as opposed to 110,936. The Social Democrats increased their share of Fourth Curia seats to seven in the elections of 1906.

173. The party lost almost 10,000 votes compared with the 1897 Fifth Curia elections (1897 = 117, 141 votes; 1901 = 107,162 votes), blaming voter disillusionment with the apparent collapse of the state political system. In the case of one of the seats, where the Laborite Josef Mender ran, it is likely that Christian Social *bürgerlich* voters also boycotted the election. See *Rp,* 5 January 1901, p. 1; 16 January 1901, pp. 1–2; *CSAZ,* 5 January 1901, p. 1; and the reports in E5 ad 5573/1901, *NÖLA.*

174. The linkage between the municipal and Crownland franchises reflected the assumption that a person eligible to vote for one self-governing taxing body—the City Council—should also be eligible to vote for the companion self-governing taxing body—the Diet. The discrepancy between the 1901 and 1902 pools of voters reflected a three-year residency rule for Diet elections. For the Diet elections, see *Statistisches Jahrbuch der Stadt Wien für das Jahr 1902,* pp. 208–9; *Rp,* 30 October 1902, p. 5; 7 November 1902, pp. 1–2; and the police reports in E2 ad 6065, Nr. 7410/1902, *Statt. Präs.*

175. For an insightful commentary on the significance of the 1902 elections, see "Die Landtagswahlen in Oesterreich und die christlichsociale Partei," *HPB,* 130 (1902): 824–35.

176. E2 ad 6065, police report of 5 November 1902, *Statt Präs., NÖLA.*

177. Police reports on the crowd violence make it clear that it occurred in spite of the best attempts of the local Social Democratic leadership to control it, but the reports also insist that bottle-throwing workers had provoked police intervention. Ibid., report of 10 November 1902. In contrast, the Social Democrats blamed the police for having provoked the clashes and for having invaded the Favoriten *Arbeiterheim* without sufficient justification. See Victor Adler, *Aufsätze, Reden, Briefe* (11 vols., Vienna, 1922–29), 11: 178–84. The campaign itself was marked by numerous clashes between Christian Social and Social Democratic sympathizers.

178. For the instrumentalization of the parliament in early Austro-Marxist thought, see Alfred Pfabigan, "Das ideologische Profil der österreichischen Sozialdemokratie vor dem Ersten Weltkrieg," in Erich Fröschl, Maria Mesner, and Helge Zoitl, eds., *Die Bewegung. Hundert Jahre Sozialdemokratie in Österreich* (Vienna, 1990), pp. 49–51.

See also Brigitte Perfahl, "Zum Marxismus-Defizit der österreichischen Sozialdemokratie 1889–1901," in *Geschichte als demokratischer Auftrag. Karl Stadler zum 70. Geburtstag* (Vienna, 1983), pp. 143–51.

179. Wolfgang Maderthaner, "Die Entwicklung der Organisationsstruktur der deutschen Sozialdemokratie in Österreich 1889 bis 1913," in idem, ed., *Sozialdemokratie und Habsburgerstaat* (Vienna, 1988), pp. 47–51.

180. *Protokoll über die Verhandlungen des Parteitages der deutschen sozialdemokratischen Arbeiterpartei in Oesterreich. Abgehalten zu Salzburg vom 26. bis zum 29. September 1904* (Vienna, 1904), p. 96; Hans Mommsen, *Die Sozialdemokratie und die Nationalitätenfrage im habsburgischen Vielvölkerstaat* (Vienna, 1963), pp. 349ff., 364; Julius Braunthal, *Victor und Friedrich Adler. Zwei Generationen Arbeiterbewegung* (Vienna, 1965), pp. 148–50.

181. The best source of socialist school-politics in Vienna is *Freie Lehrerstimme* (1896–). Otto Glöckel, *Selbstbiographie* (Zurich, 1939), has useful descriptive information on school conditions and teacher attitudes before 1900. A contemporary assessment may be found in the *Festschrift zum 25-jährigen Bestande des Zentralvereines der Wiener Lehrerschaft 1896–1921* (Vienna, 1921). For overviews of Seitz's educational politics, see Gerda Wondratsch, "Karl Seitz als Schulpolitiker. Die Zeit bis zum Ersten Weltkrieg." Dissertation, University of Vienna, 1978; and Hajime Tezuka, "Die Junglehrer-Bewegung. Vorgeschichte der Schulreform Glöckels." Dissertation, University of Vienna, 1981. See also Oskar Achs and Eva Tesar, "Aspekte sozialistischer Schulpolitik am Beispiel Täublers und Furtmüllers," in Helmut Konrad and Wolfgang Maderthaner, eds., *Neuere Studien zur Arbeitergeschichte. Zum fünfundzwanzigjährigen Bestehen des Vereins für Geschichte der Arbeiterbewegung* (3 vols., Vienna, 1984), 3: 559–79; and Ernst Glaser, *Im Umfeld des Austromarxismus. Ein Beitrag zur Geistesgeschichte des österreichischen Sozialismus* (Vienna, 1981), pp. 301–17. For general policy background relating to the schools, see Helmut Engelbrecht, *Geschichte des österreichischen Bildungswesens. Erziehung und Unterricht auf dem Boden Österreichs* (5 vols., Vienna, 1982–88), 4: 77–82 and passim.

182. See the report of 1 September 1910, Z. 38228, Carton 4471, 18, *UM Präs.*

183. Lueger's father was a laboratory attendant, while Gessmann's was a mid-level civil servant, and Weiskirchner's father was a schoolteacher (as a young teacher he had taught Karl Lueger). Hierhammer and Bielohlawek are discussed in Chapter 2, but both came from very modest, *kleinbürgerlich* backgrounds. Richard Schmitz's father was a butcher turned petty municipal official; Heinl's parents were servants and house custodians, and Seipel's father was a *Fiaker* driver and later a theater concierge.

184. For Gessmann's views on the schools, see *SP*, 1902, pp. 11308–25.

185. It is possible and even likely that the staunch conservatism of Christian Social party leaders about elementary education reflected a sense that the families of their constituents were not necessarily restricted to the opportunities and social resources that the *Volksschulen* afforded students, even if *bürgerlich* children also attended those schools. One should also keep in mind that Viennese schools were segregated by class

stratification between and even within districts. Municipal statistics correlating occupational rank of fathers with numbers of schoolchildren suggest that in wealthier districts like the Neubau and Josefstadt children of bourgeois families, as opposed to children from working-class backgrounds, were dramatically overrepresented in school enrollments, whereas in poorer districts like Favoriten and Ottakring the reverse was the case. See the occupational ranking in *Statistisches Jahrbuch der Stadt Wien für das Jahr 1912* (Vienna, 1914), p. 447. Further, J. Robert Wegs has recently made the important argument that lower-middle-class families, while often residing in the same districts and sometimes even on the same streets as the working classes, were much more likely to send their children on to more advanced schooling, whether humanistic or technical, than were working-class families. See *Growing Up Working Class: Continuity and Change among Viennese Youth, 1890–1938* (University Park, Pa., 1989), p. 28. This is confirmed by the recent research of Gary B. Cohen, who finds that *kleinbürgerlich* matriculation at the University of Vienna remained consistently strong through the last part of the nineteenth century, and even surpassed that at some German universities. See his "Die Studenten der Wiener Universität von 1860 bis 1900," in Richard Georg Plaschka and Karlheinz Mack, eds., *Wegenetz europäischen Geistes II. Universitäten und Studenten* (Vienna, 1987), p. 307, as well as Cohen's impressive *Education and Middle-Class Society in Late Imperial Austria, 1848–1918* (forthcoming, Purdue University Press). Certainly the interventions that both Albert Gessmann and Robert Pattai made in early 1908 concerning the reform of the Austrian *Mittelschulen* make little sense unless one assumes that this level of schooling was of some potential interest to their party's electoral clientele. See Robert Pattai, *Das klassische Gymnasium und die Vorbereitung zu unseren Hochschulen. Reden und Gedanken* (Vienna, 1908); and Albert Gessmann, *Zur Mittelschulreform. Vortrag in der Versammlung des 'Vereins für Schulreform' am 12. Jänner 1908* (Vienna, 1908). Gessmann proposed creating a new, more progressive form of secondary school which would adopt features taken from both the *Gymnasium* and the *Realschule;* Pattai's approach was more traditional and conservative.

186. Rudolf Hornich, "Autorität als Fundamentalbegriff der Gesellschafts- und der Erziehungswissenschaft," *Erstes Jahrbuch des Vereines für christl. Erziehungswissenschaft* (Kempten, 1908), pp. 49–76.

187. The Imperial official Robert Ehrhart has offered the interesting suggestion that the nature of the education that these young schoolteachers received in their teacher-training institutes in the later 1880s and early 1890s—stressing "realistische Kenntnisse" but lacking the "mildernde Korrektive der humanistischen Studien" that could only be obtained in a *Gymnasium*—was part of the driving force behind their actions. See *Im Dienste des alten Österreich*, pp. 97–98.

188. Karl Seitz, "Persönliche Erinnerungen," Carton 77, f. 85, *NL Seitz, WSLA.* Seitz himself was placed in an orphanage by his impoverished mother, who could not care for him. His experience of social and emotional dislocation was thus not simply the result of external observations. Josef Enslein, Seitz's colleague in the *Jungen* and a

leader in the *Freie Schule* movement, also grew up in an orphanage, as did the later leader of the Social Democratic educational reform, Otto Felix Kanitz.

189. Glöckel, *Selbstbiographie,* pp. 36–37. In 1900 another member of the socialist teachers, Siegmund Kraus, conducted an informal investigation of the frequency with which school children were involved in before- or after-school jobs. The Christian Socials tried to block his efforts, but Kraus succeeded in assembling sufficient data to show how widespread (and pernicious) the phenomenon was. For a summary of his *Enquete,* see Gertrude Langer-Ostrawsky, "Wiener Schulwesen um 1900," in Ehalt, ed., *Glücklich ist,* pp. 97–102.

190. Seitz himself was known in the movement as a "Praktiker" and not as an adherent of theory.

191. *Volksbote,* 1 March 1912, p. 3, quoted in Wondratsch, "Karl Seitz," p. 82. For a summary of the views of the *Jungen,* see also the pamphlet published by Alexander Täubler under the pseudonym Adolf Mössler, *Österreichische Volksschulzustände. Ein Wort an das Volk und seine Lehrer* (Vienna, 1897).

192. Seitz always insisted that it was a major mistake of the 1869 legislation not to have separated completely religion and education and that the whole school system thus rested on faulty premises. See *FLS,* 1898, pp. 142–43.

193. When it was first created in mid-1896 the *Zentralverein* was a coalition association which included teachers sympathetic to German nationalist views, as well as the socialist *Jungen.* The two factions divided in the spring of 1898 over the issue of loyalty to "Germanic" values, and the association became a bastion of Social Democracy.

194. *FLS,* p. 152. Engelbrecht's attempt (*Geschichte,* p. 127) to minimize the signficance of this program by conflating it with *bürgerlich* pedagogy is, I believe, incorrect. It is true that the program does not yet contain the radical clarity of Enslein's or Glöckel's later pedagogical theories, but it would also be fair to say that the latter were certainly anticipated by the former. As Achs and Tesar have shown, Täubler (and, I would insist, Seitz) believed as early as 1897 that the school was not and could not be a "neutral" and "free" place for the child's individual development, but that it was necessarily embedded in a matrix of deeply "political" power relations and that the new school of the future would also have to mark out and come to terms with these relations. Achs and Tesar, "Aspekte sozialistischer Schulpolitik," p. 569, as well as Tezuka, "Die Jung-Lehrerbewegung," pp. 144–54.

195. See "Was du nicht willst," *Österreichische Schulzeitung,* 25 October 1899; and the *Erlass* of the Lower Austrian School Council, 5 November 1900, in Z. 2267, 18, *UM Präs.* Jordan's reprimand was upheld by the Ministry of Education. His agitational activities had also run afoul of the then Liberal-controlled school board in 1894, when he was reprimanded for having damaged the dignity of the teaching corps. For his own account of his career, see *Aus meinem Leben. Erinnerungen eines Achtzigjährigen* (Vienna, n.d.).

196. For example, Seitz's exegesis of a Catholic teacher-training manual prepared by Fr. S. Rudolf Hassmann, offered in the *Landtag* in December 1904, deliberately

underestimated the concern of the author with the welfare of children in the classroom. Compare Seitz's comments in *SPNÖ,* 1904, pp. 54–55, with the original text of Hassmann, *Allgemeine Erziehungslehre für Lehrer- und Lehrerinnen-Bildungsanstalten* (Vienna, 1907).

197. The *Verein der Lehrer und Schulfreunde* was the subject of an amazing array of insults from the Social Democrats, who castigated it as a product of total opportunism. Its newspaper, the *Deutsche Schulzeitung,* occasionally published intelligent essays, however. By 1904 the group had approximately 1,000 teacher members and an additional 800 members who were drawn from *bürgerlich* political circles. See *DSZ,* 1904, p. 270.

198. Johann Schmidt, *Entwicklung der katholischen Schule in Österreich* (Vienna, 1958), p. 136.

199. Anton Pelinka has recently pointed out a similar instrumentalist orientation in the work of Karl Renner on the law. See Anton Pelinka, *Karl Renner zur Einführung* (Hamburg 1989), pp. 30–37. It is enlightening to read the speeches of Seitz, Glöckel, and Täubler alongside Max Horkheimer's early essays on critical theory.

200. It is worth noting that the Liberal regime in Vienna in the early 1890s was also unsympathetic to the *Jungen.* When the young Josef Enslein dared to publish an article in the *Österreichische Schulzeitung* criticizing appointment practices of the Liberal-dominated School Board, he was transferred to a less desirable school in an outlying district as a punishment. See Josef Enslein, "Vom Unterlehrer zum Unterstaatssekretär," *AZ,* 7 March 1948, p. 3.

201. See the comments of the *Bezirkshauptmann* of Floridsdorf to Erich Kielmansegg on why he had to appoint 24 teachers as election commissioners (out of 30 such appointments) in 1902: "da sich Wirtschaftsbesitzer zu diesem Amte wenig eignen, andere Personen aber in den kleineren Landgemeinden erfahrungsgemäss überhaupt nicht vorhanden sind." And even when peasants did serve on the commissions, "dieselben dringend eines Berathers von grösserer allgemeiner Bildung bedürfen." Nr. 6820, E 2 ad 3459, *Statt. Präs., NÖLA.*

202. The Municipal School Board had 34 members, 21 of whom were political appointees elected by the City Council. Four seats were held by school teachers elected by their colleagues.

203. Tezuka, "Die Junglehrer-Bewegung," pp. 93–119. For Lueger's anti-socialism in teacher appointments, see his comments before a group of twenty *Unterlehrer* in March 1901, quoted in *SP,* 1901, p. 2173: "Ich muss Ihnen sagen, dass ich niemanden anstelle, der mit den Sozialdemokraten oder Schönerianern in Verbindung steht oder gar diesen Richtungen angehört hat, beziehungsweise noch angehört." An excellent primary source on politics in the schools is Karl Seitz's impassioned attack on Lueger and Gessmann on 11 April 1902, ibid., pp. 11231–64. Seitz noted that although teacher appointments were by law to be decided in a collegial fashion by school boards, the Christian Socials regularly ignored this rule and simply pushed nominations through en masse. Of Gessmann's autocratic powers Seitz noted: "Im Landesschulrathe kann es

ja—das sieht man einem Decret, das man in der Hand hat, nicht an—präsidial gemacht worden sein, oder collegialisch: das aber bleibt sich ganz gleich: Section, Collegium oder Präsidium, der niederösterreichische Landesschulrath heisst immer Dr. Albert Gessmann" (p. 11251).

204. Detailed chronicles of many of the persecutory acts can be found in *Festschrift zum 25-jährigen Bestande des Zentralvereines der Wiener Lehrerschaft*, pp. 13–22; and Tezuka, pp. 164–222.

205. Kielmansegg's letter transmitting a draft of a parliamentary response, submitted to Hartel, 30 October 1901, Z. 2402, *UM Präs.*

206. The official charge is in G. Z. 1904, 21 March 1901, Carton 84, *NL Seitz*. The *Landesschulrat* was the official administrative body responsible for supervising public education in the Crownland, including Vienna. Its membership was set by provincial law, and included four deputies from the Diet and four members of the Viennese City Council. The majority of its 25 members were Imperial appointees. The *Landesschulrat* had appellate authority in approving minor disciplinary actions taken by the Municipal School Board and initiating authority for major disciplinary decisions. See Ferdinand Frank, *Enzyklopädisches Handbuch der Normalien für das österreichische Volksschulwesen mit Einschluss der Lehrerbildung und gewerblichen Fortbildungsschulen* (Vienna, 1910), pp. 78–79, 167–69.

207. See the reports by Kielmansegg in E1 ad 2012, Nr. 2786, 7 May 1900; Nr. 3766, 7 May 1900; and especially A8, Nr. 1683, 23 April 1901, *NÖLA*, as well as Lueger's notification to Seitz, 27 April 1901, Carton 84, *NL Seitz*. Hartel and Kielmansegg recognized, however, the dubious procedures sometimes used by the local school authorities. See A8 ad 6770, memoranda of 17 October 1900 and 28 January 1901, which should be read along side of Hartel's response to an interpellation by Seitz on Lueger's politics of teacher appointments in *SP*, 1902, p. 10073.

208. See Nr. 6479, 14 February 1911, Carton 4471, *UM Präs*. For a typical Christian Social reaction to Hawel's work (*Die Politiker* [Vienna, 1904]) see the commentary in the *ÖFZ*, 24 January 1904, p. 2.

209. *Rp*, 6 June 1903, pp. 10–11; 9 June 1903, p. 3; 17 June 1903, p. 9; 21 June 1903, p. 6; 23 June 1903, p. 3; and 26 June 1903, p. 6. The publicity of the pro-Christian Social slate of teachers was frankly opportunistic, telling their colleagues that the party would only support a new salary law in the *Landtag* once "wenn sie die Überzeugung gewinnen kann, dass sich die Lehrerschaft ihren Bestrebungen für das Volkswohl nicht mehr feindlich gegenüberstellt." 20 June 1903, p. 2. See also Leopold Tomola's warning that "Solange Seitz oder die von ihm empfohlenen Genossen die Vertreter der Wiener Lehrerschaft sind, solange wird die Bürgerschaft den Wünschen unseres Standes taube Ohren schenken." *DSZ*, 5 (1903): 223.

210. When the press obtained a copy of the letter which Gessmann sent to clerics asking about the reliability of local teachers, this provoked anger even among teachers otherwise sympathetic to the Christian Socials. See Oskar Achs, ed., *Otto Glöckel. Ausgewählte Schriften und Reden* (Vienna, 1985), p. 70. Heinrich Giese, the director of a

Catholic teacher-training institute in Vienna, later confessed in 1909 that "ich habe 2 Jahre lang arbeiten müssen, um die Lehrer ruhig zu bringen." See the file "Bösbauer Angelegenheit," Carton 69, *CPW.*

211. *AZ,* 22 October 1908, p. 8. The newspaper insisted that 165 of 804 *Unterlehrer* and 216 of 645 middle-level teachers were appointed or promoted for political reasons; and all appointments to *Bürgerschuldirektor* or *Oberlehrer* reflected political patronage. Seitz noted in 1902 that city authorities often refused to fill vacancies, even if there were applicants, until they were certain of the prospective candidate's political loyalty. For example, in March 1902, 17 *Unterlehrer* positions were left vacant because the party could not find younger teachers who would agree to support the Christian Socials. *SP,* 1902, p. 11260. Nor was nepotism absent in these decisions. See, for example, the case of Josef Gregorig's son, who after several failed attempts at promotion to *Bürgerschullehrer* finally made the cut, under dubious circumstances, in 1898. *FLS,* 1898, pp. 436–37.

212. After some zigzaging even Albert Gessmann agreed that this decision was the correct one because "it is a question of punishing a gross violation of duty. The conditions among the schoolteachers require a strong response." See the "Protokoll der Sitzung des k.k. niederösterr. Landesschulrathes vom 10. April 1899," Z. 22835, Carton 4470, *UM Präs.*Rauscher disappeared from the political scene after the 1900 Council elections.

213. The files of the *UM* are filled with such cases. See for example the case of Franz Kubicek, who was passed over in promotion because local school inspectors found that he treated the children too roughly, used disciplinary tactics too readily, and lectured in a dull manner. Or that of Franz Klein, who was passed over for a salary raise because he was a poor teacher who did not understand how to present instruction in an attractive manner and who therefore had difficulties in controlling his class. Z. 27264, 22/23 June 1910, Carton 4471.

214. See the summary report which Kielmansegg submitted to the Ministry of Education on 29 October 1901 on disciplinary actions against teachers in Lower Austria. Z. 2485, Carton 297.

215. The laws consisted of four different pieces of legislation. One revised the funding procedures for new school construction and maintenance, enhancing the prerogatives of the Crownland government; a second revised provisions for the administrative management of the school system, systematically enhancing the power of elected officials against state officials or the teaching corps; the third revised the procedures by which teachers were appointed, the conditions under which they worked, and the procedures by which they could be disciplined; and the fourth raised teacher salaries by an average of about 10 percent. See *SPNÖ,* 1904, pp. 292–95; and Seitz's critique on pp. 316–30. For a convenient summary, see Oskar Goldbach, "Die neuen Landesschulgesetze für Niederösterreich verglichen mit den bisher geltenden n.ö. Landesgesetzen," *DSZ,* 6 (1904): 304–17. See also *AZ,* 19 October 1904, pp. 4–5, and 21 October 1904, pp. 1–2.

216. See Hartel to Kielmansegg, 17 September 1904, and the "Ergebnisse der am 12. September 1904 im k. k. Ministerium für Kultus und Unterricht über den Entwurf des Landes-Ausschusses Regierungsrates Dr. Gessmann . . . abgehaltenen Beratung," I/ 3d Nr. 2393, 1904, *Statt. Präs., NÖLA*. This file also contains massive protests by Liberals and Social Democrats against the bills.

217. *Die Gemeinde-Verwaltung der Stadt Wien im Jahre 1905* (Vienna, 1907), p. 401. In 1908–9, 744 public school teachers participated in various courses at the *Lehrerakademie*. The teaching staff consisted of the thirteen professors attached to the Seminar, as well as seventeen other teachers and the part-time service of nine university professors. The *Lehrerakademie* component was added as a result of the final negotiations with the government in December.

218. Ludwig Battista, "Die pädagogische Entwicklung des Pflichtschulwesens und der Lehrerbildung von 1848–1948," in *100 Jahre Unterrichtsministerium 1848–1948. Festschrift des Bundesministeriums für Unterricht in Wien* (Vienna, 1948), p. 152; Rudolf Hornich, "Die Bedeutung Willmanns für unsere Zeit," *Österreichische Pädagogische Warte*, 14 (1919): 67–70; Josef Zeif, "Was verdankt die Pädagogik der Lebensarbeit Willmanns?" ibid., pp. 70–77.

219. Hornich received a doctorate in philosophy from the University of Vienna in 1890. He became the director of the teacher-training institute in St. Pölten in 1905. During the war he edited *Das neue Österreich,* a monthly journal on which Ignaz Seipel, Heinrich Lammasch, and Albert Gessmann collaborated and which offered a quiet alternative to the pro-German national proclivities of other sections of the Christian Social party.

220. For Gessmann's final comments, *SPNÖ,* p. 415. The Emperor sanctioned the laws on 25 December 1904, after the Christian Socials were forced to make what they claimed were only modest revisions in the bills. The most important change was to restore full voting rights to the regional school inspectors on the *Landesschulrat*. Although the socialists claimed this as a victory, it was a concession that Gessmann was in fact willing to make because of assurances that, in the future, the government would appoint as school inspectors men who were at least neutral towards and in some cases positively sympathetic to the Christian Social party.

221. Ibid., pp. 104, 106. The German Ambassador Wedel, who was in contact with Koerber, noted that some of Lueger's subordinates (most likely Gessmann) immediately realized the stupidity of Lueger's insult ("verschiedene seiner einflussreichen Anhänger machten kein Hehl daraus, dass er eine sehr grosse Dummheit begangen habe"). A 16885, 24 October 1904, Oest. 70/Bd. 42, *PAAA.*

222. The files relating to the celebration are in *H.A. Akten, Kleine Bestände,* Schachtel 1–4 (Mappe 8/9), 1904, *WSLA.*

223. See Weiskirchner's memorandum to all city employees, 7 October 1904, ibid.

224. *Die Gemeinde-Verwaltung der Stadt Wien im Jahre 1905* (Vienna, 1907), p. 82.

225. The money collected for the *Stiftung* was deposited in the Bankhaus Th. Plewa & Sohn, who argued to Weiskirchner that "Infolge des Umstandes, dass der

grösste Theil unserer ausgebreiteten Clientele der christlichsozialen Partei angehört, glauben wir mit bestem Erfolge wirken zu können." Letter to Weiskirchner, 28 July 1904, ibid.

226. Nor were all artisan masters necessarily poor. When the deputy ward chairman of the Landstrasse, Karl Wenzl, died in 1907, he left property worth 165,000 crowns to establish a foundation to help artisan masters. Wenzl was himself an artisan. See *Die Gemeinde-Verwaltung der Stadt Wien im Jahre 1908* (Vienna, 1910), p. 75.

227. See "Gemeinsame Sitzung der deutschen Executive mit dem n.ö. Landesausschusse," 11 October 1904, *VGAB*. These debates make it clear that the campaign against Lueger was centrally controlled by the socialist party leadership.

228. See the police report to Kielmansegg, 20 October 1904, XIV/219, Z. 2652/ 2689, 1904, *Statt. Präs., NÖLA;* as well as *AZ,* 8 October 1904, pp. 2–3; 10 October 1904, pp. 1–2; 16 October 1904, p. 1.

229. Report of 22 October 1904, *Statt. Präs.*

230. "[I]n einem Teile der Bevölkerung eine sichtlich zunehmende Erregung Platz gegriffen hat, welche eine die öffentliche Ruhe und Ordnung gefährdende Störung dieses Teiles der geplanten Festlichkeiten besorgen liess." Habrda to the fest's executive committee, 19 October 1904.

231. This is apparent from the lists of acknowledgments in the *H.A. Akten.* Compare these with the claims in *DV,* 16 October 1904 (M), p. 7. In this respect Koerber did the party a favor by prohibiting the march, as Gessmann and Weiskirchner most likely realized.

232. This was in the form of a motion expressing the party's "sharpest reproof" against Koerber and Kielmansegg. See *SPNÖ,* 1904, pp. 253–72, 274–86, as well as Wedel's report, including his reference to the "Entrüstungskomödie" in the Lower Austrian Diet, A 16885, 24 October 1904.

233. *DV,* 24 October 1904 (M), pp. 1–3; *AZ,* 24 October 1904, pp. 1–3; and the police report, 23 October 1904, XIV/219, *NÖLA.* Kielmansegg tried to dodge the issue of why the government had prohibited the Christian Social parade, but not the socialist march, by arguing that the socialists had, technically speaking, not constituted a parade. *SPNÖ,* 1904, p. 427.

234. "Ein Nach- und Abschiedswort," *DZ,* 1 January 1905, p. 2.

CHAPTER TWO

1. See Kielmansegg, *Kaiserhaus,* pp. 400–407; and Wedel's report in A 16650, 19 September 1905, Oest. 70/Bd. 43, *PAAA.* Numerous accounts testify that Lueger seemed to grow more insatiable for public accolades and deference as time went on, perhaps to the weakening of his public accessibility. See, for example, Beskiba, *Aus meinen Erinnerungen,* pp. 25, 109; and Scheicher, *Erlebnisse,* 4: 414–15.

2. *DR,* 10 May 1906, p. 4. For a similar commentary on Lueger's "imperial" ambitions, see Jakob Reumann's description of Lueger's regime as a "kleiner Hofstaat" with the mayor playing the role of a "kleiner Potentat." *AB,* 1908, p. 3019.

3. As recounted in Seitz's "Persönliche Erinnerungen," pp. 66–67.

4. For the unification of Floridsdorf to Vienna, see *Die Gemeinde-Verwaltung der Stadt Wien im Jahre 1904* (Vienna, 1906), pp. 2–8; and Kielmansegg, *Kaiserhaus,* pp. 384–85, 396. For the financial and policy background to the negotiations between the city and the government, see Kielmansegg's report in Z. 8364, 27 November 1904, and the *Vortrag* prepared for Franz Joseph (draft), dated 30 November 1904, Z. 8364, Carton 1569, 11/1, *MI Präs.*

5. Michael Hainisch's tribute to Weiskirchner's management of Vienna might or might not be expanded to include Lower Austria, but it would be difficult to argue that the province was worse off under the Christian Socials than under the Liberals. See his *75 Jahre aus bewegter Zeit. Lebenserinnerungen eines österreichischen Staatsmannes,* ed. Friedrich Weissensteiner (Vienna, 1978), pp. 224–25. See also the commendatory comments in Felix Oppenheimer, *Die Wiener Gemeindeverwaltung und der Fall des liberalen Regimes in Staat und Kommune* (Vienna, 1905), pp. 72–95.

6. *WF,* 5 January 1904, pp. 1–2.

7. Joseph Schöffel, *Erinnerungen aus meinem Leben* (Vienna, 1905), esp. pp. 281–86, 317–34; and his "Meine Antwort," *Die Fackel,* Nr. 189, 30 November 1905, pp. 1–17.

8. Albert Gessmann, "Die politische Lage in Österreich," *Rp,* 1 January 1904, p. 2. For an interesting analysis of the way in which the Christian Socials could expand, which may have influenced and reflected Gessmann's thinking, see the pamphlet by Anton Bach, *Österreichs Zukunft und die Christlich-Sozialen. Eine Stimme zur Wahlreform* (Vienna, 1906), esp. pp. 57–60. See also Friedrich Austerlitz's brilliant diatribe against Gessmann, which catches well the more ambitious nature of his, as opposed to Lueger's, vision for the party, "Gessmann als Erzieher," *K,* 2 (1908–9): 97–101. Gerald Stourzh has suggested to me that Austerlitz was deliberately imitating the title of Julius Langbehn's *Rembrandt als Erzieher.*

9. For the attempt to allow confessionally divided classrooms in September 1898 see the files in Nr. 3838, 7 February 1899, Carton 4470, *UM Präs.* At issue was an attempt in ten schools, out of a total of 399 public schools, to create some parallel classes for Catholic and Jewish children, although in each of the ten schools there was no general division of the children. That is, in each of the ten schools the children also attended some classes that were not divided along confessional lines. The Ministry of Education decided it would allow such divisions only in case "dass sich in Ansehung des Religionsunterrichtes bei Entwurf des Stundenplanes technische Schwierigkeiten ergeben."

10. "Wiener Wahlen," *Rp,* 8 May 1904, p. 1.

11. See Franz Schuhmeier's comments about Jewish political behavior in *Volkstribüne,* 13 December 1905, p. 2.

12. For the 1902 Leopoldstadt election, see Jordan's own admission in *Aus meinem Leben,* pp. 105–9. For 1910, see the court testimony of Johann Bergauer, given in the Hierhammer-Stahlich libel trial, in *AZ,* 15 February 1912, p. 9 and *NFP,* 15 February

1912 (M), p. 12, as well as *DV,* 1 May 1910 (M), p. 3. See also the report in Mayer, *Ein jüdischer Kaufmann,* pp. 357–58, relating to negotiations in 1908 about a "deal" between Jews and Christian Socials; it fell through, however.

13. "Unser Bürgermeister!" *ÖW,* 21 (1904): 197–98.

14. *WF,* 5 May 1904, p. 2.

15. "Sonderbar ist, dass gerade der Verein 'Christliche Familie' am wenigsten unterstützt und gefördert wird. . . . obwohl der Verein seit 15 Jahren eifrig kämpft, findet er doch noch immer keine Anerkennung, keine Unterstützung." Ibid., 5 May 1907, pp. 1–2. The membership of this group averaged 100–400 in each district, but with highly variable commitment and energy. The majority of members were tradesmen (with a substantial membership of women), but white-collar workers and privately wealthy individuals also joined on occasion. See the sample membership list from the Josefstadt branch for 1904 in Walter Sauer, *Katholisches Vereinswesen in Wien. Zur Geschichte des christlichsozial-konservativen Lagers vor 1914* (Salzburg, 1980), p. 119. The actual effects of the putative boycott of Jewish shops has never been adequately surveyed. Sigmund Mayer reports in *Die Wiener Juden. Kommerz, Kultur, Politik 1700–1900* (Vienna, 1918), p. 474, that the boycotts initially hurt many small Jewish dealers, but they subsided more quickly and had less impact than those instigated in Bohemia and Moravia.

16. Mayer, *Ein jüdischer Kaufmann,* p. 357. See also Wächter, "Die Gemeindebetriebe," p. 220, who reported in 1909 that "Das Schicksal will es, dass trotz alledem viele Lieferungen nichtarischer Provenienz durch Strohmänner, Zwischenhändler an die Gemeinde kommen, sehr zum Ärger der eifrigen Antisemiten in der Partei. Bemerkt muss werden, dass die Parteiführer in den letzten Jahren sehr viel Wasser in ihren Wein gegossen haben. . . ."

17. Bach, *Österreichs Zukunft ,* pp. 51–52.

18. Scheicher, *Erlebnisse,* 4: 359: "Der Antisemitismus der Partei ist den Juden nicht besonders gefährlich geworden." For a modern and judicious evaluation, see Pauley, *From Prejudice to Persecution,* pp. 45–49.

19. Lueger, Gessmann, and Weiskirchner all voted in favor of Josef Sturm, who won by a 9 to 5 vote. *AZ,* 11 January 1908, p. 3. Ferdinand Skaret argued in May 1907 that the Christian Social party leadership had long wanted to dump Schneider, but that he knew too much and could make trouble for the party. See *AZ,* 18 May 1907, p. 5.

20. Weiskirchner to Lueger, 21 March 1908, I.N. 40883, *Handschriftensammlung.*

21. See *NFP,* 5 February 1904 (M), p. 9; *Rp,* 6 February 1904, p. 5; *ÖW,* 21 (1904): 298, 316, the latter commentator seeing Albert Gessmann as responsible for Gregorig's purge. Gregorig had delivered his attack at a meeting of the *Bund der Antisemiten,* a fringe radical group.

22. For the background, see *DZ,* 17 March 1904, pp. 2–5; as well as the three handwritten protocols of the meetings of the "Commission zur Prüfung der Angelegenheit Gregorig-Zatzka" from 17, 22, and 24 March 1904, Z. 3477, Präsidialbüro, Carton 252, *MD.* The commission was bipartisan, since August Nechansky, one of the surviving

Liberals in the City Council, was also a member. Although commission members found nothing formally illegal about Zatzka's activities, it was clear to all of them that Zatzka had come very close to serious conflicts of interest.

23. The speech occurred during the annual budget debates and is in *AB*, 1902, pp. 2298–2301. It followed tough critiques of the Christian Social regime by Donath Zifferer (pp. 2271–80), Franz Schuhmeier (pp. 2280–87), and Jakob Reumann (pp. 2290–95), who accused the Christian Socials of financial bungling, if not dishonesty, of conducting budget proceedings that were a "comedy" and a "scandal," and they made no bones about their contempt for their Christian Social opponents. Any reasonable exegesis of this speech would have to set it into the raucous tone of debates in which it was given, not simply pull it out of context. To suggest that Bielohlawek was threatening the Jews of Vienna with personal or bodily harm is to misread his remarks and misunderstand the man. He was, however, clearly and unapologetically threatening them with political elimination, even though he made his main target, as Lueger usually did, what he deemed to be the insulting and patronizing behavior of the Liberal newspaper corps led by the *Neue Freie Presse*. Bielohlawek and Zifferer clashed again, two years later, in libel proceedings resulting from Zifferer's sarcastic remark at a political rally about Bielohlawek's alleged love of champagne. See *NFP,* 31 May 1904 (M), pp. 10–11.

24. *AZ,* 30 March 1909, p. 6; 10 June 1911, p. 1. Details about Bielohlawek's life—both professional and personal—also emerged in his trial with Franz Zipperer in September 1910 (see below, Chapter 5, note 122). His administrative accomplishments were reviewed in *DV,* 2 July 1918, p. 5. When the Minister of Public Works, Ottokar von Trnka, proposed in January 1914 that Bielohlawek receive a high Imperial order for his work in encouraging artisan industries, the only dissenting voice was that of Justice Minister Victor von Hochenburger, who asked if a "personality" of such a social background should be granted this honor. The rest of the Cabinet ignored this objection and voted Bielohlawek the medal. "Ministerratsprotokoll," 26 January 1914, *AVA*.

25. See Kraus's ironic commentary on Bielohlawek in *Die Fackel,* Nr. 245, 28 February 1908, and Nr. 250, 14 April 1908. Granted Kraus's extremely ambivalent relationship to his own Jewish identity and to the Viennese Jewish community, his observations about Bielohlawek are still quite insightful.

26. Bielohlawek's pride in his administrative work came through quite explicitly in his speech to the Diet in early 1912 on his budget requests, *SPNÖ,* pp. 836–43. Upon Bielohlawek's death, Paul von Vittorelli, the president of the *Oberlandesgericht* for Lower Austria and the last Imperial Minister of Justice, wrote to Alois Liechtenstein that "In langjähriger enger Fühlung auf dem Gebiete des Kinderschutzes und der Jugendfürsorge hatte ich Gelegenheit, die vortrefflichen seltenen Eigenschaften des Verewigten kennen und schätzen zu lernen und haben mich die schönen Erfolge, die er auch auf diesem Gebiete dank seinem klaren Erfassen der Verhältnisse und wahren Bedürfnisse, durch rastlosen Eifer, weit vorausblickende Umsicht und grosse Tatkraft erzielte, stets mit wahrer Freude und Genugtuung erfüllt." *DV,* 4 July 1918 (M), p. 5.

27. *NWT,* 1 July 1918, pp. 5–6. See also *NFP,* 1 July 1918 (M), p. 6.

28. See his long, thoughtful account of his views on the war, given in October 1917 at the fourth *Mandataren-Konferenz* of the party, Z. 1338, Carton 75, *CPW*. For a reflection on his career, see Heinl, *Über ein halbes Jahrhundert*, pp. 107–8.

29. "Landesausschuss Bielohlawek gestorben," *AZ*, 1 July 1918, p. 3.

30. See Herta Hafner, "Vizebürgermeister Heinrich Hierhammer—ein bürgerlicher Aufsteiger," in *Christliche Demokratie*, 6 (1988): 185–96; and idem, "Heinrich Hierhammer. Vizebürgermeister von Wien 1905–1918. Ein bürgerlicher Aufsteiger." *Diplomarbeit*, University of Vienna, 1988.

31. Quoted in Hafner, "Heinrich Hierhammer," p. 13.

32. Ibid., pp. 27, 50–51.

33. "'Ein Spruch unserer Weisen lautet: Der Tod des Gerechten versöhnt. Möge Dein Tod—und (zu Vizebürgermeister Hierhammer gewendet) es sind ja die Anzeichen dafür vorhanden—die Morgenröte einer Versöhnung zwischen sämtlichen Bürgern unserer Stadt bedeuten. Sei gesegnet Sonnenthal.' Herr Hierhammer hat hierauf Herrn Stiassny warm die Hand gedrückt." *AZ*, 9 April 1909, pp. 2, 7. Adolf Sonnenthal was a famous actor who also served as the director of the *Burgtheater* from 1887 to 1890.

34. *NWT*, 14 July 1907, p. 3.

35. The post of second vice-mayor came open upon Joseph Strobach's death in May 1905. Josef Neumayer succeeded Strobach as first vice-mayor, and Neumayer's position had then to be filled. Leopold Steiner was initially selected by the Christian Social *Bürgerklub* for the job, but he suddenly withdrew his name, citing reasons of ill health. No one in Vienna believed this excuse, and the real reason was that Lueger had insisted that Steiner give up his well-paying job as Oberkurator of the Lower Austrian Mortgage Institute, which Steiner refused to do. See *DV*, 22 May 1905 (A), p. 6; and Hafner, "Heinrich Hierhammer," p. 11.

36. Compare "Das betrogene Wien," *AT*, 26 May 1905, pp. 1–2; "Das Schweigen der Rassenantisemiten Wiens," ibid., 27 May 1905, p. 2; and "Der jüdische Vizebürgermeister von Wien," ibid., 7 June 1905, p. 1, with the uncharacteristically meek reportage in *DV*, 24 May 1905 (A), p. 2, which merely reprinted the surprised and not altogether unhappy reactions of the press in Vienna and Berlin. A native of Vienna, Josef Porzer was born in 1847 and was a contemporary of Lueger's at the University of Vienna. A quiet, unassuming, yet competent lawyer, he manifested absolute loyalty to Lueger and was also a crony of Gessmann, which may have been the primary reason he became vice-mayor. The editors of the *Fremdenblatt* took the Porzer nomination as a sign that "Dr. Lueger stark genug ist, um sich über gewisse vordem herrschende Geschmacksrichtungen, vor denen er sich widerstrebend verneigen musste, hinwegzusetzen." 24 May 1905 (M), p. 1. For another view, see Beskiba, *Aus meinen Erinnerungen*, pp. 27–29.

37. *SP*, 1905, p. 30002.

38. Lueger: "Sie werden als ein, wie ich sehe, ruhig und scharf Beobachtender bemerkt haben, dass ich in den letzten drei Jahren meinen ganzen Einfluss aufgeboten habe, um die Bewegung in ein ruhigeres Fahrwasser zu bringen"; and "Sie können darob beruhigt sein. Ich werde das seit drei Jahren eingeschlagene Verfahren nicht mehr

verlassen." As reported in Adler, "Eine Erinnerung an Bürgermeister Dr. Lueger," pp. 4, 5. Sigmund Mayer reported similarly in 1910 that "Inzwischen ist diese Tendenz [towards moderation] innerhalb der Christlichsozialen noch deutlicher hervorgetreten. Nur selten fällt im Abgeordnetenhaus ein Wort gegen die Juden, die Boykottierungen haben aufgehört. Statt der antisemitischen werden wir neben der 'Agrar-Partei' eine klerikale des Mittelstandes oder vielleicht gar nur eine Art 'Tammany Hall' vor uns haben, die um ihre Existenz kämpft." *Ein jüdischer Kaufmann,* p. 359. This trend did not go unnoticed in more vigilant anti-Semitic circles. One German nationalist voter complained at a rally in the Josefstadt in 1910 of the Christian Socials that "in ihren Reihen herrsche nicht mehr der alte antisemitische Geist und die alte Frische, die er früher bei ihren Wählerversammlungen wahrgenommen habe." *DV,* 27 April 1910 (M), p. 5.

39. *AZ,* 11 March 1910, p. 3. See also Wilhelm Stiassny's own memoir of Lueger in the *Neues Wiener Abendblatt,* 10 March 1910, p. 2, where Stiassny admitted that Lueger had become more conciliatory toward the Jewish community as the years wore on, that he had tried to direct his party into more moderate paths, and had also responded positively to requests from the leaders of the *Israelitische Kultusgemeinde.* Josef Scheicher observed that Lueger became more conciliatory over time, but implied that this was owing to his frail health and aging. *Erlebnisse,* 4: 301. Finally, note Robert Scheu's observation that "Es war des Volkes unendliches Ergötzen, als er schliesslich sogar die Juden bezauberte und mit sich versöhnte." "Karl Lueger," *Die Fackel,* Nr. 301/02, 6 May 1910, p. 45.

40. See the "Klubsitzung," 21 und 22 June 1910," Carton 90, *CPK.* On the Leykam firm, see Franz Mathis, *Big Business in Österreich. Österreichische Grossunternehmen in Kurzdarstellungen* (Munich, 1987), pp. 186–87. See also the accusations of private and official dealings with Jews by Christian Social politicians in *DR,* 3 May 1906, p. 4.

41. See *AZ,* 21 June 1908, pp. 9–10; 24 June 1908, p. 9; *AB,* 1908, p. 1545.

42. *Arbeitgeber-Zeitung,* 18 January 1908, p. 1. For a classic interpretation of this transformation, see Otto Bauer, "Das Ende des christlichen Sozialismus," *Werkausgabe* (9 vols., Vienna, 1975–80), 8: 515–24. It is also worth remembering, as William McCagg reminds us, that Jews in higher financial circles became more deliberately circumspect about their relative public visibility after the mid-1890s, so that their willingness to "import" politically alien creatures, like self-serving Christian Social politicians, as front men may not be all that surprising. See William O. McCagg, Jr., *A History of the Habsburg Jews, 1670–1918* (Bloomington, 1989), pp. 196–97.

43. See Z. 290, 806, Carton 71, *CPW.*

44. For the complex range of Jewish reactions to political anti-Semitism, see the important works by McCagg, Jr., *A History,* pp. 196–98; Steven Beller, *Vienna and the Jews 1867–1938. A Cultural History* (Cambridge, 1989), esp. pp. 201–6; Marsha L. Rozenblit, *The Jews of Vienna, 1867–1914: Assimilation and Identity* (Albany, 1983), pp. 175–93; Hannah S. Decker, *Freud, Dora, and Vienna 1900* (New York, 1991), pp.

15, 30–31; and Robert S. Wistrich, *The Jews of Vienna in the Age of Franz Joseph* (Oxford, 1989), pp. 205–343, the latter a particularly important and illuminating contribution to scholarship. See also the intelligent comments in Jane Wiegenstein, "Artists in a Changing Environment: The Viennese Art World, 1860–1918." Dissertation, Indiana University, 1980, pp. 190ff. In spite of the heroic endeavors of these authors—all of them fine scholars—I personally feel that we still face some large gaps in our understanding of the psychological and social history of the Viennese Jews between 1895 and 1918. A special desideratum would be an exploration of the world of those Jews who converted from Judaism to Christianity, and/or who married gentiles.

45. The *Alldeutsches Tagblatt* was more candid than most papers when it argued that, even during the Liberal era, municipal politicians would not have nominated a Jew for high city office because of "der latente, trotz aller judenliberalen Phrasen immer vorhandene Antisemitismus der Wiener." 25 May 1905, p. 2.

46. For the situation in Upper Austria, for example, Harry Slapnicka has argued that "[e]s fehlt allerdings gleichzeitig der starke Antisemitismus der Wiener Christlichsozialen. Dieser tritt eigentlich nur vorübergehend bei Ebenhoch deutlich in Erscheinung." *Christlichsoziale in Oberösterreich. Vom Katholikenverein 1848 bis zum Ende der Christlichsozialen 1934* (Linz, 1984), p. 153; and idem, *Oberösterreich unter Kaiser Franz Joseph (1861 bis 1918)* (Linz, 1982), p. 199. In contrast is the situation in Salzburg, where Hanns Haas argues a stronger appearance of anti-Semitism obtained: Heinz Dopsch and Hans Spatzenegger, eds., *Geschichte Salzburgs. Stadt und Land. Band II. Neuzeit und Zeitgeschichte. 2. Teil* (Salzburg, 1988), pp. 823, 933.

47. See the *Christliche Wiener Frauen-Zeitung*, 5 April 1897, pp. 7–8.

48. See Heinrich Hierhammer's recollections of the women's political utility in Hafner, "Heinrich Hierhammer," p. 100.

49. This weekly newspaper routinely printed a melange of short political articles, pious religious essays, clerical sermons, selections from the weekly Sunday gospel, and once a month provided its female readers with patterns for dressmaking and with advice on maintaining personal health and hygiene and on avoiding alcoholism.

50. For an interesting political speech by the President of the Brünn chapter of the *Bund*, Wilhelmine Novak, which combined "domestic" and political concerns while also pleading for coexistence between Czechs and Germans, see *ÖFZ*, 5 November 1905, pp. 4–5.

51. For a review of the activities of the *Bund*, see "Zehn Jahre Christlicher Wiener Frauenbund," *DV*, 1 July 1907 (M), pp. 3–4. Its secretary and the editor of its paper was a man, Franz Klier, who, according to Beskiba, was much disliked by his putative clients. See *Aus meinen Erinnerungen*, pp. 31ff. Speeches at its events tended to be gender defined; male guests spoke on political issues, females on religious and "domestic" issues, but occasionally a talk was given by a woman on a clearly political issue, so the dividing line was not rigidly set.

52. This is especially clear in the *Bund*'s preference for helping "arme, mittellose

Familien." Members were encouraged to donate money because "das Herz könnte einem oft brechen darüber" that so much poverty existed in Vienna. "An mildtätige Menschenfreunde!" *ÖFZ*, 30 April 1905, p. 6.

53. This is clear if one reads systematically the weekly *Ortsgruppen* notices in the *Österreichische Frauen-Zeitung*. The membership base of the *Frauenbund* is difficult to ascertain since published claims were most certainly inflated, but it was somewhat larger than that of the *Verein "Christliche Familie."* The latter had between 2,000 and 3,000 activists, with others occasionally co-opted for specific social events. Marianne Hainisch estimated the *Frauenbund*'s membership at 13,000 in 1901 (Marianne Hainisch, "Die Geschichte der Frauenbewegung in Österreich," in *Handbuch der Frauenbewegung*. Vol. 1 [Berlin, 1901], p. 179). More recently, Walter Sauer reports that the *Frauenbund* claimed 20,000 members in 1905 (Sauer, p. 114). Its members were assumed to be "Bürgersfrauen" who would employ domestic servants. See "Wo junge Dienstmädchen zuerst dienen sollen?" *ÖFZ*, 21 February 1904, p. 6.

54. See Hans Plecher, *Victor Silberer. Ein Lebensbild* (Vienna, 1916), p. 12. It is illuminating to compare press coverage of this event. See for example *DV*, 7 May 1907 (M), p. 5; 28 May 1907 (M), pp. 6–7; and *NFP*, 7 May 1907 (M), p. 9; 28 May 1907 (M), pp. 9–11.

55. See *Fremdenblatt*, 21 May 1905 (M), pp. 23–28; 22 May 1905 (M), pp. 8–12. This event raised 200,000 crowns on a single day.

56. Hafner, "Heinrich Hierhammer," p. 95.

57. Ibid., p. 94.

58. Heinl, *Über ein halbes Jahrhundert*, p. 24. See also Hainisch, *75 Jahre aus bewegter Zeit*, p. 235.

59. The standard work is William A. Jenks, *The Austrian Electoral Reform of 1907* (New York, 1950).

60. See, for example, Ludwig Brügel, *Geschichte der österreichischen Sozialdemokratie* (5 vols., Vienna, 1922–25), 4: 370–72, as well as Braunthal, *Victor und Friedrich Adler*, pp. 160–61.

61. Whiteside, *The Socialism of Fools*, p. 242.

62. Throughout this book, unless otherwise noted, I use the general term "German national" to refer to the parties that after 1907 had united under the umbrella of the *Deutscher Nationalverband* (the People's Party, the Agrarians, and the Progressives). At various times and on certain terms the German Radicals were also members. Unless otherwise noted, when I use the term "pan-German" I refer either to Schönerer's and Wolf's factions before 1907 and to Wolf's and Pacher's Radicals after 1907 or to political clubs sympathetic to the extreme views of these groups. For the tortuous history of the *Verband*, which reconstituted itself in various forms, see Diethild Harrington-Müller, *Der Fortschrittsklub im Abgeordnetenhaus des österreichischen Reichsrats 1873–1910* (Vienna, 1972), pp. 54–57, and Lothar Höbelt, *Kornblume und Kaiseradler. Die deutschfreiheitlichen Parteien Altösterreichs 1882–1918* (Vienna, 1993), which provides an authoritative history of these groups.

63. The growth in party clubs after 1907 is itself somewhat misleading in that the abolition of the *Grossgrundbesitz* and *Handelskammer* curias in the new parliament left a considerable deficit in party-committed seats (while the total number of seats increased from 435 to 516). See Bach, *Österreichs Zukunft,* for an appeal that the Christian Socials should assume the larger dimensions of a state people's party. For the Social Democrats, of course, their putative comprehensiveness in terms of class was a matter of record, but the 1905–6 reforms gave them additional incentives to enhance a transclass identity through the agency of anticlericalism. See below, Chapter 4.

64. For a review of the educational backgrounds of the deputies elected in 1911 elections see "Die Wirkung des allgemeinen Stimmrechtes auf das Bildungsniveau des österreichischen Abgeordnetenhaus," Carton 19, *Kabinettskanzlei, Geheimakten.* This anonymous survey showed that only half of those elected had attended a university or other institution of higher learning, and that the disparity was even greater among German and Czech deputies. Equally interesting, of the 187 deputies who had served in the army, only 70 had been officers. Sixty-one had been noncommissioned officers, and 56 enlisted men.

65. See his speech in Feldsberg in *DZ,* 8 January 1905, p. 3.

66. *Rp,* 1 February 1905, p. l; 16 February 1905, pp. 6–7; 22 March 1905, p. l; 20 June 1905, p. l; 29 July 1905, p. l; 12 September 1905, p. l; 13 September 1905, p. 1.

67. Eggenburg was a place of minor symbolic importance in 1905 to the Christian Social party since it had been the first Lower Austrian *Gemeinde* to hold local elections under a new election code passed by the *Landtag* for small rural towns. The Christian Socials swept control of the town away from a coalition of German nationalists and ersatz Progressives. See "Ein symptomatischer Wahlsieg," *DZ,* 5 January 1905 (M), p. 1, which proudly asserted that "Unsere Gegner in Niederösterreich sind fertig— vollständig abgetan." The much-touted "Eggenburg Program" was a propaganda vehicle for Gessmann (via his crony Julius Axmann) to lambaste the Hungarians and portray the Christian Socials as having strong Imperial interests, and hence ambitions. The actual meeting at Eggenburg was conceived by Gessmann as a planning session on rural electoral strategies for the party in Lower Austria, and thus was only indirectly related to "Viennese" political interests. See *DZ,* 17 September 1905, p. 3; 18 September 1905, pp. 1–2. The high point of the anti-Magyar fulminations came when Lueger pompously threatened to withhold Christian Social votes on the defense budget if any concessions were made to the Hungarian nationalists on the Army issue. See also the interesting commentary in A 16650, 19 September 1905, Oest. 70/Bd. 43, *PAAA.*

68. See the "Vorstandsprotokolle" of 16, 21, 29 and 30 September 1905, and of 21, 23, 26, 28, 29, and 31 October 1905, *VGAB.* I disagree here with Jenks, p. 40, who imputes to the Social Democrats a consistency of strategy as well as a consistency of policy. The Viennese party always demanded universal suffrage, but it was not until October 31 that it decided to move for it by what might be viewed by the Cabinet as irrevocable acts. On October 23 (after a month of dealing with mundane party business, which the more mercurial Czech Social Democrats in Prague found outrageous [see

Braunthal, *Victor und Friedrich Adler,* pp. 153–54]) the Party Executive decided on a big demonstration for the reopening of parliament, which would involve Viennese workers taking a half-day off. This was hardly a revolutionary act. The news from St. Petersburg arriving on October 31 dramatically changed the situation, culminating in a tough manifesto adopted by the Party Congress on November 1 and followed by mass demonstrations and a decision to demand a complete cessation of work on the opening day of parliament. See *Protokoll über die Verhandlungen des Gesamtparteitages der Sozialdemokratischen Arbeiterpartei in Österreich. Abgehalten zu Wien vom 29. Oktober bis 2. November 1905* (Vienna, 1905), pp. 120–25, 138. The police noted that by 5 P.M. on October 31 propaganda was being distributed in various Viennese factories stating that the Czar had been forced to grant suffrage reforms in Russia, and asking how long Austria would have to wait. The Ministry of Internal Affairs noted in a confidential report to Kielmansegg on 12 November that only since the news of the Russian Revolution had the franchise reform movement grown violent and the workers' mood ugly, XIV/220, Nr. 2784, *Statt. Präs., NÖLA.* For these events, see also William J. McGrath, *Dionysian Art and Populist Politics in Austria* (New Haven, 1974), pp. 226–31; and Mommsen, *Die Sozialdemokratie und die Nationalitätenfrage,* pp. 362–88.

69. *SP,* 1905, pp. 31777–84. See also Lueger's vague commitment in *Rp,* 28 September 1905, p. 9. Interesting, and suggestive for the indecision which the crisis provoked at the Rathaus, was the fact that Kunschak's Laborite faction was the only Christian Social group to protest publicly against the apparent discrepancy between Imperial policy in Hungary and in Austria. See *Rp,* 27 September 1905, p. 4.

70. Éva Somogyi, ed., *Die Protokolle des gemeinsamen Ministerrates der österreichisch-ungarischen Monarchie 1896–1907* (Budapest, 1991), p. 456.

71. Brügel, *Geschichte,* 4: 365. On the Emperor's role in the final decision, see Kielmansegg, *Kaiserhaus,* p. 325, and Sieghart, *Die letzten Jahrzehnte einer Grossmacht,* pp. 83–84. On his later involvement, see Max von Beck, "Der Kaiser und die Wahlreform," in Eduard von Steinitz, ed., *Erinnerungen an Franz Joseph I. Kaiser von Österreich. Apostolischer König von Ungarn* (Berlin, 1931), pp. 199–224. The street violence on November 2 is described in a police report of 3 November 1905 in XIV/220, *Statt. Präs., NÖLA.*

72. See "Ein Appell an Doktor Lueger," *Vaterland,* 15 October 1905, p. 2. Compare the response in the *DV,* 15 October 1905 (M), p. 3, with that in the *Rp,* 17 October 1905, p. 2.

73. The *Reichspost* openly came out for the reform on November 3 (p. 2). Kunschak's labor faction had voted a ringing endorsement on October 25.

74. *DV,* 20 October 1905 (M), p. 2.

75. The rally was attended by 15,000 people. The party tried to preempt public opinion by condemning the "terroristische Treiben der Sozialdemokraten" and the tolerance shown them by the government, but its embarrassment in once again being upstaged by the Reds was most likely their chief motive. XIV/220, Nr. 3808/53, report of 26 November 1905, *Statt. Präs.*

76. Adler, Bretschneider, and Winarsky visited the Police President Habrda on November 18 and presented him with a complete plan for the march. Adler took personal responsibility for the march's orderliness. He also agreed that the party would provide its own guards and would not blockade streetcar traffic. Habrda tried to persuade Adler to forbid the waving of red flags, but Adler dismissed this as illegal and politically impossible, since his supporters would do it anyway. Report of 18 November 1905. Another report to Kielmansegg on the 18th noted that the police were now convinced the parade would not be the signal to begin a general strike, and that the leadership was repressing such rhetoric in its subordinate cadres, but this change in mood and attitude came *after* Adler had become convinced that the Cabinet would move on the issue of universal suffrage. The parade on November 28 must be seen, thus, as confirmatory and self-justifying, not only as the "threat" which it is often construed as. For Lueger's interview with Kielmansegg, see the latter's report to the *MI Präs.*, 20 November 1905, in XIV/220, Nr. 2357, 1905, *Statt. Präs.* Lueger demanded, however, that the police provide extra protection for the city gasworks, and noted that he would not stop streetcar service on the Ringstrasse.

77. The Social Democrats went so far as to ask Lueger, in his capacity as mayor, to allow them to use the Volkshalle in the Rathaus for a suffrage rally. At a meeting of the leadership on 9 November 1905, Ludwig Wutschel reported that Lueger had agreed and that the rally could go forward. "Executivkomitee u. Parteivertretung," 9 November 1905, *VGAB.*

78. Herrmann to Kielmansegg, 24 November 1905, *Statt Präs., NÖLA.* On Herrmann see *Jahrbuch der österreichischen Industrie 1910* (Vienna, 1910), p. 293. For similar letters see *DV,* 15 November 1905 (M), p. 15; 26 November 1905 (M), p. 5.

79. "Ich habe früher nie ein Hehl daraus gemacht und verberge meine Überzeugung heute schon gar nicht; die Gessmann-Gautsch Form des Wahlrechtes hat mir nie gepasst." *Erlebnisse,* 6: 274–75. Scheicher's opposition to the law was criticized by Josef Schraffl in *Rp,* 19 October 1906, p. 1.

80. Pattai to Auersperg, C/51/22a, *NL Auersperg, HHSA.* I am grateful to Dr. Lothar Höbelt for bringing this citation to my attention. Not surprisingly, Pattai and Auersperg collaborated with the right nationalist *Reichsverein der deutschen Arbeiterpartei* during the last year of the First World War. Neck, *Arbeiterschaft,* 2: 275. See also Pattai's comments, to the effect that the master artisans would lose influence, in *CSAZ,* 19 May 1906, pp. 1–2 and *DV,* 1 January 1907 (M), p. 9. For Schneider's opposition, see *CSAZ,* 7 April 1906, p. 3. See also *WGGT,* XII (1906): Nr. 154/55, p. 4.

81. See Z. 3832, report of 28 November 1905, *Statt. Präs., NÖLA.*

82. *DV,* 29 November 1905 (M), p. 8; *DZ,* 29 November 1905, p. 5; *Rp,* 29 November 1905, p. 4.

83. See, for example, the story recounted in the *ÖFZ,* 3 December 1905, p. 4, as well as the commentary in *DZ,* 29 November 1905 (A), p. 2.

84. *Protokoll über die Verhandlungen,* p. 121; Brügel, *Geschichte,* 4: 356, 358; *AZ,* 1 November 1905, p. 9.

85. *DZ,* 6 December 1905, p. 6; *DV,* 6 December 1905 (M), pp. 5–6.

86. *AB*, 1905, p. 2610.

87. *Fremdenblatt*, 8 December 1905 (M), p. 6. Victor Adler presented a similar intepretation of Lueger's motives on 10 December. *NFP*, 11 December 1905 (M), p. 5. Alois Liechtenstein indirectly said much the same: at a meeting of the *Christlicher Wiener Frauenbund* he was reported as arguing that he believed "es als notwendig, dass auch die christlichsoziale Partei demonstrierende Versammlungen abhalte, um der Regierung zu zeigen, dass diese Partei nicht weniger mächtig sei als die Sozialdemokratie. . . . Es müsse darum auch die alte agitatorische Kraft der Christlichsozialen wieder zum Leben erweckt werden." *ÖFZ*, 3 December 1905, p. 4.

88. The Tyrolian *Bauernverein*, a centerpoint of Christian Social agitation, voted unanimously on 7 October to call for universal suffrage. *DV*, 11 October 1905 (A), p. 2. See also Richard Schober, *Geschichte des Tiroler Landtages im 19. und 20. Jahrhundert* (Innsbruck, 1984), pp.199–214.

89. See *SP*, Session 17: Schöpfer: 1905, pp. 32262–64; 1906, pp. 39552–54, 40231–32; Schraffl: 1905, pp. 32011–20; 1906, pp. 35150–59, 35645–46, 39444–47, 40151–53, 40328–34, 40445–49; Jodok Fink: 1906, pp. 34909–11, 40065–70, 40153–54, 40485–86.

90. *Kaiserhaus*, pp. 326–27. The debates of the committee are in *SP*, 1906, *Beilage* 2727. They do not justify Braunthal's later assertion that Victor Adler "hatte in diesen dreiundsechzig Sitzungen allein den Kampf zu führen" (p. 161). If universal suffrage had a patrimony, it was Gessmann's as much as Adler's.

91. Ernst Vergani later asserted that Gessmann had to force Lueger to accept the final version of the suffrage law and went so far as to "blame" the whole suffrage reform project on Gessmann. See *CSAZ*, 16 July 1910, p. l; *NFP*, 16 February 1912 (M), p. 14.

92. Liechtenstein to Beck, 23 July 1906, Carton 36, *NL Beck*.

93. See the files in *CPK*, Carton 36, which contain the drafts prepared for Gessmann and Weiskirchner by *Magistratssekretär* Karl Pawelka, whom the Social Democrats regularly accused of being as corrupt as his political sponsors. Not surprisingly, Pawelka ended his career as *Magistratsdirektor*, serving from November 1916 until the Social Democrats forced him into retirement in June 1919. In 1907 he was the director of the section of the *Magistrat* responsible for assembling voter registration lists and supervising elections. See also Kielmansegg, *Kaiserhaus*, pp. 327, 410–11.

94. See Pawelka's critique of Viennese Liberal proposals to strengthen state control of election procedures in Vienna, *Abänderungsvorschläge der Wiener freiheitlichen Parteien zu den Regierungsvorlagen betreffend die Wahlreform und den Schutz der Wahlfreiheit*, especially his comments on sections 9 to 20, dated 6 June 1906, Carton 36, *CPK*.

95. See Pawelka's *Bericht über die Mandatsverteilung für Wien*, which provided the scheme Gessmann eventually used in assigning seats throughout Vienna. Gessmann's justification of *Wahlpflicht* is in *Landesausschuss Bericht - Niederösterreich*, V Session, Beilage Nr. 1905, December 1906, in Carton 36, *CPK*. This file suggests Pawelka may have also drafted this document for Gessmann. See also *Rp*, 15 September 1906, p. 2

(which suggests a trade-off between a reduced residency requirement and *Wahlpflicht*) and 3 October 1906, pp. 9–10.

96. *SP,* 1905, pp. 31783–84.

97. See below, Chapter 6.

98. Victor Mataja, "Gewerbeverfassung," *Österreichisches Staatswörterbuch,* 2d ed. (4 vols., Vienna, 1905–9), 2: 463–74 provides an overview of current trade law as of 1905.

99. The *Wiener Gewerbe-Genossenschaftstag* saw the government's 1901 draft as "einen Versuch zur totalen Entmündigung des Gewerbebestandes." 8 (October 1901): 1.

100. In testimony in January 1899 before the parliamentary *Gewerbe* committee Di Pauli argued that "das Gewerbe nicht immer Schutz und Patronanz von der Regierung erwarten solle, sondern dass die Selbstthätigkeit und Mithilfe der Gewerbetreibenden der erste Faktor sei, an welchen appelliert werden müsse." *Rp,* 29 January 1899, p. 5.

101. The debates of the parliamentary committee are reprinted in *WGGT,* 12 (1905): Nr. 137–42.

102. Ibid., 13 (December 1906/January 1907): 5.

103. The text is in *RGBl,* 1907, Nr. 26. For useful summaries of the 1907 commercial reforms, see *Die Gemeinde-Verwaltung der Stadt Wien im Jahre 1907,* pp. 371–78; and *Die Gemeinde-Verwaltung der Stadt Wien im Jahre 1908,* pp. 369–74. For a hostile but intelligent commentary, see Rudolf Kobatsch, "Die Gewerbegesetznovelle vom 5. Februar 1907," *ZVSV,* 17 (1908): 276–315.

104. Section 104b of the new *Ordnung,* for example, provided for the creation of official *Gesellenprüfungskommissionen.* The *Magistrat* organized the one based in Vienna, staffing it with Christian Social artisan leaders, with Josef Schlechter as chairman. *Der Gewerbefreund,* 15 October 1908, p. 14.

105. In December 1908, for example, Richard Weiskirchner established an official advisory council (*Gewerberat*) for the artisan trades in the Ministry of Commerce, to operate in parallel with the *Industrierat* and the *Arbeitsbeirat.* See ibid., 1 April 1909, p. 2.

106. *Rp,* 2 June 1906. p. 2.

107. Schneider himself thought that in spite of the *Herrenhaus*'s modifications, the law was a "giant success." *WGGT,* 13 (December 1906/January 1907), p. 2.

108. The Social Democrats were among the first to recognize this shift. See, for example, the *AZ*'s coverage of Gessmann's speech to a congress of export dealers in Prague, 16 June 1908, p. 5.

109. For the economic upswing after 1903, see Eduard März, *Austrian Banking and Financial Policy. Creditanstalt at a Turning Point, 1913–1923,* trans. Charles Kessler (New York, 1984), pp. 3–15. März points out that "the economy's dynamism was all the more remarkable for its having to struggle against 'home-made' limitations" (p. 9).

110. *Rp,* 20 February 1908, p. 10.

111. These projects included a program to sponsor exports of Viennese fashions, the creation of artisanal *Musterlage* in Vienna, presentations at the Leipzig Trade Fair, dis-

play exhibitions of Viennese craft products at various major European cities, and the creation of various trade-specific *Erwerbs- und Wirtschaftsgenossenschaften.*

112. See Heinl, *Über ein halbes Jahrhundert,* pp. 26–32; and *DV,* 3 July 1918, p. 11.

113. See, for example, reports of the dedication ceremonies for the new Handelskammer building in *Rp,* 13 October 1907, p. 6; and the ten-year celebration of the *Bund österreichischer Industrieller* in *DV,* 16 November 1907 (M), p. 7.

114. *Rp,* 23 August 1908, p. 9. See also his speech at the *I. Reichshandwerkertag* in Graz in September 1908, where he emphasized technological modernization as crucial to solving artisan problems. Ibid., 21 September 1908, p. 5.

115. "Grössere Ziele," ibid., 3 July 1907, pp. 1–2.

116. See *AZ,* 11 February 1909, p. 10; 27 February 1909, p. 10; 1 March 1909, p. 5. For contextual developments of labor mobilization and employer opposition in Vienna after 1900, see Gerhard Meissl, "Gewerkschaft und industrielle Arbeitsbeziehungen 1889–1914," in Maderthaner, ed., *Sozialdemokratie und Habsburgerstaat,* pp. 64–77; idem, "Klassenkampf oder Harmonieduselei? Auf dem österreichischen Weg zur Massengewerkschaft (1890–1914)," in *Die Bewegung,* pp. 95–103, esp. 98.

117. The career of the local Christian Social artisan politician Johann Pabst was typical here. Born in 1860 and orphaned early in childhood, Pabst was an autodidact with a primary-school education who worked first in a pharmaceutical laboratory and then had the ambition and energy to set himself up as a retail merchant. He managed to make an economic and political success of himself, and in 1894 he was elected as chairman of the guild of small retail merchants in Vienna. In 1897 Pabst was selected to be a Councillor in the commerce section of the Viennese Chamber of Commerce. He was appointed to the *Arbeitsbeirat* in 1905, elected to parliament in 1907, and joined the *Gewerberat* in 1909.

118. See its journal, *Der Gewerbefreund,* as well as *Beiträge zur Geschichte des deutschösterreichischen Gewerbebundes* (Vienna, 1928). For its program, "Organisation," *Der Gewerbefreund,* 1 January 1909, pp. 1–2. For its real financial state, see the reports in Z. 937–38, 986, 1018, Carton 73; Z. 1482 and Z. 1505, Carton 76, *CPW.*

119. Heinl, *Über ein halbes Jahrhundert,* pp. 36–37. See also Karl Renner's comments on the modification of older protectionist mentalities in "Politische Windstille," *K,* 4 (1910–11): 193–200.

120. "Dem Gewerbestande kann eigentlich auf dem Gebiete nur geholfen werden durch eine ordentliche geregelte Darlehensgewährung, durch Veranstaltung von Austellungen usw., aber mit dem bisherigen System, dass lauter Gesetze gemacht werden . . . dass der eine dies und der andere jenes nicht machen darf, wo der eine den anderen knebelt und schliesslich nichts herauskommt, muss gebrochen werden. Ich muss bei dieser Gelegenheit erklären, dass das System der Zwangsgenossenschaften nach meinen Erfahrungen sich ebenfalls im Interesse des Gewerbestandes nicht bewährt." *SP,* 1910, p. 2984. For the response, see *DV,* 16 June 1910 (M), pp. 3–4, 26 June 1910 (M), pp. 4–5; 6 July 1910 (M), pp. 8–9. Richard Weiskirchner also warned the artisans

not to rely exclusively on protective legislation and to place more emphasis on export creation and technical modernization. See *Rp,* 3 July 1910, pp. 1–2.

121. Karl Renner, "Ein Zerrbild der Autonomie. Als Prolog zu den Wiener Gemeinderatswahlen," *AZ,* 4 February 1912, p. 3.

122. It was not surprising that one artisan leader, Josef Schlechter, would protest against the fact that "in Wien ein politisches Strebertum sich breit macht, dass eine Anzahl Leute alle bezahlten Mandate an sich zu reissen bestrebt sind," thus depriving honest artisans of their chance at political office. *WGGT,* 14 (February/March, 1907): 5. For similar public criticism of the party leadership see *WF,* 5 May 1907, pp. 1–2.

123. For the state of Kunschak's organization in 1905, see the reports at the congress held in Salzburg, in *CSAZ,* 19 August 1905, pp. 1–6. The actual number of 'Christian Social' workers was one of the political mysteries of fin de siècle Vienna, which neither the police nor the Social Democrats, nor probably even Kunschak, could accurately know. Published statistics of actual membership in his club or its affiliated organizations claimed 26,000 members in Lower Austria (including Vienna) in 1907, which is probably exaggerated, owing to double-counting and other tricks. *CSAZ,* 5 October 1907, p. 2. The alleged number of workers in Christian Social or Catholic labor organizations was approximately 90,000 in 1909, compared to over 500,000 for the socialists, and the latter's data are certainly more reliable. *CSAZ,* 6 February 1909, pp. 2–3. Kunschak's support was concentrated in city industries, which by 1914 employed over 30,000 people and where he had a natural advantage over the Social Democrats, and among lower-ranking *Angestellten,* as well as marginal groups like the *Hausbesorger* and *Portiers,* who did not feel themselves as members of the political "working-class." See the examples of membership in ibid., p. 2. Election statistics for *Gehilfenversammlung* elections in the craft trades, not to mention the industrial unions, consistently demonstrated huge socialist majorities.

124. On the problematic relationship of the group to the mother party, see ibid., 30 January 1904, pp. 1–2 ("Durch Dick und Dünn?"); on its lack of mandates in 1907, 5 October 1907, p. 2. In the 1908 *Landtag* elections Kunschak was given 7 of 48 candidatures.

125. See Anton Orel, "Die Gewerbenovelle und die Lehrlinge," *CSAZ,* 19 January 1907, pp. 2–3; and "Die christlichsoziale Partei für die Gewerbeschulreform," 12 October 1907, p. 2. For its revision see "Zur Gewerbeschulreform," 23 January 1909, pp. 1–2; *AZ,* 17 January 1909, p. 3. For examples of Laborite criticism of city and provincial wage, employment and social policies, see *AZ,* 9 May 1903, p. 4; 20 June 1903, p. 5; 12 September 1903, p. 1; 24 October 1903, p. 1; 5 March 1904, p. 6; 17 September 1904, pp. 5–6. For typical attacks on the *Hausherren,* see 18 February 1905, pp. 3; and 4 December 1909, p. 1.

126. Karl Megner, *Beamte. Wirtschafts- und sozialgeschichtliche Aspekte des k.k. Beamtentums* (Vienna 1985), pp. 128–31, discusses the reasons behind the delay.

127. On the history of the Austrian *Beamten* movement, see Emil Lederer, "An-

gestellten- und Beamtensozialpolitik," *ASSP,* 33 (1911): 975–84; idem, "Bewegung der öffentlichen Beamten und Beamtensozialpolitik," ibid., 35 (1912): 895–913; 37 (1913): 660–69.

128. Megner, *Beamte,* pp. 207–08; *Der Staatsbeamte,* 1906, pp. 169–73.

129. *Der Staatsbeamte,* 1906, pp. 4–11, 21–29, 37–41, 53, 73, 137–39, 153, 170, 190–91. For the early history of the *Dienstpragmatik* controversy, see Lederer, "Angestellten- und Beamtensozialpolitik," pp. 975–83.

130. "Mögen Sie das erreichen, was die Wiener Stadtbeamten schon haben." *DZ,* 10 December 1905, p. 7. For the agitation among the postal employees in late 1906 and early 1907, see the files in Z. 246, XIV/220, *Statt. Pras., NÖLA.* On 9 November 1906 Bienerth wrote to Kielmansegg that the government had heard that the postal officials were threatening a strike or passive resistance, which would be a "grosse Schädigung der staatlichen Interessen," as well as disadvantaging the population at large.

131. *SP,* 1907, *Beilagen* 2776–77. See also *Rp,* 23 January 1907, p. 6; 29 January 1907, p. 1; Megner, *Beamte,* pp. 133–34. The final law is in *RGBl,* 1907, Nr. 34.

132. *SP,* 1907, p. 41908.

133. Party propagandists made a special point of emphasizing the Christian Socials' contribution to the success of this legislation during the 1907 campaign. See "Die Christlichsozialen und die Beamtenfrage," *Der Reichsratswähler,* 12 April 1907, p. 2.

134. So too did a law providing additional Congrua support for the Austrian lower clergy, which also enjoyed the strong support of the Christian Social delegation. All three units of the old anti-Semitic coalition from 1891–95—artisans, white-collar employees, lower-order clerics—were now in place. *Rp,* 24 January 1907, pp. 6, 9–10; 25 January 1907, p. 9. The 1907 law improved the revisions to Congrua rates that were undertaken in 1898. Max von Hussarek was the author of both of these laws.

135. "In dieser Richtung wird eine Besserung nach beiden Seiten erst dann eintreten, wenn in unsere Dienstorganisation ein vollständig neuer Zug kommt. Die ganze Staatsverwaltung, wie sie dermalen geführt wird, ist verzopft, verzopft im höchsten Grade. Wir haben eine Unzahl von Beamten, könnten aber vielleicht mit einem aliquoten Teil dieser Beamtenschaft dasselbe leisten. Vielleicht wäre sogar dem Publikum damit viel mehr gedient und wir könnten die wenigeren Beamten besser bezahlen." *SP,* p. 41908.

136. For the campaign, see Z. 3037, 6 April 1907; Z. 3290, 13 April 1907; Z. 3460, 20 April 1907; Z. 3297, 4 May 1907; Z. 4092, 9 May 1907, Carton 2242, 34/2, *MI Präs.* See also Jan Havránek, "Soziale Struktur und politisches Verhalten der grossstädtischen Wählerschaft im Mai 1907 — Wien und Prag im Vergleich," in Isabella Ackerl, Walter Hummelberger, and Hans Mommsen, eds., *Politik und Gesellschaft im Alten und Neuen Österreich. Festschrift für Rudolf Neck zum 60. Geburtstag* (2 vols., Vienna, 1981), 1: 150–66, esp. 160–61.

137. See the police reports in Z. 3460, 20 April 1907, Carton 2242, 34/2, *MI Präs;* and I/2B2, Nr. 138, 1907: 22 March 1907, 19 April 1907, 25 April 1907, *Statt. Präs., NÖLA.* The Christian Socials had prudently accorded the municipal *Beamten* a new

salary-promotion structure based on time in grade, as well as a generous Christmas bonus in late 1906, which Weiskirchner used to applaud the party's record in dealing with the local civil service. *DV,* 1 January 1907 (M), p. 4. In four of the seven districts in which independent *Beamten* candidates ran, there was no other credible bourgeois opposition to the Christian Socials. As the police noted, this meant that the Liberals were throwing their remaining support behind these candidacies, and thus, that many of the votes they received were not necessarily "civil service" votes at all. The small number of votes which these men collected (4,565 in all seven districts) could only have been a small fraction of the total white-collar vote in a city with an electorate of over 366,000 men. Havránek (p. 164) estimates the number of *Beamten* and *Angestellten* voters in Vienna at 72,000 in 1907, but also assumes that all those voting for *Beamten* candidates were themselves *Beamten,* but this was not necessarily the case. Further, Havránek's own distribution of the registered *Beamten* voters by district suggests that the Christian Socials merited support from these voters in districts where they were highly concentrated and in which there were no civil-service challenges. The Christian Socials always assumed that Lueger's era was the high point of their ability to attract the white-collar vote. See Christian Fischer, "Die Christlichsozialen und die Festbesoldeten-Bewegung," *VW,* 9 (1918): 158–63; as well as Robert Danneberg, "Wer sind die Wiener Wähler?" *K,* 6 (1912–13): 397–410.

138. For Kielmansegg's calculations, see Z. 9664, 2 October 1907, Carton 2194, 31, *MI Präs.* On the mood of the artisanal leaders, see the debates in *WGGT,* 14 (February/ March 1907): 1–6. For an example of white-collar *Freidenker* rhetoric during the campaign, see *"Los!" Organ der radikalen Partei,* 15 and 22 April 1907.

139. On socialist strategy and organization, see the report in I/2B2, Nr. 138, 30 January 1907, *Statt. Präs., NÖLA;* and the "Instruktion für die Bezirks- und Lokalvertrauensmänner," included in the report of 14 January 1907. See also Ellenbogen's report at the "Parteivertretung" on 28 February 1907, *VGAB,* which presented a schematic list of how much money each socialist candidate should receive to cover electoral costs based on the likelihood of his actually winning. The socialists also had problems in arranging an acceptable slate, since Czechs in Favoriten demanded one of the ward's two seats for their own, which Victor Adler categorically refused. See "Gesamtexecutive," 12 January 1907, *VGAB;* and the police report of 14 February 1907, Z. 181/ 7, *NÖLA.*

140. For the results in rural Lower Austria, see *Der Bauernbündler,* Nr. 8 (1907), pp. 1–5. On Stöckler, see the confidential report of the *Bezirkshauptmann* in Amstetten to Kielmansegg, 16 May 1907, I/2B2, Nr. 1444, *Statt. Präs., NÖLA.* For the context of his rise to power, see Johann Prammer, "Konservative und Christlichsoziale Politik im Viertel ob dem Wienerwald 1848–1918." Dissertation, University of Vienna, 1973, esp. pp. 310–17, 373ff.

141. The *Landeskulturrat* was a regional council that was charged with encouraging agricultural and economic development in the Crownland. It consisted of 32 members,

the majority of whom were Christian Social politicians from rural electoral districts. In the First Republic its work was taken over by the *Niederösterreichische Landwirtschafts- kammer,* which was established in February 1922.

142. Jukel was born in 1865, a year before Josef Stöckler. He attended a *land- wirtschaftliche Lehranstalt* in Mödling before becoming an estate manager and eventu- ally a proprietor in Schönau an der Triesting in Lower Austria. In 1900 he was elected to the village council and in 1902 to the Lower Austrian Diet. In 1906 he became mayor of Schönau. He was also a reserve lieutenant in the Imperial army.

143. See the reports from officials in Mistelbach, 15 May 1907; Baden, 19 May 1907; Gänserdorf, 15 May 1907; Neunkirchen, 15 May 1907; Pöggstall, 15 May 1907; Tulln, 16 May 1907; Waidhofen a.d. T., 15 May 1907; Zwettl, 16 May 1907; and Baden, 29 August 1907, in I/2B2, Nr. 1444, *Statt. Präs., NÖLA.*

144. *Erlebnisse,* 5: 163–64. For a similar evaluation, see Karl Renner, "Die Wand- lungen der Christlichsozialen," *K,* 2 (1908–9): 8–9, and Karl Gutkas, *Geschichte des Landes Niederösterreich* (3 vols., Vienna, 1957–62), 3: 160, who calls the political mat- uration represented by the *Bauernbund* a part of a "decisive process of regeneration for the peasantry."

145. On the Bund's founding, see *Der Bauernbündler,* Nr. 1, 1906, pp. 1–4. On its background, see Therese Kraus, "Die Entstehung des 'Niederösterreichischen Bauern- bundes'." Dissertation, University of Vienna, 1950.

146. For the program, see *Der Bauernbündler,* Nr. 4 (1907), pp. 2–3. The legal statutes of the association were drafted by Gessmann's younger colleagues Friedrich Gaertner and Eduard Heinl. See Heinl, *Über ein halbes Jahrhundert,* p. 17.

147. See especially Ernst Brückmüller, *Landwirtschaftliche Organisationen und ge- sellschaftliche Modernisierung* (Salzburg, 1977); and Gavin Lewis, "The Peasantry, Rural Change and Conservative Agrarianism. Lower Austria at the Turn of the Cen- tury," *Past & Present,* 81(November 1978): 119–43.

148. *LV,* 18 May 1907, p. 3. Beck to Coudenhove (copy), May 18, 1907, Carton 34, *NL Beck.*

149. See Eulenburg's report on his conversation with Franz Joseph in A 13358, 13 November 1897, Oest. 70/Bd. 31, *PAAA.*

150. On Sieghart see the judicious evaluation in Alfred Ableitinger, "Rudolf Sieg- hart (1866–1934) und seine Tätigkeit im Ministerratspräsidium." Dissertation, Univer- sity of Graz, 1964. See also the sympathetic but fair portrait in Ehrhart, *Im Dienste des Alten Österreich,* pp. 133–42. Sieghart's correspondence with Beck in the *NL Beck* (reprinted in Margarete Sieghart, "Rudolf Sieghart und das Ministerium Beck [Juni 1906 bis November 1908]," *Österreich in Geschichte und Literatur,* 16 [1972]: 465–75, 540–57) reveals his agility and culpability in trading material favors for votes in parlia- ment on a range of issues. So too, for that matter, does Beck's correspondence: Beck wrote to Coudenhove, for example, that if Count Emerich Chotek proved willing to support the Cabinet in the *Herrenhaus* vote on the electoral reform, "ermächtige ich

Dich, ihm den geheimen Rat in sichere Aussicht zu stellen." Beck to Coudenhove, 15 December 1906, Carton 34, *NL Beck.*

151. See "Klubsitzung," 21/22 June 1910, Carton 90, *CPK.* Gessmann's estimates were not far from those of the competition, for Wilhelm Ellenbogen reported that the socialists spent 225,000 crowns on the June 1911 parliamentary elections. "Parteivertretung und Kontrolle 23. Juni 1911," *VGAB.*

152. See Josef Redlich, *Österreichische Regierung und Verwaltung im Weltkriege* (Vienna, 1925), pp. 76–77.

153. A 8562, 25 May 1907, Oest. 91/Bd. 14, *PAAA.*

154. Ebenhoch to Franz Ferdinand, 2 February 1910, Carton 14, *NL Franz Ferdinand.* Ebenhoch supported Sieghart for the governorship of the *Bodenkreditanstalt* in early 1910, a move which Franz Ferdinand found deplorable, in spite of Josef Redlich's speculation that the Archduke secretly supported the appointment (which the letters of Brosch show was definitely not the case). See also Sieghart, *Die letzten Jahrzehnte,* pp. 161–62. Others in the party elite were equally sympathetic (and beholden) to Sieghart: Brosch reported to Franz Ferdinand of Alois Liechtenstein "so wie Gessmann ist er von Sieghart ganz entzückt, nennt ihn den grössten Freund der Christlichsozialen." 16 December 1909, C 73, ibid., Carton 10. See also, below, Chapter 6, pp. 334–35.

155. "Bürgermeister Dr. Lueger über die Wahlen," *Rp,* 17 May 1907, p. 1.

156. The Christian Socials voted on 12 November with the other German parties against the Pacak motion.

157. *SP,* 1897, p. 1625.

158. For the negotiations between Baernreither and Di Pauli in October 1897, which paint a portrait of Di Pauli as an unscrupulous opportunist, see the former's detailed account in an unpublished section of his Diary, Nr. 2, ff. 10–22, *NL Baernreither,* Carton 4; as well as Sutter, *Sprachenverordnungen,* 2: 113. Baernreither thought that he had the Catholics' agreement but that at the last moment pressure from Badeni and Ebenhoch's unpredictability ruined the negotiations. On the history of the Catholic conservative/Christian Social feud, see Norbert Miko, "Die Vereinigung der Christlichsozialen Reichspartei und des Katholisch-Konservativen Zentrums im Jahre 1907." Dissertation, University of Vienna, 1949; Walter Stöger, "Das Verhältnis der Konservativen zur Christlichsozialen Partei." Dissertation, University of Vienna, 1949; and Slapnicka, *Christlichsoziale in Oberösterreich.*

159. On Baernreither's resignation and the appointment of Di Pauli, see Lichnowsky's insightful reports in A 11498, 5 October 1898, and A 11550, 6 October 1898, Oest. 70/ Bd. 33; and A 11397, 3 October 1898, Oest. 88/Bd. 3, *PAAA.* An unwillingness to ally with their former anticlerical persecutors was a standard explanation given by the clericals against joining the German-national opposition against the government. But Ebenhoch was also contemptuous of the fragmentation among the Germans and clearly thought that more might be gained materially in terms of cultural and economic policy, and in terms of patronage control for his party, by staying with the Cabinet. He

was, thus, consistent in his opportunistic pragmatism of supporting the extremes of a Franz Thun and a Rudolf Sieghart. For the bishops, other motives came into play, most clearly involving their status prerogatives. On Ebenhoch, see also Eulenburg's comments in his report in A 417, 11 January 1899, Oest.70/Bd. 33. For recent surveys of clerical-conservative politics, which although concentrating on Tyrol are relevant for other Crownlands as well, see Richard Schober, "Das Verhältnis der Katholisch-Konservativen zu den Christlichsozialen in Tirol bis zu den Reichsratswahlen von 1907," *Tiroler Heimat,* 38 (1974): 139–73, and 39 (1975): 155–93; and idem, "Ein Bischof im Kreuzfeuer der Tiroler Christlichsozialen und Konservativen. Der Rücktritt des Fürstbischofs von Brixen Dr. Simon Aichner (1904)," *Österreich in Geschichte und Literatur,* 20 (1976): 387–405. See also Josef Fontana, *Geschichte des Landes Tirol. Band 3. Vom Neubau bis zum Untergang der Habsburgermonarchie (1848–1918)* (Bolzano 1987), pp. 281–309. The political situation in Salzburg has recently received a fine exposition by Hanns Haas in *Geschichte Salzburgs,* pp. 901–34.

160. See Schober, "Ein Bischof im Kreuzfeuer," p. 389; and Eulenburg's analysis in A 5161, 27 April 1898, Oest. 86/2/Bd. 11, *PAAA.*

161. On Schöpfer see Anton Klotz, *Dr. Aemilian Schöpfer. Priester und Volksmann* (Innsbruck, 1936) and Joseph Stifter, "Dr. Aemilian Schöpfer und der Bruderstreit in Tyrol." Dissertation, University of Vienna, 1949. Schöpfer was a professor of theology at the Brixen seminary who first entered regional politics in 1888. Already in the late 1880s he was active in establishing the *Brixener Chronik* and in provoking the ire of local conservatives for his often audacious comments about conservative lethargy. He and Ebenhoch engaged in a spirited exchange in 1889 over the latter's support for the Taaffe regime, leading Ebenhoch to publish several polemical pamphlets in self-defense.

162. This is contained in a draft letter to the Pope condemning the Christian Socials, dated 1 June 1903 and reprinted in Paul Molisch, ed., *Briefe zur deutschen Politik in Österreich von 1848 bis 1918* (Vienna, 1934), pp. 370–74.

163. Schöpfer helped to organize the first Tyrolean *Bauerntag* in January 1897. He was able to resist attempts by local peasant leaders to create an independent peasant political movement outside of the traditional party structure, and with Josef Schraffl was instrumental in organizing the *Tiroler Bauernbund* in November 1904. See Stifter, "Aemilian Schöpfer," pp. 75–79; Fontana, *Geschichte des Landes Tirols,* pp. 287–88, 314–15; and the detailed survey in Benedikt Erhard, *Bauernstand und Politik. Zur Geschichte des Tiroler Bauernbundes* (Vienna, 1981), pp. 52–135.

164. Following the conservative defeats in 1901 the remnant of the *Katholische Volkspartei* and other fragments of the old Hohenwart club reunited to form the *Zentrumsklub.* See Kolmer, *Parlament,* 8: 142.

165. Ebenhoch had been elected *Landeshauptmann* of Upper Austria in 1898. For a detailed survey of Ebenhoch's political career, see Susanne Gipp, "Dr. Alfred Ebenhoch (1855–1912)." Dissertation, University of Vienna, 1974. See also Slapnicka, *Christlichsoziale,* pp. 126–82.

166. They had appeared together at various public functions in the 1890s, including

a gathering sponsored by the Catholic student associations in November 1894. See *Rp*, 15 November 1894, p. 2. Ebenhoch had also strongly supported Lueger during the latter's conflict with the Crown over his confirmation as mayor of Vienna.

167. See *Rp*, 13 September 1904, p. 1; 22 October 1904, pp. 1–2; Slapnicka, *Christlichsoziale*, p. 150.

168. Schober, "Ein Bischof im Kreuzfeuer," pp. 396–401. Lueger and Liechtenstein visited Koerber to inform him that the appointment of Altenweisel would be considered a "casus belli" for the party in Tyrol. See also "Die Intransigenten," *Rp*, 13 October 1904, pp. 1–2.

169. *Rp*, 8 May 1904, p. 1.

170. Ibid., 23 September 1904, p. 1; Alois Adler, "Die christlichsoziale Bewegung in der Steiermark von den ständischen Anfängen zur Volkspartei." Dissertation, University of Graz, 1956, pp. 150–53.

171. *Rp*, 25 February 1906, p.6; 24 March 1906, p. 1; and his speech on March 22 in parliament, *SP*, 1906, pp. 35581–93.

172. *SP*, 1906, p. 40179. For the background, see Jenks, *The Austrian Electoral Reform of 1907*, pp. 79–87. Both in Tyrol and in Lower Austria the Christian Socials were hostile to the *Grossgrundbesitz*, in its Liberal and Catholic varieties, not merely because of its politically reactionary character and its parliamentary unreliability, but because in the event of its abolition the geographical areas which de facto the landowners represented—rural communities— would be replaced by peasant *Landgemeinden*, whose votes the party would most certainly garner. Their tactical anti-aristocratism had, therefore, a rational-instrumental purpose.

173. *Rp*, 13 November 1906, p. 7.

174. See the comments of Alois Liechtenstein on the need for unity in *Rp*, 30 October 1906, p. 7.

175. See *Rp*, 17 October 1906, p. 1; 15 November 1906, p. 1; 12 February 1907, p. 2; for early Christian Social suspicions, see "Der Hock-Block in Böhmen," *Rp*, 8 January 1907, pp. 1–2.

176. *LV*, 12 December 1906, pp. 2–3.

177. See *Rp*, 16 January 1907, p. 2, in reaction to the Leoben program of the *Deutsche Volkspartei*.

178. *LV*, 5 March 1907, p. 3.

179. Alfred Ebenhoch, "Das Zentrum und der deutsche Block," ibid., 14 February 1907, p. 1.

180. "Unser Program," ibid., 3 May 1907, p. 7.

181. *Rp*, 4 May 1907, p. 1.

182. *V*, 25 May 1907, p. 1; *Rp*, 24 May 1907, p. 6.

183. For the political situation in Salzburg in 1907, see *Geschichte Salzburgs*, pp. 931–33.

184. *Rp*, 2 June 1907, p. 6; *V*, 2 June 1907, pp. 1–2; *LV*, 4 June 1907, pp. 1–2. Scheicher alludes to the inner-club opposition of the clericals in *Erlebnisse*, 5: 296–97.

185. The *Reichspost,* doubtlessly speaking for Gessmann, argued against Eben-hoch's notion of a looser parliamentary union for a more systematic party structure: "Doktor Ebenhoch scheint an ein gemeinsames Exekutivkomitee seiner Gruppe und der christlich-sozialen Partei zu denken. Das eine ist sicher, dass der Zusammenschluss umso dauernder and aussichtsvoller sein wird, je mehr ein Zweiseelenleben unmöglich gemacht und. . . . eine wirkliche Einheit geschaffen wird, die nicht nur zeitweise tak-tisch, sondern auch innerlich geschlossen operiert." 26 May 1907, p. 1.

186. Gessmann drew heavily upon resources he controlled as the leader of the Pro-vincial Executive Committee to establish this office. The official title of the secretariat was *Sekretariat der christlichsozialen Parteileitung Österreichs (Sektion Wien).* See Heinl, *Über ein halbes Jahrhundert,* p. 17; *Eduard Heinl. Ein Leben für Österreich* (Vienna, 1955), pp. 31–32; and the detailed attacks in *DV,* 7 June 1911 (Mi), p. 1, and 9 June 1911 (Mi), p. 1. For an example of their interventions, see Nr. 1089, 20 October 1908, M. Abt. 119, Carton 4/3, *WSLA.*

187. On the new parliamentary club statute, see *Rp,* 19 June 1907, p. 6, and *LV,* 19 June 1907, p. 2.

188. Morsey to Beck, 2 June 1907, *NL Beck,* Carton 36; as well as Funder's recollec-tions in Miko, "Vereinigung," pp. 346–47. Morsey admitted to Beck that even if he tried to keep the Styrian delegation out of the merger, the pressure of the Catholic clergy in the province would push his confederates into joining the *Reichspartei.*

189. His avarice was surpassed only by his stupidity: after presenting these com-plaints, Morsey proceeded to ask Beck for a seat in the *Herrenhaus.*

190. Gessmann to Funder, 4 January 1912, *NL Funder.* For Steiner's comments, see "Klubsitzung," 18 May 1910, Carton 90, *CPK.* Scheicher also alludes to Lueger's lack of enthusiasm for the merger in *Erlebnisse,* 5: 296. Sieghart, although aware of Morsey's ability to cause trouble, was dismissive of his integrity, suggesting to Beck that he could be bought off with a lucrative administrative board position: "Morsey ist absolut nicht zu fürchten. Wer so verhasst und so als Maulwurf bekannt ist, kann nicht viel schaden. Übrigens bin ich dafür, ihm jetzt eine gut dotierte Verwaltungsratstelle zu verschaffen." Sieghart to Beck, 12 August 1907. Unfortunately for Beck, Morsey was able to cause considerable difficulties over the Wahrmund Affair the following year.

191. *Rp,* 12 June 1907, p. 6. The adjective also conveyed a clear anti-Semitic refer-ence to the Jewish origins of Hock, Kuranda, and Ofner. When the German national parties resumed unity talks in late May, the exclusion of the Viennese parliamentarians Hock and Kuranda cast a shadow over the proceedings. That their exclusion from the prospective *Deutschnationalverband* occurred at Christian Social request is possible, but it is very unlikely this was the only reason.

192. Ebenhoch to Lueger, 3 June 1907, I.N. 40958 and 13 June 1907, I.N. 40942, *Handschriftensammlung.* See also Beck to Franz Ferdinand, 15 June 1907, Carton 9, *NL Franz Ferdinand,* where Beck describes Weiskirchner as the government's can-didate.

193. *DV,* 5 June 1907 (M), pp. 1–2.

194. *Rp,* 29 June 1907, p. 1.

195. *NFP,* 25 September 1909 (M), p. 7; 28 September 1909 (M), p. 8.

196. *Rp,* 9 June 1907, pp. 1–2.

197. *DV,* 20 June 1907 (A), p. 1.

198. Ebenhoch to Altenweisel, 2 March 1910, cited in Miko, "Vereinigung," p. 337.

199. On the background, see Harrington-Müller, *Der Fortschrittsklub,* pp. 53–56, 64.

200. See *Rp,* 27 June 1907, p. 10; *SP,* 1907, pp. 95–98, as well as Konrad Walcher, *Die Politik der Christlichsozialen im neuen Reichsrate. Eine Übersicht über die Tätigkeit der christlichsozialen Vereinigung in dem ersten Sessionsabschnitt der XVIII. Legislaturperiode vom 17. Juni–24. Juli 1907* (Vienna, 1908).

201. Sieghart to Beck, 13 August 1907, *NL Beck.*

202. "Der Portefeuille-Drang ist stark genug um allein zu wirken." Sieghart to Beck, 12 August 1907, ibid.

203. Franz Ferdinand to Brosch, 3 February 1909, reprinted in Leopold von Chlumecky, *Erzherzog Franz Ferdinands Wirken und Wollen* (Berlin, 1929), p. 324.

204. *DZ,* 28 November 1905, p. 1.

205. See "Stand der socialdemokratischen Bewegung in Österreich und deren Bekämpfung," in Franz M. Schindler, ed., *Sociale Vorträge gehalten bei dem Wiener socialen Vortrags-Curse 1894* (Vienna, 1895), pp. 110–18; as well as the *AZ*'s responses on 14 August 1894, p. 1; 31 August 1894, p. 2; and 7 September 1894, p. 2.

206. *Rp,* 16 February 1907, p. 5.

207. "Wahlmanifest der christlich-sozialen Reichspartei," *Rp,* 12 March 1907, pp. 10–11.

208. For example, Friedrich Funder and Leopold Kunschak ran in Styria; Richard Weiskirchner and Karl Stroh in Moravia; Julius Axmann in Silesia; Karl Lueger, Albert Gessmann, Josef Mender, Franz Bittner, and Franz Spalowsky in Bohemia. In all cases the contests were hopeless.

209. *Rp,* 24 May 1907, p. 1 ("Deutschösterreich—das sind wir").

210. *Rp,* 5 May 1907, p. 2.

211. Beck to Coudenhove, 18 May 1907, *NL Beck.*

212. Beck to Coudenhove, 3 May 1907.

213. *Rp,* 30 December 1906, p. 1; 9 January 1907, p. 1; 26 January 1907, pp. 1–2. Gessmann was later quite explicit about the all-encompassing nature of the new party. In March 1910 he called the Christian Socials an "allumfassende Volkspartei" which brought together "die Gesamtheit des Volkes." See "Klubsitzung," 10 March 1910, Carton 96, *CPK.*

214. *Rp,* 28 May 1907, pp. 1–2.

215. See Gregory's analysis in "Annual Report on Austria-Hungary for the Year 1907," p. 51, FO 371/398, *PRO.*

216. On the question of the *Zentrum* and ministerialism, see Klaus Epstein, *Matthias Erzberger and the Dilemma of German Democracy* (Princeton, 1959), pp. 34–36, 89–90.

217. See Gessmann's invitation to Spahn to join him on a tour of Vienna's suburbs and spend an evening with him at the State Opera, 7 September 1908, Nr. 79, *NL Spahn*.

218. Gaertner's personal files in the *Verwaltungsarchiv* describe him as a person of extraordinary talent and administrative competence, which was demonstrated by his conduct during the war: "Seine Vertrautheit mit den Problemen der Lebensmittelversorgung, seine Initiative und vielfach erprobte Gewandheit waren auch dafür bestimmend, dass er wiederholt zu einschlägigen Verhandlungen nach Deutschland entsendet und zur Mitwirkung an der Organisation der rumänischen Cerealienbezüge herangezogen wurde, welche Aufgaben er in der erfolgreichsten Weise durchführte." *K. K. Ministerrats-Präsidium*, Z. 5003, 3 August 1917. See also his personal files in the *Deutschösterreichische Staatskanzlei, 1918–1919, Archiv der Republik*.

219. On Gaertner, see Ehrhart, *Im Dienste des alten Österreich*, p. 156; Josef Redlich, *Schicksalsjahre Österreichs 1908–1919. Das politische Tagebuch Josef Redlichs*, ed. Fritz Fellner (2 vols., Graz, 1953–54), 1: 12, 47, 54; Kielmansegg, *Kaiserhaus*, p. 358; *NÖB*, 1: 398; and the obituaries in *NFP* and *Rp* on 7 and 8 February 1931. How he first came into contact with Gessmann is uncertain, but Eugen Schwiedland may have played a mediating role, for Gaertner studied with Schwiedland in 1904–6. Ernst Vergani reported that Gaertner had been a friend of Gessmann's son, Albert, Jr., who may have helped him gain entry to the civil service in the fall of 1907. Gaertner's most notable work was his dissertation for Alfred Weber on "Der Ausbau der Sozialversicherung in Oesterreich," published in the *ASSP*, 29 (1909): 417–43, 759–833. See also his "Die genossenschaftliche Kreditorganisation des Kleingewerbes und Kleingrundbesitzes in Oesterreich," ibid., 24 (1907): 630–56; and his "Die Brotversorgung in Oesterreich," ibid., 43 (1916–17): 610–64.

220. *Germania*, 26 May 1907, p. 1. This article is untitled, but Gaertner is the likely author.

221. "Vielleicht ist heute doch schon der Zeitpunkt für Wandlungen gekommen, vielleicht hat der Nationalitätenkampf in den sieben mageren Jahren der Obstruktion seinen Höhepunkt erreicht. Vielleicht ist das allseits bewiesene Prinzip, dass man wohl Parteien, nicht aber Nationen niederstimmen kann, tiefer in das Volk gedrungen. Dann könnten wirtschaftliche und sociale Probleme über dem Sprachenkampf heraufsteigen. Schon müssen nationale Parteien strengster Observanz wirtschaftliche Fragen in ihr Programm aufnehmen. Neue Gestaltungen werfen ihre Schatten, und Abg. Ebenhoch sagte die Schlagworte des Kampfes der Zukunft voraus: 'Hie Christentum! Hie Sozialdemokratie!'" "Alte und neue Probleme in Oesterreich," *Germania*, 15 October 1905, p. 1.

222. Ibid., 26 May 1907, p. 1.

223. Vergani variously described Gaertner as Gessmann's "spiritus rector" and as his "politischer Ratgeber." *DV*, 12 June 1910 (M), p. 2; 21 July 1910 (Mi), p. 1; 7 June

1911 (M), p. 1. He also accused Gaertner of being Jewish. Gaertner's personal files list him as a Roman Catholic, and his university records report him as having Dr. Julius Bondy, a Viennese lawyer, as his *Vormund.*

224. Calculated from the lists in *SP,* 1907, pp. 17–50.

225. See "Vergleichende Darstellung der bei den Reichsratswahlen der Jahre 1907 und 1911 für die Christlichsozialen abgegebenen Stimmen," Carton 96, *CPK.*

226. See Richard Charmatz, *Deutsch-Oesterreichische Politik. Studien über den Liberalismus und über die auswärtige Politik Österreichs* (Leipzig, 1907), pp. 312–32. Akers Douglas of the English Embassy noted in 1910, on the natural hegemony which agrarians were able to sustain under the new franchise, with the covert help of the Hungarians on economic issues: "Though the great landlords are also heavily taxed, and their power is not quite so great as it was, the high protection of agriculture and the undiminished importance of this industry to Austria-Hungary still assures them considerable authority. In the large towns the 'industrials' have gained in influence, but the results of universal suffrage have, it appears, to some extent disappointed the expectations of trade and industrial circles, for certain representative bodies, such as the Chamber of Commerce, have lost their votes, and whilst the increase of electors has benefited the working classes of the towns it has, of course, also added to the representation of agriculturists." "Annual Report on Austria-Hungary for the Year 1910," p. 30, FO 881/9771, *PRO.*

227. I/2B2, Nr. 138, police report of 21 February 1907, *Statt. Präs., NÖLA.*

228. Karl Hilgenreiner, "Vorwärts? Eine kirchenpolitische Studie," *Rp,* 1 January 1904, pp. 5–6.

229. "Die christlich-soziale Partei der österreichischen Deutschen ist in trefflicher Verwirklichung das, was das deutsche Zentrum sein möchte: eine grosse deutsche christliche Reichspartei." Martin Spahn, "Die christlich-soziale Partei der Deutschen Österreichs," *Hochland,* 5 (1908): 544–59, here 544.

230. Gessmann to Spahn, 12 August 1908, Nr. 79, *NL Spahn.*

CHAPTER THREE

1. On the background to the 1907 *Ausgleich,* see Alexander Spitzmüller, "Die staatsfinanziellen Vereinbarungen im österreichisch-ungarischen Ausgleiche," *ZVSV,* 17 (1908): 374–98; Friedrich Gaertner, "Der österreichisch-ungarische Ausgleich," *ASSP,* 25 (1907): 52–147, 338–444; L. D. Carnegie, "Report for the Year 1907–08 on the Finances of Austria-Hungary," *Diplomatic and Consular Reports,* No. 4109 (London, 1908), pp. 2–30; Sieghart, *Die letzten Jahrzehnte,* pp. 104–22; Johann Christoph Allmayer-Beck, *Ministerpräsident Baron Beck. Ein Staatsmann des alten Österreich* (Vienna, 1956), pp. 162–94; Chlumecky, *Erzherzog Franz Ferdinands Wirken und Wollen,* pp. 302ff; Jürgen Nautz, ed., *Unterhändler des Vertrauens. Aus den nachgelassenen Schriften von Sektionschef Dr. Richard Schüller* (Vienna, 1990), p. 111; and Géza Andreas von Geyr, *Sándor Wekerle 1848–1921. Die politische Biographe eines ungarischen Staatsmannes der Donaumonarchie* (Munich, 1993), pp. 234–39. For an inter-

esting evaluation of the meaning of the *Ausgleich,* see März, *Austrian Banking,* pp. 93–96.

2. See Alexander Spitzmüller-Harmersbach, *Der letzte österreichisch-ungarische Ausgleich und der Zusammenbruch der Monarchie. Sachliches und Persönliches* (Berlin, 1929), p. 13.

3. For the Archduke's views of the the problem of guarantees, see Rudolf Neck, "Der Protest Franz Ferdinands gegen die ungarischen Verfassungsgarantien von 1907," *MÖSTA,* 12 (1959): 433–37; Allmayer-Beck, *Baron Beck,* pp. 183–89; and the letters of Franz Ferdinand to Beck warning him of dire consequences if concessions were offered on 9 May 1907 and 26 June 1907. *NL Beck.*

4. Brosch's efforts to detect conspiracies merely fed the Thronfolger's suspicions. See Brosch to Franz Ferdinand, 21 December 1907, C 27 and 2 February 1908, C 30, Carton 10, *NL Franz Ferdinand.*

5. See Beck's contribution to the debates in *SP,* 1907, pp. 2254–59.

6. For the official text, see *SP,* Session 18, 1907, Beilagen Nr. 396 and 397.

7. For summaries, see the Extra-Ausgabe of the *Rp,* 16 October 1907, pp. 1–5; and *NFP,* 16 October 1907 (A), pp. 2–3, as well as Goschen's report in *BDFA,* vol. 34, pp. 178–79.

8. *Rp,* 16 September 1907, p. 4.

9. *Rp,* 17 September 1907, p. 2; *NFP,* 16 September 1907 (M), p. 3.

10. Allmayer-Beck, *Baron Beck,* p. 193.

11. "Kein Ausgleich?" *Rp,* 21 September 1907, pp. 1–2.

12. The bill also included the imposition of a three-year residency requirement (as opposed to the one year mandated in the national franchise). The secret negotiations among Gessmann, Beck, and Kielmansegg (in which Marchet was also involved) are charted in Z. 783, 28 February 1907; Z. 1456, 18 February 1907; Z. 783, 3 March 1907; Z. 8080, 9 August 1907; Z. 9007, 11 September 1907; Carton 2194, 31, *MI Präs.;* and in I/2C4, N. 2282, 1907, *Statt. Präs., NÖLA.* They commenced as early as February 1907 with Gessmann contacting Bienerth on his plans. In a repeat performance of the 1900 municipal franchise, Gessmann started out by proposing a franchise based only on universal suffrage. Kielmansegg was naturally less than happy about Gessmann's strategy to make the Lower Austrian *Regierung* suffer the adverse publicity for withdrawing this first draft, so that for a time it seemed as if Gessmann would be forced to either go with the first draft, or not bring it in at all. For the party's official explanation of why the first, more comprehensive draft was withdrawn, see *Rp,* 12 September 1907, p. 3; and Hermann Bielohlawek, "Die Unzufriedenen Genossen," *Rp,* 22 September 1907, p. 1. In the end Kielmansegg had to admit that Gessmann's manipulations were not "unklug" (Z. 9177, 16 September 1907) and that the worst the Christian Socials would have to fear would be 8 to 10 socialists elected, against 80 or so Christian Socials. The final results proved Gessmann even more successful than Kielmansegg had thought.

13. For the debates in late September, see *SPNÖ,* 1907, pp. 627–88. The most brilliant critique of the Christian Socials' tactics was offered by Karl Seitz (pp. 632–41).

14. The *AZ* noted the extraordinary haste, coming during a period when the Emperor was allegedly ill, of the sanction of the law. *AZ,* 30 October 1907, p. 1.

15. *Rp,* 21 September 1907, p. 2.

16. See *Rp,* 14 October 1907, p. 2; and Gessmann's retrospective apologetic in Bolzano on the unselfserving motives behind the party's entry, in *NFP,* 7 January 1908 (M), p. 4.

17. See the interviews in *Rp,* 17 October 1907, pp. 1–2.

18. "Der österreichisch-ungarische Ausgleich," *Österreichische Rundschau,* 13 (1907): 165 ("Wenn Österreich von Ungarn gewisse Verbesserungen des gegenwärtigen Verhältnisses oder der im Jahre 1905 getroffenen Vereinbarungen erzielen wollte, musste es dafür auch einen Gegenwert bieten, und wir können vollkommen beruhigt sein, dass die in dieser Richtung gebrachten Opfer nicht allzu gross sind").

19. Ebenhoch to Lueger, 10 October 1907, I.N. 40945, *Handschriftensammlung.*

20. *SP,* 1907, pp. 2157–59.

21. *Rp,* 26 October 1907, p. 2.

22. On Prášek see Czedik, *Zur Geschichte,* 3: 234.

23. For the background, with accompanying acerbic commentary, see *AZ,* 26 October 1907, p. 6; 1 November 1907, p. 3; 3 November 1907, p. 1; and 13 November 1907, pp. 5–6, the latter on Karel Kramář's role in the crisis.

24. Brosch to Franz Ferdinand, 7 November 1907, C 14, *NL Franz Ferdinand.* Brosch spoke with Lueger on the morning of the 7th, and this letter summarizes the conversation, together with Brosch's reflections on Lueger's motives. See also Scheicher's recollections of these events in *Erlebnisse,* 5: 265–68.

25. Gaertner, "Der österreichisch-ungarische Ausgleich," p. 444. The *Ausgleich* received final approval by the *Abgeordnetenhaus* on 17 December 1907.

26. *Rp,* 9 November 1907, p. 1 ("Wäre es nach dem Wunsche der christlichsozialen Partei gegangen und hätte diese nicht ihre parteimässigen Wünsche den allgemeinstaatlichen Interessen unterzuordnen brauchen, dann wäre vor Beginn 1908 kein Christlich-Sozialer als Mitglied der Regierung in Betracht gekommen und der Ausgleich wäre vielleicht nicht gegen sie, aber ohne die aktive Mithilfe der christlichsozialen Partei gemacht worden"). As equivocal and misleading as Funder could often be, there is no reason to doubt that this was in fact Gessmann's long-term strategy—let Beck take the heat for the *Ausgleich* and then step in after the dirty work had been done to collect the ex post facto reward.

27. As late as November 7, Brosch came up with three different scenarios as to how the ministerial assignments would take shape. The *AZ* even had to change its forecasts within the same news edition (compare *AZ,* 8 November 1907, pp. 1 and 2).

28. See *AZ,* 10 November 1907, p. 1; 11 November 1907, p. 3. Gessmann was now described as the "Parteidiktator."

29. See Lueger's comments (in pencil) on a letter of Weiskirchner's to Lueger, 25 February 1908, I.N. 40872, *Handschriftensammlung,* as well as Gerhard Rauch, "Die christlichsoziale Vereinigung und die Katholisch-Konservativen Oberösterreichs 1907–1914." Dissertation, University of Vienna, 1964, p. 37.

30. On Ebenhoch's tenure as agriculture minister, see Gipp, "Dr. Alfred Ebenhoch," pp. 184–97; and *Rp,* 17 November 1908, p. 1.

31. See Franz Ferdinand to Brosch, 3 February 1909, reprinted in Chlumecky, *Franz Ferdinands Wirken und Wollen,* p. 324. Paul Nikitsch, a Court assistant to the Thronfolger, also wrote to Brosch when rumors were spreading that Bienerth might invite Ebenhoch to return to his former post at Agriculture that the Archduke would oppose this. Letter of 20 January 1909, *NL Franz Ferdinand.* Ebenhoch merited the ire of the Feudal circles for his support of small proprietors' rights against nobles' hunting prerogatives.

32. Brosch to Franz Ferdinand, 7 November 1907. For Gessmann's self-description ("Ich bin halt einmal ein Agitator"), see *Rp,* 14 November 1907, p. 2.

33. *Rp,* 9 November 1907, p. 1; 13 November 1907 p. 2 (which refers to the new ministry as a "Ministerium für Sozialpolitik"); 29 November 1907, p. 12; 1 December 1907, p. 6; 8 January 1908, p. 7.

34. "Der Organisationsentwurf für das neue Arbeitsministerium," *NFP,* 5 January 1908 (M), pp. 4–5.

35. Gessmann: "Wir sind nicht Männer des Rückschrittes, wie man uns so vielfach hinzustellen beliebt, sondern gerade das Gegenteil, Männer durchaus moderner Gesinnung und erfüllt von den grossen Aufgaben, die unserer Zeit gestellt sind." *Rp,* 26 November 1907, p. 7; and "Denn wir würden traurige Leute sein, wenn wir an allen Forderungen der modernen Zeit blind vorübergehen würden." *NFP,* 15 January 1908 (M), p. 7.

36. *Rp,* 15 November 1907, p. 5; the *AZ* quoted the enthusiastic evaluation of Gessmann in *Die Industrie,* an industrialists' journal, for his anti-Marxism. 6 February 1908, p. 5.

37. See "Das Ministerium Gessmann," *AZ,* 12 November 1907, p. 1; and "Die Errichtung eines neuen Ministeriums," *AZ,* 10 November 1907, p. 3.

38. See Allmayer-Beck, *Baron Beck,* pp. 237–38. On the subtle interaction of the Social Democrats with the Ministries, see Redlich, *Österreichische Regierung,* pp. 78–79; Ehrhart, *Im Dienste des alten Österreich,* pp. 227–28; as well as Tschirschky's later report with similar accusations against Gautsch in A 16196, 10 October 1911, Oest. 91/Bd. 16, *PAAA.* The private correspondence of Victor Adler during the war, in the Social Democratic Party Archive in *AVA,* suggests a similar series of informal connections. See, for example, his letters to Karl Kautsky, 12 April 1918, and to Johann Schober, 19 April 1918, *SD-Parteistellen,* Carton 12.

39. "Protokoll der Sitzung des deutschen Parteivorstandes am 4. Februar 1915" and the "Protokoll der gemeinsamen Sitzung des Parteivorstandes mit der Landesparteivertretung am 8. März 1915," *VGAB.*

40. For a good expression of socialist fears see "Gessmann-Rede," *AZ,* 15 January 1908, p. 1.

41. *Rp,* 12 November 1907, p. 2; 19 November 1907, p. 2.

42. *Rp,* 16 January 1908, p. 2. Simultaneously Richard Weiskirchner came forward with a proposal to appoint parliamentary *Sektionschefs* in the various ministries— which would have opened many more high ministerial positions to party politicians. *Rp,* 15 January 1908, p. 3.

43. *NFP,* 26 January 1908 (M), p. 7.

44. *AZ,* 30 January 1908, p. 3; *NFP,* 29 January 1908 (A), p. 1; 30 January 1908 (A), pp. 1–2.

45. *NFP,* 29 January 1908 (A), p. 1.

46. *Rp,* 1 February 1909, p. 2; for the final scope of the Ministry, see *NFP,* 6 February 1908 (M), p. 2; and the report on its early history prepared for Franz Ferdinand in 1914 by Bardolff in Nr. 8, 27 January 1914, Carton 204, *MKFF.* See also Brigitte Pellar, "Staatliche Institutionen und gesellschaftliche Interessengruppen in der Auseinandersetzung um den Stellenwert der Sozialpolitik und um ihre Gestaltung. Das k.k. arbeitsstatistische Amt im Handelsministerium und sein ständiger Arbeitsbeirat 1898–1917." Dissertation, University of Vienna, 1982, pp. 458–69; as well as Walter Goldinger, "Die Zentralverwaltung in Cisleithanien—Die zivile gemeinsame Zentralverwaltung," in Adam Wandruszka and Peter Urbanitsch, eds., *Die Habsburgermonarchie 1848–1918. Band II. Verwaltung und Rechtswesen* (Vienna, 1975), pp. 148–57.

47. *Rp,* 6 February 1908, p. 1. The *AZ,* in contrast, took satisfaction in the fact that social affairs had been left in the hands of the Commerce Ministry. 9 February 1908, p. 1.

48. *AZ,* 7 February 1908, p. 2.

49. Weiskirchner to Lueger, 25 February 1908, I.N. 40872, *Handschriftensammlung.*

50. Ebenhoch to Lueger, 24 February 1908, I.N. 40946.

51. See the remarks by Adler in *SP,* 1908, pp. 4123–34.

52. *SP,* 1908, pp. 4134–42 (Drexel) and pp. 4168–78 (Redlich). Redlich argued: "Die Regierung muss parlamentarisch sein. . . . Ich bitte dieses Ministerium, das ich noch für ein parlamentarisches halte, in der Richtung der Kräftigung des parlamentarischen Gedankens zu arbeiten."

53. See Goldinger, "Die Zentralverwaltung," p. 149.

54. Ebenhoch to Lueger, 24 February 1908, I.N. 40947; and 14 March 1908, I.N. 40947; *Rp,* 25 March 1908, p. 5; 27 March 1908, p. 2.

55. On the party's continuing anti-Magyarism, see Clarke to Carnegie, 20 December 1907, FO 371/388, *PRO.*

56. See "Der Ausbau unser Kriegsmarine," *Rp,* 25 January 1908, p. 2. Earlier in the month Schlegel, along with other parliamentarians, had been the guest of the Naval High Command on a public-relations tour of fleet facilities in the Adriatic. For his career, see Alfred Schlegel, "Josef Schlegel—ein österreichischer Patriot," in *Für Kir-*

che und Heimat. Festschrift Franz Loidl zum 80. Geburtstag (Vienna, 1985), pp. 328–58.

57. See "Die Parade der Wiener Knabenhorte," *Wiener Bilder,* 10 July 1907, p. 4. Opelt encountered substantial and explicit hostility to his schemes from a variety of expert commentators at the 1907 congress on child welfare in Vienna. See the *Protokoll über die Verhandlungen des Ersten Österreichischen Kinderschutzkongresses in Wien, 18. bis 20. März 1907* (Vienna, 1907), pp. 211–19. For the general background see Engelbrecht, *Geschichte,* pp. 142–44; Eduard Liechtenstein, "Die Entwicklung der Jugendfürsorge in Österreich seit dem I. Kinderschutzkongresse vom Jahre 1907," in Josef M. Baernreither, ed., *Gutachten, Berichte und Materialien zu den Verhandlungsgegenständen des Zweiten Österreichischen Kinderschutzkongresses in Salzburg, 1913* (Vienna, 1913), pp. 82–85; and Wilhelm Bong, *Christus und die Arbeiterwelt. Meine Erlebnisse als Handwerksbursche und Fabriksarbeiter* (Vienna, 1911), pp. 94–98.

58. See Leopold Tomola's suspicions about Opelt in *AB,* 1908, p. 3040 ("Die Verwechslung mit den Oppelt'schen Horten bringt uns viel Schaden und doch sind wir es, die beständig die Behörden aufmerksam machen, wie unpädagogisch gerade diese Horte geleitet sind"). Tomola also reported that the Social Democratic district organization in Simmering also operated a military *Hort.* Eduard Liechtenstein (p. 83) argued that by 1913 some of the military orientation of the Opelt groups had dissipated, as they began to concentrate on other forms of training activities for the boys in their charge.

59. The leader of the veterans' movement in the party was the parliamentary deputy from the Stubenviertel, Josef von Baechlé, who was also the president of the municipal *Knabenhorte* association.

60. On the *Zentrum's* complex and ambivalent policies toward military appropriations, see Karl Bachem, *Vorgeschichte, Geschichte und Politik der Deutschen Zentrumspartei* (9 vols., Cologne, 1927–32): 6: 251–57, 299–302, 351–52; 7: 133–35, 138–39, 391–93. On Zabern, 7: 404–9. For Bachem's phrase "loyale Politik," see 7: 390. Bachem noted of the *Flottenverein's* behavior towards the *Zentrum:* "kein Mittel konfessioneller Verhetzung gegen das Zentrum war ihm zu bedenklich" (6: 402).

61. See *Stenographische Sitzungs-Protokolle der Delegation des Reichsrates,* Session 42, 1908, p. 609.

62. *SP,* 1907, pp. 2392–93.

63. "Protokoll," 27 October 1907, *Gemeinsame Ministerratsprotokolle,* P. A. XL, Carton 306; *DV,* 28 October 1907 (A), pp. 1–2.

64. *Rp,* 2 February 1908, p. 1; 5 February 1908, pp. 4–5.

65. *Stenographische Sitzungs-Protokolle der Delegation des Reichsrates,* 1908, p. 697; *AZ,* 4 March 1908, p. 1; *NFP,* 2 March 1908 (N), p. 1; 3 March 1908 (M), p. 3; 4 March 1908 (M), pp. 5–6; 5 March 1908 (M), pp. 2–3.

66. *Rp,* 11 March 1908, p. 10; *NFP,* 10 March 1908 (A), pp. 1–2; Liechtenstein to

Lueger, 9 March 1908, I.N. 40878, *Handschriftensammlung.* See also Goschen to Grey, 14 March 1908, FO 371/398, *PRO.*

67. Franz Ferdinand to Brosch, 11 January 1908, reprinted in Chlumecky, pp. 246–47.

68. Brosch to Franz Ferdinand, 2 February 1908, C 30, *NL Franz Ferdinand.*

69. Ebenhoch to Lueger, 22 March 1908, I.N. 40951, as well as 14 March 1908, I.N. 40947, *Handschriftensammlung.* For Hungarian reaction, see *NFP,* 12 March 1908 (A), pp. 1–2.

70. "Protokoll," 17/21 May 1908, *Gemeinsame Ministerratsprotokolle,* P. A. XL, Carton 307. For a provocative portrait of Wekerle, see the comments of Ehrhart in *Im Dienste des alten Österreich,* pp. 198–99. See also the quite insightful discussion of Hungarian defensiveness about Austrian meddling, in the "Annual Report on Austria-Hungary for the Year 1909," pp. 27–31, FO 881/9593, *PRO.*

71. Goschen interpreted the final result as a suitable compromise on the part of both sides, since in the end the Hungarians did end up supporting raises for the officer corps. See his report to Grey, 25 May 1908, FO 371/398.

72. *Rp,* 24 May 1908, p. 1; *NFP,* 23 May 1908 (M), pp. 1–2.

73. Brosch to Franz Ferdinand, 14 May 1908, C 33, *NL Franz Ferdinand.*

74. Brosch to Franz Ferdinand, 18 May 1908, C 36 and 22 May 1908, C 37, ibid.

75. *Rp,* 25 May 1908, p. 1.

76. Brosch to Franz Ferdinand, 23 May 1908, C 38; 25 May 1908, C 40, *NL Franz Ferdinand.*

77. *SP,* 1908, Anhang II, 2850/I.

78. *AZ,* 28 May 1908, p. 1; *NFP,* 28 May 1908 (M), p. 4.

79. For the background, see Allmayer-Beck, *Baron Beck,* pp. 227–46; and "Eine Geschichte des Ministeriums Becks," *DV,* 8 November 1908 (M), p. 3. Copies of the proposed legislation for Bohemia developed by Beck and Bienerth are in Carton 14, *NL Beck.*

80. *NFP,* 6 October 1908 (M), p. 8; *AZ,* 7 October 1908, p. 7.

81. *Die Tätigkeit des Sozialdemokratischen Verbandes im Abgeordnetenhaus. XVIII. Session 18 (17. Juni 1907 bis 5. Februar 1909)* (Vienna, 1909), pp. 53–54; "Der Streit um die Gerichtssprache in Böhmen," *Rp,* 11 March 1908, p. 3. The municipal governments of 86 Czech towns retaliated by refusing to accept any government or personal documents written in German. *Rp,* 3 April 1908, p. 2.

82. "Das Vordrängen der czechischen Amtssprache," *NFP,* 20 January 1908 (N), p. 3. For the general background of the *innere Amtssprache* problem, see Karl Gottfried Hugelmann, ed., *Das Nationalitätenrecht des alten Österreich* (Vienna, 1934), pp. 335–44.

83. See Klimscha's transcription of instructions he received in a telephone conversation with Beck, 17 May 1908, *NL Beck,* Carton 34.

84. See Tschirschky's report in A 17279, 19 October 1908, Oest. 70/Bd. 46, *PAAA.*

85. *AZ,* 2 July 1908, p. 5; 3 July 1908, p. 1.

86. *AZ,* 10 September 1908, pp. 1, 4; 11 September 1908, p. 3. Allmayer-Beck's brief description of these riots in *Baron Beck,* p. 239, sustains the author's argument that Beck fell only because of a personal conspiracy mounted against him, not because the basic assumptions governing his rule had failed.

87. On Laibach, see *NFP,* 21 September 1908 (N), pp. 1–2; 22 September 1908 (A), p. 1; and Goschen to Grey, FO 371/399, *PRO.* On the events in Prague, see *NFP,* 19 October 1908 (N), pp. 4–6; 20 October 1908 (M), pp. 8–9.

88. *NFP,* based on an interview in the *Österreichische Volkszeitung,* 24 September 1908 (A), pp. 1–2. See also the police report on the speeches by Otto Lecher and Emanuel Weidenhoffer at the meeting of the *Südmark* on 12 October 1908, *MI Präs.,* 15/3, Carton 1634, Z. 9839. The meeting was attended by 1,500 people, who heard Weidenhoffer demand that the Germans should pull out of the Cabinet.

89. *NFP,* 25 September 1908 (M), pp. 1–5; 26 September 1908 (M), pp. 2–5. Even this uproar had a precedent: the Czechs, who as the majority party controlled the Präsidium of the *Landtag,* had refused to appoint a petty German official to its staff, which enraged the Germans.

90. *NFP,* 30 September 1908 (A), pp. 1–2; and Chiari's criticism of Beck on September 22 in *Rp,* 23 September 1908, p. 2.

91. Beck's strategy in submitting the proposals is outlined in detail in his letter to Coudenhove, 13 October 1908, *NL Beck.* For German reaction, see Adolf Bachmann, "Die Wahlreformvorlage der Regierung für den Böhmischen Landtag," *NFP,* 10 October 1908 (M), pp. 2–3, and 13 October 1908 (M), pp. 2–3. As early as September 19 Beck asked Coudenhove to keep an eye on "die subversive Tätigkeit des Hofrates Bachmann." Letter of 19 September 1908, *NL Beck.* Allmayer-Beck ignores (pp. 238–41) a central fact of this controversy, namely, that the Germans rejected the electoral reform proposal even more vigorously than did the Feudals, since he is intent on showing that a conspiracy engineered by Franz Ferdinand and Czernin was behind the dissidence which finally erupted in late September. Aside from Beck's own after-the-fact complaints to Marchet, however (Beck to Marchet, 9 December 1908, Carton 19, *NL Marchet),* the only evidence cited for this view is the comment in the Baernreither's Diary, Nr. 9, which refers to Lobkowitz's handling of a session before the electoral reform proposals were brought in, not after.

92. A 17279, 19 October 1908, Oest. 70/Bd. 46, *PAAA.*

93. *Rp,* 17 October 1908, p. 4. Beck informed Coudenhove on 18 October that "Die böhmischen Kollegen, und in erster Linie Prášek, wollen das Kabinett verlassen, selbst um den Preis einer schweren inneren Krisis und einer Rückwirkung derselben auf die auswärtigen Verhältnisse."

94. Memoir on the Bienerth negotiations, 1908, Carton 1, *NL Gross.*

95. "Volk und Partei," *Rp,* 3 July 1908, pp. 1–2. The Wahrmund Affair is considered below, in Chapter 4.

96. Ebenhoch to Lueger, 24 February 1908, I.N. 40946; 15 March 1908, I.N. 40952; 21 March 1908, I.N. 40950, *Handschriftensammlung.*

97. For Tyrol, see Baron Biegeleben's comments to Franz Ferdinand, 30 April 1908, Carton 10, *NL Franz Ferdinand.*

98. Brosch to Franz Ferdinand, 17 October 1908, C 46, Carton 10.

99. Ebenhoch to Lueger, 30 October 1908, I.N. 40957, *Handschriftensammlung.*

100. Allmayer-Beck, *Baron Beck,* p. 244.

101. "Die Stellungnahme der christlichsozialen Partei," *Rp,* 6 November 1908, p. 3.

102. *Fremdenblatt,* 6 November 1908, p. 3.

103. *Rp,* 22 October 1908, p. 1; *NFP,* 22 October 1908 (M), pp. 5–6.

104. See Axmann's subsequent comments in *Stenographische Sitzungs-Protokolle der Delegation des Reichsrates,* Session 43, 1908, pp. 235–37; as well as *Rp,* 25 October 1908, p. 2.

105. The files of the *Ministerium für öffentliche Arbeiten, Präsidialakten,* 1908 (Büro Gessmann), Carton 1, *AVA,* contain many such petitions and requests. So many job petitioners emerged that Gessmann had a "standard rejection" form prepared to respond to the requests. For Christian Social cronyism, see particularly Z. 354 and 394/1908.

106. See the report of Schwiedland to Bardolff, discussed below in Chapter 6.

107. Kielmansegg reported that immediately after Gessmann's resignation in 1908 he told him that he would never again accept a ministry which (in Kielmansegg's words) "auf dem man doch von anderen durchaus abhängig sei." These ambiguous remarks make sense in the context of Schwiedland's exposé: the "anderen" were the officials in his own and other ministries whose actions Gessmann could not influence or command as he was accustomed to doing in the Lower Austrian government. *Kaiserhaus,* p. 416.

108. The most reliable sources for this campaign are the reports submitted to the Lower Austrian Statthalterei, I/2 C4 ("Landtagswahlen 1908-Bewegung"), *Statt. Präs., NÖLA.* For a socialist evaluation, see Victor Adler, "Die Landtagswahlen in Niederösterreich," *K,* 2 (1908–9): 49–53.

109. For the final results see *AZ,* 27 October 1908, pp. 2–6; *NFP,* 27 October 1908 (M), pp. 6–7.

110. I/2 C4, 9 September 1908, *Statt. Präs., NÖLA.* See also *Rp,* 13 October 1908, p. 6.

111. *Rp,* "Ein Tag der Ehre," 27 October 1908, pp. 1–2.

112. See, for example, Gessmann to Funder, 12 February 1912, *NL Funder;* and below, Chapter 6.

113. See Gessmann's speech "Die Hauptaufgaben unserer Gewerbepolitik," *Rp,* 20 May 1908, p. 4.

114. *Rp,* 8 November 1908, p. 1.

115. Published mid-August, 1908. A copy is in *NL Schmitz,* Carton 7.

116. Circular of Beck to the Cabinet, 20 June 1908, Z. 1282, Carton 3, *Ministerium für öffentliche Arbeiten Präs.,* 1908 (Büro Gessmann).

117. Gessmann to Spahn, 4 November 1908, Nr. 79, *NL Spahn*.

118. On the political history of the insurance legislation, see *Rp*, 4 November 1908, pp. 7–8 and the bitter comments by the Social Democrats in *Die Tätigkeit des Sozialdemokratischen Verbandes*, p. 55 ("Bienerth war schon als Minister des Innern in der Regierung Beck Gessmanns Günstling gewesen. Er hatte die christlichsozialen Schandtaten bei den niederösterreichischen Landtageswahlen ruhig geschehen lassen und Herrn Gessmanns Wünsche bei der Vorbereitung der Sozialversicherungsvorlage gehorsam erfüllt."). For an older survey, see Ludwig Brügel, *Soziale Gesetzgebung in Österreich von 1848 bis 1919* (Vienna, 1919). For a more recent discussion, see Herbert Hofmeister's essay on Austrian social insurance in Peter A. Köhler and Hans F. Zacher, eds., *The Evolution of Social Insurance 1881–1981* (London, 1982), esp. pp. 312–15, 321–22.

119. In his "Der Ausbau" Friedrich Gaertner surveyed the range of initial reactions to the government's bill, particularly in the *Arbeitsbeirat*. On the *Arbeitsbeirat*, see the dissertation by Brigitte Pellar, "Staatliche Institutionen und gesellschaftliche Interessengruppen."

120. The final draft is in *SP*, 1908, *Beilage* 1160.

121. See Gaertner's commentary in "Der Ausbau der Sozialversicherung," esp. pp. 831–33, and his unsubtle critique of socialist partisanship in the *Krankenkassen:* "Es ist eine allgemeine Erscheinung, dass junge Selbstverwaltungskörper gewissen Gefahren ausgesetzt sind, die bei der staatlichen Verwaltung nur in geringem Masse auftreten. . . . Bei diesen macht sich das Bestreben geltend, bei Besetzungen zunächst solche Anwärter zu berücksichtigen, die das Vertrauen der herrschenden Majorität besitzen. . . . Es tritt ein Nachlassen der Unparteilichkeit und des Pflichtbewusstseins ein, welches das Ansehen des öffentlichen Dienstes erschüttert," etc. (p. 831). Coming from a supporter of the Christian Social machine in Vienna, this comment was more than slightly disingenuous. For a similar attempt in Germany to undercut socialist penetration of self-administrating councils, see the circular of Bethmann Hollweg in October 1908, cited in Gerhard A. Ritter, *Sozialversicherung in Deutschland und England* (Munich, 1983), p. 57. For the political views of the Social Democrats, see Matthias Eldersch, "Die neue Sozialversicherungsvorlage," *K*, 5 (1911–12): 127–32. See also Everhard Holtmann, "Arbeiterbewegung, Staat und Sozialpolitik in der Spätzeit der Habsburgermonarchie. Strukturelle Bedingungen österreichischer Sozialgesetzgebung zwischen 1890 und 1914," in *Politik und Gesellschaft im Alten und Neuen Österreich*, 1: 239–54.

122. *Rp*, 10 November 1908, p. 1.

123. *Rp*, 15 January 1908, p. 3. For peasant interest see *Der Bauernbündler*, Nr. 11 (1907), pp. 1–2; Nr. 17 (1908), pp. 1–2; Nr. 26 (1908), p. 4; for the master artisans, *Der Gewerbefreund*, 15 January 1909, p. 6, as well as the debates in *Bericht über die Verhandlungen des Reichs-Fachverbandes der Einzelverbände der Kleidermachergenossenschaften Österreichs. Abgehalten in Wien am 6., 7. und 8. September 1908* (Vienna, 1908), pp. 26–31.

124. This switch was first mentioned in *Rp,* 7 November 1908, p. 3, and *NWT,* 8 November 1908, p. 2; and confirmed at a public meeting of the party elite reported in *DV,* 11 November 1908 (M), p. 2.

125. *Rp,* 6 November 1908, p. 5; Tschirschky to Bülow, A 18650, 8 November 1908, Oest. 88/Bd.7, *PAAA.* The *DV* published a communiqué from the Christian Social news service "Austria" on the 3rd, which implied that the leadership would support Beck only if he could guarantee an end to the Bohemian crisis. *DV,* 3 November 1908 (A), p. 2.

126. *NFP,* 6 November 1908 (M), pp. 3–4. The postulates included demands for a second Czech university, for the reopening of the Bohemian *Landtag* on Czech terms, and for the full recognition by the Germans of the Stremayr language ordinances.

127. A copy of these demands, dated 6 November 1908, is in Carton 1, *NL Gross.* A *Kreis* was to be an administrative district larger than and inclusive of the district *(Bezirk),* but smaller than a Crownland. Since it is awkward to translate the word as "circle," I leave it in German.

128. *DV,* 13 November 1908 (M), p.1.

129. Memoir on the Bienerth negotiations, Carton 1, *NL Gross.*

130. Kielmansegg, *Kaiserhaus,* pp. 356ff.

131. Tschirschky reported that the Christian Socials had put Liechtenstein's name forward for the Minister-Presidency, but had then recognized the latter's modest abilities and lack of experience hardly qualified him for the job.

132. *NWT,* 10 November 1908, p. 2, reporting an interview that a "high-placed" Christian Social official in Vienna had had with *Národní listy* in Prague.

133. *Rp,* 4 October 1908, p. 6. According to Kielmansegg, Gessmann had a secret meeting with Archduke Franz Ferdinand immediately before the party assembly where, according to Kielmansegg, Gessmann came to an agreement with the Archduke to throw the party's votes against Beck. Yet Kielmansegg also suggests that Gessmann had his own reasons for wanting Beck out and Bienerth in, following from his long-standing friendship with the latter, whom Gessmann felt he could control much more effectively than he could Beck and from his dissatisfaction with ministerial life. Kielmansegg does not argue that Gessmann was simply acting on the Archduke's "orders." See *Kaiserhaus,* pp. 359, 399, 416.

134. For Bienerth's proposals see *Rp,* 13 November 1908, p. 3; *NFP,* 13 November 1908 (M), p. 3.

135. See "Grosse Parteien," *Die Zeit,* 7 November 1908 (M), pp. 1–2.

136. Memoir on the Bienerth negotiations, *NL Gross; NFP,* 13 November 1908 (M), p. 3.

137. *Fremdenblatt,* 13 November 1098 (M), p. 1.

138. See Tschirschky's detailed report on the negotiations in A 19180, 15 November 1908, Oest. 88/ Bd. 7, *PAAA.*

139. These comments are based on the handwritten memoir in Carton 1, *NL Gross;*

on the reports in *NFP,* 13 November 1908 (A), pp. 1–2, and 14 November 1908 (M), pp. 1–4; *Die Zeit,* 14 November 1908 (M), pp. 1–3; and *Fremdenblatt,* 14 November 1908 (M), pp. 1–3.

140. *Die Zeit,* 14 November 1908 (M), p. 2.

141. *DV,* 13 November 1908 (M), p. 1.

142. Redlich to Baernreither, 19 December 1908, Carton 49, *NL Baernreither.*

143. The most vigorous proponent of this interpretation is Allmayer-Beck in his *Baron Beck.*

144. Beck to Coudenhove, 12 November 1908, Carton 34, *NL Beck.* For a similar explanation, also originating with Beck himself, see the fragment of Johann Chlumecky's diary, reprinted in Chlumecky's *Erzherzog Franz Ferdinands Wirken und Wollen,* pp. 304–5. Beck realized that Aehrenthal had also played a role in his fall, as a result of a series of jurisdictional and policy collisions in 1908 between the two men. Whether Aehrenthal's enmity took the form of pressure on the Christian Socials or of anti-Beck comments to the Emperor (which is more likely) is difficult to reconstruct. In the difficult negotiations with Wekerle in May 1908 over the issue of military salaries, Aehrenthal had generally sided with Beck, but according to Ehrhart, Beck thought Aehrenthal's annexation scheme in the autumn of 1908 "sorglos, oberflächlich, nicht sattsam durchdacht und schon gar nicht hinlänglich vorbereitet." Ehrhart, *Im Dienste des alten Österreich,* p. 206.

145. Sieghart, *Die letzten Jahrzehnte,* p. 141.

146. *Rp,* 8 November 1908, p. 1.

147. Tschirschky described this conflation of interests between the party and Belvedere well when he wrote: "Sie [the Christian Socials] haben das Gefühl ihrer Macht bekommen, wissen sich durch den Thronfolger gestützt und verlangen ausschlaggebende Stellung im neuen Ministerium." A 18650, 8 November 1908, Oest. 88/ Bd. 7. Robert Ehrhart offers an analysis similar to the one presented here, arguing that both the Thronfolger and the Christian Socials had their own distinct yet parallel reasons for wanting Beck out: "das identische Ergebnis paralleler Gedankengänge." Ehrhart dismisses the idea that the Christian Socials simply followed the Belvedere's orders: "Der Kulissentratsch behauptete, die Frontänderung der Christlichsozialen sei von dem Erzherzog-Thronfolger veranlasst worden. Die Leute stellten sich eben mit Vorliebe die politischen Vorgänge in sehr einfachen Linien vor, ungefähr wie in den Shakespearischen Königsdramen." *Im Dienste des alten Österreich,* p. 210.

148. For example, *Rp,* 13 November 1908, p. 3; 14 November 1908, p. 1.

149. Bienerth has had neither a biographer nor a systematic exploration of his regime. Among the later Minister-Presidents he thus remains the most obscure. The sources for such a study are rich, however, particularly the archives of the Militärkanzlei of the Archduke Franz Ferdinand, and Franz Ferdinand's *NL* in *HHSA,* as well as the Christian Social party archive in *AVA.* Among evaluations by contemporaries, the hostile portrait by Kielmansegg, *Kaiserhaus,* pp. 353–64, should be compared with the

more sympathetic views of Ehrhart, *Im Dienste des alten Österreich,* pp. 210–17, and Czedik, *Zur Geschichte,* 4: 4–79.

150. See, for example, Brosch's reports on Bienerth's cooperativeness on the Hungarian crisis and on upcoming appointments to the *Herrenhaus,* 30 June 1909, C 71, and 2 December 1909, C 72; and Bienerth's apology for not having been able to stop the appointment of Sieghart to the Bodenkreditanstalt, 18 March 1910, C 105. See also Ehrhart, *Im Dienste des alten Österreich,* p. 212.

151. See *Die Tätigkeit des Sozialdemokratischen Verbandes,* pp. 58–61. The party voted against the budget bill itself, however. From a different perspective see Tschirschky's report in A 20186, 3 December 1908, Oest. 70/ Bd. 46, *PAAA* ("die Regierungsgewalt versagt zur Zeit fast vollkommen").

152. See *SP,* 1908, pp. 8062–8102, 8112–66, 8179–8221. Also, *Schicksalsjahre,* 1: 4.

153. Bienerth's legislation consisted of two bills, one regulating the language of official business in Bohemia by designating 238 German, Czech, and "mixed" judicial districts; the other creating a system of 20 *Kreis* administrative units under the Bohemian *Statthalterei,* also designated by principal *Amtssprache.* The language provisions for the court jurisdictions were slightly more favorable to the Czechs than the Germans, but since the draft did recognize the territorialist principle, granting Germans a vague legal recognition of their cultural status quo, their reaction was mildly favorable, and the Czechs' strongly negative. One German politician, Rudolf Sommer, recognized the law's implications immediately: the new *Kreis* governments were in fact "einen Schritt weiter auf der Bahn zur Erreichung eines ganz eigenen deutschen Landes innerhalb Böhmens. . . ." Interview in the *NFP,* 3 February 1909 (A), p. 7. This possibility, however distant, was exactly what enraged the Czechs. On Bienerth's draft legislation, "Die Vorlagen über die nationale Verfassung," *NFP,* 3 February 1909 (A), pp. 2–4; and Anton Pergelt, "Die Sprachengesetzvorlagen," ibid., 4 February 1909 (M), pp. 2; for commentaries, see Karl Gottfried Hugelmann, "Das Nationalitätenrecht nach der Verfassung von 1867," in Hugelmann, ed., *Das Nationalitätenrecht,* pp. 255–57; and Redlich, *Schicksalsjahre,* 1: 5, 32.

154. For the initial German reception of the ministry, see "Das neue Ministerium," *NFP,* 9 February 1909 (A), p. 1; and Stephan Licht, "Das Ministerium Bienerth, Biliniski und Weiskirchner," ibid., 10 February 1909 (M), p. 2. Hochenburger was a former *Volkspartei* leader from Graz in the *Abgeordnetenhaus* between 1897 and 1901, who had actively opposed Badeni. Since he was formally retired from politics, however, he could be used by Bienerth without giving the Germans an actual share of Cabinet power or raising the specter of formal parliamentarization.

155. See A 20732, 10 December 1908, Oest. 88/Bd. 7, *PAAA* (which suggests that the German-Polish coalition without the Czechs was being planned as early as the beginning of December); and ibid., A 2722, 10 February 1909 ("durch diese beiden Männer erhält das Kabinett den Charakter einer polnisch-deutschen Kombination"); for

Bienerth's self-designation of his new government as a "Mittelstufe zwischen bureau-
kratischer und parlamentarischer Regierung," see the interview in *NFP,* 11 February
1909 (M), p. 1.

156. A 2722, 10 February 1909, Oest. 88/Bd. 7, *PAAA.* On Bienerth's lack of a
reliable parliamentary majority, in spite of the generally loyal support of the Christian
Socials, see Brosch to Franz Ferdinand, 30 June 1910, Cl32: "Die österr. Regierung
ist jedoch schwach, verfügt über keine verlässliche Majorität und kann eine weitere
Belastungsprobe des Zusammenhaltens der Mehrheit nicht riskieren."

157. Redlich to Baernreither, 19 December 1908 ("Freiherr von Bienerth ist als Tak-
tiker noch in jener Epoche stecken geblieben, die man die parlamentarische Steinzeit
nennen könnte").

158. *NFP,* 11 July 1919 (M), p. 5; *Schicksalsjahre,* 1: 20. For the background of the
Bank controversy, see Brosch to Franz Ferdinand, 25 May 1909, C 67, *NL Franz Ferdinand.*

159. "Annual Report on Austria-Hungary for the Year 1909," p. 21, FO 881/9593.
Marchet described his impressions of Bienerth and his Cabinet to Baernreither at this
juncture: "Die ganze Regierung, vom Haupt angefangen, hat keine Geltung und keine
Tatkraft, sondern ist keusch oder, wie gewiss Haerdtl, grob oder wie Stürgkh kleinlich
bureaukratisch—von den anderen, vielleicht mit Ausnahme von Weiskirchner überhaupt nicht zu reden. . . ." Letter of 15 July 1909, Carton 48, *NL Baernreither.*

160. *Schicksalsjahre,* 1: 23, 39. As early as August 1909 Marchet wrote to Baernreither commenting that "Gross and Sylvester glauben absolut nicht an B[ienerth]s Zukunft und wahrscheinlich er auch nicht." Marchet to Baernreither, 20 August 1909,
Carton 48, *NL Baernreither.*

161. Entry of 8 November 1909.

162. The House did vote for a cosmetic compromise that established a special committee to consider all national desiderata and report back within three months. See *SP,*
1909, pp. 530, 554–55.

163. On the history of Austrian commercial policy, especially in the context of Austro-Hungarian relations, see John Komlos, *The Habsburg Monarchy as a Customs
Union: Economic Development in Austria-Hungary in the Nineteenth Century*
(Princeton, 1983). On the concessions of the Cabinet to the agrarians, see "Das agrarische Geschenk für die Handelsverträge," *NFP* 14 December 1909 (M), pp. 14–15.

164. For the June 1909 debates, see the protocols of the "Klubsitzungen" of 22 and
30 June 1909, in Carton 96, Mappe 1, *CPK.* For the December debates, see the reports
of the sessions of 15, 17, and 22 December 1909, ibid. See also *NFP,* 13 December
1909 (M), p. 9; 14 December 1909 (M), pp. 4–5; *Rp,* 23 December 1909, p. 4.

165. A 21015, 20 December 1909, Oest. 91/Bd. 16, *PAAA.*

166. *Schicksalsjahre,* 1: 39–40. Gessmann's posturing may have masked more
Machiavellian agreements. Ottokar Pražák, a former minister in the Beck Cabinet, later
intimated that it had been Gessmann who had persuaded the Czechs to end their obstructionism with promises of changes in the Cabinet congenial to the Slavs. Certainly

Gessmann was one of those responsible for the dismissal of Gustav Schreiner as German *Landsmannminister* in February 1910, thus eliminating a source of anti-Czech provocations in the Cabinet. See *NFP,* 12 May 1910 (M), p. 5.

167. A 21067, 22 December 1909, and A 21015, 20 December 1909, Oest. 91/Bd. 16, *PAAA*. For similar, if slightly more sober, evaluations by the Bavarian minister in Vienna, Tucher, see Z. 548, 22 December 1909, *BHSA*.

168. "Klubsitzung," 17 December 1909.

169. For Redlich see *Schicksalsjahre,* 1: 40. For Viennese Liberal reaction, which was similar to Tschirschky's, see "Volkstäuschung und Parlamentsrettung," *NFP,* 20 December 1909 (N), p. 1 ("Die Majorität des Reichsrates ist slavisch und klerikal und wird nicht zögern, den ganzen Staat slavisch und klerikal einzurichten"); and "Die Geschäftsordnungsreform gegen die Deutschen," ibid., 19 December 1909 (M), p. 2. For Gessmann's remarks, see *AZ,* 11 May 1910, p. 2.

170. *SP,* pp. 1680–1722, 1730–86, 1800–836; *Die Tätigkeit des Sozialdemokratischen Verbandes im Abgeordnetenhause. 3. Heft. (XX. Session, 20. Oktober 1909 bis 6. Juli 1910)* (Vienna, 1910), pp. 31–32, 53–55; Czedik, *Zur Geschichte,* 4: 83–87.

171. For later commentaries on the social insurance program, see Wilhelm Winkler, "Gewerbe und Landwirtschaft in der Invaliden- und Altersversicherung der österreichischen Sozialversicherungsvorlage," *ZVSV,* 19 (1910): 602–19; idem, "Studien zur österreichischen Sozialversicherungsvorlage," ibid., 20 (1911): 415–46; and Franz Schmitt, "Umfang und System der Invaliden- und Altersversicherung nach der österreichischen Sozialversicherungsvorlage," ibid., 573–614, the former questioning the equity of combining agriculture and industry into one unified program, the latter a critique of the government's proposal for insurance for the independents.

172. See *SP,* 1910, pp. 2158–73; 2187–2236, 2262–2316. The original government draft is in *Beilagen,* Nr. 702, 24 February 1909.

173. *AZ,* 20 May 1910, p. 3.

174. *AZ,* 5 July 1910, p. 3; 6 July 1910, p. 4.

175. *Schicksalsjahre,* 1: 67.

176. See the reports Pö 58, Carton 50, 1911; and Nr. 2678, Carton 146, 1914, *MKFF.*

177. "Klubsitzung," 17 June 1910. "Die Christlichsozialen würden zwar, dank Gessmanns, mit der Regierung gehen, fürchten aber, dass sie als Verräter am Deutschtum gebrandmarkt werden, wenn sie die italienische Universität in Wien zulassen." Brosch to Franz Ferdinand, 11 June 1910, C 121; as well as 15 June 1910, C 123, and 15 July 1910, C 142, *NL Franz Ferdinand.* Franz Ferdinand initially rejected any Italian location, but eventually agreed to Bienerth's compromise of putting the Faculty in Vienna for the first few years, and then shifting it to Gradisca. For Bienerth's compromise, see "Das Provisorium 'Wien'," *NFP,* 12 June 1910 (M), p. 5. The views of the Germans are represented in ibid., 17 June 1910 (M), pp. 2–3. See also Ehrhart, *Im Dienste des alten Österreich,* pp. 215–16.

178. See "Klubsitzung," 7 July 1910, Carton 90, *CPK.*

179. A 5488, 31 March 1911, Oest. 91/Bd. 16, *PAAA*. As early as February 1910

the Christian Social parliamentary commission complained "dass vielfach sowohl vonseite der Zentralstellen wie der einzelnen Regierungsorgane den auf das Volkswohl abzielenden Bestrebungen der Partei ein geringeres Entgegenkommen zuteil werde, als dies anderen Parteien gegenüber der Fall sei." "Parlamentarische Kommission," 14 February 1910, Carton 96, *CPK; Rp*, 15 February 1910, p. 2.

180. For the Viennese feuds, and general problem of corruption in the party, see below, Chapter 5.

181. See "Klubsitzung," 24 November 1910, Carton 90, *CPK*.

182. Brosch to Franz Ferdinand, 23 September 1910, C 147; *Schicksalsjahre*, 1: 71.

183. On the price inflation, see the report in Nr. 6074, 17 January 1913, Carton 113, *MKFF;* Otto Bauer, *Die Teuerung* (Vienna 1910); "Report on the Foreign Trade of Austria-Hungary for the year 1910," *Diplomatic and Consular Reports. Austria-Hungary.* No. 4777 (London, 1911); and the detailed comments in the Foreign Office's annual report for 1910, pp. 29–31; for 1911, pp. 35–37, and for 1912, pp. 47–48, FO 881/ 9771, 881/9998 and 881/10244. All of the above reports blame a conjunction of high tariffs, inadequate domestic production, cartel controls, and natural disasters. For statistical data on the price increases, see Josef Rain, "Die Bekämpfung der Lebensmittelteuerung," in *Stenographischer Bericht über die Beratungen des VIII. österreichischen Städtetages am 20. Oktober 1911* (Vienna, 1912), pp. 65–103, which has detailed information on the evolution of Viennese consumer prices from 1896 to 1911.

184. For Rain's comments, see *Stenographischer Bericht,* p. 9.

185. Brosch to Franz Ferdinand, 23 September 1910, C 147. Weiskirchner, in particular, opposed a strong anti-Hungarian line in the Christian Social press. 28 September 1910, C 148.

186. On Hohenblum and his *Zentralstelle,* see Karl Renner, *Die Ära Hohenblum— der Ruin unserer Staats- und Volkswirtschaft!* (Vienna, 1913).

187. *SP,* 1910, pp. 3919–25. See also *AZ,* 25 November 1910, p. 3; and "Kunschak oder Reumann?" ibid., 27 November 1910, p. 1.

188. "Der fröhliche Weiskirchner," *AZ,* 26 November 1910, pp. 1–2, as well as Jakob Reumann's reponse in *SP,* 1910, pp. 4051–75.

189. *SP,* 1910, pp. 4071–78.

190. For the three motions, see ibid., p. 4252.

191. Ibid., 1910, pp. 4220–21.

192. Ibid., p. 4225.

193. Gessmann's comments at the session on 26 November: "Klubsitzung," 26 November 1910, Carton 90, *CPK.*

194. See "Klubsitzung," 24 November 1910 and 26 November 1910.

195. Ibid., p. 10.

196. This was apparent on a range of issues, especially those involving taxation, where both sides were anxious to prevent tax increases which would enlarge the curial electorate and hence prove disadvantageous to their electoral operations. On foreign policy unanimity also generally prevailed.

197. See *NFP,* 17 June 1910 (M), pp. 6–7.

198. See Weiskirchner's comments in the "Klubsitzung," 15 June 1910, Carton 90, *CPK*.

199. See "Klubsitzung," 10 February 1911. On Heilinger see also Scheicher's comments in *Erlebnisse*, 5: 418–421.

200. The relevant archival material on the Pantz controversy is to be found in a special file, Mappe XVII, in Carton 96, *CPK*. See also Rupert J. Klieber, "Die Genese der christlichsozialen Partei Salzburgs: (Politischer) Katholizismus in der Provinz zwischen 1899 und 1919." Dissertation, University of Salzburg, 1991, pp. 315–21.

201. See supplementary protocol to the "Klubsitzung," 3 December 1909.

202. See "Gruppe V der christlichsozialen Vereinigung. Angelegenheit R.v. Pantz," 1 March 1910, ibid.; "Resolution gefasst in der Sitzung der Vertreter der n.ö Landgemeinden am 8. November 1910," ibid., Mappe XVII. For an example of one of Pantz's peasant rallies against Hohenblum, see *NFP*, 18 April 1910 (M), p. 5.

203. Pantz and Kemetter to Gessmann, 22 November 1910, Carton 96, *CPK; SP,* 1910, pp. 4109–20.

204. Nothing better demonstrated the growing power of the agrarians in the party as the meeting of the "Parlamentarische Kommission" on 30 December 1910, where Weiskirchner was forced to offer a personal repudiation of Pantz and Kemetter when he asked the party to support him in his desire to remain at the Commerce Ministry. For an overview of the controversy, see the long, self-justifying letter of Pantz and Kemetter to Liechtenstein, 14 January 1911, ibid.

205. See "Klubsitzung," 12 December 1911, and the transcript of the letter drafted by Jodok Fink and Johann Hauser to Pantz repudiating the latter's behavior, Carton 90, *CPK*. Throughout 1911 the feud occupied the club's attention. Once the Viennese faction, many of the members of which were not unsympathetic to Pantz, had been decimated in the June 1911 election, the now dominant *Bauernbund* leaders in the parliamentary leadership had no difficulty in settling accounts. On Kemetter's involvment in Catholic student politics and his debt to Gessmann's patronage, see Scheicher's sympathetic comments in *Erlebnisse*, 5: 428–38; and Gerhard Hartmann, *Im Gestern bewährt, im Heute bereit. 100 Jahre Carolina. Zur Geschichte des Verbandskatholizismus* (Graz, 1988), pp. 45–47, 174. Scheicher noted an intolerance of new ideas as a principal (and unhappy) characteristic of the peasant representatives in the party after 1907, coupled with their consciousness of possessing enormous power within the delegation, given their safe seats. See also the report on Pantz in "Nachrichten aus Oesterreich-Ungarn, Rumänien und den Balkanländern," Nr. 73, 11 December 1911, Pö 68, Carton 50, *MKFF*. On Neunteufel, see Hartmann, *Im Gestern bewährt,* pp. 203, 212, and Manfred Gaar, "Franz Hagenhofer. Das Wirken eines steirischen Bauernführers." Dissertation, University of Graz, 1974, pp. 113–31. Neunteufel was a Christian Social journalist and former regional party chairman of the Christian Social party in Styria (and, like Kemetter, a former member of the "Austria Wien" Catholic student fraternity at the University of Vienna) who feuded with Franz Hagenhofer, the leader of the Styrian *Bauernbund,* and seceded from the party in 1911.

206. See Funder's letter, 22 March 1911, Carton 90, *CPK*.

207. Czedik, *Zur Geschichte*, 4: 100.

208. See "Klubsitzung," 17 January 1911, Carton 90, *CPK*. Bienerth would have preferred to shift Weiskirchner from the Commerce Ministry since, as Brosch noted, "he has failed [there]," but kept him on at the insistence of the Christian Socials, and because there seemed no other appropriate place to put him. Brosch to Franz Ferdinand, 4 January 1911, C 168.

209. Redlich, *Schicksalsjahre*, 1: 67; Czedik, *Zur Geschichte*, 4: 146–47.

210. "Klubsitzung," 9 March 1911, Carton 90, *CPK* ("Abg. Schraffl meint, dass diese Angelegenheit wieder ein Beispiel sei, wie wir unsere Ideen von den Sozi ausbeuten lassen um ihnen dann nachzulaufen").

211. "Eine Regierung ohne Pläne, ohne Begabung, ohne Gedanken." *Schicksalsjahre*, 1: 81.

212. For the background, see *Die Tätigkeit des Sozialdemokratischen Verbandes im Abgeordnetenhause. 4. Heft (XX. Session, 12. Oktober 1910 bis 31. März 1911)* (Vienna, 1911), pp. 31–38; *Schicksalsjahre*, 1: 79–82; and Tschirschky's detailed report in A 5440, 1 April 1911, Oest. 91/Bd. 16, *PAAA*.

213. "Klubsitzung," 29 March 1911, Carton 90, *CPK*. Kielmansegg argues in his memoirs that Albert Gessmann was the éminence grise of Bienerth's ministry, but as Gessmann admitted to the Christian Social club, he was unable to stop Bienerth from calling new elections in 1911. *Kaiserhaus*, pp. 356–57.

214. A 5488, 31 March 1911, Oest. 91/Bd. 16, *PAAA*.

215. A 5497, 31 March 1911, ibid.

216. For the 1911 elections, see below, Chapter 5.

CHAPTER FOUR

1. Ernst Schneider frequently complained of the decline in anti-Semitic practices in the party after 1900, as did Felix Hraba and Josef Scheicher. See *Rp*, 14 March 1908, p. 8; 11 March 1908, p. 7; and the more general griping in *Erlebnisse*, 3/2: 289–90; 5: 181, 183; 6: 361–63, 373, 400–01. Complaints from lower level party functionaries, to the effect that the Rathaus *did not* enforce a strict anti-Jewish commercial policy, suggested that their unhappiness had a real referent. See, for example, the letter to Josef Strassgraber from Währing, explaining the exigencies of government contracts policy in response to the latter's complaint about Jews receiving contracts. Z. 273, 23 July 1912, Carton 71, *CPW*. See below, Chapter 7, for war-time complaints.

2. *Rp*, 6 December 1926, p. 3. Just as Lueger's memory was later invoked and distorted by the Nazis, who tried to make him into an arch-anti-Semite, so too was he later celebrated and misrepresented by Catholics as an arch-Catholic. Jakob Fried's frankness in this instance was thus refreshing.

3. Kuppe, *Lueger*, p. 409.

4. "Zwei Toastreden Dr. Lueger's," *Rp*, 18 October 1899, p. 5.

5. Walter Sauer, *Katholisches Vereinswesen in Wien. Zur Geschichte des christlich-sozial-konservativen Lagers vor 1914* (Salzburg, 1980), esp. pp. 40–43. A fundamental

problem inherent in Sauer's treatment is, however, that not all associations or clubs that called themselves "Christian" were necessarily "Catholic." The associations founded between 1891 and 1901 that Sauer lists on pp. 256–312 range from clubs devoted to church music and the cult of various saints to Christian Social electoral clubs, social clubs in honor of Karl Lueger, and economic interest-group associations, like the *Österreichischer Kellnerbund* and the *Verkehrsbund*. Certainly all of these can be broadly grouped under the rubric "Christian," but whether all of their members actually understood and felt themselves to be practicing Catholics is quite a different matter.

6. See Georg Harrasser, ed., *Aus dem Tagebuch eines Sodalen. Tagebuchblätter des Kongregationspräfekten Johann Leb aus den Jahren 1860–1920* (Innsbruck, 1925); Josef Leb, *P. Heinrich Abel, S. J. Der Männerapostel Wiens. Ein Lebensbild* (Innsbruck, 1926); and Margarethe Richer, "Pater Heinrich Abel, S.J." Dissertation, University of Vienna, 1947. See also Michael Mitterauer, "'Nur diskret ein Kreuzzeichen'. Zu Formen des individuellen und gemeinschaftlichen Gebets in der Familie," in Andreas Heller, Therese Weber, and Oliva Wiebel-Fanderl, eds., *Religion und Alltag. Interdisziplinäre Beiträge zu einer Sozialgeschichte des Katholizismus in lebensgeschichtlichen Aufzeichnungen* (Vienna, 1990), pp. 154–204.

7. See Sauer, *Katholisches Vereinswesen in Wien*, pp. 37, 74–76, 123. See also Aemilian Schöpfer's comparison of Vienna in the 1880s and in the 1900s, in terms of the popularity of the clergy, in "Ein Bahnbrecher religiöser Volksbewegung in der Grossstadt. Zum Tode des P. Heinrich Abel, S.J.," *Das Neue Reich*, 9 (1926): 189–90.

8. It is an open (and difficult) question to estimate the rate of religious observance by Viennese, even by those adults sympathetic to the Christian Socials. Robert Prantner reports that in 1920 the Christian Socials were known as the "Partei der 10 Prozent praktizierenden Katholiken." See his *Kreuz und weisse Nelke. Katholische Kirche und Christlichsoziale Partei im Spiegel der Presse (1918–1932)* (Vienna, 1984), p. 113. Similarly, Heinrich Swoboda admitted that "es kann nicht verschwiegen werden, dass trotz all dieser Anstrengungen die Unkenntnis in religiösen Dingen sowohl in den Sphären der Intelligenz wie der unteren Hunderttausende durchaus nicht besiegt erscheint." *Grossstadtseelsorge. Eine pastoraltheologische Studie* (Regensburg, 1909), p. 142. Joseph Ernst Mayer described the pastoral milieu of the late Empire in "Die Seelsorge," in Ferdinand Klostermann, Hans Kriegl, Otto Mauer, and Erika Weinzierl, eds., *Kirche in Österreich 1918–1965* (2 vols., Vienna, 1966), 1: 85–88. For contemporary statistics on Austrian Catholicism, see Paul Michael Zulehner, *Religion ohne Kirche? Das religiöse Verhalten von Industriearbeitern* (Vienna, 1969); idem, *Religion im Leben der Österreicher. Dokumentation einer Umfrage* (Vienna, 1981); and Franz Leitner, *Kirche und Parteien in Österreich nach 1945. Ihr Verhältnis unter dem Gesichtspunkt der Äquidistanzdiskussion* (Paderborn, 1988), esp. pp. 67–75.

9. Lueger's respect for the hierarchical discipline of the Church was extremely tentative, in spite of his propagandistic trips to Rome. As Max von Millenkovich-Morold stresses, "[d]ie höhere Geistlichkeit blieb ihm trotzdem wenig geneigt." *Vom Abend zum Morgen. Aus dem alten Österreich ins neue Deutschland* (Leipzig, 1940), pp. 225–

27. See also Scheicher, *Erlebnisse,* 4: 164, 412–13; and Gerhard Silberbauer, *Öster-reichs Katholiken und die Arbeiterfrage* (Graz, 1966), pp. 127–31.

10. The party's official manifesto made no reference to Catholicism. See *Rp,* 18 May 1900, pp. 9–10. Similarly, Kunschak's manifesto for the Fourth Curia voters used words like "Religion" and "christliche Grundsätze" but also avoided the word "Catholic." *Rp,* 27 May 1900, p. 9. The *Rp* evaluated the victory of the party as one in which the "christliches Volk" would take great satisfaction, and with which "die Herren Anti-Christen schliesslich werden abfinden müssen." Again, not one word about Catholicism or Catholics. "Ein Siegestag," 27 May 1900, p. 1.

11. Albert Maria Weiss, *Lebensweg und Lebenswerk. Ein modernes Prophetenleben* (Freiburg, 1925) p. 383.

12. *HPB,* 146 (1910): 873. See also Martin Spahn's comments in "Die christlich-soziale Partei der Deutschen Österreichs," pp. 544–59.

13. Lueger's alleged quip to Pater Abel—"Ich leiste die Roharbeit und Sie machen die Männer zu ganzen Katholiken"—summarizes his understanding of his own role. *Rp,* 24 November 1926, p. 4. That he felt himself in some way to be a "Catholic" is undeniable. At the same time it is also revealing that Lueger was not a special friend of Abel, and only once attended the latter's annual pilgrimage to Mariazell. See Josef Leb, *P. Heinrich Abel,* p. 66. Whether Lueger's civic-cultural identity as a Catholic was also expressive of heartfelt or even passionate religious feelings is dubious. Scheicher, who is probably the most reliable on this subject, describes him as evincing a kind of earnest deism, believing in the "Herrgott," and not worrying much about anything else religious. See *Erlebnisse,* 5: 406, as well as the more cynical views in Beskiba, *Aus meinen Erinnerungen,* pp. 23–24 (which may also be at least partially correct). The editor of Johann Leb's diary reports of that arch-Catholic man that "Er war ein An-hänger der Partei Luegers, betete viel für sie, wählte sie, aber völlig identifiziert hat er sich nie mit ihr. Sie war ihm zu wenig katholisch." *Aus dem Tagebuch eines Sodalen,* p. 167.

14. *Christliche Demokratie,* 5 (1987): 151.

15. "Klubsitzung," 17 July 1911, *CPK,* Carton 90.

16. It is important to differentiate between attitudes towards the official Church and private religious sentiments in working-class households. See Wegs, *Growing up Work-ing Class,* pp. 144–45, and Wolfgang Maderthaner, "Kirche und Sozialdemokratie. As-pekte des Verhältnisses von politischem Klerikalismus und sozialistischer Arbei-terschaft bis zum Jahre 1938," in *Neuere Studien zur Arbeitergeschichte,* 3: 538–39. However, priestly journals like the *Correspondenzblatt* were filled with reports of the hostility of working-class men to the clergy and to the institutional practices of the Church. For accounts emphasizing the gulf between the working class and the Church, see Erich Bodzenta, "Die geschichtliche Entwicklung des Verhältnisses der Arbei-terschaft zur Kirche," in Karl Rudolf, ed., *Die Kirche und die Welt des Arbeiters* (Vi-enna, 1957), pp. 9–29; Swoboda, *Grossstadtseelsorge,* pp. 121–47; Bong, *Christus und die Arbeiterwelt.* For earlier and ultimately unsuccessful efforts by the Viennese clergy

to reactivate a broad climate of religious sympathy in the city, see the excellent study by William D. Bowman, "Priests, Parish, and Religious Practice: A Social History of Catholicism in the Archdiocese of Vienna, 1800–1870." Dissertation, The Johns Hopkins University, 1990.

17. Scheicher, *Erlebnisse,* 5: 182–83. Even a sympathetic historian like Gerhard Silberbauer is forced to admit that "Die Einstellung des Klerus zu den Arbeitervereinen zeigte, dass der Mehrzahl der Geistlichen trotz des guten Willens ein echtes Verständnis für die Arbeiterschaft nach wie vor abging, dass man über 'halbsoziale Spielereien' meist doch nicht hinauskam." *Österreichs Katholiken,* p. 141.

18. See *HPB,* 136 (1905): 911; 146 (1910): 375. This refrain is also found in Heinrich Abel's *Wetterleuchten. Meteorologische Schwankungen in der religiös-politischen Atmosphäre Österreichs* (Vienna, 1908), p. 23 ("Freilich mit der Rekatholisierung des Volkes hielt die Rückkehr der Intelligenz und Halbintelligenz zum praktischen Christentum nicht gleichen Schritt").

19. On the *Reichspost,* see Gottfried Pfaffenberger, "Die 'Reichspost' und die christlich-soziale Bewegung." Dissertation, University of Vienna, 1948; and Funder, *Vom Gestern,* passim.

20. Funder notes that Gessmann was not raised as a practicing Catholic. *Vom Gestern,* p. 271.

21. Sieghart, *Die letzten Jahrzehnte,* p. 272. For a similar portrait, see Millenkovich-Morold, *Von Abend zum Morgen,* pp. 247–48.

22. See Heinl, *Über ein halbes Jahrhundert,* p. 40; Hainisch, *75 Jahre,* pp. 224–25; and (for Robert Pattai) Julius Sylvester, *Vom toten Parlament und seinen letzten Trägern* (Vienna, 1928), p. 28. For a contemporary analysis of these two streams, see *AZ,* 1 October 1909, p. 3, commenting on the tensions between city councilman Adolf Gussenbauer and Viennese clerical interests.

23. See below, Chapter 7.

24. John W. Boyer, "Freud, Marriage and Late Viennese Liberalism: A Commentary from 1905," *JMH,* 50 (1978): 72–102.

25. For interesting reflections on church and state in late nineteenth-century Austria, see Robert Musil, "The Religious Spirit, Modernism, and Metaphysics," in *Precision and Soul. Essays and Addresses,* ed. Burton Pike and David S. Luft (Chicago, 1990), pp. 21–25.

26. For a comparative perspective relating to the "cultural socialist" orientations of the two movements which focuses on the interwar period, see Michael Scholing and Franz Walter, "Der 'Neue Mensch.' Sozialistische Lebensreform und Erziehung in der sozialdemokratischen Arbeiterbewegung Deutschlands und Österreichs," in Richard Saage, ed., *Solidargemeinschaft und Klassenkampf. Politische Konzeptionen der Sozialdemokratie zwischen den Weltkriegen* (Frankfurt, 1986), pp. 250–73, esp. p. 259.

27. Within a huge literature, see especially Ernst Glaser, *Im Umfeld des Austromarxismus. Ein Beitrag zur Geistesgeschichte des österreichischen Sozialismus* (Vienna, 1981) and Josef Weidenholzer, *Auf dem Weg zum 'Neuen Menschen.' Bildungs- und*

Kulturarbeit der österreichischen Sozialdemokratie in der Ersten Republik (Vienna, 1981). Most recently see Helmut Gruber, *Red Vienna: Experiment in Working-Class Culture, 1919–1934* (New York, 1991).

28. It is interesting to note that "Junker" rhetoric was used by the Austrian socialist movement in the context of the fight for universal suffrage, when Austro-German and Polish nobles in the *Herrenhaus* were seen as opposing the reform. See the protocol of the "Erweiterte Gesammtparteivertretungs-Sitzung," 4 May 1906, *VGAB*, where the question was posed whether Prince Hohenlohe would have the energy "den Widerstand der widerspenstigen Junker zu brechen."

29. Adler, *Aufsätze, Reden und Briefe*, 11: 67. See also Paul Michael Zulehner, *Kirche und Austromarxismus. Eine Studie zur Problematik Kirche-Staat-Gesellschaft* (Vienna, 1967), pp. 200–216.

30. See the account of the socialist rally held in the Sophiensaal on December 15, in *AZ*, 16 December 1904, pp. 3–4; as well as 8 March 1905, pp. 3–4; 11 March 1905, p. 5; and 21 March 1905, p. 4. Like the later debate over the validity of the *Freie Schule*, this collaboration provoked the hostility of Sudeten Social Democrats, who strongly opposed cooperation with German national or other *Freisinnig* types. The *Freiheit*, a socialist paper in Teplitz, was extremely negative about the Viennese *Los von Rom* campaign since it was apt "die Arbeiter über die wirklichen Bedingungen des Klassenkampfes hinwegzutäuschen." *Freiheit*, 4 March 1905, pp. 1–2. See also Albertin, "Nationalismus und Protestantismus," pp. 168–77; and Gerhard Steger, *Rote Fahne, schwarzes Kreuz. Die Haltung der Sozialdemokratischen Arbeiterpartei Österreichs zu Religion, Christentum und Kirchen. Von Hainfeld bis 1934* (Vienna, 1987) pp. 92, 168–69.

31. Rudolf Köstler interpreted this situation as a consequence of the fact that other issues—mainly the nationality question—left Austrians with little interest in church-state problems: "Es besteht hier keine religiöse Empfindsamkeit, weil der religiöse Gegensatz hinter dem nationalen weit zurücktritt." See his "Die Neuerungen Papst Pius' X und das österreichische öffentliche Recht," *Österreichische Zeitschrift für öffentliches Recht*, 3 (1916–18): 489. See also Peter Leisching, "Die römisch-katholische Kirche in Cisleithanian," pp. 62–63 ("Die politischen Interessen verlagerten sich aus dem Bereich der Kultuspolitik immer mehr auf nationale und soziale Belange") in Adam Wandruszka and Peter Urbanitsch, eds., *Die Habsburgermonarchie 1848–1918. Band IV. Die Konfessionen* (Vienna, 1985).

32. See Ernst Victor Zenker, *Kirche und Staat unter besonderer Berücksichtigung der Verhältnisse in Österreich* (Vienna, 1909), esp. pp. 94–96. See also Millenkovich-Morold, *Vom Abend zum Morgen*, pp. 224–26.

33. Mischler, "Der Haushalt der österreichischen Landschaften," p. 586, who connects the rapid expansion of the expenditures by the Lower Austrian *Landesverwaltung* with the "interests of the Christian Social party."

34. Quoted in Zulehner, *Kirche*, p. 190. Gerhard Steger in his *Rote Fahne, schwarzes Kreuz*, pp. 36–37, offers some very tentative statistics that may demonstrate the party's

increasing preoccupation with religion, especially after 1904. These data suggest a sub-stantial increase in sensitivity by the editors of the *Arbeiter-Zeitung* toward the religious question broadly conceived. During the period 1904–13 the paper published almost twice as many articles relating to religion and the churches as in the period 1894–1903. Steger finds a similar pattern for parliamentary work, ibid., pp. 148–49.

35. It is interesting to note that the first time the *Bildung* issue was put on the agenda of a socialist party congress was in Reichenberg in 1909, and it was explicitly presented as a project to which the party, with the 1907 electoral reform behind it, now had the need and opportunity of devoting time and energy: "In der letzten Berichtsperiode konnten wir endlich darangehen, die Bildungsarbeit in der Partei systematisch zu för-dern. An Versuchen, namentlich in Wien, hat es auch in früheren Jahren nicht gefehlt. Aber ihre Erfolge waren nur gering. Die starke Zunahme an Mitgliedern, welche die Partei nach dem Wahlerfolg [in 1907] zu verzeichnen hatte, machte es dringend not-wendig, der sozialistischen Erziehung der Arbeiterklasse grössere Aufmerksamkeit zu schenken als bisher." *Protokoll über die Verhandlungen des Parteitages der deutschen sozialdemokratischen Arbeiterpartei in Oesterreich. Abgehalten in Reichenberg vom 19. September bis 24. September 1909* (Vienna, 1909), p. 31. The debates at the con-gress focused on *Bildung* for adult workers, but the terms of the debate and its categori-zation as problem of a "Kultur" and "Erziehung" had obvious consequences for and parallels to the party's increasing interest in public school education for children.

36. See especially Robert Danneberg's comments in ibid., p. 138.

37. Karl Renner, "Die Wandlungen der Christlichsozialen," *K,* 2 (1908–9): 5.

38. The initial request to establish the association came in a petition to the Ministry of Internal Affairs, dated 22 November 1904 and signed by Ludo Hartmann, Julius Ofner, Josef Enslein, and others. See Z. 51874/1904, 15/4, *MI Präs.* For the history of the *Freie Schule* see Wolfgang Speiser, *Paul Speiser und das Rote Wien* (Vienna, 1979), pp. 24–36; Glöckel, *Selbstbiographie,* pp. 47–50; Glaser, *Im Umfeld des Austromarxis-mus,* pp. 301ff.; idem, "Zur Geschichte des Vereins 'Freie Schule'," *Archiv. Mitteilungs-blatt des Vereins für die Geschichte der Arbeiterbewegung,* Oct./Dec., 1978; and Te-zuka, "Die Junglehrer-Bewegung," pp. 314–39. For earlier *Freidenker* efforts in the Social Democratic party in the 1890s, which anticipated the *Freie Schule,* see Hugo Pepper, "Die frühe österreichische Sozialdemokratie und die Anfänge der Arbeiter-kultur," in *Sozialdemokratie und Habsburgerstaat,* pp. 79–99. For a judicious evalua-tion of the importance of the *Freie Schule,* see Zulehner, *Kirche,* pp. 45–54.

39. For the founding statement and the initial signatories, see *FLS,* 12 March 1905, pp. 49–52. A copy of the "Statuten des Vereins 'Freie Schule' in Wien" are in Carton 17, *NL Marchet.* The association published a monthly newsletter, the *Mitteilungen des Vereines "Freie Schule"* (Vienna, 1906–14) which contains much relevant information about its various initiatives.

40. See the police report, 12 February 1906, Z. 12457/1906, 15/4, *MI Präs.*

41. See Friedrich Wichtl, *Weltfreimaurerei, Weltrevolution, Weltrepublik. Eine Un-tersuchung über Ursprung und Endziele des Weltkrieges* (Munich, 1922), pp. 72–74,

542 Notes to Pages 174–77

and Franz Stauracz, "Der Verein 'Freie Schule', seine Protektoren und seine Ziele," *CB*, 1905, pp. 867–71.

42. For membership statistics, see *Pädagogischer Jahresbericht*, 63 (1911): 51–52.

43. "Das Programm des Vereines ist der Kampf gegen den Gewissenszwang in der Schule, der Kampf für eine freie, fortgeschrittene Unterrichtsmethode, keineswegs aber der Kampf gegen die Religion oder eine bestimmte Religion." See *NFP*, 19 March 1906 (A), p. 4.

44. Hartmann to Mach, 27 June 1912, *NL Mach*. In 1908 Hartmann sent Mach the greetings of the *Freie Schule* on the occasion of his seventieth birthday. Hartmann to Mach, 20 February 1908. The range of Hartmann's anticlerical activities has never been adequately surveyed. As early as 1902 he was organizing protests against a Catholic university in Salzburg and arranging for a series of summer lectures which were to constitute a free German summer university in Salzburg, as a way of pursuing "unseren Kampf gegen den Klerikalismus" and the "immer erwünschte, immer bedrohte und immer notwendigere Kulturgemeinschaft zwischen Deutschland und Deutsch-Österreich." Hartmann to Lujo Brentano, 18 November 1902, *NL Brentano*. The popular lecture series organized by Hartmann at the *Volksheim* in Vienna in 1900 was another mode of implicit anticlerical praxis, although the Austrian Social Democratic leadership initially viewed this project with some hesitation. For Hartmann, see Günter Fellner, *Ludo Moritz Hartmann und die österreichische Geschichtswissenschaft. Grundzüge eines paradigmatischen Konfliktes* (Salzburg, 1985).

45. See Friedrich Jodl, "Zum Jubiläum des österreichischen Reichsvolksschulgesetzes," in Wilhelm Börner, ed., *Vom Lebenswege. Gesammelte Vorträge und Aufsätze von Friedrich Jodl* (2 vols., Stuttgart, 1916–17), 2: 524–54.

46. On Jodl, see Walter Schmied-Kowarzik, "Friedrich Jodl," *Archiv für Geschichte der Philosophie*, 27 (1912): 474–89; idem, "Friedrich Jodls Weltanschauung," *Zeitschrift für Philosophie und philosophische Kritik*, 154 (1914): 129–33; and Wilhelm Börner, *Friedrich Jodl. Eine Studie* (Stuttgart, 1911). For a review of the intellectual background, see Friedrich Stadler, "Wissenschaft ins Volk! Popularisierungsbestrebungen im Wiener Kreis und 'Verein Ernst Mach' von der Jahrhundertwende bis zum Ende der Ersten Republik," in Konrad and Maderthaner, *Neuere Studien zur Arbeitergeschichte*, 3: 619–46.

47. "Religion and Modern Science," *The Monist*, 3 (1892–93): 329–51.

48. Leisching, "Die römisch-katholische Kirche," p. 178.

49. See Paul von Hock, *Der Zwang zu den religiösen Übungen in der Schule. Eine Darstellung der rechtlichen Seite dieser Frage* (Vienna, n.d. [1908]).

50. See Paul Speiser, *Die bisherigen Ergebnisse des Kampfes der Freien Schule gegen den Zwang zu religiösen Übungen*, printed as an appendix to Hock, *Der Zwang*, pp. 13–18. Later the *Unterrichtsministerium* adopted a policy of recognizing the municipal fines, but then releasing the parents by acts of amnesty from actually paying them, thereby refusing to come to terms with the actual case at hand. See Hock's comments at the private business meeting of the *Verein* on 25 March 1916, in Z. 7327, 27 March

1916, Carton 2082, 22, *MI Präs.* For the letter to Seitz, see Adolf Deutsch to Seitz, [January 1909], Carton 10, *NL Seitz.* Seitz's *Nachlass* also contains letters appealing to him for assistance by teachers who had been disciplined or even transferred because of anticlerical activities.

51. Enslein, "Vom Unterlehrer zum Unterstaatssekretär." On Enslein, see Speiser, *Paul Speiser und das Rote Wien,* pp. 31–33; "Nun müssen sich die Wege trennen," *FLS,* March, 1950, pp. 1–2; "Josef Enslein und die 'Freie Schule'," ibid., p. 5.

52. The curriculum of the *Freie Schule* obviously had parallels elsewhere in Europe and America, including some of John Dewey's innovations at the Laboratory School of the University of Chicago.

53. See Josef Enslein, "Der Unterrichtsbetrieb an der 'Freien Schule'," *NFP,* 24 August 1909 (A), pp. 1–2. Certainly Catholic authorities feared precisely this more radical program on the part of the *Freie Schule.* See the general letter of the Austrian bishops, dated October 1906, in *Wiener Diözesanblatt,* 1906, p. 243.

54. See *NFP,* 12 February 1909 (M), pp. 5–6; 13 February 1909 (M), pp. 1–2; 14 February 1909 (M), pp. 8–9; 18 February 1909 (A), pp. 2–3, 6.

55. *NFP,* 22 August 1909 (M), pp. 6–7; 23 August 1909 (M), pp. 5–6; 24 August 1909 (M), pp. 1–2; 24 August 1909 (A), pp. 1–2; 25 August 1909 (M), pp. 1–2; 25 August 1909 (A), p. 1; 26 August 1909 (M), pp. 2–3; and 31 August 1909 (M), p. 6. At issue were conflicting interpretations of Section 70 of the *Reichsvolksschulgesetz* and Section 6 of the Law of 25 May 1868.

56. When Bienerth was contemplating a cabinet shuffle, Brosch, on behalf of Franz Ferdinand, urged him to retain Stürgkh in view of his success at the post. Brosch to Franz Ferdinand, 4 January 1911, C 168, Carton 11, *NL Franz Ferdinand.* For Stürgkh's tenure as Minister of Education, see Alexander Fussek, "Minister-Prasident Karl Graf Stürgkh." Dissertation, University of Vienna, 1959, pp. 19–22; Sieghart, *Die letzten Jahrzehnte,* p. 151; and Baernreither's acerbic comments in *Fragmente eines politischen Tagebuches,* pp. 266–70. For Christian Social satisfaction with his performance as Minister of Education, see *Rp,* 1 November 1911 (M), pp. 1–2.

57. *Sammlung der Erkenntnisse des k.k. Verwaltungsgerichtshofes,* 34 (1910): 1078–90.

58. Up to this point the legal proprietor of the schools was the *Verein "Freie Schule,"* but formal control was now transferred directly to Enslein, since the leaders of the association wanted to preserve the fiction that, in an official capacity, they had not backed down before the clerical menace, in this case the Archbishop of Vienna. See *Mitteilungen des Vereines "Freie Schule,"* June 1911, p. 101.

59. On Wolny, see Siegfried Karl, "Josef Wolny. Ein Leben für Kirche und Schule." Dissertation, University of Vienna, 1966.

60. Z. 5324, 5 January 1912, Carton 2510, 13, *UM Pras.*

61. Karl, "Josef Wolny," pp. 123–27.

62. This fact emerged as part of the evidence presented in the Josefstadt District Court trial. See *Mitteilungen,* May, 1913, p. 79.

63. Enslein was consistent—he also refused to pay a teacher assigned by the *Israelitische Kultusgemeinde* to instruct the school's Jewish students.

64. See Z. 8506, 21 February 1913, Carton 2510, 13, *UM Präs.* The Provincial School Council first rejected Wolny's claims in late January 1911. It delivered a second and final decision on 9 December 1912. The Ministry of Education confirmed the Council's decision on 25 February 1913. See also Karl, "Josef Wolny," pp. 107–9.

65. The full decision of the District Court is reprinted in the *Mitteilungen,* May, 1913, pp. 75–82.

66. Wolny's appeal to the Court was in the form of a challenge against the negative decision of the Ministry of Education. See Z. 25529, 28 May 1913, *UM Präs.* See also *Sammlung der Erkenntnisse,* 38 (1914): 808–11; as well as the self-satisfied commentary "Pater Wolny am Grabe seiner Hoffnungen," in *Mitteilungen,* June 1914, pp. 98–99.

67. Karl, "Josef Wolny," pp. 118, 122.

68. Ignaz Seipel, *Der Kampf um die österreichische Verfassung* (Vienna, 1930), p. 96 ("Auf diesem Gebiet handelt es sich ja nicht nur um verschiedene staatsrechtliche Auffassungen, nicht nur um Parteiprogramme, sondern hier stehen schon die Weltanschauungen selbst einander gegenüber").

69. For the history of the *Freidenker,* see Steger, *Rote Fahne,* pp. 223–37.

70. *Schicksalsjahre,* 1: 87–88 ("Sind nur gut als lebendige Proteste gegen die Lueger-Diadochen, sind nicht etwas an und für sich").

71. See I/2b2, Z. 138, report of 7 February 1907, *Statt. Präs., NÖLA;* as well as *'Los!' Organ der radikalen Partei,* 15 April 1907, pp. 1–2. On Zenker, see his autobiography, *Ein Mann im sterbenden Oesterreich.* Zenker edited several small left-wing periodicals, after having served as a correspondent for the *Neue Freie Presse.* He clashed with the Christian Socials soon after the party took control of the city, with the result that the *Stadtrat* forbade him to enter the City Council's chambers.

72. On Zenker's election in 1911, see I/2b2, Z. 2045, police report of 27 June 1911, *Statt. Präs., NÖLA;* and *AZ,* 18 June 1911, p. 3, and 20 June 1911, p. 2. In his account of this election in his autobiography, Zenker avoided mentioning the electoral pact between the Social Democrats and the Viennese radicals in 1911, undoubtedly because he was anxious in 1934 to emphasis a constant and persistent hatred of Austrian socialism. See *Ein Mann im sterbenden Österreich,* pp, 119–20, 219, 245, 262.

73. Zenker's most important critical works were *Die Gesellschaft* (2 vols., Berlin, 1899–1903); *Soziale Ethik* (Leipzig, 1905); and *Kirche und Staat.* For his debt to Gumplowicz and Ratzenhofer and his self-characterization as a positivist, see *Ein Mann im sterbenden Österreich,* p. 113. Zenker was also an avid student of Herbert Spencer. Ibid., pp. 98–99.

74. On Gumplowicz, see William M. Johnston, *The Austrian Mind. An Intellectual and Social History 1848–1938* (Berkeley, 1972), pp. 323–28.

75. See Adolf Joffe's critique of *Soziale Ethik* in *Die neue Zeit,* 24 (1906): 804–5.

Gumplowicz, in contrast, reviewed the book quite favorably in *Österreichische Rundschau*, 6 (1906): 308–9.

76. See esp. *Soziale Ethik*, pp. 75–103.

77. "Wir haben gesehen, dass sich in unseren Tagen nicht bloss das theoretische Interesse für die Probleme der Sittlichkeit erweitert und vertieft hat, sondern dass auch in allen Ländern unseres Kulturkreises ein vielleicht unklares, aber doch ehrliches Streben sich geltend macht, die erkannten Grundsätze wahrer Sittlichkeit im Volke selbst praktisch zur Geltung zu bringen. So schwierig die Aufgabe sein mag, welche sich die Freimauerei, die Ethische Bewegung, das Freidenkertum gesetzt hat . . . Eines beweisen sie doch unwiderleglich und als Eines muss sie doch jeder sittliche und lebensgläubige Mensch mit Enthusiasmus begrüssen, als ehrlichen Ausdruck eines starken, überquellenden sittlichen Bedürfnisses, das unsere Zeit erfüllt." *Soziale Ethik*, pp. 272–73.

78. For Zenker's anti-Semitism, see *Ein Mann im sterbenden Österreich*, pp. 22–23, 62–69, 94–97, 121–22.

79. Ibid., pp. 133–35.

80. *SP*, 1912, p. 5433. Zenker also had the audacity to chastise publicly Gustav Gross, the leader of the *Deutscher Nationalverband*, for failing to support his marriage-law crusade. Ibid., 1913, p. 7292.

81. Zenker to Seton-Watson, March 1913, *Robert Seton-Watson Papers*. I am indebted to the late Professor Hugh Seton-Watson for permission to use this collection.

82. Hartmann to Jodl, 23 January 1905, I.N. 133.105, *Handschriftensammlung*.

83. Hock to Marchet, n.d., Carton 17, *NL Marchet*.

84. *Schicksalsjahre*, 1: 146–47.

85. *NFP*, 19 March 1906 (A), p. 4. The Liberal Eduard Leisching thought of Hartmann's preoccupation with the *Freie Schule* that "Ich hielt dieses Eintreten für einen ebenso grossen politischen Fehler, wie die vorausgegangene, von [Georg] Schönerer betriebene 'Los-von-Rom Bewegung'." Leisching, *Ein Leben*, p. 88.

86. *Stenographisches Protokoll der Jahres-Hauptversammlung des Vereines 'Freie Schule' vom 22. März 1908* (Vienna, 1908), p. 5.

87. See Dorschalk to Seitz, 13 December 1908, Carton 10, *NL Seitz*.

88. See Z. 4183, 11 May 1907; Z. 5519, 8 June 1907; Z. 6860, 9 July 1907; Z. 7195, 14 July 1907, Carton 2082, 22, *MI Präs*.

89. Z. 8282/1907, ibid.

90. Z. 1144, 4 March 1908, and Z. 1009, 18 January 1908, filed in Z. 1144, ibid.

91. Z. 4506, 26 April 1908, ibid.

92. For the speeches, see Z. 7327, 27 March 1916, ibid. Many of Glöckel's arguments were reprised in his *Das Tor der Zukunft* (Vienna, 1917), a speech he gave before the Association in January 1917 and which was issued as a separate pamphlet.

93. Z. 6997, 26 March 1916.

94. Zenker, *Ein Mann im sterbenden Österreich*, p. 125.

95. Redlich to Bahr, 23 March 1918, in Fritz Fellner, ed., *Dichter und Gelehrter. Hermann Bahr und Josef Redlich in ihren Briefen 1896–1934* (Salzburg, 1980), p. 321.

96. See Glaser, *Im Umfeld des Austromarxismus,* p. 306; Speiser, *Paul Speiser,* pp. 75–76.

97. Hartmann, *Im Gestern bewährt,* pp. 96–97.

98. *Rp,* 25 October 1907. p. 1; 26 October 1907, p. 6; Walter Höflechner, *Die Baumeister des künftigen Glücks. Fragment einer Geschichte des Hochschulwesens in Österreich vom Ausgang des 19. Jahrhunderts bis in das Jahr 1938* (Graz, 1988), p. 21; Andreas Mölzer, "Zur Grazer Studentengeschichte. Der Gegensatz zwischen katholischen und national-freiheitlichen Korporationen in Graz von den Anfängen bis zum Jahre 1938 im Lichte der Studentenunruhen des Jahres 1932," in Walter Höflechner, ed., *Beiträge und Materialien zur Geschichte der Wissenschaften in Österreich* (Graz, 1981), pp. 484–85.

99. The official Catholic version of Lueger's speech is in the *Bericht über den VI. Allgemeinen österreichischen Katholikentag in Wien. 16. bis 19. November 1907* (Vienna, 1908), pp. 32–33. For press accounts see *Rp,* 17 November 1907, p. 35 and *AZ,* 18 November 1907, p. 3. See also the version of the speech printed in Peter Hofrichter, "Die österreichischen Katholikentage des 20. Jahrhunderts (bis 1933)." Dissertation, University of Vienna, 1966, pp. 53–54. That the main goal of Lueger's speech was enhanced political control of the universities by his own political party and not a racial diatribe against Jewish students or faculty was recognized by virtually all serious political participants in the subsequent debates about this controversy. Lueger subsequently wrote to ten university professors arguing that "meine Ausführungen bezogen sich beinahe ausschliesslich auf die Skandalszenen, deren Schauplatz die deutschen Universitäten in Österreich gewesen sind." *NWT,* 21 November 1907, p. 3. Robert Kann has wisely observed that "Weder der Nationalismus noch der Liberalismus sahen es als ihre Sache an, zu bedenken, dass nicht alles, was Lueger in seinen Werbereden sagte, wörtlich zu nehmen war." Robert A. Kann, "Hochschule und Politik im österreichischen Verfassungsstaat (1867–1918)," in Gerhard Botz, Hans Hautmann, and Helmut Konrad, eds., *Geschichte und Gesellschaft. Festschrift für Karl R. Stadler zum 60. Geburtstag* (Vienna, 1974), p. 516.

100. The phrase is in Ludo M. Hartmann's letter to Walter Goetz, 14 May 1907, *NL Goetz.* In general see Rüdiger vom Bruch, *Wissenschaft, Politik und öffentliche Meinung. Gelehrtenpolitik im Wilhelminischen Deutschland (1890–1914)* (Husum, 1980), pp. 114–27. Ludo Hartmann played a major role in organizing the Salzburg congress.

101. See especially Jürgen Kämmerer, ed., *Heinrich Ritter von Srbik. Die wissenschaftliche Korrespondenz des Historikers 1912–1945* (Boppard am Rhein, 1988), pp. 102–11, 186.

102. For the Catholics, see Ernst Bruckmüller, "Die Verbindungen des CV in Österreich vor dem Ersten Weltkrieg: Gründungsphase und erste Konsolidierung," in Gerhard Hartmann, ed. *Der CV in Österreich. Seine Entstehung, seine Geschichte, seine Bedeutung* (Vienna, 1977), pp. 1–36; and Hartmann, *Im Gestern bewährt;* for the Zion-

ists and Jewish Nationalists, see Marsha L. Rozenblit, "The Assertion of Identity. Jewish Student Nationalism at the University of Vienna before the First World War," in *Year Book of the Leo Baeck Institute*, 27 (1982): 171–86.

103. Whiteside, *The Socialism of Fools*, p. 272, argues that pan-German extremism among university students began to decline after 1900, but the incidence of student rioting in 1907–9 suggests that this may not have been an irrevocable trend.

104. John Hagg, "Students at the University of Vienna in the First World War," *CEH*, 17 (1984): 299–302, as well as Helge Zoitl, *"Student kommt von Studieren!"* Zur *Geschichte der sozialdemokratischen Studentenbewegung in Wien* (Vienna, 1992). See also Karl Renner's testimony in *An der Wende zweier Zeiten. Lebenserinnerungen von Karl Renner* (2d ed., Vienna, 1946), pp. 267–68.

105. It is obviously difficult to make broad claims about the political views of hundreds of university professors, and substantial differences might be found between the theological and medical faculties and the philosophical and legal faculties. But I believe that Walter Höflechner's assessment of the situation in Graz that "Die Professoren waren zum grössten Teil wie die Studenten deutschnational eingestellt, auch wenn sie sich natürlich antiösterreichischen Radikalismen nicht anschlossen; aber viele gehörten doch studentischen Verbindungen als Alte Herren an, waren ihre Ehrenmitglieder und nahmen auch an ihren Veranstaltungen immer wieder teil" is close to the target, and likely applicable to Innsbruck and Vienna as well. "Zur Geschichte der Universität Graz," in *Tradition und Herausforderung. 400 Jahre Universität Graz* (Graz, 1985), pp. 39–40. Höflechner's comments in *Die Baumeister des künftigen Glücks,* p. 12, support this reading.

106. See esp. Bruch, *Wissenschaft*, pp. 112–13. One prominent Viennese academic, Josef Pernter, who was the director of the meteorological institute at the University of Vienna, refused to join in the chorus of protest against Lueger. In a long article in the *Reichspost* he lambasted the hypocrisy of his colleagues who, he insisted, used their Liberal values to mask distinctly anti-Catholic prejudices. For Pernter, it was comical that professors who owed their jobs to a Liberal-oriented civil service would now cry foul when new political parties decided to make an issue of the silent politicization of the universities that was embedded in the previous thirty years of Austrian history ("Wenn die Universitäten heute eine Domäne des Liberalismus sind, so wurde diese Stellung nur möglich durch die Eroberung der Universitäten durch die politisch-liberale Partei"). His remarks were reprinted in "Der Krach an den österreichischen Universitäten," *HPB*, 141 (1908): 664–66.

107. Karl Liebknecht's assertion in 1910 (Haag, p. 302) that Austrian universities enjoyed a more open atmosphere than their Prussian counterparts was thus true, but it was not a condition that all professors found happy or comfortable.

108. For student politics in Austria, see Paul Molisch, *Politische Geschichte der deutschen Hochschulen in Österreich von 1848 bis 1918* (2d ed., Vienna, 1939); Johann Ramminger, "Nationalismus und Universität: Die Genese des Nationalismus und die cisleithanischen Universitäten 1859–1900." Dissertation, University of Vienna,

1981; and John Haag, "Students at the University of Vienna in the First World War."
For student illiberalism at German universities in the later nineteenth century, see the
excellent study by Konrad Jarausch, *Students, Society and Politics in Imperial Germany. The Rise of Academic Illiberalism* (Princeton, 1982), particularly pp. 367–92,
which offers a detailed report on the widespread and systematic discrimination against
Catholics at most Reich universities. Similar conditions often prevailed in what was a
nominally Catholic state—Austria.

109. *DV,* 25 November 1907 (M), p. 3; *Rp,* 2 December 1907 (M), p. 2.

110. See Tucher's report of 6 December 1907, Nr. 604, *BHSA.* It is interesting, in
line with Tucher's comments, to compare Gessmann's speech at a banquet in honor of
Catholic university students on 18 November 1907, with Lueger's bombast. Gessmann
avoided polemics, merely stressing the need of Catholic intellectuals to involve themselves in public affairs and encouraging upward political mobility on the part of Catholic university students. See *Rp,* 20 November 1907, p. 9.

111. See *AZ,* 21 November 1907, p. 3.

112. *The Times,* 26 November 1907, p. 5. The immediate reference was a comment
Lueger had made about Radetzky, but Steed clearly had the other scandal in mind as
well. Steed's ambivalence about Lueger and the Christian Socials (whom he constantly
referred to as "Clericals") was matched only by his disdain for the Liberal press. Ultimately he judged both on the basis of his own preeminent standard of public virtue—
whether they were of advantage or disadvantage for England's standing on the Conti-
nent. Steed was bitter about what he took to be "Clerical" conspiracies against his work
in Vienna, following upon his trenchant criticisms of various Vatican policies during
his tenure as *Times* correspondent in Rome. See Steed to Moberly Bell, 11 November
1908, Box 178, *Steed Papers.* He reported to Valentine Chirol in 1905 that he considered Lueger to be an "arch-demagogue" but one whose presence—as a component of
what Steed saw as a larger strategy of Franz Ferdinand's—was the best "antidote to
Pangermanism." See Steed to Chirol, 6 October 1905, Box 177, *Steed Papers.* At the
same time Steed's decided anti-Semitism manifested itself when he wrote privately
about what he saw as the nefarious pro-German and anti-English politics of Jews in the
world of Viennese journalism who, he felt, were to a man crypto-Prussian patriots anxious to deliver the Monarchy to the Hohenzollerns: "five years of experience here has
taught me one thing—for some hitherto unexplained reason, interest, clannishness, un-
conscious linguistic or racial fanaticism, every Jew in this part of the world is a strong
pro-German who looks toward Berlin as the Mussulman towards Mecca . . . in their
heart of hearts they are pro-German to a man." Steed to Moberly Bell, 24 February
1908, Box 178, *Steed Papers.*

113. *AZ,* 22 November 1907, p. 2.

114. *AZ,* 26 November 1907, p. 7; *NFP,* 26 November 1907 (M), pp. 2–3.

115. Amira to Brentano, 20 November 1907, *NL Brentano.*

116. *SP,* 1907, pp. 2689–90.

117. *SP,* pp. 3046–47.

118. *SP,* pp. 2872–83.

119. On Masaryk's political and religious philosophy, see the recent evaluation by Hanus J. Hajek, *T. G. Masaryk Revisited: A Critical Assessment* (Boulder, 1983), esp. pp. 90–125, as well as Frederick M. Barnard, "Humanism and Titanism: Masaryk and Herder," and Hillel J. Kieval, "Masaryk and Czech Jewry: the Ambiguities of Friendship," the last two in Stanley B.Winters, ed., *T. G. Masaryk (1850–1937). Volume 1. Thinker and Politician* (London, 1990), pp. 23–43 and 302–27. See also Roman Szporluk, *The Political Thought of Thomas G. Masaryk* (Boulder, 1981); Zbynek A. B. Zeman, *The Masaryks—The Making of Czechoslovakia* (London, 1976); and Roland J. Hoffmann, *T. G. Masaryk und die tschechische Frage* (Munich, 1988), pp. 369–88. Masaryk's most systematic treatment of religious phenomena is in *Modern Man and Religion* (London, 1938), first published in Czech in 1896–98.

120. Max von Hussarek's brief account of Austrian church-state relations—*Grundriss des Staatskirchenrechts* (2d ed., Leipzig, 1908)—offers a good introduction not only to the substantive issues but to the remarkable reconciliation that was slowly taking place between church authorities and the Austrian administrative state by the first decade of the new century. For the latest scholarly opinion, see Leisching, "Die römisch-katholische Kirche."

121. *SP,* 1907, pp. 2881–82.

122. *SP,* pp. 2938–48.

123. On Mayr, see Hermann J. W. Kuprian, "Zwischen Wissenschaft und Politik: Die politische Entwicklung Michael Mayrs von 1907 bis 1922." Dissertation, University of Innsbruck, 1985, pp. 165–88, as well as Hainisch, *75 Jahre,* pp. 231–34. On Drexel, see Hermann Deuring, *Prälat Dr. Karl Drexel* (Dornbirn, 1956).

124. It said much about the prominence of the Alpine Catholics in the party's cultural politics that the committee on university affairs within the parliamentary delegation consisted of Mayr, Drexel, August Kemetter, Franz Stumpf, and Wilhelm Miklas—none of them elected from Viennese districts, none of them members of the old-line leadership, and all of them "Catholic" in personal political views, and all real or honorary members of a Catholic university student group. See *Rp,* 23 May 1908, p. 8.

125. *SP,* 1907, pp. 2908–18; 3019–34. Mayr's speech at the Catholic Congress in November asserted the same hope for equity, not hegemony. He invoked Ludwig Windthorst in arguing that "Die Wissenschaft und ihre Lehre ist frei und wer sie angreift, ist mein Feind. Aber die Wissenschaft darf nicht für eine einzige Richtung monopolisiert werden!" *Bericht,* p. 189.

126. *SP,* 1907, pp. 2995–98. Lueger's last-minute return to the Jews as a way of getting himself off the "clerical" hook convinced few of his listeners, since the primary logic of his Congress speech had been pro-Catholic far more than anti-Jewish. It stood in remarkable parallel to his attack on the Jews in December 1905—when all else failed, the Jews were available as a plausible rhetorical dodge. This was the discourse of a political bully caught up short before his German national compatriots in the *Nationalverband,* not of a racial anti-Semite.

127. On Wahrmund, see Matthias Höttinger, "Der Fall Wahrmund." Dissertation, University of Vienna, 1949. Höttinger's dissertation is generally unfavorable toward Wahrmund. See also the excellent summaries in Fontana, *Geschichte des Landes Tirol,* pp. 270–78, and in Hartmann, *Im Gestern bewährt,* pp. 94–120. For the pace of events in the affair I have followed Gustav Marchet's own handwritten manuscript on the "Wahrmund-Affaire" in Carton 8, *NL Marchet.*

128. The most elaborate presentation of Wahrmund's polemical views is the uncensored version of his *Katholische Weltanschauung und freie Wissenschaft* (Munich, 1908), esp. pp. 28–45. See also his *Ultramontan. Eine Abwehr in vier Artikeln* (Munich, 1908) and Wahrmund's exposition of his version of the final stages of the controversy, *Lehrfreiheit? Akten und Erläuterungen zum Fall Wahrmund* (Munich, 1909).

129. See Gregory's "Memorandum" in Goschen to Grey, 26 June 1908, No. 83, Vol. 398, FO371, *PRO.* Steed described Gregory as "a strong Catholic" who "took several opportunities of asking my opinion on ecclesiastical questions." Steed to Moberly Bell, 11 November 1908, Box 179, *Steed Papers.*

130. For a prudent evaluation of the larger issues of the controversy, as well as its foreign policy implications, see Friedrich Engel-Janosi, *Österreich und der Vatikan 1846–1918* (2 vols., Graz, 1958–60), 2: 86–103.

131. See Peter Hofrichter, "Modernismus in Österreich, Böhmen und Mähren," in Erika Weinzierl, ed., *Der Modernismus. Beiträge zu seiner Erforschung* (Graz, 1974), p. 180.

132. *SP,* 1902, pp. 10408–9, responding to an interpellation brought in by the Catholic Conservatives on 13 March 1902, ibid., p. 10294.

133. Höttinger, "Der Fall Wahrmund," pp. 16–17.

134. Ibid., p. 23.

135. See Wahrmund, *Katholische Weltanschauung und freie Wissenschaft.*

136. See Beck's letter of 13 March 1908 to Theodor Kathrein, asking that Kathrein use his influence to try to calm emotions in Tirol, in Richard Schober, ed., *Theodor Freiherr von Kathrein (1842–1916). Landeshauptmann von Tirol. Briefe und Dokumente zur katholisch-konservativen Politik um die Jahrhundertwende* (Innsbruck, 1992), pp. 310–11. See also the careful account of the Affair's local repercussion in Tyrol in Schober, *Geschichte des Tiroler Landtages,* pp. 223–25.

137. See Redlich's delicate comments on Marchet's handling of the affair in *SP,* 1908, p. 5554. See also the analysis of Marchet's policies in Czedik, *Zur Geschichte,* 3: 207–13.

138. See Marchet, "Wahrmund Affaire," p. 1.

139. Tschirschky to Bülow, A 8029, 22 May 1908, Oest. 70/Bd. 46, *PAAA.*

140. Amira to Brentano, 30 March 1908, *NL Brentano.*

141. See Engel-Janosi, *Österreich und der Vatikan,* 2: 90–96; Richard Schober, "Belmonte und Aehrenthal. Österreichisch-vatikanische Beziehungen im Schatten der Wahrmundaffäre," *MÖSA,* 27 (1974): 295–335.

142. *AZ,* 19 March 1908, p. 4, noted with glee the embarrassment Gessmann found

himself in over the Nuncio's intervention. For Christian Social reaction, see *Rp,* 18 March 1908, pp. 1–2. In a letter to Beck in early April, Morsey called Albert Gessmann "indolent" about the Wahrmund affair. See his letter of 4 April 1908, Carton 16, *NL Marchet.*

143. Marchet, "Wahrmund Affaire," p. 3; Höttinger, "Der Fall Wahrmund," pp. 61–2; Ebenhoch to Lueger, 24 February 1908, I.N. 40946, *Handschriftensammlung.* When the Budget Committee of the *Abgeordnetenhaus* finally voted on the appropriations for the universities on the 27th, the Christian Socials were surprisingly moderate toward Marchet, voting with the Coalition in support of the budget. See *Rp,* 28 March 1908 (M), pp. 3–4. This successful reimposition of discipline against those who wanted to embarrass Marchet occurred at the party meeting on March 26.

144. See Kathrein's private notes on the decision in Schober, ed., *Theodor Freiherr von Kathrein,* p. 318.

145. *AZ,* 17 May 1908, p. 3; Mölzer, "Zur Grazer Studentengeschichte," p. 485; Hartmann, *Im Gestern bewährt,* pp. 110–14. Aldrian was a law student who also served as secretary of the Styrian *Bauernverein,* which explains the forceful intervention of Hagenhofer and his colleagues.

146. Weiskirchner to Lueger, 19 February 1908, I.N. 40866, *Handschriftensammlung.*

147. Morsey to Beck, 11 April 1908, quoted in Höttinger, "Der Fall Wahrmund," p. 66. Ebenhoch's comments to Lueger suggest, however, that Morsey was isolated even within his own party. Letters of 24 February 1908, I.N 40946, and 15 March 1908, I.N. 40952, *Handschriftensammlung.*

148. Morsey, "Der Wahrmundfall und das Kabinett Beck," *Rp,* 17 May 1908 (M), pp. 1–2.

149. See *Rp,* 20 May 1908 (M), p. 4. On the afternoon of May 20, hours after the above commentary in the *Reichspost* appeared, the Christian Social news service "Austria" issued a further communiqué categorically denying that the party intended to replace Marchet with Hussarek and giving the impression that rumormongers were distorting the party's basically moderate stance. See *AZ,* 21 May 1908, p. 4. Since the party rarely engaged in this kind of squabbling publicly, one may reasonably assume it reflected serious internal differences. On Beck's role in conciliating the party in late May, see Goschen to Grey, 21 May 1908, No. 74, FO 371/398.

150. See Tschirschky's report in A 8029, 22 May 1908, Oest. 70/Bd.46, *PAAA.* Tschirschky did not note in this report the heavy pressure on the party from Brosch and Franz Ferdinand to use the Wahrmund Affair and the contestations over the military salary problem in the Delegations to dump Beck. Brosch had planted an anti-Beck article in the *Reichspost* on the morning of May 15 ("Auf verfehltem Kurse," p. 1) thinking to test the waters to see if the majority of the party leadership would abandon Beck. Brosch to Franz Ferdinand, 14 May 1908, C33, Carton 10, *NL Franz Ferdinand.* In spite of a week of intensive politicking, Brosch was forced to report on May 23 that the party showed no signs of uniting behind a movement against Beck. Lueger, ac-

cording to Brosch, was too sick to play a role, and both Gessmann and Ebenhoch wanted to preserve their seats in the Cabinet. See Brosch to Franz Ferdinand, 23 May and 25 May 1908, C 38, C 40. See also the insightful comments of Heinrich Tucher on Franz Ferdinand and the party in his report of 22 May 1908, Nr. 215, *BHSA.*

151. Höttinger, "Der Fall Wahrmund," pp. 106–7. Marchet had already assembled the rectors of the various Austrian universities on 13 June to force their (uncomfortable) public approbation for the government's strategy.

152. The final agreement between Marchet and Wahrmund was signed in the presence of Beck and Julius Sylvester on 17 June. See Wahrmund, *Lehrfreiheit?* pp. 18–20, for Wahrmund's own protocol of the negotiations.

153. The terms of the settlement with Wahrmund were the subject of bitter contestation later, during 1908 and 1909. Wahrmund insisted that he had been promised that his final destination was Vienna, and that the appointment at the German university in Prague was merely temporary. On Wahrmund's later career, see Höttinger, "Der Fall Wahrmund," pp. 108–15, 119.

154. Wahrmund to Amira, 10 July 1908, *NL Amira.*

155. Masaryk later reprinted this speech as *Freie wissenschaftliche und kirchlich gebundene Weltanschauung und Lebensauffassung. Die kirchenpolitische Bedeutung der Wahrmund-Affäre* (Vienna, 1908). For a recent evaluation of the speech, see Hoffmann, *T. G. Masaryk,* pp. 377–88.

156. See *SP,* 1908, pp. 5549–60.

157. This perspective was evident in most of Redlich's political writings before the war, emerging most powerfully in his work for the administrative reform commission. See below, Chapter 6, as well as his speech in parliament on 27 June 1907, *SP,* 1907, pp. 125–31. After the war Redlich offered a much more pessimistic and restrictively deterministic interpretation, which portrayed the late Imperial political system as being caught between the covert anti-parliamentarism of Stürgkh and the overt anti-constitutionalism of the Thronfolger. See *Österreichische Regierung,* esp. pp. 98–112. Josef Redlich's letters to Hermann Bahr, recently published in an excellent edition by Fritz Fellner, provide a telling commentary on the politics of the *Deutscher National-verband* in late Imperial politics. See especially the letters of 7 July 1917, 26 August 1917, and 17 September 1917 in *Dichter und Gelehrter,* pp. 237–38, 252–55, and 259–60. Even before the war Redlich was astounded by the rigid and unchanging intellectual framework of the German *bürgerlich* politicians. He wrote in despair to Baernreither in late 1908: "Nichts ist schwerer, als meinen politischen Freunden im Parlamente einen neuen politischen Gedanken oder eine kleine Wendung zu einer neuen Richtung einzugeben." Letter of 19 December 1908, Carton 49, *NL Baernreither.* And again in 1910: "Unsere ganzen Parteien und Politiker sind in den letzten Jahren—das gilt auch vor allem von uns Deutschen—so auf das Negative eingerichtet, dass ich mir schwerlich vorstellen kann, wie diese Elemente auf einmal positiv schöpferisch wirken sollen. Der Druck der Demagogie und die österreichische Gewohnheit, nur für den nächsten Tag

zu sorgen, haben es dahin gebracht, dass jedermann ängstlich an den bewährten Schablonen festhält." Letter of 10 August 1910, Carton 47, ibid.

158. "Memorandum," p. 3 in Goschen to Grey, No. 83.

159. Goschen to Grey, 19 March 1908, No. 44.

160. Gessmann to Funder, 12 February 1912, *NL Funder.*

161. *SP,* 1908, pp. 5179–83.

162. *SP,* 1908, p. 5489. For Beck's own vision which he aptly termed a "System der Konzentration," see the major speech on 19 December 1907 in ibid., 1907, pp. 3677–80.

163. *SP,* 1908, pp. 5301–5.

164. Adler insisted in 1913 to Theodor Thomas: "Ich selbst bin ein Gegner jeder Vermischung und jeden Zusammenarbeitens mit Gegnern." Adler to Thomas, 9 December 1913. See also Zulehner, *Kirche,* p. 210, who speaks of "die Skepsis Viktor Adlers der Freidenkerbewegung gegenüber."

165. *SP,* 1908, pp. 5717–18.

166. *SP,* pp. 6769–80.

167. See Michael Schacherl, "Gemeinsamer Kampfboden?" *K,* 1 (1907–8), 347–52; Josef Strasser, "Was kann die 'Freie Schule' noch leisten?" ibid., 493–98.

168. Strasser made similar complaints, this time on the issue of bourgeois nationalism, at the 1909 party congress. See *Protokoll über die Verhandlungen,* p. 172.

169. Karl Seitz, "Freie Schule und Sozialdemokratie," *K,* 1 (1907–8): 352–56.

170. See Max Adler, "Kirche und Schule," *K,* 2 (1908–9): 389–96, and Renner's rebuttal "Kulturkampf oder Klassenkampf?" ibid., pp. 438–45. For the general background see Norbert Leser, *Zwischen Reformismus und Bolschewismus. Der Austromarxismus als Theorie und Praxis* (Vienna, 1968). In his biography of Max Adler, Alfred Pfabigan discusses the content of these two essays but does not place them into the historical context which generated their debate. Renner's arguments in 1909 were an almost literal restatement of his June 1908 speech on Wahrmund, and are clearly owing to intraparty debate over the tactics of the party on the clericalism question. See Pfabigan, *Max Adler. Eine politische Biographie* (Frankfurt, 1982), pp. 76–91. Gerhard Steger in his *Rote Fahne* briefly touches on the debate on pp. 184–88. Although I respect Steger's work, the categories he employs are too mechanical to comprehend the diversity of socialist appropriation and manipulation of religious *Kultur.* It seems to me that the only way to approach this issue is temporarily—over time—and not by lumping pre-1914 and post-1918 experiences together in one undifferentiated whole.

171. Both were published under the pseudonym of "Karl Mann": "Bourgeoisie und Klerikalismus," *K,* 1 (1907–8): 385–89; and "Proletariat und Religion," ibid., pp. 537–42. For the cultural matrix of laboring society, as opposed to that of the Austro-Marxist intelligentsia, see Dieter Langewiesche, *Zur Freizeit des Arbeiters. Bildungsbestrebungen und Freizeitgestaltung österreichischer Arbeiter im Kaiserreich und in der Ersten Republik* (Stuttgart, 1979); and Wegs, *Growing Up Working Class.* For Germany,

see the valuable work of Vernon L. Lidtke, *The Alternative Culture. Socialist Labor in Imperial Germany* (New York, 1985). Otto Bauer was in fact using anticlericalism as one possible bridge between *Alltagskultur* of the masses and the more subtle cultural actionism of the Austro-Marxist intelligentsia, thereby connecting what some recent analysts have argued is essentially unconnectable.

172. Peter Loewenberg has noted in his insightful essay on Victor and Friedrich Adler that "Renner . . . was in many ways the spokesman for Victor Adler's parliamentary tactics." See Peter Loewenberg, *Decoding the Past. The Psychohistorical Approach* (New York, 1983), pp. 151–52. See also the important essay by Hans Mommsen, "Victor Adler und die Politik der österreichischen Sozialdemokratie im Ersten Weltkrieg," in *Politik und Gesellschaft im Alten und Neuen Österreich,* 1: 378–408. For parallel movements in the ideas of utopia, see Kenneth R. Calkins, "The Uses of Utopianism: The Millenarian Dream in Central European Social Democracy Before 1914," *CEH,* 15 (1982): 124–48.

173. "Unsere Verbündeten vom 20. Juni werden morgen unsere Feinde sein." O. B. [Otto Bauer], "Keine Blockpolitik," *K,* 4 (1910–11): 475–76.

174. See Roger Fletcher, *Revisionism and Empire. Socialist Imperialism in Germany 1897–1914* (London, 1984), pp. 81–104.

175. See Zulehner, *Kirche,* pp. 216–39; Josef Weidenholzer, *Auf dem Weg zum "Neuen Menschen,"* passim.

176. Anson Rabinbach, *The Crisis of Austrian Socialism. From Red Vienna to Civil War 1927–1934* (Chicago, 1983). See also Steger, *Rote Fahne, schwarzes Kreuz,* pp. 297–312.

177. Ernesto Laclau and Chantal Mouffe, *Hegemony and Socialist Strategy. Towards a Radical Democratic Politics* (London, 1985), p. 28. See also the insightful observations of Alfred Georg Frei, *Rotes Wien. Austromarxismus und Arbeiterkultur. Sozialdemokratische Wohnungs- und Kommunalpolitik 1919–1934* (Berlin, 1984), pp. 46–48.

178. Mataja to Seipel, 3 April 1928, *NL Seipel.*

179. Seipel to Mataja, 10 April 1928, ibid.

180. On the party's foreign policy in 1908–9 see Heribert Husinsky, "Die 'Reichspost' und die österreichische Balkanpolitik in den Jahren 1908/1909." Dissertation, University of Vienna, 1947, esp. pp. 147–223. Fritz Csoklich argues that Lueger was a strong supporter of Aurel Popovici's federalist schemes ("Das Nationalitätenproblem," p. 104). For a statement of the party's Greater-Austrian aspirations, which recognized the inevitable subordination of German and Hungarian ruling elites in the Monarchy to a more equitable federative structure, see "Grossösterreich," *Rp,* 30 August 1908, pp. 1–2.

181. Csoklich goes so far as to refer to the party's "weitgehende Programmlosigkeit in nationalen Fragen." "Das Nationalitätenproblem," p. 164.

182. Friedrich Funder was later quite explicit about the political distance that stood between "Germans" in Vienna and their sometime brethren in Bohemia and Moravia:

Sudeten nationalism appeared to the Viennese as an "unfruchtbares Lieblingsthema politischer Advokaten und lebensfremder Professoren." *Vom Gestern*, p. 201. Nor were the Social Democrats oblivious to the Czech element of the Christian Social electorate: "Ebenso ist es kaum zufällig dass man so viele tschechische Namen in den Reihen der christlichsozialen Partei findet. Die Nachkommen der tschechischen Einwanderer . . . füllen die Reihen dieser arbeiterfeindlichen Partei." Franz Tomášek, "Nationale Minderheitenschulen als soziale Erscheinung," *K*, 3 (1909–10): 109.

183. *Schriften des Vereins für Sozialpolitik*, 132 (1910): 9–13. The annual reports of the city administration under Lueger, in the *Gemeinde Verwaltung der Stadt Wien* series, offer a detailed view of the largesse of the party on occasions of public "representations." Although the socialists criticized these expenditures as waste, the Christian Socials saw them as proof of the party's public generosity and the city's economic well-being.

184. See Wedel's comments in A 14996, 8 October 1903, Oest. 86/2/Bd. 13; and the arrogant remarks in A 16885, 24 October 1904, Oest. 70/ Bd.42: "Für Deutschland hat das Überhandnehmen der christlichsozialen Bewegung insofern eine grössere Bedeutung, als sie uns feindliche oder wenigstens unfreundliche Tendenzen verfolgt. Dr. Lueger ist nicht unser Freund . . . seine Gefolgschaft aber ist uns abgeneigt aus konfessionellen Gründen, wegen unserer höheren Intelligenz und Aufklärung und wegen unserer geschlossenen Macht, in der sie eine zukünftige Bedrohung Oesterreichs wittern."

185. For the Mommsen episode, see *AB*, 1897, pp. 2246–47; and Lothar Wickert, *Theodor Mommsen. Eine Biographie* (4 vols., Frankfurt, 1959–80), 4: 74–6. For Lueger's trip to Rumania, see *DZ*, 17 June 1906, pp. 4–5; 19 June 1906, p. 3; A 10733, 15 June 1906; A 10824, 18 June 1906; A 11725, 30 June 1906, Oest. 86/2/Bd.15, *PAAA*. For Eulenburg, see the report of his conversation with Baron Bánffy in A 10418, 28 August 1897, Oest. 70/Bd. 30, where the two waxed ecstatic about the common interest Germany and Hungary had in preventing a strengthening of the "Slavic element." For the party's involvement with the Croatians, see Brosch's "Auskunft im Rathaus," 24 March 1908, and "Besprechung mit Minister Gessmann," 3 April 1908, Carton 206, *MKFF.*

186. See the insightful reflections on this problem in Erhard Busek and Emil Brix, *Projekt Mitteleuropa* (Vienna, 1986), esp. p. 121. It is incorrect to argue as Gerhard Hartmann does (*Im Gestern bewährt*, p. 154), following both Csoklich and Sutter, that up to the Badeni crisis the Christian Socials had a true Imperial mission, which they then abandoned for a German-national orientation. Rather, the party was always essentially a German party, because it was a Viennese party, and an Imperial party because it was dedicated to achieving a realistic (which meant both fair and equitable) settlement among the various national political groups in the Monarchy. Those who make that kind of argument fail to understand the constant way in which the "national" issue was mediated and filtered through the political culture of Vienna. Lueger's views on the nationality question did not change in the way Hartmann assumes. As late as December 1899 he observed with regret at a meeting of parliamenatary leaders that "[d]er Kampf

zwischen Deutschen und Slawen führt nur zur Schwächung Österreichs. Es gibt keine Debatte im Hause, in die nicht der deutsch-czechische Streit hineinschlägt." This observation led him in turn to urge the Czechs to abandon their obstructionism and allow both sides to find a modus vivendi over time in the context of a working parliament. See Schober, ed., *Theodor Freiherr von Kathrein*, pp. 531–32.

187. *Rp*, 23 March 1907, p. 5. See also 5 December 1906, p. 9; and 16 February 1907, p. 5.

188. See "Verhandlungsschrift über die Sitzung des Bürgerklubs vom 18. Juli 1917," Carton 37, *CPW*.

189. For a fine review of the effectiveness of *Umgangssprache* as a mode of evaluating nationality, see Emil Brix, *Die Umgangssprachen in Altösterreich zwischen Agitation und Assimilation. Die Sprachenstatistik in den zisleithanischen Volkszählungen 1880 bis 1910* (Vienna, 1982), esp. pp. 67–101.

190. See *SP*, 1901, p. 1582. At the oath-taking ceremony for new *Bürger* in October 1909 Lueger commented that "in der Wahrung des deutschen Charakters der Stadt Wien liegt nicht eine Feindseligkeit gegen irgendeine Nation. Sie können mir glauben, dass ich keinen Unterschied kenne zwischen den Angehörigen der verschiedenen Nationen, wenn sie wirklich treue Österreicher sind." *NFP*, 7 October 1909 (M), p. 4.

191. See A 13996, 20 August 1909, Oest. 70/Bd. 47, *PAAA*.

192. *DR*, 3 May 1906, p. 1. Leopold Tomola made explicit the connection between learning German and getting a decent job: "Nun werden Sie mir doch zugeben, dass in Wien als ein wahrhaft qualifizierter Mensch nur der gelten kann, der der deutschen Sprache mächtig ist. Es gibt keinen in diesem Hause, der behaupten kann, dass er es in Wien ohne Kenntnis der deutschen Sprache zu irgend etwas tüchtigen bringen kann. Der Arbeiter, der nur tschechisch spricht, kann sich nur als Taglöhner verwenden lassen." *SP*, 1908, pp. 5825–26.

193. *NFP*, 12 May 1910 (M), p. 10; *Rp*, 12 May 1910, p. 8; *DV*, 12 May 1910 (M), p. 3. Nagler was apparently put up to the slur by Adolf Gussenbauer, who was known as an extremist Slav-baiter.

194. See the rumors reported in "Dr. Luegers würdige Erben," *AT*, 21 March 1914, pp. 1–2, which pan-German baiting aside, seem likely to have a core of truth. See also *SMZ*, 24 January 1910, p. 2.

195. John and Lichtblau have observed that "Des weiteren erlaubte die Metropole des Vielvölkerstaats längere Phasen von Teilangepasstheit, ohne das Gefühl persönlicher Würde zu verlieren." Michael John and Albert Lichtblau, *Schmelztiegel Wien. Zur Geschichte und Gegenwart von Zuwanderung und Minderheiten* (Vienna, 1990), p. 385.

196. For an insightful statement of this problem, see Moritz Csáky, "Die Pluralität als Kriterium der österreichischen Identität," *Christliche Demokratie*, 7 (1989): 373–80, esp. 375, 378–79. It should be noted, however, that pluralism did not exclude social or cultural hierarchy; Czech was, for example, a "Dienstbotensprache" in a way that German was not.

197. See *SP,* 1909, pp. 430–31. Miklas spoke on 25 November 1909 against a motion of urgency submitted on 20 October by Karel Kramář and others regarding the protection of national minorities.

198. For recent work on the Viennese Czech community, see particularly Monika Glettler, *Die Wiener Tschechen um 1900. Strukturanalyse einer nationalen Minderheit in der Grossstadt* (Munich, 1972); Karl M. Brousek, *Wien und seine Tschechen. Integration und Assimilation einer Minderheit im 20. Jarhrhundert* (Vienna, 1980); Arnold Suppan, *Die österreichischen Volksgruppen. Tendenzen ihrer gesellschaftlichen Entwicklung im 20. Jahrhundert* (Munich, 1983), pp. 70–80; and Michael John, "Migration, Ethnizität und Urbanität. Zur Haltung der österreichischen Arbeiterbewegung in der Habsburgermonarchie," in *Die Bewegung,* pp. 165–85.

199. Glettler's thoughtful and articulate portrait of Lueger's regime (pp. 310–37) is drawn in very negative terms, confusing, I think, short-term political tactics and occasional blustering with the basic thrust of the city administration's treatment of resident Czechs. So too is the otherwise exemplary treatment in John and Lichtblau, *Schmelztiegel Wien,* pp. 277ff. This is surprising, for later in the same book the authors argue (quite rightly) that market-driven pressures to integrate themselves and thus to be able to prosper encouraged voluntary linguistic assimilation on the part of Czechs moving to the city, far more than external "German" coercion (p. 385). More typical of Lueger's views were his remarks in the City Council when two Christian Social politicians tried to use the anti-German riots in Laibach in September 1908 to provoke trouble by entering an anti-Slavic interpellation insulting the Slovenes, who had received emergency help from the city of Vienna after a recent earthquake. Lueger was angered by this tactic, commenting that "Ich glaube aber, dass es nicht gut ist wenn wir Öl ins Feuer schütten. Insbesondere bitte ich aber zu unterlassen, Werke der Wohltätigkeit in den Nationalitätenkampf einzubeziehen. . . . Ich will keinen Slovenen dadurch zum Deutschen und keinen Deutschen zum Slovenen machen, das eine aber will ich, dass sich endlich einmal die Nationalitäten in unserem Vaterlande vertragen mögen." *AB,* 1908, p. 2247. For a similar remark two weeks before see *NFP,* 4 September 1908 (M), p. 5.

200. See Funder, *Vom Gestern,* p. 461. The darling of late nineteenth-century "liberalism" in Austria, the *Neue Freie Presse,* was far more vindictive about "the Czechs" than Karl Lueger ever was.

201. In her "Minority Culture in a Capital City: The Czechs in Vienna at the Turn of the Century," in Robert B. Pynsent, ed., *Decadence and Innovation. Austro-Hungarian Life and Art at the Turn of the Century* (London, 1989), p. 54, Monika Glettler uses the example of the new *Bürgereid* as evidence of general discrimination against the local Czechs by Lueger. However, she ignores the (to my mind) crucial fact that this oath was not a generally administered oath of municipal citizenship, which all adult males in Vienna had to swear, but rather that it was both voluntary and explicitly partisan-political, since the whole institution of the *Bürgerschaft* was viewed by the Christian Socials in these terms. The only men required to take this oath were those selected to become honorific Christian Social *Bürger* by the City Council. As I indi-

cated in Chapter 1, this assemblage, although nominally a "municipal" institution, was actually an important electoral cadre group of the Christian Social party. It is not surprising that, given the pressure Lueger felt from Schönerer and the radical pan-Germans in 1899–1900, and facing strong accusations that the Christian Socials were a crypto-Slavic party, he would exploit the rhetorical cover of a pro-"German" oath, which he knew would be administered only to his own party's most likely supporters. Nor could the party even assume that the oath meant much, for later evidence from 1911 suggested that some of those who took the oath turned around and listed Czech as their *Umgangssprache* on the 1910 census! See Brix, *Die Umgangssprachen*, pp. 126, 139.

202. The figure was 23.8 percent for those Czechs who used Czech as their primary language, as opposed to 45 percent for the Jewish community. John, "Migration, Ethnizität und Urbanität," p. 173.

203. For an autobiographical testimony that reflects this mentality of functional assimilation, see the oral history memoir of Anna Simonek, recalling her father, Rudolf Simonek, in John and Lichtblau, *Schmelztiegel Wien*, pp. 386–87.

204. In rebutting in November 1897 Theodor Mommsen's accusation that Vienna was weak in defending German rights, Lueger explicitly argued that the most powerful contribution the city made to German culture was its capacity to nurture voluntary assimilation: "Der Herr Professor . . . hat keine Ahnung davon, was die Deutschen Wiens in der Behauptung ihrer Nationalität und dem Schutze derselben geleistet haben. Uns kommt nicht mehr jener Zufluss zugute, der in früheren Zeiten das Deutschtum Wiens gestärkt hat. Aus dem deutschen Lande kommen die wenigsten Einwohner nach Wien, aber ungezählte Tausende kommen aus den slavischen Ländern nach Wien, und diese Slaven haben wir ohne Geschrei durch unsere Liebenswürdigkeit zu Deutschen gemacht! Vernünftige Leute werden dabei bleiben. . . . Die Stürme werden den Slaven den Mantel ihrer Nationalität nicht nehmen, im Gegenteil, sie werden sich immer stärker in denselben hüllen und wir werden dann den Nationalitätenkampf in Wien haben. Die Sonne der Liebenswürdigkeit, die Wiener, bewegen den Tschechen, den Slaven, den Mantel abzulegen, und diese werden so Deutsche, wie wir alle. Das mögen sich gewisse Herren merken. Diesem reichsdeutschen Professor aber rufe ich zu: Hände weg von Österreich!" *AB*, 1897, pp. 2246–47.

205. "Hier herrschen nicht Hohenzollern, sondern Habsburg-Lothringen und werden so lange herrschen, als überhaupt ein Österreicher existiert. Ich bleibe bei unserem alten Programm: Gut deutsch, gut österreichisch, gut christlich immer und immerdar!" *NFP*, 19 October 1909 (M), p. 6.

206. For the history of the Komenský school movement, see Glettler, *Die Wiener Tschechen*, pp. 95–110. For the nationalist threat facing the party in 1909, see Prammer, "Konservative und christlichsoziale Politik," pp. 376–81, who interprets the Christian Socials' heightened sensitivity to the national question after 1909 as resulting from a fear of being outflanked by radical nationalist agitators in Vienna and Lower Austria.

207. See, for example, the communiqué drafted at the meeting of the Christian So-

cial parliamentary club on 16 September 1909 in *NFP,* 17 September 1909 (M), p. 3; and the debates in Mappe 2, Carton 96, *CPK.* See also Hauser's comments in the *Linzer Volksblatt,* quoted in *NFP,* 7 September 1909 (M), p. 7.

208. See Lueger's bitter comment about his experiences with the German School Association: "Klubsitzung," 4 June 1909, Carton 96, *CPK* ("Der Deutsche Schulverein ist immer gegen mich").

209. For a demographic portrait of the Czech community, see Glettler, *Die Wiener Tschechen,* pp. 25–72, and Michael John, "Migration, Ethnizität und Urbanität," pp. 172–75. On the ethnic constitution of the metropolitan population at large, see Gustav Otruba and L. S. Rutschka, "Die Herkunft der Wiener Bevölkerung in den letzten hundertfünfzig Jahren," *Jahrbuch des Vereines für Geschichte der Stadt Wien,* 13 (1957): 227–74; Gustav Otruba, "Wiens Bevölkerung. Nationale Herkunft und soziale Entwicklung," *Der Donauraum,* 13 (1968): 12–42; and the new compendium by Lichtblau and John, *Schmelztiegel Wien.*

210. See Wilhelm Winkler, *Die Tschechen in Wien* (Vienna, 1919), p. 22. See also Otto Bauer's insightful description of the Czech community in "Der Separatismus in Wien," *Werkausgabe,* 7: 1004–7.

211. For the technical procedures (and problems) governing the census see Brix, *Die Umgangssprachen,* pp. 30–34.

212. See Eduard Stepan, "Die czechische Bewegung in Wien und Niederösterreich II," *NFP,* 4 August 1909 (M), p. 3. For comparable data for the period 1908–12, see the *Statistisches Jahrbuch der Stadt Wien für das Jahr 1912* (Vienna, 1914), p. 444. By 1912 the number of Czech speakers had declined to 10,415.

213. See especially Franz Tomášek's comments on the assimilatory power of the public schools in his "Nationale Minderheitenschulen," p. 109. In 1912 Otto Bauer argued that because of changes in the cultural background of younger Czechs journeying to Vienna after 1900—individuals who had been exposed to Czech national values in Bohemia or Moravia *before* they left their native villages and towns—Vienna could expect to see more demands for Czech separatism as time went on. The events of August 1914 intervened, however, so that it is impossible to say whether Bauer's predictions would have been true in the long run, or whether Viennese assimilatory mechanisms would have continued to work effectively. "Der Separatismus," p. 1005.

214. Glettler, *Die Wiener Tschechen,* p. 346.

215. Ibid., p. 101.

216. On Janča see the comments in Tschirschky's report in A 17994, 1 November 1909, Oest. 91/Bd. 16, *PAAA;* and the portrait in Glettler, *Die Wiener Tschechen,* pp. 249–67. Perhaps the best gauge of Czech anti-assimilationist opinion (Janča's constituency) in Vienna would be the voting performance for Czech-*bürgerlich* and Czech socialist (separatist) candidates in municipal elections. In the 1912 Fourth Curia City Council elections the total number of Czech votes was 13,240 out of 285,000 votes.

217. Gletter, *Die Wiener Tschechen,* pp. 347–60, offers a detailed chronicle of the joustings as they related to the school in the Landstrasse.

218. See "Die czechischen Volksschulen in Wien," *NFP,* 24 July 1909 (M), p. 5; Gletter, *Die Wiener Tschechen,* pp. 360–61.

219. "Die czechischen Vorstösse gegen Wien," *NFP,* 10 August 1909 (M), p. 6.

220. "Eine Anregung von massgebender deutscher Seite," *NFP,* 24 July 1909 (M), p. 5.

221. See "Protestversammlung gegen die Errichtung einer czechischen Schule in Meidling," *NFP,* 31 July 1909 (M), p. 6, as well as the *NFP*'s critique of alleged Christian Social hypocrisy towards the Czechs in "Die christlichsoziale Partei und die czechischen Vorstösse in Niederösterreich," *NFP,* 13 August 1909 (A), pp. 1–2; and Emanuel Weidenhoffer, "Die czechischen Vorstösse gegen Wien," *NFP,* 3 August 1909 (M), p. 2.

222. *NFP,* 13 August 1909 (A), p. 1.

223. Most recently, under the sponsorship of Julius Axmann, on 8 January 1909. For the *Lex Kolisko* see Gertrude Balzer, "Die Lex Kolisko." Dissertation, University of Vienna, 1942; Norbert Gürke, "Die deutschen Erbländer," Hugelmann, ed., *Das Nationalitätenrecht,* pp. 442–56; and Czedik, *Zur Geschichte,* 2: 108, 198. For a general overview of the political condition of the Germans in the Monarchy, see Berthold Sutter, "Die politische und rechtliche Stellung der Deutschen in Österreich 1848 bis 1918," in Adam Wandruszka and Peter Urbanitsch, eds., *Die Habsburgermonarchie 1848–1918. Band III. Die Völker des Reiches, 1. Teilband* (Vienna, 1980), pp. 154–339.

224. An impressive recent survey of legal and constitutional positions of the national groups in the Monarchy may be found in Gerald Stourzh, *Die Gleichberechtigung der Nationalitäten in der Verfassung und Verwaltung Österreichs 1848–1918* (Vienna, 1985).

225. For the October 1904 decision of the *Reichsgericht,* see Gürke, "Die deutschen Erbländer," pp. 448–50; and Stourzh, *Die Gleichberechtigung,* pp. 80–83, and the fascinating debates of the Court, reprinted in ibid., pp. 278–306. In a case involving public education in 1877 the Court had affirmed the use of Czech as a local customary language in Ober- and Unter-Themenau and in Bischofswarth.

226. See the report in A 13996, 20 August 1909, Oest. 70/Bd. 47, *PAAA.*

227. For a portrait of German nationalist extremism in Bohemia in this period, see Andrew G. Whiteside, *Austrian National Socialism before 1918* (The Hague, 1962).

228. Stepan, "Die czechische Bewegung in Wien und Niederösterreich III," *NFP,* 5 August 1909 (M), p. 3. Many of the Czech-speakers were in fact Croats.

229. *NFP,* 2 August 1909 (N), pp. 1–2; 15 August 1909 (M), pp. 7–8; *AZ,* 14 August 1909, p. 3.

230. *NFP,* 4 September 1909 (M), p. 5; *AZ,* 2 September 1909, p. 5; 4 September 1909, p. 3.

231. See the interview with Gorup in *NFP,* 1 September 1909 (M), p. 3.

232. "Parlamentarische Kommission," 13 August 1909, Carton 96, *CPK;* the text of the communiqué is in *NFP,* 14 August 1909 (M), p. 3. For an evaluation of the Glombinski initiative, see "Das Ergebnis der Konferenz der Parteiführer," *NFP,* 18 Au-

gust 1909 (M), p. 2. Lueger sought to gain the agreement of both German and Czech party leaders to establish a special subcommittee to negotiate with the Cabinet for reopening parliament in September. The Slavic Union refused to join, however.

233. See the cynical comments of Gross to Baernreither, 17 August 1909 ("Die ganze Komödie scheint von Glabinski eingeleitet worden zu sein, um sein stark gesunkenes Prestige im Klub zu heben." Carton 48, *NL Baernreither.* Note also Sylvester to Baernreither, 19 August 1909, who argued that Bienerth had no intention of recalling the House soon: "Ich glaube, Bienerth ist selbst der Ueberzeugung, dass er mit dem Reichsrate nicht fortarbeiten kann. Er zieht eben die Sache nur solange hinaus als es möglich ist"). Carton 48, ibid.

234. *NFP,* 18 August 1909 (M), p. 5.

235. *NFP,* 7 September 1909 (M), p. 6.

236. *Rp,* 12 September 1909, p. 8; *NFP,* 12 September 1909 (M), p. 8.

237. *NFP,* 25 September 1909 (M), p. 7; 28 September 1909 (M), p. 8; and Lueger's attempt to dismiss the whole affair as unimportant in *NFP,* 4 October 1909 (M), p. 5. The debate on the *Schutzvereine* at the parliamentary club meeting of 4 June 1909 makes it clear that the leadership saw *Ostmark* as a way of outflanking the pan-German defense associations, and that the principal interest of all concerned was with gaining political control of the movement, not in pushing integral nationalism. See "Klubsitzung," 4 June 1909, Carton 96, *CPK.* The founder of the *Ostmark* movement was Josef Schlegel, who although elected to parliament from Upper Austria, never outgrew his childhood and adolescence in Schönlinde and Leitmeritz in northern Bohemia. His nationalist values were not generally characteristic of the local Lower Austrian party leadership before 1908. See Prammer, "Konservative und christlichsoziale Politik," pp. 377–82.

238. On the closing of the schools, see *AZ,* 31 August 1909, p. 3. For the *NFP's* insistence that the two school controversies were not similar, see 11 September 1909 (A), pp. 1–2.

239. Redlich recorded in his diary Baernreither's impression on visiting Bienerth in early September that Bienerth feared the collapse of his government ("auf ihn macht es den Eindruck, dass Bienerth bald zu fallen fürchtet"), which may explain the latter's indecision on what course of action to take in early September. *Schicksalsjahre,* 1: 22.

240. Schreiner to Baernreither, 26 September 1909, Carton 48, *NL Baernreither.*

241. On Schreiner, see the perceptive comments in *Die Tätigkeit des Sozialdemokratischen Verbands, 3. Heft,* pp. 29–30; and Redlich's account of Schreiner's dismissal from office, *Schicksalsjahre,* 1: 51. The Christian Socials were suspicious of Schreiner since one of the latter's first acts as *Landsmannminister* in 1908 was to urge the revitalization of the *Schutzverein* movement, which the party suspected would be used against it. See *Rp,* 21 November 1908, pp. 1–2.

242. Redlich to Marchet, 17 September 1909, Carton 11, *NL Marchet.*

243. Marchet to Baernreither, 22 September 1909, Carton 48, *NL Baernreither.*

244. "Klubsitzung," 16 September 1909, Carton 96, *CPK;* and "Landtags-Klub," 16

September 1909, Carton 1, *CS Partei: NÖ Landtag; NFP,* 17 September 1909 (M), p. 3; 18 September 1909 (A), p. 2.

245. *SPNÖ,* 1909, pp. 305–6.

246. Ibid., pp. 306–15 (Seitz); 315–19 (Renner); 319–22 (Gessmann); 324–25 (Bielohlawek); 326 (Lueger).

247. Michael John describes the socialists' problems with the issue of the Czech schools in "Migration, Ethnizität und Urbanität," p. 172.

248. *AB,* 1909, pp. 2197–98.

249. *NFP,* 2 October 1909 (A), p. 2.

250. *Schicksalsjahre,* 1: 23.

251. Redlich to Baernreither, 5 October 1909, Carton 47, *NL Baernreither.*

252. See *SPNÖ,* 1909, pp. 447–48.

253. This suspicion is clear from the later comments of Eduard von Stransky on October 9. See the "Die Beratungen der deutschen Parteien im Wiener Rathause," Mappe XIII, Carton 96, *CPK.*

254. Typical was the editorial of the *NFP,* "Von der Staatssprache herunter zur Landessprache," 11 October 1909 (N), p. 1.

255. See Redlich to Baernreither, 5 October 1910, Carton 47, *NL Baernreither.*

256. "Die Beratungen der deutschen Parteien im Wiener Rathause."

257. Freudenthal and his friends were irked that they were excluded from the summit, but the prominence of those attending was as important for the meeting's success as was its agenda. See the comments of Colloredo-Mannsfeld on 14 October 1909 in *SPNÖ,* 1910, p. 637.

258. See Gessmann's speech in the Diet on 21 January 1910 in ibid., pp. 1009–12.

259. Ibid., p. 634. In March 1912 Richard Bienerth, by now Kielmansegg's replacement as Lower Austrian *Statthalter,* gave the official government interpretation which regarded the 1909 law as having no effect on the *Unterrichtssprache* question. Ibid., 1912, p. 1423.

260. Ibid., 1909, pp. 636–37, 650.

261. A 17994, 1 November 1908, Oest. 91/Bd. 15, *PAAA.*

262. See *SPNÖ,* 1910, pp. 1009–12.

263. *AZ,* 31 October 1909, pp. 3–4. Redlich reports a conversation with Žáček to the effect that the Czechs resigned only because of insulting comments by Schreiner at the *Ministerrat* on 30 October. *Schicksalsjahre,* 1: 28.

264. See *Die Tätigkeit des Sozialdemokratischen Verbandes, 3. Heft,* pp. 10–18.

265. See *Schicksalsjahre,* 1: 39–40.

266. See the protocol in Mappe XIII, Carton 96, *CPK; AZ,* 18 January 1910, p. 3.

267. *SPNÖ,* 1910, pp. 1009–17.

268. See "Conferenz der deutschen Parteiführer," dated 6 February 1910, as well as the hand-written, six-page fragment filed with this transcript, in Mappe XIII, Carton 96, *CPK.*

269. See the "Protokoll über die Sitzung des Neunerausschusses zur Beratung Deutscher Schutzgesetze, am Dienstag, den 10. Mai 1910," Carton 1, *NL Gross.*

270. *SPNÖ,* 1912, pp. 1419ff.

271. John, "Migration, Ethnizität und Urbanität," p. 172.

272. See *SPNÖ,* 1912, pp. 1423–29. For the Christian Social–German national electoral pacts for the 1912 and 1914 City Councils elections, see below, Chapter 5. The debates at the meeting of the "Parlamentarische Kommission," 30 December 1910, Mappe II/1, Carton 96, *CPK,* also suggest another motive in addition to tactical moves against the socialists. By early 1911 the leadership also feared that the pan-German *Schutzverein* movement was outflanking the Christian Socials and felt that some more aggressive policy stance had to be adopted.

273. *SPNÖ,* 1912, pp. 1437–40.

274. Ibid., p. 1440.

275. John, "Migration, Ethnizität und Urbanität," p. 172. For an overview of the dilemma of the Social Democrats on the nationality problem after 1901, see Mommsen, *Die Sozialdemokratie und die Nationalitätenfrage,* esp. pp. 362–422; Glettler, *Die Wiener Tschechen,* pp. 377–415; and Raimund Löw, *Der Zerfall der "Kleinen Internationale." Nationalitätenkonflikte in der Arbeiterbewegung des alten Österreich (1889–1914)* (Vienna, 1984). For the consequences in Vienna, see Otto Bauer, "Der Separatismus in Wien," pp. 1003–15.

276. *SP,* 1910, pp. 3729–30; "Gesamtexecutive," 12 January 1907, *VGAB.* This meeting of the Social Democratic executive is enlightening about the limits the party faced in selling international fraternity to its voters. One delegate, Pittoni, bluntly confessed that "So wie die italien. Genossen in Triest unmöglich einen Slovenen aufstellen könnten, so kann in Wien kein Tscheche aufgestellt werden."

277. See *Protokoll über die Verhandlungen,* pp. 169–72 (Strasser); pp. 178–80 (Pernerstorfer); pp. 183–85 (Otto Bauer).

CHAPTER FIVE

1. On the course of Lueger's illness, see *NFP,* 10 March 1910 (A), pp. 4–5; *NWT,* 10 March 1910, p. 8; Kurt Skalnik, *Dr. Karl Lueger. Der Mann zwischen den Zeiten* (Vienna, 1954), pp. 159–62.

2. *ÖW,* 27 (1910): 92–93; *NWT,* 31 January 1910, p. 9; *Rp,* 31 January 1910, p. 4.

3. *Arthur Schnitzler Tagebuch 1909–1912* (Vienna, 1981), p. 133.

4. Hartmann to Bauer, 14 March 1910 (postcard), *NL Bauer.*

5. "Karl Lueger," *AZ,* 11 March 1910, pp. 1–2.

6. Was this difference in charaterization—a hostile, mass-based civil society or a hostile, repressive state—altogether accidental? Or did this bespeak differences in the agendas of German and Austrian Social Democracy?

7. "Ein Bürgermeister," *Kommunale Praxis,* 10 (1910): 321–24.

8. See the insightful comments in Redlich, *Österreichische Regierung,* pp. 74–75.

9. Within the enormous literature on American machine politics and urban reform I found the following particularly helpful: Samuel P. Hays, "The Politics of Reform in Municipal Government in the Progressive Era," *Pacific Northwest Quarterly,* 55 (1964): 157–69; Richard M. Bernard and Bradley R. Rice, "Political Environment and the Adoption of Progressive Municipal Reform," *Journal of Urban History,* 1 (1975): 149–74; Martin J. Schiesl, *The Politics of Efficiency. Municipal Administration and Reform in America 1880–1920* (Berkeley, 1977); Arthur Mann, *Yankee Reformers in the Urban Age* (Cambridge, Mass., 1954); Seymour J. Mandelbaum, *Boss Tweed's New York* (New York, 1965); Melvin G. Holli, *Reform in Detroit: Hazen S. Pingree and Urban Politics* (New York, 1969); and Kenneth Fox, *Better City Government. Innovation in American Urban Politics, 1850–1937* (Philadelphia, 1977). For helpful discussions about American urban and political history in the nineteenth century I am grateful to my colleagues Kathleen Conzen, Barry Karl, and the late Arthur Mann.

10. See Schiesl, *The Politics of Efficiency,* p. 2.

11. See Amy Bridges, *A City in the Republic. Antebellum New York and the Origins of Machine Politics* (Cambridge, 1984), pp. 3–17, 24–29.

12. See Griffith, *A History of American City Government,* pp. 63–96.

13. Michael H. Frisch, "Urban Theorists, Urban Reform, and American Political Culture in the Progressive Period," *Political Science Quarterly,* 97 (1982): 295–315.

14. On Parsons, see Mann, *Yankee Reformers,* pp. 126–144. On Shaw, see Lloyd Graybar, *Albert Shaw of the Review of Reviews. An Intellectual Biography* (Lexington, 1974).

15. See Frank Parsons, *The City for the People* (Philadelphia, 1901), esp. pp. 17–254, as well as Dorothy Ross, *The Origins of American Social Science* (Cambridge, 1991), pp. 275–78.

16. Frank Goodnow, *City Government in the United States* (New York, 1904).

17. See Shaw's comments on the situation in Vienna in *Municipal Government in Continental Europe* (New York, 1895), p. 434.

18. James Weinstein, *The Corporate Ideal in the Liberal State: 1900–1918* (Boston, 1968).

19. See Barry D. Karl, *The Uneasy State. The United States from 1915 to 1945* (Chicago, 1983), p. 233. Karl's book is an important critique of received assumptions about modern American political history. On the question of "Americanization," see Mann, *Yankee Reformers,* pp. 56–62, 122–23; Arthur S. Link and Richard L. McCormick, *Progressivism* (Arlington Heights, Ill., 1983), pp. 100–101; John Higham, *Strangers in the Land: Patterns of American Nativism, 1860–1925* (New Brunswick, N.J., 1955), pp. 234–63; and Paul S. Boyer, *Urban Masses and Moral Order in America, 1820–1920* (Cambridge, Mass., 1978).

20. See *SPNÖ,* 1914, pp. 527–82, 590–626, for the Lower Austrian Diet's discussion of the bill, with Leopold Steiner (p. 569) announcing that the Viennese deputies would go along if it was clear the innovation did not apply to Vienna.

21. See Weiskirchner's and Steiner's response to a request from Alexander Sögner

of the Christian Social Lower Austrians in late 1913 urging that the Viennese reconsider their position on proportional suffrage. The Viennese leadership unanimously rejected the idea on 10 November 1913, and Weiskirchner appealed to Sögner to stop pestering the Rathaus, since "die Aufrollung dieser Frage eine bedeutende Gefahr für die Wiener Parteibewegung in sich birgt." 12 November 1913, Z. 624, Carton 72, *CPW*. Wilhelm Miklas, in contrast, was typical of the younger Lower Austrians in favoring the idea. Miklas found Weiskirchner's covert alliance with regional German nationalists against proportional suffrage reform to be quite annoying and told him so openly. Miklas to Weiskirchner, 19 November 1913, Z. 640, ibid. See also the resolution of the "Vertrauensmännerversammlung des XVII. Bezirkes," held on 25 October 1912 against proportional suffrage and in defense of the Curial system. Z 410, ibid., Carton 71; and the discussion of the law which would have instituted proportional voting for Lower Austrian municipalities at the 3 June 1914 session of the Austrian *Ministerrat.*

22. Bridges, *A City in the Republic,* pp. 148ff.

23. See Griffith, *A History of American City Government,* pp. 66–67.

24. John W. Boyer, "Conceptions of Vienna in Its Historical Literature," paper, presented at the Urban History Symposium, Chicago Historical Society, March 1984.

25. Frisch, "Urban Theorists," p. 305.

26. *DV,* 7 June 1907 (M), pp. 4–5; *Die Gemeinde-Verwaltung der Stadt Wien im Jahre 1907,* p. 42.

27. On the regulations governing the hiring and testing of middle-level career bureaucrats in Austria, see Anton Pace, ed., *Ernst Mayrhofers Handbuch für den politischen Verwaltungsdienst in den im Reichsrate vertretenen Königreichen und Ländern* (5th ed., 7 vols., Vienna, 1895–1901), 1: 200–213, esp. 208–9. The "politische Prüfung" for Viennese *Konzeptspraktikanten* was administered by the Lower Austrian *Statthalter.* See, for example, the cases in Z. 379, 1905, Carton 87; and Z. 1996, 1907, Carton 110, *MD.* These files also indicate that the *Magistrat* was interested in policing its own affairs. Note, for example, the case of a *Diurnist* who was fired for stealing, and who then applied for reinstatement. The senior officials in the *Magistrat* refused his request and Lueger supported them. Z. 94, Carton 87. Political nominations through the patronage system succeeded only on the lower levels of bureaucracy if the candidate could pass the required entrance test. See, for example, the case of Franz Frank, whose political sponsor was no one other than the Vice-Mayor Joseph Strobach, but who failed to pass the examination with a satisfactory score and was therefore rejected. Z. 47, Carton 87, 1905. Similar cases occurred in 1907 when men supported by Wenzel Kuhn, the *Vorsteher* of the 19th District, and by the city *Baurat* Schwarz for employment in the *Kanzlei-Dienst* were also found unfit because they did not pass the entrance examination. Z. 1989 and 1999, 1907, Carton 110. Obviously the Christian Socials found it possible to combine a crude level of meritocracy with an equally crude sense of patronage.

28. See Spitzmüller's obsequious comments in "*. . .und hat auch Ursach, es zu lieben,*" pp. 74–75.

29. See Glettler, *Die Wiener Tschechen,* p. 359.

30. See Josef Dworak to Weiskirchner, 16 February 1914, Z. 911, Carton 73, *CPW.*

31. For Appel's remarks, see *NFP,* 15 March 1910 (M), p. 4. For the American context, Schiesl, *The Politics of Efficiency,* pp. 189–98.

32. Griffith, *A History of American City Government,* p. 64.

33. Albert Gessmann, who had observed Liberal patronage practices during his service as an opposition member of the *Schulsection* of the City Council, delivered a blistering attack on the Liberals' hypocrisy in accusing the Christian Socials of corruption in March 1899. See *Rp,* 19 March 1899, p. 11.

34. See fols. 1–392 ("Interventionen"), Carton 19, *NL Marchet.* It should be noted that the Social Democrats were exceptional, at least before 1918, in trying to avoid entrapment in the *Protektion* racket. See, for example, the letter sent on behalf of Karl Seitz to Julius Fels (a former student of Seitz, who wanted the latter to use his influence to get him a position), 2 November 1910, *NL Seitz,* Carton 5. Seitz refused "aus prinzipiellen Gründen."

35. Redlich, *Österreichische Regierung,* pp. 66–68. Compare the comments on Sieghart's "corruption" in *Schicksalsjahre,* 1: 37–38 and 2: 23, with Redlich's own admission that he got his professorship in Vienna only because of the personal patronage of Albert Gessmann, thus confirming that some influence peddling was selectively permissible. Apparently what was good for the goose was not good for the gander. See ibid., 1: 13, and Redlich to Bahr, 19 February 1916 and 16 November 1920, in Fritz Fellner, ed., *Dichter und Gelehrter,* pp. 157, 435.

36. See especially Schlitter's comments in his Diary, entries of 15 and 22 December 1913.

37. See Milton Rakove, *We Don't Want Nobody Nobody Sent. An Oral History of the Daley Years* (Bloomington, Ind., 1979). For a discussion of corruption from a contemporary Austrian perspective, see the essays in Christian Brünner, ed., *Korruption und Kontrolle* (Vienna, 1981).

38. "Eine Auszeichnung für Stadtrat Hörmann," *DV,* 7 June 1907 (M), p. 4.

39. *SMZ,* 18 July 1910, p. 2; *NFP,* 8 July 1910 (M), pp. 1, 3; *DV,* 8 July 1910 (M), pp. 1–2; *AZ,* 24 November 1910, p. 8. See also Scheicher, *Erlebnisse,* 5: 310–12.

40. "Klubsitzung," 7 July 1910, *CPK,* Carton 90. For the socialist victory, see *CSAZ,* 12 April 1902, pp. 1–2; *Rp,* 30 April 1902, p. 1; and *AZ,* 9 March 1914, pp. 1–2.

41. Joseph Schöffel in his *Erinnerungen* alludes to several of these incidents, but also makes it clear that in much of their behavior the Christian Socials were simply emulating, if also intensifying, former Liberal practices.

42. "Klubsitzung," 21 and 22 June 1910, *CPK,* Carton 90. For another example of alleged corruption in the *Stadtrat,* see the discussion of the activities of Hans Schneider, given during a libel trial involving Alois Moissl, *AZ,* 11 October 1913, pp. 8–9.

43. "Korruption," *AZ,* 11 October 1908, pp. 1–2.

44. For Lueger, see Redlich, *Schicksalsjahre,* 1: 56; and Schöffel, *Erinnerungen,* p. 317. For Gessmann, see Eugen Schwiedland's evaluation in *MKFF,* described below, Chapter 6.

45. *SMZ,* 19 June 1911, p. 2.

46. For the 1907 elections, see *AZ,* 4 April 1907, pp. 2–3; 30 April 1907, p. 3. For the 1908 *Landtag* elections, see the extremely detailed statement of socialist accusations submitted by Karl Seitz to parliament on 12 March 1909, and reprinted in full in *SP,* Session 19, 1909, Anhang I, 52/I, pp. 922–85.

47. See Kielmansegg's report of 11 May 1907 in Carton 2243, 34/2, *MI Präs.* On Seitz's accusations of corruption in the 1908 *Landtag* elections, which the government decided not to answer but which Kielmansegg also investigated, see Z. 11890, 25 October 1909, Carton 1571, 11/1. The Internal Ministry, in contrast, in reviewing the case, found that municipal officials had been inept in constructing the electoral lists and that some cases of sloppiness, if not of actual malfeasance in dealing with ballot protests, had occurred. See Z. 4326, 1 May 1910. Interestingly, Richard Weiskirchner as Minister of Commerce was allowed a special view of this file and noted that he was "in agreement" with the ministry's evaluations.

48. Z. 2748, 12 March 1914, Carton 2197, 31.

49. Wagner to the party secretariat, 16 April 1914, Carton 73, *CPW.*

50. He was convicted in July 1913 of election fraud, much to the *Arbeiter-Zeitung*'s discomfort: *AZ,* 18 October 1913, p. 12.

51. For typically vindictive attacks on Gessmann, see *DV,* 28 May 1910 (M), pp. 1–2; 3 June 1910 (M), pp. 1–2; 5 June 1910 (M), pp. 5–6; 24 July 1910 (M), pp. 1–5; as well as *SMZ,* 4 July 1910, p. 1. For Gessmann's own defense, see his comments in "Klubsitzung," 21 and 22 June 1910, Carton 90, *CPK; Rp,* 27 April 1910, p. 7; 5 June 1910, pp. 1–2; 8 June 1910, pp. 1–2; 13 July 1910, pp. 5–6; and the extended defense published by the Christian Social party's secretariat: *Der Verleumdungsfeldzug gegen Dr. Gessmann. Vergani, 'Deutsches Volksblatt' und Baukreditbank* (Vienna, 1911). The latter tract charged that Vergani's hate campaign was the result of a misbegotten extortion scheme on his part, since Vergani tried to pressure Gessmann into giving him a share of the founding *Aktien* of the bank and Gessmann had refused. Only thereafter did the attacks begin (see *Der Verleumdungsfeldzug,* pp. 26–31). In any event, Gessmann staunchly insisted, as confirmed by the testimony of various craft leaders in the party, that he had consulted widely with the construction trades before organizing the bank, and that it met a long-standing need. Obviously he felt the bank would have the opposite effect than it did—it would portray him as a benevolent, far-sighted social engineer willing to stimulate the private financial market to help his constituents.

52. See "Klubsitzung," 21 and 22 June 1910. The party leadership had held a general conference on the same subject on June 10. See the detailed reports in *NFP,* 11 June 1910 (M), pp. 3–4, and *DV,* 11 June 1910 (M), pp. 4–5.

53. "Klubsitzung," 18 May 1910, Carton 90, *CPK.*

54. A copy of the testament, dated 8 February 1907, is in Mappe II/2, Carton 96, *CPK.* On the origins of the document, see Kuppe, *Karl Lueger,* p. 505; and Gessmann's comments in "Klubsitzung," 18 May 1910, Carton 90, *CPK.* Lueger's decision was not a state secret for long, for Klotzberg wrote to Lueger on 6 April 1907 (I.N. 40906,

Handschriftensammlung) swearing that *he* had not been the one to blabber the news of Weiskirchner's nomination to the newspaper *Die Zeit.*

55. See especially the letters of 11 October 1911, 4 January 1912, and 13 February 1912, *NL Funder.* Erich Kielmansegg noted of the two men that "eigentlich mochten beide einander nicht. Der verschlagene Charakter Gessmanns war Lueger zuwider, aber er brauchte ihn." *Kaiserhaus,* p. 416. Gessmann, in turn, once called Lueger an "old ass." Ibid., p. 398.

56. "Klubsitzung," 17 March 1910, Carton 96.

57. Letters of 13 February and 15 January 1912, *NL Funder.* See also Gessmann's comments on the "Notwendigkeit einer energischen Organisation der bürgerlichen Gesellschaftsklassen" in *DZ,* 20 November 1906 (M), p, 2.

58. "Klubsitzung," 22 December 1909, Carton 96.

59. See Gessmann's statement in the "Klubsitzung," 21 and 22 June 1910, Carton 90.

60. See Hraba's autobiographical remarks, reprinted in *AZ,* 8 October 1910, pp. 6–7.

61. See Leopold Steiner's comments in "Klubsitzung," 18 May 1910.

62. "Klubsitzung," 17 March 1910.

63. See *NFP,* 15 March 1910 (M), p. 2; "Parteisitzung," 15 March 1910, Mappe XVI, Carton 96, *CPK.*

64. *AZ,* 11 June 1910, p. 4. A later invitation to Viennese party leaders in January 1911 noted that "die Zusammensetzung der Wiener Parteileitung unter Dr. Lueger nicht festgelegt war, sondern dass einmal die und einmal wiederum andere Herren als Wiener Parteileitung zusammenberufen wurden." Mappe IV/1,Carton 96, *CPK.* On the central election committee under Lueger, see the appendix to the file "Wiener Parteileitung," 9 April 1910, ibid.

65. On the plans for the new *Reichsparteileitung,* see the materials on the session of the "Parlamentarische Kommission," 28 April 1910, Mappe II/1, Carton 96; and "Klubsitzung," 12 May 1910, Carton 90.

66. See *NFP,* 11 June 1910 (M), pp. 3–4.

67. Rumpf was first introduced to the parliamentary club in March 1909 as its new secretary. See "Klubsitzung," 16 March 1909, Carton 96, *CPK.* The membership of and the responsibilites of the various officials were described in "Das Klub-Sekretariat der christlichsozialen Vereinigung," filed with the minutes of the "Parlamentarische Komission," 28 April 1910. The secretariat adjoined the office of the Lower Austrian *Bauernbund* on Hamerlingplatz 9 in the Josefstadt. See also *AZ,* 27 March 1910, pp. 3–4, a sharp critique of the intermixing of government and party agendas in the offices on the Hamerlingplatz; and Heinl, *Über ein halbes Jahrhundert.*

68. The Social Democrats immediately leaped on the significance of Gessmann's maneuvers. See "Liechtenstein abgesetzt—Gessmann Parteiführer," *AZ,* 18 March 1910, p. 4.

69. *Schicksalsjahre,* 1: 52. Pattai had told Redlich as early as December 1909 that Weiskirchner thought the mayorship beneath him. Ibid., p. 38.

70. For Gessmann's own version, with which Weiskirchner agreed, see "Klubsit-

zung," 18 May 1910, Carton 90, *CPK.* See also Kielmansegg's comments in *Kaiserhaus,* pp. 399–400.

71. "Parteileitung," 10 March 1910, Carton 96, *CPK.*

72. Compare *Rp,* 26 February 1910, p. 7 with *DV,* 29 May 1910 (M), pp. 1–3.

73. See the court testimony of Robert Gruber, Hraba's attorney, in *AZ,* 24 November 1910, p. 8. Vergani published the will in the morning edition of the *DV* on March 10 (p. 16). Lueger's testament had then to be read aloud at two party meetings on the afternoon of the same day, one involving the parliamentary delegation, the other the *Stadtrat. NFP,* 11 March 1910 (M), p. 4; *Extrablatt,* 11 March 1910 (M), p. 3. The *Reichspost* also published the will on the 11th, but added a long commentary which tried to undercut the force of the document and which essentially nominated Gessmann for the office of mayor. See 11 March 1910, p. 2.

74. "Noch etwas mehr Klarheit," *DV,* 12 June 1910 (M), p. 2.

75. See "Die Verteilung der Beute," *AZ* 12 March 1910, p. 2; "Intimes aus der christlichsozialen Häuslichkeit," ibid., 27 March 1910, pp. 3–4. Hraba later confirmed Gessmann's machinations in his second letter to Josef Porzer of the City Council's commission to investigate Hraba's corruption charges. See the text in *AZ,* 8 October 1910, pp. 6–7; and the summary in *NFP,* 8 October 1910 (M), pp. 12–13.

76. The *AZ* caught the flavor of Gessmann's ambivalent relationship to his Viennese colleagues in "Nur nicht Gessmann!" 15 March 1910, p. 1.

77. Heinl, *Über ein halbes Jahrhundert,* p. 18: "Wir hatten grosse Schwierigkeiten, vor allem bei Lueger selbst, der vermeinte, der Organisation Genüge getan zu haben, indem er in jedem Bezirk seinen Bezirksvorsteher am Platze wusste. Im übrigen stand er auf dem Standpunkt: Die Organisation bin ich. Die Bezirksvorsteher, die autoritär walteten, wussten jeden Versuch zu einer organisatorischen Gliederung zu hintertreiben. 'Was brauchen wir ein Sekretariat?' Auch jeder Einzelne erklärte: 'Ich bin der Mann der Alles macht'."

78. *NFP,* 3 October 1909 (M), p. 12 (the Hietzing *Bezirksvertretung* rejecting its treatment by the *Magistrat* as "Hausknechte des Magistrats") and ibid., 14 December 1909 (M), p. 8. Also, 12 May 1910 (M), p. 12.

79. The personal *and* strategic implications of this animosity were apparent in a run-in Gessmann had with Robert Pattai in early 1910 in the *Landtag* over the rights of female teachers to marry. The new agrarian majority voted against Pattai and the Viennese contingent in a split that foreshadowed serious tensions in the future. See *SPNÖ,* 1910, pp. 1482–86 (Pattai); 1492–94 (Wollek); 1994–95 (Spalowsky). At the end of the debate, Seitz screamed at Gessmann that while Lueger lay ill he was allowing the peasants to take over the city of Vienna (the peasants "machen, was sie wollen!" p. 1497).

80. Hierhammer gave a critical interview to the *Illustriertes Wiener Extrablatt* on 15 March 1910 (A), p. 1, indicating his dissent from Gessmann's tactics and promising to use all his influence to get Josef Neumayer elected mayor. Vergani later insisted that it had been a delegation of *Stadtrat* leaders, appealing for his help against Gessmann,

that had motivated him to launch his preemptive strike. See *DV,* 12 June 1910 (M), pp. 1–3.

81. *NFP,* 11 March 1910 (A), p. 1. For Bienerth's personal support of Gessmann, see Tschirschky's report in A 4393, 11 March 1910, Oest. 86/2/Bd. 18, *PAAA.*

82. See *Rp,* 13 March 1910, p. 1.

83. See Silberer's criticisms of Gessmann's apparent lack of nerve in "Klubsitzung," 18 May 1910, Carton 90, *CPK.* Gessmann responded that "sein Rücktritt sei nicht Inkonsequenz, sondern richtige Erkenntnis des Parteiinteresses gewesen." But he also cautioned that "um Vergani eventuell erfolgreich bekämpfen zu können, sei es auch nötig, dass er nicht vom Rathause unterstützt werde." In his testimony to Porzer later in the year, Hraba postdated Gessmann's withdrawal to March 18 or 19, which does not square with earlier reports in either the Christian Social or opposition press.

84. See the statement published in *NFP,* 14 March 1910 (N), p. 1. Victor Silberer provoked a minor scandal in late December 1911 by publishing an inside account of Weiskirchner's duplicitous and, for Gessmann, destructive tactics. See *NWJ,* 31 December 1911, pp. 2–3, and Gessmann's bitter comments to Funder, in which he asserted that Silberer's account was accurate: Gessmann to Funder, 4 January 1912, *NL Funder:* "was Silberer da gesagt, ist ja, soweit es Weiskirchner betrifft, absolut wahr."

85. *Schicksalsjahre,* 1: 54–56 (Weiskirchner "ist bei ihm [Franz Ferdinand] jetzt in grosser Gnade. Weiskirchner bezeichnet mich als den heiligen Sebastian, der das Unterrichtsportefeuille wird ertragen müssen").

86. *NFP,* 15 March 1910 (M), pp. 3–4; *AZ,* 15 March 1910, p. 2.

87. Compare the membership list of the *Stadtrat* in 1908 in *Wiener Kommunal-Kalender und Städtisches Jahrbuch für 1908* (Vienna, n.d,), p. 159, with the data in Oswald Knauer, "Der Wiener Gemeinderat von 1861–1918. Parteibildung und Wahlen," *Wiener Geschichtsblätter,* 19 (1964): 366–77.

88. As recounted by Hraba in *AZ,* 8 October 1910, p. 7.

89. *AZ,* 22 March 1910, p. 4.

90. *AZ,* 23 May 1910 (M), p. 6. See also debates in "Klubsitzung," 27 May 1910, Carton 90, *CPK.*

91. On Hraba, see *AZ,* 19 December 1908, p. 8.

92. The text of Hraba's speech is in *AZ,* 23 March 1910, pp. 2–3.

93. See the debates and resolution on 21 March 1910 condemning Hraba in Carton 1, *CS Partei: NÖ Landtag.* This file also contains the version of Hraba's speech used by the party in its disciplinary proceedings. See also *Rp,* 22 March 1910, p. 4.

94. *NFP,* 7 April 1910 (M), pp. 2–3; 8 April 1910 (M), p. 11. Throughout the affair Kunschak was among the most vociferous proponents of Gessmann's vengeance tactics.

95. Sebastian Grünbeck of the *Stadtrat* was Hraba's principal defender, but even Heinrich Hierhammer was reported as disgusted over the mud-slinging campaign, which inevitably hit some of the anti-Gessman faction as well. See *NFP,* 11 June 1910 (M), p. 4.

96. *NFP,* 9 April 1910 (M), p. 3; 10 April 1910 (M), p. 10; *DV,* 10 April 1910 (M), p. 3.

97. See Neumayer's interview with the *NFP,* in 10 June 1910 (M), p. 3.

98. See the file of 9 April 1910, the meeting of Landtagsklub's *Städtekurie,* with both Gessmann and Hraba present. Carton 1, *CS Partei: NÖ Landtag.*

99. See Weiskirchner's remarks in the "Klubsitzungen," 18 May and 24 May 1910. Baron Fuchs complained on 24 May that "trotz allem einige Klubmitglieder hinter Vergani stehen. Der Klub habe aber die Verpflichtung dem Obmann [Gessmann] Satisfaktion zu geben." Josef Schraffl agreed, suggesting that it might even be necessary to discipline those members of the club who were covertly supporting Vergani. See "Parlamentarische Kommission," 24 May 1910, Carton 90, *CPK.* See also *Schicksalsjahre,* 1: 65. Entry of 6 June 1910 ("Ich glaube, Weiskirchner steckt hinter Verganis Zeitungsangriffen gegen Gessmann"). It would be a mistake, however, to see the hostility between Gessmann and Weiskirchner simply as a pro-agrarian as opposed to a pro-urban orientation, as Vergani and others tried to argue. Weiskirchner himself admitted that this view was "distorted" at the club meeting on May 18, 1910. Both were men of the *Reichspartei,* although as a municipal official Weiskirchner had a stronger view of Vienna as a political corporation than Gessmann.

100. *NFP,* 2 June 1910 (M), p. 8.

101. See *Rp,* 16 April 1910, p. 8; 30 April 1910, p. 7; 1 May 1910, pp. 1–2, 6; *DV,* 16 April 1910 (M), p. 4; 17 April 1910 (M), pp. 3–4; 30 April 1910 (M), pp. 1–2; 1 May 1910 (M), pp. 1–3.

102. "Klubsitzung," 12 May 1910, Carton 90, *CPK.*

103. *NFP,* 8 June 1910 (M), p. 7.

104. *NFP,* 11 June 1910 (M), pp. 3–4; *DV,* 11 June 1910 (M), pp. 4–5.

105. For the background, see "Klubsitzung," 21 and 22 June 1910.

106. *NFP,* 17 June 1910 (M), p. 2, for Hraba's statement.

107. "Klubsitzung," 21 and 22 June 1910.

108. *Rp,* 23 June 1910, pp. 8–9; *NFP,* 23 June 1910 (M), p. 3.

109. *NFP,* 2 July 1910 (M), p. 13.

110. See the debates in the "Klubsitzungen," 24 May 1910 and 27 May 1910, Carton 90, *CPK.* Gessmann's strongest and most enthusiastic supporters were the Alpinists, whose majority in the club now came to work in favor of Gessmann and against the Viennese.

111. See Vergani's letter to Liechtenstein, reprinted in *NFP,* 23 June 1910 (A), p. 4; *DV,* 23 April 1910 (M), pp. 2–3.

112. "Klubsitzung," 7 July 1910, Carton 90, *CPK.*

113. *NFP,* 9 July 1910 (M), pp. 2–3; 10 July 1910 (M), p. 3.

114. *NFP,* 9 July 1910 (A), p. 3.

115. *SMZ,* 11 July 1910, p. 5.

116. Rumpf to the office of "Austria," postmarked July 1910, Mappe X/1, Carton 96, *CPK.* The addressee is not noted, but internal evidence suggests Funder.

117. *NFP,* 8 October 1910 (M), pp. 12–13.

118. See the *Arbeiter-Zeitung's* biting commentary on these procedures, 8 October 1910, p. 6.

119. For the commission's report to the Council, see *NFP*, 15 October 1910 (M), p. 12; 19 October 1910 (M), pp. 12–13. Gessmann confessed on 21/22 June 1910 that before 1896 "Die Partei habe die Auswüchse des Grosskapitals bekämpft und sofort nach der Eroberung Wiens nach Witkowitz gehen müssen. Luegers einziger Freund [in the Viennese banking world] sei Lohnstein gewesen, der ihm allerdings viel geleistet habe. Es brauche Courage, den Dingen ins Gesicht zu leuchten." Witkowitz was the site of the Rothschilds' huge iron works in Moravia. The likely reference here is to Lueger's having to compromise with Jewish banking interests in order to get his loans placed and floated.

120. *AZ*, 14 October 1910, pp. 2–3. For party reaction to Hraba's appearance, see "Klubsitzung," 18 October 1910, Carton 1, *CS Partei: NÖ Landtag*. Anton Baumann's comments ("Da er [Hraba] frech geworden sei, hat die Kommission die bekannte Resolution beschlossen") suggested that the majority's ire was as much personal as political. Petty spite knew no bounds: at its 22 September 1910 meeting the Diet club passed a resolution by Richard Wollek forbidding members from even speaking in public with Hraba.

121. *SPNÖ*, 1910, pp. 222–26. For Steinhof, see Elisabeth Koller-Glück, *Otto Wagners Kirche am Steinhof* (Vienna, 1984); and Peter Haiko, Harald Leupold-Löwenthal, and Mara Reissberger, "Die weisse Stadt—Der Steinhof in Wien," *Kritische Berichte*, 6 (1981).

122. Bielohlawek won the case, since the court found that Zipperer could not prove his assertion that Bielohlawek had misused his public offices for personal gain, but the trial's examination of Bielohlawek's past career came at some cost to his new-found dignity, and it also afforded a wonderful view of the patronage practices of the *Stadtrat* by showing the wide array of contracts opportunities open to enterprising Christian Social politicians. See *NFP*'s detailed transcripts: 15 September 1910 (A), pp. 3–5; 16 September (A), pp. 3–5; 17 September (M), pp. 11–15; 17 September (A), pp. 3–5; 18 September (M), pp. 14–16; 19 September (N), p. 11; 20 September (M), pp. 10–14; 21 September (M), pp. 13–16; 21 September (A), pp. 4–5. The court's verdict, with a detailed opinion, is in 22 September (M), pp. 15–16.

123. *SPNÖ*, 1910, pp. 237.

124. Ibid., p. 239.

125. Ibid., p. 246, as well as his long critique on pp. 226–32.

126. See Silberer's and Müller's comments at the "Klubsitzung," 22 September 1910, *CS Partei: NÖ Landtag*. In spite of the pleas for unity and organization, Franz Spalowsky noted at this meeting that "Hraba stehe nicht allein da" and wanted all connections between the party and the Hietzing organization "Zukunft" abrogated. Vengeance still held the upper hand. A similar confession of party disorganization occurred as early as July 1910, when Anastasias Guggenburg complained to Gessmann that the parliamentary club needed more coherence, to which Gessmann responded defensively that many parliamentary deputies did not even bother to show up for club or commission discussions. "Klubsitzung," 7 July 1910.

127. See the "Klubsitzung," 8 November 1910. *CS Partei: NÖ Landtag*. The Diet

Club had also broken into semi-official agrarian and urban subgroups, which met separately on matters of special interest to them. The fragmentation of urban vs. rural which so plagued the party on the national level after 1911 was thus informally anticipated on the provincial level in Lower Austria.

128. *NFP,* 2 October 1910 (M), p. 6.

129. Neumayer did not have to mention that the municipal administrations of Czech and Polish cities had consistently boycotted the Vienna-based Austrian *Städtetag* movement when he called for closer cooperation between Austrian and Hungarian municipalities.

130. For the consequences of this shift in terms of those who sought to maintain an independent (that is, nonassimilated) Czech identity in Vienna, see Glettler, *Die Wiener Tschechen,* pp. 347ff., 368–71; and Neumayer's letter to the leadership of the *Nationalverband,* 22 October 1912, requesting the assistance of the *Verband* in his efforts to keep Vienna "German," Carton 2, *NL Gross.* For the revival of *Lex Kolisko* agitation in Vienna in 1912–13, for which the Christian Socials were not primarily responsible, see Z. 12220, 30 October 1913, Carton 2130, 22 *MI Präs.* The *Bürgerklub* formally joined the nationalist association Ostmark as a "Gründer" in May 1913. Z. 464, Carton 71, *CPW.*

131. See the club meetings on 5 and 28 October 1910, *CS Partei: NÖ Landtag.*

132. *NFP,* 3 October 1910 (N). pp. 1–2; *AZ,* 3 October 1910, pp. 1–3.

133. See "Klubsitzung," 29 March 1911, Carton 90, *CPK;* and Tschirschky's insightful commentary on the election in A 9953, 22 June 1911, Oest. 91/Bd. 16, *PAAA.*

134. See *DV,* 20 March 1911 (M), p. 3, dismissing the plan as biased toward the "clerical wing" of the party; and the files in Mappe IV/1, Carton 96, *CPK.* The Laborites received only 3 of the 27 seats, which outraged Kunschak.

135. For some high points, see *DV,* 6 June 1911 (M), p. 1; 9 June 1911 (M), p. 3; 11 June 1911 (M), pp. 1–2; *Rp,* 7 June 1911, p. 2; 8 June 1911, pp. 1–2; and 10 June 1911, p. 3; and the savage essay on "Gessmann, Vergani und Friedmann" in *AZ,* 9 June 1911, pp. 1–2.

136. *Rp,* 11 June 1911, p. 6; *AZ,* 18 June 1911, p. 2.

137. See Z. 3368, 8 April 1911, 18 April 1911, 21 April 1911, 20 May 1911, Carton 2251 34/2, *MI Präs.;* as well as "Erweiterte Sitzung der Parteivertretung, 14. Juni 1911," *VGAB.*

138. Z. 3236, 5 April 1911, 22 April 1911, 3 June 1911, Carton 2251.

139. For the results, see the official police and *Bezirkshauptmannschaft* reports in I/2b2, Nr. 2045, 1911, *Statt. Präs., NÖLA;* and the "Vergleichende Darstellung der bei den Reichsratswahlen der Jahre 1907 und 1911 für die christlichsozialen abgegebenen Stimmen," in Carton 96, *CPK.*

140. "Wiener Parteileitung," 12 April 1911, Carton 96, *CPK.*

141. See the reports in Z. 3639, 29 April 1911; 6 May 1911; 13 May 1911; 20 May 1911; 27 May 1911; 10 June 1911, in Carton 2252, 34/2, *MI Präs.;* and I/2b2, Nr. 2045, 27 April 1911, 30 May 1911, 7 June 1911, *Statt. Präs., NÖLA.*

142. Ibid., police report of 11 May 1911; *Rp,* 1 June 1911, p. 3; 6 June 1911, p. 1;

9 June 1911, p. 1; 10 June 1911, p. 1. Max Friedmann, the Liberal candidate for one of the seats in the Innere Stadt and a wealthy Jewish industrialist, put up a considerable amount of the money needed. See also *CSAZ,* 22 April 1911, pp. 1–2.

143. See *Rp,* 10 June 1911, p. 2; *AZ,* 9 June 1911, p. 1. On Pattai, *AZ,* 20 June 1911, p. 4.

144. *AZ,* 10 June 1911, p. 4; 11 June 1911, p. 5; 12 June 1911, p. 2; *Rp,* 2 June 1911, p. 2. In 1910 the Viennese police noted that the Social Democrats tried to win bourgeois voters over to their *Teuerung* protests. See Z. 9300, 11 September 1910, Carton 1634, 15/3, *MI Präs.* See also the defensive and not terribly convincing reply in *Rp* ("Was hat das Parlament für die Beamten getan?"), 7 June 1911, p. 3.

145. See *DSZ,* 1911, pp. 92–93, 106–7, 121–29, 136–41, 170–75, 193–95; *Österreichische Postbeamten-Zeitung,* 1911, pp. 117–19; *Allgemeines österreichisches Staatsbeamten-Blatt,* 1911, pp. 153–54, 173, 213–15, 229–32. The *Zentralverband* claimed most of the credit—in the sense that it had been the *Beamten* and not the "masses" that had deserted the Christian Socials in the aftermath of the elections for the latter's defeat. See the arguments in 7 July 1911, pp. 229–30.

146. See *AZ,* 11 June 1911, p. 5; 12 June 1911, p. 2; *Rp,* 9 June 1911, p. 2; *Deutsch-österreichische Lehrer-Zeitung,* 1911, pp. 26–27, 153–54, 156.

147. For sample copies of the *Blitzlichter,* see Carton 8, *NL Marchet.*

148. See *Der Reichsratswähler,* 11 May 1911.

149. This does not include votes for party renegades, who received 10,299 votes on the first ballot.

150. For the official statistical results of the Viennese elections, see *Statistisches Jahrbuch der Stadt Wien für das Jahr 1911,* pp. 126–27, and Friedrich Adler, "Fünfzehn Jahre allgemeines Wahlrecht in Wien und Niederösterreich," *K,* 5 (1911–12): 303–11. I have rounded results to the nearest thousand. Voter turnout was higher in 1911 than 1907 (357,260 as opposed to 333,874), but since more ballots were declared invalid or empty in 1911, the final aggregate of valid ballots was not as divergent (338,283 in 1911; 324,612 in 1907). Since the percentage turnout (actual voters to registered voters) was about 90 percent for both 1907 and 1911, the increase in participation in 1911 reflected the natural increase in voter registration between 1907 and 1911. Aside from voter shifts to the Social Democrats and German nationalists, almost 4,000 ballots were cast for random, nonofficial candidates, which the *Magistrat* grouped under the general category of "zersplittert." The Christian Socials lost six seats to *Deutschfortschritt-lichen* (Friedmann, Kuranda, Neumann, Hock, Denk, and Ganser), two to German nationalists (Waber and Pollauf), one to the *Sozialpolitiker* Ofner (a variant of the first category) and one to the professional anticlerical Zenker.

151. On the Gessmann-Gross negotiations, see *Rp,* 15 June 1911, p. 3; 16 June 1911, p. 1; *AZ,* 17 June 1911, p. 1; and the revealing story of Gessmann having overreached himself in *DV,* 30 June 1911 (M), p. 1. Bienerth, who had avoided involving himself in the campaign directly, was a principal mediator in these negotiations, which served to discredit him when they fell apart.

152. *Rp,* 16 June 1911, pp. 1–2; 17 June 1911, p. 3.

153. *Rp,* 21 June 1911, p. 2. For Jewish views of the campaign, see *ÖW,* 28 (1911): 310, 346–47, 361, 381, 409–10.

154. During the war Josef Sigmund calculated the effect of proportional suffrage in Vienna, based on the unfavorable vote ratios of 1911, and found that the Christian Socials would still pick up 14 seats, as opposed to 17 for the Social Democrats, and 2 for the Liberals. See his statistical table in Carton 36, *CPK.* If one uses ratios based on the 1912 Fourth Curia ballot, the distribution of parliamentary seats would have been Christian Socials 15, Social Democrats 14, Liberals 3, and Czech Nationalists 1. Tschirschky, noting the more favorable results for the Rathaus in 1912, commented to Berlin: "Gerade durch seinen übermässigen Lärm und durch die Uebertreibungen der ihm nahestehenden Wiener Blätter hatte aber der Freisinn selbst solche Wähler, die für die christlichsoziale Partei [in 1911] unzuverlässig geworden waren, dieser wieder näher gebracht. Das freisinnige Bündnis mit der Sozialdemokratie behagte den Wiener Bürgern gleichfalls nicht. . . . Auch die deutschnationalen Wählerschaften versagten dem Freisinn die Gefolgschaft und gaben, namentlich bei den Stichwahlen, für die Christlichsozialen den Ausschlag." A 8077, 6 May 1912, Oest. 70/Bd. 48, *PAAA.*

155. The hard, uncompromising stance of the Social Democrats toward their clerical enemy may be seen indirectly in the debate at the "Erweiterte Sitzung der Parteivertretung" on 14 June 1911, *VGAB,* where the leadership adopted as its slogan for the runoff elections "Gegen die Christlichsozialen!" This was carried to the point that in the few cases where dissident Christian Social candidates were pitted against each other for a run-off, the socialists ordered their voters to abstain from voting. The election also brought new faces (and a new generation) into the socialist party machine: Fritz Adler officially joined the party secretariat in May 1911 at an annual salary of 5,000 crowns. See "Parteivertretung," 9 May 1911.

156. *AZ,* 18 June 1911, p. 7.

157. *Aufsätze, Reden, Briefe,* 11: 234.

158. *AZ,* 18 June 1911, p. 6.

159. Karl Leuthner, "Der Niedergang einer Parteidespotie," *Sozialistische Monatshefte,* 13 July 1911, pp. 875–78. For similar comments by the bourgeois anticlericals, see Ernst Victor Zenker, "Der 20. Juni," *Die Wage,* 14 (1911): 586–87.

160. "Gegen den Klerikalismus," *AZ,* 17 June 1911, p. 2; and "Grossstädtischer Klerikalismus," 18 June 1911, pp. 1–2.

161. Max Adler, "'Christlichsozial'," *AZ,* 11 June 1911, pp. 2–3.

162. Austerlitz, "Gessmann als Erzieher," pp. 97–101.

163. A 9953, 22 June 1911, Oest. 91/Bd. 16, *PAAA.* The Christian Socials, in turn, privately heaped scorn on Bienerth, blaming his ineptitude for their misfortune. See Tucher's report of 30 June 1911 in *BHSA.*

164. *AZ,* 20 June 1911, p. 5.

165. See also A 10096, 23 June 1911, Oest. 91/Bd. 16, *PAAA.* On the interest-based agenda of the election, see also the perceptive comments in Emil Lederer, "An-

gestellten- und Beamtensozialpolitik," *ASSP,* 33 (1911): 980–84. In 1911 Lederer feared the Austrian *Beamten* were moving toward emulation of the Social Democrats, if not actually to an overt sympathy with them, not on cultural but on economic and military issues. By 1913, however, he had modified his views, and now argued that, if anything, *Beamten* radicalism was closer to a form of professional, anarcho-syndicalism in its avoidance of conventional political channels (other than as an outlet for narcissistic self-gratification). See "Die Bewegung der öffentlichen Beamten und Beamtensozialpolitik," ibid., 37 (1913): 666–67.

166. Gessmann to Beck, 27 June 1911, Carton 35, *NL Beck;* and Gessmann's note to Funder in *Vom Gestern,* pp. 459–60. For Funder's testament to Gessmann's extraordinary activities in 1911, see *Rp,* 11 January 1912, pp. 1–2. This article was clearly Funder's attempt to restore Gessmann's reputation in the party.

167. See Gessmann to Funder, 22 September 1911; 12 February 1912, *NL Funder.*

168. *Rp,* 8 January 1912, pp. 1–2; 9 January 1912, pp. 8–9. According to Gessmann, Weiskirchner began scheming to displace Neumayer almost immediately after his exit from the Cabinet, including a plan to take over chairmanship of the *Bürgerklub* from Steiner by pushing the latter into a vice-mayorship. Gessmann to Funder, 22 September 1911.

169. "Neumayers Sturz," *AZ,* 20 December 1912, p. 1. Soon after Weiskirchner's accession to office, he paid back his debts to those who supported his candidacy. The salaries of the three vice-mayors were raised to 12,000 crowns; those of the other members of the *Stadtrat* and the various *Bezirksvorsteher* to 6,000 crowns; and for Leopold Steiner, as the *Oberkurator* of the Lower Austrian *Hypothekenbank,* to 12,000 crowns. On the Lower Austrian side, members of the Provincial Executive Committee now received 12,300 crowns, and the *Landmarschall* 20,600. In addition, Weiskirchner's own salary was increased to 40,000 crowns, and an additional bonus was given to Josef Porzer by virtue of his appointment as deputy *Landmarschall.* All-in-all, a nice day's work. See *AZ,* 26 April 1913, p. 3.

170. A copy of the "Parteistatut der Wiener christlichsozialen Partei" is in *CPW,* Carton 76. For a commentary on its weaknesses, see Josef K. Pultar, "Erwägungen zum Statut der Wiener christlich-sozialen Partei," *VW,* 9 (1918): 70–76. On its genesis, see the reports in *DV,* 8 October 1911 (M), p. 4; 10 October 1911 (M), p. 4; 11 October 1911 (M), p. 6; and *Rp,* 19 October 1911, p. 7; 20 October 1911, p. 2; 22 October 1911, p. 8.

171. The membership reports which were generated confirm this assumption. In the Landstrasse, for example, the Laborite club (the *Christlichsozialer Arbeiter-Wählerverein*) claimed 2,200 members, while the traditional centerpoint of bourgeois power, the *Eintracht,* led by Paul Spitaler, had only 524. The latter club maintained dictatorial control of the District Election Committee, however, and Spitaler dominated the ward as *Bezirksvorsteher.* Of the 13 City Council seats in Landstrasse, Spitaler's *Eintracht* held 8, whereas the Laborites got none! Z. 345, Carton 71; and Z. 762, Carton 72, *CPW.*

172. Letter of Josef Jünger and Ignaz Ludikowsky to the party secretariat, 2 December 1912, Z. 420, ibid.

173. The archives of the *Sekretariat* are in *CPW,* Carton 70–77, *AVA.* For its organization, see Z. 251, Carton 71. For a concise survey of its activities in the first year of operations, see its "Tätigkeits-Bericht für 1912," Z. 379, Carton 71.

174. See, for example, the files in Carton 70 (1911–12), Z. 32, 35, 123, 132; Carton 71 (1912–13): Z. 208, 226.

175. See the protocol of the *erweiterten Parteirat,* 23 May 1912, Z. 226; and Z. 330, 357, 371, and 481.

176. See, for example, Z. 33, 41, 65, 83, 105, and 128, Carton 70; Z. 290, Carton 71; Z. 679, Carton 72; Z. 892 and 929, Carton 73.

177. See, for example, the "Protokoll aufgenommen von der Christlichsozialen Parteileitung am 23. März 1912," which tried to settle a feud in Margarethen between the allies of Karl Hallmann and Josef Sturm. Z. 105, Carton 70; as well as Z. 929, Carton 73.

178. On Liberal election agitation in 1912, see Z. 2386, Carton 2130, 22, *MI Präs.*

179. For Christian Social preparations, see "Tätigkeits-Bericht für 1912," pp. 6–17, as well as Z. 206 and 226, Carton 71, *CPW;* and Z. 3467, Carton 2130, 22, *MI Präs.*

180. See Pö 53, 1912, Carton 76, *MKFF.*

181. Gessmann to Weiskirchner, 20 March 1914, Z. 855, Carton 73, *CPW.*

182. For the decline of the food prices, which stabilized with good harvests in 1912–13, as well as for the general economic recovery, see *Statistisches Jahrbuch der Stadt Wien für das Jahr 1914,* pp. 590–606; "Report on the Foreign Trade of Austria-Hungary for the Year 1912," *Diplomatic and Consular Reports,* No. 5205 (London, 1913), pp. 2–7; "Commercial Review of Austria," *Daily Consular and Trade Reports,* May 9, 1913, No. 108, pp. 705–7; July 28, 1914, No. 175, pp. 529–44. Weiskirchner also had the advantage of taking office after the temporary commercial and financial recession caused by the Balkan Wars in late 1912, which led to unemployment, export blockages, and small business bankruptcies.

183. For sample coalition negotiations, see Z. 67, Carton 70; Z. 607, 650–51, 654, Carton 72; Z. 895 and 917, Carton 73. The compacts usually involved agreements by the Christian Socials to allocate job patronage and some low-level elected offices to the nationalists. See for example the "Wahlübereinkommen" signed in the Landstrasse on 20 February 1914, which allotted 6 seats on the *Bezirksvertretung* to the local nationalists, with the proviso that they must be distributed among the four rival nationalist clubs in the district. Z. 895, Carton 73. As the unsuccessful negotiations with nationalist city leaders in February 1914 demonstrated, however, there were clear limits to the concessions the party leadership would make. They refused to allow ward compromises to bind them on city-wide strategy, and they were loath to give away *Landtag* or *Reichsrat* seats. They also refused to allow the establishment of an independent nationalist club in the City Council, insisting that anyone elected join the Christian Social *Bürgerklub.* When local district leaders were circularized about their views of such compacts with

the nationalists, opinions varied, with some leaders willing to support such practices, but others arguing that the nationalist clubs in their districts were too small and disorganized to take seriously. See the reports in Z. 763/Z. 917; and *AZ,* 12 February 1914, p. 5; 19 February 1914, p. 4; and *ODR,* 20 February 1914, p. 10; 22 February 1914, pp. 1–2.

184. See Stöckler to Weiskirchner, 10 December 1913, Z. 682, Carton 72, *CPW.* By 1913 Weiskirchner and Karl Hermann Wolf, the leader of the German Radicals, were on such good terms that he was asking the mayor to get jobs for his friends. See Wolf to Weiskirchner, 22 August 1913, Z. 667, Carton 72.

185. *Christlichsoziale Landstrasser Zeitung,* 5 November 1913, p. 1.

186. Z. 12293/1912, Carton 2130, 22, *MI Präs.;* A 15073, 22 September 1911, Oest. 70/Bd. 48, *PAAA.* The party leadership had planned demonstrations since late August. See "Parteivertretung u. nied. österr. Landesparteivertretung 24. August 1911," *VGAB,* and Rudolf G. Ardelt, *Friedrich Adler. Probleme einer Persönlichkeitsentwicklung um die Jahrhundertwende* (Vienna, 1984), pp. 217–20.

187. See Weiskirchner's letter to Josef Grünbeck, president of the *Hausbesitzerverband,* assuring him that the new *Bauordnung* would contain nothing injurious to real estate interests. 26 January 1914, Z. 726, Carton 72, *CPW.* For the first year of Weiskirchner's administration, see *Die Gemeinde-Verwaltung der Stadt Wien im Jahre 1913. Bericht des Bürgermeisters Dr. Richard Weiskirchner* (Vienna, 1914). The high point of the year, according to this report, was the centennial celebration of the Battle of Nations at Leipzig, which Weiskirchner, playing on a mild German nationalist theme, ably exploited: "Der patriotischen Aufforderung des Bürgermeisters folgend, hatte die Stadt aus Anlass der Jubelfeier festlichen Schmuck angelegt. Von den Dächern der Häuser wehten Fahnen in den Reichs- und Stadtfarben und im Festkleide zog die Jugend in die Schulen, denn in sämtlichen Volks- und Bürgerschulen wurde eine würdige Feierlichkeit abgehalten." Ibid., p. 10.

188. See Franz Bittner to Weiskirchner, 20 May 1914, Z. 1012, Carton 73, *CPW.*

189. For example, (as responses) Suess to Weiskirchner, 18 October 1913, I.N. 24731; and Baernreither to Weiskirchner, 10 April 1915, I.N. 29078, *Handschriftensammlung.* See also Weiskirchner's staged visit to the Emperor to receive Franz Joseph's gratitude for the "achievements" of the new city administration. *Rp,* 8 January 1914, p. 1. Two of the three Christian Social vice-mayors showed up for the 1914 *Industriellenball. Rp,* 3 February 1914, p. 7.

190. This was then broadcast around the city by a special party *Flugblatt.* Ironically, the financial directorate had already decided to go easy on late payers, and its director, Oskar Kokstein, informed Weiskirchner that they had already anticipated his request. This small detail was not mentioned in party propaganda, however. See Z. 439, 14 February 1913, Carton 72. The party also advertised the extent of the city's purchases from craft suppliers. See the "Gemeindelieferungen durch Genossenschaften 1902–1912," Z. 516, ibid.

191. Z. 435, Carton 71, *CPW.*

192. Kielmansegg, *Kaiserhaus,* p. 363.

193. For the agenda of the former, see *Die Tätigkeit der deutschen sozialdemokratischen Abgeordneten im österreichischen Reichsrat. 1. Heft (17. Juli bis 20. Dezember 1911)* (Vienna, 1912).

194. See "Verhandlungsschrift über die Konstituierende Sitzung der Christlichsozialen Vereinigung deutscher Abgeordneter am 4. Juli 1911," Carton 90, *CPK.*

195. On the consequences of the changes, see *Rp,* 5 July 1911, pp. 1–2.

196. On Ebenhoch's resignation, see "Klubsitzung," 14 November 1911, Carton 90, *CPK.*

197. Between 1911 and 1913 a series of regional congresses were undertaken: for example, the Viennese *Parteitag* of 6 January 1912; the Lower Austrian congresses on 16 June 1912 and 18 May 1913; the Upper Austrian assembly of 17 June 1912; and a Styrian congress of the Pantz group on 19 January 1913. A *Reichsparteitag* did not take place, however.

198. "Klubsitzung," 17 July 1911, Carton 90; *Rp,* 20 July 1911, pp. 1–2.

199. "Klubsitzung," 19 Juli 1911.

200. Gessmann to Funder, 12 February, 1912, *NL Funder,* Carton 2. Stöckler had to read a statement of loyalty to the parliamentary club in late October, denying rumors of his negotiations with the agrarians and assuring his colleagues of the loyalty of the Lower Austrians. "Klubsitzung," 24 October 1911; *Rp,* 25 October 1911, p. 2.

201. See "Klubsitzung," 4 June 1913, Carton 90.

202. *DV,* 7 July 1911 (M), pp. 4–5; 27 July 1911 (M), pp. 1–2.

203. "Klubsitzung," 19 October 1911, Carton 90, *CPK.* Liechtenstein's comments were reported by von Baechlé, who then described the desolate conditions of the Viennese party. The Viennese *Parteileitung,* headed by Liechtenstein, issued a communiqué noting that the final revisions and approval of the *Bürgerklub's* draft statute would have to await the forthcoming Viennese *Parteitag,* but added that the Christian Social workers had the right to expect appropriate representation in the newly created *weiteren Parteirat.* Funder was at this meeting and advised the parliamentary club to adopt a wait-and-see attitude toward the Viennese events. Fuchs thought that the controversies in Vienna were essentially rooted in conflicts of warring personalities, but the emphasis in the communiqué on defending the rights of Kunschak's forces suggests that larger policy issues were also at stake. Two days earlier the parliamentary club had met and adopted a resolution by Wilhelm Miklas urging (and warning) the Viennese to preserve party unity in their deliberations and supporting the idea of a *Reichsparteitag.* The eight-man urban contingent also offered a motion welcoming the new statute, while also suggesting that the party's organization would have to be put on a "wide democratic basis." See "Klubsitzung," 17 October 1911.

204. Gessmann to Funder, 4 January 1912, *NL Funder.*

205. "Klubsitzung," 19 October 1911.

206. See Hauser's *Testament,* dated 15 July 1911, reprinted in Josef Honeder, "Prälat Johann Nepomuk Hauser (1866–1927)." Dissertation, University of Vienna, 1964, appendix, p. 35.

207. See "Klubsitzung," 24 October 1911, Carton 90. Ebenhoch: "Die Partei habe immer schlechte Erfahrungen gemacht. Von 'Fall zu Fall' könnte es uns gelingen, selbst die Unterstützung der Regierung zu erhalten." Johann Mayer: "Wir werden jetzt auch nicht mehr Dank haben als früher. Wir haben früher auch Wünsche gehabt, and als Regierungspartei nichts erreicht. Jetzt können wir das Gewissen des Hauses spielen." On the political anarchy of Gautsch's last weeks in office, see Tschirschky's report in A 16517, 13 October 1911, Oest. 70/Bd. 48 *PAAA* ("Hülflos steht der Ministerpräsident inmitten dieses Chaos da"). For the initial policy, see "Klubsitzung," 19 July 1911. On Gautsch's relations with the Social Democrats, which the September 1911 riots in Vienna quickly soured, see the report in A 16196, 10 October 1911, Oest. 91/Bd. 16. The negative reaction on the part of many Christian Socials may have evinced not merely their outrage at not being consulted by Gautsch but the interests of their new agrarian leadership, since Gautsch's negotiations with Kramář were, at least in Kramář's mind, leading to an anti-agrarian coalition ministry. Redlich reported on October 19 that Kramář thought "die städtischen Parteien der Tschechen wollen den Ausgleich, sie wollen mit den Deutschen gemeinsam Österreich vom agrarischen Druck befreien." *Schicksalsjahre,* 1: 104. For Christian Socials, see the "Klubsitzung," 19 October 1911.

208. On the constitution of the new Cabinet, see Alexander Fussek, "Minister-Präsident Karl Graf Stürgkh." Dissertation, University of Vienna, 1959, pp. 33ff; Frank E. Norgate, "The Internal Policies of the Stürgkh Government, November 1911–March 1914: A Study in a Holding Action." Dissertation, New York University, 1978; and Czedik, *Zur Geschichte,* 4: 340–432. On Stürgkh, see the portraits in Kielmansegg, *Kaiserhaus,* pp. 90–93; Sieghart, *Die letzten Jahrzehnte einer Grossmacht,* pp. 148–53; Ehrhart, *Im Dienste des alten Österreich,* pp. 301ff.; Joseph Maria Baernreither, *Der Verfall des Habsburgerreiches und die Deutschen. Fragmente eines politischen Tagebuches,* ed. Oskar Mitis (Vienna, 1938), pp. 266–73; and John Leslie, "The Antecedents of Austria-Hungary's War Aims: Policies and Policy-Makers in Vienna and Budapest before and during 1914," in Elisabeth Springer and Leopold Kammerhofer, eds., *Archiv und Forschung. Das Haus-, Hof- und Staatsarchiv in seiner Bedeutung für die Geschichte Österreichs und Europas* (Vienna, 1993), pp. 348–56. It is true that Hussarek was later dismissive of Christian Social parliamentary tactics after 1911 (see Helmut Rumpler, *Max Hussarek. Nationalitäten und Nationalitätenpolitik in Österreich im Sommer des Jahres 1918* [Graz, 1965], p. 11), but his presence in the ministry was bound to be reassuring to the more clerical-minded members of the party.

209. Tschirschky's claims to this effect as early as December 1911 eventually became a leitmotiv of the regime. See A 21380, 22 December 1911, Oest. 91/Bd. 16, *PAAA.*

210. See *Die Tätigkeit,* Heft 1, pp. 8–10, 23–26; *Die Tätigkeit der deutschen sozial-*

demokratischen Abgeordneten im österreichischen Reichsrat. 2. Heft (5. März bis 5. Juli 1912) (Vienna, 1912), pp. 7–10.

211. *Die Tätigkeit,* Heft 1, p. 24; "Klubsitzungen," 17 and 22 November 1911, Carton 90, *CPK.* On the harmlessness of these motions, see Franz Loser's comment on the 17th: "Abg. Loser tritt für die Freigabe der Abstimmung ein und betont, ob es nicht diskutierbar wäre, die radikalsten Anträge anzunehmen, um die Sozialdemokraten ad absurdum zu führen. Gefahr sei ja keine, dass die Beschlüsse des Hauses ausgeführt würden."

212. *Die Tätigkeit,* Heft 1, pp. 37–39. Tomschik's original request would have cost 69 million crowns, but he compromised at 38 million to gain the support of the bourgeois parties.

213. See *Die Tätigkeit,* Heft 2, pp. 49–50; *Die Tätigkeit der deutschen sozialdemokratischen Abgeordneten im österreichischen Reichsrat. 3. Heft. (24. September 1912 bis 20. Juni 1913)* (Vienna, 1913), pp. 30–31; for the Christian Socials' tactics, see "Klubsitzungen," 27 June 1912 and 2 July 1912, Carton 90, *CPK.*

214. *SP,* 1912, p. 5010. On Pantz's and Kemetter's secession, see the police report in *NÖLA,* XIV/220, Nr. 11211, 4 July 1913.

215. See the extensive series of police reports sent to the Lower Austrian *Statthalter* in XIV/220, Z. 25, 1911–1913 *NÖLA.* Each of the three German parties had an association for organizing railway employees: the *Reichsbund deutscher Eisenbahner Österreichs* (German national); the *Allgemeiner Rechtsschutz- und Gewerkschaftsverein* (Social Democratic); and the *Verkehrsbund* (Christian Social), in addition to which both the Social Democrats and the *bürgerlich* parties organized suboccupational groups as well. The largest single association was the *Allgemeiner Rechtsschutz-Verein* with 60,000 members. On policy issues the *Eisenbahner* movement was not monolithic, since the *Beamten* resented attempts to cater to the demands of the *Diener* and *Unterbeamten,* which did not respond to their salary concerns. But each group was sufficiently aggrieved of government indifference to consider radical political options, including the possibility of instigating passive resistance on the railways. It was because of this possibility of strikes that the police devoted so much attention to the Viennese *Eisenbahn* movement.

216. *Die Tätigkeit,* Heft 3, p. 30; *SP,* 1912, *Beilage* 1616.

217. See the numerous petitions in Carton 96, Mappe XVII, *CPK.*

218. "Klubsitzungen," 29 October 1912, 2 December 1912, and 27 December 1912.

219. See the letter from the president of the Christian Social *Verkehrsbund,* transmitted by Weiskirchner to the club, 12 November 1912, Carton 96, Mappe XVII, *CPK.* For the vote, see *SP,* 1912, p. 6669.

220. On the party and the Italian Legal Faculty, see the report to Franz Ferdinand in Nr. 2678, 7 April 1914, Carton 146, *MKFF;* and "Klubsitzung," 20 October 1911, Carton 90, *CPK.* For Lueger's original concerns with the canal program, see above, Chapter 1. Koerber's original proposal called for the construction of four canals or waterways—

from the Danube to the Oder, from the Danube to the Moldau, from the Danube-Oder canal to the Elbe, and from the Danube-Oder canal to the Vistula and the Dniestr. The 1912 version provided only for the construction of the Danube-Vistula-Dniestr connection by 1927. See Josef von Bachlé's motion of 5 March 1912, signed by Stöckler and several of his allies, in *SP,* 1912, *Beilage* 1112. See also the party debates in the "Klub-sitzungen" of 28 November 1911, 20 March 1912, and 28 March 1912; as well as *AZ,* 28 March 1912, pp. 3–4. The Upper Austrians were much more negative, however, and so, had such a bill come up for a vote, this too might have been publicly divisive.

221. The Cabinet had to resubmit this legislation to the *Abgeordnetenhaus* in November 1911, the previous draft having died with Bienerth's dissolution of the House in March 1911. On the later history of the social insurance bills, see *Die Tätigkeit:* Heft 1, pp. 26–27, 54; Heft 2, pp. 62–63; Heft 3, p. 58; and *Die Tätigkeit der deutschen sozialdemokratischen Abgeordneten im österreichischen Reichsrat. 4. Heft (21. Oktober 1913 bis 29. Mai 1914)* (Vienna, 1914), pp. 38–40. The final drafts of the components of the insurance bill were virtually completed by the main committee of the *Abgeordnetenhaus* by June 1914. Unfortunately, the war intervened. For Christian Social reactions, see "Klubsitzung," 6 December 1911, at which Victor Kienböck gave an overview of the new government draft for the club; as well as the discussion in "Klubsitzung," 12 March 1912. The persistent respect for and loyalty to Albert Gessmann on the part of some of the Alpinists (against the Viennese *Bürgerklub* faction) was also apparent in these discussions. Josef Schraffl supported the bill since "die jetzige Vorlage die Grundsätze und Intentionen des Vaters der Sozialversicherung Exz. Dr. Gessmann noch im wesentlichen enthalte."

222. "Klubsitzung," 10 June 1913. For the *Krankenkassen* issue, see *AZ,* 19 March 1914, p. 9.

223. On the 1912 military laws, see Gunther E. Rothenberg, *The Army of Francis Joseph* (West Lafayette, 1976), pp. 130–37, 159–66; Norgate, "The Internal Policies," pp. 109–17; and the report in A 10937, 20 June 1912, Oest. 91/Bd.16, *PAAA;* as well as Bardolff's file on the negotiations between Austria and Hungary on the military bill in Mappe c, "Brioni 1912," Carton 180, *MKFF.* For the Christian Socials, see the "Klubsitzung," 10 June 1912, which contains the remarkable communication of Baron Heinold, acting for Stürgkh, demanding that the parties observe both a strict schedule of debate in committee and in plenum on the Army Law and that they refrain from offering major amendments. Heinold demanded a final reading of the bill by June 25. The club voted on the 12th to cooperate.

224. See the memoir by Baechlé and other Christian Social politicians on the *Kriegerkorpsgesetz* in Ps. 150, 24 Oktober 1912, Carton 80, *MKFF.* The government's bill was first submitted to parliament on 10 November 1907 and thereafter languished. See *SB,* 1907, *Beilage* 507.

225. Stürgkh was alleged to be willing to support the bill, but the Emperor refused, since the Imperial Patent of 1852 strictly regulated the carrying of arms by anyone other than military or police forces. See *RGBl,* 1852, Nr. 223.

226. Leopold Steiner, as assistant chairman of the Viennese party, made a point of writing to Jodok Fink in September 1913 welcoming the "friendly relationship" between the two organizations. See Steiner to Jodok Fink, 5 September 1913, Z. 553, Carton 72, *CPW.* On the election of 1913, see *AZ,* 15 October, 1913, pp. 1–4; and the extensive files, Z. 588, Z. 607, and Z. 614, in Carton 72, *CPW.* Mataja is discussed below, in Chapter 7, in the context of Christian Social politics during the First World War.

227. For Stürgkh's tactics in coupling the *Dienstpragmatik* to the tax bill, see the "Ministerratsprotokoll," 19 October 1912, *Ministerratsprotokolle,* Carton 27. The 1912, 1913, and 1914 Cabinet protocols are, unfortunately, almost the only prewar files that survived from the 1927 *Justizpalast* fire.

228. On the history of the *kleiner Finanzplan,* see Bardolff's "Referat über den derzeitigen Stand des Finanzplanes," Z. 3157, 1913, Carton 113, *MKFF;* and *Die Tätigkeit,* Heft 4, pp. 9–25.

229. For a socialist overview, see Karl Renner, "Steuerkämpfe und Steuerreform," *K,* 7 (1913–14): 193–99.

230. This would have resulted from approximately 40 heller being added to their annual tax bill. For a statistical review of the consequences of the tax reforms on the Viennese curial system, see the report of the *Magistrat* prepared for Weiskirchner, "Wirkungen der Steuernovelle vom 23. Jänner 1914 auf das Wahlrecht," in Z. 955, Carton 73, *CPW.*

231. *Schicksalsjahre,* 1: 216–17.

232. *SP,* 1914, pp. 9466–74; "Klubsitzung," 21 January 1914, Carton 90, *CPK.* Heinrich Mataja provided a party-slanted overview of these events in *Die Abstimmung über den Finanzplan* (Vienna, 1914), which was then widely distributed to local party officials.

233. "Wir, die Klassenpartei der Arbeiter, haben den Beamten die Treue bewahrt, während ihre eigenen Vertreter sie in letzter Stunde nochmals verraten wollten." *AZ,* 22 January 1914, p. 2. Anticipating success in his tactics for the tax bill, Stürgkh secured the Cabinet's approval to sanction the *Dienstpragmatik* on 31 December 1913. See "Ministerratsprotokoll," 31 December 1913. On the *Dienstpragmatik* see Anton Pace, ed., *Die Dienstpragmatik (Gesetz über das Dienstverhältnis der Staatsbeamten u. der Staatsdienerschaft)* (Vienna, 1914), which is a useful compendium of materials on the genesis of the law, including selections from the parliamentary debates; Max Burckhard, "Der Entwurf einer Dienstpragmatik der Staatsbeamten," *NFP,* 20 April 1910 (M), pp. 1–2; and the debates in *SP,* 1912, pp. 6486–6556, particularly the discussions by Glöckel, pp. 6490–6505, and Kemetter, pp. 6516–24. The final version, as modified by the *Herrenhaus,* passed the *Abgeordnetenhaus* on 27 December 1912. For the final result, see Otto Glöckel, "Der Kampf um das Koalitionsrecht der Staatsangestellten," *K,* 6 (1912–13): 222–26; and "Ein Staatsbeamter. Der Kampf der Staatsbeamtenschaft und sein Ende," ibid., pp. 324–30. For a modern evaluation, see Karl Megner, *Beamte,* pp. 139–42.

234. See Stürgkh's arguments in the "Ministerratsprotokoll," 30 January 1914, as well as Norgate, "The Internal Policies," pp. 274–85, and Alexander Fussek, "Ministerpräsident Karl Graf Stürgkh und die parlamentarische Frage," *MÖSTA*, 17–18 (1964–65): 337–58.

235. This included a decree raising recruit levels by 30,000 over those established in 1912; a huge state loan of 375 million crowns; and Austrian financing for a new system of railways in Bosnia-Herzogovina agreed upon by the Joint Ministerial Council in November 1913.

236. The *Arbeiter-Zeitung* summarized these suspicions eloquently in "Stürgkh will nicht," 13 March 1914, p. 1, as well as "Was plant Stürgkh?" 14 March 1914, p. 1, as opposed to the sympathetic evaluations in Fussek, "Stürgkh," pp. 50–58, and Norgate, "The Internal Policies," pp. 274–75. The problem with the latter portraits of a patient, well-meaning, flexible statesman is that they are very difficult to reconcile with the behavior of Stürgkh *after* July 1914. Tschirschky had reported to Berlin the conditions under which Stürgkh might close parliament in early January. A 214, 2 January 1914, Oest. 70/Bd. 49.

237. Joseph Maria Baernreither, *Fragmente eines politischen Tagebuches. Die südslawische Frage und Österreich-Ungarn vor dem Weltkrieg,* ed. Joseph Redlich (Berlin, 1928), pp. 268–69; similarly, Redlich, *Schicksalsjahre,* 1: 221 and 231–32. For the 1913 intervention of the Thronfolger in the Bohemian negotiations, see Bardolff's draft to Stürgkh, 9 August 1913 (submitted on a "highly confidential" basis), Carton 204, *MKFF.* For a modern evaluation of Stürgkh's practices, see Gernot D. Hasiba, *Das Notverordnungsrecht in Österreich (1848–1917). Notwendigkeit und Missbrauch eines "Staatserhaltenden Instrumentes"* (Vienna, 1985), pp. 145–49.

238. Diary, entry of 13 January 1914, *NL Berchtold.* For the background, see Keith Hitchins, "The Nationality Problem in Hungary: István Tisza and the Rumanian National Party, 1910–1914," *JMH,* 53 (1981): 619–51.

239. Diary, entry of 14 March 1914; and Tschirschky's report in A 5441, 16 March 1914, Oest. 70/Bd. 49, *PAAA.*

240. *Fragmente,* p. 266.

241. Hugo Hantsch, *Leopold Graf Berchtold. Grandseigneur und Staatsmann* (2 vols., Graz, 1963), 2: 512–13. For the political situation in mid-March, see the informative report in A 5065, 11 March 1914, Oest. 91/Bd. 17.

242. See "Klubsitzung," 17 March 1914.

243. See Stefan Licht, *Der österreichische Reichsrat und der Stand seiner Arbeiten. Mitteilungen der Industriellen Vereinigung.* Nr. 20 (Vienna, 1914), pp. 10–11.

244. See his desiderata in the "Ministerratsprotokoll," 2 May 1914.

245. See "Ministerratsprotokoll," 3 June 1914.

246. Sylvester to Baernreither, 6 May and 9 May 1914, Carton 49, *NL Baernreither; Schicksalsjahre,* 1: 230. For Sylvester's memoirs, see his *Vom toten Parlament und seinen letzten Trägern* (Vienna, 1928).

247. *Schicksalsjahre,* 1: 231.

248. This is clear from the various meetings of the *Ministerrat* immediately after the closure of parliament. See especially the debates in the "Ministerratsprotokoll," 3 April 1914, See also Hasiba, *Notverordnungsrecht,* pp. 150–53.

249. Otto Bauer, "Geschichte Österreichs," in *Werkausgabe,* 1: 939.

CHAPTER SIX

1. See Gessmann to Funder, 12 October 1911, *NL Funder.*

2. In a later letter Gessmann talked of the "Borniertheit unserer Kleingewerbetreibenden u. Kleinhandelsleute," a surprising comment for one who had spent his career representing the small businessman. Gessmann to Funder, 4 January 1912, ibid. See also his comments to Redlich in *Schicksalsjahre,* 1: 150–51.

3. Karl Renner presented an eloquent analysis of the corner into which the Viennese Christian Socials had backed themselves by relying so heavily on manipulating the curial system, in *SPNÖ,* 1914, pp. 336–38.

4. "Der Niedergang einer Parteidespotie," *Sozialistische Monatshefte,* 13 July 1911, pp. 875–78.

5. *CSAZ,* 15 July 1911, pp. 1–2, and 6; Funder, *Vom Gestern,* pp. 461–62; and *Rp,* 28 June 1911, p. 3; 12 July 1911, p. 3; 18 July 1911, p. 7; 24 July 1911, pp. 2–3; 28 July 1911, p. 2.

6. *DV,* 25 July 1911 (M), p. 4; *CSAZ,* 29 July 1911, pp. 1–2; Gustav Blenk, *Leopold Kunschak und seine Zeit* (Vienna, 1966), pp. 88–91. For Kunschak's later career, see Pelinka, *Stand oder Klasse.*

7. For the Laborites and the 1912 elections, see *CSAZ,* 27 April 1912, pp. 1–3.

8. Pedagogical courses attended by hundreds of Austrian clerics were held in February 1905 and in February 1908. See Ignaz Seipel, "Pädagogischer Kurs in Wien," *Christliche Pädagogische Blätter,* 28 (1905): 67–72, and *Der zweite pädagogisch-katechetische Kurs in Wien, 16.–29. Februar 1908* (Vienna, 1908). In September 1912 a general congress on Catholic pedagogy was held in Vienna, attended by over 900 people, 226 of whom were from the city of Vienna itself. See Emerich Holzhausen, ed., *Bericht über die Verhandlungen des Kongresses für Katechetik, Wien 1912* (Vienna, 1913), pp. xxxii–xxxiii. More generally, the work of the group around Rudolf Hornich also had a strong influence on the clergy. See his *Erstes Jahrbuch des Vereins für christliche Erziehungswissenschaft* (Kempten and Munich, 1908).

9. Boyer, *Political Radicalism in Late Imperial Vienna,* chap. 3.

10. *Erlebnisse,* 1: 106–7, 108–10; 2: 457; 3/1: 237; 4: 23; 5: 163–67; and passim.

11. On the congress, see Josef Scheicher, *Der österreichische Klerustag* (Vienna, 1903). The first notice of intentions to summon a congress came in the *Correspondenzblatt* in 1899. See *CB,* 1899, pp. 277–81, 288–91, 357–60, 441–44, 749–52, 869–72; 1900, pp. 18, 146, 189–90.

12. Scheicher, *Klerustag,* pp. 19–23.

13. *Protokoll der Bischöflichen Versammlung in Wien vom 12. bis 20. November 1901*, pp. 9–11, *EBDA; Wiener Diözesanblatt*, 1902, p. 167; *Rp*, 3 August 1902, p. 4; *CB*, 1902, pp. 663–64.

14. *Rp*, 2 September 1902, p. 3; 6 September 1902, p. 9; 27 September 1902, p. 9; *CB*, 1902, pp. 662–64; *Klerustag*, pp. 152–53, 168–70.

15. On the *Jednota*, see Barbara Schmid-Egger, *Klerus und Politik in Böhmen um 1900* (Munich, 1974), pp. 32–33, 40–49; and Ludvik Nemec, "The Czech Jednota, the Avant-Garde of Modern Clerical Progressivism and Unionism," *Proceedings of the American Philosophical Society*, 112 (1968): 74–100. The *Jednota's* newspaper, *Věstník*, was modeled after the *Correspondenzblatt*. For *Pascendi*, see the survey in Erika Weinzierl, "Der Antimodernismus Pius' X.," in *Der Modernismus: Beiträge zu seiner Erforschung* (Graz, 1974), pp. 235–55. On the modernist movement in Germany, see Norbert Trippen, *Theologie und Lehramt im Konflikt: Die kirchlichen Massnahmen gegen den Modernismus im Jahre 1907 und ihre Auswirkungen in Deutschland* (Freiburg, 1977), and Oskar Schroeder, *Aufbruch und Missverständnis: Zur Geschichte der reformkatholischen Bewegung* (Graz, 1969).

16. Friedrich Funder, *Aufbruch zur christlichen Sozialreform* (Vienna, 1953); and Ignaz Seipel, "Franz Martin Schindler," *Jahrbuch der österreichischen Leo-Gesellschaft* (Innsbruck, 1924), pp. 41–48.

17. There is no modern history of the *Leo-Gesellschaft*, but its work is reviewed in Johannes Eckardt, "Zum fünfundzwanzigjährigen Bestande der österreichischen Leo-Gesellschaft," *Das Neue Österreich*, February 1917, pp. 52–58, and March 1917, pp. 52–59; and Anton Übleis, "Österreichische Leogesellschaft," *Academia*, 26 (1913–14): 457–60.

18. *Rp*, 29 October 1922, p. 2. For Schindler's influence as a teacher, see Funder, *Aufbruch*, pp. 146–51; Alfred Missong, *August Schaurhofer: Ein Wiener Sozialapostel* (Vienna, 1936), pp. 20–23; Ernst Karl Winter, *Ignaz Seipel als dialektisches Problem. Ein Beitrag zur Scholastikforschung* (Vienna, 1966), pp. 164–65; and Jakob Fried, *Erinnerungen aus meinem Leben (1885–1936)*, ed. Franz Loidl (Vienna, 1977), p. 35 ("Besonders die Bücher von Biederlack S.J. und Prälat Schindler sowie die Vorlesungen des letzteren und des Privatdozenten Dr. Seipel haben uns viele Anregungen gegeben").

19. *Die soziale Frage der Gegenwart vom Standpunkt des Christentums* (Vienna, 1905). See also *Der Lohnvertrag* (Vienna, 1893) and *Das Kapital-Zins-Problem* (Vienna, 1903). On Schindler's social theology, see Rudolf Weiler, "Katholische Soziallehre unterwegs," in *Festschrift Franz Loidl zum 65. Geburtstag*, ed. Viktor Flieder (3 vols., Vienna, 1970), 2: 354, and 368, n. 5.

20. Funder, *Aufbruch*, p. 149.

21. Seipel saw in his own work, based on Schindler's, the development of a Catholic sociology: "Inzwischen haben wir die Soziologie erfunden—ich habe darüber bei meiner Ehrenpromotion zum Dr. jur. gesprochen. Schindler hatte gleich Biederlack und den anderen Moraltheologen von damals zeitlebens soziale Fragen vorgetragen und war

kein Soziologe. . . . Aber er beobachtet freundschaftlich meinen Weg zur Soziologie und stand bei der Geburt dieser Wissenschaft Pate." Seipel to Missong, 31 March 1932, *NL Seipel.* Although he later tried to distance himself from Ehrhard, Seipel was caught up in the latter's influence before 1914, sending Ehrhard his *Habilitationsschrift* for advice on revisions and publication prospects. Compare the recollections of Wildenauer to Schmitz, 22 August 1946, *NL Funder,* with Funder, *Aufbruch,* p. 127. On Seipel's prewar theological liberalism, see Klemens von Klemperer, *Ignaz Seipel: Christian Statesman in a Time of Crisis* (Princeton, 1972), pp. 34–41.

22. Winter, *Ignaz Seipel,* pp. 165–66.

23. On Schmitz, see Fritz Braun, "Der politische Lebensweg des Bürgermeisters Richard Schmitz." Dissertation, University of Vienna, 1968. The *NL Schmitz* contains several handwritten autobiographical fragments on Schmitz's career before 1914, which are useful in reconstructing his psychological and political development. Valuable material on Schmitz is also located in the *NL Funder.*

24. Schmitz was a featured speaker at the anti-Wahrmund demonstration organized by Catholic students at the University of Innsbruck on 15 March 1908. See Hartmann, *Im Gestern bewährt,* p. 107.

25. Funder to Schmitz, 5 April 1910, *NL Schmitz.*

26. On the early history of the *Volksbund,* Sigmund Guggenberger, "Der Katholische Volksbund und die Männervereinsbewegung," in Alois Hudal, ed., *Der Katholizismus in Österreich: Sein Wirken, Kämpfen und Hoffen* (Innsbruck, 1931), pp. 280–91; Gerhard Schultes, "Das 'Katholische Aktionskomitee für Niederösterreich.' Ein Beitrag zur Vorgeschichte der Katholischen Aktion in Wien," in *Festschrift Franz Loidl,* 1: 340–78; and Louis Bosmans, *August Schaurhofer 1872–1928. Ein Leben im Dienst der christlichen Sozialarbeit* (Vienna, 1978), pp. 30–39. For its long-term impact, see Gerhard Silberbauer, *Österreichs Katholiken und die Arbeiterfrage* esp. pp. 181–88, 222ff. For the recollections of an important participant, see Fried, *Erinnerungen.*

27. On Kienböck, see Gertrude Enderle-Burcel, ed., *Christlich-Ständisch-Autoritär. Mandatare im Ständestaat 1934–1938* (Vienna, 1991), pp. 122–23.

28. For the political impact of the Catholic student societies, see Friedrich Funder, *Das weiss-blau-goldene Band: "Norica." Fünfzig Jahre Wiener katholischen deutschen Farbstudententums* (Innsbruck, 1933); Gerhard Popp, *CV in Österreich 1864–1938: Organisation, Binnenstruktur und politische Funktion* (Vienna, 1984), esp. pp. 153–61; and Hartmann, *Im Gestern bewährt,* pp. 135–213. For the recollections of a contemporary participant, see Fried, *Erinnerungen.*

29. Scheicher, *Erlebnisse,* 5: 431.

30. Gerhard Hartmann has called attention to Albert Ehrhard's lecture, given before a group of Catholic university students in January 1899 in Vienna, in which the progressive theologian challenged the students to be the bearers of the "Christian ideal" within the Austrian universities. The intellectual program developed by young activists of the *Volksbund* closely paralleled that outlined by Ehrhard. See Albert Ehrhard, *Der katho-*

lische Student und seine Ideale. Eine Programmrede (Vienna, 1899), as well as Hartmann, *Im Gestern bewährt*, pp. 52, 58, and Heinrich Drimmel, *Albert Ehrhard und seine Studenten in Wien um 1900* (Vienna, 1976).

31. *VW,* 3 (1912): 346–47; and "Soziale Studentenarbeit in Oesterreich," in *Der soziale Student. Blätter für soziale Studentenarbeit in Österreich,* Nr. 1, supplement to *VW,* 5 (1914): 1–3.

32. Hartmann, *Im Gestern bewährt,* p. 183.

33. For these membership statistics, see *VW,* 3 (1912): 346–47.

34. See the diary fragment in Carton 16 of the *NL Schmitz.* On Schmitz's view of the need for a renewed level of ideological discourse, see Braun, pp. 24–25.

35. *Rp,* 10 January 1914, p. 1. See also Schmitz's article on "Die Wiener Märzwahlen" in *VW,* 5 (1914): 78–85.

36. Otto Maresch, "Eine österreichische 'Soziale Woche'," *Hochland,* 9 (1911–12): 252.

37. See Schmitz, "Kritische Gedanken über die christliche Gewerkschaftsbewegung," *VW,* 3 (1912): 225–30; and idem, "Die soziale Organisation der christlichen Arbeiterschaft Oesterreichs," *Rp,* 11 September 1912, pp. 27–28. See also Karl Rudolf, "Die katholische Hochschüler- und Mittelschülerbewegung in Wien und Österreich," in Hudal, ed., *Der Katholizismus,* pp. 151–52.

38. The full proceedings of the symposium are in *Die Soziale Woche: Bericht über den vom "Katholischen Volksbund für Österreich" unter dem Namen "Soziale Woche" veranstalteten sozialwissenschaftlichen Kursus v. 5.–10. Sept. 1911* (Vienna, 1911).

39. *Rp,* 10 September 1911, p. 6; Leopold Kunschak, "Aus dem Werden der christlichen Arbeiterbewegung Österreichs," *VW,* 14 (1923): 284.

40. *VW,* 2 (1911): 270; Robert Danneberg, "Eine Revision des christlichen Sozialismus," *K,* 5 (1911–12): 241–46.

41. On Brauns's career, see Hubert Mockenhaupt, *Weg und Wirken des geistlichen Sozialpolitikers Heinrich Brauns* (Paderborn, 1977); for his major intellectual positions, see Hubert Mockenhaupt, ed., *Katholische Sozialpolitik im 20. Jahrhundert: Ausgewählte Aufsätze und Reden von Heinrich Brauns* (Mainz, 1976), esp. pp. 17–57. For recent discussions of the *Gewerkschaftsstreit,* which emphasize its critical role in the weakening of the Christian labor faction in the *Zentrum,* see Rudolf Brack, *Deutscher Episkopat und Gewerkschaftsstreit 1900–1914* (Cologne, 1976); Horstwalter Heitzer, *Georg Kardinal Kopp und der Gewerkschaftsstreit 1900–1914* (Cologne, 1983); and the provocative study by Wilfried Loth, *Katholiken im Kaiserreich: Der politische Katholizismus in der Krise des wilhelminischen Deutschlands* (Düsseldorf, 1984), esp. pp. 232–77.

42. *Die Soziale Woche,* pp. 16–20, 21–27, 37–39, 41–50.

43. See especially Mockenhaupt, *Weg und Wirken,* pp. 78–82; and Brauns, "Gelbe Werksgemeinschaft oder Gewerbesolidarität?" in *Katholische Sozialpolitik,* pp. 46–49.

44. For these trends, see the important essays of Margaret Anderson, "The Kulturkampf and the Course of German History"; and "Interdenominationalism, Clerical-

ism, Pluralism: The *Zentrumsstreit* and the Dilemma of Catholicism in Wilhelmine Germany."

45. *Die Soziale Woche,* pp. 30–37.

46. Ibid., pp. 37–41.

47. Ibid., pp. 39–40. A third controversial lecture was by Franz Sommeregger, a young Austrian cleric, born in 1882, who studied theology and philosophy in Klagenfurt and Rome, before turning to law and social science at the University of Berlin, where he worked with Sering and Schmoller. His dissertation research was the basis of his contribution at the *Soziale Woche: Agrarverfassung der Landgemeinde und Landeskulturpolitik in Oesterreich seit der Grundentlastung* (Klagenfurt, 1912).

48. The *Volksbund* circle was sympathetic to the *Volksverein* position in the *Gewerkschaftsstreit.* See Alfred Schappacher, "Der Streit um das Zentrum," *VW,* 5 (1914): 85–91. It should also be noted that Kunschak made significant changes to his political program in December 1913, dropping his absolute opposition to cartels and his references to the "usurious misuse" of private property. See *CSAZ,* 13 December 1913, p. 3, and Richard Schmitz's comments in *VW,* 5 (1914): 39 ("Warme Anerkennung verdient das offene Abrücken von einer gewissen phrasenhaften 'Wirtschaftspolitik,' die in vollständiger Missachtung der Tatsachen oder in bewusster Industriegegnerschaft einfachhin das Verbot der Kartelle ohne Unterschied verlangt").

49. Gessmann to Funder, 13 February 1912, *NL Funder.*

50. The memorandum on the *Volksbund* was included with a letter from Ernst Graf Marschall to Piffl, 10 November 1913, in *Bischofsakten* 1913/16, *NL Piffl.* The authors admitted that "Indifferentismus und Passivität geben weite Kreise der katholischen Bevölkerung der erfolgreichen Agitation des Freisinns und der Sozialdemokratie preis; dank derselben reicht auch die Einflusssphäre der kirchenfeindlichen Elemente (über vielfach unmerkbare Abstufungen und kaum wahrnehmbare Übergänge) weit hinein in die noch gläubig überzeugten Volksteile und macht dieselben ihren Bestrebungen dienstbar" (p. 5).

51. Between 1907 and 1909 alone Prochazka submitted thirty-four motions and nineteen interpellations in the *Abgeordentenhaus* pertaining to lower-ranking white-collar employees and petty state officials, rather than worker groups. Cf. *Index zu den stenographischen Protokollen des Hauses der Abgeordneten, XVIII. Session 1907–1909,* 1: 338–40.

52. Gessmann to Funder, 13 February 1912, *NL Funder.*

53. *DV,* 8 October 1911 (M), p. 4.

54. For Seipel's view of the *Anschluss,* see Klemperer, *Seipel,* pp. 113ff.; and for the political background, see Anton Staudinger, *Aspekte christlichsozialer Politik 1917 bis 1920* (Vienna, 1979), pp. 140–63. The discussion held in the *Bürgerklub* on 18 February 1919 revealed, in addition to a kind of passive enthusiasm, some doubts about the project even within Viennese *bürgerlich* circles. See the "Verhandlungsschrift über die Beratung des Bürgerklubkomitees vom 18. Februar 1919 betreffend die Zukunft Wiens," Carton 37, *CPW.*

55. On Orel, see Dorit Weinberger, "Die christliche Sozialreform Anton Orels." Dissertation, University of Vienna, 1966.

56. On the 1913 Catholic Congress see *Der Katholikentag der Deutschen Österreichs vom 15. bis 17. August 1913 in Linz a. D.* (Linz, 1913), pp. 164ff. For Orel's critique of the *Volksbund,* see *Die Volksbewegung,* 1 (1913): 91–93, 105–10, 127. For a survey of the conflict between the two Catholic youth movements in prewar Austria, see Gerhard Schultes, *Der Reichsbund der katholischen deutschen Jugend Österreichs: Entstehung und Geschichte* (Vienna, 1967), pp. 25–115.

57. See various integralist critiques of the main-line Christian Socials in Vienna in *Die Volksbewegung,* 1 (1913): 7, 28, 36, 44, 131–32; and *ÖKS,* 18 May 1913, pp. 1–2; 27 July 1913, p. 1; 10 August 1913, p. 2. Schmitz argued that Christian Social workers had to have their own organizations apart from employers (and, implicitly, from the Christian Social party) since "die wirtschaftlichen Gegensätze sind zu scharf geworden und der Egoismus ist im Menschen zu tief eingegraben." *Rp,* 11 September 1912, pp. 27–28.

58. For the 1913–14 dispute, see the memorandum in the *Bischofsakten* 1913/16, *NL Pifft;* as well as *Rp,* 10 October 1913, pp. 1–3; and *Die Volksbewegung,* 1 (1913): 104, 127–28; 2 (1914): 1–2, 12–13. For Piffl's support of the *Volksbund,* see Schultes, *Der Reichsbund,* pp. 102–16.

59. On Mauss, see Friedrich Engel-Janosi, *Österreich und der Vatikan 1846–1918* (2 vols.; Graz, 1958–60), 2: 144–48; Ludwig von Pastor, *Tagebücher, Briefe, Erinnerungen,* ed. Wilhelm Wühr (Heidelberg, 1950), pp. 599–600; and the unpublished commentary "Ursprung und Entwicklung des Sonntagsblattes" and the "Lebenslauf des Priesters Anton Mauss" in the *NL Nagl,* which offer a portrait of Mauss and a critique of his movement.

60. See particularly *ÖKS,* 18 May 1913, p.1; 31 August 1913, pp. 1–2; 7 September 1913, p. 4. On the Integralist movement in Austria, see the essays in Erika Weinzierl, ed., *Der Modernismus;* and Moritz Csáky, "Österreich und der Modernismus. Nach den Berichten des österreichischen Botschafters am Vatikan 1910/11," *MÖSTA,* 17–18 (1964–65): 322–36.

61. Schultes argues that Nagl preferred Orel's youth movement over Kunschak's, citing the private diary of Josef Wagner, who was a confidant of Nagl. *Der Reichsbund,* pp. 97–101. It might be questioned, however, whether Nagl simply wanted to end the feuding in order to reestablish his own discipline over Catholic associational life in the Archdiocese. See also Franz Loidl, *Franz Xaver Kardinal Nagl. Erzbischof-Koadjutor (1910/11) und Fürsterzbischof (1911/13) von Wien. Sonderabdruck aus Beiträge zur Wiener Diözesangeschichte* (Vienna, 1965–67), p. 35.

62. After Pius X's death in 1914, Piffl had less to worry about in any event. In both Prussian and Austrian ecclesiastical circles, a critical factor in choosing the new pope in August 1914 was the perception of who would control the extremism of the Integralists most effectively. See Engel-Janosi, *Österreich und der Vatikan,* 2: 182–86. For

the Emperor's sympathy for Piffl, see Tschirschky's report of 16 March 1914 in Oest. 70/ Bd. 49, *PAAA*.

63. *Rp,* 24 September 1913, p. 8.

64. *Deutsche Rundschau,* 2 August 1913, p. 6. For Schmitz's speech on the need for a "Christian legislation," see *Lienzer Nachrichten,* 21 November 1913, p. 1. See also the report in the *Allgemeiner Tiroler Anzeiger,* 15 November 1913, p. 7.

65. Ibid., 6 February 1912, pp. 6–7. Schmitz even dared to acknowledge the right of women in independent occupations to form labor organizations that would "replace the protection they [formerly] had in their families and households." *Österreichische Volkszeitung,* 19 September 1913, pp. 9–10.

66. See Schmitz's excoriation of the "so-called German national parties" in *Rp,* 21 March 1914, p. 8, and the open hostility against "Kompromisslereien" with local nationalists at the Christian Social workers' congress in December 1913, *CSAZ,* 13 December 1913, p. 1. Local German nationalists in turn blamed the "clerical" faction in the party leadership for subverting the electoral agreement in February 1914. See *AZ,* 22 February 1914, p. 10.

67. *VW,* 5 (1914): 8–9.

68. Diary fragment, 1914, *NL Schmitz.* For a similar argument, presented in a German Catholic journal in 1911, see "Zu den Neuwahlen in Österreich," *HPB,* 148 (1911): 64–65 ("Die christlichsoziale Partei vereinigte besonders in Wien als wirtschaftliche Reaktion gegen jüdische Kapitalsmacht die divergentesten Elemente. Dies war so lange möglich, als die Partei in Opposition stand. Lueger starb zu früh, um die Partei aus ihrer rein negativ-programmatischen Qualität als Reaktion herauszuarbeiten und in eine Partei mit klaren positiven Grundsätzen umzuwandeln").

69. Braun, "Lebensweg," pp. 20–21.

70. *Rp,* 7 January 1914, p. 7; 10 January 1914, pp. 1–2. Angermayer had a penchant for Teutonic celebrations. See the description of his "Sonnwendfeier" in *DV,* 19 June 1913 (M), p. 13. The purpose of the gathering was to disprove the accusation that Christianity had dissipated the "old German customs."

71. Cf. *Egerland,* 30 October 1912, p. 3, with its connection of Viennese *Freisinn* to Social Democracy. See also Schmitz, "Die Wiener Märzwahlen," *VW,* 5 (1914): 78–85; and the commentary on this essay in *AZ,* 26 April 1914, p. 5, which in response to Schmitz's calls for a reconstruction of the party asked rhetorically: "Was sagen die Weiskirchner und Funder dazu?" Heinrich Mataja later admitted (in 1916) that party regulars had been inclined to mock the *Volksbund,* as well as other "clerical" organizations, and refused to take them seriously. See his remarks to the party conference held in February 1916, p. 20, in Carton 19, *CPK.*

72. For the role of the Viennese Catholics later in 1918, see Staudinger, *Aspekte,* pp. 144, 157–59, and below, Chapter 7.

73. Seipel to Missong, 31 March 1932. For a similar comment by Jakob Fried, who succeeded Schmitz as head of the *Volksbund* in 1915, see his *Erinnerungen,* p. 80. See

also Hedwig Pfarrhofer, *Friedrich Funder. Ein Mann zwischen Gestern und Morgen* (Graz, 1978), p. 151.

74. Z. 24463, 30 October 1918, Carton 2131, 22, *MI Präs.*; Fuchs to Harrach, 5 December 1918, Carton 861, *Familienarchiv Harrach, AVA.* I am grateful to Lothar Höbelt for calling my attention to this letter.

75. On Nagl, see Edith Saurer, *Die politischen Aspekte der österreichischen Bischofsernennungen 1867–1903* (Vienna, 1968), pp. 210–22, and Loidl, "Franz Xaver Kardinal Nagl." On the politics of his appointment as coadjutor to Gruscha, see Brosch to Franz Ferdinand, 27 December 1909, C 81; and 4 January 1910, C 84; Carton 10, *NL Franz Ferdinand;* Tucher's report of 14 March 1910, Z. 110; and the Baernreither Diary, Nr. 9, f. 38, on the rebuke Lueger received from Franz Joseph for his support of Marschall. Nagl was disliked by local clerics in Vienna for his strict, authoritarian manner. For a jaundiced contemporary view of Nagl, emphasizing his authoritarianism and lavish style of living, see *SMZ,* 10 January 1910, p. 2; 10 February 1913, pp. 2–3; and 12 May 1913, p. 3.

76. Gessmann to Nagl, 18 May 1907, Carton 1, *NL Nagl.*

77. See the transcription of the speech on 4 November 1911 in Carton 2, *NL Nagl.*

78. The transcription of the speech on 14 January 1912 is in ibid.

79. For the Congress, see Karl Kammel, ed., *Bericht über den XXIII. Internationalen Eucharistischen Kongress. Wien 12. bis 15. September 1912* (Vienna, 1912).

80. Of the first fifteen congresses held between 1881 and 1904, fourteen were held in French-speaking Europe. For the history of the eucharistic congress movement, see Rudolf v. Moreau, *Die Eucharistischen Weltkongresse. Ihr Werden, Wachsen und Wirken* (Neckar, 1960).

81. On Germany, see Moreau, *Weltkongresse,* pp. 21–23.

82. See *Schicksalsjahre,* 1: 150.

83. See Funder, *Vom Gestern,* pp. 348–50, and the allegations of Nagl's distrust of the *Reichspost* over its "tone and direction" in Sauer to Piffl, 23 August, 1913, *Bischofsakten* 1913/16, *NL Piffl.*

84. The principal documents relating to the Congress's history are printed as an appendix to the *Bericht,* pp. 817–44.

85. See Schiessl to Nagl, 26 October 1911, reprinted in *Bericht,* pp. 821–22. The Foreign Office's "Annual Report" for 1912, p. 42, noted: "One of the most striking features of the congress was the devotion to the Church displayed by the Imperial House of Austria in the prominent part taken in the celebrations by the Emperor and the Imperial Family. This example was followed by all the noble houses of Austria, who assembled in large numbers in Vienna to participate in the proceedings of the congress." FO 881/10244.

86. According to Nagl, this was to be a Congress at which "da teilt uns keine Nationalität, da darf kein Parteistandpunkt die Katholiken trennen, wo es sich handelt, den Mittelpunkt der katholishen Einheit, das Allerheiligste Sakrament zu bekennen und anzubeten." *Bericht,* p. 843. The *Reichspost* dedicated heavy coverage to the Congress,

and stressed repeatedly its multinational character. See the issues of 11–16 September 1912. See also the coverage in the *HPB,* which celebrated the Congress as showing the "alte, katholische Österreich in einem fast unverblassten Glanze" and as documenting "die katholische Einigkeit der Völker in herrlicher Weise." 150 (1912): 791.

87. As in all such events, estimates of the number of participants varied, with the socialists seeking to minimalize and the Christian Socials seeking to maximize attendance. Official reports by the police to the Lower Austrian *Statthalter* estimated approximately 100,000 participants in the procession, with several hundred thousand additional spectators. See V/45–53, Nr. 2253, 1912, *NÖLA.*

88. See the final police report, dated 15 September 1912, in V/45–53, Nr. 2253, 1912, *NÖLA.* The police arrested a total of four persons on the day of the procession: one pickpocket, one drunk, and two rowdies.

89. Diary, entry of 16 September 1912, *NL Berchtold.* The *Arbeiter-Zeitung* tried to trivialize the accomplishments of the organizers, but even it had to give grudging respect to the impressiveness of the event. See 16 September 1912, p. 2.

90. See Nagl's comments in Moreau, p. 25.

91. *AZ,* 9 September 1912, p, 2. A copy of the *Josefsblätter* confiscated by the police can be found in V/45–53, Nr. 2556, *NÖLA.*

92. Hussarek was "ein Minister für öffentliche klerikale Arbeit." See the police report on the rally, 20 September 1912, in V/45–53, Nr. 2556, 1912, *NÖLA.*

93. See the heavy coverage which the *AZ* accorded to the Congress: 8 September 1912, pp. 1–2; 11 September 1912, pp. 1–2; 12 September 1912, pp. 1–2; 13 September 1912, pp. 1–3; 14 September 1912, pp. 1–3; 15 September 1912, p. 1; 16 September 1912, p. 2; 17 September 1912, p. 2.

94. See Zenker, "Glossen zum Eucharistischen Kongress," *Die Wage,* 15 (1912): 841–45, and his speech on 19 September in V/45–53, Nr. 2556, 1912, *NÖLA.*

95. See the Interpellation brought by Volkert, Leuthner, Skaret, and others in *SP,* 1912, *Anhang* IX, Nr. 2495, pp. 11498–99. The files in V/45–53, Nr. 1959, 1912, *NÖLA,* demonstrate the extent of state support for the affair, even to the point that the Lower Austrian *Statthalter* was asked to arrange for housing accommodations for visiting clerical dignitaries (which Bienerth actually did). The central ministries in Vienna even sent official circulars to their employees inviting them to attend the Congress. See Z. 7071, 5 July 1912 and Z. 7355, 16 July 1912, Carton 2147, 25, *MI Präs.*

96. I calculated this figure from a survey of the organizers' own statistics in the *Bericht.*

97. The problem of analyzing the role of religion in the constitution of Austrian political identities is complicated by the routinized functions that historic, performative forms of Catholicism played in the legitimacy of the dynastic state. As James Shedel has observed, "one did not have to be a Catholic or a Christian to appreciate the significance of the Corpus Christi procession." James Shedel, "Emperor, Church and People: Religion and Dynastic Loyalty During the Golden Jubilee of Franz Joseph," *Catholic Historical Review,* 76 (1990): 71–92, here 78.

98. See the debates of the general meeting of the *Österreichisch-Israelitische Union* in 1912, particularly the comments of Dr. Samuely to the effect that "die Zeiten auch für die Judenschaft andere geworden seien, und dass sich namentlich in Wien mehrere einander sehr heftig bekämpfende Parteien unter den Juden gebildet hätten." *ÖW*, 29 (1912): 311.

99. For working-class losses by the *Zentrum*, see Ellen Lovell Evans, *The German Center Party 1870–1933. A Study in Political Catholicism* (Carbondale, 1981), pp. 164–65; for the German liberal and conservative parties see the perceptive comments of James Sheehan in his *German Liberalism in the Nineteenth Century* (Chicago, 1978), p. 247: "Although each of the liberal and conservative parties was able to attract a certain number of these [middle-strata] voters and build them into a core of support, most of them were not strongly attached to any one party."

100. Schmitz, "Die Wiener Märzwahlen," represents this view.

101. A copy of this appeal, published by the socialist *Wahlverein Josefstadt* in 1913, is in file Z. 521, Carton 72, *CPW*.

102. Lueger's pithy comparison in 1906 of the Emperor Franz Joseph and Kaiser Wilhelm II—"Unser Kaiser kann nicht wie der deutsche Kaiser jeden Tag Reden halten, das geht nicht mehr und man muss halt mit dem zufrieden sein, was er macht, und er macht immer etwas Gutes"—was merely one occasion in which he dared to speak his mind about his Imperial master, but in terms (depending on how ironically one reads the statement) that were not unfavorable to Franz Joseph (given Wilhelm's habit of public blabbing). Characteristically, Count Wedel saw the statement as yet another example of Lueger's "üblichen Taktlosigkeiten." A 15459, 11 September 1906, Oest. 86/6/Bd. 1, *PAAA*.

103. See Gross to Franz Ferdinand, 3 December 1913, 45–2/5, Carton 146, *MKFF.*

104. For the membership of the *Herrenhaus*, see Gerald Stourzh, "Die Mitgliedschaft auf Lebensdauer im österreichischen Herrenhause, 1861–1918," *MIÖG*, 73 (1965): 63–117; for Taaffe's manipulation of *Herrenhaus* appointments, see Sieghart, *Die letzten Jahrzehnte*, pp. 184–85. For an argument that the *Herrenhaus* would become even more powerful in the face of the political self-destruction of the *Abgeordnetenhaus*, see Kritias, *Das Parlament in Oesterreich oder die innere Gefahr* (Heidelberg, 1913), pp. 11–12.

105. On the controversy over the numerus clausus, see Jenks, *The Austrian Electoral Reform of 1907*, pp. 127–34; Stourzh, "Die Mitgliedschaft," pp. 95–100.

106. On parliamentary politics during the war, see below, Chapter 7.

107. On Gross, see Theodor Czermak, *Bischof Josef Gross von Leitmeritz* (Warnsdorf, n.d.). For the background to the Gross affair, see Saurer, *Die politischen Aspekte*, pp. 223–28. Saurer minimizes the role of Archduke Franz Ferdinand in stopping Gross's candidacy, arguing that the Belvedere acted for Piffl only after Gross's nomination had become impossible for other reasons, to wit, unfavorable publicity in the Viennese press and pressure against Gross by local Viennese clerics who feared that he would prove too autocratic for their style of life. Funder, in contrast, suggests that the Archduke

played a major role in the affair from start to finish (see *Vom Gestern,* p. 355). Obviously, the two positions are not mutually contradictory; and there is no reason to doubt Funder's views on this issue.

108. See Schlitter Diary, entry of 4 June 1913.

109. On Piffl's later career, see Prantner, *Kreuz und weisse Nelke;* and Maximilian Liebmann, "Die Rolle Kardinal Piffls in der österreichischen Kirchenpolitik seiner Zeit." Dissertation, University of Graz, 1960. Piffl has yet to be the subject of an authoritative biography.

110. For the conspiracy in 1911–12 against appointing Gessmann to the *Herrenhaus,* see Gessmann to Funder, 13 February 1912, *NL Funder.*

111. Schlitter Diary, entry of 13 March 1914. In December 1909 Liechtenstein sought an audience with Franz Ferdinand to discuss the general political situation, upon which Brosch wrote to the Archduke in openly unfavorable terms about Liechtenstein, describing him (along with Gessmann) as a creature of Rudolf Sieghart's: "so wie Gessmann ist er von Sieghart ganz entzückt, nennt ihn den grössten Freund der Christlichsozialen." Liechtenstein also supported Sieghart's appointment as governor of the *Bodencreditanstalt* (against the wishes of the Thronfolger). See Brosch to Franz Ferdinand, 16 December 1909, C 73, *NL Franz Ferdinand.*

112. See Franz Ferdinand to Brosch, 3 February 1909, reprinted in Chlumecky, *Erzherzog Franz Ferdinands Wirken und Wollen,* p. 324.

113. Franz Ferdinand to Brosch, 11 January 1908, reprinted in ibid., pp. 246–47.

114. Funder, *Vom Gestern,* pp. 516–17.

115. See *Schicksalsjahre,* 1: 150–51.

116. Pastor, *Tagebücher,* p. 603.

117. Lueger's attitude toward Franz Ferdinand has been touched upon in my discussion of the fall of Beck. See also the report of Eduard Leisching on Lueger's reaction to the Thronfolger's criticism of a bridge over the Danube Canal of which Lueger was particularly proud, in Kann and Leisching, eds., *Ein Leben für Kunst und Volksbildung,* p. 172. Franz Ferdinand followed Lueger's terminal illness with great attention, receiving daily telegrams from Vienna on Lueger's condition. See also Ottokar Czernin, *Im Weltkriege* (Berlin, 1919), p. 65.

118. *Schicksalsjahre,* 1: 210.

119. See *Vom Gestern,* pp. 486ff.; and more recently Pfarrhofer, *Friedrich Funder,* pp. 51–71.

120. See, for example, Ps. 41, 9 February 1912, Carton 78, *MKFF.*

121. Embittered by what he felt to be the depressing failure of Berchtold's policies during the Balkan wars, Funder would write to Bardolff that he intended to attack Berchtold, unless expressly forbidden to do so by the Archduke. "Die Nachwelt wird einmal fragen, ob es denn in dieser unglücklichen Zeit niemand in Oesterreich gegeben hat, der die Wahrheit zu sagen und auf die Folgen hinzuweisen wagte. . . . Die Stimmung in der Bevölkerung—ich komme ja mit weiten Kreisen in Berührung—ist eine namenlos verbitterte und das bisschen Kraftbewusstsein, das bei uns noch vorhanden

war, ist jetzt noch vielen ganz herausgerissen worden." 26 March 1913, Carton 113, *MKFF.* This mentality (repeated in another letter dated 8 April 1913) must be remembered to comprehend Funder's and many others' reactions to the events of July 1914.

122. See Ps. 89, 1912, Carton 79, *MKFF.*

123. For Brosch's plans on reforming the world of Viennese journalism, see his "Programm für den Thronwechsel," first published in the *NWJ,* 30 December 1923 and 1 January 1924, and reprinted in Georg Franz, *Erzherzog Franz Ferdinand und die Pläne zur Reform der Habsburger Monarchie* (Brünn, 1943), p. 144; and Chlumecky, *Erzherzog Franz Ferdinands Wirken und Wollen,* p. 291. See also Ps. 126, Carton 80, April 29, 1912, *MKFF.* This is Bardolff's strategy, based on a plan submitted to him by Alexander Spitzmüller, to take over majority control of the board of directors of *Die Zeit* from Heinrich Kanner and turn it into "a liberal, not Jewish, anticorruptionist paper dedicated to the idea of a black-yellow Empire." Bardolff noted in his cover letter to Franz Ferdinand that it was proving difficult to eliminate all Jewish influence from the paper, and, in this context, he invoked his own construction of the memory of Karl Lueger to justify the half-way measures he was proposing: "Wie aber weiland Dr. Lueger den Antisemitismus betrieb, so ist er auch hier praktiziert. Die Juden sind da, weil man sie dermalen nicht wegbringen kann, aber sie sind nur da mit ihrem Geld und ihrer Arbeit, zu reden haben sie nichts." For another version of the plot, see Leopold von Chlumecky's "Kurze Auszüge aus meinen umfangreichen Notizen über die Frage 'Zeitungsgründung durch das Belvedere'," in *Erzherzog Franz Ferdinands Wirken und Wollen,* pp. 314–15.

124. The *Rp* was also handicapped by the fact that it published only a morning edition, and that it could not possibly match the big dailies in the detail of its coverage of Viennese news. See Leopold Steiner's comments in "Klubsitzung," 18 May 1910, and "Parlamentarische Kommission," 8 June 1910, Carton 90, *CPK.*

125. As early as October 1909 Redlich reported that Funder was having second thoughts about having associated too closely with the "Kronprinzen-Politik" of the Christian Socials toward the Belvedere. See *Schicksalsjahre,* 1: 27.

126. *Vom Gestern,* pp. 500–501; Schlitter Diary, entry of 25 April 1914.

127. *Schicksalsjahre,* 1: 231.

128. Letter of 21 June 1912, Carton 79, *MKFF.*

129. For Gross's memorandum, see 45–2/5, Carton 146, *MKFF.*

130. Funder's response is filed in the same dossier as the Gross memorandum.

131. See Otto Conrad, "Eugen Schwiedland," in *Bericht über das Studienjahr 1936/ 37. Technische Hochschule in Wien* (Vienna, 1937), pp. 45–49. Information on Schwiedland's career is available in his files at the archive of the Technische Universität, Vienna, and at the Wiener Handelskammer. Schwiedland began his career at the Handelskammer, and then moved to the Technische Hochschule, where he became an Ordinarius in 1904. Schwiedland was one of those fascinating multidisciplinary and pluralistically political men in late Imperial Vienna, who moved freely and easily between government service, the academy, and private industry, and who defied precise

labeling. A protégé of both Carl Menger and Lujo Brentano, he also had close contacts with the Christian Social party.

132. See Redlich's notes on his conversations with Schwiedland about the Christian Social leadership in *Schicksalsjahre,* 1: 5, 8, 12. Schwiedland thought that Weiskirchner's rapid rise in power had gone to his head, leading him to pretensions and poor judgment.

133. Bardolff summarized Schwiedland's views in his own report. 45–2/5, Carton 146, *MKFF.* On the Ministry's economic politics, see Bardolff's report in Nr. 204/8, 27 January 1914, Carton 204, *MKFF.* August Kemetter confirmed Schwiedland's assertions about the tensions evident between Gessmann and his ministerial officials in *SP,* 1910, p. 1856.

134. Bardolff to Gross, 21 February 1914 (draft).

135. Pastor, *Tagebücher,* p. 604.

136. See Steed to Geoffrey Robinson, 21 May 1913, *H. Wickham Steed Papers,* Box 178. Steed insisted that the Archduke had contracted syphilis twenty years before and that it had now led to "progressive paralysis which is already so far advanced as to cause grave doubt whether the brain is not on the point of being affected." For similar rumors, see Redlich, *Schicksalsjahre,* 1: 228–29. In his biography *Erzherzog Franz Ferdinand von Österreich-Este. Leben, Pläne und Wirken am Schicksalsweg der Donaumonarchie* (Graz, 1953), pp. 313ff., Rudolf Kiszling skirts the issue by referring only to the Archduke's temperamental nature.

137. Nr. 7, 31 December 1913, Carton 204, *MKFF.*

138. Schlitter Diary, 3 October 1913.

139. Schlitter reacted to the Archduke's list-keeping by noting in his diary: "Sache selbst—stinkt sehr. Erinnert mich an Kaiser Joseph II. und an Kaiser Franz." Ibid.

140. See Eichhoff's undated (but likely from 1912) statement condemning the new *Dienstpragmatik* as the result of the Cabinet bowing to the combined pressure of the *Beamten* and the parliament, as well as Bardolff's correspondence on the *Dienstpragmatik* in Carton 2, *NL Eichhoff.* See also Eichhoff's report of 11 November 1913 on the Bosnia-Herzogovinan *Landesordnung,* which was highly defensive of Crown prerogatives against political manipulation of the civil service. Pö 36, Carton 76, *MKFF* contains the records of Bardolff's effort, undertaken in September 1912 at the Archduke's command, to persuade leading members of the *Herrenhaus* to try to gut the version of the bill passed by the *Abgeordnetenhaus.*

141. Ignaz Seipel, "Kaisertum und Demokratie," *VW* 9 (1918): 225–30, here p. 229. Compare also the perceptive comments in Klemperer, *Ignaz Seipel,* pp. 105, 145–46.

142. Otto Bauer, "Deutschland und wir," in *Werkausgabe,* 7: 279–82.

143. Hans Mommsen, "Otto Bauer, Karl Renner und die sozialdemokratische Nationalitätenpolitik in Österreich, 1905–1914," in *Arbeiterbewegung und Nationale Frage* (Göttingen, 1979), pp. 195–217, and "Victor Adler und die Politik der österreichischen Sozialdemokratie im Ersten Weltkrieg," in *Politik und Gesellschaft im alten und neuen Österreich,* 1: 386, 405.

144. Andrew G. Whiteside, "The Germans as an Integrative Force in Imperial Austria: The Dilemma of Dominance," *AHY,* 3, pt. 1 (1967): 197.

145. Elizabeth Wiskemann, *Czechs and Germans* (2d ed., London, 1967), p. 35.

146. See the classic work of Adam Wandruszka, "Österreichs politische Struktur," in *Geschichte der Republik Österreich,* ed. Heinrich Benedikt (Vienna, 1954); but for a criticism of *Lager* theory, see Hermann Fritzl and Martin Uitz, "Kritische Anmerkungen zur sogenannten Lagertheorie," *ÖZP* 4 (1975): 325–32.

147. *Rp,* 16 May 1907, p.1.

148. *SP,* 1908, pp. 5550–51. Redlich was supported by Gessman in his quest for appointment to a professorship at an Austrian institution of higher education, reflecting what eventually became a subtle political friendship between the two men. Compare Redlich to Bahr, 16 November 1920, in *Dichter und Gelehrter,* p. 435.

149. Rudolf Springer [Karl Renner], *Staat und Parlament* (Vienna, 1901), pp. 13, 28–29. See also Mommsen, *Die Sozialdemokratie und die Nationalitätenfrage,* pp. 381ff.

150. Rudolf Springer [Karl Renner], *Grundlagen und Entwicklungsziele der Österreichisch-Ungarischen Monarchie* (Vienna, 1906), pp. 122, 136. Compare also the comments in Renner's *Der Kampf der Oesterreichischen Nationen um den Staat* (Leipzig, 1902), pp. 215–29.

151. Otto Bauer, "Parlamentarismus und Arbeiterschaft," *Werkausgabe,* 8: 119–31. See also Bauer's arguments in "Unser Nationalitätenprogramm und unsere Taktik," ibid., esp. p. 76, as well as the commentary in *Die Tätigkeit des Sozialdemokratischen Verbandes im Abgeordnetenhause,* p. 5.

152. Otto Bauer, "Die Lehren des Zusammenbruchs," *Werkausgabe,* 8: 256.

153. *Schicksalsjahre,* 1: 8. The Czech Catholic theologian and later Archbishop of Prague, Franz Kordač, who was hostile to the Christian Socials, used the same image in describing the party. See "Franz Kordačs Briefe ins Germanikum," p. 93.

154. See especially Stephen Skowronek, *Building a New American State. The Expansion of National Administrative Capacities 1877–1920* (Cambridge, 1982), pp. 39–84; and the insightful essay of Charles Bright, "The State in the United States during the Nineteenth Century," in *Statemaking and Social Movements.* Compare also Martin Shefter, "Party, Bureaucracy and Political Change in the United States," in *Political Parties: Development and Decay,* ed. Louis Maisel and Joseph Cooper (Beverly Hills, 1978), pp. 211–65; Theodore Lowi, "Party, Policy and Constitution in America," in *The American Party Systems: Stages of Political Development,* ed. William Nisbet Chambers and Walter Dean Burnham (New York, 1967), pp. 238–76; and Richard Hofstadter, *The Idea of a Party System. The Rise of Legitimate Opposition in the United States, 1780–1840* (Berkeley, 1969).

155. A 5441, 16 March 1914, Oest. 70/Bd. 49, *PAAA.* The reference may have been to the luxurious system of pensions, on which see *Schicksalsjahre,* 1: 88.

156. Jürgen Kocka, "Otto Hintze, Max Weber und das Problem der Bürokratie," *Historische Zeitschrift* 233 (1981): 73. Kocka adapts this phrase from Otto Hintze's

"Machtpolitik und Regierungsverfassung," in *Staat und Verfassung: Gesammelte Abhandlungen zur allgemeinen Verfassungsgeschichte*, ed. Gerhard Oestreich (2d ed., Göttingen, 1962), p. 454.

157. Redlich, *Österreichische Regierung*, p. 64.

158. Seipel to Eduard von Poppy, 28 February 1930, *NL Seipel*. See also Ignaz Seipel, "Staat und Beamtentum," in Josef Gessl, ed., *Seipels Reden in Österreich und anderwärts* (Vienna, 1926).

159. Redlich to Baernreither, 12 August 1910, Carton 47, *NL Baernreither.*

160. Compare Redlich, *Österreichische Regierung*, pp. 67–75, and Baernreither, *Fragmente eines politischen Tagebuches*, p. 267. For discussions of the history of parliamentarism in Austria, see Helmut Widder, *Parlamentarische Strukturen im politischen System* (Berlin, 1979); and Karl Ucakar, "Politische Legitimation und Parlamentarismus," *ÖZP* 9 (1980): 421–41.

161. Wagner-Jauregg to Gross, 25 November 1914, Carton 2, *NL Gross.*

162. Spitzmüller, "*. . . und hat auch Ursach, es zu lieben,*" pp. 73–75; *Schicksalsjahre*, 1: 39. Two years earlier Schmid had been the source of contention when he ran as an independent candidate in Vienna in the parliamentary elections. See *NÖLA*, Statt. Präs. XIV/220, Nr. 1562, police report of 28 May 1907. At that time his superiors tried to have him transferred to Czernowitz.

163. A 664, 5 January 1914, Oest. 70/Bd. 49, *PAAA.*

164. Spitzmüller, "*. . . und hat auch Ursach, es zu lieben,*" p. 71. Lueger did not appear personally with this proposal, but sent a crony, Franz Rienössl.

165. For its background, see *Schicksalsjahre*, 1: 35, 70, 79, 85, 89–90, 194, 196–97, 202–3, 220, 224, 293; *Dichter und Gelehrter*, pp. 74, 167–68; Wolfgang-Rüdiger Mell, "Verwaltungsreform in Österreich," in *Verwaltungshistorische Studien*, ed. Andor Csizmadia (2 vols., Pécs, 1972), 1: 193–260; and Gernot D. Hasiba, "Die Kommission zur Förderung der Verwaltungsreform (1911–1914)," *Recht und Geschichte. Festschrift Hermann Baltl zum 70. Geburtstag*, ed. Helfried Valentinitsch (Graz, 1988), pp. 237–62. For contemporary reports, see the "Exposé betreffend die Einsetzung einer Kommission zur Förderung der Verwaltungsreform," Pö 46, 1911, Carton 50, and the "Untertänigstes Referat über die bisherige Tätigkeit der Kommission zur Reform der Staatsverwaltung," in Nr. 1479, 1913, Carton 113, 45–1/25, *MKFF.* The latter overview is by Colonel Bardolff. For contemporary commentaries, see Karl Brockhausen, *Österreichische Verwaltungsreformen* (Vienna, 1911); and from the Catholic perspective, Alfred Schappacher, "Wege zur Verwaltungsreform," *VW*, 4 (1913): 144–52, and Dr. Paulus, "Verwaltungsreform im Kriege," ibid., 6 (1915): 159–72. Redlich later insisted that the commission had been conceived of along the lines of an English royal commission that might eventually lead to a "vollständige Reform des Staatswesens" (*Österreichische Regierung*, p. 81).

166. Compare *Politische Chronik*, 1911, pp. 611–14. On the *Enquete*, see the *Enquete der Kommission zur Förderung der Verwaltungsreform, veranstaltet in der Zeit vom 21. Oktober bis 9. November 1912 zur Feststellung der Wünsche der beteiligten*

Kreise der Bevölkerung in bezug auf die Reform der Inneren und Finanzverwaltung (Vienna, 1913); and Stefan Licht, *Die Ergebnisse der Enquete über die Verwaltungsreform* (Vienna, 1913).

167. See the *Erläuterungen zu den Grundzügen einer Reform der Organisation der inneren Verwaltung* (Vienna, 1914), pp. 12–15.

168. The preliminary results of the commission were published in three yearly reports, the first two of which were reprinted in the *Wiener Zeitung* (31 August 1912; 1 August 1913). Haerdtl's report was leaked to the press in early 1913. Compare *Politische Chronik,* 1913, p. 53. A detailed summary and evaluation of Haerdtl's views is in the 1913 "Referat," accompanying a copy of the report itself. Compare also Schappacher's summary of the report in "Wege zur Verwaltungsreform," and the report in the *NFP,* 21 January 1913 (M), p. 7. On Haerdtl, see Czedik, *Zur Geschichte* 4: 110–17; and Mell, pp. 197–98, and n. 21, pp. 230–31.

169. *Bericht der Kommission zur Förderung der Verwaltungsreform über die Steigerung der Kosten der staatlichen inneren Verwaltung in der Periode von 1890 bis 1911 und über Vorschläge inbezug auf vorläufige Reformen hinsichtlich der Zentralstellen und der politischen Landesbehörden* (Vienna, 1913).

170. Bardolff, "Referat," p. 3.

171. Compare Josef Redlich, *Bericht . . . über die Entwicklung und den gegenwärtigen Stand der österreichischen Finanzverwaltung sowie Vorschläge der Kommission zur Reform dieser Verwaltung* (Vienna, 1913), pp. 116–91. Redlich's proposals were adopted, with some modification, by the commission on 2 July 1913.

172. Ibid., pp. 144–46, 180–83, 191–92.

173. Ibid., p. 183.

174. See his comments on the reform of the *Beamten* in ibid., pp. 190–91, as well as his discussion of the need to run the *Finanzverwaltung* on "das ökonomische Prinzip" on p. 189. Redlich's speeches in parliament in 1909 and 1911 on administrative reform also dramatized his linkage of administrative and economic reform (*SP,* 1909, pp. 1459–74, and 1911, pp. 1217–41).

175. Edmund Bernatzik's major work was *Rechtsprechung und materielle Rechtskraft: Verwaltungsrechtliche Studien* (Vienna, 1886).

176. Edmund Bernatzik, *Vorläufige Mitteilungen des zur Ausarbeitung eines Gesetzentwurfes über die Verwaltungsrechtsprechung bestellten Referenten E. Bernatzik über die allgemeinen Gesichtspunkte des von ihm ausgearbeiteten Entwurfes* (Vienna, 1912), pp. 3–4. The new law is the *Entwurf eines Gesetzes über die Einführung einer Verwaltungsjurisdiktion,* which includes a *Motivenbericht* and the text of the law.

177. Bernatzik, *Vorläufige Mitteilungen,* pp. 3, 5.

178. Stürgkh to Bardolff, 12 March 1913, 45–1/25–2, Carton 113, *MKFF.*

179. Compare the insightful comments in Paulus, pp. 160–65, as well as Karl Brockhausen, *Zur österreichischen Verwaltungsreform* (Vienna, 1917), pp. 4–5. Redlich too may have sensed the futility of his work by 1914. Compare the comments in *Die Vorschläge Prof. Redlichs zur Reform der Finanzverwaltung: Mitteilungen der*

Industriellen Vereinigung, Nr. 23 (Vienna, 1914), pp. 32–33, 39. For opposition from the highest civil service, see also the "Interpellation des Abgeordneten Kemetter und Genossen, betreffend Bestrebungen zur Verhinderung der Verwaltungsreform," *Anhang zu den Stenographischen Protokollen,* 1912, Vol. 7, p. 9258.

180. A 664, 5 January 1914, Oest. 70/Bd. 49, *PAAA.*

181. Alexander Brosch von Aarenau's "Programm für den Thronwechsel" is reprinted in Georg Franz, *Erzherzog Franz Ferdinand und die Pläne zur Reform der Habsburger Monarchie* (Brünn, 1943), pp. 123–49. Eichhoff's plans were summarized in an article in 1926 in the *Rp.* Various drafts, some fragmentary, of the original dossier are in Carton 2, *NL Eichhoff.* See also Kiszling, *Erzherzog Franz Ferdinand,* pp. 254–57. The most recent general analysis of the plans is Robert A. Kann, *Erzherzog Franz Ferdinand Studien* (Vienna, 1976), pp. 26–46, but see also Johannes Mende, "Dr. Carl Freiherr von Bardolff." Dissertation, University of Vienna, 1984, pp. 56–60. For Brosch's comment, see Franz, *Erzherzog Franz Ferdinand,* pp. 127–28 ("Hat in Österreich je ein Streit um Kronrechte usw. stattgefunden, seitdem das Parlement so schwach ist? Vom Standpunkt der Krone ist also ein schwaches oder arbeitsunfähiges ungarisches Parlament nur wünschenswert und keineswegs als Schreckgespenst zu fürchten" [p. 128]). The most extreme opponent of parliamentarism among the Archduke's advisors was Ottokar Czernin. See Czernin's statement of 20 November 1913, reprinted in *Schicksalsjahre,* 1: 214–15, and Redlich's comment: "Denn es ist ein Dokument für die Gesinnung nicht nur des Briefschreibers, sondern des grössten Teiles unseres Hochadels, vor allem der Leute, die den Thronfolger umgeben." For a recent review of the political imagination of one prominent Austrian aristocrat, see Solomon Wank, "A Case of Aristocratic Anti-Semitism in Austria: Count Aehrenthal and the Jews, 1878–1907," *Year Book of the Leo Baeck Institute,* 30 (1985): 435–56.

182. Compare the draft of a "Manifest Seiner Majestät an die Völker des Reiches aus Anlass der Allerhöchsten Thronbesteigung," Carton 2, *NL Eichhoff.*

183. 21 October 1913, *NL Berchtold.* A good analysis of the scope of the Archduke's political activities is Samuel R. Williamson's "Influence, Power and the Policy Process: The Case of Franz Ferdinand, 1906–1914," *Historical Journal,* 17 (1974): 417–34.

184. Compare the draft proposal calling for a "Sanierung der Verwaltungsmoral," 31 December 1913, Nr. 7, Carton 204, *MKFF.* Bardolff's views of how a Minister-President should deal with both parliament and the civil service were remarkably similar to the ways a commanding officer would treat subordinates and troop units under his command. On the semiabsolutist ethos of these plans, see G. E. Schmid, "Franz Ferdinand," *Biographisches Lexikon zur Geschichte Südosteuropas* (4 vols., Munich, 1974–81), 1: 532–35. Note also the views expressed in a position paper in the *NL Eichhoff* (possibly by Eichhoff himself) of the parallelism between military and civil service as elite loyalists of the Crown: "Ebenso wie mit Rücksicht auf äussere Feinde über die Organe der bewaffneten Macht, müsse daher—angesichts subversiver Elemente und Strömungen im Innern—das Allerhöchste Verfügungsrecht wenigstens über einen solchen Kreis von Organen der Regierungsgewalt uneingeschränkt gewahrt werden,

dass die Ausübung von Regierungsakten—ohne die Möglichkeit der Geltendmachung dienstpragmatischer Rechte—jederzeit und unbedingt sichergestellt ist. Die betreffenden Beamten müssten von jeder parteimässigen Einflussnahme freigehalten und jedenfalls durch eine eigene Gesetzesbestimmung vom Wahlrechte und der Wählbarkeit ausgenommen werden." Carton 2, *NL Eichhoff*. Compare also Kann, *Erzherzog Franz Ferdinand Studien,* p. 45, who rightly notes, "dass alle föderalistischen oder Autonomiepläne des Erzherzogs in erster Linie nur einem Ziel dienten: der Stärkung der Zentralgewalt der Krone." For the Austrian bureaucracy's reaction to him, see Sieghart, *Die letzten Jahrzehnte,* p. 241.

185. Without discounting or trivializing the role that Heinrich Lammasch played in assisting Brosch in the latter's drafting of instruments for the transition, it seems unlikely that Lammasch's personal political philosophy would have governed, either in spirit or in content, the principal policies of the new regime. In this I disagree slightly with the judicious analysis in Kann, *Erzherzog Franz Ferdinand Studien,* p. 199ff. This says nothing about the actual role of Czernin (of whom Kann offers an extremely unflattering portrait), and Kann is doubtless correct that the Archduke would have acted with more caution than that prescribed by Czernin. But at the time of the Archduke's death his two closest collaborators in the *Thronbesteigung* were apparently Bardolff and Eichhoff, not Lammasch. As Czernin points out in his *Im Weltkriege,* p. 64, the Archduke's plans were not definitive. The principal value of the *Staatsstreich* plans is in their suggestive articulation of a set of cultural values and broad policy options—sketching the range of possible and desirable state acts—not in predicting the actual achievements of the new regime. For Lammasch's own account, see Marga Lammasch and Hans Sperl, eds., *Heinrich Lammasch. Seine Aufzeichnungen, sein Wirken und seine Politik* (Vienna, 1922), pp. 77–95.

186. Seton-Watson to Funder, 30 June 1914, *R. W. Seton-Watson Papers,* School of Slavonic and East European Studies, University of London.

187. Funder to Seton-Watson, 4 July 1914.

188. Seton-Watson to Funder, 21 July 1914.

189. Funder to Brosch, 13 July 1914, *NL Brosch,* B/232.

CHAPTER SEVEN

1. See, for example, the police reports in Z. 3102, 19 February 1917, Carton 2066, 22; Z. 19014, 25 September 1917, Carton 1646, 15/3; Z. 4884, 17 March 1917, Z. 4934, 23 March 1917, and Z. 8448, 19 May 1917, Carton 2131, 22, *MI Präs.* See also the report of Police President Gorup reprinted in Rudolf Neck, ed., *Arbeiterschaft und Staat im Ersten Weltkrieg 1914–1918* (2 vols., Vienna, 1964–68), 1: 250 ("Den Parteiführern fehlt es an dem entsprechenden Betätigungsfelde, ein grosser Teil der Arbeiterschaft ist mit dem massvollen Verhalten der Führer nicht einverstanden und darin liegt auch nicht zum geringen Teile die Ursache an dem starken Rückgange der Organisation . . ."). Also illuminating are the debates about the hierarchy's loss of credibility in the aftermath of Fritz Adler's trial in the "Protokoll über die gemeinsame Sitzung der Parteivertretung,

der Gewerkschaftskommission und des Wiener Vorstandes am 1. Juni 1917." *VGAB*. These trends were apparent to the Christian Social leadership. See Seipel to Lammasch, 21 January 1918 (copy), *NL Seipel* ("Die Sozialdemokratie ist aufs äusserste zerklüftet. Das wissen wir von den Vertrauensmännern aus den Versammlungen").

2. On Austrian unions and the war government, see J. Robert Wegs, *Die österreichische Kriegswirtschaft 1914–1918* (Vienna, 1979), pp. 93–105; and most recently Margarete Grandner, *Kooperative Gewerkschaftspolitik in der Kriegswirtschaft. Die freien Gewerkschaften Österreichs im ersten Weltkrieg* (Vienna, 1992).

3. Funder, *Vom Gestern*, pp. 521–22.

4. "Protokoll der Sitzung des deutschen Parteivorstandes am 17. August." *VGAB*. See also the personal conflict between Renner and Fritz Adler at the *Vorstand* meeting on 12 January 1916 over editorial policies at *Der Kampf* ([Adler speaking]: "Er und Renner stellen gegenwärtig so extreme Richtungen in der Partei dar, dass eine wirkliche Verständigung absolut ausgeschlossen erscheint").

5. See Renner's essays in *Marxismus, Krieg und Internationale. Kritische Studien über offene Probleme des wissenschaftlichen und des praktischen Sozialismus in und nach dem Weltkrieg* (2d ed., Vienna, 1918) and *Oesterreichs Erneuerung. Politisch-programmatische Aufsätze* (Vienna, 1916); Jacques Hannek, *Karl Renner und seine Zeit* (Vienna, 1957); and the comments in Peter Broucek, ed., *Ein General im Zwielicht. Die Erinnerungen Edmund Glaises von Horstenau* (3 vols., Vienna, 1980–88), 1: 498–99. For a fair contemporary survey, see Richard Nimrichter, "Volkstum, Vaterland und Internationalismus," *VW*, 9 (1918): 13–20, 119–29, 166–77, 218–24. For an excellent recent study on war socialism, see Hans Mommsen, "Victor Adler und die Politik der österreichischen Sozialdemokratie im ersten Weltkrieg," in *Politik und Gesellschaft im Alten und Neuen Österreich*, 1: 378–408, esp. pp. 395–96. See also Berthold Unfried, "Positionen der 'Linken' innerhalb der österreichischen Sozialdemokratie während des 1. Weltkrieges," *Neuere Studien zur Arbeitergeschichte*, 2: 319–60.

6. Redlich to Bahr, 24 February 1916, in *Dichter und Gelehrter*, p. 159.

7. For a good survey of Renner's wartime thought, see Anton Pelinka, *Karl Renner zur Einführung*, pp. 39–49. See also Berthold Unfried, "Entwicklungsebenen der Arbeiterbewegung in Österreich während des Ersten Weltkrieges," in *Die Bewegung*, pp. 300–312.

8. *Friedrich Adler vor dem Ausnahmegericht* (Berlin, 1919), pp. 44, 68; and the "Protokoll über die gemeinsame Sitzung der Parteivertretung, der Gewerkschaftskommission und des Wiener Vorstandes am 1. Juni 1917," *VGAB*.

9. A 19461, 12 June 1917, Oest. 70/Bd. 51, *PAAA*.

10. Renner joined the *Ernährungsamt* with the approval of the party leadership. See "Protokoll der Sitzung des deutschen Parteivorstandes am 28. November 1916."

11. "Die Erklärung der 'Linken'," in *Protokoll der Verhandlungen des Parteitages der deutschen sozialdemokratischen Arbeiterpartei in Oesterreich. Abgehalten in Wien vom 19. bis 24. Oktober 1917* (Vienna, 1917), pp. 113–17 (esp. p. 116: "In der Zeit der standrechtlichen Massenhinrichtungen hat Renner diesen Staat geradezu idealisiert, ihn

als den Hort der kleinen Nationen gefeiert, den 'übernationalen Staat' als eine höhere Staatsform hingestellt. Er hat die Illusion zu erwecken versucht, dass die Krankheit des Staats durch eine blosse Verwaltungsreform geheilt werden könne. Wir unterschätzen die Bedeutung und die Notwendigkeit einer Verwaltungsreform in Gemeinde und Kreis nicht, aber wir sind überzeugt, dass eine Reform unserer Verwaltungsorganisation nicht zureicht, das staatliche Problem zu lösen. Wie das soziale Problem nicht in blosser Verwaltungsarbeit gelöst werden kann, sondern nur durch die Eroberung der politischen Macht durch das Proletariat, so kann auch das nationale Problem nicht durch ein paar Verwaltungsgesetze gelöst werden, sondern nur durch den vollen Sieg der Demokratie"). See also Pelinka, *Karl Renner,* pp. 48–49.

12. Victor Adler summarized this shift in perception well when he admitted at the Congress that "Ja, heute leben wir in einer anderen Luft, als wir in den Jahren 1914, 1915, und 1916 gelebt haben. Dass wir uns den Verhältnissen anpassen müssen, das wird wohl jeder zugeben." *Protokoll,* p. 172. On the socialists and the Cabinet, see ibid., pp. 134, 138, and 173.

13. Bauer to Kautsky, 19 February 1913, in *Werkausgabe,* 9: 1032.

14. See the discussion of Pernerstorfer's politics during the war in Carton 19, *CPK,* and Pernerstorfer's attack on Robert Danneberg, "Der Typus Danneberg," in the *Volks-tribüne,* 28 April 1915, as well as Leon Kane, *Robert Danneberg. Ein pragmatischer Idealist* (Vienna, 1980), pp. 80–84. See also Seitz's comments in the "Protokoll der Sitzung der Parteivertretung und d. Klubs der Abgeordneten, (Nachmittagssitzung), am 13. Juli 1915": "Seitz polemisiert gegen Renner und sagt, dass er seine Strafe durch die Anerkennung Pernerstorfers erhalten habe. Auf verschiedene Zwischenrufe sagt Seitz: Pernerstorfer hat sich am weitesten von dem entfernt, was wir bisher einen Sozialdemokraten nannten." *VGAB.*

15. Redlich to Bahr, 5 February 1918, in *Dichter und Gelehrter,* p. 304.

16. Adler to Ebert, 14 November 1917, Carton 12, *NL Adler.*

17. Adler to Braun, 17 November 1917, ibid.

18. To Braun he confessed that "Mein Trost ist, dass Otto da ist. Obwohl er sehr stark Bolschewik ist, welche Mimikri sich wohl wieder verlieren wird, ist er natürlich der einzige Mensch, der in den Abendstunden, wo er frei ist, das Geschäft weiterführen kann." See also similar comments on Bauer and his own perplexities in his letter to Kautsky, 14 November 1917 ("das eine und einzige was ich mir vorgenommen, um gar keinen Preis die Einigkeit der Partei zerstören zu lassen, habe ich doch erreicht. Nicht ohne grosse auch persönliche Opfer. Jetzt ist ja alles leichter, da Otto da ist. Allerdings ist er noch ein wenig zu viel Bolschewik und muss sich an das alte Milieu erst wieder anpassen. Aber welche Erlösung es für mich ist, ihn da zu haben, kannst Du Dir kaum denken"), Carton 12.

19. "Österreichs Pflicht," *Rp,* 2 July 1914 (M), p. 1. For Mataja's early jingoism, see also Heinrich Kanner, *Kaiserliche Katastrophenpolitik. Ein Stück zeitgenössischer Geschichte* (Leipzig, 1922), pp. 422–43. For a survey of Christian Social activities dur-

ing the war, see Heinz Meier, "Die österreichischen Christlichsozialen während des ersten Weltkrieges." Dissertation, University of Vienna, 1966.

20. "Die Entscheidung," *Rp,* 26 July 1914 (M), pp. 1–2.

21. Richard v. Kralik, *Die Entscheidung im Weltkrieg. Drei Reden* (Vienna, 1914), p. 30. On Kralik, see David C. Large, "Richard von Kralik's Search for Fatherland," in *AHY,* 17/18 (1981–82): 144–55.

22. Z. 18206, 15 December 1914, Carton 2197, 31, *MI Präs.*

23. On censorship during the war, see Gustav Spann, "Zensur in Österreich während des 1. Weltkrieges 1914–1918." Dissertation, University of Vienna, 1972.

24. The literature on German society during the war is enormous. Recent contributions that I have found particularly helpful include Gerald D. Feldman, *Army, Industry and Labor in Germany, 1914–1918* (Princeton, 1966); Jürgen Kocka, *Klassengesellschaft im Krieg. Deutsche Sozialgeschichte 1914–1918* (Göttingen, 1973); and Avner Offer, *The First World War: An Agrarian Interpretation* (Oxford, 1989).

25. Various efforts were made during the war to mediate the tensions, or at least keep open the lines of communication, between Vienna and the provinces, but suspicions were never far below the surface. See for example Johann Hauser's frustration in August 1917 over the presumptuousness of Weiskirchner and his colleagues in the Rathaus: "Die Herren in den Kopf gesetzt, sie wollen den Klub führen; das Recht erreichen durch uns, die Gedanken von Ihnen. Sie haben sich geärgert, dass wir einen Beschluss ohne sie gefasst haben." "Klubsitzung," 28 August 1917.

26. "Verhandlungsschrift über die Sitzung des Bürgerklubs vom 21. September 1914," Carton 37, *CPW.* The City Council approved the measure the next day, September 22.

27. Z. 13663, 23 September 1914, Carton 1572, 11/1, *MI Präs.*

28. In May 1915 Leopold Steiner asked Weiskirchner about the possibility of recalling the Council, but the mayor insisted that since the Social Democratic and Liberal factions would not give him a ironclad guarantee that they would not violate the *Burgfriede* by bringing politics into the discussions, he refused to summon the Council. See "Verhandlungsschrift über die Sitzung des Bürgerklubs vom 3. Mai 1915."

29. *Schicksalsjahre,* 2: 115.

30. The press release, dated 4 November 1914, as well as the Sekretariat's report to Weiskirchner on 9 November 1914, are in the file "Die Gemeinde Wien während der ersten Kriegswochen," Z. 1040, Carton 73, *CPW.*

31. See "Vorstandssitzung," 13 April 1916, Carton 91, *CPK.* For *Beamten* agitation during the war, see the materials in the *NL Gross,* Carton 2, particularly the letter of Friedrich Grabscheid, the leader of the *Zentralverband der österreichischen Staatsbeamtenvereine,* to Gross, 23 September 1915, including a memorandum of the *Verband*'s demands; and the memorandum of the *Reichsbund deutscher Postler Österreichs* to Gross, 10 February 1916, claiming that the *Nationalverband* had been principally responsible for the temporary salary supplements accorded to the officials.

32. Summary reports of the sessions of the *Obmänner-Konferenz* were printed in *AB*. See also "Beschlüsse der Obmännerkonferenz 1914–1918," Carton 25, *CPW*, and *Die Tätigkeit der Wiener Gemeindeverwaltung in der Obmänner-Konferenz während des Weltkrieges* (Vienna, 1917).

33. The socialists bridled at the way the new seats were to be created: rather than take existing positions away from his cronies, Weiskirchner intended to have the government create three new seats by an Imperial decree (raising the membership from 27 to 30). The small Liberal faction eagerly accepted, but the Social Democrats refused to join the *Stadtrat* unless they received at least one (they wanted two) of the "legal" seats formerly occupied by Christian Social loyalists. See the debates in the *Bürgerklub* on 18 September 1916, 16 October 1916, and 8 June 1917 in Carton 37, *CPW;* and the Social Democratic debates on 25 September 1916, 19 October 1916, 7 December 1916, and 4 July 1918 in "Vorstandsprotokollen," *VGAB*. On the legal background, see *Die Gemeindeverwaltung der Stadt Wien in der Zeit vom 1. Jänner 1914 bis 30. Juni 1919* (Vienna, 1923), pp. 12–13. The Christian Socials reacted with staged outrage, accusing the Social Democrats of being demagogues. *Rp*, 20 September 1916 (N), pp. 2–3; 26 September 1916 (M), p. 8; 27 September 1916 (M), p. 10. In December 1916 the Christian Socials went ahead with the expansion, securing goverment approval in April 1917, whereupon two Liberals—Oskar Hein and Oswald Hohensinner—were elected to the *Stadtrat* in June 1917. The Social Democrats continued their boycott, with Jakob Reumann twice refusing election (although on the second occasion, in July 1918, a division of opinion emerged in the socialist ranks, with the municipal club wanting Reumann to take the position but being overruled by the party executive). See also *AZ,* 9 July 1918, p. 5.

34. See his comments to Lammasch on 24 December 1917 and 21 January 1918, *NL Seipel*.

35. This is evident in the comments in Z. 15129, 28 October 1914, Carton 2130, 22, *MI Präs.*

36. "Klubsitzung," 27 January 1915, Carton 91, *CPK*.

37. *SP,* 1917, p. 296.

38. For a discussion of Austrian policy toward the Polish Question, which also raises more general issues relating to war aims, see Joachim Lilla, "Innen- und Aussenpolitische Aspekte der austropolnischen Lösung 1914–16," *MÖSTA*, 30 (1977): 221–50.

39. See his patriotic speech given on 26 October 1915, reprinted in the *Wiener Kommunal-Kalender und Städtisches Jahrbuch für 1917,* pp. 945–48. For pan-German approbation of this course, see the letter of Karl Hermann Wolf to Weiskirchner, 27 October 1915, thanking the latter for his advocacy of the economic and political integration of Germany and Austria. I.N. 29250, *Handschriftensammlung.*

40. For Stürgkh's stance toward Kramář see Christoph Führ, *Das K.u.K. Armeeoberkommando und die Innenpolitik in Österreich 1914–1917* (Graz, 1968), pp. 58–63, and the files in *MKSM,* 57–3/11–7, which contains the 629-page indictment (with evidence)

against Kramář. See also Redlich's report of a conversation with Stürgkh in March 1916: "Er erzählt mir über seine dreistündige Aussage im Kramarz-Prozess, sprach sich sehr kaustisch über die Weltfremdheit unserer Militärs aus und sprach sehr vernünftig über die Tschechen . . . ," *Schicksalsjahre,* 2: 104, as well as 41. To Berchtold, Stürgkh noted that he found the Kramář treason trial an "ungeheuere Verlegenheit." Berchtold Diary, entry of 23 January 1916, Carton 5, *NL Berchtold.*

41. Redlich to Bahr, 15 November 1920, in *Dichter und Gelehrter,* p. 431. This letter is interesting for Redlich's views on the lack of "Catholicism" in the prewar Christian Social party.

42. When the parliamentary *Vorstand* resumed regular meetings in January 1915, Gessmann was invited to serve as a spokesman for political and economic affairs, even though he had no parliamentary seat. Weiskirchner also occasionally attended club meetings. In October 1916 Gessmann was made the caretaker of party affairs, along with Victor von Fuchs, when the elected Chair was absent from Vienna. See "Vorstandssitzung," 10 October 1916, Carton 91, *CPK.*

43. "Klubsitzung," 23 March 1915. When the Tyrolean Guggenberg offered a motion demanding no territorial cessions from South Tyrol, it was not brought up for a vote, and the communiqué published in the *Reichspost* on the meeting made no mention of it. According to Funder, Gessmann and Fink accepted Erzberger's arguments. *Vom Gestern,* pp. 525–27. See also Matthias Erzberger, *Erlebnisse im Weltkrieg* (Stuttgart, 1920), p. 28; Epstein, *Erzberger,* p. 126; and István Burián, *Austria in Dissolution,* trans. Brian Lunn (London, 1925), p. 50. For a recent analysis of German policy, see Alberto Monticone, *Deutschland und die Neutralität Italiens 1914–1915* (Wiesbaden, 1982).

44. Pattai to Weiskirchner, 9 March 1915, I.N. 173.475, *Handschriftensammlung.* The protocol of the Crown Council on 8 March 1915 has been reprinted in Miklós Komjáthy, ed., *Protokolle des Gemeinsamen Ministerrates der Österreichisch-Ungarischen Monarchie (1914–1918)* (Budapest, 1966), pp. 215–33. Erzberger's interventions (more accurately his meddling) in Vienna were probably counterproductive: "Baron Burián sprach dann Herrn von Tschirschky gegenüber noch den Wunsch aus, dass Deutschland jetzt seinen Einfluss auf Italien wirken lassen und auch den Fürsten Bülow hiezu. . . . der Fürst solle nicht fortfahren, wie bisher durch Entsendung von Privatpersonen einen Druck auf die österreichische Regierung zu versuchen, was in Wien nur böses Blut gemacht habe." Lerchenfeld to Hertling, 15 March 1915, in Ernst Deuerlein, ed., *Briefwechsel Hertling-Lerchenfeld* (2 vols., Boppard am Rhein, 1973), 1: 412.

45. Funder, *Vom Gestern,* pp. 532–35; *Schicksalsjahre,* 2: 275–76; Burián, *Austria in Dissolution,* pp. 67–69. The party's later dealings with the *Zentrum* politician were strained, however, by Erzberger's fantastic plan for creating a de facto papal state out of the principality of Liechtenstein in 1916, which both Piffl and the Liechtenstein family opposed. See Erzberger to Piffl, 21 April 1916 and 24 April 1916, *NL Piffl;*

Epstein, *Erzberger,* pp. 145–48; and the description of Piffl's acerbic comments in Victor Naumann, *Profile. 30 Porträt-Skizzen aus den Jahren des Weltkrieges nach persönlichen Begegnungen* (Munich, 1925), pp. 347–48.

46. "Klubsitzung," 27 January 1915; and Mataja's "Referat über die äussere Lage," as an appendix to the "Klubsitzung" of 23 March 1915, Carton 91, *CPK.*

47. *Schicksalsjahre,* 2: 98.

48. As recorded by Leopold von Andrian to Burián, 15 September 1915, Carton 499, *PA I.* See also General Salis-Seeweis's description of his German counterparts in a conversation with Conrad: "Die Deutschen sind brutal, unverfroren und rücksichtslos. Mit dem Ton des Gentleman kommt man nicht weit, das Beste ist, mit gleicher Münze zurückzuzahlen. Sie sind grosse Räuber . . . ," transcript, Kundmann Diary, entry of 4 January 1915, p. 281, *KA.*

49. Unsigned copy of a report filed on 8 November 1915, p. 4, Deut. 180/Bd. 2, *PAAA.*

50. Examples of Prussians maligning Austrian policies or institutions are so numerous as to defy citation. See, for example, Bethmann Hollweg's description of Falkenhayn's opinion of the Austrian army in his letter to Jagow, 13 October 1915, in André Scherer and Jacques Grunewald, eds., *L'Allemagne et les problèmes de la paix pendant la première guerre mondiale* (4 vols., Paris, 1962–78): 1, Nr. 147: "Österreich sei ein Kadaver, an den wir uns nicht binden könnten." Two days later he reported another conversation with Falkenhayn in which the latter argued that "Da die deutsche Armee von der österreichisch-ungarischen nichts lernen kann, würde der Vorteil [of a military convention] nur auf österreichisch-ungarischer Seite liegen, vorausgesetzt, dass die österreichisch-ungarische Armee überhaupt lernen will." 15 October 1915, Deut. 180/Bd. 1. See also Ludendorff's excoriating description of Austrian military and civil administrative practice in A 30687, 11 November 1916, Oest. 70/Bd. 51, *PAAA;* as well as Glaise-Horstenau's account of a conversation with Ludendorff in *Erinnerungen,* pp. 423–24. Matthais Erzberger later recalled that "Nach meinen Beobachtungen ist über die 'schlappen Österreicher' in den deutschen Offizierkasinos und an anderen Stellen während des Krieges mehr gelästert worden als über alle unsere Feinde zusammen." *Erlebnisse,* p. 111. In official circles the Polish question was perhaps the most embittering issue between the two sides, but Prussian contempt for the Austrian army—scarcely veiled in the latter stages of the war—was also at work. Kurt Riezler's comments on the Polish question are fully illustrative: "Unerhörte Schwierigkeit des polnischen Problems, dass das gesamte inneroesterreichische und zugleich die Frage unseres zukünftigen Verhältnisses zu Oesterreich mitumfasst. Wahrscheinlichkeit, dass dieser Krieg mit einer Erschütterung unserer Freundschaft zu Oesterreich endet, wir also den nächsten Krieg ohne Oesterreich fechten zu müssen, Gefahr laufen" (Kurt Riezler, *Tagebücher-Aufsätze-Dokumente* [Göttingen, 1972], entry of 29 August 1915, p. 298). In his reports to Munich Heinrich Tucher often mentioned tensions between Germans and Austrians or unflattering evaluations of the latter by the former; see esp. Z. 554 (13 November 1914), Z. 605 (26 November 1914), Z. 549 (3 July 1916), and

Tucher's personal letter to Hertling, 4 August 1917, *BHSA*. The humiliation under which the Austrians suffered is no better demonstrated than by a quote from a later work on the economic history of the war by Hans Loewenfeld-Russ, *Die Regelung der Volksernährung im Kriege* (Vienna, 1926), pp. 375–76, who was compelled to admit "dass die deutschen Regierungsvertreter manchmal bei solchen Verhandlungen eine herbe Kritik über die misslichen internen Verhältnisse der Donaumonarchie übten, welche Deutschland zwangen, von ihren eigenen kargen Vorräten an Österreich abzugeben, war, so sehr es für Österreichs Vertreter häufig mehr als peinlich war, begreiflich." And, for the Christian Socials, the similar remarks of Heinrich Mataja in 1918, after the Germans had once again bailed the Austrians out with emergency food shipments: "Dass wir immer wieder zu Deutschland, das nicht unbedingt in der Lage sein müsste, uns auszuhelfen, nachdem wir mehr Agrarstaat sind als jenes, betteln gehen müssen, sei für uns beschämend." Z. 15784, 26 June 1918, Carton 1648, 15/3, *MI Präs.*

51. Conrad to Ferdinand Marterer, 20 September 1915, Kundmann Diary, p. 218. See also Hans Loewenfeld-Russ, *Im Kampf gegen den Hunger. Aus den Erinnerungen des Staatssekretärs für Volksernährung 1918–1920,* ed. Isabella Ackerl (Vienna, 1986), pp. 37–38, 45, 97.

52. Redlich, *Österreichische Regierung,* pp. 247–48; Wegs, *Die österreichische Kriegswirtschaft,* pp. 24–35. See also the account of Emperor Karl's military ambitions and his dislike of the *AOK* in Glaise Horstenau's *Erinnerungen,* pp. 372, 396, 455.

53. Carl Freiherr von Bardolff, *Soldat im alten Österreich. Erinnerungen aus meinem Leben* (Jena, 1939), pp. 298–304; Richard Georg Plaschka, Horst Haselsteiner, and Arnold Suppan, *Innere Front. Militärassistenz, Widerstand und Umsturz in der Donaumonarchie 1918* (2 vols., Munich, 1974), 1: 159–66; Mende, "Karl Bardolff," pp. 103–4. See also Polzer's comments on the political abilities of most Austrian "Durchschnittsgeneräle" in Arthur Graf Polzer-Hoditz, *Kaiser Karl. Aus der Geheimmappe seines Kabinettschefs* (Zürich, 1929), p. 143. Already in August 1915, following the successful reconquest of Lemberg in June, rumors circulated in Vienna that Bardolff was plotting to set up a military-led government to replace Stürgkh, a project in which Funder was also alleged to be interested. See "Information," in Redlich, *Schicksaljahre,* 2: 57–58; Mende, "Bardolff," pp. 82–84. Neither Bardolff nor Funder mention this incident in their memoirs, but Funder did visit the Russian front in the summer of 1915 at the invitation of Bardolff. Glaise-Horstenau reports that Bardolff was out of favor with Kaiser Karl because of his close connections to the German High Command. Glaise-Horstenau, *Erinnerungen,* p. 429.

54. Richard Wollek complained in January 1917 that "Ein Sekretär kann nicht T. Fragen etc. lösen. . . . Mangel an Initiative im Klub. N. Vbd hat 30 Abgeordneten ständig in Wien, die keinen Beruf haben und sich nur der Politik widmen. Wir lauter Gänge und Bitten. Dem N. Vbd die Arbeiten nicht allein überlassen. Nat. Frage nur vom Standpunkt der Deutsch-Tschechenfrage behandelt." "Klubsitzung," 24 January 1917.

55. See Redlich to Bahr, 28 September 1917 and 13 October 1917, *Dichter und*

Gelehrter, p. 264 ("die Deutschen sind ohne jede Führung, von dem miserablen Wolf verführt und 'angeführt'") and pp. 266–69. It is also instructive that, aside from occasional contacts between Weiskirchner and Tschirschky, the German Embassy in Vienna generally ignored the Christian Social party, a fact which Matthias Erzberger found astonishing, given the fact that this was the largest German-speaking political movement in Austria. See his *Erlebnisse,* p. 112.

56. In general see Paul Molisch, *Geschichte der deutschnationalen Bewegung in Oesterreich von ihren Anfängen bis zum Zerfall der Monarchie* (Jena, 1926), pp. 238–62; as well as Höbelt, *Kornblume und Kaiseradler.* For an excellent regional study of interwar Austrian politics, which has much information on the German nationalists, see Evan Burr Bukey, *Hitler's Hometown: Linz, Austria, 1908–1945* (Bloomington, 1986).

57. "Die Tschechen sind merklich kleiner geworden und haben kein Hehl daraus gemacht, dass ihnen Pöschmann unbequem und unangenehm ist." Freisler to Gross, 30 March 1915, Carton 2, *NL Gross.*

58. See Gross's circular letter, dated 23 August 1914, Carton 4, *NL Gross.*

59. Ganser to Erler, 7 May 1913, Carton 2, *NL Gross;* and *AZ,* 13 April 1913, p. 5; 22 April 1913, p. 4.

60. Licht to Baernreither, 9 October 1914, Carton 49, *NL Baernreither.* See also Baernreither's acidic commentary to Marchet: "Der Nationalverband repräsentiert keineswegs heute die Intelligenz des deutschen Volks in Österreich. Vielfach ist man unzufrieden mit seiner Haltung u. seiner jetzigen Passivität. Viel mehr Menschen als Sie glauben beschäftigen sich mit den grossen Zukunftsfragen u. wollen vom Nationalverband nichts wissen." Letter of 8 September 1914, Carton 19, *NL Marchet.* On Gross, see Brigitte Deschka, "Dr. Gustav Gross." Dissertation, University of Vienna, 1966.

61. "Zwangig Jahre Deutscher Klub" and "Weitere Beiträge zur Geschichte des Deutschen Klubs," *Mitteilungen des Deutschen Klubs,* Folgen 8 and 9, 1928.

62. Heinrich Class, *Wider den Strom. Vom Werden und Wachsen der nationalen Opposition im alten Reich* (Leipzig, 1932), pp. 325–26; Polzer-Hoditz, *Kaiser Karl,* pp. 389–90; Günther Ramhardter, *Geschichtswissenschaft und Patriotismus. Österreichische Historiker im Weltkrieg 1914–1918* (Munich, 1973), pp. 100–101.

63. Raphael Pacher, "Weiterdenken!" *ODR,* 3 November 1914, pp. 1–2.

64. A statement, in rough typescript, which is likely attributable to them is in A 34311, 10 December 1914, Oest. 103/Bd. 7, *PAAA.* See also *Schicksalsjahre,* 2: 7–8; and Weber, "Karl Hermann Wolf," p. 316. Other Austro-German politicians, like Pantz, Friedmann, and Dobernig, also traveled to Berlin in the late autumn. Dobernig wrote to Gross urging the latter to get in touch with the leaders of the National Liberal party in Berlin, and reporting that Stürgkh was very unhappy that he had taken his trip. Letter of 29 November 1914, Carton 2, *NL Gross.* Gross apparently took the advice, for Redlich records such a trip to Berlin in early December. *Schicksalsjahre,* 1: 294.

65. For descriptions of the various *Kreise,* which often had overlapping memberships, see Deschka, "Gross," pp. 180–201; Ilse Schwarz, "Dr. Joseph Maria Baern-

reither. Versuch einer politischen Biographie." Dissertation, University of Vienna, 1966, pp. 166–79; Gertrud Bittner, "Dr. Gustav Marchet." Dissertation, University of Vienna, 1949; Heinz Lunzer, *Hofmannsthals politische Tätigkeit in den Jahren 1914–1917* (Frankfurt, 1981), pp. 57–72; and the occasional references in *Schicksalsjahre,* 2; and in Hanns Schlitter's Diary, *NL Schlitter.* See also Molisch, *Geschichte der deutschnationalen Bewegung,* pp. 240ff.

66. On the Marchet circle, as well as those around Schlitter and Baernreither, see Fritz Fellner, "Denkschriften aus Österreich. Die österreichische Mitteleuropa-Diskussion in Wissenschaft und Politik 1915/16," in *Geschichte zwischen Freiheit und Ordnung. Gerald Stourzh zum 60. Geburtstag* (Graz, 1991), pp.145–62; and Richard W. Kapp, "Divided Loyalties: The German Reich and Austria-Hungary in Austro-German Discussions of War Aims, 1914–1916," *CEH,* 17 (1984): 129ff.

67. Brass to Marchet, 19 February 1915, Carton 19, *NL Marchet.* Brass was a wealthy industrialist member of the *Herrenhaus* from Moravia who had subsidized the *Deutsche Geschäftsstelle* before the war, a private political action group devoted to nationalist propaganda.

68. Urban to Baernreither, 21 January 1915, Carton 49, *NL Baernreither.*

69. Dobernig to Marchet, 24 January 1915, Carton 19, *NL Marchet.* Karl Urban reported to Baernreither (21 January 1915) that the two politicians were "deeply offended." By the fall of 1915 Gross's ire was still evident, however, for when Baernreither sent Gross a copy of his economic analysis of German-Austrian relations, Gross responded on September 17 that "Leider kann ich aber an der Besprechung in der von Eurer Excellenz angeregten Form nicht teilnehmen, da ich aus Ihnen jedenfalls bekannten Gründen mit Marchet nicht zusammentreffen will." Carton 11, *NL Marchet.*

70. Redlich to Gross, 4 January 1913, Carton 2, *NL Gross.*

71. See the "Denkschrift der deutschböhmischen Reichsratsabgeordneten an Seine Excellenz den Herrn Ministerpräsidenten Karl Grafen Stürgkh," Carton 19, *NL Marchet.* This has been reprinted in the *Zeitschrift für Ostforschung,* 7 (1958): 519–30.

72. For the background of the tensions, see Schachermayr to Brass, 1 February 1916, Carton 11, *NL Marchet;* Heinrich d'Elvert to Gross, 18 February 1915; Schachermayr and Much to Gross, 11 February 1915; Schachermayr to Gross, 2 March 1915, Carton 4, *NL Gross.* The files also contain various law drafts prepared by the radical Germans and various drafts of Schachermayr's pronunciamento. On Schachermayr, see Bienerth's report in Z. 11188, 4 October 1913, Carton 2130, 22, *MI Präs.* Schachermayr was active before 1914 in persuading national students in Vienna to continue to honor the so-called "Waidhofen Principle" which denied dueling honors to Jewish students. Interestingly, Bienerth noted in 1913 that a number of students in the *Kyffhäuserverband* had voted recently not to continue to observe this discrimination, much to Schachermayr's consternation.

73. Schachermayr to Gross, 21 May 1915, Carton 4, *NL Gross.*

74. Schachermayr to Gross, 22 December 1915; Carl Beurle to Gross, 28 February 1916, and Beurle to Schachermayr, 29 February 1916, Carton 4, *NL Gross.* The various

drafts of Schachermayr's *Forderungen,* as well as the final *Osterbegehrschrift* of 1916 are also in this file. For the public presentation, see "Die Forderungen der Deutschen Oesterreichs," *ODR,* 16 April 1916, pp. 2–3, which stresses Karl Hermann Wolf's influence. See also Redlich, *Österreichische Regierung,* pp. 253–56, and "Weitere Beiträge zur Geschichte des Deutschen Klubs," which asserts that Schachermayr was the primary author of the document.

75. See the program, dated January, 1915 in Carton 4, *NL Gross.*

76. See the letter of the *Deutscher Volksrat für Böhmen,* 20 September 1915, Carton 11, *NL Marchet.*

77. See his "Eindrücke von der Berliner Tagung des Deutsch-österreichisch-ungarischen Wirtschaftsverbandes," presented on 13 April 1915, Carton 8, *NL Marchet.* Compare this with Medinger's less bellicose assertions in January 1916 in *Das kommende Wirtschaftsbündnis* (Prague, 1916), pp. 29–30. For a general introduction to Mitteleuropa schemes, see Henry Cord Meyer, *Mitteleuropa in German Thought and Action 1815–1945* (The Hague, 1955), pp. 174–93. For a valuable survey of German-Austrian economic relations, see also Richard W. Kapp, "The Failure of the Diplomatic Negotiations between Germany and Austria-Hungary for a Customs Union, 1915–1916." Dissertation, University of Toronto, 1977.

78. See Friedrich Naumann, "Die mitteleuropäische Wirtschaftsgemeinschaft," *Werke* (6 vols., Cologne, 1964), 4: 479–80. The text of the speech Naumann delivered at the June 1915 meeting in Vienna is in Carton 4, *NL Gross.* See also Tucher's comments in his report of 8 July 1915, Z. 589, *BHSA.*

79. See Hainisch, *75 Jahre aus bewegter Zeit,* pp. 131–32; Fellner, "Denkschriften aus Österreich," pp. 157–60. For the beginnings of the circle, see Friedjung to Baernreither, 28 March 1915, Carton 49, *NL Baernreither,* as well as Ramhardter, *Geschichtswissenschaft,* pp. 76–79. Baernreither had written to Friedjung urging that his *Denkschrift* be made public as soon as possible. Friedjung responded with glowing compliments about Baernreither's views on German-Austrian commercial relations, which eventually found their way into Baernreither's "Denkschrift über das wirtschaftspolitische Verhältnis Oesterreich-Ungarns zu Deutschland." The latter was circularized in the summer of 1915; a copy is in Carton 4, *NL Gross.* On Baernreither's views in the first years of the war, see also Masaki Miyake, "J. M. Baernreither und 'Mitteleuropa.' Eine Studie über den Nachlass Baernreither," *MÖSTA,* 17–18 (1964–65): 359–98; and Kapp, "Austro-German Discussions," pp. 130–31.

80. *Denkschrift aus Deutsch-Österreich* (Leipzig, 1915). Hainisch, Philippovich, and Uebersberger worked on the text, in addition to Friedjung. A young nationalist-oriented staff officer at the Imperial War Ministry gave Friedjung suggestions about the military section of the document. Glaise-Horstenau, *Erinnerungen,* p. 347. For the background to and contents of this pamphlet, see Paul R. Sweet, "Germany, Austria-Hungary and Mitteleuropa: August 1915–April 1916," in Hugo Hantsch and Alexander Novotny, eds., *Festschrift für Heinrich Benedikt* (Vienna, 1957), pp. 180–212; and Ramhardter, *Geschichtswissenschaft und Patriotismus,* pp. 73–99.

81. Friedjung to Hertling, 31 August 1915, in *Briefwechsel Hertling-Lerchenfeld,* pp. 554–56.

82. Lerchenfeld to Lössl, 8 November 1915, ibid., p. 553. For the impact in Berlin, see Sweet, "Germany," pp. 188–92, and p. 209, n. 26; and Ramhardter, *Geschichtswissenschaft,* pp. 88–91. Bethmann Hollweg was much more enthusiastic than the Bavarians. See Richard W. Kapp, "Bethmann-Hollweg, Austria-Hungary and Mitteleuropa 1914–1915," *AHY,* 19–20 (1983–84): 215–36.

83. Gessmann to Erzberger, 2 October 1915, in A 29435, 10 October 1915, Oest. 70/Bd. 50, *PAAA.* The addressee is not listed, but it is very likely to have been Erzberger. Redlich presciently commented to Bahr in early 1916 that, based on his impressions after another visit by Friedrich Naumann to Vienna, "für 'Mitteleuropa' wenige Aussichten der Verwirklichung bestehen: in Deutschland hat man wenig Lust dazu und noch weniger Liebe für Österreich." Redlich to Bahr, 16 February 1916, *Dichter und Gelehrter,* p. 153.

84. Friedjung to Marchet, 30 September 1915, informing Marchet that he had sent a copy of the *Denkschrift* to Conrad. Carton 19, *NL Marchet.* According to Glaise-Horstenau (*Erinnerungen,* p. 347), Conrad ignored the document, which greatly upset Friedjung.

85. Heinrich Friedjung, "Die Gegner des Bündnisses mit Deutschland," *NFP,* 17 March 1918 (M), p. 2. Friedjung had already attacked Lammasch in the *Vossische Zeitung* on March 8 (8 March 1918 [M], pp. 1–2), to which Lammasch replied in *NFP,* 16 March 1918 (M), p. 2. See also Redlich to Bahr, 13 and 23 March 1918, in *Dichter und Gelehrter,* pp. 318, 321.

86. One of the most prominent of the critics was Joseph Schumpeter. See Robert Loring Allen, *Opening Doors. The Life and Work of Joseph Schumpeter* (2 vols., New Brunswick, 1991), 1: 150–56; Stephan Verosta, "Joseph Schumpeter gegen das Zollbündnis der Donaumonarchie mit Deutschland und gegen die Anschlusspolitik Otto Bauers (1916–1919)," in Michael Neider, ed., *Festschrift für Christian Broda* (Vienna, 1976), pp. 373–404; and Berchtold's comments in his Diary entry of 26 June 1916. Hanns Schlitter, a Catholic and a friend of Alois Liechtenstein and Cardinal Piffl, expressed reservations about Friedjung's *Denkschrift:* see his Diary, entry of 25 September 1915, *NL Schlitter.* Schlitter was active in a circle of officials attached to the Austrian Foreign Office—Andrian, Colloredo, Franckenstein, Matscheko—whose views differed substantially from those of the other *Kreise,* emphasizing somewhat more the diplomatic and economic independence of the Hapsburg Monarchy. See esp. Lunzer, *Hofmannsthals politische Tätigkeit,* pp. 57ff.; Nautz, ed., *Unterhändler des Vertrauens,* pp. 114–15; and Wegs, *Die österreichische Kriegswirtschaft,* pp. 46–48.

87. Report of 30 November 1915, Carton 68 (Handelsverkehr 1908–1918), *PA I, HHSA.*

88. Delbrück to von Holtzendorff, A 33421, 2 December 1916, Deut. 180/Bd. 4, *PAAA.* This is a copy of Delbrück's letter, which Holtzendorff sent to State Secretary Zimmermann in Berlin. Delbrück's comments were part of an evaluation of an anti-

German *Denkschrift* (generated, so Delbrück believed, by a high Austrian aristocrat) which had come to his attention.

89. This fascinating document, without indication of authorship, is in Carton 19, ff. 17–47, *Kabinettskanzlei, Geheimakten.* The author's advocacy of the immediate recall of parliament and the creation of a new government led by a distinguished Austrian aristocrat and meriting widespread public respect might have come from several political factions, not the least of which some associated with the Christian Socials.

90. Beurle to Gross, 16 September 1914, Carton 4, *NL Gross.*

91. Weiskirchner to Gross, 27 October 1914, Carton 2, *NL Gross.* Gross had visited Weiskirchner a week earlier, after which Weiskirchner had summoned a meeting of the Viennese *Parteileitung,* which agreed to join the discussions. Gessmann also reported to Fink that negotiations had ensued in the late autumn. See Deuring, *Jodok Fink,* p. 184.

92. Beurle to Gross, 13 November 1914, Carton 4, *NL Gross.* Beurle viewed his fellow Upper Austrian Johann Hauser as a pro-German nationalist, a fact that may explain Ignaz Seipel's later animosity toward Hauser. Franz Rienössl reported to a meeting of the parliamentary club in early December on a conference held at the Rathaus between local Viennese leaders and Gross, Steinwender, Wolf, and Dobernig. According to Sigmund's notes, "Das Resultat sei ein geringeres gewesen." At the end of the discussion the club moved unanimously to continue to interact with the *Nationalverband* "auf dem status quo ante." "Klubsitzung," 3 December 1914. In a different context Baernreither would write to Marchet, noting of the rivalries within the Christian Social party, "diese christ-socialen Häupter sind sehr aufeinander eifersüchtig." 18 September 1915, Carton 11, *NL Marchet.*

93. See Weiskirchner to Gross, 16 March 1915, thanking him for the draft Gross had sent to him on the 7th. The various drafts of the nationalist program are in Carton 4, *NL Gross,* and in the file "Gemeinsames Programm mit Deutschnationalverband," Carton 69, *CPW.* The final version is reprinted in Redlich, *Österreichische Regierung,* pp. 249–53. Gross's 1915 views seem to have been based on his earlier foray into war aims in late August 1914.

94. Draft dated 30 July 1915, on which Weiskirchner apparently collaborated. See his notation to Sigmund "Unser Aufsatz über Programm wurde von O. Steinwender als verbessert verzeichnet und wird von ihm und seinem Klub referiert werden." (18 July 1915), Carton 69.

95. Fuchs to Gross, 10 September 1915, Carton 4, *NL Gross.* Fuchs reported to Gross that the Christian Social parliamentary club had voted this version on September 7. Czedik wrote to Marchet on 16 September that "laut Fuchs, der seit Anfang d. m. turnusmässig Obmann ist, die christl. Sozialen eine polit. Plattform bereits beschlossen haben. . . . Dieselbe sei der Deutschnationalen Gruppe (Gross) bereits mitgeteilt." Carton 19, *NL Marchet.* The protocol of the "Klubsitzung" on 7 September 1915 suggests that the final version was based on a prior draft by Weiskirchner and Gross, which the club then revised. *CPK,* Carton 91. Czedik also wrote to Baernreither on September 16

reporting his conversation with Fuchs, who argued that "Galizien müsse dualistisch zu den übrigen Provinzen gestellt werden," an indication that the Christian Socials supported a separatist scheme for Austro-Poland, but they were not willing to accept its complete divorce from the Empire. Carton 11, *NL Marchet.*

96. Fuchs subsequently asserted his party's concerns about the autonomy issue at a parliamentary executive meeting in March 1916: "Autonomiefrage bezeugen, dass bei der Beratung die Frage ausdrücklich von uns moviert wurde. Autonomie geht aus der Verschiedenheit der Länder naturnotwendig hervor. . . . Wir stehen und fallen mit der Autonomie. Ausgestaltung sehr dehnbar." "Vorstand," 14 March 1916. Paul Samassa later argued that the "Autonomie" clause had in fact been inserted by the anti-German National faction within the Christian Socials (a clear reference to Gessmann or Gessmann's supporters) in the hope that the German Nationalists would refuse to accept the provision, and that the whole project would then be wrecked. See Paul Samassa, *Die deutschösterreichische Politik während des Krieges* (Graz, 1917), p. 11 ("Nur so lässt sich die Niederlage erklären, die der Nationalverband seinerzeit bei der Vereinbarung der gemeinsamen Richtlinien in der Frage der Länderautonomie erlitt. Sie war von dem Flügel der Christlichsozialen, der dem Zusammengehen überhaupt abgeneigt war, aufgeworfen worden, um das Zustandekommen der gemeinsamen Richtlinien zu verhindern"). Obviously, the more clerically oriented members of the party might have entered these negotiations with mixed emotions, but the fact that they proceeded with the agreement once Gross and the Nationalists had given way on the clause may also have meant that they were simply keeping their options as open as possible, as any sensible politician would do under the circumstances.

97. This is clear in light of the fact that the Christian Socials had submitted their own three-point gloss on the negotiations to Stürgkh, who gave them to the Emperor on 8 September 1915, which clearly rejected any attempt to force the Austrian Slavs into compliance: "Niemand wird aber erwarten können, dass man dieses Ziel etwa mit Gewalt, durch Verfolgungen, und durch Einschränkung der berechtigten nationalen Interessen unserer Slawen erreichen könnte." Carton 21, ff. 13–15, *Kabinettsarchiv, Geheimakten.*

98. See Weiskirchner's handwritten note on the file copy of the draft, reporting that Gross, Fuchs, and he had handed the document to Stürgkh at a special audience. Stürgkh promised to make the Emperor aware of it. 30 September 1915. "Gemeinsames Programm," Carton 69, *CPW.*

99. A 29434, 6 October 1915, Oest. 70/Bd. 50, *PAAA.* See also Z. 24624, Carton 1645, 15/3, *MI Präs.,* for Christian Social exploitation of the alliance on the food issue.

100. *NFP,* 22 January 1916 (M), p. 7. Tellingly, the newspaper observed of the concessions given to the Christian Socials that "Bei diesen Verhandlungen wurde aber ausdrücklich betont, dass der Deutschnationalverband seine Forderungen, insoweit sie über diese gemeinsamen Wünschen hinausgehen, vollinhaltlich aufrecht erhält."

101. Czedik, *Zur Geschichte,* 4: 451–57; *Schicksalsjahre,* 2: 68–69, 72.

102. A copy of the *Erlass* is in Carton 2, *NL Gross.*

103. *Schicksalsjahre,* 2: 42.

104. Dobernig to Gross, 12 December 1914, Carton 2, *NL Gross.*

105. Komjáthy, *Protokolle,* pp. 233–65, esp. 259 ("Es bestehe eine starke Agitation gegen unsere wirtschaftliche Selbständigkeit. In Ungarn lasse man diesbezüglich keine Diskussion zu, wogegen in diesem Belange in Österreich eine starke Strömung wahrnehmbar sei. . . . Eine Zollunion oder dergleichen bedeute aber nicht nur die wirtschaftliche Abhängigkeit von Deutschland sondern es würden sich auch die politischen Folgen für unsere Grossmachtstellung einstellen. Er bitte deshalb die österreichische Regierung das Präveniere zu spielen und darauf Einfluss zu nehmen, dass man die Zollunion nicht gleichsam auf dem Präsentierteller Deutschland entgegenbringe. Man müsse gegen die Enunziationen hoher Beamten Stellung nehmen und ihnen nicht gestatten, sich für diese Idee zu exponieren"). Tisza followed this outburst with a private letter to Stürgkh a month later, complaining about pan-German agitation for economic union with Germany. Letter of 13 July 1915, Carton 28, *Kabinettskanzlei, Geheimakten.* For two views of different facets of Austro-German relations in 1916–18, see Imre Gonda, *Verfall der Kaiserreiche in Mitteleuropa. Der Zweibund in den letzten Kriegsjahren (1916–1918)* (Budapest, 1977); and Meyer, *Mitteleuropa in German Thought and Action.*

106. Medinger to Marchet, 13 July 1915, Carton 19, *NL Marchet.*

107. Lerchenfeld to Lössl, 8 November 1915, Nr. 226, in *Briefwechsel Hertling-Lerchenfeld,* p. 553.

108. Conrad to Burián, 21 December 1915. AOK Nr. 19380. Carton 499, *PA I.* Soon thereafter the Imperial Cabinet met (on 7 January 1916) to discuss the Monarchy's war aims. See Komjáthy, ed., *Protokolle,* pp. 352–81.

109. Diary, Nr. 17, pp. 21–26, *NL Baernreither;* "Erinnerungen des Erasmus Freiherrn von Handel," *Jahrbuch der österreichischen Leo-Gesellschaft* (Vienna, 1930), pp. 67ff.; Redlich, *Schicksalsjahre,* 2: 201–2. In his unpublished memoirs Raphael Pacher insisted that Stürgkh had promised Wolf and him the imposition of the *Octroi.* See his memoir, "Der deutsche Volksrat," reprinted in Harald Bachmann, "Der Deutsche Volksrat für Böhmen und die deutschbömische Parteipolitik," *Zeitschrift für Ostforschung,* 14 (1965): 287.

110. These proposals are discussed in detail in Führ, *Armeeoberkommando,* pp. 127–59.

111. Redlich to Bahr, 17 July 1915, in *Dichter und Gelehrter,* p. 121. (Heinrich Lammasch, according to Hermann Bahr, thought Eichhoff to be the "creator spiritus" of the General Staff, ibid., p. 176.) Not surprisingly, some of the most vigorous opposition came from the Minister of Justice, Victor von Hochenburger, over whose institutional prerogatives the military was running roughshod. See especially Führ, *Armeeoberkommando,* pp. 142–44, 146, 148–49, 151ff. Eichhoff's drafts from 1915–16 for various constitutional reforms are in *NL Handel.* Prominent among his ideas were the elimination of voting rights for state officials and a severe curbing of the rights of provincial governments in favor of centralist authority, including allowing the Imperial

governors to veto policy decisions taken by the Provincial Executive Committees. The *NL Eichhoff* contains a typed, but undated, sixteen-page elaboration of his proposals When Leon Biliński sought to have Eichhoff replaced with a Polish-speaking politician in mid-1915, he was defended by Archduke Friedrich as "ein Mann mit der ganz aussergewöhnlichen Sachkenntnis, Arbeitskraft und Energie" and as a "k.k. Beamter vorbildlichster Art." Letter to the *Militärkanzlei,* 20 July 1915, 69–2/16–4, *MKSM.*

112. *Schicksalsjahre,* 2: 96–97. Gessmann seems to have realized this, for in 1916 he argued at a club meeting that Stürgkh was a "friend" of the party's interests but that the Army High Command was clearly not. "Vorstand," 13 April 1916.

113. The Christian Socials on the other hand became increasingly suspicious of *Beamten* pressure groups during the war, both as pressure groups for and as agents of a powerful centralizing tendency directed against provincial autonomy. See Richard Wollek's comments in ibid. Nor were the military *Octroi* drafts always congruent to those of the pan-German politicians. For Stürgkh's resistance to army pressure, see also the Berchtold Diary, entry of 10 July 1915; and Führ, *Armeeoberkommando.* For Hohenlohe's constitutional visions in 1916, see the Berchtold Diary, entry of 17 May 1916.

114. On the *Ausgleich* negotiations, see József Galántai, *Hungary in the First World War* (Budapest, 1989), pp. 195–98, 219–20; and Alexander Spitzmüller-Harmersbach, *Der letzte österreichisch-ungarische Ausgleich und der Zusammenbruch der Monarchie,* esp. pp. 20–22, who reports pan-German lobbying against a long-term settlement with Hungary.

115. Gustav Gratz and Richard Schüller, *Die äussere Wirtschaftspolitik Österreich-Ungarns. Mitteleuropäische Pläne* (Vienna, 1925), pp. 9–16.

116. He might also have gained a modest weapon against Tisza's use of Hungarian food deliveries to Austria (by 1916 in steep decline against 1914 levels, in spite of vigorous Viennese protests) as political blackmail. Poland too was on Stürgkh's mind, for his statement to the joint *Ministerrat* in January 1916 on an "Austro-Polish" solution clearly indicated that he did not underestimate the problems of incorporating an enlarged semi-independent Poland into the Monarchy. Komjáthy, *Protokolle,* pp. 366–67. Stürgkh's original views of a possible settlement for Poland were presented to the *Ministerrat* of 6 October 1915. Ibid., pp. 294–97, 309–12. Schlitter reported in October 1915 that Tisza was pressuring Stürgkh to recall the Austrian parliament, possibly to prevent a pan-German settlement. Schlitter Diary, entry of 26 October 1915.

117. See Hohenlohe's comments on Stürgkh's indecisiveness in the Berchtold Diary, entry of 4 March 1916. Gessmann too complained that "Stürgkh geht an Apathie zugrunde." "Vorstand," 14 March 1916.

118. Redlich, *Schicksalsjahre,* 2: 202.

119. Redlich, *Österreichische Regierung,* pp. 249–53.

120. *NFP,* 5 March 1916 (M), p. 10. This is in the form of an interview with Pfersche.

121. Brass to Gross, 7 March 1916, Carton 4, *NL Gross.*

122. *Dichter und Gelehrter,* p. 157. For a more general statement of Pfersche's view

of German politics in Austria, in which the Christian Socials would play no useful role, see *Die Parteien der Deutschen in Österreich vor und nach dem Weltkrieg* (Munich, 1915), esp. pp. 12–13. Pfersche blamed the "Gessmann Group" for supporting a covert anti-German strategy after 1911.

123. A complaining letter from the *Deutscher Verein* in Carniola to Gross raised exactly this issue: "Die Aufstellung der Forderung der Ausgestaltung der Länderautonomie. . . . hat bei den Deutschen jener Länder, die slawische Mehrheiten besitzen, die grösste Enttäuschung und Bestürzung hervorgerufen." Ferdinand Eger to Gross, 6 September 1916, Carton 2.

124. "Nochmals die Autonomiefrage," Carton 4, *NL Gross*, ff. 673–74.

125. *Stenographisches Protokoll der Enquete über die Landesfinanzen. 7. bis 12. März 1908* (Vienna, 1908), pp. 37–41, and Liechtenstein's comments to Lueger, 9 March 1908, I.N. 40878, *Handschriftensammlung*.

126. "Vorstandssitzung," 13 April 1916, Carton 91, *CPK*.

127. Beurle to Gross, 28 February 1916, Carton 4, *NL Gross*.

128. A collection of Beurle's correspondence relating to the *Arbeitspartei*, and the hesitant reactions of various German party leaders is in the *NL Gross*, Carton 5. On Beurle, see Else Beurle, *Dr. Carl Beurle 1860–1919* (privately printed, 1960); and Kurt Tweraser, "Carl Beurle and the Triumph of German Nationalism in Austria," *German Studies Review,* 4 (1981): 403–26.

129. "Protokoll der Sitzung des deutschen Parteivorstandes am 4. Mai 1916." *VGAB.*

130. "Protokoll der Sitzung des deutschen Parteivorstandes gemeinsam mit der Gewerkschaftskommission am 16. November 1915." Ibid.

131. "Protokoll der Sitzung des deutschen Parteivorstandes am 12. Januar 1916." Ibid.; Mommsen, "Victor Adler und die Politik der Sozialdemokratie," pp. 395–96.

132. The Christian Socials were only too aware of this commonality of interest between the nationalists and the socialists. See Gessmann's comments at the "Klubsitzung," 13 April 1916.

133. "Protokoll der Sitzung des deutschen Parteivorstandes am 31. Mai 1916." *VGAB.*

134. Diary, Nr. 8 (typed), p. 112.

135. "Die Treibereien des Nationalverbandes . . . hält Gessmann für aussichtslos. . . . Die ganze Agitation der Deutschnationalen schade den Deutschen in Österreich gewaltig." *Schicksalsjahre,* 2: 91. Gessmann was usually close to Liechtenstein, and Liechtenstein also condemned Weiskirchner's sympathies toward the pan-Germans, which he saw as a tactic on Weiskirchner's part to replace Stürgkh: Schlitter reported a conversation in February 1915 in which Liechtenstein opposed a *Zollunion* with Germany and then said (in Schlitter's words), "Der Bürgermeister Weiskirchner stehe unter dem Banne der Deutschnationalen und sei Feuer und Flamme für den wirtschaftlichen Anschluss. . . . Weiskirchner sei ein Streber, von seiner ehrgeizigen Frau sehr beeinflusst, die ihn gerne als Minister-Präsidenten sehen möchte. Deshalb tue Prinz Alois Liechtenstein samt seinen Anhängern alles, um Stürgkh zu halten—'besser Stürgkh,

als der Bürgermeister'!" Schlitter Diary, entry of 6 February 1915. For Liechtenstein's public statements, see his "Österreichs Zukunft. I. Die Nationale Frage. II. Das österreichische Parlament," in *Das Neue Österreich,* April 1916, pp. 18–22; May 1916, pp. 1–6, in which he advanced the idea that the national tensions in Bohemia could be defused by allowing public officials in the predominantly German and Czech areas to know only one language, but that for service in mixed population areas and in the central ministries *Beamten* should be encouraged to learn both languages and to be motivated to do so by a system of extraordinary salary rewards attached to their base salaries.

136. Fuchs to Gross, 22 December 1915, Carton 4, *NL Gross;* and Gessmann's comments cited in *Schicksalsjahre,* 2: 91.

137. As reported in Z. 27262, 20 December 1915, Carton 2130, 22 *MI Präs.*

138. The Christian Social parliamentary club voted in the autumn of 1915 to support the recall of parliament, but public notice of this decision was censored. See Richard Wollek's recollection in *SP,* 1917, p. 65.

139. Z. 4273, 25 February 1916, Carton 2130, 22, *MI Präs.*

140. Heinrich von Wittek, "Bemerkungen zu der als 'vertraulich' bezeichneten Denkschrift der Zentrumsfraktion des Deutschen Reichstages betreffend den wirtschaftlichen Zusammenschluss der beiden verbündeten Mittelmächte," 29 February 1916, Ad. Reg., Fach 34, Carton 68, *HHSA*. Wittek was associated with Gessmann and Liechtenstein in the *Das Neue Österreich* project, preparing an essay on Austrian commerical development for the journal's special issue, *Austria Nova,* published in 1916.

141. These documents are a fascinating and as yet untold story of the war. Sigmund wrote to Wilhelm Miklas in May 1917 asking him to serve as a *Referent* on electoral reform before the full Christian Social parliamentary club and sending him draft documents, including a reform proposal that "was the work of Gessmann, Fink, and myself from 1915." Letter of 8 May 1917, Carton 19, *CPK*. The earliest version of these drafts that I have been able to identify is the election law which is in the *NL Handel,* Carton 2. In late August 1916 Stürgkh sent a copy of Christian Social proposal for a new election code to Handel, reporting that he had been given it "from the side of the Christian Socials" and asking Handel for an evaluation, but indicating no personal support for the measure. Versions of the group's proposals from 1917 are deposited in Mappe 1, Carton 36, *CPK* ("Grundgesetz über die Reichsvertretung," which also contains a long electoral code). These documents envisaged converting the *Herrenhaus* into an appointive *Oberhaus,* which would consist of 285 members, each of whom would represent a *Stand* or province. The Lower House would keep its 516 members, but they would be elected by proportional, list voting, with women receiving the vote. Gessmann, true to his parliamentarist leanings, curbed the Article 14 prerogatives of the Crown (edicts issued thus would have a maximum life of 400 days), and curbed the powers of the Upper House to veto initiatives of the Lower House (bills voted twice by a strong majority would override *Herrenhaus* amendments).

142. Friedrich Gaertner, "Dr. Albert Gessmann als Staatsmann," *Rp*, 8 July 1920, p. 2; confirmed by Funder, *Vom Gestern*, p. 524.

143. The evaluation is in Carton 2, *NL Handel*, undated, ff. 696–711. A summary of this evaluation was then returned to Sigmund, who revised the first version to take into account Handel's criticisms (which included the fact that the party had not reduced the number of parliamentary deputies from the 1907 legislation). Sigmund's revision, entitled "Abänderungen zu dem von der christlichsozialen Partei der Regierung überreichten Entwurfe einer neuen Reichsrats-Wahlordnung," is dated 17 September 1916, Carton 36, *CPK*. The files in the party archive relating to wartime electoral reform contain numerous hand-written and typed notes by Sigmund on the advantages of introducing proportional suffrage.

144. Hornich set the tone with his introductory essay "Was will das Neue Österreich," April 1916, pp. 2–5. See also Ramhardter, *Geschichtswissenschaft*, pp. 141–44.

145. Josef Sigmund, "Ziel der Deutschen in Österreich," April 1915, Z. 1113, Carton 74, *CPW*. This draft was apparently sent to Eduard Heinl. Sigmund later served as a principal co-author of the first Christian Social draft for a constitution for the Republic, which was submitted to the *Nationalversammlung* in May 1919. See Georg Schmitz, *Die Vorentwürfe Hans Kelsens für die österreichische Bundesverfassung* (Vienna, 1981), pp. 42–43.

146. Sigmund, most likely in collaboration with Gessmann, also experimented with the construction of a new legal relationship for the Empire as a whole, drafting a "Gesetz. . .über die Vertretung des österreichisch-ungarischen Staatenbundes." A full handwritten draft of this document is in Carton 36, *CPK*. The draft provided for the creation of a true federal government, consisting of a *Bundesrat* whose members were to be delegates from Austria, Hungary, and Croatia, and a *Bundesregierung*, chaired by the Imperial Minister of Foreign Affairs as Federal Chancellor.

147. Schlitter Diary, entries of 6 February, 12 February, and 13 July 1915.

148. Seipel to Lammasch, 30 December 1918, *NL Seipel*. See also Gessmann's flattering evaluation of Piffl in *Schicksalsjahre*, 2: 91.

149. On Bösbauer's unsavory political past, see the transcripts of interviews which the Christian Social party's investigating committee conducted with various local political figures in 1909. "Bösbauer Angelegenheit," Carton 69, *CPW*. For the *Neue Zeitung's* funding, see Beck to Coudenhove, 6 September 1908, *NL Beck*, who reported that Prince Zdenko Lobkowitz, who later became the adjutant of Kaiser Karl, had spent 60,000 crowns in support of the paper by 1908.

150. To cite merely one of Bösbauer's many outrages, the Catholic lawyer Max Anton Löw reported in 1909 that the former was behind a slander campaign against Franz Martin Schindler: "Bösbauer sagte auch über den Prälaten Schindler habe er einen ganzen Faszikel Materiale, das sei einer der gemeinsten Schwindler die es gibt." "Bösbauer Angelegenheit," p. 10.

151. Copies of both memoranda are in various *Nachlässe*. I used the copies in Carton 33, *NL Beck*. The origins and authorship of these memoranda have long been a

mystery. Redlich recorded the first memorandum as having been authored by Funder, but Fritz Fellner reports that Funder denied in the 1950s having had anything to do with it. *Schicksalsjahre,* 2: 56, n. 44; 58–60. Paul Molisch requested clarification from Beck in the 1920s, apparently with little success. See Molisch to Beck, 22 May 1929, Carton 36, *NL Beck.* The key lay with Gessmann, who wrote to Erzberger on 2 October explaining the conspiracy. Erzberger in turn passed Gessmann's letter on to the German Foreign Office. Tschirschky disliked Gessmann as an alleged pro-Slavic politician, and was only too willing to believe the worst about him. See A 29435, 10 October 1915, Oest. 70/Bd. 50, *PAAA.*

152. On Beck's innocence, see Marchet to Beck, 25 September 1915, Carton 36; and Baernreither to Beck, 28 September 1915, Carton 33, *NL Beck.*

153. *Schicksalsjahre,* 2: 144. For a discussion of rumors about a new German *Einheitspartei* in the summer of 1916, see "Spectator Austriacus," "Politischer Brief," *Das Neue Österreich,* (September 1916), pp. 1–6. Gessmann articulated some of his ideas for a postwar economic settlement in a speech delivered in early October 1916, in which he forecast both greater self-regulation by industry and commerce and greater policy control by the state. See *Rp,* 9 October 1916, pp. 6–7.

154. Redlich, *Österreichische Regierung,* pp. 256–57.

155. "Vorstandssitzung," 18 July 1916, Carton 91, *CPK;* Benesch to Beck, 24 July 1916, who reported that the censor eliminated notice of the resolution in the newspapers. Carton 33, *NL Beck.* See also Tucher's comments in Z. 630, 31 July 1916.

156. Benesch to Beck, 27 July 1916; *Schicksalsjahre,* 2: 131–33; "Protokoll der deutschen Parteivertretung," 27 July 1916, *VGAB;* "Streng vertraulicher Bericht. Eine gemeinsame Beratung der Parteien des Herrenhauses und des Abgeordnetenhauses," Z. 1249, Carton 75, *CPW.*

157. "Klubsitzung," 22 August 1916, Carton 91, *CPK.*

158. *SP,* 1917, p. 192. This sense of embattled and embarrassed marginality was also apparent on the Left. When Friedrich Austerlitz dared to make derogatory comments about the future prospects of the parliament at the November 1916 *Reichskonferenz* of the Social Democratic party, arguing that the Austrian parliament had counted for nothing and could count for nothing, he met determined resistance from the caucus of the Social Democratic parliamentary deputies. See *Arbeiterschaft,* 1: 156.

159. See the police report of 23 October 1916, reprinted in *Arbeiterschaft,* 1: 123, as well as *Friedrich Adler vor dem Ausnahmegericht,* p. 29. The deputies of the *Nationalverband* were not easily able to escape public pressure for recall. On September 14 a poorly attended meeting of the *Verband* narrowly voted to support the recall of parliament (19 in favor, 16 against, with 12 abstentions), but characteristically the delegates from Bohemia, and Wolf's Radicals, strongly opposed the motion. *Rp,* 15 September 1916, p. 5.

160. *Schicksalsjahre,* 2: 148.

161. *Rp,* 11 October 1916, p. 6; 12 October 1916, p. 3. Three days later Stöckler spoke at a meeting of the *Bauernbund* where he insisted that "Der Bauernstand . . .

bedarf dringend einer parlamentarischen Tribüne. Der Bürgerstand und der Mittelstand überhaupt wird diese Forderung gewiss unterstützen." Ibid., 14 October 1916, p. 5.

162. "Verhandlungsschrift über die Sitzung des Bürgerklubs vom 16. Oktober 1916."

163. Schraffl to Gross, 13 October 1916, Carton 5, *NL Gross*. The Christian Socials were primarily interested in cooperation on food questions. See also *Die Tätigkeit*, p. 12.

164. *Friedrich Adler vor dem Ausnahmegericht*, p. 17. For the background, see Douglas D. Alder, "Assassination as Political Efficacy. Two Case Studies from World War I," *East European Quarterly*, 12 (1978–79): 209–31.

165. When the socialist leadership met with Koerber on 14 November to discuss the date of the recall of parliament, there was general agreement that this should not occur before February 1917. "Protokoll der Sitzung des deutschen Parteivorstandes am 16. November 1916," *VGAB*.

166. At this meeting Gross agreed to support the joint motion but gave a long speech decrying the weakness of the parties and their likely inability to effect substantial changes, to which Leon Biliński observed that "das vom Abg. Dr. Gross vorgebrachte Memorandum des Deutschnationalverbandes in Wirklichkeit alles darzeige, was gegen eine Einberufung des Parlaments sprechen könnte." *ODR*, 25 October 1916, pp. 2–3. A copy of Gross's speech on October 23 is in Carton 4, *NL Gross*, ff. 628–29. The Christian Socials in contrast supported the motion without equivocation, and Funder explicitly disassociated the party from Gross's pessimism. See *Rp*, 25 October 1916, pp. 1–2; *Z*, 24 October 1916, pp. 4–5; "Protokoll der Sitzung des deutschen Parteivor-stands am 23. Oktober 1916," *VGAB*.

167. The *Reichspost* quickly issued a denial that the Christian Socials had known about Gross's resolution beforehand. *Rp*, 10 November 1916, p. 6; 11 November 1916, p. 4; and *ODR*, 11 November 1916, pp. 2–3. The Christian Social parliamentary club, meeting on November 10, approved the joint resolution of the 9th, but also worked out modalities for summoning a *Reichsparteitag* in anticipation of parliament. When the recall of parliament seemed imminent, the Christian Socials agreed to join a joint action committee with the *Nationalverband*. See the session of the "Parlamentarische Kommission," 8 December 1916.

168. Koerber essentially fell from power because he was too closely associated with Emperor Franz Joseph. By early December Koerber was receiving harsh criticism in the pan-German press. See *ODR*, 6 December 1916, p. 2; 13 December 1916, p. 4; 15 December 1916, p. 2. See also Harald Bachmann, "Raphael Pacher und die deutschra-dikale Bewegung in den Sudetenländern. Aus den Erinnerungen Pachers," *Bohemia*, 5 (1964): 457–58. On the conspiracies which brought down Koerber, see Tucher's reports Z. 1012 and 1013, 14 and 16 December 1916. See also Redlich's account on 16 Decem-ber 1916 in *Schicksalsjahre*, 2: 167–69. The *Reichspost* reported on the 14th (p. 3) that Koerber had met with leaders of the *Nationalverband* and refused to support their demands for a *Neuordnung* based on an *Octroi*, which in retrospect helped to push him

out of office. For the origins of the new Cabinet, see Felix Höglinger, *Ministerpräsident Heinrich Graf Clam-Martinic* (Graz, 1964), pp. 110–26.

169. See the "Vorstandssitzungen" on 15 and 19 December 1916, and the "Klubsitzung" of 24 January 1917, Carton 91, *CPK*. The leadership explicitly denied, however, that the Christian Socials were "represented" by Urban and Baernreither. *Rp,* 22 December 1916, p. 3; 29 December 1916, p. 1.

170. "Vorstandssitzung," 9 January 1917. Clam responded, for Gessmann and Weiskirchner, as well as Bishop Gross, were also appointed to the *Herrenhaus* in 1917.

171. Anti-Semitism was not merely in the streets. Berchtold related in his private diary in early 1918 the gratuitously insulting reaction of Emperor Karl to the new Hungarian Cabinet, which had three Jews as members: "Kaiser findet die Anwesenheit von 3 Hebräern im Cabinet (Vázsonyi, Földes, Szterényi) sei nicht sehr erfreulich, immerhin stünden denselben 7 'anständigen' Männer gegenüber, der Percentsatz sei also nicht so schlecht!!!" Entry of 26 January 1918, *HHSA.* Tucher made a point of referring to Josef Redlich as that "jüdische Abgeordnete" who had international-pacifistic tendencies. Z. 450, 11 July 1917.

172. His remarks came at the annual New Year's reception on 31 December 1914, hosted by Weiskirchner at the Rathaus. See *NFP,* 1 January 1915 (M), p. 16; and Ernst Till's criticism of Weiskirchner, a copy of which is in Carton 2, *NL Handel.* Weiskirchner responded to the idea with enthusiasm. Steiner did not mention that these were largely Jewish refugees, but his audience doubtlessly knew what he was talking about.

173. *Schicksalsjahre,* 2: 180; Baernreither, "Erinnerungen," Nr. 8, p. 20.

174. See Stöckler to Gross, 27 January 1917, Carton 4, *NL Gross;* and "Klubsitzung," 24 January 1917, Carton 91, *CPK.* This version was negotiated by a subcommittee on which both German National and Christian Social deputies were represented in late December 1916 and early January 1917. See Gross to Weiskirchner, 11 December 1916, Z. 1245; and Weiskirchner to Gessmann, 16 January 1917, Z. 1233, Carton 75, *CPW.*

175. This change was owing in part to Heinrich von Wittek's strong advocacy that the Empire should maintain some connection with Galicia, if only to keep access to its natural resources. See "Klubsitzung," 24 January 1917. The Social Democrats immediately noted this modification. See *Die Tätigkeit,* p. 19.

176. *Rp,* 31 January 1917, p. 5. The text was made public in *Rp,* 17 February 1917, pp. 1–2.

177. *Schicksalsjahre,* 2: 94; Baernreither, "Erinnerungen," Nr. 8., p. 21.

178. See Baernreither's prediction to Redlich in *Schicksalsjahre,* 2: 177, which proved to be a serious mistake on his part. See also *Rp,* 17 February 1917, pp. 1–2. The *Reichspost* subsequently argued (2 March 1917, p. 6; 4 March 1917, p. 5) that the Christian Socials had opposed the use of the term "Staatssprache," preferring "Verständigungssprache," but had acceded to nationalist preferences on the issue.

179. "Erinnerungen," Nr. 8, pp. 41ff. At a meeting of party leaders on 18 April Baerneither recounted that "Minister Handel habe die Sachen nicht mit genügenden

Lokalkenntnis behandelt; er [Baernreither] habe vom Grund auf 3 Monate fleissig gearbeitet." "Gemeinsamer Vollzugsausschuss," 18 April 1917, Carton 91, *CPK.*

180. For an introduction to the controversy over *landesübliche Sprachen,* see Robert A. Kann, *The Multinational Empire: Nationalism and National Reform in the Habsburg Monarchy, 1848–1918.* 2 vols. (New York, 1950), 1: 196–99.

181. For detailed descriptions, see "Erinnerungen," Nr. 8, pp. 40–80, and Höglinger, *Ministerpräsident,* pp. 132–57.

182. "Erinnerungen," pp. 68–74.

183. *Schicksalsjahre,* 2: 178; Führ, *Armeeoberkommando,* pp. 132–38.

184. Typed copies of these interviews, as well as notes from an interview with Fuchs on 12 February, who was equally defensive of autonomy, are in Carton 8, *NL Baernreither.*

185. Copies of the actual drafts of the school legislation are in Carton 4, *NL Gross.* See also "Staatsschule?" *VW,* 8 (1917): 55–62; "Randglossen zum Streit für und wider die Länderautonomie," *Rp,* 5 January 1917, pp. 1–2. When invited to write on "Verwaltungsrecht und Autonomie der Länder" for the special issue of *Das Neue Österreich* in 1916, Gessmann offered a cogent, reasoned defense of *Selbstverwaltung,* admitting that the Czechs and Poles were among its most urgent supporters. *Austria Nova* (Vienna, 1916), pp. 215–22.

186. "Vorstandssitzung," 7 February 1917. Stöckler repeated his criticisms at a club meeting on March 7, arguing that any assault on autonomy was an attack on the party and on the state itself.

187. *Rp,* 21 February 1917, p. 5.

188. "Klubsitzung," 7 March 1917. Also apparent was a deep and abiding distrust of the *Nationalverband:* Stöckler: "Heute wird das Parlament allgemein gewünscht, daher alle Mittel. Das wäre die wichtigste Frage, die wir mit dem N.Vbd. zu verhandeln hätten. Wenn N.Vbd. nichts ernstlich tue, dann können wir keine gemeinsame Sache machen!" Mataja: "Das unbedingte Mitgehen mit N. für uns nicht vorteilhaft" and "Wiederholt von den Älteren darauf hingewiesen worden, dass der N. Vbd. unzuverlässig."

189. Hauser to Gross, 10 March 1917, Carton 2, *NL Gross.* The Viennese police noticed the parting of ways: "Beim Deutschen National Verbande und bei den Christlich-Sozialen macht sich in diesem Belange ein Auseinandergehen der Meinungen bemerkbar. Während die Majorität des Deutschen National Verbandes unter dem Einflusse der Deutschradikalen an der Fixierung der deutschen Staatssprache, der Kreiseinteilung Böhmens und der Sonderstellung Galiziens als der Grundlagen einer Einberufung des Parlaments festhält, ist die christlich soziale Partei der Überzeugung, dass die Reform der Geschäftsordnung eine genügende Vorbedingung sei." Report of 23 March 1917, reprinted in *Arbeiterschaft,* 1: 247–48. See also Staudinger, *Aspekte,* pp. 7–8.

190. See the report of Karl Brockhausen in the issue on "Länderautonomie," *Öster-*

reichische Zeitschrift für öffentliches Recht, 3 (1916): 3–18, esp. 13. Brockhousen was quoting with approval an opinion rendered by Heinrich Friedjung.

191. Report of Rudolf von Herrnritt, ibid., p. 43.

192. It is also worth noting that in the various draft documents which Sigmund and Gessmann generated on electoral and constitutional reform in 1915–17 (see above, note 141), the new structure of governance was invoked on behalf of the "Länder und Nationen Österreichs," a phrase that accorded to the Crownlands equal political and moral status along with the ethnic or linguistic nations.

193. See, for example, *Rp,* 11 March 1917, p. 2, and 17 April 1917, p. 2.

194. "'Vorschlag der christlichsozialen Arbeiterschaft Österreichs über die Neuordnung der österreichisch-ungarischen Monarchie nach dem Kriege," Z. 1247, Carton 75, *CPW.* Kunschak and his colleagues claimed that they had originally wanted to abolish the Dualism and consolidate the Monarchy into one democratic and federal state of ethnic *Reichsländer,* but that they would accept a weakened Dualism with a *Reichsparlament* possessing authority over a wide range of domestic social and economic legislation. The proposal insisted upon proportional suffrage for elections to its various parliamentary bodies, and also contained the novel idea of popular plebiscites on important legislation. Not surprisingly, the sections on the nationality problem were the weakest in the document, almost to the point of incoherence.

195. See Seipel's comments on Hauser's lethargy toward constitutional reforms in Seipel's "Frage zur Verfassungsreform," 31 August 1919, *NL Seipel.* For a similar evaluation, see Staudinger, *Aspekte,* pp. 14–20, 24.

196. *Verfall,* p. 193; Schlitter Diary, entry of 9 March 1917.

197. "Erinnerungen," p. 83.

198. See Liechtenstein's report on two party conferences held on 1 and 8 March 1917, Z. 1207, Carton 75, *CPW.* The stenographic summary of the meeting on March 1 suggests that Gessmann was behind this initiative. Interestingly, Weiskirchner showed up at the meeting unaware of the nature of the principal agenda item. Sigmund subsequently wrote to Wilhelm Miklas (8 May 1917, Carton 19, *CPK*) asking if he would be able to assume parliamentary leadership of the electoral reform initiative and informing him that he, Sigmund, had been commissioned by the club to produce the actual draft legislation for the bill, for which he relied on an earlier draft that Gessmann, Fink, and he had produced in 1915 and submitted to Stürgkh in 1916. A copy of this "Antrag der Abgeordneten . . . und Genossen, betreffend die Abänderung der Reichsratswahlordnung," dated 30 May 1917, is in Carton 36, *CPK.* Sigmund's handwritten statistical calculations on the implications of such a reform on the national party are in Carton 69. The 1917 draft was notable for its inclusion of women as enfranchised voters—an idea whose primary sponsor was apparently Jodok Fink—and its giving male voters over forty years of age a double vote.

199. "Protokoll der Sitzung des Deutschen Parteivorstandes" for 31 March and 26 April 1917, *VGAB.* The socialists also organized a series of aggressive political rallies,

which the government tolerated, demanding recall of parliament. See *Arbeiterschaft,* 1: 255ff.

200. *Schicksalsjahre,* 2: 186, 199–200; Gary W. Shanafelt, *The Secret Enemy. Austria-Hungary and the German Alliance, 1914–1918* (Boulder, 1985), pp. 122–28, which is in general an excellent analysis of Austrian war policy. On Czernin's own views on April 1917, see *Im Weltkrieg,* pp. 198–210. See also the analysis by Ingeborg Meckling, *Die Aussenpolitik des Grafen Czernin* (Munich, 1969).

201. Wedel to Bethmann Hollweg, A 12802, 18 April 1917, Oest. 91/Bd. 17, *PAAA.* In conversations with Wedel, Czernin made clear the impact of the events in Prussia. To the Cabinet on 16 April Czernin argued that the *Octroi* would be seen by the Allies as a German dictation to Austria. Baernreither, *Verfall,* p. 196.

202. Baernreither, *Verfall,* p. 196; Bethmann Hollweg to Hertling, undated (April 1917), in *Briefwechsel Hertling-Lerchenfeld,* 2: 1021. For Czernin's views in later 1917, see the report of Krafft to Loesl, 14 August 1917, based on a conversation with Czernin on August 12. Ibid., pp. 901–6.

203. For the Emperor's quarrels with Conrad, see Glaise Horstenau, *Erinnerungen,* pp. 372ff., 396; and Helmut Hoyer, *Kaiser Karl I. und Feldmarschall Conrad von Hötzendorf. Ein Beitrag zur Militärpolitik Kaiser Karls* (Vienna, 1972), pp. 125–46. In Karl's posthumously published memoirs, the "Aufzeichnungen" which he allegedly composed during exile in Switzerland in 1921 (Erich Feigl, ed., *Kaiser Karl. Persönliche Aufzeichnungen, Zeugnisse und Dokumente* [Vienna, 1984], p. 205), Karl implied that from the very beginning of Clam's ministry he opposed the *Octroi* and prevaricated until Czernin was able to stop it. When Matthias Erzberger visited the Emperor in late April, Karl told him much the same thing, rejecting the idea that Austria could be "germanized" because (in Erzberger's words) "die Mehrheit des Volkes aus Slaven bestehe; er könne diese Völker nicht vergewaltigen." "Bericht über meine Reise nach Wien am Sonntag, 22. April und Montag, 23. April." *NL Erzberger.*

204. On the Sixtus crisis of 1918, which vastly diminished Karl's esteem and respect in Austrian political circles of all ideological and nativistic persuasions, see Shanafelt, *The Secret Enemy,* pp. 128–37, 188–91, and Robert A. Kann, *Die Sixtus Affäre und die geheimen Friedensverhandlungen Österreich-Ungarns im Ersten Weltkrieg* (Munich, 1966).

205. Baernreither, *Verfall,* p. 193; and Tucher's report of 11 March 1917, Z. 181.

206. Redlich to Bahr, 11 April 1917, *Dichter und Gelehrter,* p. 220. Foreign observers had a similar impression: "Graf Wedel sagte mir heute unter vier Augen, die Regierung in Wien habe derartig die Nerven verloren, dass sie nur den einen Wunsch habe, sobald als möglich Frieden zu schliessen, und sei es um den Preis grosser Gebietsabtretungen!" Schoen to Hertling, 17 April 1917, *Briefwechsel Hertling-Lerchenfeld,* 2: 837. Similarly, Heinrich Tucher: "Das Verhalten der Regierung wird von Revolutionsangst und Furcht vor Hungerrevolten diktiert und es ist deutlich zu erkennen, dass die Regierung seit Ausbruch der russ. Revolution mehr denn je Fühlung mit den Massen sucht

und auf die Wünsche der sozialistischen Partei gesteigerte Rücksicht nimmt." Z. 253, 31 March 1917.

207. Polzer-Hoditz, *Kaiser Karl*, pp. 395–99.

208. "Gemeinsamer Vollzugsausschuss vom 22. III. 1917," Carton 91, *CPK.*

209. *Schicksalsjahre,* 2: 201; Polzer-Hoditz, *Kaiser Karl,* pp. 398–99; Höglinger, *Clam-Martinic,* pp. 172–86.

210. Baernreither Diary, Nr. 17, p. 91, entry of 27 April 1917.

211. "Vorstandssitzung," 17 April 1917, Carton 91, *CPK.*

212. "Gemeinsamer Vollzugsausschuss," 18 April 1917, ibid. Weiskirchner added that "In diesen Zeiten ist ein Oktroi ausgeschlossen. Überzeugung allgemein wir halten den Krieg nicht aus."

213. *Rp,* 20 April 1917, pp. 1–2.

214. *SP,* 1917, pp. 34–37.

215. Schlitter Diary, 24 July/3 August 1917: "Was ist aber das alles gegen den Jammer im Innern der Monarchie! . . . . Der demokratische Schwindel hat vollends alle Kreise ergriffen und führt gewiss zur Untergrabung jeder Disziplin—das wird sich schon rächen in der Armee. Die Entente-Schlagwörte sind Mode geworden. Alles soll gleichgemacht werden und das bedeutet: Absägen aller kräftigen Stützen und allgemeine Versumpfung."

216. *SP,* 1917, p. 37.

217. Ignaz Seipel, *Gedanken zur österreichischen Verfassungsreform* (Innsbruck, 1917), pp. 4–5; Polzer-Hoditz, *Kaiser Karl,* pp. 450–52. Johann Hauser was quite frank about his aversion to the party joining the Cabinet: "Was haben wir mit parlamentarischen Ministerien für traurige Erfahrungen gemacht. Wenn wir Min. entsenden, müssen wir einen der besten entsenden, der ist dann lahm gelegt. Der Mann der entsendet wird ist verloren und wir anderen mit ihm verloren." "Klubsitzung," 22 June 1917.

218. *Schicksalsjahre,* 2: 257. Entry of 25 January 1918 ("Die Leute in Berlin sind annexionistischer denn je und rechnen jetzt mit der Flandernoffensive. Ich sehe die Situation als trostlos an: denn dieser Krieg wird nur dann enden, wenn beide Teile aufs Äusserste erschöpft sind, und Deutschland wird diese Taktik am schwersten büssen").

219. *SP,* 1917, pp. 144–50.

220. *Rp,* 24 February 1918, pp. 5–6; 2 March 1918, pp. 3–4.

221. "Die Kreisregierungen in Böhmen," *NFP,* 21 May 1918 (N), pp. 1–4; *Schicksalsjahre,* 2: 271. According to Tucher, Seidler's decision to issue the *Kreis* order was also an attempt to pacify pan-German outrage over the Sixtus Affair. Z. 276, 9 June 1918.

222. The reaction of the club to the *Kreis* decree was decidedly negative, and Mataja spoke for many of his colleagues when he observed that "Eine Sache, die den Deutschen nichts nützt und d. Tschechen aufreizt." "Klubsitzung," 24 April 1918. Hermann Bielohlawek had publicly attacked the planned *Kreiseinteilung* in late 1917 as a

"Riesengefahr für das christliche Volk" since it endangered the "Bollwerk der Selbstverwaltung." Z. 29594, 5 October 1917, Carton 1646, 15/3, *MI Präs.*

223. Hagenhofer to [Sigmund?], 11 May 1917, Carton 69, *CPW.* The addressee of the letter is not noted, but it is likely that it was Sigmund. On Hagenhofer see Gaar, "Franz Hagenhofer."

224. "Vorstandssitzung," 15 May 1917.

225. See below, pp. 430–37.

226. Karl Hilgenreiner, "Christlichsozial—was ist das?" *Bonifatius-Korrespondenz,* 12 (1918): 145–49; Elmar [Richard Schmitz], "Die Bestimmung der christlichsozialen Partei", *VW,* 9 (1918): 1–4. Schmitz informed the *Parteileitung* of the change, noting also that the *Volksbund* was creating a new, political "Referat" to deal with party issues. Schmitz to the *Parteileitung,* 24 May 1918, Z. 1488, Carton 76, *CPW.*

227. *Schicksalsjahre,* 2: 254; Weber, "Karl Hermann Wolf, " pp. 325–26. For Wolf's justifications, including his assertion that "Das Parlament ist ein Sperrblock auf dem Wege zur Erfüllung unserer Wünsche," see the police report, Z. 24146, 22 November 1917, Carton 1646, 15/3, *MI Präs.*

228. Glaise Horstenau, *Erinnerungen,* pp. 458–59.

229. *NFP,* 3 April 1918 (M), pp. 1–4.

230. *Stenographische Protokolle über die Sitzungen des Herrenhauses,* 1918, pp. 781–87 ("Was aber nun Deutschland anlangt, so muss ich folgendes bemerken: Vor allem bedarf Deutschland Grund und Boden, weil es über seine Grösse hinaus bevölkert ist; es ist aus seinen Grenzen hinausgewachsen"). For Pattai's personal involvement in the politics of the radical nationalist Right, see his speech at a rally of Walter Riehl's *Deutsche Arbeiter-Partei* on 24 April 1918, Z. 9324 and Z. 9986, Carton 1647 15/3, *MI Präs.* ("Redner feiert sodann Bismarck, den Begründer des Bündnisses, als den weitblickendsten Staatsmann. Pattai wendet sich gleichfalls gegen die Errichtung des südslavischen Staates und die Abschwenkung vom Meere.")

231. *Stenographische Protokolle über die Sitzungen des Herrenhauses,* pp. 812–17. Tucher found Lammasch an "Ultrapazifist" who was also, he believed, responsible for Karl's amnesty proclamation in July 1917. Z. 119, 1 March 1918.

232. *Rp,* 10 March 1918, p. 5.

233. Klemperer, *Ignaz Seipel;* Friedrich Rennhofer, *Ignaz Seipel. Mensch und Staatsmann. Eine biographische Dokumentation* (Vienna, 1978). Carton 12 of the *NL Funder* contains the extensive research notes collected by Richard Schmitz after 1945 for an unfinished biography of Seipel, including copies of important correspondence of Seipel.

234. *Nation und Staat* (Vienna, 1916).

235. *Nationalitätsprinzip und Staatsgedanke* (München-Gladbach, n.d. [1915]); *Gedanken zur österreichischen Verfassungsreform* (Innsbruck, 1917).

236. *Schicksalsjahre,* 2: 259, 277, 291, 295; Redlich to Bahr, 10 June 1918 ("Mit P. Augustin speiste ich vor einigen Tagen bei Meinl zusammen mit dem wirklich sehr *gescheiten* und sympatischen Professor Seipel"). *Dichter und Gelehrter,* pp. 346–47.

Tucher characterized the Lammasch-Meinl circle as one of "Hofpazifisten." Tucher to Hertling, 25 August 1917.

237. As quoted in Winter, *Ignaz Seipel,* p. 148.

238. Seipel to Lammasch, 24 December 1917, *NL Seipel.* On the "Pucher-Abende," see Missong, *August Schaurhofer,* p. 36; and Richard Schmitz's notes on the history of the *Volksbund* in Carton 12, *NL Funder.*

239. Seipel to Lammasch, 21 January 1918.

240. Seipel's Diary entry for 5 October 1917: "Über Einladung Funders einer vertraulichen Besprechung über die Verfassungsreform im Beratungszimmer der Rp. beigewohnt," attended by Wilhelm Schmidt, Richard Wollek, Aemilian Schöpfer, and Victor Kienböck, among others. The origins of the February 1918 committee are not clear. Anton Staudinger surmises that this was a belated reaction to Wilson's Fourteen Points speech of 8 January 1918, which may be true. Staudinger, *Aspekte,* p. 24. It is also likely that the strike movement of mid-January 1918 and the turmoil that threatened to rip parliament apart in early February, with Czechs and Bohemian Germans at each other's throats, played a significant role. See "Klubsitzung" and "Klubsitzung n.m.," 19 February 1918.

241. The *Grundgedanken* is reprinted in Ignaz Seipel, *Der Kampf um die österreichische Verfassung* (Vienna, 1930), pp. 38–41. See also Seipel Diary entries of 20 and 25 February 1918.

242. Seipel Diary for 20 November 1917 ("Prof. Sommeregger überbringt den ersten Entwurf einer Arbeit über die Verfassungsreform für die Partei zur Durchsicht"), as well as the entries for 25, 28, 30 November 1917; 2, 3, 5, 8, 11, 22, 25, 28, 31 December 1917; 1, 7, 13, 15, 17, 18, 23, 28 January 1918; 2, 10, 13, 15, 16, 17, 19, 21, 22, 23, 25, 26, and 28 February 1918; 2 and 14 March 1918.

243. "Vor der innerpolitischen Neuordnung," 19 February 1918, pp. 1–2; "Um die Verfassungsreform," 22 February 1918, pp. 1–2; "Die nationale Autonomie als Grundlage des Ausgleichswerkes," 23 February 1918, pp. 1–2; and "Verwaltungsreform," 28 February 1918, pp. 1–2.

244. Franz Sommeregger, "Verfassungs- und Verwaltungsreform." *CPK,* Carton 34. This version is undated, but it is certainly a revision of the draft Sommeregger first presented to Seipel, and reflects deliberations in the party's committee. It is, therefore, most likely of a later date than Seipel's *Grundfragen.*

245. "Lange Unterredung mit Mataja. Jeder Versuch, ihn jetzt zu einer prinzipiellen Stellungnahme an der Friedenssache zu bringen, gescheitert. Bin sehr deprimiert." Diary, entry of 16 September 1918.

246. On the *Volkstag,* where Wolf, Pacher, and Weiskirchner were the main speakers, see *NFP,* 17 June 1918 (N), p. 5; *ODR,* 18 June 1918, pp. 1–2; Z. 14094, 16 June 1918, Carton 2131, 22, *MI Präs.;* and Z. 1497 in Carton 76, *CPW.* In the case of Weiskirchner his bellicosity may have also been a ploy to distract public attention from the impending reduction of the bread ration by 50 percent.

247. "Ein Lichtpunkt in dieser Zeit ist nur die Zusammenkunft der Monarchen im

deutschen Hauptquartier; die dort getroffene Vereinbarung ist ein Rückhalt für die Deutschen in Oesterreich, welche ihnen eine führende Rolle zuweisen wird." Police report, Z. 14099, 13 June 1918, Carton 1648, 15/3, *MI Präs.*

248. Ignaz Seipel, "Volk und Staat," *VW,* 9 (1918): 97–103. Richard Schmitz, writing, under the pseudonym of "Elmar," had similar comments in "Die Fehlbilanz des Parlamentes und die Deutschnationalen," ibid., pp. 150–55, esp. 154. An anonymous German national politician, writing in the *NWJ* in July 1918, offered an interesting interpretation of Wolf's motives in bringing this campaign to Vienna: since the voters in Wolf's Bohemian district of Trautenau had become disillusioned by his ineffectiveness during the course of the war, Wolf hoped to switch to a more reliable Lower Austrian constituency for the postwar elections. To do this he would need the Christian Socials' support. *NWJ,* 14 July 1918, p. 2.

249. Seipel to Lammasch, 17 June 1918, *NL Seipel.*

250. Ignaz Seipel, "Frage zur Verfassungsreform." 31 August 1919. *NL Seipel.* This has been reprinted in Honeder, "Hauser," appendix, pp. 67–68. See also Banhans's comments on the differences between Seipel and Hauser in the Banhans Diary, 2: 139, *HHSA.*

251. Z. 13461, 5 June 1918, Carton 1648, 15/3, *MI Präs.*

252. Seipel Diary, 4, 5, 8, 9, and 20 August 1918 and 5, 9, 11, 12, 14, 16, and 21 September 1918.

253. Richard Schmitz, "Ziele der Volksbundarbeit. Ein Programm," *VW,* 9 (1918): 103–11.

254. Franz Sommeregger, "Zur Charakteristik des Kriegssozialismus," *VW,* 9 (1918): 210–17; Rudolf Hilferding, "Arbeitsgemeinschaft der Klassen?" *K,* 8 (1915): 321–29. Hilferding's essay did not please several members of the Executive. See Renner's and Austerlitz's negative reactions in "Protokoll der Sitzung des deutschen Parteivorstandes am 12. Jänner 1916," *VGAB.*

255. There is as yet no modern social history of Austria during the war. See, however, Arthur J. May, *The Passing of the Hapsburg Monarchy* (2 vols., Philadelphia, 1966). The volumes of the Carnegie series edited by James Shotwell remain the most detailed and reliable source of material on wartime society in Austria. Wegs, *Die österreichische Kriegswirtschaft,* offers a survey of economic policy development, concentrating on files in the *Kriegsarchiv.* Gottfried Köfner, *Hunger, Not und Korruption. Der Übergang Österreichs von der Monarchie zur Republik am Beispiel Salzburgs* (Salzburg, 1980), offers an excellent survey of basic domestic trends, seen from the Alpine lands. Reinhard Sieder's "Behind the Lines: Working-Class Family Life in Wartime Vienna," in Richard Wall and Jay Winter, eds. *The Upheaval of War: Family, Work, and Welfare in Europe 1914–1918* (Cambridge, 1988), pp. 109–38, offers a survey of working-class attitudes in Vienna during the war.

256. On food provisioning during the war see Hans Loewenfeld-Russ, *Die Regelung;* and Friedrich Gaertner, "Die Brotversorgung in Oesterreich," *ASSP,* 43 (1916/17): 610–64, as well as the detailed monthly press summaries in *British Documents on*

Foreign Affairs, Part II, Series H, Vols. 9–12. The Central Powers (Frederick, Md., 1989).

257. On the *Zentralen,* see Heinrich Wittek, "Die kriegswirtschaftlichen Organisationen und Zentralen in Österreich," *ZVSV,* N. S. 2 (1922): 24–90, 226–47; Loewenfeld-Russ, *Die Regelung,* pp. 71–84; idem, *Im Kampf,* pp. 29–31; and Wegs, *Die österreichische Kriegswirtschaft,* pp. 25–30. For the anti-Semitism, see 12 December 1917, Z. 24621, Carton 1646, 15/3, *MI Präs.* See also Gessmann's comments to Redlich in September 1916 on Stürgkh's underestimation of the potentially catastrophic food situation in *Schicksalsjahre,* 2: 143.

258. The Food Office actually dated from October 1916, but Stürgkh placed it under the control of the Ministry of Internal Affairs and gave it few explicit powers. When Koerber took office, he reestablished the office under his own control as Minister-President, and endowed it with (in theory) vast regulatory powers. See *BDFA,* vol. 10, pp. 361, 398; Loewenfeld-Russ, *Im Kampf,* pp. 43–44.

259. On the *Ernährungsamt,* see Loewenfeld-Russ, *Die Regelung,* pp. 292–96, and idem, *Im Kampf,* pp. 57–102. The President of the Food Office had the status of cabinet minister, but did not enjoy the full political prerogatives of a minister.

260. See *Rp,* 14 October 1915, p. 3, and 22 October 1915, p. 8, for two examples of many such articles. The Confidential Print reports in *BDFA* show that Allied authorities were painfully aware of Austrian and Hungarian food and supply problems throughout the war.

261. Weiskirchner then allowed the speech to be published, which enraged Tisza. See Tisza to Stürgkh, 2 April 1915, Carton 20, *Kabinettskanzlei, Geheimakten;* and *BDFA,* vol. 9, p. 177.

262. On Hungarian food policies toward Austria, see Loewenfeld-Russ, *Die Regelung,* pp. 60–65, 133, 305–6. See also the *Ministerrat* discussions of 12 December 1915, 16 October 1916, 22 March 1917, 29 June 1917, and 24 September 1917 in Komjáthy, *Protokolle,* pp. 315–51, 410–24, 471–81, 510–20, 585–99.

263. For the food impoverishment of Hungarian cities and villages, see Galántai, *Hungary,* pp. 194–95. Censorship authorities of the French Postal Service obtained a collection of 20,000 Hungarian letters, half of which were from Hungary, and most of those from rural areas. On the basis of a crude content analysis, they reported that food conditions appeared to be extremely bad. *BDFA,* vol. 11, p. 96.

264. Z. 24621, 12 December 1917, Carton 1646, 15/3, *MI Präs.* So surprised were the police by this comment that they sent a special report on the speech to the Ministry of Internal Affairs. Ironically, when Tisza visited Vienna in early September 1915, at the head of a large delegation of Hungarian officials, Weiskirchner did all he could to mobilize a sympathetic reception for him. *Wiener Kommunal-Kalender und Städtisches Jahrbuch für 1916,* pp. 1134–35; and Z. 1115, Carton 74, *CPW.* See also Hans Rotter's comments ("Ungarn behandelt uns wie ein Ausland, wie ein Staat der Trippelentente"), Z. 7487, 11 April 1915, Carton 1645.

265. Arnold Durig, "Physiologie als Unterrichtsgegenstand. Erhebungen über die

Ernährung der Wiener Bevölkerung," *Wiener Medizinische Wochenschrift,* 2 November 1918, pp. 1939–41. Weiskirchner had already argued that a gap existed between German and Austrian nutritional levels as early as 1916: Z. 9699/1916, Carton 1647, 15/3, *MI Präs.* See also Sieder, "Behind the Lines," pp. 112–17. For a comparison between German cities and London, see Richard Wall, "English and German Families in the First World War, 1914–1918," in *The Upheaval of War,* pp. 43–106.

266. Z. 4884, 17 March 1917, Carton 2131, 22, *MI Präs.*

267. "Die Stimmung im Hinterlande und die Nahrungssorgen," 17 November 1917, Z. 93–2/68, *MKSM.*

268. Z. 9832, 27 April 1918, p. 4., Carton 2131, 22, *MI Präs.*

269. Z. 607, 5 January 1916, Carton 2130.

270. Z. 11397/[May] 1916 and Z. 23460, 12 October 1916, ibid.

271. Z. 11397, 11 May 1916; Z. 21327, 21 September 1916; Z. 23460, 12 October, 1916, Carton 2030; Z. 1028, 17 January 1917; Z. 1893, 31 January 1917; Z. 3911, 7 March 1917; Z. 4884, 17 March 1917, Carton 2131.

272. Z. 3911, 7 March 1917, ibid.

273. Z. 8449, 19 May 1917, ibid.

274. Z. 5995, 11 April 1917, and Z. 6608, 21 April 1917, ibid.

275. *Schicksalsjahre,* 2: 255, entry of 17 January 1918 ("Die Kürzung der Kopfquote von Mehl bringt langsam aber sicher die soziale Bewegung und die Bewegung für den Frieden ins Rollen"). For detailed official reports on January 1918, see the documents reprinted in *Arbeiterschaft,* 2: 185–338. On the condition of the working classes in general, see Wegs, *Die österreichische Kriegswirtschaft,* pp. 93–105; and Grandner, *Kooperative Gewerkschaftspolitik,* passim.

276. Z. 6356, 16 March 1918, Carton 2131.

277. Loewenfeld-Russ, *Die Regelung,* p. 301. See, for example, the angry memorandum sent by Höfer, director of the Food Office, to the War Ministry, 3 February 1917, demanding that the Army either cease trying to confiscate oat reserves intended for the civilian sector or that it provide equivalent substitutes from its own special sources. The Army intended to use the oats for horse fodder, whereas Höfer intended them for human consumption. Z. 93–2/16–2, *MKSM.*

278. Durig, "Physiologie als Unterrichtsgegenstand," p. 1936.

279. *NFP,* 7 February 1917 (M), p. 11.

280. According to Loewenfeld-Russ, prewar Vienna had approximately 8,000 stores that sold flour, yet only 800 were selected as approved *Abgabestellen.* This meant that over 7,000 stores lost their customers. *Die Regelung,* p. 357. Loewenfeld-Russ also admits that customers who had access to a war kitchen often did not have to relinquish their ration tickets, so that the system merited the suspicion outsiders held toward it (p. 354).

281. See Franz Hoss's comments on the decline of traditional shops and the spread of illegal peddlers and black marketeers, *NFP,* 21 January 1917 (M), pp. 15–16. See

also Z. 8416, 20 April 1915, Carton 1645, 15/3, *MI Präs.*; and the petition of the *Gewerbeverein Ottakring-Neulerchenfeld,* 23 September 1915, Z. 1149, Carton 74, *CPW.* Note also Kerner's evaluation in April 1918 that "unter der derzeitigen Klubleitung das Verhältnis zwischen der christlichsozialen Partei und dem Gewerbestande eine Lockerung erlitten habe." "Verhandlungsschrift über die Hauptversammlung des Bürgerklubs vom 9. April 1918," Carton 37, *CPW.*

282. The *Arbeiter-Zeitung* estimated that less than 10 percent of the content of bread was actually edible flour. "Unser Brot," *AZ,* 17 May 1918, pp. 6–7. See also *BDFA,* vol. 12, p. 261.

283. Z. 8416, 20 April 1915, Carton 1645, 15/3, *MI Präs.*

284. Other commodities were also affected. Typical was a decree of the Lower Austrian *Statthalter* in late 1916 that peasant proprietors could retain no more than 8 kilos of peas and beans per person per year. The rest was subject to compulsory sale. *BDFA,* vol. 10, pp. 363, 402.

285. Z. 1258, 16 January 1918, Carton 1588, 11/6, *MI Präs.* Such practices inevitably became common knowledge among the public, increasing bitterness towards the civil servants.

286. Nor did small producers have substantial access to war production contracts, since most of the latter went to the larger firms. See Wilhelm Winkler, *Die Einkommensverschiebungen in Österreich während des Weltkrieges* (Vienna, 1930), p. 186.

287. On rent controls, see *NFP,* 28 January 1917 (M), pp. 16–17; Grandner, *Kooperative Gewerkschaftspolitik,* pp. 257–64; and Hösl and Pirhofer, *Wohnen in Wien,* pp. 91–95. See also Wilhelm Ellenbogen's insightful comments in *Menschen und Prinzipien,* p. 70.

288. For white-collar salary adjustments in the municipality of Vienna, see *Die Gemeindeverwaltung,* pp. 24–30. Stürgkh's resistance to the supplements for state civil servants opened a point of leverage for the War Ministry and the High Command in the summer of 1915, allowing the latter to take the railway employees' welfare "to heart" and promise them support for additional income. This led to a collision between the Minister-President and Krobatin, the War Minister. It was not the first or the last time the Army would meddle in policy areas Stürgkh properly thought his own. See *Arbeiterschaft,* 1: 32–41, as well as the files relating to a similar political offensive by the Army High Command against Stürgkh in October of 1915, which led him to ask the Ministry of Internal Affairs to draft a fourteen-page defense of the government's food-provisioning policies, dated 24 November 1915, Nr. 69–22/8, *MKSM.* The latter sought to dump some of the blame onto the autonomous cities and Crownlands: "Nicht zu übersehen ist übrigens auch das in der bisherigen Gestaltung unserer öffentlichen Einrichtungen begründete, gewiss viele Mängel aufweisende, aber nicht ohne weiteres beseitigbare System der Doppelverwaltung, vermöge dessen den autonomen Vertretungen weitgehende Verwaltungsbefugnisse zustehen, mit denen die Regierung zu rechnen hat. Gerade die Vertretungen grosser Städte verfolgen nun mitunter wirtschaftliche Sonder-

interessen bestimmter Wählerkreise. Sie bringen oft den Bemühungen der Regierung kein Verständnis und keine Bereitwilligkeit entgegen und trachten zuweilen die Regierungsmassnahmen zu umgehen."

289. See the letter of protest, dated 31 January 1916, and the response by Otto Grisogono of the Ministry of Internal Affairs, 3 February 1916, in Carton 2, *NL Gross.* On civil servant salaries during the war, see *NFP,* 11 January 1917 (M), pp. 2–3, which also contains prewar data. For civil servant unrest, see Emil Lederer, "Die Angestelltenbewegung und Sozialpolitik in Oesterreich," *ASSP,* 44 (1917–18): 896–905.

290. See *Die Gemeinde-Verwaltung* pp. 165–66. Three classes of specially colored (green, blue, and brown) ration coupons were instituted, correlated to family income, whereas more prosperous consumers merely received white coupons.

291. Z. 9832, 27 April 1918, p. 4, Carton 2131, 22, *MI Präs.*

292. Z. 9660, 12 April 1918, Carton 1588, 11/6.

293. Z. 9549, 22 April 1918, ibid., protesting against the decree of 14 April 1918, *RGBl.,* 1918, Nr. 142.

294. Z. 15530, 3 July 1918, *MI Präs.*

295. The restrictions were eventually lifted in the spring of 1917 but reimposed in 1918. *Schicksalsjahre,* 2: 190; *Verwaltungsbericht der Gemeinde Wien—Städtische Strassenbahnen—für das Jahr 1916/17* (Vienna 1918), pp. 1–2, 16–21; *Die Gemeinde-Verwaltung,* pp. 637–56. In one year (1916–17) use of the streetcar system increased almost 15 percent. On the military pressures on civilian transportation systems, see Bruno Enderes, Emil Ratzenhofer, and Paul Höger, *Verkehrswesen im Kriege* (Vienna, 1931), pp. 147–48, and 151–201. According to Wegs (pp. 110–11) military and civilian transport began to collapse by the end of 1917.

296. *NFP,* 18 January 1917 (M), p. 9.

297. On employment of women during the war, see Emmy Freundlich, "Die Frauenarbeit im Krieg," in Ferdinand Hanusch and Emanuel Adler, eds., *Die Regelung der Arbeitsverhältnisse im Kriege* (Vienna, 1927), pp. 397–418, as well as pp. 79–83, 178–80, 249–50. Of the 12,700 employees of the Viennese streetcar system in 1914, 6,000 were conscripted immediately into the Army. By 1917 about 12,000 men had been conscripted, and the system had hired over 8,000 women as wartime employees. *Die Gemeinde-Verwaltung,* p. 647, and Enderes, *Verkehrswesen,* p. 141. Freundlich argues that Social Democratic unions treated women more generously than the various *Beamten* organizations, but this is probably an exaggeration.

298. This is a consistent theme of the Confidential Print reports published in *BDFA.*

299. Z. 12123, 25 May 1918, Carton 2131, 22, *MI Präs.*

300. Z. 4884, 17 March 1917, ibid.

301. Z. 9681, 2 March 1916; Z. 9602, 2 May 1916, Carton 2130, ibid. Bienerth sought to put pressure on the schools to cope with the delinquency problem, which simply started a vicious circle, since many children could not even attend regular classes, much less be supervised in off-hours by their teachers.

302. Erwin Lazar, "Der Krieg und die Verwahrlosung von Kindern und Jugend-lichen. Heilpädagogische Rück- und Ausblicke," in Clemens Pirquet, ed., *Volksgesundheit im Krieg* (2 vols. Vienna, 1926), 1: 251–72. On the problem of juvenile crime during the war, see Franz Exner, *Krieg und Kriminalität in Österreich* (Vienna, 1927), pp. 167–96.

303. For the refugees, see Zoitl, *"Student kommt von Studieren!"* pp. 113–14.

304. On the bitter public reaction to the Jewish refugees, see Z. 8318, 12482, 13241, and 22597/1915, Carton 2130, 22, *MI Präs.*, as well as *ÖW*, 35 (1918): 505–6, 609–10. In June 1915 the War Ministry even complained that local government officials were not doing enough to protect the Galician refugees from popular hostility in Vienna.

305. Z. 24621, 11 December 1917, Carton 1646, 15/3, *MI Präs.* On the Jewish *Preistreiberei* issue, see also the arguments in Z. 1365 ("Rufe und Gegenrufe"), Z. 1552, and Z. 1591, as well as in Z. 1553, 18 September 1918, Carton 76, *CPW,* insisting that Jewish profiteers were invading the gentile-dominated real estate market and buying up houses from impoverished Christians.

306. Z. 23140, 11 October 1918, Carton 1588, 11/6, *MI Präs.* On economic corruption and corruption within the civil service, see Exner, *Krieg und Kriminalität,* pp. 40–41, 43–59. Exner argues that Austria experienced a higher rate of crimes involving theft and economic malfeasance than did Germany (p. 59).

307. On Pirquet, see Richard Wagner, *Clemens von Pirquet. His Life and Work* (Baltimore, 1968), esp. pp. 18–19, 118–51; Erna Lesky, "Clemens von Pirquet," *Wiener klinische Wochenschrift,* 67 (1955): 638–39. The autobiographical reports in Christa Hämmerle, ed., *Kindheit im Ersten Weltkrieg* (Vienna, 1993), are filled with references to the hardships endured by children of various social backgrounds during the war.

308. See Erna Lesky, "Der erste Weltkrieg: eine biologische Katastrophe Wiens," *Österreichische Ärzte-Zeitung,* 25 June 1975.

309. See Clemens Pirquet, "Ernährungszustand der Kinder in Österreich während des Krieges und der Nachkriegszeit," in *Volksgesundheit im Krieg,* 1: 151–79; and Heinrich Thausing, "Ueber eine Voraussetzung aller Tuberkulosebekämpfung," *Wiener klinische Wochenschrift,* 7 November 1918, pp. 1197–99.

310. Quoted by Pirquet in "Ernährungszustand," p. 152.

311. Z. 21469, 6 October 1915; Z. 22415, 18 October 1915; Z. 24624, 16 November 1915 ("streng vertraulich"), Carton 1645, 15/3, *MI Präs.* Also, Z. 1145, 8 November 1915, Carton 74, *CPW.*

312. Compare his speech of 7 October 1915, Z. 21682, Carton 1645, with his remarks on 7 October 1917, Z. 19949, Carton 1646.

313. Z. 7487, 11 April 1915, Carton 1645.

314. Z. 21469, 5 October 1915; Z. 21682, 8 October 1915, ibid.

315. Handwritten account of a conversation between Stürgkh and Burián, recorded by Baron Schiessl, 24 October 1915, Carton 20, *Kabinettskanzlei, Geheimakten.*

316. Z. 673, 7 January 1916, Carton 1645. Adolf Anderle complained in 1917 that "Spreche man mit dem Bürgermeister, so werde seine Ausrede sein, dass er als Bürger-

meister objektiv vorgehen müsse." "Protokoll über die 5. Juli 1917 . . . abgehaltene Besprechung," Briefordner I, *NL Mataja*.

317. See his remarks in Z. 21682, 8 October 1915; and in Z. 1115, 5 August 1915, Carton 1645, 15/3, *MI Präs.; and Z. 1180, 26 June 1916, Carton 74, *CPW*.

318. Z. 15784, 26 June 1918, Carton 1648, 15/3, *MI Präs.*

319. See Weiskirchner's comments in Z. 1587, Carton 76, *CPW;* and the "Verhandlungsschrift über die Sitzung des Bürgerklubs vom 12. April 1917," Carton 37, *CPW;* for the socialists, see the proceedings of their Lower Austrian *Parteitag* in Z. 3057, 4 February 1918, 22, *MI Präs.*, and the debates in the Executive on 31 January, 18 April, 11 July, and 16 September 1918 in the "Vorstandsprotokolle," *VGAB*. By early 1918 Weiskirchner was willing to contemplate a two-curial system, one of which would be for taxpayers and property owners, the other for the general public. Agreement could not be reached with the socialists, however, since the Christian Socials insisted on making the tax-based curia almost as large as the general curia, whereas the Social Democrats, while pressing for the total abolition of all curialism, would have accepted only a privileged curia not larger than the current Fourth Curia. They also insisted that the general curia include female voters. A draft of this proposal, dated 2 September 1918, is in *SD-Parteistellen,* Carton 23.

320. Z. 15066, 1 August 1917, Carton 2131, 22, *MI Präs.*

321. *Arbeiterschaft,* 2: 28.

322. Z. 9832, 27 April 1918 and Z. 10444, 4 May 1918, Carton 2131, 22, *MI Präs.*

323. On the relaxation of police pressure, which the Cabinet then reinstituted in mid-1918 because of excesses by the parties, see Z. 13886, 13 July 1917, Carton 1646; and Z. 10327, 15 May 1918, Carton 1647.

324. See the typescript of the proceedings of the third conference of party officials on 22 January 1917, Carton 69, *CPW*.

325. For expressions of ardent anti-Semitism by party clubs, see the memoranda in Z. 1427 (Josefstadt); Z. 1432 (Landstrasse); Z. 1446 (Leopoldstadt), all from early 1918. Carton 76, *CPW*.

326. On Mataja see Elisabeth Jelinek, "Der politische Lebensweg Dr. Heinrich Matajas." Dissertation, University of Vienna, 1970; and Rudolf Ebneth, *Die österreichische Wochenschrift "Der christliche Ständestaat." Deutsche Emigration in Österreich 1933–1938* (Mainz, 1976), pp. 47–48.

327. Seipel to Mataja, 4 July 1930, *NL Seipel.* For Mataja's early connection to Gessmann, see the accusations flung against him by Kornelius Vetter in 1910 in *DV,* 19 April 1910 (M), pp. 1–2.

328. See Mataja's "Vertraulicher Bericht über die bisherige Entwicklung der Internationalen Katholischen Union," in Briefordner II, *NL Mataja.* Mataja was in contact with Erzberger at these meetings. See also Staudinger, *Aspekte,* p. 21. As early as September 1916 Mataja implicitly criticized German war aims plans when he suggested that it would be a mistake for the Central Powers to make claims on French or Belgian territory, and that these should be restricted to the eastern front, where Russian expan-

sionism needed to be curbed. See his "Exposé über die aussenpolitische Lage von Reichsratsabgeordneten Stadtrat Dr. Heinrich Mataja," submitted on 19 October 1916 to the *Kabinettskanzlei, Geheimakten,* Carton 20.

329. See Mataja's comments at the 1916 *Parteitag,* Carton 19, pp. 13–14, *CPK;* and his critical evaluation in 1917 of his fellow Viennese in "Klubsitzung," 28 August 1917.

330. Heinrich Mataja, *Zehn politische Aufsätze aus den Jahren 1911–1913* (Vienna, 1913).

331. A summary of his remarks is in Carton 19, *CPK,* which also contains a twenty-two page draft speech on party organization by Mataja which must have been given some time after the February 1916 party congress, but which elaborates the same themes in considerably greater detail. Mataja also wrote to Spalowsky immediately after the latter spoke at the third *Mandatoren-Konferenz* in January 1917, noting that he wanted to discuss reform ideas with Spalowsky. See letter of 27 January 1917, Briefordner II, *NL Mataja.*

332. Jelinek, "Mataja," p. 20.

333. Mataja to Liechtenstein, 8 January 1917, Briefordner II.

334. "Protokoll über die am 23. Juli 1917 in Wien I. Landhaus abgehaltene Besprechung christlichsozialer politischer Vereine," Briefordner I.

335. Ibid., as well as "Protokoll über die am 11. Juli 1917 in Wien I. Landhaus abgehaltene Besprechung christlichsozialer politischer Vereine."

336. Hans Preyer, on July 5, combining personal resentment and anti-Semitism: "Die Parteileute, die 20 und 30 Jahre für die Partei gearbeitet und gelitten haben, die haben das Spiel satt, das heute getrieben wird. Unverlässliche Elemente werden begünstigt, parteitreue zurückgesetzt, die antisemitischen Grundsätze verraten. Die parteitreuen Elemente müssen sich zusammenschliessen."

337. "Protokoll über die am 18. Juli 1917 in Wien, I. Landhaus abgehaltene Besprechung christlichsozialer politischer Vereine."

338. For Christian Social anti-Semitism in the First Republic, see Anton Staudinger, "Christlichsoziale Judenpolitik in der Gründungsphase der österreichischen Republik," in *Jahrbuch für Zeitgeschichte* (Vienna, 1979), pp. 11–48.

339. The "Eingabe," dated 29 August 1917, is in Briefordner I.

340. Mataja sent this document to all the members of the *weiteren Parteirat,* so it is not difficult to imagine how one of Mataja's many enemies in the party might have obtained a copy of it.

341. Liechtenstein to Mataja, 6 September 1917, Briefordner I; and *Rp,* 12 September 1917, p. 6.

342. Mataja's draft, together with his statement of justification, are in Z. 1407, Carton 76, *CPW.*

343. The draft program, whose economic sections were co-authored by Franz Hemala and Heinrich Schmid, is in Z. 1420, ibid. The idea of women's suffrage seems to have originated from Spalowsky, who together with representatives of various small Catholic womens' clubs, proposed it to the party leadership in January 1918: Z. 1391,

2 January 1918, ibid. The final program—*Christlichsoziales Wiener Gemeindeprogramm*—did not advocate full suffrage for women, however, but only allowed them a voice in those affairs where their participation might be most useful to them and to the city as a whole.

344. See, for example, the oppositional or hesitant statements in Z. 1499, Z. 1517, and Z. 1527, Carton 76, *CPW.*

345. Mataja to the *engeren Parteirat,* 13 April 1918; and Mataja to Weiskirchner, 19 May 1918, Z. 1455 and Z. 1478, ibid. The party's *Beschwerdekommission* was established on 21 May 1918. The party tax was not officially approved and only then by a narrow majority of the *Bürgerklub* until 14 October 1918.

346. Mataja to the *engeren Parteirat,* Z. 1428, 3 March 1918. Mataja essentially demanded that Weiskirchner be censored, but a later letter to the mayor on 8 April 1918, complaining about the unwillingness of the *Parteirat* even to put the complaint on the agenda of its meetings, suggests that Mataja was using the incident as a way of prodding Weiskirchner to move more quickly on the larger issue of structural reform. The latter letter also contains an extraordinary statement of Mataja's own high self-estimation, to the point of utter arrogance. Weiskirchner, in turn, although shocked by Mataja's insults, found himself overwhelmed by the latter's energy, to the point where Mataja could impose patronage demands on Weiskirchner, to which the mayor agreed; he also gave Mataja control of the lackluster *Deutsch-österreichischer Gewerbebund,* to try to revive that half-dead trade group. Weiskirchner to Mataja, Z. 1541, 8 August 1918, and Mataja to Weiskirchner, 6 June 1918, Z. 1505.

347. "Eine furchtbare Folge der Dummheiten Czernins war der 'Deutsche Kurs', den die österreichische Regierung nun gehen musste. Ich war über ihn gewiss nicht entzückt. Aber doch war das das einzige Mittel, den furor teutonicus wenigstens zu mässigen." Karl, "Aufzeichnungen," p. 212. For the course of developments, see Helmut Rumpler, *Max Hussarek. Nationalitäten und Nationalitätenpolitik in Österreich im Sommer des Jahres 1918* (Graz, 1965), pp. 22–36.

348. Compare the resolutions adopted on 14 June and 18 June 1918 by the two parliamentary groups, reprinted in *Politische Chronik,* 1918, pp. 312–14.

349. A 31023, 19 July 1918, Oest. 70/Bd. 53.

350. *SP,* 1918, pp. 4314–21.

351. See Wedel's survey of political opinion in Vienna, telegram of 11 October 1918, Oest. 95/Bd. 25; and Nostitz's report of 6 October 1918 in Alfred Opitz and Franz Adlgasser, eds., *"Der Zerfall der europäischen Mitte." Staatenrevolution im Donauraum. Berichte der Sächsischen Gesandschaft in Wien 1917–1919* (Graz, 1990), pp. 178–79.

352. See Staudinger's analysis of this resolution in *Aspekte,* pp. 47–61.

353. Both Austerlitz and Seitz sided with Renner, with the result that Victor Adler proposed a compromise to the effect that Bauer would develop his ideas as newspaper articles. "Protokoll der Sitzung des deutschen Parteivorstandes am 11. Oktober 1918," *VGAB.*

354. The Germans learned about Karl's intentions in mid-August from General Arz von Straussenburg. See A 35638, 20 August 1918, Oest. 103/Bd. 8; as well as Arz's comments in *Zur Geschichte des grossen Krieges 1914–1918* (Vienna, 1924), pp. 313–23.

355. See Helmut Rumpler, *Das Völkermanifest Kaiser Karls vom 16. Oktober 1918. Letzter Versuch zur Rettung des Habsburgerreiches* (Vienna, 1966), as well as idem, *Max Hussarek*, pp. 102–3.

356. András Siklós, *Revolution in Hungary and the Dissolution of the Multinational State, 1918* (Budapest, 1988), p. 31; Galántai, *Hungary*, pp. 314–16.

357. A 42228, 9 October 1918; A 44539, 21 October 1918, Oest. 103/Bd. 8. Nostitz reported to Dresden on October 6 that "Der Pessimismus auch der deutschnationalen Kreise kennt jetzt hier kaum noch Grenzen." *Der Zerfall*, p. 178.

358. A 44949, 22 October 1918, Oest. 103/Bd. 9. For the diplomatic background, see Betty Miller Unterberger, *The United States, Revolutionary Russia, and the Rise of Czechoslovakia* (Chapel Hill, 1989), pp. 314–17.

359. The offer was mediated by the young military adjutant Glaise-Horstenau. See his *Erinnerungen*, p. 498–99. For Hussarek's fall, see Benndorf's report of 27 October 1918 in *Der Zerfall*, pp. 191–92.

360. See Klemperer, *Ignaz Seipel*, pp. 81ff.; Josef Redlich, "Heinrich Lammasch als Ministerpräsident," in Lammasch and Sperl, *Heinrich Lammasch;* and Heinrich Benedikt, *Die Friedensaktion der Meinlgruppe 1917/18. Die Bemühungen um einen Verständigungsfrieden nach Dokumenten, Aktenstücken und Briefen* (Graz, 1962).

361. They met on October 17 to summon the provisional assembly.

362. In general, see Georg Schmitz, *Die Vorentwürfe Hans Kelsens für die österreichische Bundesverfassung* (Vienna, 1981), pp. 11–26; Staudinger, *Aspekte*, pp. 33–95; Reinhard Owerdieck, *Parteien und Verfassungsfrage in Österreich. Die Entstehung des Verfassungsprovisoriums der Ersten Republik 1918–1920* (Munich, 1987), pp. 41–60.

363. Anton Staudinger, "Zur Entscheidung der christlichsozialen Abgeordneten für die Republik," in *Österreich November 1918. Die Entstehung der Ersten Republik* (Vienna, 1986), p. 171.

364. *Stenographische Protokolle über die Sitzungen der Provisorischen Nationalversammlung für Deutschösterreich. 1918 und 1919,* vol. 1 (Vienna, 1919), p. 6. At the parliamentary club meeting prior to this session, it was apparent that confusion and uncertainty reigned over just how the dynastic principle could be preserved, but that sentiment was still strongly in favor of the Monarchy: Mataja: "Die Partei zweifelhafte Haltung bezüglich der monarchischen Form. Eine konservative Partei darf an diesem nicht mackeln lassen. . . . Irgend etwas muss doch auch bei der christlsoz. Partei feststehen. Wir müssen positiven Inhalt haben!" Miklas: "Wir können unmöglich unseren Standpunkt der Monarchie verlassen." "Klubsitzung," 21 October 1918.

365. Karl Werkmann, *Der Tote auf Madeira* (Munich, 1923), pp. 15–16; "Untersuchung der christlich-sozialen Partei über die Umsturztage November 1918." Hauser's position—which was both difficult and ambivalent—exposed him to intraparty attacks

in 1923, to the effect that he had not sufficiently tried to defend the Emperor. See Staudinger's comments in *Österreich November 1918*, p. 272; as well as Slapnicka, *Christlichsoziale in Oberösterreich*, pp. 188–90. As late as 1932 Seipel would recall to Funder the tensions between Hauser and himself when Hauser asked Seipel to visit Karl in Eckartsau and Seipel adamantly refused. Seipel to Funder, 15 February 1932, *NL Funder.*

366. Owerdieck, *Parteien*, pp. 47–51; Staudinger, *Aspekte*, pp. 96–97.

367. *Stenographische Protokolle über die Sitzungen der Provisorischen Nationalversammlung für Deutschösterreich*, p. 17.

368. *Aspekte*, pp. 107–16.

369. Owerdieck, *Parteien*, pp. 46–48.

370. "Protokoll des zu Wien am 31. Oktober 1918 abgehaltenen Ministerrates," *AVA*; a similar, overly optimistic assessment occurred at the *Ministerrat* held on November 7, where Seipel argued that he believed "diese Nationalversammlung nicht für so gefährlich."

371. *Stenographische Protokolle über die Sitzungen der Provisorischen Nationalversammlung für Deutschösterreich*, p. 37. As early as October 21 Stöckler had cautioned his colleagues that "Wir können nicht mehr tun, wie wir wollen. Die Monarchie gehört hier nicht ins Spiel. Wir haben keine freie Hand mehr. Alle werden die Wurzen sein und alles übernehmen! Die Bauern kommen als Anarchisten nach Hause." "Klubsitzung," 21 October 1918.

372. See Brügel, *Geschichte*, 5: 393–96. The original copies of the *Staatsrat's* proceedings are in the *Archiv der Republik.*

373. Reports of 22 October 1918 and 26 October 1918, Oest. 103/Bd. 9; see also the police report of 13 November reprinted in Rudolf Neck, ed., *Österreich im Jahre 1918* (Munich, 1968) pp. 154–55, in which the public is reported to have been sympathetic to Karl's personal fate, but that his behavior had brought "die Zahl der Anhänger monarchistischer Institutionen im Volke fast ganz zum Verschwinden." Even among the Christian Socials, voices emerged defensive of the Monarchy but critical of Emperor Karl. Heinrich Mataja argued at the club meeting on October 30 that "Es liegt lediglich an der Krone die monarchische Staatsform aufrecht zu erhalten."

374. This seems to me to be the only reasonable way to interpret Seipel's comments to Lammasch in his report of November 9. See Seipel to Lammasch, 9 November 1918, reprinted in Stephan Verosta, "Ignaz Seipels Weg von der Monarchie zur Republik (1917–1919)," in *Die österreichische Verfassung von 1918 bis 1938* (Munich, 1980), pp. 22–23.

375. Police reports from 13 November indicate that the proclamation of the Republic met with widespread acceptance if not satisfaction. See *Österreich im Jahre 1918*, pp. 151–57. But the "apathy" factor in the face of exhaustion and hunger should also not be discounted. Karl Niedrist touched upon this when he argued that "90% der Bevölkerung kümmert sich nicht um Republik oder Monarchie." "Klubsitzung," 30 October 1918.

376. "Protokoll der Sitzung des Parteivorstandes . . . am 11. November 1918," *VGAB*. When the Saxon delegate Benndorf visited Victor Adler on the 8th, Adler told him that he thought last-minute attempts to revive federalist schemes (which Benndorf associated with Lammasch and Redlich) would fail and that he wanted the "Anschluss Deutsch-Österreichs als einer Republik an das Deutsche Reich." *Der Zerfall*, pp. 200–201. On 10 November Benndorf reported that the Entente was conspiring with leading politicians in Vienna ("Lammasch, Redlich, Klerikale und Mitglieder der ehemaligen K.u.K. Regierung") to hinder an *Anschluss* by reinserting German-Austria into a new multinational federal state. He claimed that Wedel shared his apprehensions. Ibid., pp. 203–4.

377. Erwin Matsch, ed., *November 1918 auf dem Ballhausplatz. Erinnerungen Ludwigs Freiherrn von Flotow, des letzten Chefs des Österreichisch-Ungarischen Auswärtigen Dienstes 1895–1920* (Vienna, 1982), p. 331; "Abends Ministerrat bis 1 Uhr nachts. Seitz und Renner drängen zur Proklamierung der Republik und zur Abdankung des Kaisers. Ich im schlechten Verzögerungskampf." Seipel Diary, entry of 10 November 1918.

378. See Banhans Diary, 2: 135–40. For the authorship of the document, see Klemperer, *Ignaz Seipel*, p. 90. The document was based on a partial first draft by Karl Renner and others, with revisions by Seipel and Redlich. *Schicksalsjahre*, 2: 317. In his "Aufzeichnungen," allegedly written in 1920–21, Karl characterized the document as illegal, executed under moral and political coercion. For confirmation of Karl's state of mind on November 12, see Flotow's comments in Matsch, ed., *November 1918*, p. 332.

379. Brügel, *Geschichte*, 5: 393–96. Renner's arguments were never more brilliant. He moved effortlessly from brutal fact—in Germany the revolution had dispensed with the *Bürgertum*, while in Austria the socialists still sought to cooperate with the peasants and urbanists—to prophecies of an imminent *Anschluss* unless Austria matched what Germany had already done.

380. "Wir müssen deshalb, was für die Ententebourgeoisie ideologischer Vorwand wäre, die Republik und das Nationalitätenprinzip in unseren Lebensinteressen vollziehen." Ibid., p. 395.

381. *Politische Chronik*, 1918, p. 600; Schober, *Geschichte des Tiroler Landtages*, p. 360.

382. On monarchism in October and early November 1918, see Honeder, "Hauser," pp. 141–74, esp. 149; Funder, *Vom Gestern*, pp. 581–91; Braun, "Richard Schmitz," pp. 39–39; and Jelinek, "Heinrich Mataja," pp. 34–38.

383. Seipel later described the circumstances under which (in his view) Jodok Fink turned against the Emperor in his memoir, "Die Stellung Hausers und Finks in den Umsturztagen 1918," printed as an appendix to Honeder, "Hauser," pp. 69–72.

384. Its official members were Schmitz, Funder, Kienböck, Hemala, Dr. Alma Motzko (née Seitz) and Dr. Hildegard Burjan, but Mataja also attended some of its meetings, as did Seipel. The presence of Motzko and Burjan, who effectively argued for women's suffrage (and who were among the first Christian Social women elected to the

City Council), is indicative of the new and more aggressive views of political organization which the *Volksbund* and the Christian Social workers forced upon the Viennese
party. Its principal records are Schmitz's *Notizbücher* A and B, Carton 16, *NL Schmitz*.
See also Funder, *Vom Gestern*, pp. 583–90, and Jelinek, "Heinrich Mataja," pp. 34–38.

385. Seipel to Missong, 31 March 1932, *NL Seipel*.

386. Compare *Rp*, 12 November 1918, p. 1, with Hauser's remarks later the same
day at the parliamentary club meeting: "Wir stehen vor ernster entscheidender Sitzung
des Nat. Rates. Bisher alle bis ins Innerste kaisertreu gewesen. Seit 14 Tagen Ereignisse
überstürzt. Bis zum Manifest noch möglich über Staatsform zu reden. Möglich wird
dies der definitiven Nat. Versammlung überlassen. Deutschland heute verloren, weil
Wilhelm nicht rechtzeitig abgedankt hat. Der Zusammenbruch Deutschlands auf Österreich selbstverständlich Rückwirkung. Tiroler N. Rat. beschlossen jetzt schon Republik
zu verkündigen; fallen seh ich Zweig auf Zweig! Jetzt gibt es nur eines, wenn wir im-
stande die Republik aufzuhalten, könnten wir dies nicht tun, weil es furchtbaren Bür-
gerkrieg provozieren würde." "Klubsitzung," 12 November 1918. See also Funder, *Vom
Gestern*, pp. 592–93.

387. "Funder wünscht von mir die Entwicklung eines Programmes in einer Reihe
von Artikeln, die ich zusagte." Seipel Diary, entry of 14 November 1918. These were
published as "Das Recht des Volkes," *Rp*, 19 November 1918; "Das Wesen des demokratischen Staates," 20 November 1918; "Die demokratische Verfassung," 21 November 1918; and "Das Volk und die künftige Staatsform," 23 November 1918. Klemperer,
Ignaz Seipel, pp. 104–9, offers an elegant summary of these essays. See also Verosta,
"Ignaz Seipels Weg," pp. 30–33.

388. Heinrich Mataja, "Das Selbstbestimmungsrecht der Völker," *Rp*, 11 October
1918, pp. 1–2. See also his speech on 2 October 1918 in *SP*, 1918, pp. 4342–43, as well
as his comments in the parliamentary club on October 1: "Es is ganz ausgeschlossen,
dass die Ämter Frieden machen. Das Schwergewicht liegt in den politischen Parteien.
Müssen es als innere Aufgabe betrachten, sonst keine vernünftigen Verhandlungen. Von
sämtlichen Parteien ist unsere Partei berufen entscheidend einzugreifen und darauf zu
drängen, dass das auch ausgeführt wird. Politische Parteien entscheidend eingreifen!"
"Klubsitzung," 1 October 1918.

CHAPTER EIGHT

1. See Weiskirchner's statement of 3 December 1918, in *AB*, 1918, p. 2334, as well
as his comments in the "Verhandlungsschrift über die Sitzung des Bürgerklubs vom 13.
November 1918," Carton 37, *CPW*.

2. Z. 1587, 16 November 1918, Carton 76, *CPW*.

3. See, for example, the letter of Archduke Friedrich to Stürgkh, 3 October 1915,
complaining about "desolate" conditions in Vienna and urging vigorous action in regard to food provisioning, and the defensive response by Stürgkh's Minister of Internal
Affairs, Heinold, who insisted that "Ich darf wohl sagen, dass die Regierung über alle

Anschuldigungen gegen den Ernst ihrer Arbeit erhaben ist, und dass sie sich einig mit den massgebenden militärischen Faktoren in dem Bestreben weiss, die Widerstandskraft Oesterreichs zu wahren." Copy of a report from Heinold to Stürgkh, dated 24 November 1915, 69–22/1 and 69–22/8, *MKSM*.

4. See the report of Archduke Friedrich to Stürgkh, 28 March 1916, 69–10/1, *MKSM*. See also Schober, *Geschichte des Tiroler Landtages*, p. 353. As early as January 1915 Niedrist was not mincing his words about the behavior of Austrian army officers. At a meeting of the Christian Social parliamentary club on 27 January 1915 he was quoted as reporting that his constituents would "heidenlos schimpfen über die Offiziere. Er wolle nicht generalisieren: aber viele sind wirklich ekelhaft. Die Sozi haben grosse Stösse Aktenmaterial gesammelt. Es wird ein Tag der Rache kommen." Carton 91, *CPK*.

5. *Stenographische Protokolle über die Sitzungen der Provisorischen Nationalversammlung für Deutschösterreich, p. 37.*

6. *See Otto Bauer to Jean Longuet, 9 January 1919, in Werkausgabe, 9: 1047–50;* and Hans Mommsen, "Victor Adler und die Politik der österreichischen Sozialdemokratie im Ersten Weltkrieg," pp. 378–408.

7. For the Social Democrats and the strikes, see *Arbeiterschaft,* 2: 185ff. See also Sieder, "Behind the Lines," pp. 109–38.

8. Mataja to the party's *engeren Parteirat,* 13 April 1918, Z. 1455, Carton 76, *CPW.*

9. "Glück und Ende der Christlichsozialen," *AZ,* 6 May 1919, p. 1.

10. Some lived a few years longer. Richard Weiskirchner retired from the *Nationalrat* in 1923; he died in 1926. Leopold Steiner died in 1927.

11. Geyer, "The State in National Socialist Germany," pp. 199, 202–3.

12. Robert A. Kann, "Das geschichtliche Erbe—Gemeinsamer Nenner und rechtes Mass," in Erika Weinzierl and Kurt Skalnik, eds., *Österreich. Die Zweite Republik* (2 vols., Graz, 1972), 1: 47–48.

13. The present writer is now at work on such a general history, which will cover the years 1867 to 1955, with a postscript on Austria's history to the present.

14. Charles S. Maier, "'Fictitious bonds . . . of wealth and law': On the theory and practice of interest representation," in Suzanne Berger, ed. *Organizing Interests in Western Europe. Pluralism, Corporatism, and the Transformation of Politics* (Cambridge, 1981), p. 53.

15. Max Adler, "Wahlenthaltung ist Reaktion!" *AZ,* 3 May 1919, p. 2.

16. See most recently, Anson Rabinbach, *The Crisis of Austrian Socialism,* as well as Norbert Leser, *Zwischen Reformismus und Bolschewismus,* and Helmut Gruber, *Red Vienna.*

17. The corporatism undergirding the modern Austrian state is not simply a substitute for or replacement of formal political or bureaucratic norms and organizations, but rather an organizational mode of stating the expectations and resolving the conflicting interests of various social constituencies in officially recognized and state-legitimated

mediatory offices that carry the presumption, not of neutrality, but of controlled and balanced partisanship. The system is marked by a structured equilibrium of power, not merely by expert disinterest.

18. Lueger's conviction of owning the city has been mentioned throughout this book. Victor Adler spoke in much the same way immediately after the Social Democratic victory of June 1911. Black Vienna had now become "Red Vienna," and the "Haupt- und Residenzstadt des Kaisers" had now become the "Haupt- und Residenzstadt des österreichischen Proletariats." See *Aufsätze, Reden, Briefe,* 11: 234–35.

19. For the reactions of one important group of adversaries to the city, see C. Earl Edmondson, *The Heimwehr and Austrian Politics, 1918–1936* (Athens, 1978).

20. *Die Gemeindeverwaltung der Bundeshauptstadt Wien in der Zeit vom· 1. Juli 1919 bis 31. Dezember 1922 unter dem Bürgermeister Jakob Reumann* (Vienna, 1927), p. 2.

21. *Seipel-Steuern oder Breitner-Steuern? Die Wahrheit über die Steuerpolitik der Gemeinde Wien* (Vienna, 1927), p. 24.

22. Alessandro Pizzorno, "Interests and Parties in Pluralism," in Berger, ed. *Organizing Interests in Western Europe,* p. 250.

23. Robert Danneberg, *Das neue Wien* (5th ed., Vienna, 1930).

24. On the attempt of the parties to direct the Revolution by appropriating the administrative authority of the Imperial civil service, see especially the intelligent essays in *Studien zur Zeitgeschichte der österreichischen Länder. Band 1: Demokratisierung und Verfassung in den Ländern 1918–1920* (St. Pölten, 1983).

25. Quoted in Klemperer, *Ignaz Seipel,* p. 156.

26. On Christian Social attitudes, see ibid., pp. 106–8, 139–45, and Richard Schmitz, "Vom Parteienstaat zum autoritären Staat," *Kalasantiner Blätter,* 46 (1933): 200–201.

27. *Stenographisches Protokoll. 1. (Eröffnungs-) Sitzung des Nationalrates der Republik Österreich,* 19 Dezember 1945, p. 4 (Seitz), p. 5 (Kunschak), p. 9 (Renner).

28. Gerald Stourzh's masterful account of the State Treaty remains the authoritative commentary on this major event. *Geschichte des Staatsvertrages 1945–1955* (3d ed., Graz, 1985).

29. Georg Wagner, "Von der Staatsidee zum Nationalbewusstsein," in Georg Wagner, ed., *Österreich. Von der Staatsidee zum Nationalbewusstsein* (Vienna, 1982), pp. 109–52; Gerald Stourzh, *Vom Reich zur Republik—Studien zum Österreichbewusstsein* (Vienna, 1990); Ernst Bruckmüller, *Nation Österreich. Sozialhistorische Aspekte ihrer Entwicklung* (Vienna 1984); and John W. Boyer, "Some Reflections on the Problem of Austria, Germany, and Mitteleuropa," *CEH,* 22 (1989): 301–15.

30. On Austrian Liberalism's complicated relationship to the Catholic Church, see John W. Boyer, "Religion and Political Development in Central Europe around 1900: A View from Vienna," *AHY,* 25 (1994): 13–57.

BIBLIOGRAPHY

ARCHIVAL SOURCES
1. *Haus-, Hof- und Staatsarchiv,* Vienna

a. Private Papers
   Nachlass Joseph Maria Baernreither
   Nachlass Karl von Banhans
   Nachlass Leopold Berchtold
   Nachlass Erzherzog Franz Ferdinand
   Nachlass Friedrich Funder
   Nachlass Gustav Gross
   Nachlass Erasmus von Handel
   Nachlass Ludo Moritz Hartmann
   Nachlass Gustav Marchet
   Nachlass Heinrich Mataja
   Nachlass Hanns Schlitter
   Nachlass Richard Schmitz

b. Government Documents

   Gemeinsame Ministerratsprotokolle, 1907–1914
   Kabinettskanzlei, Geheimakten, 1907–1914
   Ministerium des Äussern, Politisches Archiv, 1914–1918

2. *Finanzarchiv,* Vienna
    Präsidialakten, Finanzministerium, 1898–1914

3. *Allgemeines Verwaltungsarchiv,* Vienna

a. Private Papers

Nachlass Max Vladimir von Beck
Nachlass Johann Eichhoff
Nachlass Karl Seitz
Personalakten Friedrich Gaertner

b. *Ministerratspräsidium*

Ministerratsprotokolle, 1912–1918

c. Austrian Party Archives

Archive of the Christian Social Party

Christlichsozialer Parlamentsklub
Christlichsoziale Partei, Wien
Christlichsoziale Partei, NÖ Landtag
Archive of the Social Democratic Party
(*SD Parteistellen*)

Nachlass Victor Adler

d. *Präsidialakten, Ministerium des Innern,* 1898–1918

e. *Präsidialakten, Ministerium für Kultus und Unterricht,* 1898–1918

f. *Präsidialakten, Ministerium für öffentliche Arbeiten,* 1908

4. *Kriegsarchiv,* Vienna

Private Papers

Nachlass Karl von Bardolff
Nachlass Alexander Brosch von Aarenau
Nachlass Rudolf Brougier
Rudolf Kundmann Diary

Government Documents

Archive of the Militärkanzlei des Generalinspektors der gesamten bewaffneten Macht (Franz Ferdinand)
Archive of the Militärkanzlei Seiner Majestät des Kaisers

5. *Wiener Stadt- und Landesarchiv,* Vienna

a. *Magistrats-Direktion*

b. *H.A. Akten, Kleine Bestände*

c. *Nachlass Karl Seitz*

6. *Niederösterreichisches Landesarchiv,* Vienna

   a. *Statthalterei, Präsidialakten,* 1897–1918

   b. *N. Öst. Landes-Ausschuss,* 1897–1905

7. *Handschriftensammlung, Stadtbibliothek,* Vienna

   Nachlass Heinrich Friedjung
   Nachlass Karl Lueger
   Nachlass Richard Weiskirchner

8. *Erzbischöfliches Diözesanarchiv,* Vienna

   Nachlass Kardinal Nagl
   Nachlass Kardinal Piffl
   Nachlass Ignaz Seipel

9. *Verein für Geschichte der Arbeiterbewegung,* Vienna

   Vorstands-Protokolle, Social Democratic Party, 1898–1919

10. *Universitätsarchiv,* Vienna

    Personalakten Albert Gessmann

11. *Politisches Archiv des Auswärtigen Amtes,* Bonn

    Oesterreich 70, 72, 73, 86/2, 86/6, 88, 91, 95, 97, 103, 1897–1918

12. *Bayerisches Hauptstaatsarchiv,* Munich

    MAIII series, reports from Vienna, 1898–1918

13. *Handschriftenabteilung,* Bayerische Staatsbibliothek, Munich

    Nachlass Karl von Amira

14. *Bundesarchiv,* Koblenz

    Nachlass Lujo Brentano
    Nachlass Martin Spahn
    Nachlass Matthias Erzberger
    Nachlass Walter Goetz

15. *Public Record Office,* London

    FO 371 series for Austria-Hungary, 1908–1914
    FO 881 series for Austria-Hungary, 1908–1914

16. *Archives of the Times,* London

   Henry Wickham Steed Papers

17. *School of Slavonic and East European Studies,* University of London

   Robert William Seton-Watson Papers

18. *University of Georgia Library, Athens, Georgia*

   Guido Adler Papers

NEWSPAPERS AND POLITICAL JOURNALS

Alldeutsches Tagblatt
Allgemeiner Tiroler Anzeiger
*Allgemeines österreichisches Staats-
   beamten-Blatt*
Arbeiter-Zeitung
Der Bauernbündler
Christlich-soziale Arbeiter-Zeitung
Christliche Wiener Frauen-Zeitung
Christlichsoziale Landstrasser Zeitung
*Correspondenzblatt für den katholischen
   Clerus Oesterreichs*
Deutsch-österreichische Lehrer-Zeitung
Deutsche Rundschau
Deutsche Schulzeitung
Deutsche Zeitung
Deutsches Volksblatt
Evangelische Kirchen-Zeitung
Die Fackel
Freie Lehrerstimme
Freiheit
Fremdenblatt
Germania
Der Gewerbefreund
Historisch-politische Blätter
Hochland
Illustriertes Wiener Extrablatt
Die Industrie
Der Kampf
Kommunale Praxis
Lienzer Nachrichten

Linzer Volksblatt
"Los!" *Organ der radikalen Partei*
Mitteilungen des Vereines "Freie Schule"
Neue Freie Presse
Neues Wiener Journal
Neues Wiener Tagblatt
Ostdeutsche Rundschau
Österreichische Frauen-Zeitung
Österreichische Postbeamten-Zeitung
Österreichische Rundschau
Österreichische Schulzeitung
Österreichische Volkszeitung
Österreichische Wochenschrift
Österreichs katholisches Sonntagsblatt
Pädagogischer Jahresbericht
Reichspost
Der Reichsratswähler
Sonn- und Montags-Zeitung
Der Staatsbeamte
Vaterland
Die Volksbewegung
Volksbote
Volksstimme
Volkstribüne
Volkswirtschaftliche Wochenschrift
Volkswohl
Wiener Bilder
Wiener Diözesanblatt
Wiener Familienfreund
Wiener Zeitung
Die Zeit

GOVERNMENT PUBLICATIONS

Amtsblatt der Reichshaupt- und Residenzstadt Wien. Vienna, 1897–1918.

Bericht der Kommission zur Förderung der Verwaltungsreform über die Steigerung der Kosten der staatlichen inneren Verwaltung in der Periode von 1890 bis 1911 und über Vorschläge inbezug auf vorläufige Reformen hinsichtlich der Zentralstellen und der politischen Landesbehörden. Vienna, 1913.

Bernatzik, Edmund. *Vorläufige Mitteilungen des zur Ausarbeitung eines Gesetzentwurfes über die Verwaltungsrechtsprechung bestellten Referenten E. Bernatzik über die allgemeinen Gesichtspunkte des von ihm ausgearbeiteten Entwurfes.* Vienna, 1912.

Bourne, Kenneth, and D. Cameron Watt, eds. *British Documents on Foreign Affairs. Reports and Papers from the Foreign Office Confidential Print.* Part II. Series H. *The First World War, 1914–1918.* Vols. 9–12. *The Central Powers.* Frederick, Md., 1989.

Enquete der Kommission zur Förderung der Verwaltungsreform, veranstaltet in der Zeit vom 21. Oktober bis 9. November 1912 zur Feststellung der Wünsche der beteiligten Kreise der Bevölkerung in bezug auf die Reform der Inneren und Finanzverwaltung. Vienna, 1913.

Die Erbauung des Wiener städtischen Gaswerkes. Im Auftrage des Herrn Bürgermeisters Dr. Karl Lueger bearbeitet. Vienna, 1901.

Erläuterungen zu den Grundzügen einer Reform der Organisation der inneren Verwaltung. Vienna, 1914.

Festschrift herausgegeben anlässlich der Hundertjahrfeier des Wiener Stadtbauamtes. Vienna, 1935.

Die Gemeinde-Verwaltung der Stadt Wien [annual volumes covering 1897 to 1922]. Vienna, 1900–1927.

100 Jahre Unterrichtsministerium 1848–1948. Festschrift des Bundesministeriums für Unterricht in Wien. Vienna, 1948.

Mitteilungen des Vereines der Beamten der Stadt Wien. Vienna, 1899–1911.

Redlich, Josef. *Bericht des Mitgliedes der Kommission zur Förderung der Verwaltungsreform Professor Dr. Josef Redlich über die Entwicklung und den gegenwärtigen Stand der österreichischen Finanzverwaltung sowie Vorschläge der Kommission zur Reform dieser Verwaltung.* Vienna, 1913.

Sammlung der Erkenntnisse des k.k. Verwaltungsgerichtshofes. Vienna, 1898–1914.

Die städtischen Elektrizitäts-Werke und Strassenbahnen in Wien. Vienna, 1903.

Statistische Jahrbücher der Stadt Wien [annual volumes covering the years 1897–1914]. Vienna, 1899–1918.

Stenographisches Protokoll der Enquete über die Landesfinanzen. 7. bis 12. März 1908. Vienna, 1908.

Stenographische Protokolle des Niederösterreichischen Landtages. Vienna, 1897–1914.

Stenographische Protokolle über die Sitzungen des Hauses der Abgeordneten. Vienna, 1867–1918.

Stenographische Protokolle über die Sitzungen des Herrenhauses. Vienna, 1918.

Stenographische Protokolle über die Sitzungen der Provisorischen Nationalversammlung für Deutschösterreich. Vienna, 1918–19.

Stenographische Sitzungs-Protokolle der Delegation des Reichsrates. Vienna, 1908.

Stenographischer Bericht über die Beratungen des VIII. österreichischen Städtetages am 20. Oktober 1911. Vienna, 1912.

Die Tätigkeit der Wiener Gemeindeverwaltung in der Obmänner-Konferenz während des Weltkrieges. Vienna, 1917.

Verwaltungsbericht der Gemeinde Wien—Städtische Strassenbahnen—für das Jahr 1916/17. Vienna 1918.

Wiener Kommunal-Kalendar und Städtisches Jahrbuch für 1916. Vienna, 1916.

Wiener Kommunal-Kalendar und Städtisches Jahrbuch für 1917. Vienna, 1917.

CONTEMPORARY PRINTED MATERIALS

Abel, Heinrich. *Wetterleuchten. Meteorologische Schwankungen in der religiös-politischen Atmosphäre Österreichs.* Vienna, 1908.

Adler, Friedrich. "Fünfzehn Jahre allgemeines Wahlrecht in Wien und Niederösterreich." *K* 5 (1911–12): 303–11.

Adler, Guido. *Wollen und Wirken. Aus dem Leben eines Musikhistorikers.* Vienna, 1935.

Adler, Max. "Kirche und Schule." *K* 2 (1908–9): 389–96.

Adler, Victor. *Aufsätze, Reden, Briefe.* 11 vols. Vienna, 1922–29.

———. "Die Landtagswahlen in Niederösterreich." *K* 2 (1908–9): 49–53.

Arthur Schnitzler Tagebuch 1909–1912. Vienna, 1981.

Arz von Straussenburg, Arthur. *Zur Geschichte des grossen Krieges 1914–1918.* Vienna, 1924.

Austerlitz, Friedrich. "Gessmann als Erzieher." *K* 2 (1908–9): 97–101.

Austria Nova. Wege in Österreichs Zukunft. Vienna, 1916.

Bach, Anton. *Österreichs Zukunft und die Christlich-Sozialen. Eine Stimme zur Wahlreform.* Vienna, 1906.

Baernreither, Joseph Maria. *Fragmente eines politischen Tagebuches. Die südslawische Frage und Österreich-Ungarn vor dem Weltkrieg.* Edited by Joseph Redlich. Berlin, 1928.

———. *Der Verfall des Habsburgerreiches und die Deutschen. Fragmente eines politischen Tagebuches.* Edited by Oskar Mitis. Vienna, 1938.

Bardolff, Carl Freiherr von. *Soldat im alten Österreich. Erinnerungen aus meinem Leben.* Jena, 1939.

Bauer, Otto. "Bourgeoisie und Klerikalismus." *K* 1 (1907–8): 385–89.

———. "Keine Blockpolitik." *K* 4 (1910–11): 475–76.

———. "Proletariat und Religion." *K* 1 (1907–8): 537–42.

———. *Die Teuerung.* Vienna, 1910.

————. *Werkausgabe*. 9 vols. Vienna, 1975–80.

Beiträge zur Geschichte des deutschösterreichischen Gewerbebundes. Vienna, 1928.

Bericht über den VI. Allgemeinen österreichischen Katholikentag in Wien. 16. bis 19. November 1907. Vienna, 1908.

Bericht über die Verhandlungen des Reichs-Fachverbandes der Einzelverbände der Kleidermachergenossenschaften Österreichs. Abgehalten in Wien am 6., 7. und 8. September 1908. Vienna, 1908.

Bernatzik, Edmund. *Rechtsprechung und materielle Rechtskraft: Verwaltungsrechtliche Studien*. Vienna, 1886.

Beskiba, Marianne. *Aus meinen Erinnerungen an Dr. Karl Lueger*. Vienna, n.d.

Bong, Wilhelm. *Christus und die Arbeiterwelt. Meine Erlebnisse als Handwerksbursche und Fabriksarbeiter*. Vienna, 1911.

Börner, Wilhelm. *Friedrich Jodl. Eine Studie*. Stuttgart, 1911.

Brockhausen, Karl. *Österreichische Verwaltungsreformen*. Vienna, 1911.

————. *Zur österreichischen Verwaltungsreform*. Vienna, 1917.

Brügel, Ludwig. *Geschichte der österreichischen Sozialdemokratie*. 5 vols. Vienna, 1922–25.

————. *Soziale Gesetzgebung in Österreich von 1848 bis 1919*. Vienna, 1919.

Burián, István. *Austria in Dissolution*. Translated by Brian Lunn. London, 1925.

Charmatz, Richard. *Deutsch-Oesterreichische Politik. Studien über den Liberalismus und über die auswärtige Politik Österreichs*. Leipzig, 1907.

Class, Heinrich. *Wider den Strom. Vom Werden und Wachsen der nationalen Opposition im alten Reich*. Leipzig, 1932.

Czernin, Ottokar. *Im Weltkriege*. Berlin, 1919.

Danneberg, Robert. *Das neue Wien*. 5th ed. Vienna, 1930.

————. "Eine Revision des christlichen Sozialismus." *K* 5 (1911–12): 241–46.

————. "Wer sind die Wiener Wähler?" *K* 6 (1912–13): 397–410.

Denkschrift aus Deutsch-Österreich. Leipzig, 1915.

"Denkschrift der deutschböhmischen Reichsratsabgeordneten an Seine Excellenz den Herrn Ministerpräsidenten Karl Grafen Stürgkh." *Zeitschrift für Ostforschung* 7 (1958): 519–30.

Dont, Jakob, ed. *Der heraldische Schmuck der Kirche des Wiener Versorgungsheims*. Vienna, 1911.

————. *Das Wiener Versorgungsheim. Eine Gedenkschrift zur Eröffnung im Auftrage der Gemeinde Wien*. Vienna, 1904.

Eckardt, Johannes. "Zum fünfundzwanzigjährigen Bestande der österreichischen Leo-Gesellschaft." *Das Neue Österreich* (February 1917): 52–58; (March 1917): 52–59.

Ehrhard, Albert. *Der katholische Student und seine Ideale. Eine Programmrede*. Vienna, 1899.

Ehrhart, Robert. *Im Dienste des alten Österreich*. Vienna, 1958.

Eldersch, Matthias. "Die neue Sozialversicherungsvorlage." *K* 5 (1911–12): 127–32.

"Erinnerungen des Erasmus Freiherrn von Handel." *Jahrbuch der österreichischen Leo-Gesellschaft.* Vienna, 1930.

Erzberger, Matthias. *Erlebnisse im Weltkrieg.* Stuttgart, 1920.

Feigl, Erich, ed. *Kaiser Karl. Persönliche Aufzeichnungen, Zeugnisse und Dokumente.* Vienna, 1984.

Festschrift zum 25-jährigen Bestande des Zentralvereines der Wiener Lehrerschaft 1896–1921. Vienna, 1921.

Fischer, Christian. "Die Christlichsozialen und die Festbesoldeten-Bewegung." *VW* 9 (1918): 158–63.

Frank, Ferdinand. *Enzyklopädisches Handbuch der Normalien für das österreichische Volksschulwesen mit Einschluss der Lehrerbildung und gewerblichen Fortbildungsschulen.* Vienna, 1910.

Fried, Jakob. *Erinnerungen aus meinem Leben (1885–1936).* Edited by Franz Loidl. Vienna, 1977.

Friedrich Adler vor dem Ausnahmegericht. Berlin, 1919.

Funder, Friedrich. *Aufbruch zur christlichen Sozialreform.* Vienna, 1953.

———. *Vom Gestern ins Heute. Aus dem Kaiserreich in die Republik.* Vienna, 1953.

———. *Das weiss-blau-goldene Band: "Norica." Fünfzig Jahre Wiener katholischen deutschen Farbstudententums.* Innsbruck, 1933.

Gessmann, Albert. *Zur Mittelschulreform. Vortrag in der Versammlung des 'Vereins für Schulreform' am 12. Jänner 1908.* Vienna, 1908.

Glöckel, Otto. "Der Kampf um das Koalitionsrecht der Staatsangestellten." *K* 6 (1912–13): 222–26.

———. *Selbstbiographie.* Zurich, 1939.

———. *Das Tor der Zukunft.* Vienna, 1917.

Goldemund, Heinrich. *Generalprojekt eines Wald- und Wiesengürtels und einer Höhenstrasse für die Reichshaupt- und Residenzstadt Wien.* Vienna, 1905.

Hainisch, Marianne. "Die Geschichte der Frauenbewegung in Österreich." In *Handbuch der Frauenbewegung.* Edited by Helene Lang and Gertrud Bäumer. 4 vols. Berlin, 1901–2.

Harrasser, Georg, ed. *Aus dem Tagebuch eines Sodalen. Tagebuchblätter des Kongregationspräfekten Johann Leb aus den Jahren 1860–1920.* Innsbruck, 1925.

Hassmann, Rudolf. *Allgemeine Erziehungslehre für Lehrer- und Lehrerinnen-Bildungsanstalten.* Vienna, 1907.

Heinl, Eduard. *Über ein halbes Jahrhundert. Zeit und Wirtschaft.* Vienna, 1948.

Heinrich Lammasch. Seine Aufzeichnungen, sein Wirken und seine Politik. Edited by Marga Lammasch and Hans Sperl. Vienna, 1922.

Hevesi, Ludwig. "Otto Wagners Stadtmuseum." In *Altkunst-Neukunst. Wien 1894–1908.* Vienna, 1909.

Hilferding, Rudolf. "Arbeitsgemeinschaft der Klassen?" *K* 8 (1915): 321–29.

Hilgenreiner, Karl. "Christlichsozial—was ist das?" *Bonifatius-Korrespondenz* 12 (1918): 145–49.

Hock, Paul von. *Der Zwang zu den religiösen Übungen in der Schule. Eine Darstellung der rechtlichen Seite dieser Frage.* Vienna, n.d. [1908].

Holzhausen, Emerich, ed. *Bericht über die Verhandlungen des Kongresses für Katechetik, Wien 1912.* Vienna, 1913.

Hornich, Rudolf. "Autorität als Fundamentalbegriff der Gesellschafts- und der Erziehungswissenschaft." *Erstes Jahrbuch des Vereines für christl. Erziehungswissenschaft.* Kempten, 1908.

————. "Die Bedeutung Willmanns für unsere Zeit." *Österreichische Pädagogische Warte* 14 (1919): 67–70.

Hron, Karl. *Habsburgische "Los von Rom" Kaiser. Eine Studie über die antiösterreichischen Tendenzen des ultramontanen Klerikalismus.* Vienna, 1901.

Hussarek, Max von. *Grundriss des Staatskirchenrechts.* 2d ed. Leipzig, 1908.

Jodl, Friedrich. "Religion and Modern Science." *The Monist* 3 (1892–93): 329–351.

————. "Zum Jubiläum des österreichischen Reichsvolksschulgesetzes." In *Vom Lebenswege. Gesammelte Vorträge und Aufsätze von Friedrich Jodl.* Edited by Wilhelm Börner. 2 vols. Stuttgart, 1916–17.

Jordan, Eduard. *Aus meinem Leben. Erinnerungen eines Achtzigjährigen.* Vienna, n.d.

Kammel, Karl, ed. *Bericht über den XXIII. Internationalen Eucharistischen Kongress. Wien 12. bis 15. September 1912.* Vienna, 1912.

Kanner, Heinrich. *Kaiserliche Katastrophenpolitik. Ein Stück zeitgenössischer Geschichte.* Leipzig, 1922.

Der Katholikentag der Deutschen Österreichs vom 15. bis 17. August 1913 in Linz a. D. Linz, 1913.

Kielmansegg, Erich. *Kaiserhaus, Staatsmänner und Politiker. Aufzeichnungen des k.k. Statthalters Erich Graf Kielmansegg.* Edited by Walter Goldinger. Vienna, 1966.

Kralik, Richard von. *Die Entscheidung im Weltkrieg. Drei Reden.* Vienna, 1914.

Kritias, *Das Parlament in Oesterreich oder die innere Gefahr.* Heidelberg, 1913.

Kunschak, Leopold. "Aus dem Werden der christlichen Arbeiterbewegung Österreichs." *VW* 14 (1923): 246–53, 279–84.

"Die Landtagswahlen in Oesterreich und die christlichsociale Partei." *Historisch-politische Blätter* 130 (1902): 824–35.

Leb, Josef. *P. Heinrich Abel, S.J. Der Männerapostel Wiens. Ein Lebensbild.* Innsbruck, 1926.

Leuthner, Karl. "Der Niedergang einer Parteidespotie." *Sozialistische Monatshefte* 13 (July 1911): 875–78.

Licht, Stefan. *Die Ergebnisse der Enquete über die Verwaltungsreform.* Vienna, 1913.

————. *Der österreichische Reichsrat und der Stand seiner Arbeiten. Mitteilungen der Industriellen Vereinigung. Nr. 20.* Vienna, 1914.

Liechtenstein, Alois. "Österreichs Zukunft. I. Die Nationale Frage. II. Das österreichische Parlament." *Das Neue Österreich* (April 1916): 18–22; (May 1916): 1–6.

Liechtenstein, Eduard. "Die Entwicklung der Jugendfürsorge in Österreich seit dem I. Kinderschutzkongresse vom Jahre 1907." In *Gutachten, Berichte und Materialien zu den Verhandlungsgegenständen des Zweiten Österreichischen Kinderschutzkongresses in Salzburg, 1913.* Edited by Josef M. Baernreither. Vienna, 1913.

Maresch, Otto. "Eine österreichische 'Soziale Woche'." *Hochland* 9 (1911–12): 250–52.

Masaryk, Thomas G. *Freie wissenschaftliche und kirchlich gebundene Weltanschauung und Lebensauffassung. Die kirchenpolitische Bedeutung der Wahrmund-Affäre.* Vienna, 1908.

Mataja, Heinrich. *Die Abstimmung über den Finanzplan.* Vienna, 1914.

Mayer, Sigmund. *Ein jüdischer Kaufmann 1831 bis 1911. Lebenserinnerungen.* Leipzig, 1911.

Medinger, Wilhelm. *Das kommende Wirtschaftsbündnis.* Prague, 1916.

Millenkovich-Morold, Max von. *Vom Abend zum Morgen. Aus dem alten Österreich ins neue Deutschland.* Leipzig, 1940.

Missong, Alfred. *August Schaurhofer: Ein Wiener Sozialapostel.* Vienna, 1936.

Naumann, Victor. *Profile. 30 Porträt-Skizzen aus den Jahren des Weltkrieges nach persönlichen Begegnungen.* Munich, 1925.

Nimrichter, Richard. "Volkstum, Vaterland und Internationalismus." *VW* 9 (1918): 13–20, 119–129, 166–77, 218–24.

Oppenheimer, Felix. *Die Wiener Gemeindeverwaltung und der Fall des liberalen Regimes in Staat und Kommune.* Vienna, 1905.

Pace, Anton, ed. *Die Dienstpragmatik (Gesetz über das Dienstverhältnis der Staatsbeamten u. der Staatsdienerschaft).* Vienna, 1914.

———. *Ernst Mayerhofers Handbuch für den politischen Verwaltungsdienst in den im Reichsrate vertretenen Königreichen und Ländern.* 5th ed. 7 vols. Vienna, 1895–1901.

Die Parteien der Deutschen in Österreich vor und nach dem Weltkrieg. Munich, 1915.

Pastor, Ludwig von. *Tagebücher, Briefe, Erinnerungen.* Edited by Wilhelm Wühr. Heidelberg, 1950.

Pattai, Robert. *Das klassische Gymnasium und die Vorbereitung zu unseren Hochschulen. Reden und Gedanken.* Vienna, 1908.

Paulus, Dr. "Verwaltungsreform im Kriege." *VW* 6 (1915): 159–72.

Plecher, Hans. *Victor Silberer. Ein Lebensbild.* Vienna, 1916.

Protokoll der Bischöflichen Versammlung in Wien vom 12. bis 20. November 1901. Brünn, 1902.

Protokoll der Bischöflichen Versammlung in Wien von 11. bis 18. Oktober 1906. Olmütz, 1907

Protokoll über die Verhandlungen des Gesamtparteitages der sozialdemokratischen Arbeiterpartei in Oesterreich. Abgehalten zu Wien vom 9. bis zum 13. November 1903. Vienna, 1903.

Protokoll über die Verhandlungen des Parteitages der deutschen sozialdemokratischen Arbeiterpartei in Oesterreich. Abgehalten zu Salzburg vom 26. bis zum 29. September 1904. Vienna, 1904.

Protokoll über die Verhandlungen des Gesamtparteitages der sozialdemokratischen Arbeiterpartei in Oesterreich. Abgehalten zu Wien vom 29. Oktober bis 2. November 1905. Vienna, 1905.

Protokoll über die Verhandlungen des Parteitages der deutschen sozialdemokratischen Arbeiterpartei in Oesterreich. Abgehalten in Reichenberg vom 19. September bis 24. September 1909. Vienna, 1909.

Protokoll der Verhandlungen des Parteitages der deutschen sozialdemokratischen Arbeiterpartei in Oesterreich. Abgehalten in Wien vom 19. bis 24. Oktober 1917. Vienna, 1917.

Pultar, Josef K. "Erwägungen zum Statut der Wiener christlich-sozialen Partei." *VW* 9 (1918): 70–76.

Renner, Karl. *An der Wende zweier Zeiten. Lebenserinnerungen von Karl Renner.* 2nd ed. Vienna, 1946.

———. *Die Ära Hohenblum—der Ruin unserer Staats- und Volkswirtschaft!* Vienna, 1913.

———. *Grundlagen und Entwicklungsziele der Österreichisch-Ungarischen Monarchie.* Vienna, 1906.

———. *Der Kampf der Oesterreichischen Nationen um den Staat.* Leipzig, 1902.

———. "Kulturkampf oder Klassenkampf?" *K* 2 (1908–9): 438–45.

———. *Marxismus, Krieg und Internationale. Kritische Studien über offene Probleme des wissenschaftlichen und des praktischen Sozialismus in und nach dem Weltkrieg.* 2nd. ed. Vienna, 1918.

———. *Oesterreichs Erneuerung. Politisch-programmatische Aufsätze.* Vienna, 1916.

———. "Politische Windstille." *K* 4 (1910–11): 193–200.

———. *Staat und Parlament.* Vienna, 1901.

———. "Steuerkämpfe und Steuerreform." *K* 7 (1913–14): 193–99.

———. "Die Wandlungen der Christlichsozialen." *K* 2 (1908–9): 5–9.

Samassa, Paul. *Die deutschösterreichische Politik während des Krieges.* Graz, 1917.

Schacherl, Michael. "Gemeinsamer Kampfboden." *K* 1 (1907–8): 347–52.

Schappacher, Alfred. "Der Streit um das Zentrum." *VW* 5 (1914): 85–91.

———. "Wege zur Verwaltungsreform." *VW* 4 (1913): 144–52.

Scheicher, Josef. *Erlebnisse und Erinnerungen.* 6 vols. Vienna, 1907–12.

———. *Der österreichische Klerustag.* Vienna, 1903.

Scheu, Robert. "Karl Lueger." *Die Fackel,* Nr. 301/02, 1910.

Schindler, Franz Martin. *Das Kapital-Zins-Problem.* Vienna, 1903.

———. *Der Lohnvertrag.* Vienna, 1893.

———. *Die soziale Frage der Gegenwart vom Standpunkt des Christentums.* Vienna, 1905.

Schmid, Ferdinand. *Finanzreform in Oesterreich.* Tübingen, 1911.

Schmied-Kowarzik, Walter. "Friedrich Jodl." *Archiv für Geschichte der Philosophie* 27 (1912): 474–89.

———. "Friedrich Jodls Weltanschauung." *Zeitschrift für Philosophie und philosophische Kritik* 154 (1914): 129–33.

Schmitz, Richard. "Die Bestimmung der christlichsozialen Partei." *VW* 9 (1918): 1–4.

———. "Die Fehlbilanz des Parlamentes und die Deutschnationalen." *VW* 9 (1918): 150–155.

———. "Kritische Gedanken über die christliche Gewerkschaftsbewegung." *VW* 3 (1912): 225–30.

———. "Vom Parteienstaat zum autoritären Staat." *Kalasantiner Blätter* 46 (1933): 200–01.

———. "Die Wiener Märzwahlen." *VW* 5 (1914): 78–85.

———. "Ziele der Volksbundarbeit. Ein Programm." *VW* 9 (1918): 103–11.

Schnitzler, Arthur. *My Youth in Vienna.* Translated by Catherine Hutter. London, 1971.

Schöffel, Joseph. *Erinnerungen aus meinem Leben.* Vienna, 1905.

———. "Meine Antwort." *Die Fackel,* Nr. 189, 1905.

Schöpfer, Aemilian. "Ein Bahnbrecher religiöser Volksbewegung in der Grossstadt. Zum Tode des P. Heinrich Abel S.J." *Das Neue Reich* 9 (1926): 189–90.

Seipel, Ignaz. "Franz Martin Schindler." *Jahrbuch der österreichischen Leo-Gesellschaft.* Innsbruck, 1924.

———. *Gedanken zur österreichischen Verfassungsreform.* Innsbruck, 1917.

———. "Kaisertum und Demokratie." *VW* 9 (1918): 225–30.

———. *Der Kampf um die österreichische Verfassung.* Vienna, 1930.

———. *Nation und Staat.* Vienna, 1916.

———. *Nationalitätsprinzip und Staatsgedanke.* Mönchen-Gladbach, n.d. [1915].

———. "Pädagogischer Kurs in Wien." *Christliche Pädagogische Blätter* 28 (1905): 67–72.

———. "Volk und Staat." *VW* 9 (1918): 97–103.

Seipels Reden in Österreich und anderwärts. Edited by Josef Gessl. Vienna, 1926.

Seipel-Steuern oder Breitner-Steuern? Die Wahrheit über die Steuerpolitik der Gemeinde Wien. Vienna, 1927.

Seitz, Karl. "Freie Schule und Sozialdemokratie." *K* 1 (1907–8): 352–56.

Sommeregger, Franz. "Zur Charakteristik des Kriegssozialismus." *VW* 9 (1918): 210–17.

Soziale Vorträge gehalten bei dem Wiener socialen Vortrags-Curse 1894. Edited by Franz M. Schindler. Vienna, 1895.

Soziale Woche: Agrarverfassung der Landgemeinde und Landeskulturpolitik in Oesterreich seit der Grundentlastung. Klagenfurt, 1912.

Die Soziale Woche: Bericht über den vom "Katholischen Volksbund für Österreich" unter dem Namen "Soziale Woche" veranstalteten sozialwissenschaftlichen Kursus v. 5.-10. Sept. 1911. Vienna, 1911.

Spahn, Martin. "Die christlich-soziale Partei der Deutschen Österreichs." *Hochland* 5 (1908): 544–59.

Speiser, Paul. *Die bisherigen Ergebnisse des Kampfes der Freien Schule gegen den Zwang zu religiösen Übungen.* Printed as an appendix to Paul v. Hock. *Der Zwang zu den religiösen Übungen in der Schule.* Vienna, n.d.

Spitzmüller, Alexander. "*. . . und hat auch Ursach, es zu lieben.*" Vienna, 1955.

Stenographisches Protokoll der Jahres-Hauptversammlung des Vereines 'Freie Schule' vom 22. März 1908. Vienna, 1908.

Strasser, Josef. "Was kann die 'Freie Schule' noch leisten?" *K* 1 (1907–8): 493–98.

Suess, Eduard. *Erinnerungen.* Leipzig, 1916.

Swoboda, Heinrich. *Grossstadtseelsorge.* Regensburg, 1909.

Sylvester, Julius. *Vom toten Parlament und seinen letzten Trägern.* Vienna, 1928.

Die Tätigkeit des Sozialdemokratischen Verbandes im Abgeordnetenhaus. XVIII. Session 18 (17. Juni 1907 bis 5. Februar 1909). Vienna, 1909.

Die Tätigkeit des Sozialdemokratischen Verbandes im Abgeordnetenhause. 3. Heft. (XX. Session, 20. Oktober 1909 bis 6. Juli 1910). Vienna, 1910.

Die Tätigkeit des Sozialdemokratischen Verbandes im Abgeordnetenhause. 4. Heft (XX. Session, 12. Oktober 1910 bis 31. März 1911). Vienna, 1911.

Die Tätigkeit der deutschen sozialdemokratischen Abgeordneten im österreichischen Reichsrat. 1. Heft (17. Juli bis 20. Dezember 1911). Vienna, 1912.

Die Tätigkeit der deutschen sozialdemokratischen Abgeordneten im österreichischen Reichsrat. 2. Heft (5. März bis 5. Juli 1912). Vienna, 1912.

Die Tätigkeit der deutschen sozialdemokratischen Abgeordneten im österreichischen Reichsrat. 3. Heft. (24. September 1912 bis 20. Juni 1913). Vienna, 1913.

Die Tätigkeit der deutschen sozialdemokratischen Abgeordneten im österreichischen Reichsrat. 4. Heft (21. Oktober 1913 bis 29. Mai 1914). Vienna, 1914.

Täubler, Alexander. "Christlichsoziale Kirche- und Klosterfürsorge." *K* 5 (1911–12): 205–9.

———. *Österreichische Volksschulzustände. Ein Wort an das Volk und seine Lehrer.* Vienna, 1897.

Tomášek, Franz. "Nationale Minderheitenschulen als soziale Erscheinung." *K* 3 (1909–10): 109.

Der Verleumdungsfeldzug gegen Dr. Gessmann. Vergani, 'Deutsches Volksblatt' und Baukreditbank. Vienna, 1911.

Die Vorschläge Prof. Redlichs zur Reform der Finanzverwaltung. Mitteilungen der Industriellen Vereinigung. Nr. 23. Vienna, 1914.

Wahrmund, Ludwig. *Katholische Weltanschauung und freie Wissenschaft.* Munich, 1908.

———. *Lehrfreiheit? Akten und Erläuterungen zum Fall Wahrmund.* Munich, 1909.

———. *Ultramontan. Eine Abwehr in vier Artikeln.* Munich, 1908.

Walcher, Konrad. *Die Politik der Christlichsozialen im neuen Reichsrate. Eine Über-*

sicht über die Tätigkeit der christlichsozialen Vereinigung in dem ersten Sessionsabschnitt der XVIII. Legislatursperiode vom 17. Juni–24. Juli 1907. Vienna, 1908.

Der Wald- und Wiesengürtel und die Höhenstrasse der Stadt Wien. Vienna, 1905.

Weiss, Albert Maria. *Lebensweg und Lebenswerk. Ein modernes Prophetenleben.* Freiburg, 1925.

Werkmann, Karl. *Der Tote auf Madeira.* Munich, 1923.

Wichtl, Friedrich. *Weltfreimaurerei, Weltrevolution, Weltrepublik. Eine Untersuchung über Ursprung und Endziele des Weltkrieges.* Munich, 1922.

Wien am Anfang des XX. Jahrhunderts. Ein Führer in technischer und künstlerischer Richtung. Vienna, 1905.

Zeif, Josef. "Was verdankt die Pädagogik der Lebensarbeit Willmanns?" *Österreichische Pädagogische Warte* 14 (1919): 70–77.

Zenker, Ernst Victor. *Die Gesellschaft.* 2 vols. Berlin, 1899–1903.

———. "Glossen zum Eucharistischen Kongress." *Die Wage* 15 (1912): 841–45.

———. *Kirche und Staat unter besonderer Berücksichtigung der Verhältnisse in Österreich.* Vienna, 1909.

———. *Ein Mann im sterbenden Österreich. Erinnerungen aus meinem Leben.* Reichenberg, 1935.

———. *Soziale Ethik.* Leipzig, 1905.

———. "Der 20. Juni." *Die Wage* 14 (1911): 586–87.

SECONDARY SOURCES

Ableitinger, Alfred. *Ernest von Koerber und das Verfassungsproblem im Jahre 1900. Österreichische Nationalitäten- und Innenpolitik zwischen Konstitutionalismus, Parlamentarismus und oktroyiertem allgemeinem Wahlrecht.* Vienna, 1973.

Achs, Oskar, ed. *Otto Glöckel. Ausgewählte Schriften und Reden.* Vienna, 1985.

Achs, Oskar, and Eva Tesar. "Aspekte sozialistischer Schulpolitik am Beispiel Täublers und Furtmüllers." In *Neuere Studien zur Arbeitergeschichte.*

Ackerl, Isabella, Walter Hummelberger, and Hans Mommsen, eds. *Politik und Gesellschaft im Alten und Neuen Österreich. Festschrift für Rudolf Neck zum 60. Geburtstag.* 2 vols. Vienna, 1981.

Alder, Douglas D. "Assassination as Political Efficacy. Two Case Studies from World War I." *East European Quarterly* 12 (1978–79): 209–31.

Allen, Robert Loring. *Opening Doors. The Life and Work of Joseph Schumpeter.* 2 vols. New Brunswick, 1991.

Allmayer-Beck, Johann Christoph. *Ministerpräsident Baron Beck. Ein Staatsmann des alten Österreich.* Vienna, 1956.

Anderson, Margaret Lavinia. "Interdenominationalism, Clericalism, Pluralism: The *Zentrumsstreit* and the Dilemma of Catholicism in Wilhelmine Germany." *CEH* 21 (1988): 350–78.

———. "The Kulturkampf and the Course of German History." *CEH* 19 (1986): 82–115.

———. *Windthorst. A Political Biography.* Oxford, 1981.

Applegate, Celia. "Localism and the German bourgeoisie: the 'Heimat' movement in the Rhenish Palatinate before 1914." In *The German Bourgeoisie.*

———. *A Nation of Provincials: The German Idea of Heimat.* Berkeley, 1990.

Ardelt, Rudolf G. *Friedrich Adler. Probleme einer Persönlichkeitsentwicklung um die Jahrhundertwende.* Vienna, 1984.

Bachem, Karl. *Vorgeschichte, Geschichte und Politik der Deutschen Zentrumspartei.* 9 vols. Cologne, 1927–32.

Bachmann, Harald. "Der Deutsche Volksrat für Böhmen und die deutschböhmische Parteipolitik." *Zeitschrift für Ostforschung* 14 (1965): 266–94.

———. "Raphael Pacher und die deutschradikale Bewegung in den Sudetenländern. Aus den Erinnerungen Pachers." *Bohemia* 5 (1964): 447–58.

Barnard, Frederick M. "Humanism and Titanism: Masaryk and Herder." In *T. G. Masaryk (1850–1937).*

Barton, Peter F. *Evangelisch in Österreich. Ein Überblick über die Geschichte der Evangelischen in Österreich.* Vienna, 1987.

Beck, Max von. "Der Kaiser und die Wahlreform." In *Erinnerungen an Franz Joseph I. Kaiser von Österreich. Apostolischer König von Ungarn.* Edited by Eduard von Steinitz. Berlin, 1931.

Beckstein, Hermann. *Städtische Interessenpolitik. Organisation und Politik der Städtetage in Bayern, Preussen und im Deutschen Reich 1896–1923.* Düsseldorf, 1991.

Beller, Steven. *Vienna and the Jews 1867–1938. A Cultural History.* Cambridge, 1989.

Benedikt, Heinrich. *Die Friedensaktion der Meinlgruppe 1917/18. Die Bemühungen um einen Verständigungsfrieden nach Dokumenten, Aktenstücken und Briefen.* Graz, 1962.

Berger, Suzanne, ed. *Organizing Interests in Western Europe. Pluralism, Corporatism, and the Transformation of Politics.* Cambridge, 1981.

Bernard, Richard M., and Bradley R. Rice. "Political Environment and the Adoption of Progressive Municipal Reform." *Journal of Urban History* 1 (1975): 149–74.

Beurle, Else. *Dr. Carl Beurle 1860–1919.* Privately printed, 1960.

Blackbourn, David. *Class, Religion and Local Politics in Wilhelmine Germany. The Centre Party in Württemberg before 1914.* New Haven, 1980.

Blackbourn, David, and Geoff Eley. *The Peculiarities of German History. Bourgeois Society and Politics in Nineteenth-Century Germany.* Oxford, 1984.

Blackbourn, David, and Richard J. Evans, eds. *The German Bourgeoisie. Essays on the Social History of the German Middle Class from the Late Eighteenth to the Early Twentieth Century.* London, 1991.

Blenk, Gustav. *Leopold Kunschak und seine Zeit.* Vienna, 1966.

Bodzenta, Erich. "Die geschichtliche Entwicklung des Verhältnisses der Arbeiterschaft zur Kirche." In *Die Kirche und die Welt des Arbeiters*. Edited by Karl Rudolf. Vienna, 1957.

Bosmans, Louis. *August Schaurhofer 1872–1928. Ein Leben im Dienst der christlichen Sozialarbeit*. Vienna, 1978.

Botstein, Leon. *Judentum und Modernität. Essays zur Rolle der Juden in der deutschen und österreichischen Kultur 1848 bis 1938*. Vienna, 1991.

Boyer, John W. "Freud, Marriage and Late Viennese Liberalism: A Commentary from 1905." *JMH* 50 (1978): 72–102.

———. *Political Radicalism in Late Imperial Vienna: The Origins of the Christian Social Movement, 1848–1897*. Chicago, 1981.

———. "Religion and Political Development in Central Europe around 1900: A View from Vienna." *AHY* 25 (1994): 13–57.

———. "Some Reflections on the Problem of Austria, Germany, and Mitteleuropa." *CEH* 22 (1989): 301–15.

Boyer, Paul S. *Urban Masses and Moral Order in America, 1820–1920*. Cambridge, Mass., 1978.

Brack, Rudolf. *Deutscher Episkopat und Gewerkschaftsstreit 1900–1914*. Cologne, 1976.

Braunthal, Julius. *Victor und Friedrich Adler. Zwei Generationen Arbeiterbewegung*. Vienna, 1965.

Bridges, Amy. *A City in the Republic. Antebellum New York and the Origins of Machine Politics*. Cambridge, 1984.

Bright, Charles. "The State in the United States during the Nineteenth Century." In *Statemaking and Social Movements*.

Bright, Charles, and Susan Harding, eds. *Statemaking and Social Movements. Essays in History and Theory*. Ann Arbor, 1984.

Brix, Emil. *Die Umgangssprachen in Altösterreich zwischen Agitation und Assimilation. Die Sprachenstatistik in den zisleithanischen Volkszählungen 1880 bis 1910*. Vienna, 1982.

Broucek, Peter, ed. *Ein General im Zwielicht. Die Erinnerungen Edmund Glaises von Horstenau*. 3 vols. Vienna, 1980–88.

Brousek, Karl M. *Wien und seine Tschechen. Integration und Assimilation einer Minderheit im 20. Jahrhundert*. Vienna, 1980.

Bruch, Rüdiger vom. *Wissenschaft, Politik und öffentliche Meinung. Gelehrtenpolitik im Wilhelminischen Deutschland (1890–1914)*. Husum, 1980.

Brückmüller, Ernst. *Landwirtschaftliche Organisationen und gesellschaftliche Modernisierung*. Salzburg, 1977.

———. *Nation Österreich. Sozialhistorische Aspekte ihrer Entwicklung*. Vienna 1984.

———. "Die Verbindungen des CV in Österreich vor dem Ersten Weltkrieg: Gründungsphase und erste Konsolidierung." In *Der CV in Österreich. Seine Entstehung, seine Geschichte, seine Bedeutung*. Edited by Gerhard Hartmann. Vienna, 1977.

Bruckmüller, Ernst, Ulrike Döcker, Hannes Steckl, and Peter Urbanitsch, eds. *Bürgertum in der Habsburger-Monarchie.* Vienna, 1990.

Brünner, Christian, ed. *Korruption und Kontrolle.* Vienna, 1981.

Bukey, Evan Burr. *Hitler's Hometown: Linz, Austria, 1908–1945.* Bloomington, 1986.

Busek, Erhard, and Emil Brix. *Projekt Mitteleuropa.* Vienna, 1986.

Calkins, Kenneth R. "The Uses of Utopianism: The Millenarian Dream in Central European Social Democracy Before 1914." *CEH* 15 (1982): 124–48.

Caplan, Jane. *Government without Administration: State and Civil Service in Weimar and Nazi Germany.* New York, 1988.

Chlumecky, Leopold von. *Erzherzog Franz Ferdinands Wirken und Wollen.* Berlin, 1929.

Clare, George. *Last Waltz in Vienna. The Rise and Destruction of a Family, 1842–1942.* New York, 1982.

Cohen, Gary B. *The Politics of Ethnic Survival. Germans in Prague, 1861–1914.* Princeton, 1981.

———. "Die Studenten der Wiener Universität von 1860 bis 1900." In *Wegenetz europäischen Geistes II. Universitäten und Studenten.* Edited by Richard Georg Plaschka and Karlheinz Mack. Vienna, 1987.

Conrad, Otto. "Eugen Schwiedland." In *Bericht über das Studienjahr 1936/37. Technische Hochschule in Wien.* Vienna, 1937.

Csáky, Moritz. "Österreich und der Modernismus. Nach den Berichten des österreichischen Botschafters am Vatikan 1910/11." *MÖSTA* 17–18 (1964–65): 322–36.

———. "Die Pluralität als Kriterium der österreichischen Identität." *Christliche Demokratie* 7 (1989): 373–80.

Czedik, Alois. *Zur Geschichte der k.k. österreichischen Ministerien 1861–1916.* 4 vols. Teschen, 1917–20.

Czeike, Felix. *Liberale, christlichsoziale und sozialdemokratische Kommunalpolitik (1861–1934).* Vienna, 1962.

Czermak, Theodor. *Bischof Josef Gross von Leitmeritz.* Warnsdorf, 1933.

Decker, Hannah S. *Freud, Dora, and Vienna 1900.* New York, 1991.

Deuerlein, Ernst, ed. *Briefwechsel Hertling-Lerchenfeld.* 2 vols. Boppard am Rhein, 1973.

Deuring, Hermann. *Prälat Dr. Karl Drexel.* Dornbirn, 1956.

Dopsch, Heinz, and Hans Spatzenegger, eds. *Geschichte Salzburgs. Stadt und Land. Band II. Neuzeit und Zeitgeschichte. 2. Teil.* Salzburg, 1988.

Drimmel, Heinrich. *Albert Ehrhard und seine Studenten in Wien um 1900.* Vienna, 1976.

Durig, Arnold. "Physiologie als Unterrichtsgegenstand. Erhebungen über die Ernährung der Wiener Bevölkerung." *Wiener Medizinische Wochenschrift,* 2 November 1918, pp. 1939–41.

Ebneth, Rudolf. *Die österreichische Wochenschrift "Der christliche Ständestaat." Deutsche Emigration in Österreich 1933–1938.* Mainz, 1976.

Edmondson, C. Earl. *The Heimwehr and Austrian Politics, 1918–1936.* Athens, 1978.

Eduard Heinl. Ein Leben für Österreich. Vienna, 1955.

Ehalt, Hubert Ch., Gernot Heiss, and Hannes Stekl, eds. *Glücklich ist, wer vergisst...? Das andere Wien um 1900.* Vienna, 1986.

Ellenbogen, Wilhelm. *Menschen und Prinzipien. Erinnerungen, Urteile und Reflexionen eines kritischen Sozialdemokraten.* Edited by Friedrich Weissensteiner. Vienna, 1981.

Enderes, Bruno, Emil Ratzenhofer, and Paul Höger. *Verkehrswesen im Kriege.* Vienna, 1931.

Enderle-Burcel, Gertrude, ed. *Christlich-Ständisch-Autoritär. Mandatare im Ständestaat 1934–1938.* Vienna, 1991.

Engelbrecht, Helmut. *Geschichte des österreichischen Bildungswesens. Erziehung und Unterricht auf dem Boden Österreichs.* 5 vols. Vienna, 1982–88.

Engel-Janosi, Friedrich. *Österreich und der Vatikan 1846–1918.* 2 vols. Graz, 1958–60.

Epstein, Klaus. *Matthias Erzberger and the Dilemma of German Democracy.* Princeton, 1959.

Erhard, Benedikt. *Bauernstand und Politik. Zur Geschichte des Tiroler Bauernbundes.* Vienna, 1981.

Evans, Ellen Lovell. *The German Center Party, 1870–1933. A Study in Political Catholicism.* Carbondale, 1981.

Evans, Richard J. *Death in Hamburg: Society and Politics in the Cholera Years, 1830–1910.* Oxford, 1987.

Exner, Franz. *Krieg und Kriminalität in Österreich.* Vienna, 1927.

Feldbauer, Peter. *Stadtwachstum und Wohnungsnot. Determinanten unzureichender Wohnungsversorgung in Wien 1848 bis 1914.* Vienna, 1977.

Feldman, Gerald D. *Army, Industry and Labor in Germany, 1914–1918.* Princeton, 1966.

Fellner, Fritz. "Denkschriften aus Österreich. Die österreichische Mitteleuropa-Diskussion in Wissenschaft und Politik 1915/16." In *Geschichte zwischen Freiheit und Ordnung. Gerald Stourzh zum 60. Geburtstag.* Edited by Emil Brix, Thomas Fröschl, and Josef Leidenfrost. Graz, 1991.

———, ed. *Dichter und Gelehrter. Hermann Bahr und Josef Redlich in ihren Briefen 1896–1934.* Salzburg, 1980.

Fellner, Günter. *Ludo Moritz Hartmann und die österreichische Geschichtswissenschaft. Grundzüge eines paradigmatischen Konfliktes.* Salzburg, 1985.

Fletcher, Roger. *Revisionism and Empire. Socialist Imperialism in Germany, 1897–1914.* London, 1984.

Flieder, Victor., ed. *Festschrift Franz Loidl zum 65. Geburtstag.* 3 vols. Vienna, 1970.

Fontana, Josef. *Geschichte des Landes Tirol. Band 3. Vom Neubau bis zum Untergang der Habsburgermonarchie (1848–1918).* Bolzano, 1987.

Fox, Kenneth. *Better City Government. Innovation in American Urban Politics, 1850–1937.* Philadelphia, 1977.

Franz, Georg. *Erzherzog Franz Ferdinand und die Pläne zur Reform der Habsburger Monarchie*. Brünn, 1943.

Frei, Alfred Georg. *Rotes Wien. Austromarxismus und Arbeiterkultur. Sozialdemokratische Wohnungs- und Kommunalpolitik 1919–1934*. Berlin, 1984.

Freidenreich, Harriet Pass. *Jewish Politics in Vienna, 1918–1938*. Philadelphia, 1991.

Freundlich, Emmy. "Die Frauenarbeit im Krieg." In *Die Regelung der Arbeitsverhältnisse im Kriege*. Edited by Ferdinand Hanusch and Emanuel Adler. Vienna, 1927.

Frisch, Michael H. "Urban Theorists, Urban Reform, and American Political Culture in the Progressive Period." *Political Science Quarterly* 97 (1982): 295–315.

Fritzl, Hermann, and Martin Uitz. "Kritische Anmerkungen zur sogenannten Lagertheorie." *ÖZP* 4 (1975): 325–32.

Fröschl, Erich, Maria Mesner, and Helge Zoitl, eds. *Die Bewegung. Hundert Jahre Sozialdemokratie in Österreich*. Vienna, 1990.

Fuchs, Carl Johannes. "Die Entwicklung der Gemeindebetriebe in Deutschland und im Ausland." *Schriften des Vereins für Sozialpolitik* 132 (1910): 29–110.

Führ, Christoph. *Das K.u.K. Armeeoberkommando und die Innenpolitik in Österreich 1914–1917*. Graz, 1968.

Fussek, Alexander. "Ministerpräsident Karl Graf Stürgkh und die parlamentarische Frage." *MÖSTA* 17–18 (1964–65): 337–58.

Gaertner, Friedrich. "Der Ausbau der Sozialversicherung in Oesterreich." *ASSP* 29 (1909): 417–43, 759–833.

———. "Die Brotversorgung in Oesterreich." *ASSP* 43 (1916–17): 610–64.

———. "Die genossenschaftliche Kreditorganisation des Kleingewerbes und Kleingrundbesitzes in Oesterreich." *ASSP* 24 (1907): 630–56.

———. "Der österreichisch-ungarische Ausgleich." *ASSP* 25 (1907): 52–147, 338–444.

Galántai, József. *Hungary in the First World War*. Budapest, 1989.

Gall, Lothar, ed. *Stadt und Bürgertum im 19. Jahrhundert*. Munich, 1990.

Garver, Bruce M. *The Young Czech Party, 1874–1901, and the Emergence of a Multi-Party System*. New Haven, 1978.

Geehr, Richard S. *Karl Lueger. Mayor of Fin de Siècle Vienna*. Detroit, 1990.

Gerschenkron, Alexander. *An Economic Spurt That Failed. Four Lectures in Austrian History*. Princeton, 1977.

Geyer, Michael. "The State in National Socialist Germany." In *Statemaking and Social Movements. Essays in History and Theory*.

Geyr, Géza Andreas von. *Sándor Wekerle 1848–1921. Die politische Biographe eines ungarischen Staatsmannes der Donaumonarchie*. Munich, 1993.

Glaser, Ernst. *Im Umfeld des Austromarxismus. Ein Beitrag zur Geistesgeschichte des österreichischen Sozialismus*. Vienna, 1981.

———. "Zur Geschichte des 'Vereins Freie Schule'." *Archiv. Mitteilungsblatt des Vereins für die Geschichte der Arbeiterbewegung* (October/December) 1978.

Glettler, Monika. "Minority Culture in a Capital City: The Czechs in Vienna at the Turn of the Century." In *Decadence and Innovation. Austro-Hungarian Life and Art at the Turn of the Century.* Edited by Robert B. Pynsent. London, 1989.

———. *Die Wiener Tschechen um 1900. Strukturanalyse einer nationalen Minderheit in der Grossstadt.* Munich, 1972.

Goldinger, Walter. "Die Zentralverwaltung in Cisleithanien—Die zivile gemeinsame Zentralverwaltung." In Adam Wandruszka and Peter Urbanitsch, eds., *Die Habsburgermonarchie 1848–1918. Band II. Verwaltung und Rechtswesen.* Vienna, 1975.

Gonda, Imre. *Verfall der Kaiserreiche in Mitteleuropa. Der Zweibund in den letzten Kriegsjahren (1916–1918).* Budapest, 1977.

Good, David F. *The Economic Rise of the Habsburg Empire, 1750–1914.* Berkeley, 1984.

Goodnow, Frank. *City Government in the United States.* New York, 1904.

Gott erhalte Österreich. Religion und Staat in der Kunst des 19. Jahrhunderts. Eisenstadt, n.d. [1990].

Grandner, Margarete. *Kooperative Gewerkschaftspolitik in der Kriegswirtschaft. Die freien Gewerkschaften Österreichs im ersten Weltkrieg.* Vienna, 1992.

Gratz, Gustav, and Richard Schüller. *Die äussere Wirtschaftspolitik Österreich-Ungarns. Mitteleuropäische Pläne.* Vienna, 1925.

Graybar, Lloyd. *Albert Shaw of the Review of Reviews. An Intellectual Biography.* Lexington, 1974.

Griffith, Ernest. *A History of American City Government. The Conspicuous Failure, 1870–1900.* Washington, D.C., 1983.

Gruber, Helmut. *Red Vienna: Experiment in Working-Class Culture, 1919–1934.* New York, 1991.

Guggenberger, Sigmund. "Der Katholische Volksbund und die Männervereinsbewegung." In *Der Katholizismus in Österreich.*

Gutkas, Karl. *Geschichte des Landes Niederösterreich.* 3 vols. Vienna, 1957–62.

Haag, John. "Students at the University of Vienna in the First World War." *CEH* 17 (1984): 299–309.

Hafner, Herta. "Vizebürgermeister Heinrich Hierhammer—ein bürgerlicher Aufsteiger." *Christliche Demokratie* 6 (1988): 185–96.

Haiko, Peter and Renata Kassal-Mikula, eds. *Otto Wagner und das Kaiser Franz Josef-Stadtmuseum. Das Scheitern der Moderne in Wien.* Vienna, 1988.

Haiko, Peter, Harald Leupold-Löwenthal, and Mara Reissberger. "'Die weisse Stadt'— Der 'Steinhof' in Wien. Architektur als Reflex der Einstellung zur Geisteskrankheit." *Kritische Berichte* 9 (1981): 3–37.

Hainisch, Michael. *75 Jahre aus bewegter Zeit. Lebenserinnerungen eines österreichischen Staatsmannes.* Edited by Friedrich Weissensteiner. Vienna 1978.

Hajek, Hanus J. *T. G. Masaryk Revisited. A Critical Assessment.* Boulder, 1983.

Hämmerl, Christa, ed. *Kindheit im Ersten Weltkrieg.* Vienna, 1993.

Hannek, Jacques. *Karl Renner und seine Zeit.* Vienna, 1957.

Hantsch, Hugo. *Leopold Graf Berchtold. Grandseigneur und Staatsmann.* 2 vols. Graz, 1963.

Harrington-Müller, Diethild. *Der Fortschrittsklub im Abgeordnetenhaus des öster-reichischen Reichsrats 1873–1910.* Vienna, 1972.

Hartmann, Gerhard. *Im Gestern bewährt, im Heute bereit. 100 Jahre Carolina. Zur Geschichte des Verbandskatholizismus.* Graz, 1988.

Hasiba, Gernot D. "Die Kommission zur Förderung der Verwaltungsreform (1911–1914)." In *Recht und Geschichte. Festschrift Hermann Baltl zum 70. Geburtstag.* Edited by Helfried Valentinitsch. Graz, 1988.

———. *Das Notverordnungsrecht in Österreich (1848–1917). Notwendigkeit und Missbrauch eines "Staatserhaltenden Instrumentes."* Vienna, 1985.

Havránek, Jan. "Soziale Struktur und politisches Verhalten der gross-städtischen Wäh-lerschaft im Mai 1907—Wien und Prag im Vergleich." In *Politik und Gesellschaft im Alten und Neuen Österreich.*

Hawlik, Johannes. *Der Bürgerkaiser. Karl Lueger und seine Zeit.* Vienna, 1985.

Hays, Samuel P. "The Politics of Reform in Municipal Government in the Progressive Era." *Pacific Northwest Quarterly* 55 (1964): 157–69.

Heindl, Waltraud. *Gehorsame Rebellen. Bürokratie und Beamte in Österreich 1780 bis 1848.* Vienna, 1991.

Heitzer, Horstwalter. *Georg Kardinal Kopp und der Gewerkschaftsstreit 1900–1914.* Cologne, 1983.

Helmer, Oskar. *50 Jahre Erlebte Geschichte.* Vienna, 1959.

Higham, John. *Strangers in the Land: Patterns of American Nativism, 1860–1925.* New Brunswick, N.J., 1955.

Hintze, Otto. "Machtpolitik und Regierungsverfassung." In *Staat und Verfassung: Ge-sammelte Abhandlungen zur allgemeinen Verfassungsgeschichte.* Edited by Ger-hard Oestreich. 2d ed. Göttingen, 1962.

Hirschfeld, Gerhard and Lothar Kettenacker, eds. *Der "Führerstaat": Mythos und Rea-lität. Studien zur Struktur und Politik des Dritten Reiches.* Stuttgart, 1981.

Hitchens, Keith. "The Nationality Problem in Hungary: István Tisza and the Rumanian National Party, 1910–1914." *JMH* 53 (1981): 619–51.

Höbelt, Lothar. *Kornblume und Kaiseradler. Die deutschfreiheitlichen Parteien Alt-österreichs 1882–1918.* Vienna, 1993.

Hoffmann, Roland J. *T. G. Masaryk und die tschechische Frage. I. Nationale Ideologie und politische Tätigkeit bis zum Scheitern des deutsch-tschechischen Ausgleichs-versuchs vom Februar 1909.* Munich, 1988.

Höflechner, Walter. *Die Baumeister des künftigen Glücks. Fragment einer Geschichte des Hochschulwesens in Österreich vom Ausgang des 19. Jahrhunderts bis in das Jahr 1938.* Graz, 1988.

———. "Zur Geschichte der Universität Graz." In *Tradition und Herausforderung. 400 Jahre Universität Graz.* Graz, 1985.

Hofrichter, Peter. "Modernismus in Österreich, Böhmen und Mähren." In *Der Moder-nismus.*

Hofstadter, Richard. *The Idea of a Party System. The Rise of Legitimate Opposition in the United States, 1780–1840.* Berkeley, 1969.

Höglinger, Felix. *Ministerpräsident Heinrich Graf Clam-Martinic.* Graz, 1964.

Holli, Melvin G. *Reform in Detroit: Hazen S. Pingree and Urban Politics.* New York, 1969.

Holtmann, Everhard. "Arbeiterbewegung, Staat und Sozialpolitik in der Spätzeit der Habsburgermonarchie. Strukturelle Bedingungen österreichischer Sozialgesetzgebung zwischen 1890 und 1914." In *Politik und Gesellschaft im Alten und Neuen Österreich.*

Hösl, Wolfgang, and Gottfried Pirhofer. *Wohnen in Wien 1814–1938. Studien zur Konstitution des Massenwohnens.* Vienna, 1988.

Howe, Frederic. *The British City: The Beginnings of Democracy.* New York, 1907.

———. *The City, the Hope of Democracy.* New York, 1905.

Hoyer, Helmut. *Kaiser Karl I. und Feldmarschall Conrad von Hötzendorf. Ein Beitrag zur Militärpolitik Kaiser Karls.* Vienna, 1972.

Huber, A.K., ed. "Franz Kordačs Briefe ins Germanikum (1879–1816)." *Archiv für Kirchengeschichte von Böhmen-Mähren-Schlesien* 1 (1967): 62–184.

Hudal, Alois, ed. *Der Katholizismus in Österreich: Sein Wirken, Kämpfen und Hoffen.* Innsbruck, 1931.

Hugelmann, Karl Gottfried, ed. *Das Nationalitätenrecht des alten Österreich.* Vienna, 1934.

Jarausch, Konrad. *Students, Society and Politics in Imperial Germany. The Rise of Academic Illiberalism.* Princeton, 1982.

Jellinek, Georg. *Allgemeine Staatslehre.* 3d ed. Bad Homburg, 1966.

Jenks, William A. *The Austrian Electoral Reform of 1907.* New York, 1950.

John, Michael. *Hausherrenmacht und Mieterelend: Wohnverhältnisse und Wohnerfahrung der Unterschichten in Wien, 1890–1923.* Vienna, 1982.

———. "Migration, Ethnizität und Urbanität. Zur Haltung der österreichischen Arbeiterbewegung in der Habsburgermonarchie." In Fröschl, ed., *Die Bewegung.*

———. "Obdachlosigkeit—Massenerscheinung und Unruheherd im Wien der Spätgründerzeit." In Ehalt, ed., *Glücklich ist.*

John, Michael, and Albert Lichtblau. *Schmelztiegel Wien. Zur Geschichte und Gegenwart von Zuwanderung und Minderheiten.* Vienna, 1990.

Johnston, William M. *The Austrian Mind. An Intellectual and Social History, 1848–1938.* Berkeley, 1972.

Kämmerer, Jürgen, ed. *Heinrich Ritter von Srbik. Die wissenschaftliche Korrespondenz des Historikers 1912–1945.* Boppard am Rhein, 1988.

Kammerhofer, Leopold. *Niederösterreich zwischen den Kriegen. Wirtschaftliche, politische, soziale und kulturelle Entwicklung von 1918 bis 1938.* Baden, 1987.

Kane, Leon. *Robert Danneberg. Ein pragmatischer Idealist.* Vienna, 1980.

Kann, Robert A. *Erzherzog Franz Ferdinand Studien.* Vienna, 1976.

———. "Das geschichtliche Erbe—Gemeinsamer Nenner und rechtes Mass." In *Österreich. Die Zweite Republik* . Edited by Erika Weinzierl and Kurt Skalnik. 2 vols. Graz, 1972.

―――. "Hochschule und Politik im österreichischen Verfassungsstaat (1867–1918)." In *Geschichte und Gesellschaft. Festschrift für Karl R. Stadler zum 60. Geburtstag.* Edited by Gerhard Botz, Hans Hautmann, and Helmut Konrad. Vienna, 1974.

―――. *The Multinational Empire: Nationalism and National Reform in the Habsburg Monarchy, 1848–1918.* 2 vols. New York, 1950.

―――. *Die Sixtus Affäre und die geheimen Friedensverhandlungen Österreich-Ungarns im Ersten Weltkrieg.* Munich, 1966.

―――. *A Study in Austrian Intellectual History. From Late Baroque to Romanticism.* New York, 1960.

Kann, Robert A., and Peter Leisching, eds. *Ein Leben für Kunst und Bildung. Eduard Leisching 1858–1938. Erinnerungen.* Vienna, 1978.

Kapp, Richard W. "Bethmann-Hollweg, Austria-Hungary and Mitteleuropa 1914–1915." *AHY* 19–20 (1983–84): 215–36.

―――. "Divided Loyalties: The German Reich and Austria-Hungary in Austro-German Discussions of War Aims, 1914–1916." *CEH* 17 (1984): 120–39.

Karl, Barry D. *The Uneasy State. The United States from 1915 to 1945.* Chicago, 1983.

Kieval, Hillel J. "Masaryk and Czech Jewry: the Ambiguities of Friendship." In *T. G. Masaryk (1850–1937).*

Kiszling, Rudolf. *Erzherzog Franz Ferdinand von Österreich-Este. Leben, Pläne und Wirken am Schicksalsweg der Donaumonarchie.* Graz, 1953.

Klemperer, Klemens von. *Ignaz Seipel: Christian Statesman in a Time of Crisis.* Princeton, 1972.

Klotz, Anton. *Dr. Aemilian Schöpfer. Priester und Volksmann.* Innsbruck, 1936.

Knauer, Oswald. "Der Wiener Gemeinderat von 1861–1918. Parteibildung und Wahlen." *Wiener Geschichtsblätter* 19 (1964): 298–303, 366–77.

Knoll, Reinhold. *Zur Tradition der Christlichsozialen Partei. Ihre Früh- und Entwicklungsgeschichte bis zu den Reichsratswahlen 1907.* Vienna, 1973.

Kocka, Jürgen. "Bürgertum und bürgerliche Gesellschaft im 19. Jahrhundert. Europäische Entwicklungen und deutsche Eigenarten." In *Bürgertum im 19. Jahrhundert. Deutschland im europäischen Vergleich.* Edited by Jürgen Kocka. 3 vols. Munich, 1988.

―――. "German History before Hitler. The Debate about the German 'Sonderweg'." *Journal of Contemporary History* 23 (1988): 3–16.

―――. *Klassengesellschaft im Krieg. Deutsche Sozialgeschichte 1914–1918.* Göttingen, 1973.

―――. "Otto Hintze, Max Weber und das Problem der Bürokratie." *Historische Zeitschrift* 233 (1981): 65–105.

Köfner, Gottfried. *Hunger, Not und Korruption. Der Übergang Österreichs von der Monarchie zur Republik am Beispiel Salzburgs.* Salzburg, 1980.

Köhler, Peter A., and Hans F. Zacher, eds. *The Evolution of Social Insurance, 1881–1981.* London, 1982.

Koller-Glück, Elisabeth. *Otto Wagners Kirche am Steinhof.* Vienna, 1984.

Kolmer, Gustav. *Parlament und Verfassung in Österreich.* 8 vols. Vienna, 1902–14.

Komjáthy, Miklós, ed. *Protokolle des Gemeinsamen Ministerrates der Österreichisch-Ungarischen Monarchie (1914–1918).* Budapest, 1966.

Komlos, John. *The Habsburg Monarchy as a Customs Union: Economic Development in Austria-Hungary in the Nineteenth Century.* Princeton, 1983.

Konrad, Helmut, and Wolfgang Maderthaner, eds. *Neuere Studien zur Arbeitergeschichte. Zum fünfundzwanzigjährigen Bestehen des Vereins für Geschichte der Arbeiterbewegung.* 3 vols. Vienna, 1984.

Koren, Stephan. "Die Industrialisierung Österreichs—vom Protektionismus zur Integration. Entwicklung und Stand von Industrie, Gewerbe, Handel und Verkehr." In *Österreichs Wirtschaftsstruktur. Gestern-Heute-Morgen.* Edited by Wilhelm Weber. 2 vols. Berlin, 1961.

Kornberg, Jacques. *Theodor Herzl. From Assimilation to Zionism.* Bloomington, 1993.

Köstler, Rudolf. "Die Neuerungen Papst Pius' X. und das österreichische öffentliche Recht." *Österreichische Zeitschrift für öffentliches Recht* 3 (1916–18): 461–89.

Krabbe, Wolfgang R. *Die deutsche Stadt im 19. und 20. Jahrhundert. Eine Einführung.* Göttingen, 1989.

Kuppe, Rudolf. *Karl Lueger und seine Zeit.* Vienna, 1933.

Laclau, Ernesto, and Chantal Mouffe. *Hegemony and Socialist Strategy. Towards a Radical Democratic Politics.* London, 1985.

Ladd, Brian. *Urban Planning and Civic Order in Germany, 1860–1914.* Cambridge, Mass., 1990.

Langer-Ostrawsky, Gertrude. "Wiener Schulwesen um 1900." in Ehalt, ed., *Glücklich ist.*

Langewiesche, Dieter. *Zur Freizeit des Arbeiters. Bildungsbestrebungen und Freizeitgestaltung österreichischer Arbeiter im Kaiserreich und in der Ersten Republik.* Stuttgart, 1979.

Large, David C. "Richard von Kralik's Search for Fatherland." *AHY* 17/18 (1981–82): 144–55.

Lazar, Erwin. "Der Krieg und die Verwahrlosung von Kindern und Jugendlichen. Heilpädagogische Rück- und Ausblicke." In *Volksgesundheit im Krieg.*

Lederer, Emil. "Die Angestelltenbewegung und Sozialpolitik in Oesterreich." *ASSP* 44 (1917–18): 896–905.

———. "Angestellten- und Beamtensozialpolitik." *ASSP,* 33 (1911): 940–84.

———. "Bewegung der öffentlichen Beamten und Beamtensozialpolitik." *ASSP* 35 (1912): 882–913; 37 (1913): 650–69.

Leisching, Peter. "Die römisch-katholische Kirche in Cisleithanien." In Adam Wandruszka and Peter Urbanitsch, eds., *Die Habsburgermonarchie 1848–1918. Band IV. Die Konfessionen.* Vienna, 1985.

Leitner, Franz. *Kirche und Parteien in Österreich nach 1945. Ihr Verhältnis unter dem Gesichtspunkt der Äquidistanzdiskussion.* Paderborn, 1988.

Leser, Norbert. *Zwischen Reformismus und Bolschewismus. Der Austro-Marxismus als Theorie und Praxis.* Vienna, 1968.

Lesky, Erna. "Clemens von Pirquet." *Wiener klinische Wochenschrift* 67 (1955): 638–39.

———. "Der erste Weltkrieg: eine biologische Katastrophe Wiens." *Österreichische Ärzte-Zeitung,* 25 June 1975.

Leslie, John. "The Antecedents of Austria-Hungary's War Aims: Policies and Policy-Makers in Vienna and Budapest before and during 1914." In Elisabeth Springer and Leopold Kammerhofer, eds., *Archiv und Forschung. Das Haus-, Hof- und Staatsarchiv in seiner Bedeutung für die Geschichte Österreichs und Europas.* Vienna, 1993.

Lewis, Gavin. "The Peasantry, Rural Change and Conservative Agrarianism. Lower Austria at the Turn of the Century." *Past & Present* 81(November 1978): 119–43.

Lichtblau, Albert. *Wiener Wohnungspolitik 1892–1919.* Vienna, 1984.

Lidtke, Vernon L. *The Alternative Culture. Socialist Labor in Imperial Germany.* New York, 1985.

Lilla, Joachim. "Innen- und Aussenpolitische Aspekte der austropolnischen Lösung 1914–16." *MÖSTA* 30 (1977): 221–50.

Link, Arthur S., and Richard L. McCormick. *Progressivism.* Arlington Heights, Ill., 1983.

Loewenberg, Peter. *Decoding the Past. The Psychohistorical Approach.* New York, 1983.

Loewenfeld-Russ, Hans. *Im Kampf gegen den Hunger. Aus den Erinnerungen des Staatssekretärs für Volksernährung 1918–1920.* Edited by Isabella Ackerl. Vienna, 1986.

———. *Die Regelung der Volksernährung im Kriege.* Vienna, 1926.

Loidl, Franz. *Franz Xaver Kardinal Nagl. Erzbischof-Koadjutor (1910/11) und Fürsterzbischof (1911/13) von Wien.* Reprinted from *Beiträge zur Wiener Diözesangeschichte.* Vienna, 1965–67.

Loth, Wilfried. *Katholiken im Kaiserreich: Der politische Katholizismus in der Krise des wilhelminischen Deutschlands.* Düsseldorf, 1984.

Löw, Raimund. *Der Zerfall der "Kleinen Internationale." Nationalitätenkonflikte in der Arbeiterbewegung des alten Österreich (1889–1914).* Vienna, 1984.

Lowi, Theodore. "Party, Policy and Constitution in America." In *The American Party Systems: Stages of Political Development.* Edited by William Nisbet Chambers and Walter Dean Burnham. New York, 1967.

Luft, David S. *Robert Musil and the Crisis of European Culture, 1880–1942.* Berkeley, 1980.

Luft, Robert. "Politischer Pluralismus und Nationalismus. Zu Parteiwesen und politischer Kultur in der tschechischen Nation vor dem ersten Weltkrieg." *Österreichische Zeitschrift für Geschichtswissenschaften* 2 (1991): 72–87.

Lunzer, Heinz. *Hofmannsthals politische Tätigkeit in den Jahren 1914–1917.* Frankfurt, 1981.

Maderthaner, Wolfgang. "Die Entwicklung der Organisationsstruktur der deutschen Sozialdemokratie in Österreich 1889 bis 1913." In *Sozialdemokratie und Habsburgerstaat.*

———. "Kirche und Sozialdemokratie. Aspekte des Verhältnisses von politischem Klerikalismus und sozialistischer Arbeiterschaft bis zum Jahre 1938." In *Neuere Studien zur Arbeitergeschichte.*

Maier, Charles S. "'Fictitious bonds . . . of wealth and law': On the theory and practice of interest representation." In *Organizing Interests in Western Europe.*

Mandelbaum, Seymour J. *Boss Tweed's New York.* New York, 1965.

Mann, Arthur. "British Social Thought and American Reformers of the Progressive Era." *Mississippi Valley Historical Review* 42 (1955–56): 672–92.

———. *Yankee Reformers in the Urban Age.* Cambridge, Mass., 1954.

März, Eduard. *Austrian Banking and Financial Policy. Creditanstalt at a Turning Point, 1913–1923.* Translated by Charles Kessler. New York, 1984.

Masaryk, Thomas G. *Modern Man and Religion.* Translated by Ann Bibza and Václar Beneš. London, 1938.

Mathis, Franz. *Big Business in Österreich. Österreichische Grossunternehmen in Kurzdarstellungen.* Munich, 1987

Matsch, Erwin, ed. *November 1918 auf dem Ballhausplatz. Erinnerungen Ludwigs Freiherrn von Flotow, des letzten Chefs des Österreichisch-Ungarischen Auswärtigen Dienstes 1895–1920.* Vienna, 1982.

May, Arthur J. *The Passing of the Hapsburg Monarchy.* 2 vols. Philadelphia, 1966.

Mayer, Joseph Ernst. "Die Seelsorge." In *Kirche in Österreich 1918–1965.* Edited by Ferdinand Klostermann, Hans Kriegl, Otto Mauer, and Erika Weinzierl. 2 vols. Vienna, 1966.

Mayer, Sigmund. *Die Wiener Juden. Kommerz, Kultur, Politik 1700–1900.* Vienna, 1918.

McCagg, William O., Jr. *A History of the Habsburg Jews, 1670–1918.* Bloomington, 1989.

McGrath, William J. *Dionysian Art and Populist Politics in Austria.* New Haven, 1974.

Meckling, Ingeborg. *Die Aussenpolitik des Grafen Czernin.* Munich, 1969.

Megner, Karl. *Beamte. Wirtschafts- und sozialgeschichtliche Aspekte des k.k. Beamtentums.* Vienna 1985.

Meissl, Gerhard. "Gewerkschaft und industrielle Arbeitsbeziehungen 1889–1914." In *Sozialdemokratie und Habsburgerstaat.*

———. "Klassenkampf oder Harmonieduselei? Auf dem österreichischen Weg zur Massengewerkschaft (1890–1914)." In *Die Bewegung.*

Melinz, Gerhard, and Susan Zimmermann. *Uber die Grenzen der Armenhilfe: Kommunale und staatliche Sozialpolitik in Wien und Budapest in der Doppelmonarchie.* Vienna, 1991.

Mell, Wolfgang-Rüdiger. "Verwaltungsreform in Österreich." In *Verwaltungshistorische Studien*. Edited by Andor Csizmadia. 2 vols. Pécs, 1972.

Meyer, Henry Cord. *Mitteleuropa in German Thought and Action, 1815–1945*. The Hague, 1955.

Mischler, Ernst. "Der Haushalt der österreichischen Landschaften." *Jahrbuch des öffentlichen Rechts der Gegenwart* 3 (1909): 579–605.

Mitterauer, Michael. "'Nur diskret ein Kreuzzeichen'. Zu Formen des individuellen und gemeinschaftlichen Gebets in der Familie." In *Religion und Alltag. Interdisziplinäre Beiträge zu einer Sozialgeschichte des Katholizismus in lebensgeschichtlichen Aufzeichnungen*. Edited by Andreas Heller, Therese Weber, and Oliva Wiebel-Fanderl. Vienna, 1990.

Miyake, Masaki. "J. M. Baernreither und 'Mitteleuropa.' Eine Studie über den Nachlass Baernreither." *MÖSTA* 17–18 (1964–65): 359–98.

Mockenhaupt, Hubert, ed. *Katholische Sozialpolitik im 20. Jahrhundert: Ausgewählte Aufsätze und Reden von Heinrich Brauns*. Mainz, 1976.

———. *Weg und Wirken des geistlichen Sozialpolitikers Heinrich Brauns*. Paderborn, 1977.

Moeller, Robert G. "The Kaiserreich Recast? Continuity and Change in Modern German Historiography." *Journal of Social History* 17 (1983–84): 655–83.

Molisch, Paul, ed. *Briefe zur deutschen Politik in Österreich von 1848 bis 1918*. Vienna, 1934.

———. *Geschichte der deutschnationalen Bewegung in Oesterreich von ihren Anfängen bis zum Zerfall der Monarchie*. Jena, 1926.

———. *Politische Geschichte der deutschen Hochschulen in Oesterreich von 1848 bis 1918*. 2d ed. Vienna, 1939.

Mölzer, Andreas. "Zur Grazer Studentengeschichte. Der Gegensatz zwischen katholischen und national-freiheitlichen Korporationen in Graz von den Anfängen bis zum Jahre 1938 im Lichte der Studentenunruhen des Jahres 1932." In *Beiträge und Materialien zur Geschichte der Wissenschaften in Österreich*. Edited by Walter Höflechner. Graz, 1981.

Mommsen, Hans. "Otto Bauer, Karl Renner und die sozialdemokratische Nationalitätenpolitik in Österreich, 1905–1914." In *Arbeiterbewegung und Nationale Frage*. Göttingen, 1979.

———. *Die Sozialdemokratie und die Nationalitätenfrage im habsburgischen Vielvölkerstaat*. Vienna, 1963.

———. "Victor Adler und die Politik der österreichischen Sozialdemokratie im Ersten Weltkrieg." In *Politik und Gesellschaft im Alten und Neuen Österreich*.

Monticone, Alberto. *Deutschland und die Neutralität Italiens 1914–1915*. Wiesbaden, 1982.

Moreau, Rudolf v. *Die Eucharistischen Weltkongresse. Ihr Werden, Wachsen und Wirken*. Neckar, 1960.

Musil, Robert. "The Religious Spirit, Modernism, and Metaphysics." In *Precision and Soul. Essays and Addresses*. Edited by Burton Pike and David S. Luft. Chicago, 1990.

Nautz, Jürgen, ed. *Unterhändler des Vertrauens. Aus den nachgelassenen Schriften von Sektionschef Dr. Richard Schüller*. Vienna, 1990.

Neck, Rudolf. "Der Protest Franz Ferdinands gegen die ungarischen Verfassungsgarantien von 1907." *MÖSTA* 12 (1959): 433–37.

———, ed. *Arbeiterschaft und Staat im Ersten Weltkrieg 1914–1918*. 2 vols. Vienna, 1964–68.

———, ed. *Österreich im Jahre 1918*. Munich, 1968.

Nemec, Ludvik. "The Czech Jednota, the Avant-Garde of Modern Clerical Progressivism and Unionism." *Proceedings of the American Philosophical Society* 112 (1968): 74–100.

Niewyk, Donald L. "Solving the 'Jewish Problem': Continuity and Change in German Antisemitism, 1871–1945." *Year Book of the Leo Baeck Institute* 35 (1990): 335–70.

Offer, Avner. *The First World War: An Agrarian Interpretation*. Oxford, 1989.

Opitz, Alfred, and Franz Adlgasser, eds. *"Der Zerfall der europäischen Mitte." Staatenrevolution im Donauraum. Berichte der Sächsischen Gesandschaft in Wien 1917–1919*. Graz, 1990.

Otruba, Gustav. "Wiens Bevölkerung. Nationale Herkunft und soziale Entwicklung." *Der Donauraum* 13 (1968): 12–42.

Otruba, Gustav, and L. S. Rutsschka. "Die Herkunft der Wiener Bevölkerung in den letzten 150 Jahren." *Jahrbuch des Vereins für Geschichte der Stadt Wien* 13 (1957): 227–74.

Owerdieck, Reinhard. *Parteien und Verfassungsfrage in Österreich. Die Entstehung des Verfassungsprovisoriums der Ersten Republik 1918–1920*. Munich, 1987.

Parsons, Frank. *The City for the People*. Philadelphia, 1901.

Pauley, Bruce F. *From Prejudice to Persecution. A History of Austrian Anti-Semitism*. Chapel Hill, 1992.

Pelinka, Anton. *Karl Renner zur Einführung*. Hamburg, 1989.

———. *Stand oder Klasse? Die Christliche Arbeiterbewegung Österreichs 1933 bis 1938*. Vienna, 1972.

Pepper, Hugo. "Die frühe österreichische Sozialdemokratie und die Anfänge der Arbeiterkultur." In *Sozialdemokratie und Habsburgerstaat*.

Perfahl, Brigitte. "Zum Marxismus-Defizit der österreichischen Sozialdemokratie 1889–1901." In *Geschichte als demokratischer Auftrag. Karl Stadler zum 70. Geburtstag*. Edited under the direction of Helmut Konrad. Vienna, 1983.

Pesendorfer, Wolfgang. *Der Oberösterreichische Landtag. Historische Entwicklung, Wesen und Bedeutung einer Institution*. Linz, 1989.

Pfabigan, Alfred. "Das ideologische Profil der österreichischen Sozialdemokratie vor dem Ersten Weltkrieg." In *Die Bewegung*.

————. *Max Adler. Eine politische Biographie.* Frankfurt, 1982.

Pfarrhofer, Hedwig. *Friedrich Funder. Ein Mann zwischen Gestern und Morgen.* Graz, 1978.

Pichl, Eduard. *Georg Schönerer und die Entwicklung des Alldeutschtums in der Ostmark.* 3d ed. 6 vols. Oldenburg, 1938.

Pirquet, Clemens. "Ernährungszustand der Kinder in Österreich während des Krieges und der Nachkriegszeit." In *Volksgesundheit im Krieg.*

————, ed. *Volksgesundheit im Krieg.* 2 vols. Vienna, 1926.

Pizzorno, Alessandro. "Interests and Parties in Pluralism." In *Organizing Interests in Western Europe.*

Plaschka, Richard Georg, Horst Haselsteiner, and Arnold Suppan. *Innere Front. Militärassistenz, Widerstand und Umsturz in der Donaumonarchie 1918.* 2 vols. Munich, 1974.

Polzer-Hoditz, Arthur Graf. *Kaiser Karl. Aus der Geheimmappe seines Kabinettschefs.* Zürich, 1929.

Popp, Gerhard. *CV in Österreich 1864–1938: Organisation, Binnenstruktur und politische Funktion.* Vienna, 1984.

Prantner, Robert. *Kreuz und weisse Nelke. Katholische Kirche und Christlichsoziale Partei im Spiegel der Presse (1918–1932).* Vienna, 1984.

Pulzer, Peter. *The Rise of Political Anti-Semitism in Germany and Austria.* Revised edition. Cambridge, Mass., 1988.

Rabinbach, Anson. *The Crisis of Austrian Socialism. From Red Vienna to Civil War 1927–1934.* Chicago, 1983.

Rakove, Milton. *We Don't Want Nobody Nobody Sent. An Oral History of the Daley Years.* Bloomington, Ind., 1979.

Ramhardter, Günther. *Geschichtswissenschaft und Patriotismus. Österreichische Historiker im Weltkrieg 1914–1918.* Munich, 1973.

Redlich, Josef. *Emperor Francis Joseph of Austria: A Biography.* New York, 1929.

————. *Österreichische Regierung und Verwaltung im Weltkriege.* Vienna, 1925.

————. *Schicksalsjahre Österreichs 1908–1919. Das politische Tagebuch Josef Redlichs.* Edited by Fritz Fellner. 2 vols. Graz, 1953–54.

Reingrabner, Gustav. "Der Evangelische Bund und die Los-von-Rom Bewegung in Österreich." In *Evangelisch und Ökumenisch. Beiträge zum 100jährigen Bestehen des Evangelischen Bundes.* Edited by Gottfried Maron. Göttingen, 1986.

Rennhofer, Friedrich. *Ignaz Seipel. Mensch und Staatsmann. Eine biographische Dokumentation.* Vienna, 1978.

Riezler, Kurt. *Tagebücher, Aufsätze, Dokumente.* Edited by Karl Dietrich Erdmann. Göttingen, 1972.

Ritter, Gerhard A. *Sozialversicherung in Deutschland und England. Entstehung und Grundzüge im Vergleich.* Munich, 1983.

Ross, Dorothy. *The Origins of American Social Science.* Cambridge, 1991.

Rothenberg, Gunther E. *The Army of Francis Joseph.* West Lafayette, 1976.

Rozenblit, Marsha L. "The Assertion of Jewish Student Nationalism at the University of Vienna before the First World War." *Year Book of the Leo Baeck Institute* 28 (1982): 171–86.

———. *The Jews of Vienna, 1867–1914: Assimilation and Identity.* Albany, 1983.

Rudolf, Karl. "Die katholische Hochschüler- und Mittelschülerbewegung in Wien und Österreich." In *Der Katholizismus in Österreich.*

Rumpler, Helmut. *Max Hussarek. Nationalitäten und Nationalitätenpolitik in Österreich im Sommer des Jahres 1918.* Graz, 1965.

———. *Das Völkermanifest Kaiser Karls vom 16. Oktober 1918. Letzter Versuch zur Rettung des Habsburgerreiches.* Vienna, 1966.

Sauer, Walter. *Katholisches Vereinswesen in Wien. Zur Geschichte des christlichsozialkonservativen Lagers vor 1914.* Salzburg, 1980.

Saurer, Edith. *Die politischen Aspekte der österreichischen Bischofsernennungen 1867–1903.* Vienna, 1968.

Scheichl, Sigurd Paul. "The Contexts and Nuances of Anti-Jewish Language: Were All 'Antisemites' Antisemites?" In *Jews, Antisemitism and Culture in Vienna.* Edited by Ivar Oxaal, Michael Pollak, and Gerhard Botz. London, 1987.

Scherer, André, and Jacques Grunewald, eds. *L'Allemagne et les problèmes de la paix pendant la première guerre mondiale.* 4 vols. Paris, 1962–78.

Schiesl, Martin J. *The Politics of Efficiency. Municipal Administration and Reform in America, 1880–1920.* Berkeley, 1977.

Schlegel, Alfred. "Josef Schlegel—ein österreichischer Patriot." In *Für Kirche und Heimat. Festschrift Franz Loidl zum 80. Geburtstag.* Vienna, 1985.

Schmid-Egger, Barbara. *Klerus und Politik in Böhmen um 1900.* Munich, 1974.

Schmidt, Johann. *Entwicklung der katholischen Schule in Österreich.* Vienna, 1958.

Schmitt, Franz. "Umfang und System der Invaliden- und Altersversicherung nach der österreichischen Sozialversicherungsvorlage." *ZVSV* 20 (1911): 573–614.

Schmitz, Georg. *Die Anfänge des Parlamentarismus in Niederösterreich. Landesordnung und Selbstregierung 1861–1873.* Vienna, 1985.

———. *Der Landesamtsdirektor. Entstehung und Entwicklung.* Vienna, 1978.

———. *Die Vorentwürfe Hans Kelsens für die österreichische Bundesverfassung.* Vienna, 1981.

Schober, Richard. "Ein Bischof im Kreuzfeuer der Tiroler Christlichsozialen und Konservativen. Der Rücktritt des Fürstbischofs von Brixen Dr. Simon Aichner (1904)." *Österreich in Geschichte und Literatur* 20 (1976): 387–405.

———. *Geschichte des Tiroler Landtages im 19. und 20. Jahrhundert.* Innsbruck, 1984.

———, ed. *Theodor Freiherr von Kathrein (1842–1916). Landeshauptmann von Tirol. Briefe und Dokumente zur katholisch-konservativen Politik um die Jahrhundertwende.* Innsbruck, 1992.

———. "Das Verhältnis der Katholisch-Konservativen zu den Christlichsozialen in Tirol bis zu den Reichsratswahlen von 1907." *Tiroler Heimat* 38 (1974): 139–73, 39 (1975): 155–93.

Scholing, Michael, and Franz Walter. "Der 'Neue Mensch.' Sozialistische Lebensreform und Erziehung in der sozialdemokratischen Arbeiterbewegung Deutschlands und Österreichs." In *Solidargemeinschaft und Klassenkampf. Politische Konzeptionen der Sozialdemokratie zwischen den Weltkriegen.* Edited by Richard Saage. Frankfurt, 1986.

Schorske, Carl E. *Fin de siècle Vienna. Politics and Culture.* New York, 1980.

Schroeder, Oskar. *Aufbruch und Missverständnis: Zur Geschichte der reformkatholischen Bewegung.* Graz, 1969.

Schultes, Gerhard. "Das 'Katholische Aktionskomitee für Niederösterreich.' Ein Beitrag zur Vorgeschichte der Katholischen Aktion in Wien." In *Festschrift Franz Loidl zum 65. Geburtstag.*

—. *Der Reichsbund der katholischen deutschen Jugend Österreichs: Entstehung und Geschichte.* Vienna, 1967.

Seliger, Maren, and Karl Ucakar. *Wahlrecht und Wählerverhalten in Wien 1848–1932. Privilegien, Partizipationsdruck und Sozialstruktur.* Vienna, 1984.

—. *Wien, politische Geschichte 1740–1934. Entwicklung und Bestimmungskräfte grossstädtischer Politik.* 2 vols. Vienna, 1985.

Shanafelt, Gary W. *The Secret Enemy. Austria-Hungary and the German Alliance, 1914–1918.* Boulder, 1985.

Shaw, Albert. *Municipal Government in Continental Europe.* New York, 1895.

Shedel, James. "Emperor, Church and People: Religion and Dynastic Loyalty During the Golden Jubilee of Franz Joseph." *Catholic Historical Review* 76 (1990): 71–92.

Sheehan, James. *German Liberalism in the Nineteenth Century.* Chicago, 1978.

Shefter, Martin. "Party, Bureaucracy and Political Change in the United States." In *Political Parties: Development and Decay.* Edited by Louis Maisel and Joseph Cooper. Beverly Hills, 1978.

Sieder, Reinhard. "Behind the Lines: Working-Class Family Life in Wartime Vienna." In *The Upheaval of War.*

Sieghart, Margarete. "Rudolf Sieghart und das Ministerium Beck (Juni 1906 bis November 1908)." *Österreich in Geschichte und Literatur* 16 (1972): 465–78, 540–57.

Sieghart, Rudolf. *Die letzten Jahrzehnte einer Grossmacht. Menschen, Völker, Probleme des Habsburger-Reichs.* Berlin, 1932.

Siklós, András. *Revolution in Hungary and the Dissolution of the Multinational State, 1918.* Budapest, 1988.

Silberbauer, Gerhard. *Österreichs Katholiken und die Arbeiterfrage.* Graz, 1966.

Silverman, Dan P. "Nazification of the German Bureaucracy Reconsidered: A Case Study." *JMH* 60 (1988): 496–539.

Skalnik, Kurt. *Dr. Karl Lueger. Der Mann zwischen den Zeiten.* Vienna, 1954.

Skowronek, Stephen. *Building a New American State. The Expansion of National Administrative Capacities, 1877–1920.* Cambridge, 1982.

Slapnicka, Harry. *Christlichsoziale in Oberösterreich. Vom Katholikenverein 1848 bis zum Ende der Christlichsozialen 1934.* Linz, 1984.

—. *Oberösterreich unter Kaiser Franz Joseph (1861 bis 1918).* Linz, 1982.

Somogyi, Éva, ed. *Die Protokolle des gemeinsamen Ministerrates der österreichisch-ungarischen Monarchie 1896–1907.* Budapest, 1991.

Sozialdemokratie und Habsburgerstaat. Edited by Wolfgang Maderthaner. Vienna, 1988.

Speiser, Wolfgang. *Paul Speiser und das Rote Wien.* Vienna, 1979.

Spitzer, Rudolf. *Des Bürgermeisters Lueger Lumpen und Steuerträger.* Vienna, 1988.

Spitzmüller-Harmersbach, Alexander. *Der letzte österreichisch-ungarische Ausgleich und der Zusammenbruch der Monarchie. Sachliches und Persönliches.* Berlin, 1929.

———. "Die staatsfinanziellen Vereinbarungen im österreichisch-ungarischen Ausgleiche." *ZVSV* 17 (1908): 374–98.

Stadler, Friedrich. "Wissenschaft ins Volk! Popularisierungsbestrebungen im Wiener Kreis und 'Verein Ernst Mach' von der Jahrhundertwende bis zum Ende der Ersten Republik." In *Neuere Studien zur Arbeitergeschichte.*

Staudinger, Anton. "Christlichsoziale Judenpolitik in der Gründungsphase der österreichischen Republik." In *Jahrbuch für Zeitgeschichte* (Vienna, 1979): 11–48.

———. "Zur Entscheidung der christlichsozialen Abgeordneten für die Republik." In *Österreich November 1918. Die Entstehung der Ersten Republik. Protokoll des Symposiums in Wien am 24. und 25. Oktober 1978.* Vienna, 1986.

Steger, Gerhard. *Rote Fahne, schwarzes Kreuz. Die Haltung der Sozialdemokratischen Arbeiterpartei Österreichs zu Religion, Christentum und Kirchen. Von Hainfeld bis 1934.* Vienna, 1987.

Steinmetz, George. *Regulating the Social: The Welfare State and Local Politics in Imperial Germany.* Princeton, 1993.

Stourzh, Gerald. *Geschichte des Staatsvertrages 1945–1955.* 3d ed. Graz, 1985.

———. *Die Gleichberechtigung der Nationalitäten in der Verfassung und Verwaltung Österreichs 1848–1918.* Vienna, 1985.

———. "Die Mitgliedschaft auf Lebensdauer im österreichischen Herrenhause, 1861–1918." *MIÖG* 73 (1965): 63–117.

———. *Vom Reich zur Republik—Studien zum Österreichbewusstsein.* Vienna, 1990.

Studien zur Zeitgeschichte der österreichischen Länder. Band 1: Demokratisierung und Verfassung in den Ländern 1918–1920. St. Pölten, 1983.

Suppan, Arnold. *Die österreichischen Volksgruppen. Tendenzen ihrer gesellschaftlichen Entwicklung im 20. Jahrhundert.* Munich, 1983.

Sutter, Berthold. *Die Badenischen Sprachenverordnungen von 1897.* 2 vols. Graz, 1960–65.

———. "Die politische und rechtliche Stellung der Deutschen in Österreich 1848 bis 1918." In Adam Wandruszka and Peter Urbanitsch, eds., *Die Völker des Reiches, 1. Teilband. Die Habsburgermonarchie 1848–1918.* Vienna, 1980.

Sweet, Paul R. "Germany, Austria-Hungary and Mitteleuropa: August 1915- April 1916." In *Festschrift für Heinrich Benedikt.* Edited by Hugo Hantsch and Alexander Novotny. Vienna, 1957.

Szporluk, Roman. *The Political Thought of Thomas G. Masaryk*. Boulder, 1981.

Tálos, Emmerich, Ernst Hanisch, and Wolfgang Neugebauer, eds. *NS-Herrschaft in Österreich 1938–1945*. Vienna, 1988.

Trippen, Norbert. *Theologie und Lehramt im Konflikt: Die kirchlichen Massnahmen gegen den Modernismus im Jahre 1907 und ihre Auswirkungen in Deutschland.* Freiburg, 1977.

Tweraser, Kurt. "Carl Beurle and the Triumph of German Nationalism in Austria." *German Studies Review* 4 (1981): 403–26.

Ucakar, Karl. "Politische Legitimation und Parlamentarismus." *ÖZP* 9 (1980): 421–41.

Unfried, Berthold. "Entwicklungsebenen der Arbeiterbewegung in Österreich während des Ersten Weltkrieges." In *Die Bewegung*.

———. "Positionen der 'Linken' innerhalb der österreichischen Sozialdemokratie während des 1. Weltkrieges." In *Neuere Studien zur Arbeitergeschichte*.

Unterberger, Betty Miller. *The United States, Revolutionary Russia, and the Rise of Czechoslovakia*. Chapel Hill, 1989.

Verosta, Stephan. "Ignaz Seipels Weg von der Monarchie zur Republik (1917–1919)." In *Die österreichische Verfassung von 1918 bis 1938. Protokoll des Symposiums in Wien am 19. Oktober 1977*. Munich, 1980.

———. "Joseph Schumpeter gegen das Zollbündnis der Donaumonarchie mit Deutschland und gegen die Anschlusspolitik Otto Bauers (1916–1919)." In *Festschrift für Christian Broda*. Edited by Michael Neider. Vienna, 1976.

Wächter, K. T. "Die Gemeindebetriebe der Stadt Wien." *Schriften des Vereins für Sozialpolitik* 130 (1909): 95–222.

Wagner, Georg. "Von der Staatsidee zum Nationalbewusstsein." In *Österreich. Von der Staatsidee zum Nationalbewusstsein*. Edited by Georg Wagner. Vienna, 1982.

Wagner, Richard. *Clemens von Pirquet. His Life and Work*. Baltimore, 1968.

Wall, Richard. "English and German Families in the First World War, 1914–1918." In *The Upheaval of War*.

Wall, Richard, and Jay Winter, eds. *The Upheaval of War. Family, Work and Welfare in Europe, 1914–1918*. Cambridge, 1988.

Wandruszka, Adam. "Österreichs politische Struktur." In *Geschichte der Republik Österreich*. Edited by Heinrich Benedikt. Vienna, 1954.

Wank, Solomon. "A Case of Aristocratic Anti-Semitism in Austria: Count Aehrenthal and the Jews, 1878–1907." *Year Book of the Leo Baeck Institute* 30 (1985): 435–56.

Wegs, J. Robert. *Growing Up Working Class: Continuity and Change among Viennese Youth, 1890–1938*. University Park, 1989.

———. *Die österreichische Kriegswirtschaft 1914–1918*. Vienna, 1979.

Wehler, Hans-Ulrich. *Deutsche Gesellschaftsgeschichte*. 2 vols. Munich, 1987.

———. "Die Geburtsstunde des deutschen Kleinbürgertums," In *Bürger in der Gesellschaft der Neuzeit. Wirtschaft—Politik—Kultur*. Edited by Hans-Jürgen Puhle. Göttingen, 1991.

Weidenholzer, Josef. *Auf dem Weg zum 'Neuen Menschen.' Bildungs- und Kulturarbeit der österreichischen Sozialdemokratie in der Ersten Republik.* Vienna, 1981.

Weiler, Rudolf. "Katholische Soziallehre unterwegs." In *Festschrift Franz Loidl zum 65. Geburtstag.*

Weinstein, James. *The Corporate Ideal in the Liberal State: 1900–1918.* Boston, 1968.

Weinzierl, Erika. "Der Antimodernismus Pius' X." In *Der Modernismus.*

———, ed. *Der Modernismus. Beiträge zu seiner Erforschung.* Graz, 1974.

Whiteside, Andrew G. *Austrian National Socialism before 1918.* The Hague, 1962.

———. "The Germans as an Integrative Force in Imperial Austria: The Dilemma of Dominance." *AHY* 3, pt. 1 (1967): 157–200.

———. *The Socialism of Fools. Georg Ritter von Schönerer and Austrian Pan-Germanism.* Berkeley, 1975.

Wickert, Lothar. *Theodor Mommsen. Eine Biographie.* 4 vols. Frankfurt, 1959–80.

Widder, Helmut. *Parlamentarische Strukturen im politischen System. Zu Grundlagen und Grundfragen des österreichischen Regierungssystems.* Berlin, 1979.

Williamson, Samuel R., Jr. "Influence, Power and the Policy Process: The Case of Franz Ferdinand, 1906–1914." *Historical Journal* 17 (1974): 417–34.

Winkler, Wilhelm. [b. 1849]. "Gewerbe und Landwirtschaft in der Invaliden- und Altersversicherung der österreichischen Sozialversicherungsvorlage." *ZVSV* 19 (1910): 602–19.

———. "Studien zur österreichischen Sozialversicherungsvorlage." *ZVSV* 20 (1911): 415–46.

Winkler, Wilhelm [b. 1884]. *Die Einkommensverschiebungen in Österreich während des Weltkrieges.* Vienna, 1930.

———. *Die Tschechen in Wien.* Vienna, 1919.

Winter, Ernst Karl. *Ignaz Seipel als dialektisches Problem. Ein Beitrag zur Scholastik-forschung.* Vienna, 1966.

Winters, Stanley B., ed. *T. G. Masaryk (1850–1937). Volume 1. Thinker and Politician.* London, 1990.

Wiskemann, Elizabeth. *Czechs and Germans.* 2d ed. London, 1967.

Wistrich, Robert S. *Between Redemption and Perdition. Modern Antisemitism and Jewish Identity.* London, 1990.

———. *The Jews of Vienna in the Age of Franz Joseph.* Oxford, 1989.

———. *Socialism and the Jews. The Dilemmas of Assimilation in Germany and Austria-Hungary.* Rutherford, N. J., 1982.

Wittek, Heinrich. "Die kriegswirtschaftlichen Organisationen und Zentralen in Österreich." *ZVSV* N.S. 2 (1922): 24–90, 226–47.

Wohl, Robert. "French Fascism, Both Right and Left: Reflections on the Sternhell Controversy." *JMH* 63 (1991): 91–98.

Zeman, Zbynek A. B. *The Masaryks—The Making of Czechoslovakia.* London, 1976.

Zoitl, Helge. *"Student kommt von Studieren!" Zur Geschichte der sozialdemokratischen Studentenbewegung in Wien.* Vienna, 1992.

Zulehner, Paul Michael. *Kirche und Austromarxismus. Eine Studie zur Problematik Kirche-Staat-Gesellschaft.* Vienna, 1967.

———. *Religion im Leben der Österreicher. Dokumentation einer Umfrage.* Vienna, 1981.

———. *Religion ohne Kirche? Das religiöse Verhalten von Industriearbeitern.* Vienna, 1969.

UNPUBLISHED PAPERS AND DISSERTATIONS

Ableitinger, Alfred. "Rudolf Sieghart (1866–1934) und seine Tätigkeit im Ministerratspräsidium." Dissertation, University of Graz, 1964.

Adelmeier, Werner. "Ernst Vergani." Dissertation, University of Vienna, 1969.

Adler, Alois. "Die christlichsoziale Bewegung in der Steiermark von den ständischen Anfängen zur Volkspartei." Dissertation, University of Graz, 1956.

Albertin, Lothar. "Nationalismus und Protestantismus in der österreichischen Los-von-Rom Bewegung um 1900." Dissertation, University of Cologne, 1953.

Balzer, Gertrude. "Die Lex Kolisko." Dissertation, University of Vienna, 1942.

Binder, Edeltrude. "Doktor Albert Gessmann." Dissertation, University of Vienna, 1950.

Bittner, Gertrud. "Dr. Gustav Marchet." Dissertation, University of Vienna, 1949.

Botstein, Leon. "Music and Its Public. Habits of Listening and the Crisis of Musical Modernism in Vienna, 1870–1914." Dissertation, Harvard University, 1985.

Bowman, William D. "Priests, Parish, and Religious Practice: A Social History of Catholicism in the Archdiocese of Vienna, 1800–1870." Dissertation, The Johns Hopkins University, 1990.

Boyer, John W. "Conceptions of Vienna in Its Historical Literature." Paper presented at the Urban History Symposium, Chicago Historical Society, March, 1984.

Braun, Fritz. "Der politische Lebensweg des Bürgermeisters Richard Schmitz." Dissertation, University of Vienna, 1968.

Csoklich, Fritz. "Das Nationalitätenproblem in Österreich-Ungarn und die christlichsoziale Partei." Dissertation, University of Vienna, 1952.

Fertl, Karl. "Die Deutschnationalen in Wien im Gegensatz zu den Christlichsozialen bis 1914." Dissertation, University of Vienna, 1973.

Fussek, Alexander. "Minister-Präsident Karl Graf Stürgkh." Dissertation, University of Vienna, 1959.

Gaar, Manfred. "Franz Hagenhofer. Das Wirken eines steirischen Bauernführers." Dissertation, University of Graz, 1974.

Gipp, Susanne. "Dr. Alfred Ebenhoch (1855–1912)." Dissertation, University of Vienna, 1974.

Hafner, Herta. "Heinrich Hierhammer. Vizebürgermeister von Wien, 1905–1918. Ein bürgerlicher Aufsteiger." *Diplomarbeit,* University of Vienna, 1988.

Harrer, Karl. "Dr. Richard Weiskirchner." Dissertation, University of Vienna, 1950.

Hofrichter, Peter. "Die österreichischen Katholikentage des 20. Jahrhunderts (bis 1933)." Dissertation, University of Vienna, 1966.

Honeder, Josef. "Prälat Johann Nepomuk Hauser (1866–1927)." Dissertation, University of Vienna, 1964.

Höttinger, Matthias. "Der Fall Wahrmund." Dissertation, University of Vienna, 1949.

Husinsky, Heribert. "Die 'Reichspost' und die österreichische Balkanpolitik in den Jahren 1908/09." Dissertation, University of Vienna, 1947.

Jelinek, Elisabeth. "Der politische Lebensweg Dr. Heinrich Matajas." Dissertation, University of Vienna, 1970.

Kant, Ferdinand. "Der Niederösterreichische Landtag von 1902 bis 1908." Dissertation, University of Vienna, 1949.

Kapp, Richard W. "The Failure of the Diplomatic Negotiations between Germany and Austria-Hungary for a Customs Union, 1915–1916." Dissertation, University of Toronto, 1977.

Karl, Siegfried. "Josef Wolny. Ein Leben für Kirche und Schule." Dissertation, University of Vienna, 1966.

Klieber, Rupert J. "Die Genese der christlichsozialen Partei Salzburgs: (Politischer) Katholizismus in der Provinz zwischen 1899 und 1919." Dissertation, University of Salzburg, 1991.

Kraus, Therese. "Die Entstehung des 'Niederösterreichischen Bauernbundes'." Dissertation, University of Vienna, 1950.

Kuprian, Hermann J. W. "Zwischen Wissenschaft und Politik: Die politische Entwicklung Michael Mayrs von 1907 bis 1922." Dissertation, University of Innsbruck, 1985.

Leitgeb, Herwig. "Die Ministerpräsidentschaft Dr. Ernest v. Koerbers in den Jahren 1900–1904 und Oktober–Dezember 1916." Dissertation, University of Vienna, 1951.

Mende, Johannes. "Dr. Carl Freiherr von Bardolff." Dissertation, University of Vienna, 1984.

Miko, Norbert. "Die Vereinigung der Christlichsozialen Reichspartei und des Katholisch-Konservativen Zentrums im Jahre 1907." Dissertation, University of Vienna, 1949.

Norgate, Frank E. "The Internal Policies of the Stürgkh Government, November 1911–March 1914: A Study in a Holding Action." Dissertation, New York University, 1978.

Patzer, Franz. "Die Entwicklungsgeschichte der Wiener Sozialdemokratischen Gemeinderatsfraktion. Von ihren Anfängen bis zum Ausbruch des ersten Weltkrieges." Dissertation, University of Vienna, 1949.

Pellar, Brigitte. "Staatliche Institutionen und gesellschaftliche Interessengruppen in der Auseinandersetzung um den Stellenwert der Sozialpolitik und um ihre Gestaltung. Das k.k. arbeitsstatistische Amt im Handelsministerium und sein ständiger Arbeitsbeirat 1898–1917." Dissertation, University of Vienna, 1982.

Pfaffenberger, Gottfried. "Die 'Reichspost' und die christlich-soziale Bewegung." Dissertation, University of Vienna, 1948.

Prammer, Johann. "Konservative und Christlichsoziale Politik im Viertel ob dem Wienerwald 1848–1918." Dissertation, University of Vienna, 1973.

Prewitt, Kenneth. "Social Sciences and Private Philanthropy: The Quest for Social Relevance." Paper presented at the University of Chicago, September 1991.

Ramminger, Johann. "Nationalismus und Universität: Die Genese des Nationalismus und die cisleithanischen Universitäten 1859–1900." Dissertation, University of Vienna, 1981.

Rauch, Gerhard. "Die christlichsoziale Vereinigung und die Katholisch-Konservativen Oberösterreichs 1907–1914." Dissertation, University of Vienna, 1964.

Richer, Margarethe. "Pater Heinrich Abel, S.J." Dissertation, University of Vienna, 1947.

Schwarz, Ilse. "Dr. Joseph Maria Baernreither. Versuch einer politischen Biographie." Dissertation, University of Vienna, 1966.

Spann, Gustav. "Zensur in Österreich während des 1. Weltkrieges 1914–1918." Dissertation, University of Vienna, 1972.

Staudinger, Anton. *Aspekte christlichsozialer Politik 1917 bis 1920. Habilitationsschrift,* University of Vienna, 1979.

Stifter, Joseph. "Dr. Aemilian Schöpfer und der Bruderstreit in Tyrol." Dissertation, University of Vienna, 1949.

Stöger, Walter. "Das Verhältnis der Konservativen zur Christlichsozialen Partei." Dissertation, University of Vienna, 1949.

Tezuka, Hajime. "Die Junglehrer-Bewegung. Vorgeschichte der Schulreform Glöckels." Dissertation, University of Vienna, 1981.

Weber, Clemens. "Karl Hermann Wolf (1862–1941)." Dissertation, University of Vienna, 1975.

Weinberger, Dorit. "Die christliche Sozialreform Anton Orels." Dissertation, University of Vienna, 1966.

Wiegenstein, Jane. "Artists in a Changing Environment: The Viennese Art World, 1860–1918." Dissertation, Indiana University, 1980.

Wondratsch, Gerda. "Karl Seitz als Schulpolitiker. Die Zeit bis zum Ersten Weltkrieg." Dissertation, University of Vienna, 1978.

INDEX

CS = CHRISTIAN SOCIAL, SOCIALIST
SD = SOCIAL DEMOCRAT, DEMOCRATIC